Lecture Notes in Computer Science 3788

Commenced Publication in 1973
Founding and Former Series Editors:
Gerhard Goos, Juris Hartmanis, and Jan van Leeuwen

Bimal Roy (Ed.)

Advances in Cryptology – ASIACRYPT 2005

11th International Conference on the Theory
and Application of Cryptology and Information Security
Chennai, India, December 4-8, 2005
Proceedings

 Springer

Volume Editor

Bimal Roy
Indian Statistical Institute, Applied Statistics Unit
203 B.T. Road, Kolkata 700 108, India
E-mail: bimal@isical.ac.in

Library of Congress Control Number: 2005936460

CR Subject Classification (1998): E.3, D.4.6, F.2.1-2, K.6.5, C.2, J.1, G.2

ISSN   0302-9743
ISBN-10   3-540-30684-6 Springer Berlin Heidelberg New York
ISBN-13   978-3-540-30684-9 Springer Berlin Heidelberg New York

Springer is a part of Springer Science+Business Media

springeronline.com

© International Association for Cryptologic Research 2005
Printed in Germany

Typesetting: Camera-ready by author, data conversion by Scientific Publishing Services, Chennai, India
Printed on acid-free paper   SPIN: 11593447   06/3142   5 4 3 2 1 0

Preface

Asiacrypt, the annual conference of cryptology sponsored by IACR is now 11 years old. Asiacrypt 2005 was held during December 4–8, 2005, at Hotel Taj Coromandel, Chennai, India. This conference was organized by the International Association for Cryptologic Research (IACR) in cooperation with the Indian Institute of Technology (IIT), Chennai.

This year a total of 237 papers were submitted to Asiacrypt 2005. The submissions covered all areas of cryptographic research representing the current state of work in the crypto community worldwide. Each paper was blind reviewed by at least three members of the Program Committee and papers co-authored by the PC members were reviewed by at least six members. This first phase of review by the PC members was followed by a detailed discussion on the papers. At the end of the reviewing process 37 papers were accepted and were presented at the conference. The proceedings contain the revised versions of the accepted papers. In addition we were fortunate to have Prof. Andrew Yao and Prof. Bart Preneel as invited speakers.

Based on a discussion and subsequent voting among the PC members, the Best Paper Award for this year's Asiacrypt was conferred to Pascal Paillier and Damien Vergnaud for the paper entitled "Discrete-Log-Based Signatures May Not Be Equivalent to Discrete Log."

I would like to thank the following people. First, the General Chair, Prof. Pandu Rangan. Next, Springer for publishing the proceedings in the *Lecture Notes in Computer Science* series. I would also like to thank the submitting authors, the Program Committee members, the external reviewers, and the local Organizing Committee consisting of Mr. Veeraraghavan and Mr. E. Boopal. I acknowledge the partial financial support provided by Microsoft Research Labs, India. I thank Dr. Debrup Chakraborty for his help in managing the submissions and the final preparation of the proceedings. Thanks also goes to Mr. Sanjit Chatterjee for his assistance in the process.

December 2005   Bimal Roy

Asiacrypt 2005

December 3–7, 2005, Chennai, India

Sponsored by the
International Association for Cryptologic Research

in cooperation with
Indian Institute of Technology, Chennai, India

General Chair
C. Pandu Rangan, Indian Institute of Technology, Chennai, India

Program Chair
Bimal Roy, Indian Statistical Institute, Kolkata, India

Program Committee

Manindra Agarwal	Indian Institute of Technology, Kanpur, India, and National University of Singapore, Singapore
Feng Bao	Institute for Infocomm Research, Singapore
Rana Barua	Indian Statistical Institute, India
P.S.L.M. Barreto	University of São Paulo, Brazil
Alex Biryukov	Katholieke Universiteit, Leuven, Belgium
Simon R. Blackburn	Royal Holloway College, University of London, UK
Colin Boyd	Queensland University of Technology, Australia
Nicolas T. Courtois	Axalto Smart Cards, France
Cunsheng Ding	Hong Kong University of Science and Technology, Hong Kong, China
Orr Dunkelman	Technion, Israel
Jovan Golic	Telecom Italia, Italy
Lai Xue Jia	Shanghai Jiaotong University, China
Thomas Johansson	Lund University, Sweden
Chi Sung Laih	National Cheng Kung University, Taiwan
Tanja Lange	Ruhr University Bochum, Germany
Pil Joong Lee	Pohang University of Science & Technology, Korea
Arjen K. Lenstra	Lucent Technologies, USA, and Technische Universiteit Eindhoven, Netherlands
Chae Hoon Lim	Sejong University, Korea
C.E. Veni Madhavan	Indian Institute of Science, India
Alfred Menezes	University of Waterloo, Canada
Phong Q. Nguyen	CNRS/École Normale Supérieure, France
Kapil Paranjape	Institute of Mathematical Sciences, India
David Pointcheval	CNRS/École Normale Supérieure, France
Jean-Jacques Quisquater	Université Catholique de Louvain, Belgium
C. Pandu Rangan	Indian Institute of Technology, Madras, India
Vincent Rijmen	Technical University of Graz, Austria
Rei Safavi-Naini	University of Wollongong, Australia
Amit Sahai	University of California, Los Angeles, USA
Kouichi Sakurai	Kyushu University, Japan
P.K. Saxena	SAG, India
Nicolas Sendrier	INRIA, France
Hovav Shacham	Stanford University, USA
Nigel Smart	University of Bristol, UK
Douglas R. Stinson	University of Waterloo, Canada
Xiaoyun Wang	Shandong University, China
Hugh Williams	University of Calgary, Canada

External Reviewers

Michel Abdalla
Raju Agarwal
Omran Ahmadi
Sattam Al-Riyami
Daniel Augot
Roberto Avanzi
Steve Babbage
Joonsang Baek
Vittorio Bagini
Boaz Barak
Mark Bauer
S.S. Bedi
Daniel J. Bernstein
Amnon Besser
Raghav Bhaskar
A.K. Bhateja
Dan Boneh
Xavier Boyen
An Braeken
Emmanuel Bresson
Christophe De Canniere
Anne Canteaut
Dario Catalano
Juyoung Cha
Sucheta Chakraborty
Pascale Charpin
Sanjit Chatterjee
Liqun Chen
Jung Hee Cheon
Benoit Chevallier-Mames
Kookrae Cho
Kim-Kwang R. Choo
Sherman Chow
Carlos Cid
Ricardo Dahab
Blandine Debraize
Alex Dent
Claus Diem
Ratna Dutta
Andreas Enge
Chun-I Fan
Nelly Fazio
Serge Fehr

Decio Luiz Gazzoni Filho
Gerhard Frey
Pierre-Alain Fouque
Navneet Gaba
Fabien Galand
Steven Galbraith
David Galindo
Juan Garay
Pierrick Gaudry
Craig Gentry
Eu-Jin Goh
Louis Goubin
Rob Granger
Jens Groth
D.J. Guan
Indivar Gupta
Saoshi Hada
Darrel Hankerson
Yong-Sork Her
Julio Cesar L. Hernández
Jason Hinek
Yvonne Hitchcock
Andreas Hirt
Martin Hirt
Susan Hohenberger
Yoshiaki Hori
Wang Chih Hung
Yong Ho Hwang
Kenji Imamoto
Yuval Ishai
Mike Jacobson
Rahul Jain
Devendra Jha
Shaoquan Jiang
Ari Juels
Pascal Junod
Guruprasad Kar
Jonathan Katz
Chong Hee Kim
Seung Joo Kim
Shinsaku Kiyomoto
Yuichi Komano
Caroline Kudla

Sandeep Kumar
Meena Kumari
Sébastien Kunz-Jacques
Kaoru Kurosawa
Hidenori Kuwakado
Yann Laigle-Chapuy
Joseph Lano
Cedric Lauradoux
Dong Hoon Lee
Jooyoung Lee
Jung Wook Lee
Wei-Bin Lee
Stephane Lemieux
Manuel Leone
Francois Levy-dit-Vehel
Benoit Libert
Yehuda Lindell
Yu Long
Chi-Jen Lu
Ling Lu
Stefan Lucks
Subhomay Maitra
John Malone-Lee
Stephane Manuel
Keith Martin
Atefeh Mashatan
Luke McAven
Renato Menicocci
Miodrag Mihaljevic
Marine Minier
Pradeep Mishra
P.R. Mishra
Chris Mitchell
Bodo Moeller
Guglielmo Morgari
Bernard Mourrain
Yi Mu
Siguna Mueller
Frédéric Muller
Mats Naeslund
Mridul Nandi
Anderson Nascimento
Gregory Neven

Antonio Nicolosi
Juan Gonzalez Nieto
Ryuzou Nishi
Takeshi Okamoto
Tatsuaki Okamoto
Harold Ollivier
Rafi Ostrovsky
Haruki Ota
S.K. Pal
Dan Page
Pascal Pallier
Dong Jin Park
Jung Hyung Park
Young Ho Park
Raphael Pass
Kenny Paterson
Kun Peng
Slobodan Petrovic
Duong Hieu Phan
N. Rajesh Pillai
Benny Pinkas
Norbert Pramstaller
J. Radhakrishnan
Christian Rechberger
Eric Rescorla
Leo Reyzin

Gal Rouvroy
Yasuyuki Sakai
Palash Sarkar
Reg Sawilla
Ruediger Schack
Renate Scheidler
Werner Schindler
Alice Silverberg
Jae Woo Seo
Nicholas Sheppard
Jong Hoon Shin
Tom Shrimpton
M.C. Shrivastava
Andrey Sidorenko
Sanjeet Singh
Martijn Stam
Hung-Min Sun
Jac Chul Sung
Krishna Suri
Willy Susilo
Gelareh Taban
Keisuke Tanaka
Edlyn Teske
Jean-Pierre Tillich
Rajeev Thamman
Nicolas Theriault

Dongvu Tonien
Wen-Guey Tzeng
Shinegori Uchiyama
Yoshifumi Ueshige
Damien Vergnaud
Eric Verheul
Neelam Verma
Guilin Wang
Huaxiong Wang
Dai Watanabe
Brent Waters
Benne de Weger
William Whyte
Peter Wild
Christopher Wolf
Kjell Wooding
Yongdong Wu
Tianbing Xia
Pratibha Yadav
Bo-Yin Yang
Yeon Hyeong Yang
Jeong Il Yoon
Young Tae Youn
Yuliang Zheng
Huafei Zhu

Table of Contents

Algebra and Number Theory

Multiparty Computation

Zero Knowledge and Secret Sharing

Block Ciphers and Hash Functions

Bilinear Maps

Key Agreement

Provable Security

Signatures

Author Index

Discrete-Log-Based Signatures May Not Be Equivalent to Discrete Log

Pascal Paillier[1] and Damien Vergnaud[2]

[1] Gemplus Card International, Advanced Cryptographic Services,
34, rue Guynemer, 92447 Issy-les-Moulineaux Cedex, France
pascal.paillier@gemplus.com
[2] Laboratoire de Mathématiques Nicolas Oresme,
Université de Caen, Campus II, B.P. 5186,
14032 Caen Cedex, France
vergnaud@math.unicaen.fr

Abstract. We provide evidence that the unforgeability of several discrete-log based signatures like Schnorr signatures cannot be equivalent to the discrete log problem in the standard model. This contradicts in nature well-known proofs standing in weakened proof methodologies, in particular proofs employing various formulations of the Forking Lemma in the random oracle Model. Our impossibility proofs apply to many discrete-log-based signatures like ElGamal signatures and their extensions, DSA, ECDSA and KCDSA as well as standard generalizations of these, and even RSA-based signatures like GQ. We stress that our work sheds more light on the provable (in)security of popular signature schemes but does not explicitly lead to actual attacks on these.

1 Introduction

It is striking to observe that after more that two decades of active research on the matter, the standard-model security of discrete-log based signatures like Schnorr, ElGamal or DSA remains mysteriously unknown. Although dedicated proof techniques do exist in weakened models (*e.g.* the random oracle model (ROM) [19,4,8] or the generic group model (GGM) [7]), none of them provides intuition about the actual security of discrete-log signatures. Even though they have withstood concerted cryptanalytic effort fairly well, we suspect that the real-life security of many of these signature schemes is actually weaker than expected. We provide evidence that most discrete-log-based signatures defined over some prime-order group $\mathbb{G}$ cannot be equivalent to extracting discrete logs over $\mathbb{G}$ in the standard model. Our results are partial in the sense that we disprove equivalence via *algebraic* reductions. In brief, algebraic reductions can only apply group operations on group elements. This restriction is not overly restrictive as we do not know any example of a cryptographic reduction which is not algebraic. Our results suggest that most discrete-log based signature schemes just cannot reach a maximal security level *i.e.* equivalence towards their primitive problem, or that if some of them do, it is through non-algebraic reductions exploiting intricate and subtle relations within the group $\mathbb{G}$.

B. Roy (Ed.): ASIACRYPT 2005, LNCS 3788, pp. 1–20, 2005.

Most interestingly, our work highlights a possible separation between the standard model and the random oracle model in which it is well-known that forging Schnorr signatures (for instance) is equivalent to extracting discrete logs. An interpretation is that random-oracle-based proofs leave unfair advantage to security reductions by probing and modifying the adversary's internal computations and thereby letting the random oracle play a crucial role that cannot be justified in real life. Previous works have observed similar separations in specific contexts [2,18].

The Fiat-Shamir paradigm of transforming identification schemes into digital signature schemes [13] is popular because it yields efficient protocols. However all known results for the security of Fiat-Shamir-transformed signature schemes like Schnorr take place in the ROM[1]. Even worse, they impose the loss of a factor nearly q_H (the number of queries the forger makes to the random oracle) in either execution time or success probability of reductions that convert a forger into an algorithm that extracts discrete logarithms. While no proof exists that the loss of this factor is necessary, the problem seems inherent to the way signature schemes are constructed from identification protocols.

We prove in this paper that any random-oracle-based reduction from computing discrete logarithms to forging Schnorr signatures *must* lose a factor at least $\sqrt{q_H}$. This shows that a proof of equivalence in the ROM, if algebraic, *will never be tight*. We believe our work gives a new perspective as to why no efficient proof of equivalence to the discrete log problem has ever been found for Schnorr signatures despite considerable research efforts.

We emphasize that although our work disproves that Schnorr, ElGamal, DSA, GQ, etc. are maximally secure, no actual attack or weakness of either of these signature schemes arises from our impossibility results. Nothing stated here refutes that forging signatures is likely to be intractable in practice.

1.1   Our Contributions

Our results are manyfold. Introducing a simple way to simulate forgeries, we are able to relate security properties of many signature schemes (Schnorr, (Meta) ElGamal, DSA[2], ECDSA, KCDSA, GQ) to *one-more* computational problems, in a positive or *negative* sense. In the positive sense, we prove the unbreakability of these signatures (meaning that the signing key cannot be recovered) under chosen-message attacks, thereby identifying security properties that have remained unknown for these schemes.

Starting from the same simulation technique, we show that no algebraic reduction can exist that would relate the unforgeability (under any kind of attacks) of these signatures to their primitive problem. This result is extendable to the

---

[1] It is known that the Fiat-Shamir transform provides a separation between the ROM and the standard model, see [14].

[2] Note that this work constitutes the first proper security analysis of DSA and ECDSA in the standard model. Previous to this work the only known security result on DSA schemes was that of Brown on ECDSA which assumed a generic group [7].

one-more setting, meaning that there cannot exist a similar reduction to a weakened, one-more version of the primitive problem. Our impossibility proofs rely on the construction of an efficient meta-reduction relating such a reduction to the one-more problem itself. Thus, under the assumption that this problem is intractable, the fact that a polynomial meta-reduction exists forbids the existence of algebraic reductions. We note that our meta-reductions are *perfect* meaning that they preserve success probabilities perfectly. This emphasizes the strength of our impossibility results.

1.2   Roadmap

We start by providing definitional facts about discrete-log-based signature schemes, security notions for signatures, the discrete log and one-more discrete log assumptions over a group $\mathbb{G}$, reductionist security proofs and algebraic reductions. Section 3 proves that Schnorr signatures are unbreakable under a chosen-message attack. Section 4 then proves that if the one-more discrete log assumption holds, then Schnorr signatures cannot be proven equivalent to the discrete log problem and Section 5 further extends this impossibility to the one-more discrete log problem. Section 6 then applies our proof technique to other signatures schemes, slightly adapting the proof to the underlying computational problem when necessary. Lastly, Section 7 explores the case of random-oracle-based reductions and shows that any reduction of that type, if algebraic, must loose a factor close to $\sqrt{q_H}$. We conclude with a series of open questions in Section 8.

2   Preliminaries

2.1   Schnorr Signatures

Schnorr's identification protocol was introduced in the late eighties [21,20] as a means to prove knowledge of the discrete logarithm of a publicly known group element. Let $\mathbb{G} = \langle g \rangle$ be a group of prime order q and P and V denote a prover and a verifier. By engaging in the protocol, P proves to V that he knows the discrete log x of a public group element $y = g^x$. The protocol has three simple moves. (Commitment) P selects a random $k \xleftarrow{\$} \mathbb{Z}_q$, computes $r = g^k$ and sends r to V. (Challenge) V picks a random $c \xleftarrow{\$} \mathbb{Z}_q$ and sends c to P. (Response) P computes and sends $s = k + cx \bmod q$ to V. Lastly, V verifies that $g^s \cdot y^{-c} = r$ and recognizes that P knows x if the equality holds.

Schnorr signatures derive from Schnorr's identification protocol by applying the Fiat-Shamir transform [13] with respect to a hash function $H : \{0,1\}^\star \mapsto \mathbb{Z}_q$. The Fiat-Shamir-transformed protocol is changed into a signature scheme by making it non-interactive. In this respect, the signer acts like P and simulates a verifier V by computing the challenge c himself as $c = H(m, r)$. For concreteness, we detail Schnorr's signature scheme Σ_H as a tuple of probabilistic algorithms $\Sigma_H = (\text{GEN}, \text{SIGN}, \text{VER})$ defined as follows.

KEY GENERATION. GEN selects a random $x \xleftarrow{\$} \mathbb{Z}_q$. The secret key is x while the public key is $y = g^x \in \mathbb{G}$.

SIGNING PROCEDURE. Given a message $m \in \{0,1\}^*$, SIGN(m) picks a random $k \xleftarrow{\$} \mathbb{Z}_q$, computes $r = g^k$, $c = H(m,r)$ and $s = k + cx \bmod q$. The output signature is (s,c).

VERIFICATION PROCEDURE. VER$(m, (s,c))$ returns 1 if $H(m, g^s y^{-c}) = c$ and 0 otherwise.

Schnorr signatures constitute one of the most important ingredients in the design of cryptographic protocols, cryptosystems and proofs of knowledge.

2.2   Security Notions

Security notions for signature schemes are defined with respect to several types of adversaries or equivalently, as the conjunction of an adversarial goal and an attack scenario. An adversary is modeled as a probabilistic Turing machine attempting to fulfill the goal while given access to certain resources when interacting with the signature scheme.

ADVERSARIAL GOALS. We make use of three separate goals in this paper although others may also be of interest (*e.g.* signature *malleability* [19]). We say that a signature scheme is *breakable* (BK) when an adversary extracts the secret key matching a prescribed public key. The scheme is said to be *universally forgeable* (UF) when there exists an adversary $\mathcal{A}$ that returns a valid signature on a message given as input to $\mathcal{A}$. The notion of *existential forgeability* (EF) is similar but allows the adversary to choose freely the value of the signed message.

ATTACK MODELS. We consider two attack scenarios in this paper. In a *key-only attack* (KOA), the adversary is given nothing else than a public key as input[3]. In a *chosen-message attack* (CMA), the adversary is given adaptive access to signatures on messages of his choice while attempting to achieve his goal.

Security notions are obtained by coupling an adversarial goal with an attack model. We distinguish between several notions of reference for which general results are immediate, as shown on Figure 1. We refer the reader to the extensive cryptographic literature for a more formal definition of these security notions.

2.3   Discrete Logarithm Problems

DL. Solving the discrete log problem DL$[g, r]$ in a group $\mathbb{G} = \langle g \rangle$ of prime order q consists in computing $k \in \mathbb{Z}_q$ given $r = g^k \in \mathbb{G}$. Because of its random self-reducibility [19], the hardness of the discrete log problem is essentially independent from the choice of its inputs (g, r) and rather depends on the inner structure of the group $\mathbb{G}$ itself. We denote DL the problem of computing discrete

---

[3] The term *no-message attacks* is also frequently used to designate such attacks.

	Key only		Chosen message
Existential forgeries	EF-KOA $[\mathcal{S}]$	$\Rightarrow$	EF-CMA $[\mathcal{S}]$
	$\Uparrow$		$\Uparrow$
Universal forgeries	UF-KOA $[\mathcal{S}]$	$\Rightarrow$	UF-CMA $[\mathcal{S}]$
	$\Uparrow$		$\Uparrow$
Breakability	BK-KOA $[\mathcal{S}]$	$\Rightarrow$	BK-CMA $[\mathcal{S}]$
Goal vs. Attack	**Key only**		**Chosen message**

Fig. 1. Major security notions for signature schemes. $\mathcal{S}$ denotes an arbitrary signature scheme and $P_1 \Leftarrow P_2$ means that P_1 is polynomially reducible to P_2. Security notions are defined by their underlying problem e.g. UF-KOA $[\mathcal{S}]$ denotes the problem of computing a universal forgery under a key-only attack.

logs over $\mathbb{G} = \langle g \rangle$ with respect to a fixed base g. A probabilistic algorithm $\mathcal{A}$ that (ε, τ)-solves DL is such that

$$\Pr_{k \xleftarrow{\$} \mathbb{Z}_q} \left[\mathcal{A}(g^k) = k \right] \geq \varepsilon$$

where the probability is taken over the random tape of $\mathcal{A}$ and $\mathcal{A}$ stops after time at most τ. The (ε, τ)-discrete-log assumption tells that DL cannot be (ε, τ)-solved over $\mathbb{G}$. The (asymptotic) discrete log assumption tells that if DL can be (ε, τ)-solved for $\tau = \mathsf{poly}\,(\log q)$ then ε is negligible before $1/\mathsf{poly}\,(\log q)$.

THE ONE-MORE DL. The computational problem n-DL is defined as a natural extension of DL. A probabilistic algorithm $\mathcal{A}$ solving n-DL is given $n + 1$ group elements $r_0, r_1, \ldots, r_n$ as well as a limited access to a discrete log oracle $\mathsf{DL_{OM}}$. $\mathcal{A}$ is allowed to access $\mathsf{DL_{OM}}$ at most n times, thus obtaining the discrete logarithm of n group elements of his choice with respect to a fixed base g. $\mathcal{A}$ must eventually output the $n + 1$ discrete logs $k_0 = \mathsf{dl}_g\,(r_0), \ldots, k_n = \mathsf{dl}_g\,(r_n)$. An algorithm $\mathcal{A}$ is said to (ε, τ)-solve n-DL when

$$\Pr_{k_0, \ldots, k_n \xleftarrow{\$} \mathbb{Z}_q} \left[\mathcal{A}^{\mathsf{DL_{OM}}}(g^{k_0}, \ldots, g^{k_n}) = (k_0, \ldots, k_n) \right] \geq \varepsilon$$

where the probability is taken over the random tape of $\mathcal{A}$, $\mathcal{A}$ stops after time at most τ and $\mathcal{A}$ calls $\mathsf{DL_{OM}}$ at most n times. The one-more discrete log assumption tells that no probabilistic algorithm can solve n-DL with non-negligible success probability over $\mathbb{G}$ for any integer $n \geq 1$. It is easily seen that DL is contained as the special case $\mathsf{DL} \equiv 0\text{-}\mathsf{DL}$ and that $n_1\text{-}\mathsf{DL} \Leftarrow n_2\text{-}\mathsf{DL}$ whenever $n_1 \geq n_2$.

2.4 Reduction-Based Security Proofs

REDUCTIONS. Cryptographers use reductionist proofs to convince others that their schemes are computationally secure. An algorithm $\mathcal{R}$ is said to reduce a problem P_1 to a problem P_2, which we then denote by $P_1 \Leftarrow_\mathcal{R} P_2$, if $\mathcal{R}$ solves P_1

with the help of an algorithm solving P_2. Algorithm $\mathcal{R}$ is then called a *reduction* from P_1 to P_2. We write $P_1 \Leftarrow P_2$ when there exists a polynomial time reduction from P_1 to P_2, and $P_1 \equiv P_2$ when one has simultaneously $P_1 \Leftarrow P_2$ and $P_2 \Leftarrow P_1$.

ALGEBRAIC ALGORITHMS. Our method of converting a reduction $\mathcal{R}$ such that DL $\Leftarrow_\mathcal{R}$ UF-KOA $[\Sigma_H]$ into an algorithm solving the one-more discrete log problem applies whenever $\mathcal{R}$ belongs to a certain "natural" class of reductions. We refer to these as *algebraic reductions*.

In brief, a reduction algorithm $\mathcal{R}$ is *algebraic* with respect to a group $\mathbb{G}$ if $\mathcal{R}$ is limited to perform group operations on group elements. Adding $1_\mathbb{G}$ to $g \in \mathbb{G}$ is thus not permitted, even if this operation is well-defined and meaningful (if $\mathbb{G}$ is the multiplicative subgroup of a ring, for instance). $\mathcal{R}$ is free to apply arbitrary operations on other data types, but when it comes to elements of $\mathbb{G}$, the only available operations are among the (redundant) limited set

$$ S = \{(g_1, g_2) \mapsto g_1 \stackrel{?}{=} g_2, (g_1, g_2) \mapsto g_1 \cdot g_2, (g_1, \lambda) \mapsto g_1^\lambda, g_1 \mapsto g_1^{-1}\} \,. $$

For instance a reduction placed into the generic group model (GGM) or more precisely in the non-programmable GGM is an algebraic reduction[4]. However, the class of algebraic reductions encompasses *much more* algorithms and in particular may be relevant on groups where there do exist algorithms exploiting the encoding of elements. This class of reductions is not overly restrictive (in fact, we do not know any example of a cryptographic reduction which is not algebraic). The restriction of our results to algebraic reductions is far much weaker than the one made in [11] which considers only reductions supplying the adversary with a public key which is always the same as its own challenge. It is worth noting that our results extend readily to such reductions.

Algebraic algorithms were originally defined by Boneh and Venkatesan [5] in the context of rings of integers modulo $n = pq$ under the form of straight-line programs computing polynomials over the ring structure $\mathbb{Z}_n$. Here, we stick to a (somewhat more natural) definition of algebraicity towards a group structure. A formal definition of this property is that an algebraic algorithm $\mathcal{R}$ admits a polynomial time extractor Extract enabling one, given $\mathcal{R}$'s inputs $(s, g_1, \ldots, g_k) \in \{0, 1\}^* \times \mathbb{G}^k$ and random tape ϖ, to recover for any variable $h \in \mathbb{G}$ output by $\mathcal{R}$ after τ elementary steps, the coefficients α_i such that $h = g_1^{\alpha_1} \ldots g_k^{\alpha_k}$. Extract possibly has non black-box access to $\mathcal{R}$ and in particular may be given the code of $\mathcal{R}$. We require that Extract runs in time poly$(\tau, |\mathcal{R}|)$ where $|\mathcal{R}|$ denotes the code size of $\mathcal{R}$.

In the sequel, we adopt the notation $P_1 \Leftarrow_{\mathrm{ALG}} P_2$ whenever there exists an algebraic algorithm $\mathcal{R}$ such that $P_1 \Leftarrow_\mathcal{R} P_2$ and $P_1 \equiv_{\mathrm{ALG}} P_2$ when $P_1 \Leftarrow_{\mathcal{R}_1} P_2$ and $P_2 \Leftarrow_{\mathcal{R}_2} P_1$ for algebraic reductions $\mathcal{R}_1, \mathcal{R}_2$. Conversely, the notation $P_1 \not\Leftarrow_{\mathrm{ALG}} P_2$ says that there exists no algebraic algorithm $\mathcal{R}$ such that $P_1 \Leftarrow_\mathcal{R} P_2$. We define $P_1 \not\equiv_{\mathrm{ALG}} P_2$ in a similar way.

---

[4] It should be mentioned that the GGM suffers from the same separation problems as the ROM, see [10].

3 Schnorr is Unbreakable Under the One-More Discrete Log Assumption

We start by showing that Schnorr's signature scheme Σ_H defined over some group $\mathbb{G}$ is at least as hard to break that the one-more discrete log problem is hard to solve over $\mathbb{G}$. This is a *positive* security result standing in the standard model.

Theorem 1 (q_s-DL $\Leftarrow$ BK-CMA $[\Sigma_H]$). *Assume there exists an adversary $\mathcal{A}$ against Σ_H that breaks the secret key under a chosen-message attack with q_s signature queries and success probability ε. Then there exists an algorithm $\mathcal{R}$ that solves q_s-DL with probability $\varepsilon' = \varepsilon$ in similar time.*

Proof. The description of $\mathbb{G} = \langle g \rangle$ is implicitly given to all parties (this will be the case for all reductions and meta-reductions considered in this paper). Assume there exists a probabilistic algorithm $\mathcal{A}$ that takes as input $y = g^x$, requests the signature of q_s messages, and outputs the secret key x with probability ε after τ steps. We construct a reduction algorithm $\mathcal{R}$ which makes use of $\mathcal{A}$ to solve a q_s-DL instance over $\mathbb{G}$. Algorithm $\mathcal{R}$ works as follows.

$\mathcal{R}$ receives $q_s + 1$ group elements $r_0, \ldots, r_{q_s}$, defines $y = r_0$ and launches $\mathcal{A}(y, \varpi)$ over some random tape ϖ. Now whenever $\mathcal{A}$ requests the Schnorr signature of a message m_i, $\mathcal{R}$ uses r_i to compute $c_i = H(m_i, r_i)$. $\mathcal{R}$ then queries the discrete log oracle to get $s_i \leftarrow \mathsf{DL_{OM}}(r_i \cdot y^{c_i})$ and returns the signature $\sigma_i = (s_i, c_i)$. It is easily seen that this simulation is perfect.

After at most q_s signature queries, $\mathcal{A}$ returns k_0 such that $r_0 = g^{k_0}$ with probability ε in which case $\mathcal{R}$ uses k_0 to retrieve the discrete logarithm $k_i = s_i - k_0 c_i \bmod q$ of r_i for $i = 1, \ldots, q_s$. $\mathcal{R}$ then returns $(k_0, k_1, \ldots, k_{q_s})$ and therefore succeeds in solving q_s-DL with probability $\varepsilon' = \varepsilon$ after at most $\tau' = \tau + \mathsf{poly}(q_s, \mathsf{Time}(H), \log q)$ steps. $\square$

4 Schnorr Signatures are Not Unforgeable Under the Discrete Log Assumption

We now show that Schnorr signatures cannot be proven universally unforgeable under the discrete log assumption in the standard model with respect to an algebraic reduction. We actually show that if such a reduction existed then the one-more discrete log assumption would not hold over $\mathbb{G}$.

Theorem 2. *Assume that the one-more discrete log assumption holds. Then* $\mathsf{DL} \not\Leftarrow_{\mathrm{ALG}} \mathsf{UF\text{-}KOA}[\Sigma_H]$.

We give a more precise formulation of Theorem 2 in the following lemma.

Lemma 1. *Assume there exists an algebraic reduction algorithm $\mathcal{R}$ that converts an (ε, τ)-universal forger $\mathcal{A}$ under a key-only attack into an (ε', τ')-solver for the discrete logarithm and assume that $\mathcal{R}$ executes $\mathcal{A}$ at most n times. Then there exists a meta-reduction algorithm $\mathcal{M}$ that solves n-DL with success probability $\varepsilon'' = \varepsilon'$ within time $\tau'' = \tau' + \mathsf{poly}(\tau', |\mathcal{R}|, n, \mathsf{Time}(H), \log q)$.*

Proof. The rest of the section is dedicated to proving Lemma 1 and we start by giving an overview of how the proof works. Assuming the existence of an algebraic reduction $\mathcal{R}$ as above, we construct a meta-reduction $\mathcal{M}$ that solves n-DL with success probability identical to the one of $\mathcal{R}$. Algorithm $\mathcal{M}$ works as follows. Given $n + 1$ group elements $r_0, \ldots, r_n \in \mathbb{G}$, $\mathcal{M}$ launches $\mathcal{R}$ over r_0 and some arbitrary random tape. $\mathcal{M}$ then perfectly simulates at most n executions of the adversary $\mathcal{A}$ by using $r_1, \ldots, r_n$ and by making requests of discrete logarithms to oracle $\mathsf{DL_{OM}}$. If $\mathcal{R}$ outputs k_0, $\mathcal{M}$ uses its transcript information to retrieve the discrete logs k_j of the r_j's.

TRACING $\mathcal{R}$'S INTERNAL GROUP OPERATIONS. The reduction algorithm $\mathcal{R}$ takes as input a challenge discrete log instance $r_0 = g^{k_0}$ and is allowed to invoke n times the universal forger $\mathcal{A}$ with freely chosen public keys $y_i = g^{x_i}$, messages m_i and random tapes ϖ_i where $i = 1, \ldots, n$. For our meta-reduction $\mathcal{M}$ to work, however, we must dispose of a constructive way to recover the value of the x_i's from the one of $k_0 = \mathsf{dl}_g(r_0)$. This is where an additional mechanism is needed. We may either choose to dive $\mathcal{R}$ into the generic model to have access to its internal computations involving group elements, or more generally consider $\mathcal{R}$ to be algebraic and let $\mathcal{M}$ dispose of the code of $\mathcal{R}$ if necessary, *i.e.* have non black-box access to $\mathcal{R}$. In the sequel, we impose that $\mathcal{R}$ is algebraic, and provided that the code of $\mathcal{R}$ is polynomial in length, $\mathcal{M}$ is assumed to dispose of a polynomial time extraction procedure $\mathsf{Extract}(k_0, \mathtt{Transcript}) = (x_1, \ldots, x_n)$.

SIMULATION OF $\mathcal{A}$. The simulation of a universal forger $\mathcal{A}(y, m, \varpi)$ under a key-only attack is described as follows. $\mathtt{Transcript}$ and j are viewed as global variables initialized before $\mathcal{A}$ is executed for the first time.

1. Receive $(y, m, \varpi) \in \mathbb{G} \times \{0,1\}^{\star} \times \{0,1\}^{\star}$
2. Select $\delta \stackrel{\$}{\leftarrow} [0,1]$ uniformly at random
3. If $\delta > \varepsilon$ stop and output $\perp$
4. Else if $(y, m, \varpi) \mapsto (s, c) \in \mathtt{Transcript}$ for some signature (s, c), stop and output (s, c)
5. Else
   (a) Define $r = r_j$ and increment j by 1
   (b) Compute $c = H(m, r)$
   (c) Request the discrete log $s \leftarrow \mathsf{DL_{OM}}(ry^c)$
   (d) Append $(y, m, \varpi) \mapsto (s, c)$ to $\mathtt{Transcript}$
   (e) Output $\sigma = (s, c)$

DESCRIPTION OF $\mathcal{M}$. $\mathcal{M}$ takes the first group element $r_0 \in \mathbb{G}$, initializes $j = 1$ and $\mathtt{Transcript} = \emptyset$, and invokes $\mathcal{R}$ with input r_0 and arbitrary random tape. $\mathcal{M}$ then simulates the universal forger $\mathcal{A}$ as above, resulting in a perfect simulation. During simulation, $\mathcal{M}$ sends ℓ requests to oracle $\mathsf{DL_{OM}}$ for some $\ell \in [1, n]$ (therefore ℓ is the value of j after the n successive simulations of $\mathcal{A}$). Now assume $\mathcal{R}$ outputs $k_0 = \mathsf{dl}_g(r_0)$. $\mathcal{M}$ then uses its transcript information to extract

$$(x_1, \ldots, x_n) = \mathsf{Extract}(k_0, \mathtt{Transcript}) \, .$$

There are ℓ records of type $(y, m, \varpi) \mapsto (s, c)$ in Transcript. Then for $j \in [1, \ell]$, if the j-th record is of the form $(g^{x_i}, *, *) \mapsto (s, c)$ for some $i \in [1, n]$ then $\mathcal{M}$ computes $k_j = \mathsf{dl}_g(r_j) = s - c x_i \bmod q$. At this point, $\mathcal{M}$ knows $(k_0, k_1, \ldots, k_\ell)$. Now for $j = \ell+1$ to n, $\mathcal{M}$ directly requests $k_j = \mathsf{dl}_g(r_j)$ to $\mathsf{DL_{OM}}$. $\mathcal{M}$ then returns $(k_0, \ldots, k_\ell, k_{\ell+1}, \ldots, k_n)$, thereby succeeding in solving n-DL. This occurs with probability $\varepsilon'' = \varepsilon'$ and time $\tau'' = \tau' + \mathsf{poly}\left(\tau', |\mathcal{R}|, n, \mathsf{Time}(H), \log q\right)$. $\qquad\square$

5 Extension to the One-More Discrete Log Assumption

Theorem 2 shows that under the one-more discrete log assumption, no algebraic reduction exists that would reduce the discrete log problem to forging Schnorr signatures. This is a big step towards proving that coming up with forgeries is strictly easier than extracting discrete logs. One may ask whether a similar impossibility result extends to computational problems weaker than DL. We provide a positive answer to this question too by showing that if the one-more discrete log assumption holds, there can be no algebraic reduction from solving *any* one-more discrete log problem to forging signatures. In other words

Theorem 3. *Assume that the one-more discrete log assumption holds. Then*

$$t\text{-DL} \quad \not\Leftarrow_{\mathrm{ALG}} \quad \mathsf{UF\text{-}KOA}\left[\Sigma_{\mathrm{H}}\right]$$

for any integer $t \geq 0$.

Note that Theorem 3 contains Theorem 2 in the special case where $t = 0$. This shows that Schnorr signatures cannot be proven universally unforgeable under the one-more discrete log assumption with respect to an algebraic reduction, or that if they can, the one-more discrete log assumption does not hold over $\mathbb{G}$, thus rendering such a reduction useless. The following lemma captures this more precisely.

Lemma 2. *Assume there exists an algebraic reduction algorithm $\mathcal{R}$ that converts an (ε, τ)-universal forger $\mathcal{A}$ under a key-only attack into an (ε', τ')-solver for t-DL and assume that $\mathcal{R}$ executes $\mathcal{A}$ at most n times. Then there exists a meta-reduction algorithm $\mathcal{M}$ that solves $(t + n)$-DL with success probability $\varepsilon'' = \varepsilon'$ within time $\tau'' = \tau' + \mathsf{poly}\left(\tau', |\mathcal{R}|, t, n, \mathsf{Time}(H), \log q\right)$.*

Proof (of Lemma 2). The proof is very similar to the one of Lemma 1. We therefore avoid details and focus on the changes we apply to extend to the general case t-DL, $t \geq 0$. Again, from an algebraic reduction $\mathcal{R}$ as above, we construct $\mathcal{M}$ that solves $(t+n)$-DL with success probability identical to the one of $\mathcal{R}$.

EXTRACTION OF SECRET KEYS. The reduction algorithm $\mathcal{R}$ now takes as input a t-DL instance

$$\left(r_0 = g^{k_0}, r_1 = g^{k_1}, \ldots, r_t = g^{k_t}\right) \in \mathbb{G}^{t+1},$$

calls $\mathsf{DL_{OM}}$ up to t times and invokes at most n times the universal forger $\mathcal{A}$ with freely chosen public keys $y_i = g^{x_i}$, messages m_i and random tapes ϖ_i where $i = 1, \ldots, n$. Since $\mathcal{R}$ is algebraic and of polynomially bounded size, we dispose of a polynomial time extraction procedure $\mathsf{Extract}(k_0, k_1, \ldots, k_t, \mathtt{Transcript}) = (x_1, \ldots, x_n)$.

SIMULATION OF $\mathcal{A}$. The simulation of the universal forger $\mathcal{A}$ is identical to the one given in the previous section.

SIMULATION OF $\mathsf{DL_{OM}}$. Since $\mathcal{R}$ attempts to solve t-DL, we must allow $\mathcal{R}$ to send up to t requests to the discrete logarithm oracle $\mathsf{DL_{OM}}$. The meta-reduction $\mathcal{M}$ individually collects these requests, forwards them to $\mathsf{DL_{OM}}$ and sends the corresponding outputs back to $\mathcal{R}$. We may assume that $\mathcal{R}$ makes exactly t oracle calls since in the case when $\mathcal{R}$ sends strictly less than t requests during the game, $\mathcal{M}$ sends additional requests of discrete logs for randomly chosen group elements to $\mathsf{DL_{OM}}$ on behalf of $\mathcal{R}$. This simulation is obviously perfect.

OVERALL DESCRIPTION OF $\mathcal{M}$. $\mathcal{M}$ takes its first $t+1$ group elements $(r_0, \ldots, r_t)$ among $(r_0, \ldots, r_{t+n})$, initializes $\mathtt{Transcript} = \emptyset$ and $j = 1$, and invokes $\mathcal{R}$ with input $(r_0, \ldots, r_t)$ and arbitrary random tape. $\mathcal{M}$ then simulates the universal forger $\mathcal{A}$ and discrete log oracle $\mathsf{DL_{OM}}$ as above, resulting in a perfect simulation. During simulation, $\mathcal{M}$ sends $t + \ell$ requests to $\mathsf{DL_{OM}}$ for some $\ell \in [1, n]$. Now assume $\mathcal{R}$ succeeds and outputs

$$k_0 = \mathsf{dl}_g(r_0), k_1 = \mathsf{dl}_g(r_1), \ldots, k_t = \mathsf{dl}_g(r_t) .$$

$\mathcal{M}$ then uses its transcript information to extract

$$(x_1, \ldots, x_n) = \mathsf{Extract}(k_0, \ldots, k_t, \mathtt{Transcript}) .$$

There are ℓ records of type $(y, m, \varpi) \mapsto (s, c)$ in $\mathtt{Transcript}$. Then for $j \in [1, \ell]$, if the j-th record is of the form $(g^{x_i}, *, *) \mapsto (s, c)$ for some $i \in [1, n]$ then $\mathcal{M}$ computes $k_{t+j} = \mathsf{dl}_g(r_{t+j}) = s - c x_i \bmod q$. Thus $\mathcal{M}$ recovers $(k_{t+1}, \ldots, k_{t+\ell})$. Now for $j = t + \ell + 1$ to n, $\mathcal{M}$ directly requests $k_j = \mathsf{dl}_g(r_j)$ to $\mathsf{DL_{OM}}$. Then $\mathcal{M}$ returns

$$\underbrace{(k_0, k_1, \ldots, k_t)}_{\text{ouput by } \mathcal{R}} \cup \underbrace{(k_{t+1}, \ldots, k_{t+\ell})}_{\text{extracted by } \mathcal{M}} \cup \underbrace{(k_{t+\ell+1}, \ldots, k_{t+n})}_{\text{requested to } \mathsf{DL_{OM}}} = (k_0, \ldots, k_{t+n}) ,$$

thereby succeeding in solving $(t + n)$-DL. This occurs with probability $\varepsilon'' = \varepsilon'$ and execution time $\tau'' = \tau' + \mathsf{poly}(\tau', |\mathcal{R}|, t, n, \mathsf{Time}(H), \log q)$. □

SUMMARY. Because of the relations

$$\mathsf{EF\text{-}CMA}\,[\Sigma_H] \Leftarrow \{\, \mathsf{EF\text{-}KOA}\,[\Sigma_H], \mathsf{UF\text{-}CMA}\,[\Sigma_H] \,\} \Leftarrow \mathsf{UF\text{-}KOA}\,[\Sigma_H] ,$$

our impossibility results readily extend to forgeries of any kind, under any attack model. We summarize our results (also displayed on Figure 2), stating our positive and negative security proofs for Schnorr signatures assuming the one-more discrete log assumption holds:

Goal vs. Atk	Key-Only Attacks	Chosen-Message Attacks
Forgeries	$\not\equiv_{\mathrm{ALG}}$ DL and even $\not\equiv_{\mathrm{ALG}} t$-DL for $t > 0$	
Breakability	$\equiv$ DL	$\Rightarrow q_s$-DL

Fig. 2. Our results for Schnorr's signature scheme Σ_H are shown in boxes. In particular, universal and existential forgeries under any kind of attack cannot be proven equivalent to the discrete log problem via an algebraic reduction.

Theorem 1: Schnorr's scheme is unbreakable under chosen-message attacks.

Theorems 2 and 3: Universal and existential forgeries under any kind of attack cannot be proven secure under the discrete log assumption or even the one-more discrete log assumption with respect to an algebraic reduction.

6   Applications to Other Signature Schemes

We extend our results to various signature schemes, adapting our meta-reduction-based proof technique to comply with the schemes' inner design.

6.1   Guillou-Quisquater

GQ signatures were suggested by Guillou and Quisquater in [15]. Among other properties, GQ is a Fiat-Shamir-transformed signature scheme based on RSA and supports identity-based public keys.

SCHEME PARAMETERS AND KEY GENERATION. Let p, q be two large primes, set $n = pq$ and choose randomly v such that $\gcd(v, \phi(n)) = 1$. The public parameters are (n, v) as well as a hash function $H : \{0, 1\}^\star \mapsto \mathbb{Z}_v$. Now the signer chooses a secret key $x \xleftarrow{\$} \mathbb{Z}_n$. The related public key is $y = x^{-v} \bmod n$.

SIGNATURE GENERATION AND VERIFICATION. Given a message m, the signer selects $k \xleftarrow{\$} \mathbb{Z}_n$, computes $r = k^v \bmod n$, $c = H(m, r)$ and $s = kx^c \bmod n$. The signature is $\sigma = (s, c)$. To verify the signature, check whether $H(m, s^v y^c \bmod n) = c$

Because of their similarity with Schnorr, GQ signatures fit our impossibility proofs quite well. However the primitive computational problem here is not DL but rather extracting v-th roots modulo n, which we denote of course by RSA. The one-more version of RSA is easily defined with the help of an oracle RSA$_{\mathsf{OM}}$ extracting the v-th root of its argument [3]. Solving n-RSA thus consists in finding the v-th root of $n + 1$ elements of $\mathbb{Z}_n$ given no more than n invocations of RSA$_{\mathsf{OM}}$. The one-more RSA assumption says that n-RSA is intractable for $n \geq 1$.

Theorem 4. *Assume the one-more RSA assumption holds. Then (i) GQ is unbreakable under chosen-message attacks. (ii) Universal and existential forgeries under any attack cannot be proven secure under the RSA assumption or the one-more RSA assumption with respect to an algebraic reduction.*

Proof (Sketch). We rely on the same proof technique as in the proofs of Theorems 1, 2 and 3. Here, however, the simulation of the UF-KOA adversary $\mathcal{A}$ must be slightly reformulated. An overall description of our meta-reduction $\mathcal{M}$ is as follows. The reduction algorithm $\mathcal{R}$ takes as input a t-RSA instance

$$(r_0 = k_0^v \bmod n, r_1 = k_1^v \bmod n, \ldots, r_t = k_t^v \bmod n) \in \mathbb{Z}_n^{t+1} \,,$$

calls $\mathsf{RSA_{OM}}$ up to t times and calls the forger $\mathcal{A}$ at most n times with public keys $y_i = x_i^{-v} \bmod n$, messages m_i and random tapes ϖ_i where $i = 1, \ldots, n$. Since $\mathcal{R}$ is algebraic, $\mathcal{M}$ is assumed to dispose of a polynomial time extraction procedure $\mathsf{Extract}(k_0, k_1, \ldots, k_t, \mathtt{Transcript}) = (x_1, \ldots, x_n)$. Now when simulating $\mathcal{A}(y, m, \varpi)$ for new inputs (y, m, ϖ), if $\mathcal{M}$ must compute a forgery then $\mathcal{M}$ takes $r = r_j$, computes $c = H(m, r)$ and requests the v-th root $s \leftarrow \mathsf{RSA_{OM}}(ry^{-c} \bmod n)$. The simulation is perfect. After recovering $(x_1, \ldots, x_n)$ from $(k_0, \ldots, k_t)$, $\mathcal{M}$ consults its transcript and if the j-th entry is $(x_i^{-v} \bmod n, *, *) \mapsto (s, c)$ for some i then $\mathcal{M}$ computes $k_{t+j} = sx_i^c = \sqrt[v]{r_{t+j}} \bmod n$. The unused inputs $r_{t+\ell+1}, \ldots, r_{t+n}$ are sent by $\mathcal{M}$ to $\mathsf{RSA_{OM}}$ to retrieve their v-th root directly. Following this slightly modified description of $\mathcal{M}$, one gets as before $\varepsilon'' = \varepsilon'$ and $\tau'' = \tau' + \mathsf{poly}(\tau', |\mathcal{R}|, t, n, \mathsf{Time}(H), \log q)$. $\qquad\square$

6.2   DSA, ECDSA and Generic DSA

DSA is a signature scheme standardized by the NIST in 1991 [9]. The original version of DSA is based on the discrete log problem over the subgroup of $\mathbb{Z}_p^*$ of prime order $q|p-1$. ECDSA, standardized as well [1], presents the same structure but is defined over a prime-order subgroup of an elliptic curve. We consider here their generalization to arbitrary prime-order groups as suggested by Brown in [7].

SCHEME PARAMETERS AND KEY GENERATION. Again, $\mathbb{G} = \langle g \rangle$ denotes a group of prime order q. The public parameters are $(\mathbb{G}, g)$, a function $G : \mathbb{G} \mapsto \mathbb{Z}_q$ and a hash function $H : \{0, 1\}^* \mapsto \mathbb{Z}_q$. The signer chooses a secret key $x \xleftarrow{\$} \mathbb{Z}_q$. The related public key is $y = g^x \in \mathbb{G}$.

SIGNATURE GENERATION AND VERIFICATION. Given a message m, the signer selects $k \xleftarrow{\$} \mathbb{Z}_q^*$, computes $r = g^k$, $\rho = G(r)$, $u = H(m)$ and $s = k^{-1}(u + \rho x) \bmod q$. The signature is $\sigma = (\rho, s)$. To verify the signature, check whether $G\left(g^{H(m)/s} \cdot y^{\rho/s}\right) = \rho$.

Note that the original DSA corresponds to the case where $\mathbb{G} = \left(\mathbb{Z}_p^*\right)^{(p-1)/q}$, $|q| = 160$, $H = \mathrm{SHA}\text{-}1$ and $G(r) = r \bmod q$. Let E be an elliptic curve group over a finite field admitting an element P of prime order q with $|q| = 160$. ECDSA is obtained with $g = P$, $\mathbb{G} = \langle g \rangle$, $H = \mathrm{SHA}\text{-}1$ and $G(r) = x_r \bmod q$ where x_r is an integer representation of the x-coordinate of point r.

Before stating our security results, we define a variant of the one-more discrete log problem $n\text{-DL}$ as follows. $n\text{-DL}^*$ consists in computing the discrete logs with respect to a fixed base g of $n + 1$ group elements with bounded (to n) access to a discrete log oracle $\mathsf{DL_{OM}^*}$. Unlike $\mathsf{DL_{OM}}$ which was limited to the fixed base g, $\mathsf{DL_{OM}^*}$ provides discrete logarithms with respect to any base $h \in \mathbb{G}$ meaning that $\mathsf{DL}^\star_{\mathsf{OM}}(h^\alpha, h)$ returns α for any $h \in \mathbb{G}$. Although $0\text{-}\mathsf{DL}^\star \equiv \mathsf{DL} \equiv 0\text{-}\mathsf{DL}$, one only has in the general[5] case $n\text{-}\mathsf{DL}^\star \Leftarrow n\text{-}\mathsf{DL}$ for $n \geq 1$. The *one-more free-base discrete log assumption* says that $n\text{-}\mathsf{DL}^\star$ is intractable for $n \geq 1$.

Theorem 5. *Assume the one-more free-base discrete log assumption holds. Then (i) Generic DSA is unbreakable under chosen-message attacks. (ii) Universal and existential forgeries under any attack cannot be proven secure under the discrete log assumption or the one-more free-base discrete log assumption with respect to an algebraic reduction.*

Proof (Sketch). We use the same proof technique as for Theorem 1 and Lemmas 1 and 2. What we are after is a reduction $q_s\text{-}\mathsf{DL}^\star \Leftarrow \mathsf{BK\text{-}CMA}\,[\text{Generic-DSA}]$ as well as a means to simulate an $\mathsf{UF\text{-}KOA}$ adversary $\mathcal{A}$ leading to a meta-reduction $\mathcal{M}$ such that if $t\text{-}\mathsf{DL}^\star \Leftarrow_\mathcal{R} \mathsf{UF\text{-}KOA}\,[\text{Generic-DSA}]$ where $\mathcal{R}$ is limited to n executions of $\mathsf{UF\text{-}KOA}\,[\text{Generic-DSA}]$, then $n\text{-}\mathsf{DL}^\star \Leftarrow_\mathcal{M} \mathcal{R}$. We first have to show how to simulate a signing oracle without knowing the secret key. Remembering that the simulator is given group elements $\{r_j\}$ for $j \in [1, q_s]$ or $[t{+}1, t{+}n]$, the signature simulation is as follows. For a given public key $y = g^x \in \mathbb{G}$ and a message m, we define $r = r_j$ and compute $\rho = G(r)$ and $u = H(m)$. We then invoke $\mathsf{DL}^\star_{\mathsf{OM}}$ to get

$$s = \mathsf{DL}^\star_{\mathsf{OM}}\left(g^u \cdot y^\rho, r\right) \ .$$

It is easy to see that if we write $r = g^k$ then s conforms to the equation $s = k^{-1}(u + \rho x) \bmod q$. The simulator then outputs $\sigma = (\rho, s)$. The simulation is obviously perfect. We now have to show how to recover $k_j = \mathsf{dl}_g(r_j)$ from *a)* either the list of secret keys $\{x_i\}$ given to simulation number $i \in [1, q_s]$ or $[1, n]$ *b)* or from the outputs $k_0, \ldots, k_t$ of $\mathcal{R}$. Since $\mathcal{R}$ is algebraic, the key extraction procedure using $\mathtt{Transcript}$ leads case *b)* to case *a)*. Therefore, we are left with the task of recovering k_j from x_i and the transcript of our simulations. This is easily done by inverting the signature formula to recover $k_j = s^{-1}(u + \rho x_i) \bmod q$. $\quad\square$

6.3   KCDSA and Trusted ElGamal Signatures Type I

DSA and DSA-like signature schemes have been extended in many ways. We focus on a generalization called TEGTSS-I put forward by Brickell *et al.* in [6]. This extension contains the korean standard KCDSA [17] as a particular case.

SCHEME PARAMETERS AND KEY GENERATION. Let $\mathbb{G} = \langle g \rangle$ be a group of prime order q. Now define three functions $f_1 : \mathbb{Z}_q^4 \mapsto \mathbb{Z}_q$, $f_2 : \mathbb{Z}_q^3 \mapsto \mathbb{Z}_q$ and $f_3 : \mathbb{Z}_q^3 \mapsto \mathbb{Z}_q$ such that for any integers $k, x, u, \rho \in \mathbb{Z}_q$,

$$\text{if } s = f_1(k, x, u, \rho) \text{ then } f_2(s, u, \rho) + x f_3(s, u, \rho) \equiv k \mod q \ .$$

The public parameters are $(\mathbb{G}, g, f_1, f_2, f_3)$, a function $G : \mathbb{G} \mapsto \mathbb{Z}_q$ and a hash function $H : \{0,1\}^\star \mapsto \mathbb{Z}_q$. The signer chooses a secret key $x \xleftarrow{\$} \mathbb{Z}_q$. The related public key is $y = g^x \in \mathbb{G}$.

---

[5] The converse is unknown.

SIGNATURE GENERATION AND VERIFICATION. Given a message m, the signer selects $k \xleftarrow{\$} \mathbb{Z}_q^*$, computes $r = g^k$, $\rho = G(r)$, $u = H(m)$ and $s = f_1(k, x, u, \rho)$. The signature is $\sigma = (\rho, s)$. To verify the signature, compute $u = H(m)$, $\alpha = f_2(s, u, \rho)$, $\beta = f_3(s, u, \rho)$ and check whether $G\left(g^\alpha \cdot y^\beta\right) = \rho$.

KCDSA fulfils this description where $\mathbb{G} = \left(\mathbb{Z}_p^*\right)^{(p-1)/q} = \langle g \rangle$, H and G are hash functions mapping $\mathbb{Z}_p$ to $\mathbb{Z}_q$, and functions f_1, f_2, f_3 are defined by

$$f_1(k, x, u, \rho) = (k - u \oplus \rho)/x \mod q ,$$
$$f_2(s, u, \rho) = u \oplus \rho ,$$
$$f_3(s, u, \rho) = s .$$

Before stating any security property of TEGTSS-I signatures, we leave as an exercise to the reader to prove the following property.

Claim. Let f_1, f_2, f_3 be functions as above. Then there exist efficiently computable functions $\delta_1, \delta_2, \delta_3, \delta_4$ and ϵ mapping $\mathbb{Z}_q^2$ to $\mathbb{Z}_q$ and such that $\delta_1(u, \rho) \neq 0$, $\delta_3(u, \rho) \cdot \delta_4(u, \rho) \neq 0$, $\epsilon(u, \rho) \neq 0$ for any $u, \rho \in \mathbb{Z}_q$ and

$$f_1(k, x, u, \rho) = \left(\frac{\delta_1(u, \rho)k + \delta_2(u, \rho)}{\delta_3(u, \rho)x + \delta_4(u, \rho)}\right)^{\frac{1}{\epsilon(u, \rho)}} , \tag{1}$$

$$f_2(s, u, \rho) = \frac{\delta_4(u, \rho)s^{\epsilon(u, \rho)} - \delta_2(u, \rho)}{\delta_1(u, \rho)} , \tag{2}$$

$$f_3(s, u, \rho) = \frac{\delta_3(u, \rho)s^{\epsilon(u, \rho)}}{\delta_1(u, \rho)} , \tag{3}$$

where all evaluations are modulo q.

As an illustration, KCDSA yields $\delta_1(u, \rho) = 1$, $\delta_2(u, \rho) = -u \oplus \rho$, $\delta_3(u, \rho) = 1$, $\delta_4(u, \rho) = 0$ and $\epsilon(u, \rho) = 1$. Note that DSA is also a particular case if we set $\delta_1(u, \rho) = 1$, $\delta_2(u, \rho) = 0$, $\delta_3(u, \rho) = \rho$, $\delta_4(u, \rho) = u$ and $\epsilon(u, \rho) = -1$. We now state our security results. As for Generic DSA, we rely on n-DL^* and the one-more free-base discrete log assumption:

Theorem 6. *Let Σ be a signature scheme of type TEGTSS-I. Assume the one-more free-base discrete log assumption holds. Then (i) Σ is unbreakable under chosen-message attacks. (ii) Universal and existential forgeries under any attack cannot be proven secure under the discrete log assumption or the one-more free-base discrete log assumption with respect to an algebraic reduction.*

Proof (Sketch). Here again, we make use of the proofs of Theorem 1, Lemmas 1 and 2. As discussed earlier, it is necessary to show how to simulate a signing oracle without knowing the secret key. Recall the simulator is given group elements $\{r_j\}$ for $j \in [1, q_s]$ or $[t+1, t+n]$. Now the signature simulation is as follows. For a given public key $y = g^x \in \mathbb{G}$ and a message m, we define $r = r_j$ and compute

$\rho = G(r)$ and $u = H(m)$. Using our claim above, we compute $\delta_i = \delta_i(u, \rho)$ for $i \in [1, 4]$ and then invoke $\mathsf{DL}^\star_{\mathsf{OM}}$ to get

$$s = \left(\mathsf{DL}^\star_{\mathsf{OM}} \left(g^{\delta_4(u,\rho)} \cdot y^{\delta_3(u,\rho)}, r^{\delta_1(u,\rho)} \cdot g^{\delta_2(u,\rho)} \right) \right)^{\frac{1}{\epsilon(u,\rho)}} .$$

Now writing $r = g^k$, we easily see that s conforms to the signature equation $s = f_1(k, x, u, \rho) \bmod q$. The simulator then outputs $\sigma = (\rho, s)$ and the simulation is perfect. Following the same argument as in the proof of Theorem 5, we now have to show how to recover k_j from x_i and the transcript of our simulations. This directly follows from the definition of TEGTSS-I since $k_j = f_2(s, u, \rho) + x_i \cdot f_3(s, u, \rho) \bmod q$. □

6.4 Trusted ElGamal Signatures Type II

Trusted ElGamal signatures of type II form another family of discrete-log-based signatures and were also suggested by Brickell *et al.* in [6]. TEGTSS-II are similar to TEGTSS-I in that functions f_1, f_2, f_3 are defined along the same lines and the generation of the public parameters and user keys is identical.

SIGNATURE GENERATION AND VERIFICATION. Given a message m, the signer selects $k \xleftarrow{\$} \mathbb{Z}_q^*$, computes $r = g^k$, $\rho = G(r)$, $u = H(m, \rho)$ and $s = f_1(k, x, u, \rho)$. The signature is $\sigma = (\rho, s)$. To verify the signature, compute $u = H(m, \rho)$, $\alpha = f_2(s, u, \rho)$, $\beta = f_3(s, u, \rho)$ and check whether $G(g^\alpha \cdot y^\beta) = \rho$.

Therefore, TEGTSS-II signatures define $u = H(m, \rho)$ instead of $u = H(m)$ while generating or verifying the signature. It is straightforward that Theorem 6 still applies in this case. The proof is identical except that the signature simulator now defines $r = r_j$ and computes $\rho = G(r)$ and $u = H(m, \rho)$.

6.5 ElGamal and Meta-ElGamal Signatures

ElGamal signatures were suggested in 1984 [12] and generalized later by Horster, Michels and Petersen [16]. We consider here a similar generalization to arbitrary prime-order groups.

SCHEME PARAMETERS AND KEY GENERATION. Let $\mathbb{G} = \langle g \rangle$ be a group of prime order q. Define three functions $F_1, F_2, F_3 : \mathbb{G} \times \{0, 1\}^* \times \mathbb{Z}_q$ such that $F_i(r, m, s)$ is linear in s for $i \in [1, 3]$. F_1, F_2 and F_3 may involve arbitrarily many hash functions. The public parameters are $(\mathbb{G}, g, F_1, F_2, F_3)$. The signer selects a secret key $x \xleftarrow{\$} \mathbb{Z}_q$. The public key is $y = g^x \in \mathbb{G}$.

SIGNATURE GENERATION AND VERIFICATION. Given a message m, the signer selects $k \xleftarrow{\$} \mathbb{Z}_q^*$, computes $r = g^k$ and solves the linear equation

$$F_1(r, m, s) \equiv x \cdot F_2(r, m, s) + k \cdot F_3(r, m, s) \mod q \tag{4}$$

which solution is some $s \in \mathbb{Z}_q$. The signature is then $\sigma = (r, s) \in \mathbb{G} \times \mathbb{Z}_q$. To verify the signature, check whether

$$g^{F_1(r,m,s)} = y^{F_2(r,m,s)} \cdot r^{F_3(r,m,s)} .$$

Original ElGamal signatures define $\mathbb{G}$ as the subgroup of order $q|p-1$ of $\mathbb{Z}_p^*$, $F_1(r, m, s) = m$ or for long messages $F_1(r, m, s) = H(m)$ where H is a hash function mapping strings to $\mathbb{Z}_q$, $F_2(r, m, s) = r \bmod q$ and $F_3(r, m, s) = s$. We now give our results for any Meta-ElGamal scheme *i.e.* for any choice of F_1, F_2, F_3 as above. We still rely on n-DL* and the one-more free-base discrete log assumption.

Theorem 7. *Let Σ be a Meta-ElGamal signature scheme. Assume the one-more free-base discrete log assumption holds. Then (i) Σ is unbreakable under chosen-message attacks. (ii) Universal and existential forgeries under any attack cannot be proven secure under the discrete log assumption or the one-more free-base discrete log assumption with respect to an algebraic reduction.*

Proof (Sketch). As discussed above, it is enough to show how to simulate a signing oracle without knowing the secret key and recover k_j from x afterwards. Recalling that the simulator is given group elements $\{r_j\}$ for $j \in [1, q_s]$ or $[t + 1, t+n]$, the signature simulation is as follows. For a given public key $y = g^x \in \mathbb{G}$ and a message m, we define $r = r_j$ and compute (as functions of m and r) the coefficients a_1, b_1, a_2, b_2, a_3 and b_3 such that $F_i(r, m, s) = a_i s + b_i$ for $i \in [1, 3]$. We then call DL$^\star_{\mathsf{OM}}$ to get

$$s = \mathsf{DL}^\star_{\mathsf{OM}} \left(g^{a_1} y^{-a_2} r^{-a_3}, g^{-b_1} y^{b_2} r^{b_3} \right) .$$

Obviously, s conforms to the verification equation. The simulator then outputs $\sigma = (r, s)$ and the simulation is perfect. Now when $\mathcal{R}$ or $\mathcal{M}$ knows all the values of x, the transcript of the simulation involving r_j leads to specific values for (r, m, s). Then k_j is recovered as the unique solution in k of the signature equation Eq. 4.   □

7 Impossibility Results in the Random Oracle Model

All known reductions attesting the unforgeability of Fiat-Shamir-transformed signatures in the random oracle model lead to a loss factor close to q_H in terms of execution time or success probability [19]. Since a reasonable bound on the number of possible hash queries is around $q_H = 2^{80}$, this loss definitely makes these reductions loose, and subsequently imply larger keys and lowered performances. There exists no proof that this loss factor is necessary. The following theorem states however, that if the one-more discrete logarithm assumption holds then each and every algebraic reduction from computing the discrete logarithm to forging Schnorr signatures must lose at least a factor $\sqrt{q_H}$.

We note that a similar result can be extended to the one-more discrete log problems. Also, although we do not extend our work further in this direction, it is easily seen that this result applies to the random-oracle security of other signature schemes as well. We start by stating a few statistical facts.

Lemma 3 (Birthday paradox). *We consider an experiment in which n objects are drawn uniformly at random from a set of m elements. Then,*

1. *the probability of selecting the same element twice is*

$$P(m, n) = 1 - \frac{m(m-1)\ldots(m-n+1)}{m^n}.$$

2. *when $n = O(\sqrt{m})$ and as $m \to \infty$, one gets*

$$P(m, n) \to 1 - \exp\left(-\frac{n(n-1)}{2m} + O\left(\frac{1}{\sqrt{m}}\right)\right) \simeq 1 - \exp\left(-\frac{n^2}{2m}\right).$$

Lemma 4. *Let q be a rational prime number, then*

$$|\mathrm{GL}_n(\mathbb{F}_q)| = (q^n - 1)(q^n - q)(q^n - q^2)\ldots(q^n - q^{n-1}).$$

Therefore, the probability $z(n, q)$ that an $n \times n$ matrix picked at random is non-invertible is

$$z(n, q) = 1 - \frac{(q^n - 1)(q^n - q)(q^n - q^2)\ldots(q^n - q^{n-1})}{q^{n^2}} \leq \frac{n}{q}.$$

Theorem 8. *Assume there exists an algebraic reduction algorithm $\mathcal{R}$ that converts an (ε, τ, q_H)-universal forger $\mathcal{A}$ under a key-only attack in the random oracle into an (ε', τ')-solver for the discrete logarithm and assume that $\mathcal{R}$ executes $\mathcal{A}$ at most n times. Then there exists a probabilistic algorithm $\mathcal{M}$ that solves n-DL with success probability $\varepsilon'' \geq \varepsilon' \cdot \exp\left(-\frac{n^2}{2q_H}\right) \cdot \left(1 - \frac{n}{q}\right)$ within time $\tau'' = \tau' + \mathsf{poly}\,(\tau', |\mathcal{R}|, n, q_H, \log q)$.*

Proof. Assuming the existence of an algebraic reduction $\mathcal{R}$ as above, we construct a meta-reduction $\mathcal{M}$ that solves n-DL. $\mathcal{R}$ takes as input a challenge discrete log instance $r_0 = g^{k_0}$ and is allowed to invoke n times the universal forger $\mathcal{A}$ with freely chosen public keys $y_i = g^{x_i}$, messages m_i and random tapes ϖ_i where $i = 1, \ldots, n$. Without loss of generality, we may assume that the n invocations of $\mathcal{R}$, are pairwise distinct *i.e.* that two distinct executions of $\mathcal{A}$ differ in the value of the public key and/or the random tape, and/or at least one value returned by the random oracle H of $\mathcal{R}$.

SIMULATION OF $\mathcal{A}$. $\mathcal{M}$ attempts to simulate at most n executions of the adversary $\mathcal{A}$ by using the vector of group elements $r = (r_1, \ldots, r_n)$ and by making requests to the discrete-log oracle $\mathsf{DL_{OM}}$. More specifically, the i-th invocation of $\mathcal{A}$ is simulated as follows:

1. Receive $(y_i, m_i, \varpi_i) \in \mathbb{G} \times \{0, 1\}^\star \times \{0, 1\}^\star$
2. For $h \in [1, q_H]$

(a) Randomly select $\boldsymbol{\alpha}_h \xleftarrow{\$} (\mathbb{Z}_q)^n$

(b) Query H to get $c_h = H(m_i, \boldsymbol{r}^{\boldsymbol{\alpha}_h})$

3. Randomly select $\ell_i \xleftarrow{\$} [1, q_H]$

(a) Set $c_i \leftarrow c_{\ell_i}$ and $\beta_i \leftarrow \alpha_{\ell_i}$

(b) Request $s_i \leftarrow \mathsf{DL_{OM}} \left(\boldsymbol{r}^{\beta_i} \cdot y_i^{c_i} \right)$

(c) Append $(y_i, m_i, \varpi_i) \mapsto (s_i, c_i)$ and (ℓ_i, β_i) to `Transcript`

4. Pick at random $\delta \in [0, 1]$

5. If $\delta > \varepsilon$ return $\perp$

6. Else return $\sigma_i = (s_i, c_i)$

Here, if $\boldsymbol{a} = (a_1, \ldots, a_w)$ and $\boldsymbol{b} = (b_1, \ldots, b_w)$ then $\boldsymbol{a}^{\boldsymbol{b}}$ stands for $\prod_{\kappa=1}^{w} a_\kappa^{b_\kappa}$. Note that all random selections made by $\mathcal{A}$ are in fact pseudo-random in ϖ_i and all hash values c_h defined by H when the selection takes place.

EXTRACTION OF DISCRETE LOGS. Again, we assume that $\mathcal{M}$ disposes of a polynomial time extraction procedure $\mathsf{Extract}(k_0, \mathtt{Transcript}) = (x_1, \ldots, x_n)$ i.e. we consider $\mathcal{R}$ to be algebraic. Therefore, if $\mathcal{R}$ outputs k_0, $\mathcal{M}$ uses its transcript information to retrieve the discrete logs x_i of the y_i's. Now $\mathcal{M}$ attempts to solve over $\mathbb{Z}_q$ the linear system

$$\begin{cases} \beta_1 \cdot \boldsymbol{k} \equiv s_1 - c_1 \cdot x_1 \mod q \\ \quad \vdots \\ \beta_n \cdot \boldsymbol{k} \equiv s_n - c_n \cdot x_n \mod q \, , \end{cases}$$

where the unknowns are $\boldsymbol{k} = (k_1, \ldots, k_n)$ and $\boldsymbol{a} \cdot \boldsymbol{b}$ denotes the dot product of vectors. The solution $\boldsymbol{k}$ is easily found using linear algebra as soon as vectors $\beta_1, \ldots, \beta_n$ are linearly independent. Two mutually exclusive cases may occur.

1. $\forall\, i, j \in [1, n]$ with $i \neq j$, one has $\ell_i \neq \ell_j$. Then by Lemma 4, we get

$$\Pr\left[\det(\beta_1, \ldots, \beta_n) = 0\right] = z(n, q) \, .$$

Then with probability $1 - z(n, q)$, $\mathcal{M}$ recovers $\boldsymbol{k}$ and succeeds in solving n-DL.

2. $\exists\, i, j \in [1, n]$ with $i \neq j$ such that $\ell_i = \ell_j$. Then the reduction $\mathcal{M}$ may fail because it might be the case that $\beta_i = \beta_j$ while $s_i - c_i x_i \neq s_j - c_j x_j \mod q$ resulting in that the system above is not solvable. The probability of this event is unknown and depends on how $\mathcal{R}$ modified its simulation of H between two executions of $\mathcal{A}$. Since distinct executions of $\mathcal{A}$ are not identical and the values of the ℓ_i's are picked pseudo-randomly after all H queries have been made, we invoke Lemma 3 to see that a collision $\ell_i = \ell_j$ occurs with probability

$$\Pr\left[\exists\, i, j \in [1, n], \ell_i = \ell_j\right] = P(q_H, n) \, .$$

Since $\Pr[\mathcal{M} \text{ fails}] \leq \Pr[\exists\, i, j \in [1, n], \ell_i = \ell_j]$, noting ε'' the success probability of $\mathcal{M}$, we finally get

$$\varepsilon'' \geq \varepsilon' \cdot (1 - P(q_H, n)) \cdot (1 - z(n, q)) \approx \varepsilon' \cdot \exp\left(-\frac{n^2}{2q_H}\right) \cdot \left(1 - \frac{n}{q}\right).$$

The execution time of $\mathcal{M}$ is upper-bounded by $\tau' + \mathsf{poly}\,(\tau', |\mathcal{R}|, n, q_H, \log q)$.   □

Our result can be interpreted as follows. When n is smaller than $\sqrt{q_H}$, the ratio $\varepsilon''/\varepsilon'$ remains negligibly close to 1 and the algebraic reduction algorithm $\mathcal{R}$ cannot exist if n-DL is intractable over $\mathbb{G}$. However when $n \gg \sqrt{q_H}$, the ratio $\varepsilon''/\varepsilon'$ becomes rapidly negligibly close to 0 as n increases, allowing $\mathcal{R}$ to exist in the sense that having a substantial ε' does not lead us to solve n-DL with substantial success probability anymore.

8   Conclusion

We believe that our results pose new challenging questions about the standard-model security of common signature schemes. Focusing specifically on Schnorr's scheme, one might wonder what security level is actually reached in real life, as DL cannot be at reach of a *humanly conceivable* reduction. Could Schnorr signatures be proven secure under the CDH or DDH assumption? Can one prove a similar separation with these assumptions? What can be said in this regard about other signature schemes like ElGamal, DSA, GQ, etc. ?

Concerning the random oracle model, we leave it as an open problem to find a more efficient meta-reduction $\mathcal{M}$ that is, to come up with a proof that a factor close to q_H must be lost in any random-oracle-based algebraic reduction $\mathcal{R}$.

Acknowledgement

We thank the anonymous reviewers for their valuable feedback. The work described in this document has been financially supported by the European Commission through the IST Program under Contract IST-2002-507932 ECRYPT.

References

1. ANSI X9.62, *Public-Key fryptography for the financial services industry: the elliptic curve digital standard algorithm (ECDSA)*, American National Standards Institute, 1999.
2. M. Bellare, A. Boldyreva and A. Palacio. *An Un-Instantiable Random-Oracle-Model Scheme for a Hybrid-Encryption Problem*. Advances in Cryptology - Eurocrypt 2004, LNCS vol. 3027, 2004.
3. M. Bellare, C. Namprempre, D. Pointcheval, and M. Semanko, *The One-More-RSA-Inversion Problems and the security of Chaum's Blind Signature Scheme*. J. Cryptology **16** (2003), no. 3, 185–215.

4. M. Bellare and A. Palacio, *GQ and Schnorr Identification Schemes: Proofs of Security against Impersonation under Active and Concurrent Attacks*. Advances in Cryptology - CRYPTO 2002, LNCS vol. 2442, Springer, 2002, pp. 162–177.

5. D. Boneh and R. Venkatesan, *Breaking RSA may not be equivalent to factoring*. Advances in Cryptology - EUROCRYPT 1998, LNCS vol. 1233, Springer, 1998, pp. 59–71.

6. E. Brickell, D. Pointcheval, S. Vaudenay and M. Yung, *Design Validations for discrete logarithm based signature schemes*. PUBLICK KEY CONFERENCE 2000, LNCS vol. 1751, Springer, 2000, pp. 276–292.

7. D. R. L. Brown, *Generic Groups, Collision Resistance and ECDSA*, Des. Codes Cryptography **35** (2005), 119–152.

8. R. Canetti, O. Goldreich, and S. Halevi, *The Random Oracle Methodology, Revisited*. J. Assoc. Comput. Mach. **51** (2004), no. 4, 557–594.

9. FIPS 186. *Digital Signature Standard, Federal Information Processing Standards Publication 186*. US Department of Commerce/NIST, National Technical Information Service, Springfield, Virginia, 1994.

10. A. Dent, *Adapting the weaknesses of the random oracle model to the generic model*. Advances in Cryptology – ASIACRYPT 2002, LNCS vol. 2501, Springer, 2002, pp. 100–109.

11. Y. Dodis and L. Reyzin, *On the Power of Claw-Free Permutations*. Third Conference on Security in Communication Networks, SCN 2002, LNCS vol. 2576, Springer, 2003, pp. 55–73.

12. T. EL GAMAL. *A Public Key Cryptosystem and a Signature Scheme Based on Discrete Logarithms*. IEEE Transactions on Information Theory, vol. IT–31, no. 4, pp. 469–472, 1985.

13. A. Fiat and A. Shamir, *How to Prove Yourself: Practical Solutions to Identification and Signature Problems*. Advances in Cryptology - CRYPTO 1986, LNCS vol. 263, Springer, 1987, pp. 186–194.

14. S. Goldwasser and Y. Tauman, *On the (In)security of the Fiat-Shamir Paradigm*. FOCS 2003, IEEE Computer Society, 2003, pp. 102–122.

15. L. C. Guillou and J.-J. Quisquater, *A "Paradoxical" Identity-Based Signature Scheme Resulting from Zero-Knowledge*. Advances in Cryptology - CRYPTO 1988, LNCS vol. 403, Springer, 1990, pp. 216–231.

16. P. Horster, H. Petersen and M. Michels, *Meta-ElGamal signature schemes*. CCS '94: Proceedings of the 2nd ACM Conference on Computer and communications security, ACM Press, 1994, pp. 96–107.

17. KCDSA, *Digital Signature Mechanism with Appendix - Part 2 : Certificate-Based Digital Signature Algorithm (KCDSA)*, TTA.KO -12.0001, 1998.

18. J. B. Nielsen, *Separating Random Oracle Proofs from Complexity Theoretic Proofs: The Non-committing Encryption Case*. Advances in Cryptology - CRYPTO 2002, LNCS vol. 2442, Springer, 2002, pp. 111–126.

19. D. Pointcheval and J. Stern, *Security Arguments for Digital Signatures and Blind Signatures*. J. Cryptology **13** (2000), no. 3, 361–396.

20. C. P. Schnorr, *Efficient signature generation by smart cards*. J. Cryptology **4** (1991), no. 3, 161–174.

21. C. P. Schnorr, *Efficient identification and signatures for smart cards*. Advances in Cryptology - CRYPTO 1989, LNCS vol. 435, Springer, 1990, pp. 239–251.

22. V. Shoup, *Lower Bounds for Discrete Logarithms and Related Problems*. Advances in Cryptology - EUROCRYPT 1997, LNCS vol. 1233, Springer, 1997, pp. 256–266.

Do All Elliptic Curves of the Same Order Have the Same Difficulty of Discrete Log?

David Jao[1], Stephen D. Miller[2,3,*], and Ramarathnam Venkatesan[1]

[1] Microsoft Research, 1 Microsoft Way, Redmond WA 98052
{davidjao, venkie}@microsoft.com
[2] Department of Mathematics, Rutgers University,
110 Frelinghuysen Rd, Piscataway, NJ 08854-8019
[3] Einstein Institute of Mathematics, Edmond J. Safra Campus,
Givat Ram, The Hebrew University of Jerusalem,
Jerusalem 91904 Israel
miller@math.huji.ac.il

Abstract. The aim of this paper is to justify the common cryptographic practice of selecting elliptic curves using their order as the primary criterion. We can formalize this issue by asking whether the discrete log problem (DLOG) has the same difficulty for all curves over a given finite field with the same order. We prove that this is essentially true by showing polynomial time random reducibility of DLOG among such curves, assuming the Generalized Riemann Hypothesis (GRH). We do so by constructing certain expander graphs, similar to Ramanujan graphs, with elliptic curves as nodes and low degree isogenies as edges. The result is obtained from the rapid mixing of random walks on this graph. Our proof works only for curves with (nearly) the same endomorphism rings. Without this technical restriction such a DLOG equivalence might be false; however, in practice the restriction may be moot, because all known polynomial time techniques for constructing equal order curves produce only curves with nearly equal endomorphism rings.

Keywords: random reducibility, discrete log, elliptic curves, isogenies, modular forms, L-functions, generalized Riemann hypothesis, Ramanujan graphs, expanders, rapid mixing.

1 Introduction

Public key cryptosystems based on the elliptic curve discrete logarithm (DLOG) problem [22, 34] have received considerable attention because they are currently the most widely used systems whose underlying mathematical problem has yet to admit subexponential attacks (see [3, 31, 46]). Hence it is important to formally understand how the choice of elliptic curve affects the difficulty of the resulting DLOG problem. This turns out to be more intricate than the corresponding problem of DLOG over finite fields and their selection.

---

* Partially supported by NSF grant DMS-0301172 and an Alfred P. Sloan Foundation Fellowship.

B. Roy (Ed.): ASIACRYPT 2005, LNCS 3788, pp. 21–40, 2005.

To motivate the questions in this paper, we begin with two observations. First, we note that one typically picks an elliptic curve at random, and examines its group order (e.g. to check if it is smooth) to decide whether to keep it, or discard it and pick another one. It is therefore a natural question whether or not DLOG is of the same difficulty on curves over the same field with the same number of points. Indeed, it is a theorem of Tate that curves E_1 and E_2 defined over the same finite field $\mathbb{F}_q$ have the same number of points if and only if they are *isogenous*, i.e., there exists a nontrivial algebraic group homomorphism $\phi\colon E_1 \to E_2$ between them. If this ϕ is efficiently computable and has a small kernel over $\mathbb{F}_q$, we can solve DLOG on E_1, given a DLOG oracle for E_2.

Secondly, we recall the observation that DLOG on $(\mathbb{Z}/p\mathbb{Z})^*$ has *random self-reducibility*: given any efficient algorithm $A(g^x) = x$ that solves DLOG on a polynomial fraction of inputs, one can solve *any* instance $y = g^x$ by an expected polynomial number of calls to A with *random* inputs of the form $A(g^r y)$. Thus, if DLOG on $(\mathbb{Z}/p\mathbb{Z})^*$ is hard in a sense suitable for cryptography at all (e.g., has no polynomial on average attack), then all but a negligible fraction of instances of DLOG on $(\mathbb{Z}/p\mathbb{Z})^*$ must necessarily be hard. This result is comforting since for cryptographic use we need the DLOG problem to be hard with overwhelming probability when we pick inputs at random. The same random self-reduction statement also holds true for DLOG on any abelian group, and in particular for DLOG on a *fixed* elliptic curve. We consider instead the following question: given a polynomial time algorithm to solve DLOG on some positive (or non-negligible) fraction of isogenous elliptic curves over $\mathbb{F}_q$, can we solve DLOG for *all* curves in the same isogeny class in polynomial time? In this paper we show that the answer to this question is essentially yes, by proving (assuming GRH) the mixing properties of random walks of isogenies on elliptic curves. It follows that if DLOG is hard at all in an isogeny class, then DLOG is hard for all but a negligible fraction of elliptic curves in that isogeny class. This result therefore justifies, in an average case sense, the cryptographic practice of selecting curves at random within an isogeny class.

1.1   Summary of Our results

The conventional wisdom is that if two elliptic curves over the same finite field have the same order, then their discrete logarithm problems are equally hard. Indeed, this philosophy is embodied in the way one picks curves in practice. However, such a widely relied upon assertion merits formal justification. Our work shows that this simplified belief is essentially true for all elliptic curves which are constructible using present techniques, but with an important qualification which we shall now describe.

Specifically, let $S_{N,q}$ denote the set of elliptic curves defined over a given finite field $\mathbb{F}_q$, up to $\overline{\mathbb{F}}_q$-isomorphism, that have the same order N over $\mathbb{F}_q$. We split $S_{N,q}$ into *levels* (as in Kohel [23]), where each level represents all elliptic curves having a particular endomorphism ring over $\overline{\mathbb{F}}_q$. The curves in each level form the vertices of an *isogeny graph* [10, 11, 33], whose edges represent prime degree isogenies between curves of degree less than some specified bound m.

Theorem 1.1. *(Assuming GRH) There exists a polynomial $p(x)$, independent of N and q, such that for $m = p(\log q)$ the isogeny graph $\mathcal{G}$ on each level is an expander graph, in the sense that any random walk on $\mathcal{G}$ will reach a subset of size h with probability at least $\frac{h}{2|\mathcal{G}|}$ after polylog(q) steps (where the implicit polynomial is again independent of N and q).*

Corollary 1.2. *(Assuming GRH) The* DLOG *problem on elliptic curves is random reducible in the following sense: given any algorithm A that solves* DLOG *on some fixed positive proportion of curves in fixed level, one can probabilistically solve* DLOG *on any given curve in that same level with* polylog(q) *expected queries to A with random inputs.*

The proofs are given at the end of Section 4. These results constitute the first formulation of a polynomial time random reducibility result for the elliptic curve DLOG problem which is general enough to apply to typical curves that one ordinarily encounters in practice. An essential tool in our proof is the *nearly Ramanujan* property of Section 3, which we use to prove the expansion properties of our isogeny graphs. The expansion property in turn allows us to prove the rapid mixing of random walks given by compositions of small degree isogenies within a fixed level. Our method uses GRH to prove eigenvalue separation for these graphs, and provides a new technique for constructing expander graphs.

The results stated above concern a fixed level. One might therefore object that our work does not adequately address the issue of DLOG reduction in the case where two isogenous elliptic curves belong to different levels. If an attack is *balanced*, i.e., successful on each level on a polynomial fraction of curves, then our results apply. However, if only unbalanced attacks exist, then a more general equivalence may be false for more fundamental reasons. Nevertheless, at present this omission is not of much practical importance. First of all, most random curves over $\mathbb{F}_q$ belong to sets $S_{N,q}$ consisting of only one level (see Section 6); for example, in Figure 1, we find that 10 out of the 11 randomly generated curves appearing in international standards documents have only one level. Second, if the endomorphism rings corresponding to two levels have conductors whose prime factorizations differ by quantities which are polynomially smooth, then one can use the algorithms of [11, 23] to navigate to a common level in polynomial time, and then apply Corollary 1.2 within that level to conclude that DLOG is polynomial-time random reducible between the two levels. This situation always arises in practice, because no polynomial time algorithm is known which even produces a pair of curves lying on levels whose conductor difference is not polynomially smooth. It is an open problem if such an algorithm exists.

Our use of random walks to reach large subsets of the isogeny graph is crucial, since constructing an isogeny between two specific curves[1] is believed to be inherently hard, whereas constructing an isogeny from a fixed curve to a subset

---

[1] If one uses polynomial size circuits (i.e., polynomial time algorithms with exponential time pre-processing) for reductions, then one can relate DLOG on two given curves. This claim follows using the smallness of diameter of our graphs and the smoothness of the degrees of isogenies involved. We omit the details.

Curve	c_π (maximal conductor gap in isogeny class)	$P(c_\pi)$ = largest prime factor of c_π
NIST P-192	1	1
NIST P-256	3	3
NIST P-384	1	1
NIST P-521	1	1
NIST K-163	$45641 \cdot 82153 \cdot 56498081 \cdot P(c_\pi)$	86110311
NIST K-233	$5610641 \cdot 85310626991 \cdot P(c_\pi)$	15053223481672199
NIST K-283	$1697 \cdot 162254089 \cdot P(c_\pi)$	1779143207551652584836995286271
NIST K-409	$2126243987731 \cdot 22431439539154506863 \cdot P(c_\pi)$	570305533066550535333734286593
NIST K-571	$3952463 \cdot P(c_\pi)$	9021184135396238924389891($contd$) 9451926768145189936450898($contd$) 0776927700984910373365482039
NIST B-163	1	1
NIST B-233	1	1
NIST B-283	1	1
NIST B-409	1	1
NIST B-571	1	1
IPSec 3rd OG, $F_{2^{155}}$	1	1
IPSec 4th OG, $F_{2^{185}}$	1	1

Fig. 1. A table of curves recommended as international standards [16, 36]. Note that the value of c_π for each of the standards curves is small (at most 3), except for the curves in the NIST K (Koblitz curve) family. These phenomena are to be expected and are explained in Section 6. Any curve with $c_\pi = 1$ has the property that its isogeny class consists of only one level. It follows from the results of Section 1.1 that randomly generated elliptic curves with $c_\pi = 1$ (or, more generally, with smooth c_π) will have discrete logarithm problems of typical difficulty amongst all elliptic curves in their isogeny class.

constituting a positive (or polynomial) fraction of the isogeny graph is proved in this paper to be easy. Kohel [23] and Galbraith [11] present exponential time algorithms (and thus exponential time reductions) for navigating between two nodes in the isogeny graph, some of which are based on random walk *heuristics* which we prove here rigorously. Subsequent papers on Weil descent attacks [12, 32] and elliptic curve trapdoor systems [45] also use isogeny random walks in order to extend the GHS Weil descent attack [13] to elliptic curves which are not themselves directly vulnerable to the GHS attack. Our work does not imply any changes to the deductions of these papers, since they also rely on the above heuristic assumptions involving exponentially long random walks. In our case, we achieve polynomial time instead of exponential time reductions; this is possible since we keep one curve fixed, and random reducibility requires only that the other curve be randomly distributed.

2   Preliminaries

Let E_1 and E_2 be elliptic curves defined over a finite field $\mathbb{F}_q$ of characteristic p. An isogeny $\phi\colon E_1 \to E_2$ defined over $\mathbb{F}_q$ is a non-constant rational map defined over $\mathbb{F}_q$ which is also a group homomorphism from $E_1(\overline{\mathbb{F}_q})$ to $E_2(\overline{\mathbb{F}_q})$ [42, §III.4]. The degree of an isogeny is its degree as a rational map. For any elliptic curve $E\colon y^2 + a_1xy + a_3y = x^3 + a_2x^2 + a_4x + a_6$ defined over $\mathbb{F}_q$, the Frobenius endomorphism is the isogeny $\pi\colon E \to E$ of degree q given by the equation $\pi(x,y) = (x^q, y^q)$. It satisfies the equation

$$\pi^2 - \mathrm{Trace}(E)\pi + q = 0,$$

where $\mathrm{Trace}(E) = q + 1 - \#E(\mathbb{F}_q)$ is the trace of the Frobenius endomorphism of E over $\mathbb{F}_q$. The polynomial $p(X) := X^2 - \mathrm{Trace}(E)X + q$ is called the characteristic polynomial of E.

An endomorphism of E is an isogeny $E \to E$ defined over the algebraic closure $\bar{\mathbb{F}}_q$ of $\mathbb{F}_q$. The set of endomorphisms of E together with the zero map forms a ring under the operations of pointwise addition and composition; this ring is called the endomorphism ring of E and denoted $\mathrm{End}(E)$. The ring $\mathrm{End}(E)$ is isomorphic either to an order in a quaternion algebra or to an order in an imaginary quadratic field [42, V.3.1]; in the first case we say E is supersingular and in the second case we say E is ordinary. In the latter situation, the Frobenius endomorphism π can be regarded as an algebraic integer which is a root of the characteristic polynomial.

Two elliptic curves E_1 and E_2 defined over $\mathbb{F}_q$ are said to be isogenous over $\mathbb{F}_q$ if there exists an isogeny $\phi \colon E_1 \to E_2$ defined over $\mathbb{F}_q$. A theorem of Tate states that two curves E_1 and E_2 are isogenous over $\mathbb{F}_q$ if and only if $\#E_1(\mathbb{F}_q) = \#E_2(\mathbb{F}_q)$ [43, §3]. Since every isogeny has a dual isogeny [42, III.6.1], the property of being isogenous over $\mathbb{F}_q$ is an equivalence relation on the finite set of $\bar{\mathbb{F}}_q$-isomorphism classes of elliptic curves defined over $\mathbb{F}_q$. We define an isogeny class to be an equivalence class of elliptic curves, up to $\bar{\mathbb{F}}_q$-isomorphism, under this equivalence relation; the set $S_{N,q}$ of Section 1.1 is thus equal to the isogeny class of elliptic curves over $\mathbb{F}_q$ having cardinality N.

Curves in the same isogeny class are either all supersingular or all ordinary. We assume for the remainder of this paper that we are in the **ordinary case**, which is the more interesting case from the point of view of cryptography in light of the MOV attack [30]. Theorem 1.1 in the supersingular case was essentially known earlier by results of Pizer [37, 38], and a proof has been included for completeness in Appendix A.

The following theorem describes the structure of elliptic curves within an isogeny class from the point of view of their endomorphism rings.

Theorem 2.1. *Let E and E' be ordinary elliptic curves defined over $\mathbb{F}_q$ which are isogenous over $\mathbb{F}_q$. Let K denote the imaginary quadratic field containing $\mathrm{End}(E)$, and write $\mathcal{O}_K$ for the maximal order (i.e., ring of integers) of K.*

1. *The order $\mathrm{End}(E)$ satisfies the property $\mathbb{Z}[\pi] \subseteq \mathrm{End}(E) \subseteq \mathcal{O}_K$.*
2. *The order $\mathrm{End}(E')$ also satisfies $\mathrm{End}(E') \subset K$ and $\mathbb{Z}[\pi] \subseteq \mathrm{End}(E') \subseteq \mathcal{O}_K$.*
3. *The following are equivalent:*
   (a) $\mathrm{End}(E) = \mathrm{End}(E')$.
   (b) There exist two isogenies $\phi \colon E \to E'$ and $\psi \colon E \to E'$ of relatively prime degree, both defined over $\mathbb{F}_q$.
   (c) $[\mathcal{O}_K : \mathrm{End}(E)] = [\mathcal{O}_K : \mathrm{End}(E')]$.
   (d) $[\mathrm{End}(E) : \mathbb{Z}[\pi]] = [\mathrm{End}(E') : \mathbb{Z}[\pi]]$.
4. *Let $\phi \colon E \to E'$ be an isogeny from E to E' of prime degree ℓ, defined over $\mathbb{F}_q$. Then either $\mathrm{End}(E)$ contains $\mathrm{End}(E')$ or $\mathrm{End}(E')$ contains $\mathrm{End}(E)$, and the index of the smaller in the larger divides ℓ.*

5. *Suppose ℓ is a prime that divides one of $[\mathcal{O}_K : \text{End}(E)]$ and $[\mathcal{O}_K : \text{End}(E')]$, but not the other. Then every isogeny $\phi\colon E \to E'$ defined over $\mathbb{F}_q$ has degree equal to a multiple of ℓ.*

Proof. [23, §4.2]. ∎

For any order $\mathcal{O} \subseteq \mathcal{O}_K$, the conductor of $\mathcal{O}$ is defined to be the integer $[\mathcal{O}_K : \mathcal{O}]$. The field K is called the CM field of E. We write c_E for the conductor of $\text{End}(E)$ and c_π for the conductor of $\mathbb{Z}[\pi]$. Note that this is not the same thing as the arithmetic conductor of an elliptic curve [42, §C.16], nor is it related to the conductance of an expander graph [21]. It follows from [4, (7.2) and (7.3)] that $\text{End}(E) = \mathbb{Z} + c_E \mathcal{O}_K$ and $D = c_E^2 d_K$, where D (respectively, d_K) is the discriminant of the order $\text{End}(E)$ (respectively, $\mathcal{O}_K$). Furthermore, the characteristic polynomial $p(X)$ has discriminant $d_\pi = \text{disc}(p(X)) = \text{Trace}(E)^2 - 4q = \text{disc}(\mathbb{Z}[\pi]) = c_\pi^2 d_K$, with $c_\pi = c_E \cdot [\text{End}(E) : \mathbb{Z}[\pi]]$.

Following [10] and [11], we say that an isogeny $\phi\colon E \to E'$ of prime degree ℓ defined over $\mathbb{F}_q$ is "down" if $[\text{End}(E) : \text{End}(E')] = \ell$, "up" if $[\text{End}(E') : \text{End}(E)] = \ell$, and "horizontal" if $\text{End}(E) = \text{End}(E)$. The following theorem classifies the number of degree ℓ isogenies of each type in terms of the Legendre symbol $\left(\frac{D}{\ell}\right)$.

Theorem 2.2. *Let E be an ordinary elliptic curve over $\mathbb{F}_q$, with endomorphism ring $\text{End}(E)$ of discriminant D. Let ℓ be a prime different from the characteristic of $\mathbb{F}_q$.*

- *Assume $\ell \nmid c_E$. Then there are exactly $1 + \left(\frac{D}{\ell}\right)$ horizontal isogenies $\phi\colon E \to E'$ of degree ℓ.*
  - *If $\ell \nmid c_\pi$, there are no other isogenies $E \to E'$ of degree ℓ over $\mathbb{F}_q$.*
  - *If $\ell \mid c_\pi$, there are $\ell - \left(\frac{D}{\ell}\right)$ down isogenies of degree ℓ.*
- *Assume $\ell \mid c_E$. Then there is one up isogeny $E \to E'$ of degree ℓ.*
  - *If $\ell \nmid \frac{c_\pi}{c_E}$, there are no other isogenies $E \to E'$ of degree ℓ over $\mathbb{F}_q$.*
  - *If $\ell \mid \frac{c_\pi}{c_E}$, there are ℓ down isogenies of degree ℓ.*

Proof. [10, §2.1] or [11, §11.5]. ∎

It follows that the maximal conductor difference between levels in an isogeny class is achieved between a curve at the top level (with $\text{End}(E) = \mathcal{O}_K$) and a curve at the bottom level (with $\text{End}(E) = \mathbb{Z}[\pi]$).

2.1   Isogeny Graphs

We define two curves E_1 and E_2 in an isogeny class $S_{N,q}$ to have the same level if $\text{End}(E_1) = \text{End}(E_2)$. An *isogeny graph* is a graph whose nodes consist of all elements in $S_{N,q}$ belonging to a fixed level. Note that a horizontal isogeny always goes between two curves of the same level; likewise, an up isogeny enlarges the size of the endomorphism ring and a down isogeny reduces the size. Since there are fewer elliptic curves at higher levels than at lower levels, the collection of isogeny graphs under the level interpretation visually resembles a "pyramid" or a "volcano" [10], with up isogenies ascending the structure and down isogenies descending.

As in [15, Prop. 2.3], we define two isogenies $\phi\colon E_1 \to E_2$ and $\phi'\colon E_1 \to E_2$ to be equivalent if there exists an automorphism $\alpha \in \mathrm{Aut}(E_2)$ (i.e., an invertible endomorphism) such that $\phi' = \alpha\phi$. The edges of the graph consist of equivalence classes of isogenies over $\mathbb{F}_q$ between elliptic curve representatives of nodes in the graph, which have prime degree less than the bound $(\log q)^{2+\delta}$ for some fixed constant $\delta > 0$. The degree bound must be small enough to permit the isogenies to be computed, but large enough to allow the graph to be connected and to have the rapid mixing properties that we want. We will show in Section 4 that there exists a constant $\delta > 0$ for which a bound of $(\log q)^{2+\delta}$ satisfies all the requirements, provided that we restrict the isogenies to a single level.

Accordingly, fix a level of the isogeny class, and let $\mathrm{End}(E) = \mathcal{O}$ be the common endomorphism ring of all of the elliptic curves in this level. Denote by $\mathcal{G}$ the regular graph whose vertices are elements of $S_{N,q}$ with endomorphism ring $\mathcal{O}$, and whose edges are equivalence classes of horizontal isogenies defined over $\mathbb{F}_q$ of prime degree $\leq (\log q)^{2+\delta}$. By standard facts from the theory of complex multiplication [4, §10], each invertible ideal $\mathfrak{a} \subset \mathcal{O}$ produces an elliptic curve $\mathbb{C}/\mathfrak{a}$ defined over some number field $L \subset \mathbb{C}$ (called the ring class field of $\mathcal{O}$) [4, §11]. The curve $\mathbb{C}/\mathfrak{a}$ has complex multiplication by $\mathcal{O}$, and two different ideals yield isomorphic curves if and only if they belong to the same ideal class. Likewise, each invertible ideal $\mathfrak{b} \subset \mathcal{O}$ defines an isogeny $\mathbb{C}/\mathfrak{a} \to \mathbb{C}/\mathfrak{a}\mathfrak{b}^{-1}$, and the degree of this isogeny is the norm $N(\mathfrak{b})$ of the ideal $\mathfrak{b}$. Moreover, for any prime ideal $\mathfrak{P}$ in L lying over p, the reductions mod $\mathfrak{P}$ of the above elliptic curves and isogenies are defined over $\mathbb{F}_q$, and every elliptic curve and every horizontal isogeny in $\mathcal{G}$ arises in this way (see [11, §3] for the $p > 3$ case, and [12] for the small characteristic case). Therefore, the isogeny graph $\mathcal{G}$ is isomorphic to the corresponding graph $\mathcal{H}$ whose nodes are elliptic curves $\mathbb{C}/\mathfrak{a}$ with complex multiplication by $\mathcal{O}$, and whose edges are complex analytic isogenies represented by ideals $\mathfrak{b} \subset \mathcal{O}$ and subject to the same degree bound as before. This isomorphism preserves the degrees of isogenies, in the sense that the degree of any isogeny in $\mathcal{G}$ is equal to the norm of its corresponding ideal $\mathfrak{b}$ in $\mathcal{H}$.

The graph $\mathcal{H}$ has an alternate description as a Cayley graph on the ideal class group $\mathrm{Cl}(\mathcal{O})$ of $\mathcal{O}$. Indeed, each node of $\mathcal{H}$ is an ideal class of $\mathcal{O}$, and two ideal classes $[\mathfrak{a}_1]$ and $[\mathfrak{a}_2]$ are connected by an edge if and only if there exists a prime ideal $\mathfrak{b}$ of norm $\leq (\log q)^{2+\delta}$ such that $[\mathfrak{a}_1\mathfrak{b}] = [\mathfrak{a}_2]$. Therefore, the graph $\mathcal{H}$ (and hence the graph $\mathcal{G}$) is isomorphic to the Cayley graph of the group $\mathrm{Cl}(\mathcal{O})$ with respect to the generators $[\mathfrak{b}] \in \mathrm{Cl}(\mathcal{O})$, as $\mathfrak{b}$ ranges over all prime ideals of $\mathcal{O}$ of norm $\leq (\log q)^{2+\delta}$.

Remark 2.1. The isogeny graph $\mathcal{G}$ consists of objects defined over the finite field $\mathbb{F}_q$, whereas the objects in the graph $\mathcal{H}$ are defined over the number field L. One passes from $\mathcal{H}$ to $\mathcal{G}$ by taking reductions mod $\mathfrak{P}$, and from $\mathcal{G}$ to $\mathcal{H}$ by using Deuring's Lifting Theorem [8,11,24]. There is no known polynomial time or even subexponential time algorithm for computing the isomorphism between $\mathcal{G}$ and $\mathcal{H}$ [11, §3]. For our purposes, such an explicit algorithm is not necessary, since we only use the complex analytic theory to prove abstract graph-theoretic properties of $\mathcal{G}$.

Remark 2.2. The isogeny graph $\mathcal{G}$ is typically a symmetric graph, since each isogeny ϕ has a unique dual isogeny $\hat{\phi}\colon E_2 \to E_1$ of the same degree as ϕ in the opposite direction [42, §III.6]. (From the viewpoint of $\mathcal{H}$, an isogeny represented by an ideal $\mathfrak{b} \subset \mathcal{O}$ has its dual isogeny represented simply by the complex conjugate $\bar{\mathfrak{b}}$.) However, the definition of equivalence of isogenies from [15] given in 2.1 contains a subtle asymmetry which can sometimes render the graph $\mathcal{G}$ asymmetric in the supersingular case (Appendix A). Namely, if $\mathrm{Aut}(E_1)$ is not equal to $\mathrm{Aut}(E_2)$, then two isogenies $E_1 \to E_2$ can sometimes be equivalent even when their dual isogenies are not. For ordinary elliptic curves within a common level, the equation $\mathrm{End}(E_1) = \mathrm{End}(E_2)$ automatically implies $\mathrm{Aut}(E_1) = \mathrm{Aut}(E_2)$, so the graph $\mathcal{G}$ is always symmetric in this case. Hence, we may regard $\mathcal{G}$ as undirected and apply known results about undirected expander graphs (as in the following section) to $\mathcal{G}$.

3   Expander Graphs

Let $G = (\mathcal{V}, E)$ be a finite graph on h vertices $\mathcal{V}$ with undirected edges $\mathcal{E}$. Suppose G is a regular graph of degree k, i.e., exactly k edges meet at each vertex. Given a labeling of the vertices $\mathcal{V} = \{v_1, \ldots, v_h\}$, the adjacency matrix of G is the symmetric $h \times h$ matrix A whose ij-th entry $A_{ij} = 1$ if an edge exists between v_i and v_j, and 0 otherwise.

It is convenient to identify functions on $\mathcal{V}$ with vectors in $\mathbb{R}^h$ via this labeling, and therefore also think of A as a self-adjoint operator on $L^2(\mathcal{V})$. All of the eigenvalues of A satisfy the bound $|\lambda| \leq k$. Constant vectors are eigenfunctions of A with eigenvalue k, which for obvious reasons is called the trivial eigenvalue λ_{triv}. A family of such graphs G with $h \to \infty$ is said to be a sequence of *expander graphs* if all other eigenvalues of their adjacency matrices are bounded away from $\lambda_{\mathrm{triv}} = k$ by a fixed amount.[2] In particular, no other eigenvalue is equal to k; this implies the graph is connected. A *Ramanujan graph* [29] is a special type of expander which has $|\lambda| \leq 2\sqrt{k-1}$ for any nontrivial eigenvalue which is not equal to $-k$ (this last possibility happens if and only if the graph is bipartite). The supersingular isogeny graphs in Appendix A are sometimes Ramanujan, while the ordinary isogeny graphs in Section 2.1 do not qualify, partly because their degree is not bounded. Nevertheless, they still share the most important properties of expanders as far as our applications are concerned. In particular their degree k grows slowly (as a polynomial in $\log |\mathcal{V}|$), and they share a qualitatively similar eigenvalue separation: instead the nontrivial eigenvalues λ

---

[2] Expansion is usually phrased in terms of the number of neighbors of subsets of G, but the spectral condition here is equivalent for k-regular graphs and also more useful for our purposes.

can be arranged to be $O(k^{1/2+\varepsilon})$ for any desired value of $\varepsilon > 0$. Since our goal is to establish a polynomial time reduction, this enlarged degree bound is natural, and in fact necessary for obtaining expanders from *abelian* Cayley graphs [1]. Obtaining *any* nontrivial *exponent* $\beta < 1$ satisfying $\lambda = O(k^\beta)$ is a key challenge for many applications, and accordingly we shall focus on a type of graphs we call "nearly Ramanujan" graphs: families of graphs whose nontrivial eigenvalues λ satisfy that bound.

   A fundamental use of expanders is to prove the rapid mixing of the random walk on $\mathcal{V}$ along the edges $\mathcal{E}$. The following rapid mixing result is standard but we present it below for convenience. For more information, see [5, 28, 40].

Proposition 3.1. *Let G be a regular graph of degree k on h vertices. Suppose that the eigenvalue λ of any nonconstant eigenvector satisfies the bound $|\lambda| \leq c$ for some $c < k$. Let S be any subset of the vertices of G, and x be any vertex in G. Then a random walk of any length at least $\frac{\log 2h/|S|^{1/2}}{\log k/c}$ starting from x will land in S with probability at least $\frac{|S|}{2h} = \frac{|S|}{2|G|}$.*

Proof. There are k^r random walks of length r starting from x. One would expect in a truly random situation that roughly $\frac{|S|}{h} k^r$ of these land in S. The lemma asserts that for $r \geq \frac{\log 2h/|S|^{1/2}}{\log k/c}$ at least half that number of walks in fact do. Denoting the characteristic functions of S and $\{x\}$ as χ_S and $\chi_{\{x\}}$, respectively, we count that

$$\#\{\text{walks of length } r \text{ starting at } x \text{ and landing in } S\} = \langle \chi_S, A^r \chi_{\{x\}} \rangle, \tag{3.1}$$

where $\langle \cdot, \cdot \rangle$ denotes the inner product of functions in $L^2(\mathcal{V})$. We estimate this as follows. Write the orthogonal decompositions of χ_S and $\chi_{\{x\}}$ as

$$\chi_S = \frac{|S|}{h}\mathbf{1} + u \quad \text{and} \quad \chi_{\{x\}} = \frac{1}{h}\mathbf{1} + w, \tag{3.2}$$

where $\mathbf{1}$ is the constant vector and $\langle u, \mathbf{1} \rangle = \langle w, \mathbf{1} \rangle = 0$. Then (3.1) equals the expected value of $\frac{|S|}{h} k^r$, plus the additional term $\langle u, A^r w \rangle$, which is bounded by $\|u\| \|A^r w\|$. Because $w \perp \mathbf{1}$ and the symmetric matrix A^r has spectrum bounded by c^r on the span of such vectors,

$$\|u\| \|A^r w\| \leq c^r \|u\| \|w\| \leq c^r \|\chi_S\| \|\chi_{\{x\}}\| = c^r |S|^{1/2}. \tag{3.3}$$

For our values of r this is at most half of $\frac{|S|}{h} k^r$, so indeed at least $\frac{1}{2} \frac{|S|}{h} k^r$ of the paths terminate in S as was required.

   In our application the quantities k, $\frac{k}{k-c}$, and $\frac{h}{|S|}$ will all be bounded by polynomials in $\log(h)$. Under these hypotheses, the probability is at least $1/2$ that some polylog(h) trials of random walks of polylog(h) length starting from x will reach S at least once. This mixing estimate is the source of our polynomial time random reducibility (Corollary 1.2).

4   Spectral Properties of the Isogeny Graph

4.1   Navigating the Isogeny Graph

Let $\mathcal{G}$ be as in Section 2.1. The isogeny graph $\mathcal{G}$ has exponentially many nodes and thus is too large to be stored. However, given a curve E and a prime ℓ, it is possible to efficiently compute the curves which are connected to E by an isogeny of degree ℓ. These curves E' have j-invariants which can be found by solving the modular polynomial relation $\Phi_\ell(j(E), j(E')) = 0$; the cost of this step is $O(\ell^3)$ field operations [11, 11.6]. Given the j-invariants, the isogenies themselves can then be obtained using the algorithms of [10] (or [26, 27] when the characteristic of the field is small). In this way, it is possible to navigate the isogeny graph locally without computing the entire graph. We shall see that it suffices to have the degree of the isogenies in the graph be bounded by $(\log q)^{2+\delta}$ to assure the Ramanujan properties required for $\mathcal{G}$ to be an expander.

4.2 θ-Functions and Graph Eigenvalues

The graph $\mathcal{H}$ (and therefore also the isomorphic graph $\mathcal{G}$) has one node for each ideal class of $\mathcal{O}$. Therefore, the total number of nodes in the graph $\mathcal{G}$ is the ideal class number of the order $\mathcal{O}$, and the vertices $\mathcal{V}$ can be identified with ideal class representatives $\{\alpha_1, \ldots, \alpha_h\}$. Using the isomorphism between $\mathcal{G}$ and $\mathcal{H}$, we see that the generating function $\sum M_{\alpha_i, \alpha_j}(n) q^n$ for degree n isogenies between the vertices α_i and α_j of $\mathcal{G}$ is given by

$$\sum_{n=1}^{\infty} M_{\alpha_i, \alpha_j}(n)\, q^n \quad := \quad \frac{1}{e} \sum_{z \in \alpha_i^{-1}\alpha_j} q^{N(z)/N(\alpha_i^{-1}\alpha_j)}, \qquad (4.1)$$

where e is the number of units in $\mathcal{O}$ (which always equals 2 for disc$(\mathcal{O}) > 4$). The sum on the righthand side depends only on the ideal class of the fractional ideal $\alpha_i^{-1}\alpha_j$; by viewing the latter as a lattice in $\mathbb{C}$, we see that $N(z)/N(\alpha_i^{-1}\alpha_j)$ is a quadratic form of discriminant D where $D := \text{disc}(\mathcal{O})$ [4, p. 142]. That means this sum is a θ-series, accordingly denoted as $\theta_{\alpha_i^{-1}\alpha_j}(q)$. It is a holomorphic modular form of weight 1 for the congruence subgroup $\Gamma_0(|D|)$ of $SL(2,\mathbb{Z})$, transforming according to the character $\left(\frac{D}{\cdot}\right)$ (see [19, Theorem 10.9]).

Before discussing exactly which degrees of isogenies to admit into our isogeny graph $\mathcal{G}$, let us first make some remarks about the simpler graph on $\mathcal{V} = \{\alpha_1, \ldots, \alpha_h\}$ whose edges represent isogenies of degree exactly equal to n. Its adjacency matrix is of course the $h \times h$ matrix $M(n) = [M_{\alpha_i, \alpha_j}(n)]_{\{1 \leq i, j \leq h\}}$ defined by series coefficients in (4.1). It can be naturally viewed as an operator which acts on functions on $\mathcal{V} = \{\alpha_1, \ldots, \alpha_h\}$, by identifying them with h-vectors according to this labeling. We will now simultaneously diagonalize all $M(n)$, or what amounts to the same, diagonalize the matrix $A_q = \sum_{n \geq 1} M(n) q^n$ for any value of $q < 1$ (where the sum converges absolutely). The primary reason this is possible is that for each fixed n this graph is an abelian Cayley graph on the ideal class group $\text{Cl}(\mathcal{O})$, with generating set equal to those classes α_i which represent an n-isogeny. The eigenfunctions of the adjacency matrix of an abelian Cayley graph are always given by characters of the group (viewed as functions on the graph), and their respective eigenvalues are sums of these characters over the generating set. This can be seen directly in our circumstance as follows. The ij-th entry of A_q is $\frac{1}{e}\theta_{\alpha_i^{-1}\alpha_j}(q)$, which we recall depends only on the ideal class of the fractional ideal $\alpha_i^{-1}\alpha_j$. If χ is any character of $\mathrm{Cl}(\mathcal{O})$, viewed as the h-vector whose i-th entry is $\chi(\alpha_i)$, then the i-th entry of the vector $A_q\chi$ may be evaluated through matrix multiplication as

$$(A_q\chi)(\alpha_i) \;=\; \frac{1}{e}\sum_{\alpha_j\in\mathrm{Cl}(\mathcal{O})}\theta_{\alpha_i^{-1}\alpha_j}(q)\,\chi(\alpha_j) \;=\; \frac{1}{e}\left(\sum_{\alpha_j\in\mathrm{Cl}(\mathcal{O})}\chi(\alpha_j)\,\theta_{\alpha_j}(q)\right)\chi(\alpha_i),$$

(4.2)

where in the last equality we have reindexed $\alpha_j \mapsto \alpha_i\alpha_j$ using the group structure of $\mathrm{Cl}(\mathcal{O})$. Therefore χ is in fact an eigenvector of the matrix eA_q, with eigenvalue equal to the sum of θ-functions enclosed in parentheses, known as a *Hecke θ-function* (see [19, §12]). These, which we shall denote $\theta_\chi(q)$, form a more natural basis of modular forms than the ideal class θ-functions θ_{α_j} because they are in fact Hecke eigenforms. Using (4.1), the L-functions of these Hecke characters can be written as

$$L(s,\chi) \;=\; L(s,\theta_\chi) \;=\; \sum_{\text{integral ideals } \mathfrak{a}\subset K}\chi(\mathfrak{a})\,(N\mathfrak{a})^{-s} \;=\; \sum_{n=1}^{\infty}a_n(\chi)\,n^{-s},$$

$$\text{where}\quad a_n(\chi) \;=\; \sum_{\substack{\text{integral ideals } \mathfrak{a}\subset K \\ N\mathfrak{a}=n}}\chi(\mathfrak{a})$$

(4.3)

is in fact simply the eigenvalue of $e\,M(n)$ for the eigenvector formed from the character χ as above, which can be seen by isolating the coefficient of q^n in the sum on the righthand side of (4.2).

4.3 Eigenvalue Separation Under the Generalized Riemann Hypothesis

Our isogeny graph is a superposition of the previous graphs $M(n)$, where n is a prime bounded by a parameter m (which we recall is $(\log q)^{2+\delta}$ for some fixed $\delta > 0$). This corresponds to a graph on the elliptic curves represented by ideal classes in an order $\mathcal{O}$ of $K = \mathbb{Q}(\sqrt{d})$, whose edges represent isogenies of prime degree $\leq m$. The graphs with adjacency matrices $\{M(p) \mid p \leq m\}$ above share common eigenfunctions (the characters χ of $\mathrm{Cl}(\mathcal{O})$), and so their eigenvalues are

$$\lambda_\chi \;=\; \frac{1}{e}\sum_{p\leq m}a_p(\chi) \;=\; \frac{1}{e}\sum_{p\leq m}\sum_{\substack{\text{integral ideals } \mathfrak{a}\subset K \\ N\mathfrak{a}=p}}\chi(\mathfrak{a}). \qquad (4.4)$$

When χ is the trivial character, λ_{triv} equals the degree of the regular graph $\mathcal{G}$. Since roughly half of rational primes p split in K, and those which do split into two ideals of norm p, λ_{triv} is roughly $\frac{\pi(m)}{e} \sim \frac{m}{e \log m}$ by the prime number theorem. This eigenvalue is always the largest in absolute value, as can be deduced from (4.4), because $|\chi(\mathfrak{a})|$ always equals 1 when χ is the trivial character. For the polynomial mixing of the random walk in Theorem 1.1 we will require a separation between the trivial and nontrivial eigenvalues of size $1/\text{polylog}(q)$. This would be the case, for example, if for each nontrivial character χ there merely exists one ideal $\mathfrak{a}$ of prime norm $\leq m$ with $\text{Re}\,\chi(\mathfrak{a}) \leq 1 - \frac{1}{\text{polylog}(q)}$. This is analogous to the problem of finding a small prime nonresidue modulo, say, a large prime Q, where one merely needs to find any cancellation at all in the character sum $\sum_{p \leq m} \left(\frac{p}{Q}\right)$. However, the latter requires a strong assumption from analytic number theory, such as the Generalized Riemann Hypothesis (GRH). In the next section we will accordingly derive such bounds for λ_χ, under the assumption of GRH. As a consequence of the more general Lemma 5.3 we will show the following.

Lemma 4.1. *Let $D < 0$ and let $\mathcal{O}$ be the quadratic order of discriminant D. If χ is a nontrivial ideal class character of $\mathcal{O}$, then the Generalized Riemann Hypothesis for $L(s, \chi)$ implies that the sum (4.4) is bounded by $O(m^{1/2} \log |mD|)$ with an absolute implied constant.*

Proof (of Theorem 1.1). There are only finitely many levels for q less than any given bound, so it suffices to prove the theorem for q large and $p(x) = x^{2+\delta}$, where $\delta > 0$ is fixed. The eigenvalues of the adjacency matrix for a given level are given by (4.4). Recall that $|D| \leq 4q$ and $\lambda_{\text{triv}} \sim \frac{m}{e \log m}$. With our choice of $m = p(\log q)$, the bound for the nontrivial eigenvalues in Lemma 4.1 is $\lambda_\chi = O(\lambda_{\text{triv}}^\beta)$ for any $\beta > \frac{1}{2} + \frac{1}{\delta+2}$. That means indeed our isogeny graphs are expanders for q large; the random walk assertion follows from this bound and Proposition 3.1.

Proof (of Corollary 1.2). The Theorem shows that a random walk from any fixed curve E probabilistically reaches the proportion where the algorithm A succeeds, in at most $\text{polylog}(q)$ steps. Since each step is a low degree isogeny, their composition can be computed in $\text{polylog}(q)$ steps. Even though the degree of this isogeny might be large, the degrees of each step are small. This provides the random polynomial time reduction of DLOG along successive curves in the random walk, and hence from E to a curve for which the algorithm A succeeds.

5 The Prime Number Theorem for Modular Form L-Functions

In this section we prove Lemma 4.1, assuming the Generalized Riemann Hypothesis (GRH) for the L-functions (4.3). Our argument is more general, and in fact gives estimates for sums of the form $\sum_{p \leq m} a_p$, where a_p are the prime coefficients of any L-function. This can be thought of as an analog of the Prime Number Theorem because for the simplest L-function, $\zeta(s)$, $a_p = 1$ and this sum is in fact exactly $\pi(m)$. As a compromise between readability and generality, we will restrict the presentation here to the case of modular form L-functions (including (4.3)). Background references for this section include [19, 20, 35]; for information about more general L-functions see also [14, 39].

We shall now consider a classical holomorphic modular form f, with Fourier expansion $f(z) = \sum_{n=0}^{\infty} c_n e^{2\pi i n z}$. We will assume that f is a Hecke eigenform, since this condition is met in the situation of Lemma 4.1 (see the comments between (4.2) and (4.3)). It is natural to study the renormalized coefficients $a_n = n^{-(k-1)/2} c_n$, where $k \geq 1$ is the weight of f (in Section 4.2 $k = 1$, so $a_n = c_n$). The L-function of such a modular form can be written as the Dirichlet series $L(s, f) = \sum_{n=1}^{\infty} a_n n^{-s} = \prod_p (1 - \alpha_p p^{-s})^{-1} (1 - \beta_p p^{-s})^{-1}$, the last equality using the fact that f is a Hecke eigenform. The L-function $L(s, f)$ is entire when f is a cusp form (e.g. $a_0 = 0$). The Ramanujan conjecture (in this case a theorem of [6] and [7]) asserts that $|\alpha_p|, |\beta_p| \leq 1$.

Lemma 4.1 is concerned with estimates for the sums

$$S(m, f) := \sum_{p \leq m} a_p. \tag{5.1}$$

As with the prime number theorem, it is more convenient to instead analyze the weighted sum

$$\psi(m, f) := \sum_{p^k} b_{p^k} \log p \tag{5.2}$$

over prime powers, where the coefficients b_n are those appearing in the Dirichlet series for $-\frac{L'}{L}(s)$:

$$-\frac{L'}{L}(s) = \sum_{n=1}^{\infty} b_n \Lambda(n) n^{-s} = \sum_{p, k} b_{p^k} \log(p) p^{-ks},$$

i.e., $b_{p^k} = \alpha_p^k + \beta_p^k$.

Lemma 5.1. *For a holomorphic modular form f one has*

$$\psi(m, f) = \sum_{p \leq m} a_p \log p + O(m^{1/2}).$$

Proof. The error term represents the contribution of proper prime powers. Since $|b_{p^k}| \leq 2$, it is bounded by twice

$$\sum_{\substack{p^k \leq m \\ k \geq 2}} \log p = \sum_{\substack{p \leq m^{1/2} \\ 2 \leq k \leq \frac{\log m}{\log p}}} \log p \leq \sum_{p \leq m^{1/2}} \log p \frac{\log m}{\log p} \leq \pi(m^{1/2}) \log m,$$

$$\tag{5.3}$$

which is $O(m^{1/2})$ by the Prime Number Theorem.

Lemma 5.2. *(Iwaniec [20, p. 114]) Assume that f is a holomorphic modular lar cusp form of level[3] N and that $L(s, f)$ satisfies GRH. Then $\psi(m, f) = O(m^{1/2} \log(m) \log(mN))$.*

---

[3] Actually in [20] N equals the conductor of the L-function, which in general may be smaller than the level. The lemma is of course nevertheless valid.

We deduce that $S'(m, f) := \sum_{p \le m} a_p \log p = O(m^{1/2} \log(m) \log(mN))$. Finally we shall estimate the sums $S(m, f)$ from (5.1) by removing the $\log(m)$ using a standard partial summation argument.

Lemma 5.3. *Suppose that f is a holomorphic modular cusp form of level N and $L(s, f)$ satisfies GRH. Then $S(m, f) = O(m^{1/2} \log(mN))$.*

Proof. First define $\tilde{a}_p$ to be a_p, if p is prime, and 0 otherwise. Then

$$\sum_{p \le m} a_p = \sum_{p \le m} [\tilde{a}_p \log p] \frac{1}{\log p} = \sum_{n \le m} [\tilde{a}_n \log n] \frac{1}{\log n}.$$

By partial summation over $2 \le n \le m$, we then find

$$\sum_{p \le m} a_p = \sum_{n < m} S'(n, f) \left(\frac{1}{\log(n)} - \frac{1}{\log(n+1)} \right) + \frac{S'(m, f)}{\log m}$$

$$\ll \sum_{n < m} \left(n^{1/2} \log(n) \log(nN) \right) \left| \frac{d}{dn} \left((\log n)^{-1} \right) \right| + m^{1/2} \log(mN)$$

$$\ll \sum_{n < m} n^{1/2} \log(n) \log(nN) \frac{1}{n(\log n)^2} + m^{1/2} \log(mN),$$

so in fact $S(m, f) = \sum_{p \le m} a_p = O(m^{1/2} \log(mN))$.

All the implied constants in these 3 lemmas are absolute. Some useful estimates for them may be found in [2].

5.1 Subexponential Reductions Via Lindelöf Hypothesis

In the previous lemma we have assumed GRH. It seems very difficult to get a corresponding unconditional bound for $S(m, f)$. However, a slightly weaker statement can be proven by assuming only the Lindelöf hypothesis (which is a consequence of GRH). Namely, one has that $\sum_{n \le m} a_n = O_\varepsilon(m^{1/2+\varepsilon} N^\varepsilon)$, for any $\varepsilon > 0$ ([19, (5.61)]). The fact that this last sum is over all $n \le m$, not just primes, is not of crucial importance for our application. However, the significant difference here is that the dependence on N is not polynomial in $\log N$, but merely subexponential. This observation can be used to weaken the hypothesis in Theorem 1.1 and Corollary 1.2 from GRH to the Lindelöf hypothesis, at the expense of replacing "polynomial" by "subexponential."

6 Distribution of c_π

Theorem 1.1 and Corollary 1.2 are statements about individual levels. As we mentioned in Section 1.1, our random reducibility result extends between two levels as long as the levels satisfy the requirement that their conductors differ by polynomially smooth amounts. In this section we explore this extension in more detail, and explain why the above requirement is typically satisfied.

It was mentioned after Theorem 2.2 that the largest possible conductor difference is c_π, which is the largest square factor of $d_\pi = \text{Trace}(E)^2 - 4q$. In principle this factor could be as large as $2\sqrt{q}$, though statistically speaking most integers (a proportion of $\frac{6}{\pi^2} \approx .61$) are square-free, explaining why c_π is very often 1 or at least fairly small [44]. This means, for example, that most randomly selected elliptic curves have an isogeny class consisting of only one level.

When an isogeny class consists of multiple levels, we need to be able to construct vertical isogenies between levels in order to conclude that DLOG instances between the levels are randomly reducible to each other. The fastest known algorithm for constructing vertical isogenies between two levels, due to Kohel [23], has runtime $O(\ell^4)$, where ℓ is the largest prime dividing the conductor of one of the levels, but not the other. Any two levels which can be efficiently bridged via Kohel's algorithm can be considered as one unit for the purposes of random reducibility. Accordingly, polynomial time random reducibility holds within an isogeny class if c_π for that isogeny class is polynomially smooth.

With this in mind, we will now determine a heuristic estimate for the expected size of the largest prime factor $P(c_\pi)$ of c_π, i.e., the largest prime which divides d_π to order at least 2. The trace $t = \text{Trace}(E)$, when sampled over random elliptic curves, is thought to have a fairly uniform distribution over most of the Hasse interval. This serves to predict the useful heuristic that $-d_\pi = 4q - t^2$ is typically of size q (see for example [25, 41]). Assuming that, the probability that $P(c_\pi)$ exceeds β can be loosely estimated as $O(1/\beta)$. This is because roughly a fraction of $\rho = \prod_{p > \beta}^{\sqrt{q}} (1 - p^{-2})$ integers of size q have no repeated prime factor $p > \beta$. It is easy to see that $\log(\rho) = O(\sum_{n > \beta} n^{-2}) = O(1/\beta)$, so that $1 - \rho = O(1/\beta)$ as suggested.

It follows that a randomly selected elliptic curve is extremely likely to have a small enough value of $P(c_\pi)$ to allow for random reducibility throughout its entire isogeny class. This explains why in Figure 1 all of the randomly generated curves have $P(c_\pi) = 1$, except for one curve which has $P(c_\pi) = 3$.

Finally, let us consider the situation where a *non-random* curve is deliberately selected so as to have a large value of c_π. Currently the only known methods for constructing such curves is to use complex multiplication methods [3, Ch. VIII] to construct curves with a predetermined number of points chosen to ensure that c_π is almost as large as $\sqrt{d_\pi}$. Some convenient examples of such curves are the Koblitz curves listed in the NIST FIPS 186-2 document [36], which we have also tabulated in Figure 1. Since these curves all have complex multiplication by the field $K = \mathbb{Q}(\sqrt{-7})$, the discriminants of these curves are of the form $d_\pi = -7c_\pi^2$. If we assume that c_π behaves as a random integer of size $\sqrt{d_\pi}$, which is roughly $\sqrt{q}$, then the distribution of $P(c_\pi)$ is governed by the usual smoothness bounds for large integers [44], and hence is typically too large to permit efficient application of Kohel's algorithm for navigating between levels. Thus we cannot prove random reducibility from a theoretical standpoint for all of the elliptic curves within the isogeny class $S_{N,q}$ of such a specially constructed curve. However, in practice only a small subset of the elliptic curves in $S_{N,q}$ are efficiently constructible using the complex multiplication method (or any other presently known method), and this subset coincides exactly with the subcollection of levels in $S_{N,q}$ which are accessible from the top level (where $\text{End}(E) = \mathcal{O}_K$) using Kohel's algorithm. Pending future developments, it therefore remains true that all of the special curves that we can construct within an isogeny class have equivalent DLOG problems in the random reducible sense.

Acknowledgments. It is a pleasure to thank William Aiello, Michael Ben-Or, Dan Boneh, Brian Conrad, Adolf Hildebrand, Henryk Iwaniec, Dimitar Jetchev, Neal Koblitz, Alexander Lubotzky, Peter Sarnak, Adi Shamir, and Yacov Yacobi for their discussions and helpful comments. We are also indebted to Peter Montgomery for his factoring assistance in producing Figure 1.

References

1. Noga Alon and Yuval Roichman, *Random Cayley graphs and expanders*, Random Structures Algorithms **5** (1994), no. 2, 271–284.
2. Eric Bach and Jonathan Sorenson, *Explicit bounds for primes in residue classes*, Math. Comp. **65** (1996), no. 216, 1717–1735.
3. I. F. Blake, G. Seroussi, and N. P. Smart, *Elliptic curves in cryptography*, London Mathematical Society Lecture Note Series, vol. 265, Cambridge University Press, Cambridge, 2000.
4. David A. Cox, *Primes of the form $x^2 + ny^2$*, A Wiley-Interscience Publication, John Wiley & Sons Inc., New York, 1989.
5. Giuliana Davidoff, Peter Sarnak, and Alain Valette, *Elementary number theory, group theory, and Ramanujan graphs*, London Mathematical Society Student Texts, vol. 55, Cambridge University Press, Cambridge, 2003.
6. Pierre Deligne, *La conjecture de Weil. I*, Inst. Hautes Études Sci. Publ. Math. (1974), no. 43, 273–307 (French).
7. Pierre Deligne and Jean-Pierre Serre, *Formes modulaires de poids 1*, Ann. Sci. École Norm. Sup. (4) **7** (1974), 507–530 (1975) (French).
8. Max Deuring, *Die Typen der Multiplikatorenringe elliptischer Funktionenkörper*, Abh. Math. Sem. Hansischen Univ. **14** (1941), 197–272 (German).
9. Martin Eichler, *Quaternäre quadratische Formen und die Riemannsche Vermutung für die Kongruenzzetafunktion*, Arch. Math. **5** (1954), 355–366 (German).
10. Mireille Fouquet and François Morain, *Isogeny volcanoes and the SEA algorithm*, Algorithmic number theory (Sydney, 2002), 2002, pp. 276–291.
11. Steven D. Galbraith, *Constructing isogenies between elliptic curves over finite fields*, LMS J. Comput. Math. **2** (1999), 118–138 (electronic).
12. Steven D. Galbraith, Florian Hess, and Nigel P. Smart, *Extending the GHS Weil descent attack*, Advances in cryptology—EUROCRYPT 2002 (Amsterdam), 2002, pp. 29–44.
13. P. Gaudry, F. Hess, and N. P. Smart, *Constructive and destructive facets of Weil descent on elliptic curves*, J. Cryptology **15** (2002), no. 1, 19–46.
14. Stephen S. Gelbart and Stephen D. Miller, *Riemann's zeta function and beyond*, Bull. Amer. Math. Soc. (N.S.) **41** (2004), no. 1, 59–112 (electronic).
15. Benedict H. Gross, *Heights and the special values of L-series*, Number theory (Montreal, Que., 1985), 1987, pp. 115–187.

16. D. Harkins and D. Carrel, *The Internet key exchange (IKE)*, Technical Report IETF RFC 2409, November 1998. http://www.ietf.org/rfc/rfc2409.txt.

17. Jun-ichi Igusa, *Fibre systems of Jacobian varieties. III. Fibre systems of elliptic curves*, Amer. J. Math. **81** (1959), 453–476.

18. Yasutaka Ihara, *Discrete subgroups of* PL(2, $k_\wp$), Algebraic Groups and Discontinuous Subgroups (Proc. Sympos. Pure Math., Boulder, Colo., 1965), 1966, pp. 272–278.

19. Henryk Iwaniec, *Topics in classical automorphic forms*, Graduate Studies in Mathematics, vol. 17, American Mathematical Society, Providence, RI, 1997.

20. Henryk Iwaniec and Emmanuel Kowalski, *Analytic number theory*, American Mathematical Society Colloquium Publications, vol. 53, American Mathematical Society, Providence, RI, 2004.

21. M. Jerrum and A. Sinclair, *Conductance and the rapid mixing property for Markov chains: the approximation of permanent resolved*, ACM Symposium on Theory of Computing (May 1988), 235–243.

22. Neal Koblitz, *Elliptic curve cryptosystems*, Math. Comp. **48** (1987), no. 177, 203–209.

23. David Kohel, *Endomorphism rings of elliptic curves over finite fields*, University of California, Berkeley, 1996, Ph.D thesis.

24. Serge Lang, *Elliptic functions*, 2nd ed., Graduate Texts in Mathematics, vol. 112, Springer-Verlag, New York, 1987. With an appendix by J. Tate.

25. H. W. Lenstra Jr., *Factoring integers with elliptic curves*, Ann. of Math. (2) **126** (1987), no. 3, 649–673.

26. Reynald Lercier, *Computing isogenies in* $\mathbf{F}_{2^n}$, Algorithmic number theory (Talence, 1996), 1996, pp. 197–212.

27. R. Lercier and F. Morain, *Algorithms for computing isogenies between elliptic curves*, Computational perspectives on number theory (Chicago, IL, 1995), 1998, pp. 77–96.

28. Alexander Lubotzky, *Discrete groups, expanding graphs and invariant measures*, Progress in Mathematics, vol. 125, Birkhäuser Verlag, Basel, 1994.

29. A. Lubotzky, R. Phillips, and P. Sarnak, *Ramanujan graphs*, Combinatorica **8** (1988), no. 3, 261–277.

30. Alfred J. Menezes, Tatsuaki Okamoto, and Scott A. Vanstone, *Reducing elliptic curve logarithms to logarithms in a finite field*, IEEE Trans. Inform. Theory **39** (1993), no. 5, 1639–1646.

31. Alfred J. Menezes, Paul C. van Oorschot, and Scott A. Vanstone, *Handbook of applied cryptography*, CRC Press Series on Discrete Mathematics and its Applications, CRC Press, Boca Raton, FL, 1997. With a foreword by Ronald L. Rivest.

32. Alfred Menezes, Edlyn Teske, and Annegret Weng, *Weak fields for ECC*, Topics in cryptology—CT-RSA 2004, 2004, pp. 366–386.

33. J.-F. Mestre, *La méthode des graphes. Exemples et applications*, Proceedings of the international conference on class numbers and fundamental units of algebraic number fields (Katata, 1986), 1986, pp. 217–242 (French).

34. Victor S. Miller, *Use of elliptic curves in cryptography*, Advances in cryptology—CRYPTO '85 (Santa Barbara, Calif., 1985), 1986, pp. 417–426.

35. M. Ram Murty, *Problems in analytic number theory*, Graduate Texts in Mathematics, vol. 206, Springer-Verlag, New York, 2001. Readings in Mathematics.

36. National Institute of Standards and Technology, *Digital Signature Standard (DSS)*, Technical Report FIPS PUB 186-2, January 2000. http://csrc.nist.gov/publications/fips/.

37. Arnold K. Pizer, *Ramanujan graphs and Hecke operators*, Bull. Amer. Math. Soc. (N.S.) **23** (1990), no. 1, 127–137.
38. _____, *Ramanujan graphs*, Computational perspectives on number theory (Chicago, IL, 1995), 1998, pp. 159–178.
39. Zeév Rudnick and Peter Sarnak, *Zeros of principal L-functions and random matrix theory*, Duke Math. J. **81** (1996), no. 2, 269–322. A celebration of John F. Nash, Jr.
40. Peter Sarnak, *Some applications of modular forms*, Cambridge Tracts in Mathematics, vol. 99, Cambridge University Press, Cambridge, 1990.
41. Jean-Pierre Serre, *Abelian l-adic representations and elliptic curves*, McGill University lecture notes written with the collaboration of Willem Kuyk and John Labute, W. A. Benjamin, Inc., New York-Amsterdam, 1968.
42. Joseph H. Silverman, *The arithmetic of elliptic curves*, Graduate Texts in Mathematics, vol. 106, Springer-Verlag, New York, 1994.
43. John Tate, *Endomorphisms of abelian varieties over finite fields*, Invent. Math. **2** (1966), 134–144.
44. Gérald Tenenbaum, *Introduction to analytic and probabilistic number theory*, Cambridge Studies in Advanced Mathematics, vol. 46, Cambridge University Press, Cambridge, 1995. Translated from the second French edition (1995) by C. B. Thomas.
45. Edlyn Teske, *An elliptic curve trapdoor system (extended abstract)*, High primes and misdemeanours: lectures in honour of the 60th birthday of Hugh Cowie Williams, 2004, pp. 341–352.
46. Lawrence C. Washington, *Elliptic curves*, Discrete Mathematics and its Applications (Boca Raton), Chapman & Hall/CRC, Boca Raton, FL, 2003.

A   Supersingular Case

In this appendix we discuss the isogeny graphs for supersingular elliptic curves and prove Theorem 1.1 in this setting. The isogeny graphs were first considered by Mestre [33], and were shown by Pizer [37,38] to have the Ramanujan property. Curiously, the actual graphs were first described by Ihara [18] in 1965, but not noticed to be examples of expander graphs until much later. We have decided to give an account here for completeness, mainly following Pizer's arguments. The isogeny graphs we will present here differ from those in the ordinary case in that they are *directed*. This will cause no serious practical consequences, because one can arrange that only a bounded number of edges in these graphs will be unaccompanied by a reverse edge. Also, the implication about rapid mixing used for Theorem 1.1 carries over as well in the directed setting with almost no modification. It is instructive to compare the proofs for the ordinary and supersingular cases, in order to see how GRH plays a role analogous to the Ramanujan conjectures.

Every $\bar{\mathbb{F}}_q$-isomorphism class of supersingular elliptic curves in characteristic p is defined over either $\mathbb{F}_p$ or $\mathbb{F}_{p^2}$ [42], so it suffices to fix $\mathbb{F}_q = \mathbb{F}_{p^2}$ as the field of definition for this discussion. Thus, in contrast to ordinary curves, there is a finite bound g on the number of isomorphism classes that can belong to any given isogeny class (this bound is in fact the genus of the modular curve $X_0(p)$, which is roughly $\frac{p+1}{12}$). It turns out that all isomorphism classes of supersingular curves defined over $\mathbb{F}_{p^2}$ belong to the same isogeny class [33]. Because the number of supersingular curves up to isomorphism is so much smaller than the number of ordinary curves up to isomorphism, correspondingly fewer of the edges need to be included in order to form a Ramanujan graph. For a fixed prime value of $\ell \neq p$, we define the vertices of the supersingular isogeny graph $\mathcal{G}$ to consist of these g isomorphism classes, with directed edges indexed by equivalence classes of degree-ℓ isogenies as defined below. In fact, we will prove that $\mathcal{G}$ is a directed $k = \ell + 1$-regular graph satisfying the Ramanujan bound of $|\lambda| \leq 2\sqrt{\ell} = 2\sqrt{k-1}$ for the nontrivial eigenvalues of its adjacency matrix. The degree ℓ in particular may be taken to be as small as 2 or 3.

For the definition of the equivalence classes of isogenies — as well as later for the proofs — we now need to recall the structure of the endomorphism rings of supersingular elliptic curves. In contrast to the ordinary setting (Section 2), the endomorphism ring $\mathrm{End}(E)$ is a maximal order in the quaternion algebra $R = \mathbb{Q}_{p,\infty}$ ramified at p and ∞. Moreover, isomorphism classes of supersingular curves E_i isogenous to E are in 1-1 correspondence with the left ideal classes $I_i := \mathrm{Hom}(E_i, E)$ of R. As in Section 2.1, call two isogenies $\phi_1, \phi_2 \colon E_i \to E_j$ equivalent if there exists an automorphism α of E_j such that $\phi_2 = \alpha \phi_1$. Under this relation, the set of equivalence classes of isogenies from E_i to E_j is equal to $I_j^{-1} I_i$ modulo the units of I_j. This correspondence is degree preserving, in the sense that the degree of an isogeny equals the reduced norm of the corresponding element in $I_j^{-1} I_i$, normalized by the norm of $I_j^{-1} I_i$ itself. This is the notion of equivalence class of isogenies referred to in the definition of $\mathcal{G}$ in the previous paragraph. Thus, for any integer n, the generating function for the number $M_{ij}(n)$ of equivalence classes of degree n isogenies from E_i to E_j (i.e., the number of edges between vertices representing elliptic curves E_i and E_j) is given by

$$\sum_{n=0}^{\infty} M_{ij}(n)\, q^n \quad := \quad \frac{1}{e_j} \sum_{\alpha \in I_j^{-1} I_i} q^{N(\alpha)/N(I_j^{-1} I_i)}, \qquad (\mathrm{A}.1)$$

where e_j is the number of units in I_j (equivalently, the number of automorphisms of E_j). One knows that $e_j \leq 6$, and in fact $e_j = 2$ except for at most two values of j – see the further remarks at the end of this appendix. Proofs for the statements in this paragraph can be found in [15, 38].

The θ-series on the righthand side of (A.1) is a weight 2 modular form for the congruence subgroup $\Gamma_0(p)$, and the matrices

$$B(n) := \begin{pmatrix} M_{11}(n) & \cdots & M_{1g}(n) \\ \vdots & \ddots & \vdots \\ M_{g1}(n) & \cdots & M_{gg}(n) \end{pmatrix}$$

(called Brandt matrices) are simultaneously both the n-th Fourier coefficients of various modular forms, as well the adjacency matrices for the graph $\mathcal{G}$. A fundamental property of the Brandt matrices $B(n)$ is that they represent the action of the nth Hecke operator $T(n)$ on a certain basis of modular forms of weight 2 for $\Gamma_0(p)$ (see [37]). Thus the eigenvalues of $B(n)$ are given by the nth coefficients of the weight-2 Hecke eigenforms for $\Gamma_0(p)$. These eigenforms include a single Eisenstein series, with the rest being cusp forms. Now we suppose that $n = \ell$ is prime (mainly in order to simplify the following statements). The nth Hecke eigenvalue of the Eisenstein series is $n+1$, while those of the cusp forms are bounded in absolute value by $2\sqrt{n}$ according to the Ramanujan conjectures (in this case a theorem of Eichler [9] and Igusa [17]). Thus the adjacency matrix of $\mathcal{G}$ has trivial eigenvalue equal to $\ell+1$ (the degree k), and its nontrivial eigenvalues indeed satisfy the Ramanujan bound $|\lambda| \leq 2\sqrt{k-1}$.

Finally, we conclude with some comments about the potential asymmetry of the matrix $B(n)$. This is due to the asymmetry in the definition of equivalence classes of isogenies. Indeed, if $\text{Aut}(E_1)$ and $\text{Aut}(E_2)$ are different, then two isogenies $E_1 \to E_2$ can sometimes be equivalent even when their dual isogenies are not equivalent. This problem arises only if one of the curves E_i has complex multiplication by either $\sqrt{-1}$ or $e^{2\pi i/3}$, since otherwise the only possible automorphisms of E_i are the scalar multiplication maps ± 1 [42, §III.10]. In the supersingular setting, one can avoid curves with such unusually rich automorphism groups by choosing a characteristic p which splits in both $\mathbb{Z}[\sqrt{-1}]$ and $\mathbb{Z}[e^{2\pi i/3}]$, i.e., $p \equiv 1 \bmod 12$ (see [37, Prop. 4.6]). In the case of ordinary curves, however, the quadratic orders $\mathbb{Z}[\sqrt{-1}]$ and $\mathbb{Z}[e^{2\pi i/3}]$ both have class number 1, which then renders the issue moot because the isogeny graphs corresponding to these levels each have only one node.

Adapting Density Attacks
to Low-Weight Knapsacks

Phong Q. Nguyễn[1] and Jacques Stern[2]

[1] CNRS & École normale supérieure, DI, 45 rue d'Ulm, 75005 Paris, France
Phong.Nguyen@di.ens.fr
http://www.di.ens.fr/~pnguyen/
[2] École normale supérieure, DI, 45 rue d'Ulm, 75005 Paris, France
Jacques.Stern@di.ens.fr
http://www.di.ens.fr/~stern/

Abstract. Cryptosystems based on the knapsack problem were among the first public-key systems to be invented. Their high encryption/ decryption rate attracted considerable interest until it was noticed that the underlying knapsacks often had a low density, which made them vulnerable to lattice attacks, both in theory and practice. To prevent low-density attacks, several designers found a subtle way to increase the density beyond the critical density by decreasing the weight of the knapsack, and possibly allowing non-binary coefficients. This approach is actually a bit misleading: we show that low-weight knapsacks do not prevent efficient reductions to lattice problems like the shortest vector problem, they even make reductions more likely. To measure the resistance of low-weight knapsacks, we introduce the novel notion of pseudo-density, and we apply the new notion to the Okamoto-Tanaka-Uchiyama (OTU) cryptosystem from Crypto '00. We do not claim to break OTU and we actually believe that this system may be secure with an appropriate choice of the parameters. However, our research indicates that, in its current form, OTU cannot be supported by an argument based on density. Our results also explain why Schnorr and Hörner were able to solve at Eurocrypt '95 certain high-density knapsacks related to the Chor-Rivest cryptosystem, using lattice reduction.

Keywords: Knapsack, Subset Sum, Lattices, Public-Key Cryptanalysis.

1 Introduction

The knapsack (or subset sum) problem is the following: given a set $\{a_1, a_2, \ldots, a_n\}$ of positive integers and a sum $s = \sum_{i=1}^{n} m_i a_i$, where each $m_i \in \{0, 1\}$, recover the m_i's. On the one hand, it is well-known that this problem is NP-hard, and accordingly it is considered to be hard in the worst case. On the other hand, some knapsacks are very easy to solve, such as when the a_i's are the successive powers of two, in which case the problem is to find the binary decomposition of s. This inspired many public-key cryptosystems in the eighties, following the seminal work of Merkle and Hellman [10]:

B. Roy (Ed.): ASIACRYPT 2005, LNCS 3788, pp. 41–58, 2005.

The Public Key: a set of positive integers $\{a_1, a_2, \ldots, a_n\}$.

The Private Key: a method to transform the presumed hard public knapsack into an easy knapsack.

Encryption: a message $m = (m_1, m_2, \ldots, m_n) \in \{0, 1\}^n$ is enciphered into $s = \sum_{i=1}^{n} m_i a_i$.

However, with the noticeable exception of the Okamoto-Tanaka-Uchiyama (OTU) quantum knapsack cryptosystem from Crypto '00 [19], all proposed knapsack schemes have been broken (see the survey by Odlyzko [18]), either because of the special structure of the public key (like in [16,22]) leading to key-recovery attacks, or because of the so-called low-density attacks [6,3] which allow to decrypt ciphertexts.

The *density* of the knapsack is defined as $d = n/\log_2 A$ where $A = \max_{1 \leq i \leq n} a_i$. The density cannot be too high, otherwise encryption would not be injective. Indeed, any subset sum $s = \sum_{i=1}^{n} m_i a_i$ lies in $[0, nA]$, while there are 2^n ways to select the m_i's: if $2^n > nA$, that is, $d > n/(n - \log_2 n)$, there must be a collision $\sum_{i=1}^{n} m_i a_i = \sum_{i=1}^{n} m_i' a_i$, On the other hand, when the density is too low, there is a very efficient reduction from the knapsack problem to the lattice shortest vector problem (SVP): namely, Coster *et al.* [3] showed that if $d < 0.9408\ldots$ (improving the earlier bound $0.6463\ldots$ by Lagarias-Odlyzko [6]), and if the a_i's are chosen uniformly at random over $[0, A]$, then the knapsack problem can be solved with high probability with a single call to a SVP-oracle in dimension n. In practical terms, this means that n must be rather large to avoid lattice attacks (see the survey [17]): despite their NP-hardness, SVP and other lattice problems seem to be experimentally solvable up to moderate dimension. This is why several articles (e.g. [6,3,1,14]) study efficient provable reductions from problems of cryptographic interest to lattice problems such as SVP or the lattice closest vector problem (CVP).

To thwart low-density attacks, several knapsack cryptosytems like Chor-Rivest [2], Qu-Vanstone [16], Okamoto-Tanaka-Uchiyama [19] use in their encryption process a *low-weight* knapsack instead of a random knapsack: $r = \sum_{i=1}^{n} m_i^2$ is much smaller than $n/2$, namely sublinear in n. This means that the message space is no longer $\{0, 1\}^n$, but a subset with a special structure, such as the elements of $\{0, 1\}^n$ with Hamming weight k, in the case of Chor-Rivest [2] or OTU [19]. Alternatively, it was noticed by Lenstra in [7] that such schemes still work with more general knapsacks where the coefficients are not necessarily 0 or 1: this leads to the *powerline encoding* where the plaintexts are the elements $(m_1, \ldots, m_n) \in \mathbb{N}^n$ such that $\sum_{i=1}^{n} m_i = k$, where again k is much less than $n/2$. With such choices, it becomes possible to decrease the bit-length of the a_i's so as to increase the density d beyond the critical density: a general subset sum $s = \sum_{i=1}^{n} m_i a_i$ may then have several solutions, but one is able to detect the correct one because of its special structure. It was claimed that such knapsack schemes would resist lattice attacks.

OUR RESULTS. In this article, we show that low-weight knapsacks are still prone to lattice attacks in theory. Extending earlier work of [6,3,20], we provide a general framework to study provable reductions from the knapsack problem to two well-known lattice problems: the shortest vector problem (SVP) and the closest vector problem (CVP). The framework relates in a simple manner the success probability of the reductions to the number of integer points in certain high-dimensional spheres, so that the existence of reductions can be assessed based only on combinatorial arguments, without playing directly with lattices. We notice that this number of integer points can be computed numerically for any realistic choice of knapsacks, which makes it possible to analyze the resistance of any concrete choice of parameters for low-weight knapsack cryptosystems, which we illustrate on the Chor-Rivest cryptosystem. We also provide a simple asymptotic bound on the number of integer points to analyze the theoretical resistance of low-weight knapsack cryptosystems. Mazo and Odlyzko [9] earlier gave sharp bounds in certain cases which are well-suited to usual knapsacks, but not to low-weight knapsacks. As a result, we introduce the so-called *pseudo-density* $\kappa = r \log_2 n / \log_2 A$ (where $r = \sum_{i=1}^{n} m_i^2$) to measure the resistance of low-weight knapsacks to lattice attacks: if κ is sufficiently low, we establish provable reductions to SVP and CVP. This shows that the security of the Okamoto-Tanaka-Uchiyama cryptosystem [19] from Crypto '00 cannot be based on a density argument because its pseudo-density is too low: like NTRU [4], the security requires the hardness of lattice problems. However, we do not claim to break OTU, and we actually believe that this system may be secure with an appropriate choice of the parameters, due to the gap between lattice oracles and existing lattice reduction algorithms, when the lattice dimension is sufficiently high. Our work shows that the density alone is not sufficient to measure the resistance to lattice attacks: one must also take into account the weight of the solution, which is what the pseudo-density does.

RELATED WORK. Omura and Tanaka [20] showed that the Lagarias-Odlyzko reduction [6] could still apply to practical instantiations of the Chor-Rivest and Okamoto-Tanaka-Uchiyama schemes with binary encoding. However, they relied on the counting techniques of Mazo and Odlyzko [9] which are not tailored to low-weight knapsacks. Hence, they could analyze numerically the resistance of any concrete choice of the parameters, but the asymptotical behaviour was not clear. As a result, it was left open to define an analogue of density to low-weight knapsacks, and it was unknown whether or not the reduction could still work when plaintexts were non-binary strings such as in the powerline encoding. Our work shows that more general encodings like the powerline encoding do not rule out lattice attacks either.

ROAD MAP. The paper is organized as follows. In Section 2 we provide necessary background on lattices and the number of integer points in high-dimensional spheres. We study reductions from knapsacks to the closest lattice vector problem (CVP) in Section 3, in the case of binary knapsacks and low-weight knapsacks. We then extend those reductions to the shortest lattice vector problem (SVP) in Section 4. We apply our results to the OTU cryptosystem in Section 5, and to the Chor-Rivest cryptosystem in Section 6. Finally, we discuss the significance of our results on the security of low-weight knapsack cryptosystems in Section 7.

ACKNOWLEDGEMENTS. This work grew out of investigations carried out by the authors under a contract with NTT. We are grateful to NTT for requesting this research and allowing us to publish our results. The preparation of the paper has in part been supported by the Commission of the European Communities through the IST program under contract IST-2002-507932 ECRYPT. We thank Damien Stehlé and the anonymous referees for their helpful comments.

2   Background

2.1   Lattices

Let $\|.\|$ and $\langle.,.\rangle$ be the Euclidean norm and inner product of $\mathbb{R}^n$. We refer to the survey [17] for a bibliography on lattices. In this paper, by the term lattice, we actually mean an integral lattice. An integral lattice is a subgroup of $(\mathbb{Z}^n, +)$, that is, a non-empty subset L of $\mathbb{Z}^n$ which is stable by subtraction: $\mathbf{x} - \mathbf{y} \in L$ whenever $(\mathbf{x}, \mathbf{y}) \in L^2$. The simplest lattice is $\mathbb{Z}^n$. It turns out that in any lattice L, not just $\mathbb{Z}^n$, there must exist linearly independent vectors $\mathbf{b}_1, \ldots, \mathbf{b}_d \in L$ such that:

$$L = \left\{ \sum_{i=1}^{d} n_i \mathbf{b}_i \mid n_i \in \mathbb{Z} \right\}.$$

Any such d-tuple of vectors $\mathbf{b}_1, \ldots, \mathbf{b}_d$ is called a basis of L: a lattice can be represented by a basis, that is, a matrix. Conversely, if one considers d integral vectors $\mathbf{b}_1, \ldots, \mathbf{b}_d \in \mathbb{Z}^n$, the previous set of all integral linear combinations of the $\mathbf{b}_i$'s is a subgroup of $\mathbb{Z}^n$, and therefore a lattice.

The *dimension* of a lattice L is the dimension d of the linear span of L. Since our lattices are subsets of $\mathbb{Z}^n$, they must have a shortest nonzero vector: In any lattice $L \subseteq \mathbb{Z}^n$, there is at least one nonzero vector $\mathbf{v} \in L$ such that no other nonzero lattice vector has a Euclidean norm strictly smaller than that of $\mathbf{v}$. Finding such a vector $\mathbf{v}$ from an arbitrary basis of L is called the *shortest vector problem* (SVP). Another famous lattice problem is the *closest vector problem* (CVP): given a basis of $L \subseteq \mathbb{Z}^n$ and a point $\mathbf{t} \in \mathbb{Q}^n$, find a lattice vector $\mathbf{w} \in L$ minimizing the Euclidean norm of $\mathbf{w} - \mathbf{t}$.

It is well-known that as the dimension increases, CVP is NP-hard and SVP is NP-hard under randomized reductions (see [17,12] for a list of complexity references). However, in practice, the best lattice reduction algorithms give good results up to moderate dimension: we will discuss this issue in Section 7. This is why it is interesting to study the solvability of various algorithmic problems, when one is given access to a SVP-oracle or a CVP-oracle in moderate dimension. We will call the oracles only once.

2.2   Lattice Points in High-Dimensional Spheres

Following [1,9], we denote by $N(n, r)$ the number of integer points in the n-dimensional sphere of radius $\sqrt{r}$ centered at the origin: that is, $N(n, r)$ is the number of $(x_1, \ldots, x_n) \in \mathbb{Z}^n$ such that $\sum_{i=1}^{n} x_i^2 \leq r$. Clearly, we have the following induction formula (which was also given in the full version of [1]):

$$N(n,r) = \begin{cases} 1 & \text{if } n = 0 \text{ and } r \geq 0, \\ 0 & \text{if } n = 0 \text{ and } r < 0, \\ \sum_{j=-\lfloor \sqrt{r} \rfloor}^{\lfloor \sqrt{r} \rfloor} N(n-1, r-j^2) & \text{if } n > 0. \end{cases}$$

This allows to compute $N(n,r)$ numerically when n and r are not too large, since the running time is clearly polynomial in (n,r).

When n grows to infinity, sharp estimates of $N(n,r)$ are known when r is proportional to n (see [9]), in which case $N(n,r)$ is exponential in n. Two particular cases are interesting for the knapsack problem: the techniques of Mazo and Odlyzko [9] show that $N(n, n/2) \leq 2^{c_0 n}$ and $N(n, n/4) \leq 2^{c_1 n}$ where $(c_0, c_1) = (1.54724\ldots, 1.0628\ldots)$. Note that $1/c_0 = 0.6463\ldots$ is the critical density of the Lagarias-Odlyzko attack [6], while $1/c_1 = 0.9409\ldots$ is the critical density of the attack of Coster $et\ al.$ [3]. These techniques are very useful when the ratio r/n is fixed and known, but less so for more general choices of n and r.

For low-weight knapsacks, we need to upper bound $N(n,r)$ when r is sublinear in n, in which case the techniques of Mazo and Odlyzko [9] do not seem well-suited. We will use instead the following simple bound:

Lemma 1. *For all $n, r \geq 0$:*

$$N(n,r) \leq 2^r \binom{n+r-1}{r}.$$

Proof. Any vector counted by $N(n,r)$ has at most r non-zero coordinates. Therefore, it suffices to bound the number of integer points with positive coordinates, and to multiply by 2^r to take sign into account. To conclude, the number of integer points with positive coordinates and norm less than $\sqrt{r}$ is clearly bounded by the number K_n^r of combinations of r elements among n with repetition. And it is well-known that $K_n^r = \binom{n+r-1}{r}$. $\square$

Corollary 1. *For all $n, r \geq 0$:*

$$N(n,r) \leq \frac{2^r e^{r(r-1)/(2n)} n^r}{r!}.$$

Proof. It suffices to prove that $r! \binom{n+r-1}{r}/n^r \leq e^{r(r-1)/(2n)}$. We have:

$$r! \binom{n+r-1}{r} / n^r = \frac{(n+r-1)(n+r-2) \cdots (n-1)}{n^r}$$

$$\leq \prod_{k=1}^{r-1} (1 + \frac{k}{n}) \leq \prod_{k=1}^{r-1} e^{k/n} \leq e^{r(r-1)/(2n)}$$

$\square$

It follows that if both n and r grow to infinity with a sublinear $r = o(n)$, then $N(n,r) = o(n^r)$ by Stirling's estimate.

3   Reducing Knapsacks to the Closest Vector Problem

In this section, we provide a general framework to reduce the knapsack problem to the closest vector problem. This allows us to easily study the case of low-weight knapsacks, which arguably simplifies the approach of [20] based on [6]. The earlier work [6,3] only considered reductions to the shortest vector problem, but we start with the closest vector problem because it is simpler to understand, and it gives slightly stronger reductions. We will later adapt those results to the shortest vector problem.

We will distinguish two types of knapsacks. The *binary knapsack* problem is the original knapsack problem: given a set $\{a_1, a_2, \ldots, a_n\}$ of positive integers and a sum $s = \sum_{i=1}^{n} m_i a_i$, where each $m_i \in \{0, 1\}$, recover the m_i's. Because of the powerline encoding, we will also be interested in a more general knapsack problem with non-binary coefficients, which we call the *low-weight knapsack* problem: given a set $\{a_1, a_2, \ldots, a_n\}$ of positive integers and a linear combination $s = \sum_{i=1}^{n} m_i a_i$, where each $m_i \in \mathbb{Z}$ and $r = \sum_{i=1}^{n} m_i^2$ is small, recover the m_i's. The case $r = o(n)$ is of particular interest.

3.1   A General Framework

Solving the knapsack problem amounts to finding a small solution of an inhomogeneous linear equation, which can be viewed as a closest vector problem in a natural way, by considering the corresponding homogeneous linear equation, together with an arbitrary solution of the inhomogeneous equation. Let $s = \sum_{i=1}^{n} m_i a_i$ be a subset sum, where each $m_i \in \{0, 1\}$.

The link between knapsacks and lattices comes from the homogeneous linear equation. Consider indeed the set L of all integer solutions to the homogeneous equation, that is, L is the set of vectors $(z_1, \ldots, z_n) \in \mathbb{Z}^n$ such that:

$$z_1 a_1 + \cdots + z_n a_n = 0. \tag{1}$$

The set L is clearly a subgroup of $\mathbb{Z}^n$ and is therefore a lattice. Its dimension is $n - 1$. It is well-known that a basis of L can be computed in polynomial time from the a_i's (see *e.g.* [16] for one way to do so).

Using an extended gcd algorithm, one can compute in polynomial time integers $y_1, \ldots, y_n$ such that

$$s = \sum_{i=1}^{n} y_i a_i. \tag{2}$$

The y_i's form an arbitrary solution of the inhomogenous equation. Now the vector $\mathbf{v} = (y_1 - m_1, \ldots, y_n - m_n)$ belongs to L. And this lattice vector is fairly close to the vector $\mathbf{t}_1 = (y_1, \ldots, y_n)$ as the coordinates of the difference are the m_i's. The main idea is that by finding the closest vector to $\mathbf{t}_1$ in the lattice L, one may perhaps recover $\mathbf{v}$ and hence the m_i's. The success probability of our reductions will depend in a simple manner on the number of integer points in high-dimensional spheres.

3.2 Binary Knapsacks

In the case of binary knapsacks, the distance between $\mathbf{t}_1$ and $\mathbf{v}$ is roughly $\sqrt{n/2}$. But because $m_i \in \{0, 1\}$, the lattice vector $\mathbf{v}$ is even closer to the vector $\mathbf{t}_2 = (y_1 - 1/2, \ldots, y_n - 1/2)$ for which the distance is exactly $\sqrt{n/4}$. It is this simple fact which explains the difference of critical density between the Lagarias-Odlyzko reduction [6] and the reduction by Coster *et al.* [3]. The following results are straightforward:

Lemma 2. *In the case of binary knapsacks, we have:*

1. $\mathbf{v}$ *is a closest vector to* $\mathbf{t}_2$ *in the lattice* L.
2. *If* $\mathbf{v}'$ *is a closest vector to* $\mathbf{t}_2$ *in* L, *then* $\|\mathbf{v}' - \mathbf{t}_2\| = \sqrt{n/4}$ *and* $\mathbf{v}'$ *is of the form* $\mathbf{v}' = (y_1 - m'_1, \ldots, y_n - m'_n)$ *where* $s = \sum_{i=1}^{n} m'_i a_i$ *and* $m'_i \in \{0, 1\}$.

Proof. The key observation is that elements of the lattice have integer coordinates and that each coordinate contributes to the distance to $\mathbf{t}_2$ by at least $1/2$. $\square$

This gives a deterministic polynomial-time reduction from the binary knapsack problem to the closest vector problem (CVP) in a lattice of dimension $n - 1$: this reduction was sketched in the survey [17], and can be viewed as a variant of an earlier reduction by Micciancio [11], who used a different lattice whose dimension was n, instead of $n - 1$ here.

Thus, a single call to a CVP-oracle in an $(n-1)$-dimensional lattice automatically gives us a solution to the binary knapsack problem, independently of the value of the knapsack density, but this solution may not be the one we are looking for, unless the unicity of the solution is guaranteed. One particular case for which the unicity is guaranteed is Merkle-Hellman: more generally, for any *traditional* knapsack cryptosystem such that the set of plaintexts is the whole $\{0, 1\}^n$ without decryption failures, a single call to a CVP-oracle is sufficient to decrypt.

It is nevertheless interesting to know when one can guarantee the unicity of the solution for general knapsacks. But if for instance some a_i is a subset sum of other a_j's where $j \in J$, then clearly, all knapsacks involving only a_i and a_ℓ's where $\ell \notin J$ may also be decomposed differently using the a_j's where $j \in J$. This means that to guarantee unicity of solutions in a general knapsack, we may only hope for probabilistic statements, by considering random knapsacks where the a_i's are assumed to be chosen uniformly at random in $[0, A]$:

Theorem 1. *Let* $(m_1, \ldots, m_n) \in \{0, 1\}^n$. *Let* $a_1, \ldots, a_n$ *be chosen uniformly and independently at random in* $[0, A]$. *Let* $s = \sum_{i=1}^{n} m_i a_i$. *Let* L *and the* y_i's *be defined by (1) and (2). Let* $\mathbf{c}$ *be a vector in* L *closest to the vector* $\mathbf{t}_2 = (y_1 - 1/2, \ldots, y_n - 1/2)$. *Then the probability that* $\mathbf{c}$ *is not equal to* $(y_1 - m_1, \ldots, y_n - m_n)$ *is less than* $(2^n - 1)/A$.

Proof. By Lemma 2, $\mathbf{c}$ is of the form $\mathbf{c} = (y_1 - m'_1, \ldots, y_n - m'_n)$ where $s = \sum_{i=1}^{n} m'_i a_i$ and $m'_i \in \{0, 1\}$. If $\mathbf{c}$ is not equal to $(y_1 - m_1, \ldots, y_n - m_n)$, then

$\mathbf{m}' = (m'_1, \ldots, m'_n) \neq \mathbf{m} = (m_1, \ldots, m_n)$. But:

$$\sum_{i=1}^{n} (m_i - m'_i)a_i = 0. \tag{3}$$

Since $\mathbf{m} \neq \mathbf{m}'$, there exists i_0 such that $m_{i_0} \neq m'_{i_0}$. For any choice of $(a_i)_{i \neq i_0}$, there exists a unique choice of a_{i_0} satisfying (3), since $m_{i_0} - m'_{i_0} = \pm 1$. It follows that for a given $\mathbf{m}' \neq \mathbf{m}$, the probability that $(y_1 - m'_1, \ldots, y_n - m'_n)$ is equal to $\mathbf{c}$ is less than $1/A$. We conclude since the number of $\mathbf{m}'$ is $2^n - 1$. □

This shows that when the density $d = n/\log_2 A$ is < 1, there is with high probability a unique solution, and this solution can be obtained by a single call to a CVP-oracle in dimension $n - 1$.

3.3   Low-Weight Knapsacks

We showed that the hidden vector $\mathbf{v} \in L$ related to the knapsack solution was relatively close to two target vectors $\mathbf{t}_1$ and $\mathbf{t}_2$. In fact, $\mathbf{v}$ was a lattice vector closest to $\mathbf{t}_2$: the distance was $\sqrt{n/4}$. In the general binary case, this was better than $\mathbf{t}_1$ for which the distance was expected to be $\sqrt{n/2}$, provided that the Hamming weight of the knapsack was roughly $n/2$. But if the Hamming weight k is much smaller than $n/2$, then the distance between $\mathbf{m}$ and $\mathbf{t}_1$ is only $\sqrt{k}$, which is much less than $\sqrt{n/4}$. We obtain the following general result regarding low-weight knapsacks (not necessarily binary):

Theorem 2. *Let* $\mathbf{m} = (m_1, \ldots, m_n) \in \mathbb{Z}^n$. *Let* $a_1, \ldots, a_n$ *be chosen uniformly and independently at random in* $[0, A]$. *Let* $s = \sum_{i=1}^{n} m_i a_i$. *Let* L *and the* y_i *'s be defined by (1) and(2). Let* $\mathbf{c}$ *be a vector in* L *closest to the vector* $\mathbf{t}_1 = (y_1, \ldots, y_n)$. *Then the probability that* $\mathbf{c}$ *is not equal to* $(y_1 - m_1, \ldots, y_n - m_n)$ *is less than* $N(n, \|\mathbf{m}\|^2)/A$.

Proof. By definition, $\mathbf{c}$ is of the form $\mathbf{c} = (y_1 - m'_1, \ldots, y_n - m'_n)$ where $s = \sum_{i=1}^{n} m'_i a_i$ and $m'_i \in \mathbb{Z}$. Let $\mathbf{m}' = (m'_1, \ldots, m'_n)$. Because $\mathbf{c}$ cannot be farther from $\mathbf{t}_1$ than $\mathbf{v}$, $\|\mathbf{m}'\| \leq \|\mathbf{m}\|$. If $\mathbf{c}$ is not equal to $(y_1 - m_1, \ldots, y_n - m_n)$, then $\mathbf{m}' \neq \mathbf{m} = (m_1, \ldots, m_n)$: there exists i_0 such that $m_{i_0} \neq m'_{i_0}$. For any choice of $(a_i)_{i \neq i_0}$, there exists at most one choice of a_{i_0} satisfying (3). It follows that for a given $\mathbf{m}' \neq \mathbf{m}$, the probability that $(y_1 - m'_1, \ldots, y_n - m'_n)$ is the closest vector is less than $1/A$. We conclude since the number of $\mathbf{m}'$ is less than $N(n, \|\mathbf{m}\|^2)$, as $\|\mathbf{m}'\| \leq \|\mathbf{m}\|$. □

Note that $N(n, \|\mathbf{m}\|^2)$ can be evaluated numerically from Section 2.2, so that one can bound the failure probability for any given choice of the parameters.

We saw that $\mathbf{t}_1$ was better than $\mathbf{t}_2$ with low-weight knapsacks, but the choice $\mathbf{t}_1$ can be improved if $k = \sum_{i=1}^{n} m_i \neq 0$, which is the case of usual knapsacks where all the m_i's are positive. Consider indeed $\mathbf{t}_3 = (y_1 - k/n, y_2 - k/n, \ldots, y_n - k/n)$. Then $\|\mathbf{v} - \mathbf{t}_3\|^2 = \|\mathbf{m}\|^2 - k^2/n$ which is less than $\|\mathbf{v} - \mathbf{t}_1\|^2 = \|\mathbf{m}\|^2$. By replacing $\mathbf{t}_1$ with $\mathbf{t}_3$ in Theorem 2, the result becomes:

Theorem 3. *Let* $\mathbf{m} = (m_1, \ldots, m_n) \in \mathbb{Z}^n$ *and* $k = \sum_{i=1}^{n} m_i$. *Let* $a_1, \ldots, a_n$ *be chosen uniformly and independently at random in* $[0, A]$. *Let* $s = \sum_{i=1}^{n} m_i a_i$. *Let* L *and the* y_i*'s be defined by (1) and(2). Let* $\mathbf{c}$ *be a vector in* L *closest to the vector* $\mathbf{t}_3 = (y_1 - k/n, \ldots, y_n - k/n)$. *Then the probability that* $\mathbf{c}$ *is not equal to* $(y_1 - m_1, \ldots, y_n - m_n)$ *is less than* $N(n, \|\mathbf{m}\|^2 - k^2/n)/A$.

If $k = \sum_{i=1}^{n} m_i$ is proportional to n, Theorem 3 yields a significant improvement over Theorem 2: for instance, if we consider a binary random knapsack for which $k \approx n/2$, Theorem 3 involves $N(n, n/4)$ instead of $N(n, n/2)$ for Theorem 2, which is exactly the difference between the critical densities of the Lagarias-Odlyzko reduction [6] and the reduction by Coster *et al.* [3]. However, in the case of low-weight knapsacks where $k = o(n)$, the improvement becomes marginal, as k^2/n is then negligible with respect to $\|\mathbf{m}\|^2$. To simplify the presentation and the discussion, we will therefore rather consider Theorem 2.

4   Reducing Knapsacks to the Shortest Vector Problem

In the previous section, we established reductions from knapsack problems (binary and low-weight) to the closest vector problem. The original lattice attacks [6,3] on knapsacks only considered reductions to the shortest vector problem (SVP), not to CVP. In this section, we show that our reductions to CVP can be adapted to SVP, thanks to the well-known embedding or (homogenization) method introduced by Kannan (see [5,12,13]), which tries to transform an $(n-1)$-dimensional CVP to an n-dimensional SVP. In general, the embedding method is only heuristic, but it can be proved in the special case of knapsack lattices. This is interesting from a practical point of view, because CVP is often solved that way.

We adapt Theorem 2 to SVP. Again, we let $s = \sum_{i=1}^{n} m_i a_i$. Let L be the lattice defined by (1), and let the $y_i's$ be defined by (2). Let $(\mathbf{b}_1, \ldots, \mathbf{b}_{n-1})$ be a basis of L. We embed L into the n-dimensional lattice L' spanned by $(1, y_1, \ldots, y_n) \in \mathbb{Z}^{n+1}$ and the $n-1$ vectors of the form $(0, \mathbf{b}_i) \in \mathbb{Z}^{n+1}$. We let $\mathbf{m}' = (1, m_1, \ldots, m_n) \in \mathbb{Z}^{n+1}$. By definition, $\mathbf{m}' \in L'$ and its norm is relatively short. The following result lowers the probability that $\mathbf{m}'$ is the shortest vector of L'.

Theorem 4. *Let* $\mathbf{m} = (m_1, \ldots, m_n) \in \mathbb{Z}^n$. *Let* $a_1, \ldots, a_n$ *be chosen uniformly and independently at random in* $[0, A]$. *Let* $s = \sum_{i=1}^{n} m_i a_i$. *Let* L', $\mathbf{m}'$ *and the* y_i*'s be defined as previously. Let* $\mathbf{s}$ *be a shortest non-zero vector in* L'. *Then the probability that* $\mathbf{s}$ *is not equal to* $\pm\mathbf{m}'$ *is less than*

$$(1 + 2(1 + \|\mathbf{m}\|^2)^{1/2})N(n, \|\mathbf{m}\|^2)/A.$$

Proof. By definition of L', $\mathbf{s}$ is of the form $\mathbf{s} = (r, ry_1 - z_1, \ldots, ry_n - z_n)$ where $r \in \mathbb{Z}$, and $(z_1, \ldots, z_n) \in L$. Since $\mathbf{s}$ is a shortest vector:

$$\|\mathbf{s}\|^2 \leq \|\mathbf{m}'\|^2 = 1 + \|\mathbf{m}\|^2. \tag{4}$$

It follows that $r^2 \leq 1 + \|\mathbf{m}\|^2$. Let $u_i = ry_i - z_i$ and $\mathbf{u} = (u_1, \ldots, u_n)$. We have $\|\mathbf{u}\| \leq \|\mathbf{s}\|$. Notice that:

$$\sum_{i=1}^{n} (u_i - rm_i)a_i = 0. \tag{5}$$

We distinguish two cases. If $r = 0$, then $\mathbf{u} \neq 0$, and it follows that the probability of (5) being satisfied for a given $\mathbf{u} \neq 0$ is less than $1/A$. And the number of possible $\mathbf{u}$ is bounded by $N(n, \|\mathbf{m}\|^2)$. Otherwise, $r \neq 0$, and there are at most $2(1 + \|\mathbf{m}\|^2)^{1/2}$ possible values for r. If $\mathbf{s} \neq \pm\mathbf{m}'$, we claim that there exists i_0 such that $u_{i_0} - rm_{i_0} \neq 0$, in which case the probability that (5) is satisfied is less than $1/A$. Otherwise, $\mathbf{u} = r\mathbf{m}$: if $|r| > 1$, this would imply that $\|\mathbf{u}\| \geq \|\mathbf{m}\|$, and $\mathbf{s}$ would not be shorter than $\mathbf{m}'$; else $r = \pm 1$, and $\mathbf{u} = \pm\mathbf{m}$ which contradicts $\mathbf{s} \neq \pm\mathbf{m}'$. This concludes the proof.   □

Theorem 4 provides essentially the same bound on the success probability as Theorem 2, because $\|\mathbf{m}\|$ is negligible with respect to $N(n, \|\mathbf{m}\|^2)$. This means that in the case of low-weight knapsacks, there is no significant difference between the CVP and SVP cases.

Theorem 4 can be viewed as a generalization of the Lagarias-Odlyzko result [6]. Indeed, if we consider a binary knapsack of Hamming weight $\leq n/2$ (which we may assume without loss of generality), then the failure probability is less than

$$(1 + 2(1 + n/2)^{1/2})N(n, n/2)/A.$$

Since $N(n, n/2) \leq 2^{c_0 n}$ where $c_0 = 1.54724\ldots$ (see Section 2), it follows that the failure probability of the reduction to SVP is negligible provided that the density $d = n/\log_2 A$ is strictly less than $1/c_0 = 0.6463\ldots$, which matches the Lagarias-Odlyzko result [6].

We omit the details but naturally, the improvement of Theorem 3 over Theorem 2 can be adapted to Theorem 4 as well: $N(n, \|\mathbf{m}\|^2)$ would decrease to $N(n, \|\mathbf{m}\|^2 - k^2/n)$ where $k = \sum_{i=1}^{n} m_i$, provided that one subtracts k/n to both y_i and m_i in the definition of L' and $\mathbf{m}'$. In the particular case of binary knapsacks, this matches the result of Coster et al. [3]: because $N(n, n/4) \leq 2^{c_1 n}$ where $c_1 = 1.0628\ldots$, the failure probability would be negligible provided that the knapsack density is less than $1/c_1 = 0.9409\ldots$ Whereas there was almost no difference between the CVP reduction and the SVP reduction for low-weight knapsacks, there is a difference in the case for binary knapsacks: in Theorem 1, the critical density was 1 and not $1/c_1$. And that would not have changed if we had transformed the CVP-reduction of Theorem 1 (instead of that of Theorem 3) into a probabilistic reduction to SVP. This is because Lemma 2 used in Theorem 1 (but not in Theorem 3) has no analogue in the SVP setting, which explains why the result with a CVP-oracle is a bit stronger than with a SVP-oracle: there are more parasites with SVP.

In other words, the framework given in Section 3 revisits the SVP reductions of Lagarias-Odlyzko [6] and Coster et al. [3]. By applying the embedding technique, we obtain the same critical densities when transforming our CVP reductions of Theorem 2 and 3 into SVP reductions.

5   Application to the OTU Cryptosystem

In this section, we apply the results of Sections 2, 3 and 4 to the Okamoto-Tanaka-Uchiyama cryptosystem [19] from Crypto 2000.

5.1   Description of OTU

The OTU cryptosystem is a knapsack cryptosystem where the knapsack has a hidden structure based on discrete logarithms like the Chor-Rivest scheme [2], but where no information on the DL group leaks, thwarting attacks like [22]. The key generation of OTU requires the extraction of discrete logarithms: if quantum computers are available, one can apply Shor's quantum algorithm, otherwise one uses groups with a special structure (e.g. groups of smooth order) so that DL is tractable.

The knapsack $(a_1, \ldots, a_n)$ used by OTU has a special structure. Let $A = \max_{1 \leq i \leq n} a_i$. To allow decryption, it turns out that A is such that $A \geq p^k$ for some integers $p, k > 1$, and p is such that there are at least n coprime numbers $\leq p$, which implies that $p \geq n$, and therefore $A \geq n^k$, and $\log_2 A$ is at least linear in k. The OTU scheme allows two kinds of encoding:

- The binary encoding, where the plaintexts are all $(m_1, \ldots, m_n) \in \{0,1\}^n$ such that $\sum_{i=1}^n m_i = k$.
- The powerline encoding [7], where the plaintexts are all $(m_1, \ldots, m_n) \in \mathbb{N}^n$ such that $\sum_{i=1}^n m_i = k$.

There is no concrete choice of parameters proposed in [19]. However, it was pointed out on page 156 of [19] that the choice $k = 2^{(\log n)^c}$ where c is a constant < 1 would have interesting properties. We will pay special attention to that case since it is the only asymptotical choice of k given in [19], but we note from the discussion in [19–Section 3.4] that the scheme could tolerate larger values of k, up to maybe a constant times $n/\log n$. Perhaps the main drawback with larger values of k is the keysize, as the storage of the knapsack is $\Omega(nk)$ bits, which is then essentially quadratic if $k = n/\log n$. What is clear is that k is at most $O(n/\log n)$: indeed the density in OTU is $O(n/(k \log n))$, and the density must be lower bounded by a constant > 0 to ensure the hardness of the knapsack, which implies that $k = O(n/\log n)$. This means that we should study two cases: the suggested case $k = 2^{(\log n)^c}$ where c is a constant < 1, and the extreme case $k = O(n/\log n)$.

5.2   Resistance to Low-Density Attacks

The parameter A can be chosen as small as $O(p^k)$ and p can be as small as $n \log n$. For the suggested case $k = 2^{(\log n)^c}$, we have $\log A = O(k \log p) = o(n)$. It follows that the usual density $d = n/\log_2 A$ grows to infinity, which is why it was claimed in [19] that OTU prevents usual lattice attacks [6,3]. However, this density argument is misleading because the weight k is sublinear in n.

Let $\mathbf{m} = (m_1, \ldots, m_n)$ and $s = \sum_{i=1}^{n} m_i a_i$. Theorems 4 and 2 provide efficient reductions from knapsacks to SVP and CVP, provided that $N(n, \|\mathbf{m}\|^2)$ is negligible with respect to A.

With the binary encoding, we have $\|\mathbf{m}\|^2 = k$, and therefore $N(n, \|\mathbf{m}\|^2) = N(n, k)$. We know that due to the choice of k in OTU (even in the extreme case), we have $k = o(n)$ with k growing to infinity. Corollary 1 then implies that $N(n, k) = o(n^k)$, and therefore $N(n, k)/A = o(1)$ since $A \geq n^k$. Hence Theorems 4 and 2 provide efficient reductions (with success probability asymptotically close to 1) to SVP and CVP in dimension n, provided that $k = o(n)$, which is a necessary requirement for OTU.

We now show that the powerline encoding does not significantly improve the situation, even though a plaintext $\mathbf{m}$ with the powerline encoding only satisfies $k \leq \|\mathbf{m}\|^2 \leq k^2$. If $\|\mathbf{m}\|^2$ was close to k^2, rather than k, Corollary 1 on $N(n, \|\mathbf{m}\|^2)$ would not allow us to conclude, because n^{k^2} would dominate A. The following result shows that $\|\mathbf{m}\|^2$ is on the average much closer to k, as in the binary encoding:

Theorem 5. *There exists a computable constant $\alpha > 0$ such that the following holds. Let $1 \leq k \leq n$ and $y = (k-1)/n$. Let $\mathbf{m} = (m_1, \ldots, m_n) \in \mathbb{N}^n$ be chosen uniformly at random such that $\sum_{i=1}^{n} m_i = k$. Then the expected value of $\|\mathbf{m}\|^2$ satisfies:*

$$E(\|\mathbf{m}\|^2) \leq k(1 + \alpha y).$$

Proof. As in the proof of Lemma 1, let K_n^k denote the number of combinations of k elements among n with repetition: $K_n^k = \binom{n+k-1}{k} = \binom{n+k-1}{n-1}$. We have:

$$E(\|\mathbf{m}\|^2) = nE(m_i^2) = n \sum_{x=1}^{k} x^2 \frac{K_{n-1}^{k-x}}{K_n^k}$$

$$= n \sum_{x=1}^{k} x^2 \frac{k(k-1)\cdots(k-x+1) \times (n-1)}{(n+k-1)(n+k-2)\cdots(n+k-x-1)}.$$

Let:

$$s(n, x, k) = n(n-1)x^2 \frac{k(k-1)\cdots(k-x+1)}{(n+k-1)(n+k-2)\cdots(n+k-x-1)},$$

so that $E(\|\mathbf{m}\|^2) = \sum_{x=1}^{k} s(n, x, k)$. We will see that the first term dominates in this sum:

$$s(n, 1, k) = \frac{n(n-1)k}{(n+k-1)(n+k-2)} \leq k.$$

We now bound $s(n, x, k)$ for all $2 \leq x \leq k$:

$$s(n, x, k) \leq kx^2 \frac{(k-1)(k-2)\cdots(k-x+1)}{(n+k-1)(n+k-2)\cdots(n+k-x+1)}$$

$$= kx^2 \prod_{u=k-x+1}^{k-1} \frac{u}{n+u} \leq kx^2 \left(\frac{k-1}{n+k-1}\right)^{x-1}$$

$$\le kx^2 \left(\frac{y}{1+y}\right)^{x-1} \text{ with } y = \frac{k-1}{n}.$$

Hence, by separating the first two terms in the sum:

$$E(\|\mathbf{m}\|^2) \le k\left(1 + \frac{4y}{1+y} + \sum_{x=3}^{k} x^2 \left(\frac{y}{1+y}\right)^{x-1}\right).$$

Because $1 \le k \le n$, we have $0 \le y < 1$ and $0 \le y/(1+y) < 1/2$. Thus, we only need to bound the series:

$$f(y) = \sum_{x=3}^{\infty} x^2 \left(\frac{y}{1+y}\right)^{x-1}.$$

A short derivative computation shows that for any $0 \le z < 1/2$, the function $x \mapsto x^2 z^{x-1}$ decreases over $x \ge 3$, because $2 + 3\ln(1/2) < 0$. Therefore, letting $z = y/(1+y)$, we obtain for all $k > 1$:

$$f(y) \le \int_{2}^{\infty} x^2 z^{x-1} dx = \left[\frac{z^{x-1}}{\ln z}\left(x^2 - \frac{2x}{\ln z} + \frac{2}{\ln^2 z}\right)\right]_{2}^{\infty} = \frac{-z}{\ln z}\left(4 - \frac{4}{\ln z} + \frac{2}{\ln^2 z}\right).$$

Since $z \le 1/2$, it follows that one can compute an absolute constant $\beta > 0$ such that for all $k > 1$, $f(y) \le \beta z$, which in fact also holds when $k = 1$, that is, $z = 0$. Hence for all $1 \le k \le n$:

$$E(\|\mathbf{m}\|^2) \le k\left(1 + \frac{4y}{1+y} + \beta z\right) \le k(1 + (4 + \beta)y).$$

This concludes the proof with $\alpha = 4 + \beta$.   □

When $k = o(n)$, we have $y = o(1)$ and the upper bound becomes $k(1 + \alpha y) = k(1 + o(1))$, which already shows that with the powerline encoding, the expected value of $\|\mathbf{m}\|^2$ is essentially k, rather than k^2. This suggests that $N(n, \|\mathbf{m}\|^2)$ will on the average still be negligible with respect to A. But Theorem 5 allows us to give a sharper estimate. In the extreme case of OTU, we have $k = O(n/\log n)$ growing to infinity, so $y = O(1/\log n)$ and the upper bound becomes $r = k(1 + O(1/\log n))$. By Corollary 1:

$$N(n, r)/A \le \frac{2^r e^{r(r-1)/(2n)} n^r}{r! n^k}.$$

Here, $r^2/n = kO(n/\log n)(1 + O(1/\log n))/n = O(k/\log n)$ therefore:

$$2^r e^{r(r-1)/(2n)} = O(1)^k.$$

And $n^r = n^{k(1+O(1/\log n))} = n^k \times (n^{O(1/\log n)})^k \le n^k \times O(1)^k$. Hence:

$$N(n, r)/A \le \frac{O(1)^k}{r!} = o(1).$$

Thus, the reductions of Theorems 4 and 2 succeed with overwhelming probability even with the powerline encoding, even if the extreme choice of k in OTU is considered. This question was left open in [20].

Although we believe that the OTU cryptosystem may be secure with an appropriate choice of the parameters, our results indicate that in its current form, it cannot be supported by an argument based on density that would protect the system against a single call to an SVP oracle or a CVP oracle.

5.3   The Pseudo-Density

We now explain why in the case of low-weight knapsacks, Theorems 4 and 2 suggest to replace the usual density $d = n/\log_2 A$ by a pseudo-density defined by $\kappa = r\log_2 n/\log_2 A$, where r is an upper bound on $\|\mathbf{m}\|^2$, $\mathbf{m}$ being the knapsack solution.

Theorems 4 and 2 showed that a low-weight knapsack could be solved with high probability by a single call to a SVP-oracle or a CVP-oracle, provided that $N(n,r)/A$ was small. Corollary 1 shows that:

$$ N(n,r)/A \leq \frac{2^r e^{r(r-1)/(2n)}}{r!} \times \frac{n^r}{A}. $$

The left-hand term $2^r e^{r(r-1)/(2n)}/r!$ tends to 0 as r grows to ∞, provided that $r = O(n)$. The right-hand term n^r/A is $2^{r\log_2 n - \log_2 A}$. This shows that if the pseudo-density κ is ≤ 1, then the right-hand term will be bounded, and therefore the low-weight knapsack can be solved with high probability by a single call to either a SVP-oracle or a CVP-oracle. On the other hand, if the pseudo-density κ is larger than 1, it will not necessarily mean that the previous upper bound does not tend to zero, as there might be some compensation between the left-hand term and the right-hand term.

Consider for instance the case of OTU with binary encoding. For any choice of k, the pseudo-density $\kappa = k\log_2 n/\log_2 A$ is ≤ 1 because $A \geq n^k$ due to decryption requirements. Therefore there is a reduction to SVP and CVP with probability asymptotically close to 1. On the other hand, if we consider the powerline encoding with an extreme case of k, the pseudo-density becomes $\kappa = k(1+O(1/\log n))\log_2 n/\log_2 A \leq 1+O(1/\log n)$ which could perhaps be slightly larger than 1. Nevertheless, the computation of the previous section showed that $N(n,r)/A$ was still $o(1)$. Thus, the pseudo-density is a good indicator, but it may not suffice to decide in critical cases.

6   Application to the Chor-Rivest Cryptosystem

The Chor-Rivest cryptosystem [2] is another low-weight knapsack cryptosystem, which survived for a long time until Vaudenay [22] broke it, for all the parameter choices proposed by the authors in [2]. Vaudenay used algebraic techniques specific to the Chor-Rivest scheme, which do not apply to OTU. His attack recovers the private key from the public key. Schnorr and Hörner [21] earlier tried to decrypt Chor-Rivest ciphertexts by solving the underlying low-weight knapsack using an improved lattice reduction method which they introduced. They succeeded for certain choices of moderate parameters, but failed for the parameter choices proposed in [2]. Despite the fact that the Chor-Rivest scheme is broken, it is an interesting case with respect to lattice attacks, and this is why we apply our results to this scheme.

6.1 Description

We give a brief description of the Chor-Rivest cryptosystem [2]. One selects a small prime q and an integer k such that one can compute discrete logarithms in $\mathrm{GF}(q^k)$. One computes the discrete logarithms $b_1, \ldots, b_q \in \mathbb{Z}_{q^k-1}$ of certain well-chosen elements in $\mathrm{GF}(q^k)$, to ensure decryption. The elements of the knapsack are $a_i = b_i + d$ where d is an integer chosen uniformly at random in $\mathbb{Z}_{q^k-1}$. The set of plaintexts is the subset of all $(m_1, \ldots, m_q) \in \{0,1\}^q$ having Hamming weight k, and the encryption of $(m_1, \ldots, m_q)$ is:

$$s = \sum_{i=1}^{q} a_i m_i \ (\mathrm{mod} \ q^k - 1).$$

The public key consists of the q, k and the a_i's.

Strictly speaking, Chor-Rivest involves a modular knapsack problem (modulo $q^k - 1$), rather than the initial knapsack problem. The density of the Chor-Rivest knapsack is $d = q/(k \log q)$, which can therefore be rather high for appropriate choices of q and k. But all our results on the knapsack problem we have discussed can be adapted to the modular knapsack problem. First of all, notice that a modular knapsack can be transformed into a basic knapsack if one can guess the hidden multiple of $q^k - 1$ involved, that is, if one knows the integer ℓ such that:

$$s + \ell(q^k - 1) = \left(\sum_{i=1}^{q} a_i m_i \right).$$

Clearly, ℓ can be exhaustively searched, and it is very close to k. In the worst-case for our reductions to lattice problems, the number of oracle calls will increase very slightly.

Alternatively, one can adapt the lattice used in our framework. Consider a modular knapsack $s = \sum_{i=1}^{n} a_i m_i \ (\mathrm{mod} \ A)$. We replace the lattice L defined by (1) by the set L of vectors $(z_1, \ldots, z_n) \in \mathbb{Z}^n$ such that:

$$z_1 a_1 + \cdots + z_n a_n \equiv 0 \ (\mathrm{mod} \ A). \tag{6}$$

The set L is a subgroup of $\mathbb{Z}^n$ and is therefore a lattice. Its dimension is n, rather than $n - 1$. It is again well-known that a basis of L can be computed in polynomial time. This time, we compute in polynomial time integers $y_1, \ldots, y_n$ such that

$$s \equiv \sum_{i=1}^{n} y_i a_i \ (\mathrm{mod} \ A). \tag{7}$$

All of our results, such as Theorems 1–4, can then be adapted to modular knapsacks provided some obvious minor changes, which we omit. For instance, in the statements of Theorems 1–4, the uniform distribution must be over $[0, A[$, and we let $s = \sum_{i=1}^{n} a_i m_i \pmod{A}$. Naturally, equations (1) and (2) must be replaced respectively by equations (6) and (7).

6.2   Application

By definition, the pseudo-density of the Chor-Rivest knapsack (with binary encoding) is $\kappa = k \log_2 q / \log_2(q^k) = 1$. We thus conclude that the low-weight knapsack problems arising from the Chor-Rivest cryptosystem can be efficiently reduced to SVP and CVP with probability close to 1. In retrospect, it is therefore not surprising that Schnorr and Hörner [21] were able to solve certain Chor-Rivest knapsacks using lattice reduction.

Concretely, we can even compute upper bounds on the failure probability of the reduction for the parameters proposed in [2] and the ones used in [21], using numerical values of $N(n, r)$, as explained in Section 2.2. The numerical results are summarized in Tables 1 and 2. Thus, if one had access to SVP-oracles or CVP-oracles in dimension roughly 200–250, one could decrypt Chor-Rivest ciphertexts with overwhelming probability for its proposed parameters.

Table 1. Application to the Chor-Rivest parameters proposed in [2]

Value of (q, k)	(197,24)	(211,24)	(256,25)	(243,24)
Value of $N(q, k)/q^k$	2^{-57}	2^{-57}	2^{-60}	2^{-57}

Table 2. Application to the Chor-Rivest parameters attacked in [21]

Value of (q, k)	(103,12)	(151,16)
Value of $N(q, k)/q^k$	2^{-18}	2^{-29}

7   Impact on the Security of Low-Weight Knapsack Cryptosystems

We have established efficient provable reductions from the low-weight knapsack problem to two well-known lattice problems: SVP and CVP. However, we do not claim to break low-weight knapsack cryptosystems like OTU. This is because there is an experimental and theoretical gap between lattice oracles for SVP/CVP and existing lattice reduction algorithms (see [17] for a list of references), as the lattice dimension increases. The state-of-the-art in lattice reduction suggests that exact SVP and CVP can only be solved up to moderate dimension, unless the lattice has exceptional properties (such as having one extremely short non-zero vector compared to all the other vectors).

To roughly estimate the hardness of SVP/CVP in a m-dimensional lattice of volume V, lattice practitioners usually compare $V^{1/m}\sqrt{m}$ with a natural quantity related to the expected solution: for SVP, the quantity is the norm of the expected shortest vector, while for CVP, it is the distance between the target vector and the lattice. If the ratio is not large, it means that the solution is not exceptionally small: SVP and CVP become intractable in practice if the dimension is sufficiently high. In the case of a knapsack defined by integers $a_1, \ldots, a_n$, the work of [16] on the so-called orthogonal lattices show as a simple particular case that the lattice L defined by (1) has volume $V = (\sum_{i=1}^{n} a_i^2)^{1/2}/\gcd(a_1, \ldots, a_n)$. Thus, with overwhelming probability, $V \approx A = \max_i a_i$. Since the dimension of L is $n - 1$, we need to consider $V^{1/(n-1)} \approx 2^{(\log_2 A)/(n-1)} \approx 2^{1/d}$ where d is the usual knapsack density. The quantity is thus $V^{1/(n-1)}\sqrt{n-1} \approx 2^{1/d}\sqrt{n}$. When dealing with a low-weight knapsack of weight $r = \sum_{i=1}^{n} m_i^2$, this quantity is not particularly large compared to the quantity $\sqrt{r}$ corresponding ot the solution, unless r is extremely small. This indicates that by taking a sufficiently high dimension n and a not too small r (which is also important to avoid simple dimension reduction methods like [8]), the corresponding lattice problems should be hard.

One may wonder how to select the lattice dimension to guarantee the hardness of SVP and CVP in practice. Current experimental records in lattice computations seem to depend on the type of lattices. For instance, Schnorr and Hörner [21], using what is still the best lattice reduction algorithm known in practice, failed to decrypt Chor-Rivest ciphertexts for its suggested parameters, which correspond to a lattice dimension around 200–250. Bleichenbacher and Nguyen [1] reported similar problems with a dense 160-dimensional lattice. On the other hand, Nguyen [13] broke the GGH-challenge in dimension 350, but not in dimension 400. The record computation for breaking the NTRU cryptosystem [4] is a SVP computation in dimension 214 by May (see [8]), while the smallest NTRU parameter currently proposed corresponds to a 502-dimensional lattice. Thus, in order to propose concrete parameters for OTU, it would be useful to gather experimental data with the best reduction algorithms known (keeping track of recent development such as [15]). Besides, SVP and CVP instances arising from knapsack problems could serve as a useful benchmark to test and design new lattice reduction algorithms.

References

1. D. Bleichenbacher and P. Q. Nguyễn. Noisy polynomial interpolation and noisy Chinese remaindering. In *Proc. of Eurocrypt '00*, volume 1807 of *LNCS*. IACR, Springer-Verlag, 2000.

2. B. Chor and R.L. Rivest. A knapsack-type public key cryptosystem based on arithmetic in finite fields. *IEEE Trans. Inform. Theory*, 34, 1988.

3. M.J. Coster, A. Joux, B.A. LaMacchia, A.M. Odlyzko, C.-P. Schnorr, and J. Stern. Improved low-density subset sum algorithms. *Comput. Complexity*, 2:111–128, 1992.

4. J. Hoffstein, J. Pipher, and J.H. Silverman. NTRU: a ring based public key cryptosystem. In *Proc. of ANTS III*, volume 1423 of *LNCS*, pages 267–288. Springer-Verlag, 1998. Additional information and updates at http://www.ntru.com.
5. R. Kannan. Minkowski's convex body theorem and integer programming. *Math. Oper. Res.*, 12(3):415–440, 1987.
6. J. C. Lagarias and A. M. Odlyzko. Solving low-density subset sum problems. *Journal of the Association for Computing Machinery*, January 1985.
7. H.W. Lenstra, Jr. On the Chor-Rivest knapsack cryptosystem. *J. of Cryptology*, 3:149–155, 1991.
8. A. May and J. Silverman. Dimension Reduction Methods for Convolution Modular Lattices. In *Cryptography and Lattices – Proc. of CALC*, volume 2146 of *LNCS*. Springer-Verlag, 2001.
9. J. E. Mazo and A. M. Odlyzko. Lattice points in high-dimensional spheres. *Monatsh. Math.*, 110:47–61, 1990.
10. R. Merkle and M. Hellman. Hiding information and signatures in trapdoor knapsacks. *IEEE Trans. Inform. Theory*, IT-24:525–530, September 1978.
11. D. Micciancio. The hardness of the closest vector problem with preprocessing. *IEEE Trans. Inform. Theory*, 47(3):1212–1215, 2001.
12. D. Micciancio and S. Goldwasser. *Complexity of lattice problems: A cryptographic perspective*. Kluwer Academic Publishers, Boston, 2002.
13. P. Q. Nguyễn. Cryptanalysis of the Goldreich-Goldwasser-Halevi cryptosystem from Crypto '97. In *Proc. of Crypto '99*, volume 1666 of *LNCS*, pages 288–304. IACR, Springer-Verlag, 1999.
14. P. Q. Nguyễn and I. E. Shparlinski, *The Insecurity of the Digital Signature Algorithm with Partially Known Nonces*, Journal of Cryptology, vol. 15, no. 3, pp. 151–176, Springer, 2002.
15. P. Q. Nguyễn and D. Stehlé. Floating-Point LLL Revisited. In *Proc. of Eurocrypt '05*, volume 3494 of *LNCS*. IACR, Springer-Verlag, 2005.
16. P. Q. Nguyễn and J. Stern. Merkle-Hellman revisited: a cryptanalysis of the Qu-Vanstone cryptosystem based on group factorizations. In *Proc. of Crypto '97*, volume 1294 of *LNCS*, pages 198–212. IACR, Springer-Verlag, 1997.
17. P. Q. Nguyễn and J. Stern. The two faces of lattices in cryptology. In *Cryptography and Lattices – Proc. of CALC*, volume 2146 of *LNCS*. Springer-Verlag, 2001.
18. A. M. Odlyzko. The rise and fall of knapsack cryptosystems. In *Cryptology and Computational Number Theory*, volume 42 of *Proc. of Symposia in Applied Mathematics*, pages 75–88. A.M.S., 1990.
19. T. Okamoto, K. Tanaka, and S. Uchiyama. Quantum Public-Key Cryptosystems. In *Proc. of Crypto '00, LNCS*. Springer-Verlag, 2000.
20. K. Omura and K. Tanaka. Density Attack to the Knapsack Cryptosystems with Enumerative Source Encoding. In *IEICE Trans. Fundamentals*, vol. E84-A, No. 1, January (2001).
21. C. P. Schnorr and H. H. Hörner. Attacking the Chor-Rivest cryptosystem by improved lattice reduction. In *Proc. of Eurocrypt '95*, volume 921 of *LNCS*, pages 1–12. IACR, Springer-Verlag, 1995.
22. S. Vaudenay Cryptanalysis of the Chor-Rivest Cryptosystem. In *Journal of Cryptology*, vol. 14 (2001), pp 87-100.

Efficient and Secure Elliptic Curve Point Multiplication Using Double-Base Chains

Vassil Dimitrov[1,2], Laurent Imbert[1,2,3], and Pradeep Kumar Mishra[2]

[1] Advanced Technology Information Processing Systems laboratory,
University of Calgary, Canada
dimitrov@atips.ca
[2] Centre for Informations Security and Cryptography,
University of Calgary, Canada
pradeep@math.ucalgary.ca
[3] Laboratoire d'Informatique,
de Robotique et de Microélectronique de Montpellier,
CNRS UMR 5506, Montpellier, France
Laurent.Imbert@lirmm.fr

Abstract. In this paper, we propose a efficient and secure point multiplication algorithm, based on double-base chains. This is achieved by taking advantage of the sparseness and the ternary nature of the so-called double-base number system (DBNS). The speed-ups are the results of fewer point additions and improved formulæ for point triplings and quadruplings in both even and odd characteristic. Our algorithms can be protected against simple and differential side-channel analysis by using side-channel atomicity and classical randomization techniques. Our numerical experiments show that our approach leads to speed-ups compared to windowing methods, even with window size equal to 4, and other SCA resistant algorithms.

1 Introduction

Elliptic curve cryptography (ECC) [24, 21] has rapidly received a lot of attention because of its small key-length and increased theoretical robustness (there is no known subexponential algorithm to solve the ECDLP problem, which is the foundation of ECC). The efficiency of an ECC implementation mainly depends on the way we implement the *scalar* or *point multiplication*; i.e., the computation of the point $kP = P + \cdots + P$ (k times), for a given point P on the curve. A vast amount of research has been done to accelerate and secure this operation, using various representations of the scalar k (binary, ternary, non-adjacent form (NAF), window methods (w-NAF), Frobenius expansion,...), various systems of coordinates (affine, projective,...) and various randomization techniques. See [15, 4, 1] for complete presentations.

In this paper, we propose new scalar multiplication algorithms based on a representation of the multiplier as a sum of mixed powers of 2 and 3, called the *double-base number system* (DBNS). The inherent sparseness of this representation scheme leads to fewer point additions than other classical methods. For

B. Roy (Ed.): ASIACRYPT 2005, LNCS 3788, pp. 59–78, 2005.

example, if k is a randomly chosen 160-bit integer, then one needs only about 22 summands to represent it, as opposed to 80 in standard binary representation and 53 in the non-adjacent form (NAF).

In order to best exploit the sparse and ternary nature of the DBNS, we also propose new formulæ for point tripling and quadrupling for curves defined over binary fields and points in affine coordinates; and for prime fields using Jacobian coordinates. Our algorithms can be protected against side-channel attacks (SCA) by using *side-channel atomicity* [5] for simple analysis, and, in the odd case, using a point randomization method proposed by Joye and Tymen [20] for differential analysis.

2   Background

In this section, we give a brief overview of elliptic curve cryptography (see [1, 3, 4, 15] for more details) and the double-base number system.

2.1   Elliptic Curve Cryptography

Definition 1. *An elliptic curve E over a field K is defined by an equation*

$$E : y^2 + a_1 xy + a_3 y = x^3 + a_2 x^2 + a_4 x + a_6 \tag{1}$$

where $a_1, a_2, a_3, a_4, a_6 \in K$, and $\Delta \neq 0$, where Δ is the discriminant of E.

In practice, the Weierstrass equation (1) can be greatly simplified by applying admissible changes of variables. If the characteristic of K is not equal to 2 and 3, then (1) rewrites

$$y^2 = x^3 + ax + b, \tag{2}$$

where $a, b \in K$, and $\Delta = 4a^3 + 27b^2 \neq 0$.

When the characteristic of K is equal to 2, we use the *non-supersingular* form of an elliptic curve, given for $a \neq 0$ by

$$y^2 + xy = x^3 + ax^2 + b, \tag{3}$$

where $a, b \in K$ and $\Delta = b \neq 0$.

The set $E(K)$ of rational points on an elliptic curve E defined over a field K is an abelian group, where the operation (generally denoted additively) is defined by the well-known law of chord and tangent, and the identity element is the special point $\mathcal{O}$, called *point at infinity*.

If the points on the curve are represented using affine coordinates, as $P = (x, y)$, both the *point addition* (ADD) and *point doubling* (DBL) involve an expensive field inversion (to compute the slope of the chord or the tangent). To avoid these inversions, several projective systems of coordinates have been proposed in the literature. The choice of a coordinates system has to be made according to the so-called $[i]/[m]$ ratio between one field inversion and one field multiplication. It is generally assumed that $3 \leq [i]/[m] \leq 10$ for binary fields [8, 14] and 30 or more for prime fields [12]. In this paper we consider affine ($\mathcal{A}$) coordinates for curves defined over binary fields and Jacobian ($\mathcal{J}$) coordinates, where the point $P = (X, Y, Z)$ corresponds to the point $(X/Z^2, Y/Z^3)$ on the elliptic curve for curves defined over fields of odd characteristic.

As we shall see, our DBNS-based point multiplication algorithms use several primitives. In the following lines, we give a very brief description and the complexities of some previously published point arithmetic algorithms. We also propose improved primitives and new formulæ in Section 4.

In the following, we will use $[i]$, $[s]$ and $[m]$ to denote the cost of one inversion, one squaring and one multiplication respectively. We shall always leave out the cost of field additions. In binary fields, we assume that squarings are free (if normal bases are used) or of negligible cost (linear operation). Moreover, for curves defined over large prime fields, we will assume that $[s] = 0.8[m]$. Note that our algorithm can be protected against SCA (see Section 2.2) using side-channel atomicity [5], which we have shown in the case of prime fields. In this case, squarings and multiplications must be performed using the same multiplier in order to be indistinguishable, and we must consider $[s] = [m]$.

For fields of even characteristic, we use affine coordinates and we consider doublings (DBL), triplings (TPL) and quadruplings (QPL) as well as the combined double-and-add (DA), triple-and-add (TA) and quadruple-and-add (QA). It is easy to verify that ADD and DBL can be computed in $1[i] + 1[s] + 2[m]$. In [11], K. Eisenträger et al. have proposed efficient algorithms for DA, TPL and TA. By trading some inversions for a small number of multiplications, these results have been further improved when $[i]/[m] > 6$ in [6]. In Table 1 below, we give the complexities of each of these primitives. We also give the break-even points between the different formulæ.

Table 1. Costs comparisons and break-even points for DA, T and TA over binary fields using affine coordinates

Operation	[11]	[6]	break-even point
$2P \pm Q$	$2[i] + 2[s] + 3[m]$	$1[i] + 2[s] + 9[m]$	$[i]/[m] = 6$
$3P$	$2[i] + 2[s] + 3[m]$	$1[i] + 4[s] + 7[m]$	$[i]/[m] = 4$
$3P \pm Q$	$3[i] + 3[s] + 4[m]$	$2[i] + 3[s] + 9[m]$	$[i]/[m] = 5$

When Jacobian coordinates are used and the curve is defined over a prime field (or a field of odd characteristic > 3), the addition and doubling operations, that we will denote $\text{ADD}^{\mathcal{J}}$ and $\text{DBL}^{\mathcal{J}}$ in this paper, require $12[m] + 4[s]$ and $4[m] + 6[s]$ respectively. The cost of $\text{DBL}^{\mathcal{J}}$ can be reduced to $4[m] + 4[s]$ when $a = -3$ in (2). Also, if the base point is given in affine coordinates ($Z = 1$), then the cost of the so-called *mixed addition* ($\mathcal{J} + \mathcal{A} \rightarrow \mathcal{J}$) reduces to $8[m] + 3[s]$. When several doublings have to be computed, as for the computation of $2^w P$, the algorithm proposed by Itoh et al. in [16] is more efficient than w invocations of $\text{DBL}^{\mathcal{J}}$. In the general case ($a \neq -3$) it requires $4w[m] + (4w+2)[s]$. In Table 2, we summarize the complexity of these different elliptic curve primitives.

Table 2. Complexity of several elliptic curve operations in Jacobian coordinates for fields of odd characteristic $\neq 3$

Curve operation	Complexity	# Registers
$\mathrm{DBL}^{\mathcal{J}}$	$4[m] + 6[s]$	6
$\mathrm{DBL}^{\mathcal{J},\, a=-3}$	$4[m] + 4[s]$	5
$\mathrm{ADD}^{\mathcal{J}}$	$12[m] + 4[s]$	7
$\mathrm{ADD}^{\mathcal{J}+\mathcal{A}}$	$8[m] + 3[s]$	7
$w\text{-}\mathrm{DBL}^{\mathcal{J}}$	$4w[m] + (4w+2)[s]$	7

2.2 Preventing Side-Channel Analysis

Side-channel attacks (SCA) are one of the most serious threat to ECC implementations. Discovered by Kocher et al. [23, 22], these attacks can reveal a secret information by sampling and analyzing various side-channel information (e.g. timing, power consumption, electromagnetic radiations) of a device. SCA can be divided into two types: *simple attacks* which observe only one trace given by a single execution of the algorithm, and *differential attacks* which use many observations and try to reveal the secret using statistical tools. Protecting ECC implementations against SCA has itself become an interesting area of research and several countermeasures have been proposed. Interested readers can refer to [4, 1] for details.

In the current work we will use a solution proposed by Chavalier-Mames et al. in [5] to protect against simple attacks, called *side-channel atomicity*. The countermeasure is based on the simple observation that some elementary operations are side-channel equivalent in the sense that they are indistinguishable (or can be made so by clever software implementation) from the side-channel.

2.3 Double-Base Number System

The double-base number system (DBNS) [10] is a representation scheme in which every positive integer k is represented as the sum or difference of $\{2, 3\}$-integers (i.e., numbers of the form $2^b 3^t$) as

$$k = \sum_{i=1}^{m} s_i \, 2^{b_i} 3^{t_i}, \quad \text{with } s_i \in \{-1, 1\}, \text{ and } b_i, t_i \geq 0 . \tag{4}$$

Clearly, this number representation scheme is highly redundant. If one considers the DBNS with only positive signs ($s_i = 1$), then certain interesting numerical and theoretical results can be proved. For instance, 10 has exactly five different DBNS representations, 100 has exactly 402 different DBNS representations and 1000 has exactly 1 295 579 different DBNS representations. Probably, the most important theoretical result about the double-base number system is the following theorem from [9].

Theorem 1. *Every positive integer k can be represented as the sum of at most* $O\left(\dfrac{\log k}{\log \log k}\right)$ *$\{2, 3\}$-integers.*

The proof is based on Baker's theory of linear forms of logarithms and more specifically on a result by R. Tijdeman [25].

Some of these representations are of special interest, most notably the ones that require the minimal number of $\{2,3\}$-integers; i.e., an integer can be represented as the sum of m terms ($\{2,3\}$-integers), but cannot be represented as the sum of $m-1$ or less. These representations, called *canonic* representations, are extremely sparse. Some numerical facts provide a good impression about the sparseness of the DBNS. The smallest integer requiring three $\{2,3\}$-integers in its canonic DBNS representations is 23. The next smallest integers requiring 4-to-7 $\{2,3\}$-integers are 431, 18 431, 3 448 733 and 1 441 896 119 respectively. In all of the above results we have assumed only positive $(+1)$ values for the s_i's. If one considers both signs, then the theoretical difficulties in establishing the properties of this number system dramatically increase. To wit, it is possible to prove that the smallest integer that cannot be represented as the sum or difference of two $\{2,3\}$-integers is 103. The next limit is conjectured to be 4985, but to prove it rigorously, one has to prove that the Diophantine equations $\pm 2^a 3^b \pm 2^c 3^d \pm 2^e 3^f = 4985$ do not have solutions in integers.

Finding one of the canonic DBNS representations, especially for very large integers, seems to be a very difficult task. Fortunately, one can apply a greedy algorithm to find a fairly sparse representation very quickly: given $k > 0$, find the largest number of the form $z = 2^b 3^t$ less than or equal to k, and apply the same procedure with $k - z$ until reaching zero. Although the greedy algorithm sometimes fails in finding a canonic representation[1], it is very easy to implement and it guarantees a representation satisfying the asymptotic bound given by Theorem 1 (see [9]).

In this paper, we will use a slightly modified version of the greedy algorithm in order to find a DBNS representation of the scalar k of particular form, well adapted to fast and secure elliptic curve point multiplication. In the next section, we introduce the concept of double-base chains and the corresponding scalar multiplication algorithms.

3   Double-Base Chain and Point Multiplication

Let E be an elliptic curve defined over K, and let $P \neq \mathcal{O}$ be a point on $E(K)$. Assuming k is represented in DBNS, our new scalar multiplication algorithm computes the new point $kP \in E(K)$, by using the so-called *double-base chain* as defined below.

Definition 2 (Double-Base Chain). *Given $k > 0$, a sequence $(C_n)_{n>0}$ of positive integers satisfying:*

$$C_1 = 1, \quad C_{n+1} = 2^u 3^v C_n + s, \quad \text{with } s \in \{-1, 1\} \tag{5}$$

---

[1] The smallest example is 41; the canonic representation is $32 + 9$, whereas the greedy algorithm returns $41 = 36 + 4 + 1$.

for some $u, v \geq 0$, and such that $C_m = k$ for some $m > 0$, is called a double-base chain for k. The length m of a double-base chain is equal to the number of $\{2,3\}$-integers in (4) used to represent k.

Let $k > 0$ be an integer represented in DBNS as $k = \sum_{i=1}^{m} s_i 2^{b_i} 3^{t_i}$, with $s_i \in \{-1, 1\}$, where the b_i's and t_i's form two decreasing sequences; i.e., $b_1 \geq b_2 \geq \cdots \geq b_m \geq 0$ and $t_1 \geq t_2 \geq \cdots \geq t_m \geq 0$. These particular DBNS representations allow us to expand k in a Horner-like fashion such that all partial results can be reused.

We first remark that such a representation always exists (e.g., the binary representation is a special case). In fact, this particular DBNS representation is also highly redundant. Counting the exact number of DBNS representations which satisfy these conditions is indeed a very interesting problem, but the only partial results we have at the moment are beyond the scope of this paper.

If necessary, such a particular DBNS representation for k can be computed using Algorithm 1 below, which is a modified version of the greedy algorithm briefly described in Section 2.3. Two important parameters of this algorithm

---

Algorithm 1. Conversion to DBNS with restricted exponents

Input k, a n-bit positive integer; $b_{max}, t_{max} > 0$, the largest allowed binary and ternary exponents

Output The sequence $(s_i, b_i, t_i)_{i>0}$ such that $k = \sum_{i=1}^{m} s_i 2^{b_i} 3^{t_i}$, with $b_1 \geq \cdots \geq b_m \geq 0$ and $t_1 \geq \cdots \geq t_m \geq 0$

1: $s \leftarrow 1$
2: **while** $k > 0$ **do**
3:     define $z = 2^b 3^t$, the best approximation of k with $0 \leq b \leq b_{max}$ and $0 \leq t \leq t_{max}$

4:     **print** (s, b, t)
5:     $b_{max} \leftarrow b, \quad t_{max} \leftarrow t$
6:     **if** $k < z$ **then**
7:         $s \leftarrow -s$
8:     $k \leftarrow |k - z|$

---

are the upper bounds for the binary and ternary exponents in the expansion of k, called b_{max} and t_{max} respectively. Clearly, we have $b_{max} < \log_2(k) < n$ and $t_{max} < \log_3(k) \approx 0.63n$. We noticed that using these utmost values for b_{max} and t_{max} do not result in short expansion. Instead, we consider the following heuristic which leads to very good results: if $k = (k_{n-1} \ldots k_1 k_0)_2$ is a randomly chosen n-bit integer (with $k_{n-1} \neq 0$), we initially set $b_{max} = x$ and $t_{max} = y$, where $2^x 3^y$ is a very good, non-trivial (with $y \neq 0$) approximation of 2^n. (Specific values are given in Table 7 for $n = 160$.) Then, in order to get decreasing sequences for b_i's and t_i's, the new largest exponents are updated according to the values of b and t obtained in Step 3.

The complexity of Algorithm 1 mainly depends on the way we implement Step 3; finding the best approximation of k of the form $z = 2^b 3^t$. If we can afford the storage of all the mixed powers of 2 and 3, this can be implemented very easily using a search over an ordered table of precomputed values. Otherwise, we can use an efficient solution recently proposed in [2] based on continued fractions and Ostrowski's number system. In both cases, the complexity of the conversion is negligible compared to the cost of the scalar multiplication. However, it is important to remark that, in most cases, the conversion into DBNS might not be needed. Indeed, in most ECC protocols, the multiplier k is a randomly chosen integer. We can thus directly generate a random DBNS number in the required form. Also, when k is part of a secret key, the conversion into DBNS can be done offline and even further optimized, when computation time is not an issue.

In the next sections, we present two versions of the DBNS-based point multiplication algorithm. We shall refer to the even case for curves defined over binary fields, when affine coordinates are used; and to the odd case for curves defined over large prime fields (or more generally any field of odd characteristic greater than 3), when Jacobian coordinates are preferred.

3.1 Point Multiplication in Even Characteristic

In even characteristic, i.e., with $P \in E(\mathbb{F}_{2^n})$ and k defined as above, Algorithm 2 below, computes the new point kP. We remark that although $m-1$ additions are

---

Algorithm 2. Double-Base Scalar Multiplication in even characteristic

---

Input An integer $k = \sum_{i=1}^{m} s_i 2^{b_i} 3^{t_i}$, with $s_i \in \{-1, 1\}$, and such that $b_1 \geq b_2 \geq \cdots \geq$
$\quad\quad b_m \geq 0$, and $t_1 \geq t_2 \geq \cdots \geq t_m \geq 0$; and a point $P \in E(K)$
Output the point $kP \in E(K)$
 1: $Z \leftarrow s_1 P$
 2: **for** $i = 1, \ldots, m-1$ **do**
 3: $\quad$ $u \leftarrow b_i - b_{i+1}$
 4: $\quad$ $v \leftarrow t_i - t_{i+1}$
 5: $\quad$ **if** $u = 0$ **then**
 6: $\quad\quad$ $Z \leftarrow 3(3^{v-1}Z) + s_{i+1}P$
 7: $\quad$ **else**
 8: $\quad\quad$ $Z \leftarrow 3^v Z$
 9: $\quad\quad$ $Z \leftarrow 4^{\lfloor (u-1)/2 \rfloor} Z$
10: $\quad\quad$ **if** $u \equiv 0 \pmod 2$ **then**
11: $\quad\quad\quad$ $Z \leftarrow 4Z + s_{i+1}P$
12: $\quad\quad$ **else**
13: $\quad\quad\quad$ $Z \leftarrow 2Z + s_{i+1}P$
14: **Return** Z

---

required to compute kP, we never actually use the addition operation (ADD); simply because we combine each addition with either a doubling (Step 13), a tripling (Step 6) or a quadrupling (Step 11), using the DA, TA and QA primitives. Note also that the TA operation for computing $3P \pm Q$ is only used in Step 6, when $u = 0$. Another approach of similar cost is to start with all the quadruplings plus one possible doubling when u is odd, and then perform $v - 1$ triplings followed by one final triple-and-add. We present new algorithms for $4P$ and $4P \pm Q$ in Section 4.

In order to evaluate the complexity of Algorithm 2, we have to count the number of curve operations; i.e., the number of DBL, DA, TPL, TA, QPL, QA, which clearly depends on the DBNS representation of the scalar k. In fact, Algorithm 2 gives us a double-base chain for k, say K_m, that we can use to determine the number of curve operations required to evaluate kP. Let us define W_n as the number of curve operations required to compute $K_n P$ from $K_{n-1}P$. We have $K_1 = 1$ and $W_1 = 0$ (in Step 1, we set Z to P or $-P$ at no cost). Then, for $n > 1$ we have

$$W_{n+1} = \delta_{u,0}\left((v-1)T + TA\right)$$
$$+ (1 - \delta_{u,0})\left(vT + \left\lfloor \frac{u-1}{2} \right\rfloor Q + \delta_{|u|_2,0}\,QA + \delta_{|u|_2,1}\,DA\right), \quad (6)$$

where $\delta_{i,j}$ is the Kronecker delta such that $\delta_{i,j} = 1$ if $i = j$ and $\delta_{i,j} = 0$ if $i \neq j$, and $|u|_2$ denotes $u \bmod 2$ (the remainder of u in the division by 2). The total cost for computing kP from the input point P is thus given by

$$W_m = \sum_{i=1}^{m} W_i \; . \qquad (7)$$

In Section 5, we illustrate the efficiency of this algorithm by providing comparisons with classical methods and a recently proposed ternary/binary approach [6].

3.2   Point Multiplication in Odd Characteristic

For fields of odd characteristic > 3, when primitives in Jacobian coordinates are more efficient, Algorithm 3 below is used to compute kP. It takes advantage of the known w-DBL$^{\mathcal{J}}$ and ADD$^{\mathcal{J}+\mathcal{A}}$ formulæ recalled in Section 2.1 and the new TPL$^{\mathcal{J}}$, w-TPL$^{\mathcal{J}}$ and w-TPL$^{\mathcal{J}}/w'$-DBL$^{\mathcal{J}}$ proposed in Section 4. Its complexity depends on the number of doublings, triplings and mixed additions that have to be performed. Clearly, the total number of (mixed) additions is equal to the length m of the double-base chain for k, or equivalently the number of

---

Algorithm 3. Double-Base Scalar Multiplication in Odd Characteristic > 3

Input An integer $k = \sum_{i=1}^{m} s_i\, 2^{b_i} 3^{t_i}$, with $s_i \in \{-1, 1\}$, and such that $b_1 \geq b_2 \geq \cdots \geq b_m \geq 0$, and $t_1 \geq t_2 \geq \cdots \geq t_m \geq 0$; and a point $P \in E(K)$
Output the point $kP \in E(K)$
1: $Z \leftarrow s_1 P$
2: **for** $i = 1, \ldots, m-1$ **do**
3:      $u \leftarrow b_i - b_{i+1}, \quad v \leftarrow t_i - t_{i+1}$
4:      $Z \leftarrow 3^v Z$
5:      $Z \leftarrow 2^u Z$
6:      $Z \leftarrow Z + s_{i+1}P$
7: **Return** Z

$\{2,3\}$-integers in its DBNS representation. Also, the number of doublings and triplings are equal to $b_1 \leq b_{max}$ and $t_1 \leq t_{max}$ respectively. However, the field cost can be more precisely evaluated if one considers the exact complexity of each iteration, by counting the exact number of field multiplications and squarings required in Steps 4 and 5 by the consecutive calls to v-TPL and u-DBL. In Section 5, we make this complexity analysis more precise and we compare our new approach with several previous algorithms recognized for their efficiency.

4 New Point Arithmetic Algorithms

In this section we present new formulæ for point quadrupling (QPL) and combined quadruple-and-add (QA) in even characteristic, and for triplings (TPL$^{\mathcal{J}}$, w-TPL$^{\mathcal{J}}$ and w-TPL$^{\mathcal{J}}/w'$-DBL$^{\mathcal{J}}$) in odd characteristic, to be used in conjunction with the proposed point multiplication algorithms.

4.1 New Algorithms for $4P$ and $4P \pm Q$ in Even Characteristic

We remark that the trick used in [11] by Eisenträger et al., which consists in evaluating only the x-coordinate of $2P$ when computing $2P \pm Q$, can also be applied to speed-up the quadrupling (QPL) primitive. Indeed, given $P = (x_1, y_1)$, where $P \neq -P$, we have $2P = (x_3, y_3)$, where

$$\lambda_1 = x_1 + \frac{y_1}{x_1}, \quad x_3 = \lambda_1^2 + \lambda_1 + a, \quad y_3 = \lambda_1(x_1 + x_3) + x_3 + y_1,$$

and $4P = 2(2P) = (x_4, y_4)$, where

$$\lambda_2 = x_3 + \frac{y_3}{x_3}, \quad x_4 = \lambda_2^2 + \lambda_2 + a, \quad y_4 = \lambda_2(x_1 + x_4) + x_4 + y_1 .$$

We observe that the computation of y_3 can be avoided by evaluating λ_2 as

$$\lambda_2 = \frac{x_1^2}{x_3} + \lambda_1 + x_3 + 1 . \tag{8}$$

As a result, computing $4P$ over binary fields requires $2[i]+3[s]+3[m]$. Compared to two consecutive doublings, it saves one field multiplication at the extra cost of one field squaring. Note that we are working in characteristic two and thus squarings are free (normal basis) or of negligible cost (linear operation in binary fields).

For the QA operation, we evaluate $4P \pm Q$, as $2(2P) \pm Q$ using one doubling (DBL) and one double-and-add (DA), resulting in $3[i] + 3[s] + 5[m]$. This is always better than applying the previous trick one more time by computing $(((P+Q)+P)+P)+P)$ in $4[i]+4[s]+5[m]$; or evaluating $3P + (P+Q)$ which requires $4[i] + 4[s] + 6[m]$.

In [6], Ciet et al. have improved an algorithm by Guajardo and Paar [13] for the computation of $4P$; their new method requires $1[i] + 5[s] + 8[m]$. Based on their costs, QA is best evaluated as $(4P) \pm Q$ using one quadrupling (QPL) followed by one addition (ADD) in $2[i] + 6[s] + 10[m]$. In Table 3 below, we summarize the costs and break-even points between our new formulæ and the algorithms proposed in [6].

Table 3. Costs comparisons and break-even points for QPL and QA in even characteristic using affine coordinates

Operation	present work	[6]	break-even point
$4P$	$2[i] + 3[s] + 3[m]$	$1[i] + 5[s] + 8[m]$	$[i]/[m] = 5$
$4P \pm Q$	$3[i] + 3[s] + 5[m]$	$2[i] + 6[s] + 10[m]$	$[i]/[m] = 5$

4.2   New Point Tripling Formula in Odd Characteristic

In order to best exploit the ternary nature of the DBNS representation we also propose new point tripling algorithms in Jacobian coordinates, for curves defined over fields of odd characteristic ($\neq 3$).

To simplify, let us first consider affine coordinates. Let $P = (x_1, y_1) \in E(K)$ be a point on an elliptic curve E defined by (2). By definition, we have $2P = (x_2, y_2)$, where

$$\lambda_1 = \frac{3x_1^2 + a}{2y_1}, \quad x_2 = \lambda_1^2 - 2x_1, \quad y_2 = \lambda_1(x_1 - x_2) - y_1 . \tag{9}$$

We can compute $3P = 2P + P = (x_3, y_3)$, by evaluating λ_2 (the slope of the chord between the points $2P$ and P) as a function of x_1 and y_1 only. We have

$$\begin{aligned}
\lambda_2 &= \frac{y_2 - y_1}{x_2 - x_1} \\
&= -\lambda_1 - \frac{2y_1}{x_2 - x_1} \\
&= -\frac{3x_1^2 + a}{2y_1} - \frac{8y_1^3}{(3x_1^2 + a)^2 - 12x_1 y_1^2} .
\end{aligned} \tag{10}$$

We further remark that

$$\begin{aligned}
x_3 &= \lambda_2^2 - x_1 - x_2 \\
&= \lambda_2^2 - x_1 - \lambda_1^2 + 2x_1 \\
&= (\lambda_2 - \lambda_1)(\lambda_2 + \lambda_1) + x_1,
\end{aligned} \tag{11}$$

and

$$\begin{aligned}
y_3 &= \lambda_2(x_1 - x_3) - y_1 \\
&= -\lambda_2(\lambda_2 - \lambda_1)(\lambda_2 + \lambda_1) - y_1 .
\end{aligned} \tag{12}$$

Thus $3P = (x_3, y_3)$ can be computed directly from $P = (x_1, y_1)$, without evaluating the intermediate values x_2 and y_2.

By replacing x_1 and y_1 by X_1/Z_1^2 and Y_1/Z_1^3 respectively, we obtain the following point tripling formulæ in Jacobian coordinates. Given $P = (X_1, Y_1, Z_1)$, we compute $3P = (X_3, Y_3, Z_3)$ as

$$X_3 = 8Y_1^2(T - ME) + X_1E^2$$
$$Y_3 = Y_1(4(ME - T)(2T - ME) - E^3) \tag{13}$$
$$Z_3 = Z_1E,$$

where $M = 3X_1^2 + aZ_1^4$, $E = 12X_1Y_1^2 - M^2$ and $T = 8Y_1^4$.

The complexity of this new point tripling algorithm is equal to $6[s] + 10[m]$. If one uses side-channel atomicity to resist simple SCA, then this is equivalent to $16[m]$. We express $\mathrm{TPL}^{\mathcal{J}}$ in terms of atomic blocks Table 11 of Appendix A. In comparison, computing $3P$ using the doubling and addition algorithms from [5], expressed as a repetition of atomic blocks, costs $10[m] + 16[m] = 26[m]$.

As we have seen in Section 3.2, operation count of Algorithm 3 can be reduced by improving the computation of consecutive triplings; i.e., expressions of the form 3^wP. From (13), we remark that the computation of the intermediate value $M = 3X_1^2 + aZ_1^4$ requires $1[m] + 3[s]$ (we omit the multiplication by 3). If we need to compute $9P$, we have to evaluate $M' = 3X_3^2 + aZ_3^4$. Since $Z_3 = Z_1E$, we have $aZ_3^4 = aZ_1^4E^4$ (where $E = 12X_1Y_1^2 - M^2$), and aZ_1^4 and E^2 have already been computed in the previous iteration. Hence, using these precomputed subexpressions, we can compute $M' = 3X_3^2 + (aZ_1^4)(E^2)^2$, with $1[m] + 2[s]$. The same technique can be applied to save one multiplication for each subsequent tripling. Thus, we can compute 3^wP with $(15w + 1)[m]$, which is better than w invocation of the tripling algorithm. The atomic blocks version of $w\text{-TPL}^{\mathcal{J}}$ is given in Table 12 of Appendix A. Note that the idea of reusing aZ^4 for multiple doublings was first proposed by Cohen et al. in [7], where modified Jacobian coordinates are proposed. It is possible that a similar approach for repeated triplings can lead to further improvements.

From Table 2, $\mathrm{DBL}^{\mathcal{J}}$ normally requires $4[m] + 6[s]$, or equivalently 10 blocks of computation if side-channel atomicity is used. However, in our scalar multiplication algorithm, we remark that we very often invoke $w'\text{-DBL}^{\mathcal{J}}$ right after a $w\text{-TPL}^{\mathcal{J}}$ (the only exceptions occur when $u = 0$, which correspond to a series of consecutive $\{2,3\}$-integers in the expansion of k having the same binary exponents). Using subexpressions computed for the last tripling, we can save $1[s]$ for the first $\mathrm{DBL}^{\mathcal{J}}$. The next $(w' - 1)\text{-DBL}^{\mathcal{J}}$ are then computed with $(4w' - 4)[m] + (4w' - 4)[s]$. (The details of these algorithms are given in Appendix A.) We summarize the complexities of these curve operations in Table 4.

Table 4. Costs of tripling algorithms in Jacobian coordinates for curves defined over fields of odd characteristic > 3

Curve operation	Complexity	# Registers
$\mathrm{TPL}^{\mathcal{J}}$	$6[s] + 10[m]$	8
$w\text{-TPL}^{\mathcal{J}}$	$(4w + 2)[s] + (11w - 1)[m]$	10
$w\text{-TPL}^{\mathcal{J}}/w'\text{-DBL}^{\mathcal{J}}$	$(11w + 4w' - 1)[s] + (4w + 4w' + 3)[m]$	10

5   Comparisons

In this section, we compare our algorithms to the classic double-and-add, NAF and 4-NAF methods, plus some other recently proposed algorithms. More precisely, we consider the ternary/binary approach from [6] in even characteristic and two algorithms from Izu et al., published in [17] and [19] for curves defined over fields of odd characteristic. In the later case, we consider the protected version of our algorithm, combined with Joye's and Tymen's randomization technique to counteract differential attacks [20].

If we assume that k is a randomly chosen n-bit integer, it is well known that the double-and-add algorithm requires n doublings and $n/2$ additions on average. Using the NAF representation, the average density of non-zero digits is reduced to $1/3$. More generally, for w-NAF methods, the average number of non-zero digits is roughly equal to $1/(w + 1)$. Unfortunately, it seems very difficult to give such an estimate for the particular DBNS representation we are considering in this paper. In [9], it is proved that the greedy algorithm (with unbounded exponents) returns a DBNS expansion which satisfies the asymptotic bound of $O(n/\log n)$ additions, but this is probably not valid with the restriction that the exponents form two decreasing sequences. The rigorous determination of this complexity leads to tremendously difficult problems in transcendental number theory and exponential Diophantine equations and is still an open problem.

Hence, in order to estimate the average number of $\{2, 3\}$-integers required to represent k, and to precisely evaluate the complexity of our point multiplication algorithms, we have performed several numerical experiments, over 10000 randomly chosen 160-bit integers (163-bit integers for binary fields). Our results are presented in the next two sections.

5.1   Binary Fields

The average number of curve operations are presented in Table 5 for 163-bit numbers. The corresponding numbers of field operations are given in Table 6 for different ratios $[i]/[m]$, using the best complexities from Tables 1 and 3 in each case.

In Table 6, we remark that our algorithm requires fewer inversions and multiplications than the other methods, and because we are working over binary fields, squarings can be ignored. We can estimate the cost of each method, in terms

Table 5. Average number of curve operations using the binary, NAF, ternary/binary and DB-chain approaches for $n = 163$ bits

Algorithm	D	DA	T	TA	Q	QA
binary	82	81	–	–	–	–
NAF	109	54	–	–	–	–
ternary/binary	38	37	55	–	–	–
DB-chain (Algo. 2)	–	17	35	5	25	14

Table 6. Average number of field operations using the binary, NAF, ternary/binary and DB-chain approaches for $n = 163$ bits, and $[i]/[m] = 4, 8$

Algorithm	$[i]/[m] = 4$			$[i]/[m] = 8$		
	$[i]$	$[s]$	$[m]$	$[i]$	$[s]$	$[m]$
binary	244	244	407	163	244	893
NAF	217	217	380	163	217	704
ternary/binary	222	222	353	130	333	795
DB-chain (Algo. 2)	215	240	327	117	405	798

Table 7. Average number of terms and the corresponding field complexity of our new scalar multiplication algorithm obtained using 10000 randomly chosen 160-bit integers and different largest binary and ternary exponents

b_{max}	t_{max}	m	Field cost	Complexity ($\#[m]$)
57	65	44.52	$1[i] + 742.10[s] + 1226.92[m]$	1999.02
76	53	38.40	$1[i] + 740.59[s] + 1133.58[m]$	1904.17
95	41	36.83	$1[i] + 755.77[s] + 1077.48[m]$	1863.25
103	36	38.55	$1[i] + 772.42[s] + 1074.22[m]$	1876.25

of the equivalent number of field multiplications, by multiplying the number of inversions by the ratio $[i]/[m]$. By doing so, we obtain a speed-up of 21%, 13.5% and 5.4% over the binary, NAF and ternary/binary approaches respectively for $[i]/[m] = 8$; and 14.1%, 4.8% and 4.4% for $[i]/[m] = 4$.

5.2 Prime Fields

In this section, we report results for 160-bit integers. If the classic methods are used in conjunction with side-channel atomicity (which implies $[s] = [m]$), the average cost of the double-and-add method can be estimated to $159 \times 10 + 80 \times 11 + 41 = 2511[m]$; similarly, the NAF and 4-NAF methods require $2214[m]$ and $1983[m]$ respectively. The results of our numerical experiments are presented in Table 7.

In Table 7, we give the average number m of $\{2, 3\}$-integers used to represent a random 160-bit integer, and the average number of field operations performed by Algorithm 3 for different values of b_{max} and t_{max}. (This cost includes the fixed cost of Joye and Tymen's randomization.) In order to compare our algorithm with the side-channel resistant algorithms presented in [17, 19, 18], we also give the uniform cost in terms of the number of field multiplications. Note that, because we are using side-channel atomicity to prevent simple analysis, squarings cannot be optimized and must be computed using a general multiplier. We thus assume $[s] = [m]$ and $[i] = 30[m]$.

In Table 8, we summarize the complexities of these recognized methods. The figures for the algorithms from Izu, Möller and Takagi are taken from [17] and [19] assuming Coron's randomization technique which turns out to be more efficient in their case. The cost of our algorithm is taken from the third row of Table 7,

Table 8. Comparison of different scalar multiplication algorithms protected against simple and differential analysis

Algorithm	Complexity ($\#[m]$)
double-and-add	2511
NAF	2214
4-NAF	1983
Izu, Möller, Takagi 2002 [17]	2449
Izu, Takagi 2005 [19]	2629
Double-base chain (Algo. 3)	1863

with $b_{max} = 95$ and $t_{max} = 41$, which corresponds to the best non-trivial approximation to 2^{160} and leads to the best complexity.

We remark that our new algorithm outperforms all the previous recognized methods. It represents a gain of 25.8% over the double-and-add, 15.8% over the NAF, 6% over 4-NAF, 23.9% over [17] and 29.1% over [19].

6   Conclusions

In this paper, we have presented fast and secure scalar multiplication algorithms which take advantage of the sparseness and the ternary nature of the double-base number system. When Jacobian coordinates are used for curves defined over fields of odd characteristic (greater than 3), new formulæ for $\mathrm{TPL}^{\mathcal{J}}$ and $w\text{-}\mathrm{TPL}^{\mathcal{J}}$ have been proposed and expressed in atomic blocks to prevent simple analysis. Differential attacks are prevented using Joye and Tymen randomization method, but any countermeasure (allowing for mixed addition) can be integrated to our point multiplication algorithm. When working over binary fields, improved algorithms for point quadrupling and combined quadruple-and-add have been presented. Although many theoretical questions remain open about the double-base number system, e.g. the exact determination of the average number of $\{2, 3\}$-integer, or the number of DBNS representation with decreasing exponents of a given integer, we have produced a modified greedy algorithm to convert the multiplier k into the particular DBNS form required by our point multiplication algorithm. However, we want to make clear the point that in most cases, this conversion is not necessary. When k is randomly chosen, it suffices to generate directly a random, convenient DBNS number (with decreasing exponents); and when k is part of a secret key, the conversion process can be performed offline and even further optimized. We believe that the proposed point multiplication algorithms are very competitive contenders for fast and secure ECC implementations.

Acknowledgments

The authors would like to thank Tanja Lange for her invaluable comments and suggestions during the final preparation of this paper.

References

[1] R. M. Avanzi, H. Cohen, C. Doche, G. Frey, T. Lange, K. Nguyen, and F. Vercauteren. *Handbook of Elliptic and Hyperelliptic Curve Cryptography.* CRC Press, 2005.

[2] V. Berthé and L. Imbert. On converting numbers to the double-base number system. In F. T. Luk, editor, *Advanced Signal Processing Algorithms, Architecture and Implementations XIV*, volume 5559 of *Proceedings of SPIE*, pages 70–78. SPIE, 2004.

[3] I. F. Blake, G. Seroussi, and N. P. Smart. *Elliptic Curves in Cryptography.* Number 256 in London Mathematical Society Lecture Note Series. Cambridge University Press, 1999.

[4] I. F. Blake, G. Seroussi, and N. P. Smart. *Advances in Elliptic Curve Cryptography.* Number 317 in London Mathematical Society Lecture Note Series. Cambridge University Press, 2005.

[5] B. Chevalier-Mames, M. Ciet, and M. Joye. Low-cost solutions for preventing simple side-channel analysis: Side-channel atomicity. *IEEE Transactions on Computers*, 53(6):760–768, June 2004.

[6] M. Ciet, M. Joye, K. Lauter, and P. L. Montgomery. Trading inversions for multiplications in elliptic curve cryptography. Cryptology ePrint Archive, Report 2003/257, 2003.

[7] H. Cohen, A. Miyaji, and T. Ono. Efficient elliptic curve exponentiation using mixed coordinates. In K. Ohta and D. Pei, editors, *Advances in Cryptology – ASIACRYPT '98*, volume 1514 of *Lecture Notes in Computer Science*, pages 51–65. Springer-Verlag, 1998.

[8] E. De Win, S. Bosselaers, S. Vandenberghe, P. De Gersem, and J. Vandewalle. A fast software implementation for arithmetic operations in GF(2^n). In K. Kim and T. Matsumoto, editors, *Advances in Cryptology – ASIACRYPT '96*, volume 1163 of *Lecture Notes in Computer Science*, pages 65–76. Springer-Verlag, 1996.

[9] V. S. Dimitrov, G. A. Jullien, and W. C. Miller. An algorithm for modular exponentiation. *Information Processing Letters*, 66(3):155–159, May 1998.

[10] V. S. Dimitrov, G. A. Jullien, and W. C. Miller. Theory and applications of the double-base number system. *IEEE Transactions on Computers*, 48(10):1098–1106, Oct. 1999.

[11] K. Eisenträger, K. Lauter, and P. L. Montgomery. Fast elliptic curve arithmetic and improved Weil pairing evaluation. In M. Joye, editor, *Topics in Cryptology – CT-RSA 2003*, volume 2612 of *Lecture Notes in Computer Science*, pages 343–354. Springer-Verlag, 2003.

[12] K. Fong, D. Hankerson, J. Lòpez, and A. Menezes. Field inversion and point halving revisited. *IEEE Transactions on Computers*, 53(8):1047–1059, Aug. 2004.

[13] J. Guajardo and C. Paar. Efficient algorithms for elliptic curve cryptosystems. In *Advances in Cryptology – CRYPTO '97*, volume 1294 of *Lecture Notes in Computer Science*, pages 342–356. Springer-Verlag, 1997.

[14] D. Hankerson, J. Lòpez Hernandez, and A. Menezes. Software implementation of elliptic curve cryptography over binary fields. In Ç. K. Koç and C. Paar, editors, *Cryptographic Hardware and Embedded Systems – CHES 2000*, volume 1965 of *Lecture Notes in Computer Science*, pages 1–24. Springer-Verlag, 2000.

[15] D. Hankerson, A. Menezes, and S. Vanstone. *Guide to Elliptic Curve Cryptography.* Springer-Verlag, 2004.

[16] K. Itoh, M. Takenaka, N. Torii, S. Temma, and Y. Kurihara. Fast implementation of public-key cryptography on a DSP TMS320C6201. In Ç. K. Koç and C. Paar, editors, *Cryptographic Hardware and Embedded Systems – CHES '99*, volume 1717 of *Lecture Notes in Computer Science*, pages 61 – 72. Springer-Verlag, 1999.

[17] T. Izu, B. Möller, and T. Takagi. Improved elliptic curve multiplication methods resistant against side channel attacks. In A. Menezes and P. Sarkar, editors, *Progress in Cryptology – INDOCRYPT 2002*, volume 2551 of *Lecture Notes in Computer Science*, pages 269–313. Springer-Verlag, 2002.

[18] T. Izu and T. Takagi. A fast parallel elliptic curve multiplication resistant against side channel attacks. In D. Naccache and P. Paillier, editors, *Public Key Cryptography*, volume 2274 of *Lecture Notes in Computer Science*, pages 280–296. Springer-Verlag, 2002.

[19] T. Izu and T. Takagi. Fast elliptic curve multiplications resistant against side channel attacks. *IEICE Transactions Fundamentals*, E88-A(1):161–171, Jan. 2005.

[20] M. Joye and C. Tymen. Protections against differential analysis for elliptic curve cryptography – an algebraic approach. In Ç. K. Koç, D. Naccache, and C. Paar, editors, *Cryptographic Hardware and Embedded Systems – CHES 2001*, volume 2162 of *Lecture Notes in Computer Science*, pages 377 – 390. Springer-Verlag, 2001.

[21] N. Koblitz. Elliptic curve cryptosystems. *Mathematics of Computation*, 48(177):203–209, Jan. 1987.

[22] P. Kocher, J. Jaffe, and B. Jun. Differential power analysis. In M. Wiener, editor, *Advances in Cryptology – CRYPTO '99*, volume 1666 of *Lecture Notes in Computer Science*, pages 388–397. Springer-Verlag, Aug. 1999.

[23] P. C. Kocher. Timing attacks on implementations of Diffie-Hellman, RSA, DSS, and other systems. In N. Koblitz, editor, *Advances in Cryptology - CRYPTO '96*, volume 1109 of *Lecture Notes in Computer Science*, pages 104–113. Springer-Verlag, Aug. 1996.

[24] V. S. Miller. Uses of elliptic curves in cryptography. In H. C. Williams, editor, *Advances in Cryptology – CRYPTO '85*, volume 218 of *Lecture Notes in Computer Science*, pages 417–428. Springer-Verlag, 1986.

[25] R. Tijdeman. On the maximal distance between integers composed of small primes. *Compositio Mathematica*, 28:159–162, 1974.

A w-DBL$^{\mathcal{J}}$ and w-TPL$^{\mathcal{J}}$ Algorithms in Atomic Blocks

In this appendix, we give the algorithms for DBL$^{\mathcal{J}}$ (including the case when a doubling is performed right after a tripling), w-DBL$^{\mathcal{J}}$, TPL$^{\mathcal{J}}$ and w-TPL$^{\mathcal{J}}$, expressed in atomic blocks.

Table 9. The DBL$^{\mathcal{J}}$ algorithm in atomic blocks. When DBL$^{\mathcal{J}}$ is called right after w-TPL$^{\mathcal{J}}$, the blocks Δ_2, Δ_3 and Δ_4 can be replaced by the blocks Δ_2' and Δ_3' to save one multiplication.

DBL$^{\mathcal{J}}$
Input: $P = (X_1, Y_1, Z_1)$
Output: $2P = (X_3, Y_3, Z_3)$
Init: $R_1 = X_1$, $R_2 = Y_1$, $R_3 = Z_1$

Δ_1	$R_4 = R_1 \times R_1$	(X_1^2)	Δ_6	$R_2 = R_2 \times R_2$	(Y_1^2)
	$R_5 = R_4 + R_4$	$(2X_1^2)$		$R_2 = R_2 + R_2$	$(2Y_1^2)$
	$*$			$*$	
	$R_4 = R_4 + R_5$	$(3X_1^2)$		$*$	
Δ_2	$R_5 = R_3 \times R_3$	(Z_1^2)	Δ_7	$R_5 = R_1 \times R_2$	(S)
	$R_1 = R_1 + R_1$	$(2X_1)$		$*$	
	$*$			$R_5 = -R_5$	$(-S)$
	$*$			$*$	
Δ_3	$R_5 = R_5 \times R_5$	(Z_1^4)	Δ_8	$R_1 = R_4 \times R_4$	(M^2)
	$*$			$R_1 = R_1 + R_5$	$(M^2 - S)$
	$*$			$*$	
	$*$			$R_1 = R_1 + R_5$	(X_3)
Δ_4	$R_6 = a \times R_5$	(aZ_1^4)	Δ_9	$R_2 = R_2 \times R_2$	$(4Y_1^4)$
	$R_4 = R_4 + R_6$	(M)		$R_7 = R_2 + R_2$	(T)
	$*$			$*$	
	$R_5 = R_2 + R_2$	$(2Y_1)$		$R_5 = R_1 + R_5$	$(X_3 - S)$
Δ_5	$R_3 = R_3 \times R_5$	(Z_3)	Δ_{10}	$R_4 = R_4 \times R_5$	$(M(X_3 - S))$
	$*$			$R_2 = R_4 + R_7$	$(-Y_3)$
	$*$			$R_2 = -R_2$	(Y_3)
	$*$			$*$	

Δ_2'	$R_5 = R_{10} \times R_{10}$		Δ_3'	$R_5 = R_5 \times R_9$
	$R_1 = R_1 + R_1$			$R_4 = R_4 + R_6$
	$*$			$*$
	$*$			$*$

Table 10. The w-DBL$^{\mathcal{J}}$ algorithm in atomic blocks. The 10 blocks (or 9 if executed after w-TPL$^{\mathcal{J}}$) of DBL$^{\mathcal{J}}$ (Table 9) must be executed once, followed by the blocks Δ_{11} to Δ_{18} which have to be executed $w - 1$ times. After the execution of DBL$^{\mathcal{J}}$, the point of coordinates (X_t, Y_t, Z_t) correspond to the point $2P$; at the end of the $w - 1$ iterations, $2^w P = (X_3, Y_3, Z_3) = (X_t, Y_t, Z_t)$.

w-**DBL**$^{\mathcal{J}}$
Input: $P = (X_1, Y_1, Z_1)$
Output: $2^w P = (X_3, Y_3, Z_3)$
Init: (X_t, Y_t, Z_t) is the result of DBL$^{\mathcal{J}}(P)$, $R_6 = aZ_1^4$, $R_7 = 8Y_1^4$

Δ_{11}	$R_4 = R_1 \times R_1$	(X_t^2)	Δ_{15}	$R_5 = R_1 \times R_2$	(S)
	$R_5 = R_4 + R_4$	$(2X_t^2)$		*	
	*			$R_5 = -R_5$	$(-S)$
	$R_4 = R_4 + R_5$	$(3X_t^2)$		*	
Δ_{12}	$R_5 = R_6 \times R_7$	$(aZ_t^4 + 8Y_t^4)$	Δ_{16}	$R_1 = R_4 \times R_4$	(M^2)
	$R_6 = R_5 + R_5$	(aZ_t^4)		$R_1 = R_1 + R_5$	$(M^2 - S)$
	*			*	
	$R_4 = R_4 + R_6$	(M)		$R_1 = R_1 + R_5$	(X_{t+1})
Δ_{13}	$R_3 = R_2 \times R_3$	$(Y_t Z_t)$	Δ_{17}	$R_2 = R_2 \times R_2$	$(4Y_t^4)$
	$R_3 = R_3 + R_3$	(Z_{t+1})		$R_7 = R_2 + R_2$	(T)
	*			*	
	$R_1 = R_1 + R_1$	$(2X_t)$		$R_5 = R_1 + R_5$	$(X_{t+1} - S)$
Δ_{14}	$R_2 = R_2 \times R_2$	(Y_t^2)	Δ_{18}	$R_4 = R_4 \times R_5$	$(M(X_{t+1} - S))$
	$R_2 = R_2 + R_2$	$(2Y_t^2)$		$R_2 = R_4 + R_7$	$(-Y_{t+1})$
	*			$R_2 = -R_2$	(Y_{t+1})
	*			*	

Table 11. The $\mathrm{TPL}^{\mathcal{J}}$ algorithm in atomic blocks

$\mathrm{TPL}^{\mathcal{J}}$
Input: $P = (X_1, Y_1, Z_1)$
Output: $3P = (X_3, Y_3, Z_3)$
Init: $R_1 = X_1,\ R_2 = Y_1,\ R_3 = Z_1$

Γ_1	$R_4 = R_3 \times R_3$	(Z_1^2)	Γ_9	$R_8 = R_6 \times R_7$	(T)
	*			$R_7 = R_7 + R_7$	$(8Y_1^2)$
	*			*	
	*			*	
Γ_2	$R_4 = R_4 \times R_4$	(Z_1^4)	Γ_{10}	$R_6 = R_4 \times R_5$	(ME)
	*			*	
	*			$R_6 = -R_6$	$(-ME)$
	*			$R_6 = R_8 + R_6$	$(T - ME)$
Γ_3	$R_5 = R_1 \times R_1$	(X_1^2)	Γ_{11}	$R_{10} = R_5 \times R_5$	(E^2)
	$R_6 = R_5 + R_5$	$(2X_1^2)$		*	
	*			*	
	$R_5 = R_5 + R_6$	$(3X_1^2)$		*	
Γ_4	$R_9 = a \times R_4$	(aZ_1^4)	Γ_{12}	$R_1 = R_1 \times R_{10}$	$(X_1 E^2)$
	$R_4 = R_5 + R_9$	(M)		*	
	*			*	
	*			*	
Γ_5	$R_5 = R_2 \times R_2$	(Y_1^2)	Γ_{13}	$R_5 = R_{10} \times R_5$	(E^3)
	$R_6 = R_5 + R_5$	$(2Y_1^2)$		$R_8 = R_8 + R_6$	$(2T - ME)$
	*			$R_5 = -R_5$	$(-E^3)$
	$R_7 = R_6 + R_6$	$(4Y_1^2)$		*	
Γ_6	$R_5 = R_1 \times R_7$	$(4X_1Y_1^2)$	Γ_{14}	$R_4 = R_6 \times R_7$	$8Y_1^2(T - ME)$
	$R_8 = R_5 + R_5$	$(8X_1Y_1^2)$		$R_6 = R_6 + R_6$	$(2(T - ME))$
	*			$R_6 = -R_6$	$(2(ME - T))$
	$R_5 = R_5 + R_8$	$(12X_1Y_1^2)$		$R_1 = R_1 + R_4$	(X_3)
Γ_7	$R_8 = R_4 \times R_4$	(M^2)	Γ_{15}	$R_6 = R_6 \times R_8$	$(2(ME - T)(2T - ME))$
	*			$R_6 = R_6 + R_6$	$(4(ME - T)(2T - ME))$
	$R_8 = -R_8$	$(-M^2)$		*	
	$R_5 = R_5 + R_8$	(E)		$R_6 = R_6 + R_5$	$(4(ME - T)(2T - ME) - E^3)$
Γ_8	$R_3 = R_3 \times R_5$	(Z_3)	Γ_{16}	$R_2 = R_2 \times R_6$	(Y_3)
	*			*	
	*			*	
	*			*	

Table 12. The w-TPL$^{\mathcal{J}}$ algorithm in atomic blocks. The 16 blocks of TPL$^{\mathcal{J}}$ must be executed once, followed by the blocks Γ_{17} to Γ_{31} which have to be executed $w - 1$ times. After the execution of TPL$^{\mathcal{J}}$, the point of coordinates (X_t, Y_t, Z_t) correspond to the point $3P$; at the end of the $w - 1$ iterations, $3^w P = (X_3, Y_3, Z_3) = (X_t, Y_t, Z_t)$.

w-**TPL**$^{\mathcal{J}}$

Input: $P = (X_1, Y_1, Z_1)$

Output: $3^w P = (X_3, Y_3, Z_3)$

Init: (X_t, Y_t, Z_t) is the result of TPL$^{\mathcal{J}}(P)$, $R_9 = aZ_1^4$, $R_{10} = E^2$

Γ_{17}	$R_4 = R_9 \times R_{10}$	$(aZ_t^4 E^2)$	Γ_{25}	$R_6 = R_4 \times R_5$	(ME)
	*			*	
	*			$R_6 = -R_6$	$(-ME)$
	*			$R_6 = R_8 + R_6$	$(T - ME)$
Γ_{18}	$R_5 = R_1 \times R_1$	(X_t^2)	Γ_{26}	$R_{10} = R_5 \times R_5$	(E^2)
	$R_6 = R_5 + R_5$	$(2X_t^2)$		*	
	*			*	
	$R_5 = R_5 + R_6$	$(3X_t^2)$		*	
Γ_{19}	$R_9 = R_4 \times R_{10}$	(aZ_t^4)	Γ_{27}	$R_1 = R_1 \times R_{10}$	$(X_t E^2)$
	$R_4 = R_5 + R_9$	(M)		*	
	*			*	
	*			*	
Γ_{20}	$R_5 = R_2 \times R_2$	(Y_t^2)	Γ_{28}	$R_5 = R_{10} \times R_5$	(E^3)
	$R_6 = R_5 + R_5$	$(2Y_t^2)$		$R_8 = R_8 + R_6$	$(2T - ME)$
	*			$R_5 = -R_5$	$(-E^3)$
	$R_7 = R_6 + R_6$	$(4Y_t^2)$		*	
Γ_{21}	$R_5 = R_1 \times R_7$	$(4X_t Y_t^2)$	Γ_{29}	$R_4 = R_6 \times R_7$	$(8Y_t^2(T - ME))$
	$R_8 = R_5 + R_5$	$(8X_t Y_t^2)$		$R_6 = R_6 + R_6$	$(2(T - ME))$
	*			$R_6 = -R_6$	$(2(ME - T))$
	$R_5 = R_5 + R_8$	$(12X_t Y_t^2)$		$R_1 = R_1 + R_4$	(X_{t+1})
Γ_{22}	$R_8 = R_4 \times R_4$	(M^2)	Γ_{30}	$R_6 = R_6 \times R_8$	$(2(ME - T)(2T - ME))$
	*			$R_6 = R_6 + R_6$	$(4(ME - T)(2T - ME))$
	$R_8 = -R_8$	$(-M^2)$		*	
	$R_5 = R_5 + R_8$	(E)		$R_6 = R_6 + R_5$	$(4(ME - T)(2T - ME) - E^3)$
Γ_{23}	$R_3 = R_3 \times R_5$	(Z_{t+1})	Γ_{31}	$R_2 = R_2 \times R_6$	(Y_{t+1})
	*			*	
	*			*	
	*			*	
Γ_{24}	$R_8 = R_6 \times R_7$	(T)			
	$R_7 = R_7 + R_7$	$(8Y_t^2)$			
	*				
	*				

Upper Bounds on the Communication Complexity of Optimally Resilient Cryptographic Multiparty Computation

Martin Hirt[1] and Jesper Buus Nielsen[2]

[1] ETH Zurich, Deptartment of Computer Science
`hirt@inf.ethz.ch`
[2] University of Aarhus, Department of Computer Science
`buus@daimi.au.dk`[*]

Abstract. We give improved upper bounds on the communication complexity of optimally-resilient secure multiparty computation in the cryptographic model. We consider evaluating an n-party randomized function and show that if f can be computed by a circuit of size c, then $\mathcal{O}(cn^2\kappa)$ is an upper bound for active security with optimal resilience $t < n/2$ and security parameter κ. This improves on the communication complexity of previous protocols by a factor of at least n. This improvement comes from the fact that in the new protocol, only $\mathcal{O}(n)$ messages (of size $\mathcal{O}(\kappa)$ each) are broadcast during the *whole* protocol execution, in contrast to previous protocols which require at least $\mathcal{O}(n)$ broadcasts *per gate*.

Furthermore, we improve the upper bound on the communication complexity of passive secure multiparty computation with resilience $t < n$ from $\mathcal{O}(cn^2\kappa)$ to $\mathcal{O}(cn\kappa)$. This improvement is mainly due to a simple observation.

1 Introduction

1.1 Secure Multiparty Computation

Secure multiparty computation (MPC) allows a set of n players to compute an arbitrary function of their inputs in a secure way. More generally, we consider reactive computations, which are specified as a circuit with input gates, evaluation gates (e.g., AND and OR gates), random gates, and output gates.

Security is specified with respect to an adversary corrupting up to t of the players for a defined threshold t. A *passive adversary* can inspect the internal state of corrupted players, an *active adversary* can take full control over them. A protocol is t-*secure* if an adversary attacking the protocol with t corruptions can only obtain inevitable goals w.r.t. gathering information and influencing the output of the protocol. I.e. it can only learn the inputs and outputs of the corrupted players, and, if it is active, only influence the inputs of the corrupted players.

---

[*] Supported by FICS, Foundations in Cryptography and Security, Center of the Danish Research Council for Natural Sciences.

B. Roy (Ed.): ASIACRYPT 2005, LNCS 3788, pp. 79–99, 2005.

1.2   Brief History of MPC

The MPC problem dates back to Yao [Yao82]. Independently Goldreich, Micali and Wigderson and Chaum, Damgård and van de Graaf [GMW87, CDG87] presented solutions to the MPC problem. Their protocols provide cryptographic security against a computationally bounded active adversary corrupting up to $t < n/2$ of the players. Later, unconditionally secure MPC protocols were proposed by Ben-Or, Goldwasser and Wigderson [BGW88] and Chaum, Crépeau and Damgård [CCD88] for the *secure-channels model*, where perfectly secure channels are assumed between every pair of parties. These protocols have resilience $t < n/3$. Later Rabin and Ben-Or [RB89] and independently Beaver [Bea91b] presented protocols with resilience $t < n/2$ for the secure-channels model with broadcast channels.

1.3   Previous Work on the Complexity of Secure MPC

There has been substantial research on the complexity of secure MPC, both the round complexity and the communication complexity in messages and bits.

As for the round complexity of secure MPC, it is now known that in a network without any setup any functionality can be computed securely in three rounds and that there exists functionalities which cannot be computed in two rounds without setup [GIKR02]. Furthermore, it is known that after an initial setup phase, any functionality can be computed in two rounds [GIKR02, CDI05] and that there exist functionalities which cannot be computed in one round even after a setup phase. Even though the resulta in [GIKR02, CDI05] only applies to a setting where the number of parties is relatively small, the above results go a long way in resolving the exact round complexity of secure MPC.

As for the communication complexity, the picture is much more open, and we are far from knowing the exact communication complexity of secure MPC. The *communication complexity* of a protocol is measured as the total number of bits sent by all uncorrupted parties during the protocol execution.

Very few results are known about the lower bound on the communication complexity, except those which follow trivially from known lower bounds on the communication complexity of Byzantine agreement — since the model of secure MPC requires agreement on the output, Byzantine agreement is a special case of secure MPC. For the upper bound on the communication complexity, much more is known.

The seminal protocols with passive security tend to be very communication-efficient, in contrast to their active-secure counterparts, that require high communication complexities. The high communication complexities of active-secure protocols is mainly due to their intensive use of a Byzantine agreement primitive, which is to be simulated by communication-intensive broadcast protocols. The most efficient broadcast protocols for $t < n$ communicate $\Omega(n^2\ell)$ bits for broadcasting an ℓ-bit message [BGP92, CW92]. We denote the communication complexity for broadcasting an ℓ-bit message by $\mathcal{B}(\ell)$.

Over the years, several protocols have been proposed which improve the efficiency of active-secure MPC. In the cryptographic model (with $t < n/2$), all protocols presented so far [GV87, BB89, BMR90, BFKR90, Bea91a, GRR98, CDM00, CDD00] require every player to broadcast one message for each multiplication gate. For a circuit with c gates, this results in a total communication complexity of $\Omega(cn\mathcal{B}(\kappa)) = \Omega(cn^3\kappa)$, where κ denotes the security parameter of the protocol. In the secure-channels model with broadcast with $t < n/2$, things are even worse: The most efficient protocol in this model [CDD+99] requires $\Omega(n^4)$ κ-bit messages to be broadcast for every multiplication gate.

In the secure-channels model with $t < n/3$, recently more efficient protocols were proposed [HMP00, HM01]: The latter protocol requires only $\mathcal{O}(n^2)$ broadcasts in total (independently of the size of the circuit), and communicates an additional $\mathcal{O}(cn^2)$ bits in total. This result is based on the so-called *player-elimination framework*, where subsets of players with faulty majority are eliminated. This prevents corrupted players from repetitively disturbing and slowing down the computation. Unfortunately, the player-elimination framework cannot capture models with $t < n/2$: In order to reconstruct an intermediate value (a wire), at least $t + 1$ players are required. After eliminating a group of players with faulty majority, the remaining set of players does not necessarily contain $t + 1$ honest players (it might even contain only one single player), hence the remaining players cannot reconstruct intermediate results — and would have to restart the whole computation.

1.4   Contributions

We consider upper bounds on the communication complexity of active-secure MPC protocol in the cryptographic model with $t < n/2$ and passive-secure MPC protocols in the cryptographic model with $t < n$. The most efficient active-secure protocol for this model is the protocol by Cramer, Damgård and Nielsen [CDN01]. This protocol requires every player to broadcast $\mathcal{O}(1)$ κ-bit values for each multiplication gate in the circuit. When replacing the broadcast primitive by the most efficient broadcast protocol with resilience $t < n/2$ known today (but unknown at the time when [CDN01] was published), this results in an overall communication complexity of $\mathcal{O}(cn^3\kappa)$ for evaluating a circuit with c gates. The same upper bound for active security was proved by Jakobsson and Juels [JJ00] using similar techniques.

We improve the upper bound for active security by constructing a new MPC protocol for the cryptographic model with resilience $t < n/2$: The new protocol requires every player to broadcast $\mathcal{O}(1)$ κ-bit values *in total*, i.e., during the whole protocol execution. Additionally, the players communicate $\mathcal{O}(n^2\kappa)$ bits per multiplication over the normal channels. This results in a total communication complexity of $\mathcal{O}(cn^2\kappa + n\mathcal{B}(\kappa)) = \mathcal{O}(cn^2\kappa + n^3\kappa)$. If every party has just one input to the circuit, then $c \geq n$ and $\mathcal{O}(cn^2\kappa + n^3\kappa) = \mathcal{O}(cn^2\kappa)$.[1]

---

[1] For simplicity we specify all bounds in the following for circuits with $c = \Theta(n)$. Bounds for $c \leq n$ are obtained by letting $c = n$.

The new protocol follows the basic paradigm of [CDN01], enhanced with ideas of [Bea91a] and [HMP00] and several novel technical contributions. Our protocol essentially improves over the best known upper bound for active security by a factor n.

Using a simple observation about threshold homomorphic encryption-based MPC protocols we also present a passive secure protocol with resilience $t < n$, communicating only $\mathcal{O}(cn\kappa)$ bits. This improves the best known upper bound for passive security, as given by the protocol of Franklin and Haber [FH96], by a factor n.

2   Preliminaries

In this section we discuss our model of security of protocols and we sketch the technical setting for threshold homomorphic encryption based MPC. The reader familiar with these issues can safely skip this section.

2.1   Model

We consider n players that are pairwise connected with authenticated open channels and we assume synchronous communication. The adversary may corrupt any t of the players. All parties and the adversary are restricted to probabilistic polynomial time. We consider a *static* adversary, which corrupts all parties before the protocol execution.

Specifying a multiparty functionality. We assume that the task to be realized is given by an arithmetic circuit with input, addition, multiplication, randomizing and output gates, all over some ring $\mathbb{M}$. We consider reactive circuits where some input gates might appear after output gates. We assume that the circuit is divided into layers being either input layers, consisting solely of input gates, evaluation layers consisting of addition, multiplication, and randomizing gates, and output layers, consisting solely of output gates. An input gate G specifies its layer and the party that is to supply the value for the gate. A negation gate specifies its layer and a gate in a previous layer, from which it takes its input. An addition gate as well as a multiplication gate specifies its layer and two gates in a previous layer, from which it takes its input. An output gate specifies its layer and a gate in a previous layer, which is to be revealed.

The ideal evaluation. To explain the multiparty functionality specified by a reactive circuit, it is convenient to image an ideal process, where the parties are connected to a fully trusted party with secure channels. The ideal evaluation of the circuit takes place in a layer by layer manner. For each input layer, for every gate specifying P_i as the party to contribute the input, P_i sends to the trusted party an input value $v \in \mathbb{M}$ over a secure line. If no value is sent, the trusted party sets v to be 0. For each evaluation layer, the trusted party computes values of all evaluation gates according to the circuit; Randomizing gates are set to be uniformly random values $v \in_R \mathbb{M}$ and addition gates and multiplication gates are evaluated in the expected manner. For each output layer, the trusted party sends the value of all output gates in the layer to all parties.

Notice that in the ideal evaluation an adversary controlling some set of corrupted parties can only achieve inevitable goals: Of information it only learns the output and the corrupted parties' inputs and, if it is active, the only influence it can exert on the evaluation is changing the corrupted parties' inputs to the function.

The goal of a protocol for a circuit is to realize the same functionality in a real-life network.

The real-life model. We assume that the network has a *setup phase*. In the setup phase a *setup function* $s : \{0,1\}^* \rightarrow (\{0,1\}^*)^{n+1}, r \mapsto (p, s_1, \ldots, s_n)$ is evaluated on a random input, and the value p is made public. The value s_i is only given to the party P_i. The reason for having a setup phase is that we will be interested in MPC protocols with active resilience $t < n/2$, and without a setup phase not even the Byzantine agreement problem [LSP82], which is a special case of the general MPC problem, can be solved with active resilience $t < n/2$. The function s is specified as part of the general protocol. In particular, s is not allowed to depend on the circuit.

Defining security. There are many proposals on how to model the security of an n-party protocol, i.e. for what it means for a protocol to realize the ideal evaluation of a circuit. Common to most is that the real-life adversary can only obtain goals comparable to those of an ideal-model adversary, i.e. inevitable goals.

The comparison of the protocol execution to the ideal evaluation is made by requiring that the complete view of an adversary attacking the protocol execution can be simulated given only the view of an adversary attacking the ideal evaluation with the same corrupted parties. This captures exactly the idea that the information gathering and the influencing capabilities of the adversary include nothing extra to that of which the adversary is entitled. This so-called simulation approach to comparing the protocol execution to the ideal evaluation originates in the definition of zero-knowledge proof in [GMR85] by Goldwasser, Micali and Rackoff. For the MPC setting the simulation approach is introduced by Goldreich, Micali and Wigderson [GMW87] and elaborated on in a large body of later work [GL90, MR91, Bea91b, BCG93, HM00, Can00, Can01]. Of these models, the universally composable (UC) security framework of Canetti [Can01] gives the strongest security guarantees. When proving an upper bound it makes sense to consider the strongest security notion. The core model in [Can01] is asynchronous, but contains hints on how to apply it to a synchronous setting as we consider here. This was e.g. done in [DN03]. It is straight-forward to formally cast our reactive circuit model in the model of [DN03], and we can prove all our protocols secure in this model.

For the detail of proofs permitted in this extended abstract we will not need any formal details about this particular simulation model. The informal proof sketches given in subsequent sections can easily be extended to fully formal simulation proofs using by now standard proof techniques for threshold homomorphic encryption based MPC, see e.g. [CDN01, DN03].

2.2 Homomorphic Encryption Scheme

In our protocols we assume the existence of a semantically secure (in the sense of IND-CPA [BDPR98]) probabilistic public-key encryption function $E_Z : \mathbb{M} \times \mathbb{R} \to \mathbb{E}, (m, \alpha) \mapsto M$, where Z denotes the public key, $\mathbb{M}$ denotes a set of messages, $\mathbb{R}$ denotes the set of random strings, and $\mathbb{E}$ denotes the set of encryptions. We write E instead of E_Z for shorthand. The decryption function is $D_z : \mathbb{E} \to \mathbb{M}, M \mapsto m$, where z denotes the secret key. Again, we write D instead of D_z.

We require that E is a group homomorphism, i.e., $E(m_1, \alpha_1) \oplus E(m_2, \alpha_2) = E(m_1 + m_2, \alpha_1 \boxtimes \alpha_2)$ for the corresponding group operations $+$ in $\mathbb{M}$, $\boxtimes$ in $\mathbb{R}$, and $\oplus$ in $\mathbb{E}$. We require that $\mathbb{M}$ is a ring $\mathbb{Z}_M$ for $M > 1$. The other groups can be arbitrary.

In general we use capital letters to denote the encryption of the corresponding lowercase letters. For $a \in \mathbb{N}$ and $B \in \mathbb{E}$ and $\alpha \in \mathbb{R}$ we write aB as a shorthand for $B \oplus \cdots \oplus B$ with $a-1$ additions and we use α^a as a shorthand for $\alpha \boxtimes \cdots \boxtimes \alpha$ with $a-1$ multiplications. We use $A \ominus B$ to denote $A \oplus (-B)$, where $-B$ denotes the inverse of B in $\mathbb{E}$.

We define a ciphertext-randomization function $\mathbb{R} : \mathbb{E} \times \mathbb{R} \to \mathbb{E}, (M, \gamma) \mapsto (M \oplus E(0, \gamma))$. If $M = E(m, \alpha)$, then $\mathbb{R}(M, \gamma) = E(m, \alpha \boxtimes \gamma)$. If γ is uniformly random in $\mathbb{R}$ and independent of α, then $\alpha \boxtimes \gamma$ is uniformly random in $\mathbb{R}$ and independent of α, so $\mathbb{R}(M, \gamma)$ will be a new independent, uniformly random encryption of m. We say that $M' = \mathbb{R}(M, \gamma)$ is a randomization of M.

We also require that there exists a passive secure threshold function sharing of D_z between n parties. I.e. for a given threshold t we split the decryption key z in n shares $z_1, \ldots, z_n$ and there exists a share-decryption function $SD_{z_i} : \mathbb{E} \to \mathbb{S}, M \mapsto m_i$, where $\mathbb{S}$ denotes the set of message shares. And there exists a combining function $C : \mathbb{S}^{t+1} \to \mathbb{M}, (m^{(1)}, \ldots, m^{(t+1)}) \mapsto m$, with the property that if $M = E_Z(m)$ and $m^{(j)} = SD_{z_{i_j}}(M)$ for $i = 1, \ldots, t+1$ and $t+1$ distinct key shares z_{i_j}, then $m = C(m^{(1)}, \ldots, m^{(t+1)})$. We require that the semantic security holds even when the distinguisher is given any t decryption key shares prior to the distinguishing game. Furthermore, for all $M = E_Z(m)$, given M, m and any t key shares one can efficiently compute all decryption shares $m_i = D_{z_i}(M)$ for $i \in \{1, \ldots, n\}$. This requirement is made to guarantee that no subset of the parties of size at most t learns anything from the other parties' decryption shares, which they could not have computed themselves from the result of the decryption.

Realizations. The probabilistic encryption function of Paillier [Pai99], enhanced by threshold decryption [FPS00, DJ01], satisfies all required properties. This scheme has $\mathbb{M} = \mathbb{Z}_N$ for an RSA modulus N. A scheme satisfying the requirements can also be build based on the QR assumption [CDN01, KY02]. For this scheme $\mathbb{M} = \mathbb{Z}_2$.

2.3   Non-malleable Zero-Knowledge Proofs

The passive secure protocol uses only a threshold homomorphic encryption scheme as described above. To add robustness and independence of inputs to the active protocol a number of zero-knowledge proofs of correct behavior and a non-malleable proof of knowledge are needed. In the following sections we refer to these proofs when they are needed. The proofs can all be realized with three round protocols with a total of $\mathcal{O}(\kappa)$ bits of communication per proof. The scheme based on the QR assumption in addition needs the strong RSA assumption for the proofs to be realizable in $\mathcal{O}(\kappa)$ bits.

Details on how to realize the non-malleable zero-knowledge proofs can be found in e.g. [CDN01].

3   Active-Secure MPC Protocol for $t < n/2$

In this section we present our upper bound on the communication complexity of an active-secure MPC protocol. The upper bound is given by a protocol. We first give an overview on this protocol, then present the required sub-protocols, and finally analyze the security and the communication complexity.

3.1   Overview

In the protocol description we use $\mathcal{P} = \{P_1, \ldots, P_n\}$ to denote the set of parties. We assume that the parties agree on the circuit before the protocol is run. The circuit is specified over the ring $\mathbb{M}$ of the encryption scheme with input gates, addition gates, multiplication gates, randomizing gates, and output gates. The proposed protocol can easily be modified to evaluate Boolean circuits, see Section 3.7 for details. In the simplest case, when the parties wish to evaluate a deterministic function, the circuit will consist of a layer of inputs gates, then the arithmetic gates necessary to evaluate the function, and finally the output gates. However, we also consider randomized gates, set to an unknown random values, and reactive circuits, where some players may receive output *before* some (other) players provide inputs.

The proposed protocol follows Beaver's circuit randomization approach [Bea91a]: In a preparation phase, a pool of random triples (a, b, c), with $c = ab$, are generated, encrypted and distributed to all players. In the evaluation phase, for each multiplication one prepared triple is used. This approach brings two advantages: First, it might be simpler to generate random products (instead of multiplying two given values). Second, the load of the multiplication protocol is shifted to the preparation phase, where all triples are generated *in parallel*, and costs can be amortized.

More formally, the protocol proceeds in three phases:

Setup Phase: In the *setup phase* a random key pair (Z, z) is generated and the decryption key z is shared among the parties with threshold t, where $t < n/2$.

Preparation Phase: In a *preparation phase*, c_M random triples $\left(a^{(i)}, b^{(i)}, c^{(i)}\right) \in \mathbb{M}^3$ (for $i = 1, \ldots, c_M$) with $c^{(i)} = a^{(i)} b^{(i)}$ are generated, encrypted, and given to every player in $\mathcal{P}$, where c_M denotes the number of multiplication gates in the circuit. Furthermore, c_R random values $r^{(i)} \in \mathbb{M}$ (for $i = 1, \ldots, c_R$) are generated and encrypted, where c_R denotes the number of random gates in the circuit.

Evaluation Phase: In an *evaluation phase*, the gates of the circuit are processed level by level, associating to each gate a random ciphertext encrypting the (output) value of the gate. The various gates are handled as follows: For each *input gate*, the designated input party broadcasts an encryption of its input for that gate. *Addition gates* are handled non-interactively using the homomorphic properties of the encryption scheme. For each *multiplication gate* one prepared triple from the preparation phase is used as described in [Bea91a]. For each *randomizing gate*, an encryption of a prepared random value $r^{(i)}$ is used. For the *output gates*, the ciphertexts are decrypted using the threshold function sharing of D_z.

In the subsequent sections we describe the phases of the protocol in detail, and finally analyze the overall complexity of the protocol.

3.2   Setup Phase

The setup function generates $((Z, pk, H), z_1, \ldots, z_n)$, where (Z, z) is a random key pair with z split into $(z_1, \ldots, z_n)$ with threshold t, pk is a random key for a non-malleable trapdoor commitment scheme,[2] and H is a random hash function chosen from a class of collision-resistant hash functions, which is used by a protocol described in the following section. The setup function also sets up digital signatures to allow to do Byzantine Agreement (BA) for resilience $t < n/2$, as discussed in Section 2.1.

One could consider a simpler setup function which only sets up digital signature keys. This allows to realize BA for resilience $t < n/2$, which in turn allows to run a secure protocol to compute the setup function for the remaining values. Either a specialized protocol or one of the general MPC protocols. In all cases this would add a term $p = \mathcal{O}(\text{poly}(n + \kappa))$ to our bounds, where p is independent of the circuit to be evaluated, giving a bound $\mathcal{O}(cn^2\kappa + \text{poly}(n + \kappa))$.

3.3   Preparation Phase

The goal of this phase is to securely generate c_M encrypted triples $\left(A^{(i)}, B^{(i)}, C^{(i)}\right)$ $(i = 1, \ldots, c_M)$, where $a^{(i)}$ and $b^{(i)}$ are uniformly random values from $\mathbb{M}$ unknown by all parties and $c^{(i)} = a^{(i)} b^{(i)}$, and furthermore, to generate c_R encrypted random values $R^{(i)}$ $(i = 1, \ldots, c_R)$.

The preparation phase proceeds in three stages: First, c_M random factors $A^{(1)}, \ldots, A^{(c_M)}$ are generated. Second, the factors $B^{(1)}, \ldots, B^{(c_M)}$ and the

---

[2] To be used in the non-malleable zero-knowledge proofs (see [CDN01]).

products $C^{(1)}, \ldots, C^{(c_M)}$ are computed in parallel. Third, the random values $R^{(1)}, \ldots, R^{(c_R)}$ for the randomizing gates are prepared.

In each stage, every player in $\mathcal{P}$ contributes to the generation of the values. However, not all these contributions will be considered. Instead, the players in $\mathcal{P}$ agree on a subset $\mathcal{P}_{ok} \subseteq \mathcal{P}$ with the following two properties: (1) Every player in $\mathcal{P}_{ok}$ successfully verified the contribution of every other player in $\mathcal{P}_{ok}$, and (2) the majority of the players in $\mathcal{P}_{ok}$ is honest. Given both properties are satisfied, the output of the stage (so far known only to $\mathcal{P}_{ok}$) can easily be made known to the players in $\mathcal{P} \setminus \mathcal{P}_{ok}$. This interim reduction of the player set is similar to the player elimination framework of [HMP00], but opposed to this, can also be applied to settings with $t < n/2$.

For the sake of easier presentation, we use a vector notation: We denote the triples by $(\vec{A}, \vec{B}, \vec{C})$ and the random values by $\vec{R}$. Furthermore, we extend all operators on group elements also to vectors of group elements, where the semantics is component-wise application of the operator.

Prepare c_M Random Ciphertexts $\vec{A}$. We first present a protocol to generate a single random encryption A, and will then extend it to generate c_M random ciphertexts $\vec{A}$ at once. The protocol proceeds as follows:

1. Every player $P_i \in \mathcal{P}$ selects at random $a_i \in \mathbb{M}$ and computes an encryption $A_i = \mathbb{E}(a_i)$.

2. Every player $P_i \in \mathcal{P}$ sends A_i to every player $P_j \in \mathcal{P}$, and proves to P_j interactively that he knows the plaintext of A_i.

3. Every player P_i broadcasts the hash value $h_i = H(A_i)$ among all players in $\mathcal{P}$, where H denotes the collision-resistant hash function defined in the setup phase.

4. Initially we set the set of mutually agreeing players to $\mathcal{P}_{ok} = \mathcal{P}$. Then, in sequence, every player $P_j \in \mathcal{P}_{ok}$ verifies for every player $P_i \in \mathcal{P}_{ok}$ whether
   - the broadcast hash value h_i matches the received encryption A_i, i.e.,
     $$h_i \stackrel{?}{=} H(A_i), \text{ and}$$
   - the bilateral interactive proof by P_i is accepting for P_j.

   If P_j's verifications succeed for all players $P_i \in \mathcal{P}_{ok}$, then P_j broadcasts $\perp$ to confirm so. Otherwise, P_j picks the index i of some player $P_i \in \mathcal{P}_{ok}$ that failed in P_j's verification, and broadcasts i. In the latter case, both players P_i and P_j are removed from the set $\mathcal{P}_{ok}$ of agreeing players, i.e., all players set $\mathcal{P}_{ok} \leftarrow \mathcal{P}_{ok} \setminus \{P_i, P_j\}$.

5. Every player $P_j \in \mathcal{P}_{ok}$ sets $A = \bigoplus_{P_i \in \mathcal{P}_{ok}} A_i$ and sends it to every $P_i \in \mathcal{P} \setminus \mathcal{P}_{ok}$.

6. Every player $P_i \in \mathcal{P} \setminus \mathcal{P}_{ok}$ sets A as the majority of received values by players in $\mathcal{P}_{ok}$.

We first argue that at the end of the protocol, all players in $\mathcal{P}$ hold the same encryption A, and then, that the plaintext of A is unknown to the adversary. One can easily verify that all honest players in $\mathcal{P}_{ok}$ compute the same value A (otherwise they hold a collision of H). Furthermore, the majority of players in $\mathcal{P}_{ok}$ is honest (at least half of the removed players $\mathcal{P} \setminus \mathcal{P}_{ok}$ is corrupted), hence in

Step 5, the majority of players $P_j \in \mathcal{P}_{ok}$ distributes the correct value A, and all players in $\mathcal{P}$ will decide for the same value A. In order to argue about the secrecy of the plaintext of A, observe that at least one player in $\mathcal{P}_{ok}$ is honest and chooses a_i uniformly at random. Since the encryption scheme is semantically secure[3] and the proof of plaintext knowledge for a_i is zero-knowledge, the protocol reveals zero knowledge about a_i to the corrupted parties.[4] Since all (corrupted) parties $P_j \in \mathcal{P}_{ok}$ gave a non-malleable proof of plaintext knowledge of *their* contribution a_j, and this proof was accepted by all parties in $\mathcal{P}_{ok}$ (at least one of them being honest), their shares a_j are independent of the share a_i. It follows that A is an encryption of a uniformly random value $a = \sum_{i \in \mathcal{P}_{ok}} a_i$ of which the adversary has zero knowledge. This informal sketch of the security can be turned into a formal simulation proof using known proof techniques, see e.g. [CDN01, DN03].

In order to generate c_M random ciphertexts $\vec{A}$, the above protocol is slightly modified:

1. Every player $P_i \in \mathcal{P}$ selects at random $\vec{a_i} \in \mathbb{M}^{c_M}$ and computes its component-wise ciphertexts $\vec{A_i}$.
2. Every player $P_i \in \mathcal{P}$ sends $\vec{A_i}$ to every player $P_j \in \mathcal{P}$, and proves to P_j interactively that he knows the plaintext of each component of $\vec{A_i}$.
3. Every player P_i broadcasts the hash value $h_i = H(\vec{A_i})$ among all players in $\mathcal{P}$.
4. Set $\mathcal{P}_{ok} = \mathcal{P}$ and, in sequence, every player $P_j \in \mathcal{P}_{ok}$ verifies for every player $P_i \in \mathcal{P}_{ok}$ whether

    - the broadcast hash value h_i matches the received ciphertexts $\vec{A_i}$, i.e., $h_i \stackrel{?}{=} H(\vec{A_i})$, and
    - all the bilateral interactive proofs by P_i are accepting for P_j.

    If P_j's verifications succeed for all players $P_i \in \mathcal{P}_{ok}$, then P_j broadcasts $\bot$ to confirm so. Otherwise, P_j picks the index i of some player $P_i \in \mathcal{P}_{ok}$ that failed in P_j's verification, and broadcasts i. In the latter case, both players P_i and P_j are removed from the set of agreeing players, i.e., all players set $\mathcal{P}_{ok} \leftarrow \mathcal{P}_{ok} \setminus \{P_i, P_j\}$.
5. Every player $P_j \in \mathcal{P}_{ok}$ sets $\vec{A} = \bigoplus_{P_i \in \mathcal{P}_{ok}} \vec{A_i}$ and sends it to every $P_i \in \mathcal{P} \setminus \mathcal{P}_{ok}$.
6. Every player $P_i \in \mathcal{P} \setminus \mathcal{P}_{ok}$ sets $\vec{A}$ as the majority of received vectors by players in $\mathcal{P}_{ok}$.

---

[3] Notice that the fact that the decryption key is shared between the parties is no problem for the semantic security as the adversary can inspect at most t parties; Since the decryption key is shared with threshold t, the t shares known by the adversary gives zero knowledge about the decryption key.

[4] Here we colloquially distinguish between information and knowledge. Since A_i determines a_i clearly the adversary has full information about a_i. However, by the semantic security and the fact that the adversary is polynomial time bounded, it has zero *knowledge* about a_i.

The security of this protocol follows immediately from the security of the previous protocol. The communication complexity of the protocol is $\mathcal{O}(c_M n^2 \kappa + n\mathcal{B}(\kappa))$ bits.

Prepare Random Ciphertexts $\vec{B}$ and Products $\vec{C}$. The B and C values of the triples are generated similarly to the A values. For the sake of simplicity, we present solely the protocol for generating a single triple. The generalization to vectors of triples is straight-forward along the lines of the protocol for generating $\vec{A}$.

1. Every player $P_i \in \mathcal{P}$ selects at random $b_i \in \mathbb{M}$, computes $B_i = \mathbb{E}(b_i)$ and $C_i = \mathbb{R}(b_i A)$.

2. Every player $P_i \in \mathcal{P}$ sends B_i and C_i to every player $P_j \in \mathcal{P}$, and proves to P_j interactively that he knows the plaintext b_i of B_i, and that C_i is a randomization of $b_i A$.

3. Every player P_i broadcasts the hash value $h_i = H(B_i, C_i)$ among all players in $\mathcal{P}$.

4. Set $\mathcal{P}_{ok} = \mathcal{P}$ and, in sequence, every player $P_j \in \mathcal{P}_{ok}$ verifies for every player $P_i \in \mathcal{P}_{ok}$ whether
   - the broadcast hash value h_i matches the received ciphertexts (B_i, C_i), i.e., $h_i \overset{?}{=} H(B_i, C_i)$, and
   - all the bilateral interactive proofs by P_i are accepting for P_j.

   If P_j's verifications succeed for all players $P_i \in \mathcal{P}_{ok}$, then P_j broadcasts $\perp$ to confirm so. Otherwise, P_j picks the index i of some player $P_i \in \mathcal{P}_{ok}$ that failed in P_j's verification, and broadcasts i. In the latter case, both players P_i and P_j are removed from the set of agreeing player, i.e., all players set $\mathcal{P}_{ok} \leftarrow \mathcal{P}_{ok} \setminus \{P_i, P_j\}$.

5. Every player $P_j \in \mathcal{P}_{ok}$ sets $B = \bigoplus_{P_i \in \mathcal{P}_{ok}} B_i$, and $C = \bigoplus_{P_i \in \mathcal{P}_{ok}} C_i$, and sends them to every $P_i \in \mathcal{P} \setminus \mathcal{P}_{ok}$.

6. Every player $P_i \in \mathcal{P} \setminus \mathcal{P}_{ok}$ sets B and C to be the majority of received values from players in $\mathcal{P}_{ok}$.

The correctness of the resulting triple (A, B, C) follows directly from the distributive law in groups. The security of the protocol can be argued along the lines of the proof of the previous protocol.

The above protocol can be extended to vector-values in a straight-forward manner. The communication complexity of the extended protocol is $\mathcal{O}(c_M n^2 \kappa + n\mathcal{B}(\kappa))$ bits.

Prepare c_R Random Values $\vec{R}$. The random $\vec{R}$ vector is prepared exactly as the random $\vec{A}$ vector, only the corresponding $\vec{B}$ and $\vec{C}$ vectors are not generated.

3.4   Evaluation Phase

In the evaluation phase, the circuit is evaluated layer by layer. In the following, we give the protocols for evaluating the different types of gates.

Input Gates. When a party P_i is to provide an input for some gate G, the parties proceed as follows:

1. P_i computes $V_i = \mathbb{E}(v_i)$ broadcasts V_i.
2. P_i bilaterally proves (in zero-knowledge) knowledge of plaintext v_i to every player $P_j \in \mathcal{P}$.
3. Each $P_j \in \mathcal{P}$, lets $b_j = 1$ if the proof from P_i was accepted and lets $b_j = 0$ otherwise.
4. The parties in $\mathcal{P}$ run a BA with input b_j from P_j. Let the output be $b \in \{0, 1\}$.
5. If $b = 1$, then each $P_j \in \mathcal{P}$ sets the encryption for gate G to be the broadcast value V_i; Otherwise, P_j sets the encryption for gate G to be $E(0, e)$, where 0 and e denotes the neutral elements from $\mathbb{M}$ respectively $\mathbb{R}$.

After this protocol the input gate is defined to the same value by all parties. The proof of knowledge given by P_i serves the purpose of guaranteeing independence of inputs. The privacy of the protocol follows from the semantic security of the encryption scheme, using that the proofs are zero-knowledge.

Using that the communication complexity of one zero-knowledge proof is $\mathcal{O}(\kappa)$, the communication complexity for giving one input is seen to be $\mathcal{O}(\mathcal{B}(\kappa) + n\kappa + \mathcal{B}(1))$. Assuming that $\mathcal{B}(\kappa) \geq n\kappa$, this is $\mathcal{O}(\mathcal{B}(\kappa))$.

Output Gates. When the value of some gate G (with associated ciphertext M) is to be revealed towards a party P_j, the parties proceed as follows:

1. Every player $P_i \in \mathcal{P}$ computes $m_i = SD_{z_i}(M)$ and sends it to P_j.
2. Every player $P_i \in \mathcal{P}$ gives a zero-knowledge proof to every other party P_j that m_i is a correct i'th decryption share.
3. P_j collects $t + 1$ decryption shares for which the proof of correct decryption share succeeded and combine them to obtain $m = D(M)$.

Since at least $t + 1$ parties are honest, P_j will be able to collect $t + 1$ shares where the proof succeeded. By the soundness of the zero-knowledge proof all collected shares will be correct, except with negligible probability. By the way the values $(z_1, \ldots, z_n)$ were set up and the requirements on the share combining algorithm have that indeed $m = D_z(M)$.

The privacy of the protocol follows from the requirements on the threshold decryption protocol: from the result of the protocol and the key shares of the t corrupted parties, the adversary could compute the key shares of the honest parties on its own. Therefore the protocol leaks zero knowledge about the key shares of the honest parties.

The communication complexity is seen to be $\mathcal{O}(n\kappa)$ per output gate and party to learn the output. If all parties are to learn the output, the communication complexity is $\mathcal{O}(n^2\kappa)$ per output gate.

If only one party is to learn the output and the output should be private, the decryption shares sent to P_j should be sent over private channels. This does not affect the order of the communication complexity.

Addition Gates. For an addition gate G where the input gates of G has associated ciphertexts M_1 and M_2, the associated ciphertext of G is set to be

$M_G = M_1 \oplus M_2$. As the $\oplus$-operator is deterministic, all parties agree on the encryption M_G, and by the homomorphic properties of $\oplus$ it holds that $D(M_G) = D(M_1) + D(M_2)$.

Multiplication Gates. For a multiplication gate G where the two input gates have associated ciphertexts M_1 and M_2, the associated ciphertext M_G of G is computed as follows:

1. Every party $P_i \in \mathcal{P}$ picks the prepared triple (A, B, C) that is associated with the gate.
2. Every party $P_i \in \mathcal{P}$ computes $D = A \oplus M_1$ and $E = B \oplus M_2$.
3. Every party $P_i \in \mathcal{P}$ invokes the decryption protocol from Section 3.4 on D and E. Denote the results by d respectively e.
4. Every party sets $M_G = (eM_1) \ominus (dB) \oplus C$.

The above way to use a prepared triple is from [Bea91a].

We argue that the protocol maintains agreement on the associated ciphertexts. Assume that the parties agree on M_1 and M_2. By the fact that $\oplus$ is a function, the parties will agree on D and E. Therefore the decryption protocol will return correct and consistent d and e values to the parties. Using that $\ominus$ and $\oplus$ are functions it then follows that the parties will agree on M_G.

We then argue the correctness of the protocol. By the correctness of the decryption protocol and the homomorphic properties of $\oplus$ and $\ominus$ we have that $D(M_G) = em_1 - db + c = (b + m_2)m_1 - (a + m_1)b + ab = m_1 m_2$, where $m_1 = D(M_1)$ and $m_2 = D(m_2)$.

For the privacy, the only values that are revealed are d and e. However, since a and b are independent, uniformly random elements from $\mathbb{M}$ unknown to any adversary which inspects at most t parties, it follows that d and e are uniformly random and independent of m_1 and m_2 in the view of the adversary. Therefore the protocol leaks zero knowledge about m_1 and m_2.

The communication complexity per gate is that of two invocations of the decryption protocol, i.e. $\mathcal{O}(n^2 \kappa)$.

Randomizing Gates. When the circuit is evaluated, the randomizing gates should be initialized by uniformly random values. To reflect the ideal evaluation the random values used for initialization should be unknown to all parties. Therefore, to every random gate, one random encrypted value $R^{(i)}$ is associated.

3.5 Complexity Analysis

In this section we consider the complexity of the active-secure protocol. Summing the complexities stated in the presentation of the protocol gives us a total complexity of $\mathcal{O}(((c_M + c_R)n^2\kappa + n\mathcal{B}(\kappa)) + c_I\mathcal{B}(\kappa) + c_O n^2\kappa + c_M n^2\kappa)$, where c_M denotes the number of multiplication gates, c_R denotes the number of randomizing input gates, c_I denotes the number of input gates, and c_O denotes the number of output gates. This is seen to be $\mathcal{O}((c_M + c_R + c_O)n^2\kappa + n\mathcal{B}(\kappa) + c_I\mathcal{B}(\kappa))$.

In the synchronous model with $t < n/2$, broadcasting (and/or doing BA on) a total of ℓ bits can be done with complexity $\mathcal{O}(n^2\ell + n^3\kappa)$ under the strong RSA assumption and the assumption the RSA signatures are secure (c.f. [Nie03]). We have $n + c_I$ broadcasts of κ-bit messages, giving $\ell = (n + c_I)\kappa$ and (a bit informally) $n\mathcal{B}(\kappa) + c_I\mathcal{B}(\kappa) = \mathcal{O}(n^2(n + c_I)\kappa + n^3\kappa) = \mathcal{O}(c_I n^2\kappa + n^3\kappa)$. This immediately gives us the bound $\mathcal{O}((c_M + c_R + c_O + c_I)n^2\kappa + n^3\kappa)$ on the communication complexity of the overall protocol.

Theorem 1. *Under the QR assumption (or the DCR assumption), the strong RSA assumption and the assumption that RSA signatures are secure, $\mathcal{O}(cn^2\kappa)$ is an upper bound on the communication complexity of an active-secure protocol with resilience $t < n/2$ for evaluating an n-party function with arithmetic circuit complexity $c \geq n$.*

3.6   Ongoing Computations

The result for active security assumes that the size of the circuit is known before the computation starts, to allow for a preparation phase. For an on-going reactive computation, even the circuit might be specified as the computation unfolds and in particular the length of the computation might not be specified on beforehand. Our result can be extended to such a setting. We simply hold a pool of prepared triples, and each time it dries out we prepare at least twice as many triples as last time. After polynomially many activations, this gives a maximum of $\mathcal{O}(\log(\kappa))$ runs of the preparation phase and prepares at most twice as many triples as needed. This gives the bound $\mathcal{O}(cn^2\kappa + n^3\kappa\log(\kappa))$.

3.7   Boolean Circuits

The proposed protocol evaluates a circuit of arithmetic gates, where the underlying ring is the message space of the encryption scheme. We can extend the protocol to evaluate a Boolean circuit, even when the message space of the encryption scheme is larger (e.g., when using Paillier encryption). In the sequel, we present the necessary modifications for Boolean circuits over AND and NOT gates. The protocol for Boolean circuits has the same communication complexity as the protocol for arithmetic circuits.

Input gates. In the input protocol, the player providing input must prove that the input is in $\{0, 1\}$. Therefore, the zero-knowledge proof for proving plaintext knowledge is augmented by a zero-knowledge proof for proving that the plaintext is either 0 or 1.

AND-gates. As it is guaranteed that all wires are encryptions of either 0 or 1, AND-gates can be realized as multiplication gates.

NOT-gates. A NOT-gates can be computed by using the homomorphism of the encryption scheme. Given an encrypted bit B, its negation can be computed as $\mathbb{E}(1) \ominus B$. Every player can compute the encrypted value of a negation gate locally, without communicating with other players.

Randomizing gates. It must also be ensured that the output of randomizing gates are in $\{0,1\}$. If $M > 2$ (as is the case for Paillier's cryptosystem), and we want to stay within the new upper bound, a new protocol is needed for this.

0. Let $\vec{R}^{(0)} = \mathbb{E}(\vec{0}, \vec{e})$ be a constant vector of length c_R, where each element is the constant encryption $\mathbb{E}(0, e)$. Let $\mathcal{P}_{ok} = \mathcal{P}$, let $\mathcal{P}_{done} = \emptyset$, let $i_{prev} = 0$, let $i_{next} = 1$ and let Prev be an empty stack.

1. $P_{i_{next}}$ computes $\vec{R}^{(i_{next})}$ from $\vec{R}^{(i_{prev})}$ as follows: For each element $R^{(i_{prev})}$ in $\vec{R}^{(i_{prev})}$, pick $\alpha \in_R \mathbb{R}$ and $b \in_R \{0,1\}$ and, if $b = 0$, let $R^{(i_{next})} = \mathbb{E}(0, \alpha) \oplus R^{(i_{prev})}$, and if $b = 1$, let $\vec{R}^{(i_{next})} = \mathbb{E}(1, \alpha) \ominus R^{(i_{prev})}$.

2. $P_{i_{next}}$ broadcasts the hash value $h_i = H(\vec{R}^{(i_{next})})$ among all players in $\mathcal{P}$.

3. $P_{i_{next}}$ sends $\vec{R}^{(i_{next})}$ to every player $P_j \in \mathcal{P}$, and gives to P_j (for each element $R^{(i_{prev})}$) a non-malleable zero-knowledge proof of knowledge of α for which *either* $R^{(i_{next})} = \mathbb{E}(0, \alpha) \oplus R^{(i_{prev})}$ *or* $R^{(i_{next})} = \mathbb{E}(1, \alpha) \ominus R^{(i_{prev})}$.

4. The parties $\mathcal{P}$ enter a BA on whether to accept the proofs given by $P_{i_{next}}$: Each party $P_j \in \mathcal{P}$ enters with $b_j = 1$ iff in the above step it received $\vec{R}^{(i_{next})}$ such that $h_i = H(\vec{R}^{(i_{next})})$ and the bilateral proof from $P_{i_{next}}$ to P_j was accepted.

5. — If the outcome of the BA is $b = 0$, then all parties in $\mathcal{P}$ set $\mathcal{P}_{ok} = \mathcal{P}_{ok} \setminus \{i_{next}\}$ and set i_{next} to be the smallest $i \in \mathcal{P}_{ok} \setminus \mathcal{P}_{done}$.

   — If the outcome of the BA is $b = 1$, then all parties in $\mathcal{P}$ set $\mathcal{P}_{done} = \mathcal{P}_{done} \cup \{i_{next}\}$, push i_{prev} on Prev, let $i_{prev} = i_{next}$ and set i_{next} to be the smallest $i \in \mathcal{P}_{ok} \setminus \mathcal{P}_{done}$.

   In both cases, if $\mathcal{P}_{ok} \setminus \mathcal{P}_{done} = \emptyset$, then go to Step 8.

6. The party $P_{i_{next}}$ broadcasts a bit $b \in \{0,1\}$, where $b = 0$ iff $i_{prev} \neq 0$ and $P_{i_{next}}$ never received $\vec{R}^{(i_{prev})}$ such that $h_{i_{prev}} = H(\vec{R}^{(i_{prev})})$ (in Step 3).

7. — If $i_{prev} = 0$ or $P_{i_{next}}$ broadcast 1, then all parties in $\mathcal{P}$ go to Step 1.

   — If $i_{prev} \neq 0$ and $P_{i_{next}}$ broadcast 0, then all parties set $\mathcal{P}_{ok} = \mathcal{P}_{ok} \setminus \{i_{prev}, i_{next}\}$. Then i_{prev} is set to be the top of Prev (which is then popped) and i_{next} is set to be the smallest $i \in \mathcal{P}_{ok} \setminus \mathcal{P}_{done}$ (if $\mathcal{P}_{ok} \setminus \mathcal{P}_{done} = \emptyset$, then go to Step 8.) Then all parties in $\mathcal{P}$ go to Step 6.

8. All parties in $\mathcal{P}$ which knows $\vec{R}^{(i_{prev})}$ such that $h_{i_{prev}} = H(\vec{R}^{(i_{prev})})$ sends $\vec{R}^{(i_{prev})}$ to all parties.

9. All parties in $\mathcal{P}$ waits for a value $\vec{R}^{(i_{prev})}$ for which $h_{i_{prev}} = H(\vec{R}^{(i_{prev})})$ to arrive and outputs $\vec{R}^{(i_{prev})}$.

We first argue termination and agreement: It is straight-forward to verify that the procedure reaches Step 8. Since at this point $P_{i_{prev}}$ at some point broadcast $h_{i_{prev}}$ and had its proof accepted by a majority of the parties in $\mathcal{P}$, at least one honest party must have received $\vec{R}^{(i_{prev})}$ such that $h_{i_{prev}} = H(\vec{R}^{(i_{prev})})$. At least that party will echo $\vec{R}^{(i_{prev})}$ in Step 8 and thus all parties will terminate in Step 9. Since $h_{i_{prev}}$ is a broadcast value, all parties will output the same value $\vec{R}^{(i_{prev})}$ unless a collision under H is found.

We then argue that $\vec{R}^{(i_{\text{prev}})}$ is a vector of encryptions of random bits of which the adversary has zero knowledge. At termination we clearly have that $\mathcal{P}_{\text{ok}} \subseteq \mathcal{P}_{\text{done}}$. Furthermore, at termination $\mathcal{P}_{\text{ok}}$ will contain a majority of honest parties and there exists a sequence $i_0 = 0 < i_1 < \cdots < i_{l-1} < i_l \leq n$ such that $\mathcal{P}_{\text{ok}} = \{i_1, \ldots, i_l\}$ and for $m = 1, \ldots, l$, the vector $\vec{R}^{(i_m)}$ was computed by P_{i_m} from $\vec{R}^{(i_{m-1})}$ as specified in Step 1. Since the proof of knowledge ensures that each party "flips" the encryptions independently and at least one party in $\mathcal{P}_{\text{ok}}$ is honest it follows that $\vec{R}^{(i_l)}$ is a vector of encryptions of independent random bits unknown to the adversary.

Each party broadcasts (at most) κ bits in Step 2 and one bit in Step 6. Besides this n BAs are executed and each party $P_{i_{\text{next}}}$ sends the vector $\vec{R}^{(i_{\text{next}})}$ to all parties and gives the non-malleable zero-knowledge proofs of knowledge in Step 3. Assuming that $\mathcal{B}(k)$ dominates the cost of one Byzantine agreement, the total communication complexity of this is $\mathcal{O}(c_R n^2 \kappa + n\mathcal{B}(\kappa))$, as desired.

The above protocol can be seen as a strengthening of the protocol used in the original preparation phase to deal with large values being build sequentially from large contributions from all parties. Similar protocols can be used to prepare c gates for the Mix-and-Match protocol in [JJ00] with complexity $\mathcal{O}(cn^2\kappa + n\mathcal{B}(\kappa))$ and for mixing c ciphertext in anonymizing networks and voting (with n servers) with complexity $\mathcal{O}(cn^2\kappa + n\mathcal{B}(\kappa))$. In both cases an optimization over $\Theta(cn\mathcal{B}(\kappa)) = \Theta(cn^3\kappa)$.

4   Passive-Secure MPC Protocol for $t < n$

In this section we present an upper bound on the communication complexity of a passive secure MPC protocol. Again the upper bound is given by a protocol. As opposed to the active secure protocol, the passive protocol is not based on novel technical contributions but rather a neat observation.

The essential observation is that from the threshold homomorphic encryption based MPC protocol of [CDN01] each gate has a short publicly known representation, namely the associated encryption. This is opposed to e.g. secret sharing based protocols, where the representation is exactly *shared* among the parties and therefore inherently large ($\Theta(n\kappa)$). This observation allows to designate some party P_{king} which drives the protocol and evaluates the circuit gate by gate, with help of the other parties.

The protocol proceeds along the lines of the active protocol, though no preparation phase is needed anymore. The details are given below.

Setup phase. In the setup phase the setup function s generates a random key pair (Z, z), splits z into $(z_1, \ldots, z_n)$ with threshold $t = n - 1$, sets $p = Z$ and sets $s_i = z_i$ for $i = 1, \ldots, n$. Furthermore one designated party P_{king} is chosen, called the king, e.g. $P_{\text{king}} = P_1$.

Input gates. When a party P_i is to provide the input $v_i \in \mathbb{M}$, the parties proceed as follows:

1. P_i selects $\alpha_i \in_R \mathbb{R}$, computes and sends $V_i = E(v_i, \alpha_i)$ to P_{king}.
2. P_{king} sends V_i to all parties.

The privacy of the protocol follows from the semantic security of the encryption scheme.

Output gates. The value of some gate G with associated ciphertext M is revealed as follows:

1. Every party P_i computes and sends $m_i = SD_{z_i}(M)$ to P_{king}.
2. P_{king} computes $m = C(m_1, \ldots, m_n)$ and sends it to all parties.

The security of this protocol is argued along the lines of the active-secure protocol. The communication complexity is $\mathcal{O}(n\kappa)$.

If the value is to be revealed privately to only one party P_j, then the parties send their decryption shares m_i privately to P_j, who computes $m = C(m_1, \ldots, m_n)$.

Addition gates. The king computes the value of addition gates using the homomorphism of the encryption scheme.

Multiplication gates. For a multiplication gate G where the two input gates have associated ciphertexts M_1 and M_2, the associated ciphertext M_G of G is computed as follows:

1. Every party $P_i \in \mathcal{P}$ selects $a_i \in_R \mathbb{M}$, $\alpha_i, \beta_i \in_R \mathbb{R}$, computes $A_i = \mathbb{E}(a_i, \alpha_i)$ and $C_i = \mathbb{R}(a_i M_2, \beta_i)$, and sends A_i and C_i to P_{king}.
2. P_{king} computes $A = M_1 \bigoplus_{P_i \in \mathcal{P}} A_i$ and $C = \bigoplus_{P_i \in \mathcal{P}} C_i$ and sends A and C to all parties,
3. Every party $P_i \in \mathcal{P}$ computes its decryption share $a_i = SD_{z_i}(A)$ and sends it to P_{king}.
4. P_{king} decrypts $a = C(a_1, \ldots, a_n)$, computes $G_M = a M_2 \ominus C$ and send it to all parties.

The security is argued as for the active-secure protocol. The communication complexity is $\mathcal{O}(n\kappa)$.

Randomizing gates. An encryption of a random value m, unknown to the adversary, is computed as follows:

1. Every party $P_i \in \mathcal{P}$ selects $a_i \in \mathbb{M}$, $\alpha_i \in \mathbb{R}$, computes $A_i = \mathbb{E}(a_i, \alpha_i)$ and sends it to P_{king}.
2. P_{king} computes $A = \bigoplus_{P_i \in \mathcal{P}} A_i$ and sends it to all parties.

Complexity analysis. It is straight forward to verify that the total number of bits sent by the parties is $\mathcal{O}((c_I + c_M + c_O + c_R)n\kappa)$.

Theorem 2. *Under the QR assumption (or the DCR assumption), $\mathcal{O}(cn\kappa)$ is an upper bound on the communication complexity of a passive secure protocol with resilience $n - 1$ for evaluating an n-party randomized function with arithmetic circuit complexity c.*

5   Conclusions and Open Problems

We presented new upper bounds on the communication complexity of optimally resilient active-secure MPC and optimally resilient passive-secure MPC. In both cases we improved the previously best bounds by a factor n. The improvement of the bound for active security was based on a combination of previous techniques for efficient MPC along with several novel technical contributions, as opposed to the improvement of the bound for passive security, which was based on a simple observation.

Our bounds were based either on the DCR assumption or on the QR assumption (in both cases requiring, additionally the strong RSA assumption and the assumption that RSA signatures are secure for active security). Even though these assumptions are standard assumptions, they are very specific. It is an interesting open problem to achieve the same bounds under general assumptions, as e.g. the existence of one-way functions. One approach would be to investigate the efficiency of active-secure information-theoretic MPC with $t < n/2$. It is known that the player elimination framework does not apply to this threshold [HMP00, HM01]. The ideas presented here might however allow to obtain similar results in this model. The new upper bound for passive security however seems very challenging to obtain under general assumptions.

It is an interesting open problem to obtain the new bound for also adaptive security. In [DN03] an adaptively secure version of the protocol from [CDN01] was presented. However, the techniques from [DN03] do not allow to make our protocol here adaptive secure while staying within the bound $\mathcal{O}(cn^2\kappa + n^3\kappa)$. We stress that although our protocol cannot be proven adaptively secure (we cannot construct a simulator), there is no obvious way for an adaptive adversary to violate the correctness or the security of the computation. This is in contrast to some folklore trick for improving efficiency, namely to have the players agree on a small random subset of players, who then perform the whole protocol.[5] In this approach, an adaptive adversary can trivially violate both privacy and correctness of the protocol, simply by corrupting the majority (or even all) of the players in the subset, once this is randomly chosen.

Another interesting open problem is to prove non-trivial lower bounds on the communication complexity of secure MPC.

Acknowledgments

We would like to thank Ivan Damgård, Serge Fehr and Matthias Fitzi for many fruitful discussions, and the anonymous referees for their helpful comments.

---

[5] Note that is is even unclear how this subset is to be chosen such that it contains an honest majority, given that the original set of players satisfies the optimal bound $t < n/2$. Furthermore, the trick only works if n is large.

References

[BB89]   J. Bar-Ilan and D. Beaver. Non-cryptographic fault-tolerant computing in constant number of rounds of interaction. In *PODC'89*, p. 201–209, 1989.

[BCG93]   M. Ben-Or, R. Canetti, and O. Goldreich. Asynchronous secure computation (extended abstract). In *25th STOC*, p. 52–61, 1993.

[BDPR98]   M. Bellare, A. Desai, D. Pointcheval, and P. Rogaway. Relations among notions of security for publickey encryption schemes. In H. Krawczyk, ed., *Crypto '98*, p. 26–45, 1998. LNCS 1462.

[Bea91a]   D. Beaver. Efficient multiparty protocols using circuit randomization. In J. Feigenbaum, ed., *Crypto '91*, p. 420–432, 1991. LNCS 576.

[Bea91b]   D. Beaver. Secure multi-party protocols and zero-knowledge proof systems tolerating a faulty minority. *Journal of Cryptology*, 4(2):75–122, 1991.

[BFKR90]   D. Beaver, J. Feigenbaum, J. Kilian, and P. Rogaway. Security with low communication overhead (extended abstract). In A. J. Menezes and S. A. Vanstone, ed., *Crypto '90*, p. 62–76, 1990. LNCS 537.

[BGP92]   P. Berman, J. A. Garay, and K. J. Perry. Optimal early stopping in distributed consensus. In *Proceedings of the sixth International Workshop on Distributed Algorithms*, p. 221–237, 1992.

[BGW88]   M. Ben-Or, S. Goldwasser, and A. Wigderson. Completeness theorems for non-cryptographic fault-tolerant distributed computation (extended abstract). In *20th STOC*, p. 1–10, 1988.

[BMR90]   D. Beaver, S. Micali, and P. Rogaway. The round complexity of secure protocols (extended abstract). In *22nd STOC*, p. 503–513, 1990.

[Can00]   R. Canetti. Security and composition of multiparty cryptographic protocols. *Journal of Cryptology*, 13(1):143–202, winter 2000.

[Can01]   R. Canetti. Universally composable security: A new paradigm for cryptographic protocols. In *42nd FOCS*, 2001.

[CCD88]   D. Chaum, C. Crépeau, and I. Damgård. Multiparty unconditionally secure protocols (extended abstract). In *20th STOC*, p. 11–19, 1988.

[CDD⁺99]   R. Cramer, I. Damgård, S. Dziembowski, M. Hirt, and T. Rabin. Efficient multiparty computations secure against an adaptive adversary. In J. Stern, ed., *EuroCrypt '99*, p. 311–326, 1999. LNCS 1592.

[CDD00]   R. Cramer, I. Damgård, and S. Dziembowski. On the complexity of verifiable secret sharing and multiparty computation. In *22nd STOC*, p. 325–334, 2000.

[CDG87]   D. Chaum, I. Damgård, and J. van de Graaf. Multiparty computations ensuring privacy of each party's input and correctness of the result. In C. Pomerance, ed., *Crypto '87*, p. 87–119, 1987. LNCS 293.

[CDM00]   R. Cramer, I. Damgård, and U. Maurer. General secure multi-party computation from any linear secret-sharing scheme. In B. Preneel, ed., *EuroCrypt 2000*, p. 316–334, 2000. LNCS 1807.

[CDN01]   R. Cramer, I. Damgaard, and J. B. Nielsen. Multiparty computation from threshold homomorphic encryption. In *EuroCrypt 2001*, p. 280–300, 2001. LNCS 2045.

[Cra96]   R. Cramer. *Modular Design of Secure yet Practical Cryptographic Protocols*. PhD thesis, CWI and University of Amsterdam, 1996.

[CW92]   B. A. Coan and J. L. Welch. Modular construction of a byzantine agreement protocol with optimal message complexity. *Information and Computation*, 97(1):61–85, March 1992.

[Dam00]   I. Damgård. Efficient concurrent zero-knowledge in the auxiliary string model. In B. Preneel, ed., *EuroCrypt 2000*, p. 418–430, 2000. LNCS 1807.

[DCIO98] G. Di Crescenzo, Y. Ishai, and R. Ostrovsky. Non-interactive and non-malleable commitment. In *30th STOC*, p. 141–150, 1998.

[DG02]   I. Damgaard and J. Groth. Non-interactive and reusable non-maleable commitment schemes. In *34th STOC*, 2002.

[DJ01]   I. Damgård and M. Jurik. A generalisation, a simplification and some applications of Paillier's probabilistic public-key system. In K. Kim, ed., *4th Public Key Cryptography*, p. 110–136, 2001. LNCS 1992.

[DN03]   I. Damgård and J. B. Nielsen. Universally composable efficient multiparty computation from threshold homomorphic encryption. In D. Boneh, ed., *Crypto 2003*, 2003. LNCS 2729.

[FF00]   M. Fischlin and R. Fischlin. Efficient non-malleable commitment schemes. In M. Bellare, ed., *Crypto 2000*, p. 414–432, 2000. LNCS 1880.

[FH96]   M. Franklin and S. Haber. Joint encryption and message-efficient secure computation. *Journal of Cryptology*, 9(4):217–232, Autumn 1996.

[FPS00]   P.-A. Fouque, G. Poupard, and J. Stern. Sharing decryption in the context of voting or lotteries. In *Proceedings of Financial Crypto 2000*, 2000.

[GIKR02] R. Gennaro, Y. Ishai, E. Kushilevitz, and T. Rabin. On 2-round secure multiparty computation. In M. Yung, ed., *Crypto 2002*, p. 178–193, 2002. LNCS 2442.

[CDI05]   R. Cramer, I. Damgård, and Y. Ishai. Local conversion of secret-sharing schemes with applications to threshold cryptography. In *TCC 2005*, p.342–362, 2005. LNCS 3378.

[GL90]   S. Goldwasser and L. Levin. Fair computation of general functions in presence of immoral majority. In A. J. Menezes and S. A. Vanstone, ed., *Crypto '90*, p. 77–93, 1990. LNCS 537.

[GMR85]   S. Goldwasser, S. Micali, and C. Rackoff. The knowledge complexity of interactive proof-systems (extended abstract). In *17th STOC*, p. 291–304, 1985.

[GMW87]   O. Goldreich, S. Micali, and A. Wigderson. How to play any mental game or a completeness theorem for protocols with honest majority. In *19th STOC*, p. 218–229, 1987.

[GRR98]   R. Gennaro, M. Rabin, and T. Rabin. Simplified VSS and fast-track multi-party computations with applications to threshold cryptography. In *PODC'98*, 1998.

[GV87]   O. Goldreich and R. Vainish. How to solve any protocol problem - an efficiency improvement. In C. Pomerance, ed., *Crypto '87*, p. 73–86, 1987. LNCS 293.

[HM00]   M. Hirt and U. Maurer. Player simulation and general adversary structures in perfect multiparty computation. *Journal of Cryptology*, 13(1):31–60, winter 2000.

[HM01]   M. Hirt and U. Maurer. Robustness for free in unconditional multi-party computation. In J. Kilian, ed., *Crypto 2001*, p. 101–118, 2001. LNCS 2139.

[HMP00]   M. Hirt, U. Maurer, and B. Przydatek. Efficient secure multi-party computation. In T. Okamoto, ed., *ASIACRYPT 2000*, p. 143–161, 2000. LNCS 1976.

[JJ00]   M. Jakobsson and A. Juels. Mix and match: Secure function evaluation via ciphertexts. In T. Okamoto, ed., *ASIACRYPT 2000*, p. 162–177, 2000. LNCS 1976.

[KY02]   J. Katz and M. Yung. Threshold cryptosystems based on factoring. In Y. Zheng, ed., *ASIACRYPT 2002*, p. 192–205, 2002. LNCS 2501.

[LSP82]   L. Lamport, R. Shostak, and M. Pease. The Byzantine generals problem. *ACM Transactions on Programming Languages and Systems*, 4(3):381–401, July 1982.

[MR91]   S. Micali and P. Rogaway. Secure computation. In J. Feigenbaum, ed., *Crypto '91*, p. 392–404, 1991. LNCS 576.

[Nie03]   J. B. Nielsen. On protocol security in the cryptographic model. Dissertation Series DS-03-8, BRICS, Department of Computer Science, University of Aarhus, August 2003.

[Pai99]   P. Paillier. Public-key cryptosystems based on composite degree residue classes. In J. Stern, ed., *EuroCrypt '99*, p. 223–238, 1999. LNCS 1592.

[RB89]   T. Rabin and M. Ben-Or. Verifiable secret sharing and multiparty protocols with honest majority. In *21th STOC*, p. 73–85, 1989.

[Yao82]   A. C.-C. Yao. Protocols for secure computations (extended abstract). In *23rd FOCS*, p. 160–164, 1982.

Graph-Decomposition-Based Frameworks for Subset-Cover Broadcast Encryption and Efficient Instantiations

Nuttapong Attrapadung and Hideki Imai

Imai Laboratory, Institute of Industrial Science, University of Tokyo,
4-6-1 Komaba, Meguro-ku, Tokyo 153-8505, Japan
nuts@imailab.iis.u-tokyo.ac.jp, imai@iis.u-tokyo.ac.jp

Abstract. We present generic frameworks for constructing efficient broadcast encryption schemes in the subset-cover paradigm, introduced by Naor et.al., based on various key derivation techniques. Our frameworks characterize any instantiation completely to its underlying *graph decompositions*, which are purely combinatorial in nature. This abstracts away the security of each instantiated scheme to be guaranteed by the generic one of the frameworks; thus, gives flexibilities in designing schemes. Behind these are new techniques based on (trapdoor) RSA accumulators utilized to obtain practical performances.

We then give some efficient instantiations from the frameworks. Our first construction improves the currently best schemes, including the one proposed by Goodrich et.al., without any further assumptions (only pseudorandom generators are used) by some factors. The second instantiation, which is the most efficient, is instantiated based on RSA and directly improves the first scheme. Its ciphertext length is of order $O(r)$, the key size is $O(1)$, and its computational cost is $O(n^{1/k} \log^2 n)$ for any (arbitrary large) constant k; where r and n are the number of revoked users and all users respectively. To the best of our knowledge, this is the first explicit collusion-secure scheme in the literature that achieves both ciphertext size and key size independent of n simultaneously while keeping all other costs efficient, in particular, sub-linear in n. The third scheme improves Gentry and Ramzan's scheme, which itself is more efficient than the above schemes in the aspect of asymptotic computational cost.

Keywords: Broadcast Encryption, Revocation Scheme, Subset-cover, Optimal Key Storage.

1 Introduction

Broadcast encryption (BE) involves 1 broadcaster and n receivers. Each receiver is given a unique private key. The broadcaster is given a private broadcaster key. The broadcaster wishes to broadcast messages to a designated set $P \subseteq N = \{1, ..., n\}$ of receivers. Any receivers in P should be able to decrypt the broadcast message using only its private key while a coalition $F \subseteq N \smallsetminus P$ (revoked users)

B. Roy (Ed.): ASIACRYPT 2005, LNCS 3788, pp. 100–120, 2005.

should not be able to do so. Such a scheme is motivated largely by pay-TV systems, the distribution of copyrighted materials such as CD/DVD. Broadcast encryption schemes were first formalized by Fiat and Naor [13]. Since then, many variants of the basic problem were proposed. The arguably most challenging variant is the one which considers the case where P can be an arbitrary subset in N while the collusion is considered the full one, $N \smallsetminus P$, and also that the private key stored by each user is fixed from the initialization time (stateless receiver). The main goal is to construct efficient schemes that satisfy the above variant and require only small size of both the header of broadcast and the private key as a function of n or $r := n - |P|$. The *header* is the encapsulation of session key that is used to encrypt data.

An efficient solution which is considered a ground work to many consequences is the Complete (binary) Subtree scheme (CS) by Naor et al. [18]. Schemes which were considered the current state of the art (before two very recent works, see below) are: (i) Pseudo-random sequences generator (PRSG) based schemes such as the Subset Difference scheme (SD) [18], its refinement–the Layered SD scheme (LSD) [14], and their somewhat generalizations in [4]. (ii) RSA accumulator based schemes such as Asano's scheme [2], and its optimal generalizations in [3,11]. See Table 1 for the efficiency comparison. No scheme above could achieve simultaneous small header size independent of n, small key size of order $O(\log n)$, while keeping computational cost and all other costs grow only sub-linear in n.

More recently, Goodrich et al. [12] and Wang et al. [20] independently propose more efficient schemes that break the above barrier. In particular, they achieve simultaneously header size of order $O(r)$ and key size of $O(\log n)$, and computational cost of $O(n^{1/k})$ for arbitrary constant k. (In fact, in [20] only the case when $k = 1, 2$ is considered).

In this paper, we propose generic frameworks for constructing broadcast encryption and give some efficient instantiations. One of our instantiations (Instantiation 2 in Table 1) achieves not only small header size as of order $O(r)$ but also small key size as $O(1)$ with no extra non-secret storage, while keeping computational cost $O(n^{1/k} \log^2 n)$ which grows only sub-linear in n. Thus this is the first scheme that achieves header and private key size independent of n while keeping computational cost sub-linear in n, with no extra non-secret storage. The contributions in more detail are described below.

1.1   Our Contributions

In the general subset-cover paradigm of [18], which includes almost all of the above schemes, it has been *implicitly* understood that one can separate the design of such a scheme into two seemingly orthogonal problems namely: designing combinatorial set system which enables subset covering (this step determines the header size), and defining computational key derivation (this step determines the private key size and computational cost). This is first explicitly characterized by Gentry-Ramzan [11] for the case of Akl-Taylor's RSA based key derivation [1].

Table 1. Comparison among previous schemes and our instantiations. (k is an arbitrary parameter, a is an arbitrary constant).

	Header size Complexity	≤	Priv. key size	Comp. cost (bit complexity) Prime-gen	Others
CS [18]	$O(r\log(\frac{n}{r}))$		$\log n + 1$	-	$O(\log\log n)$
PRSG or OWF -based ↓					
SD [18]	$O(r)$	$2r-1$	$O(\log^2 n)$	-	$O(\log n)$
LSD [14]	$O(r)$	$2kr-k$	$O(\log^{1+1/k} n)$	-	$O(\log n)$
GST04 [12]	$O(r)$	$4kr$	$2\log n$	-	$O(n^{1/k})$
WNR04 [20]	$O(r)$	$4r$	$2\log n$	-	$O(n^{1/2})$
Instantiation 1	$O(r)$	$2kr$	$\leq \log n + 1$	-	$O(n^{1/k})$
RSA Accumulator -based ↓					
Asano [2]	$O(r\log_a(\frac{n}{r})+r)$		1	$O(2^a\log_a^5 n)$	$O(2^a\log_a^2 n)$
GR04 [11]	$O(r\log_a(\frac{n}{r})+r)$		1	$O(a\log_a^5 n)$	$O(a\log_a^2 n)$
Instantiation 3	$O(r\log_a(\frac{n}{r})+r)$		1	$O(1)$	$O(a\log n)$
$(SD)^{acc}$	$O(r)$	$2r-1$	1	$O(n\log^4 n)$	$O(n)$
Instantiation 2	$O(r)$	$2kr$	1	$O((\log^5 n)/k^5)$	$O((n^{1/k}\log^2 n)/k)$

FRAMEWORK. In this paper, we characterize the two orthogonal components in general. We then explicitly present three generic sub-frameworks for computational key derivation component (*generic* as arbitrary set systems are applicable): PRSG based technique (re-formalizing from [4] so as to be consistent with presentations here), non-trapdoor- and trapdoor- RSA Accumulator based techniques. The non-trapdoor RSA based one is a new optimal generalization of Akl-Taylor's technique and is further improved by the trapdoor RSA based one.

The main issue is that we characterize three sub-frameworks so that such instantiations in these frameworks and their resulting efficiencies will depend solely on properties related to *graph decompositions* of the set systems being instantiated; while in the same time the security will be guaranteed *automatically* from the general frameworks. The PRSG based framework will be based on *tree decomposition*, and the two RSA based frameworks will be based on *chain decomposition*; both are purely combinatorial. Therefore the whole paradigm abstracts away the computational security issues and reduces the problem to only pure combinatorics. Moreover it allows modularity in designing a scheme: it is a matter of finding a set system which yields a good header size in the first step, and then finding a graph decomposition of that set system that yields a good private key size and computational cost.

As for the generic efficiency characterization, both RSA based frameworks achieve key size of $O(1)$ for all instances. One generic property of the trapdoor based framework that makes it superior to the non-trapdoor based one is that when restricting to the same asymptotic resources and instantiating the same set system (or to be more precise, its hierarchical version and itself respectively), if the non-trapdoor based one allows n users in the scheme, then the trapdoor based one will allow n^k users for any (arbitrary large) constant k. Indeed, the costs due to prime generation are exactly the same (not only asymptotically).

EFFICIENT INSTANTIATIONS. For the combinatorial set system component, all of our schemes are based on new set systems we call Subset Incremental chain (SIC) and Layered-SIC (LSIC) which are designed so to achieve small header size as being $O(r)$ while intrinsically have graph decompositions with good properties. For the computational key derivation component, we instantiate the LSIC set system by presenting their graph decompositions, resulting in various concrete schemes upon each sub-framework as follows. We use the notation $(X)^y$ to denote an instantiation of the set system X using the y-based framework. Denote LSIC[k] as LSIC with parameter k. Note that LSIC[1] = SIC.

Instantiation 1 : (LSIC[k])^{prsg}. This scheme directly improves the scheme of [12,20] (and it is fair to compare with since the same assumption, PRSG, or equivalently one-way function, was used). In particular it can reduce some overheads, albeit only within constant terms in the worst case: the worst-case key sizes are half of those in [12,20]. Indeed the key size in our scheme is non-uniform among users; some users are even required to store only constant-size keys (cf. Theorem 4, 6, and Eq.(4)). Our scheme also reduces the computational cost from [12], but only in the average case (the worst-case costs are asymptotically the same).

Instantiation 2 : (LSIC[k])^{acc}, (LSIC[k])^{tacc}. Note that (t)acc is for (trapdoor) accumulator. The performance of this scheme is as mentioned previously. It is the first scheme that achieves header and private key size independent of n while keeping computational cost sub-linear in n, with no extra non-secret storage. The number of primes used per user is optimal as being $O(\log n)$ for (LSIC[k])^{acc} and further reduced to $O((\log n)/k)$ for (LSIC[k])^{tacc} (so that the on-the-fly prime generation cost is $O((\log^5 n)/k^5)$). Had one used the non-optimal Akl-Taylor's framework as put forth to the context of BE by [2,3,11], it would be $O(n^{1/k} \log n)$ which is super-logarithmic (and the prime generation cost would be $O(n^{1/k} \log^5 n)$).

Instantiation 3 : (LSIC[$\log_a n$])^{tacc}. This scheme improves Gentry and Ramzan's scheme [11], which itself is more efficient than the above schemes in the aspect of asymptotic computational cost. Our scheme reduces *poly-logarithmic* cost due to prime generation, which was the dominant cost, to only a *constant* one without affecting the other parameters. Among the *constant-key-size* schemes with header size $O(r \log_a(n/r) + r)$ and no extra non-secret storage, this is the first one in the literature that achieves $O(\log n)$ overall computational cost. (And in fact, ours uses only a constant number of primes). The previous improvement for this class of schemes was done by [11] to improve [2] but only in the constant term involving a. (See Table 1).

1.2   Other Related Works

Very recently, Boneh et.al. [7] propose a *public-key* broadcast encryption scheme which achieves size $O(1)$ for both header and private key. However, the size of the public key to be used by an encrypter, which is also the non-secret storage needed for the decrypter, is $O(n)$. Moreover, the computational cost is $O(n-r)$

(albeit with small coefficient). The second scheme in [7] reduces the non-secret storage size to $O(\sqrt{n})$ but with the price of the increased header size as $O(\sqrt{n})$, and not independent of n anymore. Boneh and Silverberg [6] show that n-linear maps can be used to construct an optimal public-key scheme with constant private key, public key, and header size. However, there are currently no known constructions for such a map for $n > 2$. Most recently, Jho et.al. [15] propose some efficient schemes with small header size when r is not too small. However, their schemes do not enjoy practical *asymptotic* performances as either the header size is $c_1 r + c_2 n = O(n)$ (for some constant c_1, c_2) or the key size is $\binom{n-1}{k} = O(n^k)$ (where $k \geq 2$) for their best two schemes.

2   Framework and Some Preliminaries

2.1   Framework

We refer to [18] for the definitions and the security notions for private-key broadcast encryption. Now we recap the subset-cover framework [18] separately into two components as follows.

Combinatorial Set System Component. We first redefine a set system which is useful for such a scheme in this framework called complement-cover set system. Such a set system is a family of subsets of a universe with the property that every subset of the universe can be efficiently partitioned to a union of some collection of subsets in the family.

Definition 1. (COMPLEMENT-COVER SET SYSTEM). *For a map* $c : \mathbb{Z}_{>0}^2 \to \mathbb{Z}_{>0}$, *a set system* $\mathcal{S} = \{S_1, ..., S_m\}$ *over a base set* $N = \{1, ..., n\}$ *is* c-complement-cover *if there is a polynomial-time algorithm such that upon input any subset* $R \subset N$, *outputs* $\{S_{i_1}, ..., S_{i_t}\}$ *for some* $1 \leq i_1, ..., i_t \leq m$ *such that* $N \setminus R = \bigcup_{j=1}^{t} S_{i_j}$ *and that* $t \leq c(n, |R|)$. $\square$

As usual n, r is the number of all users and revoked users respectively. Such a $c(n, r)$-complement-cover set system yields a broadcast encryption scheme in the subset-cover framework with the header size $c(n, r)$. The scheme is as follows. The broadcaster defines a subset key for each subset in the family. Each user stores a set of keys in such a way that he can derive all the keys of subsets (in the family) that he is a member. (Thus, the easiest way to do is to store them all. However to reduce the storage of keys, it would be better to store only some and derive the others from those stored keys on the fly. Such derivation patterns are predefined by the broadcaster.) To revoke the set R of users, the broadcaster just let a header to be a session key encrypted with each key of subsets in the partition of $N \setminus R$. Thus the header size is $c(n, r)$. We often denote $c_X(n, r)$ for $c(n, r)$ of the set system $\mathcal{S}_X$, where X is the name of that set system.

Computational Key Derivation Component. We formalize the specification on key derivations in the context of access control scheme as the following. Denote by $k(S)$ the subset key for $S \in \mathcal{S}$ and $p(u)$ the private key of $u \in N$.

Informally, the security of such a scheme requires that with $\mathsf{p}(u)$, one can derive $\mathsf{k}(S)$ if and only if $u \in S$; moreover, the collusion $N \smallsetminus S$ cannot derive it.

Definition 2 (ACCESS CONTROL SCHEME, AC). . *An Access Control Scheme AC for a set system S over a base set N is a 2-tuple of polynomial-time algorithms (Keygen, Derive), where:*

Keygen(1^λ): *Takes as input a security parameter 1^λ. It returns all $\mathsf{k}(S_i)$'s, all $\mathsf{p}(u)$'s, and public parameter* pub.
Derive($\langle u, \mathsf{p}(u) \rangle, S_i, \mathsf{pub}$): *Takes as input $u \in N$, the key $\mathsf{p}(u)$, $S_i \in S$, and* pub. *It returns $\mathsf{k}(S_i)$ if $u \in S_i$, or special symbol $\bot$ otherwise.*   □

Naor et al. [18] proved that BE in the subset-cover paradigm whose the access control component is secure in the sense of Key-Indistinguishability (KIND) is secure in the standard notion, namely IND-CCA1. Dodis and Katz [10] use the technique involving multiple encryption to obtain a generic scheme which is IND-CCA2-secure. Key-Intractability (KINT) can be defined analogously. These definitions are captured in the full version of this paper due to limited space here. Also note that there is a simple conversion from KINT-secure scheme to KIND-secure one. Thus KIND or KINT is sufficient for the security of the scheme.

Denote $(\mathsf{X})^{\mathsf{y}}$ to be the access control scheme for set system S_{X} that is constructed via AC framework y. Denote $\mathsf{KeySize}_{(\mathsf{X})^{\mathsf{y}}}(u)$ to be the number of keys of u (i.e., $|\mathsf{p}(u)|$, when $\mathsf{p}(u)$ is treated as a set) and $\mathsf{CompCost}_{(\mathsf{X})^{\mathsf{y}}}$ to be the worst-case computational cost for Derive. We also refer $(\mathsf{X})^{\mathsf{y}}$ as a BE scheme via the complement-cover set system S_{X}. For any y, $\mathsf{HeaderSize}_{(\mathsf{X})^{\mathsf{y}}}(n, r) = \mathsf{c}_{\mathsf{X}}(n, r)$.

2.2   Some Terminology

Viewing Set system as Poset. A set system is partially ordered by the inclusion relation ($\subset$). Interpreting a set system as a partially ordered set (poset) is useful when defining key derivations in AC. Intuitively, Derive algorithm implies that whenever $S_i \subset S_j$, anyone who can access $\mathsf{k}(S_i)$ is allowed to access $\mathsf{k}(S_j)$.

Terminology for Posets, Graphs. The terminology for posets and graphs used in this paper is quite standard one (cf.[9]) (with some exceptions, see below). Here we review some. A graph is a pair $G = (V, E)$ of sets satisfying $E \subseteq \binom{V}{2}$. V is the set of vertices (or nodes), usually denoted $V(G)$, E is the set of edges, usually denoted $E(G)$. Often, we abuse notation $v \in G$ to mean $v \in V(G)$. A tree is a connected acyclic graph. We often denote $x = \mathsf{parent}_T(y)$ if x is the parent of y in tree T. A directed graph is a pair $G = (V, E)$ of sets satisfying $E \subseteq V \times V$, i.e., an edge is an ordered pair. A directed acyclic graph (DAG) is a directed graph with no directed cycle in it. A notation of chain $x \to y \to z$ means a directed graph which $E = \{x, y, z\}, V = \{(x, y), (y, z)\}$ and is generalized naturally.

An inclusion poset S can be represented by a DAG G by setting $V = S$, $E = \{(S, S') : S \subset S'; \ S, S' \in S\}$. This is called the maximal representation, denoted $\mathsf{DAG}_{\mathsf{max}}(S)$. The minimal representation, denoted $\mathsf{DAG}_{\mathsf{min}}(S)$, is the one with $E = \{(S, S') : S \subset_c S'; \ S, S' \in S\}$ where we say $S \subset_c S'$ iff there is no $S'' \in S$ such that $S \subset S'' \subset S'$.

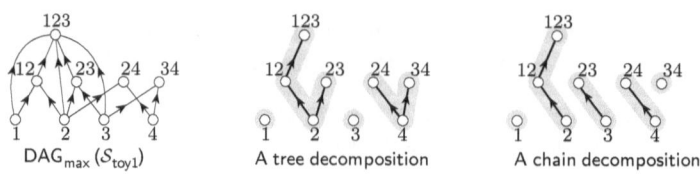

Fig. 1. Toy example 1 and its graph decompositions

In our context[1], a graph decomposition (often denoted $\mathcal{G}$) of a poset $\mathcal{S}$ is a family of connected subgraphs whose sets of nodes partition the set of all nodes in the $\mathsf{DAG}_{max}(\mathcal{S})$. (Thus we sometimes say $\mathcal{G}$ is a graph decomposition of $\mathsf{DAG}_{max}(\mathcal{S})$). When each subgraph is a tree whose edges are directed away from the root, we call it a tree decomposition (often denoted $\mathcal{T}$). When each graph is a directed chain whose edges are directed in the same direction, we call it a chain decomposition (often denoted $\mathcal{C}$). An induced graph decomposition is one in which each subgraph is an induced subgraph. Fig.1 shows graph decompositions of the set system for toy example 1, $\mathcal{S}_{toy1} = \{\{1\}, \{2\}, \{3\}, \{4\}, \{1,2\}, \{2,3\}, \{2,4\}, \{3,4\}, \{1,2,3\}\}$. From now we abuse some notations, often in figures, e.g., writing 12 or 1, 2 instead of $\{1,2\}$ if it causes no confusion. Note that every chain decomposition is a tree decomposition.

We will fix BT to be the complete binary tree of n leaves labeled $1, ..., n$ from left to right. The level of node in BT is the distance from root to it. For a fixed node, its left (resp., right) nodes are those nodes with the same level and appear on the left (resp., right). BT will be used only to help defining set systems and should not be confused with the graph representations of posets of set systems.

3   New Set Systems

3.1   Subset Incremental Chain (SIC) Set System

The SIC Set System. For $i, j \in N = \{1, ..., n\}$ and $i < j$, denote

$$i \rightarrow j := \{\{i\}, \{i, i+1\}, \ldots, \{i, \ldots, j\}\},$$
$$i \leftarrow j := \{\{j\}, \{j, j-1\}, \ldots, \{j, \ldots, i\}\},$$

and $(i \rightarrow i) = (i \leftarrow i) := \{\{i\}\}$. Consider the binary tree BT. For a node v in BT, let l_v (resp., r_v) be the leftmost (resp., rightmost) leaf under v. We define the set system SIC (of n users) by letting

$$\mathcal{S}_{\mathsf{SIC}} = \bigcup_{v \in \mathsf{BT_L}} (l_v + 1 \leftarrow r_v) \cup \bigcup_{v \in \mathsf{BT_R}} (l_v \rightarrow r_v - 1) \cup (1 \rightarrow n) \cup (2 \leftarrow n), \qquad (1)$$

where $\mathsf{BT_L}$ (resp., $\mathsf{BT_R}$) are the set of internal nodes which are left (resp., right) children. An informal visual view of $\mathcal{S}_{\mathsf{SIC}}$ is shown in Fig.2, where the union of all the collections written there is the only important information.

---

[1] Our notions for tree and chain decompositions are *not* standard ones (cf.[9]). Instead the notions introduced here might be named as *tree cover* and *path cover*, resp.

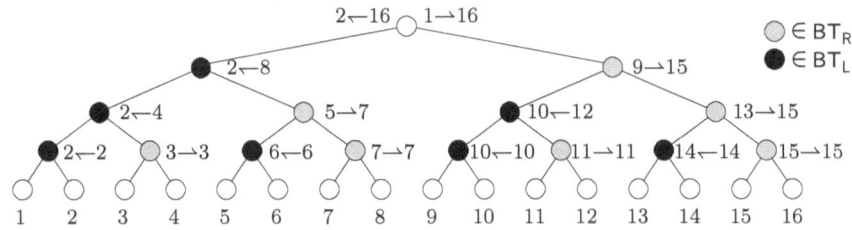

Fig. 2. Set system SIC defined by the union of all the collections written at each node

Theorem 1. $\mathcal{S}_{\mathsf{SIC}}$ *is* $(2r)$-*complement-cover set system.*

Proof. We call a set of the form $\{i, i+1, \ldots, j\}$ for some $i \leq j$ a consecutive set. We first claim that any consecutive set, say $A = \{i, \ldots, j\}$, can be partitioned to no more than 2 sets in $\mathcal{S}_{\mathsf{SIC}}$; then prove it as follows. Let a be the least common ancestor node of the leaves i and j in BT, denoted $\mathsf{lca}(i, j) = a$. Let s be the least ancestor of a which is in $\mathsf{BT_L}$ if $a \in \mathsf{BT_R}$ and which is in $\mathsf{BT_R}$ if $a \in \mathsf{BT_L}$. Let x, y be the left and right children of a. First if $i = 1$ then $A \in (1 \rightarrow n) \subseteq \mathcal{S}_{\mathsf{SIC}}$; else if $j - n$ then $A \in (2 \leftarrow n) \subseteq \mathcal{S}_{\mathsf{SIC}}$ (since $2 \leq i$). Now assume $i \neq 1$, $j \neq n$. We list all possible cases of (i, j) as follows. Let $*$ be an unspecified value.

1. If $(i = l_a; j = *; a \in \mathsf{BT_L})$ then $A \in (l_s \rightarrow r_s - 1) \subseteq \mathcal{S}_{\mathsf{SIC}}$ (since $i = l_s$; $j < r_s - 1$; and $s \in \mathsf{BT_R}$),
2. If $(i = *; j = r_a; a \in \mathsf{BT_R})$ then $A \in (l_s + 1 \leftarrow r_s) \subseteq \mathcal{S}_{\mathsf{SIC}}$ (since $j = r_s$; $l_s + 1 < i$; and $s \in \mathsf{BT_L}$),
3. If $(i = l_a; j \neq r_a; a \in \mathsf{BT_R})$ then $A \in (l_a \rightarrow r_a - 1) \subseteq \mathcal{S}_{\mathsf{SIC}}$ (since $j \leq r_a - 1$),
4. If $(i \neq l_a; j = r_a; a \in \mathsf{BT_L})$ then $A \in (l_a + 1 \leftarrow r_a) \subseteq \mathcal{S}_{\mathsf{SIC}}$ (since $l_a + 1 \leq i$),
5. If $(i \neq l_a; j \neq r_a; a \in *)$ then $A = P \cup Q$; $P = \{i, \ldots, r_x\}$, $Q = \{l_y, \ldots, j\}$, and we have $P, Q \in \mathcal{S}_{\mathsf{SIC}}$ (since
   - $\mathsf{lca}(i, r_x) = x$, thus (i, r_x) will fall to the case 2 or 4 and $P \in \mathcal{S}_{\mathsf{SIC}}$;
   - $\mathsf{lca}(l_y, j) = y$, thus (l_y, j) will fall to the case 1 or 3 thus $Q \in \mathcal{S}_{\mathsf{SIC}}$).

These proved the claim. Now we are back to the proof, it is obvious that $N \smallsetminus R$ can be partitioned to no more than r consecutive sets if 1 or $n \in R$; or to no more than $r + 1$ such sets otherwise. In the former case, the partition size to sets in $\mathcal{S}_{\mathsf{SIC}}$ is $\leq 2r$; while in the latter case (where $\{1, ..., s\}$ and $\{t, ..., n\}$ for some s, t are included in the partition), it is $\leq 1(1) + 2(r - 1) + 1(1) = 2r$. $\square$

Intuitively, SIC has graph decompositions with good properties since each collection in the union of Eq.(1) forms a chain of subset. This will become clearer in the next section. The set system LSIC below generalizes SIC.

3.2   Layered SIC (LSIC) Set Systems

The LSIC[k] Set System. We view BT consisting of subtrees (also binary and complete) of $n^{1/k}$ leaves so that there are exactly k layers of such subtrees, where

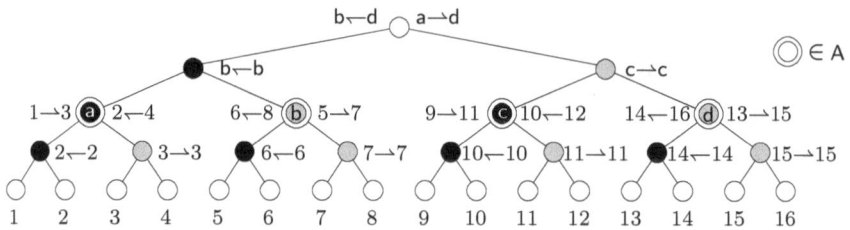

Fig. 3. Set system $\mathsf{LSIC}[k]$, $k = 2$, as the union of all collections written at each node

$k \mid \log n$. We will call such subtree an "atomic" subtree (to distinguish from other kinds of subtrees in BT). Informally, each atomic subtree contributes sets to $\mathcal{S}_{\mathsf{LSIC}}$ as in the SIC set system for that subtree, albeit each leaf in the subtree represents all the leaves under it in BT. More formally, for node z in BT, let $A_z := \{l_z, l_z + 1, ..., r_z\}$ (i.e., all the leaves under z). Let us consider the leaves u, v in an atomic subtree where v is some node on the right of u. We denote $u^{(+1)}, u^{(+2)}$ (and so on) be the next one, two (and so on) *right* leaves to u in that atomic subtree. Denote $u^{(-1)}, u^{(-2)}$ analogously. Denote

$$u \rightharpoonup v := \{A_u, A_u \cup A_{u^{(+1)}}, \ldots, A_u \cup \cdots \cup A_v\},$$
$$u \leftharpoondown v := \{A_v, A_v \cup A_{v^{(-1)}}, \ldots, A_v \cup \cdots \cup A_u\}.$$

Let l'_w, r'_w be the leftmost and rightmost leaves under w *in the atomic subtree* and not w itself; for example, $l'_{\mathsf{root}} = a, r'_{\mathsf{root}} = d$ and $l'_a = 1, r'_a = 4$ in Fig.3. Let A be the set of all nodes which are the roots of atomic subtrees but excluding the root of BT. We define $\mathsf{LSIC}[k]$ analogously to Eq.(1) by letting

$$\mathcal{S}_{\mathsf{LSIC}[k]} = \bigcup_{v \in \mathsf{BT_L} \cup A} (l'_v{}^{(+1)} \leftharpoondown r'_v) \cup \bigcup_{v \in \mathsf{BT_R} \cup A} (l'_v \rightharpoonup r'_v{}^{(-1)})$$

$$\cup (l'_{\mathsf{root}} \rightharpoonup r'_{\mathsf{root}}) \cup (l'^{(+1)}_{\mathsf{root}} \leftharpoondown r'_{\mathsf{root}}). \quad (2)$$

Intuitively, each $v \in A$ has two collections $(l'_v{}^{(+1)} \leftharpoondown r'_v), (l'_v \rightharpoonup r'_v{}^{(-1)})$ attached since it is the root of an atomic subtree, which SIC applies (cf. Eq.(1) and Fig.2).

Theorem 2. $\mathcal{S}_{\mathsf{LSIC}[k]}$ *is* $(2kr)$*-complement-cover set system for a constant* k *; and* $\mathcal{S}_{\mathsf{LSIC}[\log_a n]}$ *is* $O(r \log_a(n/r) + r)$*-complement-cover set system for a constant* a.

Note that when $k = \log_a n$, from the former claim we already have that $\mathcal{S}_{\mathsf{LSIC}[\log_a n]}$ is $(2r \log_a n)$-complement-cover, but the claim above gives a sharper bound.

Proof. First we will prove that $\mathcal{S}_{\mathsf{LSIC}[k]}$ is $(2kr)$-complement-cover. Let ST_R denote the Steiner tree of a set of leaves $R \subseteq N$, i.e., the subtree of BT that consists of all paths from the root to each leaf in R. We call a node v special if $v \in A$. We "color" a node if it is special but is not in ST_R and all of its special ancestors are in ST_R. Denote C the set of all color nodes. Hence

$N \smallsetminus R = \bigcup_{v \in C} A_v = \bigcup_{j=1}^{k} \bigcup_{v \in L_j \cap C} A_v$ where we denote L_j to be the set of all special nodes in the j-th special layer away from root (i.e., at distance $j(\log n)/k$ from the root). It suffices to prove that for each special layer j, the set $Y_j := \bigcup_{v \in L_j \cap C} A_v$ can be partitioned to at most $2r$ sets in the family $\mathcal{S}_{\mathsf{LSIC}}$. Denote x_i to be the number of uncolored special nodes in the i-th atomic subtrees from left to right in this j-th layer. From Theorem 1, it is easy to deduce that Y_j can be partitioned to at most $2(x_1 + x_2 + \cdots + x_p)$ sets in $\mathcal{S}_{\mathsf{LSIC}}$, where p is the last atomic subtree in this layer (in fact, $p = n^{(j-i)/k}$). But we have $x_1 + \cdots + x_p \leq r$ since the Steiner tree of r leaves passes through all these uncolored special nodes. This proves the claim.

Next we will prove that $\mathcal{S}_{\mathsf{LSIC}[\log_a n]}$ is $O(r \log_a(n/r) + r)$-complement-cover. We first give the definition of Stratified Subset-Difference set system with each atomic subtree of a leaves (SSD_a): $\mathcal{S}_{\mathsf{SSD}_a} = \{A_u \smallsetminus A_v : u$ is an ancestor of v in the same atomic subtree$\}$. It is known [11] that $\mathcal{S}_{\mathsf{SSD}_a}$ is $(O(r \log_a(n/r)+r))$-complement-cover. Using a similar approach as when proving Theorem 1, it is not hard to see that each $A_u \smallsetminus A_v$ can be partitioned to at most 2 sets in $\mathcal{S}_{\mathsf{LSIC}[\log_a n]}$. (The proof is omitted here due to space). Combining these we have that $\mathsf{LSIC}[\log_a n]$ has $c_{\mathsf{LSIC}[\log_a n]}(n,r) = 2c_{\mathsf{SSD}_a}(n,r) = O(r \log_a(n/r) + r)$.   □

4   Key Derivation Based on PRSG

4.1   Reformalize the PRSG Based Framework of [4]

Framework Idea (review). In this framework, we use pseudo-random sequence generators to derive keys from one subset to another. The correctness of access control schemes allows this to be done only if the first set is included in the latter (e.g.,$\{1\} \subset \{1,2\}$). Thus such derivations can be defined in correspondence with directed edges in a graph decomposition of $\mathsf{DAG}_{\max}(\mathcal{S})$, in which all the inclusion relations in $\mathcal{S}$ are included. One exception is that there should be no node with indegree > 1 in any graph in the decomposition since it would imply a collision of PRSG, which should be computable by neither broadcasters nor adversaries. Therefore, all the valid decompositions are *tree decompositions*, of which the class includes all graph decompositions of the poset that allow indegree ≤ 1 for all nodes. Each user then stores keys for subsets which he is in and are closest to the root of that tree. For the toy example 1 in Fig.1, our paradigm with the tree decomposition in the figure namely $\mathcal{T}_{\mathsf{toy1}}$ allows the user 2 to store only the keys at $2, 24$.

Note that in order to be provably secure in the KIND sense, it is mandatory to make an adaptation so that keys are not derived from another key *directly*. Instead, one should use intermediate keys denoted $\mathsf{t}(S)$ for $S \in \mathcal{S}$; how to use this is explained in the construction. This was neglected in many recent schemes that use similar one-way derivation approaches.

The Construction $(\mathsf{X})^{\mathsf{prsg}}$. This is based solely on a tree decomposition, say $\mathcal{T}$, of the poset $\mathcal{S}_{\mathsf{X}}$. The scheme applies to an arbitrary complement-cover set system X.

Keygen : (Subset keys) At a root S of a tree in T, let $t(S) \leftarrow \{0,1\}^\lambda$. For each node S (either root or non-root of a tree in T) whose all children are $S_{i_1}, ..., S_{i_d}$ where d is the outdegree of S, we define the following recurrence relation:

$$t(S_{i_1})\| \cdots \|t(S_{i_d})\|k(S) \leftarrow \mathsf{PRSG}_{d+1}(t(S)), \tag{3}$$

where $|t(S_{i_1})| = \cdots = |t(S_{i_d})| = |k(S)| = \lambda$ bits; $\mathsf{PRSG}_j : \{0,1\}^\lambda \to \{0,1\}^{j\lambda}$.
(User keys) For $u \in N$, we define $p(u) = \{t(S)|u \in S; u \notin \mathsf{parent}_G(S), G \in T\}$.
Derive : Find the tree where S is in and then use Eq.(3) to derive $k(S)$.

Characterizing Efficiency. Let $\mathsf{RN}_T(u) = |\{S \mid u \in S; u \notin \mathsf{parent}_G(S), G \in T\}|$ and call it the *reachability number* of u in T (since it is the minimal number of sufficient nodes such that when traversing from these nodes in the edge direction we meet all $S \in \mathcal{S}$ such that $u \in S$). Let $\mathsf{DD}_T = $ the depth of the deepest trees. We have

$$\mathsf{KeySize}_{(X)^{\mathsf{prsg}}}(u) = \mathsf{RN}_T(u), \quad \mathsf{CompCost}_{(X)^{\mathsf{prsg}}} = \mathsf{DD}_T. \tag{4}$$

Theorem 3. ([4]) $(X)^{\mathsf{prsg}}$ *is secure in the sense of KIND assuming secure PRSG.*

4.2   PRSG Based Instantiation for SIC, LSIC

Instantiating SIC. It suffices to define a tree decomposition of $\mathcal{S}_{\mathsf{SIC}}$ and the concrete scheme will follow automatically from the general construction of the framework. We choose the following natural one and prove that it is the optimal decomposition for SIC. For $i \leq j \in N$, define a graph $\mathsf{G}(i \rightharpoonup j)$ as $\{i\} \to \{i, i+1\} \to \cdots \to \{i, ..., j\}$; $\mathsf{G}(i \leftharpoondown j)$ as $\{j\} \to \{j, j-1\} \to \cdots \to \{j, ..., i\}$. Let

$$\mathcal{T}_{\mathsf{SIC}} = \{\mathsf{G}(l_v+1 \leftharpoondown r_v)|v \in \mathsf{BT_L}\}\cup\{\mathsf{G}(l_v \rightharpoonup r_v-1)|v \in \mathsf{BT_R}\}\cup\{\mathsf{G}(1 \rightharpoonup n), \mathsf{G}(2 \leftharpoondown n)\} \tag{5}$$

Let $\langle x \rangle$ denotes the binary representation of x. We have the following theorem.

Theorem 4. *The tree decomposition $\mathcal{T}_{\mathsf{SIC}}$ yields minimal $\max_{u \in N} \mathsf{RN}_T(u)$, indeed we have*

$$\mathsf{RN}_{\mathcal{T}_{\mathsf{SIC}}}(u) = \begin{cases} \log n + 2 - f(\langle u - 1\rangle) & ; 2 \leq u \leq n \\ 1 & ; u = 1, \end{cases}$$

where $f(y) := $ the number of the same consecutive least significant bits of y. In particular, $\max_{u \in N} \mathsf{RN}_{\mathcal{T}_{\mathsf{SIC}}}(u) = \log n + 1$. We also have $\mathsf{DD}_{\mathcal{T}_{\mathsf{SIC}}} = n$.

Proof. We define $F_v = l_v + 1 \leftharpoondown r_v$ if $v \in \mathsf{BT_L}$ and $l_v \rightharpoonup r_v - 1$ if $v \in \mathsf{BT_R}$. $\mathcal{T}_{\mathsf{SIC}}$ is really a tree decomposition since $\{F_v : v \in \mathsf{BT_L} \cup \mathsf{BT_R}\} \cup \{(1 \rightharpoonup n), (2 \leftharpoondown n)\}$ can be proved to be a pairwise non-intersecting family (somewhat straightforwardly). Next we prove the formula for $\mathsf{RN}_{\mathcal{T}_{\mathsf{SIC}}}(u)$. For $u \in N \smallsetminus \{1\}$, only possible trees in $\mathcal{T}_{\mathsf{SIC}}$ that u appears are those graphs $\mathsf{G}(F_v)$ for internal nodes v on the path from the leaf u to the root in BT, and $\mathsf{G}(1 \rightharpoonup n), \mathsf{G}(2 \leftharpoondown n)$. Each graph $\mathsf{G}(\cdot)$ that u appears contribute one key for u. Thus $\mathsf{RN}_{\mathcal{T}_{\mathsf{SIC}}}(u)$ is at most $(\log n - 1) + 2$. Let

$u, w_1, ..., w_{\log n}$, root be the nodes on that path. Due to symmetry, we assume w.l.o.g. that $w_1, ..., w_{z-1} \in \mathsf{BT_L}$ and $w_z \in \mathsf{BT_R}$. Now it is easy to see that

for $1 \le j \le z - 1$: $\mathsf{G}(F_{w_j}) = \mathsf{G}(l_{w_j} + 1 \leftarrow r_{w_j})$ does not contain $u (= l_{w_j})$;

for $j = z$ \qquad : $\mathsf{G}(F_{w_j}) = \mathsf{G}(l_{w_z} \rightarrow r_{w_z} - 1)$ contains $u(= l_{w_z})$;

for $z < j \le \log n$: $\mathsf{G}(F_{w_j})$ contains u (since $l_{w_j} < u < r_{w_j}$),

and that $z = f(\langle u - 1 \rangle)$. Thus $\mathsf{RN}_{\mathcal{T}_{\mathsf{SIC}}}(u) = (\log n - 1) + 2 - (f(\langle u - 1 \rangle) - 1)$ as desired. Now we prove that $\mathcal{T}_{\mathsf{SIC}}$ is optimal (obtaining minimal $(\max_{u \in N} \mathsf{RN}_{\mathcal{T}}(u))$ among all $\mathcal{T}$ of SIC). Observe that for all $\mathcal{T}$ of SIC, $\sum_{u \in N} \mathsf{RN}_{\mathcal{T}}(u) = \sum_{S \in \mathcal{S}_{\mathsf{SIC}}} |\{u : u \in S, u \notin \mathsf{parent}_G(S), G \in \mathcal{T}\}| \ge |\mathcal{S}_{\mathsf{SIC}}| = n \log n + 1$. Hence $\max_{u \in N} \mathsf{RN}_{\mathcal{T}}(u) \ge \lceil \frac{n \log n + 1}{n} \rceil = \log n + 1$. Our decomposition matches this bound. $\qquad \square$

The number of keys at each user is not uniform as recorded in the corollary below. While sharing some similarities with our scheme, the basic schemes in [12,20] assign one-way chains in both left and right directions at each node in BT while we use only one direction and exploit some symmetries. This can be an intuition as to why we can reduce key size at least 2 times (and up to $\log n$ in the best case, user 1). Those schemes can be considered as instantiations in our framework, but with storage-redundancies in the sense that the set systems extracted from their schemes are sets with repetition. Moreover, the scheme of [12] can also be shown to be derivation-redundant since its derivation graph as exposed in our framework contains loop edges. (See our full paper).

Corollary 5. *In the scheme* $(\mathsf{SIC})^{\mathsf{prsg}}$, *there are exactly* 2^x *users who store exactly* $x + 2$ *keys for* $0 \le x \le (\log n) - 1$ *and exactly 1 user who stores 1 key.*

Instantiating LSIC. Before describing our default tree decomposition of $\mathcal{S}_{\mathsf{LSIC}}$, denoted $\mathcal{T}_{\mathsf{LSIC}[k]}$, we first describe a more straightforward one, denoted $\mathcal{T}'_{\mathsf{LSIC}[k]}$, which is constructed, informally, as the union of all $\mathcal{T}_{\mathsf{SIC}}$ applied to each atomic subtree in BT. More formally, we can define $\mathsf{G}(u \rightarrow v)$ for u, v which are leaves in the same atomic subtree, analogously as before, by letting $\mathsf{G}(u \rightarrow v) = A_u \rightarrow A_u \cup A_{u(+1)} \rightarrow \cdots \rightarrow (A_u \cup \cdots \cup A_v)$, and analogously for $\mathsf{G}(u \leftarrow v)$. Without going into details, we can define $\mathcal{T}'_{\mathsf{LSIC}[k]}$ from Eq.(2) in an analogous way when we defined $\mathcal{T}_{\mathsf{SIC}}$ in Eq.(5) from Eq.(1).

Now $\mathcal{T}_{\mathsf{LSIC}[k]}$ is constructed by an observation that $\mathsf{G}(l'_v \rightarrow r'^{(-1)}_v)$ and $\mathsf{G}(v \rightarrow *)$ can be combined into one chain (and in particular, one tree) since the maximum element in the former, $A_{l'_v} \cup \cdots \cup A_{r'^{(-1)}_v}$, is included in A_v, the minimum element of the latter. For $v \in \mathsf{BT_R} \cup \{\text{root}\}$, let $w_1, ..., w_m$ be the sequence of nodes in $\mathsf{BT_L} \cap A$ such that $w_1 = l'_v$; for $1 \le i \le m - 1$, $w_{i+1} = l'_{w_i}$; and $l_v = l'_{w_m}$, then define $\bar{\mathsf{G}}(l'_v \rightarrow x) := \mathsf{G}(l'_{w_m} \rightarrow r'^{(-1)}_{w_m}) \rightarrow \cdots \rightarrow \mathsf{G}(l'_{w_1} \rightarrow r'^{(-1)}_{w_1}) \rightarrow \mathsf{G}(l'_v \rightarrow x)$ where x is some right node of l'_v. (Here, '$\rightarrow$' means to connect the chains). The definition for $\bar{\mathsf{G}}(x \leftarrow r'_v)$ for $v \in \mathsf{BT_L} \cup \{\text{root}\}$ can be done analogously. Now we define

$$\mathcal{T}_{\mathsf{LSIC}[k]} = \{\bar{\mathsf{G}}(l'^{(+1)}_v \leftarrow r'_v) | v \in \mathsf{BT_L}\} \cup \{\bar{\mathsf{G}}(l'_v \rightarrow r'^{(-1)}_v) | v \in \mathsf{BT_R}\}$$

$$\cup \{\bar{\mathsf{G}}(l'_{\text{root}} \rightarrow r'_{\text{root}}), \bar{\mathsf{G}}(l'^{(+1)}_{\text{root}} \rightarrow r'_{\text{root}})\}. \quad (6)$$

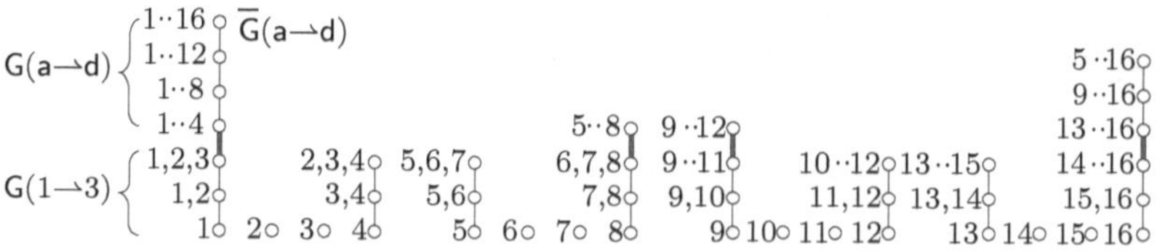

Fig. 4. The tree decomposition $\mathcal{T}_{\mathsf{LSIC}[k]}$ of the set system $\mathsf{LSIC}[k]$ (see Fig.3). A more simple decomposition $\mathcal{T}'_{\mathsf{LSIC}[k]}$ is the one without the thick red edges.

The abstraction of this decomposition may disguise the simplicity of the scheme; in Fig.4 we thus give an explicit example when $n = 16$ and $k = 2$ (cf. Fig.3).

The following theorem and corollary can be proved by an elementary counting argument based on Theorem 4. We omit the proof to the full version of this paper.

Theorem 6. *The tree decomposition* $\mathcal{T}_{\mathsf{LSIC}[k]}$ *yields*

$$\mathsf{RN}_{\mathcal{T}_{\mathsf{LSIC}[k]}}(u) = \log n + 1 + k - g_k(\langle u - 1 \rangle)$$

where $g_k(\langle x \rangle) := f(0||\langle x_1 \rangle) + f(b_1||\langle x_2 \rangle) \cdots + f(b_{k-1}||\langle x_k \rangle)$ *where we parse* $\langle x \rangle$, *with padding of 0s on the left so to have length* $\log n$ *bits, as* $\langle x_1 \rangle || \cdots || \langle x_k \rangle$ *so that each* $\langle x_i \rangle$ *has length* $(\log n)/k$ *bits;* b_j *is the least significant bit of* $\langle x_j \rangle$. *In particular,* $\max_{u \in N} \mathsf{RN}_{\mathcal{T}_{\mathsf{LSIC}[k]}}(u) = \log n + 1$. *We also have* $\mathsf{DD}_{\mathcal{T}_{\mathsf{LSIC}[k]}} = kn^{1/k}$.

As an example, user 4 will store 2 keys: $\mathsf{k}(1234), \mathsf{k}(4)$ (see Fig.4). This can be calculated as $|\mathsf{p}(4)| = 4 + 1 + 2 - (f(0||00) + f(0||11)) = 2$ (Note $\langle 4 - 1 \rangle = 0011$).

Corollary 7. *In* $(\mathsf{LSIC}[k])^{\mathsf{prsg}}$, *exactly* $\sum_{j=0}^{x-1} \binom{k}{j} C(x-1, j, (\log n)/k) 2^{x-1-j}$ *users store exactly* x *keys for* $2 \leq x \leq (\log n) + 1$ *and exactly 1 user stores 1 key where* $C(a, b, c)$ *is the number of integer compositions (ordered partitions) of* a *into* b *positive integers, each* $\leq c$.[2]

5   Key Derivation Based on Non-trapdoor RSA

5.1   The New Non-trapdoor RSA Based Framework

Framework Idea. We first briefly review the access control scheme of Akl-Taylor [1]. There, each $S \in \mathcal{S}$ is assigned a publicly known prime. The key of S is defined as $\mathsf{k}(S) = s^{\prod_{T:S \not\to T} p_T}$ modulo an RSA modulus, where s is a secret; and $S \not\to T$ means (S, T) is not an edge in $\mathsf{DAG}_{\max}(\mathcal{S})$. Each user u just stores $\mathsf{k}(\{u\})$. The terms in the exponents are arranged so that even any collusion cannot compute keys that are not supposed to be computable by them. However, the number of primes used in the above schemes are too large as $|\mathcal{S}|$. Such

---

[2] For example $C(5, 3, 2) = 3$ since $5 = 1 + 2 + 2 = 2 + 1 + 2 = 2 + 2 + 1$. The exact formula of $C(a, b, c)$ is quite complicated and is shown in [19].

primes will be stored as non-secret storage or derived on-the-fly.[3] We propose a new paradigm which makes uses of *prime powers* so that the number of primes used becomes optimal. We will see shortly that assigning prime powers depends essentially on a *chain decomposition* of $\mathsf{DAG}_{\max}(\mathcal{S})$. Indeed, the number of primes used will be exactly the number of chains; and each node in the same chain will correspond to the same prime but with a distinct power. For the toy example 1 in Fig.1, our new paradigm with the chain decomposition $\mathcal{C}_{\text{toy1}}$ will result in only 5 primes used while the Akl-taylor's needs 9 primes. We will describe how to assign those powers over primes by an incidence matrix. We formalize the notion of incidence matrices that admit a secure scheme as *maximin matrix*:

Maximin Matrix. An $n \times m$ matrix $\{a_{ij}\}$ where $a_{ij} \in \mathbb{Z}_{\geq 0}$ is called a maximin matrix for set system X if for all $S \in \mathcal{S}_\mathsf{X}$, there exists $j : 1 \leq j \leq m$ such that $\boxed{\max_{i \in S} a_{ij} < \min_{i \in N \smallsetminus S} a_{ij}.}$ We give a formal treatment of RSA functions as accumulators and our construction first, then explain later.

RSA Accumulators. We fix a function $\mathsf{f} : \mathsf{U}_\mathsf{f} \times \mathsf{E}_\mathsf{f} \to \mathsf{U}_\mathsf{f}$ to be an RSA function: $\mathsf{f}(x, e) := x^e \bmod \eta$ where $\eta = pq, p = 2p' + 1, q = 2q' + 1$ and p, q, p', q' are distinct odd primes. We restrict that U_f is the set of quadratic residues and E_f is the set of primes not equal to p', q'. We say f is generated from an RSA function generator $\mathsf{G}_{\mathsf{RSA}}(1^\lambda)$. The function f is an instance of **RSA accumulators**, first proposed in [5], which has a **quasi-commutative** property: for all $x \in \mathsf{U}_\mathsf{f}$, and $e_1, e_2 \in \mathsf{E}_\mathsf{f}$, $\mathsf{f}(\mathsf{f}(x, e_1), e_2) = \mathsf{f}(\mathsf{f}(x, e_2), e_1)$. If $E = \{e_1, ..., e_h\}$ where each $e_i \in \mathsf{E}_\mathsf{f}$, then we denote $\mathsf{f}(x, E) := \mathsf{f}(\mathsf{f}(...\mathsf{f}(x, e_1), ...), e_h)$. Note that a set E is threaten as a **multi-set**, where the repetition of members is important. We thus denote a repetition of a member e which occurs t_e times as $t_e \lhd e$. For example, $\mathsf{f}(x, \{s \lhd e_1, t \lhd e_2\}) = x^{(e_1^s \cdot e_2^t)}$.

The Construction $(\mathsf{X})^{\mathsf{acc}}$.

Keygen : Run a $\mathsf{G}_{\mathsf{RSA}}$ to obtain a description of $\mathsf{f} : \mathsf{U}_\mathsf{f} \times \mathsf{E}_\mathsf{f} \to \mathsf{U}_\mathsf{f}$. Pick a random secret $s \in \mathsf{U}_\mathsf{f}$. For $1 \leq j \leq m$, pick an element $p_j \in \mathsf{E}_\mathsf{f}$. Let pub consist of all p_j's and $\{a_{ij}\}$; indeed we let user derive prime p_j only when necessary by predetermining the intervals of those primes (see below). Let

$$\begin{aligned} \mathsf{p}(u) &= \mathsf{f}(s, \{a_{uj} \lhd p_j : 1 \leq j \leq m\}), \\ \mathsf{k}(S) &= \mathsf{f}(s, \{(\max_{i \in S} a_{ij}) \lhd p_j : 1 \leq j \leq m\}). \end{aligned} \tag{7}$$

for user $u \in N$ and set $S \in \mathcal{S}_\mathsf{X}$.

Derive : Compute $\mathsf{k}(S) = \mathsf{f}(\mathsf{p}(u), \{(\max_{i \in S} a_{ij} - a_{uj}) \lhd p_j : 1 \leq j \leq m\})$.

Theorem 8. $(\mathsf{X})^{\mathsf{acc}}$ *is KINT-secure assuming the strong RSA assumption.*

First it is easy to see that the correctness holds: Derive is computable. Next we will give an intuition as to why for each $S \in \mathcal{S}$, the collusion of all users

---

[3] In the latter, a sequence of integers $\{x_j\}$ is pre-specified by the broadcaster and p_i is defined to be the first prime in $[x_i, x_{i+1})$; the program to recognize $\{x_j\}$ has negligible size (cf. [2]). More primes imply more computational cost on-the-fly.

from $N \smallsetminus S$ cannot compute the key of S. Informally, the best they can do is to obtain the value with the same base s and the exponent term being GCD of all the exponent terms of the keys for users in $N \smallsetminus S$, which is $\prod_{j=1}^{m} p_j^{\min_{i \in N \smallsetminus S} a_{ij}}$ (by the well-known trick involving using the extended Euclid's algorithm). To be able to compute the key of S, it must divide $\prod_{j=1}^{m} p_j^{\max_{i \in S} a_{ij}}$. But this will not happen due to the property of the maximin matrix.

Constructing a Maximin Matrix. Consider a chain decomposition $\mathcal{C} = \{G_1, ..., G_m\}$ of $\mathcal{S}_X$. For each chain $G_j : S_1 \rightarrow \cdots \rightarrow S_l$, construct j-th column by letting

$$a_{ij} := \begin{cases} 0 & \text{if } i \in S_1 \\ w & \text{if } i \in S_{w+1} \smallsetminus S_w \\ l & \text{otherwise} \end{cases} \tag{8}$$

Proposition 9. *The above construction is a maximin matrix. Moreover, $\mathcal{C}$ with the minimum number of chains will imply the maximin matrix with the minimum m, the number of all primes used.*

Proof. We will prove that the construction by Eq.(8) is a maximin matrix for X. Consider arbitrary $S \in \mathcal{S}$, observe that there is a chain $G_j : S_1 \rightarrow \cdots \rightarrow S_l$ and some w, $0 \le w \le l - 1$, such that $S = S_{w+1}$ (since $\mathcal{C}$ is a chain decomposition). For all $i \in S$ we have $0 \le a_{ij} \le w$ by the construction. For all $i' \in N \smallsetminus S$ we have $w > a_{i'j}$ also by the construction. This implies $\max_{i \in S} a_{ij} \le w < \min_{i' \in N \smallsetminus S} a_{i'j}$ which is what we wanted to prove. To prove the second claim, it is sufficient to prove the converse of the first claim: from any maximin matrix for X one can construct a a chain decomposition in which the number of chains is less than or equal to the number of columns of the matrix. The proof idea is essentially the same as the first, thus we omit the detail to the full version of this paper.   □

Characterizing Efficiency. We will generate primes on the fly using the technique in [2] (cf. footnote 3). Without going into detail, this technique requires computational cost $O(\log^4 P)$ to generate one prime, and produces each prime of size $O(P \log P)$, where P is the number of all primes needed in such a scheme. In our scheme, $P = m$. Note that only when $P = O(1)$, it is worthless to use this technique; we just store the least P primes (which requires only negligible storage) so the cost for prime generation in this case is $O(1)$.

Using the notation defined earlier, we have that $\mathsf{RN}_\mathcal{C}(u)$ represents the number of chains in $\mathcal{C}$ that u appears; and $\mathsf{DD}_\mathcal{C}$ represents the length of the longest chain in $\mathcal{C}$. The number of all chains in $\mathcal{C}$ is $|\mathcal{C}|$ (and= m). We obtain:

$$\mathsf{KeySize}_{(X)^{\mathrm{acc}}}(u) = 1, \quad \mathsf{CompCost}_{(X)^{\mathrm{acc}}} = O(\mathsf{MC}_\mathcal{C}^{\mathrm{acc}} + \mathsf{PC}_\mathcal{C}^{\mathrm{acc}}),$$

where $\mathsf{MC}_\mathcal{C}^{\mathrm{acc}}(u), \mathsf{PC}_\mathcal{C}^{\mathrm{acc}}(u)$ are the cost due to Modular exponentiation and on-the-fly Prime generation for user u respectively and $\mathsf{MC}_\mathcal{C}^{\mathrm{acc}} := \max_{u \in N} \mathsf{MC}_\mathcal{C}^{\mathrm{acc}}(u)$, $\mathsf{PC}_\mathcal{C}^{\mathrm{acc}} := \max_{u \in N} \mathsf{PC}_\mathcal{C}^{\mathrm{acc}}(u)$. Such costs depend solely on $\mathcal{C}$ and can be characterized as:

$$\mathsf{MC}_\mathcal{C}^{\mathrm{acc}}(u) = O(\mathsf{DD}_\mathcal{C} \cdot (\log |\mathcal{C}|) \cdot \mathsf{RN}_\mathcal{C}(u)), \quad \mathsf{PC}_\mathcal{C}^{\mathrm{acc}}(u) = O((\log^4 |\mathcal{C}|) \cdot \mathsf{RN}_\mathcal{C}(u)).$$

The analysis are as follows. The cost of modular exponentiation for computing Derive is logarithm in the exponent term which is $\prod_{j=1}^{m} p_j^{(\max_{i \in S} a_{ij} - a_{uj})}$. To determine its complexity, observe that $\max_{i \in S} a_{ij} = a_{uj}$ for all but only $\mathsf{RN}_\mathcal{C}(u)$ terms of j due to Eq.(8) and the fact that u appears only $\mathsf{RN}_\mathcal{C}(u)$ chains. Also, observe that $\max_{i \in S} a_{ij} - a_{uj} \leq \mathsf{DD}_\mathcal{C}$ due to Eq.(8). Each p_j is $O(m \log m)$, hence has bit length $O(\log m)$. Combining these, we get $\mathsf{MC}_\mathcal{C}^{\mathrm{acc}}(u)$ as above. The cost for prime-generation above follows from the fact that the number of primes to be generated when deriving keys are $\mathsf{RN}_\mathcal{C}(u)$.

Remark 1. The MC of our scheme is asymptotically optimal among all non-trapdoor RSA-accumulator based paradigms (if there are any others) since it matches the lower bound in [11], which states that the optimal MC is of the same order as the number of subsets (in the set system) that one user is in, albeit here we calculate in bit complexity which includes the size of primes.

Remark 2. The Akl-Taylor's scheme [1] is a special case of our framework where the trivial chain decomposition (the collection of all one-node chains) is used.

5.2   Non-trapdoor RSA Based Instantiation for SIC, LSIC

Instantiating SIC, LSIC. We will state the result for LSIC so that the result for SIC can be obtained by setting $k = 1$. It suffices to define a chain decomposition of $\mathcal{S}_{\mathsf{LSIC}[k]}$ and the concrete scheme will follow automatically. We choose a chain decomposition $\mathcal{C}_{\mathsf{LSIC}[k]} = \mathcal{T}_{\mathsf{LSIC}[k]}$ defined in Eq.(6). (Note that it is obvious that $\mathcal{T}_{\mathsf{LSIC}[k]}$ was also a chain decomposition). A concrete example for $(\mathsf{SIC})^{\mathrm{acc}}$ is shown in Fig.5 for $n = 8$. As an example, the subset key $\mathsf{k}(567) = s^{(p_1^6 p_2^1 p_3^1 p_4^3 p_5^2 p_6^5 p_7^1 p_8^3)}$.

The following result follows directly from Theorem 4, 6 and the generic efficiency characterization of the framework with the fact that $|\mathcal{C}_{\mathsf{LSIC}[k]}| = n$.

Corollary 10. $\mathsf{MC}_{\mathcal{C}_{\mathsf{LSIC}[k]}}^{\mathrm{acc}} = O(kn^{1/k} \log^2 n)$ *and* $\mathsf{PC}_{\mathcal{C}_{\mathsf{LSIC}[k]}}^{\mathrm{acc}} = O(\log^5 n)$.

Scheme $(\mathsf{LSIC}[k])^{\mathrm{acc}}$ has computational cost $O(\max\{kn^{1/k} \log^2 n, \log^5 n\})$. For trillion users ($n = 10^{12}$), choose k as low as 4 we have $4n^{1/4} \log^2 n < \log^5 n$ so that the computational cost is dominant by the latter, which is roughly as in Asano's scheme (but ours enjoy exceptionally lower header size).

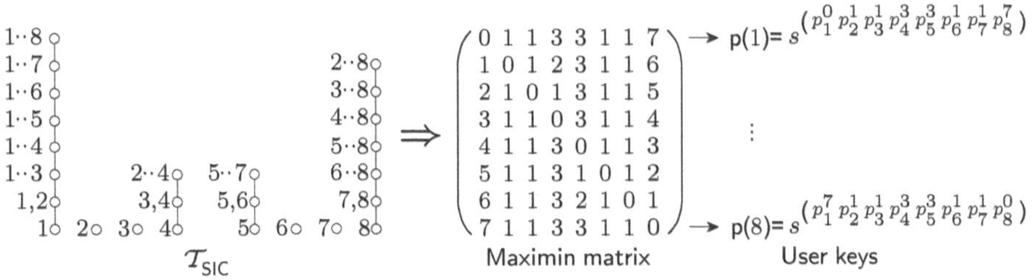

Fig. 5. Instantiating SIC ($n = 8$) by the non-trapdoor RSA accumulator based framework

Remark 3. If we instantiate with with Akl-Taylor's, its chain decomposition has $\max_{u \in N} h_u = O(n^{1/k} \log n)$, and $m = O(2^k \cdot n^{1/k}(\log n)/k)$. Thus PC $= O(n^{1/k} \log^5(n))$, which is much worse than ours, $O(\log^5 n)$. Moreover, this cost always dominates over the optimal MC for LSIC, $O(n^{1/k} \log^2 n)$.

6   Key Derivation Based on Trapdoor RSA Accumulator

6.1   The New Trapdoor RSA Based Framework

Framework Idea. The framework in this section is applicable to a class of posets that we call *tree-stratifiable posets*. Informally, such a poset of this type is defined as one which can be considered as formed by a tree hierarchy of atomic posets (not necessarily homogeneous), as shown in Fig.6. There, the graph decomposition $\mathcal{G} = \{G_x, G_y, G_z, ...\}$ is said to form a hierarchy represented by tree $\mathcal{H}$ where $V(\mathcal{H}) = \{x, y, z, ...\}$. Intuitively, such a graph decomposition is said to form a hierarchy if all the inclusion relations from every node in a lower subgraph (one with a lower index in the hierarchy), say G_y in the figure, to the next upper one in the hierarchy, G_x, are via a unique minimal node in that upper subgraph. Denote this minimal node as M_{G_y}. We will put a "dummy node" in each subgraph so that it will be the "representative" of that poset to reach that unique minimal node in the upper poset. (In the figure, the dummy node is D_{G_y} for subgraph G_y to reach M_{G_y}).

The idea for key derivations are as follows. First we define the key for each node in the highest sub-poset in the hierarchy by using the RSA-based framework in the last section. Recursively in a top-down fashion, we will define the set of keys corresponding to each lower sub-poset in the hierarchy. At some point, the set of keys for the nodes in G_x are defined. Then we define the "dummy key" for the dummy node in a next lower level sub-poset by applying a random permutation perm (w.l.o.g we will use the reverse direction) to the key of the minimal element in that upper sub-poset that it connects, that is, $k(D_{G_y}) =$ perm$^{-1}(k(M_{G_y}))$. To define keys for the other nodes in this lower sub-poset (at G_y), we will again use the RSA-based framework for that sub-poset. However, this time the key for the dummy node has been already determined, while all the keys must agree with the relations of $(G'_y)^{\text{acc}}$, where G'_y is the modified

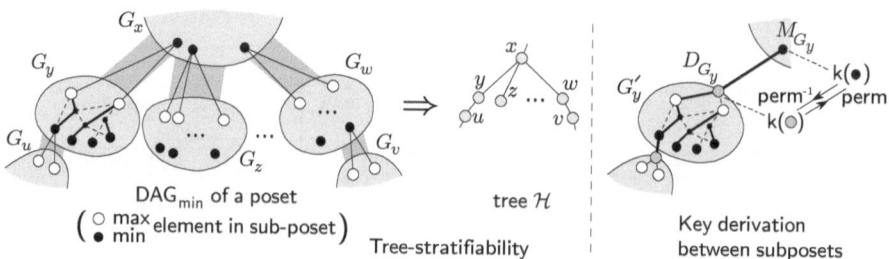

Fig. 6. The underlying idea for the trapdoor RSA based framework

subgraph that includes the dummy node, i.e., the relation of keys as defined in Eq.(7) instantiated to a poset that has G'_y as its representation. To solve this, it suffices to use the *trapdoor* of RSA. In this way, we can define keys recursively until reaching the lowest sub-posets. Users, on the other hand, do not have to use trapdoor since they only compute keys in the bottom-up fashion. Note that (perm, perm^{-1}) is a public permutation, such as any block cipher with a fixed known key. We will model perm as an ideal random permutation in the security proof (the random permuation model).

The idea of reducing the whole poset by instantiating RSA-based framework in each sub-poset results in the use of only small number of primes for the overall scheme since the same set of primes can be used across different instantiations for different sub-posets.

To formalize this, we first define some more notations. For a directed graph G, denote $V_{min}(G)$ the set of all minimal elements of poset S such that $DAG_{min}(S) = G$. $V_{max}(G)$ is defined analogously. The definition below captures what we have explained in the framework idea. Essentially, the bijection π below maps $G_x \mapsto x$.

Definition 3. (TREE-STRATIFIABLE POSET) *An inclusion poset S is called tree-stratifiable poset iff there exist an induced graph decomposition $\mathcal{G}$ of S and a tree $\mathcal{H}$ with a bijection $\pi : \mathcal{G} \rightarrow V(\mathcal{H})$ such that for each $G \in \mathcal{G}$ if we define G' by letting $V(G') = V(G) \cup \{D_G\}$ and $E(G') = E(G) \cup \{(S, D_G) : S \in V_{max}(G)\}$ where D_G is a dummy node; define $M_G := \bigcup_{S \in V_{max}(G)} S$; and define a graph $\mathcal{W}$ by letting $V(\mathcal{W}) = \bigcup_{G \in \mathcal{G}} V(G')$ and $E(\mathcal{W}) = \bigcup_{G \in \mathcal{G}} \left(E(G) \cup \{(D_G, M_G)\} \right)$, then we have that (1) for all $G \in \mathcal{G}$, $M_G \in V_{min}(\pi^{-1}(parent_{\mathcal{H}}(\pi(G))))$ and (2) $E(DAG_{min}(S)) \subseteq E(DAG_{max}(\mathcal{W}))$.* ☐

Trapdoor RSA Accumulators. A trapdoor RSA function generator G_{tRSA} is the one that works exactly the same as G_{RSA} but in addition also outputs the *trapdoor* td which is $\phi(\eta)$ where ϕ is the Euler's phi function. With td, given the description of f, any $y \in U_f$, and a (multi-)set of accumulated values E, one can efficiently compute $x \in U_f$ such that $f(x, E) = y$. Denote such x by $f_{td}(y, E^{-1})$.

Towards formalizing the construction, we "normalize" each sub-poset $G \in \mathcal{G}$ so that its base set will be $B_G = \{1, ..., |V_{min}(G')|\}$ as follows. Construct $\gamma : V(G') \rightarrow 2^{B_G}$ by first picking an injective map $\tilde{\gamma} : V_{min}(G) \rightarrow B_G$ then define for $S \in V(G')$, $\gamma : S \mapsto \{\tilde{\gamma}(U) : U \in V_{min}(G), U \subseteq S\}$. Let $\mathcal{S}_G = \gamma(V(G'))$ (the set of all images by γ from $V(G')$) be the set system with the base set B_G.

The Construction $(X)^{tacc}$. For simplicity we will consider homogeneously stratifiable poset, i.e., each $\mathcal{S}_G$ is isomorphic to each other (in the sense that its corresponding DAG is isomorphic), say the set system Y. Let $\{a_{ij}\}_{1 \leq i \leq d, 1 \leq j \leq m}$ be a maximin matrix for set system Y, where d is the cardinality of its base set.

Keygen : Run a G_{tRSA} to obtain a description of f : $U_f \times E_f \rightarrow U_f$ and trapdoor td. For $1 \leq j \leq m$, pick an element $p_j \in E_f$. Let perm and perm^{-1} be a publicly available permutation mapping $U_f \rightarrow U_f$. Let pub consist of all p_j's and $\{a_{ij}\}$. Pick a random $t \in \mathsf{U_f}$. Define keys recursively in a top-down fashion in the tree $\mathcal{H}$:

[**Top**]. At the subgraph $G_{\mathsf{root}} \in \mathcal{G}$, where root is the root of $\mathcal{H}$, by definition we have $N = M_{G_{\mathsf{root}}}$. We let $\mathsf{k}(N) = \mathsf{k}(M_{G_{\mathsf{root}}}) = t$.

[**Intermediate**]. At each atomic subgraph $G \in \mathcal{G}$, the key $\mathsf{k}(M_G)$ is previously determined. Define the key for the dummy node: $\mathsf{k}(D_G) = \mathsf{perm}^{-1}(\mathsf{k}(M_G))$. By using the trapdoor td and $\mathsf{k}(D_G)$, we solve Eq.(11) by setting $S = D_G$ (thus $\gamma(S) = B_G$) to determine the secret s_G, i.e.,

$$s_G = \mathsf{f_{td}}(\mathsf{k}(D_G), \{(\max_{i \in B_G} a_{ij}) \lhd p_j : 1 \le j \le m\}^{-1}). \tag{9}$$

Then we define the key at each element in this subgraph, $S \in V(G)$, by:

$$\mathsf{k}(S) = \mathsf{f}(s_G, \{a_{\tilde{\gamma}(S),j} \lhd p_j : 1 \le j \le m\}) \qquad \text{(for } S \in V_{\min}(G)), \tag{10}$$
$$\mathsf{k}(S) = \mathsf{f}(s_G, \{(\max_{i \in \gamma(S)} a_{ij}) \lhd p_j : 1 \le j \le m\}) \qquad \text{(for } S \in V(G)). \tag{11}$$

[**Bottom**]. For each $u \in N$, we let $\mathsf{p}(u) = \mathsf{k}(\{u\})$.

Derive : Compute from the relations given in Eq.(9),(10),(11) but in the *bottom-up* fashion by using applications of $\mathsf{f}(\cdot, \cdot)$, $\mathsf{perm}(\cdot)$ starting from $\mathsf{f}(\mathsf{p}(u), \cdot)$. Note that td is not required to do this.

Theorem 11. $(\mathsf{X})^{\mathsf{tacc}}$ *is KINT-secure in the random permutation model (*perm* as an ideal random permutation), assuming the strong RSA assumption.*

Characterizing Efficiency. If the set system X of n users is tree-stratifiable homogeneously into a set system Y of d users with the tree $\mathcal{H}$ then

$$\mathsf{KeySize}_{(\mathsf{X})^{\mathsf{tacc}}}(u) = 1, \quad \mathsf{CompCost}_{(\mathsf{X})^{\mathsf{tacc}}} = O(\mathsf{MC}_{\mathsf{X}}^{\mathsf{tacc}} + \mathsf{PC}_{\mathsf{X}}^{\mathsf{tacc}}),$$

where the cost from modular exponentiation and prime generation are depended solely on both $\mathcal{H}, \mathsf{Y}$ and only Y respectively, and can be characterized as:

$$\mathsf{MC}_{\mathsf{X}}^{\mathsf{tacc}} = h_{\mathcal{H}} \cdot \mathsf{MC}_{\mathcal{C}_{\mathsf{Y}}}^{\mathsf{acc}}, \quad \mathsf{PC}_{\mathsf{X}}^{\mathsf{tacc}} = \mathsf{PC}_{\mathcal{C}_{\mathsf{Y}}}^{\mathsf{acc}}, \tag{12}$$

where $h_{\mathcal{H}}$ is the deepest depth of $\mathcal{H}$. The first claim follows from the fact that a user has to compute Eq.(11) for at most $h_{\mathcal{H}}$ times. The second claim is from the fact that we reuse the same set of primes across sub-posets. There is also the cost due to applications of perm, which is $O(h_{\mathcal{H}})$, but this is suppressed by MC.

Generic Application. We now confine our interest to the case where $\mathcal{H}$ is the balanced completed $n^{1/k}$-ary tree of depth $h_{\mathcal{H}} = k$. This forces the base sets of Y and X to have cardinality $n^{1/k}$ and n respectively. In this case we say $\mathsf{X} = \mathsf{hier}_k(\mathsf{Y})$. The operation hier_k is well-defined and can be thought as the converse direction of tree-stratification; thus, from any poset Z one can construct a tree-stratifiable poset, namely $\mathsf{hier}_k(\mathsf{Z})$, by first scaling down the cardinality of the

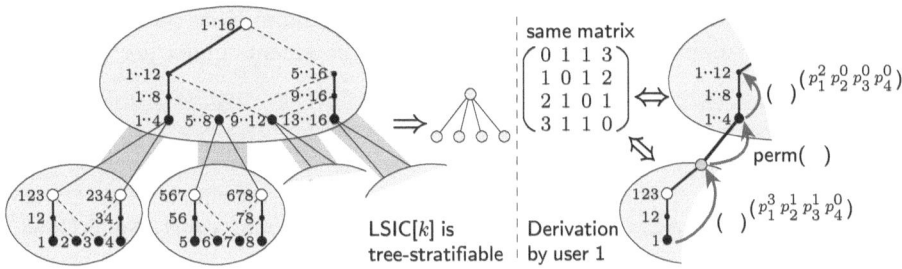

Fig. 7. Instantiating $\mathsf{LSIC}[k]$ ($n = 16, k = 2$, see Fig.3) by trapdoor RSA based framework

base set of Z to $n^{1/k}$. (Since usually any set system is originally defined in term of n). We write $\mathsf{Z}(n^{1/k})$ to emphasize the cardinality of base set. The point is that when k is a constant, Eq.(12) allows one to construct a full scheme of n users but with exactly the same asymptotic performances as those of $(\mathsf{Z}(n^{1/k}))^{\mathsf{acc}}$, which is a "scaled-down" scheme, in *both* parameters MC, PC! Moreover, if $c_{\mathsf{Z}(n)}(n,r) = O(r)$ then we can show that $c_{\mathsf{hier}_k(\mathsf{Z}(n^{1/k}))}(n,r) = O(kr) = O(r)$ (by exactly the same proof as that of Theorem 2); therefore, $\mathsf{HeaderSize}$ is also unaffected.

6.2 Trapdoor RSA Based Instantiation for LSIC

It is easy to see that $\mathsf{LSIC}[k]$ is tree-stratifiable since $\mathsf{LSIC}[k] = \mathsf{hier}_k(\mathsf{SIC}(n^{1/k}))$. (We could have define LSIC via hier operation rather than directly in Sec.3.2). An example is shown in Fig.7. From the efficiency characterization we have:

Corollary 12. (i) $\mathsf{MC}^{\mathsf{tacc}}_{\mathsf{LSIC}[k]} = O(n^{1/k}(\log^2 n)/k)$, $\mathsf{PC}^{\mathsf{tacc}}_{\mathsf{LSIC}[k]} = O((\log^5 n)/k^5)$. (ii) $\mathsf{MC}^{\mathsf{tacc}}_{\mathsf{LSIC}[\log_a n]} = O(a \log a \log n)$, $\mathsf{PC}^{\mathsf{tacc}}_{\mathsf{LSIC}[\log_a n]} = O(1)$.

Proof. See that $\mathsf{MC}^{\mathsf{acc}}_{\mathcal{C}_{\mathsf{SIC}(n^{1/k})}} = O((n^{1/k} \log^2 n)/k^2)$, $\mathsf{PC}^{\mathsf{acc}}_{\mathcal{C}_{\mathsf{SIC}(n^{1/k})}} = O((\log^5 n)/k^5)$; and $\mathsf{MC}^{\mathsf{acc}}_{\mathcal{C}_{\mathsf{SIC}(a)}} = O(a \log^2 a)$, $\mathsf{PC}^{\mathsf{acc}}_{\mathcal{C}_{\mathsf{SIC}(a)}} = O(1)$. (In fact, for the case $\mathsf{SIC}(a)$, the maximum number of primes used per user is $\log a + 1$, a small constant). □

7 Concluding Remarks

We presented three generic frameworks for constructing broadcast encryption and give some efficient instantiations. Almost all subset-cover broadcast encryption schemes based on PRSG (or one-way function) or RSA accumulator in the literature can be rewritten as instantiations in our paradigms. In fact, [18,14,17,4,12,20,15] can be viewed as PRSG-instantiated schemes and [2,3,11] are non-trapdoor-RSA-instantiated schemes from our frameworks.

The whole paradigm abstracts away the computational security issues and reduces the problem to only pure combinatorics. We leave as an open problem the question of showing any combinatorial bound from the efficiency characterization in each sub-framework. Note that the previous bounds for broadcast encryption [16] are done in the setting where no key derivation is involved.

Acknowledgements. We would like to thank Kazukuni Kobara, Ryo Nojima, and also anonymous reviewers for their valuable comments on earlier versions.

References

1. S. G. Akl, P. D. Taylor, "Cryptographic Solution to a Problem of Access Control in a Hierarchy," ACM Transactions on Computer Systems, Vol. 1, No. 3 (1983), pp. 239-248.
2. T. Asano, "A Revocation Scheme with Minimal Storage at Receivers," ASIACRYPT 2002, LNCS 2501, pp. 433-450.
3. N. Attrapadung, K. Kobara, H. Imai, "Broadcast Encryption with Short Keys and Transmissions," ACM Workshop on Digital Rights Management, 2003.
4. N. Attrapadung, K. Kobara, H. Imai, "Sequential Key Derivation Patterns for Broadcast Encryption and Key Predistribution Schemes," ASIACRYPT 2003, LNCS 2894, pp. 374-391.
5. J. Benaloh, M. de Mare,"One-way accumulators: A decentralized alternative to digital signatures," EUROCRYPT 1993, LNCS 765, pp. 274-285.
6. D. Boneh, A. Silverberg, "Applications of Multilinear Forms to Cryptography," Contemporary Mathematics, 324, pp. 7190, (2003).
7. D. Boneh, C. Gentry, B. Waters, "Collusion Resistant Broadcast Encryption With Short Ciphertexts and Private Keys," CRYPTO 2005, LNCS 3621 (to appear).
8. G. C. Chick, S. E. Tavares, "Flexible Access Control with Master Keys," CRYPTO89, LNCS 435, pp. 316-322.
9. R. Diestel, "Graph theory," 2nd ed., Graduate texts in mathematics 173, (2000).
10. Y. Dodis, J. Katz, "Chosen-Ciphertext Security of Multiple Encryption," TCC 2005, LNCS 3378, pp. 188-209.
11. C. Gentry, Z. Ramzan, "RSA Accumulator Based Broadcast Encryption," ISC 2004, LNCS 3225, pp. 73-86.
12. M. T. Goodrich, J.Z. Sun, R. Tamassia, "Efficient Tree-Based Revocation in Groups of Low-State Devices," CRYPTO 2004, LNCS 3152, pp. 511-527.
13. A. Fiat, M. Naor, "Broadcast Encryption," CRYPTO 1993, LNCS 0773, pp. 480-491.
14. D. Halevy, A. Shamir, "The LSD Broadcast Encryption Scheme," CRYPTO 2002, LNCS 2442, pp. 47-60.
15. N. Jho, J.Y. Hwang, J.H. Cheon, M.H. Kim, D.H. Lee, E.S. Yoo, "One-Way Chain Based Broadcast Encryption Schemes," EUROCRYPT 2005. LNCS 3494, pp. 559-574.
16. M. Luby, J. Staddon, "Combinatorial Bounds for Broadcast Encryption," EUROCRYPT 1998, LNCS 1403, pp. 512-526.
17. M.J. Mihaljevic, "Key Management Schemes for Stateless Receivers Based on Time Varying Heterogeneous Logical Key Hierarchy," ASIACRYPT 2003, LNCS 2894, pp. 137-154.
18. D. Naor, M. Naor and J. Lotspiech, "Revocation and Tracing Schemes for Stateless Receivers," CRYPTO 2001, LNCS 2139, pp. 41-62.
19. Z. Star, "An Asymptotic Formula in the Theory of Compositions," Aequationes Math (1976).
20. P. Wang, P. Ning, D.S. Reeves, "Storage-Efficient Stateless Group Key Revocation," ISC 2004, LNCS 3225, pp. 25-38.

Revealing Additional Information in Two-Party Computations*

Andreas Jakoby and Maciej Liśkiewicz **

Institut für Theoretische Informatik, Universität zu Lübeck, Germany
liskiewi/jakoby@tcs.uni-luebeck.de

Abstract. A two-argument function is computed privately by two parties if after the computation, no party should know anything about the
other inputs except for what he is able to deduce from his own input
and the function value. In [1] Bar-Yehuda, Chor, Kushilevitz, and Orlitsky give a complete characterisation of two-argument functions which
can be computed privately (in the information-theoretical sense) in the
Honest-But-Curious model and study protocols for "non-private" functions revealing as little information about the inputs as possible. The
authors define a measure which determines for any function f the additional information $\mathcal{E}(f)$ required for computing f and claim that f
is privately-computable if and only if $\mathcal{E}(f) = 0$. In our paper we show
that the characterisation is false: we give a privately-computable func-
tion f with $\mathcal{E}(f) \neq 0$ and another function g with $\mathcal{E}(g) = 0$ that is *not*
privately-computable. Moreover, we show some rather unexpected and
strange properties of the measure for additional information given by
Bar-Yehuda et al. and we introduce an alternative measure. We show
that for this new measure the minimal leakage of information of randomized and deterministic protocols are equal. Finally, we present some
general relations between the information gain of an optimal protocol
and the communication complexity of a function.

1 Introduction

We investigate computations of functions of two n-bit inputs x and y by two
players Alice holding x and Bob having y. For a given function f Alice (A) and
Bob (B), both with unlimited computational power, communicate to determine
$f(x, y)$ keeping as much of its input secret from the other party as possible.
In this setting two models are considered in the literature. In the first one we
assume that the players are honest but curious, that means they never deviate
from the given protocol but try to acquire knowledge about the input bits of the
other player only by observing the communication. In the second setting Alice
or Bob can be malicious, i.e. they can cheat. In this paper we study privacy in
the Honest-But-Curious setting.

---

* Supported by DFG research grant RE 672/5-1.
** On leave from Instytut Informatyki, Uniwersytet Wrocławski, Poland.

B. Roy (Ed.): ASIACRYPT 2005, LNCS 3788, pp. 121–135, 2005.

Private computation was introduced by Yao [8]. He considered the problem under cryptographic assumptions. Private computation in the information-theoretical secure setting has been introduced by Ben-Or et al. [3] and Chaum et al. [5]. Ben-Or et al. have presented a function that is not privately computable. A complete characterisation of such functions has been given independently by Kushilevitz [6] and Beaver [2]. This characterisation has been given by using so called forbidden submatrices. Let M be a matrix. We say that two row indices i and j are related ($i \sim j$) if there is a column k for which $M_{i,k} = M_{j,k}$. For example, the row indices of matrix T shown below are related while the rows of matrix T' are not related.

$$T = \begin{bmatrix} 0 & 0 \\ 0 & 1 \end{bmatrix}, \quad T' = \begin{bmatrix} 1 & 0 \\ 0 & 1 \end{bmatrix}. \tag{1}$$

We define the equivalence relation $\equiv$ to be the transitive closure of $\sim$. In a similar way, we define the relations $\sim$ and $\equiv$ on the columns of M. A matrix is forbidden if it is not monochromatic (i.e. not all elements of the matrix are the same), all its rows are equivalent with respect to $\equiv$ on rows, and all its columns are equivalent with respect to $\equiv$ on columns. Matrix T defined in (1) is a small example of a forbidden matrix and T' is an example for a not forbidden matrix. Privately-computable functions can be characterised as follows. Let M_f denote the communication matrix for the function f, i.e. an $2^n \times 2^n$ matrix such that rows and columns are indexed by n-bit inputs and for every $x, y \in \{0,1\}^n$ we have $(M_f)_{x,y} = f(x,y)$. For example T and T' in (1) are communication matrices of the two argument Boolean functions AND and XOR, respectively.

Theorem 1 ([6,2]). *In the Honest-But-Curious model a two-argument function f can be computed privately if and only if M_f does not contain any forbidden submatrix.*

Using this characterisation one can see that the majority of functions cannot be computed privately. For such functions it is natural to study the minimum amount of information about the individual inputs that must leak during their computation. There are several ways to quantify such a leakage. In [1] Bar-Yehuda et al. introduced three measures: a combinatorial measure $\mathcal{I}_c$, an information-theoretic measure $\mathcal{I}_i$, and a measure $\mathcal{I}_{c\text{-}i}$ that includes both combinatorial and information-theoretic aspects. For the measures they proved general tight bounds on minimum amount of information about the inputs that must be revealed in a computation. Moreover, they showed that sacrificing some privacy can reduce the number of messages required during the computation.

In [1] the authors define for any function f the *additional* information $\mathcal{E}(f)$ required for computing f as a difference between $\mathcal{I}_c(f)$ and $\log_2 |\text{range}(f)|$, where $|\text{range}(f)|$ denotes the cardinality of the range of function f. They claim that f is privately-computable if and only if $\mathcal{E}(f) = 0$. In our paper we show that the characterisation is false. We construct a privately-computable function f with $\mathcal{E}(f) \neq 0$. Moreover we show that for the function $f_{min}(x, y) = \min\{x, y\}$, where x and y are interpreted as integers from $\{0, 1, \ldots, 2^n - 1\}$, it holds that

$\mathcal{E}(f_{min}) = 0$. On the other hand, f_{min} cannot be computed privately since the communication matrix of f_{min}:

$$M_{f_{min}} = \begin{bmatrix} 0\,0\,0\,0\,\dots & 0 \\ 0\,1\,1\,1\,\dots & 1 \\ 0\,1\,2\,2\,\dots & 2 \\ \dots & \\ 0\,1\,2\,3\,\dots\,2^n - 1 \end{bmatrix}$$

contains a forbidden submatrix. In fact, $M_{f_{min}}$ is not monochromatic and for every $x < 2^n - 1$ we have $f_{min}(x, x) = f_{min}(x + 1, x) = f_{min}(x, x + 1) = x$ and $f_{min}(x + 1, x + 1) = x + 1$ what implies that all its rows (columns, resp.) are in the same equivalence class.

We show also some rather strange properties of the measures for revealed information $\mathcal{I}_c$, $\mathcal{I}_i$, and $\mathcal{I}_{c\text{-}i}$. For example, we show that $\mathcal{I}_c(\text{AND}) = \mathcal{I}_c(\text{XOR})$: the revealed information required for computing AND is the same as for XOR contradictory to the fact that XOR can be computed privately but AND cannot. The similar property holds for the remaining measures as well.

Furthermore, we introduce an alternative measure for the minimum revealed information, which is based on the information source defined in [4]. The revealed information of a protocol to a player is merely the logarithm of the number of different probability distributions on the communication strings a player can observe. For this measure we will show that f is a privately computable function if and only if the amount of the minimum revealed information is zero. We give some tight bounds of concrete functions and show a general lower bound for arbitrary two n-bit inputs functions.

We show that for our measure the minimal leakage of information for randomized and deterministic protocols are equal. Finally, we present some relations between the information gain of an optimal protocol and the communication complexity of a function. More precisely, we will give a lower bound for the leakage of information that is logarithmic on the communication complexity. We will show that for some specific functions this general bound is tight.

The paper is organized as follows. In the next section we give some preliminaries for communication complexity. In Section 3 we present the model of Bar-Yehuda et al. and we give there our analysis of their results. In Section 4 we discuss our measure for reviling additional information. The relation of the gain of additional information in randomized protocols and deterministic protocols is investigated in Section 5. Finally, in Section 6 we give a general relation between communication complexity and the additional information.

2 Communication Protocols

Let f be a function of two n-bit inputs x and y that are known to two parties A and B, respectively, each having unlimited computing power. The aim is to determine $f(x, y)$ by alternate transmitting messages over a noiseless binary channel according to a communication protocol. We consider two kinds of protocols: deterministic and randomised. In deterministic case each message is determined by the input known to the party and by the previously received messages. We require that in every round of communication, the set of all possible messages is prefix-free. A protocol computes f if for every (x, y) each party deduces correctly the value $f(x, y)$. Let $\mathcal{P}(x, y)$ denote the concatenation of all communication messages of a protocol $\mathcal{P}$ exchanged between A and B during the computation on an input (x, y). Let communication complexity of protocol $\mathcal{P}$, denoted by $C_\mathcal{P}$, be the maximum length of $\mathcal{P}(x, y)$, and let the communication size $CS_\mathcal{P}$ be the number of different strings $\mathcal{P}(x, y)$, over all inputs (x, y). Define the deterministic communication complexity of f, denoted by $C_D(f)$, as the smallest $C_\mathcal{P}$ over all deterministic protocols $\mathcal{P}$ computing f and analogously let the communication size $CS_D(f)$ be the smallest $CS_D(f)$ over all $\mathcal{P}$.

For the randomised protocol $\mathcal{P}$ on an input (x, y), to determine communication messages A and B can use additionally random bit strings. In this paper we consider randomised protocols where each party A and B has access to a *private* random strings R_A and R_B, respectively. In this case the communication string $\mathcal{P}(x, y)$, defined again as the concatenation of all messages transmitted during an execution of $\mathcal{P}$ on (x, y), is a random string.

For a general survey of communication complexity see e.g. Kushilevitz and Nisan [7].

3   Additional Information - The Model of Bar-Yehuda et al.

In this section we will discuss the measuring of additional information defined in [1]. First we give the definitions and the results of [1] and we show next that some of the results are false, the measures are somehow inconsistent, and they have rather unexpected and strange properties.

3.1   The Results

Let us first present the definition of privacy cost in the combinatorial setting. Next the information-theoretic measure and the measure that includes both combinatorial and information-theoretic aspects will be considered.

To define the combinatorial measure $\mathcal{I}_c(f)$ for a function f Bar-Yehuda et al. introduce a weak and a stronger definition of privacy cost. However, since the notions are equivalent to each other, we will recall the definition of $\mathcal{I}_c$ using the notion of strong privacy only. To measure information leakage during computation of f we use an auxiliary function h, which like f, is a function of two n-bit strings. The ranges of both functions can be different. Intuitively speaking, a protocol $\mathcal{P}$ for f leaks at most h, or equivalently is h-private, if during the computation of $\mathcal{P}$ on (x, y) the information learned by a party about the input of the other party can be deduced from its own input and the value $h(x, y)$.

Definition 1 ([1]). *A protocol $\mathcal{P}$ for f is strongly h-private for A if*

1. *for every $x, y \in \{0, 1\}^n$ $\mathcal{P}$ computes the value $f(x, y)$ correctly with probability 1 and*
2. *for every $x, y_1, y_2 \in \{0, 1\}^n$, $h(x, y_1) = h(x, y_2)$ implies that for all random choices r of A, $\mathcal{P}(x, y_1)$ and $\mathcal{P}(x, y_2)$ have the same distribution, namely, for every communication string s,*

$$\Pr[s = \mathcal{P}(x, y_1)|r] = \Pr[s = \mathcal{P}(x, y_2)|r],$$

where the probability is taken over the random choices of B.

Strong h-privacy for B is defined analogously. To give more intuition let us consider the Boolean function f_{equ} defined on two n-bit strings:

$$f_{equ}(x, y) = \begin{cases} 1 & \text{if } x = y, \\ 0 & \text{otherwise.} \end{cases} \tag{2}$$

Furthermore, let us consider the (deterministic) protocol of [1] for computing f_{equ} on two n-bit strings $x = x_1 x_2 \ldots x_n$ and $y = y_1 y_2 \ldots y_n$:

Protocol 1. For all $i - 1, 2, \ldots n$ do:
1. A sends x_i to B;
2. If $x_i \neq y_i$ then B transmits 0 and exit; else if $x_i = y_i$ then B transmits 1.

The protocol is strongly h_{equ}-private for both A and B, where h_{equ} is defined as follows: $h_{equ}(x, y) = \min\{i : x_i \neq y_i\}$ if $x \neq y$ and $h_{equ}(x, y) = n + 1$ otherwise. To see this, note that for the protocol $\mathcal{P}$ above and for every input (x, y) and (x, y') it holds that $\mathcal{P}(x, y) = \mathcal{P}(x, y')$ if and only if $h_{equ}(x, y) = h_{equ}(x, y')$. An analogous equivalence holds for every (x, y) and (x', y). Recall that $\mathcal{P}(x, y)$ for the deterministic protocol $\mathcal{P}$ denotes just the concatenation of all communication messages sent between A and B during the computation of $\mathcal{P}$ on (x, y).

Definition 2 ([1]). *Let h_1 and h_2 be functions of two n-bit inputs. A protocol $\mathcal{P}$ is strongly $(h_1; h_2)$-private if it is strongly h_1-private for A and strongly h_2-private for B. A protocol $\mathcal{P}$ is strongly h-private if it is strongly (h, h)-private. A function f is strongly h-private if it has a strongly h-private protocol.*

For example, f_{equ} is strongly h_{equ}-private. The revealed information $\mathcal{I}_c(f)$ and the additional information $\mathcal{E}(f)$ required for computing f are defined by

$$\mathcal{I}_c(f) = \min\{\log_2 |\operatorname{range}(h)| : f \text{ is strongly } h\text{-private }\}$$
$$\mathcal{E}(f) = \mathcal{I}_c(f) - \log_2 |\operatorname{range}(f)|.$$

Hence, for the the function f_{equ} we have:

$$\mathcal{I}_c(f_{equ}) \leq \log_2(n + 1) \quad \text{and} \quad \mathcal{E}(f) \leq \log_2(n + 1) - 2. \tag{3}$$

In [1] Bar-Yehuda et al. observe the following claim which is false as we will see in the next section.

Claim 1 ([1], p. 1932). *A function f is privately-computable if and only if $\mathcal{I}_c(f) = \log_2 |\operatorname{range}(f)|$, i.e., if and only if $\mathcal{E}(f) = 0$.*

For the min function:

$$f_{min}(x, y) = \begin{cases} x & \text{if } x \leq y, \\ y & \text{otherwise,} \end{cases} \tag{4}$$

where x and y are interpreted as integers from $\{0, 1, \ldots, 2^n - 1\}$, the authors claim that

Claim 2 ([1], p. 1933]). $0 < \mathcal{E}(f_{min}) \leq 1$.

This is not true, as we will see in the next section.

Now, we recall the definition of information-theoretic measure $\mathcal{I}_i$ and a measure that includes both combinatorial and information-theoretic aspects $\mathcal{I}_{c-i}$. In this paper we will discuss only the deterministic counterpart of these measures (denoted by $\mathcal{I}_i^{det}$ and $\mathcal{I}_{c-i}^{det}$) that refer to the leakage of information if the protocols are restricted to deterministic ones.

To define $\mathcal{I}_i^{det}$ and $\mathcal{I}_{c-i}^{det}$ one has implicitly to assume a probability distribution for the input x and y. Let us consider the input strings as a pair (X, Y) of random variables drawn from some specified distribution which is known to both parties. For a deterministic protocol $\mathcal{P}$ define

$$I_{\mathcal{P}}(X, Y) = \max\{I(X; \mathcal{P}(X, Y)|Y), I(Y; \mathcal{P}(X, Y)|X)\}$$

to be the maximum of the information gained by A or B about the input of the other party that can be deduced from the complete communication strings $\mathcal{P}(X, Y)$ and its own input. Here $I(X; Y|Z)$ denotes the conditional mutual information. The information-theoretic measure $\mathcal{I}_i^{det}$ of additional information is defined as follows

$$I_f^{det}(X, Y) = \min\{I_{\mathcal{P}}(X, Y) : \mathcal{P} \text{ is a deterministic protocol computing } f\}$$
$$\mathcal{I}_i^{det}(f) = \sup\{I_f^{det}(X, Y) : (X, Y) \text{ is distributed over } \{0, 1\}^n \times \{0, 1\}^n\}.$$

Finally define the combinatorial-information-theoretic measure $\mathcal{I}_{c-i}^{det}$ by

$$I_{\mathcal{P}} = \sup\{I_{\mathcal{P}}(X, Y) : (X, Y) \text{ is distributed over } \{0, 1\}^n \times \{0, 1\}^n\}$$
$$\mathcal{I}_{c-i}^{det}(f) = \min\{I_{\mathcal{P}} : \mathcal{P} \text{ is a deterministic protocol computing } f\}.$$

3.2   Mistakes and Inconsistencies

In the following we show that some claims of [1] are false. We start our analysis showing the following useful lemma:

Lemma 1. *For every function f of two n-bit inputs the revealed information required for computing f is bounded by n, i.e. $\mathcal{I}_c(f) \leq n$.*

Note that the lemma does not follow from the simple relation between $\mathcal{I}_c$ and deterministic communication complexity that $\mathcal{I}_c(f) \leq C_D(f)$, since $C_D(f)$ can be equal to $n + |\operatorname{range}(f)|$. On the other hand the bound stated in the lemma seems to be quite natural: One party cannot gain more than n bit of information about the input of the other party in the sense of Shannon.

Proof. Let f be a two-argument function f over $\{0,1\}^n \times \{0,1\}^n$ and let $\mathcal{P}$ be an arbitrary protocol which computes f correctly with probability 1. Define the function $g(x,y) = (x + y) \mod 2^n$ considering x and y as integer in $\{0,\dots,2^n - 1\}$. It is easy to verify that $\mathcal{P}$ is strongly g-private. In fact, for every $x_1, x_2, y_1, y_2 \in \{0,1\}^n$ with $x_1 \neq x_2$ and $y_1 \neq y_2$ we have $g(x_1,y_1) \neq g(x_1,y_2)$ and $g(x_1,y_1) \neq g(x_2,y_1)$. Hence, Condition (2) of Definition 1 is fulfilled. Because $|\operatorname{range}(g)| = 2^n$, we get

$$\mathcal{I}_c(f) = \min\{\log_2 |\operatorname{range}(h)| : f \text{ is strongly } h\text{-private }\} \leq \log_2 |\operatorname{range}(g)| = n.$$

□

As a counterexample of the characterisation given in Claim 1 consider the function $\varphi : \{0,1\}^n \times \{0,1\}^n \rightarrow \{0\} \cup \{0,1\}^n$ defined for any $n \geq 2$:

$$\varphi(x,y) = \begin{cases} y & \text{if } x = 0^n, \\ 0 & \text{otherwise.} \end{cases} \tag{5}$$

Proposition 1. *Function φ can be computed privately but $\mathcal{E}(\varphi) \neq 0$.*

Proof. Note that $0 \neq 0^n$, hence the communication matrix M_φ does not contain a forbidden submatrix: M_φ is not monochromatic and the first row of M_φ is not equivalent with any other row of the matrix. Hence by the characterisation by Kushilevitz and Beaver (Theorem 1) we know that φ can be computed privately. On the other hand according to the definition of the additional information required for computing φ and by Lemma 1 we can conclude that

$$\mathcal{E}(\varphi) = \mathcal{I}_c(\varphi) - \log_2 |\operatorname{range}(\varphi)| \leq n - \log_2(2^n + 1) < 0.$$

□

Therefore Claim 1 is false: For privately-computable function φ we have both $\mathcal{I}_c(\varphi) < \log_2 |\operatorname{range}(\varphi)|$ and $\mathcal{E}(\varphi) \neq 0$. This example shows a strange property of the definition of $\mathcal{E}(\varphi)$: *The additional information required for computing a function can be negative.*

Using again Lemma 1 one can show that Claim 2 is false:

Proposition 2. *For the function f_{min} defined in (4) it holds that*

$$\mathcal{I}_c(f_{min}) = n \quad \text{and} \quad \mathcal{E}(f_{min}) = 0.$$

Proof. By Lemma 1 we get

$$\mathcal{E}(f_{min}) = \mathcal{I}_c(f_{min}) - \log_2 |\operatorname{range}(f_{min})| \leq n - \log_2(2^n) = 0.$$

It is not difficult to show that $\mathcal{E}(f_{min}) \geq 0$. In fact, if $\mathcal{I}_c(f_{min}) < n$ then there exists a function h such that f_{min} is strongly h-private and $\log_2 |\operatorname{range}(h)| < n$. Consider $x = 2^n - 1$, then for any pair $y_1, y_2 \in \{0, 1, \ldots, 2^n - 1\}$ with $y_1 \neq y_2$ we have $f_{min}(x, y_1) \neq f_{min}(x, y_2)$. This implies the inequality $h(x, y_1) \neq h(x, y_2)$, contradicting the assumption that $\log_2 |\operatorname{range}(h)| < n$.   □

Note that the communication matrix $M_{f_{min}}$ of f_{min} contains a forbidden submatrix (see a discussion in Section 1). Hence by Theorem 1, f_{min} is not privately-computable. By Propositions 1 and 2 one can conclude

Theorem 2. *There exists a privately-computable function φ, with $\mathcal{E}(\varphi) \neq 0$ and another function f, with $\mathcal{E}(f) = 0$ that is not privately-computable.*

Now we will discuss some inconsistencies of the definitions for additional information. We will show that in fact none of these definitions suits well for measuring additional information properly. In Section 4 we will give a new definition for additional information.

For the function φ, defined in (5), let us consider two (deterministic) protocols $\mathcal{P}_1$ and $\mathcal{P}_2$ that compute φ. The protocol $\mathcal{P}_1$ works on x, y as follows: A sends 0 if $x = 0^n$ and 1 otherwise. If B receives 0 then he sends y to A and otherwise B stops the computation. In protocol $\mathcal{P}_2$, A sends 0 if $x = 0^n$ and 1 otherwise and then B sends y to A. Obviously in both cases each party can determine correctly the value of the function at the end of the communication. Note that $\mathcal{P}_1$ is private protocol in a common sense (more precisely 1-private, see e.g. [6] for the definition) while $\mathcal{P}_2$ is not private. We can say even more: Using $\mathcal{P}_2$ A gains full information about the input of B. On the other hand, both $\mathcal{P}_1$ and $\mathcal{P}_2$ are optimal with respect to $\mathcal{I}_c$. To see this, consider the function $g(x, y) = (x + y) \bmod 2^n$ used in the proof of Lemma 1. We get that both $\mathcal{P}_1$ and $\mathcal{P}_2$ are strongly g-private and the optimality follows from the obvious fact that

$$\mathcal{I}_c(\varphi) = n = |\operatorname{range}(g)|.$$

$\mathcal{I}_i^{det}$ and $\mathcal{I}_{c-i}^{det}$ measure the additional information wrong, as well. According to the definition of $I_{\mathcal{P}}$ we have for both protocols $\mathcal{P}_1, \mathcal{P}_2$

$$\begin{aligned}
I_{\mathcal{P}_i} &= \sup_{(X,Y)} I_{\mathcal{P}_i}(X, Y) \\
&= \sup_{(X,Y)} \max\{ \; H(X|Y) - H(X|\mathcal{P}_i(X,Y), Y), \\
&\qquad\qquad\qquad H(Y|X) - H(Y|\mathcal{P}_i(X,Y), X)\} \\
&= H(Y)
\end{aligned}$$

and therefore $I_{\mathcal{P}_1} = I_{\mathcal{P}_2}$. Hence neither $\mathcal{I}_i^{det}$ nor $\mathcal{I}_{c-i}^{det}$ measures *the additional* information which can be gain by a party during the computation.

Finally, let us consider the two argument functions AND and XOR. We have:

$$\mathcal{I}_{c-i}^{det}(\text{AND}) = \mathcal{I}_{c-i}^{det}(\text{XOR}) = 1.$$

But XOR can be computed privately and therefore *no* additional information can be gained during a computation of XOR. On the other hand, AND cannot be computed privately.

4 Additional Information - New Measure

In the following we will present an alternative measure for additional information, that is based on the information source defined in [4].

Definition 3. *Let $\mathcal{P}$ be a protocol for a function f which for every $x, y \in \{0,1\}^n$ computes the value $f(x,y)$ correctly with probability 1. Let $x \in \{0,1\}^n$, $z \in$ range(f) and let r be a random string provided to A. Define the information source of A on x, z, and r as the set of different probability distributions on the communication strings A, holding x and r, can observe during all computations of $\mathcal{P}$ that give the result z:*

$$\mathcal{S}_{\mathcal{P},A}(x,z,r) = \{(\mu_{x,y}(s_1), \mu_{x,y}(s_2), \ldots) : y \in \{0,1\}^n, f(x,y) = z\}$$

where $\mu_{x,y}(s_k) = \Pr[\mathcal{P}(x,y) = s_k | r]$. Define the size of the information source as

$$s_{\mathcal{P},A}(x,z) = \max_r |\mathcal{S}_{\mathcal{P},A}(x,z,r)|.$$

Analogously we define $\mathcal{S}_{\mathcal{P},B}(y,z,r)$ - the information source of B on y, z, and r and the size $s_{\mathcal{P},B}(y,z)$.

If $\mathcal{P}$ is a deterministic protocol then we will omit r in $\mathcal{S}_{\mathcal{P},A}(x,z,r)$ and write just $\mathcal{S}_{\mathcal{P},A}(x,z)$. Now we are ready to define a new *combinatorial* measure for the additional information, analogy of $\mathcal{I}_c$, that we will denote by $\mathcal{J}_c$.

Definition 4. *The additional information of $\mathcal{P}$ revealed to A is defined as*

$$J_{\mathcal{P},A} = \max\{\log_2 s_{\mathcal{P},A}(x,z) : x \in \{0,1\}^n, z \in \text{range}(f)\ \}.$$

Analogously we define $J_{\mathcal{P},B}$. The additional information that can be deduced running a protocol $\mathcal{P}$ is $J_{\mathcal{P}} = \max\{J_{\mathcal{P},A}, J_{\mathcal{P},B}\}$. The additional information required for computing f is

$$J_c(f) = \min\{J_{\mathcal{P}} : \mathcal{P} \text{ is a protocol computing } f\}.$$

We have the following characterisation of privately computable functions:

Theorem 3. *A function f is privately computable if and only if $\mathcal{J}_c(f) = 0$.*

The proof of the theorem is straightforward and we skip it here.

We can redefine the measure $\mathcal{J}_c$ in term of h-privacy used by Bar-Yehuda et al. (see Definition 2).

Definition 5. *Let h be a function of two n-bit inputs and let protocol $\mathcal{P}$ for a function f be strongly h-private. Analogously to Definition 3 and 4 let*

$$s_{\mathcal{P},A}^h(x,z) = |\{h(x,y) : y \in \{0,1\}^n, f(x,y) = z\}|$$

and

$$J_{P,A}^h = \max\{\log_2 s_{P,A}^h(x,z) : x \in \{0,1\}^n, z \in \mathrm{range}(f)\} .$$

Analogously define $s_{P,B}^h$ *and* $J_{P,B}^h$ *for B. Then* $J_P^h = \max\{J_{P,A}^h, J_{P,B}^h\}$.

Theorem 4. *For every function* f *it holds*

$$\mathcal{J}_c(f) = \min\{J_P^h : \mathcal{P} \text{ is strongly } h\text{-private protocol for } f\}.$$

Our measure modifies the definition of Bar Yehuda et al. [1] by considering the result of the function. The proof Theorem 4 uses some facts that we get from the derandomisation of an optimal protocol. We will present such a derandomisation in the next section.

Proof (of Theorem 4). Let f be a function. We show first that

$$\mathcal{J}_c(f) \le \min\{J_P^h : \mathcal{P} \text{ is strongly } h\text{-private protocol for } f\}. \qquad (6)$$

Assume h is function and $\mathcal{P}$ is a strongly h-private protocol for computing f such that J_P^h is minimum among all such functions h and protocols $\mathcal{P}$. By the definition of h-privacy we have that for every $x, y_1, y_2 \in \{0,1\}^n$, $h(x,y_1) = h(x,y_2)$ implies that for all random choices r of A, $\mathcal{P}(x,y_1)$ and $\mathcal{P}(x,y_2)$ have the same distribution. Hence, for every $x \in \{0,1\}^n$ and $z \in \mathrm{range}(f)$ we have

$$s_{P,A}(x,z) \le |\{h(x,y) : y \in \{0,1\}^n, f(x,y) = z\}| = s_{P,A}^h(x,z).$$

Similarly we have: $s_{P,B}(y,z) \le s_{P,B}^h(y,z)$. Hence both $J_{P,A} \le J_{P,A}^h$ and $J_{P,B} \le J_{P,B}^h$ are true and therefore we get $J_P \le J_P^h$. This implies that Inequality (6) is true.

To see that the inverse inequality to (6) is also true, we apply Theorem 6. Let $\mathcal{P}$ be a protocol for f such that J_P is minimal among all protocols computing f. By Theorem 6 there exists a deterministic protocol $\mathcal{P}'$ for f such that

$$J_{P'} \le J_P = \mathcal{J}_c(f).$$

Since $\mathcal{P}'$ is deterministic, we can define a function h for every $x, y \in \{0,1\}^n$ as follows: $h(x,y) = \mathcal{P}'(x,y)$. Obviously, $\mathcal{P}'$ is strongly h-private and it is true that $J_{P'}^h = J_{P'}$. Hence, by the inequality above one can conclude:

$$\min\{J_P^h : \mathcal{P} \text{ is strongly } h\text{-private protocol for } f\} \le J_{P'}^h = J_{P'} \le \mathcal{J}_c(f).$$

This completes the proof. □

Using Theorem 4 we get that $\mathcal{J}_c(f) \le \mathcal{I}_c(f)$ for every function f. However the difference can be very big: e.g. for f_{min} we have by Proposition 2 that $\mathcal{I}_c(f_{min}) = n$. On the other hand using the protocol given in [1]:

Protocol 2. For all $i = 0, 1, \ldots 2^n - 1$ or until the first 1 is transmitted do:
1. A transmits bit 1 if $x = i$ and 0 otherwise;
2. B transmits bit 1 if $y = i$ and 0 otherwise.

we get that $\mathcal{J}_c(f_{min}) \leq 1$. Since f_{min} cannot be computed privately, we obtain the equality $\mathcal{J}_c(f_{min}) = 1$.

For the equality function f_{equ} (see (2)), we get $\mathcal{I}_c(f_{equ}) \leq \log_2(n+1)$ (compare the inequalities (3)). By the fact shown in [1] that for any deterministic protocol $\mathcal{P}$ which computes f_{equ} there is $v \in \{0,1\}^n$ such that the size of the set

$$\{\mathcal{P}(x,v) : x \in \{0,1\}^n\} \cup \{\mathcal{P}(v,y) : y \in \{0,1\}^n\}$$

has at lest $n+2$ elements, we obtain for $z = 0$: $s_{\mathcal{P},A}(v,z) + s_{\mathcal{P},B}(v,z) \geq n+2$ and finally that $\mathcal{J}_c(f_{equ}) \geq \log_2(n+2)/2 > \log_2 n - 1$. Hence we get the following bounds: $\log_2 n - 1 < \mathcal{J}_c(f_{equ}) \leq \mathcal{I}_c(f_{equ}) \leq \log_2(n+1)$.

We close the section by giving a general lower bound for $\mathcal{J}_c$. Recall that a rectangle in $\{0,1\}^n \times \{0,1\}^n$ is a Cartesian product $R = V \times H$ with $V, H \subseteq \{0,1\}^n$. The rectangle R is f-constant if f is constant over R. Obviously, every protocol for $\mathcal{P}$ partitions the communication matrix M_f into f-constant rectangles. Let r_f be the largest width of an f-constant rectangle.

Theorem 5. *For every Boolean function f of two n-bit inputs*

$$\mathcal{J}_c(f) \geq n - \log_2 r_f - 2.$$

The proof of Theorem 3 of [1] works for our Theorem.

Using the general bound given in the Theorem above one can find lower bounds for Boolean functions f communication matrix of which is of the Hadamard type (see [1]). From this characterisation we get e.g. that for the n-variable inner product   mod   2 function defined as

$$f_{in}(x,y) = \sum_{i=1}^{n} x_i \cdot y_i \quad \mod 2 \tag{7}$$

it holds that $\mathcal{J}_c(f_{in}) \geq n/2 - 2$.

5   Derandomisation

In this section we will show that every randomized protocol $\mathcal{P}$ that computes the function f correctly with probability 1 can be simulated by a deterministic protocol $\mathcal{P}'$ such that the additional information that can be deduced running protocol $\mathcal{P}'$ is bounded by the additional information that can be deduced running protocol $\mathcal{P}$, i.e. $J_{\mathcal{P}'} \leq J_{\mathcal{P}}$. We will start by the derandomisation of the part of A.

Let us assume that A performing $\mathcal{P}$ starts the communication and let ℓ be an upper bound for the number of random bits used by A. In the algorithm below A simulates the t-th round of the computation of $\mathcal{P}$, with $t = 1, 2, 3, \ldots$ as follows: On a given input x A computes iteratively string c_t and a subset $\mathcal{R}_t \subseteq \{0,1\}^{\leq \ell}$ of all binary strings of lengths less or equal to ℓ, such that c_t is a complete communication string of a computation during the first t rounds and

$\mathcal{R}_t$ is a subset of all possible random strings that can be used by A. A string r is in $\mathcal{R}_t$ if there exists a computation of $\mathcal{P}$ such that the first t rounds of the computation are consistent with c_t when A on x and r. Define $\mathcal{R}_0 = \{0,1\}^{\leq \ell}$ and let c_0 be the empty string.

1. If t is odd then for every $r \in \mathcal{R}_{t-1}$ A simulates (deterministically) the t-th round of the computation of $\mathcal{P}$ on input x with the random string r that is consistent with the communication string c_{t-1} and computes a communication string for the tth round. Let w_t be lexicographically smallest among all such strings. Then A computes $\mathcal{R}_t := \{r \in \mathcal{R}_{t-1} \mid A$ sends w_t on $x, r, c_{t-1}\}$ and $c_t := c_{t-1} \circ w_t$ and sends w_t to B. For two strings v and v', by $v \circ v'$ we denote concatenation of v and v'.
2. If t is even and u_t is a message received by A from B in tth round, then $c_t := c_{t-1} \circ u_t$.

Assume that the protocol stops in round T, then it is easy to see that for every input y, every possible result z, and every random string of B, A chooses for every pair of inputs x, x' the communication string s such that it is the lexicographically smallest string with $\Pr[\mathcal{P}(x, y) = s|r], \Pr[\mathcal{P}(x', y) = s|r] > 0$. Hence, inputs x, x' that gives the same distribution on y, z, r when running $\mathcal{P}$ gives also the same distribution when running the deterministic protocol $\mathcal{P}'$.

Note that we can derandomize the part of B's protocol analogously. Hence, we can conclude:

Lemma 2. *For every protocol $\mathcal{P}$ there exists a deterministic protocol $\mathcal{P}'$ computing the same function, such that for every choice of x, y, z $s_{\mathcal{P}',A}(x, z) \leq s_{\mathcal{P},A}(x, z)$ and $s_{\mathcal{P}',B}(y, z) \leq s_{\mathcal{P},B}(y, z)$.*

Theorem 6. *For every protocol $\mathcal{P}$ there exists an deterministic protocol $\mathcal{P}'$ computing the same function, such that $J_{\mathcal{P}'} \leq J_{\mathcal{P}}$.*

This result generalises the result of Kushilevitz [6] that a protocol can be computed privately in the two party scenario iff it can be computed privately by a deterministic protocol.

Using our simulation result, we can directly deduce some bounds for the size of a minimal information source. Let s_f be the minimum size of the information source of a protocol computing f, i.e. let

$$s_f = \min_{\mathcal{P}} \max_{x,y,z} \{s_{\mathcal{P},A}(x, z), s_{\mathcal{P},B}(y, z)\}$$

(note that $\mathcal{J}_c(f) = \log_2 s_f$).

Corollary 1. $s_f \leq CS_D(f)$.

Proof. Assume that $s_f > CS_D(f)$ and let $\mathcal{P}$ be a deterministic protocol that achieve s_f and $\mathcal{P}'$ be a deterministic protocol that achieve $CS_D(f)$. Assume that $s_f = s_{\mathcal{P},A}(x, z)$ for appropriate chosen values x, z. Then the number of communication strings seen by A on input x and result z when running $\mathcal{P}$ is even higher then the number of communication strings seen by both parties when running $\mathcal{P}'$ on arbitrary inputs. Hence, the size of the information source when running $\mathcal{P}'$ is smaller than the size of the information source when running $\mathcal{P}$ – contradicting the assumption that $\mathcal{P}$ achieves the minimum size of the information source.   □

Corollary 2. $CS_D(f) = \min_{\text{deterministic } \mathcal{P} \text{ computes } f} |\bigcup_{x,z} S_{\mathcal{P},A}(x,z)|.$

Proof. Let $\mathcal{P}$ be a deterministic protocol for f such that

$$\left|\bigcup_{x,z} S_{\mathcal{P},A}(x,z)\right| = \min_{\text{deterministic } \mathcal{P}' \text{ computes } f} \left|\bigcup_{x,z} S_{\mathcal{P}',A}(x,z)\right| .$$

Since $\mathcal{P}$ is deterministic every distribution in the set $\bigcup_{x,z} S_{\mathcal{P},A}(x,z)$ rates exactly one communication string with a strictly positive probability. Furthermore, the set determines all communication strings used when running $\mathcal{P}$. The claim follows from the observation, that $\mathcal{P}$ is chosen such that the number of used communication strings is minimal.   □

6 Lower Bounds on Size of the Information Source

Corollary 1 gives a general upper bound on the minimum size of the information source s_f. This bound is not tight. In fact, it is well known (see e.g [7]) that for the equality function f_{equ} it holds that $CS_D(f_{equ}) \geq 2^n$ and $C_D(f_{equ}) = n$. On the other hand from the Protocol 1 it follows that for any optimal protocol $\mathcal{P}$ we get $s_{\mathcal{P},A}(x,z), s_{\mathcal{P},B}(y,z) \leq n$ for every x, y, z. Hence $s_{f_{equ}} \leq n < 2^n \leq CS_D(f_{equ})$. In this section we will prove a linear lower bound for the size of the information source with respect to the communication complexity, i.e. we show that for any f $s_f \in \Omega(C_D(f)/|\operatorname{range}(f)|)$. In particular for f_{equ} we get $C_D(f_{equ})/4-1 \leq s_{f_{equ}}$.

For a node v of the communication tree let X_v and Y_v denote the sets of input strings of A and B, respectively, such that on the input pairs $(x,y) \in X_v \times Y_v$ the protocol reaches v. Let $s_{\mathcal{P},A,v}(x,z)$ denote the size of the information source of the subprotocol of $\mathcal{P}$ starting in v and restricting the inputs to $X_v \times Y_v$. Let $s_{\mathcal{P},B,v}(y,z)$ be defined analogously. Finally, define

$$\operatorname{range}(v) = \{ f(x,y) \mid (x,y) \in X_v \times Y_v \} .$$

Without loss of generality let us restrict ourselves only to the protocols $\mathcal{P}$ sending no unnecessary bits for computing the function. Formally assume that all internal nodes of a communication tree of $\mathcal{P}$ have degree at least 2. We start with the following observation:

Lemma 3. *Let $\mathcal{P}$ be a deterministic protocol computing a function f and let $v_1, \ldots, v_t$ be a leaf-to-root path in the communication tree of $\mathcal{P}$. Then for all $i \in \{1, \ldots, t\}$ there exists $x \in X_{v_i}, y' \in Y_{v_i}$, and $z, z' \in \operatorname{range}(f)$ such that*

$$\max\{s_{\mathcal{P},A,v_i}(x,z), s_{\mathcal{P},B,v_i}(y',z')\} \geq \left\lceil \frac{i}{2 \cdot |\operatorname{range}(v_i)|} \right\rceil - 1 .$$

Proof. The proof follows for $i = 1$ since for every leaf v_1 of the communication tree we have $s_{\mathcal{P},A,v_1}(x, z) = s_{\mathcal{P},B,v_1}(y, z) = 0$.

Consider now an internal node v_i, with $i > 1$. Let $u_1, \ldots, u_d$ be all successors of v_i in the communication tree. Obviously, v_{i-1} is one of the nodes u_j. Let us assume, that A has to send some message in v_i, then for all $x \in X_{v_{i-1}} \subset X_{v_i}$, $y \in Y_{v_{i-1}} = Y_{v_i}$, and $z = f(x, y)$:

$$s_{\mathcal{P},A,v_i}(x, z) = \max\{1, \ s_{\mathcal{P},A,v_{i-1}}(x, z)\}.$$

On the other hand one can prove that for the information source of B we have

$$s_{\mathcal{P},B,v_i}(y, z) = \sum_{j \in \{1,\ldots,d\} \text{ with } z \in \mathrm{range}(u_j)} \max\{1, \ s_{\mathcal{P},B,u_j}(y, z)\}.$$

Therefore we can bound the quantity as follows

$$s_{\mathcal{P},B,v_i}(y, z) \geq \begin{cases} 1 + \max\{1, s_{\mathcal{P},B,v_{i-1}}(y, z)\} & \text{if } z \in \mathrm{range}(u_j) \text{ for some } u_j \neq v_{i-1} \\ \max\{1, s_{\mathcal{P},B,v_{i-1}}(y, z)\} & \text{else.} \end{cases}$$

Assume that there are k nodes on the sub-path $v_1, \ldots, v_i$ where A sends a message to B. Then there exists $z' \in \mathrm{range}(v_i)$ such that for at least

$$\left\lceil \frac{k}{|\mathrm{range}(v_i)|} \right\rceil - 1$$

of these nodes v_j it holds that $z' \in \mathrm{range}(v_{j-1}) \cap \mathrm{range}(u)$ for some direct successor $u \neq v_{j-1}$ of v_j. Note that we can show simular bounds for $s_{\mathcal{P},A,v_i}(x, z)$ and $s_{\mathcal{P},B,v_i}(y, z)$ if Bob sends a message. The claim follows immediately since either A or B has to send some message in at least $\lceil i/2 \rceil$ of the nodes $v_1, \ldots, v_i$. $\square$

As a corollary we obtain:

Corollary 3. *For every function f of two n-bit inputs it is true*

$$\frac{C_D(f)}{2 \cdot |\mathrm{range}(f)|} - 1 \ \leq \ s_f.$$

Combining the corollary above with Theorem 6 we can conclude the following lower bound on the additional information:

Theorem 7. *For every function f of two n-bit inputs we have*

$$J_c(f) \geq \log_2 C_D(f) - \log_2 |\mathrm{range}(f)| - O(1).$$

7   Conclusions

In this paper measures for revealed information required for computing f have been considered. We have analysed the measures given by Bar-Yehuda et al.

and have showed that some results presented in [1] are wrong. Moreover we have observed some unnatural properties of the measures. We have introduced a new definition for the additional information for two party protocols and have given some bounds for concrete functions for the additional information. We get e.g. that for the n-variable inner product   mod 2 function it is true that $\mathcal{J}_c(f_{in}) \geq n/2 - 2$. An interesting open problem is to show lower and upper bounds on $\mathcal{J}_c$ for another specific functions. A further task to do is to investigate a tradeoff between the additional information and the number of rounds for communication protocols.

References

1. Reuven Bar-Yehuda, Benny Chor, Eyal Kushilevitz, and Alon Orlitsky. Privacy, additional information, and communication. *IEEE Transactions on Information Theory*, 39(6):1930–1943, 1993. An early version of this paper appear in *Proc. of 5th IEEE Structure in Complexity Theory*, 1990, pp. 55–65.
2. Donald Beaver. Perfect Privacy for Two Party Protocols. Technical Report TR-11-89, Harvard University, 1989.
3. Michael Ben-Or, Shafi Goldwasser, and Avi Wigderson. Completeness theorems for non-cryptographic fault-tolerant distributed computation. In *Proc. of the 20th Ann. ACM Symp. on Theory of Computing (STOC)*, pages 1–10. ACM Press, 1988.
4. Markus Bläser, Anderas Jakoby, Maciej Liśkiewicz, and Bodo Manthey, Privacy in Non-Private Environments. Proceedings of the 10th Annual International Cryptology Conference on the Theory and Application of Cryptology and Information Security (Asiacrypt), 2004, 137-151.
5. David Chaum, Claude Crépeau, and Ivan Damgård. Multiparty unconditionally secure protocols. In *Proc. of the 20th Ann. ACM Symp. on Theory of Computing (STOC)*, pages 11–19. ACM Press, 1988.
6. Eyal Kushilevitz. Privacy and communication complexity. *SIAM Journal on Discrete Mathematics*, 5(2):273–284, 1992.
7. Eyal Kushilevitz and Noam Nisan. *Communication Complexity*. Cambridge University Press, 1997.
8. Andrew Chi-Chih Yao. Protocols for secure computations. In *Proc. of the 23rd Ann. IEEE Symp. on Foundations of Computer Science (FOCS)*, pages 160–164. IEEE Computer Society, 1982.

Gate Evaluation Secret Sharing and Secure One-Round Two-Party Computation

Vladimir Kolesnikov

Department of Computer Science,
University of Toronto, Canada
vlad@cs.utoronto.ca

Abstract. We propose *Gate Evaluation Secret Sharing* (GESS) – a new kind of secret sharing, designed for use in secure function evaluation (SFE) with minimal interaction. The resulting simple and powerful GESS approach to SFE is a generalization of Yao's garbled circuit technique.

We give efficient GESS schemes for evaluating binary gates and prove (almost) matching lower bounds. We give a more efficient information-theoretic reduction of SFE of a boolean formula F to oblivious transfer. Its complexity is $\approx \sum d_i^2$, where d_i is the depth of the i-th leaf of F.

1 Introduction

The main motivation for this work is one-round secure function evaluation (SFE). SFE is one of the core problems of cryptography. We consider the following one-round two semi-honest parties setting. Alice and Bob wish to compute a function f of their inputs x and y respectively: Alice sends the first message to Bob, Bob replies, and Alice computes $f(x, y)$. Both parties follow the prescribed protocol, but try to infer additional information from the messages they receive. This problem has been extensively studied, and very efficient solutions (with cost linear in the circuit representing f) exist (Yao's garbled circuit [3,21,24,25,27]), when Alice is polytime bounded. When Alice is computationally unlimited, only much less efficient algorithms are known [4,9,18,19,20,26].

One-round SFE is particularly interesting for several reasons. Firstly, from a practical point of view, interaction necessarily involves latencies in message deliveries, and in many practical situations waiting for messages dominates the entire computation time. Secondly, a large volume of research, e.g. [8,12,18,19], aims specifically at reducing round complexity of multiparty protocols. Investigating the two-party one-round model may help increase our understanding of general secure multiparty computation. Finally, the recently popular area of secure autonomous agent computing (see, e.g. [1,8]) relies on one-round protocols, commonly implemented via encrypted circuit constructions. A variety of very useful mobile agents computing simple functions may benefit from our improvements. One such example, discussed in [1], is that of a shopping agent that would accept a sales offer if it is below a certain threshold.

We approach the problem in a general way by reducing SFE to oblivious transfer (OT). OT is a powerful primitive, and is the subject of a vast amount of

B. Roy (Ed.): ASIACRYPT 2005, LNCS 3788, pp. 136–155, 2005.

research. It has been studied in many settings; for example, OT is instantiable with information-theoretic (IT) security (e.g. with noisy and quantum channels or a distributed sender [23]). Our SFE constructions automatically apply to all of the above (and many other) settings and will benefit from future OT research.

1.1 Our Contributions and Outline of the Work

Our main idea is a new *simple* way of evaluating circuit gates securely by using a new type of secret sharing, which we call *Gate Evaluation Secret Sharing* (GESS). Our method can be viewed as a generalization of Yao's garbled gate evaluation procedure, offering a simple and powerful approach for designing efficient SFE protocols. Our method is flexible, and not limited to $\vee, \wedge, \neg$ gates. Circuits with special purpose (e.g. non-binary) gates may be designed and implemented via GESS to achieve better efficiency for specific functions (see, e.g., Sect. 2.6).

We show how a composition of GESS schemes can be used to efficiently reduce SFE to (parallel executions of) 1-out of-2 OT. Given a boolean formula, we obtain a *one-round* reduction, meaning that an instantiation of OT results in a SFE protocol, the security and round complexity of which are that of the underlying OT. Our reduction is very efficient. Previous approaches in part suffer from the exponential (in depth) cost of evaluation of a gate, which has intuitievely appeared necessary. We break this intuition by providing a scheme for gate evaluation whose cost is only *quadratic* in the depth of the gate. Further, in our reduction, we don't "pay" for the internal gates of the formula. For a depth d circuit, this results in a factor of approximately $2^{O(\sqrt{d})}$ improvement over previous solutions: $O(2^d d^2)$ vs $\Theta(2^d 2^{\Theta(\sqrt{d})})$. (Like all other approaches, ours suffers from the fact that the number of gates may be exponential in depth. Thus, we offer polytime reduction of only NC^1 circuits.) We prove non-trivial lower bounds, showing that our constructions are almost optimal in the GESS framework.

The GESS approach is especially efficient on small circuits, since it does not use encryption. In Sect. 2.6, we demonstrate this by a new efficient protocol for the Two Millionaires problem. This protocol also serves as an example of designing and implementing custom GESS gates.

We start with describing previous approaches and giving conceptual and performance comparisons to our work (Sect. 1.2). We then present intuition for our approach and introduce the necessary formal definitions in Sect. 2 and 2.1. We present our constructions, lower bounds and performance analysis in Sect. 2.3 – 2.5. In Sect. 2.6 we present a new solution of the Two Millionaires problem.

In Sect. 3, we show how to use GESS to allow polytime SFE of polysize circuits, when Alice is polytime. In effect, we obtain another implementation of Yao's garbled circuit approach for the model with polytime Alice, offering essentially the same computational and communication complexity as its best implementations. The natural and efficient handling of the computational setting demonstrates the generality of the GESS approach. We mention that the efficiency of Yao's garbled circuit technique in the standard model can be (slightly) improved by using IT GESS on "the bottom part" of the circuit (see discussion in Sect. 3).

1.2   Comparisons with Related Previous Work

General discussion. Note the frequent use of a variety of secret sharing schemes in secure multiparty computation. They are always used, however, to share secrets *among players*. We contrast this with our novel use, where secrets are shared *among wires* and given to the player who performs reconstruction.

We note that some of the previous approaches (e.g. [9,18,19,20]) are applicable to more general representations of functions (e.g. by arithmetic formulas or branching programs (BP)). Many functions may have especially efficient representations when not restricted to boolean formulas (the setting we consider); such functions may not benefit from our constructions.

Although our reductions are efficient for polysize boolean formulas of arbitrary depth, they perform better on balanced formulas. For the latter, the complexity is quasi-linear (vs. cubic for highly unbalanced formulas) in the size of the formula. Note that it is possible ([7,6]) to rebalance any formula to obtain an equivalent log-depth balanced formula, at the cost of small increase in its size (see end of Sect. 2.4 for more discussion).

Therefore, for the remainder of this section, assume that we are given a boolean formula (or an NC^1 circuit, which can be viewed as one), which is rebalanced if it benefits the approach considered.

Let d be the depth of the formula or the circuit.

Comparing our reduction to previous constant-round approaches.

Kilian [20] was the first to show a one-round IT reduction (of complexity $\Theta(4^d)$) of SFE to OT. Kilian relies on Barrington's [2] representation of NC^1 circuits as permutation BPs. It is possible to replace Barrington's representation in Kilian's construction with a more efficient construction of Cleve [9] (see, e.g. Cramer et al. [10]). The resulting complexity is $\Theta(2^d 2^{\Theta(\sqrt{d})})$, which is the best previously known for NC^1 circuits and (re)balanced formulas.

Ishai and Kushilevitz [18,19] suggested a way of representing a circuit as a predicate on a vector of degree 3 (degree of the input variables x_i is 1) *randomizing polynomials*. Their construction assigns an (exponential in d in size) polynomial representation to each wire of the corresponding fan-out 1 circuit, and implies a one-round SFE-to-OT reduction, of complexity $\Theta(4^d)$. They also previously suggested a related *Private Simultaneous Messages* (PSM) model [17] of computation. They showed how to evaluate functions computed by BPs in the PSM model (and also in our SFE-to-OT reduction model) with resources quadratic in the size of the BP. (Recall, BPs are more powerful than permutation BPs or formulas.) For our setting, their approach implies a one-round SFE-to-OT reduction of cost $\Theta(4^d)$, using an (almost) linear in size transformation of a formula to a BP [14].

Our reduction of boolean formulas is simpler and more efficient (costing $O(2^d d^2)$) than the above approaches.

Yao's garbled circuit approach can also be used for such reduction (see, e.g. [19]). The idea is to use an IT-secure two-time encryption scheme (e.g. using one-time pad) in Yao's garbled circuit. The keys of such a scheme must be more than twice the size of the secret, causing an exponential (in d) growth of the size of secrets, even in fan-in 1 circuits[1]. The complexity of such a scheme is about $\Theta(4^d)$ (up to 2^d leaves, each of size up to 2^d). Our approach is a generalization and an improvement of this approach.

Sander, Young and Yung (SYY) ([26]) present a "fully homomorphic" encryption scheme and apply it to SFE. The encryption size grows exponentially with the number of the applied OR operations, resulting in $\Theta(8^d)$ cost of SFE. Beaver [4] suggests an optimization of the SYY pyramid and extends the approach to the multiparty setting, achieving complexity $\Theta(4^d)$. Further, using the representation of Feige, Kilian and Naor [11] of NLOGSPACE as a product of polysize matrices, he shows how to compute it in one round, bootstrapping the SYY approach, also achieving complexity $\Theta(4^d)$. Our approach is conceptually different, simpler, more composable, uses fewer assumptions, and offers complexity of at most $O(2^d d^2)$. Also, unlike SYY, we do not have the requirement of a layered circuit, which further increases our performance improvement.

Finally, we mention (but do not discuss) a variety of non-constant round solutions (e.g. [22] and [16]).

1.3   Our Setting

We are working in a setting with two semi-honest participants who use randomness in their computation. A large part of our work concerns reductions of various problems to the OT oracle. In the semi-honest model, secure reductions result in secure protocols when the called oracles are replaced by their secure implementations. Further, the oracles' implementations may be run in parallel, which, with natural OT implementations, results in secure one-round protocols. See Goldreich [15] for definitions, discussion and the composition theorem.

2   The GESS Approach

The intuition behind the GESS approach. Suppose first that the circuit C consists of a single binary gate G with two inputs, one held by Alice, and one by Bob. To transfer the value of the output wire to Alice, Bob encodes possible values of each of the two input wires and transfers to Alice two of the four encodings – one for each wire. Encoding of Alice's wire value is sent via OT. Each pair of encodings that can be possibly sent, has to allow the recovery of the corresponding to G value of the output wire, and cannot carry any other useful information. Consider the following example.

$$s'_0 \; s'_1 \quad \diagdown \!\!\!\diagup \quad s''_0 \; s''_1$$
$$\widehat{G}$$
$$0 \quad 1$$

---

[1] Note the distinction between this flavour of Yao's approach and its standard version for evaluation of polysize circuits (e.g. [3,25,24,21]). The latter is not a reduction to OT; e.g, it cannot be used to construct one-round protocols IT-secure against Alice.

Given the possible output values $0, 1$ and the semantics of the gate G, Bob generates encodings of the input wires' values $(s_0', s_1'), (s_0'', s_1'')$, such that each possible pair of encodings s_i', s_j'', where $i, j \in \{0, 1\}$, allows to reconstruct $G(i, j)$, and carries no other information. Now, if Bob sends Alice shares corresponding to their inputs, Alice would be able to reconstruct the value of the output wire, and nothing else.

This mostly corresponds to our intuition of secret sharing schemes. Indeed, the possible gate outputs play the role of secrets, which are shared and then reconstructed from the input wires encodings (shares).

Our next observation is that Bob need not share the *values* of the output wire, but instead can share their *encodings*, which, in turn, may be input shares of another gate. Thus, Alice and Bob can recursively apply the GESS approach to multi-gate circuits. For each wire, Alice will only be able to obtain one secret – the one corresponding the the value of the wire on the parties' inputs.

2.1 The Definition of Gate Evaluation Secret Sharing

We now formally state the desired properties of the secret sharing scheme. While the idea of the definition is quite simple, it is somewhat burdened with notation due to the necessary level of formalism. For simplicity, we present the definition for the case of a gate with two binary inputs and a binary output, postponing the presentation of its most general form to Appendix A (Def. 2). A simple instructive example of a GESS scheme is Constr. 2 in Sect. 2.3.

Let G be a gate with two binary inputs and a binary output. Also denote by $G : \{0, 1\} \times \{0, 1\} \mapsto \{0, 1\}$ the function computed by gate G. Let SEC be the domain of secrets. Suppose we've associated a secret $s_i \in SEC$ with each of the two possible values i of the output wire of G. In general, distributions of s_0 and s_1 may be dependent, so we talk about a *tuple* of secrets $\langle s_0, s_1 \rangle$ from a domain of tuples $TSEC \subset SEC^2$ associated with the output wire. We want to assign a share to each value of the two input wires, such that each combination of shares allows reconstruction of (only) the "right" secret. As do secrets, shares on a wire form a tuple: $\langle sh_{10}, sh_{11} \rangle \in TSH_1 \subset (SH_1)^2$ on wire 1, and $\langle sh_{20}, sh_{21} \rangle \in TSH_2 \subset (SH_2)^2$ on wire 2. In our notation, $sh_{ij} \in SH_i$ is the share of the i-th input wire ($i \in \{1, 2\}$), corresponding to the value $j \in \{0, 1\}$.

Definition 1. *(Gate evaluation Secret Sharing) A gate evaluation secret sharing scheme (GESS) for evaluating G as above (we also say GESS implementing G) is a pair of algorithms (Shr, Rec) (with implicitly defined secrets domain SEC, secrets tuples domain $TSEC$, two share domains SH_1 and SH_2 and two share tuples domains TSH_1, TSH_2), such that the following holds.*

The probabilistic share generation algorithm Shr takes as input a two-tuple of secrets $\langle s_0, s_1 \rangle \in TSEC$ and outputs two tuples of shares (one for each wire), where, $\forall i \in \{1, 2\}$, the i-th tuple $t_i \in TSH_i$ consists of two shares $sh_{ij} \in SH_i$. The deterministic share reconstruction algorithm Rec takes as input two elements $sh_1 \in SH_1$ and $sh_2 \in SH_2$ and outputs $s \in SEC$.

Let $v = \langle v_1, v_2 \rangle \in \{0,1\} \times \{0,1\}$ be a selection vector. Define the selection function $Sel(\langle sh_{10}, sh_{11} \rangle, \langle sh_{20}, sh_{21} \rangle, v) = \langle sh_{1v_1}, sh_{2v_2} \rangle$. Write $V_1 \equiv V_2$ to denote that V_1 and V_2 are distributed identically.

Shr and Rec satisfy the following conditions:

- correctness: for all random inputs of Shr and secrets tuples $\langle s_0, s_1 \rangle \in TSEC$,
  $\forall v \in \{0,1\}^2, Rec(Sel(Shr(\langle s_0, s_1 \rangle), v)) = s_{G(v)}$
- privacy (selected shares contain no information other than the value $s_{G(v)}$):
  There exists a simulator Sim, such that $\forall \langle s_0, s_1 \rangle \in TSEC$ and any $v \in \{0,1\}^2$: $Sim(s_{G(v)}) \equiv Sel(Shr(\langle s_0, s_1 \rangle), v)$

Observation 1. A simple generalization of this definition (required for discussion in Sect. 2.3 and 2.4) considers the identity gate G_I with a four-valued output wire, where each output corresponds to a pair of inputs. In this case, the secrets form a 4-tuple $\langle s_{00}, ..., s_{11} \rangle$, while there are still two two-tuples of shares. Note that we can convert GESS implementing G_I into GESS implementing any other binary gate by simply restricting some of the secrets to be equal. Denote the correspondence between a secret $s \in SEC$ and the wire value $v \in \{0,1\}$ by $s \leftrightarrow v$. Then setting $s_{01} = s_{10} = s_{11} \leftrightarrow 1, s_{00} \leftrightarrow 0$ gives the implementation of the OR, and $s_{00} = s_{01} = s_{10} \leftrightarrow 0, s_{11} \leftrightarrow 1$ – of the AND gates. NOT gates can be implemented "for free" by simply eliminating them and inverting the correspondence of the appropriate wire's values and secrets.

Observation 2. We note that, in contrast with the traditional approach of multi-secret sharing schemes, our definition allows the possibility that a single share gives out some information about a secret. It is easy to see, however, that this information must be common to every secret, since otherwise it is possible to determine whether a corresponding combination of secret/share occurred, which allows to easily construct a distinguisher breaking the privacy requirement of GESS. Further, shares of the same wire, corresponding to different values, must be distributed identically (otherwise a distinguisher exists).

The definition is given for specific input and output domains, and therefore we do not talk about polynomial bounds on Shr and Rec. However, in practice, we are interested in *ensembles* of schemes and want them to be uniform polytime algorithms. We won't insist on an ensemble of *efficient* simulators, because an efficient simulator exists if any one exists. Indeed, an efficient simulator can simply output $Sel(Shr(\langle s_0, s_1 \rangle), v)$, where at least one of the secrets s_i is equal to s, and v is any selection vector, such that $G(v) = i$.

2.2   Reduction of SFE to OT Using GESS

Suppose Alice and Bob have a circuit C, consisting of fan-out 1 gates $G_1, G_2, ...$ We formally describe a reduction of securely evaluating C on their inputs to calls to OT, resulting in a one-round protocol. Again, for simplicity of presentation we assume that all gates G_i are fan-in 2 binary gates.

Assume that for every gate G of C, there exists a GESS $GESS_G : (Shr_G, Rec_G)$ of Def. 1 with appropriate secret domains (as described below). We give explicit constructions (e.g. Constr. 2 in Sect. 2.3) of such schemes for all gates with two binary inputs. We note that GESS for every other gate can be constructed (e.g. from Constr. 1 instantiated with GESS of Constr. 2).

Construction 1. *(Reducing SFE to OT)* **Bob's precomputation.** *Bob starts with the output gate. He sets the secrets domain SEC of it to be $\{0,1\}$ and sets the secrets tuple to $\langle 0,1 \rangle$. He proceeds through gates of C recursively as follows.*

Consider a gate G. Let $TSEC$ and a secrets tuple $t = \langle s_0, s_1 \rangle \in TSEC$ are given for G. Let $GESS_G$ be a GESS scheme implementing G with secrets tuples domain $TSEC \subset SEC^2$. Bob runs Shr_G on the secrets tuple t and obtains two tuples of shares $t_1 \in TSH_1$ and $t_2 \in TSH_2$, corresponding to the first and second input wires of G respectively. Let G'_i be the i-th input gate of G ($i \in \{0,1\}$). Then Bob processes G'_i as follows. He treats the tuple of shares $t_i \in TSH_i$ of G's input wire as the tuple of secrets of G'_i, and TSH_i – as the secrets tuples domain of G'_i. Bob now applies the algorithm of this paragraph to G'_i.

Eventually, Bob obtains secrets tuples for all input wires of C. Note that Bob's choices of instances of GESS schemes for the gates of C are deterministic and built into the protocol; this explicates the corresponding Rec procedures.

Interaction. *For each input wire associated with Alice, she and Bob make (parallel) calls to OT oracles. Alice has the wire's input and Bob has the tuple of secrets as their inputs of each of the calls. For each input wire associated with Bob, Bob sends Alice the corresponding secret from that wire's tuple of secrets[2].*

Alice's computation. *Alice obtains results of the OT and the secrets corresponding to Bob's inputs. Alice proceeds, from the top down on the circuit C, as follows. For each gate, Alice knows the secrets corresponding to the inputs of the gate, and the corresponding Rec procedure. She runs Rec on the input secrets and obtains the output secret. She proceeds in this manner until she obtains the secret corresponding to the output wire. Alice outputs this secret.*

Theorem 1. *Constr. 1 is a non-cryptographic reduction (thus unconditionally secure against both Alice and Bob) of SFE of C to OT, in the semi-honest model.*

The proof of Theorem 1 is intuitive and is presented in Appendix B.

Observation 3. *A circuit C with fan-out greater than 1 can be converted into a corresponding (potentially very large) tree-circuit C' by duplicating C's subtrees where appropriate. Equivalently, one can view the secrets as being computed and propagated by Bob in parallel on the same wire. Note that we, however, need not increase the number of corresponding OT instances due to the growth of C' relative to C (until a certain efficiency threshold is reached). Rather, Bob's inputs to OT will be longer (without the increase in the total number of bits transferred). This will often result in significant computational and communication savings.*

---

[2] This message is appended to Bob's messages of the n-round instantiations of OT oracles to form an n-round protocol.

2.3   GESS for Gates with Two Binary Inputs

We now present an efficient ensemble of GESS schemes (indexed by the secrets domains) implementing any binary gate with two binary inputs. This construction is a building block of a more efficient Constr. 3. We present GESS for the 1-to-1 gate function $G : \{0,1\}^2 \mapsto \{00,01,10,11\}$, where $G(0,0) = 00, G(0,1) = 01, G(1,0) = 10, G(1,1) = 11$ (see Observation 1 for justification).

Let the secrets domain be $SEC = \{0,1\}^n$, and four (not necessarily distinct) secrets $s_{00}, ... s_{11} \in SEC$ are given; the secret s_{ij} corresponds to the value $G(i,j)$ of the output wire. Note that $|SEC| \geq 4$ need not hold; our scheme is interesting even when $|SEC| \geq 2$.

The intuition for the design of the GESS scheme is as follows. We first randomly choose two strings $R_0, R_1 \in_R SEC$ to be the shares sh_{10} and sh_{11} (corresponding to 0 and 1 of the first input wire). Now consider sh_{20} – the share corresponding to 0 of the second input wire. We want this share to produce either s_{00} (when combined with sh_{10}) or s_{10} (when combined with sh_{11}). Thus, the share $sh_{20} = B_{00}B_{10}$ will consist of two blocks. One, $B_{00} = s_{00} \oplus R_0$, is designed to be combined with R_0 and reconstruct s_{00}. The other, $B_{10} = s_{10} \oplus R_1$, is designed to be combined with R_1 and reconstruct s_{10}. Share $sh_{21} = B_{01}B_{11}$ is constructed similarly, setting $B_{01} = s_{01} \oplus R_0$ and $B_{11} = s_{11} \oplus R_1$. Note the indexing notation – the secret s_{ij} is always reconstructed using B_{ij}.

Both leftmost blocks B_{00} and B_{01} are designed to be combined with the same share R_0, and both rightmost blocks B_{10} and B_{11} are designed to be combined with R_1. Therefore, we append a 0 to R_0 to tell Rec to use the left block of the second share for reconstruction, and append a 1 to R_1 to tell Rec to use the right block of the second share for reconstruction. Finally, to hide information leaked by the order of blocks in shares, we perform the following. We randomly choose a bit b; if $b = 1$, we reverse the order of blocks in *both* shares of wire 2 and invert the appended pointer bits of the shares of wire 1. More formally:

Construction 2. *(GESS ensemble for gates with two binary inputs.)* Let $SEC = \{0,1\}^n$ and $TSEC = SEC^4$ be the secrets domains. Let the secrets tuple $\langle s_{00}, ..., s_{11} \rangle \in TSEC$ be given. The domains of shares are: $SH_1 = \{0,1\} \times SEC$ and $SH_2 = SEC^2$. Note that $TSH_1 = SH_1^2$ and $TSH_2 = SH_2^2$.

Shr chooses $b \in_R \{0,1\}, R_0, R_1 \in_R SEC$ and sets blocks
$B_{00} = s_{00} \oplus R_0, B_{01} = s_{01} \oplus R_0, B_{10} = s_{10} \oplus R_1, B_{11} = s_{11} \oplus R_1.$
Shr sets the tuples of shares $\langle sh_{10}, sh_{11} \rangle \in SH_1, \langle sh_{20}, sh_{21} \rangle \in SH_2$ as follows

	wire 1	wire 2, if $b = 0$	wire 2, if $b = 1$
wire value 0	$sh_{10} = bR_0$	$sh_{20} = B_{00}B_{10}$	$sh_{20} = B_{10}B_{00}$
wire value 1	$sh_{11} = \bar{b}R_1$	$sh_{21} = B_{01}B_{11}$	$sh_{21} = B_{11}B_{01}$

Rec proceeds as follows. On input $Sh_1 = b'r$, $Sh_2 = a_0a_1$, Rec outputs $r \oplus a_{b'}$.

Theorem 2. *For each $n \in \mathbb{N}$, Constr. 2 is a GESS scheme.*

Proof. (Sketch): To prove correctness, we need to show that no matter what the random choices of Shr and the wire values i_1, i_2 are, Rec always reconstructs $s_{G(i_1,i_2)}$. Verification of correctness is simple and is moved to Appendix D.

We now prove security. Suppose secrets $s_{00}, ..., s_{11}$ are given. This determines the distribution on the Shr generated shares. Let the input wire values i_1, i_2 be given. Then the distribution P on the corresponding pair of shares $\langle sh_{1i_1}, sh_{2i_2} \rangle$ and the secret $s = s_{G(i_1, i_2)}$ shared by the pair are determined. The goal of the simulator is, given only s, to generate a pair of shares distributed identically to P. Note that this exactly corresponds to the privacy condition $Sim(s_{G(i_1, i_2)}) \equiv Sel(Shr(s_{00}, ..., s_{11}), \langle i_1, i_2 \rangle)$ of Def. 1.

The following natural simulator $Sim(s)$ suffices. On input $s \in SEC$, Sim chooses a random bit $d \in_R \{0, 1\}$ and random strings $p, q \in_R SEC$. If $d = 0$, he outputs $(\langle d, p \rangle, \langle p \oplus s, q \rangle)$, otherwise he outputs $(\langle d, p \rangle, \langle q, p \oplus s \rangle)$. The simple proof by case analysis is presented in Appendix D.   □

The Permute and Point (PP) Technique. We note the application of the following technique: we permuted the blocks of the shares of the second wire, and appended pointers to the shares of the first wire, hiding information contained in the order of blocks. We use the same idea in all other constructions in this paper (of Sect. 2.4 and 2.6). We believe this technique is likely to be useful in many other GESS constructions; it may also have other applications.

Observation 4. *We note that the simulator Sim of Theorem 2 is the same for every gate function – it is only the secrets semantics that defines the semantics of the gate. Therefore, Sim can simulate gates without knowing what they are. Therefore, when this secret sharing scheme is plugged into the protocol of Sect. 2.2, semantics of all gates are unconditionally hidden from Alice - she only knows the wire connections of C.*

2.4   The Main Construction – GESS for AND/OR/NOT Circuits

Note the inefficiency of Constr. 2, causing the shares corresponding to the second input wire be double the size of the gate's secrets. While, in some circuits, we could avoid the exponential (in depth) secret growth by balancing the direction of greater growth toward more shallow parts of the circuit, a more efficient solution is desirable. We discuss only AND/OR circuits, since NOT gates are given for "free" (see Observation 1).

Recall, in Constr. 2 each of the two shares of the second wire consists of two blocks. Observe that in the case of OR and AND gates either left or right blocks of these two shares are equal. We use this property to reduce (relative to Constr. 2) the size of the shares when the secrets are of the above form. Our key idea is to view the shares of the second wire as being equal, except for one block.

Suppose each of the four secrets consists of n blocks and the secrets differ only in the jth block, as follows:

$$s_{00} = (\quad t_1 \quad \ldots \quad t_{j-1} \quad t_j^{00} \quad t_{j+1} \quad \ldots \quad t_n \quad), \quad \ldots$$
$$s_{11} = (\quad t_1 \quad \ldots \quad t_{j-1} \quad t_j^{11} \quad t_{j+1} \quad \ldots \quad t_n \quad),$$

where $\forall i = 1..n$: $t_i, t_j^{00}, t_j^{01}, t_j^{10}, t_j^{11} \in D$, for some domain D of size k. It is convenient to consider the *columns* of blocks, spanning across the shares. Every column (with the exception of the j-th) consists of four equal blocks. We stress that the index j is only determined by the secrets, and must not be recovered at reconstruction.We construct a GESS for gates with two binary inputs, where the size of each share of the first wire is $n(k + \lceil \log(n + 1) \rceil)$ and of the second wire is $(n + 1)k$. Further, each share of the first wire consists of n blocks of size $|D| + \lceil \log(n + 1) \rceil$, and all but one pair of corresponding blocks are equal between the shares. Each share of the second wire consists of $n + 1$ blocks of size $|D|$ and, for OR and AND gates, all but one pair of corresponding blocks are equal between the shares. Since the generated shares satisfy the above conditions on secrets, repeated application of this GESS for OR and AND gates is possible.

The scheme's intuition. For simplicity of presentation, we do not present the GESS scheme in full generality here (this is postponed to Appendix C). We show its main ideas by considering the case where the four secrets consist of $n = 3$ blocks each, and $j = 2$ is the index of the column of distinct blocks.

Our idea is to share the secrets "column-wise", that is to treat each of the three columns of blocks of the secrets as a tuple of subsecrets and share this tuple separately, producing the corresponding subshares. Consider sharing the 1-st column. All four subsecrets are equal (to $t_1 \in D$), and we share them trivially by setting both subshares of the first wire to a random string $R_1 \in_R D$, and both subshares of the second wire to be $R_1 \oplus t_1$. Column 3 is shared similarly. We share column 2 as in Constr. 2 (highlighted on the diagram), omitting the last step of appending the pointers and permutation. This preliminary assignment of shares (still leaking information due to order of blocks) is shown on the diagram.

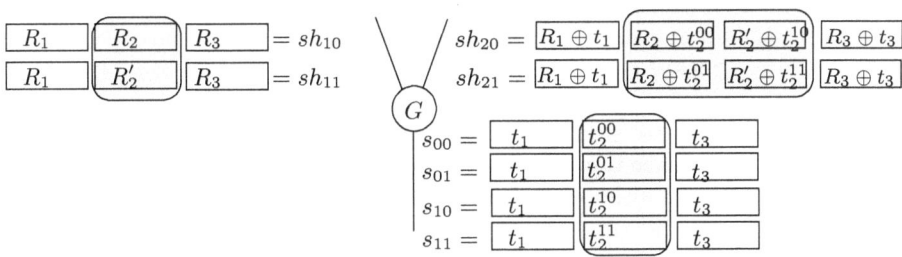

Note that the reconstruction of secrets is done by XOR'ing the corresponding blocks of the shares, and, importantly, the procedure is the same for both types of sharing we use. For example, given sh_{10} and sh_{21}, we reconstruct the secret $(R_1 \oplus (R_1 \oplus t_1),\ R_2 \oplus (R_2 \oplus t_2^{01}),\ R_3 \oplus (R_3 \oplus t_3)) = s_{01}$.

The remaining (PP) step (not shown on the diagram) is to randomly permute the order of the four columns of both shares of wire 2 and to append $(\log 4)$-bit pointers to each block of the shares of wire 1, telling Rec which block of the second share to use. Note that the pointers appended to both blocks of column 1 of wire 1 are the same. The same holds for column 3. Pointers appended to blocks of column 2 are different. For example, if the identity permutation was applied, then we will append "1" to both blocks R_1, "2" to R_2, "3" to R_2', and "4" to both blocks R_3. Because G is either an OR or an AND gate, both tuples of shares maintain the property that all but one pairs of corresponding blocks are equal between the shares of the tuple. Note that it is not a problem that the index of the column with different entries on input wire 1 is the same as that on the output wire: since the adversary never sees both shares of any wire, this index remains unconditionally hidden.

Construction 3. *(GESS for AND/OR gates) The presented construction can be naturally generalized for an arbitrary number of blocks n of size k and for arbitrary index j of the column with differing blocks. The formal presentation of this general construction is postponed to Appendix C (Constr. 6).*

Theorem 3. *For each $n, k, j \in \mathbb{N}$, Constr. 3 is a GESS scheme as defined by (a generalization of) Def. 1.*

We give the intuition of the proof and refer the reader to Appendix C for details. First, the correctness of the reconstruction is easily verifiable. Further, each of the four pairs of shares, reconstructing their corresponding secret $s \in \{s_{00}, .., s_{11}\}$, has the following structure. Let $s = (t_1, ..., t_n)$. The second share in each pair of shares is a sequence of $n + 1$ randomly chosen blocks r_i from D: $sh_2 = (r_1, ..., r_{n+1})$. The first share in each pair is a sequence of n "blocks with pointers" $sh_1 = (B_1, ..., B_n)$, as follows. $\forall i \in \{1..n\}, B_i = \langle p_i, b_i \rangle$, where $p_1, ..., p_n$ is a random permutation of a random n-element subset of $\{1..n+1\}$, and $b_i = t_i \oplus r_{p_i} \in D$. This implies the simulator $Sim(s)$, required by Def. 1.

GESS' performance. From above, if the secrets of the output wire of G consist of n blocks of size k, then the secrets of G's inputs consist of no more than $n+1$ blocks of size $k + \lceil \log(n+1) \rceil$. Similarly, d levels deeper, wires' secrets consist of no more than $n + d$ blocks of size $k + \sum_{i=1..d} \lceil \log(n + i) \rceil$. Therefore, starting with one-bit secrets $(n = 1, k = 1)$, a tree circuit will have at depth d secrets of size at most $(d+1)(d \log(d+1)+1) = d^2 \log(d+1) + d \log(d+1) + d + 1$. The shares grow very slowly: as $d \to \inf$, the "share expansion factor" — the ratio of sizes of shares to sizes of secrets of a GESS scheme for a gate G at depth d — approaches 1. Since the gates have exactly two inputs, there are at most 2^d input wires to the circuit, and the total size of Bob's secrets to be sent to Alice is $2^d(d^2 \log(d+1) + d \log(d+1) + d + 1) \approx 2^d d^2 \log d$, dominated by the 2^d term.

Rebalancing C prior to applying the above reduction may result in substantial performance improvement. Bonet and Buss [6] and Bshouty, Cleve and Eberly [7] prove the following fact (and exhibit the rebalancing procedure).

Let C be a $\{\vee, \wedge, \neg\}$-formula of leaf size m. Then for all $k \geq 2$, there is an equivalent $\{\vee, \wedge, \neg\}$-formula C', such that $depth(C') \leq (3k \ln 2) \cdot \log m$, and $leafsize(C') \leq m^\alpha$, where $\alpha = 1 + \frac{1}{1+\log(k-1)}$.

Consider a highly unbalanced C of size m. Direct application of our reduction costs $\Theta(m^3)$, more than BP based approaches [17,18,19] of cost $O(m^2)$. Rebalancing C as above, even suboptimally setting $k = 9$, results in a formula C' of size $m^{1.25}$ and depth $\approx 18.5 \log m$. Applying the reduction to C' yields a much better cost $O(m^{1.25} \log^2 m)$. An optimal (w.r.t. the cost of the GESS reduction) choice of k or better rebalancing will further improve our (but not BP's) performance.

2.5   Lower Bounds for GESS – The Optimality of Our Constructions

Let $i, j \in \{0, 1\}$. Denote by A_i (resp. B_i) the random variable of the share corresponding to the wire value i of the first (resp. second) input wire. Denote by S_{ij} the random variable of the secret corresponding to the gate output value $G(i, j)$. Let $H(\cdot)$ be Shannon entropy. We start with proving a technical lemma.

Lemma 1. *For any GESS scheme implementing a gate with binary inputs,*
$$H(A_i) + H(B_j) \geq H(S_{i(1-j)}|B_{1-j}) + H(S_{(1-i)j}|A_{1-i}) + H(S_{ij}|S_{i(1-j)}S_{(1-i)j}S_{(1-i)(1-j)}).$$

Proof. For simplicity, prove the lemma for $i = j = 0$, i.e that $H(A_0) + H(B_0) \geq H(S_{01}|B_1) + H(S_{10}|A_1) + H(S_{00}|S_{01}S_{10}S_{11})$. Other cases are analogous.

First, since $H(S_{01}|A_0 B_1) = 0$, and using the chain rule twice, obtain $H(A_0|B_1) = H(A_0 S_{01}|B_1) - H(S_{01}|A_0 B_1) = H(A_0 S_{01}|B_1) = H(S_{01}|B_1) + H(A_0|B_1 S_{01})$. Similarly, $H(B_0|A_1) = H(S_{10}|A_1) + H(B_0|A_1 S_{10})$.

By definition, A_1, B_1 do not reveal anything about S_{00} (other than what's implied by S_{11}), and, further, A_0, B_0 recover S_{00}. Then $H(S_{00}|S_{01}S_{10}S_{11}) \leq H(S_{00}|A_1 B_1 S_{01} S_{10}) \leq H(A_0 B_0|A_1 B_1 S_{01} S_{10}) \leq H(A_0|A_1 B_1 S_{01} S_{10}) + H(B_0|A_1 B_1 S_{01} S_{10}) \leq H(A_0|B_1 S_{01}) + H(B_0|A_1 S_{10})$.

Thus, $H(A_0) + H(B_0) \geq H(A_0|B_1) + H(B_0|A_1) \geq H(S_{01}|B_1) + H(A_0|B_1 S_{01}) + H(S_{10}|A_1) + H(B_0|A_1 S_{10}) \geq H(S_{01}|B_1) + H(S_{10}|A_1) + H(S_{00}|S_{01}S_{10}S_{11})$.   □

Because all shares corresponding to the same wire must be distributed identically (Observation 2), their entropies must be equal. Thus Lemma 1 implies that $\forall i_1, i_2 \in \{0, 1\} : H(A_{i_1}) + H(B_{i_2}) \geq MAX_{i,j \in \{0,1\}}(H(S_{i(1-j)}|B_{1-j}) + H(S_{(1-i)j}|A_{1-i}) + H(S_{ij}|S_{i(1-j)}S_{(1-i)j}S_{(1-i)(1-j)}))$.

Consider non-trivial gates – those that depend on both (binary) inputs. Note that the gate output need not be binary. We show the optimality of constructions for the natural case when the secrets are drawn independently at random from the same domain (with only the restrictions of secrets equality imposed by the semantics of G). In that case, by Observation 2, $H(S_{i(1-j)}|B_{1-j}) = H(S_{i(1-j)})$ and $H(S_{(1-i)j}|A_{1-i}) = H(S_{(1-i)j})$. Consider the two possible cases.

Case 1: there exist gate inputs i, j, s.t. $G(i, j)$ is not equal to the gate value on any other inputs. This is the case for most non-trivial gates (including AND and OR). In this case, $H(S_{ij}|S_{i(1-j)}S_{(1-i)j}S_{(1-i)(1-j)}) = H(S_{ij})$ and thus $\forall i_1, i_2 \in \{0, 1\} : H(A_{i_1}) + H(B_{i_2}) \geq H(S_{i(1-j)}) + H(S_{(1-i)j}) + H(S_{ij})$. This matches (within 1 bit) the upper bound given by Constr. 2.

Case 2: such i, j don't exist. Then the only non-trivial gates are XOR and ¬ XOR. GESS of Constr. 4 implements XOR and matches the lower bound of $H(S_{i(1-j)}) + H(S_{(1-i)j})$ for this case.

Construction 4. *(GESS ensemble for XOR gates.) Let $SEC = \{0, 1\}^n$ and $TSEC = SEC^2$ be the secrets domains. Let the secrets tuple $\langle s_0, s_1 \rangle \in TSEC$ be given. The domains of shares are set as follows: $SH_1 = SH_2 = SEC$.*

Shr chooses $R \in_R SEC$ and sets $sh_{10} = R, sh_{11} = s_0 \oplus s_1 \oplus R, sh_{20} = s_0 \oplus R, sh_{21} = s_1 \oplus R$.

Rec proceeds as follows. On input sh_1, sh_2, Rec outputs $sh_1 \oplus sh_2$.

Theorem 4. *For each $n \in \mathbb{N}$, Constr. 4 is a GESS as defined by Def. 1.*

The proof of Thm. 4 is very simple and is omitted.
In conclusion, for the shares A_i and B_j of the two input wires, we proved

Theorem 5. *For every GESS scheme implementing an OR or an AND gate, when all secrets are chosen at random from the same domain SEC and each has entropy H_S, $\forall i,j \in \{0,1\}$: $H(A_i) + H(B_j) \geq 3H_S$.*

Of course, the entropy of each share must be at least H_S. Then all possible gates with two binary inputs are (almost) optimally implemented by either Constr. 2 or 4. Our Constr. 3 beats the above lower bound by exploiting common informa-tion among secrets. We leave open the question of exact lower bounds for this interesting case. We stress that the share-size-to-secret-size ratio approaching 1, achieved by Constr. 3, is "near optimal".

2.6   Application of GESS: Efficient Practical Two Millionaires

We apply the GESS approach to give a new efficient solution to the two mil-lionaires problem. We design a GESS scheme for a new type of gate and use it to compute the Greater Than (GT) predicate. We use the intuitive circuit C (below) that compares bits of the parties' inputs x and y, starting with the most significant, and sets the answer bit when it encounters the difference.

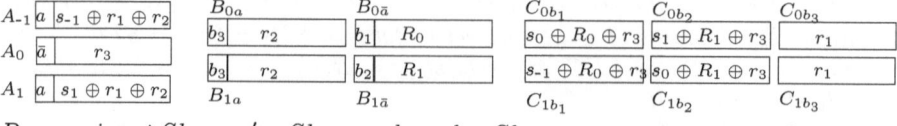

$$\text{where } T(j, x_i, y_i) = \begin{cases} j, & \text{if } j \in \{-1, 1\}, \\ -1, & \text{if } j = 0 \wedge x_i < y_i, \\ 0, & \text{if } j = 0 \wedge x_i = y_i, \\ 1, & \text{if } j = 0 \wedge x_i > y_i. \end{cases}$$

Here j is ternary input and x_i and y_i are bits. It is easy to see that C indeed computes GT: once a ternary wire is set to -1 or 1, that value is propagated to the output wire. We aim to minimize the expansion of the share corresponding to the input j. Note the double application of permute and point in Constr. 5.

Construction 5. *(GESS ensemble for T-gates.) Let $SEC = \{0,1\}^n$ and $TSEC = SEC^3$ be the secrets domains. Let the secrets tuple $\langle s_{-1}, s_0, s_1 \rangle \in TSEC$ is given. The domains of shares are set as follows: $SH_1 = \{0,1\} \times SEC$, $SH_2 = (\{0,1\}^2 \times SEC)^2$ and $SH_3 = SEC^3$.*

Shr chooses $R_0, R_1, r_1, r_2, r_3 \in_R SEC$, $a \in_R \{0,1\}$ and $b = \{b_1, b_2, b_3\}$ - a random permutation of $\{0,1,2\}$, where each b_i is suitably represented by 2 bits. Shr sets the shares $sh_{1i} = A_i$, $sh_{2i} = \langle B_{i0}, B_{i1} \rangle$, $sh_{3i} = \langle C_{i0}, C_{i1}, C_{i2} \rangle$, as shown on the following diagram.

A_{-1}	a	$s_{-1} \oplus r_1 \oplus r_2$
A_0	$\bar{a}$	r_3
A_1	a	$s_1 \oplus r_1 \oplus r_2$

B_{0a}		
b_3	r_2	
b_3	r_2	
	B_{1a}	

$B_{0\bar{a}}$		
b_1	R_0	
b_2	R_1	
	$B_{1\bar{a}}$	

C_{0b_1}	C_{0b_2}	C_{0b_3}
$s_0 \oplus R_0 \oplus r_3$	$s_1 \oplus R_1 \oplus r_3$	r_1
$s_{-1} \oplus R_0 \oplus r_3$	$s_0 \oplus R_1 \oplus r_3$	r_1
C_{1b_1}	C_{1b_2}	C_{1b_3}

Rec, on input $Sh_1 = a'r$, $Sh_2 = p_0\,b_0\,p_1\,b_1$, $Sh_3 = c_0c_1c_2$, outputs $r \oplus b_{a'} \oplus c_{p_{a'}}$.

Theorem 6. *For each $n \in \mathbb{N}$, Constr. 5 is a GESS as defined by Def. 1.*

Proof. (Sketch): Correctness of the scheme is easily verified. The simulator $Sim(s)$ chooses random $\alpha \in_R \{0,1\}, r'_0, ..., r'_4 \in_R SEC, \beta_0, \beta_1 \in_R \{0,1,2\}$, where $\beta_0 \neq \beta_1$. Let β'_i be suitable 2-bit representations of β_i. Sim outputs shares $\langle (\alpha r'_2), (\beta'_0 r'_0 \beta'_1 r'_1), (\gamma_0 \gamma_1 \gamma_2) \rangle$, where $\gamma_{\beta_\alpha} = s \oplus r'_2 \oplus r'_\alpha$, and the other two γ_i are assigned r'_3 and r'_4. The proof of equality of the generated distribution to the real execution is similar to that of previous two theorems, and is omitted.   □

Performance. Let n be the length in bits of the compared numbers. The secrets corresponding to the T-gate at level i are of length i, and thus the secrets corresponding to the corresponding x_i and y_i are of lengths $3i$ and $2i+4$. Thus, Bob needs to send $\sum_{i=1..n} 3i = 1.5n(n+1)$ bits and perform n 1-out of-2 OT's with secrets of sizes $2 + 4, ..., 2n + 4$.

The asymptotic complexity of this GT solution is worse than that of the best currently known for either setting with limited Alice (Yao's approach, see, e.g. [24]) or unlimited Alice [5,13]. Still, our solution performs better for comparing smaller numbers ($n \approx 60..70$), since we do not use encryption[3].

We note that a reduction with a complexity similar to ours (quadratic) can be obtained by using BP-based techniques of [19].

3   Extension to Evaluating Polysize Circuits

When Alice is assumed to be polynomially bounded, all polytime computable functions can be efficiently evaluated. Beaver, Micali and Rogaway [3,25], Naor, Pinkas and Sumner [24] and Lindell and Pinkas [21] suggested one-round protocols following Yao's [27] garbled circuit approach.

As discussed, the OT reduction does not allow polytime evaluation of general polysize circuits, due to the exponential growth of combined secrets size for each level of general circuits. We now informally describe a natural extension that handles this problem in the standard model. This demonstrates the generality and applicability of the GESS approach. The resulting solution is conceptually very clean, although slightly less efficient than the best known approach.

The protocol is essentially Constr. 1, with the following amendment. Bob will not propagate the secrets "up the circuit". Instead, for a gate G with output wires $w_1, ..., w_n$ and their (already computed) corresponding secrets tuples $(s_0^1, s_1^1), ..., (s_0^n, s_1^n)$, he encrypts all the secrets corresponding to each gate value *together*. More formally, he chooses two random keys k', k'' of a semantically secure private-key encryption scheme E. He computes $e_0 = E_{k'}(\langle s_0^1, ..., s_0^n \rangle), e_1 = E_{k''}(\langle s_1^1, ..., s_0^n \rangle)$ and assigns G's labels to be a random permutation of e_0, e_1. He then treats the keys as the secrets to be propagated, letting k' and k'' correspond to wire values 0 and 1 respectively. When Bob is done, he will have

---

[3] This advantage is minute with standard (public-key primitive based) OT implementations; it may be significant in other settings.

assigned secrets to each of the input wires and associated labels with each of the gates. He sends the secrets to Alice as before, additionally sending her the gate labels.

Alice obtains the secret shares for the input wires and proceeds evaluation similarly to the previous solution. The difference now is that, after having recovered a gate's secret (which is the key for one of the associated encryptions), she decrypts the corresponding encryption to recover the outgoing wires' secrets. To ensure that only one decryption succeeds, we impose an additional requirement on the encryption scheme. Informally, we need the ranges of encryptions under different keys be distinct, and that Alice is able to tell which decryption succeeded. This is a rather weak requirement, satisfied, for example, by schemes with *elusive* and *efficiently verifiable* ranges, formalized in [21]. Alice then uses the recovered secrets as shares in computing the child gate's secrets, and so on. Finally, she outputs the value of the output wire.

Theorem 7. *The above construction securely (against computationally unlimited Bob and limited Alice) reduces SFE of polysize circuits to OT, in the semihonest model.*

The proof of the theorem is rather intuitive and is presented in Appendix E.

The performance of the resulting approach is very similar to that of the currently best known solutions (e.g. [21,24]). Indeed, our wire secrets are of the same size as theirs, and thus the only difference in performance is caused by the size of the gate labels. In [24], each gate has four labels of size N each[4], where N is the security parameter. It is easy to see that each gate of our solution adds up to $6N$ bits to the collection of all gate labels (two secrets of length N expand into two shares of length $N+1$ and two shares of length $2N$, which then are encrypted and stored as labels.). Some optimization of this number is also possible. For example, we need not encrypt (and thus add the corresponding labels) for the secrets that are just larger than N. This can reduce the gate induced label size gate by up to $2N$ bits.

We further note that in our scheme we only need to use encryptions once the secret sizes grow too large (i.e some threshold larger than encryption keys). Thus our method improves the performance of the evaluation of "the bottom part" of every circuit, and can be combined with Yao's garbled circuit implementations.

Acknowledgements. The author is very grateful to Ian F. Blake, Steven Myers, Berry Schoenmakers, and, most of all, to Charles Rackoff for many criticisms and insightful discussions both on the content and presentation of this work. Special thanks to Yuval Ishai for critically reading earlier versions of this paper and for pointing out a lot of related work and interesting applications. Finally, thanks to all referees of this paper for their comments and suggestions. This research was partially supported by Ontario Graduate Scholarship (OGS).

---

[4] The authors also mention an optimization that allows using only three labels.

References

1. Joy Algesheimer, Christian Cachin, Jan Camenisch, and Gunter Karjoth. Cryptographic security for mobile code. In *SP '01: Proceedings of the IEEE Symposium on Security and Privacy*, page 2. IEEE Computer Society, 2001.
2. D A Barrington. Bounded-width polynomial-size branching programs recognize exactly those languages in NC^1. In *Proc. 18th ACM Symp. on Theory of Computing*, pages 1–5, New York, NY, USA, 1986. ACM Press.
3. D. Beaver, S. Micali, and P. Rogaway. The round complexity of secure protocols. In *Proc. 22nd ACM Symp. on Theory of Computing*, pages 503–513, 1990.
4. Donald Beaver. Minimal-latency secure function evaluation. In *Proc. EUROCRYPT 2000*, pages 335–350. Springer, 2000. Lecture Notes in Computer Science, vol. 1807.
5. Ian F. Blake and Vladimir Kolesnikov. Strong conditional oblivious transfer and computing on intervals. In *Proc. ASIACRYPT 2004*, pages 515–529, 2004.
6. Maria Luisa Bonet and Samuel R. Buss. Size-depth tradeoff for boolean formulae. *Information Processing Letters*, 11(1994):151–155.
7. N. H. Bshouty, R. Cleve, and W. Eberly. Size-depth tradeoffs for algebraic formulae. In *Proc. 32nd IEEE Symp. on Foundations of Comp. Science*, pages 334–341. IEEE, 1991.
8. Christian Cachin, Jan Camenisch, Joe Kilian, and Joy Muller. One-round secure computation and secure autonomous mobile agents. In *Proceedings of the 27th International Colloquium on Automata, Languages and Programming*, 2000.
9. R. Cleve. Towards optimal simulations of formulas by bounded-width programs. In *STOC '90: Proceedings of the twenty-second annual ACM symposium on Theory of computing*, pages 271–277, New York, NY, USA, 1990. ACM Press.
10. Ronald Cramer, Serge Fehr, Yuval Ishai, and Eyal Kushilevitz. Efficient multiparty computation over rings. In *EUROCRYPT*, pages 596–613, 2003.
11. Uri Feige, Joe Killian, and Moni Naor. A minimal model for secure computation (extended abstract). In *Proc. 26th ACM Symp. on Theory of Computing*, pages 554–563. ACM Press, 1994.
12. Pesech Feldman and Silvio Micali. An optimal probabilistic protocol for synchronous byzantine agreement. *SIAM J. Comput.*, 26(4):873–933, 1997.
13. Marc Fischlin. A cost-effective pay-per-multiplication comparison method for millionaires. In *RSA Security 2001 Cryptographer's Track*, pages 457–471. Springer-Verlag, 2001. Lecture Notes in Computer Science, vol. 2020.
14. Oliver Giel. Branching program size is almost linear in formula size. *J. Comput. Syst. Sci.*, 63(2):222–235, 2001.
15. Oded Goldreich. *Foundations of Cryptography: Volume 2, Basic Applications*. Cambridge University Press, 2004.
16. Oded Goldreich and Ronen Vainish. How to solve any protocol problem - an efficiency improvement. In *CRYPTO '87: A Conference on the Theory and Applications of Cryptographic Techniques on Advances in Cryptology*, pages 73–86, London, UK, 1988. Springer-Verlag.
17. Yuval Ishai and Eyal Kushilevitz. Private simultaneous messages protocols with applications. In *ISTCS '97: Proceedings of the Fifth Israel Symposium on the Theory of Computing Systems (ISTCS '97)*, page 174, Washington, DC, USA, 1997. IEEE Computer Society.
18. Yuval Ishai and Eyal Kushilevitz. Randomizing polynomials: A new representation with applications to round-efficient secure computation. In *Proc. 41th IEEE Symp. on Foundations of Comp. Science*, page 294. IEEE Computer Society, 2000.

19. Yuval Ishai and Eyal Kushilevitz. Perfect constant-round secure computation via perfect randomizing polynomials. In *ICALP*, pages 244–256, 2002.
20. J. Kilian. Founding cryptography on oblivious transfer. In *Proc. 20th ACM Symp. on Theory of Computing*, pages 20–31, Chicago, 1988. ACM.
21. Yehuda Lindell and Benny Pinkas.   A proof of Yao's protocol for secure two-party computation.   Cryptology ePrint Archive, Report 2004/175, 2004. http://eprint.iacr.org/.
22. Moni Naor and Kobbi Nissim. Communication preserving protocols for secure function evaluation. In *STOC '01: Proceedings of the thirty-third annual ACM symposium on Theory of computing*, pages 590–599, New York, NY, USA, 2001. ACM Press.
23. Moni Naor and Benny Pinkas. Distributed oblivious transfer. In *Proc. ASI-ACRYPT 2000*, volume 1976, pages 200–219. Springer-Verlag, 2000. Lecture Notes in Computer Science, vol. 293.
24. Moni Naor, Benny Pinkas, and Reuben Sumner. Privacy preserving auctions and mechanism design. In *1st ACM Conf. on Electronic Commerce*, pages 129–139, 1999.
25. Phillip Rogaway. *The round complexity of secure protocols*. PhD thesis, MIT, 1991.
26. Tomas Sander, Adam Young, and Moti Yung. Non-interactive cryptocomputing for NC^1. In *Proceedings 40th IEEE Symposium on Foundations of Computer Science*, pages 554–566, New York, 1999. IEEE.
27. A. C. Yao. How to generate and exchange secrets. In *Proc. 27th IEEE Symp. on Foundations of Comp. Science*, pages 162–167, Toronto, 1986. IEEE.

A   The General Definition of GESS

We give a general definition of a GESS scheme that allows to share a tuple of secrets. Let G be a gate with k inputs from domain $D_I = D_{I_1} \times \ldots \times D_{I_k}$ and one output from domain D_O. We also denote by $G : D_I \mapsto D_O$ the function computed by gate G. Let SEC be the domain of secrets and $TSEC \subset SEC^{|D_O|}$ be the domain of tuples of secrets to be shared. For simplicity of presentation and without loss of generality, assume that all domains D_{I_i} and D_O are initial sequences of non-negative numbers, e.g. $D_{I_1} = \{0, 1, 2, \ldots, |D_{I_1}| - 1\}$.

Definition 2. *(Gate evaluation Secret Sharing) A gate evaluation secret sharing scheme (GESS) for evaluating G (we also say GESS implementing G) is a pair of algorithms (Shr, Rec) (with implicitly defined secrets domain SEC, secrets tuples domain $TSEC$, k share domains $SH_1, \ldots, SH_k$ and k share tuples domains $TSH_1, \ldots, TSH_k$), such that the following holds.*

The probabilistic share generation algorithm Shr takes as input a $d_O = |D_O|$-tuple of secrets
$\langle s_0, \ldots, s_{d_O-1} \rangle \in TSEC$ *and outputs a sequence of k tuples of shares, where the i-th tuple $t_i \in TSH_i$ consists of $|D_{I_i}|$ shares $sh_{ij} \in SH_i$. The deterministic share reconstruction algorithm Rec takes as input a sequence of k elements $sh_i \in SH_i$, one from each domain, and outputs $s \in SEC$.*

Let $b = \langle b_1, \ldots, b_k \rangle \in D_I$ be a selection vector. Define the selection function $Sel(\langle sh_{10}, \ldots, sh_{1|D_{I_1}|-1} \rangle, \ldots, \langle sh_{k0}, \ldots, sh_{k|D_{I_k}|-1} \rangle, b) = \{sh_{1b_1}, \ldots, sh_{kb_k}\}$.
Shr and Rec satisfy the following conditions:

- *correctness: for all random inputs of Shr and secrets tuples $\langle s_0, ..., s_{d_O-1} \rangle \in TSEC, \forall b \in D_I, Rec(Sel(Shr(\langle s_0, ..., s_{d_O-1} \rangle), b)) = s_{G(b)}$*
- *privacy (selected shares contain no information other than the value $s_{G(b)}$): There exists a simulator Sim, such that $\forall \langle s_0, ..., s_{d_O-1} \rangle \in TSEC$ and any $b \in D_I$: $Sim(s_{G(b)}) \equiv Sel(Shr(\langle s_0, ..., s_{d_O-1} \rangle), b)$*

B Proof of Theorem 1

Proof. (Sketch): Security against Bob is trivial since he does not receive any messages. The intuition for the scheme's security against Alice is that none of the GESS implementations leak any information. To prove security, we show how to construct Sim_A, perfectly simulating the following ensemble (view of Alice): $VIEW_A(x, a) = \{x, m_{OT}, m\}$, where x and a are Alice's input and output, m_{OT} is the sequence of messages received from the OT oracles and m is the message received from Bob directly.

Sim_A first simulates wire secrets assignment as follows. He starts with the output wire, assigns its value to be a, and proceeds through gates from the bottom up as follows. Given gate G, its $GESS_G$, simulator Sim_G, and G's output wire value v, Sim_A assigns values to G's input wires according to $Sim_G(v)$.

Eventually, Sim_A assigns secrets to all input wires of C. Sim_A outputs $\{x, m'_{OT}, m'\}$, where x is Alice's input, m'_{OT} and m' are (proper representations of) the sequences of C's input wires assignments corresponding to Alice and to Bob respectively.

It is intuitive that the proposed simulator perfectly simulates Alice's view. Indeed, the vector of inputs to C defines a value assignment to each wire of the circuit, which, in turn, defines a distribution on shares/secrets obtained (received or computed) by Alice for each wire. We prove that wire assignment of Sim_A perfectly simulates the obtained secret for each wire. It is clear that Sim_A perfectly assigns the secret corresponding to the output wire by setting it to the output of the computation he obtained as its input. Further, Sim_A assigns secrets to the input wires of the output gate G. These secrets are distributed identically to the secrets that Alice reconstructs for these wires, because of the perfect simulation of Sim_G. Proceeding upward to the input wires, it is clear that Sim_A perfectly simulates all the wire assignments that Alice sees and reconstructs in the real execution.   □

C The General Construction of GESS for AND/OR Gates

Construction 6. *(Improved GESS for gates with two binary inputs.)* Let $D = \{0,1\}^k$ and $SEC = D^n$. Let secrets $s_{00}, ..., s_{11} \in SEC$ consist of n blocks of length k, and differ only in the j-th block. That is, let

$$s_{00} = (\quad t_1 \quad ... \quad t_{j-1} \quad t_j^{00} \quad t_{j+1} \quad ... \quad t_n \quad),$$
$$...$$
$$s_{11} = (\quad t_1 \quad ... \quad t_{j-1} \quad t_j^{11} \quad t_{j+1} \quad ... \quad t_n \quad),$$

where $\forall i = 1..n$: $t_i, t_j^{00}, t_j^{01}, t_j^{10}, t_j^{11} \in D$, and the index j is determined only by the secrets. Let $TSEC \subset SEC^4$ be the space of all tuples of the above form.

Shr chooses $R_1, ... R_n, R_j' \in_R D$ and a random permutation[5] $\pi : \{1..n+1\} \mapsto \{1..n+1\}$. Let $\tau = \pi^{-1}$ be the inverse of π. For $m \in \{0,1\}$, Shr sets the shares $sh_{1m} = \langle B_{m1}, ..., B_{mn} \rangle$ and $sh_{2m} = \langle C_{m1}, ..., C_{mn+1} \rangle$, as shown on the following diagram.

B_{01}	B_{0j}	B_{0n}
$\pi(1)R_1$	$\pi(j)R_j$	$\pi(n)R_n$

B_{11}	B_{1j}	B_{1n}
$\pi(1)R_1$	$\pi(n+1)R_j'$	$\pi(n)R_n$

C_{01}	$C_{0\pi(j)}$	$C_{0\pi(n+1)}$	C_{0n+1}
$R_{\tau(1)} \oplus t_{\tau(1)}$	$R_j \oplus t_j^{00}$	$R_j' \oplus t_j^{10}$	$R_{\tau(n+1)} \oplus t_{\tau(n+1)}$

C_{11}	$C_{1\pi(j)}$	$C_{1\pi(n+1)}$	C_{1n+1}
$R_{\tau(1)} \oplus t_{\tau(1)}$	$R_j \oplus t_j^{01}$	$R_j' \oplus t_j^{11}$	$R_{\tau(n+1)} \oplus t_{\tau(n+1)}$

More specifically, the blocks of both shares of the first wire will be assigned $R_1, ..., R_n$, with the exception of the jth block of the share corresponding to 1, which will be assigned R_j'. Shr then, for all i, prepends $\pi(i)$ to the ith block of both shares of the first wire, with the exception of the jth block of the second share, which gets prepended $\pi(n+1)$.

Each $\pi(i)$-th block of both shares of the second wire will be set to $R_i \oplus t_i$, with the exception of blocks $\pi(j), \pi(n+1)$. Those blocks assignment is motivated by Construction 2. Specifically, we set the $\pi(j)$-th block of the share corresponding to 0 to $R_j \oplus t_j^{00}$ and that block of the share corresponding to 1 – to $R_j \oplus t_j^{01}$. We set the $\pi(n+1)$-st block of the share corresponding to 0 to $R_j' \oplus t_j^{10}$ and that block of the share corresponding to 1 – to $R_j' \oplus t_j^{11}$. This completes the description of Shr.

Rec proceeds as follows. He obtains two shares $sh_1 = (ind_1, r_1, ..., ind_n, r_n)$ and $sh_2 = (a_1, ..., a_{n+1})$. He reconstructs the secret $s = (\sigma_1, ..., \sigma_n)$ by setting $\sigma_i = r_i \oplus a_{ind_i}$.

Theorem 8. For each $n, k, j \in \mathbb{N}$, Construction 6 is a GESS scheme as defined by Def. 1. (Note that security and correctness hold w.r.t. $TSEC$.)

Proof. (Sketch): The correctness of the reconstruction is easily verifiable. To prove security, we construct a simulator $Sim(s)$. On input $s = \sigma_1, ..., \sigma_n$, $Sim(s)$ does the following. He chooses random $r_1', ..., r_{n+1}' \in_R D$ and a random permutation $\rho : \{1..n+1\} \mapsto \{1..n+1\}$. He outputs the shares $sh_1 = (\rho(1)r_1', ..., \rho(n)r_n')$ and $sh_2 = (\sigma_{\rho^{-1}(1)} \oplus r_{\rho^{-1}(1)}', ..., \sigma_{\rho^{-1}(n+1)} \oplus r_{\rho^{-1}(n+1)}')$

We now prove that Sim perfectly simulates the real-life generated shares. The first share is distributed identically to both of the real-life generated shares of the first vector. Indeed, each r_i is distributed identically to each R_i, R_j and R_j' and $\rho(1), ..., \rho(n)$ is distributed identically to $\pi(1), ..., \pi(n)$ and to $\pi(1), ..., \pi(j-1), \pi(n+1), \pi(j+1), ..., \pi(n)$, for any j.

As for the second share, all blocks (and their positions) are generated identically to the real execution, with the exception of blocks in positions $\rho(j)$ and $\rho(n+1)$. Proof of the equality of their distribution to the corresponding blocks of the real distribution closely follows that of Construction 2 and is omitted. □

---

[5] This permutation specifies which block of the second tuple is XOR'ed with the ith block of the first tuple to obtain the ith block of the reconstructed secret.

D   Case Analysis for the Proof of Theorem 2

Proof. (Sketch): We need to consider the four possible combinations of gate input values $i_1, i_2 \in \{0, 1\}$. We show that Sim perfectly simulates the corresponding truly generated shares. Denote random variables $\langle sh_1, sh_2 \rangle = \langle b'r, a_0a_1 \rangle = Sel(Shr(s_{00}, ..., s_{11}), \langle i_1, i_2 \rangle)$. We write out only one case; others are analogous.

Case $i_1 = 0, i_2 = 0$. Thus $s = s_{G(0,0)}$.
Correctness: If $b = 0$, then $b' = 0, sh_1 = 0R_0, sh_2 = (s_{00} \oplus R_0, s_{10} \oplus R_1)$. $Rec(sh_1, sh_2) = R_0 \oplus (s_{00} \oplus R_0) = s_{00} = s$. If $b = 1$, then $b' = 1, sh_1 = 1R_0, sh_2 = (s_{10} \oplus R_1, s_{00} \oplus R_0)$. $Rec(sh_1, sh_2) = R_0 \oplus (s_{00} \oplus R_0) = s_{00} = s$.
Security: Clearly, $Sim(s)$ perfectly simulates sh_1. Further, sh_2 consists of two blocks $B_{00} = s \oplus R_0$ and $B_{10} = s_{10} \oplus R_1$. Observe that $B_{10} = s_{10} \oplus R_1$ is distributed uniformly randomly on SEC (since R_1 is random on SEC and secret). Therefore, sh_2 consists of two blocks from SEC, where one block is random on SEC and the other is equal to $s \oplus R_0$, where the non-random block is pointed by the bit b' of sh_1, Therefore $Sim(s)$ also perfectly simulates sh_2 and the pair $\langle sh_1, sh_2 \rangle$, since d is distributed identically to b'. □

E   Proof of Theorem 7

Proof. (Sketch): The reduction is trivially secure against Bob, since he does not receive any messages from Alice. To prove security against Alice, we will show how to simulate the input wires' secrets and gate labels that Bob sends to Alice, given the output of the computation. We present the proof for binary fan-in 2 circuits; a more general argument is readily obtained by natural generalization.

The simulator $Sim(x, b)$ proceeds as follows. First, it (perfectly) simulates the secret of the output wire by s.

Then, for each level of the circuit, starting from the bottom, for each gate G of the current level: given the (previously simulated) G's output wires' secrets $s_0, ..., s_{k-1}$, it simulates G's input wires' secrets and gate labels as follows. It chooses two random keys s', s'' from the key domain of the employed encryption scheme. Then it computes $e_0 = Enc_{s'}(\langle s_0, ..., s_{k-1} \rangle), e_1 = Enc_{s''}(\langle 0, ..., 0 \rangle)$ and assigns G's labels to be a random permutation of e_0, e_1. Then Sim runs the the simulator $S_G(s')$ of the secret sharing scheme of G. The simulator $S_G(s')$ produces two shares (distributed identically to real execution), each of which is the simulation of the secret of the corresponding wire.

Sim runs the above procedure on C "from the bottom up", and eventually obtains the simulations of the input wires and gate labels, which he outputs, suitably formatted.

We note the true randomness of all encryption keys and the perfect simulations of secret sharing schemes. Intuitively, the only way for an adversary to distinguish the simulation from the real execution is by distinguishing the sets of non-decrypted gate labels. However, learning anything "substantial" that way would mean breaking the semantic security of the employed encryption scheme, which can be shown by a simple hybrid argument. □

Parallel Multi-party Computation from Linear Multi-secret Sharing Schemes*

Zhifang Zhang[1], Mulan Liu[1,**], and Liangliang Xiao[2]

[1] Academy of Mathematics and Systems Science,
Key Laboratory of Mathematics Mechanization,
Chinese Academy of Sciences,
Beijing, 100080, China
{zfz, mlliu}@amss.ac.cn
[2] Institute of Software, Chinese Academy of Sciences,
Beijing, 100080, China
xllemail2004@yahoo.com.cn

Abstract. As an extension of multi-party computation (MPC), we propose the concept of secure parallel multi-party computation which is to securely compute multi-functions against an adversary with multi-structures. Precisely, there are m functions $f_1, ..., f_m$ and m adversary structures $\mathcal{A}_1, ..., \mathcal{A}_m$, where f_i is required to be securely computed against an $\mathcal{A}_i$-adversary. We give a general construction to build a parallel multi-party computation protocol from any linear multi-secret sharing scheme (LMSSS), provided that the access structures of the LMSSS allow MPC at all. When computing complicated functions, our protocol has more advantage in communication complexity than the "direct sum" method which actually executes a MPC protocol for each function. The paper also provides an efficient and generic construction to obtain from any LMSSS a multiplicative LMSSS for the same multi-access structure.

1 Introduction

The secure multi-party computation (MPC) protocol is used for n players to jointly compute an agreed function of their private inputs in a secure way, where security means guaranteeing the correctness of the output and the privacy of the players' inputs, even when some players cheat. It is fundamental in cryptography and distributed computation, because a solution of MPC problem implies in principle a solution to any cryptographic protocol problem, such as the voting problem, blind signature, and so on. After it was proposed by Yao [11] for two-party case and Goldreich, Micali, Wigderson [6] for multi-party case, it has become an active and developing field of information security.

In the MPC problem, it is common to model cheating by considering an adversary who may corrupt some subset of the players. The collection of all subsets

---

* Supported by the National Natural Science Foundation of China (No. 90304012, 90204016), 973 project (No. 2004CB318000).
** Corresponding author.

B. Roy (Ed.): ASIACRYPT 2005, LNCS 3788, pp. 156–173, 2005.

that an adversary may corrupt is called the *adversary structure*, denoted by $\mathcal{A}$, and this adversary is called an $\mathcal{A}$-adversary. So the MPC problem is to securely compute a function with respect to an adversary structure. But in practice it is sometimes needed to simultaneously compute several different functions with respect to different adversary structures, respectively. For example, in the voting problem $n = 2t+1$ $(t > 1)$ voters are to select a chairman and several fellows for a committee at the same time from m candidates. Because the position of the chairman is more important than that of fellows, the voting for the chairman is required to be secure against a (t, n) threshold adversary, while the voting for the fellows is required to be secure against a $(2, n)$ threshold adversary. Hence it makes us to propose *parallel multi-party computation* or extend MPC to parallel MPC. Precisely, in the problem of parallel multi-party computation, there are m functions $f_1, ..., f_m$ and m adversary structures $\mathcal{A}_1, ..., \mathcal{A}_m$, where f_i is required to be securely computed against an $\mathcal{A}_i$-adversary.

Obviously, secure parallel multi-party computation can be realized by designing for each function a MPC protocol with respect to the corresponding adversary structure, and then running all the protocols in a composite way. We call this the "direct sum" method. In this paper, we propose another way to realize parallel multi-party computation. It is well known that secret sharing schemes are elementary tool for studying MPC. Cramer, Damgard, Maurer [3] gave a generic and efficient construction to build a MPC protocol from any linear secret sharing scheme (LSSS). As an extension of secret sharing schemes, Blundo, De Santis, Di Crescenzo [2] proposed the general concept of *multi-secret sharing schemes* which is to share multi-secrets with respect to multi-access structures, and Ding, Laihonen, Renvall. [4] studied linear multi-secret sharing schemes. Based on Xiao and Liu's work [10] about linear multi-secret sharing schemes (LMSSS) and the construction in [3], we give a generic and efficient construction to build a parallel multi-party computation protocol from any LMSSS, provided that the access structures of the LMSSS allow MPC at all [7]. We only deal with *adaptive, passive* adversaries in the *information theoretic model*. When computing complicated functions, our protocol has more advantage in communication complexity than the "direct sum" method.

The paper is organized as follows: in Section 2 we review some basic concepts, such as LSSS, monotone span programs (MSP) and LMSSS. In Section 3 we give a clear description for the problem of secure parallel multi-party computation, and then obtain a generic protocol for it from any LMSSS. Furthermore we compare our protocol with the "direct sum" method in communication complexity. In the last section, a specific example is displayed in detail to show how our protocol works as well as its advantage.

2   Preliminaries

Since secret sharing schemes are our primary tool, first we review some basic concepts and results about them, such as linear secret sharing schemes, multi-secret sharing schemes, monotone span programs, and so on. Suppose that $P = \{P_1, ..., P_n\}$ is the set of participants and $\mathcal{K}$ is a finite field throughout this paper.

2.1 LSSS vs MSP

It is well-known that an access structure, denoted by AS, is a collection of subsets of P satisfying the monotone ascending property: for any $A' \in AS$ and $A \in 2^P$ with $A' \subset A$, it holds that $A \in AS$; and an adversary structure, denoted by $\mathcal{A}$, is a collection of subsets of P satisfying the monotone descending property: for any $A' \in \mathcal{A}$ and $A \in 2^P$ with $A \subset A'$, it holds that $A \in \mathcal{A}$. In this paper, we consider the complete situation, i.e. $\mathcal{A} = 2^P - AS$. Because of the monotone property, for any access structure AS it is enough to consider the *minimum access structure* AS_m defined as $AS_m = \{A \in AS \mid \forall B \subsetneqq A \Rightarrow B \notin AS\}$.

Suppose that S is the secret-domain, R is the set of random inputs, and S_i is the share-domain of P_i where $1 \le i \le n$. A secret sharing scheme with respect to an access structure AS is composed of the distribution function $\Pi : S \times R \rightarrow S_1 \times \cdots \times S_n$ and the reconstruction function: for any $A \in AS$, $Re = \{Re_A : (S_1 \times \cdots \times S_n)|_A \rightarrow S \mid A \in AS\}$, such that the following two requirements are satisfied.

(i) Correctness requirement: for any $A \in AS, s \in S$ and $r \in R$, it holds that $Re_A(\Pi(s,r)|_A) = s$, where suppose $A = \{P_{i_1}, ..., P_{i_{|A|}}\}$ and $\Pi(s,r) = (s_1, ..., s_n)$, then $\Pi(s,r)|_A = (s_{i_1}, ..., s_{i_{|A|}})$.

(ii) Security requirement: for any $B \notin AS$, i.e., $B \in \mathcal{A} = 2^P \setminus AS$, it holds that $0 < H(S|\Pi(S,R)|_B) \le H(S)$, where $H(\cdot)$ is the entropy function.

In the security requirement, if $H(S|\Pi(S,R)|_B) = H(S)$, we call it a perfect secret sharing scheme which we are interested in. Furthermore, a perfect secret sharing scheme is *linear* (LSSS for short), if S, R, S_i are all linear spaces over $\mathcal{K}$ and the reconstruction function is linear [1].

Karchmer and Wigderson [8] introduced monotone span programs (MSP) as linear models computing monotone Boolean functions. Usually we denote a MSP by $\mathcal{M}(\mathcal{K}, M, \psi)$, where M is a $d \times l$ matrix over $\mathcal{K}$ and $\psi : \{1, ..., d\} \rightarrow \{P_1, ..., P_n\}$ is a surjective labelling map which actually distributes to each participant some rows of M. We call d the *size* of the MSP. For any subset $A \subseteq P$, there is a corresponding characteristic vector $\overrightarrow{\delta_A} = (\delta_1, ..., \delta_n) \in \{0,1\}^n$ where for $1 \le i \le n$, $\delta_i = 1$ if and only if $P_i \in A$. Consider a monotone Boolean function $f : \{0,1\}^n \rightarrow \{0,1\}$ which satisfies that for any $A \subseteq P$ and $B \subseteq A$, $f(\overrightarrow{\delta_B}) = 1$ implies $f(\overrightarrow{\delta_A}) = 1$. We say that a MSP $\mathcal{M}(\mathcal{K}, M, \psi)$ computes the monotone Boolean function f with respect to a target vector $\overrightarrow{v} \in \mathcal{K}^l \setminus \{(0, ..., 0)\}$, if it holds that $\overrightarrow{v} \in span\{M_A\}$ if and only if $f(\overrightarrow{\delta_A}) = 1$, where M_A consists of the rows i of M with $\psi(i) \in A$ and $\overrightarrow{v} \in span\{M_A\}$ means that there exists a vector $\overrightarrow{w}$ such that $\overrightarrow{v} = \overrightarrow{w} M_A$. Beimel [1] proved that devising a LSSS with respect to an access structure AS is equivalent to constructing a MSP computing the monotone Boolean function f_{AS} which satisfies $f_{AS}(\overrightarrow{\delta_A}) = 1$ if and only if $A \in AS$.

2.2   LMSSS vs MSP

Multi-Secret sharing schemes [2] are to share multi-secrets with respect to multi-access structures. Precisely, let $AS_1, ..., AS_m$ be m access structures over P, $S^1 \times \cdots \times S^m$ be the secret-domain, $S_1, ..., S_n$ be the share-domain and R be the set of random inputs. Without loss of generality, we assume that $S^1 = \cdots = S^m = \mathcal{K}$. A linear multi-secret sharing scheme (LMSSS for short) realizing the multi-access structure $AS_1, \cdots, AS_m$ is composed of the distribution function

$$\Pi : \mathcal{K}^m \times R \longrightarrow S_1 \times \cdots \times S_n$$

$$\Pi(s^1, \cdots, s^m, r) = (\Pi_1(s^1, \cdots, s^m, r), \cdots, \Pi_n(s^1, \cdots, s^m, r)), \qquad (1)$$

and the reconstruction function $Re = \{Re_A^i : (S_1 \times \cdots \times S_n)_A \to \mathcal{K} | 1 \leq i \leq m, A \in AS_i\}$, such that the following three conditions hold:

(i) $S_1, \cdots, S_n$ and R are finitely dimensional linear spaces over $\mathcal{K}$, i.e., there exist positive integers d_k, $1 \leq k \leq n$, and l such that $S_k = \mathcal{K}^{d_k}$ and $R = \mathcal{K}^l$. Precisely, in the equality (1), we have that $\Pi_k(s^1, \cdots, s^m, r) \in \mathcal{K}^{d_k}$ for $1 \leq k \leq n$. Furthermore, denote

$$\Pi_k(s^1, \cdots, s^m, r) = (\Pi_{k1}(s^1, \cdots, s^m, r), \cdots, \Pi_{kd_k}(s^1, \cdots, s^m, r))$$

where $\Pi_{kj}(s^1, \cdots, s^m, r) \in \mathcal{K}$ and $1 \leq j \leq d_k$. Usually $d = \sum_{i=1}^n d_i$ is called the size of the linear multi-secret sharing scheme.

(ii) The reconstruction function is linear. That is, for any set $A \in AS_i$, $1 \leq i \leq m$, there exists a set of constants $\{\alpha_{kj}^i \in \mathcal{K} | 1 \leq k \leq n, P_k \in A, 1 \leq j \leq d_k\}$ such that for any $s^1, ..., s^m \in \mathcal{K}$ and $r \in R$, $s^i = Re_A^i(\Pi(s^1, ..., s^m, r)|_A) = \sum_{P_k \in A} \sum_{j=1}^{d_k} \alpha_{kj}^i \Pi_{kj}(s^1, \cdots s^m, r)$.

(iii) Security requirement: For any set $B \subset \{P_1, \cdots, P_n\}, T \subset \{S^1, \cdots, S^m\} \setminus \{S^i | B \in AS_i, 1 \leq i \leq m\}$, it holds that $H(T|B) = H(T)$, where $H(\cdot)$ is the entropy function.

Similar to the equivalence relation of LSSS and MSP, Xiao and Liu [10] studied a corresponding relation between LMSSS and MSP computing multi-Boolean functions. Let $\mathcal{M}(\mathcal{K}, M, \psi)$ be a MSP with the $d \times l$ matrix M and $f_1, ..., f_m : \{0,1\}^n \to \{0,1\}$ be m monotone Boolean functions. Suppose $\vec{v_1}, ..., \vec{v_m}$ are m linear independent l-dimension vectors over $\mathcal{K}$, then it follows that $m \leq l$. In practice, we always have $m < l$ in order to use randombits. Then $\mathcal{M}$ can compute the Boolean functions $f_1, ..., f_m$ with respect to $\vec{v_1}, ..., \vec{v_m}$ if for any $1 \leq k \leq m$ and $1 \leq i_1 < \cdots < i_k \leq m$, the following two conditions hold:

(i) For any $A \subseteq P$, $f_{i_1}(\vec{\delta_A}) = \cdots = f_{i_k}(\vec{\delta_A}) = 1$ implies that $\vec{v_{i_j}} \in span\{M_A\}$ for $1 \leq j \leq k$.

(ii) For any $A \subseteq P$, $f_{i_1}(\vec{\delta_A}) = \cdots = f_{i_k}(\vec{\delta_A}) = 0$ implies that $Rank \begin{pmatrix} M_A \\ \vec{v_{i_1}} \\ \vdots \\ \vec{v_{i_k}} \end{pmatrix} =$

$Rank\ M_A + k.$

After a proper linear transform, any MSP computing the multi-Boolean function $f_{AS_1}, \cdots, f_{AS_m}$ with respect to $\overrightarrow{v_1}, ..., \overrightarrow{v_m}$ can be converted into a MSP computing the same multi-Boolean function with respect to $\overrightarrow{e_1}, \cdots, \overrightarrow{e_m}$, where $\overrightarrow{e_i} = (0, ..., 0, \overset{i}{1}, 0, ..., 0) \in \mathcal{K}^l$ for $1 \leq i \leq m$. So without loss of generality we always assume the target vectors are $\overrightarrow{e_1}, \cdots, \overrightarrow{e_m}$.

Theorem 1. *[10] Let $AS_1, \cdots, AS_m$ be m access structures over P and $f_{AS_1}, \cdots, f_{AS_m}$ be the corresponding characteristic functions. Then there exists a linear multi-secret sharing scheme realizing $AS_1, \cdots, AS_m$ over a finite field $\mathcal{K}$ with size d if and only if there exists a monotone span program computing monotone Boolean functions $f_{AS_1}, \cdots, f_{AS_m}$ with size d.*

Actually, let $\mathcal{M}(\mathcal{K}, M, \psi)$ be a MSP computing monotone Boolean functions $f_{AS_1}, \cdots, f_{AS_m}$ with respect to $\overrightarrow{e_1}, \cdots, \overrightarrow{e_m}$, where M is a $d \times l$ matrix. Then the corresponding LMSSS realizing $AS_1, \cdots, AS_m$ over $\mathcal{K}$ is as follows: For any multi-secret $(s^1, ..., s^m) \in \mathcal{K}^m$ and random input $\overrightarrow{\rho} \in \mathcal{K}^{l-m}$, the distribution function is defined by

$$\Pi(s^1, \cdots, s^m, \overrightarrow{\rho}) = ((s^1, \cdots, s^m, \overrightarrow{\rho})(M_{P_1})^\tau, \cdots, (s^1, \cdots, s^m, \overrightarrow{\rho})(M_{P_n})^\tau),$$

where "τ" denotes the transpose and M_{P_k} denotes M restricted to those rows i with $\psi(i) = P_k$, $1 \leq i \leq d, 1 \leq k \leq n$. As to reconstruction, since $\overrightarrow{e_i} \in span\{M_A\}$ for any $A \in AS_i$, i.e., there exists a vector $\overrightarrow{v}$ such that $\overrightarrow{e_i} = \overrightarrow{v} M_A$, then

$$s^i = (s^1, \cdots, s^m, \overrightarrow{\rho})\overrightarrow{e_i}^\tau = (s^1, \cdots, s^m, \overrightarrow{\rho})(\overrightarrow{v} M_A)^\tau = (s^1, \cdots, s^m, \overrightarrow{\rho})(M_A)^\tau \overrightarrow{v}^\tau,$$

where $(s^1, \cdots, s^m, \overrightarrow{\rho})(M_A)^\tau$ are the shares held by players in A and $\overrightarrow{v}$ can be computed by every participant.

3   Parallel Multi-party Computation

3.1   Concepts and Notations

The problem of secure MPC for one function has been studied by many people and it can be stated as follows: n players $P_1, ..., P_n$ are to securely compute an agreed function $f(x_1, ..., x_n) = (y_1, ..., y_n)$ against an $\mathcal{A}$-adversary, where P_i holds private input x_i and is to get the output y_i. The security means that the correctness of the outputs and the privacy of players' inputs are always guaranteed no matter which set in $\mathcal{A}$ is corrupted by the adversary. In fact the function f can be represented as $f = (f_1, ..., f_n)$ where $f_i(x_1, ..., x_n) = y_i$ for $1 \leq i \leq n$. As the general way of treating the MPC problem, we assume that the functions involved thereafter are all of the form of f_i. So the MPC problem can be seemed as securely computing n functions with respect to the same adversary structure. As a natural extension, it is reasonable to consider securely computing multi-functions with respect to multi-adversary structures. Thus we propose the concept of *secure parallel multi-party computation*.

Precisely, there are m functions $f_1(x_1, ..., x_n), ..., f_m(x_1, ..., x_n)$ and m corresponding adversary structures $\mathcal{A}_1, ..., \mathcal{A}_m$. For $1 \leq i \leq n$, player P_i has private input $(x_i^{(1)}, x_i^{(2)}, ..., x_i^{(m)})$, where $x_i^{(j)}$ is P_i's input to the function $f_j(x_1, ..., x_n)$. So the final value of f_j is $f_j(x_1^{(j)}, x_2^{(j)}, ..., x_n^{(j)})$. An $(\mathcal{A}_1, ..., \mathcal{A}_m)$-adversary can corrupt any set in $\mathcal{A}_1 \cup \cdots \cup \mathcal{A}_m$. The n players are to securely compute the multi-function $f_1, ..., f_m$ against an $(\mathcal{A}_1, ..., \mathcal{A}_m)$-adversary, that is, for any corrupted set $B \in \mathcal{A}_{i_1} \cap \cdots \cap \mathcal{A}_{i_k}$, where $1 \leq i_1 < \cdots < i_k \leq m$ and $k \leq m$, functions $f_{i_1}, ..., f_{i_k}$ are securely computed, which includes the following two aspects:

(i) Correctness: For $1 \leq i \leq n$, P_i finally gets the correct outputs of the functions $f_{i_1}, ..., f_{i_k}$.

(ii) Privacy: The adversary gets no information about other players' (players out of B) inputs for functions $f_{i_1}, ..., f_{i_k}$, except what can be implied from the inputs and outputs held by players in B.

The problem of secure parallel multi-party computation for the multi-function $f_1, ..., f_m$ against an $(\mathcal{A}_1, ..., \mathcal{A}_m)$-adversary is essentially a direct composition of problems of secure MPC for f_j against an $\mathcal{A}_j$-adversary where $1 \leq j \leq m$. So it can be resolved by designing for each function and the corresponding adversary structure a secure MPC protocol and running them in a composite way. We call this a "direct sum" method. One of the results in [7] tells us that in the information theoretic model, every function can be securely computed against an adaptive, passive $\mathcal{A}$-adversary if and only if $\mathcal{A}$ is Q2, where Q2 is the condition that no two of the sets in the structure cover the full player set. Thus we evidently have the following proposition.

Proposition 1. *In the information theoretic model, there exists a parallel multi-party computation protocol computing m functions securely against an adaptive, passive $(\mathcal{A}_1, ..., \mathcal{A}_m)$-adversary if and only if $\mathcal{A}_1, ..., \mathcal{A}_m$ are all Q2.*

Cramer et al. [3] build a secure MPC protocol for one function based on the *multiplicative* MSP computing one Boolean function. Here we extend it to the *multiplicative* MSP computing multi-Boolean functions. Precisely, let $\mathcal{M}(\mathcal{K}, M, \psi)$ be a MSP described in Section 2. Given two vectors $\overrightarrow{x} = (x_1, ..., x_d)$, $\overrightarrow{y} = (y_1, ..., y_d) \in \mathcal{K}^d$, we let $\overrightarrow{x} \diamond \overrightarrow{y}$ be the vector containing all entries of the form $x_i \cdot y_j$ with $\psi(i) = \psi(j)$, and $< \overrightarrow{x}, \overrightarrow{y} >$ denote the inner product. For example, let

$$\overrightarrow{x} = (x_{11}, ..., x_{1d_1}, ..., x_{n1}, ..., x_{nd_n}), \quad \overrightarrow{y} = (y_{11}, ..., y_{1d_1}, ..., y_{n1}, ..., y_{nd_n}),$$

where $\sum_{i=1}^{n} d_i = d$ and $x_{i1}, ..., x_{id_i}$, as well as $y_{i1}, ..., y_{id_i}$ are the entries distributed to P_i according to ψ. Then $\overrightarrow{x} \diamond \overrightarrow{y}$ is the vector composed of the $\sum_{i=1}^{n} d_i^2$ entries $x_{ij} y_{ik}$, where $1 \leq j, k \leq d_i, 1 \leq i \leq n$, and $< \overrightarrow{x}, \overrightarrow{y} >= \sum_{i=1}^{n} \sum_{j=1}^{d_i} x_{ij} y_{ij}$. Using these notations, we give the following definition.

Definition 1. *A monotone span program $\mathcal{M}(\mathcal{K}, M, \psi)$ computing Boolean functions $f_1, ..., f_m$ with respect to $\overrightarrow{e_1}, \cdots, \overrightarrow{e_m}$ is called multiplicative, if for $1 \leq i \leq m$, there exists a $\sum_{i=1}^{n} d_i^2$-dimensional recombination vector $\overrightarrow{r_i}$, such that for any two multi-secrets $(s^1, ..., s^m), (s'^1, ..., s'^m) \in \mathcal{K}^m$ and any $\overrightarrow{\rho}, \overrightarrow{\rho}' \in \mathcal{K}^{l-m}$, it holds that*

$$s^i s'^i = < \overrightarrow{r_i}, (s^1, ..., s^m, \overrightarrow{\rho})M^\tau \diamond (s'^1, ..., s'^m, \overrightarrow{\rho'})M^\tau > .$$

In fact, when $m = 1$ the definition is the same as that of [3]. In the appendix we give an efficient and generic construction to build from any MSP a multiplicative MSP computing the same multi-Boolean function. Hence in the following we assume that the based MSP in Section 3.2 is already multiplicative.

3.2   Construction from Any LMSSS

In this section, assuming the adversary is passive and adaptive, we give a generic and efficient construction to obtain from any LMSSS a paralel multi-party computation protocol in the information theoretic model, provided that the access structures of the LMSSS allow MPC at all. Since LMSSS and MSP are equivalent, it turns out to be convenient to describe our protocol in terms of MSP's. We only describe the protocol in the case $m = 2$ and it is a natural extension for $m > 2$.

Suppose $\mathcal{A}_1$ and $\mathcal{A}_2$ are two adversary structures over P and they are both Q2. For $1 \le i \le n$, player P_i has private input $(x_i^{(1)}, x_i^{(2)})$ and they are to jointly compute functions $f_1(x_1, ..., x_n)$ and $f_2(x_1, ...x_n)$. Let $AS_1 = 2^P \setminus \mathcal{A}_1$, $AS_2 = 2^P \setminus \mathcal{A}_2$, and $\mathcal{M}(\mathcal{K}, M, \psi)$ be a multiplicative MSP computing Boolean functions f_{AS_1} and f_{AS_2} with respect to target vectors $\overrightarrow{e_1}, \overrightarrow{e_2}$, where M is a $d \times l$ matrix over $\mathcal{K}$. How to construct such a MSP is out of concern in this paper. Next we describe our protocol in three phases: input sharing, computing and outputting.

INPUT SHARING. First each player shares his private input by using the MSP $\mathcal{M}(\mathcal{K}, M, \psi)$, i.e., for $1 \le i \le n$, player P_i secretly and randomly selects $\overrightarrow{\rho_i}$ in the set of random inputs $R = \mathcal{K}^{l-2}$ and sends $(x_i^{(1)}, x_i^{(2)}, \overrightarrow{\rho_i})(M_{P_j})^\tau$ to player P_j, where $1 \le j \le n$ and $j \ne i$.

COMPUTING. Since any function that is feasible to compute at all can be specified as a polynomial size arithmetic circuit over a finite field $\mathcal{K}$ with addition gates and multiplication gates, it is enough for us to discuss how to do additions and multiplications over $\mathcal{K}$. Different from computing a single function, in parallel multi-party computation, we compute the functions simultaneously other than one after another.

Precisely, suppose f_1 contains p multiplications and f_2 contains q multiplications, where $p \le q$ and the multiplication considered here is operation between two elements. Then in each of the first p steps, we compute two multiplications coming from the two functions, respectively. In each the following $q - p$ steps, we continue to compute a multiplications of f_2 and do nothing for f_1. So after q steps we complete all the multiplications of both functions and get the intermediate results needed. Finally we compute all additions of both functions in one step. By doing so, we need less communication and random bits than the "direct sum" method. Furthermore, in order to guarantee security, all inputs and outputs of each step are multi-secret shared during computing and we call this condition the "invariant".

Example 1. Let $P = \{P_1, P_2, P_3\}$, and $f_1 = x_2^2 x_3$, $f_2 = x_1 x_2 + x_3$. For $1 \leq i \leq 3$, P_i has private input $(x_i^{(1)}, x_i^{(2)})$ which is multi-secret shared in the Input Sharing phase. Since f_1 contains two multiplications and f_2 contains one multiplication, the computing phase consists of three steps. The following table shows the computing process. Note that in the table, $x_i^{(j)}$ denotes an input value for the function f_j held by P_i, $z_i^{(j)}$ denotes an intermediate value held by an imaginary player I_i, x_i and z_i are variables and z_{ij} is the function to be computed at each step, where $1 \leq i \leq 3$ and $1 \leq j \leq 2$.

	input	*to compute*	*output*
Step 1	$(x_1^{(1)}, x_1^{(2)})$ $(x_2^{(1)}, x_2^{(2)})$ $(x_3^{(1)}, x_3^{(2)})$	$(z_{11} = x_2 x_3, z_{12} = x_1 x_2)$	$(z_1^{(1)} = x_2^{(1)} x_3^{(1)}, z_1^{(2)} = x_1^{(2)} x_2^{(2)})$
Step 2	$(x_2^{(1)}, x_2^{(2)})$ $(z_1^{(1)}, z_1^{(2)})$	$(z_{21} = x_2 z_1, z_{22} = z_1)$	$(z_2^{(1)} = x_2^{(1)} z_1^{(1)}, z_2^{(2)} = z_1^{(2)})$
Step 3	$(x_3^{(1)}, x_3^{(2)})$ $(z_2^{(1)}, z_2^{(2)})$	$(z_{31} = z_2, z_{32} = z_2 + x_3)$	$(z_3^{(1)} = z_2^{(1)}, z_3^{(2)} = z_2^{(2)} + x_3^{(2)})$

In Step 1 we do two multiplications $x_2 x_3$ and $x_1 x_2$ for f_1 and f_2, respectively; in Step 2 we do a multiplication $x_2 z_1$ for f_1 and do nothing for f_2; in Step 3, we do an addition $z_2 + x_3$ for f_2 and do nothing for f_1. It is evident that $z_3^{(1)} = x_2^{(1)} x_2^{(1)} x_3^{(1)}$ and $z_3^{(2)} = x_1^{(2)} x_2^{(2)} + x_3^{(2)}$. The invariant here means that for $1 \leq i \leq 3$, $(x_i^{(1)}, x_i^{(2)})$, $(z_i^{(1)}, z_i^{(2)})$ all keep multi-secret shared by $\mathcal{M}(\mathcal{K}, M, \psi)$ during computing.

Next we discuss how to do multiplications or additions at each step. According to the type of operations we execute respectively for the two functions at each step (*e.g.* Step 1 of Example 1), there are four cases to be considered as follows, where " \ " means that no operation is actually done and the output is one of the inputs. Without loss of generality, in the following we assume that $P = \{P_1, P_2, P_3, P_4\}$.

Case 1: $(+, +)$. First suppose that we are to compute $g_1 = x_1 + x_2$ and $g_2 = x_3 + x_4$. The inputs $(x_i^{(1)}, x_i^{(2)})$ are multi-secret shared such that each player P_j holds $(x_i^{(1)}, x_i^{(2)}, \overrightarrow{\rho_i})(M_{P_j})^\tau = (s_{i1}^{(j)}, ..., s_{id_j}^{(j)}) \in \mathcal{K}^{d_j}$ distributed by P_i where $1 \leq i \leq 4$. The output is to be multi-secret shared $(x_1^{(1)} + x_2^{(1)}, x_3^{(2)} + x_4^{(2)})$. Then P_j locally computes:

$$(x_1^{(1)}, x_1^{(2)}, \overrightarrow{\rho_1})(M_{P_j})^\tau + (x_2^{(1)}, x_2^{(2)}, \overrightarrow{\rho_2})(M_{P_j})^\tau$$
$$= (x_1^{(1)} + x_2^{(1)}, x_1^{(2)} + x_2^{(2)}, \overrightarrow{\rho_1} + \overrightarrow{\rho_2})(M_{P_j})^\tau$$
$$= (s_{11}^{(j)} + s_{21}^{(j)}, ..., s_{1d_j}^{(j)} + s_{2d_j}^{(j)}), \tag{2}$$

$$(x_3^{(1)}, x_3^{(2)}, \vec{\rho_3})(M_{P_j})^\tau + (x_4^{(1)}, x_4^{(2)}, \vec{\rho_4})(M_{P_j})^\tau$$
$$= (x_3^{(1)} + x_4^{(1)}, x_3^{(2)} + x_4^{(2)}, \vec{\rho_3} + \vec{\rho_4})(M_{P_j})^\tau$$
$$= (s_{31}^{(j)} + s_{41}^{(j)}, ..., s_{3d_j}^{(j)} + s_{4d_j}^{(j)}) . \tag{3}$$

Actually, through (2) P_j gets shares for $(x_1^{(1)} + x_2^{(1)}, x_1^{(2)} + x_2^{(2)})$ and through (3) P_j gets shares for $(x_3^{(1)} + x_4^{(1)}, x_3^{(2)} + x_4^{(2)})$. In order to guarantee security, we need to multi-secret share $(x_1^{(1)} + x_2^{(1)}, x_3^{(2)} + x_4^{(2)})$, each player must reshare his present shares. Precisely, by the reconstruction algorithm of the LMSSS, there exist $\vec{a}, \vec{b} \in \mathcal{K}^{\sum_{i=1}^n d_i}$, such that

$$x_1^{(1)} + x_2^{(1)} = \sum_{j=1}^n \sum_{k=1}^{d_j} a_{jk}(s_{1k}^{(j)} + s_{2k}^{(j)}), \quad x_3^{(2)} + x_4^{(2)} = \sum_{j=1}^n \sum_{k=1}^{d_j} b_{jk}(s_{3k}^{(j)} + s_{4k}^{(j)}) . \tag{4}$$

So each player P_j reshares $(\sum_{k=1}^{d_j} a_{jk}(s_{1k}^{(j)} + s_{2k}^{(j)}), \sum_{k=1}^{d_j} b_{jk}(s_{3k}^{(j)} + s_{4k}^{(j)}))$ through $(\sum_{k=1}^{d_j} a_{jk}(s_{1k}^{(j)} + s_{2k}^{(j)}), \sum_{k=1}^{d_j} b_{jk}(s_{3k}^{(j)} + s_{4k}^{(j)}), \vec{\rho_j}')M^\tau$ and sends each of other players a share. Finally P_j adds up all his shares obtained from the resharing, $i.e.$,

$$\sum_{i=1}^n (\sum_{k=1}^{d_i} a_{ik}(s_{1k}^{(i)} + s_{2k}^{(i)}), \sum_{k=1}^{d_i} b_{ik}(s_{3k}^{(i)} + s_{4k}^{(i)}), \vec{\rho_i}')(M_{P_j})^\tau$$
$$= (\sum_{i=1}^n \sum_{k=1}^{d_i} a_{ik}(s_{1k}^{(i)} + s_{2k}^{(i)}), \sum_{i=1}^n \sum_{k=1}^{d_i} b_{ik}(s_{3k}^{(i)} + s_{4k}^{(i)}), \sum_{i=1}^n \vec{\rho_i}')(M_{P_j})^\tau$$
$$= (x_1^{(1)} + x_2^{(1)}, x_3^{(2)} + x_4^{(2)}, \sum_{i=1}^n \vec{\rho_i}')(M_{P_j})^\tau ,$$

which is actually P_j's share for $(x_1^{(1)} + x_2^{(1)}, x_3^{(2)} + x_4^{(2)})$.

Note that if we are to compute $(x_1^{(1)} + x_2^{(1)}, x_1^{(2)} + x_2^{(2)})$ at this step, the equality (2) is enough and we do not need resharing any more. Although we only discuss adding up two items here, we can add up more items once in the same way. Furthermore, it is trivial to deal with multiplications with constants in $\mathcal{K}$, since the constant is public.

Case 2: $(\times, \times)$. Suppose we are to compute $(g_1 = x_1x_2, g_2 = x_3x_4)$. Since $\mathcal{M}(\mathcal{K}, M, \psi)$ is assumed to be multiplicative, there exist recombination vectors $\vec{r}, \vec{t} \in \mathcal{K}^{\sum_{i=1}^n d_i^2}$, such that

$$x_1^{(1)} x_2^{(1)} = < \vec{r}, (x_1^{(1)}, x_1^{(2)}, \vec{\rho_1})M^\tau \diamond (x_2^{(1)}, x_2^{(2)}, \vec{\rho_2})M^\tau >, \tag{5}$$

$$x_3^{(2)} x_4^{(2)} = < \vec{t}, (x_3^{(1)}, x_3^{(2)}, \vec{\rho_3})M^\tau \diamond (x_4^{(1)}, x_4^{(2)}, \vec{\rho_4})M^\tau > . \tag{6}$$

P_j computes $(x_1^{(1)}, x_1^{(2)}, \vec{\rho_1})(M_{P_j})^\tau \diamond (x_2^{(1)}, x_2^{(2)}, \vec{\rho_2})(M_{P_j})^\tau = (\alpha_{j1}, ..., \alpha_{jd_j^2}) \in \mathcal{K}^{d_j^2}$ and $(x_3^{(1)}, x_3^{(2)}, \vec{\rho_3})(M_{P_j})^\tau \diamond (x_4^{(1)}, x_4^{(2)}, \vec{\rho_4})(M_{P_j})^\tau = (\beta_{j1}, ..., \beta_{jd_j^2}) \in \mathcal{K}^{d_j^2}$.

From (5) and (6) we have

$$x_1^{(1)}x_2^{(1)} = \sum_{j=1}^{n}\sum_{k=1}^{d_j^2} r_{jk}\alpha_{jk}, \quad x_3^{(2)}x_4^{(2)} = \sum_{j=1}^{n}\sum_{k=1}^{d_j^2} t_{jk}\beta_{jk}. \tag{7}$$

P_j reshares $(\sum_{k=1}^{d_j^2} r_{jk}\alpha_{jk}, \sum_{k=1}^{d_j^2} t_{jk}\beta_{jk})$ by $(\sum_{k=1}^{d_j^2} r_{jk}\alpha_{jk}, \sum_{k=1}^{d_j^2} t_{jk}\beta_{jk}, \overrightarrow{\rho_j}')M^\tau$. Finally, P_j computes

$$\sum_{i=1}^{n}(\sum_{k=1}^{d_i^2} r_{ik}\alpha_{ik}, \sum_{k=1}^{d_i^2} t_{ik}\beta_{ik}, \overrightarrow{\rho_i}')(M_{P_j})^\tau$$

$$= (\sum_{i=1}^{n}\sum_{k=1}^{d_i^2} r_{ik}\alpha_{ik}, \sum_{i=1}^{n}\sum_{k=1}^{d_i^2} t_{ik}\beta_{ik}, \sum_{i=1}^{n}\overrightarrow{\rho_i}')(M_{P_j})^\tau$$

$$= (x_1^{(1)}x_2^{(1)}, x_3^{(2)}x_4^{(2)}, \sum_{i=1}^{n}\overrightarrow{\rho_i}')(M_{P_j})^\tau,$$

which is P_j's share for $(x_1^{(1)}x_2^{(1)}, x_3^{(2)}x_4^{(2)})$.

Case 3: $(+, \backslash)$ or $(\backslash, +)$. Suppose we are to compute $(g_1 = x_1 + x_2, g_2 = x_3)$. Similar to (4), we have $x_3^{(2)} = \sum_{j=1}^{n}\sum_{k=1}^{d_j} b_{jk}s_{3k}^{(j)}$. So each player P_j reshares $(\sum_{k=1}^{d_j} a_{jk}(s_{1k}^{(j)} + s_{2k}^{(j)}), \sum_{k=1}^{d_j} b_{jk}s_{3k}^{(j)})$ through

$$(\sum_{k=1}^{d_j} a_{jk}(s_{1k}^{(j)} + s_{2k}^{(j)}), \sum_{k=1}^{d_j} b_{jk}s_{3k}^{(j)}, \overrightarrow{\rho_j}')M^\tau$$

and finally computes

$$\sum_{i=1}^{n}(\sum_{k=1}^{d_i} a_{ik}(s_{1k}^{(i)} + s_{2k}^{(i)}), \sum_{k=1}^{d_i} b_{ik}s_{3k}^{(i)}, \overrightarrow{\rho_i}')(M_{P_j})^\tau = (x_1^{(1)} + x_2^{(1)}, x_3^{(2)}, \sum_{i=1}^{n}\overrightarrow{\rho_i}')(M_{P_j})^\tau,$$

which is P_j's share for $(x_1^{(1)} + x_2^{(1)}, x_3^{(2)})$.

Case 4: $(\times, \backslash)$ or $(\backslash, \times)$. It is similar to the above cases and details are omitted here.

OUTPUTTING. At the end of computing phase, we can see the final value $(f_1(x_1^{(1)}, ..., x_n^{(1)}), f_2(x_1^{(2)}, ..., x_n^{(2)}))$ is multi-secret shared by using $\mathcal{M}$. If every player is allowed to get the value, in the last phase P_i publics his share for $(f_1(x_1^{(1)}, ..., x_n^{(1)}), f_2(x_1^{(2)}, ..., x_n^{(2)}))$ where $1 \le i \le n$, then every player can compute $(f_1(x_1^{(1)}, ..., x_n^{(1)}), f_2(x_1^{(2)}, ..., x_n^{(2)}))$ by the reconstruction algorithm.

If $f_1(x_1^{(1)}, ..., x_n^{(1)})$ is required to be held only by P_1 and $f_2(x_1^{(2)}, ..., x_n^{(2)})$ is to be held only by P_2, all shares cannot be simply transmitted to P_1 and P_2. Because by doing so, P_1, resp. P_2 will also know $f_2(x_1^{(2)}, ..., x_n^{(2)})$, resp. $f_1(x_1^{(1)}, ..., x_n^{(1)})$. Fortunately, by the reconstruction algorithm, $f_1(x_1^{(1)}, ..., x_n^{(1)})$

and $f_2(x_1^{(2)}, ..., x_n^{(2)})$ are linear combinations of the shares that all players finally hold, so they can be computed through a simple MPC protocol [9] as follows, while keeping the privacy of the shares thus guaranteeing security for parallel MPC.

Since $(f_1(x_1^{(1)}, ..., x_n^{(1)}), f_2(x_1^{(2)}, ..., x_n^{(2)}))$ is multi-secret shared through $\mathcal{M}$, suppose P_i's share for it is $(s_{i1}, \cdots, s_{id_i}) \in \mathcal{K}^{d_i}$ where $1 \leq i \leq n$. Similar to the equality (4), we have that

$$f_1(x_1^{(1)}, ..., x_n^{(1)}) = \sum_{i=1}^{n} \sum_{k=1}^{d_i} a_{ik} s_{ik}, \quad f_2(x_1^{(2)}, ..., x_n^{(2)}) = \sum_{i=1}^{n} \sum_{k=1}^{d_i} b_{ik} s_{ik}.$$

In order to securely compute $f_1(x_1^{(1)}, ..., x_n^{(1)})$ such that only P_1 learns the value and other players get nothing new, we need a simple MPC protocol. Precisely, for $1 \leq i \leq n$, P_i randomly selects $r_{i1}, r_{i2}, \cdots, r_{i(n-1)} \in \mathcal{K}$ and sets $r_{in} = \sum_{k=1}^{d_i} a_{ik} s_{ik} - \sum_{j=1}^{n-1} r_{ij}$. Then P_i secretly transmits r_{ij} to P_j, $1 \leq j \leq n, j \neq i$. After that P_j locally computes $\lambda_j = \sum_{i=1}^{n} r_{ij}$ and transmits r_j to P_1 where $1 \leq j \leq n$. The process can be displayed as follows.

$$
\begin{array}{ccccc}
& P_1 & \cdots & P_n & \\
P_1 : \sum_{k=1}^{d_1} a_{1k} s_{1k} \rightarrow & r_{11} & \cdots & r_{1n} & \sum_{k=1}^{d_1} a_{1k} s_{1k} = \sum_{j=1}^{n} r_{1j} \\
P_2 : \sum_{k=1}^{d_2} a_{2k} s_{2k} \rightarrow & r_{21} & \cdots & r_{2n} & \sum_{k=1}^{d_2} a_{2k} s_{2k} = \sum_{j=1}^{n} r_{2j} \\
\cdots \qquad \cdots & \cdots & \cdots & \cdots & \cdots \\
P_n : \sum_{k=1}^{d_n} a_{nk} s_{nk} \rightarrow & r_{n1} & \cdots & r_{nn} & \sum_{k=1}^{d_n} a_{nk} s_{nk} = \sum_{j=1}^{n} r_{nj} \\
& \lambda_1 = \sum_{i=1}^{n} r_{i1} & \cdots & \lambda_n = \sum_{i=1}^{n} r_{in} &
\end{array}
$$

$$(8)$$

Finally, P_1 computes

$$\sum_{j=1}^{n} \lambda_j = \sum_{j=1}^{n} \sum_{i=1}^{n} r_{ij} = \sum_{i=1}^{n} \sum_{j=1}^{n} r_{ij} = \sum_{i=1}^{n} \sum_{k=1}^{d_i} a_{ik} s_{ik} = f_1(x_1^{(1)}, ..., x_n^{(1)}).$$

Similarly, $f_2(x_1^{(2)}, ..., x_n^{(2)})$ can be securely computed and only P_2 gets the final value.

3.3 Comparing with the "Direct Sum" Method

Since the "direct sum" method (in Section 3.1) is a natural way to realize secure parallel multi-party computation, we compare our protocol (in Section 3.2) with it. As to the security issue, note that in our protocol all inputs and outputs for every step is multi-secret shared during the protocol. For any $B \in \mathcal{A}_{i_1} \cap \cdots \cap \mathcal{A}_{i_k}$, it follows that $\{S^{i_1}, ..., S^{i_k}\} \subseteq \{S^1, ..., S^m\} \setminus \{S^i \mid B \in AS_i, 1 \leq i \leq m\}$. By the security requirement of the LMSSS, players in B get no information about $\{S^{i_1}, ..., S^{i_k}\}$ from the shares they hold, that is, the intermediate communication data held by players in B tells nothing about other players' inputs for functions $f_{i_1}, ..., f_{i_k}$. So an adversary corrupting players in B gets no information about other players' (players out of B) inputs for functions $f_{i_1}, ..., f_{i_k}$, except what can be implied from the inputs and outputs held by players in B. Hence our protocol and the "direct sum" method are of the same security.

The communication complexity is an important criterion to evaluate a protocol. By using a " non-direct sum" LMSSS, our protocol may need less communication than the "direct sum" method, and this advantage becomes more evident when computing more complicated functions, *i.e.*, the functions essentially contain more variables and more multiplications. In the next section, we show the advantage of communication complexity through a specific example.

4 Example

Suppose that $P = \{P_1, P_2, P_3, P_4, P_5\}$ is the set of players and $|\mathcal{K}| > 5$. Let $AS_1 = \{A \subset P \mid |A| \geq 2$ and $\{P_1, P_2\} \cap A \neq \varnothing\}$ and $AS_2 = \{A \subset P \mid |A| \geq 2$ and $\{P_4, P_5\} \cap A \neq \varnothing\}$ be two access structures over P. The corresponding minimum access structures are as follows:

$$(AS_1)_m = \{\{P_1, P_2\}, \{P_1, P_3\}, \{P_1, P_4\}, \{P_1, P_5\}, \{P_2, P_3\}, \{P_2, P_4\}, \{P_2, P_5\}\},$$

$$(AS_2)_m = \{\{P_4, P_5\}, \{P_1, P_4\}, \{P_2, P_4\}, \{P_3, P_4\}, \{P_1, P_5\}, \{P_2, P_5\}, \{P_3, P_5\}\}.$$

Obviously, the two corresponding adversary structures $\mathcal{A}_1 = 2^P \setminus AS_1$ and $\mathcal{A}_2 = 2^P \setminus AS_2$ are both Q2. The players are to securely compute multi-functions $f_1 = x_1 + x_2 x_3$, $f_2 = x_1 x_2$ against an $(\mathcal{A}_1, \mathcal{A}_2)$-adversary. For $1 \leq i \leq 5$, player P_i has private input $(x_i^{(1)}, x_i^{(2)})$.

By the "direct sum" method, we need to design for f_i a MPC protocol against an $\mathcal{A}_i$-adversary where $1 \leq i \leq 2$. From [3] we know that the key step is to devise LSSS with respect to AS_1 and AS_2, respectively. let

$$M_1 = \begin{pmatrix} 1\,1 \\ 2\,1 \\ 0\,1 \\ 0\,1 \\ 0\,1 \end{pmatrix}, \quad M_2 = \begin{pmatrix} 0\,1 \\ 0\,1 \\ 0\,1 \\ 1\,1 \\ 2\,1 \end{pmatrix},$$

and $\psi_1, \psi_2 : \{1, 2, \cdots, 5\} \to P$ be defined as $\psi_1(i) = \psi_2(i) = P_i$ for $1 \leq i \leq 5$. It is easy to verify that $\mathcal{M}_i(\mathcal{K}, M_i, \psi_i)$ is a multiplicative MSP computing f_{AS_i} with respect to $(1, 0) \in \mathcal{K}^2$ where $1 \leq i \leq 2$. Then the MPC protocol follows. Note that the MPC protocol for computing a single function also has input sharing phase, computing phase and outputting phase.

By the protocol in Sec3.2, first we need to design a LMSSS with respect to the multi-access structure AS_1, AS_2. Let $M =$

$$\begin{pmatrix} 1 & 0 & 1 & 1 \\ 0 & 0 & 0 & 1 \\ 0 & 0 & 0 & 1 \\ 2 & 0 & 1 & 1 \\ 0 & 0 & 1 & 1 \\ 0 & 0 & 1 & 0 \\ 0 & 1 & -2 & -1 \\ 0 & 0 & 2 & 1 \\ 0 & 1 & -1 & -1 \end{pmatrix}$$

and $\psi : \{1, 2, ..., 9\} \rightarrow$ P be defined as $\psi(1) = \psi(2) = P_1$, $\psi(3) = \psi(4) = P_2$, $\psi(5) = P_3$, $\psi(6) = \psi(7) = P_4$, $\psi(8) = \psi(9) = P_5$. It can be verified that $\mathcal{M}(\mathcal{K}, M, \psi)$ is a MSP computing f_{AS_1} and f_{AS_2} with respect to the target vectors $\vec{e_1}, \vec{e_2}$, and later we are to verify that $\mathcal{M}(\mathcal{K}, M, \psi)$ is multiplicative.

INPUT SHARING. First for $1 \leq i \leq 3$, P_i multi-secret share his private input $(x_i^{(1)}, x_i^{(2)})$ by randomly choosing $\alpha_i, \beta_i \in \mathcal{K}$ and sending $(x_i^{(1)}, x_i^{(2)}, \alpha_i, \beta_i)(M_{P_j})^\tau$ to player P_j, where $1 \leq j \leq n$. The following table shows the shares each player holds for $(x_i^{(1)}, x_i^{(2)})$ after the phase.

	$(x_1^{(1)}, x_1^{(2)})$	$(x_2^{(1)}, x_2^{(2)})$	$(x_3^{(1)}, x_3^{(2)})$
P_1	$x_1^{(1)} + \alpha_1 + \beta_1, \quad \beta_1$	$x_2^{(1)} + \alpha_2 + \beta_2, \quad \beta_2$	$x_3^{(1)} + \alpha_3 + \beta_3, \quad \beta_3$
P_2	$\beta_1, \quad 2x_1^{(1)} + \alpha_1 + \beta_1$	$\beta_2, \quad 2x_2^{(1)} + \alpha_2 + \beta_2$	$\beta_3, \quad 2x_3^{(1)} + \alpha_3 + \beta_3$
P_3	$\alpha_1 + \beta_1$	$\alpha_2 + \beta_2$	$\alpha_3 + \beta_3$
P_4	$\alpha_1, \quad x_1^{(2)} - 2\alpha_1 - \beta_1$	$\alpha_2, \quad x_2^{(2)} - 2\alpha_2 - \beta_2$	$\alpha_3, \quad x_3^{(2)} - 2\alpha_3 - \beta_3$
P_5	$2\alpha_1 + \beta_1, \quad x_1^{(2)} - \alpha_1 - \beta_1$	$2\alpha_2 + \beta_2, \quad x_2^{(2)} - \alpha_2 - \beta_2$	$2\alpha_3 + \beta_3, \quad x_3^{(2)} - \alpha_3 - \beta_3$

Denote $(x_i^{(1)}, x_i^{(2)}, \alpha_i, \beta_i)M^\tau = (s_{i1}^{(1)}, s_{i2}^{(1)}, s_{i1}^{(2)}, s_{i2}^{(2)}, s_{i1}^{(3)}, s_{i1}^{(4)}, s_{i2}^{(4)}, s_{i1}^{(5)}, s_{i2}^{(5)})$, that is, P_j holds $s_{ik}^{(j)}$ for $(x_i^{(1)}, x_i^{(2)})$ where $1 \leq k \leq d_i, 1 \leq j \leq 5$.

It can be verified that

$$x_1^{(1)} = (x_1^{(1)} + \alpha_1 + \beta_1) - (\alpha_1 + \beta_1), \quad x_1^{(2)} = (\alpha_1 + \beta_1) + \alpha_1 + (x_1^{(2)} - 2\alpha_1 - \beta_1). \quad (9)$$

$$x_2^{(1)} x_3^{(1)} = -(x_2^{(1)} + \alpha_2 + \beta_2)(x_3^{(1)} + \alpha_3 + \beta_3) + \frac{1}{2}(2x_2^{(1)} + \alpha_2 + \beta_2)(2x_3^{(1)} + \alpha_3 + \beta_3) + \frac{1}{2}(\alpha_2 + \beta_2)(\alpha_3 + \beta_3), \quad (10)$$

$$x_1^{(2)} x_2^{(2)} = (\alpha_1 + \beta_1)(\alpha_2 + \beta_2) - \alpha_1\alpha_2 + (x_1^{(2)} - 2\alpha_1 - \beta_1)(x_2^{(2)} - 2\alpha_2 - \beta_2) + (2\alpha_1 + \beta_1)(x_2^{(2)} - \alpha_2 - \beta_2) + (x_1^{(2)} - \alpha_1 - \beta_1)(2\alpha_2 + \beta_2). \quad (11)$$

The equality (9) gives the reconstruction algorithms for $\{P_1, P_3\}$ to recover $x_1^{(1)}$ and for $\{P_3, P_4\}$ to recover $x_1^{(2)}$, so as in the equality (4), we can set

$$\vec{a} = (1, 0, 0, 0, -1, 0, 0, 0, 0), \quad \vec{b} = (0, 0, 0, 0, 1, 1, 1, 0, 0).$$

The equalities (10) and (11) show the MSP $\mathcal{M}(\mathcal{K}, M, \psi)$ is multiplicative. Precisely, if we have

$$(x_1^{(1)}, x_1^{(2)}, \alpha_1, \beta_1)M^\tau \diamond (x_2^{(1)}, x_2^{(2)}, \alpha_2, \beta_2)M^\tau$$
$$= (s_{11}^{(1)}s_{21}^{(1)}, s_{11}^{(1)}s_{22}^{(1)}, s_{12}^{(1)}s_{21}^{(1)}, s_{12}^{(1)}s_{22}^{(1)}, s_{11}^{(2)}s_{21}^{(2)}, s_{11}^{(2)}s_{22}^{(2)}, s_{12}^{(2)}s_{21}^{(2)}, s_{12}^{(2)}s_{22}^{(2)}, s_{11}^{(3)}s_{21}^{(3)},$$
$$s_{11}^{(4)}s_{21}^{(4)}, s_{11}^{(4)}s_{22}^{(4)}, s_{12}^{(4)}s_{21}^{(4)}, s_{12}^{(4)}s_{22}^{(4)}, s_{11}^{(5)}s_{21}^{(5)}, s_{11}^{(5)}s_{22}^{(5)}, s_{12}^{(5)}s_{21}^{(5)}, s_{12}^{(5)}s_{22}^{(5)}),$$

then as in the equality (7) the recombination vectors are as follows:

$$\vec{r} = (-1, 0, 0, 0, 0, 0, 0, \frac{1}{2}, \frac{1}{2}, 0, 0, 0, 0, 0, 0, 0, 0),$$

$$\vec{t} = (0, 0, 0, 0, 0, 0, 0, 0, 1, -1, 0, 0, 1, 0, 1, 1, 0).$$

We transmit $22 \log |\mathcal{K}|$ bits of information in this phase. For simplicity, the functions computed in this example involve a few variables. If all variables are involved in each function, $i.e.$, variables $x_1, ..., x_5$ all appear in each function, then we need to transmit $36 \log |\mathcal{K}|$ bits in the input sharing phase, while by the "direct sum" method $40 \log |\mathcal{K}|$ bits need to be transmitted in this phase.

COMPUTING. This phase consists of two steps.

Step 1: $(\times, \times)$. The output of this step is to be the multi-secret shared $(x_2^{(1)}x_3^{(1)}, x_1^{(2)}x_2^{(2)})$. From (10) and (11), we can see that in the recombination vector $\vec{r}$ only P_1, P_2 and P_3 has nonzero coefficients, and in the recombination vector $\vec{t}$ only P_3, P_4 and P_5 has nonzero coefficients, so P_1 reshares $(u_1, v_1) = (-(x_2^{(1)} + \alpha_2 + \beta_2)(x_3^{(1)} + \alpha_3 + \beta_3), 0)$, P_2 reshares $(u_2, v_2) = (\frac{1}{2}(2x_2^{(1)} + \alpha_2 + \beta_2)(2x_3^{(1)} + \alpha_3 + \beta_3), 0)$, P_3 reshares $(u_3, v_3) = (\frac{1}{2}(\alpha_2 + \beta_2)(\alpha_3 + \beta_3), (\alpha_1 + \beta_1)(\alpha_2 + \beta_2))$, P_4 reshares $(u_4, v_4) = (0, -\alpha_1\alpha_2 + (x_1^{(2)} - 2\alpha_1 - \beta_1)(x_2^{(2)} - 2\alpha_2 - \beta_2))$ and P_5 reshares $(u_5, v_5) = (0, (2\alpha_1 + \beta_1)(x_2^{(2)} - \alpha_2 - \beta_2) + (x_1^{(2)} - \alpha_1 - \beta_1)(2\alpha_2 + \beta_2))$.

After resharing, as shares of (u_i, v_i), P_1 gets $u_i + \alpha'_i + \beta'_i$, β'_i; P_2 gets β'_i, $2u_i + \alpha'_i + \beta'_i$; P_3 gets $\alpha'_i + \beta'_i$; P_4 gets α'_i, $v_i - 2\alpha'_i - \beta'_i$ and P_5 gets $2\alpha'_i + \beta'_i$, $v_i - \alpha'_i - \beta'_i$, where $1 \le i \le 5$. Finally

P_1 computes $\sum_{i=1}^5 (u_i + \alpha'_i + \beta'_i) = x_2^{(1)}x_3^{(1)} + \sum_{i=1}^5 (\alpha'_i + \beta'_i)$, and $\sum_{i=1}^5 \beta'_i$;

P_2 computes $\sum_{i=1}^5 \beta'_i$, and $\sum_{i=1}^5 (2u_i + \alpha'_i + \beta'_i) = 2x_2^{(1)}x_3^{(1)} + \sum_{i=1}^5 (\alpha'_i + \beta'_i)$;

P_3 computes $\sum_{i=1}^5 (\alpha'_i + \beta'_i)$;

P_4 computes $\sum_{i=1}^5 \alpha'_i$, and $\sum_{i=1}^5 (v_i - 2\alpha'_i - \beta'_i) = x_1^{(2)}x_2^{(2)} - \sum_{i=1}^5 (2\alpha'_i + \beta'_i)$;

P_5 computes $\sum_{i=1}^5 (2\alpha'_i + \beta'_i)$, and $\sum_{i=1}^5 (v_i - \alpha'_i - \beta'_i) = x_1^{(2)}x_2^{(2)} - \sum_{i=1}^5 (\alpha'_i + \beta'_i)$.

It can be verified that they are the shares for $(x_2^{(1)}x_3^{(1)}, x_1^{(2)}x_2^{(2)})$ generated from $M(x_2^{(1)}x_3^{(1)}, x_1^{(2)}x_2^{(2)}, \sum_{i=1}^5 \alpha'_i, \sum_{i=1}^5 \beta'_i)^\tau$.

Step 2: $(+, \backslash)$. The output of this step is to be multi-secret shared $(x_1^{(1)} + x_2^{(1)}x_3^{(1)}, x_1^{(2)}x_2^{(2)})$. Since $(x_2^{(1)}x_3^{(1)}, x_1^{(2)}x_2^{(2)})$ is multi-secret shared after Step 1 and $(x_1^{(1)}, x_1^{(2)})$ is multi-secret shared in the Input Sharing phase, then each player adds his shares for $(x_2^{(1)}x_3^{(1)}, x_1^{(2)}x_2^{(2)})$ to his shares for $(x_1^{(1)}, x_1^{(2)})$. By the linear combinations given in (9), P_1 reshares $(p_1, q_1) = ((x_1^{(1)} + \alpha_1 + \beta_1) + x_2^{(1)} x_3^{(1)} + \sum_{i=1}^{5} (\alpha_i' + \beta_i'), 0)$, P_3 reshares $(p_3, q_3) = (-(\alpha_1 + \beta_1) - \sum_{i=1}^{5} (\alpha_i' + \beta_i'), \sum_{i=1}^{5} (\alpha_i' + \beta_i'))$ and P_4 reshares $(p_4, q_4) = (0, \sum_{i=1}^{5} \alpha_i' + x_1^{(2)} x_2^{(2)} - \sum_{i=1}^{5} (2\alpha_i' + \beta_i'))$. Finally,

P_1 computes $\displaystyle\sum_{i=1,3,4} (p_i + \alpha_i'' + \beta_i'') = x_1^{(1)} + x_2^{(1)} x_3^{(1)} + \sum_{i=1,3,4} (\alpha_i'' + \beta_i'')$, and

$\displaystyle\sum_{i=1,3,4} \beta_i''$;

P_2 computes $\displaystyle\sum_{i=1,3,4} \beta_i''$, and $\displaystyle\sum_{i=1,3,4} (2p_i + \alpha_i'' + \beta_i'') = 2(x_1^{(1)} + x_2^{(1)} x_3^{(1)}) +$

$\displaystyle\sum_{i=1,3,4} (\alpha_i'' + \beta_i'')$;

P_3 computes $\displaystyle\sum_{i=1,3,4} (\alpha_i'' + \beta_i'')$;

P_4 computes $\displaystyle\sum_{i=1,3,4} \alpha_i''$, and $\displaystyle\sum_{i=1,3,4} (q_i - 2\alpha_i'' - \beta_i'') = x_1^{(2)} x_2^{(2)} - \sum_{i=1,3,4} (2\alpha_i'' + \beta_i'')$;

P_5 computes $\displaystyle\sum_{i=1,3,4} (2\alpha_i'' + \beta_i'')$, and $\displaystyle\sum_{i=1,3,4} (q_i - \alpha_i'' - \beta_i'') = x_1^{(2)} x_2^{(2)} -$

$\displaystyle\sum_{i=1,3,4} (\alpha_i'' + \beta_i'')$.

It can be verified that they are the shares for $(x_1^{(1)} + x_2^{(1)} x_3^{(1)}, x_1^{(2)} x_2^{(2)})$ generated from $M(x_1^{(1)} + x_2^{(1)} x_3^{(1)}, x_1^{(2)} x_2^{(2)}, \sum_{i=1,3,4} \alpha_i'', \sum_{i=1,3,4} \beta_i'')^\top$.

In each step dealing with multiplications, our protocol transmits at most $36 \log |\mathcal{K}|$ bits of information. By the "direct sum" method, each time we do a multiplication it need to transmit $28 \log |\mathcal{K}|$ bits. Assume that f_1 contains p multiplications and f_2 contains q multiplications, where $p \leq q$. Then our protocol need transmit $36q \log |\mathcal{K}|$ bits to complete all multiplications, while the "direct sum" method transmits $20(p+q) \log |\mathcal{K}|$ bits. If $p = q$, we see that our protocol transmits $4p \log |\mathcal{K}|$ bits less than the "direct sum" method.

In the last step of this phase, that is, when we do additions, from the reconstruction algorithm given by (9) only P_1, P_3 and P_4 need to reshare their shares. But by the "direct sum" method, no resharing is needed when doing additions. So our protocol transmits at most $22 \log |\mathcal{K}|$ bits more than the "direct sum" method when dealing with additions. However, when both functions essentially contain large numbers of multiplications, our protocol has great advantage in communication complexity.

OUTPUTTING. Assume that all players are allowed to get the final value of both functions. Then every player publics his share for $(x_1^{(1)} + x_2^{(1)} x_3^{(1)}, x_1^{(2)} x_2^{(2)})$ and can compute the final value by the reconstruction algorithms. If $x_1^{(1)} + x_2^{(1)} x_3^{(1)}$ is assumed to be held by P_1 and $x_1^{(2)} x_2^{(2)}$ is assumed to be held by P_2, then our protocol transmits at most $20 \log |\mathcal{K}|$ bits more than the "direct sum" method according to (8). Fortunately, this disadvantage is fixed, that is, it does not depend on the functions we compute.

As a whole, our protocol needs less communication than the "direct sum" method when computing complicated functions.

References

1. Beimel, A.: Secure Schemes for Secret Sharing and Key Distribution. PhD thesis, Technion - Israel Institute of Techonlogy, 1996. Available on Internet http://www.cs.bgu.ac.il/ beimel/pub.html
2. Blundo, C., De Santis, A., Di Crescenzo, G.,: Multi-Secret sharing schemes. Advances in Crypotology-CRYPTO'94. LNCS, Vol. 839, 150-163, 1995.
3. Cramer, R., Damgard, I., Maurer, U.: General Secure Multi-Party Computation from any Linear Secret-Sharing Scheme. Proc. EUROCRYPT '00, Springer Verlag LNCS, vol. 1807, pp. 316–334. Full version available from IACR eprint archive, 2000.
4. Ding, C., Laihonen, T., Renvall, A.,: Linear multi-secret sharing schemes and error-correcting codes. Journal of Universal Computer Science, Vol.3, No.9, 1997, 1023–1036
5. Fehr, S.,: Efficient Construction of Dual MSP. manuscript 1999. Available on Internet http://homepages.cwi.nl/ fehr/papers/Feh99.pdf
6. Goldreich, O., Micali, S., Wigderson, A.: How to play ANY mental game.Proceedings of the nineteenth annual ACM conference on Theory of computing, pp.218-229, January 1987, New York, New York, United States.
7. Hirt, M., Maurer, U.,: Player simulation and general adversary structures in perfect multi-party computation. Journal of Cryptology, vol.13, NO. 1, pp.31-60, 2000.
8. Karchmer, M. and Wigderson, A.: On span programs. Proc. 8th Ann. Symp. Structure in complexity Theory, IEEE 1993, pp. 102-111.
9. Xiao, L.,: Secret sharing schemes: theory and application. PhD thesis, Academy of Mathematics and Systems Science, CAS, 2004.
10. Xiao, L., Liu, M.: Linear Multi-secret sharing schemes. Science in China Ser. F Information Sciences, vol. 48, NO.1, pp. 125-136, 2005.
11. Yao, A.: Protocols for Secure Computation. Proc. of IEEE FOGS '82, pp. 160-164, 1982.

Appendix: Construct Multiplicative MSP

Let $\mathcal{M}(\mathcal{K}, M, \psi)$ be a MSP computing f_{AS_1} and f_{AS_2} with respect to $\{\overrightarrow{e_1}, \overrightarrow{e_2}\}$. For simplicity, we use $\overrightarrow{e_1}$, resp. $\overrightarrow{e_2}$, to denote vectors with the form $(1, 0, \cdots, 0)$, resp. $(0, 1, 0, \cdots, 0)$, without distinguishing the dimensions, and the dimension can be determined from context. From [5] we can assume that the columns of M are linear independent and so $d \geq l$. Compute $\overrightarrow{w_1}, \overrightarrow{w_2}$ be such that $\overrightarrow{w_1} M = \overrightarrow{e_1}$ and $\overrightarrow{w_2} M = \overrightarrow{e_2}$, and compute $\overrightarrow{v_1}, ..., \overrightarrow{v_{d-l}}$ as a basis of the solution space to the linear functions $\overrightarrow{v} M = \overrightarrow{0}$. Then construct a matrix

$$
\widetilde{M} = \begin{pmatrix} m_{11} & \cdots & \cdots & m_{1l} & & & & \\ \vdots & \ddots & \ddots & \vdots & & & & \\ m_{d1} & \cdots & \cdots & m_{dl} & & & & \\ \overrightarrow{w_1}^{\tau} & & & & \overrightarrow{v_1}^{\tau} & \cdots & \overrightarrow{v_{d-l}}^{\tau} & \\ & \overrightarrow{w_2}^{\tau} & & & & & \overrightarrow{v_1}^{\tau} & \cdots & \overrightarrow{v_{d-l}}^{\tau} \end{pmatrix},
$$

where $\begin{pmatrix} m_{11} & \cdots & m_{1l} \\ \vdots & \ddots & \vdots \\ m_{d1} & \cdots & m_{dl} \end{pmatrix} = M$, and the blanks in $\widetilde{M}$ denote zero elements. So $\widetilde{M}$

is a $3d \times (2d - l)$ matrix over $\mathcal{K}$. Define a function $\widetilde{\psi} : \{1, ..., 3d\} \rightarrow \{1, ..., n\}$ as follows: For $1 \leq k \leq d$, $\widetilde{\psi}(k) = \psi(k)$; For $d < k \leq 2d$, $\widetilde{\psi}(k) = \psi(k - d)$; For $2d < k \leq 3d$, $\widetilde{\psi}(k) = \psi(k - 2d)$. Therefore we get a MSP $\widetilde{\mathcal{M}}(\mathcal{K}, \widetilde{M}, \widetilde{\psi})$.

Proposition 2. *The monotone span program $\widetilde{\mathcal{M}}(\mathcal{K}, \widetilde{M}, \widetilde{\psi})$ constructed above is a multiplicative MSP computing Boolean functions f_{AS_1} and f_{AS_2} with respect to target vectors $\{\vec{e_1}, \vec{e_2}\}$.*
Proof: *Let M_1^*, resp. M_2^* be the matrix composed of rows from the $(d + 1)$ th to the $2d$ th row of $\widetilde{M}$, resp. from the $(2d + 1)$ th to the $3d$ th row of $\widetilde{M}$.*

Then M_1^* and M_2^* are two $d \times (2d - l)$ matrices, and $\widetilde{M} = \begin{pmatrix} M0 \\ M_1^* \\ M_2^* \end{pmatrix}$, where $M0$

denotes the $d \times (2d - l)$ matrix generated by adding $2(d - l)$ all zero columns to the right of the original $d \times l$ matrix M. Let $AS_1^* = \{B \subset P \mid \overline{B} \notin AS_1\}$ and $AS_2^* = \{B \subset P \mid \overline{B} \notin AS_2\}$. From [5], the MSP $\mathcal{M}_1^*(\mathcal{K}, M_1^*, \psi)$, resp. $\mathcal{M}_2^*(\mathcal{K}, M_2^*, \psi)$ computes the Boolean function $f_{AS_1^*}$, resp. $f_{AS_2^*}$ with respect to the target vector $\vec{e_1}$, resp. $\vec{e_2}$.

In order to prove that $\widetilde{\mathcal{M}}(\mathcal{K}, \widetilde{M}, \widetilde{\psi})$ computes Boolean functions f_{AS_1} and f_{AS_2} with respect to target vectors $\{\vec{e_1}, \vec{e_2}\}$, we need to prove: (1) $\vec{e_1} \in span\{\widetilde{M}_A\}$ iff $A \in AS_1$; (2) $\vec{e_2} \in span\{\widetilde{M}_A\}$ iff $A \in AS_2$; (3) If $A \notin AS_1 \cup AS_2$, then $\widetilde{M}$

rejects A with respect to $\{\vec{e_1}, \vec{e_2}\}$, ie. $Rank \begin{pmatrix} \widetilde{M}_A \\ \vec{e_1} \\ \vec{e_2} \end{pmatrix} = Rank \, \widetilde{M}_A + 2$.

(1)Suppose that $A \in AS_1$. Because $\mathcal{M}(\mathcal{K}, M, \psi)$ computes f_{AS_1} with respect to $\vec{e_1}$, $\vec{e_1} \in span\{(M0)_A\} \subset span\{\widetilde{M}_A\}$. On the other hand, suppose that $\vec{e_1} \in span\{\widetilde{M}_A\}$. If $\vec{e_1} \in span\{(M0)_A\}$, then $A \in AS_1$ because $\mathcal{M}$ computes f_{AS_1} with respect to $\vec{e_1}$. Otherwise $(M_1^*)_A$ or $(M_2^*)_A$ must contribute to the generation of $\vec{e_1}$. If $(M_1^*)_A$ contributes, it is easy to see that its contribution must be $span\{\vec{e_1}\}$. So $\vec{e_1} \in span\{(M_1^*)_A\}$. Because $\mathcal{M}_1^*(\mathcal{K}, M_1^*, \psi)$ computes the Boolean function $f_{AS_1^*}$ with respect to the target vector $\vec{e_1}$, $\vec{e_1} \in span\{(M_1^*)_A\}$ implies that $A \in AS_1^*$. By the assumption $A_1 = 2^P - AS_1$ is Q2, $AS_1^* \subset AS_1$ and then $A \in AS_1$. Similarly, if $(M_2^*)_A$ contributes, its contribution must be $span\{\vec{e_2}\}$. So $\vec{e_2} \in span\{(M_2^*)_A\}$, and thus $A \in AS_2$. Because $\mathcal{M}(\mathcal{K}, M, \psi)$ computes f_{AS_2} with respect to $\vec{e_2}$, then $\vec{e_2} \in span\{\widetilde{M}_A\}$. As a result, the contribution of $(M_2^*)_A$ is included in that of $(M0)_A$. Thus we can disregard $(M_2^*)_A$ when generating $\vec{e_1}$, and we have proved that $\vec{e_1} \in span\{(M0)_A, (M_2^*)_A\}$ implies $A \in AS_1$.
(2)By the discussion similar to (1), $\vec{e_2} \in span\{\widetilde{M}_A\}$ iff $A \in AS_2$;
(3)Suppose that $A \notin AS_1 \cup AS_2$. It follows that

$$span\{(M0)_A, \vec{e_1}, \vec{e_2}\} \cap span\{(M_1^*)_A\} = span\{(M0)_A, \vec{e_1}, \vec{e_2}\} \cap span\{(M_2^*)_A\}$$
$$= span\{(M_1^*)_A\} \cap span\{(M_2^*)_A\} = 0 \ . \tag{12}$$

So

$$Rank \begin{pmatrix} \widetilde{M}_A \\ \overrightarrow{e_1} \\ \overrightarrow{e_2} \end{pmatrix} = Rank \begin{pmatrix} (M0)_A \\ \overrightarrow{e_1} \\ \overrightarrow{e_2} \end{pmatrix} + Rank \ (M_1^*)_A + Rank \ (M_2^*)_A \quad (13)$$

$$= Rank \ (M0)_A + 2 + Rank \ (M_1^*)_A + Rank \ (M_2^*)_A \quad (14)$$

$$= Rank \ \widetilde{M}_A + 2 \ , \quad (15)$$

where the equality (13) and (15) come from the equality (12), and the equality (14) comes from the fact that $\mathcal{M}$ computes f_{AS_1} and f_{AS_2} with respect to $\{\overrightarrow{e_1}, \overrightarrow{e_2}\}$.

Then we prove that $\widetilde{\mathcal{M}}(\mathcal{K}, \widetilde{M}, \widetilde{\psi})$ is multiplicative. For any $s_1, s_1' \in S^1$, $s_2, s_2' \in S^2$, and $\overrightarrow{\rho}, \overrightarrow{\rho}' \in \mathcal{K}^{2d-l-2}$, denote

$$(s_1, s_2, \overrightarrow{\rho})\widetilde{M}^\tau = (s_1, s_2, \overrightarrow{\rho})((M0)^\tau, (M_1^*)^\tau, (M_2^*)^\tau) = (\overrightarrow{u}, \overrightarrow{v}, \overrightarrow{w}) \ ,$$

where $\overrightarrow{u} = (s_1, s_2, \overrightarrow{\rho})(M0)^\tau \in \mathcal{K}^d$, $\overrightarrow{v} = (s_1, s_2, \overrightarrow{\rho})(M_1^*)^\tau \in \mathcal{K}^d$ and $\overrightarrow{w} = (s_1, s_2, \overrightarrow{\rho})(M_2^*)^\tau \in \mathcal{K}^d$. Then using the operation notations in Section 3.1, we have the following:

$$< \overrightarrow{u}, \overrightarrow{v}' >= \overrightarrow{u} \overrightarrow{v}'^\tau = (s_1, s_2, \overrightarrow{\rho})M^\tau M_1^* \begin{pmatrix} s_1' \\ s_2' \\ \overrightarrow{\rho}'^\tau \end{pmatrix}$$

$$= (s_1, s_2, \overrightarrow{\rho}) \begin{pmatrix} 1 \ 0 \cdots 0 \\ 0 \ 0 \cdots 0 \\ \vdots \ \vdots \ \ddots \ \vdots \\ 0 \ 0 \cdots 0 \end{pmatrix} \begin{pmatrix} s_1' \\ s_2' \\ \overrightarrow{\rho}'^\tau \end{pmatrix} = s_1 s_1' \ ,$$

$$< \overrightarrow{u}, \overrightarrow{w}' >= \overrightarrow{u} \overrightarrow{w}'^\tau = (s_1, s_2, \overrightarrow{\rho})M^\tau M_2^* \begin{pmatrix} s_1' \\ s_2' \\ \overrightarrow{\rho}'^\tau \end{pmatrix}$$

$$= (s_1, s_2, \overrightarrow{\rho}) \begin{pmatrix} 0 \ 0 \ 0 \cdots 0 \\ 0 \ 1 \ 0 \cdots 0 \\ 0 \ 0 \ 0 \cdots 0 \\ \vdots \ \vdots \ \vdots \ \ddots \ \vdots \\ 0 \ 0 \ 0 \cdots 0 \end{pmatrix} \begin{pmatrix} s_1' \\ s_2' \\ \overrightarrow{\rho}'^\tau \end{pmatrix} = s_2 s_2' \ .$$

Hence $\widetilde{\mathcal{M}}(\mathcal{K}, \widetilde{M}, \widetilde{\psi})$ is multiplicative.

Updatable Zero-Knowledge Databases

Moses Liskov

Computer Science Department,
The College of William and Mary,
Williamsburg, Virginia, USA
mliskov@cs.wm.edu

Abstract. Micali, Rabin, and Kilian [9] recently introduced zero-knowledge sets and databases, in which a prover sets up a database by publishing a commitment, and then gives proofs about particular values. While an elegant and useful primitive, zero-knowledge databases do not offer any good way to perform updates. We explore the issue of updating zero-knowledge databases. We define and discuss *transparent* updates, which (1) allow holders of proofs that are still valid to update their proofs, but (2) otherwise maintain secrecy about the update.

We give rigorous definitions for transparently updatable zero-knowledge databases, and give a practical construction based on the Chase et al [2] construction, assuming that verifiable random functions exist and that mercurial commitments exist, in the random oracle model. We also investigate the idea of *updatable commitments*, an attempt to make simple commitments transparently updatable. We define this new primitive and give a simple secure construction.

Keywords: zero-knowledge databases, zero-knowledge sets, transparent updates, zero-knowledge, protocols, commitments, updatable commitments.

1 Introduction

Recently, zero-knowledge databases were introduced by Micali, Rabin, and Kilian [9]. A zero-knowledge database is a finite partial function D mapping binary strings to binary strings (i.e., a set of pairs of strings (x, y) such that no two pairs have equal first entries but different second entries).[1] The *database owner* chooses D and "publishes" the zero-knowledge database in the form of a commitment that pins down the database but leaks nothing, not even its size. Once the database is committed, the set owner acts as a *prover*: on a query x, the prover gives a proof that either x lies outside D or $D(x) = y$, while still not revealing any further information about D. Commitments and proofs in a zero-knowledge database are *non-interactive* and done in the common random string model.

---

[1] Micali, Rabin, and Kilian call these simple databases "elementary" databases. All databases in this paper are of this simple type.

B. Roy (Ed.): ASIACRYPT 2005, LNCS 3788, pp. 174–198, 2005.

Zero-knowledgeness is shown by exhibiting a polynomial-time simulator that produces a full transcript distribution (i.e., the commitment and the proofs to all query strings) identical to that of the real prover, knowing only "$D(x) = y$" or "x is not in D" for each query and at the last possible moment. While it is conceptually simpler to deal with computational zero-knowledge (and in fact computationally zero-knowledge databases were provided in earlier versions of their paper [5,8]), the Micali-Rabin-Kilian solution is more desirable because it is perfect zero-knowledge. Further, it is much more efficient as it does not involve complex general purpose non-interactive zero-knowledge proofs.

Zero-knowledge databases are a powerful primitive, but they have a major disadvantage in that they are static. This seems like an undesirable property in most applications. For example, if the database were a list of people under investigation for criminal activities, updates would be a critical part of the system. Naively, the only way to update a zero-knowledge database would be to commit to its new version from scratch. However, this is undesirable in two significant ways.

- First, the running time of such an update depends on the size of D, which may be huge, even though the newest version may differ only on a single pair (x, y).
- Second, it may be that those who have seen proofs of membership or non-membership in the original set may be entitled to, or may request again, the same proofs in the new set (for example, if proofs are given due to subscription to some service). If this is the case, the owner would have to reissue old proofs, which could be a huge additional expense.

The second of these points brings up a question that is of interest: when updating such a database, should the proofs be updated as well, or should the new set be private even against those with old proofs?[2] Depending on the application in which the zero-knowledge set is used, either one may be the desirable kind of update. We distinguish these two types of updates by giving them different names:

- *opaque* updates make the updated commitment indistinguishable from a new commitment (hence, the database becomes "opaque" to the users after the update);
- *transparent* updates allow the users to determine whether their proofs are still valid, and provide a mechanism to update proofs (hence, "transparent" to proof holders).

We focus on the problem of transparent updates for two reasons: first, we believe it is the more desirable of the two, as the idea of a subscription service of some type seems to naturally fit the idea of a zero knowledge database, and second, an inefficient but adequate method exists for opaquely updatable zero-knowledge sets, namely, reconstructing the updated commitment from scratch, while no method exists for transparently updatable zero-knowledge sets.

---

[2] It is possible that neither will hold, but it seems natural that we should want one of these.

In this paper, we define the notion of transparently updatable zero-knowledge databases, and show how to construct efficient transparently updatable zero-knowledge databases both based specifically on the Micali-Rabin-Kilian construction and on the more general construction of Chase et al [2], under the additional assumption that verifiable random functions exist in the random oracle model. We also define the notion of an updatable commitment and give a computationally hiding, perfectly binding secure updatable commitment scheme.

In appendix B, we discuss the problem of opaquely updatable zero-knowledge databases.

1.1 Related Work

Zero knowledge sets were introduced in the work of Micali, Rabin, and Kilian [9]. Important precursors to zero knowledge sets appeared in earlier papers by those authors [5,8]. Chase, Healy, Lysyanskaya, Malkin, and Reyzin [2] describe the notion of *mercurial commitments*, that is, commitments that can be "hard" or "soft," an abstraction of the type of commitments used in the Micali-Rabin-Kilian construction, and show that any mercurial commitment scheme can be used to construct zero-knowledge databases. Recent work by Ostrovsky, Rackoff, and Smith [11] greatly enlarges the functionality of zero-knowledge databases by allowing more complex queries (e.g., "does the database's support intersect a given string interval?"). They first design a data structure that, without any privacy concerns, efficiently handles complex queries, and then augment it with zero-knowledge proofs so as to provide privacy, constructing zero-knowledge sets under general assumptions.

1.2 Structure of the Paper

In section 2, we give notation to be used in the rest of the paper. In section 3, we define the security properties needed for updatable zero-knowledge databases. In section 4, we summarize various primitives and previous work, and introduce the notion of updating commitments. In section 5, we give a construction for transparently updatable zero-knowledge databases. In section 6, we discuss the efficiency of our construction. We conclude and discuss open problems in section 7.

2   Notation

We shall follow in our notation from many previous papers, particularly from [9,1].

Probabilistic assignments and experiments. By $x \leftarrow M$ we indicate that the variable x is assigned according to M. If M is a finite set, we assume x is drawn from the uniform distribution on M. The notation $x_1 \leftarrow M_1; x_2 \leftarrow M_2; \ldots$ denotes the probability distribution that arises when we first assign x_1 from distribution M_1, then x_2, et cetera. If p is a predicate, then the notation $Pr[x_1 \leftarrow M_1; x_2 \leftarrow M_2; \ldots : p(x_1, x_2, \ldots)]$ denotes the probability that p is true given that distribution.

Databases. A database D is a set of pairs $\{(x_1, y_1), \ldots, (x_n, y_n)\}$ such that for any database key x there is at most one y such that $(x, y) \in D$. Each x_i and each y_i is a string of unbounded size. We denote by $[D]$ the support of D, that is, the set $\{x_1, \ldots, x_n\}$. To indicate that $x \notin [D]$ we write $D(x) = \perp$. If $x \in [D]$ we write $D(x) = y$ to indicate the unique string y such that $(x, y) \in D$. By $D(x) \leftarrow y$ we mean that D shall be changed so that $D(x) = y$. This may involve exchanging one pair (x, y') for (x, y), or adding (x, y) to the set, or if $y = \perp$, removing the pair (x, y') if any such pair is present.

Polynomial-time adversaries. For the purposes of our definitions, adversaries are specified as Turing machines that repeatedly make outputs of the form (w_i, s_i), where w_i is some query and s_i is state information the adversary will use to make the subsequent query. When we assume that such an A is a *polynomial-time adversary*, we assume that not only is A a polynomial-time algorithm, but that A will ultimately make only polynomially many queries before halting.

Adversary views. If A is an adversary, we define $\text{View}_A\{x_1 \leftarrow M_1, \ldots, x_n \leftarrow M_n\}$ to be a random variable representing the randomness, inputs, and outputs of the adversary A through the computation of the values $x_1, \ldots, x_n$ according to the given probabilistic experiment. Presumably, some of the probabilistic assignment sources M_i involve the adversary A, or the view would be trivial.

Binary trees. We use string notation to specify nodes in a binary tree. ϵ will be the root of the tree. If v is a node in the tree, $v0$ will be the left child of v while $v1$ will be the right child. Values that are stored in a tree at each node will have this string as a subscript; for example, a_ϵ would be the value of a stored at the root node ϵ. If the depth of the tree is bounded by k, the longest strings that refer to nodes in the tree will be of length k. We mean by a *prefix* of a string s any string w (including s) such that there is a string s' such that $ws' = s$. Note that if w is a prefix of s, then w will be a node that lies on the path from ϵ to s in a binary tree.

3   Definitions

Our goal in this section is to rigorously define transparently updatable zero-knowledge databases.

3.1   Mechanics

As with zero-knowledge databases, updatable zero-knowledge databases rely on a public random string σ, the *reference string*. This string must have length polynomial in k, the security parameter.

There are three types of tasks the prover will have to be able to perform. First of all, she will have to be able to commit to the database initially. Second, she will have to be able to issue proofs of membership or non-membership in the database for any key. Finally, she will have to be able to issue updates to the database.

A verifier should be able to verify proofs and to update proofs.

Transparently Updatable Database Systems. We say that a quintuple of Turing machines, (Commit, Prove, DBUpdate, Verify, PUpdate), constitute a transparently updatable database system or TUDB system if none of the machines retain state information after an execution and their computation on common inputs 1^k, a unary string called the *security parameter*, and σ, a binary string called the *reference string*, proceeds as follows:

- The database commitment algorithm is Commit. On input $(D, 1^k, \sigma)$, Commit produces two outputs: (1) a string PK, called D's *public key* (or *commitment*), and (2) a string SK, called D's *secret key*.
- The database proof algorithm is Prove. On input $(D, 1^k, \sigma, PK, SK)$, and an additional input $x \in \{0,1\}^*$, Prove outputs a string π_x, called D's *proof* about x.
- The database update algorithm is DBUpdate. On input $(D, 1^k, \sigma, PK, SK)$, an additional input $x \in \{0,1\}^*$, and a value $y \in \{0,1\}^* \cup \{\bot\}$, DBUpdate computes a new public key PK' and a new secret key SK' for the updated database in which $D(x) = y$, and a string U called the *update information* about x and y, which will be used to update proofs.
- The proof verifying algorithm is Verify. On input $(1^k, \sigma, PK)$ and an additional $x \in \{0,1\}^*$ together with its proof π_x, Verify outputs either a string $y \in \{0,1\}^*$ (meaning that it believes $y = D(x)$), $\bot$ (meaning that it believes that x is outside D's support), or *reject* (meaning that it detected cheating).
- The proof update algorithm is PUpdate. On input $(1^k, \sigma, PK, PK', U)$, and an additional $x \in \{0,1\}^*$ together with its proof π_x, PUpdate outputs either a new proof π'_x, which will be called the *updated proof about x*, $\bot$ (meaning that the update given by PK', U was about x and so the proof cannot be updated), or *reject* (meaning that it detected cheating).

3.2   Security Properties

Updatable zero-knowledge databases must satisfy certain security properties: completeness, soundness, and zero-knowledge. We first describe the desired properties informally, and then formalize our definitions.

Completeness dictates that if the prover and verifier are honest, then for any database, if the prover updates the database any number of times, then gives the verifier a proof about x, and then updates the database any number of times, the verifier may update their proof and obtain a valid one, except with negligible probability, so long as $D(x)$ was not updated after the proof was issued.

Soundness guarantees that the prover is in fact committed to a particular database. That is, given the reference string σ it should be hard for any prover to come up with a PK and any element for which it can prove two different values.

The *zero-knowledge* property of updatable zero-knowledge databases is trickier to describe. Ideally, the adversary should learn nothing more than the values of elements for which a proof has been obtained (and possibly updated), and that updates have occurred. However, we have not been able to realize this full level of security, and instead offer a weaker but acceptable notion of security. Each key x that might be included in the database will have a *pseudonym* $N(x)$. Instead of revealing only that an update has occurred, we reveal that an update has occurred about the key relating to a particular pseudonym. Thus, the pattern of updates is revealed (since the pseudonym is constant for a constant x, so repeated updates on keys can be discovered). In addition, the link between a value x and its pseudonym $N(x)$ will be revealed by Prove. However, we require that no information beyond this be revealed.

This alone does not constitute a high enough level of security: $N(x)$ could reveal information about x. One particular N that is desirable is one that answers 1 to its first input, 2 to its second distinct input, and so on. We call this pseudonym the *pattern pseudonym* N_P, as revealing $N_P(x)$ for many x is equivalent to revealing the pattern of values.

To say this more clearly, a system is zero-knowledge with respect to pseudonym N if, even given any adversary A and any database D the views of A in each of the following two experiments are indistinguishable.

1. First, a random reference string σ is chosen. Then, D is chosen by A and given to the prover, who creates an updatable zero-knowledge database based on D and σ, committing to it with PK while keeping SK private. Then the adversary adaptively chooses a sequence of strings $x_1, x_2, \ldots$ where either $x_i = \mathsf{Query}(x)$ or $x_i = \mathsf{Update}(x, y)$. When x_i is a query, the prover returns a proof π_i that either x is in the database or that x is not in the database. When x_i is $\mathsf{Update}(x, y)$, the prover updates so that $D(x) = y$ and sends PK_i, U_i to the adversary.

2. The simulator Sim, on input only the security parameter k, produces a string σ of the proper length, and a public key PK. The adversary adaptively chooses a sequence of strings $x_1, x_2, \ldots$, where either x_i is either $\mathsf{Query}(x)$ or $\mathsf{Update}(x, y)$. If $x_i = \mathsf{Query}(x)$, the simulator is told x, $N(x)$, and $D(x)$, (where D is up to date, starting with the initial D), and must compute π_i. If x_i is an update $\mathsf{Update}(x, y)$, the simulator is given $N(x)$ and must compute SK_1, PK_1, U_1, while D is updated so that $D(x) = y$. Note that the pseudonym function N is not part of the adversary or the simulator here, but rather is thought of as an oracle that is only called when the game specifies.

In the first scenario, there is no pseudonym function. In the second, the pseudonym function exists, however, the adversary is not directly aware of its presence; the adversary specifies updates $\mathsf{Update}(x, y)$ which get translated into $N(x)$ for the simulator.

The concept of pseudonyms seems inevitable in any zero-knowledge database construction. A zero-knowledge database is in some sense a committed tree, and a particular element must have a unique place to reside (so that we can prove non-membership), which can be thought of as its pseudonym. Furthermore, we cannot use zero-knowledge proofs that reveal nothing about the data structure – the user has to learn enough to allow them to update, but this seems to be the only way to avoid revealing pseudonyms. We have not been able to conceive of a system that does not use pseudonyms, or that uses them but does not reveal them.

We say a transparently updatable database is secure if it is complete, sound, and zero-knowledge with respect to the pattern pseudonym N_P. We say it is secure with respect to N if it is complete, sound, and zero-knowledge with respect to N. Thus, while we may talk about security with respect to other pseudonyms, we regard N_P as the only truly acceptable one.

Efficiency Properties. In order for us to consider an updatable zero-knowledge database efficient, we ask that:

- The running time of the procedure that generates the initial commitment may depend on the size of the database, but all other running times must be independent of the size.
- None of the sizes of the outputs other than SK may depend on the number of updates.
- None of the running times of any of the verifier algorithms may depend on the number of updates that have been performed (in a sense limiting total performance to linear in the number of updates, since some procedures are performed once per update).

3.3   Formal Definitions

We formalize our definitions in appendix A.

4   Preliminaries

Before we present our construction, we first review some crucial building blocks used in our construction. Some of our text follows closely from the preliminaries section from [9].

4.1   Updatable Commitments

Here, we define updatable commitments. In an ordinary commitment scheme, there are two algorithms: $\mathcal{C}$, which takes a message m as input and produces c and d, where c is the commitment, and d is the information used to open the commitment later, and $\mathcal{V}$, which takes a commitment c, a message m, and a decommitment d, and checks whether c was a commitment to m, using d. Note that there may also be public parameters which are inputs to all algorithms, but for clarity we simplify.

In an updatable commitment, there will be one more algorithm: $\mathcal{U}$, which takes a message m and decommitment information d, and produces a commitment c, where d will be the decommitment information used to open c. The binding property is defined in the natural way. The hiding property is essentially that commitments be indistinguishable under a chosen message attack, where the adversary may ask for commitments, updated commitments, and decommitments of his choice, so long as he doesn't ask for a decommitment of the challenge or any message derived from the challenge through updates.

Our Construction. Our construction is quite simple. Given a secure perfectly binding commitment scheme and a secure pseudorandom permutaiton P, we can construct a simple computationally hiding, perfectly binding commitment scheme as follows:

$\mathcal{C}(m)$: generate a key K for the pseudorandom permutation, a random string IV, and compute c_1, a commitment to K under the commitment scheme and d_1, the related decommitment information, and c_2, the evaluation of the pseudorandom permutation on $m \oplus IV$ with key K. Output $c = (c_1, c_2, IV)$, and $d = (K, c_1, d_1)$.

$\mathcal{V}((c_1, c_2, IV), m, (K, c_1, d_1))$: check that c_1 is a commitment to K using d_1. If not, reject. Then, check that $c_2 = P_K(m \oplus IV)$. If so, accept, if not, reject.

$\mathcal{U}(m, (K, c_1, d_1))$: compute $c_2 = P_K(m)$ and output $c = (c_1, c_2)$.

It is clear that any commitment is a commitment to one specific value, since c_1 specifies a unique K, and given that K, c_2 specifies a unique m. Furthermore, c_2 is the encryption of the one-block message m under CBC mode, so if this scheme is not hiding, then either the PRP is not pseudorandom or the underlying commitment scheme is not hiding. This is true even if K is used for many different commitments, so long as K is never revealed.

4.2 Mercurial Commitments

Mercurial commitments were introduced recently by Chase et al [2] with direct application to zero-knowledge sets and databases. A mercurial commitment is a commitment scheme in which there are two kinds of commitments and two kinds of ways to decommit.

- A "hard commitment" is a commitment to a particular value. It can only be decommitted to that value, whether the decommitment is a hard or a soft one.
- A "soft commitment" is a commitment to no value. It can never be hard-decommitted, but it can be soft-decommitted to any value.

A mercurial commitment scheme is secure when it is hiding (in the sense that the type of a commitment is kept secret as well as the value if the commitment is a hard commitment) and binding (in the sense that the committer cannot break the above rules.) Mercurial commitments have a non-interactive commitment and decommitment, but require the public random string model. In fact, they also have a trap-door property: if the public random string is chosen by a simulator, the simulator can avoid the binding properties.

4.3 Pedersen's Commitment Scheme

Pedersen's commitment scheme [12] assumes the availability of a public quadruple (p, q, g, h), where p and q are prime, $q|p-1$ and g and h are generators for G, the cyclic subgroup of Z_p^* of order q, for which computing discrete logarithms is assumed to be hard.

The commitment and verification algorithms are defined as follows, where all operations are performed modulo p:

$\mathcal{C}((p,q,g,h),m)$: randomly select $r \in Z_q$ and output (c,r), where $c = g^m h^r$ is the commitment string, and r is the (for the time being secret) proof.

$\mathcal{V}((p,q,g,h),c,m,r)$: If $c = g^m h^r$, then accept; else, reject.

This commitment scheme is perfectly hiding and computationally binding.

The mercurial commitment scheme used in [9] is based directly on this commitment scheme. Instead of using g as the base to compute g^m directly, we use a different base for each commitment: g^e for a hard commitment or h^e for a soft commitment, and publish the base that we use as part of the commitment (where e is random). A soft decommitment consists of publishing r; then, it can be checked that $c = b^m h^r$ where b is the base being used. A hard decommitment involves publishing r as well as e, so that it can also be checked that $g^e = b$.

4.4   CHLMR Zero-Knowledge Databases

The following is a summary of the general zero-knowledge database construction of Chase, Healy, Lysyanskaya, Malkin, and Reyzin [2].

ZK databases. The construction works in the public random string model, that is, there is a common random reference string σ.

In order to force every key to be of length k, we first hash them to obtain the database $\{(H(x), y)\}$. Every node in the tree can be labelled by a string $\omega \in \{0,1\}^{\leq k}$. At each node ω there will be the following values associated:

- A value v_ω. If $\omega = H(x)$ for some $x \in [D]$ then $v_\omega = H(D(x))$. If $|\omega| = k$ but $\omega \neq H(x)$ for any $x \in [D]$ then $v_\omega = H(\perp)$. If ω is an internal node, the value v_ω is defined recursively as $H(c_{\omega 0} c_{\omega 1})$ where c_ω is defined below. Essentially, the values v_ω make the tree a Merkle tree.
- A commitment c_ω which is either a soft commitment or a hard commitment to v_ω.
- Decommitment information d_ω for the commitment c_ω.

The commitment to the database is the commitment c_ϵ from the root node ϵ.

In order to prove that an element x is in the database, the set owner gives a proof consisting of:

1. $D(x)$, so that $H(D(x))$ is the value $v_{H(x)}$.
2. For every ω that is a prefix of $H(x)$, c_ω and a hard decommitment of c_ω, and
3. For every ω that is a sibling along the path from ϵ to $H(x)$, the value c_ω.

The verifier uses this to construct the values v_ω for every ω that is a prefix of $H(x)$, and then checks the hard decommitments.

In order to prove that an element x is *not* in the database, the set owner gives a proof consisting of:

1. For every ω that is a prefix of $H(x)$, c_ω and a soft decommitment of c_ω to v_ω, and
2. For every ω that is a sibling along the path from ϵ to $H(x)$, the value c_ω.

The verifier checks as before, except that the verifier uses $D(x) = \bot$, and that the decommitments are soft.

The key to the efficiency of the construction is the use of mercurial commitments. If ordinary commitments were to be used, the entire tree of depth k would have to be computed, which is clearly exponential. However, the tree is constructed so that soft commitments are used for any node that has no descendents in the data set, which allows the prover to not compute those parts of the tree ahead of time, but allows the prover to compute those parts of the tree when necessary, *and* be able to decommit.

4.5   Verifiable Random Functions

Verifiable random functions or VRFs were first presented by Micali, Rabin, and Vadhan [10], and subsequent constructions appear in [6,3]. A verifiable random function consists of four algorithms: a key generating algorithm GenVRF that produces a pair (PK, SK) on input 1^k, an algorithm ComputeVRF that computes $f_{SK}(x)$, an algorithm ProveVRF that gives proofs π that a value $y = f_{SK}(x)$ is correctly generated from x, and an algorithm VerVRF that verifies proofs, with the following informal properties:

1. If (PK, SK) are generated from GenVRF, and y is generated from ComputeVRF(SK, x) and π is generated from ProveVRF(SK, x), then VerVRF(PK, x, y, π) will accept.
2. f_{SK} is a pseudorandom function, even to an adversary that may request both outputs and outputs with proofs, so long as the two sets of queries do not overlap.
3. No adversary can produce a (PK, SK) pair for which it can give proofs that will be verified for incorrect values.

In particular, note that no adversary should be able to compute $f_{SK}(x)$ given x and PK.

5   Our Construction

We describe our construction incrementally. First, we describe how to go about updating a CHLMR database efficiently. Then, we go on to describe how to provide update information that will allow proof holders to update their proofs. Then we give a construction with an unspecified pseudonym N and prove security relative to N. We then prove security in the random oracle model and discuss issues that arise relative to implementing the random oracle.

5.1   Updating a CHLMR Database

Suppose that we wish to assign a particular value y (possibly $\perp$) to $D(x)$, for a given x, in a given CHLMR database.

Our first goal is to efficiently compute a new commitment to a CHLMR database with the updated value. This is fairly easy to do, and natural. Essentially, we just change the values at the leaf we are interested in, and update the internal nodes of the tree to maintain the required structure. To update the value $D(x)$, we regenerate the commitment $c_{H(x)}$ and from this recompute the values and commitments in the tree going up along the path from $H(x)$ to ϵ, leaving everything else the same. Now, for every prefix ω of $H(x)$, the value v_ω may change, so the value c_ω may also change. The set owner then publishes c_ϵ anew.

In order to make this fit all the properties of a ZK database, we must be careful when adding an element to the set that all its ancestors are hard commitments. Thus, when we add an element to the set that was previously not in the set, we must make commitments along the path hard commitments, even if they were previously soft commitments. In fact, we can simply make all commitments in any update hard commitments, to simplify.

5.2   A Simple Mechanism for Updating Proofs

Now, the updated database is a CHLMR database, just as was constructed before.[3] The next step is to determine what information is necessary to allow proof holders to update their proofs. Since a proof is essentially a hash path in the tree along with decommitments to the values along that path, and the only internal nodes or commitments that have changed are the ones along the path from ϵ to $H(x)$, we could just publish all the commitments at the updated internal nodes. However, this is not quite sufficient, because decommitments are necessary for the proofs to be complete. To solve this, we need to modify our mercurial commitment scheme so that it is updatable, but the requirements are a little more complex than the requirements for an updatable commitment. Specifically, we need to be able to update such that (1) the updated commitment is always a hard commitment, and (2) the holder of a decommitment (soft or hard) can update their decommitment to a new one of the same type.

Under general assumptions, the best known mercurial commitment is only computationally hiding. In order to make an updatable one, we need to combine a mercurial commitment scheme and an updatable commitment scheme as follows. Instead of publishing only the mercurial commitment c, we also publish c_H and c_S where c_H is an updatable commitment to the hard decommitment of c (or a random string if it is a soft commitment), and c_S is an updatable commitment, initially to a random string, but after any updates, to a soft decommitment of c. A hard decommitment involves opening c_H, while a soft decommitment involves opening c_S, and also giving a soft decommitment to c. This means a

---

[3] Except, some commitments might be hard that don't need to be hard commitments, but by the properties of mercurial commitments, this is an indistinguishable change.

verifier will notice a difference between opening an original commitment and opening an updated one, but this will be acceptable for our means. Updating the commitment (c, c_H, c_S) is done by replacing c with a fresh commitment and updating c_H and c_S to be commitments to their new appropriate values.

We can also make the MRK mercurial commitment updatable in this way, simply by reusing r. When we update a commitment, we always make it hard, so we also publish e. It is worth noting that this is not as hiding as we might like such a commitment to be in isolation, since (for instance) the ratio between j^m and $(g^e)^{m'}$ is revealed, and an unbounded adversary could learn information from this. This costs us perfect zero-knowledge in our construction, but under the DDH assumption, this is still hiding. We should also note that updating commitments in this way does not give a mechanism for the verifier to determine m', but, in our application, m' can be derived from other information.

5.3 Attaining Zero-Knowledge with Respect to N

Now we have a system where after an update we have a zero-knowledge database, and proofs can be updated. However, the updates do not preserve secrecy. The issue has to do with the pseudonym we use. Here, we use $H(x)$ as a pseudonym. In order to more carefully discuss the issue of our choice of pseudonym, we specify this construction by describing it in terms of an unspecified pseudonym $N(x)$.

Commit$(D, 1^k, \sigma)$: Run the database commitment algorithm but instead of using $H(x)$ to define an element's position in the tree, use $N(x)$.

Prove$(D, 1^k, \sigma, PK, SK, x)$: run the database proof algorithm, looking for x at position $N(x)$ to obtain π_x.

DBUpdate$(D, 1^k, \sigma, PK, SK, x, y)$: create a new commitment $c_{N(x)}$ to $v_{N(x)} = H(y)$. Recursively, for each ω that is a prefix of $N(x)$, update c_ω to be a hard commitment of v_ω. Compute $PK' = c_\epsilon$, update SK' by remembering all the new decommitment information, and compute $U = \{\omega, c_\omega\}$ for all prefixes ω of $N(x)$.

Verify$(1^k, \sigma, PK, x, \pi_x)$: run the proof verifying algorithm to verify π_x, using $N(x)$ instead of $H(x)$, and check the value given as $N(x)$ to be sure it is correct.

PUpdate$(1^k, \sigma, PK, PK', U, x, \pi_x)$: if U is an update about $N(x)$, output $\bot$. (Note that $N(x)$ would be known from π_x.) Otherwise, for every ω that is a prefix of $N(x)$ and is included in U, we have a decommitment to the old c_ω, so we update our decommitment. For every ω that is a sibling along the path, we change our value of c_ω to the value of c_ω given in the update U. Finally, we check our updated proof, and reject if it does not yield the same value, otherwise we outpud π_x', our updated proof.

Theorem 1. This scheme is a secure zero-knowledge transparently updatable database with respect to N.

Proof. Due to space constraints, we only provide a proof sketch here. A more detailed proof may be found in appendix C.

Completeness of this construction should be clear. Since the form of any database commitment and proof are just as in [2] except with a different scheme to assign database locations to database keys, soundness here follows from the soundness of their construction and the uniqueness of the mapping $x \mapsto N(x)$.

For zero-knowledgeness we must show a simulator that has the required properties. First of all, the simulator generates σ so that the mercurial commitment simulator can be used (that is, the simulator can break the binding property of the scheme). The simulator then generates a soft commitment c_ϵ and publishes it.

When the simulator is asked for a proof that $D(x) = y$ and is given x and $N(x)$, it simply does exactly as the CHLMR database simulator does, except that the path is a path from ϵ to $N(x)$. When the simulator is asked to update a value with a given pseudonym n, it performs an update just as DBUpdate would, using $y = \epsilon$, creating c_ω values for each ω that is a prefix of n for which c_ω was not already determined in a proof. (Note that DBUpdate does not need to know x if it knows $N(x)$.)

The values given in the proofs issued by the system are just sequences of commitments, decommitted to the correct values, so the distribution of the proofs given by the simulator and those given by the real prover are indistinguishable. The distribution of updates is also identical except that the simulator always sets $y = \epsilon$. However, the only value that depends directly on y is $c_{N(x)}$ which is a (fresh) commitment, so in fact the distribution of update strings is also indistinguishable. Thus, we achieve zero-knowledge.

5.4   Attaining Security in the Random Oracle Model

We now have a system that gives a transparently updatable zero-knowledge database with respect to N for an unspecified N. Unfortunately, we cannot simply specify $N = N_P$ and be done, because N_P cannot be computed in a way verifiable to the user. This problem can be solved by assuming the random oracle model. The idea is that we use a random oracle that may be controlled by the simulator to compute $N(x)$. It should be clear that a random oracle computed on x and a random oracle computed on $N_P(x)$ are identical. Thus, the simulator simulates the random oracle on input $N_P(x)$ by evaluating a random function on it. By doing this, the simulator may naturally compute $N(x)$ knowing only $N_P(x)$. Thus, such a simulator shows that if we use a random oracle as $N(x)$, our construction is secure.

5.5   Implementing the Random Oracle

Using the random oracle model has significant problems. First of all, random oracles are generally implemented by collision-resistant hash functions, but this cannot always be done securely. There is also an issue of pseudonym collisions, which we discuss this issue in appendix D.

Most importantly, though, we cannot simply use a public hash function here, because doing so would allow the adversary to query the pseudonym function, but it was one of our security requirements that the adversary not be able to do this. Ideally, the adversary should only be able to learn if a particular update was about x by querying the database at x.

The pseudonym function we propose to use is $H^*(x) = H(f(H(x)))$ where H is a hash function and f is a verifiable random function. We will still assume that H is a random oracle, but now, even if H is a random oracle, the adversary cannot query H^*. Before we jump into the security proof for this pseudonym, we must modify our construction slightly, because $H^*(x)$ cannot be computed by the verifier.

- In Commit we also run GenVRF and make the public key PK_f part of the public key, and keep SK_f as part of the secret key.
- In Prove$(D, 1^k\sigma, PK, SK, x)$, we also give $\pi'_x = \mathsf{ProveVRF}(SK_f, H(x))$ and $z = \mathsf{ComputeVRF}(SK_f, H(x))$.
- In Verify, we additionally run $\mathsf{VerVRF}(PK_f, H(x), z, \pi'_x)$ and check that $H^*(x) = H(z)$ before accepting.

This fits nicely into our original specification; we are simply expanding the idea of what it means to check that $H^*(x)$ is correctly computed.

Theorem 2. This construction is secure in the random oracle model.

Proof. Again, we give only a sketch of the proof, due to space constraints. See appendix C for a full proof.

Completeness is already established by our proof of Theorem 1. To prove soundness, we need only note that the pseudonym $H^*(x)$ that will be verified is unique, from the soundness property of the VRF.

Zero-knowledge is more of a challenge. We give a simulator with respect to N_P that gives us computational zero-knowledge. First, the simulator makes σ and the database commitment c_ϵ just as the previous simulator does. The simulator then runs GenVRF to generate (PK_f, SK_f), and publishes (PK_f, c_ϵ) as the database commitment.

The simulator must answer three kinds of messages: random oracle queries, database queries, and update queries. The simulator maintains two random functions, H and H', with the idea that $H'(N_P(x)) = H(f(H(x)))$. When the simulator receives an update query, it computes $H^*(x) = H'(N_P(x))$. When the simulator receives a database query, the simulator computes $H(x)$, and then computes $z = f_{SK_f}(H(x))$, and then sets $H(z) = H'(N_P(x))$ and fakes a proof that the value stored at $H^*(x) = H'(N_P(x))$ is y, just as the simulator does in theorem 1.

The illusion that $H'(N_P(x)) = H(f_{SK_f}(H(x)))$ is maintained as long as $H(z)$ is not already defined to be something else when the simulator tries to set $H(z) = H'(N_P(x))$. However, if this happens with non-negligible probability, it must be because either we have found an f-collision with non-negligible probability, or because the adversary has queried $H(z)$ separately. In either case, we can use such an adversary to break the pseudorandomness of f. Because ultimately, the zero-knowledge property of our scheme may be defeated by defeating the pseudorandomness of f, we only get computational zero-knowledge.

We note that if we restrict the adversary a bit further, we can actually remove the random oracle assumption. Specifically, if we require that whenever the adversary requests an update about x, that either the adversary has already queried the database at x, or the adversary will *never* query the database about x, then we can prove zero-knowledge without the random oracle. We can also remove the random oracle if we use general NIZK proofs. We discuss this further in appendix E.

6   Efficiency

Our proposal for the mecahnics of a transparently updatable database embeds the idea that for each update (even of a single element) to the database, a public update string is published, and that for each update string that is published, each user updates each of their proofs. Given this syntax, our performance is optimal in terms of the number of updates: each update induces additional work for both the database owner and the user, but the amount of work per update is independent from the number of updates. However, the total amount of work a user must do to maintain a proof is linear in the number of updates. In appendix F we describe some minor efficiency improvements along these lines.

7   Conclusion and Open Problems

We have given a secure construction of a transparently updatable zero-knowledge database that is both efficient and practical in the random oracle model. For our construction to be secure, we must assume the existence of a VRF, and that mercurial commitments exist. The most practical construction that arises from this work is the extension of the original Micali-Rabin-Kilian construction, which requies the discrete logarithm assumption. These two assumptions can be combined by using the VRF of Dodis and Yampolskiy [3], which relies on a more restrictive assumption than the discrete logarithm assumption.

Some open problems that may be of interest would be to construct:

- Zero-knowledge transparently updatable databases with stronger security or more general assumptions
- More efficient and/or perfect zero-knowledge opaque updates.
- Zero-knowledge databases the can be efficiently updated both transparently and opaquely.

Acknowledgements

The author sincerely and deeply thanks Susan Hohenberger, Anna Lysyanskaya, Silvio Micali, and Adam Smith for their helpful comments. The author also especially wishes to thank the anonymous program committee members who have provided useful feedback.

References

1. Manuel Blum, Alfredo De Santis, Silvio Micali, and Giuseppe Persiano. Noninteractive zero-knowledge. SIAM *Journal on Computing*, 20(6):1084 – 1118, December 1991.
2. Melissa Chase, Alex Healy, Anna Lysyanskaya, Tal Malkin, and Leonid Reyzin. Mercurial commitments with applications to zero-knowledge sets. In *Advances in Cryptology – EUROCRYPT 2005*, Lecture Notes in Computer Science. Springer-Verlag, 22 – 26 May 2005.
3. Yevgeniy Dodis and Aleksandr Yampolskiy. A verifiable random function with short proofs and keys. In Serge Vaudenay, editor, *8th International Workshop on Theory and Practice in Public Key Cryptography*, volume 3386 of *lncs*, pages 416 – 432. Springer-Verlag, 2005.
4. Oded Goldreich, Silvio Micali, and Avi Wigderson. Proofs that yield nothing but their validity or all languages in NP have zero-knowledge proof systems. *Journal of the ACM*, 38(1):691 – 729, 1991.
5. J. Kilian. Efficiently committing to databases. TR 97-040, NEC Research Institute, 1997.
6. Anna Lysyanskaya. Unique signatures and verifiable random functions from the DH-DDH separation. In Moti Yung, editor, *Advances in Cryptology – CRYPTO 2002*, Lecture Notes in Computer Science. Springer-Verlag, 2002.
7. Ralph C. Merkle. A certified digital signature. In G. Brassard, editor, *Advances in Cryptology – CRYPTO 89*, volume 435 of *Lecture Notes in Computer Science*, pages 218238. Springer-Verlag, 1990, 20 – 24 August 1989.
8. Silvio Micali and Michael Rabin. Hashing on strings, cryptography, and protection of privacy. In *Proceedings of Compression and Complexity of Sequences*, page 1, Los Alamitos, California, 11 – 13 June 1997. IEEE Computer Society.
9. Silvio Micali, Michael Rabin, and Joseph Kilian. Zero-knowledge sets. In *44th Annual Symposium on Foundations of Computer Science*, Cambridge, MA, October 2003. IEEE.
10. Silvio Micali, Michael Rabin, and Salil Vadhan. Verifiable random functions. In *40th Annual Symposium on Foundations of Computer Science*, pages 120 – 130, New York, October 1999. IEEE.
11. R. Ostrovsky, C. Rackoff, and A. Smith. Efficient proofs of consistency for generalized queries on a committed database. In *Proceedings of ICALP 2004*, 2004.
12. Torben Pryds Pedersen. A threshold cryptosystem without a trusted party (extended abstract). In D. W. Davies, editor, *Advances in Cryptology – EUROCRYPT 91*, volume 547 of *Lecture Notes in Computer Science*, pages 522-526. Springer-Verlag, 8 – 11 April 1991.

Appendix A: Formal Definitions for Opaque Updates

These definitions are closely derived from [9]. Here, we formalize the definitions described in section 3.2.

Updatable Database Simulators

Let Sim be a probabilistic polyonomial-time oracle Turing machine. We say that Sim is an updatable database *simulator* (or UDB simulator) if it computes as follows, relative to an *external* database D and pseudonym function N:

1. In its first execution, Sim^N outputs three strings, σ, PK, and SK.
2. In a subsequent execution on input SK and a triple $(x, D(x), N(x))$, $\mathsf{Sim}^N(SK, x, D(x), N(x))$ outputs a string π_x.
3. In a subsequent execution on input SK and n, $\mathsf{Sim}^N(SK, n)$ computes PK', SK', U where SK' becomes the new secret key, and PK' and U are outputs. When this happens, D may change at up to one input, namely an x such that $N(x) = n$.

Transparently Updatable Zero-Knowledge Databases
Let (Commit, Prove, DBUpdate, Verify, PUpdate) be a TUDB system where all the Turing machines in the quintuple run in probabilistic polynomial time. We say that (Commit, Prove, DBUpdate, Verify, PUpdate) is a *zero-knowledge transparently updatable database system* (or ZKTUDB system) if there exists a UDB simulator Sim and a constant c such that

1. *Completeness.* $\forall$ database $D, \exists \nu$ negligible such that $\forall k, \forall r, s, t$ such that $0 \le s \le r \le k^c$,

$Pr[\ \sigma \leftarrow \{0,1\}^{k^c}; (PK, SK) \leftarrow \mathsf{Commit}(D, 1^k, \sigma);$
$\quad x_1 \leftarrow \{0,1\}^{\le t}; y_1 \leftarrow \{0,1\}^{\le t}; \ldots; x_r \leftarrow \{0,1\}^{\le t}; y_r \leftarrow \{0,1\}^{\le t}; x \leftarrow \{0,1\}^{\le t}$
$\quad (PK', SK', U) \leftarrow \mathsf{DBUpdate}(D, 1^k, \sigma, PK, SK, (x_1, y_1)); PK \leftarrow PK'; SK \leftarrow SK';$
$\quad D(x_1) \leftarrow y_1; \ldots;$
$\quad (PK', SK', U) \leftarrow \mathsf{DBUpdate}(D, 1^k, \sigma, PK, SK, (x_s, y_s)); PK \leftarrow PK'; SK \leftarrow SK';$
$\quad D(x_s) \leftarrow y_s; \pi_x \leftarrow \mathsf{Prove}(D, 1^k, \sigma, PK, SK, x);$
$\quad (PK', SK', U) \leftarrow \mathsf{DBUpdate}(D, 1^k, \sigma, PK, SK, (x_{s+1}, y_{s+1})); SK \leftarrow SK'; D(x_{s+1}) \leftarrow y_{s+1};$
$\quad \pi_x \leftarrow \mathsf{PUpdate}(1^k, \sigma, PK, PK', U, x, \pi_x); PK \leftarrow PK';$
$\quad \ldots;$
$\quad (PK', SK', U) \leftarrow \mathsf{DBUpdate}(D, 1^k, \sigma, PK, SK, (x_r, y_r)); SK \leftarrow SK'; D(x_r) \leftarrow y_r;$
$\quad \pi_x \leftarrow \mathsf{PUpdate}(1^k, \sigma, PK, PK', U, x, \pi_x); PK \leftarrow PK';$
$\quad y \leftarrow \mathsf{Verify}(1^k, \sigma, PK, x, \pi_x):$
$\quad$ if $\exists l$ such that $s < l \le r$ and $x_l = x$ then $\pi_x = \perp$, otherwise $y = D(x)] > 1 - \nu(k).$

Here, s is the number of updates before the proof is given, and r is the number of updates total.

2. *Soundness.* $\forall x \in \{0,1\}^*$ and $\forall P'$ probabilistic polynomial time, $\exists \nu$ negligible such that $\forall k,$

$Pr[\ \sigma \leftarrow \{0,1\}^{k^c}; (PK, x, \pi_1, \pi_2) \leftarrow P'(1^k, \sigma);$
$\quad y_1 \leftarrow \mathsf{Verify}(1^k, \sigma, PK, x, \pi_1); y_2 \leftarrow \mathsf{Verify}(1^k, \sigma, PK, x, \pi_2):$
$\quad reject \notin \{y_1, y_2\} \wedge y_1 \ne y_2] \le \nu(k),$

3. *Zero-knowledge with respect to N.* $\forall A$ acceptable adversaries, $\forall k$, $\mathrm{View}(k) \approx \mathrm{View}'(k)^4$ where

---

[4] As usual, $\approx$ may refer to computational indistinguishability (in which case the system is said to be "computationally zero-knowledge"), statistical closeness ("statistical zero-knowledge"), or equality ("perfect zero-knowledge"). For computational indistinguishability, A must be a polynomial-time adversary. For statistical or perfect indistinguishability, we do not limit A's power.

$$\text{View}(k) =$$
$$\text{View}_A \{ \sigma \leftarrow \{0,1\}^{k^c}; (D, s_0) \leftarrow A(1^k, \sigma);$$
$$(PK, SK) \leftarrow \mathsf{Commit}(D, 1^k, \sigma); z_0 \leftarrow PK;$$
$$(w_1, s_1) \leftarrow A(s_0, z_0);$$
$$\text{If} \quad w_1 = \mathsf{Update}(x_1, y_1),$$
$$\quad (PK_1', SK_1', U_1) \leftarrow \mathsf{DBUpdate}(D, 1^k, \sigma, PK, SK, x_1, y_1); SK \leftarrow SK_1'; PK \leftarrow PK_1';$$
$$\quad D(x_1) \leftarrow y_1; z_1 \leftarrow (PK_1', U_1);$$
$$\text{Else} \ \ \text{if} \ w_1 = \mathsf{Query}(x_1), \ \pi_1 \leftarrow \mathsf{Prove}(D, 1^k, \sigma, PK, SK, x_1); z_1 \leftarrow \pi_1;$$
$$(w_2, s_2) \leftarrow A(s_1, z_1);$$
$$\dots \}$$

and

$$\text{View}'(k) =$$
$$\text{View}_A \{ (\sigma, PK, SK) \leftarrow \mathsf{Sim}^N(1^k); (D, s_0) \leftarrow A(1^k, \sigma);$$
$$z_0 \leftarrow PK;$$
$$(w_1, s_1) \leftarrow A(s_0, z_0);$$
$$\text{If} \quad w_1 = \mathsf{Update}(x_1, y_1),$$
$$\quad (PK_1', SK_1', U_1) \leftarrow \mathsf{Sim}^N(SK, N(x_1)); SK \leftarrow SK_1'; PK \leftarrow PK_1';$$
$$\quad D(x_1) \leftarrow y_1; z_1 \leftarrow (PK_1', U_1);$$
$$\text{Else} \ \ \text{if} \ w_1 = \mathsf{Query}(x_1), \ \pi_1 \leftarrow \mathsf{Sim}^N(SK, x_1, D(x_1), N(x_1)); z_1 \leftarrow \pi_1;$$
$$(w_2, s_2) \leftarrow A(s_1, z_1);$$
$$\dots \}$$

Appendix B: Opaquely Updatable Zero-Knowledge Databases

We define opaquely updatable zero-knowledge databases, and present a solution following ideas from Rackoff, Ostrovsky, and Smith [11] that is inefficient and relies on general non-interactive zero-knowledge proofs. We do not present any practical, efficient method better than simply committing the updated database from scratch; indeed, we view this as an important open problem.

An opaquely updatable database system (or OUDB system) is a quadruple of algorithms (Commit, Prove, DBUpdate, Verify) which satisfy the properties properties of a TUDB system, except that DBUpdate outputs only PK', SK'.

Zero-knowledge opaquely updatable databases are defined similarly to transparently updatable ones. Let (Commit, Prove, DBUpdate, Verify) be a UDB system where all the Turing machines in the quadruple run in probabilistic polynomial time. We say that (Commit, Prove, DBUpdate, Verify) is a *zero-knowledge opaquely updatable database system* (or ZKOUDB system) if there is a UDB simulator Sim and a constant c such that the following four properties are satisfied:

1. *Perfect completeness.* $\forall$ database $D, \forall r, \forall$ sequences of updates $(x_1, y_1), \dots,$ (x_r, y_r), and $\forall x \in [D] \cup \{x_1, \dots, x_r\}$,

$$Pr[\ \sigma \leftarrow \{0,1\}^{k^c}; (PK, SK) \leftarrow \mathsf{Commit}(D, 1^k, \sigma);$$
$$(PK', SK', U) \leftarrow \mathsf{DBUpdate}(D, 1^k, \sigma, PK, SK, (x_1, y_1)); PK \leftarrow PK'; SK \leftarrow SK';$$
$$D(x_1) \leftarrow y_1; \dots;$$
$$(PK', SK', U) \leftarrow \mathsf{DBUpdate}(D, 1^k, \sigma, PK, SK, (x_r, y_r)); PK \leftarrow PK'; SK \leftarrow SK';$$

$D(x_r) \leftarrow y_r; \pi_x \leftarrow \mathsf{Prove}(D, 1^k, \sigma, PK, SK);$
$y \leftarrow \mathsf{Verify}(1^k, \sigma, PK, x, \pi_x) :$
$y = D(x)] = 1.$

2. *Soundness.* ($\mathsf{Commit}, \mathsf{Prove}, \mathsf{DBUpdate}, \mathsf{Verify}$) satisfies the soundness property of a ZKTUDB.
3. *Zero-knowledge.* ($\mathsf{Commit}, \mathsf{Prove}, \mathsf{Verify}$) satisfies the zero-knowledge properties of a ZK database. We actually want zero-knowledge to hold for an adversary that can adaptively ask for queries and updates, but we capture the difference in our definition of update secrecy.
4. *Update secrecy.* For all appropriate A, $\mathrm{View}(k) \approx \mathrm{View}'(k)$ where:

$\mathrm{View}(k) =$
  $\mathrm{View}_A \{ \sigma \leftarrow \{0,1\}^{k^C}; (D, s_0) \leftarrow A(\sigma); (PK, SK) \leftarrow \mathsf{Commit}(D, 1^k, \sigma);$
  $z_0 \leftarrow PK; (w_1, s_1) \leftarrow A(s_0, z_0);$
  If $w_1 = \mathsf{Update}(x_1, y_1),$
        $(PK', SK') \leftarrow \mathsf{DBUpdate}(D, 1^k, \sigma, PK, SK, x_1, y_1); SK \leftarrow SK'; PK \leftarrow PK';$
        $D(x_1) \leftarrow y_1; z_1 \leftarrow PK';$
  Else if $w_1 = x_1, \pi_1 \leftarrow \mathsf{Prove}(D, 1^k, \sigma, PK, SK, x_1); z_1 \leftarrow \pi_1;$
  $(w_2, s_2) \leftarrow A(s_1, z_1);$
  $\ldots \}$

and

$\mathrm{View}'(k) =$
  $\mathrm{View}_A \{ \sigma \leftarrow \{0,1\}^{k^C}; (D, s_0) \leftarrow A(\sigma); (PK, SK) \leftarrow \mathsf{Commit}(D, 1^k, \sigma);$
  $z_0 \leftarrow PK; (w_1, s_1) \leftarrow A(s_0, z_0);$
  If $w_1 = \mathsf{Update}(x_1, y_1),$
        $D(x_1) \leftarrow y_1; (PK', SK') \leftarrow \mathsf{Commit}(D, 1^k, \sigma); SK \leftarrow SK'; PK \leftarrow PK';$
        $z_1 \leftarrow PK';$
  Else if $w_1 = x_1, \pi_1 \leftarrow \mathsf{Prove}(D, 1^k, \sigma, PK, SK, x_1); z_1 \leftarrow \pi_1;$
  $(w_2, s_2) \leftarrow A(s_1, z_1);$
  $\ldots \}$

Again, appropriate adversaries are polynomial-time adversaries for computational indistinguishability, and unbounded adversaries otherwise.

Opaquely Updatable Construction

To create an opaquely updatable zero-knowledge database, following Rackoff, Ostrovsky, and Smith [11], we modify the CHLMR construction as follows. Instead of sending a proof π_x to the verifier, we give $D(x)$ and a non-interactive zero-knowledge proof of knowledge relative to σ of knowledge of π_x such that π_x is a valid proof. To update, we just update the values where required, but do not publish any of the updated values. We clearly have zero-knowledge: in order to simulate, we just randomly create c_ϵ initially and each time we are asked to update we create a new random commitment, and any time we are asked to give a proof, we provide a faked non-interactive zero-knowledge proof. Furthermore, c_ϵ form a random commitment whether or not they were generated from DBUpdate, so we have update secrecy as well, and soundness and completeness follow from these same properties of CHLMR databases.

However, such non-interactive zero-knowledge proof systems are also only computational zero-knowledge. In addition, much effort was taken by Micali,

Rabin, and Kilian to avoid both computational zero-knowledge and the need for general non-interactive zero-knowledge proofs. The large amount of inefficiency added to the system may even overbalance the objection to the solution of recommitting the database from scratch. We consider it a significant open problem to construct an efficient and practical opaquely updatable zero-knowledge databases.

Appendix C: Detailed Proof of Security

Proof of Theorem 1. To prove theorem 1, we must make a minor additional asusmption, and prove several things.

First of all, note that when an update occurs, the only difference between the secret information in our construction and the secret information in a CHLMR database is that in our construction, it may be that for some internal nodes ω which have no descendents in the tree, c_ω is a hard commitment rather than a soft one. However, that is unimportant as proofs involving such an ω as a node on the path will always be of nonmembership, and so only soft decommitments will be revealed.

To prove completeness, note that when the database is updated, part of an old proof about a different element will include path elements that have changed. However, such path elements are always published as part of the update information, so they can simply be replaced. Thus, the updated proof is valid. The only possible snag we can run into is that if $N(x) = N(x')$ then an update about x' would prevent a proof about x from being properly updated. Barring this, as long as no updates have occurred about the element x since π_x was issued, π_x may be updated successfully. To deal with this issue we must assume that $N(x)$ is such that collisions are unlikely to occur. This is certainly the case for all N we use.

To prove soundness, note that if a cheating prover were to be able to produce relative to a random σ a public key PK and two valid proofs π_1 and π_2 proving different results about $D(x)$ for some particular x, then this same prover would violate the soundness of CHLMR databases.

To prove zero-knowledge, we describe the simulator. The simulator must do five things: it must create the string σ, it must provide the initial commitment, and it must provide proofs and updates when requested.

- To produce σ, PK, or to produce a proof that $D(x) = y$, the simulator runs just as the CHLMR simulator does, except using $N(x)$ instead of $H(x)$ to determine the location of key pairs.
- To produce an update on a pseudonym n, computes $v_n = H(\epsilon)$ and computes a new commitment c_n.
  The simulator then updates all the commitments along the path from ϵ to n from soft to hard commitments, with the proper values to maintain the Merkle tree structure. The simulator incorporates any new decommitment information into SK'.

Now, to prove that the view provided to the adversary in the real model is identical to that in the ideal model, we describe the view of the adversary. In the real world, the adversary sees the random string σ, and then after specifying D, the commitment c_ϵ. Then, for each proof query, the adversary sees a proof about x which consists of an appropriate value $v_{N(x)}$ and random commitments c_ω to appropriate values, forming a hash authentication path to the root. For each update query, the adversary sees a pseudonym $N(x)$, a new commitment at $N(x)$, and for each proper prefix ω of $N(x)$, a random updated commitment c_ω. Furthermore, in the case of the discrete logarithm-based scheme, the adversary also sees e for each such ω, which shows that all these commitments are hard commitments.

In the ideal world, the adversary sees the simulated σ, followed by a distribution exactly the same as in the real world, except that $c_{N(x)}$ is a commitment to $H(\epsilon)$ rather than $H(y)$. However, these commitments are hiding so this is indistinguishable from the view of the adversary in the real world. In fact, in the case of the discrete logarithm-based scheme, the views are identical, since the only difference is in what c_ω commits to where ω is a leaf, but c_ω is a perfectly hiding commitment. Furthermore, the distribution of real σ values is identical to the distribution of simulated σ values by the perfect zero-knowledge property of the Micali-Rabin-Kilian simulator.

Proof of Theorem 2. To prove that the construction using $N(x) = H(f_{SK_f}(H(x)))$ is strongly secure, we must prove that it satisfies completeness, soundness, and computational zero-knowledge with respect to N_P in the random oracle model.

Completeness is already established by the completeness proof of Theorem 1; the only difference here is that a VRF proof must be verified (note that indeed, $N(x)$ here is unlikely to have collisions). However, $N(x)$ does not change when x is updated, so this part of the proof may remain the same. To prove soundness, we need only note that the pseudonym $N(x)$ that will be verified is unique from the soundness property of the VRF.

Zero-knowledge is more of a challenge. We give a simulator with respect to N_P that gives us computational zero-knowledge. First, the simulator makes σ and the database commitment c_ϵ just as the CHLMR simulator does. The simulator then runs GenVRF to generate (PK_f, SK_f), and publishes (PK_f, c_ϵ) as the database commitment. We must be careful to note here that N_P is not available as an oracle to the simulator, but $N_P(x)$ is given without x for any update query, and $N_P(x)$ is given with x for any database query. $H^*(x)$ here refers to the value used in the construction; the actual pseudonym we are considering is $N_P(x)$.

The simulator maintains two random functions: H and H', with the idea that $H'(N_P(x)) = H(f(H(x)))$. Whenever we say the simulator must "compute" (say) $H(x)$, the simulator looks to see if it has ever set $H(x)$ to any particular value. If so, it outputs that value. If not, it generates a random value of the correct length, and notes the correspondence with x. There can never be a problem with the simulator computing a value $H(x)$ or $H'(x)$.

When the simulator receives an update query, it computes $H'(N_P(x))$, and uses this value as $H^*(x)$.

When the simulator receives a database query on $x, y, N_P(x)$, the simulator computes $H(x)$, and then computes $z = f_{SK_f}(H(x))$, and then attempts to set $H(z) = H'(N_P(x))$. That is, if H is not defined at z, $H(z)$ is set to be the value computed from $H'(N_P(x))$. Otherwise, if H' is not yet defined at $N_P(x)$, $H'(N_P(x))$ is set to be the value computed from $H(z)$. If $H(z)$ and $H'(N_P(x))$ are already defined and equal to each other, the simulator sets nothing. However, if $H(z)$ and $H'(N_P(x))$ are already defined and unequal, the simulator aborts. If the simulator does not abort, it fakes a proof that the value stored at $H^*(x) = H(z) = H'(N_P(x))$ is y, just as the MRK simulator does, and provides the value z along with $\mathsf{ProveVRF}(SK_f, H(x))$ that $z = f_{SK_f}(H(x))$.

We must prove two things. First, in cases in which the simulator doesn't abort, the adversary cannot distinguish between the simulator and the real prover. We can assume without loss of generality that the adversary will always make a database query about every value x that he asks us to update before he halts (doing so will only increase the probability that the simulator aborts). If the simulator hasn't aborted by the time the adversary halts, we can reconcile H' into H, since all values $H'(N_P(x))$ will have been set equal to $H(z)$ for some z (because the adversary has queried all points for which we have a pseudonym). Thus, this simulator is doing exactly what the simulator in our previous proof does: it accurately computes $H^*(x)$ in every case and simulates proofs and updates according to this. Thus, the view produced by such a simulator is identical to the view produced by the real prover.

Second, if the simulator aborts with non-negligible probability, we can break the security of the VRF as follows. On input a VRF public key PK_f, we act as the simulator with the given adversary in this experiment, except we give PK_f as the VRF public key instead of generating it ourselves, and we implement the simulator. Note that we only ever need to query f_{SK_f} right before we ask for a proof about it. After some number of queries, the probability that the next value we ask for will cause an abort is non-negligible, so instead of asking for $f_{SK_f}(H(x))$ that time, we pick a random z such that $H(z)$ is defined, and guess that $f_{SK_f}(H(x)) = z$. We try this with the given oracle (which is either the VRF or a random oracle), and if we are correct, we say that the oracle is a VRF, otherwise, we guess at random. If the oracle is the VRF, and an abort would have been caused, then we have a $1/p(k)$ probability of guessing the right z, where $p(k)$ is the polynomial determining how many inputs have been queried from H. Thus, if the probability of an abort at the given step is $1/q(k)$, then the probability that we break the VRF is $(1/2)(1/(p(k)q(k))) + (1/4)(1 - (1/p(k)q(k)) + 1/2(1 - \nu(k))$ which is at least $1/2 + 1/(4p(k)q(k)) - \nu(k)$ for some negligible ν.

If the probability of an abort is non-negligible, it is non-negligible at some particular query. Thus, there is some reduction that breaks the security of the VRF.

Appendix D: Pseudonym Collisions

In the work of Micali, Rabin, and Kilian, the Pedersen hash function is used to assign pseudonyms to database elements. One attractive property of using the Pedersen hash function is that if a pseudonym collision occurs, the database owner learns the discrete logarithm of h to the base g, and then may continue proving what would otherwise be impossible: for instance, that $D(x) = y$ and $D(x') = y' \neq y$ when $H(x) = H(x')$. This allows the database to have size that is unrelated to any security parameters.

If, as we propose, we replace $H(x)$ by $N(x) = H(f(H(x)))$ for some verifiable random function f, we lose this property: N could encounter collisions either from H-collisions or from f-collisions. The former would be fine while the latter would be a problem. In practice, it is acceptable to limit honest users to polynomial-size databases, in which case collisions are negligibly likely. However, we can preserve this property through some extra effort, which has a minimal impact on efficiency.

Due to space constraints, we do not give the full details of this construction. The basic idea is that we use a public-key cryptosystem, and include two public keys: one from the cryptosystem and one from a verifiable random function. Then, instead of computing $a = f(x)$, we compute $E_{PK_e}(x; a)$, that is, we encrypt a under the encryption public key, using a as the randomness. A proof consists of a and the proof that $a = f(x)$ was properly generated by the VRF. This may not be pseudorandom, but in our construction it is sufficient to have unpredictability of the full answer, and this construction does achieve that.

When we use this injective verifiable unpredictable function, we get a pseudonym function that only has collisions when they are collisions of the hash function. Thus, any pseudonym collisions can be worked around.

It is worth noting, however, that the properties of the Pedersen hash function are nice, yet we are assuming in our (main) security proof that the hash function we use is a random oracle. In our opinion, the nice properties of the Pedersen hash are worth having, and this will probably not cause a significant security problem. However, we are unwilling to assume that the Pedersen hash function is a random oracle.

Appendix E: Removing the Random Oracle Assumption

If we are willing to assume certain conditions on the adversary, we can give a construction that is secure without the random oracle assumption. The conditions are as follows:

- If the adversary first inquires about x in a database query, it may in the future ask for more database queries about x as well as updates about x.
- If the adversary first inquires about x in an update query, it may only ask for more updates about x in the future.

It may seem at first glance that we can assume this without loss of generality: any successful adversary could always make more queries, and thus, make a database query immediately before any update query so as to always comply with the conditions. The problem with this is that since the simulation is actually a game of *three* parties: the adversary, the simulator, and the functionality that provides pseudonyms, the simulator actually must interact with the functionality more than normal to handle adversaries that don't hold to these conditions, which means that the simulator must learn more, which is not acceptable. It is important that in our simulation, the *simulator* not be able to get any more information out of the pseudonym-providing functionality than the adversary would.

Given that all adversaries meet these restrictions, we remove the random oracle assumption as follows: Again, we use the pseudonym function $H^*(x) = H(f(H(x)))$. To simulate, this time without being able to control H as a random oracle, we do as follows: if x is a value that is first mentioned in a database query, we actually compute $H(f(H(x)))$. If x is a value that is first mentioned in an update query, we know that the adversary will never make a database query about this particular x, so we compute $H^*(x) = H(R(N(x)))$ where R is a random function that we maintain, and where $N(x)$ is the pseudonym of x. If the adversary can distinguish between this simulator and a real adversary then either the adversary managed to find an H-collision, (for example, if $H(x) = H(x')$, so the adversary could detect this simulator by making a database query on x and then an update query on x', which should give the same pseudonym), or all inputs that should be given to f are distinct between the two types, in which case, the probability of distinguishing is exactly the probability of distinguishing the VRF from a random function.

We should note that although the restriction on the adversary is nontrivial, such adversaries still represent a significant class of adversaries. What's more, since we use the same construction here as in Theorem 2, we have actually proved security of that construction in two different ways: one, with the random oracle model, the other, with these restrictions on the adversary.

However, we can remove the random oracle model without weakening our assumptions if we give up efficiency. Instead of using a VRF, we can simply commit to a key K for a PRP using a commitment that becomes part of the database commitment, and then use $f_K(H(x))$ as $N(x)$, and prove correctness of this using a general NIZK proof. The advantage of this is that the simulator can fake NIZK proofs of false theorems, so the simulator can simply pretend that $F(N_P(x)) = f_K(H(x))$ where F is a random function, and fake proofs when necessary.

Appendix F: Efficiency Improvements

Multi-pair Updates

Suppose the database owner wants to update the database at n pairs simultaneously. A fairly obvious method presents itself: make an update for each pair individually, and publish all the update information together. This saves space, since some updated nodes will overlap. Asymptotically, the number of nodes updated becomes $O(n(k - \log n)k)$, which represents some savings over the one-at-a-time approach, which is asymptotically $O(nk^2)$.

Multi-proof Updates

Suppose a proof owner has n proofs and an update is issued. If two proofs overlap (that is, $N(x)$ and $N(x')$ share a common prefix), the change in the updated proofs for x and x' can be computed more quickly by computing the change in the common portion of those two proofs together, then computing the change in the remaining portion of each. More generally, if a user holds n proofs, updating each separately would take time $O(nk^2)$, but by combining the work, this is reduced to time $O(n(k - \log n)k)$.

The analysis for both of these methods is based on the observation that an average case instance of n random strings will have the first $\log n$ bits in common with a newly chosen random string. Thus, if each string translates to a path of length k, the expected sum of the length of all paths is $k + k - \log 0 + \ldots + k - \log(n-1) < nk - (n/2)\log(n/2) = O(n(k - \log n))$. The additional factor of k accounts for the length of the data per node.

Simple and Tight Bounds for Information Reconciliation and Privacy Amplification

Renato Renner[1] and Stefan Wolf[2]

[1] Computer Science Department,
ETH Zürich, Switzerland
renner@inf.ethz.ch
[2] Département d'Informatique et R.O.,
Université de Montréal, QC, Canada
wolf@iro.umontreal.ca

Abstract. Shannon entropy is a useful and important measure in information processing, for instance, data compression or randomness extraction, under the assumption—which can typically safely be made in *communication theory*—that a certain random experiment is independently repeated many times. In *cryptography*, however, where a system's working has to be proven with respect to a malicious adversary, this assumption usually translates to a restriction on the latter's knowledge or behavior and is generally not satisfied. An example is quantum key agreement, where the adversary can attack each particle sent through the quantum channel differently or even carry out coherent attacks, combining a number of particles together. In information-theoretic key agreement, the central functionalities of *information reconciliation* and *privacy amplification* have, therefore, been extensively studied in the scenario of *general distributions*: Partial solutions have been given, but the obtained bounds are arbitrarily far from tight, and a full analysis appeared to be rather involved to do. We show that, actually, the general case is not more difficult than the scenario of independent repetitions—in fact, given our new point of view, even simpler. When one analyzes the possible efficiency of data compression and randomness extraction in the case of independent repetitions, then Shannon entropy H is the answer. We show that H can, in these two contexts, be generalized to two *very simple* quantities—H_0^ε and H_∞^ε, called *smooth Rényi entropies*—which are tight bounds for data compression (hence, information reconciliation) and randomness extraction (privacy amplification), respectively. It is shown that the two new quantities, and related notions, do not only extend Shannon entropy in the described contexts, but they also share central properties of the latter such as the chain rule as well as subadditivity and monotonicity.

Keywords: Information-theoretic cryptography, entropy measures, data compression, randomness extraction, information reconciliation, privacy amplification, quantum key agreement.

B. Roy (Ed.): ASIACRYPT 2005, LNCS 3788, pp. 199–216, 2005.

1   Introduction, Motivation, and Main Results

1.1   Unconditional Cryptographic Security and Key Agreement

Unconditional cryptographic security does, in contrast to *computational* security, not depend on any assumption on an adversary's computing power nor on the hardness of computational problems. This type of security is, therefore, not threatened by potential progress in algorithm design or (classical and quantum) computer engineering. On the other hand, cryptographic functionalities such as encryption, authentication, and two- or multi-party computation can generally *not* be realized in an unconditionally secure way simply from scratch. It is, therefore, a natural question under what circumstances—as realistic as possible—they *can* be realized. In particular for encryption and authentication or, more specifically, *secret-key agreement*, this question has been studied extensively: In [23] and [9], unconditional secret key agreement is realized based on the existence of noisy channels between the legitimate partners and the adversary, whereas in [15], a scenario is introduced and studied where all parties have access to pieces of information (e.g., generated by repeated realizations of a certain random experiment). On the other hand, the possibility of information-theoretic key agreement has also been studied between parties connected not only by a classical, but also a quantum channel allowing for the transmission of quantum states [22,1]. Here, the security can be shown under the condition that the laws of quantum physics are correct.

If, in a certain scenario, unconditional secret-key agreement is possible in principle, then it is a natural question what the maximum length of the generated secret key can be. To find the answer to this question has turned out to often reduce to analyzing two functionalities that form important building blocks of protocols for secret-key agreement (in any of the described settings), namely *information reconciliation* and *privacy amplification*.

Information reconciliation (see, for instance [4]) means that the legitimate partners generate identical shared strings from (possibly only weakly) correlated ones by noiseless and authenticated but public communication, hereby leaking to the adversary only a minimal amount of information about the original and, hence, the resulting string. The generated common but potentially highly compromised string must then be transformed into a virtually secret key by *privacy amplification*. On the technical level—but roughly speaking—, information reconciliation is error correction, whereas privacy amplification is hashing, e.g., by applying a universal hash function [13,2] or an extractor [16] allowing for distilling a weakly random string's min-entropy H_∞. When these two functionalities are analyzed in a context where all pieces of information stem from many independent repetitions of the same random experiment, then the analysis shows that the amount of information to be exchanged in optimal information reconciliation is the conditional Shannon entropy of, say, one party Alice's information, given the other Bob's; on the other hand, privacy amplification, in the same independent-repetitions setting, allows for extracting a string the length of which equals the conditional Shannon entropy of the shared string given the adversary's information. Hence, as often in information theory, Shannon entropy turns out to be very useful in this asymptotic model. In a (classical or quantum) *crypto-graphic* context, however, the assumption of independent repetitions typically corresponds to a restriction on the adversary's behavior, and cannot realistically be made. It has been a common belief that in this case, the analysis of the described information-reconciliation and privacy-amplification protocols—and their combination—are quite involved and lead to rather complex (functional) bounds on the (operational) quantities such as the key length. It is the main goal of this paper to show that this is, actually, not the case.

1.2   Information Reconciliation and Privacy Amplification

Information reconciliation is *error correction*: Given that Alice and Bob hold random variables X and Y, respectively, Alice wants to send a minimal quantity of information C to Bob such that given Y and C, he can perfectly reconstruct X with high probability. (More generally, protocols for information reconciliation can use two-way communication. Such interactive protocols can be computationally much more efficient than one-way protocols, but do not re-duce the minimal amount of information to be exchanged [4].) To determine the minimal amount of information to be sent from Alice to Bob such that the latter can reconstruct Alice's information with high probability reduces to the following data-compression problem.

Question 1. Given a distribution P_{XY} and $\varepsilon > 0$, what is the minimum length $H_{\text{enc}}^{\varepsilon}(X|Y)$ of a binary string $C = e(X, R)$, computed from X and some addi-tional independent randomness R, such that there exists an event Ω with proba-bility at least $1 - \varepsilon$ such that given Ω, X is uniquely determined by C, Y, and R?

Privacy amplification is *randomness extraction*: Given that Alice and Bob both know X and an adversary knows Y, Alice wants to send a message R to Bob such that from X and R, they can compute a (generally shorter) common string S about which the adversary, knowing Y and R but not X, has no in-formation except with small probability. More specifically, privacy amplification deals with the following randomness-extraction problem.

Question 2. Given a distribution P_{XY} and $\varepsilon > 0$, what is the maximum length $H_{\text{ext}}^{\varepsilon}(X|Y)$ of a binary string $S = f(X, R)$, where R is an additional random variable, such that there exists a uniformly distributed random variable U that is independent of (Y, R) together with an event Ω with probability at least $1 - \varepsilon$ such that given Ω, we have $S = U$?

The problems of determining $H_{\text{enc}}^{\varepsilon}(X|Y)$ and $H_{\text{ext}}^{\varepsilon}(X|Y)$ have been studied by several authors. Note, first of all, that in the case where the distribution in question is of the form $P_{X^n Y^n} = (P_{XY})^n$, corresponding to n independent repetitions of the random experiment P_{XY}, we have, for $\varepsilon > 0$,

$$\lim_{\varepsilon \to 0} \lim_{n \to \infty} \frac{H_{\text{enc}}^{\varepsilon}(X^n|Y^n)}{n} = \lim_{\varepsilon \to 0} \lim_{n \to \infty} \frac{H_{\text{ext}}^{\varepsilon}(X^n|Y^n)}{n} = H(X|Y) \,.$$

Interestingly, the two—*a priori* very different—questions have the same answer in this case. We will show that in general, this is not true.

Unfortunately, the assumption that the distribution has product form is generally unrealistic in a cryptographic context: In quantum key agreement, for instance, it corresponds to the assumption that the adversary attacks every particle individually, independently, and in exactly the same way. But what if she does not?

It is fair to say that the problem of optimizing privacy amplification and "distribution uniformizing" has been studied intensively in the general case and considered to be quite involved (see, for instance, [5], [6], [7], and references therein). It is our goal to show that this belief is, both for information reconciliation and privacy amplification, in fact unjustified.

An example of a previous result is that $H_{\text{ext}}^{\varepsilon}(X|Y)$ is bounded from below by the minimum, over all $y \in \mathcal{Y}$, of the so-called *collision entropies* or *Rényi entropies of order* 2, $H_2(X|Y = y)$ (see below for a precise definition) [2]. However, this bound is not tight: For instance, the adversary can be given additional knowledge that increases the H_2-entropy from her viewpoint. In fact, such "spoiling-knowledge" arguments do not only show that the H_2-bound is arbitrarily far from tight, but also that the quantity H_2 has some very counter-intuitive properties that make it hard to handle.

We define two quantities that can be computed very easily and that represent tight bounds on $H_{\text{enc}}^{\varepsilon}$ and $H_{\text{ext}}^{\varepsilon}$, respectively. In a nutshell, we show that the general case is as easy as the special independent-repetitions scenario—or even easier when being looked at it in the right way. We also observe that, in general, the answers to Questions 1 and 2 above are not at all equal.

1.3   Two New Quantities: Conditional Smooth Rényi Entropies and Their Significance

For a distribution P_{XY} and $\varepsilon > 0$, let[1]

$$H_0^{\varepsilon}(X|Y) := \min_{\Omega} \max_{y} \log |\{x : P_{X\Omega|Y=y}(x) > 0\}| \tag{1}$$

$$H_{\infty}^{\varepsilon}(X|Y) := \max_{\Omega} \min_{y} \min_{x} (-\log P_{X\Omega|Y=y}(x)) \,, \tag{2}$$

where the first minimum/maximum ranges over all events Ω with probability $\Pr[\Omega] \geq 1 - \varepsilon$.

First, we observe that these quantities are defined with respect to P_{XY} in a *very simple way* and are very easy to compute. Indeed, the involved optimization problems can easily be solved by eliminating the smallest probabilities and

---

[1] All logarithms in this paper are binary. $P_{X\Omega}(x)$ is the probability that Ω occurs and X takes the value x.

by cutting down the largest probabilities, respectively. On the other hand, they provide the answers to Questions 1 and 2 (Section 3).

Answer to Question 1. For $\varepsilon_1 + \varepsilon_2 = \varepsilon$, we have

$$H_0^\varepsilon(X|Y) \leq H_{\text{enc}}^\varepsilon(X|Y) \leq H_0^{\varepsilon_1}(X|Y) + \log(1/\varepsilon_2) \ .$$

Answer to Question 2. For $\varepsilon_1 + \varepsilon_2 = \varepsilon$, we have

$$H_\infty^{\varepsilon_1}(X|Y) - 2\log(1/\varepsilon_2) \leq H_{\text{ext}}^\varepsilon(X|Y) \leq H_\infty^\varepsilon(X|Y) \ .$$

We can say that—modulo a small error term—these results provide simple *functional* representations of the important and natural *operationally* defined quantities $H_{\text{enc}}^\varepsilon$ and $H_{\text{ext}}^\varepsilon$. In a way, H_0^ε (i.e., $H_{\text{enc}}^\varepsilon$) and H_∞^ε ($H_{\text{ext}}^\varepsilon$) are two natural generalizations of Shannon entropy to a cryptographic setting with an adversary potentially not following any rules. In particular, both H_0^ε and H_∞^ε fall back to Shannon entropy if the distribution is of the form $(P_{XY})^n$ for large n (Section 2.3). An example of an application of our results is the possibility of analyzing quantum key-agreement protocols or classical protocols based on correlated information. For instance, our results allow for deriving a simple tight bound on the efficiency of key agreement by one-way communication[2] (Section 3.3).

H_0^ε and H_∞^ε are special cases of *smooth Rényi entropies.* In Section 2.1 we give the general definition of conditional and unconditional smooth Rényi entropies of any order α, and in Section 2.2 we show that, roughly speaking, H_α^ε is, for any α ($\neq 1$), equal to either H_0^ε (if $\alpha < 1$) or H_∞^ε ($\alpha > 1$) up to an additive constant. *Unconditional* smooth Rényi entropy has been introduced in [19], applied in [18], and is, implicitly, widely used in the randomness-extraction literature (see, e.g., [21]). We will show, however, that the *conditional* quantities, introduced in this paper, are the ones that prove particularly useful in the context of cryptography.

If we have concluded that H_0^ε and H_∞^ε generalize Shannon entropy, then this is, in addition, true because they have similar properties (Section 2.4). We summarize the most important ones in a table. (Let $\varepsilon, \varepsilon', \varepsilon_1$, and ε_2 be nonnegative constants. The approximation "$\lesssim$" holds up to $\log(1/(\varepsilon - \varepsilon_1 - \varepsilon_2))$.)

Hence, all important properties of Shannon entropy also hold for the new quantities generalizing it. In contrast, note that the important chain rule, for instance, does *not* hold for the original, "non-smooth" Rényi entropies H_0, H_2, and H_∞. In fact, this drawback is one of the reasons for the somewhat limited applicability of these quantities.

---

[2] Our results thus also apply to *fuzzy extractors* [10] which are technically the same as one-way secret-key agreement schemes (where the *generation* and the *reproduction procedures* correspond to the algorithms of Alice and Bob, respectively).

	Shannon entropy H	New entropies H_0^ε and H_∞^ε
chain rule (Lemmas 4 and 5)	$H(X\|Y) = H(XY) - H(Y)$	$H_0^{\varepsilon+\varepsilon'}(XY) - H_0^{\varepsilon'}(Y) \leq H_0^\varepsilon(X\|Y)$ $\lesssim H_0^{\varepsilon_1}(XY) - H_\infty^{\varepsilon_2}(Y)$ $H_\infty^{\varepsilon_1}(XY) - H_0^{\varepsilon_2}(Y) \lesssim H_\infty^\varepsilon(X\|Y)$ $\leq H_\infty^{\varepsilon+\varepsilon'}(XY) - H_\infty^{\varepsilon'}(Y)$
sub-additivity (Lemma 6)	$H(XY) \leq H(X) + H(Y)$	$H_0^{\varepsilon+\varepsilon'}(XY) \leq H_0^\varepsilon(X) + H_0^{\varepsilon'}(Y)$ $H_\infty^\varepsilon(XY) \leq H_\infty^{\varepsilon+\varepsilon'}(X) + H_0^{\varepsilon'}(Y)$
monotonicity (Lemma 7)	$H(X) \leq H(XY)$	$H_0^\varepsilon(X) \leq H_0^\varepsilon(XY)$ $H_\infty^\varepsilon(X) \leq H_\infty^\varepsilon(XY)$

The proofs of the above properties of the new, more general, quantities are—just as are their definitions—in fact simpler than the corresponding proofs for Shannon entropy; they only apply counting arguments (instead of, for instance, the concavity of the logarithm function and Jensen's inequality). Since, on the other hand, Shannon entropy is simply a special case of the new quantities (for many independent repetitions), we obtain simpler proofs of the corresponding properties of Shannon entropy for free.

Note that although we state that all smooth Rényi entropies come down to either H_0^ε or H_∞^ε, we give *general* definitions and statements on H_α^ε for any α. This can be convenient in contexts in which the entropies have a natural significance, such as H_2 in connection with two-universal hashing [2].

2   Smooth Rényi Entropy: Definition and Properties

2.1   Definition

We start by briefly reviewing the notion of *smooth Rényi entropy* [19] and then generalize it to *conditional* smooth Rényi entropy.

Let X be a random variable on $\mathcal{X}$ with probability distribution P_X. We denote by $\mathcal{B}^\varepsilon(P_X)$ the set of non-negative functions Q_X with domain $\mathcal{X}$ such that $Q_X(x) \leq P_X(x)$, for any $x \in \mathcal{X}$, and $\sum_{x \in \mathcal{X}} Q_X(x) \geq 1 - \varepsilon$. The ε-*smooth Rényi entropy of order* α, for $\alpha \in (0, 1) \cup (1, \infty)$ and $\varepsilon \geq 0$, is defined by[3]

$$H_\alpha^\varepsilon(X) := \frac{1}{1-\alpha} \log r_\alpha^\varepsilon(X) \, ,$$

where

$$r_\alpha^\varepsilon(X) := \inf_{Q_X \in \mathcal{B}^\varepsilon(P_X)} \sum_{x \in \mathcal{X}} Q_X(x)^\alpha \, .$$

---

[3] The definition given here slightly differs from the original definition in [19]. However, it turns out that this version is more appropriate for our generalization to conditional smooth Rényi entropy (Definition 1).

For $\alpha = 0$ and $\alpha = \infty$, smooth Rényi entropy is defined by the limit values, i.e., $H_0^\varepsilon(X) := \lim_{\alpha \to 0} H_\alpha^\varepsilon(X)$ and $H_\infty^\varepsilon(X) := \lim_{\alpha \to \infty} H_\alpha^\varepsilon(X)$.

It follows directly from the definition that, for $\alpha < 1$,

$$\varepsilon \geq \varepsilon' \longleftrightarrow H_\alpha^\varepsilon(X) \leq H_\alpha^{\varepsilon'}(X)$$

holds and, similarly, for $\alpha > 1$,

$$\varepsilon \geq \varepsilon' \longleftrightarrow H_\alpha^\varepsilon(X) \geq H_\alpha^{\varepsilon'}(X) .$$

Moreover, for $\varepsilon = 0$, smooth Rényi entropy $H_\alpha^0(X)$ is equal to "conventional" Rényi entropy $H_\alpha(X)$ [20]. Similarly to conditional Shannon entropy, we define a *conditional* version of smooth Rényi entropy.

Definition 1. *Let X and Y be random variables with range $\mathcal{X}$ and $\mathcal{Y}$, respectively, and joint probability distribution P_{XY}. The conditional ε-smooth Rényi entropy of order α of X given Y, for $\alpha \in (0,1) \cup (1, \infty)$ and $\varepsilon \geq 0$, is defined by*

$$H_\alpha^\varepsilon(X|Y) := \frac{1}{1-\alpha} \log r_\alpha^\varepsilon(X|Y)$$

where

$$r_\alpha^\varepsilon(X|Y) := \inf_{Q_{XY} \in \mathcal{B}^\varepsilon(P_{XY})} \max_{y \in \mathcal{Y}} \sum_{x \in \mathcal{X}} Q_{X|Y=y}(x)^\alpha ,$$

and where $Q_{X|Y=y}(x) := Q_{XY}(x,y)/P_Y(y)$, for any $x \in \mathcal{X}$ and $y \in \mathcal{Y}$ (with the convention $Q_{X|Y=y}(x) = 0$ if $P_Y(y) = 0$).[4] For $\alpha = 0$ and $\alpha = \infty$, we define $H_0^\varepsilon(X|Y) := \lim_{\alpha \to 0} H_\alpha^\varepsilon(X|Y)$ and $H_\infty^\varepsilon(X|Y) := \lim_{\alpha \to \infty} H_\alpha^\varepsilon(X|Y)$.

For $\alpha = 0$ and $\alpha = \infty$, Definition 1 reduces to (1) and (2), respectively. Note that the *infimum* is in fact a *minimum* which is obtained by cutting away the smallest probabilities or cutting down the largest, respectively.

2.2 Basic Properties

We will now derive some basic properties of smooth Rényi entropy. In particular, we show that the smooth Rényi entropies can be split into two classes: It turns out that for any value $\alpha < 1$, $H_\alpha^\varepsilon(X|Y)$ is, up to an additive constant, equal to $H_0^\varepsilon(X|Y)$. Similarly, $H_\alpha^\varepsilon(X|Y)$, for $\alpha > 1$, is essentially $H_\infty^\varepsilon(X|Y)$.

For this, we need a generalization, to the smooth case, of the fact that

$$\alpha \leq \beta \longleftrightarrow H_\alpha(X) \geq H_\beta(X) \tag{3}$$

holds for any $\alpha, \beta \in [0, \infty]$.

Lemma 1. *Let X and Y be random variables. Then, for $\varepsilon \geq 0$ and for $\alpha \leq \beta < 1$ or $1 < \alpha \leq \beta$,*

$$H_\alpha^\varepsilon(X|Y) \geq H_\beta^\varepsilon(X|Y) .$$

---

[4] Since $\sum_x Q_{XY}(x,y)$ is generally smaller than $P_Y(y)$, the distribution $Q_{X|Y=y}(\cdot) := Q_{XY}(\cdot, y)/P_Y(y)$ is not necessarily normalized.

Proof. For any probability distribution Q on $\mathcal{X}$, the right hand side of (3) can be rewritten as

$$\sqrt[1-\alpha]{\sum_{x \in \mathcal{X}} Q(x)^\alpha} \geq \sqrt[1-\beta]{\sum_{x \in \mathcal{X}} Q(x)^\beta} . \tag{4}$$

It is easy to verify that this inequality also holds for any (not necessarily normalized) nonnegative function Q with $\sum_{x \in \mathcal{X}} Q(x) \leq 1$.

As mentioned above, the infimum in the definition of r_α^ε is actually a minimum. Hence, there exists $Q_{XY} \in \mathcal{B}^\varepsilon(P_{XY})$ such that for any $y \in \mathcal{Y}$,

$$r_\alpha^\varepsilon(X|Y) \geq \sum_{x \in \mathcal{X}} Q_{X|Y=y}(x)^\alpha$$

holds. When this is combined with (4), we find

$$\sqrt[1-\alpha]{r_\alpha^\varepsilon(X|Y)} \geq \sqrt[1-\alpha]{\sum_{x \in \mathcal{X}} Q_{X|Y=y}(x)^\alpha} \geq \sqrt[1-\beta]{\sum_{x \in \mathcal{X}} Q_{X|Y=y}(x)^\beta} .$$

Because this holds for any $y \in \mathcal{Y}$, we conclude

$$\sqrt[1-\alpha]{r_\alpha^\varepsilon(X|Y)} \geq \sqrt[1-\beta]{r_\beta^\varepsilon(X|Y)} .$$

The assertion now follows from the definition of smooth Rényi entropy. $\qquad\square$

Lemma 2 is, in some sense, the converse of Lemma 1. Since it is a straightforward generalization of a statement of [19][5], we omit the proof here.

Lemma 2. *Let X and Y be random variables. Then, for $\varepsilon \geq 0$, $\varepsilon' \geq 0$, and $\alpha < 1$, we have*

$$H_0^{\varepsilon+\varepsilon'}(X|Y) \leq H_\alpha^\varepsilon(X|Y) + \frac{\log(1/\varepsilon')}{1-\alpha}$$

and for $\alpha > 1$,

$$H_\infty^{\varepsilon+\varepsilon'}(X|Y) \geq H_\alpha^\varepsilon(X|Y) - \frac{\log(1/\varepsilon')}{\alpha-1} .$$

When Lemmas 1 and 2 are combined, we obtain the following characterization of smooth Rényi entropy $H_\alpha^\varepsilon(X|Y)$, for $\alpha < 1$, in terms of smooth Rényi entropy of order 0:

$$H_0^{\varepsilon+\varepsilon'}(X|Y) - \frac{\log(1/\varepsilon')}{1-\alpha} \leq H_\alpha^\varepsilon(X|Y) \leq H_0^\varepsilon(X|Y) .$$

Similarly, for $\alpha > 1$,

$$H_\infty^{\varepsilon+\varepsilon'}(X|Y) + \frac{\log(1/\varepsilon')}{\alpha-1} \geq H_\alpha^\varepsilon(X|Y) \geq H_\infty^\varepsilon(X|Y) .$$

If $\varepsilon = 0$, this leads to an approximation of the (conventional) Rényi entropy H_α, of any order α, in terms of the smooth Rényi entropies H_0^ε and H_∞^ε. For example, the collision entropy $H_2(X)$ cannot be larger than $H_\infty^\varepsilon(X) + \log(1/\varepsilon)$ (whereas $H_2(X) \approx 2H_\infty(X)$, for certain probability distributions P_X).

---

[5] The result of [19] corresponds to the special case where Y is a constant.

2.3 Smooth Rényi Entropy as a Generalization of Shannon Entropy

Interestingly, one obtains as an immediate consequence of the asymptotic equipartition property (AEP) (cf. [8]) that, for many independent realizations of a random experiment, smooth Rényi entropy is asymptotically equal to Shannon entropy. (Note that the same is not true at all for the usual Rényi entropies.)

Lemma 3. *Let* $(X_1, Y_1), \ldots, (X_n, Y_n)$ *be* n *independent pairs of random variables distributed according to* P_{XY}. *Then we have, for any* $\alpha \neq 1$,

$$\lim_{\varepsilon \to 0} \lim_{n \to \infty} \frac{H_\alpha^\varepsilon(X^n | Y^n)}{n} = H(X|Y) \ ,$$

where $H(X|Y)$ *is the conditional Shannon entropy.*

For a proof as well as a more detailed (non-asymptotic) version of this statement, we refer to [12].

2.4 Shannon-Like Properties of Smooth Rényi Entropy

Smooth Rényi entropy shares basic properties with Shannon entropy—this is in contrast to the usual Rényi entropies, which do not have these properties. Therefore, the smooth versions are much more natural and useful quantities in many contexts, as we will see.

Chain Rule. We first prove a property corresponding to the chain rule $H(X|Y) = H(XY) - H(Y)$ of Shannon entropy. More precisely, Lemmas 4 and 5 below are two different inequalities, which, combined, give a chain rule for smooth Rényi entropies of any order α.

Lemma 4. *Let* X *and* Y *be random variables and let* $\varepsilon \geq 0$, $\varepsilon' \geq 0$, $\varepsilon'' \geq 0$. *Then, for* $\alpha < 1 < \beta$, *we have*

$$H_\alpha^{\varepsilon+\varepsilon'+\varepsilon''}(X|Y) < H_\alpha^{\varepsilon'}(XY) - H_\beta^{\varepsilon''}(Y) + \frac{\beta - \alpha}{(1-\alpha)(\beta-1)} \log(1/\varepsilon) \ ,$$

and, similarly, for $\alpha > 1 > \beta$,

$$H_\alpha^{\varepsilon+\varepsilon'+\varepsilon''}(X|Y) > H_\alpha^{\varepsilon'}(XY) - H_\beta^{\varepsilon''}(Y) - \frac{\alpha - \beta}{(\alpha-1)(1-\beta)} \log(1/\varepsilon) \ .$$

Proof. It is easy to verify that the assertion can be rewritten as

$$\log r_\alpha^{\varepsilon+\varepsilon'+\varepsilon''}(X|Y) < \log r_\alpha^{\varepsilon'}(XY) + \frac{1-\alpha}{\beta-1} \log r_\beta^{\varepsilon''}(Y) + \frac{\beta-\alpha}{\beta-1} \log(1/\varepsilon) \ . \quad (5)$$

By the definition of $r_\alpha^{\varepsilon'}(XY)$ there exists an event Ω_1 with probability $\Pr[\Omega_1] = 1 - \varepsilon'$ such that $r_\alpha^{\varepsilon'}(XY) = \sum_{x \in \mathcal{X}, y \in \mathcal{Y}} P_{XY\Omega_1}(x, y)^\alpha$. Similarly, one can find an event Ω_2 such that $\Pr[\Omega_2] = 1 - \varepsilon''$ and $r_\beta^{\varepsilon''}(Y) = \sum_{y \in \mathcal{Y}} P_{Y\Omega_2}(y)^\beta$. Hence, the event $\Omega := \Omega_1 \cap \Omega_2$ has probability $\Pr[\Omega] \geq 1 - \varepsilon' - \varepsilon''$ and satisfies

$$\sum_{x \in \mathcal{X}, y \in \mathcal{Y}} P_{XY\Omega}(x, y)^\alpha \leq r_\alpha^{\varepsilon'}(XY)$$

as well as

$$\sum_{y \in \mathcal{Y}} P_{Y\Omega}(y)^\beta \leq r_\beta^{\varepsilon''}(Y) .$$

For any $y \in \mathcal{Y}$, let $\bar{r}_y := \sum_{x \in \mathcal{X}} P_{X\Omega | Y=y}(x)^\alpha$. Since inequality (5) is independent of the labeling of the values in $\mathcal{Y}$, we can assume without loss of generality that these are natural numbers, $\mathcal{Y} = \{1, \ldots, n\}$, for $n := |\mathcal{Y}|$, and that the values $\bar{r}_y$ are arranged in increasing order, $\bar{r}_y > \bar{r}_{y'} \longrightarrow y > y'$. Let $\bar{y} \in \mathcal{Y}$ be the minimum value such that $\Pr[Y > \bar{y}, \Omega] \leq \varepsilon$ holds. In particular,

$$\Pr[Y \geq \bar{y}, \Omega] = \Pr[Y > \bar{y} - 1, \Omega] > \varepsilon . \tag{6}$$

Let Ω' be the event that $Y \leq \bar{y}$ holds, i.e., we have $\Pr[\overline{\Omega'}, \Omega] \leq \varepsilon$ and, consequently,

$$\Pr[\Omega', \Omega] = 1 - \Pr[\overline{\Omega}] - \Pr[\overline{\Omega'}, \Omega] \geq 1 - \varepsilon - \varepsilon' - \varepsilon'' .$$

Hence, since $P_{X\Omega\Omega' | Y=y}(x) = 0$ holds for any $x \in \mathcal{X}$ and $y > \bar{y}$, we have

$$r_\alpha^{\varepsilon + \varepsilon' + \varepsilon''}(X|Y) \leq \max_{y \in \mathcal{Y}} \sum_{x \in \mathcal{X}} P_{X\Omega\Omega' | Y=y}(x)^\alpha \leq \max_{y \leq \bar{y}} \bar{r}_y \leq \bar{r}_{\bar{y}} .$$

Therefore, it remains to be proven that

$$\log \bar{r}_{\bar{y}} < \log\left(\sum_{x \in \mathcal{X}, y \in \mathcal{Y}} P_{XY\Omega}(x, y)^\alpha \right) + \frac{1 - \alpha}{\beta - 1} \log\left(\sum_{y \in \mathcal{Y}} P_{Y\Omega}(y)^\beta \right) - \frac{\beta - \alpha}{\beta - 1} \log \varepsilon .$$
$$\tag{7}$$

Let $s := \sum_{y=\bar{y}}^{n} P_Y(y)^\alpha$. Then,

$$\bar{r}_{\bar{y}} \cdot s = \sum_{y=\bar{y}}^{n} \bar{r}_{\bar{y}} P_Y(y)^\alpha \leq \sum_{y=\bar{y}}^{n} \bar{r}_y P_Y(y)^\alpha \leq \sum_{y=1}^{n} \bar{r}_y P_Y(y)^\alpha , \tag{8}$$

where the first inequality follows from the fact that $\bar{r}_y \geq \bar{r}_{\bar{y}}$ holds for all $y \geq \bar{y}$. When the definition of $\bar{r}_y$ is inserted into inequality (8), we get

$$\bar{r}_{\bar{y}} \leq \frac{1}{s} \sum_{x \in \mathcal{X}, y \in \mathcal{Y}} P_{XY\Omega}(x, y)^\alpha$$

i.e.,

$$\log \bar{r}_{\bar{y}} \leq \log\left(\sum_{x \in \mathcal{X}, y \in \mathcal{Y}} P_{XY\Omega}(x, y)^\alpha \right) - \log s . \tag{9}$$

In order to find a bound on s, let $p_y := P_{Y\Omega}(y)$, $p := \frac{\beta-\alpha}{\beta-1}$, $q := \frac{\beta-\alpha}{1-\alpha}$, and $\gamma := \frac{\alpha(\beta-1)}{\beta-\alpha}$, i.e., $\gamma p = \alpha$ and $(1-\gamma)q = \beta$. We then have $\frac{1}{p} + \frac{1}{q} = 1$ and can apply *Hölder's inequality*, yielding

$$\sqrt[p]{s} \cdot \sqrt[q]{\sum_{y\in\mathcal{Y}} P_{Y\Omega}(y)^\beta} \geq \sqrt[p]{\sum_{y=\bar{y}}^{n} (p_y)^\alpha} \cdot \sqrt[q]{\sum_{y=\bar{y}}^{n} (p_y)^\beta}$$

$$= \sqrt[p]{\sum_{y=\bar{y}}^{n} ((p_y)^\gamma)^p} \cdot \sqrt[q]{\sum_{y=\bar{y}}^{n} ((p_y)^{1-\gamma})^q}$$

$$\geq \sum_{y=\bar{y}}^{n} (p_y)^\gamma (p_y)^{1-\gamma} = \sum_{y=\bar{y}}^{n} p_y = \Pr[Y \geq \bar{y}, \Omega] > \varepsilon \ .$$

Hence,

$$\log s > p \log \varepsilon - \frac{p}{q} \log\left(\sum_{y\in\mathcal{Y}} P_{Y\Omega}(y)^\beta\right) .$$

Combining this with (9) implies (7) and, thus, concludes the proof.   □

Lemma 5. *Let X and Y be random variables and let $\varepsilon \geq 0$, $\varepsilon' > 0$. Then, for any $\alpha < 1$, we have*

$$H_\alpha^{\varepsilon+\varepsilon'}(XY) \leq H_\alpha^\varepsilon(X|Y) + H_\alpha^{\varepsilon'}(Y) \ ,$$

and, similarly, for $\alpha > 1$,

$$H_\alpha^{\varepsilon+\varepsilon'}(XY) \geq H_\alpha^\varepsilon(X|Y) + H_\alpha^{\varepsilon'}(Y) \ .$$

Proof. Let Ω be an event with $\Pr[\Omega] \geq 1 - \varepsilon$ such that

$$\max_y \sum_{x\in\mathcal{X}} P_{X\Omega|Y=y}(x)^\alpha \leq r_\alpha^\varepsilon(X|Y) \ .$$

Similarly, let Ω' be an event with $\Pr[\Omega'] \geq 1 - \varepsilon'$ such that $\Omega' \leftrightarrow Y \leftrightarrow (X, \Omega)$ is a Markov chain and

$$\sum_{y\in\mathcal{Y}} P_{Y\Omega'}(y)^\alpha \leq r_\alpha^\varepsilon(Y) \ .$$

Since $\Pr[\Omega, \Omega'] \geq 1 - \varepsilon - \varepsilon'$ holds, we have

$$r_\alpha^{\varepsilon+\varepsilon'}(XY) \leq \sum_{x\in\mathcal{X}, y\in\mathcal{Y}} P_{XY\Omega\Omega'}(x,y)^\alpha \ .$$

The assertion thus follows from

$$\sum_{x\in\mathcal{X}, y\in\mathcal{Y}} P_{XY\Omega\Omega'}(x,y)^\alpha = \sum_{x\in\mathcal{X}, y\in\mathcal{Y}} P_{Y\Omega'}(y)^\alpha P_{X\Omega|Y=y}(x)^\alpha$$

$$\leq \left(\sum_{y\in\mathcal{Y}} P_{Y\Omega'}(y)^\alpha\right)\left(\max_{y\in\mathcal{Y}} \sum_{x\in\mathcal{X}} P_{X\Omega|Y=y}(x)^\alpha\right) .   □$$

It is easy to see that the statements of Lemma 4 and Lemma 5 still hold if all entropies are conditioned on an additional random variable Z. For example, the statement of Lemma 5 then reads, for $\alpha < 1$,

$$H_\alpha^{\varepsilon+\varepsilon'}(XY|Z) - H_\alpha^{\varepsilon'}(Y|Z) \leq H_\alpha^\varepsilon(X|YZ) \tag{10}$$

and for $\alpha > 1$,

$$H_\alpha^{\varepsilon+\varepsilon'}(XY|Z) - H_\alpha^{\varepsilon'}(Y|Z) \geq H_\alpha^\varepsilon(X|YZ) . \tag{11}$$

Sub-additivity. The Shannon entropy $H(XY)$ of a pair of random variables X and Y cannot be larger than the sum $H(X)+H(Y)$. The following statement generalizes this sub-additivity property to smooth Rényi entropy. The proof of this statement is straightforward and, in fact, very similar to the (simple) proof of Lemma 5.

Lemma 6. *Let X and Y be random variables and let $\varepsilon \geq 0$. Then, for any $\alpha < 1$,*

$$H_\alpha^{\varepsilon+\varepsilon'}(XY) \leq H_\alpha^\varepsilon(X) + H_0^{\varepsilon'}(Y)$$

holds. Similarly, for $\alpha > 1$, we have

$$H_\alpha^\varepsilon(XY) \leq H_\alpha^{\varepsilon+\varepsilon'}(X) + H_0^{\varepsilon'}(Y) .$$

Monotonicity. The uncertainty on a pair of random variables X and Y cannot be smaller than the uncertainty on X alone. This is formalized by the following lemma. The proof is again similar to Lemma 5.

Lemma 7. *Let X and Y be random variables and let $\varepsilon \geq 0$. Then, for $\alpha \neq 1$, we have*

$$H_\alpha^\varepsilon(X) \leq H_\alpha^\varepsilon(XY) .$$

In particular, the smooth Rényi entropy does not increase when a function is applied:

$$H_\alpha^\varepsilon(f(X)) \leq H_\alpha^\varepsilon(X) . \tag{12}$$

Independence, Conditional Independence, and Markov Chains. Conditioning on independent randomness cannot have any effect on the entropy.

Lemma 8. *Let X and Y be independent random variables and let $\varepsilon \geq 0$, $\varepsilon' \geq 0$. Then, for any $\alpha \neq 1$, we have*

$$H_\alpha^\varepsilon(X|Y) = H_\alpha^\varepsilon(X) .$$

This statement can be generalized to random variables X, Y, and Z such that $X \leftrightarrow Z \leftrightarrow Y$ is a Markov chain:

$$H_\alpha^\varepsilon(X|YZ) = H_\alpha^\varepsilon(X|Z) .$$

When this is combined with inequalities (10) and (11), we obtain, for $\alpha < 1$,

$$H_\alpha^{\varepsilon + \varepsilon'}(XY|Z) \leq H_\alpha^\varepsilon(X|Z) + H_\alpha^{\varepsilon'}(Y|Z)$$

and, for $\alpha > 1$,

$$H_\alpha^{\varepsilon + \varepsilon'}(XY|Z) \geq H_\alpha^\varepsilon(X|Z) + H_\alpha^{\varepsilon'}(Y|Z) \ .$$

3 Smooth Rényi Entropy in Cryptography

3.1 Randomness Extraction and Privacy Amplification

The problem of extracting uniform randomness from a non-uniform source has first been studied in [3,13], and later been defined explicitly in [16]. Today, randomness extraction is a well-known and widely-used concept in theoretical computer science and, in particular, cryptography. A (strong) extractor is a function f which takes as input a random variable X and some additional uniformly distributed randomness R and is such that if X satisfies a certain entropy condition, the output $S := f(X, R)$ is almost independent of R and uniformly distributed.

For two random variables Z and W with joint distribution P_{ZW}, we define the *distance from uniform* by $d(Z|W) := \frac{1}{2}\delta(P_{ZW}, P_U \times P_W)$ where P_U is the uniform distribution on the range of Z and where $\delta(\cdot, \cdot)$ denotes the statistical distance.[6]

Definition 2. *A strong $(\tau, \kappa, \varepsilon)$-extractor on a set $\mathcal{X}$ is a function with domain $\mathcal{X} \times \mathcal{R}$ (for a set $\mathcal{R}$) and range $\mathcal{U}$ of size $|\mathcal{U}| = 2^\tau$ such that, for any random variable X on $\mathcal{X}$ satisfying $H_\infty(X) \geq \kappa$ and R uniformly distributed over $\mathcal{R}$, $d(f(X, R)|R) \leq \varepsilon$ holds.*

The following result has originally been proven in [13] based on two-universal hashing (where the randomness R is used to select a function from a two-universal[7] class of functions.). Later, similar statements have been shown in [2] and [11].[8]

Lemma 9 (Leftover hash lemma). *For any $\kappa > \tau$, there exists a strong $(\tau, \kappa, 2^{-(\kappa - \tau)/2})$-extractor.*

The following measure is closely related to *smooth entropy* as defined in [7] and [5]. For a distribution P_{XY}, it quantifies the amount of uniform randomness, conditioned on Y, which can be extracted from X.

---

[6] The *statistical distance* between two probability distributions P and Q is defined by $\delta(P, Q) := \frac{1}{2}\sum_v |P(v) - Q(v)|$.

[7] A *two-universal class of functions* from $\mathcal{Z}$ to $\mathcal{W}$ is a family $\mathcal{F}$ of functions $f : \mathcal{Z} \mapsto \mathcal{W}$ such that for any $z \neq z'$ and for f chosen at random from $\mathcal{F}$, $\Pr[f(z) = f(z')] \leq \frac{1}{|\mathcal{W}|}$.

[8] For a simple proof of Lemma 9, see, e.g., [14], p. 20.

Definition 3. *Let X and Y be random variables and let $\varepsilon \geq 0$. The ε-extractable randomness of X conditioned on Y is*

$$H^\varepsilon_{\text{ext}}(X|Y) := \max_{\mathcal{U}:\, \exists f \in \Gamma^\varepsilon_{XY}(\mathcal{X} \to \mathcal{U})} \log |\mathcal{U}| \,,$$

where $\Gamma^\varepsilon_{XY}(\mathcal{X} \to \mathcal{U})$ denotes the set of functions f from $\mathcal{X} \times \mathcal{R}$ (for some set $\mathcal{R}$) to $\mathcal{U}$ such that $d(f(X,R)|YR) \leq \varepsilon$ holds, for R independent of (X,Y) and uniformly distributed on $\mathcal{R}$.

As mentioned in the introduction, smooth Rényi entropy equals the amount of extractable uniform randomness, up to some small additive constant. Here, the lower bound follows directly from the leftover hash lemma and the definition of H^ε_∞. The upper bound, on the other hand, is a special case of the bound on one-way key agreement derived in Section 3.3.

Theorem 1. *Let X and Y be random variables and let $\varepsilon \geq 0$, $\varepsilon' \geq 0$. Then we have*

$$H^\varepsilon_\infty(X|Y) - 2\log(1/\varepsilon') \leq H^{\varepsilon+\varepsilon'}_{\text{ext}}(X|Y) \leq H^{\varepsilon+\varepsilon'}_\infty(X|Y) \,.$$

Using Lemma 2, we can, in particular, conclude that Rényi entropy of order α, for any $\alpha > 1$, is a lower bound on the number of uniform random bits that can be extracted, i.e.,

$$H_\alpha(X|Y) - \frac{\log(1/\varepsilon)}{\alpha - 1} - 2\log(1/\varepsilon') \leq H^{\varepsilon+\varepsilon'}_{\text{ext}}(X|Y) \,.$$

3.2 Data Compression, Error Correction, and Information Reconciliation

Another fundamental property of a probability distribution P is the minimum length of an encoding $C = E(X)$ of a random variable X with $P_X = P$ such that X can be retrieved from C with high probability. (A similar quantity can be defined for *a set* $\mathcal{P}$ of probability distributions.) As a motivating example, consider the following setting known as *information reconciliation* [4].[9] An entity (Alice) holds a value X which she wants to transmit to another (Bob), using τ bits of communication C. Clearly the minimum number τ of bits needed depends on the initial knowledge of Bob, which might be specified by some additional random variable Y (not necessarily known to Alice). From Bob's point of view, the random variable X is thus initially distributed according to $P_{X|Y=y}$ for some $y \in \mathcal{Y}$. Consequently, in order to guarantee that Bob can reconstruct the value of X with high probability, the error correcting information C sent by Alice must be useful for most of the distributions $P_{X|Y=y}$.

For the following, note that any probabilistic encoding function E corresponds to a deterministic function e taking as input some additional randomness R, i.e., $E(X) = e(X, R)$.

---

[9] In certain cryptographic applications, (one-way) information reconciliation schemes are also called *secure sketches* [10] (where Bob's procedure is the *recovery function*).

Definition 4. *A $(\tau, \kappa, \varepsilon)$-encoding on a set $\mathcal{X}$ is a pair of functions (e, g) together with a random variable R with range $\mathcal{R}$ where e, the* encoding function, *is a mapping from $\mathcal{X} \times \mathcal{R}$ to $\mathcal{C}$, for some set $\mathcal{C}$ of size $|\mathcal{C}| = 2^{\tau}$, and g, the* decoding *function, is a mapping from $\mathcal{C} \times \mathcal{R}$ to $\mathcal{X}$ such that, for any random variable X with range $\mathcal{X}$ satisfying $H_0(X) \leq \kappa$, $\Pr[g(e(X, R), R) \neq X] \leq \varepsilon$ holds.*

The following result has originally been shown in the context of information reconciliation [4].

Lemma 10. *For any $\tau > \kappa$, there exists a $(\tau, \kappa, 2^{-(\tau-\kappa)})$-encoding.*

For a distribution P_{XY}, the measure defined below quantifies the minimum length of an encoding $C = e(X, R)$ of X such that X can be reconstructed from C, Y, and R (with high probability).

Definition 5. *Let X and Y be random variables and let $\varepsilon \geq 0$. The ε-encoding length of X given Y is*

$$H_{\text{enc}}^{\varepsilon}(X|Y) := \min_{C:\, \exists e \in \Lambda_{XY}^{\varepsilon}(\mathcal{X} \to \mathcal{C})} \log |\mathcal{C}|$$

where $\Lambda_{XY}^{\varepsilon}(\mathcal{X} \to \mathcal{C})$ denotes the set of function e from $\mathcal{X} \times \mathcal{R}$ (for some set $\mathcal{R}$) to $\mathcal{C}$ such that there exists a decoding function g from $\mathcal{Y} \times \mathcal{C} \times \mathcal{R}$ to $\mathcal{X}$ such that $\Pr[g(Y, e(X, R), R) \neq X] \leq \varepsilon$ holds, for R independent of (X, Y) and uniformly distributed on $\mathcal{R}$.

Similarly to the amount of extractable randomness, smooth Rényi entropy can also be used to characterize the minimum encoding length.

Theorem 2. *Let X and Y be random variables and let $\varepsilon \geq 0$, $\varepsilon' \geq 0$. Then we have*

$$H_0^{\varepsilon+\varepsilon'}(X|Y) \leq H_{\text{enc}}^{\varepsilon+\varepsilon'}(X|Y) \leq H_0^{\varepsilon}(X|Y) + \log(1/\varepsilon') \ .$$

3.3   A Tight Bound for Key Agreement by One-Way Communication

As an application of Theorems 1 and 2, we prove tight bounds on the maximum length of a secret key that can be generated from partially secret and weakly correlated randomness by one-way communication.

Let X, Y, and Z be random variables. For $\varepsilon \geq 0$, define

$$M^{\varepsilon}(X; Y|Z) := \sup_{V \leftrightarrow U \leftrightarrow X \leftrightarrow (Y,Z)} H_{\infty}^{\varepsilon}(U|ZV) - H_0^{\varepsilon}(U|YV) \ . \tag{13}$$

Note that this is equivalent to[10]

$$M^{\varepsilon}(X; Y|Z) = \sup_{(U,V) \leftrightarrow X \leftrightarrow (Y,Z)} H_{\infty}^{\varepsilon}(U|ZV) - H_0^{\varepsilon}(U|YV) \ . \tag{14}$$

---

[10] To see that the measure defined by (14) is not larger than the measure defined by (13), observe that the entropies on the right-hand side of (14) do not change when the random variable U is replaced by $U' := (U, V)$. This random variable U' then satisfies $V \leftrightarrow U' \leftrightarrow X \leftrightarrow (Y, Z)$.

Consider now a setting where two parties, Alice and Bob, hold information X and Y, respectively, while the knowledge of an adversary Eve is given by Z. Additionally, they are connected by a public but authenticated one-way communication channel from Alice to Bob, and their goal is to generate an ε-secure key pair (S_A, S_B). Let $S^\varepsilon(X \to Y\|Z)$ be the maximum length of an ε-secure key that can be generated in this situation. Here, ε-secure means that, except with probability ε, Alice and Bob's keys are equal to a perfect key which is uniformly distributed and independent of Eve's information. Note that, if $\Pr[S_A \neq S_B] \leq \varepsilon_1$ and $d(S_A|W) \leq \varepsilon_2$, where W summarizes Eve's knowledge after the protocol execution, then the pair (S_A, S_B) is ε-secure, for $\varepsilon = \varepsilon_1 + \varepsilon_2$.

Theorem 3. *Let X, Y, and Z be random variables. Then, for $\varepsilon \geq 0$ and $\varepsilon' = \Theta(\varepsilon)$, we have*

$$M^{\varepsilon'}(X;Y|Z) - O(\log(1/\varepsilon')) \leq S^\varepsilon(X \to Y\|Z) \leq M^\varepsilon(X;Y|Z) .$$

Proof. We first show that the measure $M^{\varepsilon'}(X;Y|Z)$ is a *lower bound* on the number of ε-secure bits that can be generated. To see this, consider the following simple three-step protocol.

1. *Pre-processing:* Alice computes U and V from X. She sends V to Bob and keeps U.
2. *Information reconciliation:* Alice sends error-correcting information to Bob. Bob uses this information together with Y and V to compute a guess $\hat{U}$ of U.
3. *Privacy amplification:* Alice chooses a hash function F and sends a description of F to Bob. Alice and Bob then compute $S_A := F(U)$ and $S_B := F(\hat{U})$, respectively.

It follows immediately from the analysis of information reconciliation and privacy amplification that the parameters of the protocol (i.e., the amount of error correcting information and the size of the final keys) can be chosen such that the final keys have length $M^{\varepsilon'}(X;Y|Z)$ and the key pair (S_A, S_B) is ε-secure.

On the other hand, it is easy to see that *any* measure $M^\varepsilon(X;Y|Z)$ is an *upper* bound on the amount of key bits that can be generated if the following conditions, which imply that the quantity cannot increase during the execution of any protocol, are satisfied:

1. $M^\varepsilon(X;Y|Z) \geq M^\varepsilon(X';Y|Z)$ for any X' computed from X.
2. $M^\varepsilon(X;Y|Z) \geq M^\varepsilon(X;Y'|Z)$ for any Y' computed from Y.
3. $M^\varepsilon(X;Y|Z) \geq M^\varepsilon(X;YC|ZC)$ for any C computed from X.
4. $M^\varepsilon(X;Y|Z) \leq M^\varepsilon(X;Y|Z')$ for any Z' computed from Z.
5. $M^\varepsilon(S_A; S_B |W) \geq n$ if the pair (S_A, S_B) is ε-secure with respect to an adversary knowing W.

The measure $M^\varepsilon(X;Y|Z)$ defined by (13) does in fact satisfy these properties. It is thus an upper bound on the length of an ε-secure key which can be generated by Alice and Bob.

Property 1 holds since any pair of random variables U and V that can be computed from X' can also be computed from X.

Property 2 follows from $H_0^\varepsilon(A|BC) \le H_0^\varepsilon(A|B)$.

Property 3 holds since $M^\varepsilon(X; YC|ZC)$ can be written as the supremum over U and V' of $H_\infty^\varepsilon(U|ZV') - H_0^\varepsilon(U|YV')$, where V' is restricted to values of the form $V' = (V, C)$.

Property 4 follows from $H_\infty^\varepsilon(A|BC) \le H_\infty^\varepsilon(A|B)$.

Property 5 follows from $M^\varepsilon(S_A; S_B|Z) \ge H_\infty^\varepsilon(S_A|Z) - H_0^\varepsilon(S_A|S_B)$, $H_\infty^\varepsilon(S_A|Z) \ge n$, and $H_0^\varepsilon(S_A|S_B) = 0$.

$\square$

4 Concluding Remarks

We have analyzed data compression and randomness extraction in the cryptographic scenario where the assumption, usually made in classical information and communication theory, that the pieces of information stem from a large number of repetitions of a random experiment, has to be dropped. We have shown that Shannon entropy—the key quantity in independent-repetitions settings—then generalizes, depending on the context, to two different entropy measures H_0^ε and H_∞^ε. These new quantities, which are tight bounds on the optimal length of the compressed data and of the extracted random string, respectively, are very simple—in fact, simpler than Shannon information. Indeed, they can be computed from the distribution simply by leaving away the smallest probabilities or cutting down the largest ones, respectively. Moreover, the new quantities share all central properties of Shannon entropy.

An application of our results is the possibility of a simple yet general and tight analysis of protocols for quantum (see, e.g., [17]) and classical key agreement, where no assumption on an adversary's behavior has to be made. For instance, we give a simple tight bound for the possibility and efficiency of secret-key agreement by one-way communication.

It is conceivable that the new quantities have further applications in cryptography and in communication and information theory in general. We suggest as an open problem to find such contexts and applications.

Acknowledgment

The authors would like to thank Ueli Maurer for inspiring and helpful discussions.

References

1. C. H. Bennett and G. Brassard, Quantum cryptography: Public key distribution and coin tossing, *Proceedings of the IEEE International Conference on Computers, Systems, and Signal Processing*, pp. 175–179. IEEE, 1984.
2. C. H. Bennett, G. Brassard, C. Crépeau, and U. Maurer, Generalized privacy amplification, *IEEE Transactions on Information Theory*, Vol. 41, No. 6, 1915–1923, 1995.

3. C. H. Bennett, G. Brassard, and J. M. Robert, Privacy amplification by public discussion. *SIAM Journal on Computing*, Vol. 17, pp. 210–229, 1988.
4. G. Brassard and L. Salvail, Secret-key reconciliation by public discussion, *EURO-CRYPT '93*, LNCS, Vol. 765, pp. 410–423. Springer-Verlag, 1994.
5. C. Cachin, Smooth entropy and Rényi entropy, *EUROCRYPT '97*, LNCS, Vol. 1233, pp. 193–208. Springer-Verlag, 1997.
6. C. Cachin, *Entropy Measures and Unconditional Security in Cryptography*, Ph. D. Thesis, ETH Zürich, Hartung-Gorre Verlag, Konstanz, 1997.
7. C. Cachin and U. Maurer, Smoothing probability distributions and smooth entropy, *Proceedings of International Symposium on Information Theory (ISIT) '97*. IEEE, 1997.
8. T. M. Cover and J. A. Thomas, *Elements of Information Theory*. Wiley, 1991.
9. I. Csiszár and J. Körner, Broadcast channels with confidential messages, *IEEE Transactions on Information Theory*, Vol. 24, pp. 339–348, 1978.
10. Y. Dodis, L. Reyzin, and A. Smith, Fuzzy extractors: How to generate strong keys from biometrics and other noisy data, *EUROCRYPT 2004*, LNCS, Vol. 3027, pp. 523–540. Springer-Verlag, 2004.
11. J. Håstad, R. Impagliazzo, L. A. Levin, and M. Luby, A pseudorandom generator from any one-way function, *SIAM Journal on Computing*, Vol. 28, No. 4, pp. 1364–1396, 1999.
12. T. Holenstein and R. Renner, On the smooth Rényi entropy of independently repeated random experiments. manuscript, 2005.
13. R. Impagliazzo, L. A. Levin, and M. Luby, Pseudo-random generation from one-way functions (extended abstract), *Proceedings of the Twenty-First Annual ACM Symposium on Theory of Computing (STOC '89)*, pp. 12–24, 1989.
14. M. Luby and A. Wigderson, Pairwise independence and derandomization, Technical Report CSD-95-880, Computer Science Institute, Berkeley, CA, 1995. http://citeseer.ist.psu.edu/luby95pairwise.html.
15. U. M. Maurer, Secret key agreement by public discussion from common information, *IEEE Transactions on Information Theory*, Vol. 39, No. 3, pp. 733–742, 1993.
16. N. Nisan and D. Zuckerman, Randomness is linear in space, *Journal of Computer and System Sciences*, Vol. 52, pp. 43–52, 1996.
17. R. Renner, N. Gisin, and B. Kraus, Information-theoretic security proof for quantum-key-distribution protocols, *Physical Review A*, Vol. 72, 012332, 2005.
18. R. Renner and R. König, Universally composable privacy amplification against quantum adversaries, *Proc. of TCC 2005*, LNCS, Vol. 3378, pp. 407–425. Springer-Verlag, 2005.
19. R. Renner and S. Wolf, Smooth Rényi entropy and its properties, *Proceedings of International Symposium on Information Theory (ISIT) 2004*, p. 233. IEEE, 2004.
20. A. Rényi, On measures of entropy and information, *Proceedings of the 4th Berkeley Symp. on Math. Stat. and Prob.*, Vol. 1, pp. 547–561. Univ. of Calif. Press, 1961.
21. R. Shaltiel, Recent developments in explicit constructions of extractors, *Current trends in theoretical computer science. The Challenge of the New Century.*, Vol. 1, Algorithms and Complexity, 2002.
22. S. Wiesner, Conjugate coding, *SIGACT News*, Vol. 15, pp. 78–88, 1983.
23. A. D. Wyner, The wire-tap channel, *Bell System Technical Journal*, Vol. 54, No. 8, pp. 1355–1387, 1975.

Quantum Anonymous Transmissions

Matthias Christandl[1,*] and Stephanie Wehner[2,**]

[1] Centre for Quantum Computation,
Department of Applied Mathematics and Theoretical Physics,
University of Cambridge, Wilberforce Road,
Cambridge, CB3 0WA, United Kingdom
matthias.christandl@qubit.org
[2] Centrum voor Wiskunde en Informatica, Kruislaan 413,
1098 SJ Amsterdam, The Netherlands
wehner@cwi.nl

Abstract. We consider the problem of hiding sender and receiver of classical and quantum bits (qubits), even if all physical transmissions can be monitored. We present a quantum protocol for sending and receiving classical bits anonymously, which is completely traceless: it successfully prevents later reconstruction of the sender. We show that this is not possible classically. It appears that entangled quantum states are uniquely suited for traceless anonymous transmissions. We then extend this protocol to send and receive qubits anonymously. In the process we introduce a new primitive called anonymous entanglement, which may be useful in other contexts as well.

1 Introduction

In most cryptographic applications, we are interested in ensuring the secrecy of data. Sender and receiver know each other, but are trying to protect their data exchange from prying eyes. Anonymity, however, is the secrecy of identity. Primitives to hide the sender and receiver of a transmission have received considerable attention in classical computing. Such primitives allow any member of a group to send and receive data anonymously, even if all transmissions can be monitored. They play an important role in protocols for electronic auctions [32], voting protocols and sending anonymous email [10]. Other applications allow users to access the Internet without revealing their own identity [30], [14] or, in combination with private information retrieval, provide anonymous publishing [15]. Finally, an anonymous channel which is completely immune to any active attacks, would be a powerful primitive. It has been shown how two parties can use such a channel to perform key-exchange [1].

---

* Supported by the EU project RESQ IST-2001-37559, a DAAD Doktorandenstipendium and the U.K. Engineering and Physical Sciences Research Council.
** Supported by the EU project RESQ IST-2001-37559 and the NWO vici project 2004-2009. Part of this work was done while visiting CQC Cambridge.

B. Roy (Ed.): ASIACRYPT 2005, LNCS 3788, pp. 217–235, 2005.

1.1   Previous Work

A considerable number of classical schemes have been suggested for anonymous transmissions. An unconditionally secure classical protocol was introduced by Chaum [11] in the context of the Dining Cryptographers Problem. Since this protocol served as an inspiration for this paper, we briefly review it here. A group of cryptographers is assembled in their favorite restaurant. They have already made arrangements with the waiter to pay anonymously, however they are rather anxious to learn whether one of them is paying the bill, or whether perhaps an outside party such as the NSA acts as their benefactor. To resolve this question, they all secretly flip a coin with each of their neighbours behind the menu and add the outcomes modulo two. If one of them paid, he inverts the outcome of the sum. They all loudly announce the result of their computation at the table. All players can now compute the total sum of all announcements which equals zero if and only if the NSA pays. This protocol thus allows anonymous transmission of one bit indicating payment. A network based on this protocol is also referred to as a DC-net. Small scale practical implementations of this protocol are known [23]. Boykin [7] considered a quantum protocol to send classical information anonymously where the players distribute and test pairwise shared EPR pairs, which they then use to obtain key bits. His protocol is secure in the presence of noise or attacks on the quantum channel. Other anonymity related work was done by Müller-Quade and Imai [25] in the form of anonymous oblivious transfer.

In practice, two other approaches are used, which do not aim for unconditional security: First, there are protocols which employ a trusted third party. This takes the form of a trusted proxy server [3], [22], forwarding messages while masking the identity of the original sender. Secondly, there are computationally secure protocols using a chain of forwarding servers. Most notably, these are protocols based on so-called mixing techniques introduced by Chaum [10], such as Webmixes [6] and ISDN-Mixes [27]. Here messages are passed through a number of proxies which reorder the messages; hence the name MixNet. The goal of this reordering is to ensure an observer cannot match in- and outgoing messages and thus cannot track specific messages on their way through the network. Public Key Encryption is then used between the user and the different forwarding servers to hide the contents of a message. Several implemented systems, such as Mixmaster [24], PipeNet [14], Onion Routing [33] and Tor [16,35] employ layered encryption: the user successively encrypts the message with the public keys of all forwarding servers in the chain. Each server then "peels off" one layer, by decrypting the received data with its own secret key, to determine the next hop to pass the message to. The Crowds [30] system takes another approach. Here each player acts as a forwarding server himself. He either sends the message directly to the destination, or passes it on to another forwarding server with a certain probability. The aim is to make any sender within the group appear equally probable for an observer. Various other protocols using forwarding techniques are known. Since our focus lies on unconditionally secure protocols, we restrict ourselves to this brief introduction. More information can be found in the papers by Goldberg and Wagner [19], [18] and in the PhD thesis of Martin [23–Chapter 2 and 3].

Note that a DC-net computes the parity of the players inputs. Sending classical information anonymously can thus be achieved using secure multi-party computation which has received considerable attention classically [20], [12]. Quantum secure multi-party computation has been considered for the case that the players hold quantum inputs and each player receives part of the output [13]. Our protocol for sending qubits anonymously does not form an instance of general quantum secure multi-party computation, as we only require the receiver to obtain the qubit sent. Other players do not share part of this state. Instead, the receiver of the state should remain hidden.

1.2   Contribution

Here we introduce quantum protocols to send and receive classical and quantum bits anonymously. We first consider a protocol that allows n players to send and receive one bit of classical information anonymously using one shared entangled state $|\Psi\rangle = (|0\rangle^{\otimes n} + |1\rangle^{\otimes n})/\sqrt{2}$ and n uses of a broadcast channel. Given these resources, the protocol is secure against collusions of up to $n-2$ players: the collaborators cannot learn anything more by working together and pooling their resources.

The most notable property of our protocol for anonymous transmissions of classical data is that it is traceless as defined in Section 2.1. This is related to the notion of incoercibility in secure-multi party protocols [9]. Informally, a protocol is incoercible, if a player cannot be forced to reveal his true input at the end of the protocol. When forced to give up his input, output and randomness used during the course of the protocol, a player is able to generate fake input and randomness instead, that is consistent with the public transcript of communication. He can thus always deny his original input. This is of particular interest in secret voting to prevent vote-buying. Other examples include computation in the presence of an authority, such as the mafia, an employer or the government, that may turn coercive at a later point in time. In our case, incoercibility means that a player can always deny having sent. A protocol that is traceless, is also incoercible. However, a traceless protocol does not even require the player to generate any fake randomness. A sender can freely supply a fake input along with the true randomness used during the protocol without giving away his identity, i.e. his role as a sender during the protocol. This can be of interest in the case that the sender has no control over which randomness to give away. Imagine for example a burglar sneaking in at night to obtain a hard disk containing all randomness or the sudden seizure of a voting machine. As we show, the property traceless of our protocol contrasts with all classical protocols and provides another example of a property that cannot be achieved classically. The protocols suggested in [7] are not traceless, can, however, be modified to exhibit this property.

Clearly, in 2005 the group of dinner guests is no longer content to send only classical bits, but would also like to send qubits anonymously. We first use our protocol to allow two anonymous parties to establish a shared EPR pair. Finally, we use this form of anonymous entanglement to hide the sender and receiver of an arbitrary qubit. These protocols use the same resource of shared entangled states $|\Psi\rangle$ and a broadcast channel.

1.3 Outline

Section 2 states the resources used in the protocol, necessary definitions and a description of the model. In Section 2.2 we derive limitations on classical protocols. Section 3.2 then presents a quantum protocol for sending classical bits anonymously. Section 3.4 deals with the case of sending qubits anonymously and defines the notion of anonymous entanglement. Multiple simultaneous senders are considered in Section 4.

2 Preliminaries

2.1 Definitions and Model

We will consider protocols among a set of n players who are consecutively numbered. The players may assume a distinct role in a particular run of the protocol. In particular, some players might be *senders* and others *receivers* of *data items*. In our case, a data item d will be a single bit or a qubit. We use the verb *send* to denote transmission of a data item via the anonymous channel and *transmit* to denote transmission of a *message* (here classical bits) via the underlying classical message passing network[1] or via the broadcast channel given in Definition 3.

Anonymity is the secrecy of identity. Looking at data transmissions in particular, this means that a sender stays *anonymous*, if no one can determine his identity within the set of possible senders. In particular, the receiver himself should not learn the sender's identity either. Likewise, we define anonymity for the receiver. In all cases that we consider below, the possible set of senders coincides with the possible set of receivers. The goal of an *adversary* is to determine the identity of the sender and/or receiver. To this end he can choose to *corrupt* one or more players: this means he can take complete control over such players and their actions. Here, we only consider a non-adaptive adversary, who chooses the set of players to corrupt before the start of the protocol. In addition, the adversary is allowed to monitor all physical transmissions: he can follow the path of all messages, reading them as desired. Contrary to established literature, we here give the adversary one extra ability: After completion of the protocol, the adversary may *hijack* any number of players. This means that he can break into the system of a hijacked player and learn all randomness this player used during the protocol. However, he does not learn the data item d or the role this player played during the protocol. In a DC-net, for example, the randomness are the coin flips performed between two players. The adversary may then try to use this additional information to determine the identity of the sender and/or receiver. We return to the concept of hijacking in Section 2.1. In this paper, we are only interested in unconditional security and thus consider an unbounded adversary. We call a player *malicious* if he is corrupted by the adversary. A malicious player may deviate from the protocol by sending alternate messages. We call a player *honest*, if he is not corrupted and follows the protocol. If $t > 1$ players are corrupted, we also speak of a *collusion* of t players.

---

[1] A network of pairwise communication channels between the players.

Let V denote the set of all players. Without loss of generality, a *protocol* is a sequence of k rounds, where in each round the players, one after another, transmit one message. We use c_{jm} to denote the message transmitted by player m in round j. The total communication during the protocol is thus given by the sequence $C = \{c_{jm}\}_{j=1,m=1}^{k,n}$ of nk messages. Note that we do not indicate the receiver of the messages. At the beginning of the protocol, the players may have access to private randomness and shared randomness among all players, or a subset of players. In addition, each player may generate local private randomness during the course of the protocol. We use g_{jm} to denote the random string held by player m in round j. A player cannot later delete g_{jm}. Let $G_m = \{g_{jm}\}_{j=1}^{k}$ be the combined randomness held by player m. Similarly, we use $G = \{G_m\}_{m=1}^{n}$ to denote the combined randomness held by all players. Note that the data item d player m wants to send and his role in the protocol (sender/receiver/none) are excluded from G_m. In the following definitions, we exclude the trivial case where the sender or receiver are known beforehand, and where the sender is simultaneously the receiver.

It is intuitive that a protocol preserves the anonymity of a sender, if the communication does not change the a priori uncertainty about the identity of the sender. Formally:

Definition 1. *A k-round protocol P allows a sender s to be* anonymous, *if for the adversary who corrupts $t \leq n - 2$ players*

$$\max_{S} \text{Prob}[S = s | G^t, C] = \max_{S} \text{Prob}[S = s] = \frac{1}{n - t}$$

where the first maximum is taken over all random variables S which depend only on the sequence of all messages, C, and on the set of randomness held by the corrupted players, $G^t = \{G_m\}_{m \in E}$. Here, $E \subset V \backslash \{s\}$ is the set of players corrupted by the adversary; to exclude the trivial case where the sender s himself is corrupted by the adversary. A protocol P that allows a sender to be anonymous achieves *sender anonymity.*

Similarly, we define the anonymity of a receiver:

Definition 2. *A k-round protocol P allows a receiver r to be* anonymous, *if for the adversary who corrupts $t \leq n - 2$ players*

$$\max_{R} \text{Prob}[R = r | G^t, C] = \max_{R} \text{Prob}[R = r] = \frac{1}{n - t}$$

where the first maximum is taken over all random variables R which depend only on the sequence of all messages, C, and on the set of randomness held by the corrupted players, $G^t = \{G_m\}_{m \in E}$. Here, $E \subset V \backslash \{r\}$ is the set of players corrupted by the adversary; to exclude the trivial case where the receiver r himself is corrupted by the adversary. A protocol P that permits a receiver to be anonymous achieves *receiver anonymity.*

Note that protocols to hide the sender and receiver may not protect the data item sent. In particular there *could* be more players receiving the data item, even though there is only one receiver, which is determined before the protocol starts. The definition implies that the data sent via the protocol does not carry any compromising information itself.

All known protocols for sender and receiver anonymity achieving information theoretic security need a reliable broadcast channel [17]. We will also make use of this primitive:

Definition 3 (FGMR [17]). *A protocol among n players such that one distinct player s (the sender) holds an input value $x_s \in L$ (for some finite domain L) and all players eventually decide on an output value in L is said to achieve* broadcast *(or* Byzantine Agreement*) if the protocol guarantees that all honest players decide on the same output value $y \in L$, and that $y = x_s$ whenever the sender is honest.*

Informally, we say that a protocol is traceless, if it remains secure even if we make all resources available to an adversary at the end of the protocol. Consider for example the DC-net protocol discussed earlier. Imagine a curious burglar sneaking into the restaurant at night to gather all coin flips our group of cryptographers performed earlier on from the tapes of the security cameras. A protocol is traceless, if it can withstand this form of attack.

We model this type of attack by granting the adversary one additional ability. After completion of the protocol, we allow the adversary to hijack any number of players. If an adversary *hijacks* player m, he breaks into the system and learns all randomness G_m used by this player. In this paper, we allow the adversary to hijack all players after completion of the protocol. The adversary then learns all randomness used by the players, G. Nevertheless, we want him to remain ignorant about the identity of the sender and receiver. Formally,

Definition 4. *A k-round protocol P with sender s which achieves sender anonymity is* sender traceless, *if for the adversary who corrupts any $t \leq n-2$ players and, after completion of the protocol, hijacks all players*

$$\max_S \mathrm{Prob}[S = s | G, C] = \max_S \mathrm{Prob}[S = s] = \frac{1}{n - t}$$

where the first maximum is taken over all random variables S which depend only on the sequence of all messages, C, and on the set of randomness held by all players, G.

Likewise, change of sender s with receiver r, we define the property traceless for receiver anonymous protocols. Recall that G and C do not contain the data item d that was sent or the roles the players assumed during the course of the protocol.

2.2   Limitations on Traceless Protocols

Intuitively, we cannot hope to construct a classical protocol which is traceless and at the same time allows the receiver to learn what was sent: The only way data d can be send classically is by transmitting messages over the underlying network. If, however, an adversary has all information except the player's input and all communication is public, he can simply check the messages transmitted by each player to see if they "contain" d.

Theorem 1. *Let P be a classical protocol with one sender and one receiver such that for all data items $d \in D$ with $|D| \geq 2$ the following holds: the sender of d stays anonymous and the receiver knows d at the end of the protocol. Then P is not sender traceless.*

Proof. Let us assume by contradiction that the protocol is traceless. Without loss of generality, a player who is not the sender has input $d_0 \in D$ to the protocol. Let $d \in D$ be the data item that the sender s wants to send. We assume that all but one players are honest during the run of the protocol. We would like to emphasize that the only information that is not written down, is in fact the data item d of the sender.

The adversary corrupts one player. After completion of the protocol, he hijacks all players. He thus has access to all randomness and communication. Since a traceless protocol must resist the corruption of any player, it must also resist the corruption of the receiver. We therefore assume for the remainder of the proof that the adversary corrupts the receiver.

Let us consider step j in the protocol, where player m has total information g_{jm} and sends communication c_{jm}. Note that c_{jm} may only depend on the previous communication, g_{jm}, j, the number m and the role of the player m, i.e. whether m is sender, receiver or neither of them. If $m = s$, then the communication may also depend on d. Since the adversary has corrupted the receiver, and since there is only one receiver, the adversary knows that m is either a normal player or the sender. Note that since the adversary corrupted the receiver, he also knows the value of d.

After the protocol, the adversary, having access to G and C, can now calculate the messages that player m should have sent in round j depending on whether

1. m was not sender or receiver, or,
2. m was the sender and sent item d.

The messages are calculated as follows: In case 1, the adversary simulates the actions of player m as if m was neither sender nor receiver. This is possible, since the adversary has access to all randomness and all communication. In case 2, the adversary simulates the actions of m as if m was the sender and sent data item d. Let $\{f_{jm}^1\}_j, \{f_{jm}^2\}_j$ denote the set of messages resulting from the simulations of cases 1 and 2 respectively. The adversary now checks whether the set of observed messages $\{c_{jm}\}_j = \{f_{jm}^1\}_j$ or $\{c_{jm}\}_j = \{f_{jm}^2\}_j$. If the first equality holds he concludes that $s \neq m$, and for the second that $s = m$.

By assumption, the protocol is traceless for all d. Thus, the message computed for case 2) must be identical to the message computed for case 1) for all d, since otherwise the adversary could determine the sender s. This must hold for all steps j. But in this case the strategy the sender follows must be the same for both $d = d_0$ and $d \neq d_0$. Hence it cannot have been possible for r to have obtained the value of d in the first place and we have a contradiction to the assumption that the protocol achieves a transfer for all elements of a set D with $|D| \geq 2$.   □

Note that we make the assumption that there is exactly one receiver which is determined before the start of the protocol. Other players might still obtain the data item, as this is not a statement about the security of the message but merely about anonymity.

2.3   Limitations on Shared Randomness

In this section, we take a look at how many privately shared random bits are needed in order to perform anonymous transmissions. We thereby only consider unconditionally secure classical protocols based on privately shared random bits, such as for example the DC-net. In the following, we will view the players as nodes in an undirected graph. The notions of "nodes in a key-sharing graph" and "players" are used interchangeably. Similarly, edges, keys and private shared random bits are the same. Again, regard the broadcast channel as an abstract resource.

Definition 5. *The undirected graph $G = (V, E)$ is called the key-sharing graph if each node in V represents exactly one of the players and there is an edge between two nodes i and j if and only if i and j share one bit of key $r_{i,j}$.*

We first note that for any protocol P that achieves sender anonymity, where the only resource used by the n participating players is pairwise shared keys, a broadcast channel and public communication, the form of the key-sharing graph $G = (V, E)$ is important:

Lemma 1. *In any protocol P to achieve sender anonymity among n players, where the only resource available to the players is pairwise shared keys, a broadcast channel and public communication, a collusion of t players can break the sender's anonymity, if the corresponding collection of t nodes partitions the key-sharing graph $G = (V, E)$.*

Proof. t colluding nodes divide the key-sharing graph into s disjoint sets of nodes $\{S_1, \ldots, S_s\}$. Note that there is no edge connecting any of these sets, thus these sets do not share any keys. Now suppose that sender anonymity is still possible. Let $k_i \in S_i$ and $k_j \in S_j$ with $i \neq j$ be two nodes in different parts of the graph. Using a protocol achieving sender anonymity it is now possible to establish a secret bit between k_i and k_j [1]: Nodes i and j each generate n random bits: $r_i^1, \ldots, r_i^n$ and $r_j^1, \ldots, r_j^n$. Node i now announces n data of the form: "Bit b_k is r_i^k" for $1 \leq k \leq n$ using the protocol for sender anonymity. Likewise, node j announces "Bit b_k is r_j^k" for $1 \leq k \leq n$. Nodes i and j now discard all bits for which $r_i^k = r_j^k$ and use the remaining bits as a key. Note that an adversary can only learn whether $b_k = r_i^k$ or $b_k = r_j^k$ if the two announcements are the same. If $r_i^k \neq r_j^k$, the adversary does not learn who has which bit.

However, there is no channel between S_i and S_j that is not monitored by the colluding players. Thus, it cannot be possible to establish a secret bit between k_i and k_j, since the only communication allowed is classical and public [26]. This establishes the contradiction and shows that the sender's anonymity can be broken if the graph can be partitioned.   □

Furthermore, note that each player j needs to share one bit of key with at least two other players. Otherwise, his anonymity can be compromised. We can phrase this in terms of the key-sharing graph as

Corollary 1. *Each node $j \in V$ of the key-sharing graph $G = (V, E)$, used by a protocol P for anonymous transmissions, where the only resource available to the n players is pairwise shared keys, a broadcast channel and public communication, must have degree $d \geq 2$.*

Proof. Suppose on the contrary, that an arbitrary node j has degree 1: it has only one outgoing edge to another node k. Clearly, node k can partition the key-sharing graph into two disjoint sets $S_1 = \{j\}$ and $S_2 = V \setminus \{j, k\}$. By Lemma 1, node k can break j's anonymity.   □

Corollary 2. *Any protocol P that achieves sender anonymity, where no players collude and the only resource available to the n players is pairwise shared keys, a broadcast channel and public communication, needs at least n bits of pairwise shared keys.*

Proof. Consider again the key-sharing graph $G = (V, E)$. Suppose on the contrary, that only $k < n$ bits of shared keys are used. Then there must be at least one node of degree 1 in the graph. Thus, by Corollary 1 at most n bits of shared keys are necessary.   □

Corollary 3. *Any protocol P that achieves sender anonymity and is resistant against collusions of $t < n-1$ players, where the only resources available to the n players are pairwise shared keys, a broadcast channel and public communication, needs at least $n(n-1)/2$ bits of pairwise shared keys.*

Proof. Again consider the key-sharing graph G. Suppose on the contrary, that only $k < n(n-1)/2$ bits of shared keys are used. However, then there are only $k < n(n-1)/2$ edges in a graph of n nodes. Then G is not fully connected and there is a set of $t = n - 2$ colluding nodes which can partition the key-sharing graph. By Lemma 1, they can then break the sender's anonymity. Thus $n(n-1)/2$ bits of pairwise shared key are necessary to tolerate up to $t < n - 1$ colluding players.   □

2.4   Quantum Resources

We assume familiarity with the quantum model [26]. The fundamental resource used in our protocols are n-party shared entangled states of the form

$$|\Psi\rangle = \frac{1}{\sqrt{2}}(|0^n\rangle + |1^n\rangle) \equiv \frac{1}{\sqrt{2}}(|0\rangle^{\otimes n} + |1\rangle^{\otimes n}).$$

These are commonly known as generalized GHZ states [21]. By "shared" we mean that each of the n players holds exactly one qubit of $|\Psi\rangle$. They could have obtained these states at an earlier meeting or distribute and test them later on.

The key observation used in our protocols is the fact that phase flips and rotations applied by the individual players have the same effect on the global state no matter who applied them. Consider for example the phase flip defined by

$$\sigma_z = \begin{pmatrix} 1 & 0 \\ 0 & -1 \end{pmatrix}.$$

If player number i applies this transformation to his state, the global transformation is $U_i = I^{\otimes(i-1)} \otimes \sigma_z \otimes I^{\otimes(n-i)}$, where I is the identity transform. We now have $\forall i \in \{1, \ldots, n\} : U_i|\Psi\rangle = (|0^n\rangle - |1^n\rangle)/\sqrt{2}$. Note that this transformation takes place "instantaneously" and no communication is necessary.

3   Traceless Quantum Protocols

3.1   Model

To obtain traceless anonymous transmissions we allow the players to have access to a generalized GHZ state. We assume that the n players have access to the following resources:

1. n-qubit shared entangled states $|\Psi\rangle = (|0^n\rangle + |1^n\rangle)/\sqrt{2}$ on which the players can perform arbitrary measurements.
2. A reliable broadcast channel.

3.2   Sending Classical Bits

To start with, we present a protocol to send a classical bit b anonymously, if the n players share an n-qubit entangled state $|\Psi\rangle$. For now, we assume that only one person wants to send in each round of the protocol and deal with the case of multiple senders later on. We require our protocol to have the following properties:

1. (Correctness) If all players are honest, they receive the data item d that was sent by the sender. If some players are malicious, the protocol aborts or all honest players receive the same data item $\tilde{d}$, not necessarily equal to d.
2. (Anonymity) If up to $t \leq n-2$ players are malicious, the sender and receiver stay anonymous.
3. (Tracelessness) The protocol is sender and receiver traceless.

Protocol. Let's return to the original dinner table scenario described earlier. Suppose Alice, one of the dinner guests, wishes to send a bit $d \in D = \{0, 1\}$ anonymously. For this she uses the following protocol:

Protocol 1: ANON(d)
Prerequisite: Shared state $(|0^n\rangle + |1^n\rangle)/\sqrt{2}$

1: Alice applies a phase flip σ_z to her part of the state if $d = 1$ and does nothing otherwise.
2: Each player (incl. Alice):
- Applies a Hadamard transform to his/her qubit.
- Measures his/her qubit in the computational basis.
- Broadcasts his/her measurement result.
- Counts the total number of 1's, k, in the n measurement outcomes.
- If k is even, he/she concludes $d = 0$, otherwise $d = 1$.
3: The protocol aborts if one of more players do not use the broadcast channel.

Correctness. First of all, suppose all parties are honest. Since Alice applies the phase flip σ_z depending on the value of the bit d she wishes to send, the players obtain the state $(|0^n\rangle + |1^n\rangle)/\sqrt{2}$ if $d = 0$ and $(|0^n\rangle - |1^n\rangle)/\sqrt{2}$ if $d = 1$. By tracing out the other players' part of the state, we can see that no player can determine on his own whether the phase of the global state has changed. We therefore require the players to first apply a Hadamard transform H to their qubit. This changes the global state such that we get a superposition of all strings $x \in \{0,1\}^n$ with an even number of 1's for no phase flip and an odd number of 1's if a phase flip has been applied:

$$H^{\otimes n}\left(\frac{1}{\sqrt{2}}(|0^n\rangle + (-1)^d|1^n\rangle)\right) =$$

$$= \frac{1}{\sqrt{2^{n+1}}}\left(\sum_{x\in\{0,1\}^n}|x\rangle + (-1)^d\sum_{x\in\{0,1\}^n}(-1)^{|x|}|x\rangle\right)$$

$$= \frac{1}{\sqrt{2^{n+1}}}\sum_{x\in\{0,1\}^n}(1 + (-1)^{d\oplus|x|})|x\rangle,$$

where $|x|$ denotes the Hamming weight of the string x. Thus we expect an even number of 1's if $d = 0$ and an odd number of 1's if $d = 1$. The players now measure their part of the state and announce the outcome. This allows each player to compute the number of 1's in the global outcome, and thus d. If more than one player had applied a phase flip, ANON computes the parity of the players inputs. Broadcasting all measurement results needs n uses of a broadcast channel.

Now suppose that some of the players are malicious. Recall that we assume that the players use a reliable broadcast channel. This ensures an honest player obtains the same value for the announcement. Thus two honest parties will never compute a different value for the sent data item d. Further, note that it may always be possible that one or more malicious players do not use the broadcast channel. This consequently results in an abort of the protocol. We conclude that the correctness condition is satisfied.

Anonymity. As we noticed in Section 2, the resulting global state is independent of the identity of the person applying the phase flip. Since a phase flip is applied locally, no transmissions are necessary to change the global state. Subsequent transmissions are only dependent on the global state. Since this global state is invariant under an arbitrary permutation of the honest players and since the communication of the individual players depends only on their part of the states, the total communication during a run of the protocol P where player m sends d, is independent of the role of the player. If the sender is not one of the colluding players, then for the set of colluding players, all other players are equally likely to be sender. This is precisely the definition of sender anonymity. A receiver may be specified. His anonymity is then given directly as every player obtains the bit sent.

Note that a player deviating from the protocol by inverting his measurement outcome or applying a phase flip himself will only alter the outcome, but not learn the identity of the sender. The same discussion holds when the protocols is executed multiple times in succession or parallel.

Tracelessness. The most interesting property of our quantum protocol is that it is completely traceless: The classical communication during the protocol is solely dependent on the global state, which is the same no matter who the sender is. This means that Alice' communication is independent of her bit d. The randomness is now determined by the measurement results of the global state, which has already been altered according to the players inputs. Thus, the traceless condition is satisfied, because there is thus no record of Alice sending.

We believe that the tracelessness is a very intuitive property of the quantum state, as sending d simply changes the overall probability distribution of measurement outcomes instead of the individual messages of the sender. Note, however, that if we had first measured the state $|\Psi\rangle$ in the Hadamard basis to obtain classical information and then allowed the sender to invert the measured bit to send $d = 1$, our protocol would no longer be traceless. We leave no record of Alice' activity in the form of classical information. Alice can later always deny that she performed the phase flip. Whereas this is stronger than classical protocols, it also makes our protocol more prone to disruptors. Unlike in the classical scenario, we cannot employ mechanisms such as traps suggested by Chaum [11], and Waidner and Pfitzmann [38], to trace back disruptors. If one of our players is determined to disrupt the channel by, for example, always applying a phase flip himself, we are not able to find and exclude him from the network.

3.3 Anonymous Entanglement

The dinner guests realize that if they could create entanglement with any of the other players anonymously, they could teleport a quantum state to that player anonymously as well. We define the notion of anonymous entanglement, which may be useful in other scenarios as well:

Definition 6. *If two anonymous players A and B share entanglement, we speak of* anonymous entanglement (AE).

Definition 7. *If two players A and B share entanglement, where one of them is anonymous, we speak of* one-sided anonymous entanglement (one-sided AE).

It is possible to use shared entanglement together with classical communication to send quantum information using quantum teleportation [4]. Anonymous entanglement together with a protocol providing classical sender anonymity thus forms a virtual channel between two players who do not know who is sitting at the other end. This allows for easy sender and receiver anonymity for the transmission of qubits. Note that it is also possible to use anonymous entanglement to obtain a *secure* classical anonymous channel. Unlike ANON, this provides security of the data as well. Classically, such a virtual channel would have to be emulated by exchanging a key anonymously. We require that if all players are honest, the sender and recipient succeed in establishing an EPR pair. Furthermore, the protocol should achieve sender and receiver anonymity with regard to the two parts of the shared state. If one or more players are dishonest, they may disrupt the protocol.

Protocol. We use the same resource of shared states $|\Psi\rangle$ to establish anonymous entanglement for transmitting information by using an idea presented in the context of quantum broadcast [2]. More general protocols are certainly possible. For now, we assume that there are exactly two players, sender s (Alice) and receiver r (Bob), among the n players interested in sharing an EPR pair. If more players are interested, they can use a form of collision detection described later.

Protocol 2: AE
Prerequisite: Shared state $(|0^n\rangle + |1^n\rangle)/\sqrt{2}$.

1: Alice (s) and Bob (r) don't do anything to their part of the state.
2: Every player $j \in V \backslash \{s, r\}$
   - Applies a Hadamard transform to his qubit.
   - Measures this qubit in the computational basis with outcome m_j.
   - Broadcasts m_j.
3: s picks a random bit $b \in_R \{0, 1\}$ and broadcasts b.
4: s applies a phase flip σ_z to her qubit if $b = 1$.
5: r picks a random bit $b' \in_R \{0, 1\}$ and broadcasts b'.
6: r applies a phase flip σ_z to his qubit, if $b \oplus \bigoplus_{j \in V \backslash \{s,r\}} m_j = 1$.

Correctness. The shared state after the $n - 2$ remaining players applied the Hadamard transform becomes:

$$I_A \otimes I_B \otimes H^{\otimes(n-2)} \left(\frac{1}{\sqrt{2}} (|0^n\rangle + |1^n\rangle) \right) =$$

$$= \frac{1}{\sqrt{2^{n-1}}} \sum_{x \in \{0,1\}^{n-2}} (|00\rangle|x\rangle + (-1)^{|x|}|11\rangle|x\rangle).$$

All players except Alice and Bob measure this state. The state for them is thus $(|00\rangle + (-1)^{|x|}|11\rangle)/\sqrt{2}$. After Alice's phase flip the system is in state $(|00\rangle + (-1)^{|x|\oplus b}|11\rangle)/\sqrt{2}$. The sum of the measurements results gives $|x| = \bigoplus_{j\in V\setminus\{s,r\}} m_j$. Thus Bob can correct the state to $(|00\rangle + |11\rangle)/\sqrt{2}$ as desired.

Anonymity. The measurement outcomes are random. Thus, the players obtain no information during the measurement step. Likewise, the bits broadcast by Alice and Bob are random. Thus both of them remain hidden. Note that the protocol is resistant to collusions of up to $n-2$ players: The combined measurement outcomes still do not carry any information about Alice and Bob.

3.4   Sending Qubits

Let's return to the dinner table once more. After they have been dining for hours on end, Bob, the waiter, finally shows up and demands that the bill is paid. Alice, one of the dinner guests, is indeed willing to pay using her novel quantum coins, however, does not want to reveal this to her colleagues. The goal is now to transmit an arbitrary qubit and not mere classical information. As before, we ask that our protocol achieves sender and receiver anonymity and is traceless. Furthermore, if all players are honest, the receiver should obtain the qubit sent. Note that unlike in the classical case, we do not require that all honest players hold the same qubit at the end of the protocol. This would contradict the no-cloning property of quantum states. Alice now uses the shared EPR pair to send a quantum coin $|\phi\rangle$ to Bob via teleportation [26].

Protocol 3: ANONQ($|\phi\rangle$)
Prerequisite: Shared states $(|0^n\rangle + |1^n\rangle)/\sqrt{2}$

1: The players run AE: Alice and Bob now share an EPR pair: $|\Gamma\rangle = (|00\rangle + |11\rangle)/\sqrt{2}$
2: Alice uses the quantum teleportation circuit with input $|\phi\rangle$ and EPR pair $|\Gamma\rangle$, and obtains measurement outcomes m_0, m_1.
3: The players run ANON(m_0) and ANON(m_1) with Alice being the sender.
4: Bob applies the transformation described by m_0, m_1 on his part of $|\Gamma\rangle$ and obtains $|\phi\rangle$.

If all players are honest, after step 1, Alice and Bob share the state $|\Gamma\rangle = (|00\rangle + |11\rangle)/\sqrt{2}$ anonymously. The correctness condition is thus satisfied by the correctness of quantum teleportation. As discussed earlier, AE and ANON(b) do not leak any information about Alice or Bob. Since no additional information is revealed during the teleportation step, it follows that ANONQ($|\phi\rangle$) does not leak any information either and our anonymity condition is satisfied. In our example, we only wanted Alice to perform her payment anonymously, whereas Bob is known to all players. Our protocol also works, however, if Alice does not know the identity of Bob.

4   Dealing with Multiple Senders

So far, we have assumed that only a single person is sending in any one round. In reality, many users may wish to send simultaneously, leading to collisions. A user can easily detect a collision if it changes the classical outcome of the transmission. Depending on the application this may be sufficient. However, it may be desirable to detect collisions leading to the same outcome. This is important if we want to know the value of each of the bits sent and not only their overall parity.

The simplest way to deal with collisions is for the user to wait a random number of rounds, before attempting to resend the bit. This method was suggested by Chaum [11] and is generally known as ALOHA [34]. Unfortunately this approach is rather wasteful, if many players try to send simultaneously. Alternatively one could use a reservation map technique based on collision detection similar to what was suggested by Pfitzmann et al. [28]: For this one uses n applications of collision detection (of $\lceil \log n \rceil + 1$ rounds each) to reserve the following n slots.

We will now present a simple quantum protocol to detect all kinds of collisions, provided that no user tries to actively disrupt the protocol. We use the same resource, namely shared entangled states $|\Psi\rangle$. The important point of this protocol is that it is traceless.

4.1   Protocol

Before each round of communication, the n players run a ($\lceil \log n \rceil + 1$)-round test to check, whether a collision would occur. For this they require $\lceil \log n \rceil + 1$ additional states of the form $|\Psi\rangle = (|0^n\rangle + |1^n\rangle)/\sqrt{2}$. Each state is rotated before the start of the collision detection protocol. Let

$$U_j = R_z(-\pi/2^j) \otimes I^{\otimes(n-1)} = e^{i\frac{\pi}{2^{j+1}}} \begin{pmatrix} 1 & 0 \\ 0 & e^{-i\pi/2^j} \end{pmatrix} \otimes I^{\otimes(n-1)}$$

and map the jth state to $|t_j\rangle = U_j|\Psi\rangle$. This could for example be done by a dedicated player or be determined upon distribution of the entangled states $|\Psi\rangle$.

Protocol 4: Collision Detection
Prerequisite: $\lceil \log n \rceil + 1$ states $|\Psi\rangle = (|0^n\rangle + |1^n\rangle)/\sqrt{2}$

1: A designated player prepares $\lceil \log n \rceil + 1$ states by rotations:
 For $0 \le j \le \lceil \log n \rceil$, he applies $R_z(-\pi/2^j)$ to his part of one $|\Psi\rangle$ to create $|t_j\rangle$.
2: In round $0 \le j \le \lceil \log n \rceil$ each of the n players
 - Applies $R_z(\pi/2^j)$ to his part of the state $|t_j\rangle$, if he wants to send.
 - Applies a Hadamard transform to his part of the state.
 - Measures in the computational basis.
 - Announces his measurement result to all other players.
 - Counts the total number of 1's, k_j, in the measurement results.
 - If k_j is odd, concludes a collision has occurred and the protocol ends.
3: If all k_j are even, exactly 1 player wants to send.

4.2   Correctness and Privacy

Let's first take an informal look, why this works. In round j with $0 \leq j \leq \lceil \log n \rceil$, each user who wishes to send applies a rotation described by $R_z(\pi/2^j)$ to his part of the state. Note that if exactly one user tries to send, this simply rotates the global state back to the original state $|\Psi\rangle = (|0^n\rangle + |1^n\rangle)/\sqrt{2}$. If $k > 1$ users try to send, we can detect the collision in round j such that $k = 2^j m + 1$ where $m \in \mathbb{N}$ is odd: First $|t_j\rangle$ is rotated back to $|\Psi\rangle$ by the first of the k senders. The state is then rotated further by an angle of $(\pi/2^j) \cdot 2^j m = m\pi$. But

$$R_z(m\pi) = e^{-i\frac{m\pi}{2}} \begin{pmatrix} 1 & 0 \\ 0 & e^{im\pi} \end{pmatrix} = \pm i \begin{pmatrix} 1 & 0 \\ 0 & -1 \end{pmatrix}$$

applied to $|\Psi\rangle$ gives $|\Psi'\rangle = \pm i(|0^n\rangle - |1^n\rangle)/\sqrt{2}$, where we can ignore the global phase. The users now all apply a Hadamard transform to their part of the state again, measure and broadcast their measurement results to all players. As before, they can distinguish between $|\Psi\rangle$ and $|\Psi'\rangle$, by counting the number of 1's in the outcome. If the number of users who want to send in round j is not of the form $2^j m + 1$, the players may observe an even or odd number of 1's. The crucial observation is that in $\lceil \log n \rceil + 1$ rounds, the players will obtain $|\Psi'\rangle$ at least once, if more than one user wants to send, which they can detect. If no phase flip has been observed in all rounds of the collision detection protocol, the players can be sure there is exactly one sender. The key to this part of the protocol is the following simple observation:

Lemma 2. *For any integer $2 \leq k \leq n$, there exist unique integers m and j, with m odd and $0 \leq j \leq \lceil \log n \rceil$, such that $k = 2^j m + 1$.*

Proof. By the fundamental theorem of arithmetic we can write $k - 1 = 2^j m$ for unique $j, m \in \mathbb{N}$ where m is odd. We have $j \leq \lceil \log n \rceil$, since $2 \leq k \leq n$. Thus $k = 2^j m + 1$. $\qquad \square$

Corollary 4. $\lceil \log n \rceil + 1$ *rounds, using one state $(|0^n\rangle + |1^n\rangle)/\sqrt{2}$ each, are sufficient to detect $2 \leq k \leq n$ senders within a group of n players.*

Proof. Using Lemma 2 we can write $k = 2^j m + 1$ with $0 \leq j \leq \lceil \log n \rceil$. In round j the final state will be $R_z((2^j m) \cdot (\pi/2^j))|\Psi\rangle = R_z(m\pi)|\Psi\rangle = \pm i(|0^n\rangle - |1^n\rangle)/\sqrt{2}$, which the players can detect. $\qquad \square$

There exists a classical protocol already suggested by Pfitzmann et al. [37] using $O(n^2 \log n)$ bits of private shared randomness. However, this protocol is not traceless as desired by our protocol. Our protocol preserves anonymity and is traceless by the same argument used in Section 3.2.

When sending quantum states, collisions are not so easy to detect, since they do not change the outcome noticeably. The protocol to establish anonymous entanglement relies on the fact that only two players refrain from measuring. We thus require some coordination between the two players. Here, we can make use of the same collision detection protocol as we used to send classical bits: First run the collision detection protocol to determine the sender. The sender again expresses his interest in indicating that he wants to send by employing rotations. Then perform another application of collision detection for the receiver.

5 Conclusions and Future Work

We have presented a protocol for achieving anonymous transmissions using shared quantum states together with a classical broadcast channel. The main feature of this protocol is that, unlike all classical protocols, it prevents later reconstruction of the sender. This indicates that shared entangled states are very well suited to achieve anonymity. Perhaps similar techniques could also play an important role in other protocols where such a traceless property is desirable.

Our protocol is a first attempt at providing anonymous transmissions with this particular property. More efficient protocols may be possible. Perhaps a different form of quantum resource gives an additional advantage. However, we believe that our protocol is close to optimal for the given resources. We have also not considered the possibility of allowing quantum communication between the players, which could be required by more efficient protocols. It is also open whether a better form of collision detection and protection against malicious disruptors is possible. The states used for our collision detection protocol are hard to prepare if n is very large. Furthermore, using shared entangled states, it is always possible for a malicious user to measure his qubit in the computational basis to make further transmissions impossible.

So far, we have simply assumed that the players share a certain quantum resource. In reality, however, this resource would need to be established before it can be used. This would require quantum communication among the players in order to distribute the necessary states and at least classical communication for verification purposes. The original DC-net protocol suffers from a similar problem with regard to the distribution of shared keys, which is impossible to do from scratch using only classical channels [26]. Some quantum states on the other hand have the interesting property that the players can create and test the states among themselves, instead of relying on a trusted third party.

Acknowledgments

We thank Andreas Pfitzmann for sending us a copy of [28] and [27]. We also thank Ronald de Wolf, Louis Salvail and Renato Renner for useful comments. SW thanks the CQC Cambridge for their hospitality.

References

1. B. Alpern and F.B. Schneider. Key exchange using 'keyless cryptography'. *Information Processing Letters*, 16:79–1, 1983.
2. A. Ambainis, H. Buhrman, H. Röhrig, and Y. Dodis. Multiparty quantum coin flipping. In *Proceedings of CCC '03*, pages 250-259, 2003.

3. Anonymizer. Anonymizing proxy. http://www.anonymizer.com.
4. C. Bennett, G. Brassard, C. Crépeau, R. Jozsa, A. Peres, and W. Wootters. Teleporting an unknown quantum state via dual classical and Einstein-Podolsky-Rosen channels. *Physical Review Letters*, 70:1895–1899, 1993.
5. M. Ben-Or, and D. Mayers. General security definition and composability for quantum & classical protocols. quant-ph/0409062, 2004
6. O. Berthold, H. Federrath, and S. Köpsell. Web MIXes: A system for anonymous and unobservable Internet access. *Lecture Notes in Computer Science*, 2009:115–129, 2001.
7. P. Boykin. *Information Security and Quantum Mechanics: Security of Quantum Protocols*. PhD thesis, University of California, Los Angeles, 2002.
8. R. Canetti. Universally composable security: A new paradigm for cryptographic protocols. In *Electronic Colloquium on Computational Complexity (ECCC)* 016, 2001.
9. R. Canetti, and R. Gennaro. Incoercible Multiparty Computation (extended abstract). In *Proceedings of 37th IEEE FOCS*, pages 504–513, 1996
10. D. Chaum. Untraceable electronic mail, return addresses, and digital pseudonyms. *Communications of the ACM*, 24(2):84–88, 1981.
11. D. Chaum. The dining cryptographers problem: Unconditional sender and recipient untraceability. *Journal of Cryptology*, 1:65–75, 1988.
12. D. Chaum, C. Crépeau, and I. Damgard. Multiparty unconditionally secure protocols. In *Proceedings of 20th ACM STOC*, pages 11–19, 1988.
13. C. Crépeau, D. Gottesman, and A. Smith. Secure multiparty quantum computation. In *Proceedings of 34th ACM STOC*, pages 643–652, 2002.
14. W. Dei. Pipenet. http://www.eskimo.com/~weidai/pipenet.txt.
15. R. Dingledine. The free haven project: Design and deployment of an anonymous secure data haven. Master's thesis, Massachusetts Institute for Technology, 2000.
16. R. Dingledine, N. Mathewson and P. Syverson. Tor: The Second-Generation Onion Router. In *Proceedings of the 13th USENIX Security Symposium*, pages 303–320, 2004.
17. M. Fitzi, N. Gisin, U. Maurer, and O. von Rotz. Unconditional byzantine agreement and multi-party computation secure against dishonest minorities from scratch. In *Proceedings of Eurocrypt '02*, volume 2332 of *Lecture Notes in Computer Science*, pages 482–501, 2002.
18. I. Goldberg. Privacy-enhancing technologies for the internet, ii: Five years later. In *Proceedings of Privacy Enhancing Technologies, Second International Workshop (PET 2002)*, volume 2482 of *Lecture Notes in Computer Science*, pages 1–12, 2002.
19. I. Goldberg, D. Wagner, and E. Brewer. Privacy-enhancing technologies for the internet. In *Proceedings of 42nd IEEE Spring COMPCON*, 1997. http://now.cs.berkeley.edu/~daw/papers/privacy-compcon97.ps.
20. O. Goldreich, S. Micali, A. Wigderson. How to play any mental game—or—a completeness theorem for protocols with honest majority. In *Proceedings of 19th ACM STOC*, pages 218–229, 1987
21. D. M. Greenberger, M. A. Horne, and A. Zeilinger. *Bell's Theorem, Quantum Theory, and Conceptions of the Universe*. Dordrecht: Kluwer, 1989.
22. J. Helsingius. Email anonymizing server: anon.penet.fi, 1996.
23. D. Martin. *Local Anonymity in the Internet*. PhD thesis, Boston University, 1999.
24. MixMaster. Implementation of a remailer. http://mixmaster.sourceforge.net/.
25. J. Müller-Quade and H. Imai. Anonymous oblivious transfer. cs.CR/0011004, 2000.

26. M. A. Nielsen and I. L. Chuang. *Quantum Computation and Quantum Information.* Cambridge University Press, 2000.
27. A. Pfitzmann. How to implement isdns without user observability - some remarks. Technical report, Universität Karlsruhe, 1985.
28. A. Pfitzmann. *Dienstintegrierende Kommunikationsnetze mit teilnehmerueber-pruefbarem Datenschutz.* PhD thesis, Fakultaet fuer Informatik, Universität Karlsruhe, 1989.
29. B. Pfitzmann, and M. Waidner Composition and Integrity Preservation of Secure Reactive Systems In *7th ACM Conference on Computer and Communications Security,* pages 245–254, 2000.
30. M. K. Reiter and A. D. Rubin. Crowds: anonymity for Web transactions. *ACM Transactions on Information and System Security,* 1(1):66–92, 1998.
31. C. E. Shannon. A mathematical theory of communication. *Bell System Technical Journal,* 27:379–423, 623–656, 1948.
32. F. Stajano and R. J. Anderson. The cocaine auction protocol: On the power of anonymous broadcast. In *Information Hiding,* pages 434–447, 1999.
33. P. F. Syverson, D. M. Goldschlag, and M. G. Reed. Anonymous connections and onion routing. In *IEEE Symposium on Security and Privacy,* pages 44–54, 1997.
34. A. S. Tanenbaum. *Computer Networks, 3rd edition.* Prentice-Hall, 1996.
35. Tor: An anonymous Internet communication system. http://tor.eff.org
36. D. Unruh Simulatable security for quantum protocols. quant-ph/0409125
37. M. Waidner and B. Pfitzmann. Unconditional sender and recipient untraceability in spite of active attacks - some remarks. Technical report, Universität Karlsruhe, 1989.
38. M. Waidner and B. Pfitzmann. The dining cryptographers in the disco: unconditional sender and recipient untraceability with computationally secure serviceability. In *Proceedings of the workshop on the theory and application of cryptographic techniques on Advances in cryptology,* page 690, 1990.

Privacy-Preserving Graph Algorithms in the Semi-honest Model

Justin Brickell and Vitaly Shmatikov

The University of Texas at Austin, Austin TX 78712, USA

Abstract. We consider scenarios in which two parties, each in possession of a graph, wish to compute some algorithm on their *joint graph* in a privacy-preserving manner, that is, without leaking any information about their inputs except that revealed by the algorithm's output.

Working in the standard secure multi-party computation paradigm, we present new algorithms for privacy-preserving computation of APSD (all pairs shortest distance) and SSSD (single source shortest distance), as well as two new algorithms for privacy-preserving set union. Our algorithms are significantly more efficient than generic constructions. As in previous work on privacy-preserving data mining, we prove that our algorithms are secure provided the participants are "honest, but curious."

Keywords: Secure Multiparty Computation, Graph Algorithms, Privacy.

1   Introduction

In this paper, we investigate scenarios with two mutually distrustful parties, each in possession of a graph (representing, *e.g.*, a network topology, a distribution channel map, or a social network). The parties wish to compute some algorithm on their *combined* graph, but do not wish to reveal anything about their private graphs beyond that which will be necessarily revealed by the output of the algorithm in question.

For example, consider two Internet providers who are contemplating a merger and wish to see how efficient the resulting joint network would be without revealing the details of their existing networks; or two transportation companies trying to determine who has the greatest capacity to ship goods between a given pair of cities without revealing what that capacity is or which distribution channels contribute to it; or two social networking websites wishing to calculate aggregate statistics such as degrees of separation and average number of acquaintances without compromising privacy of their users, and so on.

In this paper, we construct privacy-preserving versions of classic graph algorithms for APSD (all pairs shortest distance) and SSSD (single source shortest distance). Our algorithm for APSD is new, while the SSSD algorithm is a privacy-preserving transformation of the standard Dijkstra's algorithm. We also show that minimum spanning trees can be easily computed in a privacy-preserving manner. As one of our tools, we develop protocols for privacy-preserving set union, which are results of independent interest.

B. Roy (Ed.): ASIACRYPT 2005, LNCS 3788, pp. 236–252, 2005.

We demonstrate that our constructions are significantly more efficient than those based on generic constructions for secure multi-party computation such as Yao's garbled circuits [39]. Some of the efficiency gain is due to our use of canonical orderings on graph edges. We believe that this technique may find applicability beyond the problems considered in this paper.

We prove that our constructions are secure in the *semi-honest* model. Assuming that a party correctly follows the protocol, there is no efficient adversary that can extract more information from the transcript of the protocol execution than is revealed by that party's private input and the result of the graph algorithm. Our choice of the semi-honest model follows previous work on privacy-preserving data mining such as Lindell and Pinkas' construction for a privacy-preserving version of the ID3 decision tree learning algorithm [28], and constructions by Yang *et al.* for privacy-preserving classification [38].

In general, the semi-honest model seems to be the right fit for our setting, where there is no realistic way to verify that the parties are submitting their true graphs as private inputs. The best we could hope for in the case of actively malicious participants is a protocol in which the parties first commit to their graphs, and then prove at every step of the protocol that their inputs match their commitments. This would greatly complicate the protocols without providing any protection against parties who maliciously choose their graphs in such a way that the result of the computation on the joint graph completely reveals the other party's input. We leave investigation of privacy-preserving graph algorithms in the model with malicious participants to future work.

This paper is organized as follows. We survey related work in section 2, then present our definition of privacy in section 3 and our cryptographic toolkit, including a construction for private set union, in section 4. Section 5 contains the main results of the paper: privacy-preserving APSD and SSSD algorithms. Their complexity is analyzed in section 6. Conclusions are in section 7.

2   Related Work

This paper follows a long tradition of research on privacy-preserving algorithms in the so called *secure multiparty computation* (SMC) paradigm. Informally, security of a protocol in the SMC paradigm is defined as computational indistinguishability from some *ideal functionality*, in which a trusted third party accepts the parties' inputs and carries out the computation. The ideal functionality is thus secure by definition. The actual protocol is secure if the adversary's view in any protocol execution can be simulated by an efficient simulator who has access only to the ideal functionality, *i.e.*, the actual protocol does not leak any information beyond what is given out by the ideal functionality. Formal definitions for various settings can be found, for example, in [6,7,22].

Any polynomial-time multi-party computation can be done in a privacy-preserving manner using generic techniques of Yao [39] and Goldreich, Micali, and Wigderson [23]. Generic constructions, however, are sometimes impractical due to their complexity. Recent research has focused on finding more efficient privacy-preserving algorithms for specific problems such as computation of approximations [18], auctions [33], set matching and intersection [20], surveys [19], computation of the k-th ranked element [1] and especially data mining problems such as privacy-preserving computation of decision trees [28], classification of customer data [38], and mining of vertically partitioned data [16,37].

The techniques we use in this paper are closely related to those previously used in the cryptographic version of privacy-preserving data mining, *e.g.*, by Lindell and Pinkas in their privacy-preserving transformation of the ID3 algorithm [28]. We, too, use generic Yao's protocol [39,29] as a building block. Yao's protocol can be implemented using efficient constructions for oblivious transfer [31,32] and secure function evaluation [30].

In this paper, we aim to follow the SMC tradition and provide provable cryptographic guarantees of security for our constructions. Another line of research has focused on *statistical privacy* in databases, typically achieved by randomly perturbing individual data entries while preserving some global properties [4,2,5,3,26,12,17]. A survey can be found in [36]. The proofs of security in this framework are statistical rather than cryptographic in nature, and typically permit some leakage of information, while supporting more efficient constructions. In this paradigm, Clifton *et al.* have also investigated various data mining problems [10,24,35,25], while Du *et al.* researched special-purpose constructions for problems such as privacy-preserving collaborative scientific analysis [14,13,34,15]. Recent work by Chawla *et al.* [8] aims to bridge the gap between the two frameworks and provide rigorous cryptographic definitions of statistical privacy in the SMC paradigm.

Another line of cryptographic research on privacy focuses on private information retrieval (PIR) [9,21], but the problems and techniques in PIR are substantially different from this paper.

3   Definition of Privacy

We use a simplified form of the standard definition of security in the static semi-honest model due to Goldreich [22] (this is the same definition as used, for example, by Lindell and Pinkas [28]).

Definition 1. *(computational indistinguishability): Let $S \subseteq \{0,1\}^*$. Two ensembles (indexed by S), $X \stackrel{\text{def}}{=} \{X_w\}_{w \in S}$ and $Y \stackrel{\text{def}}{=} \{Y_w\}_{w \in S}$ are computationally indistinguishable (by circuits) if for every family of polynomial-size circuits, $\{D_n\}_{n \in \mathbb{N}}$, there exists a negligible (i.e., dominated by the inverse of any polynomial) function $\mu : \mathbb{N} \mapsto [0,1]$ so that*

$$| \Pr[D_n(w, X_w) = 1] - \Pr[D_n(w, Y_w) = 1] | < \mu(|w|)$$

In such a case we write $X \stackrel{c}{\equiv} Y$.

Suppose f is a polynomial-time functionality (deterministic in all cases considered in this paper), and π is the protocol. Let x and y be the parties' respective private inputs to the protocol. For each party, define its *view* of the protocol as $(x, r^1, m_1^1, \ldots, m_k^1)$ (respectively, $(y, r^2, m_1^2, \ldots, m_l^2)$), where $r^{1,2}$ are the parties' internal coin tosses, and m_j^i is the jth message received by party i during the execution of the protocol. We will denote the ith party's view as $\mathsf{view}_i^\pi(x, y)$, and its output in the protocol as $\mathsf{output}_i^\pi(x, y)$.

Definition 2. *Protocol π securely computes deterministic functionality f in the presence of static semi-honest adversaries if there exist probabilistic polynomial-time simulators S_1 and S_2 such that*

$$\{S_1(x, f(x,y))\}_{x,y \in \{0,1\}^*} \stackrel{c}{\equiv} \{\mathsf{view}_1^\pi(x,y)\}_{x,y \in \{0,1\}^*}$$
$$\{S_2(y, f(x,y))\}_{x,y \in \{0,1\}^*} \stackrel{c}{\equiv} \{\mathsf{view}_2^\pi(x,y)\}_{x,y \in \{0,1\}^*}$$

where $|x| = |y|$.

Informally, this definition says that each party's view of the protocol can be efficiently simulated given only its private input and the output of the algorithm that is being computed (and, therefore, the protocol leaks no information to a semi-honest adversary beyond that revealed by the output of the algorithm).

4   Tools

As building blocks for our algorithms, we use protocols for privacy-preserving computation of a minimum $\min(x, y)$ and set union $S_1 \cup S_2$.

In the minimum problem, the parties have as their respective private inputs integers x_1 and x_2 which are representable in n bits. They wish to privately compute $m = \min(x_1, x_2)$. Because this problem is efficiently solved by a simple circuit containing $O(n)$ gates, it is a good candidate for Yao's generic method [39]. An implementation of this functionality with Yao's garbled circuit requires 2 communication rounds with $O(n)$ total communication complexity and $O(n)$ computational complexity.

4.1   Privacy-Preserving Set Union

In the set union problem, parties P_1 and P_2 have as their respective private inputs sets S_1 and S_2 drawn from some finite universe U. They wish to compute the set $S = S_1 \cup S_2$ in a privacy-preserving manner, *i.e.*, without leaking which elements of S are in the intersection $S_1 \cap S_2$. We will define $|S_1| = s_1$, $|S_2| = s_2$, $|S| = s$, and $|U| = u$.

In this section, we give two solutions for privacy-preserving set union: the iterative method, and the tree-pruning method. Both require communication and computational complexity that is logarithmic in u, provided s is small (note that even if we are not concerned about privacy, computing the set union requires at least $O(s \lg u)$ bandwidth, although it can be done in 1 round). Appendix B surveys several previously proposed techniques that can be used to compute the set union, but these techniques are all either linear in u (or worse), or do not fully preserve privacy.

Iterative method. The basic idea of the iterative method is to build up S one element at a time, from "smallest" to "largest." Before the protocol begins, both parties agree upon a canonical total ordering for the entire universe U. As a result, each element in U is given an integer label with $\lg u$ bits. In addition, we need a label representing ∞, for which can simply use the integer $u + 1$. The protocol proceeds as follows:

Step 1. Set $S = \emptyset$.

Step 2. P_1 selects m_1 as the canonically smallest element in S_1, or sets $m_1 = \infty$ if $S_1 = \emptyset$. P_2 likewise selects m_2 as the canonically smallest element in S_2, or sets $m_1 = \infty$ if $S_1 = \emptyset$.

Step 3. Using a protocol for private minimum, P_1 and P_2 privately compute $m = \min(m_1, m_2)$.

Step 4. If $m = \infty$, stop and return S. Otherwise, $S = S \cup \{m\}$ and the parties remove m from their input sets (it may be present in one or both). Then return to step 2.

The protocol preserves privacy because, given the output set S, a simulator can determine the value of m at each iteration. The protocol used for computing the minimum is private, so there exists an efficient algorithm that can simulate its execution to the party P_1 given its input and the output m (likewise for P_2). The simulator for the iterative method protocol uses the simulator for the minimum protocol as a subroutine, following the standard hybrid argument.

The iterative method protocol requires $s + 1$ iterations, and in each iteration the minimum of two $(\lg u)$-bit integers is privately computed. Using Yao's method, this requires a circuit with $2 \lg u$ inputs and $O(\lg u)$ gates. The $2 \lg u$ oblivious transfers can all take place in parallel, and since Yao's method requires a constant number of rounds the whole protocol takes $O(s)$ communication rounds. The total communication and computational complexity for the iterative method is $O(s \lg u)$.

Tree-pruning method. Before the tree-pruning protocol begins, the participants agree on a $(\lg u)$-bit binary label for each element in the universe (note that a canonical total ordering would automatically provide such a label). The basic idea of the protocol is that the participants will consider label prefixes of increasing length, and use a privacy-preserving BIT-OR protocol (see appendix C) to determine if either participant has an element with that prefix in his set.

Initially, the single-bit prefixes "0" and "1" are set "live." The protocol proceeds through $\lg u$ rounds, starting with round 1. In the ith round, the participants consider the set P of i-bit "live" prefixes. For each prefix $p \in P$, each participant sets his respective 1-bit input to 1 if he has an element in his set with prefix p, and to 0 if he does not have any such elements. The participants then execute a privacy-preserving BIT-OR protocol on their respective 1-bit inputs. If the result of the BIT-OR protocol is 1, then $p0$ and $p1$ are set as live $(i + 1)$-bit prefixes. Otherwise, $p0$ and $p1$ are dead prefixes.

By a simple inductive argument, the number of live prefixes in each round does not exceed $2 \cdot |S|$, because an i-bit prefix $p_i = b_1 \ldots b_i$ can be live if and only if at least one of the participants has an element whose label starts with $b_1 \ldots b_{i-1}$, and the number of such elements cannot exceed the total number of elements in the union, *i.e.*, $|S|$.

In the last round ($i = \lg u$), the length of the prefix is the same as the length of the binary labels, and the entire set P of live prefixes is declared to be the output S of the privacy-preserving set union protocol.

The tree-pruning protocol preserves privacy because, given the output set S, a simulator can determine the output of each of the BIT-OR protocols. As in the case of the iterative method protocol, we can construct a simulator for the tree-pruning protocol that uses a simulator for the BIT-OR protocol as a subroutine, and prove its correctness using a hybrid argument. The construction is simple and is omitted for brevity.

The tree-pruning protocol requires $\lg u$ iterations, and in each iteration the pairwise BIT-OR of at most $2s$ bits is computed. These computations can all take place in parallel, so the protocol requires $O(\lg u)$ communication rounds. Each iteration requires $O(s)$ communication and computational complexity, so the entire protocol has complexity $O(s \lg u)$. Both the iterative method and tree pruning protocols have the same complexity, but different numbers of rounds. The iterative method requires fewer rounds when $s = o(\lg u)$.

5   Privacy-Preserving Algorithms on Joint Graphs

We now present our constructions that enable two parties to compute algorithms on their joint graph in a privacy-preserving manner. Let G_1 and G_2 be the two parties' respective weighted graphs. Assume that $G_1 = (V_1, E_1, w_1)$ and $G_2 = (V_2, E_2, w_2)$ are complete graphs on the same set of vertices, that is, $V_1 = V_2$ and $E_1 = E_2$. Let $w_1(e)$ and $w_2(e)$ represent the *weight* of edge e in G_1 and G_2, respectively. To allow incomplete graphs, the excluded edges may be assigned weight ∞. We are interested in computing algorithms on the parties' joint *minimum* graph $\mathrm{gmin}(G_1, G_2) = (V, E, w_{min})$ where $w_{min}(e) = \min(w_1(e), w_2(e))$, since minimum joint graphs seem natural for application scenarios such as those considered in section 1.

5.1   Private All Pairs Shortest Distance (APSD)

The All Pairs Shortest Distance (APSD) problem is the classic graph theory problem of finding shortest path distances between all pairs of vertices in a graph (see, *e.g.*, [11]). We will think of APSD(G) as returning a complete graph $G' = (V, E', w')$ in which $w'(e_{ij}) = d_G(i,j)$ and V is the original edge set of G. Here $d_G(i,j)$ represents the shortest path distance from i to j in G. This problem is particularly well suited to privacy-preserving computation because the solution "leaks" useful information that can be used by the simulator.

To motivate the problem, consider two shipping companies who are hoping to improve operations by merging so that they can both take advantage of fast shipping routes offered by the other company. They want to see how quickly the merged company would be able to ship goods between pairs of cities, but they don't want to reveal all of their shipping times (and, in particular, their inefficiencies) in case the merger doesn't happen. In other words, they wish to compute $\mathrm{APSD}(G)$ where $G = \mathrm{gmin}(G_1, G_2)$.

The basic idea behind our construction is to build up the solution graph by adding edges in order from shortest to longest. The following algorithm takes as input the parties' complete graphs G_1 and G_2. The graphs may be directed or undirected, but they must have strictly positive weight functions.

1. For notational convenience we introduce a variable k, initially set to 1, that represents the iteration count of the algorithm. Color each edge in E "blue" by letting $B^{(k)}$ denote the set of blue edges in the edge set E at iteration k, and setting $B^{(0)} = E$. Let $R^{(k)}$ denote the set of "red" edges, $R^{(k)} \overset{def}{=} E - B^{(k)}$. The lengths of red edges have reached their final values and will not change as the algorithm proceeds, while the lengths of blue edges may still decrease.

2. A public graph $G_0^{(0)} = (V, E, w_0^{(0)})$ is created. Its edges are all initially weighted as $w_0^{(0)}(e) = \infty$. When the algorithm terminates after n iterations, we will have $w_0^{(n)}(e_{ij}) = d_G(i, j)$ and $B^{(n)} = \emptyset$.

3. The parties compute the following public value

$$m_0^{(k)} = \min_{e \in B^{(k-1)}} w_0^{(k-1)}(e) \tag{1}$$

and the respective private values

$$m_1^{(k)} = \min_{e \in B^{(k-1)}} w_1(e), \text{ and} \tag{2}$$

$$m_2^{(k)} = \min_{e \in B^{(k-1)}} w_2(e) \tag{3}$$

4. Now the parties *privately* compute the length of the smallest blue edge among all three graphs, $m^{(k)} = \min(\min(m_1^{(k)}, m_0^{(k)}), \min(m_2^{(k)}, m_0^{(k)}))$, using a generic protocol for private minimum (section 4). This protocol does not reveal the larger value.

5. The parties form the following public set

$$S_0^{(k)} = \{e | w_0^{(k-1)}(e) = m^{(k)}\} \tag{4}$$

and the respective private sets

$$S_1^{(k)} = \{e | w_1(e) = m^{(k)}\}, \text{ and} \tag{5}$$

$$S_2^{(k)} = \{e | w_2(e) = m^{(k)}\} \tag{6}$$

By construction, $S_0^{(k)}$, $S_1^{(k)}$, and $S_2^{(k)}$ contain only blue edges.

6. First, the parties *privately* compute the set union $S^{(k)} = S_0^{(k)} \cup S_1^{(k)} \cup S_2^{(k)}$. This is done using the privacy-preserving set union algorithm from section 4.

Next, the color of each edge $e \in S^{(k)}$ is changed from blue to red by setting $B^{(k)} = B^{(k-1)} - S^{(k)}$. Define a weight function $w_0^{\prime(k)}$ by

$$w_0^{\prime(k)}(e) = \begin{cases} m^{(k)} & \text{if } e \in S^{(k)} \\ w_0^{(k-1)}(e) & \text{otherwise} \end{cases} \tag{7}$$

7. Examine triangles with an edge $e_{ij} \in S^{(k)}$, an edge $e_{jk} \in R^{(k)}$, and an edge $e_{ik} \in B^{(k)}$. Define the weight function $w_0^{(k)}$ by fixing these triangles if they violate the triangle inequality under $w_0^{\prime(k)}$. More precisely, if $w_0^{\prime(k)}(e_{ij}) + w_0^{\prime(k)}(e_{jk}) < w_0^{\prime(k)}(e_{ik})$, then define $w_0^{(k)}(e_{ik}) = w_0^{\prime(k)}(e_{ij}) + w_0^{\prime(k)}(e_{jk})$. Do the same for triangles with an edge $e_{ij} \in R^{(k)}$, an edge $e_{jk} \in S^{(k)}$, and an edge $e_{ik} \in B^{(k)}$.

8. If there are still blue edges, go to step 3. Otherwise stop; the graph $G_0^{(k)}$ holds the solution to APSD(G).

The algorithm is proved correct in appendix A. The proof of privacy follows.

Proof (Privacy). We describe a simulator for P_1; the simulator is given P_1's input to the protocol, x, and the output of the protocol, $f(x, y) = G'$. The simulators are identical for P_1 and P_2 except for the asymmetry in the simulation of the set union and minimum subprotocols. We assume that simulators for the subprotocols exist because they are private protocols. For instance, if Yao's protocol is used then we can use the simulator in [29].

We will assume that there are n protocol rounds. The view of P_1 is

$$\{RT^m(x_1, y_1), RT^u(x_2, y_2), RT^m(x_3, y_3), \dots, RT^u(x_{2n}, y_{2n})\} \tag{8}$$

where RT^m denotes the *real transcript* of the private minimum protocol, and RT^u denotes the real transcript of the private set union protocol.

We will show in later theorems that the output of each of these protocol executions can be computed by the simulator as a polynomial function of G', which we will denote as $h_i^m(G')$ and $h_i^u(G')$. We will also show that P_1's input to each of these protocol executions can be computed as a polynomial function of x and G' which we will denote as $g_i^m(x, G')$ and $g_i^u(x, G')$. The simulator can therefore use the subprotocol simulators as subroutines, producing the simulated transcript

$$\{ST^m(g_1^m(x, G'), h_1^m(G')), \dots, ST^u(g_{2n}^u(x, G'), h_{2n}^u(G'))\} \tag{9}$$

where ST^m and ST^u denote the simulated transcripts of the minimum and union protocols, respectively.

We prove a hybrid argument over the simulated views for the minimum and set union protocols. First, define the hybrid distribution H_i in which the first i minimum/union protocols are simulated and the last $2n - i$ are real. Formally, let $H_i(x, y)$ denote the distribution:

$$\{ST^m(g_1^m(x, G'), h_1^m(G')), \dots, ST^u(g_i^u(x, G'), h_i^u(G')),$$
$$RT^m(x_{i+1}, y_{i+1}), RT^u(x_{i+2}, y_{i+2}), \dots, RT^u(x_{2n}, y_{2n})\}$$

We now prove that $H_0(x, y) \stackrel{c}{\equiv} H_{2n}(x, y)$ by showing that for all i, $H_i(x, y) \stackrel{c}{\equiv}$ $H_{i+1}(x, y)$. For the sake of contradiction, assume the opposite, and choose i so that $H_i(x, y) \stackrel{c}{\not\equiv} H_{i+1}(x, y)$. These two distributions differ in only one term, so there must be a polynomial-time distinguisher for either

$$ST^u(g_i^u(x, G'), h_i^u(G')) \text{ and } RT^u(x_i, y_i) \text{ or}$$
$$ST^m(g_i^m(x, G'), h_i^m(G')) \text{ and } RT^m(x_i, y_i)$$

However, this contradicts the privacy of the subprotocols, which implies that no such polynomial-time distinguishers exist.

We now show that for each execution of the set union and minimum subprotocols, P_1's subprotocol input and the subprotocol output are computable as functions of P_1's input and the output of the entire APSD protocol.

Theorem 1. $m^{(k)}$ is efficiently computable as a function of G'.

Proof. The edge weights found in G' are $m^{(1)} < m^{(2)} < \ldots < m^{(n)}$. Therefore $m^{(k)}$ is the kth smallest edge weight in G'.

Theorem 2. $S^{(k)}$ is efficiently computable as a function of G'.

Proof. $S^{(k)}$ is the set of edges in G' with weight $m^{(k)}$.

Theorem 3. $m_1^{(k)}$ is efficiently computable as a function of G_1 and G'.

Proof. $m_1^{(k)}$ is the smallest edge weight in G_1 that is $> m^{(k-1)}$, allowing that $m^{(0)} = 0$. This is because all edges with weight $\leq m^{(k-1)}$ are in $R^{(k-1)}$.

Theorem 4. $S_1^{(k)}$ is efficiently computable as a function of G_1 and G'.

Proof. $S_1^{(k)}$ is the set of edges in G_1 with weight $m^{(k)}$.

5.2   Private All Pairs Shortest Path

While there is only a single all pairs shortest distance solution for a given graph, there may be many all pairs shortest path solutions, because between a pair of points there may be many paths that achieve the shortest distance. As a side effect of engaging in the protocol described in section 5.1, the two participants learn an APSP solution. When defining the weight function $w_0^{(k)}$ by fixing violating triangles in $w_0'^{(k)}$ during step 7, a shortest path solution may be associated with the fixed edge. Specifically, if $w_0'^{(k)}(e_{ij}) + w_0'^{(k)}(e_{jk}) < w_0'^{(k)}(e_{ik})$, then the shortest path from i to k is through j.

In step 6 of subsequent iterations, when adding an edge $e_{ij} \in S^{(k)}$ to the set of blue edges, we can conclude that the shortest path from i to j is the edge e_{ij} itself if $e_{ij} \notin S_0^{(k)}$, or is the shortest path solution as computed above if $e_{ij} \in S_0^{(k)}$.

Note that learning this APSP solution does not imply any violation of privacy, as it is the APSP solution implied by the APSD solution.

5.3   Private Single Source Shortest Distance (SSSD)

The Single Source Shortest Distance (SSSD) problem is to find the shortest path distances from a source vertex s to all other vertices [11]. An algorithm to solve APSD also provides the solution to SSSD, but leaks additional information beyond that of the SSSD solution and cannot be considered a private algorithm for SSSD. Therefore, this problem warrants its own investigation.

Similar to the protocol of section 5.1, the SSSD protocol on the minimum joint graph adds edges in order from smallest to largest. This protocol is very similar to Dijkstra's algorithm, but is modified to take two graphs as input.

1. Set $w_1^{(0)} = w_1$ and $w_2^{(0)} = w_2$. Color all edges incident on the source s blue by putting all edges e_{si} into the set $B^{(0)}$. Set the iteration count k to 1.
2. Both parties privately compute the minimum length of blue edges in their graphs.

$$m_1^{(k)} = \min_{e_{si} \in B^{(k-1)}} w_1^{(k-1)}(e_{si}),$$

$$m_2^{(k)} = \min_{e_{si} \in B^{(k-1)}} w_2^{(k-1)}(e_{si})$$

3. Using the privacy-preserving minimum protocol, compute

$$m^{(k)} = \min(m_1^{(k)}, m_2^{(k)}).$$

4. Each party finds the set of blue edges in its graph with length $m^{(k)}$.

$$S_1^{(k)} = \{e_{si} | w_1^{(k-1)}(e_{si}) = m^{(k)}\}, \text{ and}$$

$$S_2^{(k)} = \{e_{si} | w_2^{(k-1)}(e_{si}) = m^{(k)}\}$$

5. Using the privacy-preserving set union protocol, compute

$$S^{(k)} = S_1^{(k)} \cup S_2^{(k)}.$$

6. Color the edges in $S^{(k)}$ red by setting $B^k = B^{(k-1)} - S^{(k)}$. Define a weight function $w_1'^{(k)}$ by

$$w_1'^{(k)}(e) = \begin{cases} m^{(k)} & \text{if } e \in S^{(k)} \\ w_1^{(k-1)}(e) & \text{otherwise} \end{cases} \tag{10}$$

and a weight function $w_2'^{(k)}$ by

$$w_2'^{(k)}(e) = \begin{cases} m^{(k)} & \text{if } e \in S^{(k)} \\ w_2^{(k-1)}(e) & \text{otherwise} \end{cases} \tag{11}$$

7. Similar to the APSD algorithm, form the weight function $w_1^{(k)}$ by fixing the triangles in $w_1'^{(k)}$ that violate the triangle inequality and contain edges in $S^{(k)}$. $w_{2(k)}$ is likewise formed from $w_2'^{(k)}$.

If there are still blue edges remaining, go to step 2. Otherwise stop; both parties now have a graph with each edge incident on s colored red, and with the weight of these edges equal to the shortest path distance from s to each vertex.

5.4   Minimum Spanning Tree

Suppose that two frugal telephone companies wish to merge. Each company has a cost function for connecting any pair of houses, and they want to connect every house as cheaply as possible using the resources available to the merged company. In other words, they wish to compute $\mathrm{MST}(\mathrm{gmin}(G_1, G_2))$. If they can perform this computation privately, then both companies can see the final result without revealing their entire cost functions.

Both Kruskal's and Prim's algorithms for MST are easily turned into private protocols using our techniques, because the algorithms already consider edges in order from smallest to largest. At each iteration, Kruskal's algorithm adds the shortest edge such that its addition does not form a loop. It is a simple task for each party to compute the set of edges which would not form loops, and then to privately compute the length of the shortest edge in this set. One problem arises when there are multiple edges that share this length. In the shortest path algorithms, we addressed this issue by adding all edges of appropriate length at the same time using the private set union protocol, but this will not work for MST. Instead, we can assign a canonical ordering to the edges, and at each step find the shortest length edges that are canonically "first." This will allow a simulator to determine, given the final MST, in what order the edges arrived.

6   Complexity Analysis

For each algorithm considered in this paper, we calculate the number of rounds, the total communication complexity, and the computational complexity, and compare them with the generic method. Using Yao's method on a circuit with m gates and n inputs requires $O(1)$ rounds, $O(m)$ communication, and $O(m+n)$ computational overhead. Lindell and Pinkas note in [28] that the computational overhead of the n oblivious transfers in each invocation of Yao's protocol typically dominates the computational overhead for the m gates, but for correct asymptotic analysis we must still consider the gates.

Complexity of privacy-preserving APSD. For our analysis we will assume that the edge set E has size n, and that the maximum edge length is l. The generic approach to this problem would be to apply Yao's Method to a circuit that takes as input the length of every edge in G_1 and G_2, and returns as output $G = \mathrm{APSD}(\mathrm{gmin}(G_1, G_2))$. Clearly, such a circuit will have $2n \log l$ input bits. To count the number of gates, note that a circuit to implement Floyd-Warshall requires $O(n^{3/2})$ minimums and $O(n^{3/2})$ additions. For integers represented with $\log l$ bits, both of these functionalities require $\log l$ gates, so we conclude that Floyd-Warhsall requires $O(n^{3/2} \log l)$ gates. To compute gmin requires $O(n \log l)$ gates, but this term is dominated by the gate requirement for Floyd-Warshall. We conclude that the generic approach requires $O(1)$ rounds, $O(n^{3/2} \log l)$ communication, and $O(n^{3/2} \log l)$ computational overhead.

The complexity of our approach depends on the number of protocol iterations k, which is equal to the number of different edge lengths that appear in the solution graph. In iteration i, we take the minimum of two $(\lg l)$-bit integers, and compute a set union of size s_i. Because each edge in the graph appears in exactly one of the set unions, we also know that $\sum_{i=1}^{k} s_i = n$.

First we will determine the contribution to the total complexity made by the integer minimum calculations. If we use Yao's protocol, then each integer minimum requires a constant number of communication rounds, $O(\lg l)$ inputs, and $O(\lg l)$ gates, so the k calculations together contribute $O(k)$ rounds, $O(k \lg l)$ communication complexity, and $O(k \lg l)$ computational complexity.

Complexity contribution of the set union subprotocols depends on whether we use the iterative method or the tree pruning method as described in section 4. If the iterative method is used, then the k invocations of set union require a total of $O(n)$ rounds, $O(k \lg n)$ communication complexity, and $O(k \lg n)$ computational complexity. If the tree-pruning method is used, then $O(k \lg n)$ rounds are required, but the communication and computational complexity remains the same. The asymptotically better performance of the iterative method hides the fact that each of the k rounds requires $O(\lg n)$ oblivious transfers, which are considerably more expensive than the $O(|s_i|)$ private BIT-OR computations performed in each of the $\lg u$ rounds of the tree-pruning method.

Using the iterative method for set union, and noting that $k = O(n)$, we conclude that our APSD protocol requires $O(n)$ communication rounds, $O(n \log n + n \log l)$ communication complexity, and $O(n \log n + n \log l)$ computational complexity. As compared to the generic approach, we have traded more rounds for better overall complexity.

Complexity of privacy-preserving SSSD. Complexity of SSSD is similar to that of APSD, except that the number of rounds is $k = O(v)$ and the total number of set union operations is v, where v is the number of vertices $(O(e^{1/2}))$. We conclude that our protocol requires $O(v)$ rounds, $O(v(\log v + \log l))$ oblivious transfers, and $O(v(\log v + \log e))$ gates. A generic solution, on the other hand, would require $O(v^2 \log l)$ oblivious transfers.

7   Conclusions

In this paper, we presented privacy-preserving protocols that enable two honest but curious parties to compute APSD and SSSD on their *joint graph*. A related problem is how to construct privacy-preserving protocols for graph *comparison*. Many of these problems (*e.g.*, comparison of the graphs' respective maximum flow values) reduce to the problem of privacy-preserving comparison of two values, and thus have reasonably efficient generic solutions. For other problems, such as graph isomorphism, there are no known polynomial-time algorithms even if privacy is not a concern. Investigation of other interesting graph algorithms that can be computed in a privacy-preserving manner is a topic of future research.

References

1. G. Aggarwal, N. Mishra, and B. Pinkas. Secure computation of the k-th ranked element. In *Proc. Advances in Cryptology - EUROCRYPT 2004*, volume 3027 of *LNCS*, pages 40–55. Springer-Verlag, 2004.
2. D. Agrawal and C. Aggarwal. On the design and quantification of privacy preserving data mining algorithms. In *Proc. 20th ACM SIGACT-SIGMOD-SIGART Symposium on Principles of Database Systems (PODS)*, pages 247–255. ACM, 2001.
3. R. Agrawal, A. Evfimievski, and R. Srikant. Information sharing across private databases. In *Proc. 2003 ACM SIGMOD International Conference on Management of Data*, pages 86–97. ACM, 2003.
4. R. Agrawal and R. Srikant. Privacy-preserving data mining. In *Proc. 2000 ACM SIGMOD International Conference on Management of Data*, pages 439–450. ACM, 2000.
5. M. Bawa, R. Bayardo, and R. Agrawal. Privacy-preserving indexing of documents on the network. In *Proc. 29th International Conference on Very Large Databases (VLDB)*, pages 922–933. Morgan Kaufmann, 2003.
6. D. Beaver. Foundations of secure interactive computing. In *Proc. Advances in Cryptology - CRYPTO 1991*, volume 576 of *LNCS*, pages 377–391. Springer-Verlag, 1992.
7. R. Canetti. Security and composition of multiparty cryptograpic protocols. *J. Cryptology*, 13(1):143–202, 2000.
8. S. Chawla, C. Dwork, F. McSherry, A. Smith, and H. Wee. Towards privacy in public databases. In *Proc. 2nd Theory of Cryptography Conference (TCC)*, volume 3378 of *LNCS*, pages 363–385. Springer-Verlag, 2005.
9. B. Chor, E. Kushilevitz, O. Goldreich, and M. Sudan. Private information retrieval. *J. ACM*, 45(6):965–981, 1998.
10. C. Clifton, M. Kantarcioglou, J. Vaidya, X. Lin, and M. Zhu. Tools for privacy preserving distributed data mining. *ACM SIGKDD Explorations*, 4(2):28–34, 2002.
11. T. Cormen, C. Leiserson, and R. Rivest. *Introduction to Algorithms*. MIT Press, 1990.
12. I. Dinur and K. Nissim. Revealing information while preserving privacy. In *Proc. 22nd ACM SIGACT-SIGMOD-SIGART Symposium on Principles of Database Systems (PODS)*, pages 202–210. ACM, 2003.
13. W. Du and M. Atallah. Privacy-preserving cooperative scientific computations. In *Proc. 14th IEEE Computer Security Foundations Workshop (CSFW)*, pages 273–294. IEEE, 2001.
14. W. Du and M. Atallah. Privacy-preserving cooperative statistical analysis. In *Proc. 17th Annual Computer Security Applications Conference (ACSAC)*, pages 102–112. IEEE, 2001.
15. W. Du, Y. Han, and S. Chen. Privacy-preserving multivariate statistical analysis: linear regression and classification. In *Proc. 4th SIAM International Conference on Data Mining (SDM)*, pages 222–233. SIAM, 2004.
16. C. Dwork and K. Nissim. Privacy-preserving data mining on vertically partitioned databases. In *Proc. Advances in Cryptology - CRYPTO 2004*, volume 3152 of *LNCS*, pages 528–544. Springer-Verlag, 2004.
17. A. Evfimievski, R. Srikant, R. Agrawal, and J. Gehrke. Privacy preserving mining of association rules. *Information Systems*, 29(4):343–364, 2004.

18. J. Feigenbaum, Y. Ishai, T. Malkin, K. Nissim, M. Strauss, and R. Wright. Secure multiparty computation of approximations. In *Proc. 28th International Colloquium on Automata, Languages and Programming (ICALP)*, volume 2076 of *LNCS*, pages 927–938. Springer-Verlag, 2001.
19. J. Feigenbaum, B. Pinkas, R. Ryger, and F. Saint-Jean. Secure computation of surveys. In *Proc. EU Workshop on Secure Multiparty Protocols*, 2004.
20. M. Freedman, K. Nissim, and B. Pinkas. Efficient private matching and set intersection. In *Proc. Advances in Cryptology - EUROCRYPT 2004*, volume 3027 of *LNCS*, pages 1–19. Springer-Verlag, 2004.
21. Y. Gertner, Y. Ishai, E. Kushilevitz, and T. Malkin. Protecting data privacy in private information retrieval schemes. *J. Computer and System Sciences*, 60(3):592–629, 2000.
22. O. Goldreich. *Foundations of Cryptography: Volume II (Basic Applications)*. Cambridge University Press, 2004.
23. O. Goldreich, S. Micali, and A. Wigderson. How to play any mental game. In *Proc. Annual 19th ACM Symposium on Theory of Computing (STOC)*, pages 218–229. ACM, 1987.
24. M. Kantarcioglu and C. Clifton. Privacy-preserving distributed mining of association rules on horizontally partitioned data. In *Proc. ACM SIGMOD Workshop on Research Issues in Data Mining and Knowledge Discovery (DMKD)*. ACM, July 2002.
25. M. Kantarcioglu, J. Jin, and C. Clifton. When do data mining results violate privacy? In *Proc. 10th ACM SIGKDD International Conference on Knowledge Discovery and Data Mining (KDD)*, pages 599–604. ACM, 2004.
26. H. Kargupta, S. Datta, Q. Wang, and K. Sivakumar. On the privacy preserving properties of random data perturbation techniques. In *Proc. 3rd IEEE International Conference on Data Mining (ICDM)*, pages 99–106. IEEE, 2003.
27. L. Kissner and D. Song. Privacy-preserving set operations. In *Proc. Advances in Cryptology - CRYPTO 2005 (to appear)*. Springer-Verlag, 2005.
28. Y. Lindell and B. Pinkas. Privacy preserving data mining. *J. Cryptology*, 15(3):177–206, 2002.
29. Y. Lindell and B. Pinkas. A proof of Yao's protocol for secure two-party computation. `http://eprint.iacr.org/2004/175`, 2004.
30. M. Naor and K. Nissim. Communication preserving protocols for secure function evaluation. In *Proc. 33rd Annual ACM Symposium on Theory of Computing (STOC)*, pages 590–599. ACM, 2001.
31. M. Naor and B. Pinkas. Efficient oblivious transfer protocols. In *Proc. 12th Annual Symposium on Discrete Algorithms (SODA)*, pages 448–457. ACM, 2001.
32. M. Naor and B. Pinkas. Computationally secure oblivious transfer. *J. Cryptology*, 18(1):1–35, 2005.
33. M. Naor, B. Pinkas, and R. Sumner. Privacy preserving auctions and mechanism design. In *Proc. 1st ACM Conference on Electronic Commerce*, pages 129–139. ACM, 1999.
34. H. Polat and W. Du. Privacy-preserving collaborative filtering using randomized perturbation techniques. In *Proc. 3rd IEEE International Conference on Data Mining (ICDM)*, pages 625–628. IEEE, 2003.
35. J. Vaidya and C. Clifton. Privacy-preserving association rule mining in vertically partitioned data. In *Proc. 8th ACM SIGKDD International Conference on Knowledge Discovery and Data Mining (KDD)*, pages 639–644. ACM, 2002.

36. V. Verykios, E. Bertino, I. Fovino, L. Provenza, Y. Saygin, and Y. Theodoridis. State-of-the-art in privacy preserving data mining. *SIGMOD Record*, 33(1):50–57, 2004.
37. R. Wright and Z. Yang. Privacy-preserving Bayesian network structure computation on distributed heterogeneous data. In *Proc. 10th ACM SIGKDD International Conference on Knowledge Discovery and Data Mining (KDD)*, pages 713–718. ACM, 2004.
38. Z. Yang, S. Zhong, and R. Wright. Privacy-preserving classification of customer data without loss of accuracy. In *Proc. 5th SIAM International Conference on Data Mining (SDM)*. SIAM, 2005.
39. A. Yao. How to generate and exchange secrets. In *Proc. 27th IEEE Symposium on Foundations of Computer Science (FOCS)*, pages 162–167. IEEE, 1986.

A   Proof of Private APSD Protocol Correctness

Before proving the algorithm correct, we prove some supporting lemmas.

Lemma 1. *If an edge $e \in R^k$ and $w_0^{(k)}(e) = l$ then $\forall j > k, w_0^{(j)}(e) = l$.*

Proof. Intuitively, this says that once the protocol establishes the length of a red edge, it never changes. This follows from the protocol lacking operations that alter the length of red edges.

Lemma 2. *For an edge $e \in R^{(k)}$, $w_0^{(k)}(e) \leq m^{(k)}$.*

Proof. In step 6 of iteration k, for edges $e \in S^{(k)}$ we set $w_0^{(k)}(e) = m^{(k)}$ and $e \in R^{(k)}$. Apply lemma 1 to complete the proof.

Lemma 3. *For an edge $e \in B^{(k)}$, $w_0^{(k)}(e) > m^{(k)}$.*

Proof. First, we show that for an edge $e \in B^{(k)}$, $w_0'^{(k)}(e) > m^{(k)}$. If $w_0'^{(k)}(e) = m^{(k)}$ then $e \in S^{(k)}$ (and $e \notin B^{(k)}$). If $w_0'^{(k)}(e) < m^{(k)}$ and $e \in B^{(k)}$, then $w_0^{(k-1)}(e) < m^{(k)}$ and we would have defined a smaller $m^{(k)}$.

Now, for those edges e where we have $w_0^{(k)}(e) < w_0'^{(k)}(e)$ because of step 7, we still have $w_0^{(k)}(e) > m^{(k)}$ because the right-hand side of the assignment is strictly greater than $m^{(k)}$.

Lemma 4. *For all edges e, $e \in R^{(k)} \leftrightarrow w_0^{(k)}(e) \leq m^{(k)}$ and $e \in B^{(k)} \leftrightarrow w_0^{(k)}(e) > m^{(k)}$.*

Proof. This is an immediate consequence of lemmas 2 and 3.

Lemma 5. *For every red edge $e_{ij} \in R^{(k)}$, $w_0^{(k)}(e_{ij}) = d_G(i,j)$.*

Proof. The proof is by induction on k. For $k = 0$, the result is trivial. We will now assume that the result holds for values less than k and prove it for k.

Because of lemma 1, it is sufficient to prove that for edges $e_{ij} \in S^{(k)}$, $d_G(i,j) = m^{(k)}$. We consider two cases.

1. The shortest path from i to j in G is the edge e_{ij}.
   In this case, $d_G(i,j) = \min(w_1(e_{ij}), w_2(e_{ij}))$. To complete the proof, it's enough to show that $w_0^{(k-1)}(e_{ij}) \geq d_G(i,j)$. Suppose that in some iteration $h < k$ we set $w_0^{(h)}(e_{ij}) = w_0'^{(h)}(e_{ik}) + w_0'^{(h)}(e_{kj})$ in step 7. Then by inductive hypothesis, this implies a shorter path from i to j than the edge e_{ij} which is a contradiction.

2. The shortest path from i to j in G is through k.
   In this case, $d_G(i,j) = d_G(i,k) + d_G(k,j)$. WLOG, assume that $w_0^{(k)}(e_{ik}) \geq w_0^{(k)}(e_{kj})$. Then by lemmas 1 and 4, we have that for some $h < k$, $w_0^{(k)}(e_{ik}) = m^{(h)}$. This means that in step 7 of iteration h the protocol set $w_0^{(h)}(e_{ij}) = w_0^{(h)}(e_{ik}) + w_0^{(h)}(e_{kj})$. By the inductive hypothesis, $w_0^{(h)}(e_{ik}) = d_G(i,k)$ and $w_0^{(h)}(e_{kj}) = d_G(k,j)$. We conclude that $w_0^{(h)}(e_{ij}) = d_G(i,k) + d_G(k,j)$ and therefore that $w_0^{(k)}(e_{ij}) \leq d_G(i,k) + d_G(k,j)$. By the same argument as in the first case, we also have $w_0^{(k)}(e_{ij}) \geq d_G(i,k) + d_G(k,j)$. Therefore, $m^{(k)} = d_G(i,k) + d_G(k,j) = d_G(i,j)$.

It is now a simple task to prove algorithm correctness.

Proof (Correctness). Suppose the algorithm terminates after n iterations. Then $R^{(n)} = E$. Apply lemma 5.

B   Survey of Privacy-Preserving Set Union Protocols

Generic Yao's method. It is easy to construct a circuit for computing the set union. Each party P_p inputs one bit for every element e in the universe U. The input bit b_{pi} is set to 1 if party P_p has element e_i in his set, and 0 otherwise. The circuit consists of $|U|$ AND gates, each of which takes as inputs b_{0i} and b_{1i} and outputs $o_i = b_{0i} \wedge b_{1i}$. Then $o_i = 1$ iff element e_i is in the set union. Since this circuit has $O(u)$ inputs and $O(u)$ gates, we conclude that the computational overhead and the communication complexity are both $O(u)$.

Commutative encryption. Clifton *et al.* [10] present a simple construction for privacy-preserving set union that uses commutative encryption. Each party encrypts the elements in its set, exchanges the encrypted sets with the other party, and then encrypts the other party's encrypted elements with its own key. The double-encrypted sets are then combined. Due to commutativity of encryption, all elements in the intersection appear as duplicates. They are removed, and the remaining elements are decrypted. Scrambling the order of elements may hide which elements are in the intersection, but the size of the intersection is still revealed, thus this method is not secure in the standard sense of definition 2. This protocol requires communication and computational complexity $O(|s_1| + |s_2|)$.

Complement of set intersection. When the universe U is small, it is possible to use complementation and take advantage of the fact that $S_1 \cup S_2 = \overline{\bar{S}_1 \cap \bar{S}_2}$.

Freedman *et al.* [20] present a privacy-preserving protocol for set intersection that uses homomorphic encryption which requires $O(k)$ communication overhead and $O(k \ln \ln k)$ computation overhead, where k is the size of the set intersection. For applications considered in this paper, sets S_1 and S_2 are very small, so their complements are of size $O(u)$. As a result, this method requires $O(u \ln \ln u)$ computation, which is unacceptable.

Polynomial set representation. Kissner and Song [27] present a method for representing sets as polynomials, and give several privacy-preserving protocols for set operations using these representations. They do not provide a protocol for the standard set union problem. Instead, they give a protocol for the "threshold set union" problem, in which the inputs are multi-sets and the output is the set of elements whose multiplicity of appearance in the union exceed some threshold; the intersection of the input sets is also revealed. When applied to regular sets (as opposed to multi-sets) this protocol does not preserve privacy as the intersection is the only information one can hope to keep private.

C   Privacy-Preserving Bit-OR

First, observe that the circuit for computing OR of 2 bits consists in a single gate. Therefore, even the generic construction using Yao's protocol [39] is efficient, requiring a single *1-out-of-2* oblivious transfer.

An alternative construction without oblivious transfers is provided by a semantically secure homomorphic encryption scheme such as ElGamal. Suppose Alice and Bob want to compute OR of their respective bits b_A and b_B in a privacy-preserving manner (Alice and Bob are honest, but curious). Alice picks some cyclic group G of prime order q with generator g where the Decisional Diffie-Hellman problem is presumed hard, *e.g.*, the group of quadratic residues modulo some large prime $p = 2q + 1$, and chooses its secret key k at random from $\{0, \ldots, q-1\}$. Alice sends to Bob its public key q, g, g^k together with its ciphertext c_A, which is created as follows. If $b_A = 0$, then $c_A = (g^r, g^{kr})$, where r is randomly selected from $\{0, \ldots, q-1\}$. If $b_A = 1$, then $c_A = (g^r, g \cdot g^{kr})$.

Upon receipt of $c_A = (\alpha, \beta)$ and Alice's public key, Bob computes c_B as follows. First, it randomly picks $r' \in \{0, \ldots, q-1\}$. If $b_B = 0$, then $c_B = (\alpha^{r'}, \beta^{r'})$. If $b_B = 1$, then $c_B = (\alpha^{r'}, g^{r'} \cdot \beta^{r'})$. Bob returns c_B to Alice.

Alice computes bit b by decrypting $c_B = (\gamma, \delta)$ with its private key k, *i.e.*, $b = \frac{\delta}{\gamma^k}$. Clearly, if $b_A = b_B = 0$, then $b = 1$. In this case, Alice declares that $b_A \vee b_B = 0$. If $b \neq 1$, then Alice declares that $b_A \vee b_B = 1$.

To verify that this construction preserves privacy, observe that secrecy of b_A follows from the semantic security of ElGamal. Now suppose $b_A = 1$. If $b_B = 0$, then the decrypted plaintext $b = g^{r'}$. If $b_B = 1$, then $b = g^{2r'}$. Since B does not know r', it cannot tell the difference. Thus, A does not learn b_B if $b_A = 1$.

(We are grateful to Stas Jarecki for a helpful discussion of constructions for privacy-preserving BIT-OR).

Spreading Alerts Quietly
and the Subgroup Escape Problem

James Aspnes[1,*], Zoë Diamadi[1], Kristian Gjøsteen[2],
René Peralta[1], and Aleksandr Yampolskiy[1,**]

[1] Yale University, Department of Computer Science,
51 Prospect Street, New Haven, CT 06520, USA
{aspnes, diamadi, peralta, yampolsk}@cs.yale.edu
[2] Norwegian University of Science and Technology,
Department of Telematics, 7491 Trondheim, Norway
kristian.gjosteen@item.ntnu.no

Abstract. We introduce a new cryptographic primitive called the **blind coupon mechanism** (BCM). In effect, the BCM is an authenticated bit commitment scheme, which is AND-homomorphic. It has not been known how to construct such commitments before. We show that the BCM has natural and important applications. In particular, we use it to construct a mechanism for transmitting alerts undetectably in a message-passing system of n nodes. Our algorithms allow an alert to quickly propagate to all nodes without its source or existence being detected by an adversary, who controls all message traffic. Our proofs of security are based on a new **subgroup escape problem**, which seems hard on certain groups with bilinear pairings and on elliptic curves over the ring $\mathbb{Z}_n$.

Keywords: Blind Coupon Mechanism, AND-homomorphic Bit Commitment, Subgroup Escape Problem, Elliptic Curves Over Composite Moduli, Anonymous Communication.

1   Introduction

MOTIVATION. As more computers become interconnected, chances increase greatly that an attacker may attempt to compromise your system and network resources. It has become common to defend the network by running an Intrusion Detection System (IDS) on several of the network nodes, which we call sentinels. These sentinel nodes continuously monitor their local network traffic for suspicious activity. When a sentinel node detects an attacker's presence, it may want to alert all other network nodes to the threat. However, issuing an alert out in the open may scare the attacker away too soon and preclude the system administrator from gathering more information about attacker's rogue

---

* Supported in part by NSF grants CCR-0098078, CNS-0305258, and CNS-0435201.
** Supported by NSF grants CCR-0098078, ANI-0207399, CNS-0305258, and CNS-0435201.

B. Roy (Ed.): ASIACRYPT 2005, LNCS 3788, pp. 253–272, 2005.

exploits. Instead, we would like to propagate the alert without revealing the ids of the sentinel nodes or the fact that the alert is being spread.

We consider a powerful (yet computationally bounded) attacker who observes all message traffic and is capable of reading, replacing, and delaying circulating messages. Our work provides a cryptographic mechanism that allows an alert to spread through a population of processes at the full speed of an epidemic, while remaining undetectable to the attacker. As the alert percolates across the network, all nodes unwittingly come to possess the signal, making it especially difficult to identify the originator even if the secret key is compromised and the attacker can inspect the nodes' final states.

A NEW TOOL: A BLIND COUPON MECHANISM. The core of our algorithms is a new cryptographic primitive called a **blind coupon mechanism** (BCM). The BCM is related, yet quite different, from the notion of commitment. It consists of a set D_{SK} of **dummy coupons** and a set S_{SK} of **signal coupons** ($D_{SK} \cap S_{SK} = \emptyset$). The owner of the secret key SK can efficiently sample these sets and distinguish between their elements. We call the set of dummy and signal coupons, $D_{SK} \cup S_{SK}$, the set of **valid** coupons.

The BCM comes equipped with a **verification algorithm** $\mathcal{V}_{PK}(x)$ that checks if x is indeed a valid coupon. There is also a probabilistic **combining algorithm** $\mathcal{C}_{PK}(x, y)$, that takes as input two valid coupons x, y and outputs a new coupon which is, with high probability, a signal coupon if and only if at least one of the inputs is a signal coupon. As suggested by the notation, both algorithms can be computed by anyone who has access to the public key PK of the blind coupon mechanism.

We regard the BCM secure if an observer who lacks the secret key SK (a) cannot distinguish between dummy and signal coupons (**indistinguishability**); (b) cannot engineer a new signal coupon unless he is given another signal coupon as input (**unforgeability**); and (c) cannot distinguish randomly chosen coupons from coupons produced by the combining algorithm (**blinding**).

OUR MAIN CONSTRUCTION. Our BCM construction uses an abstract group structure (U, G, D). Here, U is a finite set, $G \subseteq U$ is a cyclic group, and D is a subgroup of G. The elements of D will represent dummy coupons and the elements of $G \setminus D$ will be signal coupons (see also Figure 1). The combining operation will simply be a group operation. To make verification possible, there

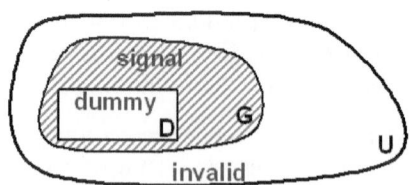

Fig. 1. Abstract group structure used in our BCM construction

will need to be an easy way to distinguish elements of G (valid coupons) from elements of $U \setminus G$ (invalid coupons).

In order for the BCM to be secure, the following two problems must be hard on this group structure:

- **Subgroup Membership Problem:** Given generators for G and D and an element $y \in G$, decide whether $y \in D$ or $y \in G \setminus D$.
- **Subgroup Escape Problem:** Given a generator for D (but not G), find an element of $G \setminus D$.

The subgroup membership problem has appeared in many different forms in the literature [11, 18, 28, 31, 33, 16, 29]. The subgroup escape problem has not been studied before. To provide more confidence in its validity, we later analyze it in the generic group model.

Notice that the task of distinguishing a signal coupon from a dummy coupon (indistinguishability) and the task of forging a signal coupon (unforgeability) are essentially the subgroup membership and subgroup escape problems. The challenge thus becomes to find a concrete group structure (U, G, D) for which the subgroup membership and the subgroup escape problems are hard.

We provide two instantiations of the group structure: one using groups with bilinear pairings, and one using elliptic curves over composite moduli.

WHY IS A BCM USEFUL? The BCM can potentially be useful in various applications. If signal coupons are used to encode a "1" and dummy coupons a "0", then a BCM can be viewed as an OR-homomorphic bit commitment scheme. The BCM is indeed **hiding** because dummy and signal coupons appear the same to an outside observer. It is also **binding** because the sets of dummy and signal coupons are disjoint. In addition, the BCM's verification function ensures the commitment is authenticated. By switching signal coupons to encode a "0" and dummy coupons to encode a "1", we get an AND-homomorphic bit commitment. As far as we know, it has not been known how to construct such commitments before. The BCM thus provides a missing link in protocol design. Using BCM together with techniques of Brassard *et al.* [7], we can obtain short non-interactive proofs of circuit satisfiability, whose length is linear in the number of AND gates in the circuit. Other potential uses include i-voting (voting over the Internet) [10].

SPREADING ALERTS WITH THE BCM. Returning to our original motivation, we demonstrate how a BCM can be used to propagate alerts quickly and quietly throughout the network. During the initial network setup, the network administrator generates the BCM's public and secret keys. He then distributes signal coupons to sentinel nodes. All other nodes receive dummy coupons. In our mechanism, nodes continuously transmit either dummy or signal coupons with all nodes initially transmitting dummy coupons. Sentinel nodes switch to sending signal coupons when they detect the attacker's presence. The BCM's combining algorithm allows dummy and signal coupons to be combined so that a node can propagate signal coupons without having to know that it has received any, and so that an attacker (who can observe all message traffic) cannot detect where or when signals are being transmitted within the stream of dummy messages.

In addition, the BCM's verification algorithm defends against Byzantine nodes [25]: While Byzantine nodes can replay old dummy messages instead of relaying signals, they cannot flood the network with invalid coupons, thereby preventing an alert from spreading; at worst, they can only act like crashed nodes.

We prove that if the underlying BCM is secure, then the attacker cannot distinguish between executions where an alert was sent and executions where no alert was sent. The time to spread the alert to all nodes will be determined by the communications model and alert propagation strategy. At any point in time, the network administrator can sample the state of some network node and check if it possesses a signal coupon.

PAPER ORGANIZATION. The rest of the paper is organized as follows. We begin with a discussion of related work in Section 2. In Section 3, we formally define the notion of a blind coupon mechanism and sketch an abstract group structure, which will allow us to implement it. Then in Section 4, we provide two concrete instantiations of this group structure using certain bilinear groups and elliptic curves over the ring $\mathbb{Z}_n$. In Section 5, we show how the BCM can be used to spread alerts quietly throughout a network. In Section 6, we analyze the hardness of the subgroup escape problem in the generic group model. Some of the proofs have been omitted due to space limitations; they can be found in the full version, available as a Yale CS technical report [3]. Conclusions and open problems appear in Section 7.

2   Related Work

Our motivating example of spreading alerts is related to the problem of anonymous communication. Below, we describe known mechanisms for anonymous communication, and contrast their properties with what can be obtained from the blind coupon mechanism. We then discuss literature on elliptic curves over a ring, which are used in our constructions.

2.1   Anonymous Communication

Two basic tools for anonymous message transmission are DC-nets ("dining-cryptographers" nets) [9,19] and mix-nets [8]. These tools try to conceal who the message sender and recipient are from an adversary that can monitor all network traffic. While our algorithms likewise aim to hide who the signal's originators are, they are much less vulnerable to disruption by an active adversary that can delay or alter messages, and they can also hide the fact that a signal is being spread through the network.

DC-nets enable one participant to anonymously broadcast a message to others by applying a dining cryptographers protocol. A disadvantage of DC-nets for unstructured systems like peer-to-peer networks is that they require substantial setup and key management, and are vulnerable to jamming. In contrast, the initialization of our alert-spreading application involves distributing only a public key used for verification to non-sentinel nodes and requires only a single secret key shared between the sentinels and the receiver, jamming is prevented by the verification algorithm, and outsiders can participate in the alert-spreading (although they cannot initiate an alert), which further helps disguise the true source. As the signal percolates across the network, all nodes change to an alert state, further confounding the identification of an alert's primary source even if a secret key becomes compromised.

The problem of hiding the communication pattern in the network was first addressed by Chaum [8], who introduced the concept of a **mix**, which shuffles messages and routes them, thereby confusing traffic analysis. This basic scheme was later extended in [40, 39]. A further refinement is a **mix-net** [1, 21, 20], in which a message is routed through multiple trusted mix nodes, which try to hide correlation between incoming and outgoing messages. Our mechanism is more efficient and produces much stronger security while avoiding the need for trusted nodes; however, we can only send very small messages.

Beimel and Dolev's [4] proposed the concept of buses, which hide the message's route amidst dummy traffic. They assume a synchronous system and a passive adversary. In contrast, we assume both an asynchronous system and very powerful adversary, who in addition to monitoring the network traffic controls the timing and content of delivered messages.

2.2   Elliptic Curves over a Ring

One of our BCM constructions is based on elliptic curves over the ring $\mathbb{Z}_n$, where $n = pq$ is a product of primes. Elliptic curves over $\mathbb{Z}_n$ have been studied for nearly twenty years and are used, *inter alia*, in Lenstra's integer factoring algorithm [27] and the Goldwasser-Kilian primality testing algorithm [17]. Other works [13, 23, 31] exported some factoring-based cryptosystems (RSA [35], Rabin [34]) to the elliptic curve setting in hopes of avoiding some of the standard attacks. The security of our BCM relies on a special feature of the group of points on elliptic curves modulo a composite: It is difficult to find new elements of the group except by using the group operation on previously known elements. This problem has been noted many times in the literature, but was previously considered a nuisance rather than a cryptographic property. In particular, Lenstra [27] chose the curve and the point at the same time, while Demytko [13] used twists and x-coordinate only computations to compute on the curve without y-coordinates. To the best of our knowledge, this problem's potential use in cryptographic constructions was first noted in [15].

2.3   Epidemic Algorithms

Our alert mechanism belongs to the class of epidemic algorithms (also called gossip protocols) introduced in [12]. In these algorithms, each process chooses to partner processes with which to communicate randomly. The drawback of gossip protocols is the number of messages they send, which is in principle unbounded if there is no way for the participants to detect when all information has been fully distributed.

3   Blind Coupon Mechanism

The critical component of our algorithms that allows information to propagate undetectably among the processes is a cryptographic primitive called a **blind coupon mechanism** (BCM). In Section 3.1, we give a formal definition of the BCM and its security properties. In Section 3.2, we describe an abstract group structure that will allow us to construct the BCM.

3.1   Definitions

Definition 1. *A **blind coupon mechanism** is a tuple of PPT algorithms* $(\mathcal{G}, \mathcal{V}, \mathcal{C}, \mathcal{D})$ *in which:*

- $\mathcal{G}(1^k)$, *the probabilistic **key generation algorithm**, outputs a pair of public and secret keys* (PK, SK) *and two strings* (d, s). *The public key defines a universe set* U_{PK} *and a set of **valid coupons** G_{PK}. The secret key implicitly defines an associated set of **dummy coupons** D_{SK} and a set of **signal coupons** S_{SK}.[1] It is the case that* $d \in D_{SK}$ *and* $s \in S_{SK}$, $D_{SK} \cap S_{SK} = \emptyset$, *and* $D_{SK} \cup S_{SK} = G_{PK}$.
- $\mathcal{V}_{PK}(y)$, *the deterministic **verification algorithm**, takes as input a coupon* y *and returns 1 if* y *is valid and 0 if it is invalid.*
- $z \leftarrow \mathcal{C}_{PK}(x, y)$, *the probabilistic **combining algorithm**, takes as input two valid coupons* $x, y \in G_{PK}$ *and produces a new coupon* z. *The output* z *is a signal coupon (with overwhelming probability) whenever one or more of the inputs is a signal coupon, otherwise it is a dummy coupon (see Figure 2).*
- $\mathcal{D}_{SK}(y)$, *the deterministic **decoding algorithm**, takes as input a valid coupon* $y \in G_{PK}$. *It returns 0 if* y *is a dummy coupon and 1 if* y *is a signal coupon.*

The BCM may be established either by an external trusted party or jointly by the application participants, running the distributed key generation protocol (*e.g.*, one could use a variant of [2]). In this paper, we assume a trusted dealer (the network administrator) who runs the key generation algorithm and distributes signal coupons to the supervisor algorithms of sentinel nodes at the start of the system execution. In a typical algorithm, the nodes will continuously exchange coupons with each other. The combining algorithm $\mathcal{C}_{PK}$ enables nodes to locally and efficiently combine their coupons with coupons of other nodes.

---

[1] Note that membership in S_{SK} and D_{SK} should not be efficiently decidable when given only PK (unlike membership in G_{PK}). However, we require that membership is always efficiently decidable when given SK.

x	y	$C(x,y)$
D_{SK}	D_{SK}	D_{SK}
D_{SK}	S_{SK}	S_{SK}
S_{SK}	D_{SK}	S_{SK}
S_{SK}	S_{SK}	S_{SK}

Fig. 2. Properties of the combining algorithm

The verification function $\mathcal{V}_{PK}$ prevents the adversary from flooding the system with invalid coupons and making it impossible for the signal to spread.

For this application, we require the BCM to have certain specific security properties.

Definition 2. *We say that a blind coupon mechanism $(\mathcal{G}, \mathcal{V}, \mathcal{C}, \mathcal{D})$ is* **secure** *if it satisfies the following requirements:*

1. **Indistinguishability:** *Given a valid coupon y, the adversary cannot tell whether it is a signal or a dummy coupon with probability better than $1/2$. Formally, for any PPT algorithm $\mathcal{A}$,*

$$\left| \Pr\left[b = b' \middle| \begin{array}{c} (PK, SK, d, s) \leftarrow \mathcal{G}(1^k); \\ x_0 \xleftarrow{\$} D_{SK}; x_1 \xleftarrow{\$} S_{SK}; \\ b \xleftarrow{\$} \{0,1\}; b' \leftarrow \mathcal{A}(1^k, PK, d, x_b) \end{array} \right] - \frac{1}{2} \right| \leq negl(k)$$

2. **Unforgeability:** *The adversary is unlikely to fabricate a signal coupon without the use of another signal coupon as input[2]. Formally, for any PPT algorithm $\mathcal{A}$,*

$$\Pr\left[y \in S_{SK} \middle| \begin{array}{c} (PK, SK, d, s) \leftarrow \mathcal{G}(1^k); \\ y \leftarrow \mathcal{A}(1^k, PK, d) \end{array} \right] \leq negl(k)$$

3. **Blinding:** *The combination $\mathcal{C}_{PK}(x,y)$ of two valid coupons x, y looks like a random valid coupon. Formally, fix some pair of keys (PK, SK) outputted by $\mathcal{G}(1^k)$. Let U_D be a uniform distribution on D_{SK} and let U_S be a uniform distribution on S_{SK}. Then, for all valid coupons $x, y \in G_{PK}$,*

$$\begin{cases} \mathrm{Dist}(\mathcal{C}_{PK}(x,y), U_D) = negl(k) & \text{if } x, y \in D_{SK}, \\ \mathrm{Dist}(\mathcal{C}_{PK}(x,y), U_S) = negl(k) & \text{otherwise.} \end{cases}$$

(Here, $\mathrm{Dist}(A, B) \stackrel{def}{=} \frac{1}{2} \sum_x |\Pr[A = x] - \Pr[B = x]|$ is the statistical distance between a pair of random variables A, B.)

To build the reader's intuition, we describe a straw-man construction of a BCM. Suppose we are given any semantically secure encryption scheme $\mathcal{E}(\cdot)$

---

[2] The adversary, however, can easily generate polynomially many dummy coupons by using $\mathcal{C}_{PK}(\cdot, \cdot)$ with the initial dummy coupon d that he receives.

and a set-homomorphic signature scheme $\mathrm{SIG}(\cdot)$ by Johnson *et al.* [22]. This signature scheme allows anyone possessing sets $x, y \subseteq \mathbb{Z}_p$ and their signatures $\mathrm{SIG}(x), \mathrm{SIG}(y)$ to compute $\mathrm{SIG}(x \cup y)$ and $\mathrm{SIG}(w)$ for any $w \subseteq x$. We represent dummy coupons by a random-length vector of encrypted zeroes; *e.g.*, $x = (\mathcal{E}(0), \ldots, \mathcal{E}(0))$. The signal coupons are represented by a vector of encryptions that contains at least one encryption of a non-zero element; *e.g.*, $y = (\mathcal{E}(0), \ldots, \mathcal{E}(0), \mathcal{E}(1))$. To prevent the adversary from forging coupons, the coupons are signed with the set-homomorphic signature. The combining operation is simply the set union: $\mathcal{C}_{PK}\big((x, \mathrm{SIG}(x)), (y, \mathrm{SIG}(y))\big) = (x \cup y, \mathrm{SIG}(x \cup y))$. The drawback of this construction is immediate: as coupons are combined and passed around the network, they quickly grow very large. Constructing a BCM with no expansion of coupons is more challenging. We describe such a construction next.

3.2   Abstract Group Structure

We sketch the abstract group structure that will allow us to implement a secure and efficient BCM. Concrete instantiations of this group structure are provided in Section 4.

Let $\Gamma = \{\Gamma_k\}$ be a family of sets of tuples (U, G, D, d, s), where U is a finite set, and G is a subset of U. G also has a group structure: it is a cyclic group generated by s. D is a subgroup of G generated by d, such that the factor group G/D has prime order $|G|/|D|$. The orders of D and G/D are bounded by 2^k; moreover, $|G|/|U| \leq negl(k)$ and $|D|/|G| \leq negl(k)$.

Let $\mathcal{G}'$ be a PPT algorithm that on input of 1^k samples from Γ_k according to some distribution. We consider Γ_k to be a probability space with this distribution.

We assume there exists an efficient, deterministic algorithm for distinguishing elements of G from elements of $U \setminus G$, and an efficient algorithm for computing the group operation in G.

- The **key generation algorithm** $\mathcal{G}(1^k)$ runs $\mathcal{G}'$ to sample (U, G, D, d, s) from Γ_k, and outputs the public key $PK = (U, G, d, k)$, the secret key $SK = |D|$, as well as d and s.

  The elements of D will represent dummy coupons, the elements of $G \setminus D$ will represent signal coupons, and the elements of $U \setminus G$ will be invalid coupons (see Figure 1).
- The **verification algorithm** $\mathcal{V}_{PK}(y)$ checks that the coupon y is in G.
- The **combining algorithm** $\mathcal{C}_{PK}(x, y)$ is simply the group operation combined with randomization. For input $x, y \in G$, sample r_0, r_1 and r_2 uniformly at random from $\{0, 1, \ldots, 2^{2k} - 1\}$, and output $r_0 d + r_1 x + r_2 y$.
- Because $|D| \cdot y = 0$ if and only if $y \in D$, the **decoding algorithm** $\mathcal{D}_{SK}$ checks if $|D| \cdot y = 0$.

The indistinguishability and unforgeability properties of the BCM will depend on the hardness assumptions described below.

Definition 3. *The **subgroup membership problem** for Γ asks: given a tuple (U, G, D, d, s) from Γ and $y \in G$, decide whether $y \in D$ or $y \in G \setminus D$.*

The subgroup membership problem is hard if for any PPT algorithm $\mathcal{A}$,

$$\left| \Pr\left[b' = b \left| \begin{array}{c} (U, G, D, d, s) \xleftarrow{\$} \Gamma_k; \\ y_0 \xleftarrow{\$} D; y_1 \xleftarrow{\$} G \setminus D; \\ b \xleftarrow{\$} \{0, 1\}; b' \leftarrow \mathcal{A}(U, G, D, d, s, y_b) \end{array} \right. \right] - \frac{1}{2} \right| \leq negl(k).^3$$

Various subgroup membership problems have been extensively studied in the literature, and examples include the Decision Diffie-Hellman problem [11], the quadratic residue problem [18], among others [28, 31, 33]. Our constructions however are more related to the problems described in [16, 29].

Definition 4. *The **subgroup escape problem** for Γ asks: given U, G, D and the generator d for D from the tuple (U, G, D, d, s) from Γ, find an element $y \in G \setminus D$.*

The subgroup escape problem is hard if for any PPT algorithm $\mathcal{A}$,

$$\Pr\left[y \in G \setminus D \left| \begin{array}{c} (U, G, D, d, s) \xleftarrow{\$} \Gamma_k; \\ y \leftarrow \mathcal{A}(U, G, D, d) \end{array} \right. \right] \leq negl(k).$$

The subgroup escape problem has to our knowledge not appeared in the literature before. It is clear that unless $|G|/|U|$ is negligible, finding elements of $G \setminus D$ cannot be hard. We show in Section 6 that if $|G|/|U|$ is negligible, the subgroup escape problem is provably hard in the generic model.

We also note that the problem of generating a signal coupon from polynomially many dummy coupons is essentially the subgroup escape problem.

Theorem 1. *Let Γ be as above. If the subgroup membership problem and the subgroup escape problem for Γ are hard, then the corresponding BCM is secure.*

Proof. Fix k and (U, G, D, d, s) sampled from Γ_k.

We prove the blinding property first, and start with the ideal case: For input $x, y \in G$, sample r_0 uniformly from $\{0, 1, \ldots, |D| - 1\}$, and r_1 and r_2 uniformly from $\{0, 1, \ldots, |G/D| - 1\}$, and output $r_0 g + r_1 x + r_2 y$.

If $x, y \in D$, the product is uniformly distributed in D, since $r_0 g$ is.

If $x \notin D$, then the residue class $r_1 x + D$ is uniformly distributed in G/D. Since $r_0 g$ is uniformly distributed in D, the product is uniformly distributed in G. The uniform distribution on G is $|D|/|G|$-close to the uniform distribution on $G \setminus D$. The same argument holds for $r_2 y$.

Finally we note that we do not need to know $|D|$ or $|G/D|$. Since we know that $|D|$ and $|G/D|$ are less than 2^k, sampling r_0, r_1, r_2 uniformly from the set

---

[3] Henceforth, we assume that groups we operate on have some concise description, which can be passed as an argument to our algorithms. We also assume that group elements can be uniquely encoded as bit strings.

$\{0, \dots, 2^{2k} - 1\}$ will produce an output distribution that is 2^{-k}-close to ideal, which proves the bound for blinding.

Next, we prove the indistinguishability property, so let $\mathcal{A}$ be an adversary against indistinguishability. We have a subgroup membership problem instance (U, G, D, d, s) and $y \in G$. We construct the public key $PK = (U, G, d, k)$, and give $\mathcal{A}$ as input PK, d and y.

If $\mathcal{A}$ answers 1, we conclude that $y \in G \setminus D$, otherwise $y \in D$. Whenever $\mathcal{A}$ is correct, we will be correct, so $\mathcal{A}$ must have negligible advantage.

Finally, we deal with forging. Let $\mathcal{A}$ be an adversary against unforgeability. We have a subgroup escape problem instance U, G and D, and a generator d for D. Again we construct the public key $PK = (U, G, d, k)$, and give $\mathcal{A}$ as input PK and d.

Our output is simply $\mathcal{A}$'s output. Whenever $\mathcal{A}$ succeeds, we will succeed, so $\mathcal{A}$ must have negligible success probability.   □

4   Constructing the BCM

We now give two instantiations of the abstract group structure (U, G, D) described in the previous section. First, we review some basic facts about elliptic curves over composite moduli in Section 4.1. Then, in Section 4.2, we describe our BCM construction that utilizes these curves. In Section 4.3, we describe an alternative BCM construction on elliptic curves equipped with bilinear pairings. These constructions can be used to undetectably transmit a one-shot signal throughout the network. In Section 4.4, we describe how the BCM's bandwidth can be further expanded.

4.1   Preliminaries

Let n be an integer greater than 1 and not divisible by 2 or 3. We first introduce projective coordinates over $\mathbb{Z}_n$. Consider the set $\tilde{U}$ of triples $(x, y, z) \in \mathbb{Z}_n^3$ satisfying $\gcd(x, y, z, n) = 1$. Let $\sim$ be the equivalence relation on $\tilde{U}$ defined by $(x, y, z) \sim (x', y', z')$ iff there exists $\lambda \in \mathbb{Z}_n^*$ such that $(x, y, z) = (\lambda x', \lambda y', \lambda z')$. Let U be the set of equivalence classes in $\tilde{U}$. We denote the equivalence class of (x, y, z) as $(x : y : z)$.

An elliptic curve over $\mathbb{Z}_n$ is defined by the equation

$$E : Y^2 Z \equiv X^3 + aXZ^2 + bZ^3 \pmod{n},$$

where a, b are integers satisfying $\gcd(4a^2 - 27b^3, n) = 1$. The set of points on $E/\mathbb{Z}_n$ is the set of equivalence classes $(x : y : z) \in U$ satisfying $y^2 z \equiv x^3 + axz^2 + bz^3 \pmod{n}$, and is denoted by $E(\mathbb{Z}_n)$. Note that if n is prime, these definitions correspond to the usual definitions for projective coordinates over prime fields. Let p and q be primes, and let $n = pq$. Let $E_p : Y^2 Z = X^3 + a_p XZ^2 + b_p Z^3$ and $E_q : Y^2 Z = X^3 + a_q XZ^2 + b_q Z^3$ be elliptic curves defined over $\mathbb{F}_p$ and $\mathbb{F}_q$, respectively. We can use the Chinese remainder theorem to find a and b yielding an elliptic curve $E : Y^2Z = X^3 + aXZ^2 + bZ^3$ over $\mathbb{Z}_n$ such that the reduction of E modulo p gives E_p and likewise for q.

It can also be shown that the Chinese remainder theorem gives a set isomorphism

$$E(\mathbb{Z}_n) \xrightarrow{\sim} E_p(\mathbb{F}_p) \times E_q(\mathbb{F}_q)$$

inducing a group operation on $E(\mathbb{Z}_n)$. For almost all points in $E(\mathbb{Z}_n)$, the usual group operation formulae for the finite field case will compute the induced group operation. When they fail, the attempted operation gives a factorization of the composite modulus n. Unless $E_p(\mathbb{F}_p)$ or $E_q(\mathbb{F}_q)$ has smooth or easily guessable order, this will happen only with negligible probability (see [14] for more details).

4.2 BCM on Elliptic Curves Modulo Composites

Let $p, q, \ell_1, \ell_2, \ell_3$ be primes, and suppose we have elliptic curves $E_p/\mathbb{F}_p$ and $E_q/\mathbb{F}_q$ such that $\#E_p(\mathbb{F}_p) = \ell_1\ell_2$ and $\#E_q(\mathbb{F}_q) = \ell_3$. Curves of this form can be found using complex multiplication techniques [5, 26].

With $n = pq$, we can find $E/\mathbb{Z}_n$ such that $\#E(\mathbb{Z}_n) = \ell_1\ell_2\ell_3$. Let U be the projective plane modulo n, let G be $E(\mathbb{Z}_n)$, and let D be the subgroup of order $\ell_1\ell_3$. The public key is $PK = (G, D, n)$, while the secret key is $SK = (p, q, l_1, l_2, l_3)$.[4]

VERIFICATION FUNCTION For any equivalence class $(x : y : z)$ in U, it is easy to decide if $(x : y : z)$ is in $E(\mathbb{Z}_n)$ or not, simply by checking if $y^2z \equiv x^3 + axz^2 + bz^3$ (mod n).

SUBGROUP MEMBERSHIP PROBLEM For the curve $E_p(\mathbb{F}_p)$, distinguishing the elements of prime order from the elements of composite order seems to be hard, unless it is possible to factor the group order [16].

Counting the number of points on an elliptic curve defined over a composite number is equivalent to factoring the number [27,24]. Therefore, the group order $E_p(\mathbb{F}_p)$ is hidden.

When the group order is hidden, it cannot be factored. It therefore seems reasonable that the subgroup of $E(\mathbb{Z}_n)$ of order $\ell_1\ell_3$ is hard to distinguish from the rest of the points on the curve, as long as the integer n is hard to factor.

SUBGROUP ESCAPE PROBLEM Anyone capable of finding a random point on the curve will with overwhelming probability be able to find a point outside the subgroup D.

Finding a random point on an elliptic curve over a field is easy: Choose a random x-coordinate and solve the resulting quadratic equation. It has rational solutions with probability close to $1/2$.

---

[4] To describe groups G and D, we publish the elliptic curve equation and the generator for D. This gives away enough information to perform group operations in G, check membership in G, and generate new elements in D (but not in G).

This does not work for elliptic curves over the ring $\mathbb{Z}_n$, since solving square roots modulo n is equivalent to factoring n. One could instead try to choose a y-coordinate and solve for the x-coordinate, but solving cubic equations in $\mathbb{Z}_n$ seems no easier than finding square roots.

One could try to find x and y simultaneously, but there does not seem to be any obvious strategy. This is in contrast to quadratic curves, where Pollard [36] gave an algorithm to find solutions of a quadratic equation modulo a composite (which broke the Ong-Schnorr-Shamir signature system [32]). These techniques do not seem to apply to the elliptic curve case.

Finding a lift of the curve over the integers does not seem promising. While torsion points are fairly easy to find, they will not exist if the curve $E/\mathbb{Z}_n$ does not have points of order less than or equal to 12. If we allow $E/\mathbb{Z}_n$ to have points of small order that are easily found, we can simply include them in the subgroup D.

Finding rational non-torsion points on curves defined over $\mathbb{Q}$ is certainly non-trivial, and seems impossibly hard unless the point on the lifted curve has small height [38]. There does not seem to be any obvious way to find a lift with rational points of small height (even though they certainly exist).

What if we already know a set of points on the curve? If we are given $P_1, P_2, P_3 \in E(\mathbb{Z}_n)$, we can find, unless the points are collinear, a quadratic curve

$$C : YZ = \alpha X^2 + \beta XZ + \gamma Z^2$$

defined over $\mathbb{Z}_n$ that passes through P_1, P_2, P_3. Considering divisors, it is easy to show that the fourth intersection point P_4 is the inverse sum of the three known points.

If points of the curve only yield new points via the group operation, and it seems hard to otherwise find points on $E(\mathbb{Z}_n)$, it is reasonable to assume that $E(\mathbb{Z}_n)$ and its subgroup, as described in the previous section, yield a hard subgroup escape problem.

4.3   BCM on Groups with Bilinear Pairings

Let p, ℓ_1, ℓ_2, and ℓ_3 be primes such that $p+1 = 6\ell_1\ell_2\ell_3$, and $p = 2 \pmod 3$. Here, l_1, l_2, l_3 must be distinct and larger than 3. The elliptic curve $E : Y^2 = X^3 + 1$ defined over $\mathbb{F}_p$ is supersingular and has order $p + 1$. Because $\mathbb{F}_{p^2}^*$ has order $p^2 - 1 = (p+1)(p-1)$, there is a modified Weil pairing $\hat{e} : E(\mathbb{F}_p) \times E(\mathbb{F}_p) \to \mathbb{F}_{p^2}^*$. This pairing is known to be bilinear: $\hat{e}(aP, bQ) = \hat{e}(P, Q)^{ab}$ for all $P, Q \in E(\mathbb{F}_p)$ and $a, b \in \mathbb{Z}_p$. It can be computed as described in [6].

Let $U = E(\mathbb{F}_p)$, and let G and D be the subgroups of $E(\mathbb{F}_p)$ of order $\ell_1\ell_2$ and ℓ_1, respectively. We also let P be a point in $E(\mathbb{F}_p)$ of order $6\ell_1\ell_2\ell_3$, and let R be a point of order $6\ell_3$ in $E(\mathbb{F}_p)$, say $R = \ell_1\ell_2 P$. The public key is $PK = (G, D, p, R)$ and the secret key is $SK = (l_1, l_2, l_3)$. The pairing $\hat{e}$ allow us to describe G in the public key without giving away secret information.

VERIFICATION FUNCTION. We claim that for any point $Q \in E(\mathbb{F}_p)$, $Q \in G$ if and only if $\hat{e}(Q, R)$ is equal to 1. If $Q \in G$, then Q has order $\ell_1\ell_2$ and for some integer s, $Q = 6s\ell_3 P$. Then

$$\hat{e}(Q, R) = \hat{e}(6s\ell_3 P, \ell_1\ell_2 P) = \hat{e}(P, P)^{6s\ell_1\ell_2\ell_3} = 1.$$

So the point R and the pairing $\hat{e}$ allows us to determine if points are in G or in $U \setminus G$.

SUBGROUP MEMBERSHIP PROBLEM. Distinguishing the subgroup D (the points of order ℓ_1) from G (the points of order $\ell_1\ell_2$) can easily be done if the integer $\ell_1\ell_2\ell_3$ can be factored. In general, factoring seems to be the best way to distinguish the various subgroups of $E(\mathbb{F}_p)$.

Because we do not reveal any points of order ℓ_2 or $\ell_2\ell_3$, it seems impossible to use the pairing to distinguish the subgroup D in this way. (Theorem 1 of [16] assumes free sampling of any subgroup, which is why it and the pairing cannot be used to distinguish the subgroups of $E(\mathbb{F}_p)$.) It therefore seems reasonable to assume that the subgroup membership problem for G and D is hard, which will provide indistinguishability.

SUBGROUP ESCAPE PROBLEM. For a general cyclic group of order $\ell_1\ell_2\ell_3$, it is easy to find elements of order $\ell_1\ell_2$ if ℓ_3 is known. Unless ℓ_3 is known, it is hard to find elements of order $\ell_1\ell_2$, and knowing elements of order ℓ_1 does not help.

For our concrete situation, factoring the integer $\ell_1\ell_2\ell_3$ into primes seems to be the best method for solving the problem. If the primes ℓ_1, ℓ_2 and ℓ_3 are chosen carefully to make the product $\ell_1\ell_2\ell_3$ hard to factor, it seems reasonable to assume that the subgroup escape problem for U, G and D is hard.

4.4   Extending the BCM's Bandwidth

The blind coupon mechanism allows to undetectably transmit a single bit. Although this is sufficient for our network alert application, sometimes we may want to transmit longer messages.

TRIVIAL CONSTRUCTION. By using multiple blind coupon schemes over different moduli in parallel, we can transmit longer messages. Each m-bit message $x = x_1 \ldots x_m$ is represented by a vector of coupons $\langle c_1, \ldots, c_{2m} \rangle$, where each c_i is drawn from a different scheme. Each processor applies his algorithm in parallel to each of the entries in the vector, verifying each coupon independently and applying the appropriate combining operation to each c_i.

A complication is that an adversary given a vector of coupons might choose to propagate only some of the c_i, while replacing others with dummy coupons. We can enable the receiver to detect when it has received a complete message by representing each bit x_i by two coupons: c_{2i-1} (for $x_i = 0$) and c_{2i} (for $x_i = 1$). A signal coupon in either position tells the receiver both the value of the bit and that the receiver has successfully received it.

Alas, we must construct and run $\Omega(m)$ blind coupon schemes in parallel to transmit m bits.

BETTER CONSTRUCTION. Some additional improvements in efficiency are possible. As before, our group structure is (U, G, D). Suppose our cyclic group G has order $n_0 p_1 \cdots p_m$, where p_i are distinct primes. Let D be the subgroup of G of order n_0.

An m-bit message $x = x_1 \ldots x_m$ is encoded by a coupon $y \in G$, whose order is divisible by $\prod_{i : x_i = 1} p_i$. For all i, we can find an element $g_i \in G$ of order $n_0 p_i$. We can thus let $y = g_1^{r_1 x_1} \cdots g_m^{r_m x_m}$ for random $r_1, \ldots, r_m \in \{0, 1, \ldots, 2^{2k} - 1\}$.

When we combine two coupons y_1 and y_2, it is possible that the order of their combination $\mathcal{C}_{PK}(y_1, y_2)$ is less than the l.c.m. of their respective orders. However, if the primes p_i are sufficiently large, this is unlikely to happen.

In Section 4.2, n_0 is a product of two moderately large primes, while the other primes can be around 2^{80}. For the construction from Section 4.3, n_0 is prime, but every prime must be fairly large to counter elliptic curve factorization.

This technique allows us to transmit messages of quite restricted bandwidth. It remains an open problem whether some other tools can be used to achieve higher capacity without a linear blow-up in message size.

5   Spreading Alerts with the BCM

In this section, we show how the BCM can be used to spread an alert quietly and quickly throughout a network.

To summarize these results briefly, we consider a very general message-passing model in which each node P_i has a "split brain," consisting of an **update algorithm** $\mathcal{U}_i$ that is responsible for transmitting and combining coupons, and a **supervisor algorithm** $\mathcal{S}_i$ that may insert a signal coupon into the system at some point. The supervisor algorithm $\mathcal{S}_i$ of sentinel nodes initially hands out dummy coupons until attacker's presence is detected when it switches to sending signal coupons. Meanwhile, regular nodes' $\mathcal{S}_i$ always doles out dummy coupons. The update algorithm $\mathcal{U}_i$ in each node may behave arbitrarily; the intent is that it represents an underlying strategy for spreading alerts whose actions do not depend on whether the process is transmitting a dummy or signal coupon.

The nodes carry out these operations under the control of a PPT **attacker** $\mathcal{A}$ (who wants to remain undetectable) that can observe all the external operations of the nodes and may deliver any message to any node at any time, including messages of its own invention. (To save space, we omit a formal description of the model from this extended abstract, deferring details to the full paper.)

We show first that, assuming the BCM is secure, the attacker can neither detect nor forge alerts (with non-negligible probability) despite its total control over message traffic. This result holds no matter what update algorithm is used by each node; indeed, it holds even if the update half of each node colludes actively with the adversary. We then give examples of some simple strategies for spreading an alert quickly through the network with some mild constraints on the attacker's behavior.

5.1   Security

Let us begin with the security properties we want our alert-spreading mechanism to have. In the following, we let $\hat{c}_i^t$ be the indicator variable for the event that the supervisor half of node P_i supplies a signal coupon at time t. (This is the only information we need about the behavior of S_i.) We write $\Xi(PK, SK, \mathcal{A}, \{\mathcal{U}_i\}, \{\hat{c}_i^t\})$ for the probability distribution on protocol executions given the specified public key, secret key, attacker, update algorithms, and supervisor behaviors.

Definition 5. *A set of update algorithms $\{\mathcal{U}_i\}$ is **secure** if, for any adversary algorithm $\mathcal{A}$, and any $T = poly(k)$, we have:*

1. **Undetectability:** *Given two distributions on executions, one in which no signal coupons are injected by supervisors and one in which some are, the adversary cannot distinguish between them with probability greater than $1/2$. Formally, let $\hat{c}_i^{0,t} = 0$ for all i, t and let $\hat{c}_i^{1,t}$ be arbitrary. Then for any PPT algorithm $\mathcal{D}$,*

$$\left| \Pr\left[b = b' \;\middle|\; \begin{array}{l} (PK, SK, d, s) \leftarrow \mathcal{G}(1^k); \\ b \xleftarrow{\$} \{0,1\}; \\ \xi \xleftarrow{\$} \Xi\left(PK, SK, \mathcal{A}, \{\mathcal{U}_i\}, \{\hat{c}_i^{b,t}\}\right); \\ b' \leftarrow \mathcal{D}(1^k, PK, d, \{\hat{c}_i^{1,t}\}, \xi) \end{array} \right] - \frac{1}{2} \right| \leq negl(k).$$

2. **Unforgeability:** *The adversary cannot cause any process to transmit a signal coupon unless one is supplied by a supervisor. Formally, if $\hat{c}_i^t = 0$ for all i, t, then there is no PPT algorithm $\mathcal{A}$ such that*

$$\Pr\left[\exists (s, r, m, c) \in \xi \wedge (c \in S_{SK}) \;\middle|\; \begin{array}{l} (PK, SK, d, s) \leftarrow \mathcal{G}(1^k); \\ \xi \xleftarrow{\$} \Xi(PK, SK, \mathcal{A}, \{\mathcal{U}_i\}, \{\hat{c}_i^t\}); \end{array} \right] \leq negl(k).$$

Security of the alert-spreading mechanism follows immediately from the security of the underlying blind coupon mechanism. The essential idea behind undetectability is that because neither the adversary nor the update algorithms can distinguish between dummy and signal coupons distributed by the supervisor algorithms, there is no test that can detect their presence or absence. For unforgeability, the inability of the adversary and update algorithms to generate a signal coupon follows immediately from the unforgeability property of the BCM.

Theorem 2. *An alert-spreading mechanism is secure if the underlying blind coupon mechanism is secure.*

Proof (sketch). We show first undetectability and then unforgeability.

Undetectability. Suppose that the alert-spreading mechanism does not satisfy undetectability, *i.e.* that there exists a set of update algorithms $\{\mathcal{U}_i\}$, an adversary $\mathcal{A}$, and pattern $\{\hat{c}_i^{1,t}\}$ of signal coupons that can be distinguished from only dummy coupons by some PPT algorithm $\mathcal{D}$ with non-negligible probability.

Let us use this fact to construct a PPT algorithm $\mathcal{B}$ that violates indistinguishability. Let y be the coupon input to $\mathcal{B}$. Then $\mathcal{B}$ will simulate an execution ξ of the alert-spreading protocol by simulating the adversary $\mathcal{A}$ and the appropriate update algorithm $\mathcal{U}_i$ at each step. The only components of the protocol that $\mathcal{B}$ cannot simulate directly are the supervisor algorithms $\mathcal{S}_i$, because $\mathcal{B}$ does not have access to signal coupons provided to the supervisor algorithms of sentinel nodes. But here $\mathcal{B}$ lets $c_i^t = \mathcal{C}(d, d)$ when $\hat{c}_i^{1,t} = 0$ and lets $c_i^t = \mathcal{C}(y, y)$ when $\hat{c}_i^{1,t} = 1$. By the blinding property of the BCM, if $y \in D_{SK}$, then all coupons c_i^t will be statistically indistinguishable from uniformly random dummy coupons, giving a distribution on executions that is itself statistically indistinguishable from $\Xi\left(PK, SK, \mathcal{A}, \{\mathcal{U}_i\}, \{\hat{c}_i^{0,t}\}\right)$. If instead $y \in S_{SK}$, then c_i^t will be such that the resulting distribution on executions will be statistically indistinguishable from $\Xi\left(PK, SK, \mathcal{A}, \{\mathcal{U}_i\}, \{\hat{c}_i^{1,t}\}\right)$. It follows from the indistinguishability property of the BCM that no PPT algorithm $\mathcal{D}$ can distinguish between these two distributions with probability greater than $1/2 + negl(k)$.

Unforgeability. The proof of unforgeability is similar. Suppose that there is some adversary and a set of update functions that between them can, with non-negligible probability, generate a signal coupon given only dummy coupons from the supervisor algorithms. Then a PPT algorithm $\mathcal{B}$ that simulates an execution of this system and returns a coupon obtained by combining all valid coupons sent during the execution forges a signal coupon with non-negligible probability, contradicting the unforgeability property of the BCM.

□

5.2   Performance

It is not enough that the attacker cannot detect or forge alerts: a mechanism that used no messages at all could ensure that. To ensure that all non-faulty nodes eventually receive an alert, we must specify both a strategy for the nodes' update algorithms and place restrictions on the attacker's ability to discard messages. In the full paper, we give two simple examples of how alerts might be spread in practice: a synchronous flooding algorithm that spreads an alert to all nodes in time proportional to the diameter of the network (after removing faulty nodes), and a simple asynchronous epidemic algorithm that spreads the alert in time $O(n \log n)$ in a complete network of n nodes, where at most a constant fraction of nodes is faulty. In each case the behavior of the update algorithms is straightforward: invalid incoming coupons are discarded, while valid incoming coupons are combined with previous coupons.

6   Generic Security of the Subgroup Escape Problem

We prove that the subgroup escape problem is hard in the generic group model [37] when the representation set is much larger than the group.

Let G be a finite cyclic group and let $U \subseteq \{0, 1\}^*$ be a set such that $|U| \geq |G|$. In the generic group model, elements of G are encoded as unique random strings.

We define a random injective function $\sigma : G \to U$, which maps group elements to their string representations. Algorithms have access to an oracle that on input of $x \pm y$ returns $\sigma(\sigma^{-1}(x) \pm \sigma^{-1}(y))$ when both $x, y \in \sigma(G) \subseteq U$, and otherwise the special symbol $\bot$. An algorithm can use the oracle to decide whether $x \in U$ is in $\sigma(G)$ or not by sending the query $x + x$ to the oracle. If $x \notin \sigma(G)$, the reply will be $\bot$.

Theorem 3. *Let D be a subgroup of $G \subseteq U$. Let g be a generator of D. Let $\mathcal{A}$ be a generic algorithm that solves the subgroup escape problem. If $\mathcal{A}$ makes at most q queries to the group oracle, then*

$$\Pr\left[y \in G \setminus D \;\middle|\; \mathcal{A}(1^k, \sigma(g)) = \sigma(y) \right] \leq \frac{q(|G| - |D|)}{(|U| - q)}.$$

Proof. The algorithm can only get information about σ through the group oracle. If the input to the oracle is two elements known to be in $\sigma(D)$, then the adversary learns a new element in $\sigma(D)$.

To have any chance of finding an element of $\sigma(G \setminus D)$, the adversary must use the group oracle to test elements that are not known to be in $\sigma(D)$.

Suppose that after i queries, the adversary knows a elements in $\sigma(D)$ and b elements of $U \setminus \sigma(G)$ $(a + b \leq i)$. For any z outside the set of tested elements, the probability that $z \in \sigma(G \setminus D)$ is exactly $(|G| - |D|)/(|U| - b)$ (note that it is independent of a).

Therefore, the probability that the adversary discovers an element in $\sigma(G \setminus D)$ with $i+1$ query is at most $(|G|-|D|)/(|U|-i)$. For up to q queries, the probability that at least one of the tested elements are in $\sigma(G \setminus D)$ is at most

$$\sum_{i=1}^{q} \frac{|G| - |D|}{|U| - i} \leq q \cdot \frac{|G| - |D|}{|U| - q}.$$

For a sufficiently large universe U, this probability is negligible. $\qquad\square$

7   Conclusion

We have defined and constructed a blind coupon mechanism, implementing a specialized form of a signed, AND-homomorphic encryption. Our proofs of security are based on the novel subgroup escape problem, which seems hard on certain groups given the current state of knowledge. Our scheme can be instantiated with elliptic curves over $\mathbb{Z}_n$ of reasonable size which makes our constructions practical. We have demonstrated that the BCM has many natural applications. In particular, it can be used to spread an alert undetectably in a variety of epidemic-like settings despite the existence of Byzantine processes and a powerful, active adversary.

Acknowledgments

We are grateful to Yevgeniy Dodis for his helpful comments regarding this work.

References

1. M. Abe. Mix-networks on permutation networks. In *Advances in Cryptology - ASIACRYPT '99*, volume 1706 of *Lecture Notes in Computer Science*, pages 258–273. Springer-Verlag, 1999.
2. J. Algesheimer, J. Camenisch, and V. Shoup. Efficient computation modulo a shared secret with applications to the generation of shared safe prime products. In *Advances in Cryptology - Proceedings of CRYPTO 2002*, volume 2442 of *Lecture Notes in Computer Science*, pages 417–432. Springer-Verlag, 2002.
3. J. Aspnes, Z. Diamadi, K. Gjøsteen, R. Peralta, and A. Yampolskiy. Spreading alerts quietly and the subgroup escape problem. Technical Report YALEU/DCS/TR-1326, Yale University, August 2005. Available at `ftp://ftp.cs.yale.edu/pub/TR/tr1326.pdf`.
4. A. Beimel and S. Dolev. Buses for anonymous message delivery. In *Second International Conference on FUN with Algorithms*, pages 1–13. Carleton Scientific, 2001.
5. I. F. Blake, G. Seroussi, and N. P. Smart. *Elliptic Curves in Cryptography*, volume 265 of *London Mathematical Society Lecture Note Series*. Cambridge University Press, 1999.
6. D. Boneh and M. Franklin. Identity-based encryption from the Weil pairing. *Lecture Notes in Computer Science*, 2139:213–229, 2001.
7. G. Brassard, D. Chaum, and C. Crépeau. Minimum disclosure proofs of knowledge. *Journal of Computer and System Sciences*, 37(2):156–189, 1988.
8. D. Chaum. Untraceable electronic mail, return address and digital pseudonyms. *Communications of the ACM*, 24(2):84–88, 1981.
9. D. Chaum. The dining cryptographers problem: Unconditional sender and recipient untraceability. *Journal of Cryptology*, 1:65–75, 1988.
10. D. Chaum, P. Y. Ryan, and S. A. Schneider. A practical, voter-verifiable election scheme. Technical Report CS-TR-880, School of Computing Science, University of Newcastle, December 2004.
11. R. Cramer and V. Shoup. Universal hash proofs and a paradigm for adaptive chosen ciphertext secure public-key encryption. In L. R. Knudsen, editor, *Proceedings of EUROCRYPT 2002*, volume 2332 of *Lecture Notes in Computer Science*, pages 45–64. Springer-Verlag, 2002.
12. A. Demers, D. Greene, C. Hauser, W. Irish, J. Larson, S. Shenker, H. Sturgis, D. Swinehart, and D. Terry. Epidemic algorithms for replicated database maintenance. In F. B. Schneider, editor, *Proceedings of the 6th Annual ACM Symposium on Principles of Distributed Computing*, pages 1–12, Vancouver, BC, Canada, Aug. 1987. ACM Press.
13. N. Demytko. A new elliptic curve based analogue of RSA. In *Advances in Cryptology - Proceedings of EUROCRYPT 93*, volume 765 of *Lecture Notes in Computer Science*, pages 40–49. Springer-Verlag, 1993.
14. S. D. Galbraith. Elliptic curve Paillier schemes. *Journal of Cryptology*, 15(2):129–138, 2002.
15. K. Gjøsteen. *Subgroup membership problems and public key cryptosystems*. PhD thesis, NTNU, May 2004.
16. K. Gjøsteen. Symmetric subgroup membership problems. In S. Vaudenay, editor, *Proceedings of Public Key Cryptography 2005*, volume 3386 of *LNCS*, pages 104–119. Springer-Verlag, 2005.

17. S. Goldwasser and J. Kilian. Primality testing using elliptic curves. *Journal of the Association for Computing Machinery*, 46:450–472, 1999.
18. S. Goldwasser and S. Micali. Probabilistic encryption. *Journal of Computer and System Sciences*, 28:270–299, April 1984.
19. P. Golle and A. Juels. Dining cryptographers revisited. In *Advances in Cryptology - Proceedings of EUROCRYPT 2004*, pages 456–473, 2004.
20. M. Jakobsson. A practical Mix. In *Advances in Cryptology - Proceedings of EUROCRYPT 98*, volume 1403 of *Lecture Notes in Computer Science*, pages 448–461. Springer-Verlag, 1998.
21. M. Jakobsson. Flash mixing. In *Proceedings of the Eighteenth Annual ACM Symposium on Principles of Distributed Computing*, pages 83–89. ACM, 1999.
22. R. Johnson, D. Molnar, D. X. Song, and D. Wagner. Homomorphic signature schemes. In *CT-RSA*, pages 244–262, 2002.
23. K. Koyama, U. M. Maurer, T. Okamoto, and S. A. Vanstone. New public-key schemes based on elliptic curves over the ring z_n. In *Advances in Cryptology - Proceedings of CRYPTO 91*, volume 576 of *Lecture Notes in Computer Science*, pages 252–266, 1992.
24. N. Kunihiro and K. Koyama. Equivalence of counting the number of points on elliptic curve over the ring Z_n and factoring n. In Nyberg [30].
25. L. Lamport, R. Shostack, and M. Pease. The Byzantine generals problem. *ACM Transactions on Programming Languages and Systems*, 4(3):382–401, 1982.
26. G.-J. Lay and H. G. Zimmer. Constructing elliptic curves with given group order over large finite fields. In L. M. Adleman and M.-D. A. Huang, editors, *ANTS*, volume 877 of *Lecture Notes in Computer Science*, pages 250–263. Springer-Verlag, 1994.
27. H. W. Lenstra, Jr. Factoring integers with elliptic curves. *Annals of Mathematics*, 126:649–673, 1987.
28. D. Naccache and J. Stern. A new public key cryptosystem based on higher residues. In Nyberg [30], pages 308–318.
29. J. M. G. Nieto, C. Boyd, and E. Dawson. A public key cryptosystem based on the subgroup membership problem. In S. Quing, T. Okamoto, and J. Zhou, editors, *Proceedings of ICICS 2001*, volume 2229 of *Lecture Notes in Computer Science*, pages 352–363. Springer-Verlag, 2001.
30. K. Nyberg, editor. *Advances in Cryptology - EUROCRYPT '98*, volume 1403 of *Lecture Notes in Computer Science*. Springer-Verlag, 1998.
31. T. Okamoto and S. Uchiyama. A new public-key cryptosystem as secure as factoring. In Nyberg [30], pages 308–318.
32. H. Ong, C.-P. Schnorr, and A. Shamir. An efficient signature scheme based on quadratic equations. In *proceedings of ACM Symposium on Theory of Computing*, ACM, pages 208–216, 1984.
33. P. Paillier. Public-key cryptosystems based on composite degree residue classes. In J. Stern, editor, *Proceedings of EUROCRYPT '99*, volume 1592 of *Lecture Notes in Computer Science*, pages 223–238. Springer-Verlag, 1999.
34. M. Rabin. Digitalized signatures and public-key functions as intractable as factorization. Technical Report MIT/LCS/TR-212, Laboratory for Computer Science, Massachusetts Institute of Technology, January 1979.
35. R. Rivest, A. Shamir, and L. Adleman. A method for obtaining digital signatures and public-key cryptosystems. *Communications of the ACM*, 21(2):120–126, 1978.
36. C. P. Schnorr and J. Pollard. An efficient solution of the congruence $x^2 + ky^2 \equiv m \pmod{n}$. *IEEE Transactions on Information Theory*, 33(5):702–709, 1987.

37. V. Shoup. Lower bounds for discrete logarithms and related problems. In W. Fumy, editor, *Proceedings of EUROCRYPT '97*, volume 1233 of *Lecture Notes in Computer Science*, pages 256–266. Springer-Verlag, 1997.
38. J. H. Silverman. Computing rational points on rank 1 elliptic curves via *L*-series and canonical heights. *Mathematics of computation*, 68(226):835–858, April 1999.
39. P. F. Syverson, D. M. Goldschlag, and M. G. Reed. Anonymous connections and Onion routing. *IEEE Journal on Selected Areas in Communications: Special Issue on Copyright and Privacy Protection*, 16(4):482–494, 1998.
40. P. F. Syverson, M. G. Reed, and D. M. Goldschlag. Onion routing access configurations. In *DISCEX2000:Proceedings of the DARPA information survivability conference and exposition*, pages 34–40. IEEE CS Press, 2000.

A Sender Verifiable Mix-Net and a New Proof of a Shuffle

Douglas Wikström

Royal Institute of Technology (KTH),
KTH, Nada, SE-100 44 Stockholm, Sweden
dog@nada.kth.se

Abstract. We introduce the first El Gamal based mix-net in which each mix-server partially decrypts and permutes its input, i.e., no re-encryption is necessary. An interesting property of the construction is that a sender can verify non-interactively that its message is processed correctly. We call this *sender verifiability*.

The mix-net is provably UC-secure against static adversaries corrupting any minority of the mix-servers. The result holds under the decision Diffie-Hellman assumption, and assuming an ideal bulletin board and an ideal zero-knowledge proof of knowledge of a correct shuffle.

Then we construct the first proof of a decryption-permutation shuffle, and show how this can be transformed into a zero-knowledge proof of knowledge in the UC-framework. The protocol is sound under the strong RSA-assumption and the discrete logarithm assumption.

Our proof of a shuffle is not a variation of existing methods. It is based on a novel idea of independent interest, and we argue that it is at least as efficient as previous constructions.

1 Introduction

The notion of a mix-net was invented by Chaum [10]. Properly constructed a mix-net takes a list of cryptotexts and outputs the cleartexts permuted using a secret random permutation. Usually a mix-net is realized by a set of mix-servers organized in a chain that collectively execute a protocol. Each mix-server receives a list of encrypted messages from the previous mix-server, transforms them, using partial decryption and/or random re-encryption, reorders them, and outputs the result. The secret permutation is shared by the mix-servers.

1.1 Previous Work

Chaum's original "anonymous channel" [10,40] enables a sender to send mail anonymously. When constructing election schemes [10,17,42,47,39] a mix-net can be used to ensure that the vote of a given voter cannot be revealed. Abe gives an efficient construction of a general mix-net [2], and argues about its properties. Jakobsson has written (partly with Juels) more general papers on the topic of mixing [30,31,32] focusing on efficiency. There are two known approaches to

B. Roy (Ed.): ASIACRYPT 2005, LNCS 3788, pp. 273–292, 2005.

proving a correct shuffle efficiently. These are introduced by Furukawa et al. [19,20,21], and Neff [37,38] respectively. Groth [27] generalizes Neff's protocol to form an abstract protocol for any homomorphic cryptosystem.

Desmedt and Kurosawa [13] describe an attack on a protocol by Jakobsson [30]. Similarly Mitomo and Kurosawa [36] exhibit a weakness in another protocol by Jakobsson [31]. Pfitzmann has given some general attacks on mix-nets [44,43], and Michels and Horster give additional attacks in [35]. Wikström [48] gives several attacks for a protocol by Golle et al. [26]. He also gives attacks for the protocols by Jakobsson [31] and Jakobsson and Juels [33]. Abe [3] has independently found related attacks.

Canetti [9], and independently Pfitzmann and Waidner [45] proposed security frameworks for reactive processes. We use the former universal composability (UC) framework. Both frameworks have composition theorems, and are based on older definitional work. The initial ideal-model based definitional approach for secure function evaluation is informally proposed by Goldreich, Micali, and Wigderson in [22]. The first formalizations appear in Goldwasser and Levin [24], Micali and Rogaway [34], and Beaver [5]. See [8,9] for an excellent background on these definitions.

Wikström [49] defines the notion of a mix-net in the UC-framework, and provides a construction that is provably secure against static adversaries under the decisional Diffie-Hellman assumption. The scheme is practical only when the number of mix-servers is small.

1.2   Contributions

We introduce a new type of El Gamal based mix-net in which each mix-server only decrypts and permutes its input. No re-encryption is necessary. This allows an individual sender to verify non-interactively that its message was processed correctly, i.e., the scheme is *sender verifiable*. Although some older constructions have this property, our is the first provably secure scheme.

Then we give the first proof of a decrypt-permutation shuffle of El Gamal cryptotexts. There are two known approaches, [37,27] and [19], to construct such a protocol, but our solution is based on a novel idea of independent interest, and we argue that it is at least as efficient as previous schemes.

We also give the first transformation of a proof of a shuffle into an efficient zero-knowledge proof of knowledge in the UC-framework. An important technical advantage of the new decrypt and permute construction is that witnesses are much smaller than for previous shuffle relations.

Combined, our results give a mix-net that is provably UC-secure against static adversaries corrupting any minority of the mix-servers. The mix-net is efficient for any number of mix-servers, improving the result in Wikström [49].

1.3   Outline of the Paper

The paper is organized as follows. Notation is introduced in Section 2. In Section 3 we define the ideal mix-net functionality. A partial result in this direction is given in Section 4, where we describe a sender verifiable mix-net and discuss sender verifiability. In Section 5 we describe a zero-knowledge proof of knowledge that a mix-server processes its input correctly. Then in Section 6 we transform this into a realization of an ideal zero-knowledge functionality in the UC-framework. Proofs of all claims are given in the full version [50] of this paper.

2   Notation

Throughout, $S_1, \ldots, S_N$ denote senders and $M_1, \ldots, M_k$ mix-servers. All participants are modeled as interactive Turing machines. We abuse notation and use S_i and M_j to denote both the machines themselves and their identity. We denote the set of permutations of N elements by Σ_N. We use the term "randomly" instead of "uniformly and independently at random". A function $f : \mathbb{N} \to [0,1]$ is said to be negligible if for each $c > 0$ there exists a $K_0 \in \mathbb{N}$ such that $f(K) < K^{-c}$ for $K > K_0 \in \mathbb{N}$. A probability $p(K)$ is overwhelming if $1 - p(K)$ is negligible.

We assume that G_q is a group of prime order q with generator g for which the Decision Diffie-Hellman (DDH) Assumption holds. Informally, it means that it is infeasible to distinguish the distributions $(g^\alpha, g^\beta, g^{\alpha\beta})$ and $(g^\alpha, g^\beta, g^\gamma)$ when $\alpha, \beta, \gamma \in \mathbb{Z}_q$ are randomly chosen. This implies that also the Discrete Logarithm (DL) assumption holds, namely that it is infeasible to compute the logarithm in base g of a random element in G_q. For concreteness we let G_q be a subgroup of prime order q of the multiplicative group $\mathbb{Z}_p^*$ for some prime p. When we say that an element in $\mathbb{Z}_q$ is prime, we mean that its representative in $\{0, \ldots, q-1\}$ is a prime when considered as an integer.

We review the El Gamal [14] cryptosystem employed in G_q. The private key x is generated by choosing $x \in \mathbb{Z}_q$ randomly. The corresponding public key is (g, y), where $y = g^x$. Encryption of a message $m \in G_q$ using the public key (g, y) is given by $E_{(g,y)}(m, r) = (g^r, y^r m)$, where r is chosen randomly from $\mathbb{Z}_q$, and decryption of a cryptotext on the form $(u, v) = (g^r, y^r m)$ using the private key x is given by $D_x(u, v) = u^{-x} v = m$.

We also use an RSA modulus $\mathbf{N} = \mathbf{pq}$, where $\mathbf{p}$ and $\mathbf{q}$ are safe primes. We denote by $QR_\mathbf{N}$ the group of squares in $\mathbb{Z}_\mathbf{N}^*$ and adopt the convention that any element $\mathbf{b}$ in $QR_\mathbf{N}$ is written in boldface. We assume that the strong RSA-assumption holds for such rings. Informally, it means that given random $(\mathbf{N}, \mathbf{h})$, where $\mathbf{h} \in QR_\mathbf{N}$, it is infeasible to find a non-trivial eth root $\mathbf{b}$ of $\mathbf{h}$, i.e., an $e \neq \pm 1$ such that $\mathbf{b}^e = \mathbf{h}$. This differs from the RSA-assumption in that e is not fixed.

The primary security parameter K_1 is the number of bits in q. Several other security parameters are introduced later in the paper. We denote by PRG a pseudo-random generator (cf. [23]). We denote by Sort the algorithm that given a list of strings as input outputs the same set of strings in lexicographical order.

2.1   The Universally Composable Security Framework

We analyze the security of our protocols in the Universally Composable (UC) security framework of Canetti [9]. There are several variants and extensions of this framework, but we consider a plain model with asynchronous authenticated communication. In the full version [50] we give a formal definition of this model. Here we only indicate how our notation differs from the standard [9].

The notion of a communication model, $\mathcal{C}_\mathcal{I}$, used below is not explicit in Canetti [9]. It works as a router between participants and between participants and ideal functionalities. Given the input $((A_1, B_1, C_1, \ldots), \ldots, (A_s, B_s, C_s, \ldots))$ it interprets A_j as the receiver of $(B_j, C_j, \ldots)$. The adversary cannot read the correspondence with ideal functionalities, but it has full control over when a message is delivered.

Our results hold for both blocking and non-blocking adversaries, where a blocking adversary is allowed to block the delivery of a message indefinitely.

Definition 1. *We define* $\mathcal{M}_l$ *to be the set of* static adversaries *that corrupt less than* l *out of* k *participants of the mix-server type, and arbitrarily many participants of the sender type.*

Throughout we implicitly assume that a message handed to an ideal functionality that is not on the form prescribed in its definition is returned to the sender immediately. In particular this includes verifying membership in G_q when appropriate. We use the same convention for definitions of protocols.

3   The Ideal Mix-Net

Although other definitions of security of mix-nets have been proposed, the most natural definition is given by Wikström [49] in the UC-framework. He formalizes a trusted party that waits for messages from senders, and then when a majority of the mix-servers request it, outputs these messages but in lexicographical order. For simplicity it accepts only one input from each sender. We prove security relative this functionality.

Functionality 1 (Mix-Net). The ideal functionality for a *mix-net*, $\mathcal{F}_{MN}$, running with mix-servers $M_1, \ldots, M_k$, senders $S_1, \ldots, S_N$, and ideal adversary $\mathcal{S}$ proceeds as follows

1. Initialize a list $L = \emptyset$, and set $J_P = \emptyset$ and $J_M = \emptyset$.
2. Repeatedly wait for new inputs and do
   (a) Suppose $(S_i, \mathsf{Send}, m_i)$, $m_i \in G_q$, is received from $\mathcal{C}_\mathcal{I}$. If $i \notin J_P$, set $J_P \leftarrow J_P \cup \{i\}$, and append m_i to L. Then hand $(\mathcal{S}, S_i, \mathsf{Send})$ to $\mathcal{C}_\mathcal{I}$.
   (b) Suppose (M_j, Run) is received from $\mathcal{C}_\mathcal{I}$. Set $J_M \leftarrow J_M \cup \{j\}$. If $|J_M| > k/2$, then sort the list L lexicographically to form a list L', hand $((\mathcal{S}, M_j, \mathsf{Output}, L'), \{(M_l, \mathsf{Output}, L')\}_{l=1}^k)$ to $\mathcal{C}_\mathcal{I}$ and ignore further messages. Otherwise, hand $\mathcal{C}_\mathcal{I}$ the list $(\mathcal{S}, M_j, \mathsf{Run})$.

4   A Sender Verifiable El Gamal Based Mix-Net

In recent El Gamal based mix-nets, e.g. [38,20,49], the mix-servers form a chain, and each mix-server randomly permutes, partially decrypts, and *re-encrypts* the output of the previous mix-server. In older constructions decryption is instead carried out jointly at the end of the chain. Our construction is different in that each mix-server *partially decrypts* and *sorts* the output of the previous mix-server. Thus, no cryptotext is re-encrypted and the permutation is not random, but determined by the lexicographical order of the cryptotexts.

Let us consider why re-encryption is often considered necessary. In several previous mix-nets each mix-server M_j holds a secret key $x_j \in \mathbb{Z}_q$ corresponding to a public key $y_j = g^{x_j}$. A joint public key $y = \prod_{j=1}^{k} y_j$ is used by a sender S_i to compute a cryptotext $(u_{0,i}, v_{0,i}) = (g^{r_i}, y^{r_i} m_i)$ of a message m_i for a random $r_i \in \mathbb{Z}_q$. The mix-servers take turns and compute

$$(u_{j,i}, v_{j,i})_{i=1}^{N} = \left(g^{s_{j,i}} u_{j-1,\pi_j(i)}, \left(\prod_{l=j+1}^{k} y_l \right)^{s_{j,i}} v_{j-1,\pi_j(i)} / u_{j-1,\pi_j(i)}^{x_j} \right)_{i=1}^{N} ,$$

for random $s_{j,i} \in \mathbb{Z}_q$ and $\pi_j \in \Sigma_N$, i.e., each mix-server permutes, partially decrypts and re-encrypts its input. In the end $(v_{k,i})_{i=1}^{N} = (m_{\pi(i)})_{i=1}^{N}$ for some random joint permutation π. The reason that re-encryption is necessary with this type of scheme is that otherwise the first component $u_{0,i}$ of each cryptotext remains unchanged during the transformation, which allows anybody to break the anonymity of all senders. For the older type of construction it is obvious why re-encryption is necessary.

4.1 Our Modification

We modify the El Gamal cryptosystem to ensure that also the first component $u_{j-1,i}$ is changed during partial decryption. Each mix-server is given a secret key $(w_j, x_j) \in \mathbb{Z}_q^2$ and a corresponding public key $(z_j, y_j) = (g^{w_j}, g^{x_j})$. To partially decrypt and permute its input it computes

$$(u_{j-1,i}^{1/w_j}, v_{j-1,i} u_{j-1,i}^{-x_j/w_j})_{i=1}^{N} , \tag{1}$$

from L_{j-1}, and sorts the result lexicographically. The result is denoted by $L_j = (u_{j,i}, v_{j,i})_{i=1}^{N}$. Note that both components of each cryptotext are transformed using the secret key of the mix-server. For this transformation to make any sense we must also modify the way the joint key is formed. We define

$$(Z_{k+1}, Y_{k+1}) = (g, 1) \quad \text{and} \quad (Z_j, Y_j) = (Z_{j+1}^{w_j}, Y_{j+1} Z_{j+1}^{x_j}) . \tag{2}$$

The joint keys must be computed jointly by the mix-servers. A sender encrypts its message using the public key (Z_1, Y_1), i.e., $(u_{0,i}, v_{0,i}) = (Z_1^{r_i}, Y_1^{r_i} m_i)$ for some random r_i. The structure of the keys are chosen such that a cryptotext on the form $(u_{j-1,i}, v_{j-1,i}) = (Z_j^{r_i}, Y_j^{r_i} m_i)$ given as input to mix-server M_j satisfies

$$(u_{j-1,i}^{1/w_j}, v_{j-1,i} u_{j-1,i}^{-x_j/w_j}) = (Z_j^{r_i/w_j}, Y_j^{r_i} Z_j^{-r_i x_j/w_j} m_i)$$
$$= ((Z_j^{1/w_j})^{r_i}, (Y_j Z_j^{-x_j/w_j})^{r_i} m_i) = (Z_{j+1}^{r_i}, Y_{j+1}^{r_i} m_i) .$$

Thus, each mix-server M_j transforms a cryptotext $(u_{j-1,i}, v_{j-1,i})$ encrypted with the public key (Z_j, Y_j) into a cryptotext $(u_{j,i}, v_{j,i})$ encrypted with the public key (Z_{j+1}, Y_{j+1}). Note that $\text{Sort}(\{v_{k,i}\}_{i=1}^N) = \text{Sort}(\{m_i\}_{i=1}^N)$, since $Y_{k+1} = 1$.

There are several seemingly equivalent ways to set up the scheme, but some of these do not allow a reduction of the security of the mix-net to the DDH-assumption. The relation in Equation (1) is carefully chosen to allow a reduction.

4.2   Sender Verifiability

An important consequence of our modification is that a sender can compute $(Z_{j+1}^{r_i}, Y_{j+1}^{r_i} m_i)$ and verify that this pair is contained in L_j for $j = 1, \ldots, k$. Furthermore, if this is not the case the sender can easily prove to any outsider which mix-server behaved incorrectly. We call this *sender verifiability*, since it allows a sender to verify that its cryptotext is processed correctly by the mix-servers. This is not a new property. In fact Chaum's original construction [10] has this property, but our construction is the first provably secure scheme with this property.

We think that sender verifiability is an important property that deserves more attention. The verification process is unconditional and easily explained to anybody with only a modest background in mathematics, and a verification program can be implemented with little skills in programming. This means that in the main application of mix-nets, electronic elections, a sender can convince herself that her vote was processed correctly. We stress that this verification does not guarantee anonymity or correct processing of any other cryptotext. Thus, a proof of the overall security of the mix-net is still required.

The reader may worry that sender verifiability allows a voter to point out its vote to a coercer. This is the case, but the sender can do this in previous mix-nets as well by pointing at its message in the original list L_0 of cryptotexts and revealing the randomness used during encryption, so this problem is not specific to our scheme. Furthermore, our scheme becomes coercion-free whenever the sender does not know the randomness of its cryptotext, as other El Gamal based mix-nets, but sender verifiability is then lost.

4.3   A Technical Advantage

There is also an important technical consequence of the lack of re-encryption in the mixing process. The witness of our shuffle relation consists of a pair (w_j, x_j), which makes it easy to turn our proof of knowledge into a secure realization of the ideal functionality $\mathcal{F}_{\text{ZK}}^{R_{\text{DP}}}$. This should be contrasted with all previous shuffle relations, where the witness contains a long list of random exponents used to re-encrypt the input that must somehow be extracted by the ideal adversary in the UC-setting.

A potential alternative to our approach is to formalize the proof of a shuffle as a proof of membership [7] in the UC-framework. However, a proof of membership is not sufficient for the older constructions where decryption is carried out jointly at the end of the mixing chain. The problem is that the adversary could corrupt the last mix-server M_k and instruct it to output L_0 instead of a re-encryption and permutation of L_{k-1}. This would obviously break the anonymity of all senders. The malicious behavior is not detected, since the ideal proof of membership only expects an element in the language and no witness from corrupted parties, and L_0 is a re-encryption and permutation of L_{k-1}. Interestingly, it seems that the adversary cannot attack the real protocol if the proof of membership of a correct shuffle is implemented using a proof of knowledge in the classical sense.

It is an open question if a proof of membership suffices for mix-nets where each mix-server *partially decrypts* and then re-encrypts and permutes its input.

4.4   Preliminaries

We describe the mix-net in a hybrid model as defined in the UC-framework. This means that the mix-servers and senders have access to a set of ideal functionalities introduced in this section. We assume the existence of an authenticated bulletin board. All parties can write to it, but no party can erase any message from it. A formal definition is given in [49,50]. We also assume an ideal functionality corresponding to the key set-up sketched in Section 4.1. This is given below.

Functionality 2 (Special El Gamal Secret Key Sharing). The ideal *Special El Gamal Secret Key Sharing over G_q*, $\mathcal{F}_{SKS}$, with mix-servers $M_1, \ldots, M_k$, senders $S_1, \ldots, S_N$, and ideal adversary $\mathcal{S}$.

1. Initialize sets $J_j = \emptyset$ for $j = 0, \ldots, k$.
2. Until $|J_0| = k$, repeatedly wait for inputs. If $(M_j, \mathtt{MyKey}, w_j, x_j)$ is received from $\mathcal{C}_{\mathcal{I}}$ such that $w_j, x_j \in \mathbb{Z}_q$ and $j \notin J_0$. Set $J_0 \leftarrow J_0 \cup \{j\}$ compute $z_j = g^{w_j}$ and $y_j = g^{x_j}$, and hand $(\mathcal{S}, \mathtt{PublicKey}, M_j, w_j, z_j)$ to $\mathcal{C}_{\mathcal{I}}$.
3. Set $(Z_{k+1}, Y_{k+1}) = (g, 1)$ and $(Z_j, Y_j) = (Z_{j+1}^{w_j}, Y_{j+1}Z_{j+1}^{x_j})$. Then hand $((\mathcal{S}, \mathtt{PublicKeys}, (Z_j, Y_j, z_j, y_j)_{j=1}^k), \{(S_i, \mathtt{PublicKeys}, (Z_j, Y_j, z_j, y_j)_{j=1}^k)\}_{i=1}^N, \{(M_l, \mathtt{Keys}, w_l, x_l, (Z_j, Y_j, z_j, y_j)_{j=1}^k)\}_{l=1}^k)$ to $\mathcal{C}_{\mathcal{I}}$.
4. Until $|J_0| = k$, repeatedly wait for inputs. If $(M_j, \mathtt{Recover}, M_l)$ is received from $\mathcal{C}_{\mathcal{I}}$, set $J_l \leftarrow J_l \cup \{j\}$. If $|J_l| > k/2$, then hand $((\mathcal{S}, \mathtt{Recovered}, M_l, w_l, x_l), \{(M_j, \mathtt{Recovered}, M_l, w_l, x_l)\}_{j=1}^k)$ to $\mathcal{C}_{\mathcal{I}}$, and otherwise hand $(\mathcal{S}, M_j, \mathtt{Recover}, M_l)$ to $\mathcal{C}_{\mathcal{I}}$.

The above functionality can be securely realized by letting each mix-server secret share its secret key using Feldman's [15] verifiable secret sharing scheme. Note that the functionality explicitly allows corrupted mix-servers to choose their keys in a way that depends on the public keys of uncorrupted mix-servers. The special joint keys would then be computed iteratively using Equation (2), and during this process each mix-server would prove that it does this correctly using standard methods.

Each mix-server partially decrypts each cryptotext and sorts the resulting cryptotexts. Thus, proving correct behavior corresponds to proving knowledge of a secret key (w, x) such that the cryptotexts (u_i, v_i) input to a mix-server are related to the cryptotexts (u'_i, v'_i) it outputs by the following relation.

Definition 2 (Knowledge of Correct Decryption-Permutation). *Define for each N a relation $R_{\text{DP}} \subset (G_q^3 \times G_q^{2N} \times G_q^{2N}) \times (\mathbb{Z}_q \times \mathbb{Z}_q)$, by*

$$((g, z, y, \{(u_i, v_i)\}_{i=1}^N, \{(u_i', v_i')\}_{i=1}^N), (w, x)) \in R_{\text{DP}}$$

precisely when $z = g^w$, $y = g^x$ and $(u_i', v_i') = (u_{\pi(i)}^{1/w}, v_{\pi(i)} u_{\pi(i)}^{-x/w})$ for $i = 1, \ldots, N$ and $\pi \in \Sigma_N$ such that the list $\{(u_i', v_i')\}_{i=1}^N$ is sorted lexicographically.

To avoid a large class of "relation attacks" [44,43,48] no sender can be allowed to construct a cryptotext of a message related to the message encrypted by some other sender. Thus, each sender is required to prove knowledge of the randomness it uses to form its cryptotexts. This corresponds to the following relation.

Definition 3 (Knowledge of Cleartext). *Define a relation $R_C \subset G_q^4 \times \mathbb{Z}_q$ by $((Z, Y, u, v), r) \in R_C$ precisely when $\log_Z u = r$.*

Formally, we need a secure realization of the following functionality parameterized by the above relations.

Functionality 3 (Zero-Knowledge Proof of Knowledge). Let $\mathcal{L}$ be a language given by a binary relation R. The ideal *zero-knowledge proof of knowledge* functionality $\mathcal{F}_{\text{ZK}}^R$ of a witness w to an element $x \in \mathcal{L}$, running with parties $P_1, \ldots, P_k$

1. Upon receipt of $(P_i, \text{Prover}, x, w)$ from $\mathcal{C}_{\mathcal{I}}$, store w under the tag (P_i, x), and hand $(\mathcal{S}, P_i, \text{Prover}, x, R(x, w))$ to $\mathcal{C}_{\mathcal{I}}$.
2. Upon receipt of $(M_j, \text{Question}, P_i, x)$ from $\mathcal{C}_{\mathcal{I}}$, let w be the string stored under the tag (P_i, x) (the empty string if nothing is stored), and hand $((\mathcal{S}, M_j, \text{Verifier}, P_i, x, R(x, w)), (M_j, \text{Verifier}, P_i, R(x, w)))$ to $\mathcal{C}_{\mathcal{I}}$.

In [49] a secure realization π_C of $\mathcal{F}_{\text{ZK}}^{R_C}$ is given, under the DDH-assumption, which is secure against $\mathcal{M}_{k/2}$-adversaries.

The functionality $\mathcal{F}_{\text{ZK}}^{R_{\text{DP}}}$ is securely realized in Section 6.

4.5   The Mix-Net

We now give the details of our mix-net. It executes in a hybrid model with access to the ideal functionalities described above.

Protocol 1 (Mix-Net). The mix-net protocol $\pi_{\text{MN}} = (S_1, \ldots, S_N, M_1, \ldots, M_k)$ consists of senders S_i, and mix-servers M_j.

SENDER S_i. Each sender S_i proceeds as follows.

1. Wait for $(\text{PublicKeys}, (Z_j, Y_j, z_j, y_j)_{j=1}^k)$ from $\mathcal{F}_{\text{SKS}}$.
2. Wait for an input (Send, m_i), $m_i \in G_q$. Then choose $r_i \in \mathbb{Z}_q$ randomly and compute $(u_i, v_i) = E_{(Z_1, Y_1)}(m_i, r_i) = (Z_1^{r_i}, Y_1^{r_i} m_i)$. Then hand $(\text{Prover}, (Z_1, Y_1, u_i, v_i), r_i)$ to $\mathcal{F}_{\text{ZK}}^{R_C}$, and hand $(\text{Write}, (u_i, v_i))$ to $\mathcal{F}_{\text{BB}}$.

MIX-SERVER M_j. Each mix-server M_j proceeds as follows.

1. Choose $w_j, x_j \in \mathbb{Z}_q$ randomly and hand $(\texttt{MyKey}, w_j, x_j)$ to $\mathcal{F}_{\text{SKS}}$.
2. Wait for $(\texttt{Keys}, (w_j, x_j), (Z_j, Y_j, z_j, y_j)_{j=1}^k)$ from $\mathcal{F}_{\text{SKS}}$, where $w_j, x_j \in \mathbb{Z}_q$ and $Z_j, Y_j, z_j, y_j \in G_q$.
3. Wait for an input $(\texttt{Run})$, and then hand $(\texttt{Write}, \texttt{Run})$ to $\mathcal{F}_{\text{BB}}$.
4. Wait until more than $k/2$ different mix-servers have written $\texttt{Run}$ on $\mathcal{F}_{\text{BB}}$, and let the last entry of this type be $(c_{\text{Run}}, M_i, \texttt{Run})$.
5. Form the list $L_* = \{(u_\gamma, v_\gamma)\}_{\gamma \in I_*}$, for some index set I_*, by choosing for $\gamma = 1, \ldots, N$ the entry $(c, S_\gamma, (u_\gamma, v_\gamma))$ on $\mathcal{F}_{\text{BB}}$ with the smallest $c < c_{\text{run}}$ such that $u_\gamma, v_\gamma \in G_q$, if present.
6. For each $\gamma \in I_*$ do the following,
   (a) Hand $(\texttt{Question}, S_\gamma, (Z_1, Y_1, u_\gamma, v_\gamma))$ to $\mathcal{F}_{\text{ZK}}^{R_C}$.
   (b) Wait for $(\texttt{Verifier}, S_\gamma, b_\gamma)$ from $\mathcal{F}_{\text{ZK}}^{R_C}$.
   Then form $L_0 = \{(u_{0,i}, v_{0,i})\}_{i=1}^{N'}$ consisting of pairs (u_γ, v_γ) such that $b_\gamma = 1$.
7. For $l = 1, \ldots, k$ do
   (a) If $l \neq j$, then do
      i. Wait until an entry $(c, M_l, (\texttt{List}, L_l))$ appears on $\mathcal{F}_{\text{BB}}$, where L_l is on the form $\{(u_{l,i}, v_{l,i})\}_{i=1}^{N'}$ for $u_{l,i}, v_{l,i} \in G_q$.
      ii. Hand $(\texttt{Question}, M_l, (g, z_l, y_l, L_{l-1}, L_l))$ to $\mathcal{F}_{\text{ZK}}^{R_{\text{DP}}}$, and wait for $(\texttt{Verifier}, M_l, b_l)$ from $\mathcal{F}_{\text{ZK}}^{R_{\text{DP}}}$.
      iii. If $b_l = 0$, then hand $(\texttt{Recover}, M_l)$ to $\mathcal{F}_{\text{SKS}}$, and wait for $(\texttt{Recovered}, M_l, (w_l, x_l))$ from $\mathcal{F}_{\text{SKS}}$. Then compute

$$L_l = \{(u_{l,i}, v_{l,i})\}_{i=1}^{N'} = \text{Sort}(\{(u_{l-1,i}^{1/w_l}, v_{l-1,i} u_{l-1,i}^{-x_l/w_l})\}_{i=1}^{N'}) \ .$$

   (b) If $l = j$, then compute

$$L_j = \{(u_{j,i}, v_{j,i})\}_{i=1}^{N'} = \text{Sort}(\{(u_{j-1,i}^{1/w_j}, v_{j-1,i} u_{j-1,i}^{-x_j/w_j})\}_{i=1}^{N'}) \ ,$$

   Finally hand $(\texttt{Prover}, (g, z_j, y_j, L_{j-1}, L_j), (w_j, x_j))$ to $\mathcal{F}_{\text{ZK}}^{R_{\text{DP}}}$, and hand $(\texttt{Write}, (\texttt{List}, L_j))$ to $\mathcal{F}_{\text{BB}}$.
8. Output $(\texttt{Output}, \text{Sort}(\{v_{k,i}\}_{i=1}^{N'}))$.

Theorem 1. *The ideal functionality $\mathcal{F}_{\text{MN}}$ is securely realized by π_{MN} in the $(\mathcal{F}_{\text{BB}}, \mathcal{F}_{\text{SKS}}, \mathcal{F}_{\text{ZK}}^{R_C}, \mathcal{F}_{\text{ZK}}^{R_{\text{DP}}})$-hybrid model with respect to $\mathcal{M}_{k/2}$-adversaries under the DDH-assumption in G_q.*

5   A New Efficient Proof of a Shuffle

We want to securely realize the ideal functionality $\mathcal{F}_{\text{ZK}}^{R_{\text{DP}}}$. It turns out that a useful step in this direction is to construct a statistical zero-knowledge proof for the relation R_{DP}, i.e., a proof of the decryption-permutation shuffle. First we explain the key ideas in our approach. Then we give a detailed description of our protocol. Finally, we explain how it can be turned into a public coin protocol.

5.1   Our Approach

The protocol for proving the relation R_{DP} is complex, but the underlying ideas are simple. To simplify the exposition we follow Neff [37,38] and consider the problem of proving that a list of elements in G_q are exponentiated and permuted. More precisely, let $y, u_1, \ldots, u_N, u'_1, \ldots, u'_N \in G_q$ be defined by $y = g^x$ and $u'_i = u^x_{\pi(i)}$ for a permutation π. Only the prover knows x and π and it must show that the elements satisfy such a relation. We also omit numerous technical details. In particular we remove several blinding factors, hence the protocols are not zero-knowledge as sketched here.

Extraction Using Linear Independence. The verifier chooses a list $P = (p_i)_{i=1}^N \in \mathbb{Z}_q^N$ of random primes and computes $U = \prod_{i=1}^N u_i^{p_i}$. Then it requests that the prover computes $U' = \prod_{i=1}^N (u'_i)^{p_{\pi(i)}}$, proves that $U' = U^x$ and that it knows a permutation π such that $U' = \prod_{i=1}^N (u'_i)^{p_{\pi(i)}}$.

The idea is then that if a prover succeeds in doing this it can be rewound and run several times with different random vectors P_j, giving different U_j and U'_j, until a set $P_1, \ldots, P_N$ of linearly independent vectors in $\mathbb{Z}_q^N$ are found. Linear independence implies that there are coefficients $a_{l,j} \in \mathbb{Z}_q$ such that $\sum_{j=1}^N a_{l,j} P_j$ equals the lth unity vector e_l, i.e., the vector with a one in the lth position and all other elements zero. We would then like to conclude that

$$u_l^x = \left(\prod_{j=1}^N U_j^{a_{l,j}} \right)^x = \prod_{j=1}^N (U'_j)^{a_{l,j}} = \prod_{j=1}^N \left(\prod_{i=1}^N (u'_i)^{P_{j,\pi^{-1}(i)}} \right)^{a_{l,j}} = u'_{\pi(l)} \ , \qquad (3)$$

since that would imply that the elements satisfy the shuffle-relation.

Proving a Permutation of Prime Exponents. The prover can use standard techniques to prove knowledge of integers $\rho_1, \ldots, \rho_N$ such that $U' = \prod_{i=1}^N (u'_i)^{\rho_i}$, but it must also prove that $\rho_i = p_{\pi(i)}$ for some permutation π.

Suppose that $\prod_{i=1}^N p_i = \prod_{i=1}^N \rho_i$ over $\mathbb{Z}$. Then unique factorization in $\mathbb{Z}$ implies that each ρ_i equals some product of the p_i and -1. If in addition we demand that $\rho_i \in [-2^K+1, 2^K-1]$, no such product can contain more than one factor. This implies that every product must contain exactly one factor. Thus, $\rho_i = \pm p_{\pi(i)}$ for some permutation π. If we also have $\sum_{i=1}^N p_i = \sum_{i=1}^N \rho_i$, then we must clearly have $\rho_i = p_{\pi(i)}$.

We observe that proving the above is relatively simple over a group of unknown order such as the group $\mathrm{QR}_\mathbf{N}$ of squares modulo an RSA modulus $\mathbf{N}$. The prover forms commitments

$$\mathbf{b}_0 = \mathbf{g} \ , \quad (\mathbf{b}_i, \mathbf{b}'_i)_{i=1}^N = (\mathbf{h}^{t_i} \mathbf{b}_{i-1}^{P_{\pi(i)}}, \mathbf{h}^{t'_i} \mathbf{g}^{P_{\pi(i)}})_{i=1}^N \ ,$$

with random t_i and t'_i and proves, using standard methods, knowledge of ρ_i, τ_i, τ'_i such that

$$U' = \prod_{i=1}^N (u'_i)^{\rho_i} \ , \quad \mathbf{b}_i = \mathbf{h}^{\tau_i} \mathbf{b}_{i-1}^{\rho_i} \ , \quad \text{and} \quad \mathbf{b}'_i = \mathbf{h}^{\tau'_i} \mathbf{g}^{\rho_i} \ . \qquad (4)$$

Note that $\mathbf{b}_N = \mathbf{h}^\tau \mathbf{g}^{\prod_{i=1}^N \rho_i}$ for some τ, so the verifier can check that $\prod_{i=1}^N \rho_i = \prod_{i=1}^N p_i$ by asking the prover to show that it knows τ such that $\mathbf{b}_N/\mathbf{g}^{\prod_{i=1}^N p_i} = \mathbf{h}^\tau$. We then note that a standard proof of knowledge over a group of unknown order also gives an upper bound on the bit-size of the exponents, i.e., it implicitly proves that $\rho_i \in [-2^K + 1, 2^K - 1]$. Finally, since $\prod_{i=1}^N \mathbf{b}'_i = \mathbf{h}^{\tau'} \mathbf{g}^{\sum_{i=1}^N \rho_i}$ for a $\tau' = \sum_{i=1}^N \tau'_i$, the verifier can check that $\sum_{i=1}^N \rho_i = \sum_{i=1}^N p_i$ by asking the prover to show that it knows τ' such that $\prod_{i=1}^N \mathbf{b}'_i/\mathbf{g}^{\sum_{i=1}^N p_i} = \mathbf{h}^{\tau'}$.

Fixing a Permutation. In Equation (3) above it is assumed that a fixed permutation π is used for all prime vectors $P_1, \ldots, P_N$. Unfortunately, this is not necessarily the case, i.e., the permutation used in the jth proof may depend on j and we should really write π_j.

To solve this technical problem we force the prover to commit to a fixed permutation π before it receives the prime vector P. The commitment is on the form $(w_i)_{i=1}^N = (g^{r'_i} g_{\pi^{-1}(i)})_{i=1}^N$. The verifier then computes $W = \prod_{i=1}^N w_i^{p_i}$ and the prover proves that $W = g^{r'} \prod_{i=1}^N g_i^{p_i}$ in addition to Equations (4). The idea is that the prover must use π to permute the p_i or find a non-trivial representation of $1 \in G_q$ using $g, g_1, \ldots, g_N$, which is infeasible under the DL-assumption.

5.2 An Honest Verifier Statistical Zero-Knowledge Computationally Convincing Proof of Knowledge of a Decryption-Permutation

In this section we describe our proof of a shuffle in detail. Although we consider a decrypt-permutation relation, our approach can be generalized to a proof of a shuffle for the other shuffle relations considered in the literature. In the full version [50] we detail such shuffles, including a shuffle of Paillier [41] cryptotexts.

We introduce several security parameters. We use K_1 to denote the number of bits in q, the order of the group G_q, and similarly K_2 to denote the number of bits in the RSA-modulus $\mathbf{N}$. We use K_3 to denote the number bits used in the random primes mentioned above. At some point in the protocol the verifier hands a challenge to the prover. We use K_4 to denote the number of bits in this challenge. At several points exponents must be padded with random bits to achieve statistical zero-knowledge. We use K_5 to denote the number of additional random bits used to do this. We assume that the security parameters are chosen such that $K_3 + K_4 + K_5 < K_1, K_2$, and $K_5 < K_3 - 2$. Below the protocol we explain how the informal description above relates to the different components of the protocol.

Protocol 2 (Proof of Decryption-Permutation). The common input consists of an RSA modulus $\mathbf{N}$ and $\mathbf{g}, \mathbf{h} \in \mathrm{QR}_\mathbf{N}$, generators $g, g_1, \ldots, g_N \in G_q$, a public key $(z, y) \in G_q^2$, and two lists $L = (u_i, v_i)_{i=1}^N$ and $L' = (u'_i, v'_i)_{i=1}^N$ in G_q^{2N}. The private input to the prover consists of $(w, x) \in \mathbb{Z}_q^2$ such that $(z, y) = (g^w, g^x)$ and $(u'_i, v'_i) = (u_{\pi(i)}^{1/w}, v_{\pi(i)}/u_{\pi(i)}^{x/w})$ for a permutation $\pi \in \Sigma_N$ such that L' is lexicographically sorted.

1. The prover chooses $r'_i \in \mathbb{Z}_q$ randomly, computes $(w_i)_{i=1}^N = (g^{r'_i} g_{\pi^{-1}(i)})_{i=1}^N$, and hands $(w_i)_{i=1}^N$ to the verifier.
2. The verifier chooses random primes $p_1, \ldots, p_N \in [2^{K_3-1}, 2^{K_3} - 1]$, and hands $(p_i)_{i=1}^N$ to the prover.
3. Both parties compute $(U, V, W) = (\prod_{i=1}^N u_i^{p_i}, \prod_{i=1}^N v_i^{p_i}, \prod_{i=1}^N w_i^{p_i})$.
4. The prover chooses the following elements randomly $k_1, k_2, k_3, k_4, k_5 \in \mathbb{Z}_q$, $l_1, \ldots, l_7, l_{r'}, l_{1/w}, l_{x/w}, l_w, l_x \in \mathbb{Z}_q$, $t_i, t'_i \in [0, 2^{K_2+K_5} - 1]$, $s_i, s'_i \in [0, 2^{K_2+K_4+2K_5} - 1]$, $r_i \in [0, 2^{K_3+K_4+K_5} - 1]$ for $i = 1, \ldots, N$, $s \in [0, 2^{K_2+NK_3+K_4+K_5+\log_2 N} - 1]$, and $s' \in [0, 2^{K_2+K_5+\log_2 N} - 1]$. Then the prover computes

$$(b_1, b_2) = (g^{k_1} U^{1/w}, g^{k_2} U^{x/w}) \tag{5}$$

$$(b_3, b_4, b_5) = (g_1^{k_3} g^{1/w}, g_1^{k_4} b_3^x, g_1^{k_5} b_3^w) \tag{6}$$

$$(\beta_1, \beta_2) = (g^{l_1} U^{l_{1/w}}, g^{l_2} U^{l_{x/w}}) \tag{7}$$

$$(\beta_3, \beta_4) = (g_1^{l_3} g^{l_{1/w}}, g_1^{l_6} g^{l_{x/w}}) \tag{8}$$

$$(\beta_5, \beta_6, \beta_7, \beta_8, \beta_9) = (g_1^{l_4} b_3^{l_x}, g^{l_x}, g_1^{l_5} b_3^{l_w}, g^{l_w}, g_1^{l_7}) \tag{9}$$

$$(\alpha_1, \alpha_2, \alpha_3) = \left(g^{l_1} \prod_{i=1}^N (u'_i)^{r_i}, g^{-l_2} \prod_{i=1}^N (v'_i)^{r_i}, g^{l_{r'}} \prod_{i=1}^N g_i^{r_i} \right) \tag{10}$$

$$\mathbf{b}_0 = \mathbf{g} \tag{11}$$

$$(\mathbf{b}_i, \mathbf{b}'_i)_{i=1}^N = (\mathbf{h}^{t_i} \mathbf{b}_{i-1}^{p_{\pi(i)}}, \mathbf{h}^{t'_i} \mathbf{g}^{p_{\pi(i)}})_{i=1}^N \tag{12}$$

$$(\boldsymbol{\gamma}_i, \boldsymbol{\gamma}'_i)_{i=1}^N = (\mathbf{h}^{s_i} \mathbf{b}_{i-1}^{r_i}, \mathbf{h}^{s'_i} \mathbf{g}^{r_i})_{i=1}^N \tag{13}$$

$$(\boldsymbol{\gamma}, \boldsymbol{\gamma}') = (\mathbf{h}^s, \mathbf{h}^{s'}) , \tag{14}$$

and $((b_i)_{i=1}^5, (\beta_i)_{i=1}^9, (\alpha_1, \alpha_2, \alpha_3), (\mathbf{b}_i, \mathbf{b}'_i)_{i=1}^N, (\boldsymbol{\gamma}_i, \boldsymbol{\gamma}'_i)_{i=1}^N, (\boldsymbol{\gamma}, \boldsymbol{\gamma}'))$ is handed to the verifier.

5. The verifier chooses $c \in [2^{K_4-1}, 2^{K_4} - 1]$ randomly and hands c to the prover.
6. Define $t = t_N + p_{\pi(N)}(t_{N-1} + p_{\pi(N-1)}(t_{N-2} + p_{\pi(N-2)}(t_{N-3} + p_{\pi(N-3)}(\ldots))))$, $t' = \sum_{i=1}^N t'_i$, $r' = \sum_{i=1}^N r'_i p_i$, $k_6 = k_4 + k_3 x$, and $k_7 = k_5 + k_3 w$. The prover computes

$$
\begin{aligned}
(f_i)_{i=1}^7 &= (ck_i + l_i)_{i=1}^7 & \text{mod } q \\
(f_{1/w}, f_{x/w}) &= (c/w + l_{1/w}, cx/w + l_{x/w}) & \text{mod } q \\
(f_w, f_x) &= (cw + l_w, cx + l_x) & \text{mod } q \\
f_{r'} &= cr' + l_{r'} & \text{mod } q \\
(e_i, e'_i)_{i=1}^N &= (ct_i + s_i, ct'_i + s'_i)_{i=1}^N & \text{mod } 2^{K_2+K_4+2K_5} \\
(d_i)_{i=1}^N &= (cp_{\pi(i)} + r_i)_{i=1}^N & \text{mod } 2^{K_3+K_4+K_5} \\
e &= ct + s & \text{mod } 2^{K_2+NK_3+K_4+K_5+\log_2 N} \\
e' &= ct' + s' & \text{mod } 2^{K_2+K_5+\log_2 N}
\end{aligned}
$$

Then it hands $(((f_i)_{i=1}^7, f_{1/w}, f_{x/w}, f_w, f_x, f_{r'}), (e_i, e'_i)_{i=1}^N, (d_i)_{i=1}^N, (e, e'))$ to the verifier.

7. The verifier checks that $b_i, \beta_i, \alpha_i \in G_q$, and that L' is lexicographically sorted and that

$$(b_1^c \beta_1, b_2^c \beta_2) = (g^{f_1} U^{f_1/w}, g^{f_2} U^{f_x/w}) \tag{15}$$

$$(b_3^c \beta_3, b_4^c \beta_4) = (g_1^{f_3} g^{f_1/w}, g_1^{f_6} g^{f_x/w}) \tag{16}$$

$$(b_4^c \beta_5, y^c \beta_6) = (g_1^{f_4} b_3^{f_x}, g^{f_x}) \tag{17}$$

$$(b_5^c \beta_7, z^c \beta_8, (b_5/g)^c \beta_9) = (g_1^{f_5} b_3^{f_w}, g^{f_w}, g_1^{f_7}) \tag{18}$$

$$(b_1^c \alpha_1, (V/b_2)^c \alpha_2, W^c \alpha_3) = \left(g^{f_1} \prod_{i=1}^{N} (u_i')^{d_i}, g^{-f_2} \prod_{i=1}^{N} (v_i')^{d_i}, g^{f_{r'}} \prod_{i=1}^{N} g_i^{d_i} \right) \tag{19}$$

$$(\mathbf{b}_i^c \boldsymbol{\gamma}_i, (\mathbf{b}_i')^c \boldsymbol{\gamma}_i')_{i=1}^{N} = (\mathbf{h}^{e_i} \mathbf{b}_{i-1}^{d_i}, \mathbf{h}^{e_i'} \mathbf{g}^{d_i})_{i=1}^{N} \tag{20}$$

$$(\mathbf{g}^{-\prod_{i=1}^{N} p_i} \mathbf{b}_N)^c \boldsymbol{\gamma} = \mathbf{h}^e \tag{21}$$

$$\left(\mathbf{g}^{-\sum_{i=1}^{N} p_i} \prod_{i=1}^{N} \mathbf{b}_i' \right)^c \boldsymbol{\gamma}' = \mathbf{h}^{e'} . \tag{22}$$

Equations (5)-(9) are used to prove that $(b_1, V/b_2) = (g^{\kappa_1} U^{1/w}, g^{-\kappa_2} V/U^{x/w})$ using standard Schnorr-like proofs of knowledge of logarithms. Equations (12) contain commitments corresponding to those in the outline of our approach. Equations (13) are used to prove knowledge of exponents τ_i, τ_i', ρ_i such that $(\mathbf{b}_i, \mathbf{b}_i') = (\mathbf{h}^{\tau_i} \mathbf{b}_{i-1}^{\rho_i}, \mathbf{h}^{\tau_i'} \mathbf{g}^{\rho_i})$. We remark that the verifier need not check that $\mathbf{b}_i, \mathbf{b}_i', \boldsymbol{\gamma}_i, \boldsymbol{\gamma}_i', \boldsymbol{\gamma}, \boldsymbol{\gamma}' \in QR_\mathbf{N}$ for our analysis to go through. Equations (14) are used to prove that $\prod_{i=1}^{N} \rho_i = \prod_{i=1}^{N} p_i$ and $\sum_{i=1}^{N} \rho_i = \sum_{i=1}^{N} p_i$, i.e., that ρ_i in fact equals $p_{\pi(i)}$ for some permutation π. Equation (10) is used to prove that $(b_1, V/b_2)$ also equals $(g^{k_1} \prod_{i=1}^{N} (u_i^{1/w_j})^{p_i}, g^{-k_2} \prod_{i=1}^{N} (v_i/u_i^{x_j/w_j})^{p_i})$. If the two ways of writing b_1 and b_2 are combined we have

$$(U^{1/w}, V/U^{x/w}) = \left(\prod_{i=1}^{N} (u_i^{1/w_j})^{p_i}, \prod_{i=1}^{N} (v_i/u_i^{x_j/w_j})^{p_i} \right) ,$$

which by the argument in Section 5.1 implies that $((g, z, y, L, L'), (w, x)) \in R_{DP}$.

5.3 Security Properties

Formally, the security properties of our protocol are captured by the following.

Proposition 1 (Zero-Knowledge). *Protocol 2 is honest verifier statistical zero-knowledge.*

The protocol could be modified by adding a first step, where the verifier chooses $(\mathbf{N}, \mathbf{g}, \mathbf{h})$ and $(g_1, \ldots, g_N)$. This would give a computationally sound proof of knowledge. However, in our application we wish to choose these parameters jointly and only once, and then let the mix-servers execute the proof with these parameters as common inputs. Thus, there may be a negligible portion of the parameters on which the prover can convince the verifier of false statements. Because of this we cannot hope to prove that the protocol is a proof of knowledge in the formal sense. Damgård and Fujisaki [12] introduce the notion of a computationally convincing proof of knowledge to deal with situations like these. We do not use the notion of "computationally convincing proofs" explicitly in our security analysis, but the proposition below implies that our protocol satisfies their definition.

We consider a malicious prover A which is given $\boldsymbol{\Gamma} = (\mathbf{N}, \mathbf{g}, \mathbf{h})$ and $\bar{g} = (g, g_1, \ldots, g_N)$ as input and run with internal randomness r_p. The prover outputs an instance $I_A(\boldsymbol{\Gamma}, \bar{g}, r_p)$, i.e., public keys $z, y \in G_q$ and two lists $L, L' \in G_q^{2N}$ and then interacts with the honest verifier on the common input consisting of $(\boldsymbol{\Gamma}, \bar{g}, z, y, L, L')$. Denote by $T_A(\boldsymbol{\Gamma}, \bar{g}, r_p, r_v)$ the transcript of such an interaction when the verifier runs with internal randomness r_v. Let Acc be the predicate taking a transcript T as input that outputs 1 if the transcript is accepting and 0 otherwise. Let $L_{R_{DP}}$ be the language corresponding to the decryption-permutation relation R_{DP}. We prove the following proposition.

Proposition 2 (Soundness). *Suppose the strong RSA-assumption and the DL-assumption are true. Then for all polynomial-size circuit families $A = \{A_K\}$ it holds that $\forall c > 0$, $\exists K_0$, such that for $K_1 \geq K_0$*

$$\Pr_{\boldsymbol{\Gamma}, \bar{g}, r_p, r_v} [\mathrm{Acc}(T_A(\boldsymbol{\Gamma}, \bar{g}, r_p, r_v)) = 1 \wedge I_A(\boldsymbol{\Gamma}, \bar{g}, r_p) \notin L_{R_{DP}}] < \frac{1}{K_1^c} .$$

5.4 Generation of Primes from a Small Number of Public Coins

In our protocol the verifier must generate vectors in $\mathbb{Z}_q^N$ such that each component is a "randomly" chosen prime in $[2^{K_3-1}, 2^{K_3}-1]$. We define a generator PGen that generates prime vectors from public coins. Let $p(n)$ be the smallest prime at least as large as n. Our generator PGen takes as input N random integers $n_1, \ldots, n_N \in [2^{K_3-1}, 2^{K_3} - 1]$ and internal randomness r, and defines $p_i = p(n_i)$. To find p_i it first redefines n_i such that it is odd by incrementing by one if necessary. Then it executes the Miller-Rabin primality test for $n_i, n_i + 2, n_i + 4, \ldots$ until it finds a prime. We put an explicit bound on the running time of the generator by bounding the number of integers it considers and the number of iterations of the Miller-Rabin test it performs in total. If the generator stops due to one of these bounds it outputs $\perp$. If $N \geq K_3$, the bound corresponds to $\frac{6K_3^4}{K_1^3}N$ exponentiations modulo a K_1-bit integer. The generator can be used in the obvious way to turn the protocol above into a public-coin protocol. The verifier sends $(n_1, \ldots, n_N, r)$ to the prover instead of $p_1, \ldots, p_N$ and the prover and verifier generates the primes by computing $(p_1, \ldots, p_N) = \mathsf{PGen}(n_1, \ldots, n_N, r)$. A result by Baker and Harman [4] implies that the resulting distribution is close to uniform.

Theorem 2 (cf. [4]). *For large integers n there exists a prime in $[n - n^{0.535}, n]$.*

Corollary 1. *For all primes $p \in [2^{K_3-1}, 2^{K_3} - 1]$, $\Pr[p(n) = p] \leq 2^{-0.465(K_3-1)}$, where the probability is taken over a random choice of $n \in [2^{K_3-1}, 2^{K_3} - 1]$*

The corollary gives a very pessimistic bound. It is commonly believed that the theorem is true with 0.465 replaced by any constant less than one. Furthermore, Cramér argues probabilistically that there is a prime in every interval $[n - \log^2 n, n]$. See Ribenboim [46] for a discussion on this.

We must argue that the generator fails with negligible probability. There are two ways the generator can fail. Either it outputs $p_1, \ldots, p_N$, where $p_i \neq p(n_i)$ for some i, or it outputs $\bot$.

Lemma 1. *The probability that* $\mathsf{PGen}(n_1, \ldots, n_N, r) \neq (p(n_1), \ldots, p(n_N))$ *conditioned on* $\mathsf{PGen}(n_1, \ldots, n_N, r) \neq \bot$ *is negligible.*

Unfortunately, the current understanding of the distribution of the primes does not allow a strict analysis of the probability that $\mathsf{PGen}(n_1, \ldots, n_N, r) = \bot$. Instead we give a heuristic analysis in Cramér's probabilistic model of the primes.

Definition 4 (Cramér's Model). *For each integer n, let X_n be an independent binary random variable such that* $\Pr[X_n = 1] = 1/\ln n$. *An integer n is said to be prime* if $X_n = 1$.*

The idea is to consider the primality of the integers as a typical outcome of the sequence $(X_n)_{n \in \mathbb{Z}}$. Thus, when we analyze the generator we assume that the primality of an integer n is given by X_n, and our analysis is both over the internal randomness of PGen and the randomness of X_n.

Lemma 2. *In Cramér's model the probability that* $\mathsf{PGen}(n_1, \ldots, n_N, r) = \bot$ *is negligible.*

We stress that zero-knowledge and soundness of the modified protocol are not heuristic. The zero-knowledge property holds for arbitrarily distributed *integers* p_i. Soundness follows from Lemma 1. It is only completeness that is argued heuristically. Although this is not always clear, similar heuristic arguments are common in the literature, e.g. to generate safe primes and to encode arbitrary messages in G_q. We assume that Lemma 2 is true from now on.

Although we now have a public-coin protocol it requires many random bits. This can be avoided by use of a pseudo-random generator PRG as suggested by Groth [28]. Instead of choosing $n_1, \ldots, n_N$ randomly and sending these integers to the prover, the verifier chooses a random seed $s \in [0, 2^{K_1} - 1]$ and hands this to the prover. The prover and verifier then computes $(n_1, \ldots, n_N) = \mathsf{PRG}(s)$ and computes the primes from the integers as described above. The output $(p_1, \ldots, p_N)$ may not appear to the prover as random, since he holds the seed s. However, we prove in the full version [50] that if we define $P_j = \mathsf{PGen}(\mathsf{PRG}(s))$ and let $P_1, \ldots, P_{j-1} \in \mathbb{Z}_q^N$ be any linearly independent vectors, the probability that $P_j \in \mathrm{Span}(P_1, \ldots, P_{j-1})$ or $p_{j,i} = p_{j,l}$ for some $i \neq l$ is negligible for all $1 \leq j \leq N$. This is all we need in our application.

Universal Verifiability and Random Oracles. If the Fiat-Shamir heuristic is applied to a proof of a shuffle, any outsider can check, non-interactively, that a mix-server behaves correctly. If the verification involves no trusted parameters the resulting mix-net is called "universally verifiable". In our protocol the RSA parameters $(\mathbf{N}, \mathbf{g}, \mathbf{h})$ must be trusted by the verifier and we do not see how these can be generated from public coins. Thus, if the Fiat-Shamir heuristic is applied to our protocol the result is not really universally verifiable.

However, we can achieve universal verifiability under the root assumption in class groups with prime discriminant. A class group is defined by its discriminant Δ. It is conjectured that finding non-trivial roots in a class group with discriminant $\Delta = -p$ for a prime p is infeasible (cf. [29]). The idea would be to generate a prime p of suitable size from random coins handed to the prover by the verifier in the first round. Then the integer part of the protocol would be executed in the class group defined by $\Delta = -p$. With this modification the protocol gives a universally verifiable mix-net.

5.5   Complexity

Comparing the complexity of protocols is tricky, since any comparison must take place for equal security rather than for equal security parameters. The only rigorous method to do this is to perform an exact security analysis of each protocol and choose the security parameters accordingly. Various optimization and pre-computing techniques are also applicable to different degrees in different protocols and in different applications. Despite this we argue informally, but carefully, in the full paper [50] that the complexity of our protocol is at least as good as that of the most efficient previous proofs of a shuffle.

More precisely, our protocol requires 5 rounds as the previously known most round efficient proof of a shuffle [21] involving decryption. Furthermore, for practical parameters, e.g. $K_1 = 2048$, $K_2 = 1024$, $K_4 = 160$, $K_3 = 100$, and $K_5 = 50$, the complexity is less than $2.5N$ and $1.6N$ general exponentiations in G_q for the prover and verifier. With optimizations as in [21] this corresponds to $0.5N$ and $0.8N$ general exponentiations in G_q, which indicates that the protocol is at least as fast as that in [21].

6   Secure Realization of $\mathcal{F}_{\mathrm{ZK}}^{R_{\mathrm{DP}}}$

In this section we transform the proof of a shuffle into a secure realization of $\mathcal{F}_{\mathrm{ZK}}^{R_{\mathrm{DP}}}$ in a $(\mathcal{F}_{\mathrm{RSA}}, \mathcal{F}_{\mathrm{CF}}, \mathcal{F}_{\mathrm{BB}})$-hybrid model, where $\mathcal{F}_{\mathrm{RSA}}$ is an RSA common reference string functionality, and $\mathcal{F}_{\mathrm{CF}}$ is a coin flipping functionality.

Functionality 4 (RSA Common Reference String). The ideal *RSA Common Reference String*, $\mathcal{F}_{\mathrm{RSA}}$, with mix-servers $M_1, \ldots, M_k$ and ideal adversary $\mathcal{S}$ proceeds as follows.

1. Generate two random $K_2/2$-bit primes $\mathbf{p}$ and $\mathbf{q}$ such that $(\mathbf{p} - 1)/2$ and $(\mathbf{q} - 1)/2$ are prime and compute $\mathbf{N} = \mathbf{pq}$. Then choose $\mathbf{g}$ and $\mathbf{h}$ randomly in $\mathrm{QR}_{\mathbf{N}}$. Finally, hand $((\mathcal{S}, \mathtt{RSA}, \mathbf{N}, \mathbf{g}, \mathbf{h}), \{(M_j, \mathtt{RSA}, \mathbf{N}, \mathbf{g}, \mathbf{h})\}_{j=1}^k)$ to $\mathcal{C}_{\mathcal{I}}$.

There are protocols [6,16] for generating a joint RSA modulus, but these are not analyzed in the UC-framework, so for technical reasons we cannot apply these directly. If these protocols cannot be used to give a UC-secure protocol, general methods [11] can be used since this need only be done once.

Functionality 5 (Coin-Flipping). The ideal *Coin-Flipping functionality*, $\mathcal{F}_{\mathrm{CF}}$, with mix-servers $M_1, \ldots, M_k$, and adversary $\mathcal{S}$ proceeds as follows.

1. Set $J_K, = \emptyset$ for all K.
2. On reception of $(M_j, \mathtt{GenerateCoins}, K)$ from $\mathcal{C}_{\mathcal{I}}$, set $J_K \leftarrow J_K \cup \{j\}$. If $|J_K| > k/2$, then set $J_K \leftarrow \emptyset$ choose $c \in \{0,1\}^K$ and hand $((\mathcal{S}, \mathtt{Coins}, c), \{(M_j, \mathtt{Coins}, c)\}_{j=1}^k)$ to $\mathcal{C}_{\mathcal{I}}$.

It is not hard to securely realize the coin-flipping functionality using a UC-secure verifiable secret sharing scheme (cf. [1]). Each mix-server M_j chooses a random string c_j of K bits and secretly shares it. Then all secrets are reconstructed and c is defined as $\oplus_{j=1}^k c_j$.

Finally, we give the protocol which securely realizes $\mathcal{F}_{\mathrm{ZK}}^{R_{\mathrm{DP}}}$. This is essentially a translation of Protocol 2 into a multiparty protocol in the UC-setting.

Protocol 3 (Zero-Knowledge Proof of Decryption-Permutation). The protocol $\pi_{\mathrm{DP}} = (M_1, \ldots, M_k)$ consists of mix-servers M_j and proceeds as follows.

MIX-SERVER M_j. Each mix-server M_j proceeds as follows.

1. Wait for $(\mathrm{RSA}, \mathbf{N}, \mathbf{g}, \mathbf{h})$ from $\mathcal{F}_{\mathrm{RSA}}$. Then hand $(\mathtt{GenerateCoins}, NK_1)$ to $\mathcal{F}_{\mathrm{CF}}$ and wait until it returns $(\mathtt{Coins}, (g_1', \ldots, g_N'))$. Then map these strings to elements in G_q by $g_i = (g_i')^{(p-1)/q} \bmod p$ (recall that $G_q \subset \mathbb{Z}_p^*$).
2. On input $(\mathtt{Prover}, (g, z, y, L, L'), (w, x))$, where $((g, z, y, L, L'), (w, x)) \in L_{R_{\mathrm{DP}}}$
   (a) Hand $(\mathtt{Prover}, (g, z, 1, 1), w)$ and $(\mathtt{Prover}, (g, y, 1, 1), x)$ to $\mathcal{F}_{\mathrm{ZK}}^{R_C}$.
   (b) Denote by W the first message of the prover in Protocol 2. Then hand $(\mathtt{Write}, \mathtt{W}, W)$ to $\mathcal{F}_{\mathrm{BB}}$.
   (c) Then hand $(\mathtt{GenerateCoins}, K_1)$ to $\mathcal{F}_{\mathrm{CF}}$ and wait until it returns $(\mathtt{Coins}, s)$. Then set $P = \mathsf{PGen}(\mathsf{PRG}(s))$. If $P = \bot$ go to Step 2c, otherwise let P be the primes used by the prover in Protocol 2.
   (d) Denote by C the second message of the prover in Protocol 2. Hand $(\mathtt{Write}, \mathtt{C}, C)$ to $\mathcal{F}_{\mathrm{BB}}$. Then hand $(\mathtt{GenerateCoins}, K_4 - 1)$ to $\mathcal{F}_{\mathrm{CF}}$ and wait until it returns $(\mathtt{Coins}, c')$. Let $c = c' + 2^{K_4 - 1}$ be the final challenge in Protocol 2.
   (e) Denote by R the third message of the prover in Protocol 2. Hand $(\mathtt{Write}, \mathtt{R}, R)$ to $\mathcal{F}_{\mathrm{BB}}$.
3. On input $(\mathtt{Question}, M_l, (g, z, y, L, L'))$, where $L, L' \in G_q^{2N}$ and $(z, y) \in G_q$
   (a) Hand $(\mathtt{Question}, M_l, (g, z, 1, 1))$ to $\mathcal{F}_{\mathrm{ZK}}^{R_C}$ and wait until it returns $(\mathtt{Verifier}, M_l, b_{z,l})$. Then hand $(\mathtt{Question}, M_l, (g, y, 1, 1))$ and wait until it returns $(\mathtt{Verifier}, M_l, b_{y,l})$. If $b_{z,l} b_{y,l} = 0$ output $(\mathtt{Verifier}, M_l, 0)$.
   (b) Then wait until $(M_l, \mathtt{W}, W)$ appears on $\mathcal{F}_{\mathrm{BB}}$. Hand $(\mathtt{GenerateCoins}, K_1)$ to $\mathcal{F}_{\mathrm{CF}}$ and wait until it returns $(\mathtt{Coins}, s)$. Then set $P = \mathsf{PGen}(\mathsf{PRG}(s))$. If $P = \bot$ go to Step 3b, otherwise let P be the primes used by the verifier in Protocol 2.

(c) Wait until $(M_l, \mathtt{C}, C)$ appears on $\mathcal{F}_{\mathrm{BB}}$. Then hand $(\mathtt{GenerateCoins}, K_4 - 1)$ to $\mathcal{F}_{\mathrm{CF}}$ and wait until it returns $(\mathtt{Coins}, c')$, and until $(M_l, \mathtt{R}, R)$ appears on $\mathcal{F}_{\mathrm{BB}}$. Let $c = c' + 2^{K_4-1}$ be the final challenge in Protocol 2. Then verify (W, P, C, c, R) as in Protocol 2 and set $b_j = 1$ or $b_j = 0$ depending on the result.

(d) Hand $(\mathtt{Write}, \mathtt{Judgement}, M_l, b_j)$ to $\mathcal{F}_{\mathrm{BB}}$ and wait until $(M_{l'}, \mathtt{Judgement}, M_l, b_{l'})$ appears on $\mathcal{F}_{\mathrm{BB}}$ for $l' \neq j$. Set $b = 1$ if $|\{b_{l'} \mid b_{l'} = 1\}| > k/2$ and otherwise $b = 0$. Output $(\mathtt{Verifier}, M_l, L, L', b)$.

Theorem 3. *The ideal functionality $\mathcal{F}_{\mathrm{ZK}}^{R_{\mathrm{DP}}}$ is securely realized by π_{DP} in the $(\mathcal{F}_{\mathrm{ZK}}^{R_{\mathrm{C}}}, \mathcal{F}_{\mathrm{CF}}, \mathcal{F}_{\mathrm{RSA}}, \mathcal{F}_{\mathrm{BB}})$-hybrid model with respect to $\mathcal{M}_{k/2}$-adversaries under the DL-assumption and the strong RSA-assumption.*

Corollary 2. *The composition of π_{MN}, π_{C}, π_{DP}, securely realizes $\mathcal{F}_{\mathrm{MN}}$ in the $(\mathcal{F}_{\mathrm{SKS}}, \mathcal{F}_{\mathrm{CF}}, \mathcal{F}_{\mathrm{RSA}}, \mathcal{F}_{\mathrm{BB}})$-hybrid model with respect to $\mathcal{M}_{k/2}$-adversaries under the DDH-assumption and the strong RSA-assumption.*

As indicated in the body of the paper all assumptions except the assumption of a bulletin board can be eliminated. The assumption of a bulletin board can only be eliminated for blocking adversaries (cf. [49]).

7   Conclusion

We have introduced a novel way to construct a mix-net, and given the first provably secure sender verifiable mix-net. We have also introduced a novel approach to construct a proof of a shuffle, and shown how this can be used to securely realize the ideal zero-knowledge proof of knowledge functionality for a decrypt-permutation relation. Combined, this gives the first universally composable mix-net that is efficient for any number of mix-servers.

Acknowledgments

I thank Johan Håstad for excellent advise, in particular for discussing efficient generation of the primes. I also thank Mårten Trolin for discussions.

References

1. M. Abe, S. Fehr, *Adaptively Secure Feldman VSS and Applications to Universally-Composable Threshold Cryptography*, to appear at Crypto 2004. (full version at Cryptology ePrint Archive, Report 2004/118, http://eprint.iacr.org/, May, 2004).
2. M. Abe, *Universally Verifiable mix-net with Verification Work Independent of the Number of Mix-centers*, Eurocrypt '98, pp. 437-447, LNCS 1403, 1998.
3. M. Abe, *Flaws in Some Robust Optimistic Mix-Nets*, In Proceedings of Information Security and Privacy, 8th Australasian Conference, LNCS 2727, pp. 39-50, 2003.

4. R. C. Baker and G. Harman, *The difference between consecutive primes*, Proc. Lond. Math. Soc., series 3, 72 (1996) 261–280.
5. D. Beaver, *Foundations of secure interactive computation*, Crypto '91, LNCS 576, pp. 377-391, 1991.
6. D. Boneh, and M. Franklin, *Efficient generation of shared RSA keys*, Crypto' 97, LNCS 1233, pp. 425-439, 1997.
7. J. Buus Nielsen, *Universally Composable Zero-Knowledge Proof of Membership*, manuscript, http://www.brics.dk/~buus/, April, 2005.
8. R. Canetti, *Security and composition of multi-party cryptographic protocols*, Journal of Cryptology, Vol. 13, No. 1, winter 2000.
9. R. Canetti, *Universally Composable Security: A New Paradigm for Cryptographic Protocols*, http://eprint.iacr.org/2000/067 and ECCC TR 01-24. Extended abstract appears in 42nd FOCS, IEEE Computer Society, 2001.
10. D. Chaum, *Untraceable Electronic Mail, Return Addresses and Digital Pseudonyms*, Communications of the ACM - CACM '81, Vol. 24, No. 2, pp. 84-88, 1981.
11. R. Canetti, Y. Lindell, R. Ostrovsky, A. Sahai, *Universally Composable Two-Party and Multi-Party Secure Computation*, 34th STOC, pp. 494-503, 2002.
12. I. Damgård, E. Fujisaki, *A Statistically-Hiding Integer Commitment Scheme Based on Groups with Hidden Order*, Asiacrypt 2002, LNCS 2501, pp. 125-142, 2002.
13. Y. Desmedt, K. Kurosawa, *How to break a practical MIX and design a new one*, Eurocrypt 2000, pp. 557-572, LNCS 1807, 2000.
14. T. El Gamal, *A Public Key Cryptosystem and a Signature Scheme Based on Discrete Logarithms*, IEEE Transactions on Information Theory, Vol. 31, No. 4, pp. 469-472, 1985.
15. P. Feldman, *A practical scheme for non-interactive verifiable secret sharing*, 28th FOCS, pp. 427-438, 1987.
16. P. Fouque and J. Stern, *Fully Distributed Threshold RSA under Standard Assumptions*, Cryptology ePrint Archive, Report 2001/008, 2001.
17. A. Fujioka, T. Okamoto and K. Ohta, *A practical secret voting scheme for large scale elections*, Auscrypt '92, LNCS 718, pp. 244-251, 1992.
18. E. Fujisaki, T. Okamoto, *Statistical Zero Knowledge Protocols to Prove Modular Polynomial Relations*, Crypto 97, LNCS 1294, pp. 16-30, 1997.
19. J. Furukawa, K. Sako, *An efficient scheme for proving a shuffle*, Crypto 2001, LNCS 2139, pp. 368-387, 2001.
20. J. Furukawa, H. Miyauchi, K. Mori, S. Obana, K. Sako, *An implementation of a universally verifiable electronic voting scheme based on shuffling*, Financial Cryptography '02, 2002.
21. J. Furukawa, *Efficient, Verifiable Shuffle Decryption and its Requirements of Unlinkability*, PKC 2004, LNCS 2947, pp. 319-332, 2004.
22. O. Goldreich, S. Micali, and A. Wigderson, *How to Play Any Mental Game*, 19th STOC, pp. 218-229, 1987.
23. O. Goldreich, *Foundations of Cryptography*, Cambridge University Press, 2001.
24. S. Goldwasser, L. Levin, *Fair computation of general functions in presence of immoral majority*, Crypto '90, LNCS 537, pp. 77-93, 1990.
25. S. Goldwasser, S. Micali, *Probabilistic Encryption*, Journal of Computer and System Sciences (JCSS), Vol. 28, No. 2, pp. 270-299, 1984.
26. P. Golle, S. Zhong, D. Boneh, M. Jakobsson, A. Juels, *Optimistic Mixing for Exit-Polls*, Asiacrypt 2002, LNCS, 2002.
27. N. Groth, *A Verifiable Secret Shuffle of Homomorphic Encryptions*, PKC 2003, pp. 145-160, LNCS 2567, 2003.

28. N. Groth, *Personal Communication*, 2004.
29. J. Buchmann, S. Hamdy, *A Survey on IQ Cryptography*, In Public-Key Cryptography and Computational Number Theory, Walter de Gruyter, pp. 1-15, 2001.
30. M. Jakobsson, *A Practical Mix*, Eurocrypt '98, LNCS 1403, pp. 448-461, 1998.
31. M. Jakobsson, *Flash Mixing*, In Proceedings of the 18th ACM Symposium on Principles of Distributed Computing - PODC '98, pp. 83-89, 1998.
32. M. Jakobsson, A. Juels, *Millimix: Mixing in small batches*, DIMACS Techical report 99-33, June 1999.
33. M. Jakobsson, A. Juels, *An optimally robust hybrid mix network*, In Proceedings of the 20th ACM Symposium on Principles of Distributed Computing - PODC '01, pp. 284-292, 2001.
34. S. Micali, P. Rogaway, *Secure Computation*, Crypto '91, LNCS 576, pp. 392-404, 1991.
35. M. Michels, P. Horster, *Some remarks on a reciept-free and universally verifiable Mix-type voting scheme*, Asiacrypt '96, pp. 125-132, LNCS 1163, 1996.
36. M. Mitomo, K. Kurosawa, *Attack for Flash MIX*, Asiacrypt 2000, pp. 192-204, LNCS 1976, 2000.
37. A. Neff, *A verifiable secret shuffle and its application to E-Voting*, In Proceedings of the 8th ACM Conference on Computer and Communications Security - CCS 2001, pp. 116-125, 2001.
38. A. Neff, *Verifiable Mixing (Shuffling) of ElGamal Pairs*, preliminary full version of [37], http://www.votehere.com/documents.html, Mars, 2005.
39. V. Niemi, A. Renvall, *How to prevent buying of votes in computer elections*, Asiacrypt'94, LNCS 917, pp. 164-170, 1994.
40. W. Ogata, K. Kurosawa, K. Sako, K. Takatani, *Fault Tolerant Anonymous Channel*, Information and Communications Security - ICICS '97, pp. 440-444, LNCS 1334, 1997.
41. P. Paillier, *Public-Key Cryptosystems Based on Composite Degree Residuosity Classes*, Eurocrypt '99, LNCS 1592, pp. 223-238, 1999.
42. C. Park, K. Itoh, K. Kurosawa, *Efficient Anonymous Channel and All/Nothing Election Scheme*, Eurocrypt '93, LNCS 765, pp. 248-259, 1994.
43. B. Pfitzmann, *Breaking an Efficient Anonymous Channel*, Eurocrypt '94, LNCS 950, pp. 332-340, 1995.
44. B. Pfitzmann, A. Pfitzmann, *How to break the direct RSA-implementation of mixes*, Eurocrypt '89, LNCS 434, pp. 373-381, 1990.
45. B. Pfitzmann, M. Waidner, *Composition and Integrity Preservation of Secure Reactive Systems*, 7th Conference on Computer and Communications Security of the ACM, pp. 245-254, 2000.
46. P. Ribenboim, *The new book of prime number records*, 3rd ed., ISBN 0-38794457-5, Springer-Verlag, 1996.
47. K. Sako, J. Killian, *Reciept-free Mix-Type Voting Scheme*, Eurocrypt '95, LNCS 921, pp. 393-403, 1995.
48. D. Wikström, *Five Practical Attacks for "Optimistic Mixing for Exit-Polls"*, In proceedings of Selected Areas of Cryptography (SAC), LNCS 3006, pp. 160-174, 2003.
49. D. Wikström, *A Universally Composable Mix-Net*, Proceedings of First Theory of Cryptography Conference (TCC '04), LNCS 2951, pp. 315-335, 2004.
50. D. Wikström, *A Sender Verifiable Mix-Net and a New Proof of a Shuffle*, Cryptology ePrint Archive, Report 2005/137, 2005, http://eprint.iacr.org/.

Universally Anonymizable Public-Key Encryption

Ryotaro Hayashi and Keisuke Tanaka

Dept. of Mathematical and Computing Sciences,
Tokyo Institute of Technology, 2-12-1 Ookayama,
Meguro-ku, Tokyo 152-8552, Japan
{hayashi9, keisuke}@is.titech.ac.jp

Abstract. We first propose the notion of universally anonymizable public-key encryption. Suppose that we have the encrypted data made with the same security parameter, and that these data do not satisfy the anonymity property. Consider the situation that we would like to transform these encrypted data to those with the anonymity property without decrypting these encrypted data. In this paper, in order to formalize this situation, we propose a new property for public-key encryption called universal anonymizability. If we use a universally anonymizable public-key encryption scheme, not only the person who made the ciphertexts, but also anyone can anonymize the encrypted data without using the corresponding secret key. We then propose universally anonymizable public-key encryption schemes based on the ElGamal encryption scheme, the Cramer-Shoup encryption scheme, and RSA-OAEP, and prove their security.

Keywords: encryption, anonymity, key-privacy, ElGamal, Cramer-Shoup, RSA-OAEP.

1 Introduction

The classical security requirement of public-key encryption schemes is that it provides privacy of the encrypted data. Popular formalizations such as indistinguishability or non-malleability, under either the chosen-plaintext or the chosen-ciphertext attacks are directed at capturing various data-privacy requirements.

Bellare, Boldyreva, Desai, and Pointcheval [1] proposed a new security requirement of encryption schemes called "key-privacy" or "anonymity." It asks that an encryption scheme provides (in addition to privacy of the data being encrypted) privacy of the key under which the encryption was performed. That is, if an encryption scheme provides the key-privacy, then the receiver is anonymous from the point of view of the adversary.

In addition to the notion of key-privacy, they provided the RSA-based anonymous encryption scheme, RSA-RAEP, which is a variant of RSA-OAEP (Bellare and Rogaway [2], Fujisaki, Okamoto, Pointcheval, and Stern [7]). Recently, Hayashi, Okamoto, and Tanaka [10] proposed the RSA-based anonymous encryption scheme by using the RSACD function. Hayashi and Tanaka [11] constructed

B. Roy (Ed.): ASIACRYPT 2005, LNCS 3788, pp. 293–312, 2005.

	RSA-OAEP	Sampling Twice [11]	RSA-RAEP [1]	RSACD [10]	Expanding
anonymity	No	Yes	Yes	Yes	Yes
# of mod. exp. to encrypt (average / worst)	1 / 1	2 / 2	$1.5 / k_1$	1.5 / 2	1 / 1
# of random bits to encrypt (average / worst)	k_0	$2k_0 + k + 3$ / $2k_0 + k + 3$	$1.5k_0 / k_1 k_0$	$1.5k_0 / 1.5k_0$	$k_0 + 160$ / $k_0 + 160$
size of ciphertexts	k	k	k	k	$k + 160$

Fig. 1. The costs of the encryption schemes

the RSA-based anonymous encryption scheme by using the sampling twice technique. In [11], they also mentioned the scheme with the expanding technique for comparison, however, there is no security proof.

With respect to the discrete-log based schemes, Bellare, Boldyreva, Desai, and Pointcheval [1] proved that the ElGamal and the Cramer-Shoup encryption schemes provide the anonymity property when all of the users use a common group.

In this paper, we consider the following situation. In order to send e-mails, all members of the company use the encryption scheme which does not provide the anonymity property. They consider that e-mails sent to the inside of the company do not have to be anonymized and it is sufficient to be encrypted the data. However, when e-mails are sent to the outside of the company, they want to anonymize them for preventing the eavesdropper on the public network.

A trivial answer for this problem is that all members use the encryption scheme with the anonymity property. However, generally speaking, we require some computational costs to create ciphertexts with the anonymity property. In fact, the RSA-based anonymous encryption schemes proposed in [1,10,11], which are based on RSA-OAEP, are not efficient with respect to the encryption cost or the size of ciphertexts, compared with RSA-OAEP (See Figure 1. Here, k, k_0, k_1 are security parameters and we assume that N is uniformly distributed in $(2^{k-1}, 2^k)$.). Since the members do not require to anonymize the e-mails, it would be better to use the standard encryption scheme within the company.

We propose another way to solve this. Consider the situation that not only the person who made the ciphertexts, but also anyone can transform the encrypted data to those with the anonymity property without decrypting these encrypted data. If we have this situation, we can make an e-mail gateway which can transform encrypted e-mails to those with the anonymity property without using the corresponding secret key when they are sent to the outside of the company.

Furthermore, we can use this e-mail gateway in order to guarantee the anonymity property for e-mails sent to the outside of the company. The president of the company may consider that all e-mails sent to the outside of the company should be anonymized. In this case, even if someone tries to send e-mails to the outside of the company without anonymization, the e-mails passing through the e-mail gateway are always anonymized.

In this paper, in order to formalize this idea, we propose a special type of public-key encryption scheme called a *universally anonymizable public-key encryption scheme.* A universally anonymizable public-key encryption scheme consists of a standard public-key encryption scheme $\mathcal{PE}$ and two additional algorithms, that is, an anonymizing algorithm $\mathcal{UA}$ and a decryption algorithm $\mathcal{DA}$ for anonymized ciphertexts. We can use $\mathcal{PE}$ as a standard encryption scheme which is not necessary to have the anonymity property. Furthermore, in this scheme, by using the anonymizing algorithm $\mathcal{UA}$, anyone who has a standard ciphertext can anonymize it with its public key whenever she wants to do that. The receiver can decrypt the anonymized ciphertext by using the decryption algorithm $\mathcal{DA}$ for anonymized ciphertexts. Then, the adversary cannot know under which key the anonymized ciphertext was created.

To formalize the security properties for universally anonymizable public-key encryption, we define three requirements, the key-privacy, the data-privacy on standard ciphertexts, and that on anonymized ciphertexts.

We then propose the universally anonymizable public-key encryption schemes based on the ElGamal encryption scheme, the Cramer-Shoup encryption scheme, and RSA-OAEP, and prove their security.

We show the key-privacy property of our schemes by applying an argument in [1] with modification. The argument in [1] for the discrete-log based scheme depends heavily on the situation where all of the users employ a common group. However, in our discrete-log based schemes, we do not use the common group for obtaining the key-privacy property. Therefore, we cannot straightforwardly apply their argument to our schemes. To prove the key-privacy property of our schemes, we employ the idea described in [5] by Cramer and Shoup, where we encode the elements of QR_p (a group of quadratic residues modulo p) where $p = 2q+1$ and p, q are prime to those of $\mathbb{Z}_q$. This encoding plays an important role in our schemes. We also employ the expanding technique. With this technique, if we get the ciphertext, we expand it to the common domain. This technique was proposed by Desmedt [6]. In [8], Galbraith and Mao used this technique for the undeniable signature scheme. In [13], Rivest, Shamir, and Tauman also used this technique for the ring signature scheme.

The organization of this paper is as follows. In Section 2, we review the definitions of the Decisional Diffie-Hellman problem, the families of hash functions, and the RSA family of trap-door permutations. In Section 3, we formulate the notion of universally anonymizable public-key encryption and its security properties. We propose the universally anonymizable public-key encryption scheme based on the ElGamal encryption scheme in Section 4, that based on the Cramer-Shoup encryption scheme in Section 5, and that based on RSA-OAEP in Section 6.

2   Preliminaries

2.1   The Decisional Diffie-Hellman Problem

In this section, we review the decisional Diffie-Hellman Problem.

Definition 1 (DDH). *Let $\mathcal{G}$ be a group generator which takes as input a security parameter k and returns (q, g) where q is a k-bit integer and g is a generator of a cyclic group G_q of order q. Let D be an adversary. We consider the following experiments:*

Experiment $\mathbf{Exp}_{\mathcal{G},D}^{\text{ddh-real}}(k)$

$(q,g) \leftarrow \mathcal{G}(k); \; x,y \overset{R}{\leftarrow} \mathbb{Z}_q$

$X \leftarrow g^x; \; Y \leftarrow g^y; \; T \leftarrow g^{xy}$

$d \leftarrow D(q,g,X,Y,T)$

return d

Experiment $\mathbf{Exp}_{\mathcal{G},D}^{\text{ddh-rand}}(k)$

$(q,g) \leftarrow \mathcal{G}(k); \; x,y \overset{R}{\leftarrow} \mathbb{Z}_q$

$X \leftarrow g^x; \; Y \leftarrow g^y; \; T \overset{R}{\leftarrow} G_q$

$d \leftarrow D(q,g,X,Y,T)$

return d

The advantage of D in solving the Decisional Diffie-Hellman (DDH) problem for $\mathcal{G}$ is defined by

$$\mathbf{Adv}_{\mathcal{G},D}^{\text{ddh}}(k) = \left| \Pr[\mathbf{Exp}_{\mathcal{G},D}^{\text{ddh-real}}(k) = 1] - \Pr[\mathbf{Exp}_{\mathcal{G},D}^{\text{ddh-rand}}(k) = 1] \right|.$$

We say that the DDH problem for $\mathcal{G}$ is hard if the function $\mathbf{Adv}_{\mathcal{G},D}^{\text{ddh}}(k)$ is negligible for any algorithm D whose time-complexity is polynomial in k.

The "time-complexity" is the worst case execution time of the experiment plus the size of the code of the adversary, in some fixed RAM model of computation.

2.2 Families of Hash Functions

In this section, we describe the definitions of families of hash functions and universal one-wayness.

Definition 2 (Families of Hash Functions). *A family of hash functions* $\mathcal{H} = (\mathcal{GH}, \mathcal{EH})$ *is defined by two algorithms. A probabilistic generator algorithm* $\mathcal{GH}$ *takes the security parameter* k *as input and returns a key* K. *A deterministic evaluation algorithm* $\mathcal{EH}$ *takes the key* K *and a string* $M \in \{0,1\}^*$ *and returns a string* $\mathcal{EH}_K(M) \in \{0,1\}^{k-1}$.

Definition 3 (Universal One-Wayness). *Let* $\mathcal{H} = (\mathcal{GH}, \mathcal{EH})$ *be a family of hash functions and let* $C = (C_1, C_2)$ *be an adversary. We consider the following experiment:*

Experiment $\mathbf{Exp}_{\mathcal{H},C}^{\text{uow}}(k)$

$(x_0, \mathsf{si}) \leftarrow C_1(k); \; K \leftarrow \mathcal{GH}(k); \; x_1 \leftarrow C_2(K, x_0, \mathsf{si})$

if $((x_0 \neq x_1) \wedge (\mathcal{EH}_K(x_0) = \mathcal{EH}_K(x_1)))$ then return 1 else return 0

Note that si *is the state information. We define the advantage of* C *via*

$$\mathbf{Adv}_{\mathcal{H},C}^{\text{uow}}(k) = \Pr[\mathbf{Exp}_{\mathcal{H},C}^{\text{uow}}(k) = 1].$$

We say that the family of hash functions $\mathcal{H}$ is universal one-way if $\mathbf{Adv}_{\mathcal{H},C}^{\text{uow}}(k)$ is negligible for any algorithm C whose time-complexity is polynomial in k.

2.3 The RSA Family of Trap-Door Permutations

In this section, we describe the definitions of the RSA family of trap-door permutations denoted by RSA and θ-partial one-wayness of RSA.

Definition 4 (The RSA Family of Trap-Door Permutations). *The RSA family of trap-door permutations* RSA $= (K, E, I)$ *is described as follows. The key generation algorithm K takes as input a security parameter k and picks random, distinct primes p, q in the range $2^{\lceil k/2 \rceil - 1} < p, q < 2^{\lceil k/2 \rceil}$ and $2^{k-1} < pq < 2^k$. It sets $N = pq$ and picks $e, d \in \mathbb{Z}^*_{\phi(N)}$ such that $ed = 1 \pmod{\phi(N)}$. The public key is (N, e, k) and the secret key is (N, d, k). The evaluation algorithm is $E_{N,e,k}(x) = x^e \bmod N$ and the inversion algorithm is $I_{N,d,k}(y) = y^d \bmod N$.*

Definition 5 (θ-Partial One-Wayness of RSA**).** *Let $k \in \mathbb{N}$ be a security parameter. Let $0 < \theta \le 1$ be a constant. Let A be an adversary. We consider the following experiment:*

> Experiment $\mathbf{Exp}^{\theta\text{-pow-fnc}}_{\mathsf{RSA},A}(k)$
>
> $((N, e, k), (N, d, k)) \leftarrow K(k);\ x \xleftarrow{R} \mathbb{Z}^*_N;\ y \leftarrow x^e \bmod N$
>
> $x_1 \leftarrow A(pk, y)$ where $|x_1| = \lceil \theta \cdot |x| \rceil$
>
> if $\left((x_1 \| x_2)^e \bmod N = y \text{ for some } x_2\right)$ return 1 else return 0

Here, "$\|$" denotes concatenation. We define the advantage of the adversary via

$$\mathbf{Adv}^{\theta\text{-pow-fnc}}_{\mathsf{RSA},A}(k) = \Pr[\mathbf{Exp}^{\theta\text{-pow-fnc}}_{\mathsf{RSA},A}(k) = 1]$$

where the probability is taken over K, $x \xleftarrow{R} \mathbb{Z}^*_N$, and A. We say that RSA *is θ-partial one-way if the function $\mathbf{Adv}^{\theta\text{-pow-fnc}}_{\mathsf{RSA},A}(k)$ is negligible for any adversary A whose time complexity is polynomial in k.*

Note that when $\theta = 1$ the notion of θ-partial one-wayness coincides with the standard notion of one-wayness. Fujisaki, Okamoto, Pointcheval, and Stern [7] showed that the θ-partial one-wayness of RSA is equivalent to the (1-partial) one-wayness of RSA for $\theta > 0.5$.

3   Universally Anonymizable Public-Key Encryption

In this section, we propose the definition of universally anonymizable public-key encryption schemes and its security properties.

3.1   The Definition of Universally Anonymizable Public-Key Encryption Schemes

We formalize the notion of universally anonymizable public-key encryption schemes as follows.

Definition 6. *A universally anonymizable public-key encryption scheme $\mathcal{UAPE} = ((\mathcal{K}, \mathcal{E}, \mathcal{D}), \mathcal{UA}, \mathcal{DA})$ consists of a public-key encryption scheme $\mathcal{PE} = (\mathcal{K}, \mathcal{E}, \mathcal{D})$ and two other algorithms.*

- *The key generation algorithm $\mathcal{K}$ is a randomized algorithm that takes as input a security parameter k and returns a pair (pk, sk) of keys, a public key and a matching secret key.*

- *The encryption algorithm $\mathcal{E}$ is a randomized algorithm that takes the public key pk and a plaintext m and returns a standard ciphertext c.*
- *The decryption algorithm $\mathcal{D}$ for standard ciphertexts is a deterministic algorithm that takes the secret key sk and a standard ciphertext c and returns the corresponding plaintext m or a special symbol $\perp$ to indicate that the standard ciphertext is invalid.*
- *The anonymizing algorithm $\mathcal{UA}$ is a randomized algorithm that takes the public key pk and a standard ciphertext c and returns an anonymized ciphertext c′.*
- *The decryption algorithm $\mathcal{DA}$ for anonymized ciphertexts is a deterministic algorithm that takes the secret key sk and an anonymized ciphertext c′ and returns the corresponding plaintext m or a special symbol $\perp$ to indicate that the anonymized ciphertext is invalid.*

We require the standard correctness condition. That is, for any (pk, sk) outputted by $\mathcal{K}$ and $m \in \mathcal{M}(pk)$ where $\mathcal{M}(pk)$ denotes the message space of pk, we have $m = \mathcal{D}_{sk}(\mathcal{E}_{pk}(m))$ and $m = \mathcal{DA}_{sk}(\mathcal{UA}_{pk}(\mathcal{E}_{pk}(m)))$.

In the universally anonymizable public-key encryption scheme, we can use $\mathcal{PE} = (\mathcal{K}, \mathcal{E}, \mathcal{D})$ as a standard encryption scheme. Furthermore, in this scheme, by using the anonymizing algorithm $\mathcal{UA}$, anyone who has a standard ciphertext can anonymize it whenever she wants to do that. The receiver can decrypt the anonymized ciphertext by using the decryption algorithm $\mathcal{DA}$ for anonymized ciphertexts.

3.2   Security Properties of Universally Anonymizable Public-Key Encryption Schemes

We now define security properties with respect to universally anonymizable public-key encryption schemes.

Data-Privacy. We define the security property called *data-privacy* of universally anonymizable public-key encryption schemes. The definition is based on the indistinguishability for standard public-key encryption schemes.

We can consider two types of data-privacy, that is, the data-privacy on standard ciphertexts and that on anonymized ciphertexts. We first describe the definition of the data-privacy on standard ciphertexts.

Definition 7 (Data-Privacy on Standard Ciphertexts). *Let $b \in \{0, 1\}$ and $k \in \mathbb{N}$. Let $A_{\text{cpa}} = (A_{\text{cpa}}^1, A_{\text{cpa}}^2)$, $A_{\text{cca}} = (A_{\text{cca}}^1, A_{\text{cca}}^2)$ be adversaries that run in two stages and where A_{cca} has access to the oracles $\mathcal{D}_{sk_0}(\cdot)$, $\mathcal{D}_{sk_1}(\cdot)$, $\mathcal{DA}_{sk_0}(\cdot)$, and $\mathcal{DA}_{sk_1}(\cdot)$. Note that si is the state information. It contains pk, m_0, m_1, and so on. For $\text{atk} \in \{\text{cpa}, \text{cca}\}$, we consider the following experiment:*

Experiment $\mathbf{Exp}_{\mathcal{UAPE}, A_{\text{atk}}}^{\text{dataS-atk-}b}(k)$
$(pk, sk) \leftarrow \mathcal{K}(k); \ (m_0, m_1, \mathsf{si}) \leftarrow A_{\text{atk}}^1(pk); \ c \leftarrow \mathcal{E}_{pk}(m_b); \ d \leftarrow A_{\text{atk}}^2(c, \mathsf{si})$
return d

Note that $m_0, m_1 \in \mathcal{M}(pk)$. Above it is mandated that A_{cca}^2 never queries the challenge c to either $\mathcal{D}_{sk_0}(\cdot)$ or $\mathcal{D}_{sk_1}(\cdot)$. It is also mandated that A_{cca}^2 never queries either the anonymized ciphertext $\tilde{c} \in \{\mathcal{U}A_{pk_0}(c)\}$ to $\mathcal{D}A_{sk_0}(\cdot)$ or $\tilde{c} \in \{\mathcal{U}A_{pk_1}(c)\}$ to $\mathcal{D}A_{sk_1}(\cdot)$. For atk $\in \{cpa, cca\}$, we define the advantage via

$$\mathbf{Adv}_{\mathcal{U}\mathcal{A}\mathcal{P}\mathcal{E}, A_{atk}}^{dataS\text{-}atk}(k) = \left| \Pr[\mathbf{Exp}_{\mathcal{U}\mathcal{A}\mathcal{P}\mathcal{E}, A_{atk}}^{dataS\text{-}atk\text{-}1}(k) = 1] - \Pr[\mathbf{Exp}_{\mathcal{U}\mathcal{A}\mathcal{P}\mathcal{E}, A_{atk}}^{dataS\text{-}atk\text{-}0}(k) = 1] \right|.$$

We say that the universally anonymizable public-key encryption scheme $\mathcal{U}\mathcal{A}\mathcal{P}\mathcal{E}$ provides the data-privacy on standard ciphertexts against the chosen plaintext attack (respectively the adaptive chosen ciphertext attack) if $\mathbf{Adv}_{\mathcal{U}\mathcal{A}\mathcal{P}\mathcal{E}, A_{cpa}}^{dataS\text{-}cpa}(k)$ (resp. $\mathbf{Adv}_{\mathcal{U}\mathcal{A}\mathcal{P}\mathcal{E}, A_{cca}}^{dataS\text{-}cca}(k)$) is negligible for any adversary A whose time complexity is polynomial in k.

In the above experiment, if the challenge is c, then anyone can compute $\mathcal{U}A_{pk_0}(c)$. Therefore, in the CCA setting, we restrict the oracle access to $\mathcal{D}A$ as described above.

We next describe the definition of the data-privacy on anonymized ciphertexts.

Definition 8 (Data-Privacy on Anonymized Ciphertexts). *Let* $b \in \{0, 1\}$ *and* $k \in \mathbb{N}$. *Let* $A_{cpa} = (A_{cpa}^1, A_{cpa}^2)$, $A_{cca} = (A_{cca}^1, A_{cca}^2)$ *be adversaries that run in two stages and where* A_{cca} *has access to the oracles* $\mathcal{D}_{sk_0}(\cdot)$, $\mathcal{D}_{sk_1}(\cdot)$, $\mathcal{D}A_{sk_0}(\cdot)$, *and* $\mathcal{D}A_{sk_1}(\cdot)$. *For atk* $\in \{cpa, cca\}$, *we consider the following experiment:*

$$\begin{aligned}
&\text{Experiment } \mathbf{Exp}_{\mathcal{U}\mathcal{A}\mathcal{P}\mathcal{E}, A_{atk}}^{dataA\text{-}atk\text{-}b}(k) \\
&\quad (pk, sk) \leftarrow \mathcal{K}(k); \ (m_0, m_1, \mathsf{si}) \leftarrow A_{atk}^1(pk) \\
&\quad c \leftarrow \mathcal{E}_{pk}(m_b); \ c' \leftarrow \mathcal{U}A_{pk}(c); \ d \leftarrow A_{atk}^2(c', \mathsf{si}) \\
&\quad \text{return } d
\end{aligned}$$

Note that $m_0, m_1 \in \mathcal{M}(pk)$. Above it is mandated that A_{cca}^2 never queries the challenge c' to either $\mathcal{D}A_{sk_0}(\cdot)$ or $\mathcal{D}A_{sk_1}(\cdot)$. For atk $\in \{cpa, cca\}$, we define the advantage via

$$\mathbf{Adv}_{\mathcal{U}\mathcal{A}\mathcal{P}\mathcal{E}, A_{atk}}^{dataA\text{-}atk}(k) = \left| \Pr[\mathbf{Exp}_{\mathcal{U}\mathcal{A}\mathcal{P}\mathcal{E}, A_{atk}}^{dataA\text{-}atk\text{-}1}(k) = 1] - \Pr[\mathbf{Exp}_{\mathcal{U}\mathcal{A}\mathcal{P}\mathcal{E}, A_{atk}}^{dataA\text{-}atk\text{-}0}(k) = 1] \right|.$$

We say that the universally anonymizable public-key encryption scheme $\mathcal{U}\mathcal{A}\mathcal{P}\mathcal{E}$ provides the data-privacy on anonymized ciphertexts against the chosen plaintext attack (resp. the adaptive chosen ciphertext attack) if $\mathbf{Adv}_{\mathcal{U}\mathcal{A}\mathcal{P}\mathcal{E}, A_{cpa}}^{dataA\text{-}cpa}(k)$ (resp. $\mathbf{Adv}_{\mathcal{U}\mathcal{A}\mathcal{P}\mathcal{E}, A_{cca}}^{dataA\text{-}cca}(k)$) is negligible for any adversary A whose time complexity is polynomial in k.

Remark 1. In the CPA setting, if there exists an algorithm which breaks the data-privacy on anonymized ciphertexts, then we can break that on standard ciphertexts by applying the anonymizing algorithm to the standard ciphertexts and passing the resulting anonymized ciphertexts to the adversary which breaks the data-privacy on anonymized ciphertexts. Therefore, in the CPA setting, it is sufficient that the universally anonymizable public-key encryption scheme provides the data-privacy of standard ciphertexts.

On the other hand, in the CCA setting, the data privacy on standard ciphertexts does not always imply that on anonymized ciphertexts, since the oracle access of the adversary attacking the data privacy on standard ciphertexts is restricted more strictly than that on anonymized ciphertexts.

Key-Privacy. We define the security property called *key-privacy* of universally anonymizable public-key encryption schemes. If the scheme provides the key-privacy, the adversary cannot know under which key the anonymized ciphertext was created.

Definition 9 (Key-Privacy). *Let $b \in \{0, 1\}$ and $k \in \mathbb{N}$. Let $A_{\mathrm{cpa}} = (A_{\mathrm{cpa}}^1, A_{\mathrm{cpa}}^2)$, $A_{\mathrm{cca}} = (A_{\mathrm{cca}}^1, A_{\mathrm{cca}}^2)$ be adversaries that run in two stages and where A_{cca} has access to the oracles $\mathcal{D}_{sk_0}(\cdot)$, $\mathcal{D}_{sk_1}(\cdot)$, $\mathcal{DA}_{sk_0}(\cdot)$, and $\mathcal{DA}_{sk_1}(\cdot)$. For atk $\in$ {cpa, cca}, we consider the following experiment:*

Experiment $\mathbf{Exp}_{\mathcal{UAPE}, A_{\mathrm{atk}}}^{\mathrm{key\text{-}atk\text{-}}b}(k)$
   $(pk_0, sk_0) \leftarrow \mathcal{K}(k);\ (pk_1, sk_1) \leftarrow \mathcal{K}(k)$
   $(m_0, m_1, \mathsf{si}) \leftarrow A_{\mathrm{atk}}^1(pk_0, pk_1);\ c \leftarrow \mathcal{E}_{pk_b}(m_b);\ c' \leftarrow \mathcal{UA}_{pk_b}(c);\ d \leftarrow A_{\mathrm{atk}}^2(c', \mathsf{si})$
   return d

Note that $m_0 \in \mathcal{M}(pk_0)$ and $m_1 \in \mathcal{M}(pk_1)$. Above it is mandated that A_{cca}^2 never queries the challenge c' to either $\mathcal{DA}_{sk_0}(\cdot)$ or $\mathcal{DA}_{sk_1}(\cdot)$. For atk $\in$ {cpa, cca}, we define the advantage via

$$\mathbf{Adv}_{\mathcal{UAPE}, A_{\mathrm{atk}}}^{\mathrm{key\text{-}atk}}(k) = \left| \Pr[\mathbf{Exp}_{\mathcal{UAPE}, A_{\mathrm{atk}}}^{\mathrm{key\text{-}atk\text{-}1}}(k) = 1] - \Pr[\mathbf{Exp}_{\mathcal{UAPE}, A_{\mathrm{atk}}}^{\mathrm{key\text{-}atk\text{-}0}}(k) = 1] \right|.$$

We say that the universally anonymizable public-key encryption scheme $\mathcal{UAPE}$ provides the key-privacy against the chosen plaintext attack (resp. the adaptive chosen ciphertext attack) if $\mathbf{Adv}_{\mathcal{UAPE}, A_{\mathrm{cpa}}}^{\mathrm{key\text{-}cpa}}(k)$ (resp. $\mathbf{Adv}_{\mathcal{UAPE}, A_{\mathrm{cca}}}^{\mathrm{key\text{-}cca}}(k)$) is negligible for any adversary A whose time complexity is polynomial in k.

Bellare, Boldyreva, Desai, and Pointcheval [1] proposed a security requirement of encryption schemes called "key-privacy." Similar to the above definition, it asks that the encryption provides privacy of the key under which the encryption was performed. In addition to the property of the universal anonymizability, there are two differences between their definition and ours.

In [1], they defined the encryption scheme with some *common-key* which contains the common parameter for all users to obtain the key-privacy property. For example, in the discrete-log based schemes such that the ElGamal and the Cramer-Shoup encryption schemes, the common key contains a common group G, and the encryption is performed over the common group for all uses.

On the other hand, in our definition, we do not prepare any common key for obtaining the key-privacy property. In the universally anonymizable public-key encryption scheme, we can use the standard encryption scheme which is not necessary to have the key-privacy property. In addition to it, anyone can anonymize the ciphertext by using its public key whenever she want to do that, and the adversary cannot know under which key the anonymized ciphertext was created.

The definition in [1], they considered the situation that the message space was common to each user. Therefore, in the experiment of their definition, the adversary chooses only one message m from the common message space and receives a ciphertext of m encrypted with one of two keys pk_0 and pk_1.

In our definition, we do not use common parameter and the message spaces for users may be different even if the security parameter is fixed. In fact, in Sections 4 and 5, we propose the encryption schemes whose message spaces for users are different. Therefore, in the experiment of our definition, the adversary chooses two messages m_0 and m_1 where m_0 and m_1 are in the message spaces for pk_0 and pk_1, respectively, and receives either a ciphertext of m_0 encrypted with pk_0 or a ciphertext of m_1 encrypted with pk_1. The ability of the adversary with two messages m_0 and m_1 might be stronger than that with one message m.

We say that a universally anonymizable public-key encryption scheme $\mathcal{UAPE}$ is CPA-secure (resp. CCA-secure) if the scheme $\mathcal{UAPE}$ provides the data-privacy on standard ciphertexts, that on anonymized ciphertexts, and the key-privacy against the chosen plaintext attack (resp. the adaptive chosen ciphertext attack).

4 ElGamal and Its Universal Anonymizability

In this section, we propose a universally anonymizable ElGamal encryption scheme.

4.1 The ElGamal Encryption Scheme

Definition 10 (ElGamal). *The ElGamal encryption scheme* $\mathcal{PE}^{EG} = (\mathcal{K}^{EG}, \mathcal{E}^{EG}, \mathcal{D}^{EG})$ *is as follows. Note that* $\mathcal{Q}$ *is a QR-group generator with a safe prime which takes as input a security parameter* k *and returns* (q, g) *where* q *is* k-*bit prime,* $p = 2q + 1$ *is prime, and* g *is a generator of a cyclic group* QR_p *(a group of quadratic residues modulo* p*) of order* q*.*

Algorithm $\mathcal{K}^{EG}(k)$	Algorithm $\mathcal{E}^{EG}_{pk}(m)$	Algorithm $\mathcal{D}^{EG}_{sk}(c_1, c_2)$
$(q, g) \leftarrow \mathcal{Q}(k)$	$r \xleftarrow{R} \mathbb{Z}_q$	$m \leftarrow c_2 \cdot c_1^{-x}$
$x \xleftarrow{R} \mathbb{Z}_q;\ y \leftarrow g^x$	$c_1 \leftarrow g^r$	return m
return $pk = (q, g, y)$ and $sk = x$	$c_2 \leftarrow m \cdot y^r$	
	return (c_1, c_2)	

The ElGamal encryption scheme is secure in the sense of IND-CPA if the DDH problem for $\mathcal{Q}$ is hard.

4.2 Universal Anonymizability of the ElGamal Encryption Scheme

We now consider the situation that there exists no common key, and in the above definition of the ElGamal encryption scheme, each user chooses an arbitrary prime q where $|q| = k$ and $p = 2q + 1$ is also prime, and uses a group of quadratic residues modulo p. Therefore, each user U_i uses a different groups G_i for her encryption scheme and if she publishes the ciphertext directly (without anonymization) then the scheme does not provide the key-privacy. In fact, the adversary simply checks whether the ciphertext y is in the group G_i, and if $y \notin G_i$ then y was not encrypted by U_i. To anonymize the standard ciphertext of the ElGamal encryption scheme, we consider the following strategy in the anonymizing algorithm.

1. Compute a ciphertext c over each user's prime-order group.
2. Encode c to an element $\bar{c} \in \mathbb{Z}_q$ (the encoding function).
3. Expand $\bar{c}$ to the common domain (the expanding technique).

We describe the encoding function and the expanding technique.

The Encoding Function. Generally speaking, it is not easy to encode the elements of a prime-order group of order q to those of $\mathbb{Z}_q$. We employ the idea described in [5] by Cramer and Shoup. We can encode the elements of QR_p where $p = 2q + 1$ and p, q are prime to those of $\mathbb{Z}_q$.

Let p be safe prime (i.e. $q = (p-1)/2$ is also prime) and $QR_p \subset \mathbb{Z}_p^*$ a group of quadratic residues modulo p. Then we have $|QR_p| = q$ and $QR_p = \{1^2 \bmod p,\ 2^2 \bmod p, \cdots,\ q^2 \bmod p\}$. It is easy to see that QR_p is a cyclic group of order q, and each $g \in QR_p \backslash \{1\}$ is a generator of QR_p.

We now define a function $F_q : QR_p \rightarrow \mathbb{Z}_q$ as

$$F_q(x) = \min\left\{\pm x^{\frac{p-1}{4}} \bmod p\right\}.$$

Noticing that $\pm x^{\frac{p-1}{4}} \bmod p$ are the square roots of x modulo p, the function F_q is bijective and we have $F_q^{-1}(y) = y^2 \bmod p$. We call the function F_q an *encoding function*. We also define a *t-encoding function* $\bar{F}_{q,t} : (QR_p)^t \rightarrow (\mathbb{Z}_q)^t$. $\bar{F}_{q,t}$ takes as input $(x_1, \cdots, x_t) \in (QR_p)^t$ and returns $(y_1, \cdots, y_t) \in (\mathbb{Z}_q)^t$ where $y_i = F_q(x_i)$ for each $i \in \{1, \cdots, t\}$. It is easy to see that $\bar{F}_{q,t}$ is bijective and we can define $\bar{F}_{q,t}^{-1}$.

The Expanding Technique. This technique was proposed by Desmedt [6]. In [8], Galbraith and Mao used this technique for the undeniable signature scheme. In [13], Rivest, Shamir, and Tauman also used this technique for the ring signature scheme.

In the expanding technique, we expand $\bar{c} \in \mathbb{Z}_q$ to the common domain $\{0, 1\}^{k+k_b}$. In particular, we choose $t \xleftarrow{R} \{0, 1, 2, \cdots, \lfloor (2^{k+k_b} - \bar{c})/q \rfloor\}$ and set $c' \leftarrow \bar{c} + tq$.

Then, for any q where $|q| = k$, if $\bar{c}$ is uniformly chosen from $\mathbb{Z}_q$, then the statistical distance between the distribution of the output c' by the expanding technique and the uniform distribution over $\{0, 1\}^{k+k_b}$ is less than $1/2^{k_b-1}$. In the following, we set $k_b = 160$.

Our Scheme. We now propose our universally anonymizable ElGamal encryption scheme. Our scheme provides the key-privacy against the chosen plaintext attack even if each user chooses an arbitrary prime q where $|q| = k$ and $p = 2q+1$ is also prime, and uses a group of quadratic residues modulo p.

Definition 11. *Our universally anonymizable ElGamal encryption scheme* $\mathcal{UAPE}^{\mathsf{EG}} = ((\mathcal{K}^{\mathsf{EG}}, \mathcal{E}^{\mathsf{EG}}, \mathcal{D}^{\mathsf{EG}}), \mathcal{UA}^{\mathsf{EG}}, \mathcal{DA}^{\mathsf{EG}})$ *consists of the ElGamal encryption scheme* $\mathcal{PE}^{\mathsf{EG}} = (\mathcal{K}^{\mathsf{EG}}, \mathcal{E}^{\mathsf{EG}}, \mathcal{D}^{\mathsf{EG}})$ *and two algorithms described as follows.*

Algorithm $\mathcal{UA}_{pk}^{\mathsf{EG}}(c_1, c_2)$	Algorithm $\mathcal{DA}_{sk}^{\mathsf{EG}}(c_1', c_2')$
$(\bar{c}_1, \bar{c}_2) \leftarrow \bar{F}_{q,2}(c_1, c_2)$	$\bar{c}_1 \leftarrow c_1' \bmod q; \ \bar{c}_2 \leftarrow c_2' \bmod q$
$t_1 \xleftarrow{R} \{0, 1, 2, \cdots, \lfloor (2^{k+160} - \bar{c}_1)/q \rfloor\}$	$(c_1, c_2) \leftarrow \bar{F}_{q,2}^{-1}(\bar{c}_1, \bar{c}_2)$
$t_2 \xleftarrow{R} \{0, 1, 2, \cdots, \lfloor (2^{k+160} - \bar{c}_2)/q \rfloor\}$	$m \leftarrow \mathcal{D}_{sk}^{\mathsf{EG}}(c_1, c_2)$
$c_1' \leftarrow \bar{c}_1 + t_1 q; \ c_2' \leftarrow \bar{c}_2 + t_2 q$	return m
return (c_1', c_2')	

4.3 Security

In this section, we prove that our universally anonymizable ElGamal encryption scheme $\mathcal{UAPE}^{\mathsf{EG}}$ is CPA-secure assuming that the DDH problem for $\mathcal{Q}$ is hard.

We can easily see that our scheme provides the data-privacy on standard ciphertexts against the chosen plaintext attack if the DDH problem for $\mathcal{Q}$ is hard. More precisely, we can prove that if there exists a CPA-adversary attacking the data-privacy on standard ciphertexts of our scheme with advantage ϵ, then there exists a CPA-adversary attacking the indistinguishability of the ElGamal encryption scheme with the same advantage ϵ.

Note that this implies our scheme provides the data-privacy on anonymized ciphertexts against the chosen plaintext attack if the DDH problem for $\mathcal{Q}$ is hard.

We now prove our scheme provides the key-privacy against the chosen plaintext attack. To prove this, we use the idea of Halevi [9].

Lemma 1 (Halevi [9]). *Let* $\mathcal{PE} = (\mathcal{K}, \mathcal{E}, \mathcal{D})$ *be a (standard) encryption scheme that is CCA secure (resp. CPA secure) for the indistinguishability (data-privacy). Then a sufficient condition for* $\mathcal{PE}$ *to be also CCA secure (resp. CPA secure) for the key-privacy (defined by Bellare, Boldyreva, Desai, and Pointcheval) if the statistical distance between the two distributions*

$$D_0 = \{(pk_0, pk_1, \mathcal{E}_{pk_0}(m)) : (pk_0, sk_0), (pk_1, sk_1) \leftarrow \mathcal{K}(k); \ m \xleftarrow{R} \mathcal{M}(pk_0)\}$$
$$D_1 = \{(pk_0, pk_1, \mathcal{E}_{pk_1}(m)) : (pk_0, sk_0), (pk_1, sk_1) \leftarrow \mathcal{K}(k); \ m \xleftarrow{R} \mathcal{M}(pk_1)\}$$

is negligible.

This lemma shows the relation between the indistinguishability and the key-privacy for *standard* encryption scheme. We can apply this lemma to our universally anonymizable encryption scheme. That is, if the universally anonymizable encryption scheme $\mathcal{UAPE} = ((\mathcal{K}, \mathcal{E}, \mathcal{D}), \mathcal{UA}, \mathcal{DA})$ provides the data-privacy on *anonymized* ciphertexts against CCA (resp. CPA) and the statistical distance between the two distributions

$$D_0' = \{(pk_0, pk_1, \mathcal{UA}_{pk_0}(\mathcal{E}_{pk_0}(m))) \colon (pk_0, sk_0), (pk_1, sk_1) \leftarrow \mathcal{K}(k); \ m \overset{R}{\leftarrow} \mathcal{M}(pk_0)\}$$
$$D_1' = \{(pk_0, pk_1, \mathcal{UA}_{pk_1}(\mathcal{E}_{pk_1}(m))) \colon (pk_0, sk_0), (pk_1, sk_1) \leftarrow \mathcal{K}(k); \ m \overset{R}{\leftarrow} \mathcal{M}(pk_1)\}$$

is negligible, then $\mathcal{UAPE}$ provides the key-privacy against CCA (resp. CPA).

By using this, in order to prove that our scheme provides the key-privacy against the chosen plaintext attack, all we have to do is to see that the two distributions D_0' and D_1' derived by our scheme satisfy the property defined above. It is easy to see that the statistical distance between D_0' and D_1' is less than $2 \times (1/2^{159})^2$.

In conclusion, our universally anonymizable ElGamal encryption scheme is CPA-secure assuming that the DDH problem for $\mathcal{Q}$ is hard.

5   Cramer-Shoup and Its Universal Anonymizability

In this section, we propose a universally anonymizable Cramer-Shoup encryption scheme.

5.1   The Cramer-Shoup Encryption Scheme

Definition 12 (Cramer-Shoup). *The Cramer-Shoup encryption scheme* $\mathcal{PE}^{CS} = (\mathcal{K}^{CS}, \mathcal{E}^{CS}, \mathcal{D}^{CS})$ *is defined as follows. Let* $\mathcal{H} = (\mathcal{GH}, \mathcal{EH})$ *be a family of hash functions. Note that* $\mathcal{Q}$ *is a QR-group generator with a safe prime.*

Algorithm $\mathcal{K}^{CS}(k)$	Algorithm $\mathcal{E}_{pk}^{CS}(m)$	Algorithm $\mathcal{D}_{sk}^{CS}(u_1, u_2, e, v)$
$(q, g) \leftarrow \mathcal{Q}(k); \ K \leftarrow \mathcal{GH}(k)$	$r \overset{R}{\leftarrow} \mathbb{Z}_q$	$\alpha \leftarrow \mathcal{EH}_K(u_1, u_2, e)$
$g_1 \leftarrow g; \ g_2 \overset{R}{\leftarrow} QR_p$	$u_1 \leftarrow g_1^r; \ u_2 \leftarrow g_2^r$	if $(u_1^{x_1+y_1\alpha} u_2^{x_2+y_2\alpha} = v)$
$x_1, x_2, y_1, y_2, z \overset{R}{\leftarrow} \mathbb{Z}_q$	$e \leftarrow h^r m$	then $m \leftarrow e/u_1^z$
$c \leftarrow g_1^{x_1} g_2^{x_2}; \ d \leftarrow g_1^{y_1} g_2^{y_2}$	$\alpha \leftarrow \mathcal{EH}_K(u_1, u_2, e)$	else $m \leftarrow \perp$
$h \leftarrow g_1^z$	$v \leftarrow c^r d^{r\alpha}$	return m
$pk \leftarrow (q, g_1, g_2, c, d, h, K)$	return (u_1, u_2, e, v)	
$sk \leftarrow (x_1, x_2, y_1, y_2, z)$		
return (pk, sk)		

Cramer and Shoup [5] proved that the Cramer-Shoup encryption scheme is secure in the sense of IND-CCA2 assuming that $\mathcal{H}$ is universal one-way and the DDH problem for $\mathcal{Q}$ is hard. Lucks [12] recently proposed a variant of the Cramer-Shoup encryption scheme for groups of unknown order. This scheme is secure in the sense of IND-CCA2 assuming that the family of hash functions in the scheme is universal one-way, and both the Decisional Diffie-Hellman problem in QR_N (a set of quadratic residues modulo N) and factoring N are hard.

5.2 Universal Anonymizability of the Cramer-Shoup Encryption Scheme

We propose our universally anonymizable Cramer-Shoup encryption scheme. Our scheme provides the key-privacy against the adaptive chosen ciphertext attack even if each user chooses an arbitrary prime q where $|q| = k$ and $p = 2q + 1$ is also prime, and uses a group of quadratic residues modulo p.

Note that in our scheme we employ the encoding function and the expanding technique appeared in Section 4.

Definition 13. *Our universally anonymizable Cramer-Shoup encryption scheme* $\mathcal{UAPE}^{CS} = ((\mathcal{K}^{CS}, \mathcal{E}^{CS}, \mathcal{D}^{CS}), \mathcal{UA}^{CS}, \mathcal{DA}^{CS})$ *consists of the Cramer-Shoup encryption scheme* $\mathcal{PE}^{CS} = (\mathcal{K}^{CS}, \mathcal{E}^{CS}, \mathcal{D}^{CS})$ *and two algorithms described as follows.*

Algorithm $\mathcal{UA}_{pk}^{CS}(u_1, u_2, e, v)$
$\quad (\bar{u}_1, \bar{u}_2, \bar{e}, \bar{v}) \leftarrow \bar{F}_{q,4}(u_1, u_2, e, v)$
$\quad t_1 \xleftarrow{R} \{0, 1, 2, \cdots, \lfloor (2^{k+160} - \bar{u}_1)/q \rfloor\}$
$\quad t_2 \xleftarrow{R} \{0, 1, 2, \cdots, \lfloor (2^{k+160} - \bar{u}_2)/q \rfloor\}$
$\quad t_3 \xleftarrow{R} \{0, 1, 2, \cdots, \lfloor (2^{k+160} - \bar{e})/q \rfloor\}$
$\quad t_4 \xleftarrow{R} \{0, 1, 2, \cdots, \lfloor (2^{k+160} - \bar{v})/q \rfloor\}$
$\quad u'_1 \leftarrow \bar{u}_1 + t_1 q; \; u'_2 \leftarrow \bar{u}_2 + t_2 q$
$\quad e' \leftarrow \bar{e} + t_3 q; \; v' \leftarrow \bar{v} + t_4 q$
$\quad$ return (u'_1, u'_2, e', v')

Algorithm $\mathcal{DA}_{sk}^{CS}(u'_1, u'_2, e', v')$
$\quad \bar{u}_1 \leftarrow u'_1 \bmod q; \; \bar{u}_2 \leftarrow u'_2 \bmod q$
$\quad \bar{e} \leftarrow e' \bmod q; \; \bar{v} \leftarrow v' \bmod q$
$\quad (u_1, u_2, e, v) \leftarrow \bar{F}_{q,4}^{-1}(\bar{u}_1, \bar{u}_2, \bar{e}, \bar{v})$
$\quad m \leftarrow \mathcal{D}_{sk}^{CS}(u_1, u_2, e, v)$
$\quad$ return m

5.3 Security

In this section, we prove that our universally anonymizable Cramer-Shoup encryption scheme $\mathcal{UAPE}^{EG}$ is CCA-secure assuming that the DDH problem for $\mathcal{Q}$ is hard and $\mathcal{H}$ is universal one-way.

We can prove that our scheme provides the data-privacy on standard ciphertexts against the adaptive chosen ciphertext attack if the DDH problem for $\mathcal{Q}$ is hard and $\mathcal{H}$ is universal one-way. More precisely, we can prove that if there exists a CCA-adversary A attacking the data-privacy on standard ciphertexts of our scheme with advantage ϵ, then there exists a CCA2-adversary B attacking the indistinguishability of the Cramer-Shoup encryption scheme with the same advantage ϵ. In the reduction of the proof, we have to simulate the decryption oracles for anonymized ciphertexts for A. If A makes a query $c' = (u'_1, u'_2, e', v')$ to $\mathcal{DA}_{sk_0}(\cdot)$, we simply compute $c = (u'_1 \bmod q_0, u'_2 \bmod q_0, e' \bmod q_0, v' \bmod q_0)$ and decrypt c by using the decryption algorithm $\mathcal{D}_{sk_0}(\cdot)$ for standard ciphertexts for B. We can simulate $\mathcal{DA}_{sk_1}(\cdot)$ in a similar way.

In order to prove that our scheme provides the key-privacy and the data-privacy on anonymized ciphertexts against the adaptive chosen ciphertext attack, we need restriction as follows.

We define the set of ciphertexts $EC_{CS}((u'_1, u'_2, e', v'), pk)$ called "equivalence class" as

$$EC_{\mathsf{CS}}((u_1', u_2', e', v'), pk) = \{(\breve{u}_1, \breve{u}_2, \breve{e}, \breve{v}) \in (\{0,1\}^{k+160})^4 |$$
$$\breve{u}_1 = u_1' \pmod{q} \wedge \breve{u}_2 = u_2' \pmod{q} \wedge \breve{e} = e' \pmod{q} \wedge \breve{v} = v' \pmod{q}\}.$$

If $c' = (u_1', u_2', e', v') \in (\{0,1\}^{k+160})^4$ is an anonymized ciphertext of m under $pk = (q, g_1, g_2, c, d, h, K)$ then any element $\breve{c} = (\breve{u}_1, \breve{u}_2, \breve{e}, \breve{v}) \in EC_{\mathsf{CS}}(c', pk)$ is also an anonymized ciphertext of m under pk. Therefore, when c' is a challenge anonymized ciphertext, the adversary can ask an anonymized ciphertext $\breve{c} \in EC_{\mathsf{CS}}(c', pk_0)$ to the decryption oracle $\mathcal{DA}_{sk_0}^{\mathsf{CS}}$ for anonymized ciphertexts, and if the answer of $\mathcal{DA}_{sk_0}^{\mathsf{CS}}$ is m_0 then the adversary knows that c' is encrypted by pk_0 and the plaintext of c' is m_0.

Furthermore, the adversary can ask $(u_1' \bmod q_0, u_2' \bmod q_0, e' \bmod q_0, v' \bmod q_0)$ to the decryption oracle $\mathcal{D}_{sk_0}^{\mathsf{CS}}$ for standard ciphertexts. If the answer of $\mathcal{D}_{sk_0}^{\mathsf{CS}}$ is m_0, then the adversary knows that c' is encrypted by pk_0 and the plaintext of c' is m_0.

To prevent these attacks, we add some natural restriction to the adversaries in the definitions of the key-privacy and the data-privacy on anonymized ciphertexts. That is, it is mandated that the adversary never queries either $\breve{c} \in EC_{\mathsf{CS}}(c', pk_0)$ to $\mathcal{DA}_{sk_0}^{\mathsf{CS}}$ or $\breve{c} \in EC_{\mathsf{CS}}(c', pk_1)$ to $\mathcal{DA}_{sk_1}^{\mathsf{CS}}$. It is also mandated that the adversary never queries either $(u_1' \bmod q_0, u_2' \bmod q_0, e' \bmod q_0, v' \bmod q_0)$ to $\mathcal{D}_{sk_0}^{\mathsf{CS}}$ or $(u_1' \bmod q_1, u_2' \bmod q_1, e' \bmod q_1, v' \bmod q_1)$ to $\mathcal{D}_{sk_1}^{\mathsf{CS}}$.

We think these restrictions are natural and reasonable. Actually, in the case of undeniable and confirmer signature schemes, Galbraith and Mao [8] defined the anonymity on undeniable signature schemes with the above restriction. In [11], Hayashi and Tanaka also employed the same restriction in order to prove the anonymity of their encryption scheme. Incidentally, Canetti, Krawczyk, and Nielsen [4] proposed a relaxed notion of CCA security, called Replayable CCA (RCCA). In their security model, the schemes which require restriction such as equivalence class for proving their CCA security satisfy a variant of RCCA, pd-RCCA (publicly-detectable replayable-CCA) secure.

If we add these restrictions then we can prove that our scheme provides the data-privacy on anonymized ciphertexts against the adaptive chosen ciphertext attack if the DDH problem for $\mathcal{Q}$ is hard and $\mathcal{H}$ is universal one-way. More precisely, we can prove that if there exists a CCA-adversary attacking the data-privacy on anonymized ciphertexts of our scheme with advantage ϵ, then there exists a CCA-adversary attacking the data-privacy on standard ciphertexts of our scheme with the same advantage ϵ.

We now prove our scheme provides the key-privacy against the adaptive chosen ciphertext attack. If we add the restrictions described above, we can prove this in a similar way as that for our universally anonymizable ElGamal encryption scheme. Note that the statistical distance between D_0' and D_1' (See Section 4.3.) is less than $2 \times (1/2^{159})^4$.

In conclusion, our universally anonymizable Cramer-Shoup encryption scheme is CCA-secure assuming that the DDH problem for $\mathcal{Q}$ is hard and $\mathcal{H}$ is universal one-way.

6   RSA-OAEP and Its Universal Anonymizability

In this section, we propose a universally anonymizable RSA-OAEP scheme.

6.1   RSA-OAEP

Definition 14 (RSA-OAEP). *RSA-OAEP* $\mathcal{PE}^{\mathsf{RO}} = (\mathcal{K}^{\mathsf{RO}}, \mathcal{E}^{\mathsf{RO}}, \mathcal{D}^{\mathsf{RO}})$ *is as follows. Let k, k_0 and k_1 be security parameters such that $k_0 + k_1 < k$. This defines an associated plaintext-length $n = k - k_0 - k_1$. The key generation algorithm $\mathcal{K}^{\mathsf{RO}}$ takes as input a security parameter k and runs the key generation algorithm of* RSA *to get N, e, d. It outputs the public key $pk = (N, e)$ and the secret key $sk = d$. The other algorithms are depicted below. Let $G : \{0,1\}^{k_0} \rightarrow \{0,1\}^{n+k_1}$ and $H : \{0,1\}^{n+k_1} \rightarrow \{0,1\}^{k_0}$ be hash functions. Note that $[x]^\ell$ denotes the ℓ most significant bits of x, and $[x]_{\ell'}$ denotes the ℓ' least significant bits of x.*

Algorithm $\mathcal{E}_{pk}^{\mathsf{RO}}(m)$	Algorithm $\mathcal{D}_{sk}^{\mathsf{RO}}(c)$
$r \xleftarrow{R} \{0,1\}^{k_0}$	$s \leftarrow [c^d \bmod N]^{n+k_1}$; $t \leftarrow [c^d \bmod N]_{k_0}$
$s \leftarrow (m \| 0^{k_1}) \oplus G(r)$	$r \leftarrow t \oplus H(s)$
$t \leftarrow r \oplus H(s)$	$m \leftarrow [s \oplus G(r)]^n$; $p \leftarrow [s \oplus G(r)]_{k_1}$
$c \leftarrow (s \| t)^e \bmod N$	if $(p = 0^{k_1})$ $z \leftarrow m$ else $z \leftarrow \perp$
return c	return z

Fujisaki, Okamoto, Pointcheval, and Stern [7] proved that OAEP with partial one-way permutations is secure in the sense of IND-CCA2 in the random oracle model. They also showed that RSA is one-way if and only if RSA is θ-partial one-way for $\theta > 0.5$. Thus, RSA-OAEP is secure in the sense of IND-CCA2 in the random oracle model assuming RSA is one-way.

6.2   Universal Anonymizability of RSA-OAEP

A simple observation that seems to be folklore is that if one publishes the ciphertext of the RSA-OAEP scheme directly (without anonymization) then the scheme does not provide the key-privacy. Suppose an adversary knows that the ciphertext c is created under one of two keys (N_0, e_0) or (N_1, e_1), and suppose $N_0 \leq N_1$. If $c \geq N_0$ then the adversary bets it was created under (N_1, e_1), else the adversary bets it was created under (N_0, e_0). It is not hard to see that this attack has non-negligible advantage.

To anonymize ciphertexts of RSA-OAEP, we do not have to employ the encoding function and we only use the expanding technique.

Definition 15. *Our universally anonymizable RSA-OAEP scheme $\mathcal{UAPE}^{\mathsf{RO}} = ((\mathcal{K}^{\mathsf{RO}}, \mathcal{E}^{\mathsf{RO}}, \mathcal{D}^{\mathsf{RO}}), \mathcal{UA}^{\mathsf{RO}}, \mathcal{DA}^{\mathsf{RO}})$ consists of RSA-OAEP $\mathcal{PE}^{\mathsf{RO}} = (\mathcal{K}^{\mathsf{RO}}, \mathcal{E}^{\mathsf{RO}}, \mathcal{D}^{\mathsf{RO}})$ and two algorithms described as follows.*

Algorithm $\mathcal{UA}_{pk}^{\mathsf{RO}}(c)$	Algorithm $\mathcal{DA}_{sk}^{\mathsf{RO}}(c')$
$\alpha \xleftarrow{R} \{0, 1, 2, \cdots, \lfloor (2^{k+160} - c)/N \rfloor\}$	$c \leftarrow c' \bmod N$
$c' \leftarrow c + \alpha N$	$z \leftarrow \mathcal{D}_{sk}^{\mathsf{RO}}(c)$
return c'	return z

6.3   Security

In this section, we prove that our universally anonymizable RSA-OAEP scheme $\mathcal{UAPE}^{\mathsf{RO}}$ is CCA-secure in the random oracle model assuming RSA is one-way.

We can prove that our scheme provides the data-privacy on standard ciphertexts against the adaptive chosen ciphertext attack in the random oracle model assuming RSA is θ-partial one-way for $\theta > 0.5$. More precisely, if RSA-OAEP is secure in the sense of IND-CCA2 then our scheme provides the data-privacy on standard ciphertexts against the adaptive chosen ciphertext attack. The proof is similar to that for our universally anonymizable Cramer-Shoup encryption scheme.

In order to prove that our scheme provides the key-privacy and the data-privacy on anonymized ciphertexts against the adaptive chosen ciphertext attack, we need the restrictions similar to those for our universally anonymizable Cramer-Shoup encryption scheme. We define the equivalence class for our universally anonymizable RSA-OAEP scheme as

$$EC_{\mathsf{RO}}(c', pk) = \{\check{c} \in \{0,1\}^{k+160} | \check{c} = c' \ (\mathrm{mod}\ N)\}$$

where $pk = (N, e)$ and it is mandated that the adversary never queries either $\check{c} \in EC_{\mathsf{RO}}(c', pk_0)$ to $\mathcal{DA}^{\mathsf{RO}}_{sk_0}$ or $\check{c} \in EC_{\mathsf{RO}}(c', pk_1)$ to $\mathcal{DA}^{\mathsf{RO}}_{sk_1}$. It is also mandated that the adversary never queries either $c' \bmod N_0$ to $\mathcal{D}^{\mathsf{RO}}_{sk_0}$ or $c' \bmod N_1$ to $\mathcal{D}^{\mathsf{RO}}_{sk_1}$.

If we add these restrictions then we can prove that our scheme provides the data-privacy on anonymized ciphertexts against the adaptive chosen ciphertext attack in the random oracle model assuming RSA is θ-partial one-way for $\theta > 0.5$ in a similar way as that for our universally anonymizable Cramer-Shoup encryption scheme.

Furthermore, if we add the restrictions described above, then we can prove that our scheme provides the key-privacy against the adaptive chosen ciphertext attack in the random oracle model assuming RSA is θ-partial one-way for $\theta > 0.5$. More precisely, we show the following theorem [1].

Theorem 1. *For any adversary A attacking the key-privacy of our scheme under the adaptive chosen ciphertext attack, and making at most q_{dec} queries to decryption oracle for standard ciphertexts, q'_{dec} queries to decryption oracle for anonymized ciphertexts, q_{gen} G-oracle queries, and q_{hash} H-oracle queries, there exists a θ-partial inverting adversary B for RSA, such that for any k, k_0, k_1, and $\theta = \frac{k-k_0}{k}$,*

$$\mathbf{Adv}^{\mathrm{key\text{-}cca}}_{\mathcal{UAPE}^{\mathsf{RO}}, A}(k) \leq 8q_{\mathrm{hash}} \cdot ((1 - \epsilon_1) \cdot (1 - \epsilon_2))^{-1} \cdot \mathbf{Adv}^{\theta\text{-}\mathrm{pow\text{-}fnc}}_{\mathsf{RSA}, B}(k)$$

$$+ q_{\mathrm{gen}} \cdot (1 - \epsilon_2)^{-1} \cdot 2^{-k+2}$$

---

[1] Halevi [9] noted that we cannot apply Lemma 1 directly to the schemes analyzed in the random oracle model.

where $\epsilon_1 = \frac{2}{2^{k/2-3}-1} + \frac{1}{2^{159}}$, $\epsilon_2 = \frac{2q_{\text{gen}}+q_{\text{dec}}+q'_{\text{dec}}+2q_{\text{gen}}(q_{\text{dec}}+q'_{\text{dec}})}{2^{k_0}} + \frac{2(q_{\text{dec}}+q'_{\text{dec}})}{2^{k_1}} + \frac{2q_{\text{hash}}}{2^{k-k_0}}$, *and the running time of* B *is that of* A *plus* $q_{\text{gen}} \cdot q_{\text{hash}} \cdot O(k^3)$.

In conclusion, since RSA is θ-partial one-way if and only if RSA is one-way for $\theta > 0.5$, our universally anonymizable RSA-OAEP scheme is CCA-secure in the random oracle model assuming RSA is one-way.

6.4   Proof of Theorem 1

The proof is similar to that for RSA-RAEP. We construct the partial inverting algorithm M for the RSA function using a CCA-adversary A attacking the key-privacy of our encryption scheme. We describe the partial inverting algorithm M for RSA using a CCA-adversary A attacking the anonymity of our encryption scheme. M is given $pk = (N, e, k)$ and a point $y \in \mathbb{Z}_N^*$ where $|y| = k = n+k_0+k_1$. Let $sk = (N, d, k)$ be the corresponding secret key. The algorithm is trying to find the $n + k_1$ most significant bits of the e-th root of y modulo N.

1) M picks $\mu \xleftarrow{R} \{0, 1, 2, \ldots, \lfloor(2^{k+160} - y)/N\rfloor\}$ and sets $Y \leftarrow y + \mu N$.
2) M runs the key generation algorithm of RSA with security parameter k to obtain $pk' = (N', e', k)$ and $sk' = (N', d', k)$. Then it picks a bit $b \xleftarrow{R} \{0, 1\}$, and sets $pk_b \leftarrow (N, e)$ and $pk_{1-b} \leftarrow (N', e')$. If the above y does not satisfy $y \in (\mathbb{Z}_{N_0}^* \cap \mathbb{Z}_{N_1}^*)$ then M outputs Fail and halts; else it continues.
3) M initializes four lists, called G-list, H-list, Y_0-list, and Y_1-list to empty. It then runs A as follows. Note that M simulates A's oracles G, H, $\mathcal{D}_{sk_0}$, and $\mathcal{D}_{sk_1}$ as described below.
   3-1) M runs $A_1(pk_0, pk_1)$ and gets (m_0, m_1, si) which is the output of A_1.
   3-2) M runs $A_2(Y, \text{si})$ and gets a bit $d \in \{0, 1\}$ which is the output of A_2.
4) M chooses a random element on the H-list and outputs it as its guess for the $n + k_1$ most significant bits of the e-th root of y modulo N.

M simulates A's oracles G, H, $\mathcal{D}_{sk_0}$, and $\mathcal{D}_{sk_1}$ as follows:

- When A makes an oracle query g to G, then for each (h, H_h) on the H-list, M builds $z = h\|(g \oplus H_h)$, and computes $y_{h,g,0} = z^{e_0} \bmod N_0$ and $y_{h,g,1} = z^{e_1} \bmod N_1$. For $i \in \{0, 1\}$, M checks whether $y = y_{h,g,i}$. If for some h and i such a relation holds, then we have inverted y under pk_i, and we can still correctly simulate G by answering $G_g = h \oplus (m_i\|0^{k_1})$. Otherwise, M outputs a random value G_g of length $n + k_1$. In both cases, M adds (g, G_g) to the G-list. Then, for all h, M checks if the k_1 least significant bits of $h \oplus G_g$ are all 0. If they are, then it adds $y_{h,g,0}$ and $y_{h,g,1}$ to the Y_0-list and the Y_1-list, respectively.
- When A makes an oracle query h to H, M provides A with a random string H_h of length k_0 and adds (h, H_h) to the H-list. Then for each (g, G_g) on the G-list, M builds $z = h\|(g \oplus H_h)$, and computes $y_{h,g,0} = z^{e_0} \bmod N_0$ and $y_{h,g,1} = z^{e_1} \bmod N_1$. M checks if the k_1 least significant bits of $h \oplus G_g$ are all 0. If they are, then it adds $y_{h,g,0}$ and $y_{h,g,1}$ to the Y_0-list and the Y_1-list, respectively.

- When for $i \in \{0,1\}$, A makes an oracle query $\hat{y} \in \mathbb{Z}_{N_i}^*$ to $\mathcal{D}_{sk_i}$, M checks if there exists some $y_{h,g,i}$ in the Y_i-list such that $\hat{y} = y_{h,g,i}$. If there is, then it returns the n most significant bits of $h \oplus G_g$ to A. Otherwise it returns $\bot$ (indicating that $\hat{y}$ is an invalid ciphertext).
- When for $i \in \{0,1\}$, A makes an oracle query $\hat{Y} \in \{0,1\}^{k+160}$ to $\mathcal{D}\mathcal{A}_{sk_i}$, M checks if there exists some $y_{h,g,i}$ in the Y_i-list such that $\hat{Y} \bmod N_i = y_{h,g,i}$. If there is, then it returns the n most significant bits of $h \oplus G_g$ to A. Otherwise it returns $\bot$ (indicating that $\hat{Y}$ is an invalid anonymized ciphertext).

In order to analyze the advantage of M, we define some events. For $i \in \{0,1\}$, let $w_i = y^{d_i} \bmod N_i$, $s_i = [w_i]^{n+k_1}$, and $t_i = [w_i]_{k_0}$.

- DSBad denotes the event that
    - A $\mathcal{D}_{sk_0}$ query is not correctly answered, or
    - A $\mathcal{D}_{sk_1}$ query is not correctly answered.
- DABad denotes the event that
    - A $\mathcal{D}\mathcal{A}_{sk_0}$ query is not correctly answered, or
    - A $\mathcal{D}\mathcal{A}_{sk_1}$ query is not correctly answered.
- DBad = DSBad $\vee$ DABad.
- YBad denotes the event that $y \notin (\mathbb{Z}_{N_0}^* \cap \mathbb{Z}_{N_1}^*)$.
- AskR denotes the event that (r_0, G_{r_0}) or (r_1, G_{r_1}) is on the G-list at the end of step 3-2.
- AskS denotes the event that (s_0, H_{s_0}) or (s_1, H_{s_1}) is on the H-list at the end of step 3-2.

We let $\Pr[\cdot]$ denote the probability distribution in the game defining advantage and $\Pr_1[\cdot]$ the probability distribution in the simulated game where $\neg$YBad occurs. We can bound $\Pr_1[\mathsf{AskS}]$ in a similar way as in the proof of the anonymity for RSA-RAEP [1], and we have

$$\Pr_1[\mathsf{AskS}] \geq \frac{1}{2} \cdot \Pr_1[\mathsf{AskR} \wedge \mathsf{AskS}|\neg\mathsf{DBad}] \cdot \Pr_1[\neg\mathsf{DBad}|\neg\mathsf{AskS}].$$

We next bound $\Pr_1[\mathsf{AskR} \wedge \mathsf{AskS}|\neg\mathsf{DBad}]$. Let $\epsilon = \mathbf{Adv}_{\mathcal{UAPE}^{\mathrm{RO}},A}^{\mathrm{key\text{-}cca}}(k)$. The proof of the following lemma is similar to that for RSA-RAEP.

Lemma 2.

$$\Pr_1[\mathsf{AskR} \wedge \mathsf{AskS}|\neg\mathsf{DBad}] \geq \frac{\epsilon}{2} \cdot \left(1 - 2q_{\mathrm{gen}} \cdot 2^{-k_0} - 2q_{\mathrm{hash}} \cdot 2^{-n-k_1}\right) - 2q_{\mathrm{gen}} \cdot 2^{-k}.$$

We next bound $\Pr_1[\neg\mathsf{DBad}|\neg\mathsf{AskS}]$. It is easy to see that $\Pr_1[\neg\mathsf{DBad}|\neg\mathsf{AskS}] \leq \Pr_1[\neg\mathsf{DSBad}|\neg\mathsf{AskS}] + \Pr_1[\neg\mathsf{DABad}|\neg\mathsf{AskS}]$, and the proof of the following lemma is similar to that for RSA-RAEP.

Lemma 3.

$$\Pr_1[\mathsf{DSBad}|\neg\mathsf{AskS}] \leq q_{\mathrm{dec}} \cdot \left(2 \cdot 2^{-k_1} + (2q_{\mathrm{gen}} + 1) \cdot 2^{-k_0}\right),$$
$$\Pr_1[\mathsf{DABad}|\neg\mathsf{AskS}] \leq q_{\mathrm{dec}}' \cdot \left(2 \cdot 2^{-k_1} + (2q_{\mathrm{gen}} + 1) \cdot 2^{-k_0}\right).$$

By applying Lemmas 2 and 3, we can bound $\Pr_1[\mathsf{AskS}]$ as

$\Pr_1[\mathsf{AskS}]$

$\geq \frac{1}{2} \cdot \left(\frac{\epsilon}{2} \cdot \left(1 - \frac{2q_{\mathrm{gen}}}{2^{k_0}} - \frac{2q_{\mathrm{hash}}}{2^{n+k_1}}\right) - \frac{2q_{\mathrm{gen}}}{2^k}\right) \cdot \left(1 - (q_{\mathrm{dec}} + q'_{\mathrm{dec}}) \cdot \left(\frac{2}{2^{k_1}} + \frac{2q_{\mathrm{gen}}+1}{2^{k_0}}\right)\right)$

$\geq \frac{\epsilon}{4} \cdot \left(1 - \frac{2q_{\mathrm{gen}}+q_{\mathrm{dec}}+q'_{\mathrm{dec}}+2q_{\mathrm{gen}}(q_{\mathrm{dec}}+q'_{\mathrm{dec}})}{2^{k_0}} - \frac{2(q_{\mathrm{dec}}+q'_{\mathrm{dec}})}{2^{k_1}} - \frac{2q_{\mathrm{hash}}}{2^{k-k_0}}\right) - \frac{q_{\mathrm{gen}}}{2^k}.$

We next bound the probability that $\neg\mathsf{YBad}$ occurs.

Lemma 4.

$$\Pr[\mathsf{YBad}] \leq \frac{2}{2^{k/2-3}-1} + \frac{1}{2^{159}}.$$

Proof (Lemma 4). Let $N = pq$ and $N' = p'q'$. We define a set $S[N]$ as $\{\tilde{Y}|\tilde{Y} \in [0, 2^{k+160}) \wedge (\tilde{Y} \bmod N) \in \mathbb{Z}_N^*\}$. Then, we have

$\Pr[\mathsf{YBad}]$

$= \Pr[y \overset{R}{\leftarrow} \mathbb{Z}_N^*;\ \mu \overset{R}{\leftarrow} \{0,1,2,\ldots,\lfloor(2^{k+160}-y)/N\rfloor\};\ Y \leftarrow y + \mu N :\ Y \notin S[N']]$

$\leq \Pr[Y' \overset{R}{\leftarrow} S[N] :\ Y' \notin S[N']] + 1/2^{159}$

since the distribution of Y' is statistical indistinguishable from that of Y, and the statistically distance is less than $1/2^{159}$.

Since $2^{160} \cdot \phi(N) \leq |S[N]| \leq 2^{k+160}$, we have

$$\Pr[Y' \overset{R}{\leftarrow} S[N] :\ Y' \notin S[N']] \leq \frac{2^{k+160}-|S[N']|}{|S[N]|} \leq \frac{2^{k+160}-|S[N']|}{2^{160}\cdot\phi(N)}.$$

Furthermore, we have

$$\begin{aligned}
2^{k+160} - |S[N']| &= \left|\{Y'|Y' \in [0, 2^{k+160}) \wedge (Y' \bmod N') \notin \mathbb{Z}_{N'}^*\}\right| \\
&\leq \left|\{Y'|Y' \in [0, 2N' \cdot 2^{160}) \wedge (Y' \bmod N') \notin \mathbb{Z}_{N'}^*\}\right| \\
&= 2^{161} \times \left|\{Y'|Y' \in [0, N') \wedge Y' \notin \mathbb{Z}_{N'}^*\}\right| \\
&= 2^{161}(N' - \phi(N')).
\end{aligned}$$

Noticing that $2^{\lceil k/2\rceil-1} < p, q, p', q' < 2^{\lceil k/2\rceil}$ and $2^{k-1} < N, N' < 2^k$, we have

$$\begin{aligned}
\Pr[Y' &\overset{R}{\leftarrow} S[N] :\ Y' \notin S[N']] \\
&\leq \frac{2^{161}(N'-\phi(N'))}{2^{160}\cdot\phi(N)} \leq \frac{2(p'+q')}{N-p-q} \leq \frac{2(2^{\lceil k/2\rceil}+2^{\lceil k/2\rceil})}{2^{k-1}-2^{\lceil k/2\rceil}-2^{\lceil k/2\rceil}} \leq \frac{2}{2^{k/2-3}-1}.
\end{aligned}$$

Assuming $\neg\mathsf{YBad}$ occurs, we have by the random choice of b and symmetry, that the probability of M outputting s is at least $\frac{1}{2q_{\mathrm{hash}}} \cdot \Pr_1[\mathsf{AskS}]$. Thus,

$$\mathbf{Adv}_{\mathrm{RSA},B}^{\theta\text{-pow-fnc}}(k) \geq (1 - \Pr[\mathsf{YBad}]) \cdot \left(\frac{\Pr_1[\mathsf{AskS}]}{2q_{\mathrm{hash}}}\right).$$

Substituting the bounds for the above probabilities and re-arranging the terms, we get the claimed result.

Finally, we estimate the time complexity of M. It is the time complexity of A plus the time for simulating the random oracles. In the random oracle simulation, for each pair $((g, G_g), (h, H_h))$, it is sufficient to compute $y_{h,g,0} = z^{e_0} \bmod N_0$ and $y_{h,g,1} = z^{e_1} \bmod N_1$. Therefore, the time complexity of M is that of A plus $q_{\mathrm{gen}} \cdot q_{\mathrm{hash}} \cdot O(k^3)$.

References

1. M. Bellare, A. Boldyreva, A. Desai, and D. Pointcheval. Key-Privacy in Public-Key Encryption. In Boyd [3], pages 566–582. Full version of this paper, available via http://www-cse.ucsd.edu/users/mihir/.
2. M. Bellare and P. Rogaway. Optimal Asymmetric Encryption – How to Encrypt with RSA. In A. De Santis, editor, *Advances in Cryptology – EUROCRYPT '94*, volume 950 of *LNCS*, pages 92–111, 1994. Springer-Verlag.
3. C. Boyd, editor. *Advances in Cryptology – ASIACRYPT 2001*, volume 2248 of *LNCS*, 2001. Springer-Verlag.
4. R. Canetti, H. Krawczyk, and J. B. Nielsen. Relaxing Chosen-Ciphertext Security. In D. Boneh, editor, *Advances in Cryptology – CRYPTO 2003*, volume 2729 of *LNCS*, pages 565–582, 2003. Springer-Verlag.
5. R. Cramer and V. Shoup. A Practical Public Key Cryptosystem Provably Secure against Adaptive Chosen Ciphertext Attack. In H. Krawczyk, editor, *Advances in Cryptology – CRYPTO '98*, volume 1462 of *LNCS*, pages 13–25, 1998. Springer-Verlag.
6. Y. Desmedt. Securing traceability of ciphertexts: Towards a secure software escrow scheme. In L. C. Guillou and J.-J. Quisquater, editors, *Advances in Cryptology – EUROCRYPT '95*, volume 921 of *LNCS*, pages 147–157, 1995. Springer-Verlag.
7. E. Fujisaki, T. Okamoto, D. Pointcheval, and J. Stern. RSA-OAEP is Secure under the RSA Assumption. In J. Kilian, editor, *Advances in Cryptology – CRYPTO 2001*, volume 2139 of *LNCS*, pages 260–274, 2001. Springer-Verlag.
8. S. D. Galbraith and W. Mao. Invisibility and Anonymity of Undeniable and Confirmer Signatures. In M. Joye, editor, *Topics in Cryptology – CT-RSA 2003*, volume 2612 of *LNCS*, pages 80–97, 2003. Springer-Verlag.
9. S. Halevi. A Sufficient Condition for Key-Privacy. IACR Cryptology ePrint Archive, http://eprint.iacr.org/2005/005.pdf, 2005.
10. R. Hayashi, T. Okamoto, and K. Tanaka. An RSA Family of Trap-door Permutations with a Common Domain and its Applications. In F. Bao, R. H. Deng, and J. Zhou, editors, *Public Key Cryptography – PKC 2004*, volume 2947 of *LNCS*, pages 291–304, 2004. Springer-Verlag.
11. R. Hayashi and K. Tanaka. The Sampling Twice Technique for the RSA-based Cryptosystems with Anonymity. In S. Vaudenay, editor, *Public Key Cryptography – PKC 2005*, volume 3386 of *LNCS*, pages 216–233, 2005. Springer-Verlag.
12. S. Lucks. A Variant of the Cramer-Shoup Cryptosystem for Groups of Unknown Order. In Y. Zheng, editor, *Advances in Cryptology – ASIACRYPT 2002*, volume 2501 of *LNCS*, pages 27–45, 2002. Springer-Verlag.
13. R. L. Rivest, A. Shamir, and Y. Tauman. How to Leak a Secret. In Boyd [3], pages 552–565.

Fast Computation of Large Distributions and Its Cryptographic Applications*

Alexander Maximov and Thomas Johansson

Dept. of Information Technology, Lund University, Sweden,
P.O. Box 118, 221 00 Lund, Sweden
{movax, thomas}@it.lth.se

Abstract. Let $X_1, X_2, \ldots, X_k$ be independent n bit random variables. If they have *arbitrary* distributions, we show how to compute distributions like $\Pr\{X_1 \oplus X_2 \oplus \cdots \oplus X_k\}$ and $\Pr\{X_1 \boxplus X_2 \boxplus \cdots \boxplus X_k\}$ in complexity $O(kn2^n)$. Furthermore, if $X_1, X_2, \ldots, X_k$ are *uniformly* distributed we demonstrate a large class of functions $F(X_1, X_2, \ldots, X_k)$, for which we can compute their distributions efficiently.

These results have applications in linear cryptanalysis of stream ciphers as well as block ciphers. A typical example is the approximation obtained when additions modulo 2^n are replaced by bitwise addition. The efficiency of such an approach is given by the bias of a distribution of the above kind. As an example, we give a new improved distinguishing attack on the stream cipher SNOW 2.0.

Keywords: cryptanalysis, complexity, algorithms, convolution, approximations, large distributions, pseudo-linear functions.

1 Introduction

Linear cryptanalysis is one of the most powerful techniques for cryptanalysis. It can be regarded as a generic attack. It is for example the fastest known attack on DES. More recently, we have seen that linear cryptanalysis also plays a major role in the area of stream ciphers. Many recent proposals have been analyzed through the idea of replacing nonlinear operations by linear ones, and then hoping that obtained linear equations are correct with a probability slightly larger than otherwise expected. Actually, the best known attacks on many recent stream cipher proposals are linear attacks. This includes stream ciphers like Scream [1], SNOW [2,3], SOBER [4,5], RC4 [6], A5/1 [7], and many more.

Most work in linear cryptanalysis on block ciphers are based on bitwise linear approximations. To oversimplify, we find a sum of certain plaintext bits, ciphertext bits and key bits such that this sum is zero with a probability $1/2 + \epsilon$,

---

* The work described in this paper has been supported in part by Grant VR 621-2001-2149, and in part by the European Commission through the IST Program under Contract IST-2002-507932 ECRYPT. The information in this document reflects only the author's views, is provided as is and no guarantee or warranty is given that the information is fit for any particular purpose. The user thereof uses the information at its sole risk and liability.

B. Roy (Ed.): ASIACRYPT 2005, LNCS 3788, pp. 313–332, 2005.

where ϵ is usually small. By getting access to a large number of different plaintext/ciphertext pairs we can eventually find out the value of the sum of key bits. This results in a key recovery attack.

In linear attacks on stream ciphers, it is mostly the case that a linear approximation will give us a set of keystream symbols that sum to zero with probability $1/2 + \epsilon$. Since no key bits are involved in the expression, this gives us a distinguishing attack. In some linear attacks on stream ciphers, one has moved from the binary alphabet to instead consider a sum of variables defined over a larger set. For example, we can consider a sum of different bytes from keystream sequence if it is byte oriented. Distinguishers based on symbols from a larger alphabet have been considered in for example [8,9,10].

It is clear that moving to a larger alphabet gives improved results. However, the computational complexity of finding the result increases. To be a bit more specific, assume for example that the operation $X_1 \boxplus X_2$ is replaced by $X_1 \oplus X_2$, where $\boxplus$ denotes mod 2^n addition. The usefulness of such an approximation is given by the distribution $\Pr\{(X_1 \boxplus X_2) \oplus (X_1 \oplus X_2) = \gamma\}$. However, the complexity of computing this distribution can be large. For example, for $n = 32$ bits a straight forward approach would require complexity 2^{64}, an impossible size to implement.

Several previous papers studied related problems. For example, in [11] differential properties of addition, such as $\mathtt{DC}^+(\alpha, \beta \rightarrow \gamma) := \Pr\{(x \boxplus y) \oplus ((x \oplus \alpha) \boxplus (y \oplus \beta)) = \gamma\}$, were studied in details, including different useful and efficient computational algorithms. There are a few other results where different classes of similar functions (mostly related to differential properties) were achieved, e.g., in [12,13,14], and others. However, these papers focus only on a small class of functions, which can be regarded as a subclass of the functions studied in this paper, refered to as pseudo-linear functions. Moreover, our main concern is the algorithms on large distribution tables, i.e., to provide a practical tool for cryptanalysis over large distributions (or a large alphabet). When, for example, the probability space is $|\Omega| = 2^{32}$, our algorithms and data structures allow us to store and perform the most common operations over such huge distributions, with a reasonable time on a usual PC.

Consider $X_1, X_2, \ldots, X_k$ to be independent n bit random variables. If they have *arbitrary* distributions, we show how to compute distributions like $\Pr\{X_1 \oplus X_2 \oplus \cdots \oplus X_k\}$ and $\Pr\{X_1 \boxplus X_2 \boxplus \cdots \boxplus X_k\}$ in complexity $O(kn2^n)$. For example, we compute the distribution $\Pr\{(X_1 \boxplus X_2) \oplus (X_1 \oplus X_2) = \gamma\}$ in complexity $2^{37} \cdot c$ for some small c. The presented algorithms makes use of techniques from Fast Fourier Transform and Fast Hadamard Transform. Although some of these techniques were also mentioned in a recent paper [15], we include the full approach for completeness. We show how they can be performed when more complicated data structures are used, introduced due to a high memory complexity.

Next, if $X_1, X_2, \ldots, X_k$ are *uniformly* distributed we demonstrate a large class of functions $F(X_1, X_2, \ldots, X_k)$, for which we can compute the distribution $\Pr\{F(X_1, X_2, \ldots, X_k) = \gamma\}$ efficiently. Here, the algorithms are based on performing a combinatorial count in a bitwise fashion, taking the "carry depth" into account. These results give us efficient methods of calculating distributions of *certain* functions $F(X_1, X_2, \ldots, X_k)$. Fortunately, this includes many functions that appear in linear analysis of ciphers.

As an example, we show an application in linear cryptanalysis of stream ciphers. A typical operation is the approximation obtained when additions modulo 2^n are replaced by bitwise addition. The efficiency of such an approach is given by the bias of a distribution of the above kind. In our example, we give a new improved distinguishing attack on the stream cipher SNOW 2.0.

In Section 2 we define a pseudo-linear class of functions and derive an algorithm to calculate their distributions. In Section 3 we show how a convolution of several distributions can be calculated efficiently. In Section 4 an application example of our approach to attack SNOW 2.0 is given. Finally, we summarize our results and make conclusions.

2   A Pseudo-Linear Function Modulo 2^n and Its Distribution

For notation purposes we denote n-bit variables by a capital letter X, and 1-bit variables by a small letter x. Individual bits of X in a vector form are represented as $X = \overline{x_{n-1} \ldots x_1 x_0}$. By $X[a : b]$ we denote an integer number of the form $\overline{x_b \ldots x_{a+1} x_a}$. If $Y = \overline{y_{m-1} \ldots y_0}$, then $X || Y = \overline{x_{n-1} \ldots x_0 y_{m-1} \ldots y_0}$ is another integer number (*concatenation*). We use '$\boxplus$' and '$\boxminus$' to denote arithmetical addition and subtraction modulo 2^n, respectively. However, when the inputs to a function $F(\cdot)$ are from the ring $\mathbb{Z}_{2^n}$, we assume '$+$' to be an addition in the ring as well. Matrix multiplication is denoted as '$\times$'. When '$\cdot$' is applied to two vectors, then it denotes element-by-element multiplication of corresponding positions from the vectors.

2.1   A Pseudo-Linear Function Modulo 2^n

Let $\mathcal{X}$ be a set of k uniformly distributed n-bit (nonnegative) integer random variables $\mathcal{X} = \{X_1, \ldots, X_k\}$, $X_i \in \mathbb{Z}_{2^n}$. Let $\mathcal{C}$ be a set of n-bit constants $\mathcal{C} = \{C_1, \ldots, C_l\}$. Let T_i be some symbol or expression on $\mathcal{X}$ and $\mathcal{C}$. We define *arithmetic*, *Boolean*, and *simple* terms as follows.

Definition 1. *Given $\mathcal{X}$ and $\mathcal{C}$ we say that: (1) $\mathcal{A}$ is an 'arithmetic term', if it has only the arithmetic $+$ operator between the input terms (e.g., $\mathcal{A} = T_1 + T_2 + \ldots$); (2) $\mathcal{B}$ is a 'Boolean term' if it contains only bitwise operators such as NOT, OR, AND, XOR, and others (e.g., $\mathcal{B} = (\overline{T_1} \oplus T_2) | T_3 \& \overline{T_4} \ldots$); (3) $\mathcal{S}$ is a 'simple term' if it is a symbol either from $\mathcal{X}$ or $\mathcal{C}$ (e.g., $\mathcal{S} = X_i$).* ☐

Next, we define a *pseudo-linear function modulo 2^n*.

Definition 2. *$F(X_1, \ldots, X_k)$ is called a 'pseudo-linear function modulo 2^n' (PLFM) on $\mathcal{X}$ if it can recursively be expressed in arithmetic ($\mathcal{A}$), Boolean ($\mathcal{B}$),* *and simple (S) terms* [1]. *We also refer the number of* $\mathcal{A}$, $\mathcal{B}$, *and* $\mathcal{S}$ *terms to be* a, b, *and* s, *respectively.*   □

Note, if a given function contains a subtraction $\boxminus$, then it can easily be substituted by $\boxplus$ using

$$X \boxminus Y \equiv X \boxplus (\text{NOT } Y) \boxplus 1 \mod 2^n, \tag{1}$$

which is valid in the ring modulo 2^n. Note that the number of $\mathcal{A}$-terms does not grow during the substitution

As an example, let us consider a linear approximation of a modulo sum of the following kind '$X_1 \boxplus X_2 \boxplus X_3 \rightarrow X_1 \oplus X_2 \oplus X_3 \oplus N$', where N is the noise variable introduced due to the approximation. The expression for the noise variable is a PLFM: $N = F(X_1, X_2, X_3) = (X_1 + X_2 + X_3) \oplus X_1 \oplus X_2 \oplus X_3$.

Finding the distribution of such an approximation could be the bottleneck in cryptanalysis work. The trivial algorithm for solving this problem would be as follows.

```
1.   Loop for all  (X₁, X₂, X₃) ∈ ℤ₂ⁿ³
2.       T[(X₁ ⊞ X₂ ⊞ X₃) ⊕ X₁ ⊕ X₂ ⊕ X₃] + +;
```

After termination of the algorithm we have $\Pr\{N = \gamma\} = T[\gamma]/2^{3n}$. The complexity of this classical solution when the variables are 32-bits integers, is $O(2^{96})$, infeasible for a common PC. Instead, we suggest another principle to solve this problem, as follows.

```
1.   for  γ = 0 ... 2ⁿ − 1
2.       T[γ]  =  some combinatorial function.
```

In the upcoming section we show how this combinatorial function is constructed.

2.2   Algorithm for Calculating the Distribution for a PLFM

The problem we are considering in this subsection is the following. Given a PLFM $F(X_1, X_2, \ldots, X_k)$ on $\mathcal{X}$ and $\mathcal{C}$, we want to calculate the probability $\Pr\{F(X_1, X_2, \ldots, X_k) = \gamma\}$, for a fixed value γ, in an efficient way.

Let some arithmetic term $\mathcal{A}$ have k^+ operators '+', i.e., $\mathcal{A} = T_0 + T_1 + \ldots + T_k$, where T_j are some other terms, possibly $\mathcal{B}$ or $\mathcal{S}$. Then, considering 1-bit inputs, the evaluation of the $\mathcal{A}$ term can, potentially, produce the *local* maximum carry value $\omega_{max} = \lfloor \frac{k^+ + 1}{2} \rfloor$. This carry value at some bit t can influence on the next bits of the sum at positions $t+1, t+2$, etc. Therefore, the maximum carry value σ_{max} at every bit t of the sum for $\mathcal{A}$ is then derived as the minimum integer solution for the equation $\sigma_{max} = \lfloor (k^+ + 1 + \sigma_{max})/2 \rfloor$. Thus, for every arithmetic term $\mathcal{A}_i$ the *maximum local carry value* is

$$\sigma_{imax} = k_i^+, \tag{2}$$

where k_i^+ is the number of additions in $\mathcal{A}_i$.

---

[1] Note that a PLFM is a T-function [16], but not vice versa.

For any t-bit truncated input tuple $(X_1, \ldots, X_k)$ to the function $F(\cdot)$ we can define *a tuple of local carry values* for each of the $\mathcal{A}_i$-terms, as follows:

$$\Psi|_t = (\sigma_1, \sigma_2, \ldots, \sigma_a)|_t, \tag{3}$$

where σ_i is the corresponding local carry value for the $\mathcal{A}_i$-term, when the inputs are t-bit truncated, and it can also be expressed as

$$\sigma_i|_t = \left(\sum_{j=0}^{k_i^+} (T_{i,j}(X_1, \ldots, X_k) \mod 2^t) \right) \text{div } 2^t, \tag{4}$$

when $\mathcal{A}_i = T_{i,0} + \ldots + T_{i,k_i^+}$.

Assume there is an oracle $P_t(\Psi_0, \gamma)$ which can tell us the number of choices of the tuple $(X_1[0:t-1], \ldots, X_k[0:t-1])$ out of $2^{t \cdot k}$ possible combinations, such that for each choice the function F produces a required vector of local carry values $\Psi|_t = \Psi_0$, and the condition $F(X_1, \ldots, X_k) = \gamma \mod 2^t$ is satisfied, i.e. $F(X_1, \ldots, X_k)[0:t-1] = \gamma[0:t-1]$. The probability we are seeking can now be written as

$$\Pr\{F(X_1, \ldots, X_k) = \gamma\} = \frac{1}{2^{k \cdot n}} \sum_{\Psi} P_n(\Psi, \gamma). \tag{5}$$

It remains to show how to construct the oracles $P_t(\Psi_0, \gamma)$. Assume we know the answer $P_t(\Psi_0, \gamma)$ for every Ψ_0. When $\Psi|_t = \Psi_0$ is fixed, then, by trying all combinations for t^{th} bits of the inputs, i.e., testing each k-bit vector $(X_1[t:t], \ldots, X_k[t:t])$, we can calculate the exact value of $F(X_1, \ldots, X_k)[t:t]$, as well as the exact resulting local carries vector $\Psi|_{t+1}$. Clearly, the oracle $P_{t+1}(\Psi', \gamma)$ makes calls to $P_t(\Psi_0, \gamma)$, for various values of Ψ_0. That relation is linear, and can easily be represented in a matrix form. For this purpose, let us introduce a one-to-one *index mapping function* $\text{Index}(\Psi) : (\sigma_1 \times \sigma_2 \times \ldots \times \sigma_a) \to \theta \in [0 \ldots \theta_{\max} - 1]$, as follows.

$$\text{Index}(\Psi) = ((\sigma_1 \cdot (\sigma_{2\max} + 1) + \sigma_2) \cdot (\sigma_{3\max} + 1) + \sigma_3) \cdot \ldots$$
$$\theta_{\max} = \prod_{j=1}^{a} (\sigma_{j\max} + 1) = \prod_{j=1}^{a} (k_j^+ + 1). \tag{6}$$

Now, $P_t(\Psi, \gamma)$ for all Ψ can be regarded as a vector $\Big(P_t(\text{Index}^{-1}(0), \gamma), \ldots,$ $P_t(\text{Index}^{-1}(\theta_{\max} - 1), \gamma) \Big)$, also referred for simplicity as P_t, for all the consecutive valid tuples Ψ. The transformation from P_t to P_{t+1} is a linear function, i.e., it can be written as

$$P_{t+1} = M_{\gamma_t|t} \times P_t, \tag{7}$$

where $M_{\gamma_t|t}$ is some fixed *connection matrix* of size $(\theta_{\max} \times \theta_{\max})$, which, in general, is different for different t's. It depends on the tth bits of the constants involved in $F(\cdot)$, and it also depends on the value of the tth bit γ_t from the given

γ, since the oracle $P_{t+1}(\Psi, \gamma)$ must satisfy γ taken modulo 2^{t+1} as well. If the input variables are 0-truncated, then the only one vector $\Psi|_0 = (0, 0, \ldots, 0)$ of local carry values is possible, i.e., $P_0 = (1 \quad 0 \quad \ldots \quad 0)$. Therefore, we assign the oracle P_0 to be just a zero vector, but $P_0(0, \gamma) = 1$.

In this way, $2n$ such matrices have to be constructed. However, in most cases this number is much less. The algorithm to construct matrices from (7) and then calculate (5) is given as follows.

Theorem 1. *For a given PLFM $F(X_1, \ldots, X_k)$, and a fixed $\gamma \in \mathbb{Z}_{2^n}$, we have:*

$$\Pr\{F(X_1, \ldots, X_k) = \gamma\} = \frac{1}{2^{k \cdot n}} (1 \; 1 \; \ldots \; 1) \times \left(\prod_{t=n-1}^{0} M_{\gamma_t | t} \right) \times (1 \; 0 \; \ldots \; 0)^{\mathrm{T}}, \quad (8)$$

where $M_{\gamma_t | t}$ are connection matrices of size $(\theta_{\max} \times \theta_{\max})$, precomputed with the algorithm below.

Algorithm: *Construction of $2n$ matrices $M_{\gamma_t | t}$.*

1. *Input:*
   $F(X_1, \ldots, X_k)$ – *a PLFM with a arithmetical terms $\mathcal{A}_i$, each having k_i^+ operators '+', correspondingly;*
2. *Data structures:*
   $\theta_{\max} = \prod_{i=1}^{a}(k_i^+ + 1)$;
   $M_{\{0,1\}|t=[0\ldots n-1]}[\theta_{\max}][\theta_{\max}]$ – $2n$ *square matrices of size $(\theta_{\max} \times \theta_{\max})$, initialised with zeros;*
3. *Precomputation algorithm:*
   for $t = 0 \ldots n - 1$
      Temporary set the constants from $\mathcal{C}$ to be just t^{th} bit of the
         original ones, i.e., set $(C_1, \ldots, C_l) = (C_1[t : t], \ldots, C_l[t : t])$
      for $(X_1, \ldots, X_k) \in \{0, 1\}^k$ – *(all combinations for the tth bits of X's)*
         for $\theta = 0 \ldots \theta_{\max} - 1$ – *(all combinations for Ψ)*
         $(\sigma_1, \ldots, \sigma_a) = \mathtt{Index}^{-1}(\theta)$
         ^{z} Evaluate all $\mu_i = \sigma_i + \mathcal{A}_i(X_1, \ldots, X_n)$, but in $\mathcal{A}_i$ substitute
            all sub terms $\mathcal{A}_j$ with the values $(\mu_j \mod 2)$, correspondingly
         $\theta' = \mathtt{Index}(\mu_1 \text{ div } 2, \ldots, \mu_a \text{ div } 2)$ – *(a new resulting Ψ')*
         Evaluate the function $f = F(\cdot) \mod 2$, but substitute
            all terms $\mathcal{A}_j$ with the values μ_j, correspondingly
         $M_{f|t}[\theta'][\theta] := M_{f|t}[\theta'][\theta] + 1$

- *Time Complexity:* $O(n \cdot \theta_{\max} \cdot 2^k)$
- *Memory Complexity:* $O(2n \cdot \theta_{\max}^2)$

---

^{z} Variables μ_i, which correspond to the terms $\mathcal{A}_i$, should be calculated recursively.
The deepest $\mathcal{A}$ term should be calculated first, and so on.

□

Below we give an example that demonstrates all the steps of the algorithm.

Example 1. Let $k = 3$, $n = 5$. Assume that our goal is to calculate the probability $\Pr\{F(X_1, X_2, X_3) = 10110_2\}$, where:

$$F(X_1, X_2, X_3) = (X_1 \boxplus (X_2 \oplus (X_1 \boxminus X_2 \boxplus 25)))) \oplus (X_1 \text{ AND } X_3). \tag{9}$$

The first step is to cancel the operator $\boxminus$ by (1), and by rewriting the expression we get

$$F(X_1, X_2, X_3) = (\underbrace{X_1 + \overbrace{(X_2 \oplus \underbrace{(X_1 + (\overbrace{\text{ NOT } X_2}^{}) + 26)))}_{\mathcal{A}_1}}^{\mathcal{B}_2}}_{\mathcal{B}_3} \oplus (X_1 \text{ AND } X_3).$$

The function $F(\cdot)$ is a PLFM, since it can be expressed in $\mathcal{A}$ and $\mathcal{B}$ terms, marked above (the $\mathcal{S}$ terms are simply elements from the set $\{X_1, X_2, X_3, 26\}$). I.e.,

$$\mathcal{B}_1(\mathcal{X}, \mathcal{C}) = \text{ NOT } X_2$$
$$\mathcal{A}_1(\mathcal{X}, \mathcal{C}) = \underbrace{X_1 + \mathcal{B}_1(\mathcal{X}, \mathcal{C}) + 26}_{k_1^+ = 2}$$

$$\mathcal{B}_2(\mathcal{X}, \mathcal{C}) = X_2 \oplus \mathcal{A}_1(\mathcal{X}, \mathcal{C})$$
$$\mathcal{A}_2(\mathcal{X}, \mathcal{C}) = \underbrace{X_1 + \mathcal{B}_2(\mathcal{X}, \mathcal{C})}_{k_2^+ = 1}$$

1. $\theta_{\max} = (k_1^+ + 1)(k_2^+ + 1) = 3 \cdot 2 = 6$;
2. for $t = 0 \ldots 4$
3. $\quad C = 26[t : t]$
4. $\quad$ for $(X_1, X_2, X_3) \in \{0, 1\}^3$
5. $\qquad$ for $(\sigma_1, \sigma_2) = (0 \ldots 2, 0 \ldots 1)$
6. $\qquad\quad \mu_1 = \sigma_1 + X_1 + (\text{ NOT } X_2) + C$
7. $\qquad\quad \mu_2 = \sigma_2 + X_1 + (X_2 \oplus \mu_1 \mod 2)$
8. $\qquad\quad f = (\mu_2 \oplus (X_1 \text{ AND } X_3)) \mod 2$
9. $\qquad\quad M_{f|t}[(\mu_1 \text{ div } 2) \cdot 2 + (\mu_2 \text{ div } 2)]$
   $\qquad\qquad [\sigma_1 \cdot 2 + \sigma_2] + +.$

Applying Theorem 1 to construct $2n$ matrices.

$\mathcal{B}_3(\mathcal{X}, \mathcal{C}) = \mathcal{A}_2(\mathcal{X}, \mathcal{C}) \oplus (X_1 \text{ AND } X_3)$, where $F(X_1, X_2, X_3) = \mathcal{B}_3(\mathcal{X}, \mathcal{C})$.
After all computations we receive the following matrices

$$M_{\gamma_0 = 0|t=0} = \begin{pmatrix} 1 & 0 & 2 & 0 & 0 & 0 \\ 0 & 5 & 0 & 0 & 0 & 0 \\ 1 & 0 & 2 & 0 & 1 & 0 \\ 0 & 1 & 2 & 2 & 0 & 5 \\ 0 & 0 & 0 & 0 & 1 & 0 \\ 0 & 0 & 0 & 0 & 0 & 1 \end{pmatrix} \quad M_{\gamma_0 = 1|t=0} = \begin{pmatrix} 5 & 0 & 0 & 2 & 0 & 0 \\ 0 & 1 & 0 & 0 & 0 & 0 \\ 1 & 0 & 0 & 2 & 5 & 0 \\ 0 & 1 & 2 & 2 & 0 & 1 \\ 0 & 0 & 0 & 0 & 1 & 0 \\ 0 & 0 & 0 & 0 & 0 & 1 \end{pmatrix} \quad M_{\gamma_1 = 0|t=1} = \begin{pmatrix} 2 & 0 & 0 & 0 & 0 & 0 \\ 0 & 0 & 0 & 0 & 0 & 0 \\ 2 & 0 & 1 & 0 & 2 & 0 \\ 2 & 2 & 0 & 5 & 0 & 0 \\ 0 & 0 & 1 & 0 & 2 & 0 \\ 0 & 0 & 0 & 1 & 2 & 2 \end{pmatrix} \quad M_{\gamma_1 = 1|t=1} = \begin{pmatrix} 0 & 2 & 0 & 0 & 0 & 0 \\ 0 & 0 & 0 & 0 & 0 & 0 \\ 0 & 2 & 5 & 0 & 0 & 2 \\ 2 & 2 & 0 & 1 & 0 & 0 \\ 0 & 0 & 1 & 0 & 0 & 2 \\ 0 & 0 & 0 & 1 & 2 & 2 \end{pmatrix}.$$

No need to construct the matrices for $t = 2, 3, 4$, because they will repeat as $M_{*|t=2} = M_{*|t=0}$ and $M_{*|t=4} = M_{*|t=3} = M_{*|t=1}$. This happens since there are only two different combinations for any t^{th} "bit slice" of constants from the set $\mathcal{C} = \{26\}$. In particular, for every bit t we have $26[t : t] = 0$ or 1 in step 3 in the figure above. Finally, from (8) we calculate

$$\Pr\{F(X_1, X_2, X_3) = 10110_2\} = \frac{1}{2^{15}}(1\ \ 1\ \ 1\ \ 1\ \ 1\ \ 1) \times M_{1|4} \times M_{0|3} \times M_{1|2} \times$$

$$\times M_{1|1} \times M_{0|0} \times (1\ \ 0\ \ 0\ \ 0\ \ 0\ \ 0)^{\mathrm{T}} = \frac{1}{2^{15}} \cdot 404 \approx 0.0123291015625.$$

One can check this probability by the classical solution, trying all possible values for $(X_1, X_2, X_3) \in \mathbb{Z}_{2^5}^3$ and calculating the function $F(\cdot)$ directly from (9).

Preparing the matrices requires $2 \cdot 2^3 \cdot 6 = 96$ steps (2 values for t, 8 combinations for (X_1, X_2, X_3), and the number of different local carries is $\theta_{max} = 6$); each step requires one function evaluation. To calculate one probability we need to make 5 multiplications of a matrix and a vector, which takes $5 \cdot 6^2$ operations, plus one scalar product of two vectors at the end, i.e., in total 186 operations. Calculating the complete distribution for all possible γ's takes $2^5 \cdot 186 = 5952$ operations in total. Note that the classical way requires $2^{3.5} = 32768$ steps with the function evaluation each step.   □

The second example presented in Appendix A is taken from the real cryptanalysis. In that example we, additionally, demonstrate a new trick and show how time complexity can be reduced even more than in Theorem 1. With a precomputation, which usually takes a negligible time, the construction of the complete distribution can have a very small time complexity $O(\theta_{max} \cdot 2^n)$. That example also shows the advantage of using proposed technique as the computation complexity 2^{96} from the classical solution is reduced down to $2^{32.585}$.

3   Distributions of Functions with Arbitrarily Distributed Inputs

The previous section assumed $X_1, X_2, \ldots$ to be uniformly distributed, allowing a combinatorial approach. In this section we consider $X_1, X_2, \ldots$ *independent* but with *arbitrary* distributions. Despite the ideas described in this section were partly mentioned in [15], we include them for completeness.

Let us have a probability space Ω of size $q = |\Omega| = 2^n$ and two distributions D_X and D_Y over Ω for two random variables X and Y, respectively. Given the distributions D_X and D_Y we consider two major types of convolution, defined as

$$D_Z = D_X * D_Y :\Rightarrow$$

$$\Pr\{Z = Z_0\} = \sum_{\substack{\forall X_0, Y_0 \in \Omega : \\ X_0 * Y_0 = Z_0}} \Pr\{X = X_0\} \cdot \Pr\{Y = Y_0\}, \quad \forall Z_0 \in \mathbb{Z}_{2^n}, \quad (10)$$

where $*$ is either $\boxplus$ or $\oplus$.

In both cases the time complexity to calculate the resulting distribution D_Z is $O(q^2)$, i.e., quadratic. Due to such a high complexity, many attacks in cryptanalysis deal with at most 16-18-bit distributions only. Nowadays, when design of ciphers is often 32-bit oriented, it would be a challenging and useful task to perform a convolution of two 32-bit distributions, i.e., calculating $\Pr\{X+Y = \gamma\}$ for all γ when X and Y have some arbitrary distributions.

For notation purposes the distribution D_X will also be represented as a vector of size 2^n of probabilities as $[D_X] = \{p_X(0), p_X(1), \ldots, p_X(2^n - 1)\}$, where $p_X(X_0) = \Pr\{X = X_0\}$.

Convolution over $\boxplus$. If $[D_X]$ and $[D_Y]$ are represented as two polynomials with coefficients from these two vectors, then the resulting vector $[D_Z]$ has coefficients of the product of the polynomials $[D_X]$ and $[D_Y]$. Fast multiplication of two polynomials can be done via *Fast Fourier Transform (FFT)* [17], the complexity of which is $O(q \log q)$ [2]. The convolution over $\boxplus$ can now easily be calculated as

$$[D_Z] = [D_X \boxplus D_Y] = \mathrm{FFT}_n^{-1}(\mathrm{FFT}_n([D_X]) \cdot \mathrm{FFT}_n([D_Y])). \tag{11}$$

Convolution over $\oplus$. A similar idea can be applied to this type of convolution. Instead, we use *Fast Hadamard Transform (FHT)* [17].

FHT is a linear transformation of a vector of size 2^n. This transformation can also be done by a matrix multiplication $H_n \times [V]$, where H_n is a well-known Hadamard matrix. FHT, however, performs this matrix multiplication for time $O(q \log q = n \cdot 2^n)$, the same as FFT. In practice, however, FHT is much faster than FFT, since it does not need to work with complex and float numbers. Therefore, approximations of kind $\boxplus \Rightarrow \oplus$ are more preferable, than otherwise. Additionally, the implementation of FHT is extremely simple and small in C/C++, and we present it in Appendix C.

Since FHT_n^{-1} differs from FHT_n by only the coefficient 2^{-n}, then the convolution over $\oplus$ via FHT is computed as

$$[D_Z] = [D_X \oplus D_Y] = \frac{1}{2^n} \cdot \mathrm{FHT}_n(\mathrm{FHT}_n([D_X]) \cdot \mathrm{FHT}_n([D_Y])). \tag{12}$$

Finally, we point out that the convolution of a linear composition of k independent terms is derived as

$$D_{(Z = C_1 X_1 \oplus C_2 X_2 \oplus \ldots \oplus C_k X_k)} = \frac{1}{2^n} \cdot \mathrm{FHT}_n\left(\mathrm{FHT}_n([D_{C_1 X_1}]) \cdot \ldots \cdot \mathrm{FHT}_n([D_{C_k X_k}])\right),$$

where C_i are some constants. In practice, this also means that if these distribution tables for $X_1, \ldots, X_k$ are stored with precisions $\xi_1, \ldots, \xi_k$ bits after point, respectively, then for probabilities of Z the precision of only $\xi = n + \sum_{j=1}^{k} \xi_j$ bits after point should be considered (or reserved) before the FHT procedure.

In sections above several algorithms have been derived with good time complexities, which, in most cases, allow us to operate on large distributions. However, memory complexity problems become to be the main concern for implementation aspects. We have algorithms that operate with 32-bit distributions,

---

[2] The resulting polynomial $[D_X] \cdot [D_Y]$ is of degree $2q$, but its powers have to be taken modulo q. It means that the second half just need to be added to the first half of $2n$ coefficients, in order to receive $[D_Z]$. However, this is done automatically when FFT of size q is applied to $[D_X]$ and $[D_Y]$ directly.

but how to manage the memory? We present a possible solution in Appendix B, suggest our data structures for large distributions and show how typical operations can be mounted.

4   Application: 32-Bit Cryptanalysis of SNOW 2.0

A stream cipher is a cryptographic primitive used to ensure privacy on a communication channel. The SNOW family is a typical example of word-oriented KSGs based on a linear feedback shift register (LFSR). SNOW 2.0 is an improved version of SNOW 1.0 aimed to be more secure and still more efficient in performance. The most powerful attack on SNOW 2.0 was presented by Watanabe, Biryukov and De Cannie're [18] in 2003. It is a linear distinguishing attack similar to the general framework presented in [19,20] and it requires a received keystream sequence of length 2^{225} bits and has a similar time complexity.

In this section we propose an improved attack on SNOW 2.0. Whereas the attack in [18] uses a binary linear approximation approach, the new attack is based on approximations of words, i.e., 32-bit vectors. This technique is more powerful and we get a reduction of the required keystream length to 2^{202}. To make the calculation of 32-bit distributions possible we use our algorithms and data structures from Appendix B.

4.1   A Short Description of SNOW 2.0

The structure of SNOW 2.0 is shown in Figure 1. It has 128- or 256-bit secret key and a 128-bit initial vector. It is based on LFSR over $\mathbb{F}_{2^{32}}[x]$ and the feedback polynomial is given by

$$\pi(x) = \alpha x^{16} + x^{14} + \alpha^{-1}x^5 + 1, \tag{13}$$

where α is a root of the polynomial

$$y^4 + \beta^{23}y^3 + \beta^{245}y^2 + \beta^{48}y + \beta^{239} \in \mathbb{F}_{2^8}[y], \tag{14}$$

and β is a root of

$$z^8 + z^7 + z^5 + z^3 + 1 \in \mathbb{F}_2[z]. \tag{15}$$

The state of the LFSR is denoted by $(s_{t+15}, s_{t+14}, \ldots, s_t)$. Each s_{t+i} is an element of the field $\mathbb{F}_{2^{32}}$. The Finite State Machine (FSM) has two 32-bit registers, $R1$ and $R2$. The output of the FSM F_i is given by

$$F_i = (s_{t+15} \boxplus R1_t) \oplus R2_t, \quad t \geq 0, \tag{16}$$

and the keystream z_t is given by

$$z_t = F_t \oplus s_t, \quad t \geq 1. \tag{17}$$

Two registers $R1$ and $R2$ are updated as follows,

$$R1_{t+1} = s_{t+5} \boxplus R2_t,$$
$$R2_{t+1} = S'(R1_t). \tag{18}$$

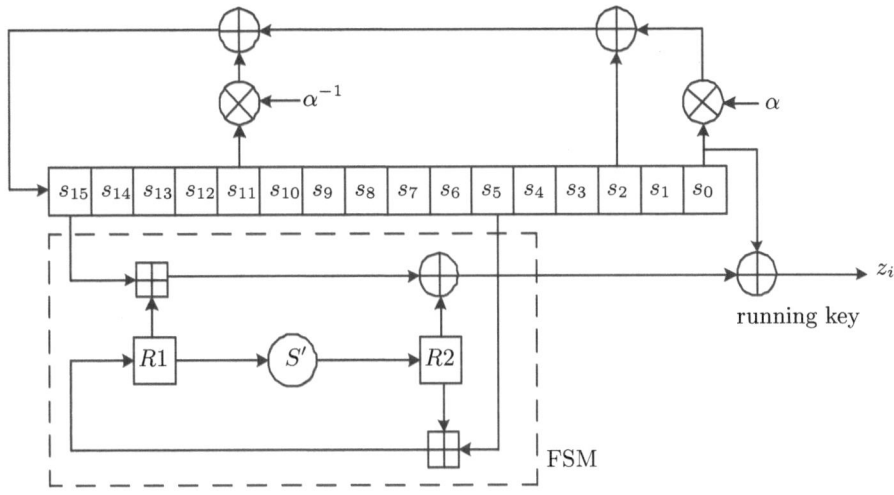

Fig. 1. The structure of SNOW 2.0

where $S'(W)$ is a one-to-one mapping transformation $S' : \mathbb{F}_{2^{32}} \to \mathbb{F}_{2^{32}}$. If a 32-bit integer W is represented as a vector of 4 8-bit bytes $W = (\,w_0\ w_1\ w_2\ w_3\,)^{\mathrm{T}}$, then

$$S'(W) = \begin{pmatrix} x & x+1 & 1 & 1 \\ 1 & x & x+1 & 1 \\ 1 & 1 & x & x+1 \\ x+1 & 1 & 1 & x \end{pmatrix} \cdot \begin{pmatrix} S_R[w_0] \\ S_R[w_1] \\ S_R[w_2] \\ S_R[w_3] \end{pmatrix}, \tag{19}$$

where S_R is the Rijndael 8-to-8-bit S-box, and the linear transformation (matrix multiplication) is done in the field $\mathbb{F}_{2^8}$ with generating polynomial

$$g(x) = x^8 + x^4 + x^3 + x + 1 \in \mathbb{F}_2[x]. \tag{20}$$

4.2   Basic Idea Behind the New Attack

The basic idea behind the new attack is to find such a linear combination of the output words z_i that is equal to 0 if the system is linear, or producing some biased noise if the system is approximated by a linear function. From the other hand, the linear combination representing the noise should be unbiased if the given sequence z_i is truly random.

Consider the feedback polynomial of the LFSR given in equation (13), i.e., $\pi(x) = \alpha x^{16} + x^{14} + \alpha^{-1}x^5 + 1$. A similar relation holds for the LFSR's output s_t at any time t, i.e.,

$$s_{t+16} \oplus \alpha^{-1}s_{t+11} \oplus s_{t+2} \oplus \alpha s_t = 0, \quad t \geq 1. \tag{21}$$

Next we make an approximation of the FSM to make it look linear. For any time $t \geq 1$ two output words z_t and z_{t+1} can be expressed as

$$\begin{cases} z_t = s_t \oplus (R1 \boxplus s_{t+15}) \oplus R2 \\ z_{t+1} = s_{t+1} \oplus S'(R1) \oplus (R2 \boxplus s_{t+5} \boxplus s_{t+16}). \end{cases} \tag{22}$$

Let us substitute $\boxplus \to \oplus$ and change $S'(R) \to R$. Then the sum $z_t \oplus z_{t+1}$ is expressed as

$$\begin{aligned} z_t \oplus z_{t+1} = \ & s_t \oplus (R1 \oplus s_{t+15} \oplus N_{c2}(R1, s_{t+15})) \oplus R2 \\ & \oplus s_{t+1} \oplus (R1 \oplus N_S(S'(R1), R1)) \\ & \oplus (R2 \oplus s_{t+5} \oplus s_{t+16} \oplus N_{c3}(R2, s_{t+5}, s_{t+16})) \\ = \ & s_t \oplus s_{t+1} \oplus s_{t+5} \oplus s_{t+15} \oplus s_{t+16} \oplus N_0(t), \end{aligned} \tag{23}$$

where $N_0(t)$ is a variable representing the error introduced by the linear approximation in time t,

$$N_0(t) = N_{c2}(R1, s_{t+15}) \oplus N_S(S'(R1), R1) \oplus N_{c3}(R2, s_{t+5}, s_{t+16}). \tag{24}$$

Here $N_{c2}(R1, s_{t+15})$ is a noise random variable introduced by the approximation of the modulo sum of two variables of the following kind "$R1 \boxplus s_{t+15} \to R1 \oplus s_{t+15} \oplus N_{c2}$". The variable $N_{c3}(R2, s_{t+5}, s_{t+16})$ is a similar approximation noise, but for the modulo sum of three variables. Finally, $N_S(S'(R1), R1))$ is the noise variable from the approximation "$S'(R1) \to R1 \oplus N_S$". Let us derive a linear relation, based on (21).

$$\begin{aligned} 0 \ \overset{Eq(21)}{=} \ & (s_{t+16} \oplus \alpha^{-1} s_{t+11} \oplus s_{t+2} \oplus \alpha s_t) \oplus (s_{t+17} \oplus \alpha^{-1} s_{t+12} \oplus_{t+3} \oplus \alpha s_{t+1}) \\ & \oplus (s_{t+21} \oplus \alpha^{-1} s_{t+16} \oplus s_{t+7} \oplus \alpha s_{t+5}) \oplus (s_{t+31} \oplus \alpha^{-1} s_{t+26} \oplus s_{t+17} \\ & \oplus \alpha s_{t+15}) \oplus (s_{t+32} \oplus \alpha^{-1} s_{t+27} \oplus s_{t+18} \oplus \alpha s_{t+16}) \\ = \ & (s_{t+16} \oplus s_{t+17} \oplus s_{t+21} \oplus s_{t+31} \oplus s_{t+32}) \oplus \alpha^{-1} \cdot (s_{t+11} \oplus s_{t+12} \\ & \oplus s_{t+16} \oplus s_{t+26} \oplus s_{t+27}) \oplus (s_{t+2} \oplus s_{t+3} \oplus s_{t+7} \oplus s_{t+17} \oplus s_{t+18}) \\ & \oplus \alpha \cdot (s_t \oplus s_{t+1} \oplus s_{t+5} \oplus s_{t+15} \oplus s_{t+16}) \\ \overset{Eq(22)}{=} \ & (z_{t+2} \oplus z_{t+3} \oplus z_{t+16} \oplus z_{t+17}) \oplus \alpha^{-1} \cdot (z_{t+11} \oplus z_{t+12}) \\ & \oplus \alpha \cdot (z_t \oplus z_{t+1}) \oplus (N_0(t+2) \oplus N_0(t+16)) \oplus \alpha^{-1} \cdot N_0(t+11) \\ & \oplus \alpha \cdot N_0(t) \ = \ \mathbf{Z}(t) \oplus \mathbf{N}(t), \end{aligned} \tag{25}$$

where $\mathbf{N}(t)$ is the 32-bit total sum of noise variables introduced by several approximations, expressed as $\mathbf{N}(t) = (N_0(t+2) \oplus N_0(t+16)) \oplus \alpha^{-1} \cdot N_0(t+11) \oplus \alpha \cdot N_0(t)$, and $\mathbf{Z}(t)$ is the "known" part calculated from the output sequence at any time t, $\mathbf{Z}(t) = (z_{t+2} \oplus z_{t+3} \oplus z_{t+16} \oplus z_{t+17}) \oplus \alpha^{-1}(z_{t+11} \oplus z_{t+12}) \oplus \alpha(z_t \oplus z_{t+1})$. Obviously, $\mathbf{N}(t) \oplus \mathbf{Z}(t) = 0$.

After all, a linear distinguishing attack can now be performed, if we know the distribution $D_{\mathbf{N}}$ of the 32-bit noise variable $\mathbf{N}$. For a sufficiently large number of received symbols from either the random distribution D_{Random}, or the distribution of the noise $D_{\mathbf{N}}$, one can construct the *type* (or *empirical distribution*) D_{Type}. We then make a decision whether the stream comes from a truly random generator or from the cipher, according to the distances from D_{Type} to $D_{\mathbf{N}}$ and D_{Random}. Note, the 32-bit noise distribution definitely contains the best binary approximation found in [18], but, clearly, it also contains some additional information, which makes the bias of the noise larger.

We will explain this procedure more in detail in the full version of the paper, but since this is a standard hypothesis testing we simply refer to e.g., [9,21].

4.3 Computational Aspects

To calculate the bias of the 32-bit noise variable $\mathbf{N}$, its distribution table has to be constructed. It can be calculates via the distribution of N_0, expressed in (24) [3]. To construct the distributions of N_{c2} and N_{c3} we use Theorem 1 (PLFM construction). The expression for N_S is a function on one variable, i.e., it takes no more than $O(2^{32})$ operations to build the distribution D_{N_S}. Next, the distribution of N_0 is calculated via FHT with the algorithm from Section 3 (convolution over $\oplus$) and Appendix B (FHT for large distributions). Afterwards, the distribution of $\alpha \cdot N_0$ and $\alpha^{-1} \cdot N_0$ was computed using algorithms described in Appendix B (function evaluation). Finally, we again use FHT to calculate the distribution of the total noise variable $D_{\mathbf{N}}$, and then calculate the bias $\epsilon = |D_{\mathbf{N}} - D_{\text{Random}}|$.

All these operations took us less than 2 weeks on a usual Pentium IV 3.4GHz, 2Gb of memory and 256Gb of HDD.

4.4 Simulation Results and Discussions

At the end of our simulations we received the distance $\epsilon = |D_{\mathbf{N}} - D_{\text{Random}}| \approx 2^{-101}$, which means that SNOW 2.0 can be distinguished from random with the known keystream of size 2^{202}, and with a similar time complexity. The advantage of our attack is presented in the following table.

Attack on SNOW 2.0	bit(s) considered	bias (ϵ)	complexity
Watanabe et. al. [18]	1	$2^{-112.25}$	2^{225}
our attack	32	2^{-101}	2^{202}

For future research work on this topic it is left to note that the expression for the noise variable $\mathbf{N}(t)$ (25) contains two parts: $N_{c3}(R2_t, s_{t+5}, s_{t+16})$ and $N_{c3}(R2_{t+11}, s_{t+16}, s_{t+27})$, which, in our simulations, were considered as independent. However, since they both use the same input s_{t+16}, they are not really independent and, theoretically, the result should be slightly improved if one consider them as dependent.

---

[3] We adopted the data structures from Appendix B for our simulations as follows: we use 2^{10} files, each containing 2^{22} points of a sub distribution. Since the precision of the probabilities have to be at least $2^{-(192\cdot4+32)}$ (four noises N_0, each containing N_S with precision 2^{-32}, N_{c2} with precision 2^{-64}, and N_{c3} with precision 2^{-96}; plus 32 bits must be reserved for FHT),each cell has to be of size at least 100 bytes. I.e., each sub distribution in the memory takes at least 400Mb. However, this estimate is conservative, and in our simulations we used almost 2Gb of operation memory.

5   Results and Conclusions

In this paper we have proposed new algorithms for computation of distributions of certain functions where the input variables are from a large alphabet. In the case when the input variables were uniformly distributed, the distribution for a class of functions called PLFM was shown to be efficiently calculated. The second case considered the same problem but for arbitrary distribution of input variables. Efficient methods of calculating the distribution of sums of variables both in $\mathbb{Z}_{2^n}$ and $\mathbb{F}_{2^n}$ were proposed, based on Fast Fourier Transform and Fast Hadamard Transform, respectively.

The cryptologic applications of the results were demonstrated by extending the linear cryptanalysis of the stream cipher SNOW 2.0 to work over a larger alphabet. We believe that there are many instances of stream ciphers as well as block ciphers, where cryptanalytic results can be improved by considering analysis over a larger alphabet. In all these cases, the algorithms derived in this paper will be essential for calculating the performance of such attacks.

We also believe that the technique considering "local carries" presented in algorithms for PLFMs can easily be transformed for finding *one* or even *all solutions* for equations like $F(X_1, \ldots, X_k) = 0$. Finding solutions for other kinds of equations, including $F(X_1, \ldots, X_k) = \gamma$ and systems of equations, is obviously converted to finding one or all solutions for an equation of the first kind. Consequently, many properties of PLFM functions can be derived, similarly as it was done for smaller classes in, e.g., [11,12,14]. More details will be included in the extended version of this paper.

A few open problems can be mentioned. Clearly, we would like to find other classes of functions where we can compute the distribution efficiently. Also, we would like to find further instances of existing ciphers where linear attacks over larger alphabets are applicable.

Acknowledgements

We thank anonymous reviewers for their useful comments that helped us to improve this paper.

References

1. S. Halevi, D. Coppersmith, and C.S. Jutla. Scream: A software-efficient stream cipher. In J. Daemen and V. Rijmen, editors, *Fast Software Encryption 2002*, volume 2365 of *Lecture Notes in Computer Science*, pages 195–209. Springer-Verlag, 2002.
2. P. Ekdahl and T. Johansson. SNOW - a new stream cipher. In *Proceedings of First Open NESSIE Workshop*, 2000.
3. P. Ekdahl and T. Johansson. A new version of the stream cipher SNOW. In K. Nyberg and H. Heys, editors, *Selected Areas in Cryptography—SAC 2002*, volume 2595 of *Lecture Notes in Computer Science*, pages 47–61. Springer-Verlag, 2002.

4. P. Hawkes and G.G. Rose. Primitive specification and supporting documentation for SOBER-t16 submission to NESSIE. In *Proceedings of First Open NESSIE Workshop*, 2000. Available at http://www.cryptonessie.org, Accessed August 18, 2005.

5. P. Hawkes and G.G. Rose. Primitive specification and supporting documentation for SOBER-t32 submission to NESSIE. In *Proceedings of First Open NESSIE Workshop*, 2000. Available at http://www.cryptonessie.org, Accessed August 18, 2005.

6. N. Smart. Cryptography: An Introduction, 2003.

7. M. Briceno, I. Goldberg, and D. Wagner. A pedagogical implementation of A5/1. Available at http://jya.com/a51-pi.htm, Accessed August 18, 2005, 1999.

8. T. Johansson and A. Maximov. A Linear Distinguishing Attack on Scream. In *Information Symposium in Information Theory—ISIT 2003*, page 164. IEEE, 2003.

9. P. Ekdahl and T. Johansson. Distinguishing attacks on SOBER-t16 and SOBER-t32. In J. Daemen and V. Rijmen, editors, *Fast Software Encryption 2002*, volume 2365 of *Lecture Notes in Computer Science*, pages 210–224. Springer-Verlag, 2002.

10. Jovan DJ. Golić and Philip Hawkes. Vectorial approach to fast correlation attacks. *Designs, Codes, and Cryptography*, 35(1):5–19, 2005.

11. Helger Lipmaa and Shiho Moriai. Efficient algorithms for computing differential properties of addition. In *Fast Software Encryption 2001*, pages 336–350. Springer-Verlag, 2002.

12. Helger Lipmaa, Johan Wallén, and Philippe Dumas. On the additive differential probability of exclusive-or. In *Fast Software Encryption 2004*, pages 317–331, 2004.

13. Alexander Maximov. On linear approximation of modulo sum. In *Fast Software Encryption 2004*, pages 483–484, 2004.

14. Helger Lipmaa. On differential properties of pseudo-hadamard transform and related mappings. In *Progress in Cryptology—INDOCRYPT 2002*, pages 48–61. Springer-Verlag, 2002.

15. Jovan Dj. Golic and Guglielmo Morgari. Vectorial fast correlation attacks. *Cryptology ePrint Archive, Report 2004/247*, 2004.

16. A. Klimov and A. Shamir. A new class of invertible mappings. In *CHES '02: Revised Papers from the 4th International Workshop on Cryptographic Hardware and Embedded Systems*, pages 470–483. Springer-Verlag, 2003.

17. T. Cormen, C. Leiserson, R. Rivest, and C. Stein. *Introduction to Algorithms*. MIT Press, 2001.

18. D. Watanabe, A. Biryukov, and C. De Canniere. A distinguishing attack of SNOW 2.0 with linear masking method. In *Selected Areas in Cryptography—SAC 2003*, pages 222–233. Springer-Verlag, 2003.

19. D. Coppersmith, S. Halevi, and C.S. Jutla. Cryptanalysis of stream ciphers with linear masking. In M. Yung, editor, *Advances in Cryptology—CRYPTO 2002*, volume 2442 of *Lecture Notes in Computer Science*, pages 515–532. Springer-Verlag, 2002.

20. J.D. Golić. Linear models for keystream generators. *IEEE Transactions on Computers*, 45(1):41–49, January 1996.

21. P. Junod. On the optimality of linear, differential and sequential distinguishers. In *Advances in Cryptology—EUROCRYPT 2003*, volume 2656 of *Lecture Notes in Computer Science*, pages 17–32. Springer-Verlag, 2003.

Appendix A: Second Example from Real Cryptanalysis

Example 2. Let us have $k = 3$ uniformly distributed independent random variables $X_1, X_2, X_3 \in \mathbb{Z}_{2^{32}}$, i.e., $n = 32$. Assume in some cryptanalysis we perform a linear approximation '$X_1 \boxplus X_2 \boxplus X_3 \rightarrow X_1 \oplus X_2 \oplus X_3 \oplus N$', where N is a noise variable introduced due to the approximation. The task is to find the bias ϵ of the noise variable N.

The expression for N is: $N = \underbrace{\overbrace{(X_1 + X_2 + X_3)}^{\mathcal{A}_1} \oplus X_1 \oplus X_2 \oplus X_3}_{\mathcal{B}_1} \mod 2^{32}$,

which is a PLFM with only one $\mathcal{A}$ term. The maximum carry-bit index value is $\theta_{max} = (k_1^+ + 1) = 3$. Since no constants are involved all matrices $M_{*|t}$ for all t's are the same. Hence, only two matrices $M_{0|0}$ and $M_{1|0}$ have to be constructed, using Theorem 1.

$$M_{\gamma_0=0|t=0} = \begin{pmatrix} 4 & 0 & 0 \\ 4 & 0 & 4 \\ 0 & 0 & 4 \end{pmatrix}, \qquad M_{\gamma_0=1|t=0} = \begin{pmatrix} 0 & 1 & 0 \\ 0 & 6 & 0 \\ 0 & 1 & 0 \end{pmatrix}. \qquad (26)$$

The probability $\Pr\{N = \gamma\}$ can now be calculated efficiently. For example, $\Pr\{N = \gamma = \text{0x72A304F8}\} = \frac{1}{2^{3 \cdot 32}}(1 \; 1 \; 1) \times \left(\prod_{t=n-1}^{0} M_{\gamma[t:t]|0}\right) \times (1 \; 0 \; 0)^{\mathrm{T}} = \frac{1}{2^{96}} \cdot 2187 \cdot 2^{51} \approx 0.266967773/2^{32}$. Note that the probability for an odd γ is 0. To calculate one probability the number of $32 \cdot 3^2 + 3 = 291$ operations is required. Hence, to calculate the complete distribution would take $291 \cdot 2^{32}$ operations.

However, this time complexity can be reduced significantly with specific data structures use, which we call "fast-tables". Each table is of size 2^{16} entries, which contain 3-dimentional vectors. These tables are precomputed as shown in Figure on the right. This precomputation requires $2^{16} \cdot 3^2 = 9 \cdot 2^{17}$ operations. The advantage is that any probability can now be derived as just one scalar product

1. *Data structures:*
      $\text{FastT}[2][0 \ldots 2^{16} - 1]$ – two 'fast-tables'
2. *Initialisation:*
      $\text{FastT}[0][0] = (1 \; 0 \; 0)$, $\text{FastT}[1][0] = (1 \; 1 \; 1)$
3. *Precomputation of the tables:*
      for $t = 0 \ldots 15$
      for $x = 1, 0$ (*note, the order is backward*)
      for $Y = 0 \ldots 2^t - 1$
      ^{z} $\text{FastT}[0][x||Y_t] = M_{x|t} \times \text{FastT}[0][Y]$
          $\text{FastT}[1][x||Y_t] = \text{FastT}[1][Y] \times M_{x|n-t-1}$

      Fast-tables precomputation algorithm.

      ^{z} Y_t is a t-bit value of Y. I.e., in C/C++ it would look like: $(x||Y_t) \Rightarrow (\text{x<<t})|\text{Y}$

$$\Pr\{N = \gamma\} = \frac{1}{2^{3 \cdot 32}} \cdot <\text{FastT}[0][\overline{\gamma_{15} \ldots \gamma_0}], \text{FastT}[1][\overline{\gamma_{16} \ldots \gamma_{31}}] >^4, \qquad (27)$$

which takes only 3 operations (instead of 291). Finally, the bias ϵ can be derived as follows:

---

[4] Note, the input for $\text{FastT}[1][\cdot]$ is bit-reversed.

1. $\epsilon = 0.5$ *(the bias for odd values of γ)*
2. for $\gamma = 0 \ldots 2^{31} - 1$ *(only even 2γ's are considered)*
3. $\epsilon + = |\Pr\{N = 2\gamma\} - 2^{-32}|$

The total time for this solution is the following sum: $2 \cdot 2^3 \cdot 3 = 48$ – to compute matrices, $9 \cdot 2^{17}$ – to precompute fast-tables, and $3 \cdot 2^{31}$ – to calculate the bias ϵ. In total $6443630640 \approx 2^{32.585}$ number of operations is required. To calculate the distribution of the noise variable N the same number of operations is needed, whereas the classical solution requires 2^{96} operations. Note, when the question is only to find the bias ϵ for some large distribution with memory limits conditions, the classical solution will fail with respect to the memory limits.   □

Appendix B: Data Structures for Large Distributions and Operations

B.1   Data Structure Proposal

Assume we want to operate on a distribution of size 2^n, but, however, the operation memory allows us to work only with a distribution of size at most 2^m, where $m < n$. If this is the case, to be able to work with large distributions of size 2^n we then propose to use *hard disk memory (HDD)*. Let

$$r = n - m,$$

then one need to create 2^r files on HDD, which we denote as $\text{File}^r_{(0\ldots 2^r-1)}$, to store one distribution table. The upper parameter r denotes the number of files to be created (2^r), and the index on the bottom is the selector of a particular file. Sometimes we will write also $\text{File}^r_{X:(A)}$ to show that this is the sub distribution file A for the random variable X. Each file stores the corresponding sub distribution of size 2^m. I.e., the probability $\Pr\{X = X_0\}$ can be accessed by

$$\Pr\{X = X_0\} = \text{File}^r_{X:(X_0[m:n-1])}[X_0 \mod 2^m]. \tag{28}$$

Note that the *upper* $r = (n - m)$ bits select the file, and the *lower* m bits are the cell index in the sub distribution.

The operation memory is regarded as *a fast memory*, whereas the HDD memory is regarded as *a very slow memory*. Working with such data structure frequent access (loading and saving) to the files on HDD should be avoided, since these operations are extremely much slower than an access to the memory. I.e., the most operations have to be done in the operation memory domain, and the number of access to the files has to be reduced as much as possible. In the next parts of this Appendix we present efficient solutions to apply common algorithms when operating on large distributions with the proposed data structures.

B.2   A PLFM Distribution Construction

For a given pseudo-linear function $F(\cdot)$ modulo 2^n its distribution can be constructed as follows.

```
1.  for A = 0...2^r − 1
2.      load sub distribution SubDist[·] ←File^r_{(A)}
3.      calculate the vector v = (1  1  ...  1) × (∏^0_{t=r−1} M_{A[t:t]|t+m})
4.      for B = 0...2^m
5.          SubDist[B]=Pr{F = AB̄}=v × (∏^0_{t=m−1} M_{B[t:t]|t}) × (1 0... 0)^T
6.      save sub distribution File^r_{(A)}←SubDist[·]
```

This algorithm requires to access each file once. Additionally, the steps 3 and 5 could be done more efficient with precomputed fast-tables (see, e.g. Appendix A).

B.3   A Function $Y = F(X)$ Evaluation Distribution

Let us have a distribution D_X of a random variable X, stored in data structures as suggested before. Let us also have a function defined on one variable $F(X)$. We need to construct the distribution of $Y = F(X)$ in an efficient way. As an example, this function could be a multiplication $\alpha \cdot X$ in some finite field, a permutation of X, a multiplication on a matrix, or some other function on X in general.

One could take the values of X consecutively, and then each time calculate Y. The problem appears when the consecutive values Y should be stored in different files. It could happen that we need to access the Y's files $O(2^n)$ times, which is expensive in time.

We suggest the following algorithm containing three stages. In the first stage the function is evaluated and the resulting Y's are separated into two files (bins), according to the upper bit value. In the second stage we perform *binary sorting* algorithm, each time dividing each bin into two new bins. The third stage accumulates probabilities from the bins and transfer the resulting sub distributions to the data structures of Y (files).

Stage I: Evaluate $Y = F(X)$ and separate into two files (narrowed distribution)

```
1. create two files (bins) f_0 = *File^1_{Y:(0)} and f_1 = *File^1_{Y:(1)}
2. for all A = 0...2^{n−m} − 1
3.      load sub distribution SubDist_X[·] ←File^r_{X:(A)}
4.      for all B = 0...2^m − 1
5.          Evaluate Y_0 = F(A||B)
6.          Save the pair f_{Y_0[n−1:n−1]} ← (SubDist_X[B], Y_0)
7. close the files f_0 and f_1
```

Stage II: Expand the files $*File^1_{Y:(A_1)} \rightarrow *File^2_{Y:(A_2)} \rightarrow \cdots \rightarrow *File^r_{Y:(A_r)}$

```
1. for k = 1...r − 1
2.      for all A = 0...2^k − 1
3.          open two files f_0 = *File^{k+1}_{Y:(A||0)} and f_1 = *File^{k+1}_{Y:(A||1)}
4.          while( not the end of the file *File^k_{Y:(A)} )
5.              read the pair (p, Y_0) ← *File^k_{Y:(A)}
6.              save the pair f_{Y_0[n−k−1:n−k−1]} ← (p, Y_0)
7.          close the files f_0 and f_1
```

Stage III: Construct $File^r_{Y:(A)}$ from $*File^r_{Y:(A)}$

```
1. for all A = 0...2^r
2.     clear SubDist_Y[0...2^m − 1]
3.     while( not the end of the file *File^r_{Y:(A)} )
4.         read the pair (p, Y_0) ← *File^k_{Y:(A)}
5.         SubDist_Y[Y_0]=SubDist_Y[Y_0]+p
6.     save sub distribution File^r_{Y:(A)}←SubDist_Y[·]
```

The complexity of this algorithm is $O((1+r)\cdot 2^n)$. However, the coefficient r in the complexity can be reduced with a small programming trick. If at the step II.3 we, instead, open 2^d files (in Windows at most 2^9 files can be open at the same time), and perform not a binary sorting but a d-tuple bits sorting at once, then the complexity will be reduced to $O((1 + r/d)\cdot 2^n)$. For example, if the number of files is 2^{16} (r=16), then with $d = 8$ we can compute the distribution of any function $F(X)$ by reading and storing distributions of size 2^n from the files only 3 times (instead of 17).

Note that in the implementation of FFT the first operation is the construction of the distribution $D_{Rev(X)}$ for the *bit reverse* of the random variable X, which is just a sub case of the general problem of this sub section. We simply define the function $Y = F(X)$ such that Y is the bit-reverse of X, and apply the algorithm above. There are other more nice and efficient solutions for this particular problem, but we only mention their existence.

B.4   Convolution over ⊕

To perform a convolution over ⊕ we need to be able to perform FHT on the proposed data structures. We propose a modified FHT algorithm, where first local FHTs for sub distributions are separately performed, and then evaluate the "convolution" over the files as follows.

```
1. for A = 0...2^r − 1
2.     load sub distribution SubDist[·] ←File^r_{(A)}
3.     FHT(m, SubDist)
4.     save sub distribution File^r_{(A)} ←SubDist[·]
5. FHT*(r, NULL) -- the same FHT as before but with another
                    butterfly function bfly*(j+k, j+k+(1<<i)).
```

The modified butterfly function bfly* is

```
1. bfly*(A, B)
2.     load   SubDist_1[·] ←File^r_{(A)}  and  SubDist_2[·] ←File^r_{(B)}
3.     for i = 0...2^m − 1
4.         bfly(SubDist_1[i], SubDist_2[i])
5.     save   File^r_{(A)} ←SubDist_1[·]  and  File^r_{(B)} ←SubDist_2[·]
```

This algorithm requires to load/save each file $r = n − m$ times. The modified butterfly function bfly* can also be implemented memoryless. It can read one value from File$^r_{(A)}$ and one value from File$^r_{(B)}$, perform the usual butterfly operation and save the results back to the files immediately. There are two additional ideas to accelerate the FHT evaluation:

(a) In steps 3 and 4 of the algorithm above only two files are processed. Instead, we could have a larger block of 2^d files opened and processed at the same time. The calculation of the batterfly function on two probabilities $\text{SubDist}_1[i]$ and $\text{SubDist}_2[i]$ can be substituted by a 'local' FHT on 2^d inputs, instead. Since the size of each file is 2^m, we need to repeat this procedure 2^m times for each group of 2^d files (inputs are taken in parallel from a group of 2^d files opened at the same time, but the number of such parallel inputs for each group is 2^m). As the result, each file is accessed around $(r+1)/d$ times;

(b) The computation can also be splittet into 2^c independent processes (2^c computers), and then the results can be merged together afterwards.

B.5   Convolution over ⊞

A convolution over ⊞ on the suggested data structures can be done in a similar way as for ⊕. In the first step we perform the *bit reversing* operation on the input distribution, as described in Appendix B.3. Afterwards, we use the same idea as in the previous sub section, based on the *parallel FFT circuit*. The description of the parallel FFT circuit can be found in the book [17].

Appendix C: Efficient FHT Implementation in C/C++

Fast Hadamard Transform (FHT) implementation in C/C++

```
// butterfly operation
template<class T> void inline bfly (T &a, T &b)
{ T tmp; tmp=a; a+=b; b=tmp-b; }

// FHTn, size of the input distribution is 2^n
template<class T> void FHT(int n, T *Dist)
{ for (int i=0; i<n; ++i)
    for (int j=0; j<(1<<n); j+=1<<(i+1) )
      for (int k=0 ; k<(1<<i); ++k)
        bfly (Dist[j+k], Dist [j+k+(1<<i)]);
}
```

An Analysis of the XSL Algorithm

Carlos Cid[1],[*] and Gaëtan Leurent[2]

[1] Information Security Group,
Royal Holloway, University of London,
Egham, Surrey TW20 0EX, United Kingdom
carlos.cid@rhul.ac.uk
[2] École Normale Supérieure,
Département d'Informatique, 45 rue d'Ulm,
Paris 75230 Cedex 05, France
gaetan.leurent@ens.fr

Abstract. The XSL "algorithm" is a method for solving systems of multivariate polynomial equations based on the linearization method. It was proposed in 2002 as a dedicated method for exploiting the structure of some types of block ciphers, for example the AES and Serpent. Since its proposal, the potential for algebraic attacks against the AES has been the source of much speculation. Although it has attracted a lot of attention from the cryptographic community, currently very little is known about the effectiveness of the XSL algorithm. In this paper we present an analysis of the XSL algorithm, by giving a more concise description of the method and studying it from a more systematic point of view. We present strong evidence that, in its current form, the XSL algorithm does not provide an efficient method for solving the AES system of equations.

Keywords: XSL algorithm, T′ method, Linearization, AES.

1 Introduction

In 2002 Courtois and Pieprzyk showed that recovering an AES encryption key was equivalent to solving a large system of multivariate quadratic equations over a small finite field [10,11]. They exploited the fact that the only non-linear component of the cipher (the S-Box) is based on the inverse map over the finite field $\mathbb{F}_{2^8}$, and were able to obtain a set of multivariate quadratic equations that completely described the S-Box transformation. By combining all equations throughout the cipher, they were able to express the full encryption transformation as a large, sparse and overdefined system of multivariate quadratic equations over $\mathbb{F}_2$ (in total 8000 equations with 1600 variables for the AES with 128-bit keys).

The problem of solving systems of multivariate quadratic equations over a finite field is known to be NP-complete, and it is widely believed that the commonly applied techniques (such as Gröbner Basis algorithms) cannot generally be used for efficiently solving systems with more than a handful of variables. However the system derived from the AES is very structured, and the hope is that a

---

[*] This author was supported by EPSRC Grant GR/S42637.

B. Roy (Ed.): ASIACRYPT 2005, LNCS 3788, pp. 333–352, 2005.

dedicated method can exploit this rich structure. With that in mind, a method called XSL was proposed in [10,11], which it was claimed could provide an efficient way to recover the encryption key for certain types of block ciphers. According to the estimates presented in [10], with the XSL algorithm one could mount a (at least theoretical) successful attack against the AES with 256-bit keys.

Around the same time, Murphy and Robshaw [13] showed how to express the AES encryption as a far simpler system of equations over $\mathbb{F}_{2^8}$. It was noticed then that, if XSL worked as predicted, this system should be easier to solve than the original one over $\mathbb{F}_2$, and in theory could provide an efficient attack against the AES with 128-bit keys [13,14].

Since the introduction of the XSL algorithm, the potential for algebraic attacks against block ciphers (and in particular the AES) has been the source of much speculation. Although it has attracted a lot of attention from the cryptographic community, currently very little is known about the effectiveness of the XSL algorithm, and of algebraic attacks in general, against block ciphers.

In this paper we present an analysis of the XSL algorithm. Based on our results we conclude that, as presented in [11], the XSL algorithm should not provide an efficient method for solving the AES system of equations.

2   Linearization Methods

The XSL algorithm was introduced in [10,11], and it is derived from an earlier algorithm called XL [8]. The XL algorithm and its many variants [7,9,11] are all based on the method of *linearization*, a well-known technique for solving large systems of multivariate polynomial equations. In this method we consider all monomials in the system as independent variables and try to solve it using linear algebra techniques. Note that the linearization method can only be successful if the number of *linearly independent* equations is approximately the same as the number of monomials in the system. The XL algorithm and its variants attempt to generate enough equations when this is not the case.

The XL is a simple algorithm: if we consider a system of m quadratic equations and n variables over a finite field $\mathbb{K}$,

$$f_1(x_1,\ldots,x_n) = 0 \ , \ \ldots \ , \ f_m(x_1,\ldots,x_n) = 0, \tag{1}$$

the algorithm simply multiplies the original equations by all monomials M_i up to a prescribed degree $D - 2$, and attempts to solve the system of all resulting equations

$$M_i \cdot f_j(x_1,\ldots,x_n) = 0 \tag{2}$$

of degree at most D by linearization.

Although not fully understood when first introduced, currently there seems to be a much better understanding of the behaviour of the XL algorithm, including its merits and limitations [1,2,3,4,12]. In particular it has been shown that some of the heuristics used in deriving the complexity of the XL algorithm [8] were too optimistic [12].

The XSL algorithm works slightly different. Whereas in the XL algorithm the equations are multiplied by all monomials up to a certain degree, in the XSL algorithm the equations are multiplied only by "carefully selected monomials". The goal here is to create fewer new monomials when generating the new equations. Additionally, there is a last step (called T' method), in which we try to obtain new linearly independent equations without creating any new monomials.

Analysis of the XSL algorithm does not seem to be an easy task, and currently very little is known about its behaviour. There are a number of reasons for this. Firstly, XSL can be considered an *ad-hoc* method, and the algorithm relies on the system presenting a somewhat special form, such as having "S-Boxes" with overdefined system of equations, repeated layers of linear equations, and so on. Secondly there are different versions of the algorithm (two attacks are given in [10], which are substantially different from the attack proposed in [11]), and in all cases, the description given leaves some room for interpretation. Furthermore, given the size of the systems involved, it is very difficult to implement and run experiments even on small examples to verify the heuristics in [10,11].

In the following sections, we give a more concise description of the XSL algorithm and study it from a more systematic point of view in an attempt to get an insight into the algorithm and better understand its behaviour.

3   The XSL Algorithm

There are different versions of the XSL algorithm. The first version was proposed in [10], where two different attacks were described: the first one eliminating the key schedule equations (but requiring a number of plaintext-ciphertext pairs), and a second, more specific attack, that used the key schedule equations (and should work with a single plaintext-ciphertext pair). Later a different version of the algorithm was introduced in [11] (called "compact XSL"). Only the first attack was described in [11], although it is straightforward to extend the method to the second attack.

In this paper we concentrate on the "compact XSL" algorithm. Although the algorithm can in theory be applied to a number of block ciphers, our analysis is focused on the AES, and we take into account the special structure of the systems derived from this cipher. The systems used are over $\mathbb{F}_2$ and always include the key schedule equations (i.e. we perform the second XSL attack).

The XSL algorithm, as described in [11], is supposed to work only on special types of ciphers; it assumes that the cipher is built with layers of small S-Boxes interconnected by linear key-dependent layers. The S-Box is such that it can be described by an overdefined set of quadratic equations. To apply the second attack (i.e. including the key schedule), the key schedule needs to have a similar structure to the encryption (which is the case for the AES).

The XSL algorithm consists of four main steps:

1. Process the existing set of equations, by choosing certain sets of monomials and equations that will be used during the later steps of the algorithm.

2. Select the value of the parameter P, and multiply the chosen equations by the product of $P - 1$ selected monomials. This is the "core" of the XSL attacks and should generate a large number of equations whose terms are the product of the monomials chosen earlier.

3. Perform the T′ method, in which some selected equations are multiplied by single variables. The goal is to generate new equations without creating any new monomials. Iterate with as many variables as necessary until the system has enough linearly independent equations to apply linearization[1].

4. Apply linearization, by considering each monomial as a new variable and performing Gaussian elimination. This should yield a solution for the system.

In the following sections we describe the first three steps, in an attempt to better understand the behaviour of the XSL algorithm. During our analysis, we illustrate the working of the algorithm on a small variant of the AES defined in [5]. The cipher used (denoted by SR(3,1,1,4)) has a 4-bit block and 3 rounds, and its operations are over the field $\mathbb{F}_{2^4}$. We note however that this small cipher is used only to assist the understanding of the algorithm's various steps; all results obtained are valid for the full AES, and we always present figures for this cipher. We use the following notation throughout this paper (similarly to [11]):

B: number of S-Boxes in each encryption round; N_r: number of encryption rounds;
$\mathcal{R}$: set of all equations; R: cardinality of $\mathcal{R}$;
$\mathcal{E}$: subset of $\mathcal{R}$ consisting of all L.I. equations; E: cardinality of $\mathcal{E}$;
$\mathcal{T}$: set of all monomials in the system; T: cardinality of $\mathcal{T}$;
$\mathcal{T}_i'$: set of monomials in the system such T': cardinality of $\mathcal{T}_i'$;
   that $x_i \cdot \mathcal{T}_i' \subseteq \mathcal{T}$; s: number of bits on the S-Box;
t: number of monomials in the S-Box equations; r: number of equations in an S-Box;
t_i': number of monomials in the S-Box equations to be used in the T′ method;
L: number of subsets of linear layer equations; S: total number of S-Boxes;
S_m: number of encryption S-Boxes; S_k: number of key schedule S-Boxes;
b_i: number of neighbouring S-Boxes for equations in the subset i;
N_b: number of columns in the data array; N_a: number of rows in the data array.

4   Step 1 - Processing of the Original Set of Equations

The processing method suggested in [11] is that for every S-Box, a basis of $t - r$ monomials is chosen and the remaining r monomials are written as linear combinations of the elements of the basis. Furthermore, the basis should be chosen such that the variables (i.e. monomials of degree 1) are not in the basis, and the constant monomial 1 is in the basis.

For the AES, we have $r = 24$ and $t = 81$, so each S-Box has a basis consisting of 57 monomials. If we denote by w_{ij} and x_{ij} the jth bit of the input and output of the ith S-Box respectively, we can choose our basis such that it consists of the

---

[1] The T′ method has also been proposed as the final step of the XL algorithm, in the so-called XL2 method [9].

monomials $x_{ij}w_{ik}$, with $j \neq k$, and 1. In our small example, we have $r = 12$ and $t = 25$, so after this processing the S-Box equations would be given by

$$
\left\{
\begin{array}{ll}
w_{10} & +w_{10}x_{11} + w_{11}x_{10} + w_{11}x_{12} + w_{12}x_{10} + w_{13}x_{11} + 1 \\
w_{11} & +w_{10}x_{11} + w_{10}x_{13} + w_{11}x_{13} + w_{12}x_{10} + w_{12}x_{13} + w_{13}x_{10} + w_{13}x_{11} \\
w_{12} & +w_{10}x_{11} + w_{10}x_{12} + w_{12}x_{11} + w_{12}x_{13} + w_{13}x_{10} + w_{13}x_{11} \\
w_{13} & +w_{10}x_{11} + w_{10}x_{12} + w_{10}x_{13} + w_{11}x_{10} + w_{11}x_{13} + w_{12}x_{10} + w_{12}x_{13} + w_{13}x_{10} \\
x_{10} & +w_{10}x_{11} + w_{10}x_{12} + w_{11}x_{10} + w_{11}x_{13} + w_{12}x_{11} + 1 \\
x_{11} & +w_{10}x_{12} + w_{10}x_{13} + w_{11}x_{10} + w_{11}x_{13} + w_{13}x_{10} + w_{13}x_{11} + w_{13}x_{12} \\
x_{12} & +w_{10}x_{13} + w_{11}x_{10} + w_{11}x_{12} + w_{11}x_{13} + w_{12}x_{10} + w_{13}x_{12} \\
x_{13} & +w_{10}x_{11} + w_{10}x_{12} + w_{10}x_{13} + w_{11}x_{10} + w_{12}x_{10} + w_{13}x_{10} + w_{13}x_{11} + w_{13}x_{12} \\
w_{10}x_{10} & +w_{10}x_{11} + w_{11}x_{10} + w_{12}x_{13} + w_{13}x_{12} + 1 \\
w_{11}x_{11} & +w_{10}x_{12} + w_{10}x_{13} + w_{11}x_{12} + w_{12}x_{10} + w_{12}x_{11} + w_{12}x_{13} + w_{13}x_{10} + w_{13}x_{12} \\
w_{12}x_{12} & +w_{10}x_{11} + w_{11}x_{10} + w_{11}x_{13} + w_{12}x_{13} + w_{13}x_{11} + w_{13}x_{12} \\
w_{13}x_{13} & +w_{10}x_{13} + w_{11}x_{12} + w_{12}x_{11} + w_{13}x_{10},
\end{array}
\right.
$$

and the basis would be given by

$$
\{\; w_{10}x_{11}, w_{10}x_{12}, w_{10}x_{13}, w_{11}x_{10}, w_{11}x_{12}, w_{11}x_{13},
$$
$$
w_{12}x_{10}, w_{12}x_{11}, w_{12}x_{13}, w_{13}x_{10}, w_{13}x_{11}, w_{13}x_{12}, 1 \;\}.
$$

The set consisting of the monomials in the bases of all the S-Boxes is used to multiply the remaining equations in the system (the linear layer equations) in step 2 of the algorithm, while the S-Box relations are used to carry out substitutions in the linear layer equations (Section 5). One of the main ideas of the XSL algorithm is that during the attack the equations are always expressed as sum of terms that are the product of monomials in the bases of P different S-Boxes.

When performing the second XSL attack, we need to do the same processing with the key schedule S-Boxes. In this case we denote by k_{ij} and s_{ij} the jth bit of the input and output of the ith key schedule S-Box, respectively. Similarly to the encryption S-Boxes, we choose our basis such that it consists of the monomials $k_{ij}s_{ik}$, with $j \neq k$, and 1. We note however the key schedule has a slightly different structure from the encryption, such that not every key variable goes through an S-Box. The suggestion in [10] is that we should introduce the so-called "artificial S-Boxes", with the necessary variables and no equations. We find this a unnecessary and somewhat cumbersome step, which makes our analysis a bit more complex. In particular, it is harder to derive accurate figures for the number of monomials and equations in the resulting system. In our opinion it is better to rewrite the key schedule system such that these "artificial S-Boxes" are no longer required (see Appendix A). Either way, the chosen form for the key schedule equations should not be relevant in the analysis that follows and does not have any significant influence on the complexity of the attack described.

The linear layer equations (from the encryption and the key schedule) are the equations that will be used directly in step 2 of the algorithm. Each equation (called "active equation") will be multiplied by monomials of the basis from some $(P - 1)$ different S-Boxes (called "passive S-Boxes"). The S-Box relations are not *explicitly* used in the algorithm, but rather in an indirect form. The linear layer equations are linear in the many variables of the system, and these variables are not in the basis of any S-Box. Thus the XSL algorithm requires us to substitute the variables by their expressions as linear combination of the monomials from the corresponding S-Box basis prior to multiplication. Again, the idea of the XSL algorithm is that during the attack the equations are always expressed as sum of terms that are the product of monomials in the bases of the S-Boxes. For example, in our small cipher the initial key addition operation is expressed by the following subsystem:

$$\begin{cases} p_0 + w_{10} + k_{00} \\ p_1 + w_{11} + k_{01} \\ p_2 + w_{12} + k_{02} \\ p_3 + w_{13} + k_{03}, \end{cases} \tag{3}$$

where the p_i variables correspond to the plaintext values. After performing the substitution of the monomials w_{1j} and k_{0j} by their respective expressions from the corresponding S-Boxes bases, the subsystem (3) is written as:

$$\begin{cases} p_0 + w_{10}x_{11} + w_{11}x_{10} + w_{11}x_{12} + w_{12}x_{10} + w_{13}x_{11}+ \\ \quad + k_{00}s_{01} + k_{01}s_{00} + k_{01}s_{02} + k_{02}s_{00} + k_{03}s_{01}, \\ p_1 + w_{10}x_{11} + w_{10}x_{13} + w_{11}x_{13} + w_{12}x_{10} + w_{12}x_{13} + w_{13}x_{10} + w_{13}x_{11}+ \\ \quad + k_{00}s_{01} + k_{00}s_{03} + k_{01}s_{03} + k_{02}s_{00} + k_{02}s_{03} + k_{03}s_{00} + k_{03}s_{01}, \\ p_2 + w_{10}x_{11} + w_{10}x_{12} + w_{12}x_{11} + w_{12}x_{13} + w_{13}x_{10} + w_{13}x_{11}+ \\ \quad + k_{00}s_{01} + k_{00}s_{02} + k_{02}s_{01} + k_{02}s_{03} + k_{03}s_{00} + k_{03}s_{01}, \\ p_3 + w_{10}x_{11} + w_{10}x_{12} + w_{10}x_{13} + w_{11}x_{10} + w_{11}x_{13} + w_{12}x_{10} + w_{12}x_{13} + w_{13}x_{10}+ \\ \quad + k_{00}s_{01} + k_{00}s_{02} + k_{00}s_{03} + k_{01}s_{00} + k_{01}s_{03} + k_{02}s_{00} + k_{02}s_{03} + k_{03}s_{00}. \end{cases}$$

The processing above is performed on all equations arising from the linear layer system (including the key schedule). This results in $(N_r + 1) \cdot B \cdot s + K_e$ quadratic equations over $\mathbb{F}_2$, with $2s \cdot S$ variables and $S \cdot (t - r - 1)$ monomials (excluding the constant monomial), where K_e is the number of key schedule equations and S is the total number of S-Boxes in the cipher. In our small example $S = 6$ and $K_e = 8$, so we have $4 \cdot 1 \cdot 4 + 8 = 24$ equations on 48 variables and 72 monomials. For the AES-128, we have $S = 10 \cdot (16 + 4) = 200$ and $K_e = 192$. Thus there are 1600 equations, 3200 variables and 11200 monomials (Appendix A).

5 Step 2 - Multiplying the Equations

In this step, the attacker selects the value of the parameter P (refer to [11] on how to compute P), and then multiplies each of the equations derived from the cipher linear layer after the substitution described above by the product of $(P-1)$ monomials from different S-Boxes. Only the monomials in the bases are used. To ensure that the equations generated contain only terms that are the product of monomials from P *different* S-Boxes, a few neighbouring S-Boxes need to be excluded (i.e. S-Boxes that have monomials in common with the active equation). This can be visualised in the diagram illustrating the encryption operation in our small example (Figure 1). For example, when multiplying the equations in the subset Lin$_2$, we should not include the monomials in S-Boxes S_2, S_3 and K_2.

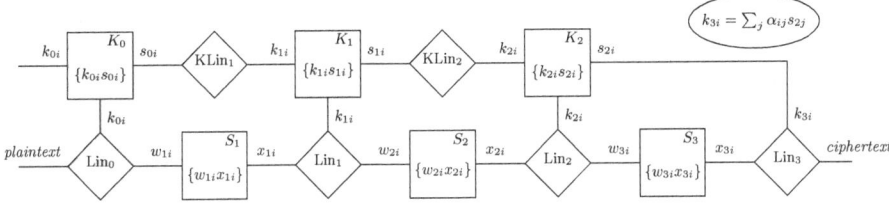

Fig. 1. S-Boxes and Linear Layers on the SR(3,1,1,4) encryption

After multiplication, we expect to have $R = \sum_{i=1}^{L} s \sum_{k=1}^{P} (t-r-1)^{k-1} \binom{S-b_i}{k-1}$ equations (though not all linearly independent), where L is the number of subsets of linear layer equations and b_i is the number of neighbouring S-Boxes for the subset i. In total, we expect to have $T = \sum_{k=0}^{P} (t-r-1)^k \binom{S}{k}$ monomials in the system (Appendix A).

As computed in the previous section, we have 1600 quadratic equations on 3200 variables and 11200 monomials for the AES-128 before multiplication[2]. So it appears that we start with an *underdefined* system, which in principle should not be solvable. Note however that, apart from the initial substitution, we have not used the S-Boxes relations yet.

It is not completely clear from the description in [11] how to include the S-Boxes equations. The authors say that "each time, in the attack we want to use one of the other r terms [not in the S-Box basis], we will write them as linear combination of the elements of the basis" [11]. Although this description leaves the method somewhat open for interpretation, we believe that the most likely way to proceed is to generate all equations via multiplication and then perform (as much as possible) substitutions of monomials not in the bases by their expressions with the corresponding linear combination of monomials in the basis. This should hopefully introduce many new equations. Note that because the initial system used by the XSL algorithm is *underdefined*, the system can only be solved if further substitutions are performed.

As before, let w_{ij} and x_{ij} be the jth bit of the input and output of the ith S-Box respectively, such that the basis consists of the monomials $x_{ij}w_{ik}$, with $j \neq k$, and 1 (note that on the key schedule S-Boxes, the variables should be k_{ij} and s_{ij}, but for simplicity we rename these variables). We denote by $[w_{ij}]$, $[x_{ij}]$ and $[x_{ij}w_{ij}]$ the expressions of these monomials as linear combination of the monomials in the S-Box basis. When performing substitutions, we need to make sure that variables are always substituted in pairs, from the same S-Box (w_{ij} and x_{ik}). This is required to ensure that the resulting new equations are still made up of terms that are the product of monomials from the bases of the S-Boxes. Furthermore, we should also make sure that the substitutions do not create monomials of degree higher than $2P$.

---

[2] Appendix A of [11] describes how to simplify the equations and reduce the number of variables. However this new format does not seem to be suitable for the XSL attack.

The relations used for substitution and generation of new equations are

$$
\begin{array}{ll}
(x_{ij}w_{ik}) \cdot (x_{ij}w_{ik}) = x_{ij}w_{ik} & \text{for any } i,j,k \\
(x_{ij}w_{ik}) \cdot (x_{ij}w_{il}) = (x_{ij}w_{ik}) \cdot [w_{il}] = [w_{ik}] \cdot (x_{ij}w_{il}) & \text{for any } i,j,k \\
(x_{ij}w_{ik}) \cdot (x_{il}w_{ik}) = (x_{ij}w_{ik}) \cdot [x_{il}] = [x_{ij}] \cdot (x_{il}w_{ik}) & \text{for any } i,j,k \quad (4)\\
x_{ij}w_{ik} = [x_{ij}] \cdot [w_{ik}] & \text{for } j \neq k \\
x_{ij}w_{ik} = [x_{ij}] \cdot [w_{ik}] \quad = [x_{ij}w_{ik}] & \text{for } j = k.
\end{array}
$$

For each S-Box, the number of relations is $s^2 + s^3 + s^3 + s(s-1) + 2s = 2s^3 + 2s^2 + s$.

Note that substitutions using any of the relations in (4) will always result in (or only be possible by) monomials made up of the product of some monomials from the *same* S-Box. However, the XSL algorithm described in [11] excludes monomials from neighbouring S-Boxes when multiplying the original equations, and so the generated equations have only terms of the form

$$
x_{i_1 j_1} w_{i_1 k_1} \cdot x_{i_2 j_2} w_{i_2 k_2} \cdot \ldots \cdot x_{i_l j_l} w_{i_l k_l}, \tag{5}
$$

with $l \leq P$ and all i_r's pairwise distinct. This means that no substitutions can be made such that the resulting new equations contain only terms that are the product of up to P monomials from *different* S-Boxes. Substitutions always introduce new monomials, and this is not intended to happen with the XSL algorithm. Without any substitutions, we never get any new expressions, and the method essentially ignores the S-Box equations. Therefore, no matter how large the parameter P is, there is no hope that the XSL algorithm (as described in [11]) can solve the initial set of equations[3].

The problem with the XSL algorithm arises from the attempt to have only monomials made up of the product of P *different* S-Boxes, and as such some S-Boxes needed to be excluded when multiplying. The simplest way to get round this situation is to allow the product of any P monomials from the bases, not necessarily from different S-Boxes, and use all S-Boxes when multiplying, including the neighbouring ones. The effect is that we should expect a larger number of monomials in the end (as well as equations), but this will also allow the substitutions, and we will be able to include the S-Boxes relations in the computations.

A more systematic way to proceed is however to add the relations (that were to be used for substitution) to the initial set of equations, and perform the algorithm without any further substitutions. Care has to be taken though, as some of the new equations have degree 4 rather than 2 (e.g. $x_{ij}w_{ik} = [x_{ij}] \cdot [w_{ik}]$), and these should be multiplied by the product of up to $P-2$ monomials only. We note also that, as the monomial $x_{ij}w_{ij}$ does not belong to the S-Box basis, we should not include some of the relations involving this monomial (for example, $x_{ij}w_{ij} = [x_{ij}w_{ij}]$) in the initial set of equations.

It can be shown that this new procedure is essentially equivalent to the previous one, and all new equations created by substitution can also be generated by applying the method to this enlarged set of equations. We call this modified method *sXL* (standing for *substitute and XL*), and examine it in the following section.

---

[3] Substitutions could still be performed by modifying the last step of XSL (T' method), but this is obviously not the way it was originally proposed.

5.1   The sXL Algorithm

The sXL algorithm seems to be the natural way to get round the flaw in the original XSL algorithm described in [11]. In the sXL algorithm, equations are first processed as described in Section 4. We then add the many new relations (4) resulting from the S-Boxes equations to the original linear layer equations, and multiply all equations in this set by the product of $(P-1)$ monomials from the bases of (not necessarily distinct) S-Boxes, for an appropriate value P.

In the initial set, there were $(N_r + 1) \cdot B \cdot s + K_e$ quadratic equations on $2s \cdot S$ variables and $S \cdot (t - r - 1)$ monomials. To this set we add

$$S \cdot (s(s-1) + s(s-1)^2 + s(s-1)^2 + s(s-1) + s) = S \cdot (2s^3 - 2s^2 + s)$$

quartic equations derived from the relations in (4) (we are excluding some relations using the monomial $x_{ij}w_{ij}$). We call this new set $\overline{S}$.

To analyse the running time of the sXL algorithm, we need to compute the minimal value P_m of the parameter P for which the method yields a solution of the system. We initially ignore the T$'$ method (Section 6).

In order to compute P_m, we introduce new variables Y_{ijk} and substitute the monomials $(x_{ij} \cdot w_{ik})$ in the equations in $\overline{S}$ by Y_{ijk}. We denote the resulting new set of equations by $S \subset \mathbb{K}[Y]$. The new variables Y_{ijk} are related by the various relations of type

$$Y_{ijk} \cdot Y_{ipq} = x_{ij}w_{ik} \cdot x_{ip}w_{iq} = x_{ij}w_{iq} \cdot x_{ip}w_{ik} = Y_{ijq} \cdot Y_{ipk}, \tag{6}$$

where we might have to use the S-Box relations if $j = q$ or $p = k$. We call this set $\mathcal{R} \subset \mathbb{K}[Y]$, and it contains $S \cdot \frac{s^2(s-1)^2}{4}$ equations.

We now consider the system of equations $S \cup \mathcal{R} \subset \mathbb{K}[Y]$, and execute the XL algorithm on this system. The algorithm is required to run to a certain degree D_m to yield a solution.

We now have the following proposition (proof is given in Appendix B):

Proposition 1. *Let $\overline{S}$ be the set consisting of the original linear layer equations together with the relations (4) resulting from the S-Boxes equations, all written as sum of terms made up of the product of monomials in the S-Boxes bases. Denote by P_m the minimal value of the parameter P for which the algorithm described above (sXL) yields a solution of the system. Similarly, let $S \cup \mathcal{R} \subset \mathbb{K}[Y]$ denote the set of equations derived from $\overline{S}$ and the relations (6) by substituting the monomials $(x_{ij} \cdot w_{ik})$ by Y_{ijk}. If D_m denotes the minimal degree for which the XL algorithm yields a solution of this system, then $P_m = D_m$.*

Proposition 1 states that the sXL algorithm is essentially equivalent to an initial substitution (substituting the monomials $(x_{ij} \cdot w_{ik})$ by Y_{ijk}), and then applying the XL algorithm to the resulting system in $\mathbb{K}[Y]$ (thus the name *sXL - substitute and XL*). For the AES-128, we start the XSL algorithm with 1600 equations, 3200 variables and 11200 monomials (i.e. an underdefined system). To run the sXL algorithm, we use the set $\overline{S}$, which contains 182400 linearly independent equations. The set $\mathcal{R}$ has 156800 linearly independent equations, and after adding all relations and substituting the monomials, the set $\mathcal{S} \cup \mathcal{R}$ has 276800 equations (each S-Box contains 1376 linearly independent equations) on 11200 variables. By Proposition 1 above and Theorem 1 from [12], we expect to run the algorithm up to degree at least $D = 51$ for the method to yield a solution. If we include the T' method as last stage (essentially running the XL2 method [9]), we expect to run the algorithm to degree at least $D = 20$. Thus in the best case, the complexity of the attack is at least

$$(\dim(\phi(\overline{U}_D)))^\omega = (\dim(U_D) - \dim(\ker \phi))^\omega$$
$$\geq \left(\sum_{i=0}^{20} \binom{11200}{i} - 156800 \cdot \sum_{i=0}^{18} \binom{11200}{i} \right)^\omega \approx 2^{492},$$

where ϕ, U_D, $\overline{U}_D$ are defined in the proof of Proposition 1 (Appendix B), and $\omega = 2.376$ is the highly optimistic Gaussian reduction exponent given in [11]. Furthermore it should be clear that there seems to be no benefit in running this method instead of simply applying XL or XL2 to the simplified AES system of 8000 equations over 1600 variables described in [10]. Using the same results from [12], we expect in this case to run the algorithm up to degree at least $D = 44$ for the XL algorithm and at least $D = 29$ for the XL2 method. Again, in the best case the complexity of the attack is at least

$$T^\omega = \left(\sum_{i=0}^{29} \binom{1600}{i} \right)^\omega \approx 2^{488}.$$

We recall that the inefficiency of the XL algorithm against the AES has already been shown in [11], and this was in fact the motivation for the proposal of the XSL algorithm. We have shown however that the XSL algorithm presented in [11] has a flaw in its description, and the natural modification (i.e. sXL) is essentially equivalent to the XL algorithm (or XL2) on a much larger system, resulting therefore in a less efficient method of attack against the AES.

6   Step 3 - The T' method

The T' method is the final stage of the XSL algorithm before linearization. We recall that to apply linearization, we require that the number of *linearly independent* equations in the system needs to be approximately the same as the number of monomials (in the notation introduced earlier, $E \approx T$). Starting with a system resulting from step 2 (which may still have T much larger than E), the T' method works by multiplying some selected equations by single variables x_i (reducing modulo $x_i^2 + x_i$ when necessary) in an attempt to obtain new linearly independent equations without creating any new monomials. The hope is that after a few iterations we have $E = T - 1$. Although the method seems to have been designed to work on systems of equations over $\mathbb{F}_2$, it is possible to modify it to work on equations over other finite fields.

Let $\mathcal{R}$ be a system of multivariate polynomial equations of degree at most D with n variables $\{x_1, x_2, \ldots, x_n\}$ over the finite field $\mathbb{K} = \mathbb{F}_2$. We assume that

$\mathcal{R}$ contains E linearly independent equations. Let $\mathcal{T}$ be the set of all monomials in the system, and T_i' be the set of monomials that can be multiplied by the variable x_i and still belong to $\mathcal{T}$, i.e. $T_i' = \{t \in \mathcal{T} | x_i \cdot t \in \mathcal{T}\}$.

Denote by T and T_i' the cardinality of the sets $\mathcal{T}$ and T_i', respectively. Assuming that $E \geq T - T_i' + C$ and $C \geq 1$, we can apply the following "algorithm" [11].

1. Perform a Gaussian elimination on the system $\mathcal{R}$ to bring it to a form in which each monomial is a known linear combination of monomials in T_i'. Since we have $E \geq T - T_i' + C$, we should have around C equations of which all monomial are in T_i'.
2. Multiply these equations by x_i, reducing modulo $x_i^2 + x_i$ when necessary. Add any new linearly independent equations to the system $\mathcal{R}$.
3. Repeat steps 1 and 2 on the resulting system with other variables x_j until $E = T - 1$.

It is expected in [11] that the number of new equations generated grows at exponential rate, and that if the initial system has a unique solution, then after a few iterations (perhaps using as little as three variables) the algorithm should generate enough equations to solve the system by linearization.

Consider the polynomials in $\mathcal{R}$ as vectors over $\mathbb{K}$ in the polynomial algebra $\mathbb{K}[x_1, \ldots, x_n]$ and $\mathcal{E}$ the vector space (of dimension E) generated by $\mathcal{R}$. With an abuse of notation, we denote the space generated by all monomials of degree at most D by $\mathcal{T}$. By using the field relation $x^2 + x = 0$ to reduce the degree of monomials when necessary, we have $T = \dim(\mathcal{T}) = \sum_{i=0}^{D} \binom{n}{i}$.

For any variable x_i, let $T_i' \subseteq \mathcal{T}$ be the subspace of $\mathcal{T}$ defined earlier. We can write

$$\mathcal{T} = T_i' \oplus \mathcal{U} \quad \text{and} \quad T_i' = \dim(T_i') = \sum_{i=0}^{D-1} \binom{n}{i} + \binom{n-1}{D-1}. \tag{7}$$

In order to apply the T' method, we need $\mathcal{E} \cap T_i' \neq \emptyset$. The vectors in $\mathcal{E} \cap T_i'$ correspond to the equations that are multiplied by the variable x_i when running the algorithm. A sufficient condition is that

$$\dim(\mathcal{E}) > \dim(\mathcal{U}) = \dim(\mathcal{T}) - \dim(T_i'), \tag{8}$$

or equivalently, that $E > T - T_i'$. We denote the subspace $\mathcal{E} \cap T_i'$ by $\mathcal{C}_i$, and its dimension by $C_i = E - T + T_i'$.

We note that the multiplication of the equations in $\mathcal{E} \cap T_i'$ by x_i induces a linear transformation $X_i : T_i' \to T_i'$. By appropriately choosing an ordered basis for T_i', X_i can be represented by the $T' \times T'$ matrix $\begin{pmatrix} 0 & 0 \\ 0 & \text{Id} \end{pmatrix}$, where Id corresponds to the $\frac{T_i'}{2} \times \frac{T_i'}{2}$ identity matrix. The image of X_i is generated by $\{x_i, x_1 x_i, x_2 x_i, \ldots, x_1 \ldots x_i \ldots x_n\}$. The T' method simply computes $X_i(\mathcal{C}_i)$ and adds the resulting vectors to the space $\mathcal{E}$. If we denote by η_k the number of new equations generated by the kth iteration of the algorithm using the variable x_{i_k}, then

$$\eta_k \leq \min(\gamma + \eta_{k-1}, \dim(\text{Im}(X_{i_k}))), \tag{9}$$

where $\gamma = E - T + T'$ for the initial system if x_{i_k} is a new variable, otherwise $\gamma = 0$. This shows that the number of new equations generated by the method does not grow at exponential rate as suggested in [11].

It should be clear that if $X_i(\mathcal{C}_i) \subseteq \mathcal{C}_i$, then the T' method applied to the variable x_i in a particular iteration of the algorithm does not generate any new linearly independent equations. We should then try other variables, as suggested in [11], in the hope that new equations are generated. These could be then added to the system, and the process could be repeated with further variables (including x_i). However, once the condition above is met by all variables, no new equations can be generated. Thus we have the following lemma.

Lemma 1. *Let $\mathcal{R}$ be a system of m multivariate equations of degree $D \geq 2$ with n variables $\{x_1, x_2, \ldots, x_n\}$ over the finite field $\mathbb{K} = \mathbb{F}_2$, and let $\mathcal{C}_i$ and X_i be the $\mathbb{K}$-subspace of $\mathbb{K}[x_1, \ldots, x_n]$ and the linear transformation with respect to the variable x_i, as defined above. If $X_i(\mathcal{C}_i) \subseteq \mathcal{C}_i$ for every $1 \leq i \leq n$, then the T' method does not generate any new linearly independent equation.*

Therefore if a system satisfies the conditions of Lemma 1 before we have enough linearly independent equations to apply linearization, the T' method surely fails. Although it is not clear how likely a system is to satisfy these conditions, in Appendix C we present an example of a small system for which the T' method does not work.

We can make some further remarks about the T' method when it is applied as the final step for XL-type algorithms. Suppose that S is the initial system of m quadratic equations with n variables over the finite field $\mathbb{F}_2$. The XL algorithm multiplies these equations by all monomials up to a prescribed degree $d = D - 2$, obtaining a much larger system $\mathcal{R}$ with $R = \sum_{i=0}^{D-2} \binom{n}{i} \cdot m$ equations. We expect to have

$$T = \sum_{i=0}^{D} \binom{n}{i} \quad \text{and} \quad T_i' = \sum_{i=0}^{D-1} \binom{n}{i} + \binom{n-1}{D-1}, \tag{10}$$

and therefore $T - T_i' = \binom{n-1}{D}$. The T' method is supposed to work as soon as the number of linearly independent equations (E) is larger than $T - T_i'$. By the results of [12], we see that this condition can only be satisfied if T' is greater-or-equal to the coefficient of the Dth term of the expected Hilbert Series of a generic algebra of type $(n + 1; m; d_1, \ldots, d_m)$.

Furthermore, given a variable x_i, the set $\mathcal{R}$ of equations can be divided into three subsets: (a) all equations obtained by multiplying monomials of degree up to $d - 1 = D - 3$, (b) all equations obtained by multiplying monomials of degree $d = D - 2$ with the variable x_i, and (c) equations obtained by multiplying monomials of degree $d = D - 2$ without x_i. Thus we can write

$$R = \sum_{i=0}^{D-2} \binom{n}{i} \cdot m = \left(\sum_{i=0}^{D-3} \binom{n}{i} + \binom{n-1}{D-3} + \binom{n-1}{D-2} \right) \cdot m \tag{11}$$

To apply the T′ method, we should first perform a Gaussian reduction on the set $\mathcal{R}$, and then multiply the equations in $\mathcal{T}_i'$ by the variable x_i in an attempt to obtain new linearly independent equations.

It is clear that all equations in (a) and (b) are in $\mathcal{T}_i'$. However, the equations in (b) are fixed by x_i and no new equations will be generated by multiplication. For equations in (a), any new equations would have been already included when running the XL algorithm, so no new linearly independent equations can be generated by multiplication either.

The only useful equations of $\mathcal{R}$ for the T′ method are therefore the ones in (c), and the method can work if applied to (at most) $\binom{n-1}{D-2} \cdot m$ equations. This fact had already been remarked in [6].

In [15] it is shown how the T′ method can be interpreted in terms of Buchberger's Gröbner Basis algorithm. The method is further discussed (in the context of the XL2 [9] algorithm) in [2,4], where some doubts are cast on the general applicability of the method. It is remarked that the T′ method may not be able to run because some of the monomials in $\mathcal{T} \setminus \mathcal{T}'$ cannot be expressed as linear combination of monomials in $\mathcal{T}'$ (and therefore cannot be reduced). In particular, this will happen if $C = E - T + T'$ is small, because as we saw above, after the XL algorithm many equations are already in $\mathcal{T}'$.

It is also noted in [2] that the method should operate with all variables instead of just two or three. In this case the XL2 method is equivalent to running the XL algorithm one degree higher and eliminating all the highest degree monomials. However it is not hard to construct examples where two variables prove to be enough.

The T′ method is perhaps the least understood part of XL-type algorithms. Experiments have proved to be inconclusive, and more study may be needed to verify whether it can be used in general as a final step of algorithms for efficiently solving systems of multivariate equations.

7   Conclusion

Since the proposal of the XSL algorithm, the potential for algebraic attacks against block ciphers, and in particular the AES, has been the source of much speculation and has attracted a lot of attention from the cryptographic community. Although not much is known about the effectiveness of algebraic attacks as a cryptanalytic technique, it is widely believed that the most promising approach is the development of *dedicated* methods for specific block ciphers. The XSL algorithm is perhaps the first attempt to exploit the particular structure of the AES system of equations. We have shown however that, as presented in [11], the XSL algorithm cannot solve the system arising from the AES. By discussing some alternatives for the algorithm, we come to the conclusion that, in its current form, it is unlikely that the algorithm can provide an efficient method for solving the AES system of equations.

References

1. Gwénolé Ars, Jean-Charles Faugère, Hideki Imai, Mitsuru Kawazoe, and Makoto Sugita. Comparison Between XL and Gröbner Basis Algorithms. In Pil Joong Lee, editor, *Advances in Cryptology - ASIACRYPT 2004*, volume 3329 of *Lecture Notes in Computer Science*, pages 338–353. Springer, 2004.
2. Jiun-Ming Chen, Nicolas Courtois, and Bo-Yin Yang. On Asymptotic Security Estimates in XL and Gröbner Bases-Related Algebraic Cryptanalysis. In *ICICS*, volume 3269 of *Lecture Notes in Computer Science*, pages 401–413. Springer, 2004.
3. Jiun-Ming Chen and Bo-Yin Yang. All in the XL Family: Theory and Practice. In *Proceedings of the 7th International Conference on Information Security and Cryptology*, volume 3506 of *Lecture Notes in Computer Science*, pages 67–86. Springer, 2004.
4. Jiun-Ming Chen and Bo-Yin Yang. Theoretical Analysis of XL over Small Fields. In *Proceedings of the 9th Australasian Conference on Information Security and Privacy*, volume 3108 of *Lecture Notes in Computer Science*, pages 277–288. Springer, 2004.
5. Carlos Cid, Sean Murphy, and Matthew Robshaw. Small Scale Variants of the AES. In H. Gilbert and H. Handschuh, editors, *Fast Software Encryption - FSE 2005*, volume 3557 of *Lecture Notes in Computer Science*, pages 145–162. Springer-Verlag, 2005.
6. Don Coppersmith. Comments on Crypto-Gram Newsletter. http://www.schneier.com/crypto-gram-0210.html, October 2002.
7. Nicolas Courtois. Algebraic Attacks over $GF(2^k)$, Applications to HFE Challenge 2 and Sflash-v2. In F. Bao et al., editor, *PKC 2004*, volume 2947 of *LNCS*, pages 201–217. Springer-Verlag, 2004.
8. Nicolas Courtois, Alexander Klimov, Jacques Patarin, and Adi Shamir. Efficient Algorithms for Solving Overdefined Systems of Multivariate Polynomial Equations. In Bart Preneel, editor, *Advances in Cryptology - EUROCRYPT 2000*, volume 1807 of *Lecture Notes in Computer Science*, pages 392–407. Springer, 2000.
9. Nicolas Courtois and Jacques Patarin. About the XL algorithm ober GF(2). In M. Joye, editor, *Progress in Cryptology - CT-RSA 2003*, pages 140–156. Springer-Verlag, 2003.
10. Nicolas Courtois and Josef Pieprzyk. Cryptanalysis of Block Ciphers with Overdefined Systems of Equations. Cryptology ePrint Archive, Report 2002/044, 2002.
11. Nicolas Courtois and Josef Pieprzyk. Cryptanalysis of Block Ciphers with Overdefined Systems of Equations. In Yuliang Zheng, editor, *Advances in Cryptology - ASIACRYPT 2002*, volume 2501 of *Lecture Notes in Computer Science*, pages 267–287. Springer, 2002.
12. Claus Diem. The XL-Algorithm and a Conjecture from Commutative Algebra. In Pil Joong Lee, editor, *Advances in Cryptology - ASIACRYPT 2004*, volume 3329 of *Lecture Notes in Computer Science*, pages 323–337. Springer, 2004.
13. Sean Murphy and Matthew Robshaw. Essential Algebraic Structure within the AES. In M. Yung, editor, *Advances in Cryptology - CRYPTO 2002*, volume 2442 of *LNCS*, pages 1–16. Springer-Verlag, 2002.
14. Sean Murphy and Matthew Robshaw. Comments on the Security of the AES and the XSL Technique. *Electronic Letters*, 39:26–38, 2003.
15. Makoto Sugita, Mitsuru Kawazoe, and Hideki Imai. Relation between XL algorithm and Gröbner Bases Algorithms. Cryptology ePrint Archive, Report 2004/112, 2004.

A   The XSL Attack on the AES-128

In this Appendix we make some computations concerning the XSL attack against the AES with 128-bit keys.

A.1   Key Schedule

The AES key schedule presents a different structure from the encryption, in that not all key variables go through an S-Box. The suggestion in [10] is that, when performing the second XSL attack, one should introduce the so-called "artificial S-Boxes", with some key variables and no equations. Instead of that, in our analysis we rewrite the key schedule system such that these "artificial S-Boxes" are no longer required.

There are $S_k = N_a N_r$ S-Boxes in the AES key schedule, and a total of $s N_a N_b (N_r + 1)$ subkeys variables, of which $s N_a N_r$ go through an S-Box during the key schedule. So we choose to introduce $s N_a N_r$ new variables, to represent the bits of the S-Box output $s_{j,3,i}$. For the AES-128, we have $N_a = N_b = 4$, $N_r = 10$, and so $S_k = 40$. A diagram for the key schedule of the AES-128 is shown in Figure 2.

The key schedule set of equations used in the XSL attack consists initially of $s N_a N_b N_r$ linear equations. We can however express all subkeys variables as linear expression of the $2 s N_a N_r$ S-Boxes variables (representing the bits of $k_{j,3,i}$ and $s_{j,3,i}$), as shown in the equations below:

$$
\begin{aligned}
k_{0,0,i} &= k_{0,3,i} + k_{1,3,i} + k_{2,3,i} + k_{3,3,i} + s_{2,3,i} + s_{1,3,i} + s_{0,3,i} \\
k_{1,0,i} &= k_{0,3,i} + k_{1,3,i} + k_{2,3,i} + k_{3,3,i} + s_{2,3,i} + s_{1,3,i} \\
k_{2,0,i} &= k_{0,3,i} + k_{1,3,i} + k_{2,3,i} + k_{3,3,i} + s_{2,3,i} \\
k_{j,0,i} &= k_{j,3,i} + k_{j-1,3,i} + k_{j-2,3,i} + k_{j-3,3,i} && \text{for } j = 3 \ldots (N_r - 1) \\
k_{0,1,i} &= k_{0,3,i} + k_{2,3,i} + s_{1,3,i} \\
k_{1,1,i} &= k_{1,3,i} + k_{3,3,i} + s_{2,3,i} \\
k_{j,1,i} &= k_{j,3,i} + k_{j-2,3,i} && \text{for } j = 2 \ldots (N_r - 1) \\
k_{0,2,i} &= k_{0,3,i} + k_{3,3,i} + s_{2,3,i} \\
k_{j,2,i} &= k_{j,3,i} + k_{j-1,3,i} && \text{for } j = 1 \ldots (N_r - 1) \\
k_{N_r,0,i} &= k_{N_r-4,3,i} + k_{N_r-3,3,i} + k_{N_r-2,3,i} + k_{N_r-1,3,i} + s_{N_r-1,3,i} \\
k_{N_r,1,i} &= k_{N_r-4,3,i} + k_{N_r-2,3,i} + s_{N_r-1,3,i} \\
k_{N_r,2,i} &= k_{N_r-4,3,i} + k_{N_r-1,3,i} + s_{N_r-1,3,i} \\
k_{N_r,3,i} &= k_{N_r-4,3,i} + s_{N_r-1,3,i}
\end{aligned}
$$

The equations above can also be used to simplify the key schedule linear layer equations relating variables from S-Boxes. These equations can be written as

$$ k_{j,3,i} = k_{j+4,3,i} + s_{j+3,3,i} \quad \text{for } j = 0 \ldots (N_r - 5). \tag{12} $$

We therefore have $N_a(N_r-4)$ sets of s linear equations, and so $K_e = N_a(N_r-4)s$. For the AES-128, we have $K_e = 192$. The number of key schedule S-Boxes needed to express the different subkeys is given in Table 1.

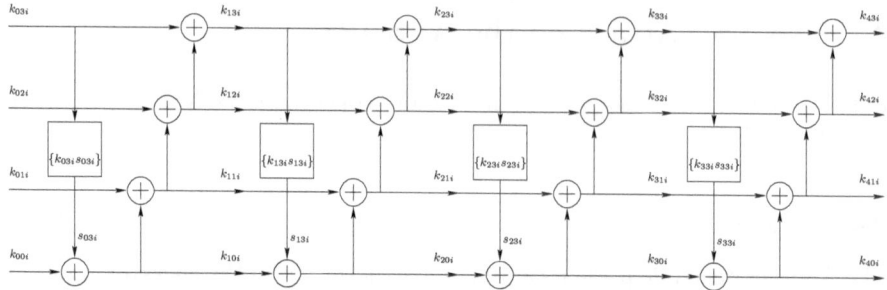

Fig. 2. Diagram for the AES-128 key schedule

Table 1. Number of S-Boxes used in equations involving $k_{j,r,i}$

j	0	1	2	3	4	5	6	7	8	9	10
$k_{j,0,i}$	4	4	4	4	4	4	4	4	4	4	4
$k_{j,1,i}$	3	3	2	2	2	2	2	2	2	2	3
$k_{j,2,i}$	3	2	2	2	2	2	2	2	2	2	2
$k_{j,3,i}$	1	1	1	1	1	1	1	1	1	1	2

A.2   Complexity of the XSL Attack on the AES-128

In this section we show that, in addition to the issues raised in Section 5, the XSL heuristics presented in [11] overestimate the number of equations generated by the algorithm[4]. Firstly, when deriving the complexity of the attacks, the XSL heuristics assume that all equations generated by the method are linearly independent. It should be clear that they are not. Even for $P = 2$, there are many relations of the type $f_i \cdot [f_j] = f_j \cdot [f_i]$. Secondly, the XSL algorithm states that neighbouring S-Boxes need to be excluded when multiplying the linear layer equations. This also needs to be taken into account when estimating the total number of equations.

The subsets of linear layer equations from the encryption have common variables with four S-Boxes from the current round, one S-Box from the next round (except in the first and last rounds, where some monomials are replaced by the plaintext or the ciphertext), and a number of key schedule S-Boxes. The number of neighbouring S-Boxes for the key schedule equations can be derived from Table 1, while the number of neighbouring S-Boxes for the encryption equations is given in Table 2.

Therefore the number of equations obtained by multiplication should be

$$R = \sum_{i=1}^{L} s \sum_{k=1}^{P} (t - r - 1)^{k-1} \binom{S - b_i}{k - 1} \tag{13}$$

---

[4] Note that although the key schedule equations were not used in [11], the way the heuristics were used to obtain the number of equations can be easily applied to the system including the key schedule.

Table 2. Number of neighbouring S-Boxes for the encryption equations (defining $w_{j,k,i}$)

j	0	1	2	3	4	5	6	7	8	9	10
$w_{j,0,i}$	5	9	9	9	9	9	9	9	9	9	8
$w_{j,1,i}$	4	8	7	7	7	7	7	7	7	7	7
$w_{j,2,i}$	4	7	7	7	7	7	7	7	7	7	6
$w_{j,3,i}$	2	6	6	6	6	6	6	6	6	6	6

instead of $Ss(t-r)^{(P-1)}\binom{S}{P-1}$ given in [11]. Likewise, the number of monomials is

$$T = \sum_{k=0}^{P}(t-r-1)^k\binom{S}{k} \tag{14}$$

instead of $(t-r)^P\binom{S}{P}$ given in [11]. For the AES-128, we have

$$S = S_m + S_k = N_a N_b N_r + N_a N_r = 200,$$
$$L = N_a N_b(N_r+1) + N_a(N_r - N_b) = 200,$$

while b_i can be obtained from Tables 1 and 2.

Using these figures and the formulas given in [11], we obtain $P = 9$, giving $T \approx 2^{100}$ and $T^\omega \approx 2^{238}$ for the second XSL attack against the AES-128. We note however that we are not taking into account the linear dependencies between these equations, and so the complexity is likely to be much higher.

We also note that, with these new figures and assuming that *almost* all R equations are linearly independent [11], the T' method seems to be irrelevant for the attack. In fact, since $T \approx 100T'$, when $P = 9$ we already have $R > T - 2$ (so there is no need for the T' method), while for $P = 8$ we are still in the situation that $R < T - T'$ (and are therefore unlikely to be able to use the T' method).

B   Relation Between sXL and XL

We present here the proof of Proposition 1 from Section 5.1.

Let $\bar{S}$ be the set of equations consisting of the original linear layer equations (after the processing described in Section 4), and the relations (4) resulting from the S-Boxes equations. All these equations are written as sum of terms made up of the product of monomials in the bases of the S-Boxes.

Let $D \in \mathbb{N}$ and $\bar{U}_D$ be the set of equations generated by running the sXL algorithm with the parameter $P = D$ on the set $\bar{S}$. Denote by $\mathbb{K}[\{x_{ij} \cdot w_{ik}\}]$ the subring of $\mathbb{K}[x,w]$ generated by the various monomials of type $(x_{ij} \cdot w_{ik})$ contained in the bases of the S-Boxes. Furthermore, let $\mathbb{K}[\{x_{ij} \cdot w_{ik}\}]_{\leq 2D}$ and $\mathbb{K}[x,w]_{\leq 2D}$ be the $\mathbb{K}$-vector spaces generated by the respective polynomials of total degree at most $2D$. It is clear that we have $\bar{U}_D \subset \mathbb{K}[\{x_{ij} \cdot w_{ik}\}]_{\leq 2D}$.

Similarly to [12], we define

$$\bar{\chi}(D) = \dim_\mathbb{K}(\mathbb{K}[\{x_{ij} \cdot w_{ik}\}]_{\leq 2D}) - \dim_\mathbb{K}(\bar{U}_D).$$

The sXL algorithm will yield a solution for the system if $\overline{\chi}(D) = 1$ (we are ignoring by now the T′ method)[5]. We denote by P_m the minimal value of D for which this relation is satisfied.

We now introduce new variables Y_{ijk} and substitute the monomials $(x_{ij} \cdot w_{ik})$ in the equations in $\overline{S}$ by Y_{ijk}. As the equations in $\overline{S}$ are either quadratic or quartic, this can be done in a straightforward way. We denote this new set of equations by $S \subset \mathbb{K}[Y]$. To this set we add the equations (6)

$$Y_{ijk} \cdot Y_{ipq} = Y_{ijq} \cdot Y_{ipk}, \tag{15}$$

contained in the set $\mathcal{R} \subset \mathbb{K}[Y]$. Let U_D be the set of equations generated by running the XL algorithm up to degree D on the set $S \cup \mathcal{R} \subset \mathbb{K}[Y]$. It is clear that we have $U_D \subset \mathbb{K}[Y]_{\leq D}$. Now we define

$$\chi(D) = \dim_{\mathbb{K}}(\mathbb{K}[Y]_{\leq D}) - \dim_{\mathbb{K}}(U_D).$$

Again, we can solve the system directly by linearization if $\chi(D) = 1$, but more generally, we only need $\chi(D) \leq D$. We denote by D_m the minimal degree D for which this relation is satisfied.

Let ϕ be the $\mathbb{K}$-homomorphism defined as

$$\phi : \mathbb{K}[Y]_{\leq D} \longrightarrow \mathbb{K}[\{x_{ij} \cdot w_{ik}\}]_{\leq 2D}$$
$$Y_{ijk} \longmapsto x_{ij} w_{ik} \ .$$

It is clear that $\phi(\mathbb{K}[Y]_{\leq D}) = \mathbb{K}[\{x_{ij} \cdot w_{ik}\}]_{\leq 2D}$ and $\phi(U_D) = \overline{U}_D$. Let V_D be the subset of $\mathbb{K}[Y]_{\leq D}$ defined as

$$V_D = \langle \prod_{l=1}^{D-2} Y_{i_l j_l k_l} \cdot \mathcal{R} \rangle. \tag{16}$$

Lemma 2. V_D is the kernel of the homomorphism ϕ.

Proof. In one direction, it is clear that $V_D \subseteq \ker \phi$. Now let $\mathcal{B} = \{M_i\}$ be the canonical basis of $\mathbb{K}[Y]_{\leq D}$ and r the number of distinct monomials of type $\phi(M_i)$. It is clear that each $\phi(M_i)$ is a non-null monomial of $\mathbb{K}[\{x_{ij} \cdot w_{ik}\}]_{\leq 2D}$, and thus r is the rank of ϕ. We can then choose $b = \#\mathcal{B} - r$ linearly independent polynomials of the form $M_i + M_j$ with $\phi(M_i) = \phi(M_j)$. Since $\dim(\ker \phi) = b$, it follows that these polynomials form a basis of $\ker \phi$.

Let $M_1 = \prod_l m_{1l}$, where $m_{1l} = \prod_r Y_{i_l j_r k_r}$ are monomials involving only variables (i.e. quadratic monomials in $\mathbb{K}[\{x_{ij} \cdot w_{ik}\}]$) from the same S-Box. It is clear that $M_2 = \prod_l m_{2l}$, with $\phi(m_{1l}) = \phi(m_{2l})$. So without loss of generality, we assume that $M_1 = m_1 = \prod_r Y_{ij_r k_r}$ and $M_2 = m_2 = \prod_l Y_{ij_l k_l}$.

If we write $\nu : j_r \to k_r$ and $M_1 = \prod_j Y_{ij\nu(j)}$, then there exists a permutation $\sigma \in S_K$ such that $M_2 = \prod_j Y_{i\sigma(j)\nu(j)}$. Write σ as a product of transpositions

[5] In fact, by renaming monomials if necessary, we should be able to successfully solve the system if $\overline{\chi}(D) \leq D$ [8].

$\sigma = \prod_p \tau_p$, where $\tau_p = (a_p, b_p)$ with $a_p, b_p \in \{k_r\}$. Denote by t_p the product $\tau_{p-1}\tau_{p-2}\ldots\tau_0$, where $t_0 = $ id and $t_\infty = \sigma$. If we call

$$Z_{jk} = \begin{cases} Y_{ijk} & \text{if } j \neq k \\ [Y_{ijk}] & \text{if } j = k \end{cases},$$

then we have

$$\prod_i Z_{i\nu(i)} + \prod_i Z_{\tau_p(i)\nu(i)} = \left(Z_{a_p\nu(a_p)}Z_{b_p\nu(b_p)} + Z_{a_p\nu(b_p)}Z_{b_p\nu(a_p)}\right) \prod_{i \neq a_p, b_p} Z_{i\nu(i)}$$

$$\prod_i Z_{t_p(i)\nu(i)} + \prod_i Z_{t_{p+1}(i)\nu(i)} = \left(Z_{a_p\nu(a_p)}Z_{b_p\nu(b_p)} + Z_{a_p\nu(b_p)}Z_{b_p\nu(a_p)}\right) \prod_{t_p(i) \neq a_p, b_p} Z_{t_p(i)\nu(i)}$$

Therefore

$$M_1 + M_2 = \prod_i Z_{t_\infty(i)\nu(i)} + \prod_i Z_{t_0(i)\nu(i)} \in \langle(Z_{\alpha\beta}Z_{\gamma\delta} + Z_{\alpha\delta}Z_{\gamma\beta}) \cdot \mathbb{K}[Y]_{\leq D-2}\rangle,$$

and $\ker \phi = V_D$. □

Therefore, according to the lemma we have

$$\frac{\mathbb{K}[Y]_{\leq D}}{V_D} \cong \mathbb{K}[\{x_{ij} \cdot w_{ik}\}]_{\leq 2D} \qquad \text{and} \qquad \frac{U_D}{V_D} \cong \overline{U}_D.$$

It follows that $\chi(D) = \overline{\chi}(D)$ and $P_m = D_m$.

C An Example for which the T′ Method Fails

In Appendix B of [11] a concrete working example for the T′ method is presented. The example consisted of a system of 8 quadratic equations with 5 variables, such that $T = 16$ and $T' = 10$. By alternately applying the method with respect to the variables x_1 and x_2, a total of 15 linearly independent equations were obtained and the system could then be solved by linearization.

Below we present an example for which the T′ method does not work. Our system has 7 linearly independent quadratic equations over $\mathbb{F}_2$ with 5 variables (so we have $E = 7$, $T = 16$ and $T' = 10$). Our system has also a unique solution ($x_2 = x_3 = x_5 = 0$, $x_1 = x_4 = 1$). In our case, however, there is only one exceeding equation, i.e. $C = E - T + T' = 1$.

$$\begin{cases} x_1x_2 + x_1x_4 + x_2x_3 + x_2x_5 + x_4x_5 + x_1 + x_3 + x_4 + x_5 + 1 = 0 \\ x_1x_2 + x_1x_3 + x_2x_5 + x_3x_5 + x_4x_5 + x_4 + 1 = 0 \\ x_2x_3 + x_3x_5 + x_3x_4 + x_2 + x_3 + x_4 + x_5 + 1 = 0 \\ x_1x_5 + x_1x_3 + x_3x_4 + x_4x_5 + x_5 = 0 \\ x_1x_5 + x_1x_3 + x_2x_4 + x_2 + x_3 = 0 \\ x_1x_3 + x_2x_4 + x_3x_5 + x_1 + x_2 + x_5 + 1 = 0 \\ x_2x_5 + x_2x_3 + x_4x_5 + x_2 + x_3 + x_5 = 0 \end{cases} \qquad (17)$$

The system (17) is such that for every variable x_i, we have $C_i \subseteq \ker(X_i)$ and therefore $X_i(C_i) = \{0\}$. So we are unable to obtain a single new equation. For example, on working with the variable x_1, we can represent the system as:

$$\begin{cases} x_2 x_3 = x_1 x_3 + x_1 x_4 + x_1 x_5 + 1 \\ x_2 x_4 = x_1 x_3 + x_1 x_5 + x_2 + x_3 \\ x_2 x_5 = x_1 x_3 + x_1 + x_3 + x_4 \\ x_3 x_4 = x_1 x_3 + x_1 x_4 + x_1 + x_2 + x_4 + 1 \\ x_3 x_5 = x_1 x_5 + x_1 + x_3 + x_5 + 1 \\ x_4 x_5 = x_1 x_4 + x_1 x_5 + x_1 + x_2 + x_4 + x_5 + 1 \\ 1 = x_1 x_2 + x_1 x_4 + x_1 + x_2 + x_4. \end{cases} \quad (18)$$

However, when multiplying the last equation by x_1 we have

$$x_1 \cdot (1 + x_1 x_2 + x_1 x_4 + x_1 + x_2 + x_4) = 0.$$

The same is valid for all the remaining variables. For example, with respect to x_2:

$$\begin{cases} x_1 x_3 = x_2 x_5 + x_1 + x_3 + x_4 \\ x_1 x_4 = x_2 x_3 + x_2 x_4 + x_2 + x_3 + 1 \\ x_1 x_5 = x_2 x_4 + x_2 x_5 + x_1 + x_2 + x_4 \\ x_3 x_4 = x_2 x_3 + x_2 x_4 + x_2 x_5 \\ x_3 x_5 = x_2 x_4 + x_2 x_5 + x_2 + x_3 + x_4 + x_5 + 1 \\ x_4 x_5 = x_2 x_3 + x_2 x_5 + x_2 + x_3 + x_5 \\ 0 = x_1 x_2 + x_2 x_3 + x_2 x_4 + x_1 + x_3 + x_4. \end{cases}$$

Again the same occurs:

$$x_2 \cdot (x_1 x_2 + x_2 x_3 + x_2 x_4 + x_1 + x_3 + x_4) = 0.$$

Therefore no new equations can be generated and the T' method fails for this system.

New Applications of Time Memory Data Tradeoffs

Jin Hong[1] and Palash Sarkar[2]

[1] National Security Research Institute,
161 Gajeong-dong, Yuseong-gu,
Daejeon, 305-350, Korea
`jinhong@etri.re.kr`
[2] Cryptology Research Group, Applied Statistics Unit,
Indian Statistical Institute, 203, B.T. Road,
Kolkata, India 700108
`palash@isical.ac.in`

Abstract. Time/memory tradeoff (TMTO) is a generic method of inverting oneway functions. In this paper, we focus on identifying candidate oneway functions hidden in cryptographic algorithms, inverting which will result in breaking the algorithm. The results we obtain on stream and block ciphers are the most important ones. For streamciphers using IV, we show that if the IV is shorter than the key, then the algorithm is vulnerable to TMTO. Further, from a TMTO point of view, it makes no sense to increase the size of the internal state of a streamcipher without increasing the size of the IV. This has impact on the recent ECRYPT call for streamcipher primitives and clears an almost decade old confusion on the size of key versus state of a streamcipher. For blockciphers, we consider various modes of operations and show that to different degrees all of these are vulnerable to TMTO attacks. In particular, we describe multiple data chosen plaintext TMTO attacks on the CBC and CFB modes of operations. This clears a quarter century old confusion on this issue starting from Hellman's seminal paper in 1980 to Shamir's invited talk at Asiacrypt 2004. We also provide some new applications of TMTO and a set of general guidelines for applying TMTO attacks.

Keywords: time memory data tradeoff.

1 Introduction

Time memory tradeoff (TMTO) algorithm is a generic method of inverting otherwise well behaved oneway functions. The technique of using TMTO to invert oneway function was introduced by Hellman in his seminal paper [16] on the topic in 1980. This topic has two parts.

TMTO Algorithms: This covers development of new TMTO algorithms including use of multiple data and investigation of theoretical issues about general TMTO algorithms. Apart from Hellman's work, other contributions to this line of research include Rivest's idea of distinguished points, Fiat-Naor [10], Babbage [4],

B. Roy (Ed.): ASIACRYPT 2005, LNCS 3788, pp. 353–372, 2005.
© International Association for Cryptologic Research 2005

Golić [12], Biryukov-Shamir [7], Oechslin [23] and Kim-Matsumoto [20]. In this work, we will use some of the relevant results from the above papers, but we will not present any new contribution to this area.

TMTO Applications: Our contribution is to this area of TMTO research. As mentioned before, TMTO is applied to invert oneway function. Therefore an important question is to identify a target oneway function on which to apply TMTO. The initial work by Hellman [16] is a *chosen plaintext* attack and applies TMTO to the oneway function which maps the keyspace to the cipherspace by encrypting an *a priori* chosen message using a blockcipher. The work of Babbage [4], Golić [12] and Biryukov-Shamir [7] applies TMTO to the oneway function which maps the internal state space to a keystream segment of a streamcipher. See [13] for an adaptation of this application to the state space of a PRNG.

We would like to point out that this clear distinction between TMTO algorithm and the oneway function on which to apply it does not appear explicitly in the literature. On the other hand, with this distinction made clear one begins to search for suitable oneway functions hidden in cryptographic algorithms on which to apply TMTO.

In this paper, we present a systematic investigation of the above line of research. We consider a wide range of cryptographic algorithms and look for candidate oneway functions for TMTO applications. Our results on stream and block ciphers are the most interesting and also turns out to be quite important as discussed below. We also consider hash functions and asymmetric algorithms and finally describe a set of guidelines for applying TMTO to cryptographic algorithm. Due to lack of space, the last description as well as some of the other details are given in the Appendix. We next describe our contributions to stream and block ciphers.

1.1   Streamcipher

As mentioned before, the works of Babbage [4], Golić [12], and Biryukov-Shamir [7] have applied TMTO to the oneway function mapping internal state to a keystream segment. A suggested countermeasure for resisting TMTO has been to use a state whose size is double that of the key size. This can be seen from the following quote from [12].

> "...doubling the memory size, from 64 to 128 bits, is very likely to push the attacks beyond the current technological limits. Note that the secret session key size need not be increased to 128 bits."

Over the last few years, this has led streamcipher designers to incorporate huge internal states. Also, most recent streamcipher proposals have quoted their huge state size as indications of resistance to TMTO attacks.

We revisit TMTO on streamciphers. Most streamciphers use an initialization vector (IV) in addition to the secret key. We show that the function mapping (key, IV) to a keystream segment of suitable length is a candidate oneway function for TMTO application. In the case where the key is longer than the IV, the algorithm becomes vulnerable to TMTO *irrespective of the size of the internal state*. Thus, huge state size *does not* guarantee resistance to TMTO attacks. This clears an almost decade old confusion on this issue. Further, our results shows that it does not make sense to increase the state size without a corresponding increase of the IV size. These results have been considered important enough to bring about a change in the recent ECRYPT call for streamcipher primitives.

Prior to our work, the only oneway function in a streamcipher considered for TMTO application was the state to keystream map. Our work shows that the (key, IV) to keystream map is another such function. It is an interesting problem to identify other possible candidate functions. Such functions may not be generic to all streamciphers (as the above two are), but may also be algorithm specific.

1.2 Blockcipher

Blockciphers are mostly used in an appropriate mode of operation. Hellman's attack applies to the ECB mode of operation. There is widespread belief in the cryptographic community that the following two points are true.

1. It is not possible to use multiple data with blockcipher tradeoffs.
2. Cipher block chaining with random IVs will foil tradeoff attacks on blockciphers.

The following quote from the invited talk by Adi Shamir at Asiacrypt 2004 [25] suggests that the first of these is a well settled fact (and not even an open problem).

> "Generic time/memory tradeoff attacks on stream ciphers ($TM^2D^2 = N^2$) are stronger than the corresponding attacks on block ciphers ($TM^2 = N^2$) since they can exploit the availability of a lot of data."

(In fact, the above statement was provided as one of the evidences that blockciphers are stronger than streamciphers.)

The second point is explicitly stated in Hellman's paper [16]. We quote the relevant portions from Hellman's paper. The first of these appears on Page 404, second column, third paragraph.

> "It should be remembered, however, that the time-memory trade-off does not work in a known plaintext attack if block chaining or cipher feedback is used. . . "

This appears even more explicitly on Page 405, second column, third paragraph of Section IV.

> "Even a block cipher can foil the time-memory trade-off in a known plaintext attack through cipher block chaining [7], [8] or other techniques which introduce memory into encipherment. . . . Again, proposed standards include provision for cipher block chaining with a random indicator."

The last sentence suggests that using CBC with a random IV will resist TMTO attacks. There is some confusion between chosen and known plaintext attacks. While the TMTO attack on the ECB mode developed by Hellman is itself a *chosen* plaintext attack, the above comments relate only to *known* plaintext TMTO attacks. We discuss this point in more details in Appendix A.

We investigate the possibility of TMTO application on various block cipher modes of operations. For every mode of operation that we consider, it turns out that there is a suitable oneway function to which *chosen plaintext* TMTO can be applied under appropriate conditions. The most interesting results are for the CBC and the CFB modes of operations. Contrary to Shamir's statement above on the use of multiple data, we show how to apply nontrivial multiple data TMTO to both the CBC and CFB modes of operations. Further, our results show that Hellman's statements above are not correct for chosen plaintext attacks (but they could still be true for known plaintext attacks). However, an algorithm which is not secure against chosen plaintext attacks cannot be considered to be secure. Hence, CBC and CFB modes of operations cannot be considered to be secure against TMTO attacks. This clears a quarter century old confusion on this issue.

Related Work: In a recent work, Biryukov [6] studies applications of multiple data TMTO. We would like to point out that the situation considered in [6] is different from the one we consider here. More specifically, Biryukov [6] considers the situation where a single message is encrypted with many keys and the corresponding ciphertexts are available to the attacker. The goal of the attacker is to obtain one of these keys. This situation applies to the ECB mode of operation of a block cipher, which is the mode usually considered for cryptanalysis of block ciphers. Detailed discussion on strengths of a block cipher in ECB mode and UNIX password hashing is presented in [6]. We would like to mention that one of the reviewers of this paper pointed out that obtaining one-out-of-many keys was earlier suggested in [12].

In contrast to [6], this work and its earlier version [17] considers the more general problem of identifying suitable oneway functions in cryptographic algorithms and possible access to multiple data. The more interesting cases considered here are streamciphers with IV, various modes of operation of block ciphers such as CBC, CFB, etcetra. We note that none of these cases are considered in [6].

Lastly, we would like to clarify some confusion regarding authorship. The work [6] and [22] has been merged and is due to appear as [5] in the proceedings of SAC'05. Thus, there is an overlap of authors between [5] and the current paper. However, the common author was in no way involved with either the preparation or the original submission of [6] to SAC'05.

2   Review of TMTO Algorithms

Time memory data tradeoff algorithms are applied to invert one-way functions. Let $f : \{0,1\}^n \rightarrow \{0,1\}^n$ be a one-way function inverting which will break a cipher. We briefly describe the existing work on methodology of applying TMTO.

A TMTO algorithm has two phases. In the offline phase, a set of tables are prepared. In the online phase, the attacker is given $y_1, \ldots, y_D$ and has to find a pre-image for one of the y_i's, i.e., for some i, the attacker has to find one x_i such that $f(x_i) = y_i$.

We put $N = 2^n$ to be the size of the search space. The pre-computation time is denoted by P and the online search time is denoted by T. The number of data points $y_1, \ldots, y_D$ is D and the memory required to store (the required fraction of) the tables is denoted by M.

The original TMTO algorithm by Hellman [16] used $D = 1$ and satisfied the so-called TMTO curve: $TM^2 = N^2$ with a typical point of $T = M = N^{2/3}$. The pre-computation time is $P = N$.

Babbage [4] and Golić [12] considered TMTO on streamciphers. The tradeoff is basically a birthday attack, and the tradeoff curve is $TM = N$, $T = D$ and $P = M = N/D$. We will call this the BG attack. A typical point on the curve is $T = M = D = P = N^{\frac{1}{2}}$.

Biryukov and Shamir described a multiple data variation of the Hellman method to obtain a new TMTO on streamciphers. The tradeoff curve of $TM^2D^2 = N^2$, $1 \leq D^2 \leq T$, $P = N/D$ was given. We will call this the BS attack. A typical point on the curve is $T = M = N^{\frac{1}{2}}$, $D = N^{\frac{1}{4}}$, $P = N^{\frac{3}{4}}$.

Permutation: If the one-way function f to be inverted is a permutation, then even for $D = 1$, one can obtain the tradeoff curve $TM = N$ with a better tradeoff of $T = M = N^{1/2}$, $D = 1$.

Multiple Data: Availability of multiple data improves the effectiveness of a TMTO attack. In many cases with $D > 1$, the pre-computation time will also be less than N. On the other hand, we need to carefully examine the scenario under which multiple data attack is applied. For example, Hellman originally applied TMTO to find the key of a blockcipher used in the ECB mode of operation. An easy extension to multiple data attack would be for the attacker to target multiple keys and be satisfied with obtaining at least one of these. A similar situation applies to streamciphers as we point out later. A more nontrivial application of multiple data attack is to be able to identify a situation where all the obtained data corresponds to one single key. In this paper, we will mostly be concerned with TMTO attacks which uses multiple data corresponding to a *single* key.

Attack complexity: The complexity of a TMTO attack is usually taken to be the sum or maximum of T, M, and D. It is customary not to take the pre-computation time P as adding to the attack complexity. This is explicitly mentioned in the following quote from Hellman[16],

> "The N operations required to compute the table are not counted because they constitute a pre-computation which can be performed at the cryptanalyst's leisure."

Similarly, Biryukov-Shamir [7], writes that the pre-computation phase "can take a very long time". Following in these steps, it has been customary to ignore pre-computation time for TMTO attacks. In the case $D = 1$, exhaustive search (or even more) pre-computation time is unavoidable. More generally, the pre-computation time is $P = N/D$ and N is of the form 2^{k+v}, where k is the key length and v is the length of associated data (IV, nonce, tweak, etcetra). If we put $D = N^a$, with $0 \le a < 1$, then $P = N^{1-a}$ and is less than 2^k if $k > \frac{1-a}{a} \times v$. Since 2^k correspond to exhaustive search time, under the last condition the pre-computation time is less than exhaustive search.

3   Streamcipher

Let us be given a streamcipher algorithm that takes a k-bit key. Our search space is the key space of size $N = 2^k$. Consider the following oneway function f which takes a single k-bit key (and no IV) as input. The cipher algorithm specifies a key load mechanism and an initialization procedure. Take the first k bits of keystream as output for the function f.

Inverting f will provide the key. This approach of applying TMTO to the key space of a streamcipher is not a new idea. Hellman [16] briefly mentions this situation as one possible application. Also, in the appendix of a more recent paper [11], this situation is more definitely mentioned in relation to BG-tradeoff.

Let us consider multiple data when applying TMTO to f. Consider the situation of a dummy terminal session. Assume that each session is encrypted with a new key, and that the first encrypted text of a session is the (fixed) login screen so that the keystream prefix of each session is always exposed. Each session we observe gives one target data point. Inverting any one of the data points, gives us the corresponding secret key. Using the BS curve, if we can observe $D = N^{1/4} = 2^{k/4}$ sessions, then we have an attack with $T = M = N^{1/2} = 2^{k/2}$ and $P = 2^{3k/4}$. Depending on the amount of available data, one could also choose other suitable points of the BS curve. In any case, under this kind of an attack scenario, no streamcipher can provide security level equal to its key length.

3.1   Streamciphers with IV

The situation with streamciphers have changed somewhat since the early work of Hellman, and modern ciphers now use a nonce or an initial vector (IV) in addition to the secret key. Resynchronization is more common in this situation, and obtaining large sets of data is more realistic.

Consider an environment where many short messages are encrypted, each with a different IV. Assume that the master key is seldom changed. This may happen with wireless communication frames, or maybe a disk encryption scheme where each sector is encrypted with a different IV. Assume some of these frames or sectors are known to us in the form of bare keystream. Since IVs are usually public, if we can obtain the master key to one of these frames, all other frames using the same master key would be readable.

We first need to define an appropriate oneway function. Consider the function

$$f : \{\text{master keys}\} \times \{\text{IVs}\} \rightarrow \{\text{keystream prefix}\}. \tag{1}$$

Function f sends a random (k-bit key, v-bit IV) pair to a $(k+v)$-bit keystream prefix. So our search space is of size $N = 2^{k+v}$. For a good cipher, this mapping should behave like a random function. We consider three cases with different data requirements. The first of these follows from the BG curve ($TM = N$; $T = D$) , while the other two follow from the BS curve $TM^2D^2 = N^2$.

1. $(P, D, M, T) = (N^{1/2}, N^{1/2}, N^{1/2}, N^{1/2})$: $P = 2^{(k+v)/2} < 2^k$ for $k > v$.
2. $(P, D, M, T) = (N^{2/3}, N^{1/3}, N^{1/3}, N^{2/3})$: $P = 2^{2(k+v)/3} < 2^k$ for $k > 2v$.
3. $(P, D, M, T) = (N^{3/4}, N^{1/4}, N^{1/2}, N^{1/2})$: $P = 2^{3(k+v)/4} < 2^k$ for $k > 3v$.

If we ignore pre-computation time, then data requirement is the minimum in the third case above. In this case, we have an attack whenever $T = M = N^{1/2}$ is less than 2^k. The last condition holds for $k > v$ and hence we can say that *if IV is any shorter than key, the streamcipher is vulnerable to a TMTO attack.*

Pre-Computation Time: If we wish to take pre-computation time into account, then the third case gives an attack for $k > 3v$. If more data is available, then using the first two cases, we get attacks under different relations between k and v. As already mentioned before, if $D = N^a$ for some $0 \le a < 1$, the pre-computation time is $P = N^{1-a}$ and is less than 2^k for $k > \frac{1-a}{a} \times v$. On the other hand, for a fixed value of k and v, if we wish to make the pre-computation time at least as expensive as exhaustive search, then we must ensure that the access to multiple data is restricted to the condition $a \le v/(k+v)$. If $a > v/(k+v)$, then we have a TMTO attack where even the pre-computation time is less than exhaustive search.

Below, we state some remarks on this and give some variations to this method.

1. Putting a restriction on how many frames are encrypted before the master key is renewed does not stop this attack completely. The attacker still gets to know one of the many master keys.
2. Making the state initialization process more complex has completely no effect on this TMTO attack. *Neither does the size of the internal state of the stream cipher affect this TMTO in any manner.*
3. The known part of keystream need not be at the very beginning. As long as they are fixed positions in the keystream, they do not even need to be continuous. The oneway function can be defined to match the known part.
4. If IV is XORed into the key before being placed into the internal state, we could set the domain of the oneway function to be at that position. In general, the domain of f should be at the point of least entropy occurring during the initialization process.
5. Using IVs in a predictable manner effectively reduces the IV space, making TMTO more efficient.

3.2   State Versus Key Size

Previous multiple data attacks on streamciphers have targeted the internal state of the cipher. It has been suggested that to resist TMTO attacks, the internal state size should be at least twice the key size. Our new attack shows that if IV is any shorter than the key, then the streamcipher is vulnerable to TMTO *irrespective* of the size of the internal state. There are two consequences.

First, simply increasing state size of a streamcipher does not make the algorithm TMTO resistant. Second, it does not make sense to increase the state size without a corresponding increase in the size of the IV. For example, if one believes that TMTO forces internal state of any streamcipher to be twice as big as key, as is requested in the ECRYPT Call for Stream Cipher Primitives [3], then one should also request IV size to be at least as big as key size.

Conversely, suppose one is on the other side of this argument, with the opinion that birthday attack based BG-tradeoff should not be taken seriously, and that BS-tradeoff with pre-computation time consideration only mandates IV size bigger than half of key size. Then one should demand state size of only 1.5 times key size.

3.3   ECRYPT Streamcipher Project

Consider a streamcipher taking 80-bit keys with 32-bit IVs. At first, this seems to be a perfectly normal use of key and IV. Actually, this is one of the mandatory parameter set for streamciphers aiming for Profile 2 of the recent ECRYPT Call for Stream Cipher Primitives [3].

Here $N = 2^{112}$ and using the BS curve $TM^2D^2 = N^2$, one sees that this is vulnerable under the tradeoff point $T = M = 2^{56}$, $D = 2^{28}$, $P = 2^{84}$. The pre-computation time is slightly more than exhaustive key search. The tradeoff point $T = 2^{74.7}$, $M = D = 2^{37.3}$, $P = 2^{74.7}$ is also applicable, and brings the offline complexity to under 80 bits. One weak point of this second approach is that the data must spread over multiple keys and the attacker recovers only one of these keys.

After a preliminary version [17] of our work was made public, members of ECRYPT STVL have posted a note [8], with the following modifications.

- 80-bit key with 32-bit IV can no longer be considered a secure parameter set for streamciphers.
- It makes no sense to increase internal state size of a streamcipher without increasing IV size.

Thus, even though our attack appears to be simple, it turns out to be important enough to bring changes to the ECRYPT call for streamcipher primitives. Actually, we were also *surprised* that such a simple and important observation as ours was actually missed by the entire large and active streamcipher community for so many years.

3.4   GSM

Our discussion so far on streamciphers has shown that security level reached by using a key of length longer than IV length, does not correspond to key length, under the framework of TMTO attacks. In this section, we turn to a more specific example. It will illustrate that the actual joint entropy of key and IV matters more than just their length.

The encryption algorithm for GSM mobile phones [1] is called A5/3. It is a modified version of OFB mode of operation based on the KASUMI blockcipher. KASUMI is a 64-bit blockcipher with key length of 128 bits.

In the use of A5/3 for GSM encryption, most part of IV is fixed to some constant value. Only a 22-bit counter part is incremented each time the IV is changed. The 128-bit key is actually a concatenation of two copies of a single 64-bit key. Only 228 bits of keystream is used after initialization with a new IV, but this is not important for us.

We can define our oneway function as

$$(\text{64-bit key}, \text{22-bit counter value}) \mapsto \text{86-bit keystream prefix}.$$

There is an initialization process making A5/3 slightly different from the usual OFB mode of operation and the feedback itself is also a bit different, but as was already commented, this is immaterial. It suffices to know the exact specification for keystream production in order to be able to apply TMTO algorithms.

In this case, $N = 2^{86}$. If we choose $D = N^{1/4}$ and $T = M$ in the curve $TM^2D^2 = N^2$, then we get an attack with the parameters $D = 2^{21.5}$ and $T = M = 2^{43}$. The precomputation time is $P = 2^{64.5}$. Since the counter used in the IV is only 22 bits long, it seems more reasonable to collect data that correspond to multiple master keys. In practice, this may have been obtained from multiple users. When one of these keys is recovered, it can be used to decrypt messages encrypted with the same key and different IVs.

The authors are not aware of the actual situation, but if only a small portion of the possible counter values are used in real life (this would happen if the counter always started from zero), i.e., if the entropy of the counter is smaller, the attacker's position is strengthened further.

3.5   Designing TMTO Resistant Streamciphers with IV

The level of threat brought about by a TMTO attack depends largely on the environment. But a good streamcipher design would be aimed at resisting these threat under any plausible environment it could be in. If one views TMTO attacks as threat to streamciphers, one of the following measures should be taken.

1. Ensure that, in every implementation of the cipher, the collective entropy of key and IV will always be at least twice that of intended security level. In particular, the length of key and IV should add up to at least twice security level and the IV should not be used in a predictable way. During the state initialization process, the collective entropy of key and IV should not be allowed to decrease below twice key size.

2. If you are designing a general purpose streamcipher, and do not know in what manner your cipher is going to be used, claim security level corresponding to half your key size. Then, arbitrary use of IV may be allowed. Entropy of internal state after initialization should not be smaller than that provided by key size.

Here, in saying that the IV usage should be random, we mean it to be un-predictable from the viewpoint of a TMTO attacker preparing a table. So, for example, as long as the starting point is chosen at random, the IV may be sup-plied through a counter for a limited period of time. This possibility was pointed out in [8] in response to an earlier version of this paper.

Pre-Computation Time: As mentioned in Section 3.1, the pre-computation time can be less than exhaustive search if $D = N^a$ with $a > v/(k + v)$. Thus, one approach to securing streamciphers against TMTO with less than exhaustive pre-computation is to ensure that the access to multiple data is restricted to at most $N^{v/(k+v)}$. Any value of k and v satisfying this condition can then be used.

4   Blockcipher Modes of Operation

In this section, we consider several non-trivial applications of multiple data cho-sen plaintext TMTO attacks to different blockcipher modes of operations. We were able to do this successfully on every mode we have considered. This seems to indicate that, in general, *all blockcipher modes of operation are vulnerable to TMTO attacks.*

4.1   ECB, CTR, OFB

For the ECB mode of operation, TMTO that utilize multiple data may be used if the attacker's objective is to recover any single one of the multiple keys that encrypted the same chosen plaintext.

Counter mode is in a very similar situation if counter usage is predictable. The counter value predicted to be used gives us a basis for the chosen plaintext attack, and when the corresponding ciphertext is given, the key may be recovered in time shorter than key exhaustive search. After this, all other text encrypted with the same key may be decrypted.

As we already saw in the GSM example, OFB mode of operation is essentially a streamcipher with IV, and arguments of the previous section apply.

4.2   CBC Mode of Operation

Consider a blockcipher where message, IV and cipher lengths are b bits. Let the key length be lb bits. (Note that l need not be an integer and we denote $\lambda = \lceil l \rceil$, $\mu = l - \lfloor l \rfloor$.) The encryption function E_k maps a b-bit string to a b-bit string. For a plaintext $m_1, m_2, \ldots$, with each $|m_i| = b$, the CBC encryption with an IV V, produces a ciphertext $c_1, c_2, \ldots$ as follows: $c_i = E_k(m_i \oplus c_{i-1})$, where we assume $c_0 = V$.

Let m be a fixed b-bit string. For example, if we are dealing with a 64-bit blockcipher, we let m be 8 ASCII space characters. This definition of m also appears in the original work by Hellman [16].

For any b-bit IV V and lb-bit key k, we define a one-way function f : $\{0,1\}^{(l+1)b} \to \{0,1\}^{(l+1)b}$ as $f(k||V) = c_1||c_2|| \cdots ||c_{\lambda+1}$ where

$$f(k||V) = \underbrace{E_k(m \oplus V)}_{c_1} || \underbrace{E_k(m \oplus c_1)}_{c_2} || \cdots || \underbrace{E_k(m \oplus c_{\lambda-1})}_{c_\lambda} || \mathsf{prefix}_{\mu b}(\underbrace{E_k(m \oplus c_\lambda)}_{c_{\lambda+1}}).$$

(Here $\mathsf{prefix}_i(x)$ denotes the i-bit prefix of the binary string x.) Then the output of f is the $(l+1)b$-bit prefix of the encryption of the plaintext M which consists of $\lambda + 1$ repetitions of the b-bit message m using the key k and IV V.

The f defined above is the target one-way function to be inverted. We incorporate multiple data in the following manner. Let $c_1 c_2 \ldots c_{D+\lambda}$ be a ciphertext obtained by encrypting a plaintext consisting of $D + \lambda$ many repetitions of the b-bit message m using an unknown key k and IV V. For $1 \le i \le D$, define $C_i = c_i \ldots c_{\lambda+i}$. Due to the self-similar structure of CBC chaining, we have the following relationships.

1. C_1 is the CBC encryption of M using key k and IV V.
2. C_2 is the CBC encryption of M using key k and IV c_1.
3. C_3 is the CBC encryption of M using key k and IV c_2.
4. In general, C_i is the CBC encryption of M using key k and IV c_{i-1}.

Then by the definition of f, we have $f(k||c_{i-1}) = D_i = \mathsf{prefix}_{(l+1)b} C_i$, for $1 \le i \le D$. Inverting f on any of the D_i's will yield k (and also c_{i-1}). If the IV V is not public, we could just ignore the first block and think of the second block as starting a CBC mode with the IV set to the first ciphertext block, decrypting from the second block onwards. Further, the repetitions of m need not be at the begining of the message. If there are $D+\lambda$ repetitions of m occurring somewhere in the message, then we can use the known ciphertext block preceding the $D+\lambda$ repetitions as the IV and obtain the required D data points.

This establishes a multiple data scenario for attacking the CBC mode of operation. Here the search space is $N = 2^{(l+1)b}$ while the key space is 2^{lb}. Assuming the curve $TM^2D^2 = N^2$ holds, an optimal point of $T = M = N^{1/2}$, $D = N^{1/4}$ yields an attack if and only if $N^{1/2} < 2^{lb}$, i.e., $2^{(l+1)b/2} < 2^{lb}$ which holds if and only if $l > 1$. Thus, $b = 128$ and $l = 2$ gives an attack. This situation corresponds to AES with message and cipher length equal to 128 bits and key length equal to 256 bits. Similarly, the parameters $b = 128$ and $l = 1.5$ gives an attack corresponding to AES with 128-bit message block and 192-bit key.

The discussion on pre-computation time is similar to that presented in Section 3.1 and hence is not repeated here.

OMAC OMAC [19] is a NIST standard for encryption and authentication. It is a one key CBC with the capability of producing an authentication tag. Ignoring the MAC, the TMTO attack on CBC also works for OMAC.

4.3   CFB and TBC Modes of Operation

CFB is the other mode of operation which Hellman remarked to be secure against known plaintext TMTO attacks. However, the situation with CFB is exactly the same with CBC, i.e., CFB is equally susceptible to chosen plaintext TMTO attacks.

As before, let E_k be the encryption function of a blockcipher with b-bit message, IV and cipher blocks and lb-bit key blocks. Given a plaintext of b-bit blocks $m_1, m_2, \ldots$, and an IV V, the CFB mode of operation produces a ciphertext $c_1, c_2, \ldots$, where $c_i = m_i \oplus E_k(c_{i-1})$. As before, we assume $c_0 = V$.

The one-way function to be inverted is defined from $(l + 1)b$-bit strings to itself in the following manner. As before, let m be a fixed b-bit message string. Then, given a lb-bit key k and a b-bit IV V, we define,

$$f(k||v) = \underbrace{m \oplus E_k(V)}_{c_1} || \underbrace{m \oplus E_k(c_1)}_{c_2} || \cdots || \underbrace{m \oplus E_k(c_{\lambda-1})}_{c_\lambda} || \mathsf{prefix}_{\mu b} \underbrace{(m \oplus E_k(c_\lambda))}_{c_{\lambda+1}}.$$

Now the entire discussion given for CBC applies. Also, the same argument applies to tweakable blockciphers [21] running in TBC mode. It suffices to use tweak in place of IV.

4.4   Other Modes of Operation

We have considered OCB [24], CMC [14], and EME [15] modes of operation. With the attacker given full power with respect to pre-computation and data availability, if key (two keys are used for CMC, but we can treat them as one long key) is any longer than IV, nonce, or tweak, these modes cannot provide security level equal to key size.

4.5   OCB

The mode OCB [24] produces MAC in addition to the ciphertext. Encryption part of OCB is similar to ECB, except that one extra key-like element is used for each block of encryption. These key-like elements are derived from a key and nonce pair, and is updated for each block of additional encryption.

From the view point of TMTO, the MAC output part is no different from the ciphertext. As before, we use the chosen plaintext attack scenario and define the oneway function to send (key, nonce) pair to (ciphertext||MAC).

4.6   CMC, EME

Let us consider the CMC [14] and EME [15] modes of operation. A tweak in addition to a key (two keys are used for CMC, but we just consider them as one long key) is used. These are two-pass encryption modes and every bit of the ciphertext depends on the whole input text. TMTO should provide the attacker with a key (in addition to the tweak). This can then be used on ciphertexts using different tweaks.

We fix a plaintext and define the oneway function f as follows. The function f takes as input a pair (key, tweak) and encrypts the plaintext to obtain the ciphertext. This is hashed (by a collision resistant hash function) to obtain a string of length equal to $|\text{key}| + |\text{tweak}|$. This string is the output of f. In the online phase, we will have a ciphertext and can hash it to obtain a string in the range of the oneway function. Finding a pre-image of the range element will provide the secret key (and also the tweak).

These modes of operations extend a small block length pseudorandom permutation to a wide block length pseudorandom permutation. The intended application is for in-place disk encryption, where the tweak is the sector address and the plaintext block consists of the contents of the corresponding sector. Thus, block length is quite large (around 512 bytes). The reason for using hash function in the definition of the oneway function is so that we do not record this long ciphertext in the table.

It is quite possible that the contents of many of the sectors are identical, which is especially true if the sectors are not in use. In such situation, we can utilize multiple data by obtaining the ciphertexts corresponding to different sector addresses (tweaks) among the sectors containing our fixed chosen plaintext. Inverting any of the points will reveal the master key (and the corresponding tweak), which can be used to decrypt other blocks.

5   Hash Function

With the demand for small hash functions increasing in relation to its possible use in RFIDs, the relatively less interesting results we have concerning hash functions may have implications on hash designed for those environments.

Simple hash We could not find reasonable application of TMTO to collision finding, but obtaining preimage or second preimage quickly with the added advantage of pre-computation time seem to be plausible attack scenarios not considered before. Applying TMTO to the oneway hash function itself, with the message space appropriately restricted, one can see that no hash function can achieve preimage resistance security level equal to its digest size.

Keyed hash and MAC Under the chosen plaintext attack model, keyed hash (or MAC) is very similar to the ECB mode of operation. Sending key to the keyed hash value of a fixed plaintext is the oneway function to be considered. Attacker's objective is to recover the key, given the keyed hash value corresponding to the chosen plaintext. Once the key is obtained, it could be used to forge other hash (or MAC) values. TMTO applies as before and security level equal to key size cannot be reached.

6   Asymmetric Algorithms

In many cases of public key algorithms, the relevant oneway functions satisfy the so-called random self reducibility property, i.e., solving one particular instance of the problem is as hard as solving a random instance of the problem. This is usually shown by converting a specific instance to a random instance. We would like to point out that this provides a natural way of applying multiple data

TMTO, even when a single data item is obtained from the application domain. This is also true for the so-called homomorphic encryption algorithms, whereby knowing the encryption of a single message, it is possible to create encryptions of many related messages.

In symmetric key algorithms, usually the security level expected of an algorithm is equal to its key size. This is far from true in the asymmetric world. Hence TMTO algorithms, the best of which only halves the security level, is less interesting here. Nevertheless, to show that TMTO is a versatile tool, we shall apply tradeoff methods to some asymmetric algorithms.

6.1   NTRUEncrypt

Let us consider the 80-bit security version of NTRU public key cryptosystem [2]. Latest parameter set [18] specify a message space of 2^{251} size. Of the 251 bits, only about $\frac{2}{3}$ is used for the actual message and the rest is filled with a randomizing value. (This situation resembles the key+IV situation considered in previous sections and shows that even *probabilistic* algorithms are not completely out of reach from TMTO.) What is important is that, for a fixed public key, once the 251-bit input is formed, the rest of the encryption process is deterministic from that point on. We can take this deterministic encryption process as our oneway function f and apply the tradeoff point $T = M = N^{2/3}$ to obtain a message recovery attack of $2^{167.3}$ complexity.

Actually, we can do better. As mentioned in Section 2, if f is a permutation, then a better tradeoff point $T = M = N^{1/2}$ applies. Notice that encryption is a bijective process (the so called wrapping failure no longer occurs for parameters presented in [18]). Hence, even though there are some complications, arguing that f is a permutation is reasonable. In such a case, attack complexity goes down to $2^{125.5}$.

We have shown that at the cost of exhaustive pre-computed encryption with a fixed public key, one can decrypt any ciphertext with online time and memory complexity $2^{125.5}$. This is larger than, but close to, the best known attack on NTRU of complexity 2^{106}, which happens to be another time memory tradeoff called the meet-in-the-middle attack. To bring multiple data into the picture, one might consider the situation where multiple encrypted messages are given to the attacker and inverting just one is good enough.

Similar arguments as given above apply to all public key encryption schemes. Also, for other public key schemes there can be alternative oneway functions to consider. For example, one may consider the function from the decryption key to the plaintext for a fixed ciphertext. It might not always be valid to consider this, but in the cases it is valid, applying TMTO to such a function will yield the decryption key. We do not discuss these issues further, since for such applications, TMTO does not appear to be a realistic threat.

6.2   Signature Schemes

Many signature schemes send a triple (m, k, r) consisting of message, key, and randomizing value to a signature (x, s). Here, x is a function of the random value r and sometimes also of m, and s is a function of all inputs.

One fixes a message m likely to be signed by the victim in the near future and apply TMTO to the function $(k, r) \mapsto (x, s)$. Depending on the relative size of k and r, this could be efficient than key exhaustive search. However, the attack complexity will not go anywhere near the claimed security level of the signature schemes. Alternatively, one could apply TMTO to the $(r, m) \mapsto x$ part first (under chosen plaintext scenario), and use the obtained r to recover k, for a more efficient attack. Thus, there are several possibilities for candidate oneway functions, possibly different from the oneway function the designer had in mind.

7 General Framework for TMTO Application

Through arguments of this paper, we have seen that TMTO can be applied to many different situations in a very versatile way. In this section, let us take for granted that TMTO is a general method for inverting well-behaved oneway functions, and explain a general method for applying it to cryptographic situations.

In all of the cryptographic situations considered in this paper, under an appropriate attack scenario, we could devise a oneway function of the following form.

$$f : K \times V \to C. \tag{2}$$

Here, K denotes the secret values the attacker is trying to obtain, and V refers to the set of auxiliary values which is, in many situations, public but not controllable by the attacker. The set C contains the output values and specific targets from this set is given to the attacker at the online stage of TMTO. What these sets refer to in the various situations considered in this paper is listed in Table 1. In some cases, V is missing from the cryptographic system, in which case we think of V as containing a single element.

Table 1. Fitting various cryptographic situations into TMTO framework

situation		K	V	C
block	ECB [16], CTR	key	-	single ciphertext block
	OFB, CBC, CFB	key	IV	ciphertext blocks
	TBC	key	nonce	ciphertext blocks
	OCB	key	nonce	ciphertext blocks + MAC
	CMC, EME	key(s)	tweak	ciphertext blocks
stream	previous [4,7,12]	state	-	keystream of state size
	simple	key	-	keystream of key size
	with IV	key	IV	keystream of (key+IV) size
hash	preimage	message	-	hash value
	keyed	key	-	hash value
public key encryption		message	randomizing value	ciphertext
signature		key	randomizing value	signature

Once a oneway function is fixed, in most cases, we will want to be able to apply f iteratively. This can be taken care of by applying a random hash

$$h : C \to K \times V. \tag{3}$$

The second thing we should consider is that most of the TMTO algorithm will apply with better success rate if $h \circ f$ is close to an injection so that a target uniquely determines the pre-image. As long as set C is larger than $K \times V$, for most cryptographic applications, this can be naturally expected of the system to some degree. If C is smaller than $K \times V$, one should find some way to deform f so that the image space is larger. We saw through chosen plaintext attack scenarios that this could easily be done by simply increasing your plaintext length so that the output is long enough. In other situations, for example, if V contains publicly known values, using a hash $h' : V \to V'$ of appropriate length and setting

$$f' : K \times V \to C' = C \times V' \qquad (k, v) \mapsto f(k, v) || h'(v) \tag{4}$$

could be another solution. One should keep in mind that the image must be some value that is either public or can be calculated from publicly available data.

We can now write up a set of guidelines for applying TMTO to a cryptographic system.

1. Identify a (oneway) function $f : K \times V \to C$, inverting which will reveal a secret information of the attacker's interest, belonging to K. This function need not be the oneway function the designer of the system based his system on.
2. K and V should be taken as small as possible, allowing it to be just big enough to reflect the actual entropy of values used.
3. If needed, adjust the function so that the entropy of function image space is equal to its input space. This will help in making the function f injective, hence raising the success probability of attack.
4. Lower attack complexity can be achieved if it is possible to devise an attack scenario where the attacker is given multiple target points in the image space of f and finding the inverse image of any one of those points is good enough.
5. Depending on the reasonable amount of target points available, apply a suitable TMTO method to obtain a secret value in K.
6. When abundant data is at hand, TMTO with $D = N^{1/4}$; $T = M = N^{1/2}$ is applicable, and the attack is meaningful whenever $|K| > |V|$. At the other extreme, with one data point and oneway function of bad characteristics, we could apply the TMTO of Fiat and Naor [10], and the attack is successful when $|K| > |V|^3$.

We can summarize all this by saying that the most difficult task of applying the TMTO to a cryptographic system is finding a plausible scenario of attack, preferably in which a large set of data is available. Once this is done, the rest of the process comes naturally.

8   Conclusion

TMTO is basically a generic oneway function inverter. To attack a specific system with these TMTO methods, it suffices to identify a suitable oneway function, inverting which will provide one with a secret. In doing this, one should open their eyes to oneway functions hiding in the system, different from the one designer of the system had in mind. Success of TMTO depends heavily on the available amount of data, so devising an appropriate scenario of attack is also crucial.

By applying generic TMTO to blockciphers in ways not tried before, we have confirmed that TMTO has security implications, not only to ECB, but to most blockcipher modes of operation. We have also shown that TMTO affects the security of every streamcipher, not only those with small internal states.

We conclude with the remark that TMTO as a general oneway function inversion technique is more powerful and versatile a tool than is currently known to the crypto community.

References

1. 3GPP TS 55.215 V6.2.0 (2003–09), A5/3 and GEA3 Specifications. Available from http://www.gsmworld.com
2. Consortium for efficient embedded security. Efficient embedded security standards (EESS) #1. Version 2.0, June 2003. Available from http://www.ceesstandards.org/
3. ECRYPT. Call for stream cipher primitives. Version 1.2, Feb. 2004. http://www.ecrypt.eu.org/stream/
4. S. H. Babbage, Improved exhaustive search attacks on stream ciphers. *European Convention on Security and Detection,* IEE Conference publication No. 408, pp. 161–166, IEE, 1995.
5. A. Biryukov, S. Mukhopadhyay and P. Sarkar, Improved time-memory trade-offs with multiple data, *Proceedings of Selected Areas in Cryptography,* 2005, to appear.
6. A. Biryukov, Some thoughts on time-memory-data tradeoffs. Cryptology ePrint Archive, Report 2005/207, http://eprint.iacr.org/2005/207, 30 June, 2005.
7. A. Biryukov and A. Shamir, Cryptanalytic time/memory/data tradeoffs for stream ciphers. *Asiacrypt 2000,* LNCS 1976, pp. 1–13, Springer-Verlag, 2000.
8. C. De Cannière, J. Lano, and B. Preneel, Comment on the rediscovery of time memory data tradeoffs. Available as a link on the *ECRYPT Call for Stream Cipher Primitives* [3] page version 1.3, April 2005.
9. Denning, *Cryptography and data security,* Addison-Wesley, 1982.
10. A. Fiat and M. Naor, Rigorous time/space tradeoffs for invering functions. *SIAM J. on Computing,* vol 29, no 3, pp. 790–803, SIAM, 1999.
11. S. Fluhrer, I. Mantin, and A. Shamir, Weakness in the key scheduling algorithm of RC4. *SAC 2001,* LNCS 2259, pp. 1–24, Springer-Verlag, 2001.
12. J. Dj. Golić, Cryptanalysis of alleged A5 stream cipher. *Eurocrypt'97,* LNCS 1233, pp. 239–255, Springer-Verlag, 1997.
13. Z. Gutterman and D. Malkhi, Hold your sessions: An attack on Java session-id generation. *CT-RSA 2005,* LNCS 3376, pp. 44–57, Springer-Verlag, 2005.
14. S. Halevi and P. Rogaway, A tweakable enciphering mode. *Crypto 2003,* LNCS 2729, pp. 482–499, Springer-Verlag, 2003.

15. S. Halevi and P. Rogaway, A parallelizable enciphering mode. *CT-RSA 2004*, LNCS 2964, pp. 292–304, Springer-Verlag, 2004.
16. M. E. Hellman, A cryptanalytic time-memory trade-off. *IEEE Trans. on Infor. Theory*, **26** (1980), pp. 401–406.
17. J. Hong and P. Sarkar, Rediscovery of time memory tradeoffs. Cryptology ePrint Archive, Report 2005/090, http://eprint.iacr.org/2005/090, 22 March, 2005.
18. N. Howgrave-Graham, J. H. Silverman, and W. Whyte, Choosing parameter sets for NTRUEncrypt with NAEP and SVES-3. *CT-RSA 2005*, LNCS 3376, pp. 118–135, Springer-Verlag, 2005.
19. T. Iwata and K. Kurosawa, OMAC: One-Key CBC MAC. *Fast Software Encryption, FSE 2003*, LNCS 2887, pp. 129–153. Springer-Verlag.
20. I.-J. Kim and T. Matsumoto, Achieving higher success probability in time-memory trade-off cryptanalysis without increasing memory size. *IEICE Trans. Fundamentals*, **E82-A**, pp. 123–129, 1999.
21. M. Liskov, R. L. Rivest, and D. Wagner, Tweakable block ciphers. *Crypto 2002*, LNCS 2442, pp. 31–46, Springer-Verlag, 2002.
22. S. Mukhopadhyay and P. Sarkar, TMTO with multiple data: Analysis and new single table trade-offs. Cryptology ePrint Archive, Report 2005/214, http://eprint.iacr.org/2005/214, 4 July, 2005.
23. P. Oechslin. Making a fast cryptanalytic time-memory trade-off. *Crypto 2003*, LNCS 2729, pp. 617–630, 2003.
24. P. Rogaway, M. Bellare, J. Black, and T. Krovetz, OCB: A block-ciper mode of operation for efficient authenticated ecryption. *8th ACM CCS*, ACM Press, pp. 196–205, 2001.
25. A. Shamir, Stream ciphers: Dead or alive? Presentation slides for invited talk given at *Asiacrypt 2004*. Available from http://www.iris.re.kr/ac04/

A   Known Versus Chosen Plaintext TMTO Attacks on Blockciphers

The issue of known and chosen plaintext attacks was briefly mentioned in Section 1.2. We continue the discussion here.

Hellman's attack on the ECB mode of operation uses a oneway function f defined as follows. Fix a message block m and define a map from key to ciphertext by $f(k) = E_k(m)$. Suppose, we are given a ciphertext c which is the encryption of m under an unknown key k, i.e., $f(k) = c$. If we can invert f on c, then we can hope to find k. Clearly, for this attack to work, we must have an encryption of m and hence the attack is actually a chosen plaintext attack (CPA).

Hellman explains that this can also be turned into a known plaintext attack (KPA) or ciphertext only attack (COA) in the following sense. Suppose m is a block which occurs very frequently, for example a string of blanks. For a *KPA*, the cryptanalyst looks for the occurence of m in the plaintext and inverts f on the corresponding ciphertext block to obtain k. For a *COA*, the cryptanalyst will look for repetitions among the encrypted message. For each frequently repeated ciphertext block, he will try to invert f. If the block encrypts m, then he finds k, else he fails. The time required for the COA increases, since many trials might have to be done before actually finding an encryption of m. Note that for successful conversion of CPA to KPA and to COA, the block m *must* occur in the (unknown) plaintext corresponding to target data. Thus, if the target data is given randomly, then the above conversions are not meaningful. Furthermore, in Hellman's CPA converted to KPA or COA, there is no way to utilise multiple data to bring down the pre-computation time.

Our attacks on the CBC and CFB modes of operations in Section 4 are *CPA*. As in Hellman, we need to fix a plaintext and then define the oneway function to be inverted. To utilise multiple data, our fixed plaintext consists of $D + \lambda$ repetitions of m. Again, as in Hellman, we need to choose m and D such that $D + \lambda$ repetitions of m is likely in an actual message. Then we can convert the CPA to KPA by inspecting the obtained plaintext for $D + \lambda$ repetitions of m. We consider the corresponding portion of $D + \lambda$ ciphertext blocks. Using the ciphertext block preceding this portion as the IV, we can use the $D + \lambda$ ciphertext blocks to obtain D data points required for the attack. Again, as in Hellman's case, this conversion is not meaningful if the data corresponding to random plaintext is given.

It might appear that for a meaningful KPA, we need a larger portion to be frequently repeated than is required by Hellman. Though this is true, the actual requirement might not be too high. For example, if $\lambda+1$ repetitions of m occur in the plaintext, we can launch an attack with $D = 1$. Having more blocks increases D and the efficiency of the attack.

Conversion of the CPA on CBC and CFB to COA is also possible, though it becomes less efficient. Suppose that we want to utilise D data points and in the pre-computation phase have prepared the tables to cover N/D data points. In the online stage, we do the following. We slide (one block at a time) a window of $D + \lambda$ blocks over the ciphertext. Each window gives us D data points and if we perform the online search of the TMTO, with a constant probability of success we will get a hit. However, the k obtained may not be the correct key since there is no guarantee that the $D + \lambda$ blocks correspond to an encryption of $D + \lambda$ repetitions of m. We can easily verify this by decrypting a portion or whole of the ciphertext using this k. On the other hand, if the window of $D + \lambda$ ciphertext blocks actually correspond to an encryption of $D+\lambda$ repetitions of m, then we have the correct key. Hence, if the unknown plaintext indeed contained $D + \lambda$ repetitions of m, then by trying out all possible windows we are assured of success. This pushes up the online time by a factor which in the worst case is equal to the number of blocks in the obtained ciphertext. This makes the attack less efficient, though it still remains meaningful under our assumption on the data.

B   When Should We Start Building a Table?

We consider the question of whether it makes sense to start the long-term pre-computation search today.

Moore's law It has been observed that processor power doubles every 1.5 years. Let us assume that this will be true for the foreseeable future. Going back to high school mathematics, we can write the processing power $p(t)$ at time t as

$$p(t) = \alpha \cdot 2^{\frac{2}{3}t}. \tag{5}$$

We will take $t = 0$ to correspond to today, in which case, constant α will be our current computational power.

Example table creation Let us consider Hellmans's TMTO on AES as an example. The pre-computation stage will be an exhaustive processing of all 128-bit keys. On a desktop PC, AES encryption runs at 488 Mbps, which translates to about 2^{47}-many 128-bit blocks per year. We should consider the keyschedule also. Assuming that it runs at about the same speed as the encryption, we can take

$$\alpha = 2^{46} \quad \text{"key} \mapsto \text{ciphertext" mappings/year.} \tag{6}$$

So how long would the table creating take? Solving for T in

$$\int_0^T 2^{46+\frac{2}{3}t}\, dt = 2^{128}, \tag{7}$$

we find that the table creation will end $T = 121.3$ years from now. This assumes that the computer is constantly upgraded.

Starting later What happens if we do nothing for 120 years, and only then start building the table? Our computation power will be $\alpha = 2^{46} \cdot 2^{\frac{2}{3}120} = 2^{126}$. Solving for T' in

$$\int_0^{T'} 2^{126+\frac{2}{3}t}\, dt = 2^{128}, \tag{8}$$

we find that the table creation will take $T' = 2.3$ years, hence ending 122.3 years from now. So we are late by one year than what was achievable. But, is finishing one year earlier really worth the trouble of upgrading the computer constantly for 120 years?

In general, given any computation that takes n years from now to complete, if one starts the computation n years later, it can be finished in less than 1.5 years from then on.

Linear Cryptanalysis of the TSC Family of Stream Ciphers

Frédéric Muller and Thomas Peyrin

DCSSI Crypto Lab,
51, boulevard de La Tour-Maubourg,
75700 PARIS-07 SP
Frederic.Muller@sgdn.pm.gouv.fr,
Thomas.Peyrin@gmail.com

Abstract. In this paper, we introduce a new cryptanalysis method for stream ciphers based on T-functions and apply it to the TSC family which was proposed by Hong *et al.*. Our attack are based on linear approximations of the algorithms (in particular of the T-function). Hence, it is related to correlation attack, a popular technique to break stream ciphers with a linear update, like those using LFSR's.

We show a key-recovery attack for the two algorithms proposed at FSE 2005 : TSC-1 in $2^{25.4}$ computation steps, and TSC-2 in $2^{48.1}$ steps. The first attack has been implemented and takes about 4 minutes to recover the whole key on an average PC. Another algorithm in the family, called TSC-3, was proposed at the ECRYPT call for stream ciphers. Despite some differences with its predecessors, it can be broken by similar techniques. Our attack has complexity of 2^{42} known keystream bits to distinguish it from random, and about 2^{66} steps of computation to recover the full secret key.

An extended version of this paper can be found on the ECRYPT website [23].

1 Introduction

1.1 Background

Together with block ciphers, stream ciphers are the second important family of symmetric encryption primitive. They work by generating a long pseudo-random sequence (generally called the keystream) from a short key. Then, a message is encrypted by a simple XOR with the keystream and the decryption works the same way. The keystream should not be distinguishable from a random sequence to make the cipher secure. Even if the cryptographic security is the main issue, the efficiency of the algorithm has also to be taken in account. Indeed, speed is the main advantage of stream ciphers over block ciphers.

Nowadays, designing a stream cipher is risky and the existence of good block ciphers has brought some issues about the future of stream ciphers [2,24]. However, some particular domains continue to be active. For example, fast software-oriented stream ciphers may still be needed, as well as hardware-oriented designs

B. Roy (Ed.): ASIACRYPT 2005, LNCS 3788, pp. 373–394, 2005.

with a small footprint for resource constrained devices. A call for primitive has recently been launched by the european ECRYPT project and many new algorithms have been proposed for this occasion [6,7].

A classical approach for stream cipher design is the use of Linear Feedback Shift Registers (LFSR). Such primitives have to be combined with nonlinear Boolean functions to break the linearity. Due to the apparition of new attacks (like algebraic attacks [1,4]), new primitives have been introduced to replace LFSR's. A nice example are the Triangular-functions (T-functions) by Klimov and Shamir [13,14]. They are a new class of mappings, with the property to be computable from Least Significant Bits (LSB) to Most Significant Bits (MSB). This is well suited for implementations, because many operations available on processors (like +,*,XOR,OR,AND) are T-functions. T-functions are not (necessarily) linear and, for appropriate choices, they can be permutations with one single cycle, which is useful for stream ciphers design. Klimov and Shamir also extended their theory to multi-word T-functions and provided some results in other domains such as block ciphers and hash functions [12,15,16,17].

The first T-function Based Stream Ciphers (TFBSC) were proposed in the original papers by Klimov and Shamir. More recently, Hong et al. proposed a new class of single cycle T-functions, which have the property to use S-boxes [10]. They described two new algorithms. The first one, TSC-1, is designed for hardware environment and the second, TSC-2, can be implemented very efficiently in software. Several attacks have also been published. At Asiacrypt 2004, Mitra and Sarkar [22] described a time-memory trade-off attack which breaks some of the algorithms proposed by Klimov and Shamir. Künzli, Junod and Meier recently found distinguishing attacks applicable to many TFBSC's [19]. Taking into account these results, Hong et al. proposed a new algorithm, called TSC-3 at the ECRYPT competition for stream cipher [7]. This algorithm is an improvement over its two predecessors, in order to thwart the published attack [11]. However, the basic construction remains roughly the same.

1.2   Contribution of the Paper

Our contribution in this paper is to present a **new cryptanalysis method for TFBSC's**. Our idea is to mount a statistical attack using **linear approximations** of the cipher. First, we linearize the behavior of the T-function by considering several consecutive steps. Next, we linearize other components, like the output function. Then we describe how to recover the secret key by combining all these linear approximations. This framework is closely related to correlation attacks against LFSR-based stream ciphers [21,25] and also to linear cryptanalysis against block ciphers [20].

It applies very efficiently to the TSC family. Indeed, we can break TSC-1 with time complexity of $2^{25.4}$ steps and data complexity of $2^{21.4}$ keystream words. Similarly, TSC-2 can be broken with $2^{44.1}$ data and $2^{48.1}$ time. We implemented the first attack against TSC-1. It needs about 4 minutes to recover the whole initial secret key (Pentium-III 700 MHz).

Table 1. Summary of attacks against the TSC family

Algorithm	Type of Attack	Time	Data
TSC-1	Distinguishing [18,19]	2^{22}	2^{22}
TSC-1	Distinguishing	2^{19}	2^{15}
TSC-1	Key-recovery attack	$2^{25.4}$	$2^{21.4}$
TSC-2	Distinguishing[19]	2^{34}	2^{34}
TSC-2	Key-recovery attack	$2^{48.1}$	$2^{44.1}$
TSC-3	Distinguishing	2^{42}	2^{42}
TSC-3	Key-recovery attack	2^{66}	2^{34}

This cryptanalysis method also applies against the ECRYPT proposal TSC-3, although some adaptations are needed. In particular, the linear approximations we use are a little bit more complicated than in the case of TSC-1 and TSC-2. We describe how to distinguish the output of TSC-3 from random data by processing about 2^{42} keystream words. This observation can be extended to a key-recovery attack with time complexity of 2^{66} and data complexity of about 2^{34} keystream bits.

These attacks are the first key recovery attacks against the TSC family (distinguishing attacks have already been pointed out in [18,19]). Table 1 summarizes all these results. We also point out some important requirements for the design of T-function based stream ciphers. In particular, the existence of good linear approximations of the T-function over several consecutive steps should be avoided.

To begin, we review the basic properties of T-functions. Secondly, we overview the existing TFBSC and the existing attacks. In Section 4, we give a general framework to attack TFBSC. Next, we describe how this framework applies to break TSC-1, TSC-2 and TSC-3.

2   Introduction to T-functions

We give a short review of T-functions results; readers can see [12] for further details.

2.1   Single-Word T-functions

Basically, a single-word T-function is a mapping on a n-bit word where the bit i of the output can depend only on bits $0, 1, \cdots, i$ of the input. For example, most arithmetic operations, like addition, subtraction and multiplication are T-functions. It is also the case of most logical operations (OR,AND,XOR). These operations are called primitive operations. They are useful because they are available on most processors and can generally be executed in one clock cycle.

Moreover, the composition of two T-functions is a T-function, which allows to design a large number of such functions. Klimov and Shamir developed tools in order to study their invertibility and their cycle structure. In particular, some families provide a great feature: a single cycle of maximal length. However, single-word T-functions are not useful by themselves as n is usually limited on modern processors (to 32 or 64 bits). To increase the state size, it is better to use, for instance 4 words of 64 bits instead of one word of 256 bits.

2.2   Multi-word T-functions

The definition of T-functions can be extended to multi-word T-functions: the bit i of any output word depends only on bits 0 to i of each input word.

More formally, let $\mathbf{x}$ represent m words of n bits each denoted by x_i with $0 \leq i < m$. We get $\mathbf{x} = (x_j)_{j=0}^{m-1}$. Also, $[x_j]_i$ will refer to the i-th bit of a word x_j, seen as an integer:

$$[x_j] = \sum_{i=0}^{n-1} [x_j]_i 2^i.$$

Then $[\mathbf{x}]_i$ denotes the **layer** of i-th bits of the m words x_i composing $\mathbf{x}$. Thus we also get:

$$[\mathbf{x}]_i = \sum_{k=0}^{m-1} [x_k]_i 2^k.$$

Here is a clear depiction:

Definition 1. *A (multi-word) $T - function$ is a map*

$$\mathbf{T} : \begin{cases} (\{0,1\}^n)^m \longrightarrow (\{0,1\}^n)^m \\ \\ \mathbf{x} \longmapsto \mathbf{T}(\mathbf{x}) = (T_k(\mathbf{x}))_{k=0}^{m-1} \end{cases}$$

sending an m-tuple of n-bit words to another m-tuple of n-bit words, where each resulting n-bit word is denoted as $T_k(\mathbf{x})$, such that for each $0 \leq i < n$, the i-th bits of the resulting words $[\mathbf{T}(\mathbf{x})]_i$ are functions of just the lower input bits $[\mathbf{x}]_0, [\mathbf{x}]_1, \ldots, [\mathbf{x}]_i$.

We can also define a mapping from n-bit words to n-bit words in which the bit i of the output depends only on bits $0, 1, \ldots, i-1$ of the input. Such mappings are called **parameters** and are useful to construct interesting T-functions.

2.3   Properties of T-functions

We focus on **multi-word** T-functions, since they are the most interesting for stream cipher design. Basically, two properties can be expected :

- **invertibility** : This avoids a loss of entropy, if the T-function is used to update the state of a stream cipher.
- **single-cycle** : It is important for security that the sequence of internal states has a large period. A single cycle of maximal length 2^{nm} is even better, but is possible only if the T-function is invertible.

Klimov and Shamir proposed a method to construct T-functions which exhibits the single-cycle property. Their analysis is based on **odd** and **even parameters** (see [15] for more details).

Another approach was recently proposed by Hong *et al* [10] : Let $\mathbf{x} = (x_k)_{k=0}^{m-1}$ and $\mathbf{y} = (y_k)_{k=0}^{m-1}$ be two multi-words and let α be a single word. We note $\mathbf{x} \oplus \mathbf{y}$ and $\alpha \cdot \mathbf{x}$ defined as :

$$\mathbf{x} \oplus \mathbf{y} = (x_k \oplus y_k)_{k=0}^{m-1} \quad \text{and} \quad \alpha \cdot \mathbf{x} = (\alpha \wedge x_k)_{k=0}^{m-1}.$$

We also note $\sim \alpha$ the bitwise complement of α.

Theorem 1. *Let S be a single cycle S-box and let α be an odd parameter. If S^o is an odd power of S and S^e is an even power of S, the mapping*

$$T(\mathbf{x}) = (\alpha(\mathbf{x}) \cdot \mathbf{S}^o(\mathbf{x})) \oplus (\sim \alpha(\mathbf{x}) \cdot \mathbf{S}^e(\mathbf{x}))$$

defines a single cycle T-function.

3   Existing TFBSC's

3.1   Klimov and Shamir's Ciphers

After introducing the concept of T-functions, Klimov and Shamir proposed several examples of TFBSC [15,16]. All are based on a similar construction.

Let C_0 be an odd number, $C_1 = \text{0x12481248}$ and $C_3 = \text{0x48124812}$. We set $a_0 = x_0$ and $a_{i+1} = a_i \wedge x_{i+1}$ for $i = 0, 1, 2$. We also have $\alpha = \alpha(\mathbf{x}) = (a_3 + C_0) \oplus a_3$. The following mapping is a single cycle T-function operating on 64-bit words:

$$T \begin{pmatrix} x_3 \\ x_2 \\ x_1 \\ x_0 \end{pmatrix} \longmapsto \begin{pmatrix} x_3 \oplus (\alpha \wedge a_2) \oplus (2x_0(x_1 \vee C_1)) \\ x_2 \oplus (\alpha \wedge a_1) \oplus (2x_0(x_3 \vee C_3)) \\ x_1 \oplus (\alpha \wedge a_0) \oplus (2x_2(x_3 \vee C_3)) \\ x_0 \oplus \alpha \qquad \oplus (2x_2(x_1 \vee C_1)) \end{pmatrix} \tag{1}$$

Mitra and Sarkar described [22] a time-memory trade-off attack on a stream cipher based on (1) with a very simple output function. They analyzed the multiplicative part of the update function and managed to recover the initial secret key in 2^{40} time, 2^{24} space and less than five 128-bit blocks of keystream.

3.2   The TSC Family

Hong *et al.* provided two TFBSC's deduced from their new single-cycle T-functions family given in Theorem 1. For all algorithms, the number of words is $m = 4$. While Klimov-Shamir's proposal are software-oriented designs (with the use of integer multiplication), the TSC family is S-box oriented. In particular, the authors have suggested an implementation method for TSC-1 and TSC-3 which could make them suitable as hardware-oriented designs.

TSC-1

TSC-1 uses 4 words of $n = 32$ bits each, hence the internal state has size 128 bits. First a single-cycle S-box S_1 operating on 4 bits is defined :

$$S_1[16] = \{3, 5, 9, 13, 1, 6, 11, 15, 4, 0, 8, 14, 10, 7, 2, 12\};$$

The following function is an odd parameter :

$$\alpha(\mathbf{x}) = (p + C) \oplus p \oplus 2s,$$

where $C = \text{0x12488421}$, $p = x_0 \wedge x_1 \wedge x_2 \wedge x_3$ and $s = x_0 + x_1 + x_2 + x_3$. According to Theorem 1 with $S^o = S_1$ and $S^e = S_1^2$, the following T-function is single-cycle :

$$T(\mathbf{x}) = (\alpha(\mathbf{x}) \cdot S_1(\mathbf{x})) \oplus (\sim \alpha(\mathbf{x}) \cdot S_1^2(\mathbf{x})). \tag{2}$$

Finally, 32 output bits are produced after application of $\mathbf{T}$ by:

$$f(\mathbf{x}) = (x_{0 \lll 9} + x_1)_{\lll 15} + (x_{2 \lll 7} + x_3), \tag{3}$$

where the symbol $\lll$ denotes left rotation. Every addition is done modulo 2^{32}. It is proven that the period of this T-function is 2^{128}.

TSC-2

TSC-2 is quite similar to TSC-1. It uses a different S-box :

$$S_2[16] = \{5, 2, 11, 12, 13, 4, 3, 14, 15, 8, 1, 6, 7, 10, 9, 0\};$$

and the following odd parameter:

$$\alpha_2(\mathbf{x}) = (p + 1) \oplus p \oplus 2s.$$

According to Theorem 1 with $S^o = Id$ and $S^e = S_2$:

$$\mathbf{x} \longmapsto \mathbf{x} \oplus (\alpha_2(\mathbf{x}) \cdot (\mathbf{x} \oplus S_2(\mathbf{x}))).$$

is single-cycle. Finally 32 keystream bits are obtained by:

$$f_2(\mathbf{x}) = (x_{0 \lll 11} + x_1)_{\lll 14} + (x_{0 \lll 13} + x_2)_{\lll 22} + (x_{0 \lll 12} + x_3).$$

TSC-3

At the ECRYPT competition for stream ciphers [11], Hong *et al.* proposed the stream cipher TSC-3. It differs from its two predecessors regarding several elements :

- First, it uses 4 words of size 40 bit each. This breaks the 32-bit oriented architecture, but it does not matter since the cipher is primarily designed for hardware implementations. In addition, this increases the state size to 160 bits. Therefore the expected level of security is 2^{80}, which can be reached by generic attacks, such as time-memory-data trade-offs [3].
- Secondly, each layer is still updated by S-boxes, but the branching function is more complex than for TSC-1 or TSC-2. Indeed, the parameter is made of 2 words p_0 and p_1. For the i-th layer, one first computes the value

$$tmp = 2 * [p_1]_i + [p_0]_i \in \{0, 3\}$$

  According to the value of tmp, $[x]_i$ is update using either S, S^2, S^5 or S^6 where S is the same S-box as in TSC-1.
- The output function is also modified in TSC-3. One first starts by initializing 4 variables y_i of 32 bits each, by removing the 8 LSB's from each x_i. Then, the y_i's are permuted depending on the value of the least significant layer of the sate, $[x]_0$. Therefore there are $2^4 = 16$ possible permutations. Afterward, the output function looks very much like the ones used in TSC-1 and TSC-2 :

$$f(\mathbf{y}) = (y_0 \lll 9 + y_1 \ggg 2) \lll 8 + (y_2 \lll 7 + y_3) \ggg 9$$

- An initialization mechanism has also been added in order to set up the state from a key and an IV of variable length. This mechanism is based on the T-function itself, but is not described here.

For more information about these elements of TSC-3, the reader should refer directly to the specifications [10] or to the ECRYPT website [6].

4   Linear Cryptanalysis Against TFBSC's

4.1   Context

Attacks based on linear approximations have many applications in cryptanalysis. For instance, Matsui's attack is the best cryptanalysis of DES [20] and more generally linear cryptanalysis has many applications for block ciphers. In the field of stream ciphers, popular attacks based on linear approximations have been developed for LFSR oriented designs and are generally referred to as **correlation attacks** [21,25]. Also linear cryptanalysis for stream ciphers has already been suggested [5,8] and has already been applied, for instance by Golic against RC4 [9].

In the case of TFBSC, the idea of using linear approximations was first introduced by Künzli, Junod and Meier. At the rump session of FSE 2005, they presented a distinguishing attack against the TSC-1 requiring about 2^{22} known keystream bits [18]. This idea is further developed in [19].

4.2   A Framework for Linear Cryptanalysis of TFBSC's

The attack we propose is composed by three steps :

1. find a **linear approximation of the T-function**. This provides a probabilistic relation between bits from the internal state of the stream cipher at different instants.
2. find a **linear approximation of the output function**. This provides a probabilistic relation between keystream bits and internal state bits.
3. **combine both approximations**. One goal may be to find relations involving keystream bits only, in order to obtain a distinguisher. But a more interesting idea is to guess some key bits in order to eliminate some terms in the approximations and therefore to **increase the bias**.

The general idea of this framework is to remove the non-linearity provided by the T-function. While steps 1 and 2 are almost always possible, it can be hard to combine the approximations in step 3.

More formally, let $[x_j]_i^t$ represent the value of the bit i from register j at time t. In the first step, we look for equations of the form :

$$\Pr\left(\bigoplus_{i,j}[x_j]_i^t = \bigoplus_{i,j}[x_j]_i^{t+\delta}\right) = \frac{1}{2}(1+\epsilon)$$

for some δ and with $|\epsilon|$ as big as possible. For the purpose of the attacks against TSC-1 and TSC-2, it turns out that we are only interested in the particular linear relations of the form :

$$[x_j]_i^t = [x_j]_i^{t+\delta}$$

This corresponds to the probability for a given bit in the internal state to flip between time t and time $t + \delta$, also called the **bit-flip probability**. While the design criteria of the TSC family [10,11] and the first known attacks [18,19] focused on these bit-flip properties, there is no reason to restrict the analysis to such particular cases. The cryptanalysis of TSC-3 (see Section 7) is a good example of attack where other types of linear approximations are needed.

The second step depends on how complex is the output function, but it is generally possible to find linear approximations for the algorithms of the TSC family. For instance, suppose we find a probabilistic linear relation between several state bits $[x_j]_i^t$ and several keystream bits $[s]_k^t$, at time t. We combine this relation with the first step, to obtain a linearized relation of the form :

$$\bigoplus_{i,j}([x_j]_i^t \oplus [x_j]_i^{t+\delta}) = \bigoplus_{k}([s]_k^t \oplus [s]_k^{t+\delta}) \tag{4}$$

which is equal to 0 with probability $0.5\,(1 + \epsilon)$ and hopefully $|\epsilon| \gg 0$.

In the third step, we try to propose distinguishing attacks and key recovery attacks based on relation (4). A useful trick for T-functions, is that when we guess the i LSB's of each register in the initial state, we can predict these i LSB's at every instant because of the triangular structure.

5   The TSC-1 Case

In this section, we apply our framework to the TSC-1 case and show an efficient key-recovery attack. We explain the attack by following the three steps of our framework.

5.1   First Step

We want to approximate the behavior of the state-update function between time t and time $t + \delta$. By looking at the update function (2), we observe that the i-th layer's update depends on one parameter bit only, $[\alpha(\mathbf{x})]_i$. Depending on this bit, the 4 bits of the layer are updated using either S_1 or S_1^2 :

$$[\mathbf{T}(\mathbf{x})]_i = \begin{cases} S_1^2([\mathbf{x}]_i) & \text{if } [\alpha(\mathbf{x})]_i = 0 \\ \\ S_1([\mathbf{x}]_i) & \text{if } [\alpha(\mathbf{x})]_i = 1 \end{cases}$$

We assume that the parameter is uniformly distributed. Then

$$\Pr\left([\alpha(\mathbf{x})]_i = 0\right) = \Pr\left([\alpha(\mathbf{x})]_i = 1\right) = \frac{1}{2}$$

for $i \neq 0$. This property has been verified experimentally. We construct a binary tree describing the update of the i-th layer (see Figure 1). We start from an unknown 4-bit value a and each branch corresponds to a value of $[\alpha(\mathbf{x})]_i$. After j advances, there are 2^j leaves in the tree, each corresponding to a power of

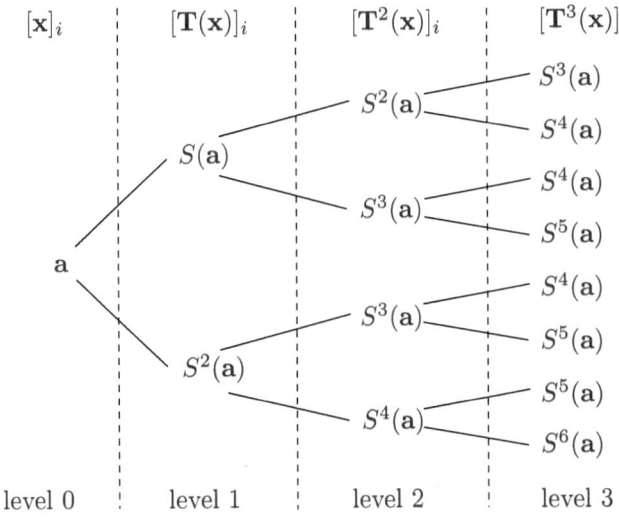

Fig. 1. Possible Evolutions of the i-th layer for TSC-1

S_1. Let K_i^j be the number of occurrence of S_1^i at the level j of the tree. The coefficients K_i^j can be computed by the formula:

$$K_i^j = \binom{j}{i-j} \text{ with } i \geq j.$$

Using these coefficients, we can compute the probabilities of each output value after j advances, for each value of a. Then, we search for linear approximations between bits of the i-th layer at time t and at time $t + j$. In the case of TSC-1, we restrict our analysis to particular linear approximations where the same bit is considered twice (known as bit-flip probabilities). The authors of TSC-1 took them into account for the design, so the S-box has probability $1/2$ to flip each input bit. The same holds for all powers S_1^i of the S-box, except for $i = 4, 8, 12$ and 16. So nothing will be observed at the level 1 in the tree, but at further levels, the "weak" powers may appear with high coefficients. We explored the tree at depth j and computed the bit-flip probabilities for several values of j. The results are given in Table 2 (due to some symmetry properties, the probability is the same for the 4 input bits). We observe that the strongest bias are obtained with $j = 3, 5, 8, 11$. An example of good linear approximation is :

$$\Pr\left([x_i]_1^t \oplus [x_i]_1^{t+3} = 1\right) \simeq 0.64 = \frac{1}{2}(1 + 0.28).$$

for all $i = 0, \ldots, 3$.

In Table 7 of the Appendix, we give experimental results. They show that the observed bias match the theoretical analysis. Therefore the **initial assumption that the parameter bits are uniformly distributed is satisfied**. The only exception concerns the LSB of the registers. Indeed, the parameter bit is constant at position 0, so the previous assumption no longer holds. This analysis explains what Künzli *et al.* observed [18] with $j = 8$ and 11, although the best bias is obtained with $j = 3$.

5.2   Second Step

In this step, we want to "linearize" the behavior of the output function of TSC-1 defined by (3). This function uses addition and left rotation on 32-bit words.

Table 2. TSC-1 : Bit Flip Probabilities for Different Depth j of the Tree

j	P	$|\epsilon|$	j	P	$|\epsilon|$
1	0.5000	0.0000	9	0.5264	0.0528
2	0.5937	0.1874	10	0.4143	0.1714
3	0.6406	0.2812	11	0.3993	0.2014
4	0.5078	0.0156	12	0.4849	0.0302
5	0.4219	0.1562	13	0.5587	0.1174
6	0.4473	0.1054	14	0.5507	0.1014
7	0.5479	0.0958	15	0.4972	0.0056
8	0.5996	0.1992	16	0.4717	0.0566

Left rotation is already linear, so we only have to linearize the additions. This can be naturally done by introducing a **carry bit**. For instance, when adding two integers a_0 and a_1, we can express the i-th bit of the result by the linear expression :

$$[a_0]_i \oplus [a_1]_i \oplus R_i$$

where R_i depends on layers $< i$.

Consider the addition of n integers of 32 bits called $a_0, \ldots, a_{n-1}$. We note $A = \sum_{k=0}^{n-1} a_k$ and $R(i)$ the i-th carry. For $n = 2$ terms, the carry is simply one bit, but more generally, it is an integer formally defined by :

$$R(i) = \frac{\sum_{k=0}^{n-1}(a_k \bmod 2^i) - (\sum_{k=0}^{n-1}(a_k \bmod 2^i)) \bmod 2^i}{2^i}.$$

with $R(0) = 0$. The linearized expression of the i-th bit of A is given by :

$$[A]_i = \left[\sum_{k=0}^{n-1} a_k \right]_i = [R(i)]_0 \oplus \bigoplus_{k=0}^{n-1} [a_k]_i. \tag{5}$$

In the case of TSC-1, the output function is composed by an addition with 2 terms $(E = x_0 \lll 9 + x_1)$ and an addition with 3 terms $(S = E_{\lll 15} + x_2 \lll 7 + x_3)$ where S represents the output. Hence, using linearized relations (5), for any bit i we have:

$$\begin{cases} [E]_i = [x_0]_{(i+23)} \oplus [x_1]_{(i)} \oplus [R_E(i)]_0 \\ \\ [S]_i = E_{(i+17)} \oplus [x_2]_{(i+25)} \oplus [x_3]_{(i)} \oplus [R_S(i)]_0 \end{cases}$$

where R_E and R_S represent the carry for the 2-term and 3-term addition respectively. All indexes are taken modulo 32. We can note that $R_E(i) \in \{0,1\}$ and $R_S(i) \in \{0,1,2\}$. Finally, we obtain :

$$[S]_i = [x_0]_{(i+8)} \oplus [x_1]_{(i+17)} \oplus [R_E(i+17)]_0 \oplus [x_2]_{(i+25)} \oplus [x_3]_{(i)} \oplus [R_S(i)]_0.$$

which is a **linear approximation of the output function**.

We would like to XOR this relation at two instants t and $t + \delta$ for instance with $\delta = 3$, since this is the value identified in the first step. We already now the bit-flip probabilities of the register bits. Now the problem is to determine the bit-flip probabilities of the carry bits between t and $t + 3$.

5.3   Bit Flip Property of Carries

Basically, each input bit in the additions E and S is flipped with a known probability, different from 0.5. As a consequence, we may expect that the carries also flip with probabilities different from 0.5. The goal of this Section is to evaluate this probability.

We define the "general carry" as $[R_G(i)] = [R_E(i+17)] \oplus [R_S(i)]$. We also call $X_{R_G}(i) = [R_G(i)]_0^t \oplus [R_G(i)]_0^{t+3}$ and $X_j(i) = [x_j]_i^t \oplus [x_j]_i^{t+3}$. From the previous section, we get :

$$[S]_i^t \oplus [S]_i^{t+3} = X_{R_G}(i) \oplus X_0(i+8) \oplus X_1(i+17) \oplus X_2(i+25) \oplus X_3(i)$$

From the first step, we know that $\Pr(X_j(i) = 1) = \frac{1}{2}(1 + \epsilon_i^j)$. The biases ϵ_i^j are given in Table 7 in the Appendix. So the only remaining term is $X_{R_G}(i)$. Experimentally, we observed that

$$\Pr(X_{R_G}(i) = 1) = \frac{1}{2}(1 + \epsilon_i^G) \text{ with } |\epsilon_i^G| \gg 0$$

and that ϵ_i^G apparently depends on the position i considered. Unfortunately, we also observed that the two "internal" carries $R_S(i)$ and $R_E(i)$ are not independent, so it is not possible to handle them separately.

To explain this bias, we model the phenomenon as a **Markov chain**. Indeed, carries at layer $i+1$ are computed only from the carries at layer i and from the terms in the addition, so we do not need to remember what happened previously. We implemented a recursive algorithm to evaluate the following probability, starting from the least significant bit $i = 0$:

$$\Pr_i(a,b,c,d) = \Pr \ (\ (R_S(i)^t = a) \wedge (R_S(i)^{t+3} = b)$$
$$\wedge (R_E(i+17)^t = c) \wedge (R_E(i+17)^{t+3} = d))$$

for all possible $a, b, c, d \in \{0, 1, 2\}^2 \times \{0, 1\}^2$. To compute $\Pr_{i+1}(a, b, c, d)$, we examine all cases at layer i : we try all values of the terms in the addition, we try all values of the carries at layer i, and we compute the new carries. Each event at layer i is associated with its corresponding probability, and we increment accordingly the probabilities of layer $i + 1$. After examining all cases, we know $\Pr_{i+1}(a, b, c, d)$. Then, we increment i and jump to the next layer [1].

In the end, we obtain the bit-flip probability of the general carry by :

$$\Pr(X_{R_G}(i) = 1) = \sum_{a,b,c,d|\text{LSB}(a) \oplus \text{LSB}(b) \oplus c \oplus d = 1} \Pr_i(a, b, c, d).$$

The experiments on TSC-1 returned the same probabilities as our computation by a Markov chain. These results are listed in the rightmost column of Table 7 (see the Appendix). We now have biased linear approximations which involve only TSC-1's output bits and internal state bits, so we can continue to the third step.

---

[1] There is a slight technicality, since the layer 0 actually depends from the layer 31 due to the left rotation, so we do not know how to initialize the recursion. Actually, probabilities are quite independent from the initial value, so we can handle this difficulty.

5.4   Third Step

Distinguishing Attacks

It is easy to use a bias on the output of a stream cipher for a distinguishing attack : one just produces enough keystream bits and checks if the bias is satisfied or not. For a bias ε, it it well known that about ε^{-2} samples are needed. As an example, Künzli *et al.* pointed out a distinguisher requiring 2^{22} output bits for TSC-1 [18]. Similarly, our previous analysis provides a distinguishing attack. For example, consider the layer $i = 1$ of the output. We have

$$[S]_1^t \oplus [S]_1^{t+3} = X_{R_G}(1) \oplus X_0(9) \oplus X_1(18) \oplus X_2(26) \oplus X_3(1)$$

Assuming the terms are independent, the bias are just multiplied, so

$$\Pr\left([[S]_1^t \oplus [S]_1^{t+3} = 1\right) = 0.5 \left(1 + \varepsilon_D\right)$$

with :

$$\varepsilon_D = \epsilon(X_0(9)) \times \epsilon(X_1(18)) \times \epsilon(X_2(26)) \times \epsilon(X_3(1)) \times \epsilon(X_{R_G}(1))$$
$$= 0.2834 * 0.2824 * 0.2732 * 0.2812 * (-0.0874)$$
$$= -2^{-10.86}$$

using Table 7 in the Appendix. This gives a data complexity of $\epsilon_D^{-2} \simeq 2^{21.7}$ keystream bits, which is slightly better than [19].

Key Recovery Attacks

As pointed out in Section 4.2, if we guess the i LSB's of each register in the initial state, we can predict these bits at any moment. This idea can be used to **eliminate many terms in the linear approximations**.

First, let us guess the LSB of each register. There are $2^4 = 16$ possibilities. For any instant t, we can predict these LSB and thus eliminate all terms of the form $X_i(0)$ in the linear approximations. For instance, we can predict $[S]_0^t \oplus [S]_0^{t+3} \oplus X_3(0)$ which is biased with

$$\epsilon = -0.2826 * 0.2818 * 0.2826 * 0.1906 = -2^{-7.86}$$

according to Table 7 of the Appendix. This bias will be observed only for the correct guess. So, with a sufficient amount of data, we can find which of the 16 guesses is correct. The process can be repeated to successively guess all layers of the initial state, starting from the least significant ones.

The complexity of guessing each layer depends on the best bias that can be found. For the first step of the attack, the bias is $\epsilon = -2^{-7.86}$ so we need

$$M = \epsilon^{-2} = 2^{15.72}$$

keystream bits to find the correct guess. The time complexity is about

$$T = 2^{15.72} \times 2^4 = 2^{19.72}$$

Table 3. Possible Attack Schedule for TSC-1

round	bit position attacked	register attacked	number of known terms	bias obtained	time complexity
0	0	3	1	$2^{-7.86}$	$2^{19.72}$
1	1	3	1	$2^{-9.03}$	$2^{22.06}$
2	9	2	1	$2^{-9.41}$	$2^{22.82}$
3	10	2	1	$2^{-9.29}$	$2^{22.58}$
4	11	2	1	$2^{-9.33}$	$2^{22.66}$
5	12	2	1	$2^{-9.39}$	$2^{22.78}$
6	13	2	1	$2^{-9.31}$	$2^{22.62}$
7	7	3	2	$2^{-7.48}$	$2^{18.96}$
8	0	0	2	$2^{-6.04}$	$2^{16.08}$
9	1	0	2	$2^{-7.21}$	$2^{18.42}$
10	10	3	2	$2^{-7.47}$	$2^{18.94}$
11	11	3	2	$2^{-7.46}$	$2^{18.92}$
12	19	2	2	$2^{-7.49}$	$2^{18.98}$
13	20	2	2	$2^{-7.51}$	$2^{19.02}$
14	21	2	2	$2^{-7.50}$	$2^{19.00}$
15	15	3	3	$2^{-4.81}$	$2^{13.62}$
16	8	0	3	$2^{-6.07}$	$2^{16.14}$
17	9	0	3	$2^{-5.76}$	$2^{15.52}$
18	10	0	3	$2^{-5.64}$	$2^{15.28}$
19	11	0	3	$2^{-5.63}$	$2^{15.26}$
20	12	0	3	$2^{-5.69}$	$2^{15.38}$
21	13	0	3	$2^{-5.66}$	$2^{15.32}$
22	14	0	3	$2^{-5.64}$	$2^{15.28}$
23	15	0	4	$2^{-2.94}$	$2^{9.88}$
24	24	3	4	$2^{-3.84}$	$2^{11.68}$
25	0	2	4	$2^{-2.39}$	$2^{8.78}$
26	1	2	4	$2^{-3.52}$	$2^{11.04}$
27	10	1	4	$2^{-3.82}$	$2^{11.64}$
28	11	1	4	$2^{-3.81}$	$2^{11.62}$
29	12	1	4	$2^{-3.82}$	$2^{11.64}$
30	13	1	4	$2^{-3.83}$	$2^{11.66}$
31	14	1	4	$2^{-3.82}$	$2^{11.64}$

steps. If we stop the attack after this step, we obtain a distinguishing attack which is slightly better than [19]. At each step, we can choose between several linear approximations (one for each of the 32 keystream bits). We always pick the position which gives the best results (see Table 3 for more details). Note that after guessing the layer 7, we can eliminate two terms in the linear approximations, so the complexity drops. Similarly, the complexity drops after the layer 15 (3 terms are eliminated) and after the layer 23 (4 terms are eliminated). The full cost of the attack is dominated by the first layers (layer number 2 in particular). The total complexity is of $2^{21.4}$ data and $2^{25.4}$ time.

6   The TSC-2 Case

The attack against TSC-2 is similar to the attack against TSC-1. The only difficulty is that the bit-flip probability for the register x_0 is almost balanced, because the authors have used a particular S-box. Unfortunately, due to some second order effects, we can still obtain good linear approximations of the T-function. Details can be found in the extended version of this paper [23].

The resulting complexity is of $2^{48.1}$ time and $2^{44.1}$ data to recover the secret key. This result is worse than for TSC-1, mostly because the output function is quite complicated (6 terms are used instead of 4), so the observed bias is much smaller.

7   The TSC-3 Case

Since TSC-3 has some particular features compared to the two previous algorithms, the application of the attack is not exactly the same. However, it roughly follows the same framework.

7.1   First Step

The updating of any layer $[x]_i$ of the state can still be represented in a **tree-oriented fashion**, although it is no longer a binary tree (each node has 4 branches). Let us first suppose that the parameter words are uniformly distributed. Then, after applying the T-function, $[T(x)]_i$ has probability $1/4$ to be equal to any of the $S^j([x]_i)$, for $j = 1, 2, 5, 6$. Similarly, after t updates, one can easily compute the probability for $[T^t(x)]_i$ to be equal to each power of the S-box[2]. This is summarized in Table 4. Then we can apply essentially the same

Table 4. Exploration of the tree for TSC-3: Probability that $[T^t[x]]_i = S^j([x]_i)$

j	0	1	2	3	4	5	6	7	8	9	10	11	12	13	14	15
$t=0$	1	0	0	0	0	0	0	0	0	0	0	0	0	0	0	0
$t=1$	0	1/4	1/4	0	0	1/4	1/4	0	0	0	0	0	0	0	0	0
$t=2$	0	0	1/16	1/8	1/16	0	1/8	1/4	1/8	0	1/16	1/8	1/16	0	0	0
$t=3$	0.047	0.047	0.016	0.016	0.047	0.047	0.016	0.047	0.141	0.141	0.047	0.047	0.141	0.141	0.047	0.016
$t=4$	0.039	0.063	0.094	0.063	0.023	0.031	0.047	0.031	0.023	0.063	0.094	0.063	0.039	0.094	0.141	0.094

analysis than for TSC-1 and TSC-2. However, here we are not interested only in bit-flip properties. Linear relations involving one input bit and another output bit may be of interest, because the registers are permuted in the output function, so we may compare bits belonging to different registers in the next steps of the attack. So we focus on the linear relations of the form :

$$[x_j]_i^t = [x_{j'}]_i^{t+\delta} \tag{6}$$

for two different register indexes $j, j' \in \{0, 3\}$ and for some depth δ. While the S-box of TSC-3 (the same as the one used in TSC-1) has good bit-flip properties, such advanced linear approximations have not been taken into account by the designers.

---

[2] Remember that $S^{16} = I$.

Table 5. Probability that $[x_j]_i^t = [x_{j'}]_i^{t+\delta}$

Case $\delta = 1$

Input \ Output	$[x_0]_i^t$	$[x_1]_i^t$	$[x_2]_i^t$	$[x_3]_i^t$
$[x_0]_i^{t+1}$	0.5	0.53125	0.46875	0.5
$[x_1]_i^{t+1}$	0.46875	0.5	0.5	0.46875
$[x_2]_i^{t+1}$	0.5	0.53125	0.5	0.53125
$[x_3]_i^{t+1}$	0.53125	0.5	0.46875	0.5

Case $\delta = 2$

Input \ Output	$[x_0]_i^t$	$[x_1]_i^t$	$[x_2]_i^t$	$[x_3]_i^t$
$[x_0]_i^{t+2}$	0.515625	0.515625	0.5	0.5
$[x_1]_i^{t+2}$	0.5	0.515625	0.46875	0.5
$[x_2]_i^{t+2}$	0.5	0.5	0.515625	0.515625
$[x_3]_i^{t+2}$	0.5	0.5	0.5	0.515625

Case $\delta = 3$

Input \ Output	$[x_0]_i^t$	$[x_1]_i^t$	$[x_2]_i^t$	$[x_3]_i^t$
$[x_0]_i^{t+3}$	0.51172	0.49610	0.51172	0.50391
$[x_1]_i^{t+3}$	0.50391	0.51172	0.49610	0.51172
$[x_2]_i^{t+3}$	0.49610	0.48828	0.51172	0.49610
$[x_3]_i^{t+3}$	0.48828	0.49610	0.50391	0.51172

From Table 4, it is easy to derive the probability that relation (6) holds, for any pair of positions (j, j'). These results do not depend on which layer i we consider although some side effects are observed at the least significant positions[3]. The results for certain values of δ are given in Table 5. They have been verified experimentally, by running the cipher on a random initial state.

7.2   Second Step

In the case of TSC-3, the output function is not directly applied to the state registers, but to 4 registers y_0, y_1, y_2 and y_3 which are truncated and permuted copies of the state registers x_0, x_1, x_2 and x_3. First we linearize the output function as we did for TSC-1 and TSC-2 :

$$[S]_i = [y_0]_{(i+17)} \oplus [y_1]_{(i+26)} \oplus [y_2]_{(i+2)} \oplus [y_3]_{(i+9)} \oplus [R_G(i)]_0$$

where $R_G(i)$ is the "general carry", defined as before. Then, we replace the bits from the registers y_i by the appropriate bits from the state registers x_i. Because of the truncation and the permutation, we have $[y_j]_i = [x_{\pi(j)}]_{i+8}$ where π is a 4-bit permutation determined by the layer $[x]_0$ of the internal state. The

---

[3] Contrarily to TSC-1 or TSC-2, these side effects are not bothering for TSC-3, since layers 0 to 7 are discarded by the output function.

linear approximations depend on this permutation. Suppose that we are in the particular case where :

$$[x]_0^t = 4$$

Then the next value of this layer is :

$$[x]_0^{t+1} = 1$$

Looking at the permutations π associated with these particular values, we get

$$[S]_i^t = [x_0]_{(i+25)}^t \oplus [x_1]_{(i+34)}^t \oplus [x_3]_{(i+10)}^t \oplus [x_2]_{(i+17)}^t \oplus [R_G(i)]_0^t$$

and

$$[S]_i^{t+1} = [x_1]_{(i+25)}^{t+1} \oplus [x_0]_{(i+34)}^{t+1} \oplus [x_2]_{(i+10)}^{t+1} \oplus [x_3]_{(i+17)}^{t+1} \oplus [R_G(i)]_0^{t+1}$$

Using the Table 5, we observe that :

$$\Pr([x_0]_{(i+25)}^t = [x_1]_{(i+25)}^{t+1}) = 0.46875$$
$$\Pr([x_1]_{(i+34)}^t = [x_0]_{(i+34)}^{t+1}) = 0.53125$$
$$\Pr([x_3]_{(i+10)}^t = [x_2]_{(i+10)}^{t+1}) = 0.53125$$
$$\Pr([x_2]_{(i+17)}^t = [x_3]_{(i+17)}^{t+1}) = 0.46875$$

These 4 probabilities are of the form $0.5\,(1 \pm 2^{-4})$. We tried to consider other values of $[x]_0$ than 4, but it seems to be the best choice, since the highest probabilities in Table 5 appear. Combining the two relations at instants t and $t+1$, we get :

$$[S]_i^t \oplus [S]_i^{t+1} = [R_G(i)]_0^t \oplus [R_G(i)]_0^{t+1}$$

with probability $0.5\,(1+\varepsilon)$ and $|\varepsilon| = (2^{-4})^4 = 2^{-16}$.

Like for TSC-1 and TSC-2, the carries from the additions involved in the output function are not independent from each other. So it is not easy to express simply the probability that $[R_G]$ changes between t and $t+1$. Like before, modeling this phenomenon by a Markov chain could provide more precise results, but we choose to measure the probability experimentally for the sake of simplicity. Results for several values of i are given in Table 6. For some well-chosen positions (typically those were one of the carries is guaranteed to be 0), the probability deviates significantly from 0.5. We observed biases as high as $\epsilon \simeq 2^{-3}$ for "good" positions such as $i = 8$ or $i = 23$. As a consequence,

$$[S]_{23}^t \oplus [S]_{23}^{t+1}$$

is equal to 0 with probability of $0.5\,(1+\varepsilon)$ and $|\varepsilon| \simeq 2^{-16} \times 2^{-3} = 2^{-19}$.

This bias is only valid when $[x_0]^t = 4$, which is the case for exactly one position over 16 in the keystream sequence. It is straightforward to determine which positions should be analyzed if we guess the 4 LSB's of the initial state. In the next section, we show how to exploit this bias for distinguishing and key-recovery attacks.

Table 6. TSC-3 : Bias measured experimentally on the Carry

Position	$\Pr([R_G]_i^t \oplus [R_G]_i^{t+1})$	Position	$\Pr([R_G]_i^t \oplus [R_G]_i^{t+1})$
$i = 0$	0.5001	$i = 16$	0.4993
$i = 1$	0.4921	$i = 17$	0.4998
$i = 2$	0.4968	$i = 18$	0.4997
$i = 3$	0.4989	$i = 19$	0.4998
$i = 4$	0.5001	$i = 20$	0.5003
$i = 5$	0.5003	$i = 21$	0.5002
$i = 6$	0.5004	$i = 22$	0.4996
$i = 7$	0.4999	$i = 23$	0.4452
$i = 8$	0.4442	$i = 24$	0.4862
$i = 9$	0.4871	$i = 25$	0.4962
$i = 10$	0.4967	$i = 26$	0.4995
$i = 11$	0.4999	$i = 27$	0.5003
$i = 12$	0.4996	$i = 28$	0.5005
$i = 13$	0.4997	$i = 29$	0.4997
$i = 14$	0.5002	$i = 30$	0.4996
$i = 15$	0.4997	$i = 31$	0.5007

7.3 Third Step

If we exploit positions 8 or 23 of the output word, we showed in the previous section a bias of the order of $\varepsilon = 2^{-19}$. This can be used to distinguish TSC-3's output sequence from random data, provided $\varepsilon^{-2} = 2^{38}$ samples are given. Since only one position out of 16 in the output sequence is useful, it means that :

$$M = 16 \times 2^{38} = 2^{42}$$

output words are needed. In addition, we must try all values for the initial state's LSB, so the time complexity is about

$$T = 2^4 \times 2^{38} = 2^{42}$$

computation steps.

To mount a key-recovery attack, we start by guessing the 9 least significant layers of the initial state (36 bits in total), in order to predict $[x]_8^t$ for all t. This layer is also the least significant layer of the registers y_i, and it turns out that it is also used in one of the "best" linear approximations : $[S]_{23}^t \oplus [S]_{23}^{t+1}$.

Therefore, we can eliminate one term in this approximation which increases the bias from 2^{-19} to 2^{-15}. Once we found the correct guess for these 36 state bits, it is straightforward to continue the attack, like we did for TSC-1 and TSC-2. The first step is clearly the most expensive, because we must guess 36 bits at the same time. So, the time complexity is

$$T = 2^{36} \times (2^{15})^2 = 2^{66}$$

computation steps. The data complexity of this attack is only :

$$M = 16 \times 2^{30} = 2^{34}$$

output words.

These two attacks show that the stream cipher TSC-3 does not reach the expected security level.

8   Criteria for Future Design

First, we can notice that the 3 separate steps in our linear cryptanalysis framework are always possible, to some extent.

- The periodicity of the least significant layers in multi-word T-functions is always small, by construction. The periodicity of the i-th layer is always 2^{mi} at most for a state of m words. Therefore the following linear relation always holds with probability 1 :

$$[x_j]_i^t \oplus [x_j]_i^{t+2^{mi}} = 0$$

  Other approximations can exist depending on the nature of the T-function, as illustrated in the case of the TSC family.
- For any choice of the output function, there exist linear approximations between input and output bits. Unless the function is very complex (but it is generally not the case, because the output function needs to be fast), it is likely that approximations with good probability can even be found.
- If the approximations of step 1 and step 2 can be combined, it is generally feasible to exploit these biased relations into a key-recovery attack.

Therefore the difficulty does not lie in finding linear approximations or exploiting them, but on combining all approximations to describe the complete cipher. This is something we did not manage to do for Klimov and Shamir's proposal for instance [16]. It is likely that T-function will receive a lot of attention in the future for stream cipher design. To prevent the application of linear cryptanalysis, we suggest to use several safeguards.

- Never use the least significant half of the registers in the output function, because of the small periodicity (this countermeasure was already applied by Klimov and Shamir in several proposals, and TSC-3 has also taken a step in this direction compared to its two predecessors).
- Use rotations in the output function in order to combine the bits from all registers. The output function of TSC-1 or TSC-3 is probably too simple, which makes the analysis easier.
- Try to avoid simple linear approximations for the T-functions over several consecutive steps. For the S-box based T-functions proposed by Hong et al., it is an open problem to say if this is possible. It seems that the current proposals do not provide enough diffusion, but maybe for an appropriate instantiation, the existence of good linear approximations may be avoided. This is an interesting topic for future research.
- Try to take advantage of the "complex" operations which are available on processors. For instance, we believe it is a good idea to use the integer multiplication, when possible, even in the output function.

All these countermeasures may have a negative impact on the encryption speed, but this must be put into the balance with the increased level of security.

9 Conclusion and Comments

In this paper, we give a general framework of linear cryptanalysis for stream ciphers using a T-function. The idea consists in linearizing separately the T-function and the output function, and then connecting both approximations. We successfully applied it to the TSC family of stream ciphers but we believe it can have many applications against this emerging family.

We managed to find a key recovery attack requiring $2^{21.4}$ data with $2^{25.4}$ time for TSC-1, and $2^{44.1}$ data with $2^{48.1}$ time for TSC-2. The attack against TSC-1 has been implemented and requires about 4 minutes of analysis on an average PC. Thus, TSC-1 and TSC-2 are not secure enough for stand-alone use.

An advanced version of our attack also allows to break TSC-3, one of the stream ciphers recently proposed for the ECRYPT project. This attack is very interesting because the designers took into account distinguishing attacks by Künzli *et al.* and added countermeasures. However, our general framework still allows to break the cipher. TSC-3 can be distinguished from random by processing 2^{42} output words, and its secret key can be recovered with 2^{66} computation steps and 2^{34} known output words.

For future designs of stream ciphers, we suggest to benefit from complex operations that allow T-functions. For instance, integer multiplication has good diffusion properties and prevents good linear approximations. Moreover, we recommend never to use LSB's of the state registers in the output function.

References

1. F. Armknecht and M. Krause. Algebraic Attacks on Combiners with Memory. In D. Boneh, editor, *Advances in Cryptology – Crypto'03*, volume 2729 of *Lectures Notes in Computer Science*, pages 162–175. Springer, 2003.
2. S. Babbage. Stream Ciphers: What Does the Industry Want ? In *State of the Art of Stream Ciphers* workshop (SASC'04), 2004.
3. A. Biryukov and A. Shamir. Cryptanalytic time/memory/data tradeoffs for stream ciphers. In T. Okamoto, editor, *Advances in Cryptology – Asiacrypt'00*, volume 1976 of *Lectures Notes in Computer Science*, pages 1–13. Springer, 2000.
4. N. Courtois and W. Meier. Algebraic Attacks on Stream Ciphers with Linear Feedback. In E. Biham, editor, *Advances in Cryptology – Eurocrypt'03*, volume 2656 of *Lectures Notes in Computer Science*, pages 345–359. Springer, 2003.
5. C. Ding, G. Xiao, and W. Shan. *The Stability Theory of Stream Ciphers*, volume 561 of *Lectures Notes in Computer Science*. Springer, 1991. see Section 3.3.
6. ECRYPT Network of Excellence in Cryptology.
   http://www.ecrypt.eu.org/index.html.
7. ECRYPT Stream Cipher Project. See http://www.ecrypt.eu.org/stream/.
8. J. Golić. Linear Cryptanalysis of Stream Ciphers. In B. Preneel, editor, *Fast Software Encryption – 1994*, volume 1008 of *Lectures Notes in Computer Science*, pages 154–169. Springer, 1995.
9. J. Golić. Linear Statistical Weakness of Alleged RC4 Keystream Generator. In W. Fumy, editor, *Advances in Cryptology – Eurocrypt'97*, volume 1233 of *Lectures Notes in Computer Science*, pages 226–238. Springer, 1997.

10. J. Hong, D. Lee, Y. Yeom, and D. Han. A New Class of Single Cycle T-functions. In H. Gilbert and H. Handschuh, editors, *Fast Software Encryption – 2005*, volume 3557 of *Lectures Notes in Computer Science*, pages 68–82. Springer, 2005.

11. J. Hong, D. Lee, Y. Yeom, D. Han, and S. Chee. T-function Based Stream Cipher TSC-3. ECRYPT Stream Cipher Project Report 2005/031, 2005. http://www.ecrypt.eu.org/stream.

12. A. Klimov. *Applications of T-functions in Cryptography*. PhD thesis, Weizmann Institute of Science, 2004. http://www.wisdom.weizmann.ac.il/ ask/.

13. A. Klimov and A. Shamir. A New Class of Invertible Mappings. In B. Kaliski, Ç. Koç, and C. Paar, editors, *Cryptographic Hardware and Embedded Systems (CHES) – 2002*, volume 2523 of *Lectures Notes in Computer Science*, pages 470–483. Springer, 2002.

14. A. Klimov and A. Shamir. Cryptographic Applications of T-functions. In M. Matsui and R. Zuccherato, editors, *Selected Areas in Cryptography – 2003*, volume 3006 of *Lectures Notes in Computer Science*, pages 248–261. Springer, 2004.

15. A. Klimov and A. Shamir. New Cryptographic Primitives Based on Multiword T-Functions. In B. Roy and W. Meier, editors, *Fast Software Encryption – 2004*, volume 3017 of *Lectures Notes in Computer Science*, pages 1–15. Springer, 2004.

16. A. Klimov and A. Shamir. The TFi Family of Stream Ciphers, 2004. Handout given at the SASC'04 workshop.

17. A. Klimov and A. Shamir. New Applications of T-functions in Block Ciphers and Hash Functions. In H. Gilbert and H. Handschuh, editors, *Fast Software Encryption – 2005*, volume 3557 of *Lectures Notes in Computer Science*, pages 18–31. Springer, 2005.

18. S. Künzli, P. Junod, and W. Meier. Attacks Against TSC. Rump Session at *Fast Software Encryption* (FSE'05), 2005.

19. S. Künzli, P. Junod, and W. Meier. Distinguishing Attacks on T-Functions. In *International Conference on Cryptology in Malaysia (MyCrypt 2005)*, 2005. To appear.

20. M. Matsui. Linear Cryptanalysis Method for DES Cipher. In T. Helleseth, editor, *Advances in Cryptology – Eurocrypt'93*, volume 765 of *Lectures Notes in Computer Science*, pages 386–397. Springer, 1993.

21. W. Meier and O. Staffelbach. Fast Correlations Attacks on Certain Stream Ciphers. In *Journal of Cryptology*, pages 159–176. Springer, 1989.

22. J. Mitra and P. Sarkar. Time-Memory Trade-Off Attacks on Multiplications and T-functions. In P. Lee, editor, *Advances in Cryptology - Asiacrypt'04*, volume 3329 of *Lectures Notes in Computer Science*, pages 468–482. Springer, 2004.

23. F. Muller and T. Peyrin. Linear Cryptanalysis of TSC Stream Ciphers - Applications to the ECRYPT proposal TSC-3. ECRYPT Stream Cipher Project Report 2005/042, 2005. http://www.ecrypt.eu.org/stream.

24. A. Shamir. Stream Ciphers: Dead or Alive ? Invited talk presented at Asiacrypt'04, 2004.

25. T. Siegenthaler. Correlation-immunity of Nonlinear Combining Functions for Cryptographic Applications. In *IEEE Transactions on Information Theory*, volume 30, pages 776–780, 1984.

Appendix

Table 7. TSC-1 for $t/t + 3$: Bit Flip Probabilities of the Registers and of the LSB of the General Carry

bit position	register 0	register 1	register 2	register 3	LSB(R_G)
0	0.5000	0.5000	0.5000	0.5000	0.5953
1	0.6406	0.6406	0.6406	0.6406	0.4563
2	0.6479	0.6479	0.6479	0.6479	0.4948
3	0.6446	0.6446	0.6446	0.6446	0.5247
4	0.6442	0.6442	0.6442	0.6442	0.5328
5	0.6427	0.6427	0.6427	0.6427	0.5343
6	0.6356	0.6356	0.6356	0.6356	0.5356
7	0.6412	0.6412	0.6412	0.6412	0.5352
8	0.6413	0.6413	0.6413	0.6413	0.5263
9	0.6417	0.6416	0.6416	0.6417	0.5337
10	0.6417	0.6417	0.6417	0.6417	0.5355
11	0.6364	0.6364	0.6364	0.6364	0.5357
12	0.6408	0.6408	0.6409	0.6409	0.5354
13	0.6412	0.6411	0.6412	0.6412	0.5352
14	0.6416	0.6416	0.6415	0.6416	0.5354
15	0.6417	0.6416	0.6416	0.6417	0.4348
16	0.6364	0.6364	0.6364	0.6363	0.4952
17	0.6408	0.6409	0.6409	0.6408	0.5253
18	0.6412	0.6412	0.6412	0.6412	0.5332
19	0.6416	0.6416	0.6417	0.6416	0.5349
20	0.6364	0.6364	0.6364	0.6364	0.5355
21	0.6409	0.6408	0.6408	0.6409	0.5359
22	0.6412	0.6412	0.6412	0.6413	0.5355
23	0.6365	0.6365	0.6365	0.6365	0.5360
24	0.6408	0.6408	0.6408	0.6409	0.5349
25	0.6413	0.6413	0.6413	0.6413	0.5266
26	0.6366	0.6365	0.6366	0.6366	0.5333
27	0.6409	0.6408	0.6408	0.6409	0.5351
28	0.6414	0.6413	0.6413	0.6412	0.5357
29	0.6365	0.6366	0.6365	0.6365	0.5357
30	0.6408	0.6409	0.6408	0.6408	0.5355
31	0.6412	0.6412	0.6412	0.6412	0.5351

A Practical Attack on the Fixed RC4 in the WEP Mode

I. Mantin

NDS Technologies, Israel

imantin@nds.com

Abstract. In this paper we revisit a known but ignored weakness of the RC4 keystream generator, where secret state info leaks to the generated keystream, and show that this leakage, also known as Jenkins' correlation or the RC4 glimpse, can be used to attack RC4 in several modes. Our main result is a practical key recovery attack on RC4 when an IV modifier is concatenated to the beginning of a secret root key to generate a session key. As opposed to the WEP attack from [FMS01] the new attack is applicable even in the case where the first 256 bytes of the keystream are thrown and its complexity grows only linearly with the length of the key. In an exemplifying parameter setting the attack recovers a 16-byte key in 2^{48} steps using 2^{17} short keystreams generated from different chosen IVs. A second attacked mode is when the IV succeeds the secret root key. We mount a key recovery attack that recovers the secret root key by analyzing a single word from 2^{22} keystreams generated from different IVs, improving the attack from [FMS01] on this mode. A third result is an attack on RC4 that is applicable when the attacker can inject faults to the execution of RC4. The attacker derives the internal state and the secret key by analyzing 2^{14} faulted keystreams generated from this key.

Keywords: RC4, Stream ciphers, Cryptanalysis, Fault analysis, Side-channel attacks, Related IV attacks, Related key attacks.

1 Introduction

RC4 is the most widely used stream cipher in software applications. Among numerous applications it is used to protect Internet traffic as part of the SSL and is integrated into Microsoft Windows. It was designed by Ron Rivest in 1987 and kept as a trade secret until it leaked out in 1994. RC4 has a secret internal state which is a permutation of all the $N = 2^n$ possible n bits words, associated with two indices in it, when in practical applications $n = 8$, and thus RC4 has a huge state of $log_2(2^8! \times (2^8)^2) \approx 1700$ bits.

In this paper we revisit a known but previously ignored property of RC4, which we denote as the *Glimpse property* also known as Jenkins' correlations. The glimpse is a leakage of information from RC4 secret state to the generated keystream, where every keystream word hints on a state word through the correlation $S[j] = i - z$ which occurs with doubled probability (1/128 instead of

B. Roy (Ed.): ASIACRYPT 2005, LNCS 3788, pp. 395–411, 2005.

© International Association for Cryptologic Research 2005

1/256), when i is a known index of RC4 state, z is the hinting keystream word and $S[j]$ is the hinted entry of the secret internal state.

The glimpse property was first mentioned in the web page of Jenkins ([Jen96]) and was first brought to formal literature in [MS01] in 2001. In Chapter 7 of [Man01] Mantin analyzed the glimpse property, defined a generalized version of the correlation and discovered small biases in the keystream that stem from it. However, due to the fact that the glimpse discovers a negligible part of the internal state (one byte out of 1700) and the fact that it does so with biased but still small probability, that was the last trial for exploiting this property to attack RC4.

In this paper we revisit the glimpse in RC4 and RC4-like stream ciphers, analyze its origin and discuss the ways a cryptanalyst can use it. We define a generalized version of the glimpse and discuss the availability of the generalized correlations in RC4 and RC4-like ciphers.

Our main result is a practical key recovery attack on RC4 that works even when the common recommendation of throwing a 256-byte prefix of the keystream is adopted. The attack works in a mode of operation where an initial value (IV) is concatenated to the beginning of the root key and works in both the chosen IV and known IV models. The attack allows some data-time tradeoff that depends on the length of the root key. For example, some parameter setting for a 16-byte key allows the attacker to recover the key in 2^{48} steps using 2^{17} data or with 2^{32} steps using 2^{20} data. In the known (random) IV model the data complexity of the attack requires an additional multiplicative factor of $N = 256$ in order to have a sufficient number of "good" IVs.

In the second part of the work we present the *fork* model where many instances of RC4 are available to the attacker with almost equal state and show that in this model an attacker can use the glimpse property to recover RC4 internal state. We show two realizations of this model; the first is where the IV modifier is concatenated to a end of a secret root key in order to generate many independent RC4 keystreams from a single secret root key. In this mode we mount a chosen and known (random) IV attacks that recover the secret key by analyzing 2^{22} keystreams that were generated from this key and different IVs. Another realization of this model is where the attacker injects faults into the execution of RC4 and distorts the generated keystream. In that case we mount a fault attack that uses 2^{14} faulty keystreams to recover the internal state and the secret key.

The rest of the paper is organized in the following way: In Sect. 2 we describe RC4 and previous cryptanalysis. In Sect. 3 we re-present the glimpse property and analyze its origin and availability. In Sect. 4 we describe key recovery attacks on RC4 in the preceding IV mode when the first 256 bytes are thrown. In Sect. 5 we present the *Fork* model and use the glimpse property to mount an attack on RC4 in this model. In Sect. 6 we adjust the fork model attack to mount a key recovery attack on the succeeding IV mode. In Sect. 7 we adjust the fork model attack to mount an efficient fault attack on RC4. We summarize our work in Sect. 8.

KSA($K[0 \ldots \ell - 1]$)	PRGA(K)
Initialization:	Initialization:
$\quad$ For $i = 0 \ldots N - 1$	$\quad i = 0$
$\quad\quad S[i] = i$	$\quad j = 0$
$\quad j = 0$	$\quad S = KSA(K)$
Scrambling:	Generation loop:
$\quad$ For $i = 0 \ldots N - 1$	$\quad i = i + 1$
$\quad\quad j = j + S[i] + K[i \bmod \ell]$	$\quad j = j + S[i]$
$\quad\quad Swap(S[i], S[j])$	$\quad Swap(S[i], S[j])$
	$\quad$ Output $z = S[S[i] + S[j]]$

Fig. 1. The Key Scheduling Algorithm and the Pseudo-Random Generation Algorithm

2   RC4 and Its Security

2.1   Description of RC4

RC4 consists of 2 parts (described in Fig. 1): A key scheduling algorithm KSA which turns a variable-size key (with typical size of 5-32 bytes) into an initial permutation S of $\{0, \ldots, N - 1\}$, and an output generation part PRGA which uses this permutation to generate a pseudo-random keystream.

The PRGA initializes two indices i and j to 0, and then loops over four simple operations which increment i as a counter, increment j pseudo randomly, exchange the two values of S pointed to by i and j, and output the value of S pointed to by $S[i] + S[j]$[1].

2.2   Previous Analysis of RC4

Cryptanalysis of RC4 is divided into two main parts, analysis of the initialization of RC4 and analysis of the keystream generation. The first part focuses on the KSA, the PRGA initialization and the integration of both, whereas the last focuses on the internal state and the round operation of the PRGA.

Due to the simplicity of the initialization part and the major difference between the typical key sizes and the effective size of RC4 state, this part was subject to extensive analysis and indeed numerous significant weaknesses were discovered of many types, including classes of weak keys ([Roo95]), patterns that appear twice and three times the expected probability (the second byte bias [MS01]), propagation of key patterns through the KSA to the initial permutation and through the PRGA initialization to the prefix of the stream (the invariance weakness [FMS01]), related key attacks ([GW00]), statistical biases in different prefixes of the generated stream ([FMS01] and [PP04]) and analysis of the biased distribution of RC4 initial permutation ([Mir02] and [Man01]). However, the most devastating attack on RC4 was described in [FMS01] where RC4 was proved to have serious related-key vulnerabilities, exposing several implementations of RC4 to practical key recovery attacks, where the effected implementations are those that employ trivial key-IV combination methods such as

---

[1] Here and in the rest of the paper all the additions are carried out modulo N.

concatenation or exclusive-or. A subsequent work by Stubblefield et-al ([SIR01]) implemented the attack on the security protocols of the international standard for wireless LAN communication 802.11b (WEP) that used RC4 in the IV concatenation mode, and these protocols were declared as broken.

This attack had a great impact on the trust of cryptographers and security designers in RC4 and the common practice for using RC4 today includes hardening of the initialization process by omitting some prefix of the keystream, usually 256 bytes as recommended by RSA laboratories in [RSA01]. This hardening neutralizes most of the attacks and weaknesses that were discovered in RC4 initialization. However, this mode still has some weaknesses, including a biased distribution of the PRGA initial permutation ([Mir02]) and statistical biases in the first bytes that are emitted after the 256th round ([PP04]).

Statistical analysis of the keystream generation part gave rise to several weaknesses and biased patterns in RC4 keystreams. Golić ([Gol97]) and Fluhrer and McGrew ([FM00]) designed distinguishers of RC4 streams from random streams that require $2^{44.7}$ and $2^{30.6}$ keystream words respectively. Subsequently Mantin improved these results in [Man05] and designed a 2^{28} distinguisher. In his paper he also described several families of patterns denoted in [Man05] as recyclable patterns, which occur in RC4 keystreams with extremely high probability that is several times the probability in random streams, and described an algorithm that uses these patterns to predict in some rare cases bits and full bytes of RC4 with success probabilities that are close to 1.

Several other classes of RC4 partial states were defined and analyzed in [FM00], [MS01] and [PP03] as such that create unique patterns in the output stream and allow a viewer of the output stream to recover parts of the internal state with more than trivial probability (chapter 2 of [Man01] contains an overview of these classes). The cycles structure of RC4 state progression was also analyzed in [MT98] and [Fin94], where the last describes short cycles that are unreachable by RC4. [KM+98], [MT98] and [Gol00] describe state recovery attacks through backtracking with complexity that is less than the square root of an exhaustive search over all possible states. However, due to the hugeness of the state (1700 bits for $n = 8$), these attacks are completely impractical as they require more than 2^{700} steps. Mantin in [Man05] describes an approach that under some circumstances can improve this attack significantly through using the recyclable patterns.

Two variants of RC4 were recently proposed, both slightly more complex than the original RC4 and are claimed to be more secure than it. RC4A ([PP04]) was designed by Paul and Preneel and works with two RC4 tables. The generation stage of RC4A is slightly more efficient than RC4's, but the initialization stage requires at least twice the effort of RC4 initialization. VMPC ([Zol04]) was designed by Zoltak and includes several changes to the KSA, the IV integration method, the PRGA initialization, the round operation and the output selection method. Maximov described in [Max05] distinguishers for both variants, requiring 2^{54} data for VMPC and 2^{58} data for RC4A and Tsunoo et-al subsequently described in [TS+05] a prefix distinguishers for VMPC and RC4A keystream generators, requiring 2^{23} keystream prefixes for RC4A and 2^{24} keystream prefixes for VMPC. A regular distinguisher (as opposed to a prefix distinguisher) of RC4A was shown in [Man05] that needs a keystream of 2^{29} keywords and is an adjusted variant of the RC4 distinguisher mentioned in this work.

The trend of side-channel attacks had not skipped RC4. Hoch and Shamir made in [HS04] an exhaustive fault analysis of many stream ciphers including RC4 and found them all vulnerable to key recovery attack in this model. In particular their attack on RC4 requires 2^{16} faults. Biham et-al proposed in [BGN05] two other fault attacks on RC4; in the impossible fault attack is based on using faults to force the cipher to enter the impossible states known as Finney's states ([Fin94]). In the differential fault attack, the attacker compares many faulty keystreams to a non-faulty keystream and identifies the three permutation entries that are used in the first round, the second round, etc. Several variants and optimizations for this attack are described and the best configuration of the attack requires 2^{10} faults and key resets.

2.3 Notations

In vast majority of RC4 implementations $N = 256$ and $n = 8$. In many cases we simplify expressions by using numbers instead of parameters. Whenever appropriate, we mention this conversion.

For a positive integer X we use the notation $[X]$ to specify the domain of indices modulo X, i.e., $[X] = \{0, 1, \dots, X - 1\}$. We denote the domain of permutations of $[X]$ as $\mathcal{P}[X]$.

We use the notations i_t, j_t and S_t for the indices i and j and the permutation S after round t, where the rounds are indexed in accordance with i, i.e., $i_t = t$. Thus the KSA has rounds $0, \dots, 255$ and the PRGA has rounds $1, 2, \dots$. We use the same indexing for both the KSA permutations and the PRGA permutations and whenever there might be a confusion, we use the notations $S^{(KSA)}$ and $S^{(PRGA)}$ respectively.

The output function $Z : \mathcal{P}[X] \times [X] \times [X] \to [X]$ is defined on RC4 states as $Z(S, i, j) \stackrel{def}{=} S[S[i] + S[j]]$. We denote output words with z and index them in the same manner as i and j, i.e., $z_t = Z(S_t, i_t, j_t)$.
We denote the KSA key as K and its length as ℓ_K.

3   The Glimpse

The glimpse property as was first introduced in [Jen96] is defined in Theorem 1.

Theorem 1 (The Glimpse Main Theorem). *Let $i \in [N]$. Then*

$$\mathbb{P}_{j \in R[N], S \in R\mathcal{P}[N]}[S[j] = i - Z(S, i, j)] \approx 2/N \tag{1}$$
$$\mathbb{P}_{j \in R[N], S \in R\mathcal{P}[N]}[S[i] = j - Z(S, i, j)] \approx 2/N \tag{2}$$

In other words, when z is the output then

$$\mathbb{P}[S[j] = i - z] \approx \mathbb{P}[S[i] = j - z] \approx 2/N$$

The proof of Theorem 1 appears in the discussion of useful states in Sect. 2.3 of [Man01], and we only bring the intuition behind one of them (the second stems from symmetry). In the case where $i = S[i] + S[j]$, the correlation occurs with probability 1 since

$$Z(S, i, j) = S[S[i] + S[j]] = S[i] = i - S[j] \tag{3}$$

In the other case $(i \neq S[i] + S[j])$, the correlation occurs with a probability of $1/N$ and thus the overall probability is

$$1/N \cdot 1 + (1 - 1/N) \cdot 1/N \approx 2/N \tag{4}$$

A generalized version of the glimpse was proved in Sect. 7 of [Man01], where different relations between i and z hint on corresponding relations between $S[i]$ and $S[j]$. This generalization is given in Theorem 2.

Theorem 2. *Let f be a $[N] \to [N]$ function and let $h_f(x) \stackrel{def}{=} f(x) + x$. Suppose that h_f is on-to-one in the domain $[N]$ and onto $[N]$. Then for every $i \in [N]$,*

$$\mathbb{P}_{j \in_R [N], S \in_R \mathcal{P}[N]}[S[j] = f(S[i]) | i = h_f(Z(S, i, j))] \approx 2/N \tag{5}$$

The original glimpse is a special case with the degenerated function $f(x) \stackrel{def}{=} i - z$ and $h_f(z) = i$. The base condition $i = h_f(Z(S, i, j))$ occurs always and thus the probability of the derived condition $[S[j] = f(S[i])]$ is always $2/N$. Thus many relations between the index i and the output word z imply corresponding relations between the permutation entries that are used.

In Sect. A of the appendix we discuss the availability of the glimpse and show that it exists in many other output selection functions. Notice that since the index j is secret, the output hints on a value in an unknown location. However, the value in this location was in a known location i immediately before this round and furthermore, this is the same value that was used to update j in this round. These facts underline the analysis in the rest of the paper.

4   Attacking the Truncated RC4

One of the most popular IV combination methods for RC4 and other stream ciphers is a concatenation of the IV to the root key in order to obtain a one-time session key. This mode of operation was attacked by Fluhrer et-al in [FMS01] both in the case where the IV is concatenated to the end of the root key (we denote this mode as the succeeding IV mode) and in the case where the IV is concatenated to the beginning of the root key (we denote this mode as the preceding IV mode). Their attack on the preceding IV mode was found applicable to the RC4 implementation in WEP and it is sometimes referred to as the WEP attack or the FMS attack. The attack recovers the bytes of the root key one at a time, where in the iterative step IVs are selected that cause leakage of information from the target keyword into the first word of the generated keystream[2]. Since the publication of this attack in 2001 the common practice in implementations of RC4 is to throw a prefix of 256 bytes from the keystream and thus prevent access of the attacker to the first output word and foil the attack. We denote this usage mode of RC4 as *the truncated RC4*.

In this section we present a new attack on the truncated RC4. The attack resembles the FMS attack in many aspects, where instead of using the leakage of the keyword to the first output word, we use the glimpse property to redirect the leakage to the 257th keystream word and thus overcome the omission of the first keystream words.

The rest of this section is organized as follows. We first describe the WEP attack and the way in which particular keywords leak to the first keystream word. Afterwards we present a new leakage scenario where keyword info leaks to the 257th keystream word. We describe how the attack uses this leakage scenario to recover the root key and end with complexity analysis and a comparison to the WEP attack.

4.1   The WEP Attack

We denote the root key as RK and the session key that is combined from RK and an IV as SK. We denote the length of these keys by $|RK|$ and $|SK|$ respectively and the length of the IV by ℓ_{IV} and thus $|SK| = |RK| + \ell_{IV}$.

The attack recovers the keywords one at a time. The iterative step of the attack assumes knowledge of some prefix of the RC4 keywords, and uses the first word of each of several keystreams to derive the next keyword (which we denote below as the target keyword). The attack starts with the known IV as a basis, and repeatedly applies the iterative step in order to recover all the keywords in the root key. The keystreams from which first words are taken to recover the target keyword, are carefully selected according to the IV that was used to generate them.

The Iterative Step. The iterative step for the $(x+1)^{th}$ keyword $SK[x]$ (which is $RK[x - \ell_{IV}]$) as the target keyword simulates the first x steps of the KSA using the x known keywords in order to recover the permutation after x rounds S_{x-1}. The KSA uses the next keyword, which is the target keyword, to calculate the value of j in the next step j_x and thus this keyword can be easily derived from j_x. Since the swap in round x occurs in locations $i_x = x$ and j_x, $S_x[x] = S_{x-1}[j_x]$ and knowing S_{x-1}, $S_x[x]$ leads to j_x and further on to the target keyword.

The first output value is $S[S[1] + S[S[1]]]$ and thus only three permutation entries are used for this calculation; the ones in locations 1, $S[1]$ and $S[1] + S[S[1]]$. When these locations are lower than or equal to x after round x they are guaranteed not to be visited by i during the subsequent $N - x$ rounds and

---

[2] The attack is therefore a Known Plaintext Attack (KPA). Stubblefield et-al subsequently showed that the first plaintext byte in typical WEP applications is a constant header and thus the KPA model is realistic.

with high probability of more than $e^{-3} \approx 5\%$ (using Lemma 1, which is proved in Appendix B) no to be visited by the pseudo-random index j during these rounds. In that case, the first keystream word can be deduced with high probability from the values that are at these locations in the permutation S_x. Furthermore, when in addition $S[1] + S[S[1]] = x$ (in [FMS01] it was denoted as the resolved condition) the first keystream word z_1 is exactly $S_x[x]$, from which the target keyword can be derived.

Formally, when $1, S[1] < x$ and $S[1] + S[S[1]] = x$, then with probability of at least 5%

$$
\begin{aligned}
SK[x] = \quad & j_x - j_{x-1} - S_{x-1}[x] \qquad = \\
= \; & S_{x-1}^{-1}[S_x[x]] - j_{x-1} - S_{x-1}[x] \quad \overset{w.p.\ 1/e^3}{=} \\
= \; & S_{x-1}^{-1}[z_1] - j_{x-1} - S_{x-1}[x]
\end{aligned}
\tag{6}
$$

Thus when IVs are selected that cause S_{x-1} to satisfy the resolved condition, the above calculation points to the correct target keyword with probability of about 5%. Using this observation Fluhrer et-al recovered the target keyword through employing a simple voting mechanism where every first keystream word gives a vote to a keyword candidate.

Analysis of the WEP Attack. In [FMS01] it was estimated that in order to mount the attack for a particular keyword the attacker needs about 60 votes from which an average number of three votes go to the correct target keyword. In order to guarantee the 5% probability, these votes must come from situations where the resolved condition was satisfied and thus in the chosen IV model the number of IVs that are needed is 60 per keyword.

In the known IV model the situation is more complicated where the attacker must wait for IVs that lead to the resolved condition, which under reasonable randomness assumptions have a fraction of $\frac{x}{N^2}$ and thus the $(x + 1)^{th}$ keyword requires $60N^2/x$ IVs. Since the data can be reused for different iterative steps the main complexity parameter for the attack is the maximal number of IVs for a keyword, which is $60 \cdot N^2/\ell_{IV}$. A somewhat surprising result is that the attack works better when longer IVs are used.

4.2   The New Attack

We present a similar leakage from the target keyword in two stages, to $S_1^{(PRGA)}[1]$ and through it to the 257th keystream word z_{257}.

We first describe the way $S_x[x]$ reaches location 1 of S. Suppose that after round $x - 1$ of the KSA we have $S_{x-1}[1] = x$. In the next round some arbitrary value Y, pointed to by j, is swapped into location x. This Y leads to the target keyword in the same manner as in the WEP attack (known S_{x-1}, Y leads to j_x, j_x leads to $SK[x]$). Suppose that during the remaining $N - x$ KSA rounds the values x and Y remain at locations 1 and x. The probability of this event is at least $1/e^2$ (using Lemma 1). In the first round of the PRGA round we get

$$i_1 = 1 \tag{7}$$

$$j_1 = j_0 + S_0^{(PRGA)}[1] = S_x^{(KSA)}[1] = x \tag{8}$$

$$S_1^{(PRGA)}[1] = S_0^{(PRGA)}[j_1] = S_x^{(KSA)}[x] = Y \tag{9}$$

Thus with probability $1/e^2$ target keyword info leaks into $S_1^{(PRGA)}[1]$. In the next 255 rounds of the PRGA i traverses locations $2, \ldots, 255, 0$ and with probability $1/e$ (again we use Lemma 1) the index j also skips location 1 and then $S_{256}^{(PRGA)}[1] = S_1^{(PRGA)}[1] = Y$. However, the glimpse property causes information on this particular byte to leak to the next keystream word and thus we complete a leakage chain from the target keyword to z_{257}.

Combining these observations with the glimpse probabilities we get (probabilities are presented over the equality sign)

$$i_{257} - z_{257} \stackrel{2/N}{=} S_{256}^{(PRGA)}[1] \stackrel{1/e}{=} S_1^{(PRGA)}[1] \stackrel{1/e^2}{=} Y \tag{10}$$

Thus we reach a probability of $2e^{-3}/N$ for the complete scenario to occur and in this case the correct target keyword is

$$SK[x] = S_{x-1}^{-1}[i_{257} \quad z_{257}] \quad j_{x-1} \quad S_{x-1}[x] \tag{11}$$

Notice that when the chain breaks, there is still a probability of $1/N$ to have a lucky guess and thus the overall probability for a successful guess is

$$\mathbb{P}[\ SK[x] = S_{x-1}^{-1}[i_{257} - z_{257}] - j_{x-1} - S_{x-1}[x]] \approx$$

$$\approx \quad \frac{2}{e^3 N} \cdot 1 + (1 - \frac{2}{e^3 N}) \cdot \frac{1}{N} =$$

$$= \quad \frac{1}{N} + \frac{2}{e^3 N} \cdot (1 - \frac{1}{N}) \approx$$

$$\approx \quad \frac{1}{N} \cdot (1 + \frac{2}{e^3}) \approx 1.1 \cdot \frac{1}{N} \tag{12}$$

Simulations we carried out show that this analysis is somewhat optimistic and that the actual probability for a correct guess (given that the IV conditions are satisfied) is $1.075 \cdot 1/N$.

4.3   Complexity Analysis

Next we compare the attack parameters and probabilities to those of the WEP attack. The probability of having a "good" IV *increases* from $\frac{x}{N^2}$ in the WEP attack to $1/N$ (need only $S_{x-1}[1] = x$). However, the advantage in the voting process significantly decreases from 5% to $1.075/256$. Thus the voting in this attack is much harder than in the WEP attack, even though a larger fraction of the IVs are "good" and this voting requires almost one million "good" IVs (see Fig. 2) for recovering the target keyword with a probability that is close to 1.

However, a smarter key recovery algorithm can tolerate some errors in the guessing. The algorithm can guess C possible values for every keyword and check all the

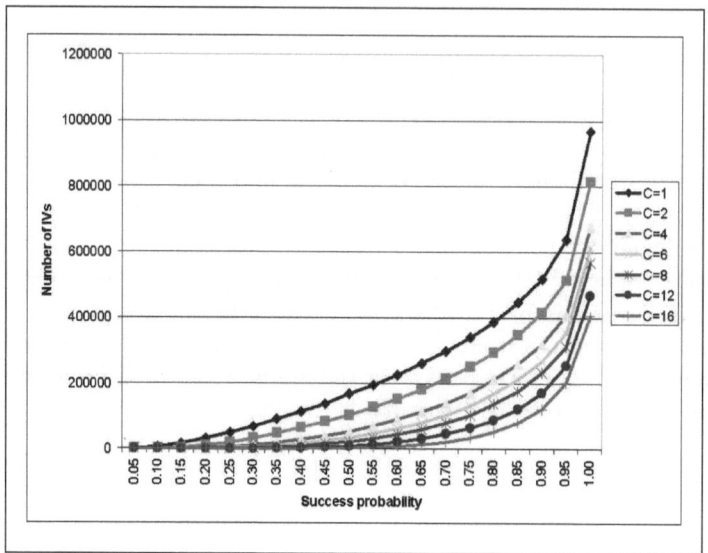

Fig. 2. The number of IVs that are required for different success probabilities (for the attack on the Truncated RC4). The different graphs are for different selections of the branching factor C.

possible C^{ℓ_K} branches, where a typical value for C is 4-5. Typical RC4 keys are 16 bytes or below, which makes the number of possibilities checked by the algorithm no more than $5^{16} \approx 2^{37}$. This attack can be further optimized by using a smart branching strategy that instead of using a fixed branching factor, selects the number of branches according to the result of the voting, e.g., avoiding branching when a single value sticks out clearly as the correct keyword. However, in this extended abstract we limit the discussion to the simple case of a fixed branching factor.

In Fig. 2 we show the number of samples of "good" IVs that are required for different success probabilities and different selections of the branching factor C. For example, for $C = 8$ the attack requires a practical amount of 2^{17} "good" IVs in order to get a success probability of 80% for recovery of every keyword. The selection of C depends heavily on the key length, where large C's can be used only when the key is short. For example, for a 16-byte key, using $C = 8$ implies a time complexity of $8^{16} = 2^{48}$ and using $C = 4$ the time complexity drops to 2^{32}.

In the known (random) IV model the data complexity increases by a factor of N, which is the expected number of IVs until a "good" one is found. With the above parameter setting the data complexity for a known IV attack grows to 2^{25} whereas the time complexity remains the same 2^{48}.

5   The Fork Model

In this section we discuss a situation where many identical instances of RC4 diverge at a certain point, i.e., at a certain point they have the same state

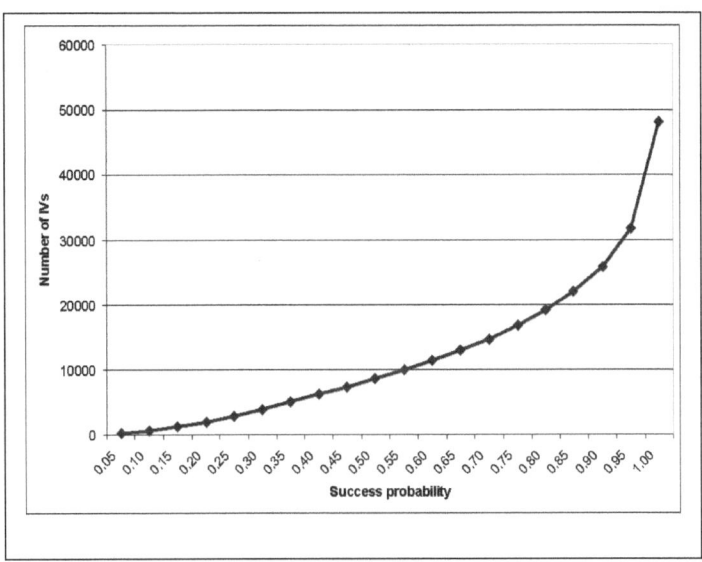

Fig. 3. The number of IVs that are required for different success probabilities (for the attack on RC4 in the fork model)

(permutation and indices) and afterwards some small change to the state occurs, causing each of the instances to evolve differently. A small change in this context may be a change in j and possibly change to a small number of permutation entries. We show that in this model, given a sufficient number of instances the permutation at the divergence point can be recovered.

The attack goes iteratively over the permutation entries and recovers one permutation value at a time. Let S be the permutation in the divergence point and let t be an index for which the attacker wants to reveal $S[t] = x$. The attacker waits until the round where the index i reaches location t and looks at the keystream word that was emitted at that point. If the attacker is lucky, the value x remains in location t until that round (we denote this event as A) and due to the glimpse property the emitted value will be biased towards $i - S[j] = i - x$ (we denote the event where $z = i - x$ by B). Using Lemma 1 (which is proved in Appendix B) we estimate the probability of A with $p_A = 1/e$ and the glimpse property guarantees that the event B occurs with probability $2/N$. Assuming independence of the events and uniform distribution of the output when both event do not occur (when one event does not occur the probability if 0) we get

$$
\begin{aligned}
\mathbb{P}[x = i - z] &= \mathbb{P}[A, B] + \mathbb{P}[\neg A, \neg B] \cdot 1/N = \\
&= 2/N \cdot p_A + (1 - 2/N) \cdot (1 - p_A) \cdot 1/(N - 1) \approx \\
&\approx 2/N \cdot p_A + (1 - p_A) \cdot 1/N = \\
&= 1/N \cdot (1 + p_A) \approx \\
&\approx 1/N \cdot (1 + 1/e)
\end{aligned}
\tag{13}
$$

This probability was verified through simulations and indeed the correct x value has a significant advantage on other guesses. Through using a voting mechanism where votes are given to values $i - z$, the correct value of x is expected to noticeably stick out. In Fig. 3 we analyze the number of iterations that are required for recovery of x under these circumstances. After 20,000 iterations, every permutation entry is recovered with success probability of 80%. The iterative step is repeated for each of the permutation entries and under reasonable assumptions of independency the same data can be reused for each of the locations.

Notice that in the case where 80% of the guesses are correct, there are still 50 permutation entries that are guessed incorrectly. However, the attacker can avoid guesses that have only small advantage and use only those with high level of confidence. As was shown in [KM+98] having a significant part of the permutation provides the critical mass for completion of the state recovery task.

6   Attacking the Succeeding IV Mode

While presenting a practical key recovery attack for the preceding IV mode, Fluhrer et-al only showed is [FMS01] several sets of weak keys for the succeeding IV mode.

However, this mode of operation "almost" realizes the fork model, where the first rounds of the KSA use an identical part of the key (the root key) whereas the following rounds use different part of the key (IVs). The "almost" is due to the fact that the KSA does not output words and thus the first leakage occurs only in the beginning of the PRGA, i.e., after $N - \ell_K$ rounds that ruin $N - \ell_K$ entries from the divergence permutation.

However, this hurdle can be overcome through appropriate adjustments. In order to reveal a single permutation entry, the attacker can direct the leakage of this value to a fixed location ℓ_K, which leaks through the ℓ_K^{th} keystream word.

In every step of the attack, the attacker fixes $IV[0]$ and uses varying values for the rest of the IV. After ℓ_K rounds of using words of the root key, The index j in round ℓ_K depends on the "keyword" $IV[0]$ in an additive manner and thus every value $IV[0]$ implies a different j_{ℓ_K}, a different value in location ℓ_K after round ℓ_K and eventually a leakage of a different permutation entry to the ℓ_K^{th} keystream word.

Thus for every value of $IV[0]$ a new value leaks to the keystream. Notice that the keywords are used in an additive manner and thus any increase of $IV[0]$ causes a similar increase in j at the corresponding round and eventually the attacker learns the permutation at the divergence point, but with a fixed shift that depends on the unknown j_{ℓ_K-1}, and needs to try all possible 256 shifts in order to recover the correct permutation. Notice that j_{ℓ_K-1} is unknown at this stage and thus every step of the attack (with a fixed $IV[0]$) exposes a permutation entry from an unknown location. Thus the attacker needs to try all possible values for j_{ℓ_K-1} in order to complete the recovery of the permutation.

Since every stage of the attack needs IVs with different $IV[0]$, data cannot be reused for the different stages and a multiplicative factor of N should be considered when evaluating the amount of data that is needed for the attack, i.e., instead of recovering the permutation with 2^{14} keystreams and IVs the attack needs 2^{22} keystreams and IVs. The number of steps is proportional to the amount of IVs.

Notice that the attack is somewhat wasty as it always works with one location out of the ℓ_K locations that leak information to the keystream. This attack can thus be further optimized for at least partial reuse of the data. The optimized attack uses only N/ℓ_K values for $IV[0]$ that have additive differences of ℓ_K between them, and each of these values is reused for recovering ℓ_K permutation entries. This optimization improves the data complexity of the attack by a factor of ℓ_K and thus for a 16-byte key, the data complexity of the attack drops to 2^{20}. However, this optimization works only in the chosen IV model.

The last step of the attack is a recovery of the root key from the permutation. An efficient implementation of this stage is described in the appendix of [FMS01].

7   Fault Attack on RC4

In this section we describe a fault attack on RC4 that is based on realization of the fork model.

7.1   The Attack Model

We assume that the attacker can apply several types of faults to the cryptographic device; In a data fault the attacker causes some bit flipping changes to RAM or internal registers. In a flow Fault the attacker causes small changes to the flow of the executed program, e.g., skipping an instruction, changing the address of accessed memory, etc.

Following [HS04] we assume that the attacker has only limited control over the fault, that he can select the fault area but not a particular bit and that he has no knowledge on which fault eventually occurred and when exactly had it happened. As usually assumed in fault analysis, we assume that the attacker can reset the system with the same key, i.e., cause the system to get back to the original configuration, cancelling the previously made faults and reuse the same key. This model is somewhat conservative, but more realistic than a model where the attacker is more powerful.

7.2   The Attack

The objective of the attack is to recover the initial permutation of RC4 S_0, which is the output of the KSA and the input of the PRGA. Other permutations can be recovered through similar approach. The attacker injects to the PRGA process faults that change the progression of j, where in order to do that, the attacker needs to inject either a fault to j or a fault to one of the entries of S that are located closely after the index i.

The identical part of the instances is the execution until the fault and the divergence is in the fault. By reusing the analysis from Sect. 5 we conclude that the number of faults that are required for recovery of the state that precede the fault is 2^{14}.

8   Summary

In this paper we presented several new attacks of RC4, all relying on a combination of a leakage of state information to the keystream with a slow evolution of the state, both of which are inherent properties of RC4 fundamental mechanisms. Since the leakage is from a "moving target" part of the state we could not exploit it to attack the keystream generation of RC4 and the applicability of the attack is limited to particular modes of operation.

We proved the common belief that throwing 256 words removes all the vulnerabilities of RC4 initialization to be faulty by showing that the preceding IV mode remains weak even in this case. Despite of the fact that the attack is applicable only for a particular key-IV combination method, we believe that similar attacks on equivalent key-IV combination methods such as exclusive-or and succeeding IV, are not out of reach. RC4 KSA is intolerably sensitive to related key analysis and minimal control is sufficient for an attacker to direct this leakage to desired places.

RSA Security recommends in [RSA01] on employing *at least one* of omitting 256 bytes and employing stronger key-IV combination method. From our findings this recommendation turns to be insufficient as it "allows" modes of operation that are completely insecure. Our recommendation is to avoid using RC4 without employing both strengthening methods or at least to throw a longer prefix of the keystream as proposed by Mironov in [Mir02] .

In addition, we presented attacks on the succeeding IV mode than are stronger than previously known ones and a new fault attack that is comparable to known ones in its complexity.

References

[Fin94]   Hal Finney: An RC4 Cycle that Can't Happen. (1994)
[Roo95]   Andrew Roos: A Class of Weak Keys in the RC4 Stream Cipher. Posted to sci.crypt (1995)
[Jen96]   Robert J. Jenkins: Isaac and RC4.
           http://burtleburtle.net/bob/rand/isaac.html.
[Gol97]   Jovan Dj. Golić: Linear Statistical Weakness of Alleged RC4 Keystream Generator. EUROCRYPT 1997: 226-238
[KM+98]   Lars R. Knudsen, Willi Meier, Bart Preneel, Vincent Rijmen and Sven Verdoolaege: Analysis Methods for (Alleged) RC4. ASIACRYPT 1998: 327-341
[MT98]   Serge Mister, Stafford E. Tavares: Cryptanalysis of RC4-like Ciphers. Selected Areas in Cryptography 1998: 131-143
[Gol00]   Jovan Dj. Golić: Iterative Probabilistic Cryptanalysis of RC4 Keystream Generator. ACISP 2000: 220-233

[GW00]   Alexander L. Grosul and Dan S. Wallach: a Related-Key Cryptanalysis of
            RC4. Technical Report TR-00-358, Department of Computer Science, Rice
            University (2000)
[FM00]   Scott R. Fluhrer and David A. McGrew: Statistical Analysis of the Alleged
            RC4 Keystream Generator. FSE 2000: 19-30
[MS01]   Itsik Mantin and Adi Shamir: A Practical Attack on Broadcast RC4, FSE
            2001: 152-164
[FMS01]   Scott R. Fluhrer, Itsik Mantin and Adi Shamir: Weaknesses in the Key
            Scheduling Algorithm of RC4. Selected Areas in Cryptography 2001: 1-24
[Man01]   Itsik Mantin: The Security of the Stream Cipher RC4. Master Thesis (2001)
            The Weizmann Institue of Science
[SIR01]   Adam Stubblefield, John Ioannidis, Aviel D. Rubin: Using the Fluhrer,
            Mantin, and Shamir Attack to Break WEP. NDSS 2002
[RSA01]   RSA Security Response to Weaknesses in Key Scheduling Algorithm of RC4.
            Technical Report, RSA Data Security (2001)
[Mir02]   Ilya Mironov: (Not So) Random Shuffles of RC4. CRYPTO 2002: 304-319
[PP03]   Souradyuti Paul, Bart Preneel: Analysis of Non-fortuitous Predictive States
            of the RC4 Keystream Generator. INDOCRYPT 2003: 52-67
[PP04]   Souradyuti Paul, Bart Preneel: A New Weakness in the RC4 Keystream
            Generator and an Approach to Improve the Security of the Cipher. FSE
            2004: 245-259
[Zol04]   Bartosz Zoltak: VMPC One-Way Function and Stream Cipher. FSE 2004:
            210-225
[HS04]   Jonathan J. Hoch, Adi Shamir: Fault Analysis of Stream Ciphers. CHES
            2004: 240-253
[BGN05]   Eli Biham, Louis Granboulan, Phong Q. Nguyen: Impossible Fault Analysis
            of RC4 and Differential Fault Analysis of RC4. FSE 2005: 359-367
[Max05]   Alexander Maximov: Two Linear Distinguishing Attacks on VMPC and
            RC4A and Weakness of RC4 Family of Stream Ciphers. FSE 2005: 342-358
[Man05]   Itsik Mantin: Predicting and Distinguishing Attacks on RC4 Keystream
            Generator, EUROCRYPT 2005: 491-506
[TS+05]   Yukiyasu Tsunoo, Teruo Saito, Hiroyasu Kubo, Maki Shigeri, Tomoyasu
            Suzaki, and Takeshi Kawabata: The Most Efficient Distinguishing Attack
            on VMPC and RC4A, SKEW 2005

A   Availability of the Glimpse

The existence of the glimpse stems from the usage of permutation access of depth
two when selecting the output value. In Conjecture 1 we generalize the glimpse
in a different direction than Theorem 2 and claim that the glimpse will exist for
almost any output selection function of depth two.

We begin with defining a general output selection function. Let $f, g : [N] \to [N]$ be invertible functions and denote the corresponding inverse functions by F and G respectively. Let $h : [N] \times [N] \to [N]$ be a 2-parameter function that is invertible in each of its parameters, and let H_1 and H_2 be the inverse functions of h where

$$\forall X, Y \in [N], \ H_1(X, h(X,Y)) = Y, H_2(h(X,Y), Y) = X$$

Conjecture 1 (The Generalized Glimpse Conjecture).
Let $Z(S, i, j) \stackrel{def}{=} f(S[h(S[g(i)], S[j])])$ be an output selection function of an RC4-like keystream generator. Then,

$$\mathbb{P}_{j \in_R [N], S \in_R \mathcal{P}[N]}[S[j] = H_1(F(Z(S, i, j)), g(i))] \approx 2/N \qquad (14)$$

We will give the intuition behind Conjecture 1. In order to simplify the expressions we define $Z' \stackrel{def}{=} F \circ Z$ and $i' \stackrel{def}{=} g(i)$ and thus given that $Z'(S, i, j) \stackrel{def}{=} S[h(S[i'], S[j])]$ we need to show that

$$\mathbb{P}_{j \in_R [N], S \in_R \mathcal{P}[N]}[S[j] = H_1(Z'(S, i, j), i')] \approx 2/N \qquad (15)$$

We define two functions over the domain of RC4 states and two corresponding events. The internal dependency function $IDF(S, i', j)$ is defined as $h(S[i'], S[j])$ and the event where $i' = IDF(S, i', j)$ is denoted as A_{IDF}. The external dependency function $EDF(S, i', j)$ is defined as $H_1(Z'(S, i', j), i')$ and the event where $S[j] = EDF(S, i', j)$ is denoted as A_{EDF}. Our arguments follow the original proof of the glimpse.

We observe two cases. In the first case A_{IDF} occurs. In that case A_{EDF} occurs with probability 1 in the same manner as the original glimpse

$$z' \stackrel{def}{=} Z'(S, i, j) = S[h(S[i'], S[j])] = S[i'] \qquad (16)$$
$$i' = h(S[i'], S[j]) = h(z', S[j]) \qquad (17)$$
$$S[j] = H_1(z', i') = H_1(F(Z(S, i, j)), g(i)) \qquad (18)$$

In the other case, $IDF(S, i, j)$ is almost random and with the uncertainty in S and j causes a distribution that is very close to uniform for z'. Thus the probability of A_{EDF} is $1/N \cdot 1 + (1 - 1/N) \cdot 1/N \approx 2/N$.

B   RC4 State Evolution

RC4 permutation evolves fairly rapidly with the generation, where on every round two values change locations. The index i progresses in a predictive manner traversing the permutation sequentially and thus guarantees that no location or value is left untouched during a sequence of N rounds (it is possible that a value is swapped with itself). The index j adds pseudo-randomness to the state progression by jumping between the permutation entries in a seemingly unpredicted manner. However, when concentrating on a sequence that is shorter than N rounds, there are permutation entries which are guaranteed not to be visited by the index i, and these entries have relatively high probability not to be touched also by j during this sequence of rounds.

We formalize this situation in Lemma 1 and quote its proof from [Man05].

Lemma 1 (The Evolution Lemma). *Let $\mathcal{I}$ be a set of r permutation locations. Suppose that RC4 is in a state where the predictable course of the index i in the next k rounds avoids visiting $\mathcal{I}$. Then the probability of the permutation S k rounds later to have the values in $\mathcal{I}$ unchanged is approximately $e^{-kr/N}$.*

Proof. The index i does not reach any of the indices in $\mathcal{I}$. The index j progresses in a pseudo-random manner and reaches each of the r positions in each of the k rounds with probability $1/N$. Failing in these kr trials results with having the set $\mathcal{I}$ untouched and the probability of this event to occur is $(1-1/N)^{kr} \approx e^{-kr/N}$.

$\square$

In the special case where $r = 1$ and $k \leq N$ we have a bound of $1/e$ for the probability of a single value, located more than k entries ahead of i to remain in place during the following k rounds.

A Near-Practical Attack Against
B Mode of HBB

Joydip Mitra

Managemant Development Institute,
Post Box 60, Mehrauli Road, Sukhrali,
Gurgaon, Haryana, India 122001
joydip@mdi.ac.in

Abstract. Stream cipher Hiji-Bij-Bij (HBB) was proposed by Sarkar at Indocrypt'03. This cipher uses cellular automata (CA). The algorithm has two modes: a basic mode (B) and a self-synchronizing mode (SS). This article presents the first attack on B mode of HBB using 128 bit secret key. This is a known-pliantext guess-then-determine attack. The main step in the attack guesses 512 bits of unknown out of the 640 bits of the initial internal state. The guesses are done sequentially and the attack uses a breadth-first-search-type algorithm so that the time complexity is 2^{50}.

Keywords: cryptanalysis, known-plaintext attack, HBB, stream cipher.

1   Introduction

A typical stream cipher generates a long sequence of pseudo-random numbers, known as key-streams, from a given seed (a secret key). The plaintext message M is then XORed with the key stream to generate the ciphertext C. Thus, a steam cipher handles each bit of plaintext separately.

In this article, we will concentrate on the stream cipher HBB, proposed by Sarkar in Indocrypt'03 [1]. This is the first stream cipher replacing LFSR by CA. This is a classical masking-type stream cipher, i.e. it evolves a linear and a non-linear generator and XORs selected portions of these to produce the key stream. Thus, the design methodology is classical and there are other ciphers like SNOW which use the same principle. The non-linear part has some nice provable properties. These are aimed at resisting correlation and low diffusion attacks. The linear portion ensures a sequence of vectors with long period. Again, there are ciphers like SNOW [4] and TURING [5] which use such sequence generators. So, weakness in HBB is possibly in the way CA is used. The design has certain flaws that are to be considered while suggesting new ciphers involving CA. Ours is a guess-then-determine known-plaintext attack. The FSE'05 attack [2] was an algebraic attack. The present attack exploits structural weaknesses in greater depth than previously done. Some salient features of our attack are as follows:

(1) Exploits weakness in the use of CA. (2) Exploits the linearity in the mixing of the linear part to the non-linear part. (3) Proves an interesting property of the

B. Roy (Ed.): ASIACRYPT 2005, LNCS 3788, pp. 412–424, 2005.

nonlinear update function: Fixing the first 32 bits of the output of the nonlinear update function ensures that there are 2^{24} choices for each of the four 32-bit blocks of the input. While by itself this is not a weakness, this is combined with the first two properties to get an efficient attack.

The HBB cipher has two modes: basic mode (B) and self-synchronizing mode (SS). So far two articles have been found in the literature dealing with cryptanalysis of HBB. (Other articles on this topic are not known to the author.) Joux and Muller [2] have shown that the SS mode of HBB is not secured. They have also attacked the B mode. Their attack requires more than 2^{50} bits of known plaintext and more than 2^{142} time. Vlastimil Klima [3] has presented another attack, marginally faster than the one in [2], on B mode. His attack requires 34 blocks of known plaintext, i.e. 34×2^7 bits of known plaintext and its time complexity is 2^{140}. Thus, so far the B mode of HBB, using 128-bit secret key, seemed secured. The present work attacks only the B mode of HBB. This attack requires 225 blocks of consecutive plaintext to be known. It guesses 512 bits of internal state in a *sequential* manner, so that the time complexity does not exceed 2^{50}. Thus, the present attack is a near-practical one and shows that the B mode of HBB using even 128 bit secret key is also not secured.

The rest of the article is organized as follows: Section 2 describes one round of B mode of HBB. (Understanding of cellular automata (CA) is not required to follow this attack. Hence CA is not discussed.) Section 3 describes our first attack having time complexity 2^{61} for finding the initial internal state of 640 bits. Next, in Section 4, we improve this attack to get the unknown 640 bits of initial internal state in 2^{50} time. Finally we present our conclusion in Section 5, followed by references.

One reviewer has pointed out that some of the ideas used in the attack has earlier occurred in [7,8,9].

2   One Round of HBB

We start by describing one round of B mode of HBB encryption. We use two 256-bit constants given by:

$\mathcal{R}_0 = (\ 80ffaf46977969e971553bb599be6b2b \ 4b3372952308c787b84c7cce36d501e6 \ )_{16}$
$\mathcal{R}_1 = (\ dd18c62b153df31ac98e86c1910fee24 \ 2942d51b4201eb3dc1d1a85f57b8919b \ )_{16}$

And, a 128-bit string x will also be written as a 4×32 matrix

$$x = \begin{bmatrix} x_0 \\ x_1 \\ x_2 \\ x_3 \end{bmatrix}$$

where, $x = x_0 \| x_1 \| x_2 \| x_3$ and each x_i is a 32-bit string.

One Round of HBB Encryption One round of HBB encryption, i.e. encryption of i-th message block M_i, $i \geq 0$, is described as follows:

Algorithm 1. HBB Encrypt
Input: Plaintext M_i
Output: Ciphertext C_i
Internal State at the beginning of encryption:
   a) Non-linear core : $N_{i-1} = N_{i-1,0} \| \ldots \| N_{i-1,3}$
   b) Linear core   : $L_{i-1} = L_{i-1,0} \| \ldots \| L_{i-1,15}$
   /* each substring is 32-bit long */
Update internal state and compute key stream K_i and ciphertext C_i
   1. Update Linear Core /* $L_i = \text{NextState}(L_{i-1})$ */
      1.1 $LX_{i-1} = L_{i-1,0} \| \ldots \| L_{i-1,7}$; $LY_{i-1} = L_{i-1,8} \| \ldots \| L_{i-1,15}$;
      1.2 $LX_i = (LX_{i-1} \ll 1) \oplus (LX_{i-1} \gg 1) \oplus (LX_{i-1} \wedge \mathcal{R}_0)$;
      1.3 $LY_i = (LY_{i-1} \ll 1) \oplus (LY_{i-1} \gg 1) \oplus (LY_{i-1} \wedge \mathcal{R}_1)$;
      1.4 $L_i = LX_i \| LY_i$;
   2. Half-update Non-Linear Core /* $NZ_i = \text{updateNLC}(N_{i-1})$ */
      2.1 $NV_i = \text{NLSub}(N_{i-1})$;/* replace each byte by its image */
      2.2 $NW_i = \text{Delta}(NV_i)$;
             /* replace each word by XOR of other three words */
      2.3 $NX_i = \text{RotateLeft}(NW_i)$; /* rotate j-th word by $8 * j + 4$ bits */
      2.4 $NY_i = \text{FastTranspose}(NX_i)$;
             /* replace each 4×4 sub-matrix by its transpose */
      2.5 $NZ_i = \text{NLSub}(NY_i)$;
   3. Compute Key-Stream K_i
      $K_{i,0} = NZ_{i,0} \oplus L_{i,0}$; $K_{i,1} = NZ_{i,1} \oplus L_{i,7}$;
      $K_{i,2} = NZ_{i,2} \oplus L_{i,8}$; $K_{i,3} = NZ_{i,3} \oplus L_{i,15}$;
   4. Compute N_i /* updated non-linear core */
      $N_{i,0} = NZ_{i,0} \oplus L_{i,3}$; $N_{i,1} = NZ_{i,1} \oplus L_{i,4}$;
      $N_{i,2} = NZ_{i,2} \oplus L_{i,11}$; $N_{i,3} = NZ_{i,3} \oplus L_{i,12}$;
   5. Compute Ciphertext C_i
      $C_i = M_i \oplus K_i$;
Internal State at the end of encryption: N_i and L_i

3   A Simple Attack on HBB

Ours is a known-plaintext attack and we will assume that the key streams K_i
for $0 \le i \le 224$ are known. (This is equivalent to knowing (M_i, C_i) pair for
$0 \le i \le 224$.) From the knowledge of these key streams, using a guess-then-
determine attack, we will determine the entire internal state (L_0, N_0) (related
to encryption of first message block M_0). Sketch of our attack is given below.

Algorithm 2: Sketch of Attack against HBB
Assumption: Key streams K_i, for $0 \le i \le 224$, are known.
   1. Determine LX_0 /* unknown 256 bits */
   2. Determine LY_0 /* unknown 256 bits */
   3. Compute $N_0 = K_0 \oplus (L_{0,0} \| L_{0,7} \| L_{0,8} \| L_{0,15}) \oplus (L_{0,3} \| L_{0,4} \| L_{0,11} \| L_{0,12})$
   4. Proceed forward and break the rest of the cipher.

So, the complexity of attack is really the complexity of finding the unknown 512 bits of the linear core L_0. The method for determining LX_0 and LY_0 will be similar and will have same time complexities. So, we will only discuss attack against LX_0. Time complexity of our attack will be twice the time complexity of the attack against LX_0. Idea behind the attack against LX_0 is presented below.

Let us write $LX_0 = \ell \| b_0 b_1 \ldots b_{223}$ where ℓ is a 32-bit string and each b_i is a bit. We first note that, knowing $\ell \| b_0 \ldots b_{t-1}$ we can compute $L_{i,0}$ for $0 \leq i \leq t$ uniquely. (See Algorithm A1, Appendix A for pseudocode.) Since $K_{i,0}$ are known for $0 \leq i \leq t$, we also know $NZ_{i,0} = L_{i,0} \oplus K_{i,0}$ for $0 \leq i \leq t$. But if $NZ_{i,0}$ is fixed, then $N_{i-1,0}$ can have only 2^{24} possible choices. (This result is proved in Section 3.1.) For every fixed i, the set of all such possible choices of $N_{i,0}$ will be denoted by $\mathcal{N}_{i,0}$. For every $i = 0, \ldots t-1$, from $NZ_{i,0}$ (unique) and $N_{i,0}$ (one of 2^{24} choices) we get $L_{i,3} = NZ_{i,0} \oplus N_{i,0}$ (2^{24} choices). The set of all possible (2^{24}) choices of $L_{i,3}$ will be denoted by $\mathcal{L}_{i,3}$. Thus, we have,

$$\mathcal{L}_{i,3} = \{NZ_{i,0} \oplus N_{i,0} \; : \; N_{i,0} \in \mathcal{N}_{i,0}\}$$

Next we consider the update function of the linear core. Given a choice x of $L_{i,3}$, we know the middle 30 bits of corresponding choice y of $L_{i+1,3}$. We will write $x \Rightarrow y$ to denote this. So, given $\mathcal{L}_{0,3}$, an x_1 is a *valid* choice of $L_{1,3}$ only if for some $x_0 \in \mathcal{L}_{0,3}$ we get $x_0 \Rightarrow x_1$. But $\mathcal{L}_{1,3}$ is already obtained and we know that $x_1 \notin \mathcal{L}_{1,3}$ is *not* a valid choice of $L_{1,3}$. Hence, given $\mathcal{L}_{0,3}$ and $\mathcal{L}_{1,3}$, the valid choices of $L_{1,3}$ are given by the set

$$\mathcal{L}_{1,3}^V | \mathcal{L}_{0,3} = \{x_1 \in \mathcal{L}_{1,3} \; : \; x_0 \Rightarrow x_1 \text{ for some } x_0 \in \mathcal{L}_{0,3}\}$$

The super-script "V" stands for "valid". Similarly, given $\mathcal{L}_{0,3}$, $\mathcal{L}_{1,3}$ and $\mathcal{L}_{2,3}$, the valid choices of $L_{2,3}$ will be given by the set

$$\begin{aligned}
\mathcal{L}_{2,3}^V | \mathcal{L}_{0,3} &= \{x_2 \in \mathcal{L}_{2,3} \; : \; x_0 \Rightarrow x_1 \Rightarrow x_2 \text{ for some } x_0 \in \mathcal{L}_{0,3}, \; x_1 \in \mathcal{L}_{1,3}\} \\
&= \{x_2 \in \mathcal{L}_{2,3} \; : \; x_1 \Rightarrow x_2 \text{ for some } x_1 \in \mathcal{L}_{1,3}^V | \mathcal{L}_{0,3}\}
\end{aligned}$$

We now define the following sets

$$\mathcal{N}_{i,0}^V = \{x \oplus NZ_{i,0} \; : \; x \in \mathcal{L}_{i,3}^V | \mathcal{L}_{0,3}\}$$

As a convention, we take $\mathcal{N}_{0,0}^V = \mathcal{N}_{0,0}$. Proceeding this way we can find $\mathcal{N}_{i,0}^V$ for $0 \leq i \leq t-1$ and for a wrong choice of $\ell \| b_0 \ldots b_{223}$, the set $\mathcal{N}_{223,0}^V$ will be empty. This constitutes an attack against LX_0. The idea is summarized below.

Algorithm 3: Idea behind first attack against LX_0

Guess $\ell \| b_0 \ldots b_{t-1}$					
Compute	$L_{0,0}$	$L_{1,0}$	$\ldots$	$L_{t-1,0}$	$L_{t,0}$ (unique choice)
Compute	$NZ_{0,0}$	$NZ_{1,0}$	$\ldots$	$NZ_{t-1,0}$	$NZ_{t,0}$ (unique choice)
Compute	$\mathcal{N}_{0,0}$	$\mathcal{N}_{1,0}$	$\ldots$	$\mathcal{N}_{t-1,0}$	$\mathcal{N}_{t,0}$ (2^{24} choices)
Compute	$\mathcal{N}_{0,0}^V$	$\mathcal{N}_{1,0}^V$	$\ldots$	$\mathcal{N}_{t-1,0}^V$	(shrinking sets)

Certain finer points are to be noted. First, if at any stage $\mathcal{N}_{i,0}^V = \phi$ then $\mathcal{N}_{223,0}^V = \phi$. So, we need not compute $\mathcal{N}_{223,0}^V$ to declare a choice $\ell \| b_0 \ldots b_{223}$ of LX_0 to be wrong, and we can guess these bits in LX_0 *sequentially*. Second, we can compute $\mathcal{N}_{i,0}^V$ without computing $\mathcal{L}_{i,3}^V | \mathcal{L}_{0,3}$ and without explicitly computing even $\mathcal{N}_{i,0}$. (This computation and reason for doing this are explained in section 3.2.) Third point is a more important one. Suppose ℓ in LX_0 is fixed and suppose for all possible choices of $b_0 \ldots b_{t-1}$, we have computed the sets $\mathcal{N}_{t,0}^V$. These sets can be kept in a binary tree T. Root of T will be ℓ. For every other non-leaf node $y \in T$, its left (right) child will be the string $y \| 0$ ($y \| 1$). The node represented by x in T, with $|x| = 32 + t$ bits, will contain the set $\mathcal{N}_{t-1,0}^V$ for $x = \ell \| b_0 \ldots b_{t-1}$ *only if* $\mathcal{N}_{t-1,0}^V \neq \phi$. Thus T may have 2^t nodes at level t. The actual number may be less if some of the sets $\mathcal{N}_{t-1,0}^V$ are empty. (Level of root is zero.) Now from each of the sets $\mathcal{N}_{t-1,0}^V$ at level t of T, and for each choice of $b_t = 0, 1$, we will compute $\mathcal{N}_{t,0}^V$. But the resulting set will be added to the tree only if it is non-empty. It will be argued that this breadth-first type processing of sets can be done in 2^{48} time giving LX_0.

Below the two sections (3.1 and 3.2) contain our results and algorithms to be used in the subsequently explained attack and its complexity (Section 3.3).

3.1 Determine $N_{i-1,0}$ from $NZ_{i,0}$

Suppose we know $NZ_{i,0}$ for some $i \geq 1$. Since,

$$NY_{i,0} = \text{NLSub}^{-1}(NZ_{i,0})$$

we can find out $NY_{i,0} = (y_{31} \ldots y_0)$. Since FastTranspose transposes every 4×4 sub-matrix of its input, it is an idempotent function. Thus using $NY_i = \text{FastTranspose}(NX_i)$ we get $NX_i = \text{FastTranspose}(NY_i)$ and hence,

$$NX_i = \begin{bmatrix} y_{31} & y_{27} & y_{23} & y_{19} & y_{15} & y_{11} & y_7 & y_3 \\ y_{30} & y_{26} & y_{22} & y_{18} & y_{14} & y_{10} & y_6 & y_2 \\ y_{29} & y_{25} & y_{21} & y_{17} & y_{13} & y_9 & y_5 & y_1 \\ y_{28} & y_{24} & y_{20} & y_{16} & y_{12} & y_8 & y_4 & y_0 \end{bmatrix} {}_* {}_* {}_* {}_* {}_* {}_* {}_* {}_*$$

where every " $*$ " represents an unknown 4×3 matrix of bits. But NX_i was calculated as RotateLeft(NW_i) and so, NW_i can be computed as

$$NW_i = \text{RotateRight}(NX_i)$$

where j-th word of NX_i is given a circular rotation by $8 * j + 4$ bits. Hence,

$$NW_i = \begin{bmatrix} y_3 & y_{31} & y_{27} & y_{23} & y_{19} & y_{15} & y_{11} & y_7 \\ y_{10} & y_6 & y_2 & y_{30} & y_{26} & y_{22} & y_{18} & y_{14} \\ y_{17} & y_{13} & y_9 & y_5 & y_1 & y_{29} & y_{25} & y_{21} \\ y_{24} & y_{20} & y_{16} & y_{12} & y_8 & y_4 & y_0 & y_{28} \end{bmatrix} {}_* {}_* {}_* {}_* {}_* {}_* {}_* {}_*$$

where every " $*$ " represents an unknown 4×3 matrix of bits. Next, we note that "Delta" is also an idempotent operation, and hence, $NV_i = \text{Delta}(NW_i)$. So, if we write $NV_{i,0} = v_{31} \ldots v_0$ then,

$$v_{31} = y_{10} \oplus y_{17} \oplus y_{24}$$
$$v_{27} = y_6 \oplus y_{13} \oplus y_{20}$$
$$v_{23} = y_2 \oplus y_9 \oplus y_{16}$$
$$v_{19} = y_{30} \oplus y_5 \oplus y_{12}$$
$$v_{15} = y_{26} \oplus y_1 \oplus y_8$$
$$v_{11} = y_{22} \oplus y_{29} \oplus y_4$$
$$v_7 = y_{18} \oplus y_{25} \oplus y_0$$
$$v_3 = y_{14} \oplus y_{21} \oplus y_{28}$$

Thus, given $NZ_{i,0}$, we know 8 specified bits of $NV_{i,0}$. In particular, we know 2 bits of every byte of $NV_{i,0}$. Finally note that, $N_{i-1,0} = \text{NLSub}^{-1}(NV_{i,0})$ and hence, given $NZ_{i,0}$ we know 8 bits of image (NLSub) of $N_{i-1,0}$. To make this formal, let us define two functions $g_1(x)$, $g_2(x) : \{0,1\}^{32} \to \{0,1\}^8$ as follows:

Function $g_1(x)$
1. Compute $y = \text{NLSub}(x) = y_{31} \ldots y_0$
2. Compute $a = y_{31} y_{27} y_{23} y_{19} y_{15} y_{11} y_7 y_3$
3. Return a

Function $g_2(x)$
1. Compute $y = \text{NLSub}^{-1}(x) = y_{31} \ldots y_0$
2. **for** $j = 0, \ldots, 7$ **do**
3. $a_j = y_{14+4j} \oplus y_{21+4j} \oplus y_{28+4j}$ (subscripts are computed mod 32)
4. **end-do**
5. Compute $a = a_7 a_6 a_5 a_4 a_3 a_2 a_1 a_0$
6. Return a

Also, for $a \in \{0,1\}^8$, define the following sets:

$$\mathcal{N}^*(a) = \{x \in \{0,1\}^{32} : g_1(x) = a\} \tag{1}$$

Then, using functions g_1, g_2 and sets $\mathcal{N}^*(a)$, we have the following proposition:

Proposition 1. *Given $NZ_{i,0}$, there are exactly 2^{24} choices of $N_{i-1,0}$ given by:*

$$\mathcal{N}_{i-1,0} = \mathcal{N}^*(g_2(NZ_{i,0}))$$

In particular, every byte of $N_{i-1,0}$ can have 2^6 choices.

3.2 Compute $\mathcal{N}_{t+1,0}^V$ from $\mathcal{N}_{t,0}^V$

For k-bit strings $x = x_{k-1} \ldots x_0$ and $r = r_{k-1} \ldots r_0$, with $k > 2$, define the following:

1. $m(x)$ will denote the string obtained from x by deleting its MSB and LSB.
2. $f(x,r) = (x_{k-2} \ldots x_0 \| 0) \oplus (0 \| x_{k-1} \ldots x_1) \oplus (x \wedge r)$.

Using this notation, $y\prime \in \mathcal{L}^V_{t+1,3}|\mathcal{L}_{0,3}$ if and only if $y\prime \in \mathcal{L}_{t+1,3}$ and, for some choice $x\prime \in \mathcal{L}^V_{t,3}|\mathcal{L}_{0,3}$, we get

$$m(f(x\prime, r)) = m(y\prime) \tag{2}$$

with r chosen suitably from definition of EvolveCA function given in HBB [1].

Lemma 1. *Fix* $y = y_{31} \ldots y_0$. *Then* $y \in \mathcal{N}^V_{t+1,0}$ *if and only if* $y \in \mathcal{N}_{t+1,0}$ *and for some* $x \in \mathcal{N}^V_{t,0}$ *and some* $\epsilon_{31}, \epsilon_0 \in \{0,1\}$,

$$\epsilon_{31}\|m(f(x \oplus NZ_{t,0}, r)) \oplus m(NZ_{t+1,0})\|\epsilon_0 = y \tag{3}$$

Proof. The proof follows using equation 2.

To check if $y \in \mathcal{N}_{t+1,0}$, we use the fact that,

$$\mathcal{N}_{t+1,0} = \mathcal{N}^*(g_2(NZ_{t+2,0})) = \{y \ : \ g_1(y) = g_2(NZ_{t+2,0})\}$$

So, we can compute $\mathcal{N}^V_{t+1,0}$ as follows: Initialize sets $D1[j]$, $0 \leq j < 256$ as empty sets. For each $x \in \mathcal{N}^V_{t,0}$ and for every $\epsilon_{31}, \epsilon_0 \in \{0,1\}$, we compute y as in equation 3. Then insert y to the set $D1[g1(y)]$. Once we have exhausted $\mathcal{N}^V_{t,0}$, we set $\mathcal{N}^V_{t+1,0}$ as $D1[g2(NZ_{t+2,0})]$. The pseudocode is given below.

Algorithm 4. Computation of $\mathcal{N}^V_{t+1,0}$ from $\mathcal{N}^V_{t,0}$
```
0.  for v1 = 0 to 255 do
1.      D1(v1) ← φ /* set initialized by φ */
2.  end-do
3.  for every x ∈ N^V_{t,0} do
4.      z ← m(f(x ⊕ NZ_{t,0}, r)) ⊕ m(NZ_{t+1,0})
5.      for (ε_{31}, ε_0) ∈ {0,1}² do
6.          Set y ← ε_{31}‖z‖ε_0
7.          Add y to the set D1[g1(y)]
8.      end-do
9.  end-do
10. N^V_{t+1,0} ← D1[g2(NZ_{t+2,0})]
```

This computation of $\mathcal{N}^V_{t+1,0}$ has two major advantages: First, we do not need to maintain the set $\mathcal{N}_{t+1,0}$ (having 2^{24} elements) explicitly and hence no time is required to handle such sets. Second advantage is that we can compute the sets $D1[v]$ for $0 \leq v < 256$ without the knowledge of $NZ_{t+2,0}$. This is going to be useful while finding the value of LX_0.

3.3   Algorithm to Determine LX_0

All valid choices of LX_0 will be found and will constitute a list FX. Writing $LX_0 = L_{0,0}\|b_0b_1 \ldots b_{223}$, we can find FX as union of sets $FX(\ell)$ that represents all valid choices of LX_0 with $L_{0,0} = \ell$. For a given value ℓ of $L_{0,0}$, we will now construct the set $FX(\ell)$. Suppose, we have a list $F0(t)$ of tuples $(y, n_0, n_1, D[y])$ having the following interpretation:

1. n_0 represents $NZ_{t,0}$ when $\ell\|b_0\ldots,b_t = y$,
2. n_1 represents $NZ_{t+1,0}$ when $\ell\|b_0\ldots,b_t = y$, and
3. $D[y]$ represents $\mathcal{N}_{t,0}^V$ when $\ell\|b_0\ldots b_t = y$.

Then, y is an invalid choice of $\ell\|b_0\ldots,b_t$ if $D[y]$ is empty. So, we also put the restriction on $F0(t)$ that it will contain only those tuples $(y, n_0, n_1, D[y])$ for which $D[y]$ is non-empty. With this interpretation, clearly $FX(\ell) = F0(223)$. If for some $t < 223$ the set $F0(t)$ is empty, then the set $F0(223)$ is also empty. Hence, the following steps will compute $FX(\ell)$ for $L_{0,0} = \ell$.

Step 1 Build list $F0(0)$

Using $K = K_{0,0}$, compute $n_0 = NZ_{0,0} = L_{0,0} \oplus K$ and, initialize the list $F0$ by ϕ. Next take, $K = K_{1,0}$ and for each $b = b_0 \in \{0,1\}$, set $y \leftarrow \ell\|b$, compute $L_{1,0}$ from $\ell\|b$, and then compute

$$n_1 = NZ_{1,0} = L_{1,0} \oplus K$$

Define $D[y] = \mathcal{N}^*(g_2(n1))$ and add the following tuple to the list $F0(0)$:

$$(y,\ n0,\ n1,\ D[y])$$

provided the set $D[y]$ is non-empty. Thus, $F0(0)$ now looks like the following:

$$F0(0) = \{(\ell\|0, n_0, n_1, D[\ell\|0]),\ (\ell\|1, n_0, n_1, D[\ell\|1])\}$$

The set $D[\ell\|0]$ represents $\mathcal{N}_{0,0}^V$ for $L_{0,0} = \ell$ and $b_0 = 0$. The other sets in the list $F0(0)$ has similar interpretations. This completes our computation of $F0(0)$. In the remaining steps, we will build list $F0(t + 1)$ from $F0(t)$.

Step 2 Set $t \leftarrow 0$.

Step 3 Compute $F0(t + 1)$ from $F0(t)$

For each tuple in $F0(t)$, we first generate sets $D1(v1)$ for $0 \leq v1 < 256$ using Algorithm 3. Then for every value of $b \in \{0,1\}$, we compute the corresponding $\mathcal{N}_{t+1,0}^V$ as follows:

1. Compute $L_{t+2,0}$ from $y\|b$ as in Algorithm A2, Appendix A.
2. Compute $NZ_{t+2,0} = L_{t+2,0} \oplus K_{t+2,0}$,
3. Set $D[y\|b] = D1(g_2(NZ_{t+2,0}))$,
4. Add a tuple $(y\|b, n_1, NZ_{t+2,0}, D[y\|b])$ to $F0(t+1)$ only if $D[y\|b]$ is non-empty.

Note that, $y\|b$ represents a valid choice of $\ell\|b_0\ldots b_t b_{t+1}$ if and only if the set $D[y\|b]$ is non-empty. For such valid choices of $\ell\|b_0\ldots b_t b_{t+1}$, the corresponding tuples are put in a list $F0(t + 1)$. Once, we have exhausted all the elements in the list $F0(t)$, we have generated $F0(t + 1)$. Again, elements in $F0(t + 1)$ will have interpretations (similar to that) given in the beginning of this step. Finally, this computation of $F0(t + 1)$ from $F0(t)$ is presented in the following algorithm.

Algorithm 5. Compute $F0(t+1)$ from $F0(t)$

  0. **for** each $(y, n_0, n_1, D[y]) \in F0(t)$ **do**

    1.   Compute $D1(0), \ldots, D1(255)$ from D[y] using Algorithm 3.

    2.   **for** $b \in \{0, 1\}$ **do**

    3.   Compute $n_2 = NZ_{t+2,0}$ from y, b and $K_{t+2,0}$.

    4.   Set $D[y\|b] = D1[g_2(n_2)]$.

    5.   **if** $D[y\|b]$ is non-empty

    6.   **then** Add tuple $(y\|b, n_1, n_2, D[y\|b])$ to $F0(t+1)$.

    7.   **end-if**

    8.   **end-do**

  9. **end-do**

Step 4 $t \leftarrow t + 1$

Step 5 Check for loop

    If now $t < 223$ and the list $F0(t)$ is non-empty, go to Step 3.

Step 6 Compute $FX(\ell)$

    Set $FX(\ell) \leftarrow F0(t)$.

We now argue that this process does not lead to handling of infinite sets. We have seen *empirically* that for every choice of $NZ_{0,0}$, $NZ_{1,0}$ and $NZ_{2,0}$, the set $D[\ell\|b_0 b_1]$ has less than 2^{21} elements for each possible choice of $\ell\|b_0 b_1$. In other words, the size of $D[\ell\|b_0 b_1]$ is at most 1/8-th of the size of $D[\ell\|b_0]$. But for every b_0, there are two choices of b_1. Hence, if η_t denotes the total number of 32-bit strings contained in the $D[\ ]$ sets of list $F0(t)$, then

$$\eta_1 \leq \frac{1}{4}\eta_0 = 2^{-2}\eta_0$$

Proceeding this way, we will have $\eta_t \leq 2^{-t}\eta_0$. Note that, $F0(0)$ contains two tuples, each of which contains a set $D[\ ]$ of 2^{24} elements. Thus, $\eta_0 = 2^{24} + 2^{24} = 2^{25}$. So, the total number of 32-bit strings contained in all $F0(t)$ for $0 \leq t \leq 223$ is

$$\sum_{t=0}^{223} \eta_t < \sum_{t \geq 0} \eta_t = \eta_0 \sum_{t \geq 0} 2^{-2t} < 2^{26}$$

Now, from Algorithms 4 and 5, it is clear that, during the computation of $F0(t+1)$ from $F0(t)$, each string from each set $D[\ ]$ in $F0(t)$ will be processed only once. And for each such processing, we will consider four possible choices of ϵ_{31} and ϵ_0. Hence the total number of computation of strings in the entire process of finding $FX(\ell)$ is given by

$$4 \times \sum_{t=0}^{223} \eta_t < 4 \times 2^{26} = 2^{28} \tag{4}$$

Now note that there are 2^{32} choices of ℓ and so, we have proved the following:

Proposition 2. *For every fixed value of ℓ, the set $FX(\ell)$ can be computed in less than 2^{28} time. And so, time complexity of finding the set FX is $2^{32} \times 2^{28} = 2^{60}$. In other words, time complexity of finding LX_0 is 2^{60}.*

Since each element in $F0(t)$ gives rise to at most two tuples in $F0(t+1)$, and since $F0(0)$ has two tuples, number of tuples in $F0(t)$ will be at most 2^{t+1}. The $D[\ ]$ sets in all these tuples will together contain $\eta_t = 2^{25-2t}$ strings. Hence for $t > 8$, some sets $D[\ ]$ are bound to be empty. For example, for $k = 10$, the list $F0$ is supposed to contain at most 2^{11} tuples, and the $D[\ ]$ sets will have at most 2^5 strings. So, $F0(10)$ can not contain more than 2^5 valid tuples (with corresponding non-empty set $D[\ ]$). Thus, the list $F0(\ )$ will go on shrinking for $t > 8$. Hence, we are going to get a singleton set FX.

Complexity of First Attack Against HBB: By Proposition 2, LX_0 can be found in 2^{60} time. Time complexity for finding LY_0 will be the same and so, time complexity of our first attack against B–mode of HBB has time complexity:

$$2^{60} + 2^{60} = 2^{61}.$$

4   A Faster Attack

This attack is almost same as the first attack, except for computation of the set $\mathcal{N}_{t,0}^V$. We first note the following: Fix $t \geq 0$. Let $N_{t,0} = H \| L$ where H (L) is a 16-bit string and "$\|$" represents concatenation of strings. Then, by Proposition 1, H (L) will have 2^{12} choices. We will denote the collection of all such choices of H (L) by $\mathcal{HN}_{t,0}$ ($\mathcal{LN}_{t,0}$) and write $N_{t,0} = \mathcal{HN}_{t,0} \| \mathcal{LN}_{t,0}$. We will now mimic the computation of $\mathcal{N}_{t,0}^V$ from the sets $\mathcal{N}_{i,0}$ $0 \leq i \leq t+1$. In the same way, we can compute the set $\mathcal{HN}_{t,0}^V$ from the sets $\mathcal{HN}_{i,0}$ $0 \leq i \leq t+1$. The pseudocode is given in Algorithm A3, Appendix A. Similarly, we can compute $\mathcal{LN}_{t,0}^V$. (For pseudocode, see Algorithm A4, Appendix A.) Clearly, $\mathcal{N}_{t,0}^V$ will be a subset of $\mathcal{HN}_{t,0}^V \| \mathcal{LN}_{t,0}^V$. If for any t, one of the sets $\mathcal{HN}_{t,0}^V$ or $\mathcal{LN}_{t,0}^V$ is empty, so will be $\mathcal{N}_{t,0}^V$. So, we will only compute $\mathcal{HN}_{t,0}^V$ for $t \geq 0$. The computation follows similar steps as in Section 3.3. Thus, our faster attack can be described by the following algorithm:

Algorithm 6. Sketch of faster attack

Guess $\ell \| b_0 \ldots b_{t-1}$					
Compute	$L_{0,0}$	$L_{1,0}$ $\ldots$	$L_{t-1,0}$	$L_{t,0}$	(unique choice)
Compute	$NZ_{0,0}$	$NZ_{1,0}$ $\ldots$	$NZ_{t-1,0}$	$NZ_{t,0}$	(unique choice)
Compute	$\mathcal{HN}_{0,0}$	$\mathcal{HN}_{1,0}$ $\ldots$	$\mathcal{HN}_{t-1,0}$	$\mathcal{HN}_{t,0}$	(2^{12} choices)
Compute	$\mathcal{HN}_{0,0}^V$	$\mathcal{HN}_{1,0}^V$ $\ldots$	$\mathcal{HN}_{t-1,0}^V$		(shrinking sets)

For computations of $\mathcal{HN}_{t,0}^V$, we introduce the following functions:

Function $g_3(x)$: $\{0,1\}^{16} \to \{0,1\}^4$
1. Compute $y = \mathrm{NLSub}(x) = y_{15} \ldots y_0$
2. Compute $a = y_{15} y_{11} y_7 y_3$
3. Return a

Function $g_4(x) : \{0,1\}^{32} \to \{0,1\}^4$
1. Compute $y = \mathrm{NLSub}^{-1}(x) = y_{31} \ldots y_0$
2. **for** $j = 0, \ldots, 7$ **do**
3. $a_j = y_{14+4j} \oplus y_{21+4j} \oplus y_{28+4j}$ (subscripts are computed mod 32)
4. **end-do**
5. Compute $a = a_7 a_6 a_5 a_4$
6. Return a

Function $g_5(x) : \{0,1\}^{32} \to \{0,1\}^4$
1. Compute $y = \mathrm{NLSub}^{-1}(x) = y_{31} \ldots y_0$
2. **for** $j = 0, \ldots, 7$ **do**
3. $a_j = y_{14+4j} \oplus y_{21+4j} \oplus y_{28+4j}$ (subscripts are computed mod 32)
4. **end-do**
5. Compute $a = a_3 a_2 a_1 a_0$
6. Return a

Now for $a \in \{0,1\}^4$, defining the sets $\mathcal{J}^*(a) = \{x \in \{0,1\}^{16} : g_3(x) = a\}$, we get the following from Proposition 1:

$$\mathcal{HN}_{i-1,0} = \mathcal{J}^*(g_4(NZ_{i,0})) \text{ and, } \mathcal{LN}_{i-1,0} = \mathcal{J}^*(g_5(NZ_{i,0}))$$

where each set $\mathcal{J}^*(\ )$ contains 2^{12} elements. The pseudocodes are given in Algorithm A3 and A4 of Appendix A. We have seen *empirically* that, for $t \geq 0$,

$$\frac{\text{size of } \mathcal{HN}^V_{t+1,0}}{\text{size of } \mathcal{HN}^V_{t,0}} < \frac{1}{2\sqrt{2}} \quad \text{and,} \quad \frac{\text{size of } \mathcal{LN}^V_{t+1,0}}{\text{size of } \mathcal{LN}^V_{t,0}} < \frac{1}{2\sqrt{2}}$$

So, in this revised faster attack, each initial tuple contains one set, of cardinality 2^{12} (as opposed to 2^{24} elements in the first attack). Define π_t to be the sum of cardinalities of all surviving $\mathcal{HN}^V_{t,0}$ sets, for all values of $\ell \| b_0 \ldots b_t$ with fixed ℓ. Then, $\pi_t \leq \frac{1}{\sqrt{2}} \pi_{t-1}$. So, the complexity of finding $FX(\ell)$ for a given ℓ is

$$4 \times \sum_{t=0}^{223} \pi_t < 4 \times 2^{13} \times \sum_{t=0}^{223} \left(\frac{1}{\sqrt{2}}\right)^t \leq 2^{17}$$

as opposed to 2^{28} (equation 4) for the first attack. So, this revised attack is faster than the first attack by a margin of $2^{11} (= 2^{28}/2^{17})$. In other words, the time required to find L_0 is given by: $2^{61}/2^{11} = 2^{50}$.

5   Conclusion

We have presented an attack against the B mode of HBB. The time complexity of the attack is 2^{50} requiring 225 blocks of plaintext to be known. Thus, HBB using even 128-bit secret key is also not secured. We think there are certain design weaknesses in HBB shown by our attack: (1) Improper use of CA generator.

knowing any p bits of the CA at any point of time ensures that one knows $p - 2$ bits of the CA in the next time point. This is crucial and previously unobserved property of the CA. Compared to an LFSR, it is this property that makes CA much more susceptible to guess-then-determine attacks. This is a lesson on the secure CA usage. (2) The key stream is produced by XORing a portion of the linear and the nonlinear part. Further the nonlinear part is updated by mixing a separate portion of the linear part into it. While this mixing is necessary, the manner in which it is done is not correct. The linear part is simple XORed into the nonlinear part creating a weakness that can again be exploited in a guess-then-determine attack. (This property allows the recent algebraic attack on HBB.) On the other hand, SNOW also updates the nonlinear part by mixing with the linear part. But this mixing is effected by an addition modulo 2^{32}. In fact, as has been recently observed that if this addition is replaced by a XOR, SNOW also becomes weak and susceptible to algebraic attacks [6]. (3) Too much of the state is revealed by HBB. In order to achieve efficiency, the entire nonlinear part is mixed with a portion of the linear part to produce the 128-bit keystream block. Again this is an undesirable thing to do and makes the verification stage of the guess-then-determine attack easier. Thus, to develop a cipher using CA, a designer should avoid the above pitfalls.

If an LFSR is used instead of a CA, then the described attack will not hold. Whether the attack can be modified to also hold for LFSR is still an open problem. Implementation of the attack can be obtained from the author.

References

1. Palash Sarkar. Hiji-Bij-Bij: A New Stream Cipher with a Self-Synchronizing Mode of Operation. In T. Johansson and S. Maitra, editors, *Progress in Cryptology - INDOCRYPT'03, volume 2904 of Lecture Notes in Computer Science, pages 36-51, Springer Verlag.*
2. Antoine Joux and Frederic Muller: Two Attacks against the HBB Stream Cipher. In *FSE'05, pages 341-353.*
3. Vlastimil Klima: Cryptanalysis of Hiji-bij-bij (HBB). In *Cryptology ePrint Archive: Report 2005/003.*
4. P. Ekdahl and T. Johansson: A new version of the stream cipher SNOW. In K. Nyberg and H Heys, editors, *Selected Areas in Cryptography, 9th Annual International Workshop, SAC 2002, volume 2595 of Lecture Notes in Computer Science, pages 47-61. Springer-Verlag, Berlin, 2003.*
5. G. Rose and P. Hawkes: Turing: a fast software stream cipher. In *Rump session of Crypto 2002, http://people.qualcomm.com/ggr/QC/Turing.tgz*
6. Olivier Billet, Henri Gilbert: Resistance of SNOW 2.0 Against Algebraic Attacks. In *CTRSA 2005, pages 19-28.*
7. J. Golic: Cryptanalysis of three mutually clock-controlled stop/go shift registers. In *IEEE Trans. Information Theory, vol. 46, pages 1081-1090, May 2000.*
8. J. Golic, A. Clark and E. Dawson: Generalized inversion attack on nonlinear filter generators. In *IEEE Trans. Computers, vol. 49, pages 1100-1109, Oct. 2000.*
9. J. Golic: Multibit cascades may be vulnerable to inversion attack. In *Electronics Letters, vol. 36(18), pages 1536-1538, Aug. 2000.*

Appendix A

Algorithm A1. Compute $L_{i,0}$ $0 \leq i \leq t$ from $\ell \| b_0 \ldots b_{t-1}$
1. $\mathcal{R}_{0,t} \leftarrow$ most significant $32 + t$ bits of $\mathcal{R}_0$
2. $x \leftarrow \ell \| b_0 \ldots b_{t-1}$; $L_{0,0} = \ell$;
3. **for** $i = 0$ to $t - 1$ **do**
4. $x \leftarrow (x \ll 1) \oplus (x \gg 1) \oplus (x \wedge \mathcal{R}_{0,t})$;
5. $L_{i+1,0} =$ most significant 32 bits of x ;
6. **end-do**

Algorithm A2. Compute $L_{t+2,0}$ from $\ell \| b_0 \ldots b_{t+1}$
1. $x \leftarrow \ell \| b_0 \ldots b_t b_{t+1}$;
2. **for** $i = 0$ to $t + 1$ **do**
3. $x \leftarrow (x \ll 1) \oplus (x \gg 1) \oplus (x \wedge \mathcal{R}_{0,t+1})$;
4. **end-do**
5. $L_{t+2,0} =$ most significant 32 bits of x ;

Algorithm A3. Computation of $\mathcal{HN}_{t+1,0}^V$ from $\mathcal{HN}_{t,0}^V$
  1.   **for** $v1 = 0$ to 15 **do**
  2. $HD1(v1) \leftarrow \phi$ /* set initialized by ϕ */
  3.   **end-do**
  4. $NZ_{t+1,0} = nz_{t+1,1} \| nz_{t+1,0}$ /* each sub-string has 16 bits */
  5. $NZ_{t,0} = nz_{t,1} \| nz_{t,0}$ /* each sub-string has 16 bits */
  6.   **for** every $x \in \mathcal{HN}_{t,0}^V$ **do**
  7. $z \leftarrow m(f(x \oplus nz_{t,1}, r1)) \oplus m(nz_{t+1,1})$
  8.   **for** $(\delta_{31}, \delta_{16}) \in \{0,1\}^2$ **do**
  9.   Set $z^* \leftarrow \delta_{31} \| z \| \delta_{16}$
  10.   Add z^* to the set $HD1(g_3(z^*))$
  11.   **end-do**
  12.   **end-do**
  13. $\mathcal{HN}_{t+1,0}^V \leftarrow HD1(g_4(NZ_{t+2,0}))$

Algorithm A4. Computation of $\mathcal{LN}_{t+1,0}^V$ from $\mathcal{LN}_{t,0}^V$
  1.   **for** $v1 = 0$ to 15 **do**
  2. $LD1(v1) \leftarrow \phi$ /* set initialized by ϕ */
  3.   **end-do**
  4. $NZ_{t+1,0} = nz_{t+1,1} \| nz_{t+1,0}$ /* each sub-string has 16 bits */
  5. $NZ_{t,0} = nz_{t,1} \| nz_{t,0}$ /* each sub-string has 16 bits */
  6.   **for** every $x \in \mathcal{LN}_{t,0}^V$ **do**
  7. $z \leftarrow m(f(x \oplus nz_{t,0}, r0)) \oplus m(nz_{t+1,0})$
  8.   **for** $(\delta_{15}, \delta_0) \in \{0,1\}^2$ **do**
  9.   Set $z^* \leftarrow \delta_{15} \| z \| \delta_0$
  10.   Add z^* to the set $LD1(g_3(z^*))$
  11.   **end-do**
  12.   **end-do**
  13. $\mathcal{LN}_{t+1,0}^V \leftarrow LD1(g_5(NZ_{t+2,0}))$

Here, $r1$ and $r0$ are chosen suitably from $\mathcal{R}_0$ (Section 2).

New Improvements of Davies-Murphy Cryptanalysis

Sébastien Kunz-Jacques and Frédéric Muller

DCSSI Crypto Lab,
51, boulevard de La Tour-Maubourg,
75700 PARIS-07 SP
{Sebastien.Kunz-Jacques, Frederic.Muller}@sgdn.pm.gouv.fr

Abstract. In this paper, we revisit the famous Davies-Murphy cryptanalysis of DES. First we improve its complexity down to the analysis of 2^{45} chosen plaintexts, by considering 6 distributions instead of 7. The previous improvement of the attack by Biham and Biryukov costed 2^{50} known plaintexts. This new result is better than differential cryptanalysis but slightly worse than linear cryptanalysis. Secondly, we explore the link between this attack and other cryptanalysis techniques, in particular linear cryptanalysis.

1 Introduction

DES (Data Encryption Standard) is a popular encryption algorithm published in the late 70's by the American National Bureau of Standards (NBS) for governmental use [12]. DES is a block cipher encrypting blocks of data of length 64 bits under a secret key of length 56 bits. DES quickly became a popular cipher and is still widely used today. Although it has been replaced by the more recent AES [13], DES is still an attracting topic for cryptographers. Indeed 64-bit block algorithms remain in use in many cryptographic devices and the migration to AES is quite slow.

Given the large amount of research on the topic, DES has surprisingly well resisted to cryptanalysis. In practice, the best way of attacking DES is by brute force on the 56 bits of the key. This is feasible with large resources and can be achieved using a dedicated hardware or a large cluster of standard machines [7]. Another topic of analysis has been the research of shortcut attacks (faster than exhaustive search). Several results have been published since the early 90's :

- **Differential Cryptanalysis** [4] has been the first published theoretical cryptanalysis of DES. This technique, proposed by Biham and Shamir, requires to encrypt (under the same key) 2^{47} chosen plaintexts.
- **Linear Cryptanalysis** [11] was published shortly after by Matsui. It is slightly more efficient than Differential Cryptanalysis, since it requires about 2^{43} known plaintexts. This attack was implemented by Matsui and the experience was repeated afterwards and even slightly improved [8,9,15].

B. Roy (Ed.): ASIACRYPT 2005, LNCS 3788, pp. 425–442, 2005.

Table 1. Summary of Cryptanalysis of DES

Cryptanalysis Technique	Time Complexity	Data Complexity
Exhaustive Search	2^{56}	1 known plaintext
Linear Cryptanalysis [11]	2^{43}	2^{43} known plaintexts
Bi-Linear Cryptanalysis [5]	$\simeq 2^{43}$	$\simeq 2^{43}$ known plaintexts
Differential Cryptanalysis [4]	2^{47}	2^{47} chosen plaintexts
Davies-Murphy Cryptanalysis [3,6]	2^{50}	2^{50} known plaintexts
This paper	2^{45}	2^{45} chosen plaintexts

- **Bi-Linear Cryptanalysis** [5] was published recently at Crypto 2004. It is an extension of Linear Cryptanalysis using some particular quadratic approximations instead of linear ones. Its complexity is roughly the same as Linear Cryptanalysis and the two techniques appear to be closely related.
- **Davies-Murphy Cryptanalysis** [6] is a dedicated attack against DES. The starting point was the observation by Davies that adjacent pairs (and triplets) of S-boxes in DES produced unbalanced output. At first, it was believed the attack was slower than exhaustive search. However, in 1995, Biham and Biryukov [3] demonstrated how to improve these results. Their resulting attack costs 2^{50} known plaintexts, which is worse than Linear or Differential cryptanalysis, but still represents a theoretical break of DES.
- There exists other attacks like differential-linear attack or partitioning attacks.

In this paper, we propose a further improvement of the Davies-Murphy cryptanalysis. Our new attack requires to encrypt and process 2^{45} chosen plaintexts, in order to recover the secret key. Therefore our results place the attack between linear cryptanalysis and differential cryptanalysis in terms of complexity (see Table 1).

Also, our improved attack is very closely related to linear cryptanalysis (we use a biased linear combination of intermediate bits). It is already well known (with Biham's work [2] in particular) that Matsui's attack and Davies-Murphy attack are closely related. In Section 4, we further explore this relation in the general case. We prove that linear distinguishers become almost optimal after several convolutions, which explains the convergence observed between the complexities of both attacks. It also shows that Davies-Murphy cryptanalysis cannot significantly outperform linear cryptanalysis.

2   DES and Davies-Murphy Cryptanalysis

2.1   DES

DES [12] was published in 1977. It is a Feistel cipher (see Figure 1) with 16 rounds. DES operates on a 64-bit block of data, which is split in two halves of equal length.

The round function F of DES (also see Figure 2) first expands the state from 32 to 48 bits using a linear expansion E. Then a 48-bit subkey K is added

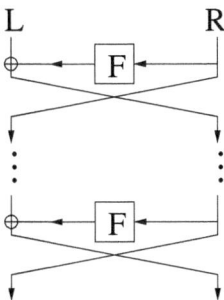

Fig. 1. General Structure of a Feistel cipher

bitwise to the state before a layer S of S-boxes is applied. This layer is built with 8 different S-boxes applied in parallel, each taking 6 input bits and producing 4 output bits. Therefore the layer S reduces the state size from 48 to 32 bits. Finally the state is permuted with a function P. Therefore

$$F(x) = P \circ S(K \oplus E(x))$$

Even though this round function is not bijective, the Feistel network remains invertible by construction. However a consequence of the non-invertibility is that for a given key, some outputs are produced more often than others by the round function F. This causes a natural imbalance in the cipher. The general idea of Davies-Murphy cryptanalysis is to take advantage of this property.

2.2 Pairs of Adjacent S-Boxes

Any pair of adjacent S-box of DES "shares" two input bits (see Figure 2). To detail this phenomenon, we focus on the pair of S-boxes (S_1, S_2) and call (V_1, V_2) the corresponding outputs. We want to observe the distribution of (V_1, V_2) for a fixed key and a random round input.

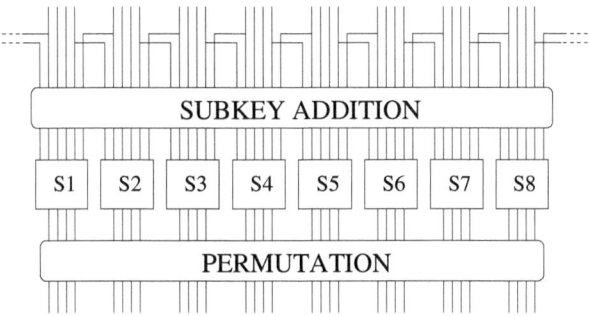

Fig. 2. The round function F of DES

The Output of Adjacent S-Boxes is Not Balanced

Let $\{x_i\}_{i=1...32}$ be the round input bits and $\{k_i\}_{i=1...48}$ the bits of the subkey K. It directly follows from the specifications of DES that the input of S_1 - denoted $A = (a_1, ..., a_6)$ - is

$$A = (x_{32}, x_1, x_2, x_3, x_4, x_5) \oplus (k_1, k_2, k_3, k_4, k_5, k_6)$$

Similarly, the input of S_2 - denoted $B = (b_1, ..., b_6)$ - is

$$B = (x_4, x_5, x_6, x_7, x_8, x_9) \oplus (k_7, k_8, k_9, k_{10}, k_{11}, k_{12})$$

An important observation is that x_4 and x_5 are used twice : once in A and once in B. Suppose that the x_i's are random, then A and B are also random, except they have to verify the constraints :

$$a_5 \oplus b_1 = k_5 \oplus k_7 \tag{1}$$

$$a_6 \oplus b_2 = k_6 \oplus k_8 \tag{2}$$

Hence for a pair of adjacent S-boxes, like (S_1, S_2), the output distribution depends on two key bits $s = k_5 \oplus k_7$ and $t = k_6 \oplus k_8$.

The Imbalance Depends on 1 Key Bit Only

DES S-boxes have a very particular form. Indeed, when the leftmost and rightmost input bits are fixed, each S_i performs a permutation of the remaining 4 input bits. A subtle consequence of this property is that the distribution of (V_1, V_2) does not depend on (s, t) but only on $s \oplus t$. In this section, we explain why this property is true.

Fix a target output called (z_1, z_2). Each z_i has exactly 4 preimages due to the row structure of the DES S-boxes. Hence there are 4 inputs of S_1 (one in each row of the S-box) such that $V_1 = z_1$. Similarly 4 inputs of S_2 yield $V_2 = z_2$. The total number of preimages of (z_1, z_2) is thus $4 \times 4 = 16$ where each solution is formed with an input of S_1 combined with an input of S_2. Let $N_{(s,t)}$ be the number among these 16 solutions that also satisfy the constraints (1) and (2) on s and t. Clearly,

$$N_{(0,0)} + N_{(0,1)} + N_{(1,0)} + N_{(1,1)} = 16 \tag{3}$$

For a fixed key, the probability $p(z_1, z_2)$ to obtain the output (z_1, z_2) is related to the quantity $N_{(s,t)}$ by the formula

$$p_{(s,t)}(z_1, z_2) = N_{(s,t)} \times 2^{-10}$$

Besides we can use symmetry arguments : since the bit a_6 is used to index the rows of the S-box S_1, it is well balanced among all preimages. So exactly half of the 4 S_1-preimages of z_1 satisfy $a_6 = 1$. Since all preimages of (z_1, z_2) are obtained by choosing independently a S_1-preimage of z_1 and a S_2-preimage of z_2, then $t = a_6 \oplus b_2$ is balanced among these 16 preimages and :

$$N_{(0,0)} + N_{(1,0)} = N_{(0,1)} + N_{(1,1)} = 8 \tag{4}$$

Using the same symmetry argument on the bit b_1 we see that

$$N_{(0,0)} + N_{(0,1)} = N_{(1,0)} + N_{(1,1)} = 8 \tag{5}$$

Putting together (4) and (5) we deduce :

$$N_{(0,0)} = N_{(1,1)}$$
$$N_{(0,1)} = N_{(1,0)}$$

Hence the output distribution of adjacent S-boxes depends only on the key-dependent bit k defined as

$$k = s \oplus t = k_5 \oplus k_6 \oplus k_7 \oplus k_8$$

An Example

Two output distributions are therefore possible for (S_1, S_2) depending on the key-dependent bit k. Call $\mathcal{D}_0$ (resp. $\mathcal{D}_1$) the distribution corresponding to the case $k = 0$ (resp. $k = 1$). For instance $\mathcal{D}_1(z_1, z_2)$ is the probability that the output of (S_1, S_2) is (z_1, z_2) when $k = 1$.

The full distribution is represented in Table 2. It is interesting to notice that $\mathcal{D}_0$ and $\mathcal{D}_1$ are symmetric : they sum up to the uniform distributions. Denote by a single variable x the eight bits of (z_1, z_2). Then :

$$\frac{\mathcal{D}_0(x) + \mathcal{D}_1(x)}{2} = \frac{1}{256}$$

Hence, although the output is not balanced for a fixed key, it is globally balanced over all keys.

2.3 The Resulting Imbalance on 16 Rounds

Since DES is a Feistel cipher, the XOR of plaintext and ciphertext is the XOR of 8 round outputs (see Figure 1). We focus on the output of adjacent S-boxes, like

Table 2. Output distributions for (S_1, S_2). Values in the table should be divided by 1024.

z_2 \ z_1	00	01	02	03	04	05	06	07	08	09	10	11	12	13	14	15	00	01	02	03	04	05	06	07	08	09	10	11	12	13	14	15
00	4	4	4	4	4	4	4	4	4	4	4	4	4	4	4	4	4	4	4	4	4	4	4	4	4	4	4	4	4	4	4	4
01	5	5	4	3	4	4	3	4	3	4	6	4	4	5	3	3	3	3	4	5	4	4	5	4	5	4	2	4	4	3	5	5
02	2	2	4	6	4	4	6	4	6	4	0	4	4	2	6	6	6	6	4	2	4	4	2	4	2	4	8	4	4	6	2	2
03	4	4	4	4	4	4	4	4	4	4	4	4	4	4	4	4	4	4	4	4	4	4	4	4	4	4	4	4	4	4	4	4
04	4	4	4	4	4	4	4	4	4	4	4	4	4	4	4	4	4	4	4	4	4	4	4	4	4	4	4	4	4	4	4	4
05	3	3	4	5	4	4	5	4	5	4	2	4	4	3	5	5	5	5	4	3	4	4	3	4	3	4	6	4	4	5	3	3
06	4	4	4	4	4	4	4	4	4	4	4	4	4	4	4	4	4	4	4	4	4	4	4	4	4	4	4	4	4	4	4	4
07	5	5	4	3	4	4	3	4	3	4	6	4	4	5	3	3	3	3	4	5	4	4	5	4	5	4	2	4	4	3	5	5
08	5	5	4	3	4	4	3	4	3	4	6	4	4	5	3	3	3	3	4	5	4	4	5	4	5	4	2	4	4	3	5	5
09	4	4	4	4	4	4	4	4	4	4	4	4	4	4	4	4	4	4	4	4	4	4	4	4	4	4	4	4	4	4	4	4
10	6	6	4	2	4	4	2	4	2	4	8	4	4	6	2	2	2	2	4	6	4	4	6	4	6	4	0	4	4	2	6	6
11	3	3	4	5	4	4	5	4	5	4	2	4	4	3	5	5	5	5	4	3	4	4	3	4	3	4	6	4	4	5	3	3
12	5	5	4	3	4	4	3	4	3	4	6	4	4	5	3	3	3	3	4	5	4	4	5	4	5	4	2	4	4	3	5	5
13	3	3	4	5	4	4	5	4	5	4	2	4	4	3	5	5	5	5	4	3	4	4	3	4	3	4	6	4	4	5	3	3
14	3	3	4	5	4	4	5	4	5	4	2	4	4	3	5	5	5	5	4	3	4	4	3	4	3	4	6	4	4	5	3	3
15	4	4	4	4	4	4	4	4	4	4	4	4	4	4	4	4	4	4	4	4	4	4	4	4	4	4	4	4	4	4	4	4
							Case $k = 0$																Case $k = 1$									

S_1 and S_2.[1] For these 8 bits, unbalanced distributions (like the one described in Table 2) are produced at each round. After XORing these outputs, the result is a **convolution** of several distributions of the form $\mathcal{D}_k$.

At first, one could expect the convolution of t output distributions to depend on t key-dependent bits, $i.e.$ one bit per distribution. However it can easily be shown that only the parity of these t bits matters. For instance, consider the distribution $\mathcal{D}_1 \times \mathcal{D}_1$ obtained by the convolution of $\mathcal{D}_1$ with itself.

$$\mathcal{D}_1 \times \mathcal{D}_1(x) = \sum_a \mathcal{D}_1(a)\, \mathcal{D}_1(a \oplus x)$$

$$= \sum_a \left(\frac{2}{256} - \mathcal{D}_0(a) \right) \left(\frac{2}{256} - \mathcal{D}_0(a \oplus x) \right)$$

$$= \frac{4}{256} - \frac{2}{256} - \frac{2}{256} + \sum_a \mathcal{D}_0(a)\, \mathcal{D}_0(a \oplus x)$$

$$= \sum_a \mathcal{D}_0(a)\, \mathcal{D}_0(a \oplus x)$$

$$= \mathcal{D}_0 \times \mathcal{D}_0(x)$$

So it is equivalent to compose $\mathcal{D}_0$ with itself or $\mathcal{D}_1$ with itself. More generally only matters the parity of the t key-dependent bits involved. By extension, we simply denote $\mathcal{D}_0^t$ (resp. $\mathcal{D}_1^t$) the distribution after t convolutions when the parity bit is 0 (resp. 1). If an attacker can efficiently distinguish these two distributions, he learns one bit of information about the key. However, this analysis requires a large amount of pairs (plaintext, ciphertext) because distributions are almost uniform after a few convolutions.

2.4   Application to Cryptanalysis

The problem of distinguishing two distributions is a classical topic in the literature, since it is related to many cryptanalysis problems (see [1] for example). In the particular case of DES, the problem is to distinguishing $\mathcal{D}_0^8$ from $\mathcal{D}_1^8$. One of these two distributions should be observed when XORing 8 appropriate bits from the plaintext and the ciphertext.

Davies and Murphy estimated in [6] the number of samples necessary to distinguish theses 2 distributions. For several pairs of adjacent S-boxes, these results are summarized in Table 3. The results depend highly on which pair is considered. In particular, (S_7, S_8) is the most favorable pair for the attack, although it falls short above the 2^{56} limit. Therefore it was first believed that Davies-Murphy cryptanalysis could not break DES.

Later, further improvements of Davies-Murphy cryptanalysis have been proposed. Biham and Biryukov suggested to use 7 convolutioned distributions instead of 8. So their approximation no longer takes into account the full DES but only 15 rounds and accordingly an additional analysis is needed to handle the

---

[1] After the permutation P, the corresponding bits are $2, 9, 13, 17, 18, 23, 28$ and 31.

Table 3. Number of known plaintext needed for a 97% success rate

Pair of S-boxes	$(1,2)$	$(2,3)$	$(3,4)$	$(4,5)$	$(5,6)$	$(6,7)$	$(7,8)$	$(8,1)$
Complexity	$2^{66.0}$	$2^{69.3}$	$2^{85.6}$	$2^{70.6}$	$2^{71.6}$	$2^{66.0}$	$2^{56.6}$	$2^{77.3}$

first (or last) round. The resulting attacks works by processing only 2^{50} known plaintexts, which is better than exhaustive search.

More recently, other extensions of Davies-Murphy Cryptanalysis were published. Pornin analyzed how to improve the resistance against the attack [14], and Kunz-Jacques et al. suggested to use the attack for side channel analysis [10].

3 Improving Davies-Murphy Cryptanalysis

In this section, we propose a new improvement of Davies-Murphy cryptanalysis. Our general idea is to use the convolution of only 6 distributions of round outputs (Davies and Murphy used 8 distributions [6], Biham and Biryukov only 7 distributions [3]). Therefore we approximate the behavior of only 13 rounds of DES. We take into account the 3 remaining rounds, but chosen plaintext is then needed, and several additional algorithmic tricks must be used.

3.1 General Framework

Like many statistical cryptanalysis, our attack is decomposed in three main phases.

- First we identify an internal object in the cipher that does not behave randomly. This statistical imbalance can be used to distinguish its behavior from a random one. Generally, such an object needs to be predictable from the plaintext, the ciphertext and eventually several key bits.
- Then we encrypt a large number of (chosen) messages and remember only a small part of information about each result. Typically, we store the number of occurrences of a small pattern of plaintext/ciphertext bits.
- Finally, we reconstruct the internal object from the collected data. This phase generally contains some partial exhaustive search and the statistical properties of the object are used as a stopping condition. Eventually we want to retrieve the secret key faster than exhaustive search.

3.2 The Internal Object

Davies-Murphy cryptanalysis targets the distribution of 8 bits from the round output, which are obtained from 2 adjacent S-boxes. After t convolutions, the resulting distribution is denoted $\mathcal{D}_0^t$ or $\mathcal{D}_1^t$ depending on the value of a key-dependent parity bit. Previous papers [3,6] require to distinguish between these two distributions. Our attack has two important differences.

Table 4. Comparison of several distinguishers for Davies-Murphy cryptanalysis

Pair of S-boxes		$(1, 2)$	$(2, 3)$	$(3, 4)$	$(4, 5)$	$(5, 6)$	$(6, 7)$	$(7, 8)$	$(8, 1)$
Opt. Dist.	$t = 1$	$2^{4.4}$	$2^{4.1}$	$2^{6.8}$	$2^{4.7}$	$2^{5.4}$	$2^{5.1}$	$2^{4.2}$	$2^{5.7}$
Best. Lin. Dist. $t = 1$		2^{8}	$2^{8.83}$	$2^{10.83}$	$2^{8.83}$	$2^{8.83}$	2^{8}	$2^{6.83}$	$2^{9.66}$
Opt. Dist.	$t = 6$	$2^{47.9}$	$2^{49.6}$	2^{62}	$2^{50.9}$	$2^{51.9}$	$2^{47.9}$	$2^{40.8}$	$2^{55.9}$
Best. Lin. Dist. $t = 6$		2^{48}	2^{53}	2^{65}	2^{53}	2^{53}	2^{48}	2^{41}	2^{58}
Opt. Dist.	$t = 8$	2^{64}	$2^{67.3}$	$2^{83.6}$	$2^{68.6}$	$2^{69.6}$	2^{64}	$2^{54.6}$	$2^{75.3}$
Best. Lin. Dist. $t = 8$		2^{64}	$2^{70.6}$	$2^{86.6}$	$2^{70.6}$	$2^{70.6}$	2^{64}	$2^{54.6}$	$2^{77.3}$

First we need to distinguish one of these two distributions (it does not matter whether the parity bit is 0 or 1 due to symmetry properties) from a uniform distribution. Secondly, to reduce the cost of the data collection, we propose to focus on the linear combination of these 8 bits with the strongest bias. Naturally, such a **linear distinguisher** cannot be more efficient than the **optimal distinguisher**, but it requires the storage of only 1 bit of information (instead of 8 bits) which turns out to be crucial for the data collection and data analysis phase.

Table 4 compares the samples needed by the optimal distinguisher and the best linear distinguisher for a fixed probability of success.

The complexities obtained are very similar for both distinguishers. This comparison is further developed in Section 4. Here we are interested by $t = 6$ and target the most favorable pair of S-box, *i.e.* (S_7, S_8). We computed that the best linear combination λ is

$$\lambda(X) = x_5 \oplus x_7 \oplus x_{12} \oplus x_{21} \oplus x_{22} \oplus x_{27} \oplus x_{32}$$

where $X = (x_1, \ldots, x_{32})$ is the output of the round function F. We have

$$Pr[\lambda(X) = 1] = 0.5 \, (1 \pm 2^{-3.4}) = 0.5 \pm 0.046875$$

depending on the key. After 6 convolutions, we have

$$Pr[\lambda(X)' = 1] = 0.5 \, (1 \pm (2^{-3.4})^6) = 0.5 \, (1 \pm 2^{-20.5})$$

The amount of data needed for the corresponding distinguisher is about 2^{41} samples.

3.3   The Data Collection

In the following we do not take into account the initial and the final permutation of DES. Let $(p_i)_{i \in 1, \ldots, 64}$ denote the plaintext bits. The left branch of the plaintext is called $p_L = (p_1, \ldots, p_{32})$ and the right branch $p_R = (p_{33}, \ldots, p_{64})$. Similar notations are used for the ciphertext bits c_i. In this data collection phase, we encrypt n messages that verify

PLAINTEXT

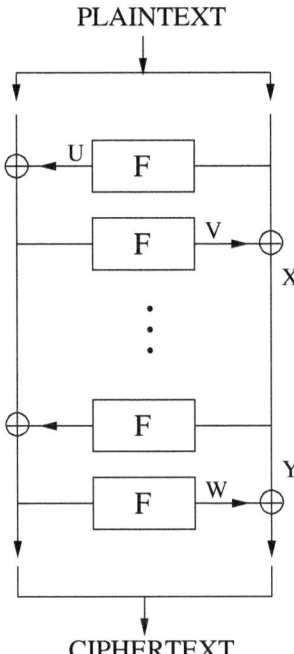

CIPHERTEXT

Fig. 3. Summary of the data collection phase

- The left branch of the plaintext p_L is chosen at random
- 14 bits of the right branch are also random : $(p_{50}, \ldots, p_{63})$. These bits are involved only in S-boxes S_5, S_6, S_7 and S_8.
- The 18 remaining plaintext bits are set to an arbitrary but constant value.

Given the degrees of freedom, n cannot exceed 2^{46}. For each encryption, we store the following piece of information

- The bit $\lambda(p_R) \oplus \lambda(c_R)$
- The 14 bits $(p_{50}, \ldots, p_{63})$ from the plaintext, which are involved in the S-boxes S_5, S_6, S_7 and S_8 of the first round.
- The 10 bits $(p_1, p_{24}, \ldots, p_{32})$ from the plaintext, which are involved in the S-boxes S_7 and S_8 of the second round.
- The 10 bits $(c_1, c_{24}, \ldots, c_{32})$ from the ciphertext, which are involved in the S-boxes S_7 and S_8 of the last round.

Hence we have a pattern of $1 + 14 + 10 + 10 = 35$ bits to store. For sake of efficiency, we only store the number of occurrences of each pattern in a table. This requires a table of size 2^{35}, where each entry in the table is a counter[2].

This data collection phase is detailed in Figure 3. X and Y denote two intermediate states in the right branch of the Feistel. U is the output of the

---

[2] Two bytes should be sufficient to store the counter, since each pattern occurs in average $2^{45} \times 2^{-35} = 1024$ times.

1-st round, V the output of the 2-nd round and W the output of the 16-th round. $X \oplus Y$ is the XOR of 6 round outputs so $\lambda(X \oplus Y)$ is not uniformly distributed according to the results of Section 3.2. However this object is not directly accessible. The purpose of storing these pieces of information about each message is to later predict $\lambda(X \oplus Y)$ in the data analysis phase.

3.4   The Data Analysis

We want to predict $\lambda(X \oplus Y)$ from the data collected previously. For that purpose, we use the following relation :

$$\lambda(X \oplus Y) = \lambda(p_R) \oplus \lambda(c_R) \oplus \lambda(V) \oplus \lambda(W) \tag{6}$$

Notation U_i, V_i and W_i is used to denote the bits from U, V and W.

The general idea of the attack is to perform an exhaustive search on a portion of the key bits. The pattern bits previously stored allow to determine the value of $\lambda(V)$ and $\lambda(W)$ in each case. Hence we determine all the terms involved in (6) and eventually predict how many times $\lambda(X \oplus Y)$ is equal to 1 among the samples. For the correct guess, this number should be significantly far from half of the samples.

Unfortunately, such a direct approach is way too expensive. Hence we need to decompose the attack in several steps. At each step, we only guess a few key bits, derive some intermediate information, and immediately get rid of what is no longer needed in the initial pattern.

Let us detail the first step. The starting point is the table built in the data collection phase. We refer to it as T_0. Guess the following 6 bits from the secret key : $(K_7, K_{21}, K_{22}, K_{39}, K_{53}, K_{63})$. They are XORed to the bits $(c_{28}, c_{29}, c_{30}, c_{31}, c_{32}, c_1)$ before S-box S_8 at round 16. Hence we can determine S_8's output and in particular the combination $W_5 \oplus W_{21} \oplus W_{27}$, which is a portion of the term $\lambda(W)$. After this step, 4 bits from the ciphertext are no longer needed. Thus we replace T_0 by a new table T_1 of size only 2^{31} where the number of occurrences of the following 31-bit pattern is stored :

- The bit $\lambda(p_R) \oplus \lambda(c_R) \oplus W_5 \oplus W_{21} \oplus W_{27}$
- The 14 bits $(p_{50}, \ldots, p_{63})$ from the plaintext
- The 10 bits $(p_1, p_{24}, \ldots, p_{32})$ from the plaintext
- The 6 bits $(c_{24}, \ldots, c_{29})$ from the ciphertext, which are involved in the S-box S_7 of the last round.

In the second step, we guess 6 additional key bits which are involved in S_7 at round 16 : $K_4, K_6, K_{23}, K_{28}, K_{29}, K_{46}$. Up to this point, 12 key bits have been guessed. Then we use the remaining 6 ciphertext bits in T_1 to predict $W_7 \oplus W_{12} \oplus W_{22} \oplus W_{32}$. Now we know all of $\lambda(W)$ and can get rid of all ciphertext bits. Hence we replace T_1 by a new table T_2 where the number of occurrences of the following 25-bit pattern is stored :

- The bit $\lambda(p_R) \oplus \lambda(c_R) \oplus \lambda(W)$
- The 14 bits $(p_{50}, \ldots, p_{63})$ from the plaintext
- The 10 bits $(p_1, p_{24}, \ldots, p_{32})$ from the plaintext

Table 5. Successive steps of the data analysis phase

Step	Key bits guessed	Total bits guessed	Old table	New table	Time complexity
0	-	0	-	2^{35}	2^{35}
1	$7, 21, 22, 39, 53, 63$	6	2^{35}	2^{31}	2^{41}
2	$4, 6, 23, 28, 29, 46$	12	2^{31}	2^{25}	2^{43}
3	$37, 54$	14	2^{25}	2^{23}	2^{39}
4	$5, 30, 47$	17	2^{23}	2^{19}	2^{40}
5	$15, 20, 38, 61$	21	2^{19}	2^{15}	2^{40}
6	$13, 14, 31, 45, 55, 62$	27	2^{15}	2^{11}	2^{42}
7	3 internal bits	30	2^{11}	2^{7}	2^{41}
8	4 internal bits	34	2^{7}	2^{1}	2^{41}

Similarly, the next steps of the analysis allow us to predict the term $\lambda(V)$ in relation (6). To that purpose, we first need to predict some bits of U. These steps are detailed in Appendix A.

Table 5 summarizes the successive steps of this data analysis phase. At each step, the complexity corresponds to the number of bits guessed multiplied by the size of the table to manipulate. The maximal complexity reached during the analysis is of 2^{43}.

After step 8, we have guessed a total of 34 bits, among which 27 are directly key bits. So we know how many times $\lambda(X \oplus Y)$ is equal to 1 using the relation (6) and the content of table T_8. Then we can apply our statistical distinguisher to determine the correct guess among the $2^{34} - 1$ wrong guesses.

3.5   Finishing the Attack

How to finish the attack depends on the exact probability of success of the linear distinguisher, and thus on the number of samples n. Generally one assumes that both distributions occur with the same probability. Then, the probability P_{fa} of false alarm (*i.e.* the probability that a wrong guess is identified as correct) is the same as the probability P_{nd} of non-detection of the correct key (*i.e.* the probability that a correct guess is identified as wrong). But here we need to identify one correct guess among $2^{34} - 1$ wrong guesses, so the crucial point is to have a low probability of false alarms. Therefore we propose several trade-offs. First, we set P_{nd} to 50%. Then we have $P_{fa} = \phi(\sqrt{d})$ where d is a parameter computed from the number of samples n (see Section 4 for more details) and ϕ is defined as

$$\phi(t) = \frac{1}{\sqrt{2\pi}} \int_{-\infty}^{-t} e^{-\frac{1}{2}u^2} du$$

Secondly, we set $P_{nd} = 15.86\%$. This gives $P_{fa} = \phi(\sqrt{d} - 1)$. Table 6 presents various numeric applications. The number of samples n cannot exceed 2^{46} because we do not have enough degrees of freedom. It is not possible to completely

Table 6. Probability of false alarm depending on n and the scenario

n	d	Case $P_a = P_{nd}$	$P_{nd} = 50\%$	$P_{nd} = 15.86\%$
2^{41}	1	30.85%	15.86%	50%
2^{42}	2	23.98%	7.86%	22.94%
2^{43}	4	15.86%	2.28%	15.86%
2^{44}	8	7.86%	$2^{-8.74}$	3.37%
2^{45}	16	2.28%	$2^{-14.95}$	$2^{-9.53}$
2^{46}	32	$2^{-8.74}$	$2^{-26.95}$	$2^{-19.25}$

eliminate false alarms as P_{fa} is always greater than 2^{-34}. But false alarms can be discarded by guessing the remaining key bits and testing each candidate with a couple (plaintext, ciphertext). Since 34 key bits are guessed in the core of the attack[3], there are only $56 - 34 = 22$ bits left to guess.

Suppose we pick $n = 2^{45}$ samples and fix the probability of non-detection to 50%, then the number of false alarms is

$$P_{fa} \times 2^{34} = 2^{19.05}$$

Guessing the remaining 22 bits brings the complexity up to $2^{41.05}$ candidates. One couple (plaintext, ciphertext) is then enough to identify the full secret key.

3.6 Summary

- The memory complexity of the attack is always the size of T_0, *i.e* a table containing 2^{35} entries of 2 bytes each.
- The time complexity of the attack is at least the complexity of the data analysis, *i.e.* 2^{43} steps of computation.
- The data complexity of the attack can range between $n = 2^{41}$ and $n = 2^{46}$ chosen plaintexts. In all cases, the key recovery is faster than exhaustive search, but the exact complexity depends on n.
- For example, when $n = 2^{45}$, the full secret key can be recovered with probability of 50% after 2^{41} trial DES encryptions. This is the trade-off we suggest to use.

4 Link Between Davies-Murphy Cryptanalysis and Linear Cryptanalysis

It is known since Biham's work [2] that there exists an underlying linear attack with similar complexity as Davies-Murphy's attack. In this paper, we also use a biased linear combination of bits, in order to improve the Davies-Murphy attack. Therefore a natural question is to explain the link between both techniques, in the general case.

---

[3] 7 are only intermediate bits, but they give a condition on a few key bits. Hence their entropy is equivalent to 7 key bits in practice.

An important parameter is the data complexity ratio between the optimal distinguisher (used in the Davies-Murphy original cryptanalysis) and the best *linear* distinguisher for outputs of pairs of adjacent S-boxes. As seen in Table 4, the more rounds are applied, the closer the complexities are. In this section, we explain this phenomenon and account for the exact values of the ratios observed in Table 4. We show that, due to the effects of the convolutions, the same phenomenon will always be observed, independently of the original distribution. To some extent, this shows that linear cryptanalysis is always optimal.

4.1   Optimal vs Best Linear Distinguishers

Suppose we have a random variable X that follows a distribution $\mathcal{D}$ or the uniform distribution $\mathcal{U}$. (in the Davies-Murphy case, $\mathcal{D} = \mathcal{D}_0^t$ or $\mathcal{D}_1^t$ for some t). Let $\mathcal{S} = \{0, \ldots, 2^n\}$ be the image set of X. Our goal is to distinguish between theses two distributions. Basically, there are two approaches : we can use the best (optimal) distinguisher, or we can restrict the analysis to linear distinguishers only.

Optimal Distinguisher. It is well known (see [1] for instance) that the optimal distinguisher between $\mathcal{D}$ and $\mathcal{U}$ has probability of error

$$P_e = \frac{1}{\sqrt{2\pi}} \int_{-\infty}^{-\frac{\sqrt{d}}{2}} e^{-\frac{1}{2}u^2} du$$

when the number of samples n is related to the parameter d by

$$n = \frac{d}{\Delta(\mathcal{D})}$$

and $\Delta(\mathcal{D})$ is the Squared Euclidean Imbalance (SEI) of $\mathcal{D}$ from $\mathcal{U}$. If for any $x \in \mathcal{S}$, $\mathcal{D}(x)$ denotes the probability that $X = x$, the SEI is computed as

$$\Delta(\mathcal{D}) = |\mathcal{S}| \sum_x \left(\mathcal{D}(x) - \frac{1}{2^n} \right)^2$$

Linear Distinguisher. Consider a linear combination $\lambda(X)$ of the bits of X. Suppose that, when X follows $\mathcal{D}$, it satisfies :

$$Pr_{\mathcal{D}}[\lambda(X) = 1] = \frac{1}{2}(1 + \varepsilon)$$

then it is well known that about $n = \varepsilon^2$ samples are needed to detect this bias. We introduce the usual notation

$$LP(\lambda) = (Pr_{\mathcal{D}}[\lambda(X) = 1] - Pr_{\mathcal{D}}[\lambda(X) = 0])^2 = \varepsilon^2$$

The question is to determine the $LP_{max} = \max_\lambda \{LP(\lambda)\}$ of the best linear distinguisher for a given distribution $\mathcal{D}$. By definition, it requires more data than the optimal distinguisher, but we are interested into the ratio between the two complexities.

Relation Between $\Delta(\mathcal{D})$ and LP_{max}. Using the Fourier transform (see Section 2.4 of [1]), one shows that

$$\Delta(\mathcal{D}) = \sum_{\lambda \neq 0} LP(\lambda) \tag{7}$$

Therefore we can derive the following bound for the ratio between the two data complexities :

$$LP_{max} \leq \Delta(\mathcal{D}) \leq (2^n - 1)LP_{max}$$

It can be shown that both bounds are actually tight, so the best linear distinguisher can be significantly worse (up to a factor of 2^n) than the optimal distinguisher. However, in Davies-Murphy cryptanalysis, we are dealing with particular distributions.

4.2 The Case of Davies-Murphy Cryptanalysis

The target distribution $\mathcal{D}_i^t$ in this case is obtained after t convolutions. In practice, when t grows, the ratio apparently gets small (see Table 4). In this Section, we explain the ratios observed. Since linear biases are just multiplied after each convolution, (7) can be re-expressed as :

$$\Delta(\mathcal{D}_i^t) = \sum_{\lambda \neq 0} LP(\lambda)^t \tag{8}$$

where $LP(\cdot)$ are computed with respect to the base distribution $\mathcal{D}_i$ (by symmetry it does matter whether the parity bit i is 0 or 1).

Suppose now that there are $m \leq 2^n - 1$ linear forms whose LP is equal to LP_{max}, and that all other λ are such that

$$LP(\lambda) \leq \alpha \, LP_{max}$$

for some $0 \leq \alpha < 1$. Then (8) yields

$$m \, (LP_{max})^t \leq \Delta(\mathcal{D}_i^t) \leq (m + \alpha^t(2^n - 1 - m)) \, (LP_{max})^t$$

When t is big enough, then $\alpha^t \ll 1$ and

$$\Delta(\mathcal{D}_i^t) \simeq m \, (LP_{max})^t \tag{9}$$

We can compute LP_{max} and m in the case of DES. These results are summarized in Table 7.

In practice, the approximation of equation (9) accurately predicts the maximum linear bias and the loss between optimal and linear distinguishers. The weakest couples of DES S-boxes w.r.t. linear distinguishers are the ones that have a small number of linear forms reaching the maximum bias LP_{max}. For the best pair of S-boxes (S_7, S_8), LP_{max} is only reached once, so the ratio between both distinguishers is almost 1 after 6 convolutions. Hence, replacing the optimal distinguisher with the best linear one does not result in a significant deterioration.

Table 7. Difference Between Optimal and Linear Distinguisher Explained

Pair of S-boxes		$(1,2)$	$(2,3)$	$(3,4)$	$(4,5)$	$(5,6)$	$(6,7)$	$(7,8)$	$(8,1)$
m		1	10	8	4	2	1	1	4
$\log_2(m)$		0	3.3	3	2	1	0	0	2
LP_{max}		2^8	$2^{8.83}$	$2^{10.83}$	$2^{8.83}$	$2^{8.83}$	2^8	$2^{6.83}$	$2^{9.66}$
Opt. Dist. $\Delta(\mathcal{D}^6)$	$t=6$	$2^{47.9}$	$2^{49.6}$	2^{62}	$2^{50.9}$	$2^{51.9}$	$2^{47.9}$	$2^{40.8}$	$2^{55.9}$
Best. Lin. Dist. LP^6_{max}	$t=6$	2^{48}	2^{53}	2^{65}	2^{53}	2^{53}	2^{48}	2^{41}	2^{58}
Expected value from (9)	$t=6$	$2^{47.9}$	$2^{52.9}$	2^{65}	$2^{52.9}$	$2^{52.9}$	$2^{47.9}$	$2^{40.8}$	$2^{57.9}$
Opt. Dist. $\Delta(\mathcal{D}^8)$	$t=8$	2^{64}	$2^{67.3}$	$2^{83.6}$	$2^{68.6}$	$2^{69.6}$	2^{64}	$2^{54.6}$	$2^{75.3}$
Best. Lin. Dist. LP^8_{max}	$t=8$	2^{64}	$2^{70.6}$	$2^{86.6}$	$2^{70.6}$	$2^{70.6}$	2^{64}	$2^{54.6}$	$2^{77.3}$
Expected value from (9)	$t=8$	2^{64}	$2^{70.6}$	$2^{86.6}$	$2^{70.6}$	$2^{70.6}$	2^{64}	$2^{54.6}$	$2^{77.3}$

4.3 Summary

A consequence of the convolutions involved in Davies-Murphy cryptanalysis is that distributions become very quickly "smooth". Therefore the complexity of the optimal distinguisher can increase very quickly after several rounds, while the complexity of a linear distinguisher increases more regularly.

Hence, using a linear distinguisher becomes almost optimal after several convolutions. This explains the phenomenon that Biham observed in [2] and it also explains why we obtained good results in this paper, while restricting our analysis to linear distinguishers. This observation is independent of the initial distribution, so it would make no difference if used other S-boxes for instance. However, the linear characteristic used in our attack has some nice properties :

- it is iterative
- it uses only output bits of the round function
- the same linear form is used at every round

These properties allow us to concentrate on one half of the Feistel network, reducing the effective number of rounds to consider down from 16 to 8 (algorithmic tricks further reduce this number to 6). Therefore, although this linear characteristic is not the best one known for DES, its a particular form may be helpful to optimize the data analysis phase.

5 Conclusion

In this paper, we improve the famous Davies-Murphy cryptanalysis of DES, by using 6 round output distributions (instead of 7 or 8 like in previous papers on the topic [3,6]). Several trade-offs are possible, but we describe a key-recovery attack with complexity of 2^{45} chosen plaintexts. This positions the attack at the second rank of cryptanalysis of DES : slightly better than Biham and Shamir's differential cryptanalysis but slightly worse than Matsui's linear cryptanalysis.

In addition, we have shown that using linear distinguishers for the Davies-Murphy cryptanalysis was almost an optimal choice, because of the particular structure of the attack. Therefore Davies-Murphy cryptanalysis is closely related to a particular family of linear attacks, where the linear mask involves only the round output. This allows for efficient optimizations of the data collection and data analysis. At the same time, it shows that it is unlikely to (significantly) outperform Matsui's attack with further algorithmic improvements.

References

1. T. Baignères, P. Junod, and S. Vaudenay. How Far Can We Go Beyond Linear Cryptanalysis? In P-J. Lee, editor, *Advances in Cryptology – Asiacrypt'04*, volume 3329 of *Lectures Notes in Computer Science*, pages 432–450. Springer, 2004.

2. E. Biham. On Matsui's Linear Cryptanalysis. In A. De Santis, editor, *Advances in Cryptology – Eurocrypt'94*, volume 950 of *Lectures Notes in Computer Science*, pages 341–355. Springer, 1995.

3. E. Biham and A. Biryukov. An Improvement of Davies' Attack on DES. In A. De Santis, editor, *Advances in Cryptology – Eurocrypt'94*, volume 950 of *Lectures Notes in Computer Science*, pages 461–467. Springer, 1995.

4. E. Biham and A. Shamir. Differential Cryptanalysis of the Full 16-round DES. In E.F. Brickell, editor, *Advances in Cryptology – Crypto'92*, volume 740 of *Lectures Notes in Computer Science*, pages 487–496. Springer, 1992.

5. N. Courtois. Feistel Schemes and Bi-linear Cryptanalysis. In M. Franklin, editor, *Advances in Cryptology – CRYPTO'04*, volume 3152 of *Lectures Notes in Computer Science*, pages 23–40. Springer, 2004.

6. D. Davies and S. Murphy. Pairs and Triplets of DES S-Boxes. *Journal of Cryptology*, 8(1):1–25, 1995.

7. DES Cracker Project. See
   http://www.eff.org/Privacy/Crypto/Crypto_misc/DESCracker/.

8. P. Junod. On the Complexity of Matsui's Attack. In S. Vaudenay and A. Youssef, editors, *Selected Areas in Cryptography – 2001*, volume 2259 of *Lectures Notes in Computer Science*, pages 199–211. Springer, 2001.

9. L. Knudsen and J-E. Mathiassen. A Chosen-Plaintext Linear Attack on DES. In B. Schneier, editor, *Fast Software Encryption – 2000*, volume 1978 of *Lectures Notes in Computer Science*, pages 262–272. Springer, 2001.

10. S. Kunz-Jacques, F. Muller, and F. Valette. The Davies-Murphy Power Attack. In P.-J. Lee, editor, *Advances in Cryptology – Asiacrypt'04*, volume 3329 of *Lectures Notes in Computer Science*, pages 451–467. Springer, 2004.

11. M. Matsui. Linear Cryptanalysis Method for DES Cipher. In T. Helleseth, editor, *Advances in Cryptology – Eurocrypt'93*, volume 765 of *Lectures Notes in Computer Science*, pages 386–397. Springer, 1993.

12. National Bureau of Standards (NBS), U.S. *FIPS 46, "Data Encryption Standard", Federal Information Processing Standards Publication 46*, 1977.

13. National Institute of Standards and Technology (NIST). Advanded Encryption Standard (AES) FIPS Publication 197, November 2001. Available at http://csrc.nist.gov/publications/fips/fips197/fips-197.pdf.

14. T. Pornin. Optimal Resistance Against the Davies and Murphy Attack. In K. Ohta and D. Pei, editors, *Advances in Cryptology – Asiacrypt'98*, volume 1514 of *Lectures Notes in Computer Science*, pages 148–159. Springer, 1998.
15. T. Shimoyama and T. Kaneko. Quadratic Relation of S-box and Its Application to the Linear Attack of Full Round DES. In H. Krawczyk, editor, *Advances in Cryptology – Crypto'98*, volume 1462 of *Lectures Notes in Computer Science*, pages 200–211. Springer, 1998.

A   Detailed Steps of the Data Analysis Phase

A.1   Step 3

In the step number 3, we guess the key bits involved in S_5 at the first round. Luckily, 4 of these bits $(K_4, K_{22}, K_{28}, K_{39})$ are already known. Thanks to the key scheduling properties, only K_{37} and K_{54} need to be guessed. We know the plaintext bits involved in S_5 (part of it are arbitrary constants, the rest is contained in the pattern of table T_2). So we can predict S_5's output and in particular the bit U_{24}. 2 plaintext bits are no longer needed and the new table T_3 contains the number of occurrences of the 23-bit pattern formed by :

- The bit $\lambda(p_R) \oplus \lambda(c_R) \oplus \lambda(W)$
- The 12 bits $(p_{52}, \ldots, p_{63})$ from the plaintext
- The 9 bits $(p_1, p_{25}, \ldots, p_{32})$ from the plaintext
- The intermediate bit $p_{24} \oplus U_{24}$

A.2   Step 4

In the step number 4, we guess the key bits involved in S_6 at the first round. Luckily, 3 of these bits (K_{23}, K_{29}, K_{53}) are already known. Thanks to the key scheduling properties, only K_5, K_{30} and K_{47} need to be guessed. We predict S_6's output and in particular the bits U_{27} and U_{32}. 4 plaintext bits are no longer needed and the new table T_4 contains the number of occurrences of the 19-bit pattern formed by :

- The bit $\lambda(p_R) \oplus \lambda(c_R) \oplus \lambda(W)$
- The 8 bits $(p_{56}, \ldots, p_{63})$ from the plaintext
- The 7 bits $(p_1, p_{25}, p_{26}, p_{28}, p_{29}, p_{30}, p_{31})$
- The 3 intermediate bits $(p_{24} \oplus U_{24}, p_{27} \oplus U_{27}, p_{32} \oplus U_{32})$

A.3   Step 5

In the step number 5, we guess the key bits involved in S_7 at the first round. Luckily, 2 of these bits (K_{21}, K_{63}) are already known. Thanks to the key scheduling properties, only K_{15}, K_{20}, K_{38} and K_{61} need to be guessed. We predict S_7's output and in particular the bit U_{30}. 4 plaintext bits are no longer needed and the new table T_5 contains the number of occurrences of the 15-bit pattern formed by :

- The bit $\lambda(p_R) \oplus \lambda(c_R) \oplus \lambda(W)$
- The 4 bits $(p_{60}, \ldots, p_{63})$ from the plaintext
- The 6 bits $(p_1, p_{25}, p_{26}, p_{28}, p_{29}, p_{31})$
- The 4 intermediate bits $(p_{24} \oplus U_{24}, p_{27} \oplus U_{27}, p_{30} \oplus U_{30}, p_{32} \oplus U_{32})$

A.4   Step 6

In the step number 6, we guess the key bits involved in S_8 at the first round. Hence we need to guess $K_{13}, K_{14}, K_{31}, K_{45}, K_{55}$ and K_{62}. Then we predict S_8's output and in particular the bit U_{25}. 4 plaintext bits are no longer needed and the new table T_6 contains the number of occurrences of the 11-bit pattern formed by :

- The bit $\lambda(p_R) \oplus \lambda(c_R) \oplus \lambda(W)$
- The 5 bits $(p_1, p_{26}, p_{28}, p_{29}, p_{31})$
- The 5 intermediate bits $(p_{24} \oplus U_{24}, p_{25} \oplus U_{25}, p_{27} \oplus U_{27}, p_{30} \oplus U_{30}, p_{32} \oplus U_{32})$

A.5   Step 7

In the step number 7, we guess the missing input bits of S-box S_7 at the second round. The actual input is

$$(p_{24} \oplus U_{24}, \ldots, p_{29} \oplus U_{29}) \oplus (K_{53}, K_{13}, K_{30}, K_{55}, K_6, K_{11})$$

Thanks to the key scheduling properties, we already know 4 of these key bits. Besides we already know 3 intermediate bits of the form $p_i \oplus U_i$. The missing U_i's are not known but they depend only on the key and the fixed plaintext bits, so their value is the same for all samples. So we can guess the 3 bits $(U_{26}, U_{28} \oplus K_6, U_{29} \oplus K_{11})$ and predict S_7's output. Then, we determine $V_7 \oplus V_{12} \oplus V_{22} \oplus V_{32}$. The new table T_7 contains the number of occurrences of the 7-bit pattern formed by :

- The bit $\lambda(p_R) \oplus \lambda(c_R) \oplus \lambda(W) \oplus V_7 \oplus V_{12} \oplus V_{22} \oplus V_{32}$
- The 4 bits $(p_1, p_{28}, p_{29}, p_{31})$
- The 2 intermediate bits $(p_{30} \oplus U_{30}, p_{32} \oplus U_{32})$

A.6   Step 8

In the step number 8, we guess the missing input bits of S-box S_8 at the second round. Thanks to the key scheduling properties, all key bits involved $(K_5, K_6, K_{23}, K_{37}, K_{47}$ and $K_{54})$ are already known. Hence we just need to guess the 4 missing input bits : $U_1, U_{28}, U_{29}, U_{31}$. in order to predict S_8's output and in particular $V_5 \oplus V_{21} \oplus V_{27}$. Hence we know the value of $\lambda(V)$. The new table T_8 contains the number of occurrences of the bit :

- The bit $\lambda(p_R) \oplus \lambda(c_R) \oplus \lambda(W) \oplus \lambda(V)$

A Related-Key Rectangle Attack
on the Full KASUMI

Eli Biham[1], Orr Dunkelman[1,*] Nathan Keller[2]

[1]Computer Science Department, Technion,
Haifa 32000, Israel
{biham, orrd}@cs.technion.ac.il
[2]Einstein Institute of Mathematics, Hebrew University,
Jerusalem 91904, Israel
nkeller@math.huji.ac.il

Abstract. KASUMI is an 8-round Feistel block cipher used in the confidentiality and the integrity algorithms of the 3GPP mobile communications. As more and more 3GPP networks are being deployed, more and more users use KASUMI to protect their privacy. Previously known attacks on KASUMI can break up to 6 out of the 8 rounds faster than exhaustive key search, and no attacks on the full KASUMI have been published.

In this paper we apply the recently introduced related-key boomerang and rectangle attacks to KASUMI, resulting in an attack that is faster than exhaustive search against the full cipher. We also present a related-key boomerang distinguisher for 6-round KASUMI using only 768 adaptively chosen plaintexts and ciphertexts encrypted or decrypted under four related keys.

Recently, it was shown that the security of the entire encryption system of the 3GPP networks cannot be proven using only the "ordinary" assumption that the underlying cipher (KASUMI) is a Pseudo-Random Permutation. It was also shown that if we assume that KASUMI is also secure with respect to differential-based related-key attacks then the security of the entire system can be proven. Our results show that theoretically, KASUMI is not secure with respect to differential-based related-key attacks, and thus, the security of the entire encryption system of the 3GPP cannot be proven at this time.

1 Introduction

KASUMI [31] is a 64-bit block cipher used in the confidentiality and the integrity algorithms of the 3GPP mobile communications. KASUMI was developed through the collaborative efforts of the 3GPP organizational partners. It is a slight modification of the known block cipher MISTY1 [27], optimized for implementation in hardware.

---

* The research presented in this paper was supported by the Clore scholarship programme.

B. Roy (Ed.): ASIACRYPT 2005, LNCS 3788, pp. 443–461, 2005.

The security of the entire 3GPP mobile network relies on the security of the underlying block cipher KASUMI. Initial examination of the modes of operation used in the 3GPP networks showed that if KASUMI is a Pseudo-Random Permutation (PRP), then the entire network is provably secure [20,16]. However, it appeared that the proof was incorrect [17]. Moreover, it was shown that assuming only that the underlying cipher is a PRP, the security of the modes of operation cannot be proven [17]. In [18], Iwata and Kohno showed that if KASUMI is a PRP and is also secure with respect to differential-based related-key attacks, then the modes in which KASUMI is used can be proven secure. This result shows that the strength of KASUMI with respect to related-key attacks is crucial to the security of the entire mobile network.

KASUMI accepts 128-bit keys and consists of eight Feistel rounds. Previous results on KASUMI include an impossible differential attack on a 6-round version of the cipher presented by Kühn [25] and a related-key differential attack on a 6-round version of the cipher presented by Blunden and Escott [12]. There are no known attacks applicable to the full 8-round KASUMI.

In this paper we apply the recently introduced related-key boomerang and rectangle attacks to the full 8-round KASUMI and to reduced-round versions of the cipher.

The *boomerang attack* [33] is an adaptive chosen plaintext and ciphertext attack built over differential cryptanalysis [9]. The cipher is treated as a cascade of two sub-ciphers, and a short differential is used in each of these two sub-ciphers. These two differentials are combined in an elegant way to suggest some property of the entire cipher with high probability that can be detected using adaptive chosen plaintext and ciphertext queries.

The boomerang attack was further developed in [21] into a chosen plaintext attack called the *amplified boomerang attack*. The transformation uses birthday paradox techniques to eliminate the adaptive nature of the attack by encrypting large sets of plaintexts. After the encryption of the plaintexts, the attacker searches for quartets of plaintexts that behave as if they were constructed in the boomerang process. The transformation to a chosen plaintext attack (instead of an adaptive chosen plaintexts and ciphertexts attack) has price both in a much larger data complexity, and in a much more complicated algorithm for the identification of the right quartets. After its introduction, the amplified boomerang attack was further developed into the *rectangle attack* [6]. The rectangle attack utilizes a more careful analysis that shows that the probability of a right quartet is significantly higher than suggested by the amplified boomerang attack. Also an optimized algorithm for finding and identifying the right quartets was given in [7]. The boomerang and the rectangle attacks were used to attack several reduced-round versions of block ciphers, including the AES, Serpent, SHACAL-1, COCONUT98 (the full cipher), SC2000, Khufu and FEAL.

Related-key attacks were introduced by Biham [2] in 1993. This technique assumes that the attacker is able to request the encryptions of plaintexts under two related keys: an unknown key and a key (also unknown) that is related to it in some known way. Under this assumption, the attacker uses the relations between the keys and various weaknesses of the cipher to derive information about the two keys. In [2] a related-key attack was applied to a modified variant of DES [28], to LOKI [13] and to Lucifer [29]. In [22] Kelsey et al. combined the related-key technique with differential cryptanalysis [9]. In the related-key differential attack, the attacker requests the encryption of pairs of plaintexts with some chosen difference under the unknown key and under a related key such that the difference between the keys is chosen by the attacker. Related-key differential attacks were used to attack several full/reduced versions of block ciphers, including AES [14], KASUMI [31], and others (see the attacks of [19,12,22]).

The related-key boomerang and rectangle attacks were presented by Kim et al. [23,24] and independently by Biham et al. [8]. These attacks are a combination of the boomerang/rectangle technique with the related-key differential technique. In the attack, the attacker examines quartets of plaintexts encrypted under four differentially related keys. The key differences are used to improve the two differentials used for the boomerang (or the rectangle) distinguisher. Related-key boomerang and rectangle attacks were used to attack reduced versions of AES [14], IDEA [26] and SHACAL-1 [15] and the full COCONUT98 [32].

In this paper we present a key recovery related-key rectangle attack on the entire 8-round version of KASUMI. The attack requires $2^{54.6}$ chosen plaintexts encrypted under four related keys and has time complexity of $2^{76.1}$ encryptions. We also present a related-key boomerang distinguisher of 6-round KASUMI. The distinguisher requires 768 adaptive chosen plaintexts and ciphertexts encrypted under four related keys and has a negligible time complexity. We summarize our results along with previously known results on KASUMI in Table 1.[1]

Our results do not practically compromise the security of the 3GPP mobile networks. However, our results show that KASUMI cannot be considered secure against differential-based related-key attacks. Therefore, the security of the entire mobile network cannot be proven at this stage.

This paper is organized as follows: In Section 2 we give a brief description of the structure of KASUMI. In Section 3 we describe the related-key boomerang and rectangle attacks. In Section 4 we present a related-key rectangle attack on the full KASUMI. Section 5 contains a related-key boomerang distinguisher of 6-round KASUMI. Finally, Section 6 summarizes the paper.

---

[1] We note that several generic attacks that apply to any block cipher with 64-bit block and 128-bit keys, such as exhaustive key search, key-collision, and time-memory-data tradeoffs, may be used to attack the cipher. For example, a key-collision attack on this cipher has time complexity of 2^{64} encryptions using 2^{64} known plaintexts, each encrypted under a different key [3]. For time-memory-data tradeoff attacks using four different keys as in our attack, the overall time complexity (including preprocessing) is very close to the time complexity of an exhaustive key search. A time-memory-data tradeoff attack using a fixed known plaintext encrypted under a large number of 2^{43} keys can be performed with on-line computation of 2^{84} encryptions and preprocessing of 2^{85} encryptions [11].

Table 1. Summary of the Attacks on KASUMI

Attack	Number of		Complexity		Source
	Rounds	Keys	Data	Time	
Higher-Order Differential	$4^\dagger$	1	$2^{10.5}$ CP	$2^{22.11}$	[30]
Related-Key Differential	6	1	$2^{18.6}$ RK-CP	$2^{113.6}$	[12]
Impossible Differential	6	1	2^{55} CP	2^{100}	[25]
Related-Key Boomerang Distinguisher	6	4	768 RK-ACPC	1	Section 5.2
Related-Key Boomerang Key Recovery	6	34	2^{13} RK-ACPC	2^{13}	Section 5.3
Basic Related-Key Rectangle	8	4	2^{53} RK-CP	2^{102}	Section 4.2
Improved Related-Key Rectangle	8	4	$2^{54.6}$ RK-CP	$2^{76.1}$	Section 4.4
Related-Key Boomerang	8	4	$2^{45.2}$ RK-ACPC	$2^{78.7}$	Section 4.4

RK – Related-key, CP – Chosen plaintext, ACPC – Adaptive chosen plaintext and ciphertext
Time complexity is measured in encryption units.
† – this attack is on a version of the cipher without the FL functions.

2 The KASUMI Cipher

KASUMI [31] is a 64-bit block cipher that has a key size of 128 bits. KASUMI was designed as a modification of MISTY1 [27], optimized for implementation in hardware. Therefore, most of the components of KASUMI are similar to the respective components of MISTY1.

KASUMI has a recursive structure. Each of its eight Feistel rounds is composed of an FO function which is a 3-round 32-bit Feistel construction, and of an FL function that mixes a 32-bit subkey with the data. The order of the two functions changes each round (in odd rounds the FL function is first, and in the even rounds the FO function is first).

The FO function also has a recursive structure. Each of the three rounds of the FO functions consists of a key mixing stage and of an application of the FI function, yet another three-round Feistel construction. The FI functions use two non-linear S-boxes $S7$ and $S9$ (where $S7$ is a 7-bit to 7-bit permutation and $S9$ is a 9-bit to 9-bit permutation) and accept an additional 16-bit subkey, which is mixed with the data. In total, a 96-bit subkey enters FO in each round — 48 subkey bits used in the FI functions and 48 subkey bits in the key mixing stages.

Table 2. KASUMI's Key Schedule Algorithm

Round	$KL_{i,1}$	$KL_{i,2}$	$KO_{i,1}$	$KO_{i,2}$	$KO_{i,3}$	$KI_{i,1}$	$KI_{i,2}$	$KI_{i,3}$
1	$K_1 \lll 1$	K_3'	$K_2 \lll 5$	$K_6 \lll 8$	$K_7 \lll 13$	K_5'	K_4'	K_8'
2	$K_2 \lll 1$	K_4'	$K_3 \lll 5$	$K_7 \lll 8$	$K_8 \lll 13$	K_6'	K_5'	K_1'
3	$K_3 \lll 1$	K_5'	$K_4 \lll 5$	$K_8 \lll 8$	$K_1 \lll 13$	K_7'	K_6'	K_2'
4	$K_4 \lll 1$	K_6'	$K_5 \lll 5$	$K_1 \lll 8$	$K_2 \lll 13$	K_8'	K_7'	K_3'
5	$K_5 \lll 1$	K_7'	$K_6 \lll 5$	$K_2 \lll 8$	$K_3 \lll 13$	K_1'	K_8'	K_4'
6	$K_6 \lll 1$	K_8'	$K_7 \lll 5$	$K_3 \lll 8$	$K_4 \lll 13$	K_2'	K_1'	K_5'
7	$K_7 \lll 1$	K_1'	$K_8 \lll 5$	$K_4 \lll 8$	$K_5 \lll 13$	K_3'	K_2'	K_6'
8	$K_8 \lll 1$	K_2'	$K_1 \lll 5$	$K_5 \lll 8$	$K_6 \lll 13$	K_4'	K_3'	K_7'

$X \lll i$ — X rotated to the left by i bits

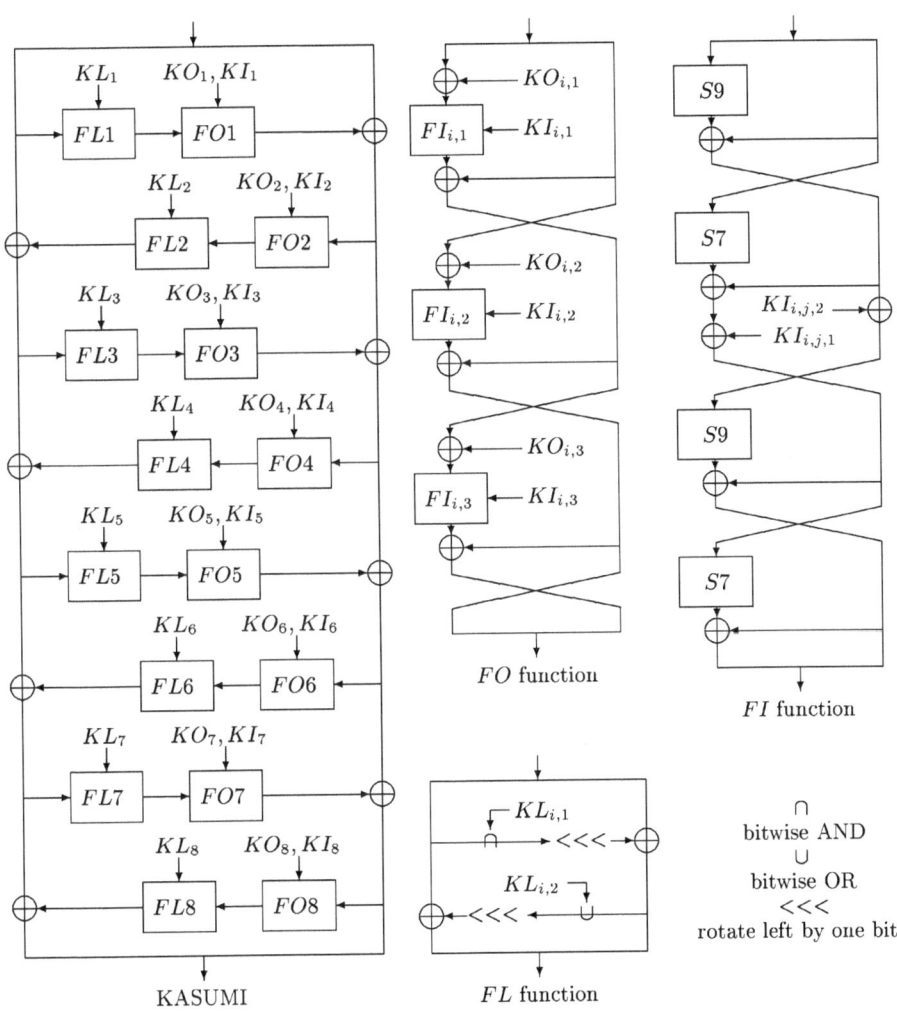

Fig. 1. Outline of KASUMI

The FL function accepts 32-bit input and two 16-bit subkey words. One subkey word affects the data using the OR operation, while the second one affects the data using the AND operation. We outline the structure of KASUMI and its parts in Figure 1.

One of the major differences between KASUMI and MISTY1 is in the key schedule. In KASUMI, the subkeys are derived from the key in a linear way: The 128-bit key K is divided into eight 16-bit words: $K_1, K_2, \ldots, K_8$. Each K_i is used to compute $K_i' = K_i \oplus C_i$, where the C_i's are known and fixed constants. The constants C_i are interleaved with the key bits in order to avoid weak-key classes based on fixing key bits to be zero. Such weak keys were found in IDEA [26] (see for example [10]) and in other ciphers as well.

Table 3. KASUMI's Key Schedule Constants

Round	1	2	3	4	5	6	7	8
Constant	C_1	C_2	C_3	C_4	C_5	C_6	C_7	C_8
Value	0123_x	4567_x	$89AB_x$	$CDEF_x$	$FEDC_x$	$BA98_x$	7654_x	3210_x

In each round, eight words are used as the round subkey (up to some in-word rotations). Therefore, the 128-bit subkey of each round is a linearly dependent of the secret key in a very simple way. We give the exact key schedule of KASUMI in Table 2 and list the values of the constants in Table 3.

3   Related-Key Boomerang and Related-Key Rectangle Attacks

In this section we describe the related-key boomerang and related-key rectangle attacks. First, we outline the boomerang/rectangle attacks and the related-key differential attacks separately. Then, we describe the combination that forms the related-key boomerang and related-key rectangle attacks.

3.1   The Boomerang and the Rectangle Attacks

The main idea behind the boomerang attack [33] is to use two short differentials with high probabilities instead of one long differential with a low probability. We assume that a block cipher $E : \{0,1\}^n \times \{0,1\}^k \to \{0,1\}^n$ can be described as a cascade $E = E_1 \circ E_0$, such that for E_0 there exists a differential $\alpha \to \beta$ with probability p, and for E_1 there exists a differential $\gamma \to \delta$ with probability q. We note that the second differential $\gamma \to \delta$ for E_1 is actually used in the backward direction, i.e., decryption, but as we are dealing with differentials (and not truncated differentials), then this does not change the probability of the differential.

The distinguisher is based on the following boomerang process:

- Ask for the encryption of a pair of plaintexts (P_1, P_2) such that $P_1 \oplus P_2 = \alpha$ and denote the corresponding ciphertexts by (C_1, C_2).
- Calculate $C_3 = C_1 \oplus \delta$ and $C_4 = C_2 \oplus \delta$, and ask for the decryption of the pair (C_3, C_4). Denote the corresponding plaintexts by (P_3, P_4).
- Check whether $P_3 \oplus P_4 = \alpha$.

The boomerang attack uses the first characteristic $(\alpha \to \beta)$ for E_0 with respect to the pairs (P_1, P_2) and (P_3, P_4), and uses the second characteristic $(\gamma \to \delta)$ for E_1 with respect to the pairs (C_1, C_3) and (C_2, C_4).

For a random permutation the probability that the last condition is satisfied is 2^{-n}. For E, the probability that the pair (P_1, P_2) is a right pair with respect to the first differential $(\alpha \to \beta)$ is p. The probability that both pairs (C_1, C_3) and (C_2, C_4) are right pairs with respect to the second differential is q^2. If all these are right pairs, then $E_1^{-1}(C_3) \oplus E_1^{-1}(C_4) = \beta = E_0(P_3) \oplus E_0(P_4)$. Thus, with probability p, $P_3 \oplus P_4 = \alpha$. The total probability of this quartet of plaintexts and ciphertexts to satisfy the boomerang conditions is $(pq)^2$.

The attack can be mounted for all possible β's and γ's simultaneously (as long as $\beta \neq \gamma$). Therefore, a right quartet for E is encountered with probability no less than $(\hat{p}\hat{q})^2$, where:

$$\hat{p} = \sqrt{\sum_\beta \text{Pr}^2[\alpha \to \beta]}, \qquad \text{and} \qquad \hat{q} = \sqrt{\sum_\gamma \text{Pr}^2[\gamma \to \delta]}.$$

The complete analysis is given in [33,6,7].

As the boomerang attack requires adaptive chosen plaintexts and ciphertexts, many of the techniques that were developed for using distinguishers in key recovery attacks cannot be applied. This led to the introduction of chosen plaintext variants of the boomerang attack called the *amplified boomerang attack* [21] and the *rectangle attack* [6]. The transformation of the boomerang attack into a chosen plaintext attack is quite standard, as it can be achieved by birthday-paradox arguments. The key idea behind the transformation is to encrypt many plaintext pairs with input difference α, and to look for quartets that conform to the requirements of the boomerang process.

Given the same decomposition of E as before, and the same basic differentials, the analysis in [6] shows that out of N plaintext pairs, the number of right quartets is expected to be $N^2 2^{-n} \hat{p}^2 \hat{q}^2$. We note, that the main reduction in the probability follows from the fact that unlike the boomerang attack, in the rectangle attack the event $E_0(P_1) \oplus E_0(P_3) = \gamma$ occurs with probability 2^{-n}.

3.2   Related-Key Differentials

Related-key differentials [22] were used for cryptanalysis several times in the past. Recall, that a regular differential deals with some plaintext difference ΔP and a ciphertext difference ΔC such that

$$\text{Pr}_{P,K}[E_K(P) \oplus E_K(P \oplus \Delta P) = \Delta C]$$

is high enough (or zero [5]).

A related-key differential is a triplet of a plaintext difference ΔP, a ciphertext difference ΔC, and a key difference ΔK, such that

$$\text{Pr}_{P,K}[E_K(P) \oplus E_{K \oplus \Delta K}(P \oplus \Delta P) = \Delta C]$$

is useful (high enough or zero).

3.3   Related-Key Boomerang Attacks

Let us assume that we have a related-key differential $\alpha \to \beta$ of E_0 under a key difference ΔK_{ab} with probability p. Assume also that we have another related-key differential $\gamma \to \delta$ for E_1 under a key difference ΔK_{ac} with probability q.

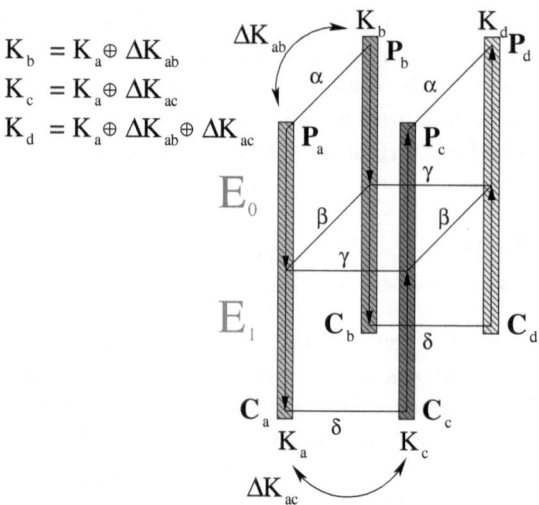

$$K_b = K_a \oplus \Delta K_{ab}$$
$$K_c = K_a \oplus \Delta K_{ac}$$
$$K_d = K_a \oplus \Delta K_{ab} \oplus \Delta K_{ac}$$

Fig. 2. A Related-Key Boomerang Quartet

The related-key boomerang process involves four different unknown (but related) keys — K_a, $K_b = K_a \oplus \Delta K_{ab}$, $K_c = K_a \oplus \Delta K_{ac}$, and $K_d = K_a \oplus \Delta K_{ab} \oplus \Delta K_{ac}$. The attack is performed by the following algorithm:

- Choose a plaintext P_a at random, and compute $P_b = P_a \oplus \alpha$.
- Ask for the ciphertexts $C_a = E_{K_a}(P_a)$ and $C_b = E_{K_b}(P_b)$.
- Compute $C_c = C_a \oplus \delta$ and $C_d = C_b \oplus \delta$.
- Ask for the plaintexts $P_c = E_{K_c}^{-1}(C_c)$ and $P_d = E_{K_d}^{-1}(C_d)$.
- Check whether $P_c \oplus P_d = \alpha$.

See Figure 2 for an outline of such a quartet.

It is easy to see that for a random permutation, the probability that the last condition is satisfied is 2^{-n}. For E the probability that this condition is satisfied is $p^2 q^2$. Hence, the related-key boomerang attack can be used for distinguishing and key recovery attacks for this cipher.

The attack can use many differentials for E_0 and E_1 simultaneously (just like in a regular boomerang attack), as long as all related-key differentials used in E_0 have the same key difference ΔK_{ab} and the same input difference α, and that all related-key differentials used in E_1 have the same key difference ΔK_{ac} and the same output difference δ. Thus, the probability of a quartet to be a right one is $\hat{p}^2 \hat{q}^2$.

In the case of KASUMI, the key schedule algorithm is linear. Therefore, given a key difference, all subkey differences are known, and can be easily used in the related-key model.

3.4   Related-Key Rectangle Attack

The transformation of the related-key boomerang attack into a related-key rectangle attack is similar to the transformation of the boomerang attack to the rectangle attack. The related-key rectangle distinguisher is as follows:

- Choose N plaintext pairs $(P_a, P_b = P_a \oplus \alpha)$ at random and ask for the encryption of P_a under K_a and of P_b under K_b. Denote the set of these pairs by S.
- Choose N plaintext pairs $(P_c, P_d = P_c \oplus \alpha)$ at random and ask for the encryption of P_c under K_c and P_d under K_d. Denote the set of these pairs by T.
- Search a pair of plaintexts $(P_a, P_b) \in S$ and a pair of plaintexts $(P_c, P_d) \in T$, and their corresponding ciphertexts (C_a, C_b) and (C_c, C_d), respectively, satisfying:
  - $P_a \oplus P_b = P_c \oplus P_d = \alpha$
  - $C_a \oplus C_c = C_b \oplus C_d = \delta$

The analysis of the related-key rectangle attack is similar to the one of the rectangle attack (with the same modifications that were presented at the related-key boomerang attack). Starting with N plaintext pairs in S and N plaintext pairs in T, we expect to find $N^2 2^{-n}(\hat{p}\hat{q})^2$ right quartets. For a random permutation the number of "right quartets" is about $N^2 2^{-2n}$, so as long as $\hat{p}\hat{q} > 2^{-n/2}$ we can use the rectangle attack to distinguish between a random permutation and the attacked cipher. This distinguisher can be later used for a key recovery attack.

4   Related-Key Rectangle Attack on KASUMI

In this section we devise a related-key rectangle attack on the entire KASUMI. We start with a short description of the related-key differentials used in this attack, then describe a basic attack without full optimization, and its analysis. Finally, we describe the optimizations that reduce the complexities to our final results.

4.1   Related-Key Differentials of KASUMI

As mentioned earlier, KASUMI's round function is composed of two main functions: the FO function and the FL function. A non-zero input difference to the FO function can become almost any output difference, with approximately the same probability. However, non-zero differences to the FL-function propagate with much higher probabilities.

For the rectangle attack we use two related-key differentials. The first related-key differential is for rounds 1–4, while the second is used in rounds 5–7.

4.1.1   A 4-Round Related-Key Differential for Rounds 1–4   This 4-round related-key differential is an extension by one round of the related-key differential presented in [12]. The key difference is $\Delta K_{ab} = (0, 0, 1, 0, 0, 0, 0, 0)$, i.e., only the third key word has a non-zero difference $K_3' = 0001_x$. The plaintext difference of the differential is $\alpha = (0_x, 0020\ 0000_x)$. It was shown in [12] that with probability $1/4$, the difference after three rounds is equal to α as

well. The input difference of the FO function in the fourth round is non-zero $(0020\ 0000_x)$. The key difference of the fourth round is introduced only at the end of the FO function (precisely, in $FI_{4,3}$). Hence, the non-zero difference propagates through all the parts of FO, and the output difference of the round function is distributed almost uniformly. Therefore, we shall use the differentials $\alpha = (0_x, 0020\ 0000_x) \rightarrow (y, 0020\ 0000_x)$ for all the possible values of y. In the worst case, all the y values are equiprobable. Thus, when using all the 2^{32} possible values, each of them is expected to occur with probability 2^{-32}. Hence, each differential of the form $\alpha = (0_x, 0020\ 0000_x) \rightarrow (y, 0020\ 0000_x)$ has probability 2^{-34}. The effective probability of the differentials when using all these differentials simultaneously is $\hat{p} = \sqrt{2^{32} \cdot (2^{-34})^2} = \sqrt{2^{-36}} = 2^{-18}$. If the y values are not equiprobable, then the value of $\hat{p}$ is higher.

As observed in [12], the attacker can select two bits of the plaintext in order to double the probability of the differential: The attacker assigns one bit of the plaintext to be one (thus fixing one bit of the output of the OR operation in $FL1$) and one bit of the plaintext to be zero (thus fixing one bit of the output of the AND operation in $FL1$). More precisely, let $P = (P_{LL}, P_{LR}, P_{RL}, P_{RR})$, where P_{LL} is the 16 plaintext bits that enter the AND operation of the FL function in the first round, and P_{LR} are the remaining bits of the left half of the plaintext. The attacker sets the least significant bit of P_{LL} and the second least significant bit of P_{LR} to $P_{LL}^0 = 0$ and $P_{LR}^1 = 1$, where the superscript $x \in \{0,1\}$ denotes the x'th bit of that quarter of the plaintext. This selection ensures that the characteristic holds with probability 1 in the first round (instead of $1/2$), despite of the key difference. Therefore, the probability of the differential $\alpha = (0_x, 0020\ 0000_x) \rightarrow (y, 0020\ 0000_x)$ is increased from 2^{-34} to 2^{-33}, and the effective probability of the first part of the rectangle is increased to $\hat{p} = \sqrt{2^{32} \cdot (2^{-33})^2} = \sqrt{2^{-34}} = 2^{-17}$.

It is possible to rotate all the words of the key difference ΔK_{ab} and the characteristic by the same number of bits, without changing the probability of the characteristic. Hence, the above characteristic can be replaced by 15 other characteristics.

4.1.2   A 3-Round Related-Key Differential for Rounds 5–7

The 3-round related-key differential used in rounds 5–7 is the 3-round differential of [12] shifted by four rounds. The key difference is $\Delta K_{ac} = (0, 0, 0, 0, 0, 0, 1, 0)$. Again, it is possible to rotate the difference in K_7' and the corresponding values in the characteristic, to obtain a new characteristic with the same probability.

The differential is $\gamma = (0_x, 0020\ 0000_x) \rightarrow (0_x, 0020\ 0000_x) = \delta$ with probability $q = \hat{q} = 1/4$.

4.2   The Basic Related-Key Rectangle Attack on KASUMI

The attack on KASUMI treats the cipher as a cascade of three parts: E_0 consists of the first four rounds, E_1 consists of rounds 5–7, and E_f the round after the distinguisher (round 8), which is used for analysis. Let K_a, $K_b = K_a \oplus \Delta K_{ab}$,

$K_c = K_a \oplus \Delta K_{ac}$, and $K_d = K_c \oplus \Delta K_{ab}$ be the unknown related keys that we want to retrieve.

For E_0 we use the 4-round differential with $\hat{p} = 2^{-17}$ presented earlier, whose key difference is $\Delta K_{ab} = (0,0,1,0,0,0,0,0)$ and whose input difference is $\alpha = (0_x, 0020\ 0000_x)$. For E_1 we use the 3-round differential with $\hat{q} = 2^{-2}$ presented earlier, whose key difference is $\Delta K_{ac} = (0,0,0,0,0,1,0,0)$ and whose output difference is $\delta = (0_x, 0020\ 0000_x)$.

If we encrypt $N = 2^{51}$ pairs of plaintexts under K_a and K_b, and the same number of pairs under K_c and K_d, we expect to find $N^2 = 2^{102}$ quartets, of which about $N^2 \cdot 2^{-64} \cdot 2^{-34} \cdot 2^{-4} = 2^{102} \cdot 2^{-102} = 1$ are right rectangle quartets.

In the attack we identify the right quartets out of all possible quartets, and then analyze them to retrieve the subkey of round 8. This analysis is performed in the following way:

1. **Data Collection Phase:**
   (a) Ask for the encryption of 2^{51} pairs of plaintexts (P_a, P_b), where $P_b = P_a \oplus \alpha$, $P^0_{a_{LL}} = 0$, and $P^1_{a_{LR}} = 1$, and where P_a is encrypted under K_a and P_b is encrypted under K_b. Insert each pair into a hash table indexed by the 64-bit value of $(C_{a_{RL}}, C_{a_{RR}}, C_{b_{RL}}, C_{b_{RR}})$.
   (b) Ask for the encryption of 2^{51} pairs of plaintexts (P_c, P_d), where $P_d = P_c \oplus \alpha$, $P^0_{c_{LL}} = 0$, and $P^1_{c_{LR}} = 1$, and where P_c is encrypted under K_c and P_d is encrypted under K_d. For each pair, access the hash table in the entry corresponding to the value $(C_{c_{RL}} \oplus 0020_x, C_{c_{RR}}, C_{d_{RL}} \oplus 0020_x, C_{d_{RR}})$. For each pair (P_a, P_b) found in this entry, apply Step 2 on the quartet (P_a, P_b, P_c, P_d).

The $(2^{51})^2$ possible quartets are filtered according to a condition on 64 bits on the difference of the ciphertexts, leading to about 2^{38} quartets that enter Step 2. In the following step, we treat all remaining quartets as right quartets. The analysis of a quartet is done by guessing 32 bits of the key $(KO_{8,1}, KI_{8,1})$, and trying to deduce $KL_{8,2}$. In most cases there is a contradiction, e.g., one of the pairs suggests something which is impossible, or the two pairs disagree on some key bit.

2. **Analyzing Quartets:**
   (a) For each quartet (C_a, C_b, C_c, C_d), guess the 32-bit value of $KO_{8,1}$ and $KI_{8,1}$. Assume that this is a right quartet. For the two pairs (C_a, C_c) and (C_b, C_d) use the value of the guessed key to compute the input and output differences of the OR operation in the last round of both pairs. For each bit of this 16-bit OR operation of $FL8$, the possible values of the corresponding bit of $KL_{8,2}$ are given in Table 4. On average $(8/16)^{16} = 2^{-16}$ values of $KL_{8,2}$ are suggested by each quartet and guess of $KO_{8,1}$ and $KI_{8,1}$.
   (b) For each quartet and values of $KO_{8,1}, KI_{8,1}$ and $KL_{8,2}$ suggested in Step 2(a), guess the 32-bit value of $KO_{8,3}$ and $KI_{8,3}$, and use this information to compute the input and output differences of the AND operation in both pairs. For each bit of the 16-bit AND operation of $FL8$, the

Table 4. Possible Values of $KL_{8,2}$ and $KL_{8,1}$

OR — $KL_{8,2}$					AND — $KL_{8,1}$				
	(X_2', Y_2')					(X_2', Y_2')			
(X_1', Y_1')	(0,0)	(0,1)	(1,0)	(1,1)	(X_1', Y_1')	(0,0)	(0,1)	(1,0)	(1,1)
(0,0)	{0,1}	—	1	0	(0,0)	{0,1}	—	0	1
(0,1)	—	—	—	—	(0,1)	—	—	—	—
(1,0)	1	—	1	—	(1,0)	0	—	0	—
(1,1)	0	—	—	0	(1,1)	1	—	—	1

* The two bits of the differences are denotes by (input difference, output difference): (X_1', Y_1') for one pair and (X_2', Y_2') for the other.

possible values of the corresponding bit of $KL_{8,1}$ are given in Table 4. On average $(8/16)^{16} = 2^{-16}$ values of $KL_{8,1}$ are suggested by each quartet and guess of $KO_{8,1}, KI_{8,1}, KO_{8,3}$, and $KI_{8,3}$ and the computed value of $KL_{8,2}$.

3. **Finding the Right Key:** For each quartet and value of $KO_{8,1}, KI_{8,1}$, $KO_{8,3}, KI_{8,3}$ and the value of $KL_{8,1}$ and $KL_{8,2}$ suggested in Step 2, guess the remaining 32 bits of the key, and perform a trial encryption.

4.3 Analysis of the Attack

We first analyze Step 2(a), and show that given the input and output differences of the OR operation in the two pairs of the quartet, the expected number of suggestions for the key $KL_{8,2}$ is 2^{-16}. This means that the $2^{38} \cdot 2^{32} = 2^{70}$ (quartet, subkey guesses) tuples suggest $2^{70} \cdot 2^{-16} = 2^{54}$ subkey guesses for 48-bit value.

Let us examine a difference in some bit j. There are four combinations of input difference and output difference for this bit for each pair. Table 4 lists the key bits that the two pairs suggest for the respective key bit.

There are nine entries that contain no value. For example, a difference 0 may never cause a difference 1 by any function. Another possible contradiction happens when one pair suggests that the key bit is 0, while the second pair suggests that the key bit is 1. The total number of possible key bits is 8 out of 16 entries. Thus, on average there is $1/2$ a possibility for each bit. In total, for the 16 bits there are $(1/2)^{16} = 2^{-16}$ possibilities on average. A similar analysis can be applied to Step 2(b).

As noted earlier, the expected number of (quartet, subkey guesses) tuples that enter Step 2(b) is 2^{54}. For each of these tuples, we guess 32 additional bits, resulting in $2^{54} \cdot 2^{32} = 2^{86}$ (quartet, subkey guesses) tuples. As step 2(b) is similar to Step 2(a), then after its execution, the expected number of (quartet, subkey guesses) tuples is $2^{86} \cdot 2^{-16} = 2^{70}$, while the guessed subkey has 96 bits in total.

Step 2(a) can be implemented using only a few logical operations. The test whether a pair suggests a contradiction (a zero difference in the input with corresponding non-zero difference in the output) can be performed as follows: Let X' be the word of input differences and let Y' be the word of output differences.

Compute $Z = \overline{X'} \wedge Y'$, where $\overline{X'}$ is the bitwise complement of X'. If Z is non-zero then there is some bit in X' which is zero, while the corresponding bit in Y' is 1. Thus, we can check using two logical operation whether one of the pairs suggests a contradiction of this kind.

We can also find which bits of the key a key suggests. For the OR operation, the bits that a pair suggests is the bits for which X' has 1, and the value of $KL_{8,2}$ in these bits is the same as in $\overline{Y'}$. To check whether the two pairs suggest contradicting values for the key, it suffices to check whether $(X_1' \wedge X_2') \wedge (Y_1' \oplus Y_2') \neq 0$. A similar method can be used on Step 2(b) (after updating the relevant expression to take into consideration the AND operation). Further optimizations of the generation of the list of possible values of $KL_{8,2}$ and $KL_{8,1}$ can be made using table lookups.

Step 3 goes over all 2^{70} suggestions for the 96 bits of the key, and tries to complete the remaining 32 bits by an exhaustive search. This can easily be performed due to the linear key schedule of KASUMI. The time complexity of this step is 2^{102} trial encryptions.

As the complexity of Step 3 is dominant, the total complexity of this attack is 2^{102} trial encryptions. This complexity is further reduced in the next subsection.

4.4   Improvements of the Attack

Step 3 can be improved by using counting techniques. In case we encrypt three times the data ($2^{52.6}$ plaintexts encrypted under four different keys), we expect to have nine right quartets. Instead of completing the missing key bits by an exhaustive key search, we count how many (quartet, subkey guesses) tuples suggest each value of the 96 bits of $KO_{8,1}$, $KI_{8,1}$, $KO_{8,3}$, $KI_{8,3}$, $KL_{8,1}$ and $KL_{8,2}$. Only few possible wrong key values are expected to get more than five suggestions. On the other hand, the right key has probability 88.4% to have at least this number of suggestions. Therefore, we identify which 96-bit values have more than five suggestions, and exhaustively search over the remaining bits of these cases. The time complexity of this attack is dominated by Step 2(b). The data complexity of the attack is $2^{54.6}$ related-key chosen plaintexts and the time complexity of the attack is equivalent to $2^{86.2}$ full KASUMI encryptions.

Another improvement of the attack is based on the observation that Step 2(b) can be implemented in two substeps. In the first one, we guess $KO_{8,3}$ and the 9 bits of $KI_{8,3,2}$, and find the value of only 9 bits of $KL_{8,1}$. Hence, we generate $9 \cdot 2^{54} \cdot 2^{25} = 2^{82.2}$ (quartet, subkey guesses) where the subkey guess is of 73 bits. As this improvement first deals only with 9 bits of $KL_{8,1}$, the expected number of remaining (quartet, subkey guesses) values is $2^{73.2}$. Then, we perform the second substep on the 7 remaining bits of $KI_{8,3,1}$ and of $KL_{8,1}$. The time complexity of the attack is now dominated by the first substep of Step 2(b), whose complexity is equivalent to about $2^{79.2}$ KASUMI encryptions.

Our last improvement uses the fact that Step 2(b) (and even its first substep) partially depends on Step 2(a). After Step 2(a) there are 2^{54} tuples of the form (quartet, subkey guesses), where the subkey guess is of 48 bits. However, Step 2(b) uses only 32 bits of the guessed subkey, i.e., the value of $KO_{8,1}$ and

$KI_{8,1}$. As mentioned earlier, a given quartet suggests about 2^{16} values for the 48 bits of $KO_{8,1}, KI_{8,1}, KL_{8,2}$. However, it suggests about $2^{12.9}$ values for 32 bits of $KO_{8,1}, KI_{8,1}$.

This observation is used to reduce the complexity of the attack: The purpose of Step 2(a) is now to find the list of about $2^{12.9}$ values for $KO_{8,1}, KI_{8,1}$ that a quartet suggests, and then Step 2(b) finds the list of about $2^{12.9}$ values for $KO_{8,3}, KI_{8,3}$. Only then, in Step 3, we take into consideration the possible values of $KL_{8,1}$ and $KL_{8,2}$. This reduces the time complexity of the attack to $2^{76.1}$ KASUMI encryptions.

The attack can also be transformed into a related-key boomerang attack that requires $2^{43.2}$ adaptive chosen plaintexts and ciphertexts (encrypted under four different keys). The attack is performed starting at the decryption direction, and thus it is a chosen ciphertext attack with adaptively chosen plaintexts. The time complexity of this related-key boomerang attack is $2^{78.1}$ encryptions.

5   The Related-Key Boomerang Attack on 6-Round KASUMI

In this section we present a related-key boomerang attack on 6-round KASUMI. The attack is on the first six rounds (rounds 1–6). It finds 16 bits of the key using only 768 adaptive chosen plaintexts and ciphertexts.

5.1   Another 3-Round Differential of KASUMI

In this subsection we present four related-key conditional characteristics [1] for rounds 4–6 of KASUMI. We describe the conditional characteristics in the backward direction as this is the direction in which we use them. These characteristics can be easily adapted to hold for any three consecutive rounds starting with an even round, either in the forward or in the backward direction.

The key difference of all these conditional characteristics is $\Delta K_{ac} = (0, 0, 0, 0, 0, 1, 0, 0)$. Unlike regular characteristics, conditional characteristics depend on the value of some key bit. The four conditional characteristics we use depend on the same key bit. Two of them assume that the value of this key bit is 0, while the two other assume that the value is 1. Let $\delta_0 = (0020\ 0000_x, 0_x)$, $\delta_1 = (0020\ 0040_x, 0_x)$, and $\delta' = (0001\ 0000_x, 0_x)$. The two conditional characteristics that depend on the value zero are $\delta_0 \to \delta_0$ and $\delta_0 \oplus \delta' \to \delta_0$. The two conditional characteristics that depend on the value one are $\delta_1 \to \delta_1$ and $\delta_1 \oplus \delta' \to \delta_1$ (the index of the subscript of δ denotes the value of the key bit). All these conditional characteristics have probability 1/4.

Given a pair with a ciphertext difference of the conditional characteristic, then during the decryption the zero input difference is preserved in round 6 by the $FO6$, and with probability 1/2 it is also the output difference of $FL6$ (there is a subkey difference in one bit that is canceled with probability 1/2). In round 5, we hope to achieve a difference of $0020\ 0000_x$ after $FL5$, which is then canceled with the key difference in $KO5,1$. This is where the conditional property of the characteristics is used. In order to achieve the desired output difference of $FL5$, the conditional characteristic depends on the value of the key bit that is ANDed in $FL5$. There is an active bit in the data, and if the value of the key bit is 1, then this difference is preserved. Otherwise, if the value is 0, then the AND operation has a zero output difference. Thus, for a given value of this key bit, exactly two out of the four characteristics yield a difference $0020\ 0000_x$ after $FL5$ (this part of the conditional characteristic has probability 1), whereas for the other two characteristics this difference is impossible. Therefore, in our attack we use all four characteristics in parallel, and know that two of them pass round 5 with a zero output difference with probability 1.

In round 4, the zero difference is preserved by the $FO4$ function. Again, it has probability $1/2$ to be preserved also by $FL4$, and probability $1/2$ of not being preserved. Thus, the input difference of the characteristic is either the output difference (δ_1 or δ_2), or the output difference XORed with δ'.

Hence, either each of the first two conditional characteristics have probability $1/4$, or the other two have probability $1/4$. For each such case the effective probability based on the two characteristics is $\hat{q} = \sqrt{(1/4)^2 + (1/4)^2} = 1/\sqrt{8}$. The successful conditional characteristics are determined by the value of the fifth bit of K_5 (i.e., K_5^4).

We note that all these conditional characteristics can be rotated along with the key difference, to produce 15 similar sets of characteristics with the same effective probability.

5.2   A Related-Key Boomerang Distinguisher on 6-Round KASUMI

In this subsection we present a related-key boomerang distinguisher of 6-round KASUMI. The distinguisher is mounted on rounds 1–6 of KASUMI, but it can be easily adapted to rounds 2–7 or to rounds 3–8 as well.

Denote by E a reduced version of KASUMI consisting of the first six rounds of the cipher. We describe E as a cascade $E = E_1 \circ E_0$, where E_0 corresponds to rounds 1–3 and E_1 corresponds to rounds 4–6. The attack exploits the characteristic $\alpha = (0_x, 0020\ 0000_x) \rightarrow (0_x, 0020\ 0000_x)$ of E_0 with probability $1/4$, as well as the four characteristics $\delta_0 \rightarrow \delta_0$, $\delta_0 \oplus \delta' \rightarrow \delta_0$, $\delta_1 \rightarrow \delta_1$, and $\delta_1 \oplus \delta' \rightarrow \delta_1$ of E_1 with probability $1/4$. The key difference used in E_0 is $\Delta K_{ab} = (0,0,1,0,0,0,0,0)$, and the key difference of all the characteristics of E_1 is $\Delta K_{ac} = (0,0,0,0,0,1,0,0)$.

The attack essentially performs two standard related-key boomerang distinguishers, one for each possible value of the key bit K_5^4. A small improvement that we use, is to save some of the data by reusing some of the plaintexts generated in the attack. The attack algorithm is as follows:

1. Choose M pairs of plaintexts $(P_{a,i}, P_{b,i})$ (for $1 \le i \le M$) such that $P_{a,i} \oplus P_{b,i} = \alpha$. Ask for the encryption of the pairs such that in each pair, $P_{a,i}$ is encrypted under K_a and $P_{b,i}$ is encrypted under the related-key $K_b = K_a \oplus \Delta K_{ab}$. Denote the corresponding ciphertexts by $(C_{a,i}, C_{b,i})$.

2. For $1 \leq i \leq M$, calculate $C_{c,i} = C_{a,i} \oplus \delta_0$ and $C_{d,i} = C_{b,i} \oplus \delta_0$. Ask for the decryption of the pairs $(C_{c,i}, C_{d,i})$ such that in each pair, $C_{c,i}$ is decrypted under $K_c = K_a \oplus \Delta K_{ac}$ and $C_{d,i}$ is decrypted under $K_d = K_a \oplus \Delta K_{ab} \oplus \Delta K_{ac}$. Denote the corresponding plaintexts by $(P_{c,i}, P_{d,i})$.

3. For $1 \leq i \leq M$, calculate $C_{e,i} = C_{a,i} \oplus \delta_1$ and $C_{f,i} = C_{b,i} \oplus \delta_1$. Ask for the decryption of the pairs $(C_{e,i}, C_{f,i})$ such that in each pair $C_{e,i}$ is decrypted under K_c and $C_{f,i}$ is decrypted under K_d. Denote the corresponding plaintexts by $(P_{e,i}, P_{f,i})$.

4. Check whether $P_{c,i} \oplus P_{d,i} = \alpha$ and count the number of such occurrences.

5. Check whether $P_{e,i} \oplus P_{f,i} = \alpha$ and count the number of such occurrences.

6. If one of the two counters from Steps 4 and 5 is greater than zero, then output "6-Round KASUMI". Otherwise, output "Not 6-Round KASUMI".

The total probability of the boomerang process of this distinguisher is $(1/4)^2 \cdot (1/\sqrt{8})^2 = 1/128$, either for quartets counted in Step 4 or for quartets counted in Step 5. Therefore, for $M = 256$ we expect to find two right quartets in Step 4 or Step 5 (either for the quartets $(P_{a,i}, P_{b,i}, P_{c,i}, P_{d,i})$ or for the quartets $(P_{a,i}, P_{b,i}, P_{e,i}, P_{f,i})$). Filtering of these pairs is expected to be very effective as for a random permutation the probability of the event $P_{c,i} \oplus P_{d,i} = \alpha$ (or the event $P_{e,i} \oplus P_{f,i} = \alpha$) is 2^{-64}.

The boomerang distinguisher can be improved using the following observation: Just like in the rectangle attack, by fixing two plaintext bits ($P_{a_{LL}}^0 = 0, P_{a_{LR}}^1 = 1$), the probability of the first characteristic in the encryption direction is $1/2$ (instead of $(1/4)^2$). Therefore, if we choose all the $(P_{a,i}, P_{b,i})$ according to this additional requirement, the probability of the characteristic in rounds 1–3 in the forward direction doubles.

The overall probability of this boomerang process in this case is doubled to $1/64$. Thus, $M = 128$ suffices for a success rate of about 86%. Hence, our distinguisher requires a total of $3 \cdot 128 \cdot 2 = 768$ adaptively chosen plaintexts and ciphertexts such that 256 chosen plaintexts are encrypted and 512 adaptively chosen ciphertexts are decrypted. The time complexity of the attack is negligible.

5.3   Related-Key Boomerang Key Recovery Attack on 6-Round KASUMI

We note that the boomerang distinguisher can be also used for a key recovery attack. As mentioned earlier, the set of characteristics (of E_1) for which the attack succeeds depends on the value of a single key bit of K_5. Thus, the value of this key bit can be detected by observing which one of the sets of characteristics of E_1 is successful. Similar attacks can be mounted by taking other single bits of K_6 to have key difference in E_1. That way, all 16 bits of K_5 can be retrieved by performing the attack 16 times, each time with another key difference. The rest of the key can be retrieved using auxiliary techniques.

---

[2] The actual probability is slightly higher, i.e., $5/8$, and the probability of the first characteristic in the decryption direction is $5/16$.

This variant of the attack requires 256 chosen plaintexts encrypted under two keys (K_a and K_b), and sixteen times the decryption of 512 adaptive chosen ciphertexts decrypted under two related keys. The total data complexity of the attack is 2^{13} adaptive chosen plaintexts and ciphertexts encrypted under 34 keys. The time complexity of the attack is less than 2^{13} KASUMI encryptions.

6 Summary and Conclusions

In this paper we apply the related-key boomerang and related-key rectangle attacks to the KASUMI block cipher. Our attacks are first attacks on the full cipher. The related-key rectangle attack requires $2^{54.6}$ chosen plaintexts encrypted under four keys ($2^{52.6}$ plaintexts encrypted under each key). The time complexity is equivalent to $2^{76.1}$ KASUMI encryptions.

We also present an efficient related-key boomerang distinguisher on 6-round KASUMI requires 768 adaptive chosen plaintexts and ciphertexts, using four related keys.[3] This attack can be converted to a key recovery attack that requires 2^{13} adaptive chosen plaintexts and ciphertexts encrypted under 34 related keys, and finds 16 key bits with time complexity of less than 2^{13} KASUMI encryptions.

Previous works show that the security of the KASUMI block cipher with respect to related-key attacks is significant for proving that the modes of operations used in the 3GPP networks are secure. Our results show that KASUMI cannot be considered secure with respect to differential-based related-key attacks. Therefore, the currently existing security proofs of the protocols of the 3GPP network should be revised to reflect this situation.

Acknowledgments

It is a pleasure to thank Elad Barkan for useful references, and to Tetsu Iwata for providing us with a clear understanding of the model and requirements of the security proofs. The valuable comments made by the anonymous referees are also appreciated.

References

1. Ishai Ben-Aroya, Eli Biham, *Differential Cryptanalysis of Lucifer*, Advances in Cryptology, proceedings of EUROCRYPT '93, Lecture Notes in Computer Science 773, pp. 187–199, Springer-Verlag, 1994.
2. Eli Biham, *New Types of Cryptanalytic Attacks Using Related Keys (Extended Abstract)*, Journal of Cryptology, Vol. 7, No. 4, pp. 229–246, Springer-Verlag, 1994.
3. Eli Biham, *How to decrypt or even substitute DES-encrypted messages in 2^{28} steps*, Information Processing Letters, Vol. 84, No. 3, pp. 117–124, Elsevier, 2002.

---

[3] We expect to be able to reduce this complexity even further, but decided to save some of our time.

4. Eli Biham, Alex Biryukov, Adi Shamir, *Miss in the Middle Attacks on IDEA and Khufu*, proceedings of Fast Software Encryption 6, Lecture Notes in Computer Science 1636, pp. 124–138, Springer-Verlag, 1999.

5. Eli Biham, Alex Biryukov, Adi Shamir, *Cryptanalysis of Skipjack Reduced to 31 Rounds*, Advances in Cryptology, proceedings of EUROCRYPT '99, Lecture Notes in Computer Science 1592, pp. 12–23, Springer-Verlag, 1999.

6. Eli Biham, Orr Dunkelman, Nathan Keller, *The Rectangle Attack – Rectangling the Serpent*, Advances in Cryptology, proceedings of EUROCRYPT '01, Lecture Notes in Computer Science 2045, pp. 340–357, Springer-Verlag, 2001.

7. Eli Biham, Orr Dunkelman, Nathan Keller, *New Results on Boomerang and Rectangle Attacks*, proceedings of Fast Software Encryption 9, Lecture Notes in Computer Science 2365, pp. 1–16, Springer-Verlag, 2002.

8. Eli Biham, Orr Dunkelman, Nathan Keller, *Related-Key Boomerang and Rectangle Attacks*, Advances in Cryptology, proceedings of EUROCRYPT '05, Lecture Notes in Computer Science 3494, pp. 507–525, Springer-Verlag, 2005.

9. Eli Biham, Adi Shamir, *Differential Cryptanalysis of the Data Encryption Standard*, Springer-Verlag, 1993.

10. Alex Biryukov, Jorge Nakahara J., Bart Preneel, Joos Vandewalle, *New Weak-Key Class of IDEA*, proceedings of Information and Communications Security 4, Lecture Notes in Computer Science 2513, pp. 315–326, Springer-Verlag, 2002.

11. Alex Biryukov, Sourav Mukhopadhyay, Palash Sarkar, *Improved Time-Memory Trade-offs with Multiple Data* preproceedings of Selected Areas in Cryptography 2005, pp. 113-131, 2005, to appear in LNCS.

12. Mark Blunden, Adrian Escott, *Related Key Attacks on Reduced Round KASUMI*, proceedings of Fast Software Encryption 8, Lecture Notes in Computer Science 2355, pp. 277–285, Springer-Verlag, 2002.

13. Lawrence Brown, Josef Pieprzyk, Jennifer Seberry, *LOKI — A Cryptographic Primitive for Authentication and Secrecy Applications*, Advances in Cryptology, proceedings of AUSCRYPT '90, Lecture Notes in Computer Science 453, pp. 229–236, Springer-Verlag, 1990.

14. Joan Daemen, Vincent Rijmen, *The design of Rijndael: AES — the Advanced Encryption Standard*, Springer-Verlag, 2002.

15. Helena Handschuh, David Naccache, *SHACAL*, preproceedings of NESSIE first workshop, Leuven, 2000.

16. Dowon Hong, Ju-Sung Kang, Bart Preneel, Heuisu Riu, *A Concrete Security Analysis for 3GPP-MAC*, proceedings of Fast Software Encryption 10, Lecture Notes in Computer Science 2887, pp. 154–169, Springer-Verlag, 2003.

17. Tetsu Iwata, Kaoru Kurosawa, *On the Correctness of Security Proofs for the 3GPP Confidentiality and Integrity Algorithms*, proceedings of Cryptography and Coding — 9th IMA International Conference, Lecture Notes in Computer Science 2898, pp. 306–318, Springer-Verlag, 2003.

18. Tetsu Iwata, Tadayoshi Kohno, *New Security Proofs for the 3GPP Confidentiality and Integrity Algorithms*, proceedings of Fast Software Encryption 11, Lecture Notes in Computer Science 3017, pp. 427–445, Springer-Verlag, 2004.

19. Goce Jakimoski, Yvo Desmedt, *Related-Key Differential Cryptanalysis of 192-bit Key AES Variants*, proceedings of Selected Areas in Cryptography 2003, Lecture Notes in Computer Science 3006, pp. 208–221, Springer-Verlag, 2004.

20. Ju-Sung Kang, Sang Uk Shin, Dowon Hong, Okyeon Yi, *Provable Security of KASUMI and 3GPP encryption mode*, Advances in Cryptology, proceedings of ASIACRYPT '01, Lecture Notes in Computer Science 2248, pp. 255–271, Springer-Verlag, 2001.

21. John Kelsey, Tadayoshi Kohno, Bruce Schneier, *Amplified Boomerang Attacks Against Reduced-Round MARS and Serpent*, proceedings of Fast Software Encryption 7, Lecture Notes in Computer Science 1978, pp. 75–93, Springer-Verlag, 2000.
22. John Kelsey, Bruce Schneier, David Wagner, *Related-Key Cryptanalysis of 3-WAY, Biham-DES, CAST, DES-X, NewDES, RC2, and TEA*, proceedings of Information and Communication Security 1997, Lecture Notes in Computer Science 1334, pp. 233–246, Springer-Verlag, 1997.
23. Jongsung Kim, Guil Kim, Seokhie Hong, Sangjin Lee, Dowon Hong, *The Related-Key Rectangle Attack — Application to SHACAL-1*, proceedings of ACISP 2004, Lecture Notes in Computer Science 3108, pp. 123–136, Springer-Verlag, 2004.
24. Seokhie Hong, Jongsung Kim, Guil Kim, Sangjin Lee, Bart Preneel, *Related-Key Rectangle Attacks on Reduced Versions of SHACAL-1 and AES-192*, proceedings of Fast Software Encryption 12, Lecture Notes in Computer Science 3557, pp. 368–383, Springer-Verlag, 2005.
25. Ulrich Kühn, *Cryptanalysis of Reduced-Round MISTY*, Advances in Cryptology, proceedings of EUROCRYPT '01, Lecture Notes in Computer Science 2045, pp. 325–339, Springer-Verlag, 2001.
26. Xuejia Lai, James L. Massey, *A Proposal for a New Block Cipher Encryption Standard*, Advances in Cryptology, proceeding of EUROCRYPT '90, Lecture Notes in Computer Science 473, pp. 389–404, Springer-Verlag, 1991.
27. Mitsuru Matsui, *Block encryption algorithm MISTY*, proceedings of Fast Software Encryption 4, Lecture Notes in Computer Science 1267, pp. 64–74, Springer-Verlag, 1997.
28. US National Bureau of Standards, *Data Encryption Standard*, Federal Information Processing Standards Publications No. 46, 1977.
29. Arthur Sorkin, *Lucifer, a Cryptographic Algorithm*, Cryptologia, Vol. 8, No. 1, pp. 22–41, 1984.
30. Hidema Tanaka, Chikashi Ishii, Toshinobu Kaneko, *On the Strength of KASUMI without FL Functions against Higher Order Differential Attack*, proceedings of Information Security and Cryptology 3, Lecture Notes in Computer Science 2015, pp. 14–21, Springer-Verlag, 2001.
31. 3rd Generation Partnership Project, Technical Specification Group Services and System Aspects, 3G Security, *Specification of the 3GPP Confidentiality and Integrity Algorithms; Document 2: KASUMI Specification*, V.3.1.1, 2001.
32. Serge Vaudenay, *Provable Security for Block Ciphers by Decorrelation*, proceedings of Annual Symposium on Theoretical Aspects of Computer Science '98, Lecture Notes in Computer Science 1373, pp. 249–275, Springer-Verlag, 1998.
33. David Wagner, *The Boomerang Attack*, proceedings of Fast Software Encryption 6, Lecture Notes in Computer Science 1636, pp. 156–170, 1999.

Some Attacks Against a Double Length Hash Proposal

Lars R. Knudsen[1] and Frédéric Muller[2]

[1] Department of Mathematics, Technical University of Denmark,
DK-2800 Kgs. Lyngby, Denmark
Lars.R.Knudsen@mat.dtu.dk
[2] DCSSI Crypto Lab,
51, boulevard de La Tour-Maubourg 75700 PARIS 07 SP
Frederic.Muller@sgdn.pm.gouv.fr

Abstract. At FSE 2005, Nandi *et al* proposed a method to turn an n-bit compression function into a $2n$-bit compression function. In the black-box model, the security of this double length hash proposal against collision attacks is proven, if no more than $\Omega(2^{2n/3})$ oracle queries to the underlying n-bit function are made.

We explore the security of this hash proposal regarding several classes of attacks. We describe a collision attack that matches the proven security bound and we show how to find preimages in time 2^n. For optimum security the complexities of finding collisions and preimages for a $2n$-bit compression function should be respectively of 2^n and 2^{2n}. We also show that if the output is truncated to $s \leq 2n$ bits, one can find collisions in time roughly $2^{s/3}$ and preimages in time roughly $2^{s/2}$.

These attacks illustrate some important weaknesses of the FSE 2005 proposal, while none of them actually contradicts the proof of security.

1 Introduction

1.1 Hash Functions

Cryptographic hash functions are important primitives in cryptology. They are used in a wide range of applications including message integrity, authentication schemes or public key encryption schemes. Most importantly, they are used to speed up digital signature schemes, which otherwise would be slow and unlikely to be implemented widely. A cryptographic hash function takes an input of arbitrary size and produces an output, also called the hash value, of a fixed, predetermined size. In practice there is a limit for the length of the input, but typically this is chosen big enough for all practical applications. The important properties of a cryptographic hash function are :

- *collision-resistance* : it should be difficult to find a pair $x \neq x'$ of inputs to the hash function H such that $H(x) = H(x')$
- *2nd preimage-resistance* : it should be difficult, for a given x to find $x' \neq x$ such that $H(x) = H(x')$

B. Roy (Ed.): ASIACRYPT 2005, LNCS 3788, pp. 462–473, 2005.

– *preimage-resistance* : it should be difficult, for a given y to find x such that $H(x) = y$

There are generic attacks which apply to any hash function. If the size of the hash value is n bits, then it is well-known that collisions can be found in time $2^{n/2}$ and preimages can be found in time 2^n. For 2nd preimages, the complexity of generic attacks ranges between $2^{n/2}$ and 2^n, depending on the length of the target message. Recent results by Kelsey and Schneier show that the complexity can be only $2^{n/2}$ if the length of the target message is also $2^{n/2}$ [10]. In general, hash functions are built by iterating a basic function called the **compression function**. Attacks can target either the full hash function or the compression function only, although there are connections between both approaches.

1.2   Recent Results in Attacking Hash Functions

Many advances have been made recently for hash function cryptanalysis :

- Some important weaknesses have been shown for popular algorithms. It is the case of MD4 [7,17], MD5 [19], SHA-0 [2,4,20] and SHA-1 [18], for which it was shown how to find collisions much faster than $2^{n/2}$. These results illustrate some weaknesses of the underlying compression functions.
- The generic construction itself could be at risk. Most hash functions are iterative and are built using the Merkle-Damgård method [6,12]. Recent results suggest that this construction is not necessarily a good choice [9,10].
- Computing power is always growing. Attacks with complexity 2^{64} are already accessible using distributed computing. And attacks with complexity 2^{80} may also soon be feasible. Therefore hash functions with output size ≤ 160 bits are not a good choice for long term security.

In light of all this, more work is probably needed for hash function design. In particular, it is believed that a good solution is to increase the size of the internal state. This idea has been independently proposed by Lucks [11], Hirose [8] and Nandi *et al.*[14]. Unfortunately the output size of most available compression functions is not large enough, so one needs to design compression functions with an increased output length. Rather than building a new primitive from scratch, Nandi *et al.* suggested to use a secure n-bit compression function, in order to build a larger compression function (of size $2n$-bit for example). The small compression function could then be instantiated with one of the available function, or with a block cipher in the Davies-Meyer construction. An interesting argument for this new construction is that its security has been proven, using some assumptions on the underlying "small" compression function.

1.3   Our Results

In this paper, we focus on the security of the new double length hash proposal of FSE 2005 [14] against all usual attacks. Regarding the proven security, the authors have only focused on collision attacks, so one may hope to find (second) preimage attacks without contradicting the security proof. Another interesting open problem is to find a collision attack that matches the security proof claimed in [14].

First, we show that a collision can be found for this proposal in time $2^{2n/3}$, which fits the proven security bound (but a generic attack on a $2n$-bit function would cost 2^n). Secondly, we show that preimages can be found in 2^n, while the best generic attack on a $2n$-bit compression function costs 2^{2n}.

An interesting question is how these results would apply to a full hash function built using the FSE 2005 compression function. Iterated constructions generally require the compression function to be collision-resistant in order to guarantee the security of the full hash function. This is the case of the popular Merkle-Damgård construction [6,12]. Another example was given at Crypto'05, where Coron *et al.* revisited the Merkle-Damgård construction [5]. In their analysis, the compression function is modeled as a random oracle.

Sometimes the iterative structure even allows to find better attacks against the full hash than against the compression function alone, as demonstrated in [9,19]. However we did not take into account such scenarios.

1.4   Notions of Security for Truncated Hash

We introduce new notions of security for compression functions and hash functions. These notions are the **near-preimage resistance** and the **near-collision resistance**. The idea is that it should remain difficult to find collisions or preimages on a truncated version of the function. It is often easier to find "near" attacks than attacks against the full hash. This was illustrated in the case of the SHA family where Biham and Chen first described near collisions [1] before "real" collision attacks were later demonstrated [2,18].

There are important motivations for taking into account near-collision and near-preimage attacks in practice. First, truncating the output diminishes the size of the hash value. This can be critical to reduce data storage or to reduce the communication complexity (case of MAC's for instance). When it is estimated that s bits are a sufficient level of security, it is customary to truncate the output. In some case, this even helps to prevent some attacks (it makes more difficult to detect internal collisions in MAC algorithms, for instance).

Secondly, another motivation is that new hash functions may need to remain compatible backward with former applications. For instance, an output of size 160 bits may be needed for compatibility with systems that previously implemented SHA-1. Therefore it is likely that new designs may end up being truncated for practical purpose. A nice illustration of hash function truncation is given by the SHA-2 family [15] : intermediate hash sizes (224 bits and 384 bits) are obtained by truncation of the larger hash sizes (256 bits and 512 bits).

It is expected that the best attacks against truncated hash function remain generic attacks. If the output size is reduced from n to s bits, then the best collision attack should cost $2^{s/2}$ steps and the best preimage attack should cost 2^s steps. In their original paper, Biham and Chen [1] considered near preimages where the **truncated positions are freely chosen by the attacker**. With these additional degrees of freedom, the task of the attacker is easier, because he can first test several messages and choose the truncated positions only afterwards. For example, it is very easy to find a near preimage for SHA with $s = 80$ when the attacker can choose the truncated positions. However, such scenarios are not very realistic in practice, so **we only focus on near attacks where the truncated positions are predetermined**.

On the one hand, the security of a truncated hash function is unlikely to drop dramatically compared to the full version. Suppose that one can find preimages in time T for a s-bit truncated output. Then, for a given n-bit challenge y, an attacker can simply truncate y to s bits and obtain a preimage x for the truncated value. Then, s bits of the initial challenge are already satisfied by x, and the attacker can simply hope that the remaining $n - s$ bits also satisfy the challenge. Therefore a preimage attack for the full hash should cost :

$$T' = T \times 2^{n-s}$$

However there is no guarantee. The previous relation is true for most designs, but there may also exist special designs where this is not true.

On the other hand, truncated the hash function may improve the level of security. This situation has been observed for MAC algorithms where truncation sometimes prevents the detection of internal collisions. Therefore, it is interesting to analyze how the complexity of an attack changes when the output is truncated. For instance, the FSE 2005 double length hash proposal [14] has a security regarding collision attacks proven with a bound of $2^{2n/3}$. Thus, it is very tempting to truncate its output to

$$2 \times (2n/3) = 4n/3$$

bits only, since it appears to be the highest security one can achieve. Unfortunately, in that case, we show that collision attacks would become much easier than $2^{2n/3}$. More generally, when the hash output is truncated to $s < 2n$ bits, we show how to find collisions in time $2^{s/3}$ and preimages in time $2^{s/2}$.

2   Description of the Double Length Compression Function

A compression function is a function $F : \{0,1\}^m \rightarrow \{0,1\}^n$ where $m > n$. Suppose that F requires t calls to either

- a block cipher of block size l.
- a smaller compression function with inputs of l bits

Then, the **rate** r of F is generally defined as the ratio :

$$r = \frac{m - n}{tl}$$

It represents the amount of data compressed for each application of the block cipher (or the smaller function). Achieving a compression function with a ratio $r = 1$ and which is practical seems to be a very difficult task [3]. In their paper,

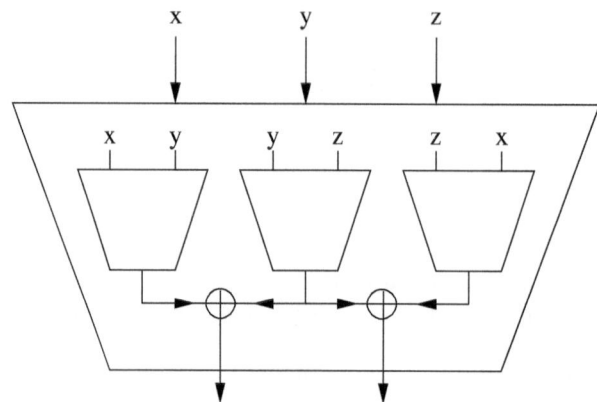

Fig. 1. The double length 1/3-rate construction of FSE 2005

Nandi *et al.* [14] introduce two new constructions of respective rates $r = 1/3$ and $r = 2/3$. The attacks against both proposals are essentially the same, so we consider first the compression function of rate $1/3$.

Let $f_i : \{0,1\}^{2n} \rightarrow \{0,1\}^n$ be independent random functions, for $i = 1, 2, 3$. We define the double-length compression function $F : \{0,1\}^{3n} \rightarrow \{0,1\}^{2n}$ by :

$$F(x, y, z) = (F_1(x, y, z) \mid F_2(x, y, z))$$
$$= (f_1(x, y) \oplus f_2(y, z) \mid f_2(y, z) \oplus f_3(z, x))$$

This function has a rate of $1/3$: it compresses one block of n bits with 3 evaluations of the "small" f_i functions. This construction is also illustrated in Figure 1.

Similarly, a function with rate $2/3$ is proposed in [14]. The idea is to instantiate all the f_i's with a block cipher using keys of length $2n$ bits, in the Davies-Meyer construction. This allows to compress an input of $4n$ bits into an output of $2n$ bits, thereby improving the ratio from $1/3$ to $2/3$. This construction could be instantiated with AES-256 for instance.

3   Collisions

In [14], it is proven that no collision can be exhibited for the proposed $2n$-bit compression function with less than $\Omega(2^{2n/3})$ queries to the three underlying n-bit functions. In addition, it is described how to match this bound.

First, we quickly remind the attack proposed by the designers. Then we argue that the number Q of oracle queries is not the proper way to estimate the complexity of a collision attack. We denote the actual time and memory needed for the attack by T and M : while the original attack is such that $Q = 2^{2n/3}$, the authors of [14] do not give many details about its complexity. Apparently their attack requires $T = M = 2^n$. Using additional tricks, we propose a better attack which satisfies $Q = T = M = 2^{2n/3}$. We do not take into account constant and logarithmic factors to evaluate the complexities of all attacks.

3.1   The Original Attack

Let us pick at random $2^{n/3}$ values for x, y and z. We call these values x_i, y_i and z_i for $i = 1 \ldots 2^{n/3}$. Compute for all pairs (i, j),

$$A_{i,j} = f_1(x_i, y_j)$$

Then store all results in a table $T_A(i, j)$ with $2^{2n/3}$ entries. Similarly, compute

$$B_{i,j} = f_2(y_i, z_j)$$

and store in a table $T_B(i, j)$. Finally, compute

$$C_{i,j} = f_3(z_i, x_j)$$

and store in a table $T_C(i, j)$. At this point $Q = 3 \times 2^{2n/3}$ queries have been made to the n-bit compression functions.

Now consider all triplets (x_i, y_j, z_k). There are 2^n such triplets and the compression function F produces $2n$-bit outputs. So the birthday paradox tells us that, with good probability, two triplets will give a collision on F. One table lookup to T_A, one to T_B and one to T_C are sufficient to evaluate each $F(x_i, y_j, z_k)$, so no new oracle query is needed. After computing the 2^n outputs, we store them in a table and sort it, in order to detect if an element appears twice. Therefore a collision is expected to be found with $Q = 2^{2n/3}$ and $T = M = 2^n$.

3.2   A Better Attack

While the notion of oracle queries is useful for a security proof, it is not relevant in practice : specifications of a hash function are typically public, so an attacker can evaluate off-line the functions f_i. It is therefore not natural to make a distinction between the time needed for the Q oracle queries and the rest of the analysis. According to the security proof of [14] any generic attack needs to evaluate at least $2^{2n/3}$ times one of the n-bit compression functions. Therefore

$$T > 2^{2n/3}$$

for any generic collision attack. In this section, we describe how to reach this lower bound. Fix one of the inputs of F, for instance let $y = y_0$. Then, consider $2^{2n/3}$ random values of x and z. We denote these values by x_i and z_i for $i = 1 \ldots 2^{2n/3}$. Compute, for all i,

$$A_i = f_1(x_i, y_0)$$

and store the results in a table T_A. Similarly, compute for all i

$$B_i = f_2(y_0, z_i)$$

and store the results in a table T_B. Both tables have $2^{2n/3}$ entries.

Next, fix an arbitrary $2n/3$-bit pattern α and compute all pairs of elements $(A_i \in T_A, B_j \in T_B)$ such that $A_i \oplus B_j$ starts by α in its $2n/3$ least significant bits. There are

$$\frac{2^{2n/3} \times 2^{2n/3}}{2^{2n/3}} = 2^{2n/3}$$

such pairs. They can be obtained with $2^{2n/3}$ computation. This merging of T_A and T_B under the constraint of the pattern α can be done by first XORing α to all the elements of T_A, then sorting T_B, and finally searching for a collision between the two tables. This costs $2^{2n/3}$ in time and memory. Such merging algorithms have been known for a long time by the folklore but have been thoroughly studied by Wagner in [16]. The resulting table is noted $T = T_A \bowtie_\alpha T_B$.

Finally, compute F for the $2^{2n/3}$ triplets (x_i, y_0, z_j) corresponding to elements of T. It is guaranteed that the $2n$-bit output always starts by the prefix α. Hence the probability of collision among two such triplets is $2^{-4n/3}$ instead of 2^{-2n}. Since there are $2^{2n/3}$ triplets to test, the birthday paradox tells us that a collision is expected. To summarize, our improved collision attack requires about

$$T = 2^{2n/3}$$

computations steps, which is an optimal result, according to the security proof of [14]. The memory required is of the order of $M = 2^{2n/3}$.

For an ideal compression function with a $2n$-bit output, finding a collision should require the computation of 2^n function values. Therefore the FSE hash proposal is not optimal. Also, one might be tempted to truncate the output of the F_i-functions, e.g., to $2n/3$ bits each, thereby obtaining a hash result of $s = 4n/3$ bits. However, as we shall show next, this enables one to find collisions in time less than $2^{2n/3}$.

3.3   Near-Collisions

If the output of F is truncated to $s \leq 2n$ we show how to find a near-collision with $T = 2^{s/3}$, that is, two inputs to F which are equal in s fixed bit-positions.

When F_1 and F_2 are truncated by the same number of bits, the method is exactly similar to the one above, replacing $2n$ by s.

Fix the input y of F to a value y_0. Then, consider $2^{s/3}$ random values of x and z. We denote these values by x_i and z_i for $i = 1, \ldots, 2^{s/3}$. Compute, for all i, $A_i = f_1(x_i, y_0)$ and store the results in a table T_A. Similarly, compute for all i $B_i = f_2(y_0, z_i)$ and store the results in a table T_B. Both tables have $2^{s/3}$ entries. In both tables, we truncate the outputs of f_1 and f_2 as it is done in F. Then, we fix an arbitrary $s/3$-bit pattern β on the $s/2$ remaining bits, and merge T_A and T_B according to this pattern. We use the same algorithm as in Section 3.2. The result is a table $T = T_A \bowtie_\alpha T_B$ containing :

$$\frac{2^{s/3} \times 2^{s/3}}{2^{s/3}} = 2^{s/3}$$

elements of $s/2$ bits. Finally, we apply F to all triplets (x_i, y, z_j) of T. It is guaranteed that the first $s/3$ bits of all outputs of F_1 are equal to β. Hence the probability of having a collision among two such triplets in all the s bits is only $2^{-2s/3}$ instead of 2^{-s}. Since there are $2^{s/3}$ triplets to test, the birthday paradox tells us that a collision is expected.

Now suppose F_1 is truncated to s_1 bits and F_2 is truncated to s_2 bits, with $s = s_1 + s_2$. The pattern β has length $s/3$ bits, while the elements in T have length s_1 bits. So when $s_1 < s/3$ we may have problems in the previous algorithm. In that case, we need to exchange the roles of F_1 and F_2, but the idea remains essentially the same.

To summarize, independently of how the truncation is made, we find a near-collision in s bits with about $T = 2^{s/3}$ computation. The memory required is also of the order of $M = 2^{s/3}$. The number of oracle queries is also of $Q = 2^{s/3}$.

4   Preimages

For a $2n$-bit compression function, it is expected that 2^{2n} evaluations should be needed in order to find an input x that maps to $y = F(x)$ for a given challenge y. This requirement is generally expressed as preimage resistance. Unfortunately, the hash proposal of [14] does not satisfy this property. In this section, we describe a preimage attack with complexity of 2^n steps.

4.1   The Preimage Attack

Let h be a given target of length $2n$ bits. Our goal is to find a preimage (x, y, z) such that $F(x, y, z) = h$. We can rewrite h as (h_1, h_2) and re-express our goal as :

$$F_1(x, y, z) = f_1(x, y) \oplus f_2(y, z) = h_1 \tag{1}$$
$$F_2(x, y, z) = f_2(y, z) \oplus f_3(z, x) = h_2 \tag{2}$$

The basic idea is to consider many triplets (x, y, z), and to first eliminate those which do not satisfy (1). Actually, merging algorithms can again be used to check this constraint efficiently. If there are enough remaining candidates, one is expected to satisfy (2).

More precisely, let us fix an arbitrary y and compute, for all possible x, $A_x = f_1(x, y)$. Results are stored in a table T_A with 2^n entries. Similarly, we compute all $B_z = f_2(y, z)$ and store the results in a table T_B. Using a merging algorithm [16] as in Section 3.2, we compute

$$T = T_A \bowtie_{h_1} T_B$$

T contains all pairs of (A_x, B_z) such that $A_x \oplus B_z = h_1$, so there should be :

$$\frac{2^n \times 2^n}{2^n}$$

entries. The corresponding time complexity is about 2^n. By construction, all triplets (x, y, z) in table T satisfy relation (1). Then we compute $F_2(x, y, z)$ for each of them. We expect that h_2 will be reached, since the probability for a random triplet to satisfy (2) is 2^{-n}. Therefore T should contain one preimage by F for the target $h = (h_1, h_2)$.

To summarize, we propose a preimage attack against the proposal of [14] with time complexity of $T = 2^n$ computation steps. In addition, the memory requirement is about $M = 2^n$. The number of oracle queries to the function f_i's is also about 2^n.

For an ideal compression function of $2n$ bits, finding a preimage should require about 2^{2n} computation. As was the case for collisions, it is next shown that truncating the output of the hash function will not give ideal security for the truncated construction.

4.2   Near-Preimages

Let h be a given target of length $s < 2n$ bits. We can find a preimage (x, y, z) such that $F(x, y, z)$ truncated to s bits yields h in time roughly $2^{s/2}$. If both functions F_i's are truncated to $s/2$ bits, then the method is in essence the same as in the previous section, simply replace n by $s/2$.

Suppose that both halves of the hash proposal are not truncated equally. For instance, F_1 is truncated to s_1 bits and F_2 to s_2 bits, with

$$s_1 + s_2 = s$$

Without loss of generality, we suppose that $s_1 > s/2 > s_2$. In this case, we fix an arbitrary value of y and consider $2^{s/2}$ arbitrary values of x and z. We compute all $f_1(x, y)$ and store in table T_A and similarly compute all $f_2(y, z)$ into a table T_B. As in the previous section, we truncate the elements in both tables, and then use a merging algorithm. We verify the constraint on the s_1 bits of h_1. The result is a table

$$T = T_A \bowtie_{h_1} T_B$$

of size

$$\frac{2^{s/2} \times 2^{s/2}}{2^{s_1}} = 2^{s-s_1} = 2^{s_2}$$

At this point, we are sure to hit the target h_1 for all triplets of T. Since there are 2^{s_2} such triplets, one of them should also hit the target h_2 and therefore provide a valid preimage.

Therefore, if the double length hash is truncated to s bits (it does not matter which bits of the output are removed), then a preimage attack costs only $2^s/2$.

5   Application to the 2/3 Rate Compression Function

[14] also specifies a rate 2/3 compression function and gives an example of an implementation of the scheme using a block cipher as the underlying cryptographic primitive. Here we give only the generic description of the proposal using randomly chosen functions as building blocks.

Let $f_i : \{0,1\}^{3n} \to \{0,1\}^n$ be independent random functions, for $i = 1, 2, 3$. Define the compression function $F : \{0,1\}^{4n} \to \{0,1\}^{2n}$

$$
\begin{aligned}
F(x,y,z,w) &= (F_1(x,y,z,w) \mid F_2(x,y,z,w)) \\
&= (f_1(x,y,w) \oplus f_2(y,z,w) \mid f_2(y,z,w) \oplus f_3(x,z,w))
\end{aligned}
$$

This function has a rate of $2/3$: it compresses two blocks of n bits with three evaluations of the f-functions. Note however that this scheme is not directly comparable to the first schemes presented above, since the underlying functions are of a different nature.

Nonetheless, the collision and preimage attacks presented earlier also apply to this variant. This is easy to observe : by fixing the value of w in the rate $2/3$ scheme, one gets exactly the rate $1/3$ scheme. It follows easily that all the attacks described in the previous sections also apply to the implementation of the proposal using a block cipher.

6   Some General Considerations

There is one important property of the compression function of [14] that makes our attacks possible : two of three of the underlying subfunctions f_i can be attacked independently, by fixing one input variable. Another important observation is that (part of) the output is the sum of the outputs of smaller subfunctions. This opens the door for techniques more efficient than the usual birthday attack. Consider a compression function of the form

$$
h(x) = h_1(x_1 \mid y) \oplus h_2(x_2 \mid y),
$$

where x_1 can be varied independently of x_2 and vice versa. Then in a search for a collision on h, one is looking for values x_1, x_1', x_2, x_2', such that

$$
h_1(x_1 \mid y) \oplus h_2(x_2 \mid y) \oplus h_1(x_1' \mid y) \oplus h_2(x_2' \mid y) = 0,
$$

a solution to which is known to be faster than the birthday attack [16].

One possible way to remove this freedom for an attacker could be to use subfunctions whose outputs depend on all (three) input variables. We can do so in a rate $1/3$ construction using the subfunctions of the (insecure) rate $2/3$ proposal of [14]. Let $f_i : \{0,1\}^{3n} \to \{0,1\}^n$ be independent random functions, for $i = 1, 2, 3$. Define the compression function $F : \{0,1\}^{3n} \to \{0,1\}^{2n}$

$$
F(x,y,z) = (f_1(x,y,z) \oplus f_2(x,y,z) \mid f_2(x,y,z) \oplus f_3(x,y,z))
$$

Evidently this reduces to a construction of the form

$$
F(x,y,z) = (g_1(x,y,z) \mid g_2(x,y,z)).
$$

The construction of secure double length compression function of this form is further investigated in recent papers by Lucks [11] and Nandi [13].

Table 1. Summary of all attacks against [14]

Type of Attack	Time	Memory	Oracle Query
Collision [14]	2^n	2^n	$2^{2n/3}$
Collision	$2^{2n/3}$	$2^{2n/3}$	$2^{2n/3}$
Near-collision (s bits)	$2^{s/3}$	$2^{s/3}$	$2^{s/3}$
Preimage	2^n	2^n	2^n
Near-preimage (s-bits)	$2^{s/2}$	$2^{s/2}$	$2^{s/2}$

7   Conclusion

In this paper, we have investigated a new double block length hash function proposed at FSE 2005 by Nandi *et al.*. Their idea is to turn a "small", secure, n-bit compression function into a $2n$-bit compression function. The advantage of their method is to offer a proof of security regarding collisions attacks.

Although, we do not contradict this security proof, we show that this construction is not fully satisfying. Indeed, its security level is much worse than a generic $2n$-bit compression function. Table 1 summarizes all these results.

In addition, we have introduced new notions of security for compression functions, *i.e.* **near-collision** and **near-preimage** resistance. These notions are important, because it is quite usual that hash function outputs are truncated for practical purposes. One could be tempted to truncate the output of [14] to $4n/3$ bits or less, in order to fit to the proven security bound. Our results show that this would be a bad idea because it would deteriate the security of the construction below $2^{2n/3}$.

References

1. E. Biham and R. Chen. Near-Collisions of SHA-0. In M. Franklin, editor, *Advances in Cryptology – CRYPTO'04*, volume 3152 of *Lectures Notes in Computer Science*, pages 290–305. Springer, 2004.
2. E. Biham, R. Chen, A. Joux, P. Carribault, C. Lemuet, and W. Jalby. Collisions of SHA-0 and Reduced SHA-1. In R. Cramer, editor, *Advances in Cryptology – Eurocrypt'05*, volume 3494 of *Lectures Notes in Computer Science*, pages 36–57. Springer, 2005.
3. J. Black, M. Cochran, and T. Shrimpton. On the Impossibility of Highly-Efficient Blockcipher-Based Hash Functions. In R. Cramer, editor, *Advances in Cryptology – Eurocrypt'05*, volume 3494 of *Lectures Notes in Computer Science*, pages 526–541. Springer, 2005.
4. F. Chabaud and A. Joux. Differential Collisions in SHA-0. In H. Krawczyk, editor, *Advances in Cryptology – CRYPTO'98*, volume 1462 of *Lectures Notes in Computer Science*, pages 56–71. Springer, 1998.

5. J-S. Coron, Y. Dodis, C. Malinaud, and P. Puniya. Merkle-Damgård Revisited: How to Construct a Hash Function. In V. Shoup, editor, *Advances in Cryptology – Crypto'05*, volume 3621 of *Lectures Notes in Computer Science*, pages 430–448. Springer, 2005.

6. I. Damgård. A Design Principle for Hash Functions. In G. Brassard, editor, *Advances in Cryptology – Crypto'89*, volume 435 of *Lectures Notes in Computer Science*, pages 416–427. Springer, 1990.

7. H. Dobbertin. Cryptanalysis of MD4. In D. Gollmann, editor, *Fast Software Encryption – 1996*, volume 1039 of *Lectures Notes in Computer Science*, pages 53–69. Springer, 1996.

8. S. Hirose. Provably Secure Double-Block-Length Hash Functions in a Black-Box Model. In C. Park and S. Chee, editors, *Information Security and Cryptology – ICISC'04*, volume 3506 of *Lectures Notes in Computer Science*. Springer, 2005.

9. A. Joux. Multicollisions in Iterated Hash Functions. Application to Cascaded Constructions. In M. Franklin, editor, *Advances in Cryptology – CRYPTO'04*, volume 3152 of *Lectures Notes in Computer Science*, pages 306–316. Springer, 2004.

10. J. Kelsey and B. Schneier. Second Preimages on n-Bit Hash Functions for Much Less than 2^n Work. In R. Cramer, editor, *Advances in Cryptology – Eurocrypt'05*, volume 3494 of *Lectures Notes in Computer Science*, pages 474–490. Springer, 2005.

11. S. Lucks. Design Principles for Iterated Hash Functions. Cryptology ePrint Archive, Report 2004/253, 2004. http://eprint.iacr.org/.

12. R. Merkle. One Way Hash Functions and DES. In G. Brassard, editor, *Advances in Cryptology – Crypto'89*, volume 435 of *Lectures Notes in Computer Science*, pages 428–446. Springer, 1990.

13. M. Nandi. Designs of Efficient Secure Large Hash Values. Cryptology ePrint Archive, Report 2004/296, 2004. http://eprint.iacr.org/.

14. M. Nandi, W. Lee, K. Sakurai, and S. Lee. Security analysis of a 2/3-rate double length compression function in black-box model. In H. Gilbert and H. Handschuh, editors, *Fast Software Encryption – FSE'05*, volume 3557 of *Lectures Notes in Computer Science*, pages 243–254. Springer, 2005.

15. National Institute of Standards and Technology (NIST). Secure Hash Standard FIPS Publication 180-2, August 2002. Available at http://csrc.nist.gov/publications/fips/fips180-2/fips180-2.pdf .

16. D. Wagner. A Generalized Birthday Problem. In M. Yung, editor, *Advances in Cryptology – Crypto'02*, volume 2442 of *Lectures Notes in Computer Science*, pages 288–303. Springer, 2002. Extended Abstract.

17. X. Wang, X. Lai, D. Feng, H. Chen, and X. Yu. Cryptanalysis of the Hash Functions MD4 and RIPEMD. In R. Cramer, editor, *Advances in Cryptology – Eurocrypt'05*, volume 3494 of *Lectures Notes in Computer Science*, pages 1–18. Springer, 2005.

18. X. Wang, Y. Yin, and H. Yu. Finding Collisions in the Full SHA1. In V. Shoup, editor, *Advances in Cryptology – Crypto'05*, volume 3621 of *Lectures Notes in Computer Science*, pages 17–36. Springer, 2005.

19. X. Wang and H. Yu. How to Break MD5 and Other Hash Functions. In R. Cramer, editor, *Advances in Cryptology – Eurocrypt'05*, volume 3494 of *Lectures Notes in Computer Science*, pages 19–35. Springer, 2005.

20. X. Wang, H. Yu, and Y. Yin. Efficient Collision Search Attacks on SHA0. In V. Shoup, editor, *Advances in Cryptology – Crypto'05*, volume 3621 of *Lectures Notes in Computer Science*, pages 1–16. Springer, 2005.

A Failure-Friendly Design Principle
for Hash Functions

Stefan Lucks

University of Mannheim, Germany
http://th.informatik.uni-mannheim.de/people/lucks/

Abstract. This paper reconsiders the established Merkle-Damgård design principle for iterated hash functions. The internal state size w of an iterated n-bit hash function is treated as a security parameter of its own right. In a formal model, we show that increasing w quantifiably improves security against certain attacks, even if the compression function fails to be collision resistant. We propose the wide-pipe hash, internally using a w-bit compression function, and the double-pipe hash, with $w = 2n$ and an n-bit compression function used twice in parallel.

Keywords: hash function, provable security, multi-collision, failure-friendliness.

1 Introduction

A cryptographic hash function $H : \{0, 1\}^* \to \{0, 1\}^n$ maps an infinite set of inputs to the finite set of n-bit hash values. While collisions (inputs $X \neq Y$ with $H(X) = H(Y)$) necessarily exist, a hash function should be *collision resistant*: given H, it should be infeasible for an adversary to *actually find* any collisions. But what if a hash function fails to be collision resistant? This paper deals with *failure-friendly* hash functions providing *some* security even if collision resistance has failed. It has been inspired by recent advances in collision finding [25,26,27,28,1].

The design of today's cryptographic hash functions ubiquitously follows the Merkle/Damgård (MD) structure [16,6], iterating some underlying compression function. The hash function is collision resistant, if the compression function is. However, if computing a compression function collision is somehow feasible, the hash function may fail worse than expected. E.g., finding *multiple collisions* should be way more expensive than finding plain (2-)collisions – but Joux [11] disproved this for the MD design. Also, MD hash functions completely fail to defend against *2nd collision* attacks: If $H(M) = H(N)$ for any two messages M, N, then $H(M||S) = H(N||S)$ for all $S \in \{0, 1\}^n$. (Technically, this assumes M and N to be "extended messages", see below.) In other words, given a single collision, an adversary can easily construct many more collisions. This has long been known, but recently been exploited to turn "random" collisions (as, e.g., for MD5 [26]) into "meaningful" ones [12,17,14,15]. Even a 2nd preimage like scenario is possible [7]: given any two texts T_1 and T_2, Daum and Lucks presented two corresponding PostScript files with identical MD5 hashes.

B. Roy (Ed.): ASIACRYPT 2005, LNCS 3788, pp. 474–494, 2005.

Our Contributions. This paper describes and analyses *failure-friendly* iterated hash functions. The goal is to defend against certain classes of attacks even if collision resistance fails. We propose and analyse variants of the Merkle-Damgård design, *increasing the internal state to $w > n$ bits*. The *wide-pipe* hash is quite similar to the Merkle-Damgård hash, except for using a "largish" w-bit compression function to finally generate $n < w$ bits of output. The *double-pipe* hash sets $w = 2n$ and employs one single n-bit compression function, used twice in parallel for each message block. In random and standard model settings, we prove the security of our schemes against K-**collision** attacks (for $K \geq w$), and K-way **preimage** and **2nd preimage** attacks (for $K \geq 1$). Additionally, we discuss and semi-formally verify the resistance against **2nd collision** attacks.

Related Proposals. The double-pipe hash may remind the readers of the RIPEMD-family of hash functions [22,8], also calling two compression functions in parallel. The hash functions specified in [22,8] combine both n-bit compression values into a single n-bit state, strictly following the Merkle-Damgård design principle, thus being as failure-unfriendly as any Merkle-Damgård hash function. But [8] also outlines some double-width variants of RIPEMD-128 and -160, which we refer to as RIPEMD-256 and -320. RIPEMD-256 and -320 can almost be viewed as instantiation of our design principle – except for the following:

- By outputting **both** compression values at the end, RIPEMD-256 and -320 use the two n-bit compression functions like a single $2n$-bit compression function – again following the Merkle-Damgård design, thus, e.g., being entirely vulnerable to 2nd collision attacks.
- RIPEMD-256 and -320 were proposed as a a convenience feature for applications requiring a $2n$-bit hash "without needing a larger security level" [8]. On the other hand, our double-pipe construction has been designed *to improve the security* against certain attacks.

We propose a *generic and failure-friendly* design principle providing *provable security* under reasonable assumptions. Assuming a "good" n-bit compression function,[1] our analysis would justify the usage of, say, a failure-friendly variant of RIPEMD-320 with $2n = 320$ internal state bits and $n = 160$ output bits.

Recently, Coron et al. [5] also analysed variants of the Merkle-Damgård design in a fashion similar to the current paper. One of the proposals in [5] is rather similar to our wide-pipe design. However, [5] aims for variably-sized random oracles, based on an (extremely strong) ideal compression function (i.e., a fixed-size random oracle). This is orthogonal to our approach of taking possible compression function weaknesses into account. Nandi et. al. [18] proposed and analysed a rather different "2/3 rate double length compression function". Both [5] and [18] restrict their analysis to the random and Shannon oracle, while the current paper also provides some analyses in the standard model. Also, none of the constructions in [5,18] resemble the current paper's double-pipe hash design.

---

[1] Note that [8] took great care to ensure that both compression functions behave "differently enough". Somewhat surprisingly, our results indicate that it would even be OK to use the same compression function twice, instead of two different functions.

Road map. We first describe Merkle-Damgård hashing and introduce notations, abstractions, and attacks. Section 2 describes and analyses the wide-pipe hash, a modified Merkle-Damgård design with an extended internal state size. Section 3 modifies the wide-pipe hash, introducing and analysing the double-pipe hash. Section 4 investigates the security of a "weakened" double-pipe hash, based on a common construction for compression functions; see Appendix A for the proofs. Section 5 deals with extension attacks and Section 6 discusses our results and their implications. Appendix B provides examples for our hash constructions.

1.1 The Merkle-Damgård (MD) Principle for Iterated Hashing

A hash function H takes a message $M \in \{0,1\}^*$ to compute $H(M) \in \{0,1\}^n$. (In practice, the length $|M|$ of M may be bounded by some huge constant.) An iterated hash H is based on a compression function C with a fixed number of input bits and splits M into fixed-sized chunks $M_1, M_2, \ldots, M_L \in \{0,1\}^m$. The final chunk M_L may contain additional information, such as $|M|$. $(M_1, \ldots M_L)$ is the "expanded message". Assume a compression function $C : \{0,1\}^n \times \{0,1\}^m \to \{0,1\}^n$ and a fixed *initial value* H_0. Given $M \in \{0,1\}^*$, one computes the MD hash as follows:

– Expand M to $(M_1, \ldots, M_L) \in \{0,1\}^{mL}$. (*MD strengthening:* The last block
   M_L takes the length $|M|$ in bits. Thus, if $|M| \neq |M'|$, then $M_L \neq M'_{L'}$.)
– For $i \in \{1, \ldots, L\}$: compute $H_i := C(H_{i-1}, M_i)$.
– Finally: output H_L.

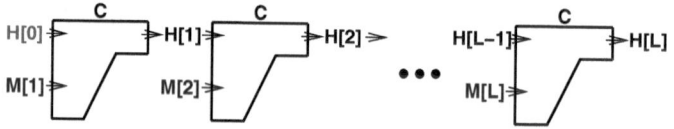

Fig. 1. The Merkle-Damgård (MD) Hash

Note that the MD hash function does not provide any resistance against *2nd collision attacks*: consider messages $M \neq M'$ with expansions $(M[1], \ldots, M[L])$ and $(M'[1], \ldots, M'[L])$. If M and M' collide, then $H[L] = H'[L]$ for $H[L] = C(\cdot, M[L])$ and $H'[L] = C(\cdot, M'[L])$, and therefore *all* expanded messages $(M[1], \ldots, M[L], S[1], \ldots, S[T])$ and $(M'[1], \ldots, M'[L], S[1], \ldots, S[T])$ also collide.

1.2 Notation, Abstractions, and Attacks

Random Oracles. A *fixed-size random oracle* is a function $f : \{0,1\}^a \to \{0,1\}^b$, chosen uniformly at random. For interesting sizes a and b, it is infeasible to implement f, or to store its truth table. Thus, we assume a public oracle which, given $x \in \{0,1\}^a$, computes $y = f(x) \in \{0,1\}^b$. A *variably-sized random oracle* is a random function $g : \{0,1\}^* \to \{0,1\}^b$, accessible by a public oracle.

Equivalently, g is an infinite set of fixed-size random oracles $g_a : \{0,1\}^a \rightarrow \{0,1\}^b$ for $a \in \{0,1,2\ldots\}$. We view a fixed-size random oracle as an *ideal compression function*, and a variably-sized random oracle as an *ideal hash function*.

Shannon Oracle. An *ideal block cipher* is some invertible random oracle $E : \{0,1\}^n \times \{0,1\}^m \rightarrow \{0,1\}^n$, such that for each $M \in \{0,1\}^m$, for the function $E(\cdot, M) = E_M(\cdot)$ an inverse $E^{-1}(\cdot, M)$ exists. Apart from that, E is uniformly chosen at random. Given x and M, one can ask a Shannon oracle for $y = E(x, M)$, and, given y and M, one can ask the oracle for $x = E^{-1}(y, M)$.

Adversary. As usual in the context of the Shannon and random oracle models, we consider a computationally unbounded adversary with access to either a Shannon or a random oracle. The adversary's "running time" is determined by her number of oracle queries. Our adversaries are probabilistic algorithms, and we concentrate on the expected running time (i.e., the expected number of oracle queries). We will describe the running time asymptotically. When necessary for clarity, we use the symbols O ("big-Oh", for "the expected running time is asymptotically *at most*") and Ω ("big-Omega", for "... *at least*"). [2]

Classes of Attacks. Informally, a real hash function H should behave like an ideal one (i.e., like a random oracle). This would not be useful for a formal definition, though (see [4]). Instead, one considers somewhat simpler security goals for $H : \{0,1\}^* \rightarrow \{0,1\}^n$. We consider the following classes of attacks:

K-**collision** for $K \geq 2$: Find K different M^i, with $H(M^1) = \cdots = H(M^K)$.
K-**way (2nd) preimage** for $K \geq 1$: Given Y (or M with $H(M) = Y$), find K
    different messages M^i, with $H(M^i) = Y$ (and $M^i \neq M$).
2nd collision: Given any collision $A \neq B$ with $H(A) = H(B)$, find C, D with
    $C \notin \{A, B, D\}$ and $H(C) = H(D)$.

The first two classes include "traditional" 2-collisions, 1-way preimages and 1-way 2nd preimages. Some applications need protection against the large-K-variants, e.g., [10,23,3]. The third class deals with a very natural assumption for "good" hash functions: even if the adversary somehow – with a great deal of luck, by doing much computational work, or by a mixture of both – has found *one* collision, it should still be *hard* to find *another one*. The poor defence of established hash functions against such attacks has been elaborated above.

Facts. Our analysis uses the following facts:

1. **Fact:** *Finding a K-collision for a fixed size random oracle $C : \{0,1\}^{n+m} \rightarrow \{0,1\}^n$ or for a variably-sized random oracle Model $H : \{0,1\}^* \rightarrow \{0,1\}^n$ takes time $\Omega(2^{(K-1)n/K})$, and finding a K-way preimage or a K-way 2nd preimage for H or C takes time $\Omega(K2^n)$.*
2. **Fact:** *Given a collision $A \neq B$ with $C(A) = C(B)$ for a fixed size random oracle $C\{0,1\}^{n+m} \rightarrow \{0,1\}^n$ (or $H(A) = H(B)$ for a variably-sized random oracle $H\{0,1\}^* \rightarrow \{0,1\}^n$), finding a 2nd collision $C \neq D$, $C \notin \{A, B\}$ for C (or H) takes time $\Omega(2^{n/2})$.*

---

[2] Recall $f = O(g)$, if a constant c exists, such that $f(n) \leq cg(n)$ holds for all large enough n, and $f = \Omega(g)$, if a c exists such that $f(n) \geq cg(n)$ for all large enough n.

Initial Values. Like the MD hash, our hash functions depend on the compression function(s) <u>and</u> an initial value (IV). One can set the IV to some fixed ("random") constant. But for our analysis, we will even allow the adversary to actually choose the IV.[3] This makes our results all the more meaningful.

Standard Model Formalism. For a fixed hash function $H : \{0,1\}^* \to \{0,1\}^n$, trivial algorithms to "find" collisions exist: given any $M \neq M'$ with $H(M) = H(M')$, output M and M'. Collision resistance implies the non-existence of algorithms to "find" collisions. Thus, for a standard model proof of collision resistance, we must refine our formalism. Instead of a fixed hash function, we actually consider a *hash function family* $H : \mathcal{I} \times \{0,1\}^* \to \{0,1\}^n$. Here, $\mathcal{I}$ is a finite nonempty set of indices (or "keys"). We assume an index $i^* \in \mathcal{I}$ being chosen uniformly at random, write $H(\cdot)$ instead of $H(i^*, \cdot)$ and consider the fixed hash function $H : \{0,1\}^* \to \{0,1\}^n$ as a *random member* of its family.

Fix some RAM model of computation. In any attack game, the adversary is given i^* as its first input. We measure the adversary's *expected running time* over uniformly distributed random i^* (and the adversary's internal coin flips, if applicable). To capture a trivial adversary using huge tables, the running time of any program is assumed to be at least linear in the program size.

We formalise compression functions C exactly like hash functions: assume a family $C : \mathcal{I}_C \times \{0,1\}^\alpha \to \{0,1\}^\beta$ and an index $i^C \in \mathcal{I}_C$ chosen uniformly at random, write $C(\cdot)$ instead of $C(i^C, \cdot)$, and consider the fixed compression function $C : \{0,1\}^\alpha \to \{0,1\}^\beta$ as a random member of its family. An adversary's running time is taken over random i^C. If H is defined by iterating C, a random member of the hash family H is defined by i^C and some random initial value H_0, i.e., $i^* = (i^C, H_0)$. Similarly, if H is constructed by applying C' and C'', then $i^* = (i^{C'}, i^{C''}, H_0)$. Recall that in our attacks we even allow the adversary to choose H_0. The adversary can make this choice *after* being given i^C or $(i^{C'}, i^{C''})$.

2   The Wide-Pipe Hash: A Modified MD Hash

Constructing a collision-resistant compression function with $w > n$ output bits may be simpler than constructing an n-bit compression function with the same level of collision resistance. The *wide-pipe hash* uses such a w-bit compression function to generate an n-bit hash value at the end. [4] This approach defeats Joux' attack – and even provides security against *all* generic K-collision attacks (which treat the compression function as a random oracle). Let $H_0 \in \{0,1\}^w$ be a (random) *initial value*. Using **two compression functions**

$$C' : \{0,1\}^w \times \{0,1\}^m \to \{0,1\}^w \quad \text{and} \quad C'' : \{0,1\}^w \to \{0,1\}^n,$$

we compute the <u>wide-pipe hash</u> H:

- For $i \in \{1, \ldots, L\}$: compute $H_i := C'(H_{i-1}, M_i)$.
- Finally: set $H(M) = C''(H_L)$.

---

[3] This is similar to the "aSec" and "aPre" notions of hash function security from [24].
[4] This idea has independently been proposed by Finney in a mailing list [9].

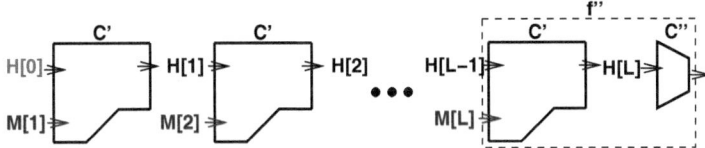

Fig. 2. The Wide-Pipe Hash

For technical reasons, we need to distinguish between different kinds of collisions. Consider $M \neq N$ with $H(M) = H(N)$. M and N are expanded to sequences $(M_1, \ldots, M_L) \neq (N_1, \ldots, N_{L'})$. Denote H_i^M and H_j^N for the internal hash values when computing $H(M)$ and $H(N)$. We define

Final collisions: $H_L^M \neq H_{L'}^N$ but $C''(H_L^M) = C''(H_{L'}^N)$.
Internal collisions: $H_L^M = H_{L'}^N$. (Note that an internal collision implies a collision for C', i.e., $(H_i^M, M_i) \neq (H_i^N, N_i)$ with $C'(H_i^M, M_i) = C'(H_i^N, N_i)$.)
Final K-collisions: Any K-collision M^1, ..., M^K (with $H(M^1) = \cdots = H(M^K)$) is *final*, if all 2-collisions (M^i, M^j) (with $i \neq j$) are final.

2.1   Resistance Against K-Collision Attacks

Observe that Joux finds 2^k-collisions in time $\min\{k * 2^{w/2}, 2^{n(2^k-1)/2^k}\}$. This tightly describes the security of H, up to the (logarithmic) factor k. Define the composition $f'' : \{0,1\}^w \times \{0,1\}^m \rightarrow \{0,1\}^n$ of C' and C'' by $f''(H, M) = C''(C'(H, M))$, as indicated in Figure 2. Make the following two assumptions:

  1. C' is collision resistant, and   **2.** f'' is K-collision resistant.

Under these assumptions, we prove the K-collision resistance of H.[5] For the concrete security analysis, we assume that finding a collision for C' takes at least time T', and finding a K-collision for f'' at least time $T''(K)$.

Lemma 1. *An adversary needs $\Omega(\min\{T', T''(K)\})$ units of time to find a K-collision for the wide-pipe Hash H, even if she can choose H_0.*

Proof. Any final K-collision is equivalent to a K-collision for f''. On the other hand, if a K-collision for H is not a final K-collision, then an internal collision has been found. For all H_0, finding an internal collision is equivalent to finding a collision for C'. Thus, finding a K-collision for H is at least as hard as finding either a K-collision for f'', or a collision for C.   □

In the random oracle model, H **is as secure against multi-collision attacks as an ideal hash** for $w \geq 2n$.

---

[5] It would seem natural to assume the K-collision resistance of C''. Indeed, f'' is K-collision resistant if C' is collision resistant and C'' is K-collision resistant. But even if C'' is K-collision vulnerable, f'' can still be K-collision resistant. E.g., model C' as a random oracle and set C'' to be the plain truncation of w-bit inputs to n-bit outputs. For $\log_2(K) \leq w - n$, C'' is trivially K-collision weak, but f'' is not.

Theorem 2. *Consider the wide-pipe hash H. Allow the adversary to choose H_0.*

1. *Model C' and C'' as independent random oracles. The adversary needs time $\Omega(\min\{2^{w/2}, 2^{n(K-1)/K}\})$ to find a K-collision for H.*
2. *Define $C'' : \{0,1\}^w \to \{0,1\}^n, C''(x_1,\ldots,x_w) = (x_1,\ldots,x_n)$ as the n-bit truncation of its w-bit input. Model C' as a random oracle. The adversary needs time $\Omega(\min\{2^{w/2}, 2^{n(K-1)/K}\})$ to find a K-collision for H.*

Proof. Due to Lemma 1, finding a K-collision takes time $\Omega(\min\{T', T''(K)\})$. By Fact 1, $T' = \Omega(2^{w/2})$. If C'' is an independent random oracle, then $T''(K) = \Omega(2^{n(K-1)/K})$. If C'' just truncates, then f'' can be viewed as a random oracle with n output bits. Again, this gives $T''(K) = \Omega(2^{n(K-1)/K})$. $\qquad\square$

2.2   Resistance Against K-Way (2nd) Preimage Attacks

Joux' (2nd) preimage attack also works for the wide-pipe hash. Its time $O(k * 2^{w/2} + 2^n)$ tightly bounds the security of H, up to the (logarithmic) k. Let T' be a lower bound for finding collisions for C' (as before) and assume that finding K-way preimages for f'' takes at least time $P''(K)$.

Lemma 3. *Consider the wide-pipe hash H. Allow the adversary to choose H_0.*

1. *The adversary needs time $\Omega(P''(1))$ to find a single preimage for H.*
2. *She needs time $\Omega(\min\{T', P''(K)\})$ to find a K-way preimage for H.*

Proof. Finding a preimage for H implies finding a preimage for f''. Finding a K-way preimage for H either implies finding at least one internal collision – and thus a collision for C' – or a K-way preimage for f''. $\qquad\square$

In the random oracle model, we also consider 2nd preimage attacks.

Theorem 4. *Consider the wide-pipe hash H. Model C' and C'' as independent random oracles. An adversary allowed to choose H_0 needs*

1. *time $\Omega(2^n)$ to find a single preimage for H,*
2. *time $\Omega(\min\{2^{w/2}\})$ to find a K-way preimage for H, and*
3. *time $\Omega(\min\{2^{w/2}, K2^n\})$ to find a K-way 2nd preimage for H.*

Proof. The first two bounds are direct consequences of Lemma 3 and Fact 1. Now consider 2nd preimages: given a random $X \in \{0,1\}^w$, we are searching for one or more different $X^i \in \{0,1\}^w$ with $C''(X) = C''(X^i)$. We choose an arbitrary message M with the expansion $M_1, \ldots, M_L$, query the C'-oracle for the internal hash values $H_1, \ldots, H_L$, and define

$$C''' : \{0,1\}^w \to \{0,1\}^n : \quad \begin{cases} C'''(H_L) = C''(X), \\ C'''(X) = C''(H_L), \\ C'''(Z) = C''(Z) & \text{if } Z \notin \{X, H_L\}. \end{cases}$$

Note that with overwhelming probability $X \neq H_L$. Now we run the adversary to find single or multiple 2nd preimages for M, replacing C'' by C'''. Observe that

X is a random value, and, since C' is a random oracle, H_L is random, too. Thus, C''' is a uniformly distributed random function just like C'' – the adversary can't distinguish between C'' and C'''. Our little manipulation (replacing C'' by C''' for the adversary) does not affect the adversary's probability of success or running time. We write H''' for the wide-pipe hash function using C' and C'''.

If the adversary succeeds, she finds 2nd preimage(s) M^i with $H'''(M) = H'''(M^i)$. We write L^i for the length of the expansion of M^i (in chunks). Consider the inputs $H_{L^i}^i$ for C'''. If $H_{L^i}^i = H_L$, we have found a collision for C'. Else, $H_{L^i}^i$ is a 2nd preimage for C''.   □

Increasing w improves the security of H against multiple (2nd) preimage attacks. But an adversary whose running time exceeds $2^{w/2}$ can still run Joux' attack and benefit from the iterated structure of H. In fact, no hash function with some fixed internal state size w can be as secure against multiple (2nd) preimage attacks as an ideal hash.

3   The Double-Pipe Hash

There is one drawback for the wide-pipe design: its compression function C' needs a larger output and finding collisions for C' must be much harder than finding collisions for the hash function itself. It would be interesting to use a compression function which only has to satisfy essentially the same security requirements as the hash. For instance, if we assume the internal compression function of, SHA-1, RIPEMD-160, or SHA-256 to be as secure as an ideal 160-bit (256-bit for SHA-256) compression function, can we construct some variant to improve security? Note that the SHA-1 and RIPEMD-160 compression functions can be written as $C : \{0,1\}^{160} \times \{0,1\}^{512} \rightarrow \{0,1\}^{160}$, their SHA-256 counterpart as $C : \{0,1\}^{256} \times \{0,1\}^{512} \rightarrow \{0,1\}^{256}$. Thus, the following construction would be applicable to all of them: Using *one single narrow-pipe* compression function $C : \{0,1\}^n \times \{0,1\}^{n+m} \rightarrow \{0,1\}^n$, with $m \geq n$ and two distinct (random) *initial values* $H_0' \neq H_0'' \in \{0,1\}^n$, we compute the double-pipe hash H^{D}:

- For $i \in \{1, \ldots, L-1\}$: compute
  - $H_i' := C(H_{i-1}', H_{i-1}''\|M_i)$ and
  - $H_i'' := C(H_{i-1}'', H_{i-1}'\|M_i)$
- Finally: $H^{\mathrm{D}}(M) := C(H_{L-1}', H_{L-1}''\|M_L)$

So in $H^{\mathrm{D}}(M)$, we have replaced the wide-pipe chaining values $H_{i-1} \in \{0,1\}^w$ by pairs $(H_{i-1}', H_{i-1}'') \in (\{0,1\}^n)^2$. In each iteration, the value $H_i' = C(H_{i-1}', H_{i-1}''\|M_i)$ – one half of the new chaining value – functionally depends on both halfs H_{i-1}' and H_{i-1}'' of the old chaining value (similarly for H_i''). This is vital for the security of the double-pipe hash. Otherwise, $H^{\mathrm{D}}(M)$ would degenerate into the cascade of two hash functions, thus being vulnerable to Joux' attack.

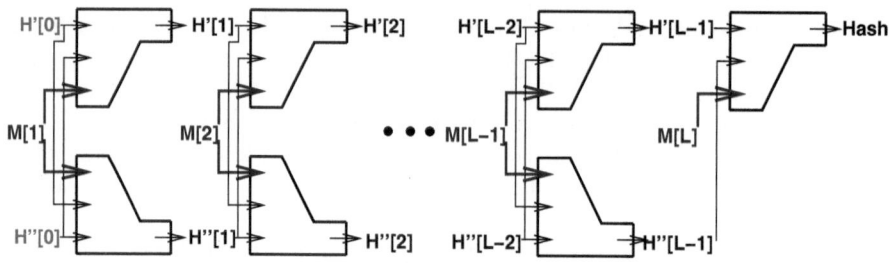

Fig. 3. The Double-Pipe Hash

3.1   Security Against Multiple Collision Attacks

In principle, the double-pipe hash is a special case of the wide-pipe hash with
$w = 2n$ and $C'(H', H''||M) = (\, C(H'_{i-1}, H''_{i-1}||M_i),\ C(H''_{i-1}, H'_{i-1}||M_i)\,)$, where
$C''(H', H'') = H'$ simply truncates $2n$ input bits to n output bits. (Thus, we
do not need to compute the value $H''_L := C(H'_{L-1}, H''_{L-1}||M_L)$, as indicated
in Figure 3.) Similarly to our analysis of the wide-pipe design, we distinguish
internal collisions from final ones. The improved security of the wide-pipe hash
over the plain MD hash depends on internal collision resistance being much
stronger than final collision resistance. Unfortunately, this reasoning does not
hold for the double-pipe construction. Finding internal collisions with $H' = H''$
and $G' = G''$ may be as "easy" as finding collisions for C, i.e., as finding final
collisions. To deal with this, we define two special cases of internal collisions, in
addition to considering K-collisions, and make the following three assumptions:

1. It is infeasible to find a **strict (internal) collision** for C, i.e., two triples
   $(H', H'', M) \neq (G', G'', N)$ with $H' \neq H''$ and $G' \neq G''$, but
   $C(H'', H'||M) = C(G'', G'||N)$ and $C(H', H''||M) = C(G', G''||N)$.
2. It is infeasible to find an **(internal) cross collision** for C: a triple (H', H'', M), with $H' \neq H''$ but $C(H', H''||M) = C(H'', H'||M_i)$.
3. It is infeasible to find K-collisions for C.

We will prove H^D to be secure under the above three assumptions. While
dealing with strict or cross collisions is unusual in cryptography, these assumptions appear to be natural and reasonable. We analyse the feasibility of finding
strict or cross collisions for a random oracle C. For the concrete security analysis, we assume that finding strict collisions takes at least time T_S, finding cross
collisions at least time T_X, and finding K-collisions at least time $T(K)$.

Theorem 5. *If we model the compression function C as a random oracle, then
finding cross collisions for C needs time $T_X = \Omega(2^n)$, and finding strict collisions
for C needs time $T_S = \Omega(2^n)$,*

Proof. First, consider T_X. Any triple (H', H'', M) can only be part of a cross
collision, if $H' \neq H''$ and $C(H', H''||M) = C(H'', H'||M)$, i.e., with a probability
of 2^{-n} (for $H' \neq H''$). Thus, we expect to make $T_X = \Omega(2^n)$ oracle queries to
find a cross collision.

Now consider T_S. For any triple (G', G'', M) with $G' \neq G''$, the pair $(H', H'') \in \{0,1\}^{2n}$ with $H' = C(G', G''||M)$ and $H'' = C(G'', G'||M)$ is a uniformly distributed $2n$-bit random value, chosen independently from all the other $C(\cdot, \cdot||\cdot)$-values. If the adversary chooses q different triples (G', G'', M) and makes q queries to the C-oracle, then her probability to succeed is $\sum_{0 \leq j < q} j/2^{2n} = \Omega(q^2/2^{2n})$. Thus, we expect to make $T_S = q = \Omega(2^n)$ oracle queries to find a strict collision. $\square$

Lemma 6. *Consider H^D. Allow the adversary to choose $H_0' \neq H_0''$.*

1. *Any internal collision for H^D reduces to a strict or to a cross collision.*
2. *The adversary needs time $\Omega(\min\{T_S, T_X, T(K)\})$ to find a K-collision.*

Proof. For the first claim, observe that the initial values H_0' and H_0'' are different. Any non-strict internal collision implies a triple $(H_{i-1}', H_{i-1}'', M_i)$ with $H_{i-1}' = H_{i-1}''$. This implies the existence of a cross-colliding triple (H_j', H_j'', M_{j+1}), with $j \leq i-2$, $H_j' \neq H_j''$, and $H_{j+1}' = C(H_j', H_j''||M_{j+1}) = C(H_j'', H_j'||M_{j+1}) = H_{j+1}''$. Thus, any non-strict internal collision implies a cross collision.

For claim 2, we argue as in the proof of Lemma 1. A K-collision for H^D either reduces to a final K-collision (taking time $T(K)$), or to an internal collision. By the first claim, an internal collision is either strict (taking time T_S), or is a cross collision (taking time T_X). $\square$

Theorem 7. *Consider H^D, and model C as a random oracle. An adversary who can choose $H_0' \neq H_0''$ needs time $\Omega(2^{n(K-1)/K})$ to find K-collisions.*

Proof. The result follows from Theorem 5, Lemma 6, and Fact 1. $\square$

3.2 Resistance Against K-Way (2nd) Preimage Attacks

Our treatment of K-way (2nd) preimage attacks is quite similar to Section 2.2. Let T_S and T_X be defined as above and assume finding preimages for C to take at least time $P(1)$.

Lemma 8. *Consider H^D. Allow the adversary to choose $H_0' \neq H_0''$.*

1. *To find a single preimage, the adversary needs time $\Omega(P(1))$.*
2. *To find K-way preimages, the adversary needs time $\Omega(\min\{T_S, T_X, T(K)\})$.*

Proof. Claim 1: See proof of Lemma 3 with $f''(\cdot, \cdot||\cdot) := C(\cdot, \cdot||\cdot)$. Claim 2 follows from claim 1 of Lemma 6. Note that a K-way preimage also is a K-collision. $\square$

Theorem 9. *Consider the double-pipe hash H^D. Model the compression function C as a random oracle. An adversary who can choose H_0 needs time $\Omega(2^n)$ for finding a single or K-way preimage or a single or K-way 2nd preimage.*

The proof of Theorem 9 is quite similar to the proof of Theorem 12 below.

Our results indicate that in the random oracle model, **the double-pipe hash H^D is asymptotically as secure as the wide-pipe hash with $w = 2n$.**

4   Davies-Meyer (DM) Compression Functions

If we trust an existing MD-hash to meet its security goal, it seems reasonable to use its compression function as the building-block C for the double-pipe hash. But most practical hash (or rather, compression) functions (including the SHA-family of hash functions, see Table 1) suffer from a specific structural weakness: They use a block cipher like function $E : \{0,1\}^{n+m} \times \{0,1\}^n \to \{0,1\}^n$, i.e., that for each "key" $K \in \{0,1\}^{n+m}$ the function $E(K, \cdot)$ permutates over $\{0,1\}^n$, and both $E(M, \cdot)$ and its inverse can efficiently be computed. A **DM compression function** $C : \{0,1\}^n \times \{0,1\}^{n+m} \to \{0,1\}^n$ is defined as follows:

$$C(H_{i-1}, M_i) = E(M_i, H_{i-1}) + H_{i-1}.$$

(Here "$+$" is any group operation over $\{0,1\}^n$.) The ability to efficiently compute $E_M^{-1}(\cdot)$ can be useful for the adversary, see e.g. Kelsey and Schneier [13] for examples. Thus, we have to extend our formalism for the security proofs accordingly – by considering a Shannon oracle, instead of a random oracle.

4.1   Double-Pipe Hash with DM Compression Function

Some generic attacks against hash functions don't apply in the random oracle model, but are feasible in the Shannon model [13]. Fortunately, this does not pose a problem for the double-pipe hash. Those parts of our analysis of the double-pipe hash which do not assume random oracles are still relevant and applicable.[6] However, trusting those parts of our analysis which treat C as a random oracle would be risky. For this reason, we additionally analyse the double-pipe hash in the Shannon-model. See Appendix A for the proofs of the Theorems below.

Theorem 10. *Consider a DM compression function C. If we model E by a Shannon oracle, then $T_X = \Omega(2^n)$ and $T_S = \Omega(2^n)$.*

Theorem 11. *Consider H^D with a DM compression function C. If we model E by a Shannon oracle, then finding K-collisions takes time $\Omega(2^{(n-1)(K-1)/K})$.*

Theorem 12. *Consider H^D with a DM compression function C. If we model E by a Shannon oracle, then finding a single or K-way preimage or a single or K-way 2nd preimage takes time $P(1) = \Omega(2^n)$.*

5   Resistance Against 2nd Collision Attacks

Note that our definition of a 2nd collision attack assumes the adversary to be given the first collision essentially "for free". This is difficult to handle in the standard model. Thus, we concentrate on the random oracle model.

---

[6] Observe that the "DM compression function" is the function C with some specific non-random property. Given such C, the definition of H^D is the same.

In general, our hash designs do not protect against 2nd collision attacks: given an *internal collision*, attacking the wide-pipe or double-pipe hash is as easy as attacking the MD hash. Our design rationale, however, has been to defend against internal collisions, leaving final collisions as the "dotted line", where the hash function is likely to break (if it breaks at all). This is the foundation for the security proofs in the previous sections. In the remainder of this section, we thus focus on the specific case that the adversary is only given a *final collision*.

5.1   Wide-Pipe Hash: 2nd Collision Resistance

Consider the following attack: *fix* H_0, *choose* two incomplete expanded messages $(M_1, \ldots, M_{L-1})$ and $(N_1, \ldots, N_{L'-1})$, defining some pre-final internal states H_{L-1}^M and $H_{L'-1}^N$, *receive* a first collision and finally *provide* a 2nd collision. The first collision is defined by $M_L, N_{L'}$ such that the hash collides, but C' does not:

$$f''(H_{L-1}^M, M_L) = f''(H_{L'-1}^N, N_{L'-1}) \quad \text{but} \quad C'(H_{L-1}^M, M_L) = C'(H_{L'-1}^N, N_{L'-1})$$

In this section, we consider an attack game giving the adversary even more freedom: *choose* any H_{L-1}^M and $H_{L'-1}^N$, *receive* $M_L, N_{L'}$ for a first collision as above, and *provide* any four messages $A, B, C, D \in \{0,1\}^*$, $A \neq B$, $C \neq D$, $H(A) = H(B)$, $H(C) = H(D)$, with $C \notin \{A, B, D\}$.

Theorem 13. *Consider the wide-pipe hash H. Model C' as a random oracle. If C'' either is an independent random oracle, or the n-bit truncation of its w-bit input, the adversary needs time $\Omega(2^{n/2})$ to win the 2nd collision game for H.*

Proof (Sketch). Recall that we have got a first collision for f'', but no collision for C'. Finding messages $A, B, C, D \in \{0,1\}^*$ as required implies finding

- an internal collision (a collision for C'), taking time $\Omega(2^{w/2}) > \Omega(2^{n/2})$,
- or a 2nd collision for f'', namely intermediate hashes H_A, H_B, H_C, H_D
  $\in \{0,1\}^w$, and final message blocks $M_A, M_B, M_C, M_D \in \{0,1\}^m$ with
  $(H_A, M_A) \neq (H_B, M_B)$,
  $(H_C, M_C) \notin \{(H_A, M_A), (H_B, M_B), (H_D, M_D)\}$,
  $f''(H_A, M_A) = f''(H_B, M_B)$, and $f''(H_C, M_C) = f''(H_D, M_D)$.

We argue that finding a 2nd collision for f'' would take time $\Omega(2^n)$. If the 2nd collision for f'' includes a collision for C', then we need time time $\Omega(2^{w/2})$ to find it. Else, the 2nd collision is still as hard to find as a 2nd collision for any n-bit random oracle – both when C'' is an independent random oracle and when C'' plainly truncates –, thus taking time $\Omega(2^{n/2})$, see Fact 2.   □

5.2   The Double-Pipe Hash: 2nd Collision Resistance

We adapt the attack game from above to the double-pipe hash: *choose* four arbitrary pairs $G' \neq G''$, $H' \neq H'' \in \{0,1\}^n$, *receive* $M, N \in \{0,1\}^m$ with $C(G', G''\|M) = C(H', H''\|N)$, and *provide* $A, B, C, D \in \{0,1\}^*$, with $A \neq B$, $C \neq D$, $H^D(A) = H^D(B)$, $H^D(C) = H^D(D)$, and $C \notin \{A, B, D\}$.

Theorem 14. *Consider the double-pipe hash H^D. Model C as a random oracle. The adversary needs time $\Omega(2^{n/2})$ to win the 2nd collision game for H^D.*

Proof (Sketch). As above, finding such $A, B, C, D \in \{0,1\}^*$ with $A \neq B$ and $C \notin \{A, B, D\}$, implies finding

- either an **internal collision**, taking time $\Omega(2^n)$ ($\to$ Lemma 6, Theorem 5)
- or **intermediate hashes** $H'_A, H''_A, H'_B, H''_B, H'_C, H''_C, H'_D, H''_D \in \{0,1\}^n$ and **final message blocks** $M_A, M_B, M_C, M_D \in \{0,1\}^m$ with

$$(H'_A, H''_A \| M_A) \neq (H'_B, H''_B \| M_B),$$
$$(H'_C, H''_C \| M_C) \notin \{ (H'_A, H''_A \| M_A), (H'_B, H''_B \| M_B), (H'_D, H''_D \| M_D) \},$$
$$C(H'_A, H''_A \| M_A) = C(H'_B, H''_B \| M_B), \quad \text{and}$$
$$C(H'_C, H''_C \| M_C) = C(H'_D, H''_D \| M_D).$$

The intermediate hashes and message blocks constitute a 2nd preimage for C. According to Fact 2, finding such a 2nd preimage takes time $\Omega(2^{n/2})$.   □

Theorem 15. *Consider H^D with a DM compression function C. Model E by a Shannon oracle. Winning the 2nd collision game takes time $\Omega(2^{n/2})$.*

See Appendix A for a sketch of the proof.

6   Discussion

A Variant of the double-pipe hash. To reduce the set of cryptographic assumptions, Preneel [21] proposed to use $C : \{0,1\} \times \{0,1\}^n \times \{0,1\}^{n+m} \to \{0,1\}^n$ with one extra bit of input. Set $H'_i := C(0, H'_{i-1}, H''_{i-1} \| M_i)$, $H''_i := C(1, H''_{i-1}, H'_{i-1} \| M_i)$, and finally $\text{Hash}(M) := C(0, H'_{L-1}, H''_{L-1} \| M_L)$. Proofs of security for this variant of the double-pipe hash are very similar to the proofs for H^D itself, but without the need to assume finding cross collisions to be infeasible.
Two Independent Security Parameters. The main lesson from [11,13] and the current paper is that *the internal state size w of an iterated hash function should be seen as a security parameter of its own right.*

Any security architect choosing parameters for a cryptographic hash should choose both w and n according to her specific security requirements. For an application where even a single hash collision would be the ultimate disaster, $w = n$ suffices. If, on the other hand, additional multi-collisions or (multiple or single) preimages or 2nd preimages or feasible 2nd collisions would turn things from bad to worse, $w \gg n$ is recommendable, due to an improved failure mode.

2nd Collision Resistance. For applications such as digital signatures, 2nd collision resistance can have a *huge impact on practical security*. Our constructions are reasonably 2nd collision resistant. E.g., a double-pipe hash using the MD5 compression function would fail collision resistance due to [26], but for the double-pipe hash, this attack could only be used to generate final collisions. Accordingly, this double-pipe hash still defeats known exploits that make collisions "meaningful" [12,17,14,15,7].

Cascading. The idea to improve the security of hash functions by cascading has been discussed for a long time, see, e.g., [20]. Cascading looks like an obvious technique to improve the security of hash functions – but due to Joux' attack, cascading iterated hash functions is not that useful. On the other hand, the double-pipe construction can be seen as a cascade of compression functions. To this end, our double-pipe construction provides a *theoretically sound* technique to *cascade compression functions instead of the complete hash functions*.

Summary. This paper takes an abstract and proof-centric look at the design of hash functions. Similarly to [2], we consider our work a "feasible and useful step for understanding the security" of iterated hash functions, thereby complementing the attack-centric approach [11,13]. In the spirit of Merkle [16] and Damgård [6], this paper shows how to compose "good" hash functions, given "good" compression functions. We provide standard model explanations, what it means for the compression function to be "good". Additionally, we analyse the security of our constructions in the random oracle and Shannon model.

Acknowledgement. The author thanks Frederik Armknecht, John Kelsey, Ulrich Kühn, Arjen Lenstra, Bart Preneel, and the anonymous reviewers for their suggestions, discussions, and inspirations.

References

1. E. Biham, R. Chen, A. Joux, P. Carribault, C. Lemuet, W. Jalby. Collisions of SHA-0 and reduced SHA-1. Eurocrypt 2005, LNCS 3494, 36–57.
2. J. Black, P. Rogaway, T. Shrimpton. Black-box analysis of the block-cipher based hash-function construction from PGV. Crypto 02, LNCS 2442, 320-335.
3. E. Brickell, D. Pointcheval, S. Vaudenay, M. Yung. Design validation for discrete logarithm based signature schemes. PKC 2000, LNCS 1751, 276–292
4. R. Canetti, O. Goldreich, S. Halevi. The random oracle methodology, revisited. 30th STOC 1998, 209–218.
5. J. Coron, Y. Dodis, C. Malinaud, P. Punyia. Merkle-Damgård revisited: how to construct a hash function. Accepted for Crypto 2005.
6. I. Damgård. A design principle for hash functions. Crypto 89, LNCS 435, 416–427.
7. M. Daum, S. Lucks. The story of Alice and her boss. Eurocrypt 05 rump session. http://th.informatik.uni-mannheim.de/people/lucks/HashCollisions/
8. H. Dobbertin, A. Bosselaers, B. Preneel. RIPEMD-160, a strengthened version of RIPEMD. FSE 1996, LNCS 1039, 71-82. See also http://www.esat.kuleuven.ac.be/bosselae/ripemd160.html
9. H. Finney. More problems with hash functions. The cryptography mailing list. 24 Aug 2004. http://lists.virus.org/cryptography-0408/msg00124.html
10. M. Girault, J. Stern. On the length of cryptographic hash-values used in identification schemes. Crypto 94, LNCS 839, 202–215
11. A. Joux. Multicollisions in iterated hash functions, application to cascaded constructions. Crypto 04, LNCS 3152, 306–316.
12. D. Kaminski. MD5 to be considered harmful someday. Dec. 2004. http://www.doxpara.com/md5_someday.pdf

13. J. Kelsey. B. Schneier. Second preimages on n-bit hash functions in much less than 2^n work. Eurocrypt 2005, LNCS 3494, 474–490.
14. A. Lenstra, B. de Weger. On the possibility of constructing meaningful hash collisions for public keys. To appear at ACISP 2005.
15. A. Lenstra, B. de Weger, X. Wang. Colliding X.509 certificates. Cryptology eprint archive report 2005/067. http://eprint.iacr.org/2005/067/
16. R. Merkle. One-way hash functions and DES. Crypto 89, LNCS 435, 428–446.
17. O. Mikle. Practical attacks on digital signatures using MD5 message digest. Cryptology eprint archive report 2004/356. http://eprint.iacr.org/2004/356/
18. M. Nandi, W. Lee, K. Sakurai, S. Lee. Security analysis of a 2/3-rate double length compression function in the black box model. FSE 2005, LNCS 3557, 243–254.
19. National Institute of Standards and Technology (NIST). Secure hash standard. FIPS 180-2. August 2002.
20. B. Preneel. Analysis and design of cryptographic hash functions. PhD thesis, Katholieke Universiteit Leuven, 1993.
21. B. Preneel. Private communication. Hash Function Workshop, Krakow, 2005.
22. RIPE integrity primitives for secure information systems. Final report of RACE integrity primitives evaluation (RIPE RACE 1040). LNCS 1007, 1995.
23. R. Rivest, A. Shamir. PayWord and MicroMint – two simple micropayment schemes. CryptoBytes, Vol. 2, # 1 (1996), 7–11.
24. P. Rogaway and T. Shrimpton. Cryptographic Hash-Function Basics: Definitions, Implications, and Separations for Preimage Resistance, Second-Preimage Resistance, and Collision-Resistance. FSE 2004, LNCS 3017, 371-388.
25. X. Wang, X. Lai, D. Feng, H. Cheng, X. Yu. Cryptoanalyisis of the hash functions MD4 and RIPEMD. Eurocrypt 2005, LNCS 3494, 1–18.
26. X. Wang, H. Yu. How to break MD5 and other hash functions. Eurocrypt 2005, LNCS 3494, 19–35.
27. X. Wang, H. Yu, Y. L. Yin. Efficient collision search attacks on SHA0. Accepted for Crypto 2005.
28. X. Wang, Y. L. Yin, H. Yu. Finding collisions in the full SHA1. Accepted for Crypto 2005.

Appendix

A   Security of Double-Pipe Hash with Davies-Meyer

A.1   Conventions

In this section, we analyse the security of the double-pipe hash with a Davies-Meyer compression function. The adversary A has access to a Shannon oracle for E and E^{-1}. Similarly to [2], we assume:

- A never asks a query for which the response is already known. Namely, if A asks for $E_k(x)$ and receives y, she neither asks for $E_k^{-1}(y)$, nor for $E_k(x)$ again. Similarly, if she has asked for $E_k^{-1}(y)$ and received x.
- Recall that for the type of attacks we consider, a successful adversary always outputs one or more messages M^i, which either collide or constitute some (2nd) preimages. Before finishing, the adversary makes all the oracle calls to compute all hash values $H(M^i)$.

- We define a <u>simulator</u>, to respond to A's oracle queries:
  - Initially:
    * set $i := 0$; clear the logbook;
    * for all (k, x): mark $E_k(x)$ as undefined;
  - At any time, $\overline{\text{DOMAIN}}(E_k)$ denotes the set of points x where $E_k(x)$ is still undefined. Similarly we write $\overline{\text{RANGE}}(E_k)$, for the set of points y where $E_k^{-1}(y)$ is still undefined.
  - Responding to an oracle query $E_k(x)$:
    * set $i := i + 1$
    * randomly choose y from $\overline{\text{RANGE}}(E_k)$
    * append $(x_i, k_i, y_i) := (x, k, y)$ to the logbook;
    * respond y;
  - Responding to an oracle query $E_k^{-1}(y)$:
    * set $i := i + 1$
    * randomly choose x from $\overline{\text{DOMAIN}}(E_k)$
    * append $(x_i, k_i, y_i) := (x, k, y)$ to the logbook;
    * respond x;
  For our proofs, we will discuss the logbook entries (x_i, k_i, y_i).

This is without loss of generality: any adversary not following the first two conventions can easily be transformed into an equivalent one following them. And an adversary following the first two conventions cannot distinguish the simulator from a "true" Shannon oracle.

A.2   Internal Collisions

Theorem 10.   *Consider a DM compression function C. If we model E by a Shannon oracle, then $T_X = \Omega(2^n)$ and $T_S = \Omega(2^n)$.*

Proof. For the proof, we assume that the adversary does not make more than $q \leq 2^{n-1}$ queries. This is technically correct, since $2^{n-1} = \Omega(2^n)$.

Time T_X to find cross collisions: a cross collision is described by $H'_{i-1} \neq H''_{i-1}$, M_i with

$$C(H'_{i-1}, H''_{i-1} \| M_i) = H'_i = H''_i = C(H''_{i-1}, H'_{i-1} \| M_i). \qquad (1)$$

In time q, we can check at most $q/2$ such triples $(H'_{i-1}, H''_{i-1}, M_i)$ for cross collisions. Now we argue that for $q \leq 2^{n-1}$, for each such triple the probability p_x to satisfy Equation 1 is at most $1/2^{n-1}$. This implies that the expected number of oracle queries we need to make before we get the first cross collision is $T_X = \Omega(2^n)$, as claimed.

We still have to show $p_x \leq 2^{n-1}$. If the adversary's answer involves a cross collision, then, by the above conventions, the simulator's logbook contains two triples (x_a, k_a, y_a) and (x_b, k_b, y_b) with $a \neq b$,

$$\begin{aligned} x_a &= H'_{i-1}, \quad k_a = (H''_{i-1} \| M_i), \qquad y_a = E_{k_a}(x_a), \\ x_b &= H''_{i-1}, \quad k_b = (H'_{i-1} \| M_i), \text{ and } y_b = E_{k_b}(x_b). \end{aligned}$$

Thus, we can rewrite Equation 1 as

$$\overbrace{E_{k_a}(x_a)+x_a}^{y_a} = \overbrace{E_{k_b}(x_b)+x_b}^{y_b},$$

which corresponds to

$$y_a + x_a = y_b + x_b. \tag{2}$$

If (w.l.o.g.) $a < b$, then either y_b or x_b is a uniformly distributed random value from a huge subset of $\{0,1\}^n$:

- If the b-th oracle query has been $E_{k_b}(x_b)$, then y_b is a random value from $\overline{\text{RANGE}}(E_{k_b})$.
- Else x_b is a random value from $\overline{\text{DOMAIN}}(E_{k_b})$.

Since $|\overline{\text{RANGE}}(E_{k_b})| = |\overline{\text{DOMAIN}}(E_{k_b})| = 2^n - b + 1 \geq 2^n - q$, and due to $q \leq 2^{n-1}$, we get $p_x \leq 1/2^{n-1}$, as claimed.

Time T_S to find strict collisions: for triples (G', G'', M) with $G' \neq G''$, we consider pairs $(H', H'') \in \{0,1\}^{2n}$, where

$$H' = C(G', G''\|M) \quad \text{and} \quad H'' = C(G'', G'\|M). \tag{3}$$

A strict collision consists of such a triple (G', G'', M) and another triple $(F', F'', N) \neq (G', G'', M)$ with

$$C(F', F''\|N) = H' \quad \text{and} \quad C(F'', F'\|N) = H''. \tag{4}$$

After q oracle queries, there are $\Omega(q^2)$ pairs $((G', G'', M),(F', F'', N))$ of triples. We claim that for $q \leq 2^{n-1}$, the probability p_s to satisfy Equation 4 is $p_s \leq 1/2^{2(n-1)}$. Hence, the expected number of oracle queries to get a strict collision is $T_S = \Omega(2^n)$.

It remains to prove $p_s \leq 1/2^{2(n-1)}$. Consider a triple (x_a, k_a, y_a) with $x_a = G'$, $k_a = (G''\|M)$, and $y_a = E_{k_a}(x_a)$ from the simulator's logfile. We only have a chance for a strict collision if the logfile contains another triple (x_b, k_b, y_b) with $x_b = G''$, $k_b = (G'\|M)$, and $y_b = E_{k_b}(x_b)$. Note that x_b and k_b are uniquely determined by x_a and k_a, and vice versa. Equation 3 can then be rewritten as

$$H' = E_{k_a}(x_a) + x_a = y_a + x_a \quad \text{and} \quad H'' = E_{k_b}(x_b) + x_b = y_b + x_b.$$

A strict collision implies another triple (F', F'', N) to satisfy Equation 4. This corresponds to two more triples (x_c, k_c, y_c) and (x_d, k_d, y_d) on the server's logfile with

$$H' = y_a + x_a = y_c + x_c \tag{5}$$

$$H'' = y_b + x_b = y_d + x_d. \tag{6}$$

Both equations are of the same type as Equation 2. As in that context, we argue that due to $q \leq 2^{n-1}$ the probability for Eq. 5 to hold is no more than $1/2^{n-1}$; similarly for Eq. 6. More importantly, the conditional probability to satisfy Eq. 6, assuming Eq. 5 is at most $1/2^{n-1}$. Thus, the joint probability p_s for *both* Eq. 5 *and* Eq. 6 is $p_s \leq 1/2^{2(n-1)}$. □

A.3 Resistance Against K-Collision Attacks

Theorem 11. *Consider H^D with a DM compression function C. If we model E by a Shannon oracle, then finding K-collisions takes time $\Omega(2^{(n-1)(K-1)/K})$.*

Proof. Due to the first claim of Lemma 6 and Theorem 10, we know that an internal collision would take time $\Omega(2^n)$. Thus, in time $\Omega(2^{(n-1)(K-1)/K})$ we cannot expect to find any internal collision. The only chance to find a K-way collision for H is finding a final K-collision, which takes time $T(K)$. In the remainder of this proof, we show $T(K) = \Omega(2^{(n-1)(K-1)/K})$. As in the proof of Theorem 10, we assume $q \leq 2^{n-1} = \Omega(2^n)$.

A final K-collision consists of K different triples with (G^i, H^i, M^i) with

$$C(G^1, H^1 || M^1) = \cdots = C(G^K, H^K || M^K).$$

By the above conventions, this implies that there are K triples $(x_1, k_1, y_1), \ldots, (x_K, k_K, y_K)$ in the simulator's logbook with

$$\overbrace{E_{k_1}(x_1)}^{y_1} + x_1 = \cdots = \overbrace{E_{k_K}(x_K)}^{y_K} + x_K.$$

These are K sums $x_i + y_i$, and similarly to the proof of Theorem 10, for each such sum either x_i or y_i has been chosen from a huge subset $\{0,1\}^n$. Since $q \leq 2^{n-1}$, the size of this subset exceeds $2^n - q \geq 2^{n-1}$. For this reason, we expect to make $T(K) = \Omega(2^{(n-1)(K-1)/K})$ Shannon oracle queries for a K-collision.   □

A.4 Resistance Against K-way (2nd) Preimage Attacks

Theorem 12. *Consider H^D with a DM compression function C. If we model E by a Shannon oracle, then finding a single or K-way preimage or a single or K-way 2nd preimage takes time $P(1) = \Omega(2^n)$.*

Proof. As in some of the proofs above, we assume $q \leq 2^{n-1}$.

Finding K-way (2nd) preimages isn't faster than finding single (2nd) preimages. Thus, we concentrate on single ones.

First, we start with singe preimages. Due to Lemma 8, finding a single preimage for the hash H^D takes time $\Omega(P(1))$, i.e., is asymptotically not faster than finding a preimage for the compression function $C(K, X) = E_K(X) + X$. Let a target Z be given, and an adversary is trying to find K and X with $C(K, X) = E_K(X) + X = Z$. By the above conventions, this corresponds to an entry (x_i, k_i, y_i) in the simulator's logbook with $x_i + y_i = Z$, and either x_i or y_i has been chosen from a huge subset of $\{0,1\}^n$ of size $> 2^n - q \geq 2^{n-1}$. Thus, for each query to the Shannon oracle, the probability to find a preimage for Z is at most 2^{n-1}, and we expect to make $P(1) = \Omega(2^n)$ such queries to find such a preimage.

Now consider 2nd preimages: assume an algorithm to find 2nd preimages for H^{D}. Consider we are given (K, N) and searching for some 2nd preimage $(K', N') \neq (K, N)$ with

$$C(K', N') = E_{K'}(N') + N' = E_K(N) + N = C(K, N).$$

The following technique resembles the proof of Theorem 4. We choose some message M, expand it to $(M_1, \ldots, M_L)$ and accordingly compute the internal hashes $H'_1, H''_1, \ldots, H'_{L-1}, H''_{L-1}$. Assume $(K, N) \notin \{(H'_i, H''_i \| M_i), (H''_i \| H'_i \| M_i) \mid 1 \leq i < L\}$ (this holds with overwhelming probability).

Set $N^{-1} := E_K^{-1}(Z - N)$ and define the function $E' : \{0, 1\}^n \times \{0, 1\}^{n+m} \rightarrow \{0, 1\}^n$:

$$
\begin{aligned}
E'_K(N) &= Z - N \\
E'_K(N^{-1}) &= E_K(N) \\
E'_Q(R) &= E_Q(R) \text{ for } (Q, R) \notin \{(K, N), (K, N^{-1})\}.
\end{aligned}
$$

Now we run the adversary, replacing the (Shannon-) oracle for E and E^{-1} by an oracle for E' and its inverse. Observe that for the adversary $H^{\mathrm{D}}(M) = Z$ holds. Further, both E and E' are random permutations over $\{0, 1\}^n$, so the adversary's chances of success are not affected by the change from E to E'.

Assume the adversary succeeds in finding a 2nd preimage $\overline{M}$ for M. Write $(\overline{M_1}, \ldots, \overline{M_{\overline{L}}})$ for the expansion of $\overline{M}$ and $\overline{H'_1}, \overline{H''_1}, \ldots, \overline{H'_{\overline{L}-1}}, \overline{H''_{\overline{L}-1}}$ for the internal hashes.

- If $(\overline{H'_{\overline{L}-1}}, \overline{H''_{\overline{L}-1}}, \overline{M_{\overline{L}}}) = (H'_{L-1}, H''_{L-1}, M_L)$, then the adversary has found an internal collision. From above, we know that this needs time $\min\{T_X, T_S\} = \Omega(2^n)$.
- Otherwise, $(\overline{H'_{\overline{L}-1}}, \overline{H''_{\overline{L}-1}}, \overline{M_{\overline{L}}})$ is a preimage for Z. From above, we know that this takes time $P(1) = \Omega(2^n)$.

Thus, in order to find a 2nd preimage for H, the adversary either has to find an internal collision, or a 2nd preimage for C, and solving either problem takes time $\Omega(2^n)$. □

A.5 2nd Collision Resistance

Theorem 15. *Consider H^{D} with a DM compression function C. Model E by a Shannon oracle. Winning the 2nd collision game takes time $\Omega(2^{n/2})$.*

Proof (Sketch). Recall the proof of Theorem 14. A 2nd collision for H^{D} either implies an internal collision or a 2nd preimage for C. Finding an internal collision reduces to strict or internal collisions, thus taking time $\Omega(2^n)$ ($\rightarrow$ Theorem 10).

We still have to show that finding 2nd collisions for C takes time $\Omega(2^{n/2})$. From Theorem 11, we know that finding (first) collisions (i.e., K-collisions with

$K = 2$) takes time $\Omega(2^{n/2})$. In the proof of Theorem 11, finding such collisions for C is shown equivalent to the following task:

$$\text{find} \quad x_1, k_1, x_2, k_2 \quad \text{with} \quad E_{k_1}(x_1) + x_1 = E_{k_2}(x_2) + x_2,$$
$$\text{and} \quad (x_1, k_1) \neq (x_2, k_2).$$

Similarly, finding 2nd collisions for C is equivalent to the task:

$$\text{given} \quad x_a, k_a, x_b, k_b \quad \text{with} \quad E_{k_a}(x_a) + x_a = E_{k_b}(x_b) + x_b$$
$$\text{with} \quad (x_1, k_1) \neq (x_2, k_2),$$
$$\text{find} \quad x_c, k_c, x_d, k_d \quad \text{with} \quad E_{k_c}(x_c) + x_c = E_{k_d}(x_d) + x_d,$$
$$\text{and} \quad (x_a, k_a) \neq (x_b, k_b),$$
$$\text{and} \quad (x_c, k_c) \notin \{ (x_a, k_a), (x_b, k_b), (x_c, k_c) \}.$$

Regarding the second task, we replace the family E of permutations by a modified family E':

- Randomly choose x_a, k_a, x_b, k_b. Assume $k_a \neq k_b$ (this is overwhelmingly probable).
- Compute $y^* := E_{k_b}(x_b) + x_b - x_a$ and $x^* := E_{k_a}(y^*)$.
- Set $E'_{k_a}(x_a) := y^*$ and $E'_{k_a}(x^*) := E_{k_a}(x_a)$. Otherwise, E' behaves identical to E.
- Observe $E'_{k_a}(x_a) + x_a = E'_{k_b}(y_b)$. Given such x_a, k_a, x_b, k_b, solve the second collision task for E' instead of E. The solution is x_c, k_c, x_d, k_d as above.

With significant probability, we have $\{(x_c, k_c), (x_d, k_d)\} \cap \{(x_a, k_a), (x^*, k_a)\} = \{\}$. In this case, our 2nd collision for E' is a first collision for E. Thus, our proof reveals a technique to efficiently find collisions for C, if one can find 2nd collisions. Due to Theorem 11, finding such collisions takes time $\Omega(2^{n/2})$.   □

B   Examples

The SHA standard. Two of the five SHA-∗ hash functions [19], namely SHA-224 and -384, have already been designed according to this paper's "wide-pipe" paradigm, see Table 1. Of course, the authors of SHA-224 and -384 where to reuse existing compression functions, but they could have done so – improving the hash function's performance – by truncating the internal hash values to 224 or 348 bit and extending the message chunk size by 256-224=32 or 512-348=128 bit. Our results provides some formal ("after the fact") justification for the design of SHA-224 and -348.

A natural choice for the parameters w and n would, however, be $w = 2n$. As an *example for the wide-pipe hash*, we could set $C' :=$ (SHA-512 compression function) and $C'' :=$ (SHA-256 compression function) to define a 256-bit hash with an internal hash size of $w = 512$. For large messages, this 256-bit hash would be about as fast as SHA-512. As an *example for a 256-bit double-pipe hash*, consider $C :=$ (SHA-256 compression function). The size of a SHA-256

Table 1. SHA standard hash functions and their parameters [19]

	final hash size n [bit]	internal hash size w [bit]	message chunk size [bit]	uses compression function from
SHA-1	160	160	512	(own)
SHA-224	224	256	512	SHA-256
SHA-256	256	256	512	(own)
SHA-384	384	512	1024	SHA-512
SHA-512	512	512	1024	(own)

message chunk is $m + n = 512$, so the size of a double-pipe message chunk would be $m = 512 - n = 256$ bit. For large messages, double-piped SHA-256 would be about four times slower than plain SHA-256. Similarly, a double-piped SHA-1 hash would be about three times slower than plain SHA-1.[7]

AES-based example for the double-pipe hash. Consider an AES-based MD hash $H_{\mathrm{AES}}^{\mathrm{MD}}$, using the AES block cipher in Davies-Meyer mode. The block size of $H_{\mathrm{AES}}^{\mathrm{MD}}$ is the AES block size: 128 bit. For applications which do not require collision resistance, it may be fine to use a 128-bit hash. But resistance against multi-collision attacks or 2nd preimage attacks could be a concern for these applications – and from the Joux and the Kelsey-Schneier attacks, we know that $H_{\mathrm{AES}}^{\mathrm{MD}}$ is much less resistant against these attacks than we would expect from a 128-bit hash. For a well funded and motivated adversary, it is possible to find, say, a 2^{16}-collision for $H_{\mathrm{AES}}^{\mathrm{MD}}$. This weakness does not much depend on the AES key size (either 128 bit, 192 bit, or 256 bit).

In contrast to $H_{\mathrm{AES}}^{\mathrm{MD}}$, its double-pipe counterpart (only defined for the AES key size of 256 bit) provides much better protection against these attacks, assuming the AES itself does not suffer from some still unknown cryptanalytic weaknesses. Even finding a 3-collision for a double-pipe 128-bit hash would take more than 2^{80} units of running time and therefore seems to be infeasible today. The price for the improved security is a performance penalty by a factor of four, similarly to double-piped SHA-256.

---

[7] Note that sharing initial values between different hash functions is never recommendable. Thus, H_0' and H_0'' should not be taken from [19].

Identity-Based Hierarchical Strongly Key-Insulated Encryption and Its Application

Yumiko Hanaoka[1], Goichiro Hanaoka[2], Junji Shikata[3], and Hideki Imai[2,4]

[1] NTT DoCoMo, Inc
yamamotoyumi@nttdocomo.co.jp
[2] Research Center for Information Security,
National Institute of Advanced Industrial Science and Technology
hanaoka-goichiro@aist.go.jp
[3] Graduate School of Environment and Information Sciences,
Yokohama National University
shikata@mlab.jks.ynu.ac.jp
[4] Institute of Industrial Science, University of Tokyo
imai@iis.u-tokyo.ac.jp

Abstract. In this paper, we discuss non-interactive updating of decryption keys in identity-based encryption (IBE). In practice, key revocation is a necessary and inevitable process and IBE is no exception when it comes to having to manage revocation of decryption keys without losing its merits in efficiency. Our main contribution of this paper is to propose novel constructions of IBE where a decryption key can be renewed without having to make changes to its public key, i.e. user's identity. We achieve this by extending the hierarchical IBE (HIBE). Regarding security, we address semantic security against adaptive chosen ciphertext attacks for a very strong attack environment that models all possible types of key exposures in the random oracle model. In addition to this, we show method of constructing a partially collusion resistant HIBE from arbitrary IBE in the random oracle model. By combining both results, we can construct an IBE with non-interactive key update from only an arbitrary IBE.

1 Introduction

Background. As to our best of knowledge, current public key infrastructures involve complex construction of *certification authorities* (CA), consequently requiring expensive communication and computation costs for certificate verification. In 1984, Shamir introduced an innovative concept called *identity-based encryption* (IBE) [25](later actualized in [7]) where any public key is determined as an arbitrary string, e.g. user's name, e-mail address, etc. which simplifies certificate management in public key infrastructures. In this paper, we address non-interactive updating of user's decryption key in IBE. Revocation and renewal of decryption key is a necessary process carried out in practice, and so, designing of IBE which allows renewal and updating of decryption keys without losing its merits in efficiency will have considerable implications in the practical

B. Roy (Ed.): ASIACRYPT 2005, LNCS 3788, pp. 495–514, 2005.

crypto-infrastructure. One application of IBE is of a mobile phone scenario, in which case, phone number represents the user identity. It will be both simple and convenient for the mobile phone users to be able to communicate and identify each other by their phone numbers only. The users will also want to keep their phone numbers as fixed identities, and therefore, it is necessary to be able to renew and update the decryption key in a way its corresponding public key will be unchanged. As you can see, in practical situations as seen in this scenario, such problem of IBE can be critical. Our main objective is to solve this problem.

Our Results. Our main contribution of this paper is to propose novel constructions of IBE where a decryption key can be renewed without having to make changes to its public key, i.e. user's identity. We start by discussing the impossibility of dealing with such a problem in the conventional IBE model, followed by introducing a new IBE model which makes this possible. Based on the new model, we construct a new IBE in which a decryption key can be updated "non-interactively", that is, *allow user to renew and update his decryption key without any help from the central authority, and most importantly, without having to change his identity.* In our scheme, similar to [13], we assume a *private device* (PD). PD is not connected to the network except at each fixed time period when the decryption key is updated. A *helper key* stored in the PD generates a key-update information which is used to update the decryption key. All secret operations are done by the user alone. Our scheme can be regarded as the first construction of an identity-based version of *strongly secure* key insulated encryption [13]. Here, we mean "strongly" by a system whose security is guaranteed even when its PD is physically compromised. Our scheme is different from [13] in a way that the PD is divided into multiple levels forming a hierarchical structure improving its security.

In brief, our proposed schemes are constructed by extending the hierarchical identity-based encryption schemes (HIBE) [24,22]. Straightforward extension of HIBE, however, will be completely vulnerable for our attack model. Our major contribution of this paper is the proposal of two secure constructions of IBE that can renew and update the decryption key non-interactively: (1) a generic construction based on any HIBE, and (2) a specific construction based on Gentry-Silverberg HIBE [22]. In the generic construction, only an arbitrary (chosen plaintext secure) HIBE is used to build a chosen ciphertext secure IBE with non-interactive key update. The merit of such scheme is the flexibility it has in selecting the underlying assumption which can be determined depending on the requirement of the system. As a by-product, the same method used in the generic construction can also be used to build a (standard) strongly secure key-insulated encryption from an arbitrary (H)IBE and a standard public key encryption. On the other hand, the specific construction is constructed by directly extending the Gentry-Silverberg HIBE [22]. Although being more efficient than the generic scheme, the specific scheme is based on the bilinear Diffie-Hellman (BDH) assumption [7,8] and flexibility may become a concern when designing new constructions in terms of security. In addition to our main contribution, we also show a construction of a partially collusion resistant HIBE built from only an arbitrary IBE. This can be applied to the above result (i.e. generic scheme) to give a construction of IBE with non-interactive key update built from only an arbitrary IBE. Note that we mean "partial collusion resistant" in a sense that we argue based on the security definition in [24] and not in [22]. Security of our schemes is proved in the random oracle model.

Applications: Mobile Phone Scenario. Now let's consider the suitability of introducing a private device (PD) in the mobile phone scenario (see also **Background.**). At first glance, it seems like a hassle to having to use the PD whenever you need to update your decryption key, although, it is not as you might think so. As a mobile phone user, it is your routine job to re-charge your battery every now and then. Now, assume a PD-BC (i.e. a private device that can function also as a battery charger). PD-BC can provide a convenient mean to update the decryption key since updating can be done at the same time you re-charge the battery (which you have to do it anyways). The security of the system is also guaranteed even if the PD-BC is compromised. Here, we introduced a mobile phone scenario, but this is just one of many attractive applications of IBE. Whoever is in high risk of losing the decryption key (e.g. laptop PC user) can benefit from this system. To further improve the security, PD can be stratified into multiple levels. Each level has its own device which updates the device of a level below, each level with varying updating periods. We let the lowest level PD be the least secure device (i.e. PD-BC) of which the keys are updated more frequently than the ones in the higher levels. Security of the devices in each level also increases as the level of the hierarchy goes higher. As an example, the least secure device, PD-BC, updates the decryption key everyday and the helper key stored in the PD-BC is updated (using the PD of a level higher) every 2-3 months. Since lower level PDs are used more frequently, they must be kept in places more handy (e.g. at home or work place) and higher level PDs which are used not as frequently be kept somewhere not as convenient but physically safer (e.g. safe). Our IBE system can guarantee the security even if any level PD is compromised even of the highest one.

Related Works. The problem of revocability of private keys in identity-based schemes was initially discussed by Shinozaki, Itoh, Fujioka and Tsujii [26]. Baek and Zheng [2] showed an application of threshold decryption method to IBE. It does decrease the possibility of getting the keys to be exposed in the first place, however, it does not deal with what it can do after key exposure has actually occured. In [16], Dodis and Yung proposed an interesting idea that refreshes the private keys in HIBE. Their scheme provides a solution to the problem of *gradual* key exposure in which the private key is assumed to slowly compromise over time. Boneh and Franklin in their paper ([7], Section 1.1.1) showed the first generalized method for key revocation in IBE schemes. In their scheme, a privileged Private Key Generator (PKG) generates each user's decryption key where its corresponding public key is set to be the concatenation of user identity and fixed length of time the key is available, e.g. "`recipient@xxx.xxx` ‖ `2005.01.01-2005.12.31`". In such a setting, the public key, despite of whether it is revoked or not, is renewed regularly by the PKG, and also, the renewal interval must be set short (e.g. per day) to alleviate the damage caused by key exposures. Therefore, having to set the interval short and require frequent contacts with the PKG implies increase in the total communication and computation cost, consequently, losing one of primary advantages of IBE (i.e. low costs in communication and computation). Further, it needs to work out a way to establish a secure channel between the PKG and the user. For instance, it needs to compensate for additional transmission for key issuing and also has to deal with complicated transactions if the secret information used to setup the secure channel is exposed. Moreover, forward security must be considered. It is, hence, not desirable to have to require frequent communication via secure channel with the PKG in IBE as it implicates loss of primary advantages of IBE.

While, on the other hand, as a solution to key exposure and revocation problem in conventional public key systems, Dodis, Katz, Xu and Yung [13] proposed a scheme called *key-insulated encryption*. As said earlier, this scheme also assumes a PD in which it stores the *helper key*. The helper key assists the user to renew his decryption key by generating secrets necessary to update the key. Here, the public key is fixed. In [14,15], Dodis, Franklin, Katz, Miyaji and Yung further improved [13] with an additional property, forward security. Notice that being able to renew the decryption key without having to make any changes to the corresponding public key as in the key-insulated encryption scheme, is the very technique, desired in IBE. Possible harmonization of the advantages of the two schemes; an identity-based version of a (strongly secure) key-insulated encryption scheme has never been constructed before. Also, there has never been a construction built of a hierarchical version of key-insulated encryption where the PD is organized in a hierarchical tree structure. Besides the related works shown so far, there are other interesting researches done on the topic of key exposure and revocation as well, for example, [21,1], but both are looked from a non identity-based perspective.

We mentioned earlier that our IBE with non-interactive key update is constructed by extending the HIBE [24,22]. HIBE is a powerful cryptographic tool and also forms the basis of various cryptographic techniques, e.g. [11]. However, all methods known to construct HIBE [24,22,11,4,6] require specific assumptions in elliptic curve cryptography, e.g. the BDH problem [7,8] as the underlying assumption and therefore lacks flexibility in selecting the underlying assumption. (While for IBE, besides BDH, there is also a construction based on quadratic residuosity problem [10].) There is also an open problem for a generic construction of HIBE based on arbitrary IBE and is one of important research topics in this area.

2   Model and Definitions

Overview of the Model. Before we start discussing the details of the actual construction of our IBE scheme, recall earlier how we said it was impossible to construct an IBE that allows an essential property as key revocation if based on the model of conventional IBE. To be more specific, it is impossible, based on the conventional IBE model, for the user to *immediately* revoke and renew his decryption key *only* at times he needs to renew the decryption key without losing the advantage of IBE in terms of communication cost, since in the conventional IBE, a public parameter distributed at system set up phase and the user's identity are the only parameters used to encrypt a message.

Recall that we said earlier, [7] showed the first generalized method for key revocation based on the conventional IBE model. Their scheme, however, required to establish a secure channel between a user and a PKG which also needed to be available at all times. Moreover, the burden on the PKG was heavy which required the PKG to periodically renew the users' decryption keys at fixed and frequent time intervals. Their model is simple and generally does not have any problem using it and may be practical for some applications. However, there are other situations where their assumption is neither preferred nor available.

We introduce a new model of IBE that can renew and update the decryption keys non-interactively (i.e without any loss in communication cost). We introduce a *private device* (PD) which stores the helper key used to renew the decryption key at regular time intervals without requiring interactions with other entities. We further improve the security by giving hierarchical construction in the PD, letting the keys of each level be renewed using the devices of a level higher (See **Applications: Mobile Phone Scenario** in Sec. 1.). Our model can be regarded as both hierarchical and identity-based extension of key-insulated encryption [13]. Similar to [13], we address *random-access key-update*, namely, allowing one-step renewal of current decryption key to any of the decryption keys of any time period (even the past keys). Random-access key-update lets any ciphertext of any time period to be decrypted at any time.

Model. In our model, private devices are structured hierarchically into ℓ-levels, and for $i = 1, \cdots, \ell$, *i-th level helper key* is stored in the i-th level device. Decryption key is stored in the 0-level PD (i.e. mobile phone). Key-update information is generated using the *i-th level helper key* which is used to renew the $(i-1)$-th level helper key for $i = 2, \cdots, \ell$. Decryption key is renewed using the helper key of the 1st-level PD (i.e. PD-BC). To make things simple, we consider $\ell = 2$: 1st- and 2nd-level PD corresponds to PD-BC and PD that updates PD-BC helper key, respectively. (Note that this can be generalized for arbitrary $\ell \geq 1$.)

Now, let $T_0(\cdot)$ and $T_1(\cdot)$ map *time* to corresponding time periods for decryption key and 1st-level helper key, respectively. For example, assuming that decryption key and 1st-level helper key is updated every day and every 2-3 months, respectively, we have $T_0(2005/\text{Aug.}/26\text{th}/17 : 00) = 2005/\text{Aug.}/26\text{th}$ and $T_1(2005/\text{Aug.}/26\text{th}/17 : 00) = 2005/\text{Jul.-Sep.}$. In addition, we let $T_2(\cdot)$ be a function such that for all $\texttt{time}$, $T_2(\texttt{time}) = 0$. At time, $\texttt{time}$, user updates his decryption key if 1st-level helper key is valid for the time period $T_1(\texttt{time})$, and a 1st-level helper key can be updated at any time. Def. 1 formally addresses this.

Definition 1 (IKE). A 2-level *identity-based key-insulated encryption scheme (IKE)* IKE consists of 8 algorithms: $\mathsf{IKE} = (\mathsf{PGen}_{\mathsf{IKE}}, \mathsf{Gen}_{\mathsf{IKE}}, \Delta\text{-}\mathsf{Gen}^i_{\mathsf{IKE}}, \mathsf{Upd}^i_{\mathsf{IKE}}\,(i = 1, 2), \mathsf{Enc}_{\mathsf{IKE}}, \mathsf{Dec}_{\mathsf{IKE}})$ and each are described as follows.

$\mathsf{PGen}_{\mathsf{IKE}}$. The *public-parameter generation algorithm* $\mathsf{PGen}_{\mathsf{IKE}}(1^k)$ where k is the security parameter and outputs a master key s and a public parameter p. Note that $\mathsf{PGen}_{\mathsf{IKE}}$ and $\mathsf{Gen}_{\mathsf{IKE}}$ are used by the PKG only.

$\underline{\mathsf{Gen}_{\mathsf{IKE}}}$. The *user-secret generation algorithm* $\mathsf{Gen}_{\mathsf{IKE}}$ takes s, p and user's identity U as inputs, and outputs U's initial private keys (d_0^0, d_0^1, d_0^2) where d_0^0 is the U's initial decryption key, and d_0^i $(i = 1, 2)$ are stored in U's i-th level PD as initial i-th helper key.

$\underline{\Delta\text{-}\mathsf{Gen}_{\mathsf{IKE}}^i}$. A helper key stored in the 1st-level PD and $\Delta\text{-}\mathsf{Gen}_{\mathsf{IKE}}^1$ are used to generate the key-update information required to renew the decryption key. Similarly, a helper key stored in the 2nd-level PD and $\Delta\text{-}\mathsf{Gen}_{\mathsf{IKE}}^2$ are used to generate the key-update information required to renew the 1st-level helper key. More specifically, for $i = 1, 2$, the *key-update information generation algorithm* $\Delta\text{-}\mathsf{Gen}_{\mathsf{IKE}}^i$ takes d_t^i, p, U and time as inputs, and outputs key-update information $\delta_{T_{i-1}(\texttt{time})}^{i-1}$ only if $t = T_i(\texttt{time})$.

$\underline{\mathsf{Upd}_{\mathsf{IKE}}^i}$. U's decryption key, key-update information $\delta_{T_0(\texttt{time})}^0$ and $\mathsf{Upd}_{\mathsf{IKE}}^1$ are used to generate U's decryption key for time. Similarlly, U's 1st-level helper key, key-update information $\delta_{T_1(\texttt{time})}^1$ and $\mathsf{Upd}_{\mathsf{IKE}}^2$ are used to generate U's 1st-level helper key for time. More specifically, for $i = 1, 2$, the *key-update information generation algorithm* $\mathsf{Upd}_{\mathsf{IKE}}^i$ takes d_t^{i-1}, p and $\delta_{T_{i-1}(\texttt{time})}^{i-1}$ as inputs for any t, and outputs a new key $d_{T_{i-1}(\texttt{time})}^{i-1}$ for time period $T_{i-1}(\texttt{time})$.

$\underline{\mathsf{Enc}_{\mathsf{IKE}}}$. The *encryption algorithm* $\mathsf{Enc}_{\mathsf{IKE}}$ inputs m, U, p and time where m is a plaintext, U is the user identity and time indicates the time at which m is encrypted, and outputs ciphertext $\langle c, \texttt{time} \rangle$.

$\underline{\mathsf{Dec}_{\mathsf{IKE}}}$. The *decryption algorithm* $\mathsf{Dec}_{\mathsf{IKE}}$ inputs $\langle c, \texttt{time} \rangle$, d_t^0 and p, and outputs m or $\perp$ where $\perp$ indicates failure. $\mathsf{Dec}_{\mathsf{IKE}}$ correctly recovers the plaintext only if $t = T_0(\texttt{time})$.

Security Definition. Security of IKE is based on the assumption that adversary does not (illegally) obtain all of the target user's keys all at once. Recall that helper keys of different levels in the hierarchy are managed differently (most likely stored at different places). It is unlikely for such an event to occur, i.e. an adversary to obtain all of the keys of all levels all at once, considering that PDs are disconnected from the network most of the time. We also like to remind that it gets much harder to steal the keys as the levels in the hierarchy increase this is because PDs in the higher levels are connected to the network less frequently and also managed in places physically much safer.

We consider an attack model based on the standard IND-ID-CCA setting in [7,8] plus the next case: when an adversary is allowed access to any of target user's keys and also the helper keys but excluding the combinations of keys that can trivially lead to the target key from the definition of IKE. Next, we give some examples of key exposures for our security definition.

EXAMPLES OF KEY EXPOSURES. We consider a 2-level IKE: decryption key is renewed every day, 1st-level helper key is renewed every three months and 2nd-level helper key is never updated. Then, any ciphertext for 2005/Dec./31st should not be decrypted by dishonest means even for the following cases:

1. Exposures of the victim's 1st-level helper keys for 2005/Jan.-Mar., $\cdots$, 2005/ Jul.-Sep. and decryption keys for 2005/Jan./1st, $\cdots$, 2005/Dec./30th

2. Exposures of the victim's 2nd-level helper key and decryption keys for 2005/ Jan./1st, $\cdots$, 2005/Dec./30th
3. Exposures of the victim's 2nd-level helper key and 1st-level helper keys for 2005/Jan.-Mar., $\cdots$, 2005/Oct.-Dec.

Again, we exclude the combinations of keys that can trivially determine the target key, for example, exposures of both the victim's 1st-level helper key for 2005/Oct.-Dec. and decryption key for 2005/Dec./30th. It is obvious that a decryption key for 2005/Dec./31st is easily computable from the definition of IKE. We do not consider these cases.

Next, we formally address the security definition. In our attack model, adversary is allowed access to the following four types of oracles: (1) *key generation oracle* $\mathsf{KG}(\cdot, s, p)$, which on input U, returns U's initial decryption keys (d_0^0, d_0^1, d_0^2) and (2) *left-or-right encryption oracle* $\mathsf{LR}(\cdot, \cdot, \cdot, \cdot, p, b)$ [3], which for given U, time and equal length messages m_0, m_1, returns *challenge ciphertext* $c := \mathsf{Enc}_{\mathsf{IKE}}(m_b, U, p, \mathtt{time})$ where $b \in_R \{0, 1\}$, and models encryption requests of an adversary of a user identity and a message pair of his choice. The third is a (3) *decryption oracle* $\mathsf{D}(\cdot, \cdot, s, p)$ which on input U and $\langle c, \mathtt{time} \rangle$, returns decryption result of c with the corresponding decryption key d_t^0 where $t = T_0(\mathtt{time})$. This models chosen ciphertext attack. With these three oracles, KG, LR and D, the standard IND-ID-CCA setting can be modeled. In addition to the above, we introduce a (4) *key issue oracle* $\mathsf{KI}(\cdot, \cdot, \cdot, s, p)$ which on input i, U and $\mathtt{time}$, returns d_t^i where $t = T_i(\mathtt{time})$. This models partial exposure of honest user's keys including the victim's keys. The adversary may query the four oracles adaptively in any order he wants subject to the restriction that he makes only one query to LR. Let U^* be the user's identifier of this query, and let $\langle c^*, \mathtt{time}^* \rangle$ denote the challenge ciphertext returned by LR in response to this query. Also, the adversary is not allowed to ask KG and KI for queries which can trivially determine U^*'s decryption key for $\mathtt{time}^*$ from the definition of IKE. The adversary succeeds the attack by guessing the value b, and the scheme is considered to be secure if any probabilistic polynomial time adversary has success probability negligibly close to $1/2$.

Definition 2 (KE-CCA security). Let IKE be a 2-level identity-based key-insulated encryption scheme. Define adversary A's succeeding probability as:

$$\mathsf{Succ}_{A,\mathsf{IKE}} := \Pr[(s, p) \leftarrow \mathsf{PGen}_{\mathsf{IKE}}(1^k); b \in_R \{0, 1\};$$
$$b' \leftarrow A^{\mathsf{KG}(\cdot, s, p), \mathsf{LR}(\cdot, \cdot, \cdot, \cdot, p, b), \mathsf{D}(\cdot, \cdot, s, p), \mathsf{KI}(\cdot, \cdot, \cdot, s, p)} : b' = b]$$

where U^* is never asked to $\mathsf{KG}(\cdot, s, p)$ and $(U^*, \langle c^*, \mathtt{time} \rangle)$ is never asked to $\mathsf{D}(\cdot, \cdot, s, p)$ such that $T_0(\mathtt{time}) = T_0(\mathtt{time}^*)$. A can ask KI for any keys of any users if there exists a "special level" $j \in \{0, 1, 2\}$ such that

- $\mathsf{KI}(j, U^*, \mathtt{time}, s, p)$ is never asked for any $\mathtt{time}$, and
- $\mathsf{KI}(i, U^*, \mathtt{time}, s, p)$ is never asked for any $(i, \mathtt{time})$ such that $i < j$ and $T_i(\mathtt{time}) = T_i(\mathtt{time}^*)$.

Then, IKE is *KE-CCA secure* (KE-CCA stands for *key exposure & chosen cipher-text attack*) if, for any probabilistic polynomial time adversary A, $|\mathsf{Succs}_{A,\mathsf{IKE}} - 1/2|$ is negligible. (Note that a "special level" is a level in which the PD of U^* is not compromised. Also, recall 0-level PD is the user's terminal, i.e. the mobile phone.)

Exposure of Key-Update Information. If we look closer into the security of IKE, it can be realized that exposure of key-update information should also be considered in addition to the above discussion. Although, we can also see that it is obvious that if $\delta^i_{T_i(\texttt{time})}$ can be computed from $d^i_{T_i(\texttt{time})}$ and d^i_t for any `time` and t, then, exposure of key-update information can be simulated by using KI. Hence, if this property holds, then the security definition so far discussed will be sufficient (by itself) even when exposure of the key-update information is considered. As a matter of fact all of our constructions satisfy this property.

3   Straightforward IKE from HIBE Is Insecure

Although HIBE and IKE are alike in some sense, it is not as simple as bringing HIBE as building blocks to construct KE-CCA secure IKE. We give further discussion on this later, but first, we clarify the relation between HIBE and IKE.

Brief Review of HIBE. HIBE distributes the workload of the PKG in IBE by organizing the PKGs in a hierarchical tree structure. Security definition of an HIBE follows. This definition runs parallel with [22] which is the hierarchical extension of Boneh and Franklin's IBE [7,8]. Note that 1-level HIBE refers to a standard IBE. A user in an HIBE hierarchy is defined as a tuple of identities: $(D^{t-1}.D^{t-2}.\cdots.D^0)$ where t denotes depth of the hierarchy. The user's ancestors in the hierarchy tree include the root-PKG and users/sub-PKGs whose identities are $\{(D^{t-1}.D^{t-2}.\cdots.D^i : 0 \leq i \leq t-1)\}$.

Definition 3 (HIBE). *A t-level hierarchical identity-based encryption (HIBE)* HIBE consists of $3+t$ algorithms: $\mathsf{HIBE} = (\mathsf{PGen}_{\mathsf{HIBE}}, \mathsf{Gen}^i_{\mathsf{HIBE}}\ (1 \leq i \leq t), \mathsf{Enc}_{\mathsf{HIBE}}, \mathsf{Dec}_{\mathsf{HIBE}})$ and are defined as follows:

$\mathsf{PGen}_{\mathsf{HIBE}}$. The *public-parameter generation algorithm* $\mathsf{PGen}_{\mathsf{HIBE}}(1^k)$ where k is the security parameter, outputs root-master key s and public parameter p. $\mathsf{PGen}_{\mathsf{HIBE}}$ is used only by the root-PKG.

$\mathsf{Gen}^i_{\mathsf{HIBE}}$. The *user-secret generation algorithm* $\mathsf{Gen}^t_{\mathsf{HIBE}}$ inputs D^{t-1}, s and p, and outputs D^{t-1}'s key $s_{D^{t-1}}$. Similarly, $\mathsf{Gen}^{t-i+1}_{\mathsf{HIBE}}$ takes $D^{t-1}.D^{t-2}.\cdots.D^{t-i}$, $s_{D^{t-1}.D^{t-2}.\cdots.D^{t-i+1}}$ and p as inputs, and outputs $D^{t-1}.D^{t-2}.\cdots.D^{t-i}$'s key $s_{D^{t-1}.D^{t-2}.\cdots.D^{t-i}}$ for $2 \leq i \leq t$. Here, for $1 \leq i \leq t-1$, $s_{D^{t-1}.D^{t-2}.\cdots.D^{t-i}}$ is the sub-master key which enables $D^{t-1}.D^{t-2}.\cdots.D^{t-i}$ to generate his descendant's keys, and $s_{D^{t-1}.D^{t-2}.\cdots.D^0}$ is the decryption key of $D^{t-1}.D^{t-2}.\cdots.D^0$.

$\mathsf{Enc}_{\mathsf{HIBE}}$. The *encryption algorithm* $\mathsf{Enc}_{\mathsf{HIBE}}$ takes m, $D^{t-1}.D^{t-2}.\cdots.D^0$ and p as inputs where m is a plaintext and $D^{t-1}.D^{t-2}.\cdots.D^0$ is the receiver's identity, and outputs a ciphertext c.

$\mathsf{Dec_{HIBE}}$. The *decryption algorithm* $\mathsf{Dec_{HIBE}}$ takes c, $s_{D^{t-1}.D^{t-2}.\cdots.D^0}$ and p as inputs, and outputs m or $\bot$ which means failure. $\mathsf{Dec_{HIBE}}$ recovers the plaintext only if c is encrypted correctly using $D^{t-1}.D^{t-2}.\cdots.D^0$ as an encryption key.

Security of an HIBE is defined as follows. An adversary adaptively selects a target user's identity and equal length messages m_0, m_1 and submits to a *left-or-right encryption* oracle LR which returns ciphertext of m_b such that $b \in_R \{0,1\}$ for a target user. The adversary also have access to a *decryption oracle* D which gives decryption results of any ciphertext except for the challenge ciphertext from LR. There is also a *key generation oracle* KG which exposes any user key except for the target's and its ancestors'. HIBE is *secure* if an adversary correctly determines b with probability at most $1/2 + neg$ where neg is negligible. HIBE is IND-HID-CCA (resp. IND-HID-CPA) if unlimited access to D and KG (resp. only KG) is allowed [22]. HIBE is IND-wHID-CCA (resp. IND-wHID-CPA) if unlimited access (resp. no access) to D is allowed while the number of queries to KG is bounded as follows [24]: unlimited access is allowed for at least one level in the hierarchy, but for the rest of the levels, the number of queries do not exceed the threshold value w such that $w = O(\mathsf{poly}(k))$. See Appendix A for more details.

An Insecure IKE from HIBE. Consider the following (insecure) construction of a 2-level IKE based on a 3-level HIIBE: In the initial phase, PKG generates $(s, p) := \mathsf{PGen_{HIBE}}(1^k)$ and user U's 2nd-level helper key $d_0^2 := \mathsf{Gen_{HIBE}^3}(U, s, p)$. At $\mathtt{time}$, U generates his 1st-level helper key $d_{T_1(\mathtt{time})}^1 := \mathsf{Gen_{HIBE}^2}(T_1(\mathtt{time}), d_0^2, p)$ and decryption key $d_{T_0(\mathtt{time})}^0 := \mathsf{Gen_{HIBE}^1}(T_0(\mathtt{time}), d_{T_1(\mathtt{time})}^1, p)$. For a message m for U at $\mathtt{time}$, a ciphertext c is generated as $c = \mathsf{Enc_{HIBE}}(m, U.T_1(\mathtt{time}).T_0(\mathtt{time}), p)$. Renewal of decryption keys in IBE from HIBE is described in [24] as well.

We show a straightforward construction of an IKE from HIBE which is insecure (i.e. not KE-CCA secure). The above (insecure) construction does not satisfy the security of 2. and 3. of the EXAMPLES OF KEY EXPOSURES. from the previous section. Namely, if the 1st-level PD (or the PD-BC) is stolen at $\mathtt{2005/Oct./1st/0:00}$, then confidentiality of the ciphertexts generated during period $\mathtt{2005/Oct.\text{-}Dec.}$ is lost. Morover, exposure of the 2nd-level helper key can alone compromise the security for any time period. Therefore, a straightforward construction of IKE from HIBE is not KE-CCA secure.

4   Generic Construction

Basic Idea. As shown in the previous section, straightforward construction of an IKE from HIBE is vulnerable, and for such a system, loss of only one of users' PDs implies compromisation of the entire system. In this section, we show a generic construction of a secure IKE built from three distinct HIBEs. Here's the general idea: each of three HIBEs each plays a part to mutually secure the different types of key exposures, consequently, protecting the system totally, guaranteeing its security even if a PD is compromised. We extend a technique called *multiple encryption* proposed in [28] to construct a KE-CCA secure IKE from HIBE. It is important to note that the original [28] scheme is applied only

$PGen_{IKE}(1^k):$
  $(s_h, p_h) \leftarrow PGen_{HIBE_h}(1^k),\ 1 \le h \le 3$
  choose $H_h,\ 1 \le h \le 3$
return $s := (s_1, s_2, s_3)$
  $p := (p_1, p_2, p_3, H_1, H_2, H_3)$

$Gen_{IKE}(s, p, U):$
  parse $s = (s_1, s_2, s_3)$
  $s_{h,U} \leftarrow Gen^h_{HIBE_h}(U, s_h, p_h),\ 1 \le h \le 3$
  $d_0^0 := (s_{1,U}, \cdot, \cdot),\ d_0^1 := (s_{2,U}, \cdot),\ d_0^2 := s_{3,U}$
return (d_0^0, d_0^1, d_0^2)

$\Delta\text{-}Gen^1_{IKE}(d_t^1, p, U, \texttt{time}):$
  parse $d_t^1 = (\sigma_2, \sigma_3)$
  $\sigma'_h \leftarrow Gen_{HIBE_h}(T_0(\texttt{time}), \sigma_h, p_h),\ h = 2, 3$
return $\delta^0_{T_0(\texttt{time})} := (\sigma'_2, \sigma'_3)$

$\Delta\text{-}Gen^2_{IKE}(d_0^2, p, U, \texttt{time}):$
  parse $d_0^2 = \sigma_3 (= s_{3,U})$
  $\sigma'_3 \leftarrow Gen_{HIBE_3}(T_1(\texttt{time}), \sigma_3, p_3)$
return $\delta^1_{T_1(\texttt{time})} := \sigma'_3$

$Upd^1_{IKE}(d_t^0, p, \delta^0_{T_0(\texttt{time})}):$
  parse $d_t^0 = (\sigma_1, \sigma_2, \sigma_3)$
  parse $\delta^0_{T_0(\texttt{time})} = (\sigma'_2, \sigma'_3)$
return $d^0_{T_0(\texttt{time})} := (\sigma_1, \sigma'_2, \sigma'_3)$

$Upd^2_{IKE}(d_t^1, p, \delta^1_{T_1(\texttt{time})}):$
  parse $d_t^1 = (\sigma_2, \sigma_3)$
  parse $\delta^1_{T_1(\texttt{time})} = \sigma'_3$
return $d^1_{T_1(\texttt{time})} := (\sigma_2, \sigma'_3)$

$Enc_{IKE}(m, U, p, \texttt{time}):$
  $\overline{m}_1, \overline{m}_2 \in_R \{0,1\}^n,\ \overline{m}_3 := m \oplus \overline{m}_1 \oplus \overline{m}_2$
  $r_1, r_2, r_3 \in_R \{0,1\}^{k_1}$
  $R_h := H_h(m, \overline{m}_h, r_1, r_2, r_3),\ 1 \le h \le 3$
  $U_1 := U,\ U_2 := U.T_0(\texttt{time}),\ U_3 := U.T_1(\texttt{time}).T_0(\texttt{time})$
  $c_h := Enc_{HIBE_h}(\overline{m}_h \| r_h, U_h, p_h; R_h),\ 1 \le h \le 3$
  return $\langle c, \texttt{time} \rangle := \langle (c_1, c_2, c_3), \texttt{time} \rangle$

$Dec_{IKE}(\langle c', \texttt{time} \rangle, d_t^0, p):$
  output $\perp$ and halt if $t \neq T_0(\texttt{time})$
  parse $c' = (c'_1, c'_2, c'_3)$
  parse $d_t^0 = (\sigma_1, \sigma_2, \sigma_3)$
  $(\overline{m}'_h \| r'_h) \leftarrow Dec_{HIBE_h}(c'_h, \sigma_h, p_h),\ 1 \le h \le 3$
  $m' := \oplus_{1 \le h \le 3} \overline{m}'_h$
  validity check by re-encryption
  return m'

Fig. 1. Generic Construction of KE-CCA Secure IKE from IND-HID-CPA HIBE

to standard public key encryption, so, straightforward adoption of this scheme, again, does not immediately imply a secure IKE.

Construction. Fig. 1 shows a generic construction of KE-CCA secure IKE from any HIBE where each of HIBEs has only *chosen plaintext security*, i.e. IND-HID-CPA (See Appendix A). Here, we give supplementary explanation of the Fig. 1 and give discussion on our generic construction in more details.

Let $HIBE_h = (PGen_{HIBE_h}, Gen^i_{HIBE_h}\ (1 \le i \le h), Enc_{HIBE_h}, Dec_{HIBE_h})$ be h-level HIBE for $1 \le h \le 3$ and construct a 2-level IKE $IKE = (PGen_{IKE}, Gen_{IKE}, \Delta\text{-}Gen^i_{IKE}, Upd^i_{IKE}\ (i = 1, 2), Enc_{IKE}, Dec_{IKE})$ as follows.

$PGen_{IKE}$ sets up the master keys and public parameters of $HIBE_h$ and cryptographic hash functions $H_h : \{0,1\}^{2n+3k_1} \to \mathcal{COIN}$ for $1 \le h \le 3$ where n denotes the size of a message of IKE. $\mathcal{COIN}$ is the internal coin-flipping space of

$\mathsf{Enc}_{\mathsf{HIBE}_h}$ assuming that $n + k_1$ is the size of a message in HIBE_h.[1] The security analysis will view H_h as random oracles. $\mathsf{Gen}_{\mathsf{IKE}}$ generates U's secrets of HIBE_h for $1 \leq h \leq 3$ as U's initial key for IKE. Δ-$\mathsf{Gen}^1_{\mathsf{IKE}}$ generates decryption keys of HIBE_2 and HIBE_3 for identities $U.T_0(\texttt{time})$ and $U.T_1(\texttt{time}).T_0(\texttt{time})$, respectively, as the "differential" of the U's previous key and of the next renewed key at $\texttt{time}$. Then, $\mathsf{Upd}^1_{\mathsf{IKE}}$ generates U's decryption key of IKE for $\texttt{time}$ by combining the differential with the U's previous key. Similarly, Δ-$\mathsf{Gen}^2_{\mathsf{IKE}}$ generates a sub-master key of HIBE_3 for $U.T_1(\texttt{time})$, and $\mathsf{Upd}^2_{\mathsf{IKE}}$ generates U's 1st-level helper key of IKE for $\texttt{time}$ by combining U's previous key and Δ-$\mathsf{Gen}^2_{\mathsf{IKE}}$'s output. $\mathsf{Enc}_{\mathsf{IKE}}$ *securely* integrates the three encryption algorithms of h-level HIBE for $1 \leq h \leq 3$. First, a plaintext m is divided into three shares $\overline{m}_1, \overline{m}_2, \overline{m}_3$, and each $\overline{m}_h$ ($1 \leq h \leq 3$) is encrypted by h-level HIBE HIBE_h for identity U_h where $U_1 := U$, $U_2 := U.T_0(\texttt{time})$ and $U_3 := U.T_1(\texttt{time}).T_0(\texttt{time})$. Here, the technique in [28] is applied (but not straightforwardly, as mentioned earlier) to securely integrating the three underlying HIBEs. $\mathsf{Dec}_{\mathsf{IKE}}$ recovers each of the three shares and composes them to recover the plaintext. It also checks the validity of the ciphertext by re-encryption. Namely, $R'_h := H_h(m', \overline{m}'_h, r'_1, r'_2, r'_3)$ and $\nu_h \leftarrow \mathsf{Enc}_{\mathsf{HIBE}_h}(\overline{m}'_h\|r'_h, U_h, p_h; R'_h)$ are computed for $1 \leq h \leq 3$, unless $\nu_h = c'_h$, for all h, output $\perp$, otherwise output m'. This scheme can easily be generalized to an ℓ-level IKE for arbitrary $\ell \geq 1$.

Definition 4 (γ-uniformity [20]). Let $\mathsf{HIBE} = (\mathsf{PGen}_{\mathsf{HIBE}}, \mathsf{Gen}^i_{\mathsf{HIBE}} (1 \leq i \leq t),$ $\mathsf{Enc}_{\mathsf{HIBE}}, \mathsf{Dec}_{\mathsf{HIBE}})$ be t-level HIBE. For given $D^{t-1}.D^{t-2}. \cdots .D^0$, x, y and z, define

$$\gamma(D^{t-1}.D^{t-2}. \cdots .D^0, x, y, z)$$
$$:= \Pr[r \leftarrow_R \mathcal{COIN} : z = \mathsf{Enc}_{\mathsf{HIBE}}(x, D^{t-1}.D^{t-2}. \cdots .D^0, y; r)],$$

where $\mathcal{COIN}$ is the internal coin-flipping space for $\mathsf{Enc}_{\mathsf{HIBE}}$. We say that HIBE is γ-*uniform* if $\gamma(D^{t-1}.D^{t-2}. \cdots .D^0, x, y, z) \leq \gamma$ for any $D^{t-1}.D^{t-2}. \cdots .D^0$, x, y and z.

Theorem 1. *The above scheme is a KE-CCA secure 2-level IKE in the random oracle model, assuming that HIBE_h ($1 \leq h \leq 3$) are IND-HID-CPA HIBEs. More precisely, suppose there is an adversary A who can break the above scheme with probability $1/2 + \epsilon_A$ with run time at most t_A. Suppose A makes at most q_{KG}, q_{KI}, q_{D}, q_{H_1}, q_{H_2}, q_{H_3} queries to KG, KI, D, H_1, H_2, H_3, respectively. Then, there is another adversary B who can break at least one of HIBE_h ($1 \leq h \leq 3$) in the sense of IND-HID-CPA with probability $1/2 + \epsilon_B$, and running time t_B is:*

$$\epsilon_B \geq \frac{1}{3}\epsilon_A - \frac{1}{3}\frac{q_{H_1} + q_{H_2} + q_{H_3}}{2^{k_1}} - \frac{1}{6}q_{\mathsf{D}}\gamma_{max},$$
$$t_B \leq t_A + 2\tau_{ENC} + (2q_{\mathsf{KG}} + 5q_{\mathsf{KI}})\tau_{GEN}$$
$$+ q_{\mathsf{D}}((q_{H_1} + q_{H_2} + q_{H_3})\tau_{ENC} + q_{H_1}q_{H_2}q_{H_3} \cdot O(k)),$$

---

[1] For simplicity, we assume for all HIBE_h, spaces of coin-flipping and messages to be $\mathcal{COIN}$ and $\{0,1\}^{n+k_1}$, respectively.

assuming that $\gamma_{max} = \max(\gamma_1, \gamma_2, \gamma_3)$, HIBE_i *is* γ_i-*uniform, and running time of* $\mathsf{Gen}^i_{\mathsf{HIBE}_h}$ *and* $\mathsf{Enc}_{\mathsf{HIBE}_h}$ *are at most* τ_{GEN} *and* τ_{ENC}, *respectively, for any* h *and* i.

Proof. See Appendix B.   □

Random Oracle. If we want to eliminate random oracle, multiple encryption technique in [12] can be extended instead of the one we used of [28] to construct a KE-CCA secure IKE, assuming that underlying HIBEs are all IND-HID-CCA in the standard model, e.g. [11,4,5,6,27], while the above construction using [28] requires only IND-HID-CPA HIBEs. Furthermore, by applying a similar method to our proposed scheme, we can construct another KE-CCA secure IKE from HIBE with only one-wayness under chosen plaintext attacks.

"Standard" Strongly Key-Insulated Encryption. By extending the multiple encryption technique mentioned in the above, we can construct a generic construction of a strongly secure key-insulated encryption [13] from a chosen plaintext secure IBE and a chosen plaintext secure standard public key encryption. This method can also be applied to the Cocks IBE [10] to construct a strongly secure key-insulated encryption. (The Boneh-Franklin IBE based scheme was proposed earlier in [9]).

5   Efficient Construction from Bilinear Mapping

Basic Idea. In the previous section, we showed a construction of KE-CCA secure IKE using HIBE as a black-box. Here, we propose a construction of KE-CCA secure IKE by directly extending Gentry-Silverberg HIBE (GS-HIBE) [22] and Fujisaki-Okamoto conversion [19,20]. The major difference between our two construction is as follows: in our specific construction, h-level HIBEs for $1 \leq h \leq 3$ are being integrated using a homomorphic property of pairing, while our generic construction is based on multiple encryption [28]. Our specific construction is more efficient than the generic construction. Note that since our specific construction is based on a specific assumption, i.e. BDH assumption, it may lack flexibility in designing new construction in terms of security.

Construction. As shown in Fig. 2, a 2-level IKE $\mathsf{IKE} = (\mathsf{PGen}_{\mathsf{IKE}}, \mathsf{Gen}_{\mathsf{IKE}}, \Delta\text{-}\mathsf{Gen}^i_{\mathsf{IKE}}, \mathsf{Upd}^i_{\mathsf{IKE}}$ $(i = 1, 2), \mathsf{Enc}_{\mathsf{IKE}}, \mathsf{Dec}_{\mathsf{IKE}})$ can be constructed using bilinear mapping. Here, we give supplementary explanation of the Fig. 2 and give discussion on our specific construction in more details.

   $\mathsf{PGen}_{\mathsf{IKE}}$ generates two cyclic groups G_1 and G_2 of prime order q and an efficiently computable mapping $\hat{e} : G_1 \times G_1 \rightarrow G_2$ such that $\hat{e}(aP, bQ) = \hat{e}(P, Q)^{ab}$ for all $P, Q \in G_1$ and any positive integers a, b. This does not send all pairs in $G_1 \times G_1$ to the identity in G_2. Also, $\mathsf{PGen}_{\mathsf{IKE}}$ chooses cryptographic hash functions $H_1 : \{0,1\}^* \rightarrow G_1$, $H_2 : G_2 \rightarrow \{0,1\}^{n+k_1}$ and $H_3 : \{0,1\}^n \times \{0,1\}^{k_1} \rightarrow Z_q$, where n denotes the size of the message space. The security analysis will view H_1, H_2, H_3 as random oracles. It further generates master key s and its corresponding public paramter Q. $\mathsf{Gen}_{\mathsf{IKE}}$, $\Delta\text{-}\mathsf{Gen}^i_{\mathsf{IKE}}$ and $\mathsf{Upd}^i_{\mathsf{IKE}}$ $(i = 1, 2)$ are the

$\mathsf{PGen}_{\mathsf{IKE}}(1^k)$:	$\mathsf{Gen}_{\mathsf{IKE}}(s, p, U)$:
set up G_1, G_2, $\hat{e}$, $P \in G_1$	$P_U := H_1(U) \in G_1$
$s_1^0, s_2^1, s_3^2 \in_R Z_q$	$S_1^0 := s_1^0 P_U$, $S_2^1 := s_2^1 P_U$, $S_3^2 := s_3^2 P_U$
$Q := (s_1^0 + s_2^1 + s_3^2)P$	$d_0^0 := (S_1^0, (\cdot, \cdot), (\cdot, \cdot, \cdot))$
choose H_1, H_2, H_3	$d_0^1 := (S_2^1, (\cdot, \cdot))$
return $s := (s_1^0, s_2^1, s_3^2)$	$d_0^2 := S_3^2$
$\quad p := (G_1, G_2, \hat{e}, P, Q, H_1, H_2, H_3)$	return (d_0^0, d_0^1, d_0^2)

$\Delta\text{-}\mathsf{Gen}_{\mathsf{IKE}}^1(d_t^1, p, U, \mathtt{time})$:	$\Delta\text{-}\mathsf{Gen}_{\mathsf{IKE}}^2(d_0^2, p, U, \mathtt{time})$:
parse $d_t^1 = (S_2^1, (S_3^1, Q_3^1))$	parse $d_0^2 = S_3^2$
$s_2^0, s_3^0 \in_R Z_q$	$s_3^1 \in_R Z_q$
$P_{t_0} := H_1(U.T_1(\mathtt{time}).T_0(\mathtt{time}))$	$P_{t_1} := H_1(U.T_1(\mathtt{time}))$
$\hat{S}_h^0 := S_h^1 + s_h^0 P_{t_0}$, $\hat{Q}_h^0 := s_h^0 P$, $h = 2, 3$	$\hat{S}_3^1 := S_3^2 + s_3^1 P_{t_1}$, $\hat{Q}_3^1 := s_3^1 P$
return $\delta_{T_0(\mathtt{time})}^0 := ((\hat{S}_2^0, \hat{Q}_2^0), (\hat{S}_3^0, \hat{Q}_3^0, Q_3^1))$	return $\delta_{T_1(\mathtt{time})}^1 := (\hat{S}_3^1, \hat{Q}_3^1)$

$\mathsf{Upd}_{\mathsf{IKE}}^1(d_t^0, p, \delta_{T_0(\mathtt{time})}^0)$:	$\mathsf{Upd}_{\mathsf{IKE}}^2(d_t^1, p, \delta_{T_1(\mathtt{time})}^1)$:
parse $d_t^0 = (S_1^0, (S_2^0, Q_2^0), (S_3^0, Q_3^0, Q_3^1))$	parse $d_t^1 = (S_2^1, (S_3^1, Q_3^1))$
parse $\delta_{T_0(\mathtt{time})}^0 = ((\hat{S}_2^0, \hat{Q}_2^0), (\hat{S}_3^0, \hat{Q}_3^0, \hat{Q}_3^1))$	parse $\delta_{T_1(\mathtt{time})}^1 = (\hat{S}_3^1, \hat{Q}_3^1)$
return $d_t^0 := (S_1^0, (\hat{S}_2^0, \hat{Q}_2^0), (\hat{S}_3^0, \hat{Q}_3^0, \hat{Q}_3^1))$	return $d_{T_1(\mathtt{time})}^1 := (S_2^1, (\hat{S}_3^1, \hat{Q}_3^1))$

$\mathsf{Enc}_{\mathsf{IKE}}(m, U, p, \mathtt{time})$:
  $P_U := H_1(U)$, $P_{t_1} := H_1(U.T_1(\mathtt{time}))$, $P_{t_0} := H_1(U.T_1(\mathtt{time}).T_0(\mathtt{time}))$
  $\mu \in_R \{0,1\}^n$, $r := H_3(\mu, m)$, $g := \hat{e}(Q, P_U)$
  $c := \langle rP, rP_{t_1}, rP_{t_0}, (m||\mu) \oplus H_2(g^r) \rangle$
  return $\langle c, \mathtt{time} \rangle$

$\mathsf{Dec}_{\mathsf{IKE}}(\langle c', \mathtt{time} \rangle, d_t^0, p)$:
  parse $c' = \langle V, V_{t_1}, V_{t_0}, W \rangle$
  parse $d_t^0 = (S_1^0, (S_2^0, Q_2^0), (S_3^0, Q_3^0, Q_3^1))$
  $(m'||\mu') := W \oplus H_2(\frac{\hat{e}(S_1^0 + S_2^0 + S_3^0, V)}{\hat{e}(Q_2^0 + Q_3^0, V_{t_0})\hat{e}(Q_3^1, V_{t_1})})$
  validity check by re-encryption
  return m'

Fig. 2. KE-CCA Secure IKE from Bilinear Mapping

same as in the generic construction based on [22]. Based on the homomorphic property of pairing, $\mathsf{Enc}_{\mathsf{IKE}}$ and $\mathsf{Dec}_{\mathsf{IKE}}$ integrates three HIBE encryptions into one. Although, not mentioned in Fig. 2, to protect from active attacks, $\mathsf{Dec}_{\mathsf{IKE}}$ outputs $\perp$ and halts if (i) $t \neq T_0(\mathtt{time})$ or (ii) $(V, V_{t_1}, V_{t_0}, W) \notin G_1^3 \times \{0,1\}^{n+k_1}$ or (iii) re-encryption of m' for U, $\mathtt{time}$ and μ' is not identical to $\langle c', \mathtt{time} \rangle$.

Theorem 2. *The above scheme is a KE-CCA secure 2-level IKE in the random oracle model assuming that a computational BDH (CBDH) problem [7,8] is hard to solve. More precisely, we suppose there is an adversary A who breaks the above scheme with probability $1/2 + \epsilon_A$ with run time at most t_A. Also, suppose that A makes at most q_{KG}, q_{KI}, q_{D}, q_{H_2}, q_{H_3} queries to KG, KI, D, H_2, H_3, respectively. Then, there is another adversary who can solve the CBDH problem* *with probability ϵ_{cbdh} and running time t_{cbdh} where*

$$\epsilon_{cbdh} \geq \frac{6}{e^3 q_{H_2}(3 + q_{\mathsf{KG}} + q_{\mathsf{KI}})^3} \cdot (\epsilon_A - \frac{q_{H_3}}{2^{k_1}} - \frac{q_D}{2q}),$$

$$t_{cbdh} \leq O(t_A + (2q_{\mathsf{KG}} + 5q_{\mathsf{KI}})\tau_{EXP} + q_D(\tau_{\hat{e}} + q_{H_3}\tau_{EXP} + q_{H_2}q_{H_3} \cdot O(k))),$$

assuming time for exponentiation over G_1 is at most τ_{EXP}, and time for pairing computation is at most $\tau_{\hat{e}}$.

Proof of the theorem is given in the full version of this paper [23].

Efficiency. In a pairing based scheme, the dominant factor that decides its total computation cost is the number of pairing computation carried out. For the above construction of KE-CCA secure IKE from bilinear mapping, only one and three pairing computations are required for encryption and decryption, respectively. On the other hand, for the generic construction (shown in the previous section) using [22] as the underlying HIBE, the numbers of pairing computation for encryption and decryption are three and six, respectively.

6   Generic HIBE from Any IBE

As seen from our discussion given so far, HIBE serves as important role as building blocks of various cryptographic schemes including the ones that we have proposed. In this section, we show a generic construction of HIBE from arbitrary IBE that also provides a partial solution to an open problem of HIBE. We can, for example, bring the Cocks IBE [10] to construct an HIBE, also implying that hereafter a new construction of an IBE is ever proposed, it can also be converted to construct an HIBE. For the security definition, we introduce partial collusion resistance (i.e. IND-wHID-CCA) [24] instead of full collusion resistance (i.e. IND-HID-CCA) [22]. The security definition is more relaxed but our contribution is significant as this is the first generic HIBE construction built from an arbitrary IBE. In this section, for simplicity, we show a construction of a 2-level HIBE, but it can also be extended for a t-level HIBE for $t > 2$.

Security Definition. Our construction of a generic HIBE proposed here is based on the security definition of [24]. Particularly, for our 2-level construction of HIBE, it is collusion free for the users (in the lower domain), but has polynomial-sized collusion threshold w for the sub-PKGs (in the higher domain), where $w = O(\mathsf{poly}(k))$ and k is a security parameter.

Cover Free Family. We use cover free family (CFF) [17] as a building block, similar to the generic construction of key-insulated encryption [13]. Reminding that, method used in [13] only addresses chosen plaintext security, and cannot be applied straightforwardly to construct a chosen ciphertext secure HIBE.

Definition 5 (CFF). Let $L := \{\ell_1, \ell_2, \cdots, \ell_u\}$ and $F = \{F_1, \cdots, F_v\}$ be a family of subsets of L. We call (L, F) an (u, v, w)-*cover free family* (CFF) if for all $F_i \in F$, $F_i \not\subset F_{j_1} \cup \cdots \cup F_{j_w}$ for any $F_{j_\kappa}(\neq F_i) \in F$, $\kappa \in \{1, ..., w\}$.

$\mathsf{PGen_{HIBE}}(1^k)$:

      generate (u, v, w)-CFF (L, F)

      $(s_i, p_i) \leftarrow \mathsf{PGen_{IBE}}(1^k)$, $1 \leq i \leq u$

      choose $H : \{0,1\}^* \rightarrow F$ and $H_i : \{0,1\}^{2n+\hat{u}k_1} \rightarrow \mathcal{COIN}$, $1 \leq i \leq u$

return $s := \{s_i\}_{1 \leq i \leq u}$ and $p := (H, \{p_i, H_i\}_{1 \leq i \leq u})$

$\mathsf{Gen^2_{HIBE}}(D^1, s, p)$:	$\mathsf{Gen^1_{HIBE}}(D^1.D^0, s_{D^1}, p)$:
parse $s = \{s_i\}_{1 \leq i \leq u}$	parse $s_{D^1} = \{s_i\}_{i \in F_{D^1}}$
$F_{D^1} := H(D^1) \in F$	$s_{i,D^1.D^0} \leftarrow \mathsf{Gen_{IBE}}(D^1.D^0, s_i, p_i)$, $i \in F_{D^1}$
return $s_{D^1} := \{s_i\}_{i \in F_{D^1}}$	return $s_{D^1.D^0} := \{s_{i,D^1.D^0}\}_{i \in F_{D^1}}$

$\mathsf{Enc_{HIBE}}(m, D^0.D^1, p)$:

      $F_{D^1} := H(D^1) \in F$

      $\overline{m}_i \in_R \{0,1\}^n$, $i \in F_{D^1}$ such that $\oplus_{i \in F_{D^1}} \overline{m}_i = m$

      $r_i \in_R \{0,1\}^{k_1}$, $i \in F_{D^1}$

      $c_i \leftarrow \mathsf{Enc_{IBE}}(\overline{m}_i || r_i, D^0.D^1, p_i; H_i(m, \overline{m}_i, R))$, $i \in F_{D^1}$

     return $c := \{c_i\}_{i \in F_{D^1}}$

$\mathsf{Dec_{HIBE}}(c', s_{D^1.D^0}, p)$:

      parse $c' = \{c'_i\}_{i \in F_{D^1}}$

      parse $s_{D^1.D^0} = \{s_{i,D^1.D^0}\}_{i \in F_{D^1}}$

      $(\overline{m}'_i || r'_i) \leftarrow \mathsf{Dec_{IBE}}(c'_i, s_{i,D^1.D^0}, p_i)$, $i \in F_{D^1}$

      $m' := \oplus_{i \in F_{D^1}} \overline{m}'_i$

      validity check by re-encryption

     return m'

Fig. 3. Generic Construction of Partially Collusion Resistant HIBE

It should be noted that there exist nontrivial constructions of CFF with $u = O(w^2 \log v)$ and $\#F_i = O(w \log v)$ $(1 \leq i \leq v)$. In the following, we assume $\#F_1 = \#F_2 = \cdots = \#F_v = \hat{u}$ for some $\hat{u}$ and $\#\{F_i | \ell_j \in F_i \in F\} \geq \lceil v\hat{u}/u \rceil$ for all $\ell_j \in L$. Concrete methods for generating CFF are given in [18].

Construction. Fig. 3 shows a generic construction of a chosen ciphertext secure 2-level HIBE with partial collusion resistance from an arbitrary IND-ID-CPA IBE using CFF. Here, we give supplementary explanation of the Fig. 3 and give discussion on our generic construction of HIBE in more details.

Let $\mathsf{IBE} = (\mathsf{PGen_{IBE}}, \mathsf{Gen_{IBE}}, \mathsf{Enc_{IBE}}, \mathsf{Dec_{IBE}})$ be standard IBE (i.e. 1-level HIBE). Then, 2-level HIBE $\mathsf{HIBE} = (\mathsf{PGen_{HIBE}}, \mathsf{Gen^i_{HIBE}}$ $(i=1,2), \mathsf{Enc_{HIBE}}, \mathsf{Dec_{HIBE}})$ can be constructed as follows.

$\mathsf{PGen_{HIBE}}$ generates (u, v, w)-CFF (L, F) and u pairs of master key and public parameter of IBE where $L = \{1, \cdots, u\}$, $u = O(\mathsf{poly}(k))$, $v = O(\exp(k))$ and $w = O(\mathsf{poly}(k))$. For hash functions, n denotes the size of a message of HIBE, and $\mathcal{COIN}$ represents the internal coin-flipping space of $\mathsf{Enc_{IBE}}$, assuming that $n + k_1$ is the size of a message in IBE. The security analysis will view H and H_i $(1 \leq i \leq u)$ as random oracles. $\mathsf{Gen^2_{HIBE}}$ picks master keys corresponding to F_{D^1}. $\mathsf{Gen^1_{HIBE}}$ generates IBE decryption keys by using $s_{D^1} = \{s_i\}_{i \in F_{D^1}}$. $\mathsf{Enc_{HIBE}}$ encrypts m with encryption algorithms which correspond to F_{D^1} where R is a concatenation of all r_i arranged in increasing order of i for $i \in F_{D^1}$. Dec$_{\text{HIBE}}$ decrypts all c'_i for $i \in F_{D^1}$. Then, it re-encrypts m' with $\overline{m}'_i$ and r'_i. Unless the encryption result is identical to c', Dec$_{\text{HIBE}}$ outputs $\perp$, otherwise, outputs m'.

Theorem 3. *The above scheme is* IND-*w*HID-CCA *in the random oracle model, with a restriction that an adversary is allowed to query sub-PKGs' keys at most w times, assuming that* IBE *is* IND-ID-CPA. *More precisely, assume an adversary A who breaks the above scheme with probability $1/2 + \epsilon_A$ with run time at most t_A and that A makes at most q_{KG}, q_{D}, q_{H_i} queries to* KG, D, H_i $(1 \le i \le u)$, *respectively. Then, there is another adversary B who can break* IBE *in the sense of* IND-ID-CPA *with probability $1/2 + \epsilon_B$ and running time t_B where*

$$\epsilon_B \ge \frac{\hat{u}}{u^2}\left(\epsilon_A - \frac{q_{all}}{2^{k_1}} - \frac{\gamma q_{\text{D}}}{2}\right),$$

$$t_B \le t_A + \hat{u}\tau_{ENC} + q_{\text{KG}}\hat{u}\tau_{GEN} + q_{\text{D}}(q_{\Sigma}\tau_{ENC} + q_{\Pi} \cdot O(k)),$$

and $q_{all} := \sum_{1 \le i \le u} q_{H_i}$, $q_{\Sigma} := \max_{\{i_1, \cdots, i_{\hat{u}}\} \subseteq \{1, \cdots, u\}}(\sum_{i \in \{i_1, \cdots, i_{\hat{u}}\}} q_{H_i})$ and $q_{\Pi} := \max_{\{i_1, \cdots, i_{\hat{u}}\} \subseteq \{1, \cdots, u\}}(\prod_{i \in \{i_1, \cdots, i_{\hat{u}}\}} q_{H_i})$, assuming that IBE *is γ-uniform, and running time of* Gen$_{\text{IBE}}$ *and* Enc$_{\text{IBE}}$ *is at most τ_{GEN} and τ_{ENC}, respectively.*

Proof of the theorem is given in the full version of this paper [23].

Acknowledgment

We would like to thank Steven Galbraith, Craig Gentry and Phil MacKenzie for their helpful comments and discussions. We also thank anonymous reviewers for their invaluable comments.

References

1. S.S. Al-Riyami and K.G. Paterson, "Certificateless public key cryptography," Proc. of Asiacrypt'03, pp.452-473, 2003.
2. J. Baek and Y. Zheng, "Identity-based threshold decryption," Proc. of PKC'04, pp.262-276, 2004.
3. M. Bellare, A. Desai, E. Jokipii and P. Rogaway, "A concrete security treatment of symmetric encryption," Proc. of FOCS'97, pp.394-403, 1997.
4. D. Boneh and X. Boyen, "Efficient selective-ID secure identity-based encryption without random oracles," Proc. of Eurocrypt'04, pp.223-238, 2004.
5. D. Boneh and X. Boyen, "Secure identity based encryption without random oracles," Proc. of Crypto'04, pp.443-459, 2004.
6. D. Boneh, X. Boyen and E.-J. Goh, "Hierarchical identity based encryption with constant size ciphertext." Proc. of Eurocyrpt'05, pp.440-456, 2005.
7. D. Boneh and M. Franklin, "Identity-based encryption from the Weil pairing," Proc. of Crypto'01, pp.213-229, 2001.
8. D. Boneh and M. Franklin, "Identity-based encryption from the Weil pairing," SIAM J. of Computing, vol. 32, no. 3, pp.586-615, 2003 (full version of [7]).
9. M. Bellare and A. Palacio, "Protecting against key exposure: strongly key-insulated encryption with optimal threshold," available at http://eprint.iacr.org/2002/064/ .

10. C. Cocks, "An identity based encryption scheme based on quadratic residues," Proc. of IMA Int. Conf. 2001, Coding and Cryptography, pp. 360-363, 2001.

11. R. Canetti, S. Halevi and J. Katz, "A forward secure public key encryption scheme," Proc. of Eurocrypt'03, pp.255-271, 2003.

12. Y. Dodis and J. Katz, "Chosen-ciphertext security of multiple encryption," Proc. of TCC'05, pp.188-209, 2005.

13. Y. Dodis, J. Katz, S. Xu and M. Yung, "Key-insulated public key cryptosystems," Proc. of Eurocrypt'02, pp.65-82, 2002.

14. Y. Dodis, M. Franklin, J. Katz, A. Miyaji and M. Yung, "Intrusion-resilient public-key encryption," Proc. of CT-RSA'03, pp.19-32, 2003.

15. Y. Dodis, M. Franklin, J. Katz, A. Miyaji and M. Yung, "A generic construction for intrusion-resilient public-key encryption," Proc. of CT-RSA'04, pp.81-98, 2004.

16. Y. Dodis and M. Yung, "Exposure-resilience for free: the hierarchical ID-based encryption case," Proc. IEEE Security in Storage Workshop 2002, pp.45-52, 2002.

17. P. Erdös, P. Frankl and Z. Furedi, "Families of finite sets in which no sets is covered by the union of two others," J. of Combin. Theory Ser. A 33, pp.158-166, 1982.

18. P. Erdös, P. Frankl and Z. Furedi, "Families of finite sets in which no sets is covered by the union of r others," Israel Journal of Math., 51, pp.79-89, 1985.

19. E. Fujisaki and T. Okamoto, "How to enhance the security of public-key encryption at minimum cost," Proc. of PKC'99, pp.53-68, 1999.

20. E. Fujisaki and T. Okamoto, "Secure integration of asymmetric and symmetric encryption schemes," Proc. of Crypto'99, pp.537-554, 1999.

21. C. Gentry, "Certificate-based encryption and the certificate revocation problem," Proc. of Eurocrypt'03, pp.272-293, 2003.

22. C. Gentry and A. Silverberg, "Hierarchical ID-based cryptography," Proc. of Asiacrypt'02, pp.548-566, 2002.

23. Y. Hanaoka, G. Hanaoka, J. Shikata and H. Imai, "Identity-based hierarchical strongly key-insulated encryption and its application," available at http://eprint.iacr.org/2004/338/.

24. J. Horwitz and B. Lynn, "Toward hierarchical identity-based encryption," Proc. of Eurocrypt'02, pp.466-481, 2002.

25. A. Shamir, "Identity-based cryptosystems and signature schemes," Proc. of Crypto'84, pp.47-53, 1985.

26. S. Shinozaki, T. Itoh, A. Fujioka and S. Tsujii, "Provably secure key-update schemes in identity-based systems," Proc. of Eurocrypt'90, pp.16-30, 1990.

27. B. Waters, "Efficient identity based encryption without random oracles," Proc. of Eurocrypt'05, pp.114-127, 2005.

28. R. Zhang, G. Hanaoka, J. Shikata and H. Imai, "On the security of multiple encryption or CCA-security + CCA-security = CCA-security?" Proc. of PKC'04, pp.360-374, 2004.

Appendix A: Formal Security Definitions for HIBE

Here, we give a formal security definition of hierarchical identity-based encryption (HIBE). The definition runs parallel with [22] and [24] which is the hierarchical extension of Boneh and Flanklin's IBE [7,8].

Regarding chosen ciphertext attacks, we address the following three types of oracles: First, is a *key generation oracle* KG which on input $D^{t-1}.D^{t-2}.\cdots.D^i$, returns $D^{t-1}.D^{t-2}.\cdots.D^i$'s secret $s_{D^{t-1}.D^{t-2}.\cdots.D^i}$ for $0 \leq i \leq t-1$. Next, is a *left-or-right encryption oracle* LR which for a given user $D^{*,t-1}.D^{*,t-2}.\cdots.D^{*,0}$ and equal length messages m_0, m_1, picks $b \in_R \{0,1\}$ and returns a *challenge ciphertext* $c := \mathsf{Enc}_{\mathsf{HIBE}}(D^{*,t-1}.D^{*,t-2}.\cdots.D^{*,0}, m_b, p)$. This models an encryption request of an adversary who can pick a target's identity and a message pair of his choice. Finally, the adversary is allowed access to a *decryption oracle* D, which on input $D^{t-1}.D^{t-2}.\cdots.D^0$ and a ciphertext c, returns a decryption result of c using $s_{D^{t-1}.D^{t-2}.\cdots.D^0}$. This models the chosen ciphertext attack. Also, if considering only chosen plaintext attacks, any access to D is prohibited while accesses to KG and LR remain permitted. An adversary may query the three oracles adaptively in any order he wants, subject to the restriction that he makes only one query to the left-or-right oracle. Let $D^{*,t-1}.D^{*,t-2}.\cdots.D^{*,0}$ be the user's identifier of this query and let c^* denote the challenge ciphertext returned by the left-or-right oracle in response to this query. The adversary succeeds by guessing the value b. A HIBE is considered secure, if any probabilistic polynomial time adversary has success probability negligibly close to $1/2$.

Definition 6. Let $\mathsf{HIBE} = (\mathsf{PGen}_{\mathsf{HIBE}}, \mathsf{Gen}^i_{\mathsf{HIBE}} \ (1 \leq i \leq t), \mathsf{Enc}_{\mathsf{HIBE}}, \mathsf{Dec}_{\mathsf{HIBE}})$ be a hierarchical identity-based encryption scheme. Define adversary A's succeeding probability in the above chosen ciphertext attack game as:

$$\mathsf{Succ}_{A,\mathsf{HIBE}} := \Pr[(s,p) \leftarrow \mathsf{PGen}_{\mathsf{HIBE}}(1^k); b \in_R \{0,1\};$$
$$b' \leftarrow A^{\mathsf{KG}(\cdot,s,p),\mathsf{LR}(\cdot,\cdot,\cdot,s,p),\mathsf{D}(\cdot,\cdot,s,p)} : b' = b],$$

where any element in $\{(D^{*,t-1}.D^{*,t-2}.\cdots.D^{*,i} : 0 \leq i \leq t-1)\}$ is never asked to KG and A is not allowed to query $\mathsf{D}(D^{*,t-1}.D^{*,t-2}.\cdots.D^{*,0}, c^*, s, p)$ if c^* is returned by LR. Then, HIBE is

- <u>IND-HID-CCA</u> if $|\mathsf{Succ}_{A,\mathsf{HIBE}} - 1/2|$ is negligible for any probabilistic polynomial time adversary A (particularly, we call IND-ID-CCA if $t = 1$),
- <u>IND-HID-CPA</u> if $|\mathsf{Succ}_{A,\mathsf{HIBE}} - 1/2|$ is negligible for any probabilistic polynomial time adversary A who is not allowed to submit any query to D at all (particularly, we call IND-ID-CPA if $t = 1$),
- <u>IND-wHID-CCA</u> if $|\mathsf{Succ}_{A,\mathsf{HIBE}} - 1/2|$ is negligible for any probabilistic polynomial time adversary A who is allowed to submit queries to KG at most w times for given layers in the hierarchy (A is also allowed to submit unlimited number of queries to KG for at least one layer),
- <u>IND-wHID-CPA</u> if $|\mathsf{Succ}_{A,\mathsf{HIBE}} - 1/2|$ is negligible for any probabilistic polynomial time adversary A who is allowed to submit queries to KG at most w times for given layers in the hierarchy, but no query to D is permitted (A is also allowed to submit unlimited number of queries to KG for at least one layer).

Next, we give concrete examples for the above IND-wHID-CCA and IND-wHID-CPA. Suppose we have a 2-level HIBE which includes a root-PKG layer, a sub-PKG layer and a user layer. The sub-PKG layer is set as the special layer in which the number of queries from the adversary is bounded. In the IND-wHID-CCA (or IND-wHID-CPA) setting, an adversary is allowed to ask the sub-PKGs' keys for at most w times while allowing unlimited number of user's decryption keys to be exposed. In addition to KG, the adversary is allowed access to D also when considering the IND-wHID-CCA setting.

Appendix B: Proof of Theorem 1

Here, we prove KE-CCA security for our generic construction. We construct an adversary B who can break at least one of underlying HIBEs in the sense of IND-HID-CPA by using another adversary A who is able to break KE-CCA security of the proposed IKE.

For given public parameters p_h $(1 \leq h \leq 3)$ which corresponds to HIBE_h, respectively, B chooses $i' \in \{0, 1, 2\}$ and computes $\mathsf{PGen}_{\mathsf{HIBE}_h}(1^k) = (s'_h, p'_h)$ for $1 \leq h \leq 3$, $h \neq i' + 1$. Also, B sets (p_1, p'_2, p'_3), (p'_1, p_2, p'_3) and (p'_1, p'_2, p_3) for $i' = 0, 1$ and 2, respectively, as (part of) public parameter of IKE and sends it to A. On A's requests for the oracles, B answers to them following the next simulation:

SIMULATION OF LR. For an LR oracle query $U^*, \texttt{time}^*, m_0, m_1$ from A, B simulates IKE's LR oracle as follows. First, B sets $a = i' + 1$. For all h $(1 \leq h \leq 3$, $h \neq a)$, B picks $\overline{m}_h \in_R \{0, 1\}^n$ and $r_h \in_R \{0, 1\}^{k_1}$ such that $\oplus_{1 \leq h \leq 3, h \neq a} \overline{m}_h = \alpha$ for $\alpha \in_R \{0, 1\}^n$. Also, B sets $\overline{m}_{a,0} = m_0 \oplus \alpha$ and $\overline{m}_{a,1} = m_1 \oplus \alpha$. Then, B picks $r_{a,j} \in_R \{0, 1\}^{k_1}$ for $j = 0, 1$, and sets $U_1^* = U^*$, $U_2^* = U^*.T_0(\texttt{time}^*)$ and $U_3^* = U^*.T_1(\texttt{time}^*).T_0(\texttt{time}^*)$. Also, B sends U_a^*, $(\overline{m}_{a,0}||r_{a,0})$, $(\overline{m}_{a,1}||r_{a,1})$ to B's own LR oracle which corresponds to HIBE_a, and the oracle returns challenge ciphertext c_a^*. Next, B encrypts $(\overline{m}_h||r_h)$ by the encryption algorithm of HIBE_h with p'_h and U_h^*, and produces challenge ciphertexts c_h^* for $1 \leq h \leq 3$, $h \neq a$. Finally, B returns $\langle (c_1^*, c_2^*, c_3^*), \texttt{time}^* \rangle$ to A. Note that B's goal is to distinguish the underlying plaintext of c_a^*.

SIMULATION OF H_h. For H_h $(1 \leq h \leq 3)$ oracle queries, B returns random values if the query has never been asked before, otherwise B returns the same value as before. If a H_h query is identical to $(m_{b'}, \overline{m}_h, \omega_1, \omega_2, \omega_3)$ such that $\omega_a = r_{a,b'}$ and $\omega_h = r_h$ $(1 \leq h \leq 3$, $h \neq a)$ for some $b' \in \{0, 1\}$ (here, $\overline{m}_a$ means $\overline{m}_{a,b'}$), B outputs $\langle b', a \rangle$ and halts.

SIMULATION OF KG. It is clear that for any of the KG queries, B can answer it perfectly by asking B's own KG oracles. More precisely, on A's request for a KG oracle query $U(\neq U^*)$, B can ask U to B's KG oracle corresponding to HIBE_a, as well as run user-secret generation algorithms of HIBE_h with master key s'_h for $1 \leq h \leq 3$, $h \neq a$. Then, B produces d_0^i for $0 \leq i \leq 2$ by using these results and return (d_0^0, d_0^1, d_0^2).

SIMULATION OF KI. Interestingly, answers to A's KI oracle query can be perfectly simulated by B when i' is the "special level" (see Def. 2) chosen by A. Namely, B can perfectly answer any KI oracle query by using B's own KG oracles which corresponds to HIBE_a and master keys s'_h $(1 \leq h \leq 3$, $h \neq a)$ which correspond to HIBE_h. It should be noticed that the simulation is perfect even if $U = U^*$.

SIMULATION OF D. On A's D query for U and $\langle c, \text{time} \rangle$, B searches for the combinations of A's previous queries made to H_1, H_2, H_3 such that each of the combinations consists of the next three queries ψ_1, ψ_2, ψ_3, where for $1 \leq i \leq 3$, query ψ_i is asked to H_i and ψ_i forms $(m, \overline{m}_i, r_1, r_2, r_3)$ for some n-bit strings $m, \overline{m}_i$ and k_1-bit strings r_1, r_2, r_3 such that $\oplus_{1 \leq i \leq 3} \overline{m}_i = m$ (note that m, r_1, r_2 and r_3 are common for all ψ_1, ψ_2 and ψ_3). If there exists such a combination whose corresponding ciphertext (for U and time) is identical to $\langle c, \text{time} \rangle$, then B returns m. Otherwise, B returns $\perp$.

When A outputs b', B also outputs $\langle b', a \rangle$ as an answer for the IND-HID-CPA game for HIBE_a.

Now, we estimate B's succeeding probability. Simulations of LR, H_h ($1 \leq h \leq 3$), and KG are perfect. Simulation of KI fails only when i' is not the special level chosen by A. Therefore, if we let $1/2 + \epsilon_A$ be the succeeding probability of A, then B's succeeding probability can be estimated to be $1/2 + \epsilon_B$ where

$$\epsilon_B \geq \frac{1}{3}(\frac{1}{2} + \epsilon_A - \Pr[\text{H-Ask}]) \cdot \Pr[\neg \text{D-Fail}] + \frac{2}{3} \cdot \frac{1}{2} - \frac{1}{2},$$

where H-Ask denotes an event that $(m_{\overline{b}}, \overline{m}_h, \omega_1, \omega_2, \omega_3)$ such that $\omega_a = r_{a,\overline{b}}$ and $\omega_j = r_j$ ($j \neq a$) is asked to H_h for some h, and D-$Fail$ denotes an event that B rejects a D query which should not be rejected.

Since it is informtion-theoretically impossible to find $r_{a,\overline{b}}$, we have $\Pr[\text{H-Ask}] \leq 1 - (1 - 1/2^{k_1})^{q_{H_1} + q_{H_2} + q_{H_3}}$ where q_{H_i} ($1 \leq i \leq 3$) are the numbers of queries made to H_i. Simulation of D fails only when A submits a ciphertext which should not be rejected, but its corresponding H_i oracle query is not asked. Therefore, $\Pr[\neg \text{D-Fail}] \geq (1 - \gamma_{max})^{q_D}$ where q_D is the number of queries for D, $\gamma_{max} = \max(\gamma_1, \gamma_2, \gamma_3)$ assuming that HIBE_i is γ_i-uniform.

Hence, we have

$$\epsilon_B \geq \frac{1}{3}(\frac{1}{2} + \epsilon_A - (1 - (1 - \frac{1}{2^{k_1}})^{q_{H_1} + q_{H_2} + q_{H_3}}))(1 - \gamma_{max})^{q_D} + \frac{2}{3} \cdot \frac{1}{2} - \frac{1}{2}$$

$$\geq \frac{1}{3}\epsilon_A - \frac{1}{3}\frac{q_{H_1} + q_{H_2} + q_{H_3}}{2^{k_1}} - \frac{1}{6}q_D\gamma_{max}.$$

Also, if letting t_A be A's running time, then B's running time can be estimated to be t_B, where

$$t_B \leq t_A + 2\tau_{ENC} + (2q_{KG} + 5q_{KI})\tau_{GEN}$$
$$+ q_D((q_{H_1} + q_{H_2} + q_{H_3})\tau_{ENC} + q_{H_1}q_{H_2}q_{H_3}O(k)),$$

assuming that the number of queries made to KG and KI is q_{KI} and q_{KI}, respectively, and running time of $\mathsf{Gen}^i_{\mathsf{HIBE}_h}$ and $\mathsf{Enc}_{\mathsf{HIBE}_h}$ are at most τ_{GEN} and τ_{ENC}, respectively, for any h and i. Therefore, ϵ_A is negligible if ϵ_B, $1/2^{k_1}$ and γ_{max} are all negligible, and hence, our proposed generic construction of IKE is KE-CCA secure. $\square$

Efficient and Provably-Secure Identity-Based Signatures and Signcryption from Bilinear Maps

Paulo S.L.M. Barreto[2], Benoît Libert[3,*],
Noel McCullagh[1,**], and Jean-Jacques Quisquater[3]

[1] School of Computer Applications,
Dublin City University,
Ballymun, Dublin 9, Ireland
noel.mccullagh@computing.dcu.ie

[2] PCS, Escola Politécnica, Universidade de São Paulo,
Av. Prof. Luciano Gualberto, tr. 3, n. 158, s. C1-46,
BR 05508-900, São Paulo(SP), Brazil
pbarreto@larc.usp.br

[3] UCL, Microelectronics Laboratory, Crypto Group,
Place du Levant, 3, B-1348, Louvain-La-Neuve, Belgium
Telephone : +32(0)10 47.80.62, Fax : +32(0)10 47.25.98
libert,quisquater@dice.ucl.ac.be

Abstract. In this paper we describe a new identity-based signcryption (IBSC) scheme built upon bilinear maps. This scheme turns out to be more efficient than all others proposed so far. We prove its security in a formal model under recently studied computational assumptions and in the random oracle model. As a result of independent interest, we propose a new provably secure identity-based signature (IBS) scheme that is also faster than all known pairing-based IBS methods.

1 Introduction

Two fundamental services of public key cryptography are privacy and authentication. Public key encryption schemes aim at providing confidentiality whereas digital signatures must provide authentication and non-repudiation. Nowadays, noticeably, many real-world cryptographic application require those distinct goals to be simultaneously achieved. This motivated Zheng [39] to provide the cryptographer's toolbox with a novel cryptographic primitive which he called 'signcryption.' The purpose of this kind of cryptosystem is to encrypt and sign data in a single operation which has a computational cost less than that of doing both operations sequentially. Proper signcryption schemes should provide confidentiality as well as authentication and non-repudiation. As in conventional encryption schemes, recovering the plaintext from a signcrypted message must be

---

* This author's work was supported the DGTRE's First Europe Program of the Walloon Region in Belgium.
** This author wishes to thank Enterprise Ireland for their support with this research under grant IF/2002/0312/N.

B. Roy (Ed.): ASIACRYPT 2005, LNCS 3788, pp. 515–532, 2005.

computationally infeasible without the recipients private key; as in conventional digital signatures, it must be computationally infeasible to create signcrypted texts without the senders private key.

Identity based cryptography has become a very fashionable area of research for the last couple of years. The concept was originally introduced in 1984 by Shamir [34] whose idea was that users within a system could use their online identifiers (combined with certain system-wide information) as their public keys. This greatly reduces the problems with key management that have hampered the mass uptake of public key cryptography on a per individual basis. While identity-based signature schemes (IBS) rapidly emerged [20,23] after 1984 (see [5] for a thorough study of them), and despite another bandwidth-consuming proposal [18], it is only in 2001 that bilinear mappings over elliptic curve were found to yield the first fully practical identity-based encryption (IBE) solution [10]. Those bilinear maps, or pairings, subsequently turned out to yield a plenty of cryptographic applications [2] among which several recent outstanding results on identity-based encryption [7,8,21,36].

Several identity-based signcryption algorithms have been proposed so far, e.g. [11,14,16,17,26,27,30,33,37]. Within this handful of results, only [11,14,16,17,26,37] consider schemes supported by formal models and security proofs in the random oracle model [6]. Among them, Chen and Malone-Lee's proposal [14] happens to yield the most efficient construction.

The main contribution of this paper is to propose a new identity-based signcryption scheme that even supersedes [14] from an efficiency point of view at the expense of a security resting on stronger assumptions. The new construction can benefit from the most efficient pairing calculation techniques for a larger variety of elliptic curves than previous schemes. Indeed, recent observations [35] pinpointed problems arising when many provably secure pairing based protocols are implemented using asymmetric pairings and ordinary curves. Our proposal avoids those problems thanks to the fact that it does not require to hash onto an elliptic curve cyclic subgroup. As a result of independent interest, we discovered a new identity-based signature that happens to be faster at verification than previously known IBS schemes.

This paper is organized as follows. Section 2 presents the basic security theoretic concepts of bilinear map groups and the hard problems underlying our proposed algorithms. We describe our identity-based signature scheme and prove its security in section 3. We propose a new identity-based signcryption scheme in section 4, and compare its efficiency to various schemes in section 5. We draw our conclusions in section 6.

2   Preliminaries

2.1   Bilinear Map Groups and Related Computational Problems

Let k be a security parameter and p be a k-bit prime number. Let us consider groups $\mathbb{G}_1$, $\mathbb{G}_2$ and $\mathbb{G}_T$ of the same prime order p and let P, Q be generators of respectively $\mathbb{G}_1$ and $\mathbb{G}_2$. We say that $(\mathbb{G}_1, \mathbb{G}_2, \mathbb{G}_T)$ are *bilinear map groups* if there exists a bilinear map $e : \mathbb{G}_1 \times \mathbb{G}_2 \to \mathbb{G}_T$ satisfying the following properties:

1. Bilinearity: $\forall\ (S, T) \in \mathbb{G}_1 \times \mathbb{G}_2,\ \forall\ a, b \in \mathbb{Z},\ e(aS, bT) = e(S, T)^{ab}$.
2. Non-degeneracy: $\forall\ S \in \mathbb{G}_1,\ e(S, T) = 1$ for all $T \in \mathbb{G}_2$ iff $S = \mathcal{O}$.
3. Computability: $\forall\ (S, T) \in \mathbb{G}_1 \times \mathbb{G}_2,\ e(S, T)$ is efficiently computable.
4. There exists an efficient, publicly computable (but not necessarily invertible) isomorphism $\psi : \mathbb{G}_2 \to \mathbb{G}_1$ such that $\psi(Q) = P$.

Such bilinear map groups are known to be instantiable with ordinary elliptic curves such as those suggested in [29] or [4]. In this case, the trace map can be used as an efficient isomorphism ψ as long as $\mathbb{G}_2$ is properly chosen [35]. With supersingular curves, symmetric pairings (i.e. $\mathbb{G}_1 = \mathbb{G}_2$) can be obtained and ψ is the identity.

The computational assumptions for the security of our schemes were previously formalized by Boneh and Boyen [9,7] and are recalled in the following definition.

Definition 1 ([9,7]). *Let us consider bilinear map groups* $(\mathbb{G}_1, \mathbb{G}_2, \mathbb{G}_T)$ *and generators* $P \in \mathbb{G}_1$ *and* $Q \in \mathbb{G}_2$.

The **q-*Strong Diffie-Hellman*** *problem (q-SDHP) in the groups* $(\mathbb{G}_1, \mathbb{G}_2)$ *consists in, given a* $(q + 2)$-*tuple* $(P, Q, \alpha Q, \alpha^2 Q, \dots, \alpha^q Q)$ *as input, finding a pair* $\left(c, \frac{1}{c+\alpha}P\right)$ *with* $c \in \mathbb{Z}_p^*$.

The **q-*Bilinear Diffie-Hellman Inversion*** *problem (q-BDHIP) in the groups* $(\mathbb{G}_1, \mathbb{G}_2, \mathbb{G}_T)$ *consists in, given* $(P, Q, \alpha Q, \alpha^2 Q, \dots, \alpha^q Q)$, *computing* $e(P, Q)^{1/\alpha} \in \mathbb{G}_T$.

3   A New Identity-Based Signature

We here present a new identity-based signature that is significantly more efficient all known pairing based IBS schemes as its verification algorithm requires a single pairing calculation. This efficiency gain is obtained at the expense of letting the security rely on a stronger assumption than other provably secure pairing based IBS [12,15,24].

Setup: given a security parameter k, the PKG chooses bilinear map groups $(\mathbb{G}_1, \mathbb{G}_2, \mathbb{G}_T)$ of prime order $p > 2^k$ and generators $Q \in \mathbb{G}_2$, $P = \psi(Q) \in \mathbb{G}_1$, $g = e(P, Q)$. It then selects a master key $s \xleftarrow{R} \mathbb{Z}_p^*$, a system-wide public key $Q_{pub} = sQ \in \mathbb{G}_2$ and hash functions $H_1 : \{0,1\}^* \to \mathbb{Z}_p^*$, $H_2 : \{0,1\}^* \times \mathbb{G}_T \to \mathbb{Z}_p^*$. The public parameters are

$$\mathsf{params} := \{\mathbb{G}_1, \mathbb{G}_2, \mathbb{G}_T, P, Q, g, Q_{pub}, e, \psi, H_1, H_2\}$$

Keygen: for an identity ID, the private key is $S_{\mathsf{ID}} = \frac{1}{H_1(\mathsf{ID})+s}P$.

Sign: in order to sign a message $M \in \{0,1\}^*$, the signer

1. picks a random $x \xleftarrow{R} \mathbb{Z}_p^*$ and computes $r = g^x$,
2. sets $h = H_2(M, r) \in \mathbb{Z}_p^*$,
3. computes $S = (x + h)S_{\mathsf{ID}}$.

The signature on M is $\sigma = (h, S) \in \mathbb{Z}_p^* \times \mathbb{G}_1$.

Verify: a signature $\sigma = (h, S)$ on a message M is accepted iff

$$h = H_2(M, e(S, H_1(\mathsf{ID})Q + Q_{pub})g^{-h}).$$

The scheme can be thought of as an identity-based extension of a digital signature discussed in two independent papers [9,38]. More precisely, the method for obtaining private keys from identities is a simplification of a method suggested by Sakai and Kasahara ([33]).

In [25], Kurosawa and Heng described an identity-based identification (IBI) protocol that implicitly suggests an IBS described in appendix E and which can be proven secure under the same assumption as our proposal. It turns out that ours is slightly faster than the Kurosawa-Heng IBS in the signature generation.

At Eurocrypt'04, Bellare, Namprempre and Neven established a framework [5] for proving the security of a large family of identity-based signatures and they only found two schemes to which their framework does not apply. The present one does not either fall into the category of schemes to which it applies. Indeed, it can be showed that our IBS does not result from the transformation of any convertible standard identification or signature scheme (in the sense of [5]) unless the q-SDHP is easy. A direct security proof is thus needed.

3.1   Security Results

We recall here the usual model [5,12,15,19,24] of security for identity-based signatures which is an extension of the usual notion of existential unforgeability under chosen-message attacks [22].

Definition 2 ([12]). *An IBS scheme is **existentially unforgeable** under adaptive chosen message and identity attacks if no probabilistic polynomial time (PPT) adversary has a non-negligible advantage in this game:*

1. *The challenger runs the setup algorithm to generate the system's parameters and sends them to the adversary.*
2. *The adversary $\mathcal{F}$ performs a series of queries to the following oracles:*
   - *Key extraction oracle: returns private keys for arbitrary identities.*
   - *Signature oracle: produces signatures on arbitrary messages using the private key corresponding to arbitrary identities.*
3. *$\mathcal{F}$ produces a triple $(\mathsf{ID}^*, M^*, \sigma^*)$ made of an identity ID^*, whose private key was never extracted, and a message-signature pair (M^*, σ^*) such that (M^*, ID^*) was not submitted to the signature oracle. She wins if the verification algorithm accepts the triple $(\mathsf{ID}^*, M^*, \sigma^*)$.*

The next lemmas establish the security of the scheme under the q-SDH assumption. Lemma 1 [12] allows to only consider a weaker attack where a forger is challenged on a given identity chosen by the challenger. The proof of lemma 2 relies on the forking lemma [31,32].

Lemma 1 ([12]). *If there is a forger $\mathcal{F}_0$ for an adaptively chosen message and identity attack having advantage ϵ_0 against our scheme when running in a time t_0 and making q_{h_1} queries to random oracle h_1, then there exists an algorithm $\mathcal{F}_1$ for an adaptively chosen message and given identity attack which has advantage $\epsilon_1 \le \epsilon_0\left(1 - \frac{1}{2^k}\right)/q_{h_1}$ within a running time $t_1 \le t_0$. Moreover, $\mathcal{F}_1$ asks the same number key extraction queries, signature queries and H_2-queries as $\mathcal{F}_0$ does.*

Lemma 2. *Let us assume that there is an adaptively chosen message and given identity attacker $\mathcal{F}$ that makes q_{h_i} queries to random oracles H_i $(i = 1, 2)$ and q_s queries to the signing oracle. Assume that, within a time t, $\mathcal{F}$ produces a forgery with probability $\epsilon \ge 10(q_s + 1)(q_s + q_{h_2})/2^k$. Then, there exists an algorithm $\mathcal{B}$ that is able to solve the q-SDHP for $q = q_{h_1}$ in an expected time*

$$t' \le 120686 q_{h_2}(t + O(q_s \tau_p))/(\epsilon(1 - q/2^k)) + O(q^2 \tau_{mult})$$

where τ_{mult} denotes the cost of a scalar multiplication in $\mathbb{G}_2$ and τ_p is the cost of a pairing evaluation.

Proof. See appendix A. □

The combination of the above lemmas yields the following theorem.

Theorem 1. *Let us assume that there exists an adaptively chosen message and identity attacker $\mathcal{F}$ making q_{h_i} queries to random oracles H_i $(i = 1, 2)$ and q_s queries to the signing oracle. Assume that, within a time t, $\mathcal{F}$ produces a forgery with probability $\epsilon \ge 10(q_s + 1)(q_s + q_{h_2})/2^k$. Then, there exists an algorithm $\mathcal{B}$ that is able to solve the q-SDHP for $q = q_{h_1}$ in an expected time*

$$t' \le 120686 q_{h_1} q_{h_2}(t + O(q_s \tau_p))/(\epsilon(1 - q/2^k)) + O(q^2 \tau_{mult})$$

where τ_{mult} and τ_p respectively denote the cost of a scalar multiplication in $\mathbb{G}_2$ and the required time for a pairing evaluation.

4   Fast Identity-Based Signcryption

4.1   Formal Model of Identity-Based Signcryption

The formal structure that we shall use for identity-based signcryption schemes is the following.

Setup: is a probabilistic algorithm run by a private key generator (PKG) that takes as input a security parameter to output public parameters params and a master key mk that is kept secret.

Keygen: is a key generation algorithm run by the PKG on input of params and the master key mk to return the private key S_{ID} associated to the identity ID.

Sign/Encrypt: is a probabilistic algorithm that takes as input public parameters params, a plaintext message M, the recipient's identity ID_R, and the sender's private key S_{ID_S}, and outputs a ciphertext $\sigma = \mathsf{Sign/Encrypt}(M, S_{ID_S}, ID_R)$.

Decrypt/Verify: is a deterministic decryption algorithm that takes as input a ciphertext σ, public parameters params, the receiver's private key S_{ID_R} and (optionally) a sender's identity ID_S before returning a valid message-signature pair (M, s) or a distinguished symbol $\perp$ if σ does not decrypt into a message bearing signer ID_S's signature.

Unlike recent works of [11,14] that present two-layer designs of probabilistic signature followed by a deterministic encryption, our construction is a single-layer construction jointly achieving signature and encryption on one side and decryption and verification on the other side. Although the description of our scheme could be modified to fit a two-layer formalism, we kept the monolithic presentation without hampering the non-repudiation property as, similarly to [11,14], our construction enables an ordinary signature on the plaintext to be extracted from any properly formed ciphertext using the recipient's private key. The extracted message-signature pair can be forwarded to any third party in such a way that a sender remains committed to the content of the plaintext.

Unlike models of [11,14] that consider anonymous ciphertexts, the above one assumes that senders' identities are sent in the clear along with ciphertexts. Actually, receivers do not need to have any a priori knowledge on whom the ciphertext emanates from in our scheme but this simply allows more efficient reductions in the security proofs. A simple modification of our scheme yields anonymous ciphertexts and enables senders' identities to be recovered by the Decrypt/Verify algorithm (which only takes a ciphertext and the recipient's private key as input).

Definition 3. *An identity-based signcryption scheme (IBSC) satisfies the **message confidentiality** property (or adaptive chosen-ciphertext security: IND-IBSC-CCA) if no PPT adversary has a non-negligible advantage in the following game.*

1. *The challenger runs the Setup algorithm on input of a security parameter k and sends the domain-wide parameters params to the $\mathcal{A}$.*
2. *In a find stage, $\mathcal{A}$ starts probing the following oracles:*
   - *Keygen: returns private keys associated to arbitrary identities.*
   - *Sign/Encrypt: given a pair of identities ID_S, ID_R and a plaintext M, it returns an encryption under the receiver's identity ID_R of the message M signed in the name of the sender ID_S.*
   - *Decrypt/Verify: given a pair of identities (ID_S, ID_R) and a ciphertext σ, it generates the receiver's private key $S_{ID_R} = $ Keygen(ID_R) and returns either a valid message-signature pair (M, s) for the sender's identity ID_S or the $\perp$ symbol if, under the private key S_{ID_R}, σ does not decrypt into a valid message-signature pair.*
3. *$\mathcal{A}$ produces two plaintexts $M_0, M_1 \in \mathcal{M}$ and identities ID_S^* and ID_R^*. She may not have extracted the private key of ID_R^* and she obtains $C = $ Sign/Encrypt$(M_b, S_{ID_S^*}, ID_R^*, $ params$)$, for a random a bit $b \xleftarrow{R} \{0, 1\}$.*
4. *In the guess stage, $\mathcal{A}$ asks new queries as in the find stage. This time, she may not issue a key extraction request on ID_R^* and she cannot submit C to the Decrypt/Verify oracle for the target identity ID_R^*.*
5. *Finally, $\mathcal{A}$ outputs a bit b' and wins if $b' = b$.*

$\mathcal{A}$'s advantage is defined as $Adv(\mathcal{A}) := 2 \times \Pr[b' = b] - 1$.

The next definition, given in [11], considers non-repudiation w.r.t. signatures embedded in ciphertexts rather than w.r.t. ciphertexts themselves.

Definition 4. *An identity-based signcryption scheme (IBSC) is said to be **existentially signature-unforgeable** against adaptive chosen messages and ciphertexts attacks (ESUF-IBSC-CMA) if no PPT adversary can succeed in the following game with a non-negligible advantage:*

1. *the challenger runs the Setup algorithm on input k and gives the system-wide public key to the adversary $\mathcal{F}$.*
2. *$\mathcal{F}$ issues a number of queries as in the previous definition.*
3. *Finally, $\mathcal{F}$ outputs a triple $(\sigma^*, \mathsf{ID}_S^*, \mathsf{ID}_R^*)$ and wins the game if the sender's identity ID_S^* was not corrupted and if the result of the Decrypt/Verify oracle on the ciphertext σ^* under the private key associated to ID_R^* is a valid message-signature pair (M^*, s^*) such that no Sign/Encrypt query involved M^*, ID_S^* and some receiver ID_R' (possibly different from ID_R^*) and resulted in a ciphertext σ' whose decryption under the private key $S_{\mathsf{ID}_R'}$ is the alleged forgery $(M^*, s^*, \mathsf{ID}_S^*)$.*

The adversary's advantage is its probability of victory.

In both of these definitions, we consider insider attacks [1]. Namely, in the definition of message confidentiality, the adversary is allowed to be challenged on a ciphertext created using a corrupted sender's private key whereas, in the notion of signature non-repudiation, the forger may output a ciphertext computed under a corrupted receiving identity.

4.2   The Scheme

Our scheme is obtained from an optimized combination of our IBS scheme with the most basic version of the Sakai-Kasahara IBE ([33,13]) which is only secure against chosen-plaintext attacks when used as an encryption-only system. This allows performing the signature-encryption operation without computing a pairing whereas only two pairings have to be computed upon decryption/verification.

Setup: given k, the PKG chooses bilinear map groups $(\mathbb{G}_1, \mathbb{G}_2, \mathbb{G}_T)$ of prime order $p > 2^k$ and generators $Q \in \mathbb{G}_2$, $P = \psi(Q) \in \mathbb{G}_1$, $g = e(P, Q) \in \mathbb{G}_T$. It then chooses a master key $s \overset{R}{\leftarrow} \mathbb{Z}_p^*$, a system-wide public key $Q_{pub} = sQ \in \mathbb{G}_2$ and hash functions $H_1 : \{0,1\}^* \to \mathbb{Z}_p^*$, $H_2 : \{0,1\}^* \times \mathbb{G}_T \to \mathbb{Z}_p^*$ and $H_3 : \mathbb{G}_T \to \{0,1\}^n$. The public parameters are

$$\text{params} := \{\mathbb{G}_1, \mathbb{G}_2, \mathbb{G}_T, P, Q, g, Q_{pub}, e, \psi, H_1, H_2, H_3\}$$

Keygen: for an identity ID, the private key is $S_{\mathsf{ID}} = \frac{1}{H_1(\mathsf{ID})+s} Q \in \mathbb{G}_2$.

Sign/Encrypt: given a message $M \in \{0,1\}^*$, a receiver's identity ID_B and a sender's private key S_{ID_A},

1. Pick $x \xleftarrow{R} \mathbb{Z}_p^*$, compute $r = g^x$ and $c = M \oplus H_3(r) \in \{0,1\}^n$.
2. Set $h = H_2(M, r) \in \mathbb{Z}_p^*$.
3. Compute $S = (x + h)\psi(S_{\mathsf{ID}_A})$.
4. Compute $T = x(H_1(\mathsf{ID}_B)P + \psi(Q_{pub}))$.

The ciphertext is $\sigma = \langle c, S, T \rangle \in \{0,1\}^n \times \mathbb{G}_1 \times \mathbb{G}_1$.

Decrypt/Verify: given $\sigma = \langle c, S, T \rangle$, and some sender's identity ID_A,

1. Compute $r = e(T, S_{\mathsf{ID}_B})$, $M = c \oplus H_3(r)$, and $h = H_2(M, r)$.
2. Accept the message iff $r = e(S, H_1(\mathsf{ID}_A)Q + Q_{pub})g^{-h}$. If this condition holds, return the message M and the signature $(h, S) \in \mathbb{Z}_p^* \times \mathbb{G}_1$.

If required, the anonymity property is obtained by scrambling the sender's identity ID_A together with the message at step 1 of Sign/Encrypt in such a way that the recipient retrieves it at the first step of the reverse operation. This change does not imply any computational penalty in practice but induces more expensive security reductions. In order for the proof to hold, ID_A must be appended to the inputs of H_2.

4.3   Security Results

The following theorems claim the security of the scheme in the random oracle model under the same irreflexivity assumption as Boyen's scheme [11]: the signature/encryption algorithm is assumed to always take distinct identities as inputs (in other words, a principal never encrypts a message bearing his signature using his own identity).

Theorem 2. *Assume that an IND-IBSC-CCA adversary $\mathcal{A}$ has an advantage ϵ against our scheme when running in time τ, asking q_{h_i} queries to random oracles H_i $(i = 1, 2, 3)$, q_{se} signature/encryption queries and q_{dv} queries to the decryption/verification oracle. Then there is an algorithm $\mathcal{B}$ to solve the q-BDHIP for $q = q_{h_1}$ with probability*

$$\epsilon' > \frac{\epsilon}{q_{h_1}(2q_{h_2} + q_{h_3})}\left(1 - q_{se}\frac{q_{se} + q_{h_2}}{2^k}\right)\left(1 - \frac{q_{dv}}{2^k}\right)$$

within a time $\tau' < \tau + O(q_{se} + q_{dv})\tau_p + O(q_{h_1}^2)\tau_{mult} + O(q_{dv}q_{h_2})\tau_{exp}$ where τ_{exp} and τ_{mult} are respectively the costs of an exponentiation in $\mathbb{G}_T$ and a multiplication in $\mathbb{G}_2$ whereas τ_p is the complexity of a pairing computation.

Proof. See appendix B.   □

Theorem 3. *Assume there exists an ESUF-IBSC-CMA attacker $\mathcal{A}$ that makes q_{h_i} queries to random oracles H_i $(i = 1, 2, 3)$, q_{se} signature/encryption queries and q_{dv} queries to the decryption/verification oracle. Assume also that, within a time τ, $\mathcal{A}$ produces a forgery with probability $\epsilon \geq 10(q_{se} + 1)(q_{se} + q_{h_2})/2^k$. Then, there is an algorithm $\mathcal{B}$ that is able to solve the q-SDHP for $q = q_{h_1}$ in expected time*

$$\tau' \leq 120686q_{h_1}q_{h_2}\frac{\tau + O((q_{se} + q_{dv})\tau_p) + q_{dv}q_{h_2}\tau_{exp}}{\epsilon(1 - 1/2^k)(1 - q/2^k)} + O(q^2\tau_{mult})$$

where τ_{mult}, τ_{exp} and τ_p denote the same quantities as in theorem 2.

Proof. See appendix C.   □

We now restate theorem 2 for the variant of our scheme with anonymous ciphertexts. The simulator's worst-case running time is affected by the fact that, when handling Decrypt/Verify requests, senders'identities are not known in advance. The reduction involves a number of pairing calculations which is quadratic in the number of adversarial queries.

Theorem 4. *Assume that an IND-IBSC-CCA adversary $\mathcal{A}$ has an advantage ϵ against our scheme when running in time τ, asking q_{h_i} queries to random oracles H_i $(i = 1, 2, 3)$, q_{se} signature/encryption queries and q_{dv} queries to the decryption/verification oracle. Then there is an algorithm $\mathcal{B}$ to solve the q-BDHIP for $q = q_{h_1}$ with probability*

$$\epsilon' > \frac{\epsilon}{q_{h_1}(2q_{h_2} + q_{h_3})}\left(1 - q_{se}\frac{q_{se} + q_{h_2}}{2^k}\right)\left(1 - \frac{q_{dv}}{2^k}\right)$$

within a time $\tau' < \tau + O(q_{se} + q_{dv}q_{h_2})\tau_p + O(q_{h_1}^2)\tau_{mult} + O(q_{dv}q_{h_2})\tau_{exp}$ where τ_{exp}, τ_{mult} and τ_p denote the same quantities as in previous theorems.

Proof. See appendix D. □

Theorem 3 can be similarly restated as its reduction cost is affected in the same way.

A formal proof of *ciphertext anonymity* in the model of [11] will be given in the full version of this paper for the anonymous version of the scheme.

We concede that even the latter variant does not feature all the properties of the systems of Boyen ([11]) or Chen-Malone-Lee ([14]). For example, it does not have the *ciphertext unlinkability* property ([11,14]): it seems infeasible for anyone to use his private key to embed a given message-signature pair into a proper ciphertext intended to himself. We were also unable to formally establish the *ciphertext authentication property* according to which a ciphertext is always signed and encrypted by the same person and cannot be subject to a kind of 'man-in-the-middle' attack. Nevertheless, the scheme does seem to have this property because of the same reason that precludes the ciphertext unlinkability property.

Overall, we believe that the scheme does satisfy the main requirements that might be desired in practice. In our opinion, it suffices to implement most practical applications and its great efficiency renders it more than interesting for identity-based cryptography.

5   Efficiency Discussions and Comparisons

In [35], Smart and Vercauteren pointed out problems that arise when several pairing based protocols are implemented with asymmetric pairings. They showed the difficulty of finding groups $\mathbb{G}_2$ allowing the use of the most efficient pairing calculation techniques for ordinary curves [3] if arbitrary strings should be *efficiently* hashed onto them and efficient isomorphism $\psi : \mathbb{G}_2 \to \mathbb{G}_1$ must be available at the same time. As a consequence, several protocols have to be implemented with groups for which no efficient isomorphism $\psi : \mathbb{G}_2 \to \mathbb{G}_1$ is computable and their security eventually has to rely on somewhat unnatural assumptions.

Except [33] that has no security proof (and actually has several known security problems [28]), all known identity-based signcryption schemes would require to hash onto $\mathbb{G}_2$ if they were instantiated with asymmetric pairings. Our scheme avoids this problem since it does not require to hash onto a cyclic group. It thus more easily benefits from optimized pairing calculation algorithms. For example, section 4 of [35] yields an example of group $\mathbb{G}_2$ for which techniques of [3] can be used and where efficient isomorphisms are available.

We now assess the comparative efficiency of several identity-based signcryption schemes, implemented according to their original descriptions. Table 1 summarises the number of relevant basic operations underlying several identity-based signcryption and signature schemes, namely, $\mathbb{G}_T$ exponentiations, scalar point

Table 1. Efficiency comparison

signcryption scheme	Sign/Encrypt				Decrypt/Verify			
	exp	mul	pairings	time (ms)	exp	mul	pairings	time (ms)
Boyen ([11])	1	3	1†	9.37		2	4†	12.66
Chow-Yiu-Hui-Chow¶ ([16])		2	2⋆	7.24		1	4⋆	11.88
Libert-Quisquater¶♠ ([26])		2	2⋆	7.24		1	4⋆	11.88
Nalla-Reddy◇⋈ ([30])	1	2	1†	8.43	1		3†	9.06
Malone-Lee♣ ([27])		3	1‡	5.47	1		3	9.06
Chen-Malone-Lee ([14])		3	1‡	5.47	1		3	9.06
Sakai-Kasahara♣ ([33])	2	1+1§		6.41	1		2	9.37
Libert-Quisquater⋈ ([26])		3	1‡	5.47	1		2	6.41
ours	1	2		2.65	1		2	6.09

signature scheme	Sign				Verify			
	exp	mul	pairings	time (ms)	exp	mul	pairings	time (ms)
Chow-Yiu-Hui-Chow ([16])		2	1‡	3.60			2†	6.41
Heß([24])	1	2		2.50	1		2†	6.41
Cha-Cheon ([12])		2		1.87			2	6.41
ours		2		1.56			1	3.60

(†) One pairing is precomputable, incurring for each user a storage cost of one $\mathbb{G}_T$ element for each other user in the system.

(‡) One pairing is precomputable, incurring for each user a storage cost of one $\mathbb{G}_T$ element for each other user in the system, plus one $\mathbb{G}_T$ exponentiation.

(⋆) Two pairings are precomputable, incurring for each user a storage cost of one $\mathbb{G}_T$ element for each user in the system, plus two $\mathbb{G}_T$ exponentiations.

(§) One of the scalar multiplications is done in $\langle Q \rangle$ rather than $\langle P \rangle$ where (P, Q) generates $E[p]$.

(¶) Universally verifiable scheme (i.e. supports public ciphertext validation).

(♣) These schemes suffer from security problems as mentioned in [26,28].

(♠) This scheme does not provide insider-security for the message-confidentiality criterion.

(◇) This scheme has no security proof.

(⋈) This construction can only authenticate messages from the receiver's point of view.

multiplications, and pairing evaluations, and compares the observed processing times (in milliseconds) for a supersingular curve of embedding degree $k = 6$ over $\mathbb{F}_{3^{97}}$, using implementations written in C++ and run on an Athlon XP 2 GHz. Subtleties in the algorithms determine somewhat different running times even when the operation counts for those algorithms are equal. We see from these results that our proposed algorithms rank among the fastest schemes.

6 Conclusion

We have described efficient and provably secure signature and signcryption schemes that are faster than any pairing-based scheme previously proposed in the literature. The latter can be instantiated with either named or anonymous ciphertexts and is more convenient than previous proposals for implementations with asymmetric pairings.

References

1. J.-H. An, Y. Dodis, and T. Rabin. On the security of joint signature and encryption. In *Eurocrypt'02*, volume 2332 of *LNCS*, pages 83–107. Springer, 2002.
2. P. S. L. M. Barreto. The pairing based crypto lounge. http://planeta.terra.com.br/informatica/paulobarreto/pblounge.html.
3. P. S. L. M. Barreto, B. Lynn, and M. Scott. On the selection of pairing-friendly groups. In *SAC'03*, volume 3006 of *LNCS*, pages 17–25. Springer, 2003.
4. P. S. L. M. Barreto and M. Naehrig. Pairing-friendly elliptic curves of prime order. Cryptology ePrint Archive, Report 2005/133, 2005. http://eprint.iacr.org/2005/133.
5. M. Bellare, C. Namprempre, and G. Neven. Security proofs for identity-based identification and signature schemes. In *Eurocrypt'04*, volume 3027 of *LNCS*, pages 268–286. Springer, 2004.
6. M. Bellare and P. Rogaway. Random oracles are practical: A paradigm for designing efficient protocols. In *1st ACM Conference on Computer and Communications Security*, pages 62–73, Fairfax, USA, 1993. ACM Press.
7. D. Boneh and X. Boyen. Efficient selective-ID secure identity based encryption without random oracles. In *Eurocrypt'04*, volume 3027 of *LNCS*, pages 223–238. Springer, 2004.
8. D. Boneh and X. Boyen. Secure identity based encryption without random oracles. In *Crypto'04*, volume 3152 of *LNCS*, pages 443–459. Springer, 2004.
9. D. Boneh and X. Boyen. Short signatures without random oracles. In *Eurocrypt'04*, volume 3027 of *LNCS*, pages 56–73. Springer, 2004.
10. D. Boneh and M. Franklin. Identity-based encryption from the Weil pairing. In *Crypto'01*, volume 2139 of *LNCS*, pages 213–229. Springer, 2001.
11. X. Boyen. Multipurpose identity-based signcryption: A swiss army knife for identity-based cryptography. In *Crypto'03*, volume 2729 of *LNCS*, pages 383–399. Springer, 2003.
12. J. C. Cha and J. H. Cheon. An identity-based signature from gap Diffie-Hellman groups. In *PKC'03*, volume 2567 of *LNCS*, pages 18–30. Springer, 2003.

13. L. Chen and Z. Cheng. Security proof of Sakai-Kasahara's identity-based encryption scheme. Cryptology ePrint Archive, Report 2005/226, 2005. http://eprint.iacr.org/2005/226.

14. L. Chen and J. Malone-Lee. Improved identity-based signcryption. In *PKC'05*, volume 3386 of *LNCS*, pages 362–379. Springer, 2005.

15. J. H. Cheon, Y. Kim, and H. J. Yoon. A new id-based signature with batch verification. Cryptology ePrint Archive, Report 2004/131, 2004. http://eprint.iacr.org/2004/131.

16. S. S. M. Chow, S. M. Yiu, L. C. K. Hui, and K. P. Chow. Efficient forward and provably secure ID-based signcryption scheme with public verifiability and public ciphertext authenticity. In *6th International Conference on Information Security and Cryptology – ICISC'03*, volume 2971 of *LNCS*, pages 352–369. Springer, 2003.

17. S. S. M. Chow, T. H. Yuen, L. C. K. Hui, and S. M. Yiu. Signcryption in hierarchical identity based cryptosystem. In *20th International Conference on Information Security (SEC'05)*. IFIP TC11, 2005.

18. C. Cocks. An identity based encryption scheme based on quadratic residues. In *8th IMA International Conference*, volume 2260 of *LNCS*, pages 360–363. Springer, 2001.

19. Y. Dodis, J. Katz, S. Xu, and M. Yung. Strong key-insulated signature schemes. In *PKC'03*, volume 2567 of *LNCS*, pages 130–144. Springer, 2003.

20. A. Fiat and A. Shamir. How to prove yourself: Practical solutions to identification and signature problems. In *Crypto'86*, volume 0263 of *LNCS*, pages 186–194. Springer, 1986.

21. C. Gentry and A. Silverberg. Hierarchical ID-based cryptography. In *Asiacrypt'02*, volume 2501 of *LNCS*, pages 548–566. Springer, 2002.

22. S. Goldwasser, S. Micali, and R. Riverst. A digital signature scheme secure against adaptive chosen message attacks. *SIAM Journal of Computing*, 17(2):281–308, 1988.

23. L. Guillou and J.-J. Quisquater. A "paradoxical" identity-based signature scheme resulting from zero-knowledge. In *Crypto'88*, volume 0403 of *LNCS*, pages 216–231. Springer, 1988.

24. F. Heß. Efficient identity based signature schemes based on pairings. In *SAC'02*, volume 2595 of *LNCS*, pages 310–324. Springer, 2003.

25. K. Kurosawa and S.-H. Heng. Identity-based identification without random oracles. In *ISH'05*, LNCS. Springer, 2005. To appear.

26. B. Libert and J.-J. Quisquater. New identity based signcryption schemes from pairings. In *IEEE Information Theory Workshop*, Paris, France, 2003. http://eprint.iacr.org/2003/023.

27. J. Malone-Lee. Identity-based signcryption. Cryptology ePrint Archive, Report 2002/098, 2002. http://eprint.iacr.org/2002/098.

28. N. McCullagh and P. S. L. M. Barreto. Efficient and forward-secure identity-based signcryption. Cryptology ePrint Archive, Report 2004/117, 2004. http://eprint.iacr.org/2004/117.

29. A. Miyaji, M. Nakabayashi, and S. Takano. New explicit conditions of elliptic curve traces for FR-reduction. *IEICE Transactions on Fundamentals*, E84-A(5):1234–1243, 2001.

30. D. Nalla and K. C. Reddy. Signcryption scheme for identity-based cryptosystems. Cryptology ePrint Archive, Report 2003/066, 2003. http://eprint.iacr.org/2003/066.

31. D. Pointcheval and J. Stern. Security proofs for signature schemes. In *Eurocrypt'96*, volume 1992 of *LNCS*, pages 387–398. Springer, 1996.

32. D. Pointcheval and J. Stern. Security arguments for digital signatures and blind signatures. *Journal of Cryptology*, 13(3):361–396, 2000.
33. R. Sakai and M. Kasahara. ID based cryptosystems with pairing on elliptic curve. In *SCIS'03*, Hamamatsu, Japan, 2003. http://eprint.iacr.org/2003/054.
34. A. Shamir. Identity based cryptosystems and signature schemes. In *Crypto'84*, volume 0196 of *LNCS*, pages 47–53. Springer, 1984.
35. N. P. Smart and F. Vercauteren. On computable isomorphisms in efficient pairing based systems. Cryptology ePrint Archive, Report 2005/116, 2005. http://eprint.iacr.org/2005/116.
36. B. Waters. Efficient identity-based encryption without random oracles. In *Eurocrypt'05*, volume 3494 of *LNCS*, pages 114–127. Springer, 2005.
37. T. H. Yuen and V. K. Wei. Fast and proven secure blind identity-based signcryption from pairings. In *CT-RSA'05*, volume 3376 of *LNCS*, pages 305–322. Springer, 2003.
38. F. Zhang, R. Safavi-Naini, and W. Susilo. An efficient signature scheme from bilinear pairings and its applications. In *PKC'04*, volume 2947 of *LNCS*, pages 277–290. Springer, 2004.
39. Y. Zheng. Digital signcryption or how to achieve cost (signature & encryption) << cost(signature) + cost(encryption). In *Crypto'97*, volume 1294 of *LNCS*, pages 165–179. Springer, 1997.

A   Proof of Lemma 2

Proof. We first show how to provide the adversary with a consistent view and we then explain how to apply the forking lemma.

Algorithm $\mathcal{B}$ takes as input $(P, Q, \alpha Q, \alpha^2 Q, \ldots, \alpha^q Q)$ and aims to find a pair $(c, \frac{1}{c+\alpha}P)$. In a setup phase, it builds a generator $G \in \mathbb{G}_1$ such that it knows $q - 1$ pairs $(w_i, \frac{1}{w_i + \alpha}G)$ for $w_1, \ldots, w_{q-1} \in_R \mathbb{Z}_p^*$. To do so,

1. It picks $w_1, w_2, \ldots, w_{q-1} \xleftarrow{R} \mathbb{Z}_p^*$ and expands $f(z) = \prod_{i=1}^{q-1}(z + w_i)$ to obtain $c_0, \ldots, c_{q-1} \in \mathbb{Z}_p^*$ so that $f(z) = \sum_{i=0}^{q-1} c_i z^i$.
2. It sets generators $H = \sum_{i=0}^{q-1} c_i(\alpha^i Q) = f(\alpha)Q \in \mathbb{G}_2$ and $G = \psi(H) = f(\alpha)P \in \mathbb{G}_1$. The public key $H_{pub} \in \mathbb{G}_2$ is fixed to $H_{pub} = \sum_{i=1}^{q} c_{i-1}(\alpha^i Q)$ so that $H_{pub} = \alpha H$ although $\mathcal{B}$ does not know α.
3. For $1 \le i \le q - 1$, $\mathcal{B}$ expands $f_i(z) = f(z)/(z + w_i) = \sum_{i=0}^{q-2} d_i z^i$ and

$$\sum_{i=0}^{q-2} d_i \psi(\alpha^i Q) = f_i(\alpha)P = \frac{f(\alpha)}{\alpha + w_i}P = \frac{1}{\alpha + w_i}G. \tag{1}$$

The pairs $(w_i, \frac{1}{\alpha + w_i}G)$ are computed using the left member of (1).

$\mathcal{B}$ is then ready to answer $\mathcal{F}$'s queries along the course of the game. It first initializes a counter ℓ to 1 and launches $\mathcal{F}$ on the input (H_{pub}, ID^*) for a randomly chosen challenge identity $\mathsf{ID}^* \xleftarrow{R} \{0, 1\}^*$. For simplicity, we assume that queries to H_1 are distinct, and that any query involving an identifier ID is preceded by the random oracle query $H_1(\mathsf{ID})$.

- H_1-queries on an identity $\mathsf{ID} \in \{0,1\}^*$: $\mathcal{B}$ returns a random $w^* \xleftarrow{R} \mathbb{Z}_p^*$ if $\mathsf{ID} = \mathsf{ID}^*$. Otherwise, $\mathcal{B}$ answers $w = w_\ell \in \mathbb{Z}_p^*$ and increments ℓ. In both cases, $\mathcal{B}$ stores (ID, w) (where $w^* = w$ or w_ℓ) in a list L_1.
- Key extraction queries on $\mathsf{ID} \neq \mathsf{ID}^*$: $\mathcal{B}$ recovers the matching pair (ID, w) from L_1 and returns the previously computed $(1/(\alpha + w))G$.
- Signature query on a message-identity pair (M, ID): $\mathcal{B}$ picks $S \xleftarrow{R} \mathbb{G}_1$, $h \xleftarrow{R} \mathbb{Z}_p^*$, computes $r = e(S, Q_{\mathsf{ID}})e(G, H)^{-h}$, where $Q_{\mathsf{ID}} = H_1(\mathsf{ID})H + H_{pub}$, and backpatches to define the value $H_2(M, r)$ as $h \in \mathbb{Z}_p^*$ ($\mathcal{B}$ aborts in the unlikely event that $H_2(M, r)$ is already defined).

We have explained how to simulate $\mathcal{F}$'s environment in a chosen-message and given identity attack. We are ready to apply the forking lemma that essentially says the following: consider a scheme producing signatures of the form (M, r, h, S), where each of r, h, S corresponds to one of the three moves of a honest-verifier zero-knowledge protocol. Let us assume that a chosen-message attacker $\mathcal{F}$ forges a signature (M, r, h, S) in a time t with probability $\epsilon \geq 10(q_s + 1)(q_s + q_h)/2^k$ (k being a security parameter so that h is uniformly taken from a set of 2^k elements) when making q_s signature queries and q_h random oracle calls. If the triples (r, h, S) can be simulated without knowing the private key, then there exists a Turing machine $\mathcal{F}'$ that uses $\mathcal{F}$ to produce two valid signatures (m, r, h_1, S_1), (m, r, h_2, S_2), with $h_1 \neq h_2$, in expected time $t' \leq 120686 q_h t/\epsilon$.

In our setting, from a forger $\mathcal{F}$, we build an algorithm $\mathcal{F}'$ that replays $\mathcal{F}$ a sufficient number of times on the input (H_{pub}, ID^*) to obtain two suitable forgeries $\langle M^*, r, h_1, S_1 \rangle$, $\langle M^*, r, h_2, S_2 \rangle$ with $h_1 \neq h_2$.

The reduction then works as follows. The simulator $\mathcal{B}$ runs $\mathcal{F}'$ to obtain two forgeries $\langle M^*, r, h_1, S_1 \rangle$, $\langle M^*, r, h_2, S_2 \rangle$ for the same message M^* and commitment r. At this stage, $\mathcal{B}$ recovers the pair (ID^*, w^*) from list L_1. We note that $w^* \neq w_1, \ldots, w_{q-1}$ with probability at least $1 - q/2^k$. If both forgeries satisfy the verification equation, we obtain the relations

$$e(S_1, Q_{\mathsf{ID}^*})e(G, H)^{-h_1} = e(S_2, Q_{\mathsf{ID}^*})e(G, H)^{-h_2},$$

with $Q_{\mathsf{ID}^*} = H_1(\mathsf{ID}^*)H + H_{pub} = (w^* + \alpha)H$. Then, it comes that

$$e((h_1 - h_2)^{-1}(S_1 - S_2), Q_{\mathsf{ID}^*}) = e(G, H),$$

and hence $T^* = (h_1 - h_2)^{-1}(S_1 - S_2) = \frac{1}{w^* + \alpha}G$. From T^*, $\mathcal{B}$ can proceed as in [9] to extract $\sigma^* = \frac{1}{w^* + \alpha}P$: it first obtains $\gamma_{-1}, \gamma_0, \ldots, \gamma_{q-2} \in \mathbb{Z}_p^*$ for which $f(z)/(z + w^*) = \gamma_{-1}/(z + w^*) + \sum_{i=0}^{q-2} \gamma_i z^i$ and eventually computes

$$\sigma^* = \frac{1}{\gamma_{-1}}\left[T^* - \sum_{i=0}^{q-2} \gamma_i \psi(\alpha^i Q)\right] = \frac{1}{w^* + \alpha}P$$

before returning the pair (w^*, σ^*) as a result.

It finally comes that, if $\mathcal{F}$ forges a signature in a time t with probability $\epsilon \geq 10(q_s + 1)(q_s + q_{h_2})/2^k$, $\mathcal{B}$ solves the q-SDHP in expected time

$$t' \leq 120686 q_{h_2}(t + O(q_s \tau_p))/(\epsilon(1 - q/2^k)) + O(q^2 \tau_{mult})$$

where the last term accounts for the cost of the preparation phase. $\square$

B   Proof of Theorem 2

Proof. Algorithm $\mathcal{B}$ takes as input $\langle P, Q, \alpha Q, \alpha^2 Q, \ldots, \alpha^q Q \rangle$ and attempts to extract $e(P, Q)^{1/\alpha}$ from its interaction with $\mathcal{A}$.

In a preparation phase, $\mathcal{B}$ selects $\ell \stackrel{R}{\leftarrow} \{1, \ldots, q_{h_1}\}$, elements $I_\ell \stackrel{R}{\leftarrow} \mathbb{Z}_p^*$ and $w_1, \ldots, w_{\ell-1}, w_{\ell+1} \ldots, w_q \stackrel{R}{\leftarrow} \mathbb{Z}_p^*$. For $i = 1, \ldots, \ell-1, \ell+1, \ldots, q$, it computes $I_i = I_\ell - w_i$. As in the technique of [9] and in lemma 2, it sets up generators $G_2 \in \mathbb{G}_2$, $G_1 = \psi(G_2) \in \mathbb{G}_1$ and another $\mathbb{G}_2$ element $U = \alpha G_2$ such that it knows $q-1$ pairs $(w_i, H_i = (1/(w_i + \alpha))G_2)$ for $i \in \{1, \ldots, q\} \backslash \{\ell\}$. The system-wide public key Q_{pub} is chosen as

$$Q_{pub} = -U - I_\ell G_2 = (-\alpha - I_\ell)G_2$$

so that its (unknown) private key is implicitly set to $x = -\alpha - I_\ell \in \mathbb{Z}_p^*$. For all $i \in \{1, \ldots, q\} \backslash \{\ell\}$, we have $(I_i, -H_i) = (I_i, (1/(I_i + x))G_2)$.

$\mathcal{B}$ then initializes a counter ν to 1 and starts $\mathcal{A}$ on input of (G_1, G_2, Q_{pub}). Throughout the game, we assume that H_1-queries are distinct, that the target identity ID_R^* is submitted to H_1 at some point and that any query involving an identity ID comes after a H_1-query on ID:

- H_1-queries (let us call ID_ν the input of the νth one of such queries): $\mathcal{B}$ answers I_ν and increments ν.
- H_2-queries on input (M, r): $\mathcal{B}$ returns the defined value if it exists and a random $h_2 \stackrel{R}{\leftarrow} \mathbb{Z}_p^*$ otherwise. To anticipate possible subsequent Decrypt/Verify requests, $\mathcal{B}$ additionally simulates random oracle H_3 on its own to obtain $h_3 = H_3(r) \in \{0,1\}^n$ and stores the information $(M, r, h_2, c = M \oplus h_3, \gamma = r \cdot e(G_1, G_2)^{h_2})$ in L_2.
- H_3-queries for an input $r \in \mathbb{G}_T$: $\mathcal{B}$ returns the previously assigned value if it exists and a random $h_3 \stackrel{R}{\leftarrow} \{0,1\}^n$ otherwise. In the latter case, the input r and the response h_3 are stored in a list L_3.
- Keygen queries on an input ID_ν: if $\nu = \ell$, then $\mathcal{B}$ fails. Otherwise, it knows that $H_1(\mathsf{ID}_\nu) = I_\nu$ and returns $-H_\nu = (1/(I_\nu + x))\, G_2 \in \mathbb{G}_2$.
- Sign/Encrypt queries for a plaintext M and identities $(\mathsf{ID}_S, \mathsf{ID}_R) = (\mathsf{ID}_\mu, \mathsf{ID}_\nu)$ for $\mu, \nu \in \{1, \ldots, q_{h_1}\}$: we observe that, if $\mu \neq \ell$, $\mathcal{B}$ knows the sender's private key $S_{\mathsf{ID}_\mu} = -H_\mu$ and can answer the query according to the specification of Sign/Encrypt. We thus assume $\mu = \ell$ and hence $\nu \neq \ell$ by the irreflexivity assumption. Observe that $\mathcal{B}$ knows the receiver's private key $S_{\mathsf{ID}_\nu} = -H_\nu$ by construction. The difficulty is to find a random triple $(S, T, h) \in \mathbb{G}_1 \times \mathbb{G}_1 \times \mathbb{Z}_p^*$ for which

$$e(T, S_{\mathsf{ID}_\nu}) = e(S, Q_{\mathsf{ID}_\ell})e(G_1, G_2)^{-h} \tag{2}$$

where $Q_{\mathsf{ID}_\ell} = I_\ell G_2 + Q_{pub}$. To do so, $\mathcal{B}$ randomly chooses $t, h \stackrel{R}{\leftarrow} \mathbb{Z}_p^*$ and computes $S = t\psi(S_{\mathsf{ID}_\nu}) = -t\psi(H_\nu)$, $T = t\psi(Q_{\mathsf{ID}_\ell}) - h\psi(Q_{\mathsf{ID}_\nu})$ where $Q_{\mathsf{ID}_\nu} = I_\nu G_2 + Q_{pub}$ in order to obtain the desired equality $r = e(T, S_{\mathsf{ID}_\nu}) = e(S, Q_{\mathsf{ID}_\ell})e(G_1, G_2)^{-h} = e(\psi(S_{\mathsf{ID}_\nu}), Q_{\mathsf{ID}_\ell})^t e(G_1, G_2)^{-h}$ before patching the hash value $H_2(M, r)$ to h ($\mathcal{B}$ fails if H_2 is already defined but this only happens with probability $(q_{se} + q_{h_2})/2^k$). The ciphertext $\sigma = \langle M \oplus H_3(r), S, T \rangle$ is returned.

- Decrypt/Verify queries on a ciphertext $\sigma = \langle c, S, T \rangle$ for identities $(\mathsf{ID}_S, \mathsf{ID}_R) = (\mathsf{ID}_\mu, \mathsf{ID}_\nu)$: we assume that $\nu = \ell$ (and hence $\mu \neq \ell$ by the irreflexivity assumption), because otherwise $\mathcal{B}$ knows the receiver's private key $S_{\mathsf{ID}_\nu} = -H_\nu$ and can normally run the Decrypt/Verify algorithm. Since $\mu \neq \ell$, $\mathcal{B}$ has the sender's private key S_{ID_μ} and also knows that, for all valid ciphertexts, $\log_{S_{\mathsf{ID}_\mu}}(\psi^{-1}(S) - hS_{\mathsf{ID}_\mu}) = \log_{\psi(Q_{\mathsf{ID}_\nu})}(T)$, where $h = H_2(M, r)$ is the hash value obtained in the Sign/Encrypt algorithm and $Q_{\mathsf{ID}_\nu} = I_\nu G_2 + Q_{pub}$. Hence, we have the relation

$$e(T, S_{\mathsf{ID}_\mu}) = e(\psi(Q_{\mathsf{ID}_\nu}), \psi^{-1}(S) - hS_{\mathsf{ID}_\mu}) \tag{3}$$

which yields $e(T, S_{\mathsf{ID}_\mu}) = e(\psi(Q_{\mathsf{ID}_\nu}), \psi^{-1}(S))e(\psi(Q_{\mathsf{ID}_\nu}), S_{\mathsf{ID}_\mu})^{-h}$. We observe that the latter equality can be tested without inverting ψ as $e(\psi(Q_{\mathsf{ID}_\nu}), \psi^{-1}(S)) = e(S, Q_{\mathsf{ID}_\nu})$. The query is thus handled by computing $\gamma = e(S, Q_{\mathsf{ID}_\nu})$, where $Q_{\mathsf{ID}_\mu} = I_\mu G_2 + Q_{pub}$, and searching through list L_2 for entries of the form $(M_i, r_i, h_{2,i}, c, \gamma)$ indexed by $i \in \{1, \ldots, q_{h_2}\}$. If none is found, σ is rejected. Otherwise, each one of them is further examined: for the corresponding indexes, $\mathcal{B}$ checks if

$$e(T, S_{\mathsf{ID}_\mu})/e(S, Q_{\mathsf{ID}_\nu}) = e(\psi(Q_{\mathsf{ID}_\nu}), S_{\mathsf{ID}_\mu})^{-h_{2,i}} \tag{4}$$

(the pairings are computed only once and at most q_{h_2} exponentiations are needed), meaning that (3) is satisfied. If the unique $i \in \{1, \ldots, q_{h_2}\}$ satisfying (4) is detected, the matching pair $(M_i, \langle h_{2,i}, S \rangle)$ is returned. Otherwise, σ is rejected. Overall, an inappropriate rejection occurs with probability smaller than $q_{dv}/2^k$ across the whole game.

At the challenge phase, $\mathcal{A}$ outputs messages (M_0, M_1) and identities $(\mathsf{ID}_S, \mathsf{ID}_R)$ for which she never obtained ID_R's private key. If $\mathsf{ID}_R \neq \mathsf{ID}_\ell$, $\mathcal{B}$ aborts. Otherwise, it picks $\xi \xleftarrow{R} \mathbb{Z}_p^*$, $c \xleftarrow{R} \{0,1\}^n$ and $S \xleftarrow{R} \mathbb{G}_1$ to return the challenge $\sigma^* = \langle c, S, T \rangle$ where $T = -\xi G_1 \in \mathbb{G}_1$. If we define $\rho = \xi/\alpha$ and since $x = -\alpha - I_\ell$, we can check that

$$T = -\xi G_1 = -\alpha\rho G_1 = (I_\ell + x)\rho G_1 = \rho I_\ell G_1 + \rho\psi(Q_{pub}).$$

$\mathcal{A}$ cannot recognize that σ^* is not a proper ciphertext unless she queries H_2 or H_3 on $e(G_1, G_2)^\rho$. Along the guess stage, her view is simulated as before and her eventual output is ignored. Standard arguments can show that a successful $\mathcal{A}$ is very likely to query H_2 or H_3 on the input $e(G_1, G_2)^\rho$ if the simulation is indistinguishable from a real attack environment.

To produce a result, $\mathcal{B}$ fetches a random entry (M, r, h_2, c, γ) or $\langle r, . \rangle$ from the lists L_2 or L_3. With probability $1/(2q_{h_2} + q_{h_3})$ (as L_3 contains no more than $q_{h_2} + q_{h_3}$ records by construction), the chosen entry will contain the right element $r = e(G_1, G_2)^\rho = e(P, Q)^{f(\alpha)^2\xi/\alpha}$, where $f(z) = \sum_{i=0}^{q-1} c_i z^i$ is the polynomial for which $G_2 = f(\alpha)Q$. The q-BDHIP solution can be extracted by noting that, if $\gamma^* = e(P, Q)^{1/\alpha}$, then

$$e(G_1, G_2)^{1/\alpha} = \gamma^{*(c_0^2)} e\left(\sum_{i=0}^{q-2} c_{i+1}(\alpha^i P), c_0 Q\right) e\left(G_1, \sum_{j=0}^{q-2} c_{j+1}(\alpha^j)Q\right).$$

In an analysis of $\mathcal{B}$'s advantage, we note that it only fails in providing a consistent simulation because one of the following independent events:

E_1: $\mathcal{A}$ does not choose to be challenged on ID_ℓ.
E_2: a key extraction query is made on ID_ℓ.
E_3: $\mathcal{B}$ aborts in a Sign/Encrypt query because of a collision on H_2.
E_4: $\mathcal{B}$ rejects a valid ciphertext at some point of the game.

We clearly have $\Pr[\neg E_1] = 1/q_{h_1}$ and we know that $\neg E_1$ implies $\neg E_2$. We also already observed that $\Pr[E_3] \leq q_{se}(q_{se} + q_{h_2})/2^k$ and $\Pr[E_4] \leq q_{dv}/2^k$. We thus find that

$$\Pr[\neg E_1 \wedge \neg E_3 \wedge \neg E_4] \geq \frac{1}{q_{h_1}}\left(1 - q_{se}\frac{q_{se} + q_{h_2}}{2^k}\right)\left(1 - \frac{q_{dv}}{2^k}\right).$$

We obtain the announced bound by noting that $\mathcal{B}$ selects the correct element from L_2 or L_3 with probability $1/(2q_{h_2} + q_{h_3})$. Its workload is dominated by $O(q_{h_1}^2)$ multiplications in the preparation phase, $O(q_{se} + q_{dv})$ pairing calculations and $O(q_{dv}q_{h_2})$ exponentiations in $\mathbb{G}_T$ in its emulation of the Sign/Encrypt and Decrypt/Verify oracles. □

C Proof of Theorem 3

Proof. The proof is almost similar to the one of theorem 1. Namely, it shows that a forger in the ESUF-IBSC-CMA game implies a forger in a chosen-message and *given* identity attack. Using the forking lemma [31,32], the latter is in turn shown to imply an algorithm to solve the q-Strong Diffie-Hellman problem. More precisely, queries to the Sign/Encrypt and Decrypt/Verify oracles are answered as in the proof of theorem 2 and, at the outset of the game, the simulator chooses public parameters in such a way that it can extract private keys associated to any identity but the one which is given as a challenge to the adversary. By doing so, thanks to the irreflexivity assumption, it is able to extract clear message-signature pairs from ciphertexts produced by the forger (as it knows the private key of the receiving identity ID_R^*). □

D Proof of Theorem 4

Proof. The simulator is the same as in theorem 2 with the following differences (recall that senders' identities are provided as inputs to H_2).

- H_2-queries on input (ID_S, M, r): $\mathcal{B}$ returns the previously defined value if it exists and a random $h_2 \xleftarrow{R} \mathbb{Z}_p^*$ otherwise. To anticipate subsequent Decrypt/Verify requests, $\mathcal{B}$ simulates oracle H_3 to obtain $h_3 = H_3(r) \in \{0,1\}^{n+n_0}$ (where n_0 is the maximum length of identity strings) and stores $(\mathsf{ID}_S, M, r, h_2, c = (M\|\mathsf{ID}_S) \oplus h_3, \gamma = r \cdot e(G_1, G_2)^{h_2})$ in list L_2.

- Decrypt/Verify queries: given a ciphertext $\sigma = \langle c, S, T \rangle$ and a receiver's identity $\mathsf{ID}_R = \mathsf{ID}_\nu$, we assume that $\nu = \ell$ because otherwise $\mathcal{B}$ knows the receiver's private key. The simulator $\mathcal{B}$ does not know the sender's identity ID_S but knows that $\mathsf{ID}_S \neq \mathsf{ID}_\nu$. It also knows that, for the private key S_{ID_S}, $\log_{S_{\mathsf{ID}_S}}(\psi^{-1}(S) - h S_{\mathsf{ID}_S}) = \log_{\psi(Q_{\mathsf{ID}_\nu})}(T)$, and hence

$$e(T, S_{\mathsf{ID}_S}) = e(\psi(Q_{\mathsf{ID}_\nu}), \psi^{-1}(S) - h S_{\mathsf{ID}_S}), \tag{5}$$

where $h = H_2(\mathsf{ID}_S, M, r)$ is the hash value obtained in the Sign/ Encrypt algorithm and $Q_{\mathsf{ID}_\nu} = I_\nu G_2 + Q_{pub}$. The query is handled by searching through list L_2 for entries of the form $(\mathsf{ID}_{S,i}, M_i, r_i, h_{2,i}, c, \gamma_i)$ indexed by $i \in \{1, \dots, q_{h_2}\}$. If none is found, the ciphertext is rejected. Otherwise, each one of these entries for which $\mathsf{ID}_{S,i} \neq \mathsf{ID}_\nu$ is further examined by checking whether $\gamma_i = e(S, H_1(\mathsf{ID}_{S,i})Q + Q_{pub})$ and

$$e(T, S_{\mathsf{ID}_{S,i}})/e(S, Q_{\mathsf{ID}_\nu}) = e(\psi(Q_{\mathsf{ID}_\nu}), S_{\mathsf{ID}_{S,i}})^{-h_{2,i}}. \tag{6}$$

(at most $3q_{h_2} + 1$ pairings and q_{h_2} exponentiations must be computed), meaning that equation (5) is satisfied and that the ciphertext contains a valid message signature pair if both relations hold. If $\mathcal{B}$ detects an index $i \in \{1, \dots, q_{h_2}\}$ satisfying them, the matching pair $(M_i, \langle h_{2,i}, S \rangle)$ is returned. Otherwise, σ is rejected and such a wrong rejection again occurs with an overall probability smaller than $q_{dv}/2^k$. □

E   The Kurosawa-Heng Identity-Based Signature

We describe here the IBS scheme that can be derived from a modification of the Kurosawa-Heng [25] identity-based identification scheme using the Fiat-Shamir heuristic [20].

Setup and **Keygen** are the same as in our scheme described in section 3. The public parameters are
$$\mathsf{params} := \{\mathbb{G}_1, \mathbb{G}_2, \mathbb{G}_T, P, Q, g, Q_{pub}, e, \psi, H_1, H_2\}.$$
We also define $Q_{\mathsf{ID}} = H_1(\mathsf{ID})Q + Q_{pub}$.
Sign: to sign a message $M \in \{0,1\}^*$, the signer does the following:
1. picks $x \xleftarrow{R} \mathbb{Z}_p^*$ and computes $r = e(P, Q_{\mathsf{ID}})^x \in \mathbb{G}_T$,
2. sets $h = H_2(M, r) \in \mathbb{Z}_p^*$,
3. computes $S = xP + h S_{\mathsf{ID}}$.

The signature on M is $\sigma = (h, S) \in \mathbb{Z}_p^* \times \mathbb{G}_1$.
Verify: a signature $\sigma = (h, S)$ on a message M is accepted iff
$$h = H_2(M, e(S, Q_{\mathsf{ID}})g^{-h}).$$

The above IBS can be proven secure under the q-Strong Diffie-Hellman assumption. Even in its optimized version where $e(P, H_1(\mathsf{ID})Q + Q_{pub})$ is pre-computed by the signer, its signature generation algorithm happens to be slightly more expensive than our scheme's one which requires a simple scalar multiplication at step 3.

Verifier-Local Revocation Group Signature Schemes with Backward Unlinkability from Bilinear Maps

Toru Nakanishi and Nobuo Funabiki

Department of Communication Network Engineering,
Okayama University, 3-1-1 Tsushima-Naka,
Okayama 700-8530, Japan
{nakanisi, funabiki}@cne.okayama-u.ac.jp

Abstract. An approach of membership revocation in group signatures is verifier-local revocation (VLR for short). In this approach, only verifiers are involved in the revocation mechanism, while signers have no involvement. Thus, since signers have no load, this approach is suitable for mobile environments. Although Boneh and Shacham recently proposed a VLR group signature scheme from bilinear maps, this scheme does not satisfy the backward unlikability. The backward unlikability means that even after a member is revoked, signatures produced by the member before the revocation remain anonymous. In this paper, we propose VLR group signature schemes with the backward unlinkability from bilinear maps.

1 Introduction

A *group signature scheme* [10,8,1,15,2,9,16,13,6,7,14] allows a group member to anonymously sign a message on behalf of a group, where a group manager controls the membership of members. Then, often a third party can cancel the anonymity of signatures to trace the signers. Some schemes support membership revocation [15,2,9,16,6,7], where the membership of a member can be disabled without influencing the other members.

This paper focuses on the membership revocation. The simplest revocation method is that the manager changes the group public key and secret keys of all members except the revoked member to re-distribute the keys [2]. However, the other members' loads are enormous. A better solution is to broadcast a small public membership message to all signers and verifiers, as in [9,16,6]. Although the costs of signers are better, the signer still has to obtain some data depending on the size of the group (or the number of revoked members) whenever signing. On the other hand, there is another approach [15,2,7], where some revocation messages are only sent to verifiers, although the verifiers need the computational cost depending the number of revoked members. Since the signers' costs are lower, this type is suitable for mobile environments where mobile hosts anonymously communicate with the servers. We refer to this type as *Verifier-Local Revocation* (VLR for short) group signature scheme, as in [7].

B. Roy (Ed.): ASIACRYPT 2005, LNCS 3788, pp. 533–548, 2005.

In [15,2], VLR group signature schemes based on the strong RSA assumption are proposed. However, the schemes have some drawbacks on efficiency. The first scheme of [15] and the scheme of [2] suffer from the inefficiency of signing, due to the used inefficient zero-knowledge proofs. The second scheme of [15] forces a signer to compute $O(T)$ exponentiations at every time interval, where T is the total number of time intervals. Since the revocation can be performed only at the beginning of each time interval, T should be large. This means the signer's heavy load.

In [7], a VLR group signature scheme based on bilinear maps is proposed by Boneh and Shacham. The advantage of this scheme is that signatures are short, since the elliptic curves can be adopted. On the other hand, the schemes of [15,2] have an advantage over [7], *backward unlinkability*. This property means that even after a member is revoked, signatures produced by the member before the revocation remain anonymous. However, in the scheme of [7], all the signatures produced from the revoked member are linkable. This means that the anonymity of signatures produced before the revocation is compromised. In some cases that all signatures from an illegal person should be traced, the linkability is useful, as well as *traceable signatures* in [13]. However, the linkability is undesirable in most cases. In case a member leaves voluntarily, the anonymity of signatures before leaving should be ensured. This is the same in case a member's secret key is stolen.

In this paper, we propose VLR group signature schemes from bilinear maps, which moreover satisfy the backward unlinkability. In the schemes, the concept of time intervals is adopted, as [15]. For each member, there are revocation tokens of all intervals $1, \ldots, T$. When a revocation happens at interval j^*, the revocation tokens of the member at all $j \geq j^*$ are sent to verifiers. Then, signatures after j^* (including j^*) can be detected, while signatures before j^* remain anonymous. Therefore, the backward unlinkability holds. Since the proposed schemes adopt only efficient zero-knowledge proofs, signing process is efficient. Moreover, a signer does not need any computation depending on T.

We first propose a basic VLR group signatures scheme, and prove the security. In the basic scheme, a group manager publishes revocation tokens at every interval. Thus, the total data of the revocation tokens published up to a proceeded interval becomes very long. Therefore, we propose an extended scheme, where the total data size is reduced at the sacrifice of the signer's slight cost.

2   Model and Security Definitions

We show a model of VLR group signature scheme with backward unlinkability, which is extended from a model of VLR group signature scheme proposed in [7].

Definition 1. *A VLR group signature scheme with backward unlinkability consists of the following algorithms:*

KeyGen(n, T)**:** *It is a probabilistic algorithm on inputs n, which is the number of members, and T, which is the number of time intervals. It outputs a group public key gpk, an n-element vector of members' secret keys* **gsk** $=$

$(\boldsymbol{gsk}[1], \ldots, \boldsymbol{gsk}[n])$, and an $n \times T$-element vector of revocation tokens $\boldsymbol{grt} = (\boldsymbol{grt}[1][1], \ldots, \boldsymbol{grt}[n][T])$, where $\boldsymbol{grt}[i][j]$ indicates the token of member i at time interval j.

Sign$(gpk, j, \boldsymbol{gsk}[i], M)$**:** This takes as inputs the group public key gpk, the current time interval j, a secret key $\boldsymbol{gsk}[i]$, and a message $M \in \{0,1\}^*$, and outputs the signature σ.

Verify$(gpk, j, RL_j, \sigma, M)$**:** This takes as inputs gpk, j, a set of the revocation tokens RL_j at the time interval j, a signature σ, and the message M. Then, it outputs either valid or invalid. The validity means that σ is a correct signature on M at interval j w.r.t. gpk, and that the signer is not revoked at the interval j.

Remark 1. In practice, algorithm **KeyGen** is performed by a trusted group manager. The manager gives each $\boldsymbol{gsk}[i]$ to each group member indexed by i, who can compute a group signature using algorithm **Sign**. Furthermore, at each interval j, the manager distributes revocation list RL_j, which consists of tokens $\boldsymbol{grt}[i][j]$ for all revoked members at j, to verifiers. The verifiers can verify a group signature using algorithm **Verify**.

Then, the security requirements, *Correctness*, *Traceability*, and *BU-anonymity*, are defined as follows, which are also extended from [7].

Definition 2 (Correctness). *Correctness requires that for all* $(gpk, \boldsymbol{gsk}, \boldsymbol{grt}) =$ **KeyGen**(n, T), *all* $j \in [1, T]$, *all* RL_j, *all* $i \in [1, n]$, *and all* $M \in \{0,1\}^*$,

$$\textbf{Verify}(gpk, j, RL_j, \textbf{Sign}(gpk, j, \boldsymbol{gsk}[i], M), M) = \text{valid} \iff \boldsymbol{grt}[i][j] \notin RL_j.$$

As well as [7], we introduce implicit tracing algorithm: For any interval j, using the revocation token $\boldsymbol{grt}[i][j]$ of all members, the implicit tracing algorithm can trace the signer from a valid signature-message pair (σ, M).

The following traceability requirement captures the unforgeability of group signatures, introduced first by [3]. Consider the following traceability game between an adversary $\mathcal{A}$ and a challenger, where $\mathcal{A}$ tries to forge a signature that cannot be traced to one of members corrupted by $\mathcal{A}$.

Setup: The challenger runs **KeyGen**(n, T), and obtains $gpk, \boldsymbol{gsk}$, and $\boldsymbol{grt}$. He provides $\mathcal{A}$ with gpk and $\boldsymbol{grt}$, and sets U with empty.

Queries: $\mathcal{A}$ can query the challenger about the following.

    Signing: $\mathcal{A}$ requests a signature on an arbitrary message M for an arbitrary member i at an arbitrary interval j. The challenger responds the corresponding signature.

    Corruption: $\mathcal{A}$ requests the secret key of an arbitrary member i. The challenger adds i to U, and responds the key.

Output: Finally, $\mathcal{A}$ outputs a message M^*, an interval j^*, a set $RL_{j^*}^*$ of revocation tokens, and a signature σ^*.

Then, $\mathcal{A}$ wins if (1) **Verify**$(gpk, j^*, RL_{j^*}^*, \sigma^*, M^*) = $ valid, and (2) σ^* traces to a member outside of the coalition, i.e, $U \setminus RL_{j^*}^*$ or the trace is failure, and (3) $\mathcal{A}$ did not obtain σ^* by making a signing query at M^*.

Definition 3 (Traceability). *Traceability requires that for all PPT $\mathcal{A}$, the probability that $\mathcal{A}$ wins the traceability game is negligible.*

The following BU-anonymity requirement captures the anonymity with the backward unlinkability. Consider the following BU-anonymity game.

Setup: The challenger runs **KeyGen**(n, T), and obtains $gpk, \boldsymbol{gsk}$, and $\boldsymbol{grt}$. He provides $\mathcal{A}$ with gpk.

Queries: At the beginning of every interval $j \in [1, T]$, the challenger announces the beginning of j to $\mathcal{A}$, where j is incremented. At the current interval j, $\mathcal{A}$ can query the challenger about the following.

    Signing: $\mathcal{A}$ requests a signature on an arbitrary message M for an arbitrary member i at the current interval j. The challenger responds the corresponding signature.

    Corruption: $\mathcal{A}$ requests the secret key of an arbitrary member i.

    Revocation: $\mathcal{A}$ requests the revocation of an arbitrary member i at the current interval j. The challenger responds $\boldsymbol{grt}[i][j]$.

Challenge: $\mathcal{A}$ outputs a message M and two members i_0 and i_1. The corruption of i_0 and i_1 must not be requested. Furthermore, the revocations of i_0 and i_1 must not be requested before the current interval j_0 (including j_0). The challenger chooses $\phi \in_R \{0, 1\}$, and responds the signature on M of member i_ϕ at the current interval j_0.

Restricted queries: Similarly, $\mathcal{A}$ can make the signing queries, corruption queries, and revocation queries, while the time interval is incremented. However, $\mathcal{A}$ cannot query the corruptions of i_0 and i_1, and the revocations of i_0 and i_1 at the interval j_0 (Note that the revocations of i_0 and i_1 after j_0 is permitted).

Output: Finally, $\mathcal{A}$ outputs a bit ϕ' indicating its guess of ϕ.

If $\phi' = \phi$, $\mathcal{A}$ wins. We define the advantage of $\mathcal{A}$ as $|\Pr[\phi' = \phi] - 1/2|$.

Definition 4 (BU-anonymity). *BU-anonymity requires that for all PPT $\mathcal{A}$, the advantage of $\mathcal{A}$ on the BU-anonymity game is negligible.*

3   Preliminaries

3.1   Bilinear Groups

Our scheme utilizes bilinear groups and bilinear maps as follows:

1. G_1, G_2 and G' are multiplicative cyclic groups of prime order p,
2. g_1 is a generator of G_1, and g_2 is a generator of G_2,
3. ψ is an efficiently computed isomorphism from G_2 to G_1, with $\psi(g_2) = g_1$,
4. e is an efficiently computed bilinear map: $G_1 \times G_2 \to G'$, i.e., (1) for all $u \in G_1, v \in G_2$ and $a, b \in Z$, $e(u^a, v^b) = e(u, v)^{ab}$, and (2) $e(g_1, g_2) \neq 1$.

Hereafter, for simplicity, we consider only the case of $G_1 = G_2$, and we set $G = G_1 = G_2$, and $g = g_1 = g_2$. Our scheme can be extended to the case of $G_1 \neq G_2$, as [7].

3.2   Assumptions

Our scheme is based on the q-SDH assumption [6,7] and the DBDH assumption [4] in G.

Definition 5 (q-SDH assumption). *For all PPT algorithm $\mathcal{A}$, the probability*

$$\Pr[\mathcal{A}(g, g^\gamma, \ldots, g^{(\gamma^q)}) = (g^{(1/\gamma+x)}, x) \wedge x \in Z_p^*]$$

is negligible, where $\gamma \in_R Z_p^*$.

Definition 6 (Decision BDH (DBDH) assumption). *For all PPT algorithm $\mathcal{A}$, the probability*

$$|\Pr[\mathcal{A}(g, g^a, g^b, g^c, e(g,g)^{abc}) = 0] - \Pr[\mathcal{A}(g, g^a, g^b, g^c, e(g,g)^d) = 0]|$$

is negligible, where $a, b, c, d \in_R Z_p^*$.

3.3   Proving Relations on Representations

As well as [6,7], we adopt signatures converted by Fiat-Shamir heuristic (using a hash function) from zero-knowledge proofs of knowledge (PK), where a signer can convince a verifier of knowledge with relations on representations. We call the signatures SPKs. The SPKs we adopt are the generalization of the Schnorr signature, and the underlying PKs are basically derived from [11,12,8]. We introduce the following notation.

$$SPK\{(x_1, \ldots, x_t) : R(x_1, \ldots, x_t)\}(M),$$

which means a signature of message M by a signer who knows secret values $x_1, \ldots, x_t$ satisfying a relation $R(x_1, \ldots, x_t)$. In this paper, the following SPKs on G, G' are utilized.

SPK **of representation:** An SPK proving the knowledge of a representation of $C \in G$ to the bases $g_1, g_2, \ldots, g_t \in G$ on message M is denoted as

$$SPK\{(x_1, \ldots, x_t) : C = g_1^{x_1} \cdots g_t^{x_t}\}(M).$$

This can be also constructed on group G'.

SPK **of representations with equal parts:** An SPK proving the knowledge of representations of $C, C' \in G$ to the bases $g_1, \ldots, g_t \in G$ on message M, where the representations include equal values as parts, is denoted as

$$SPK\{(x_1, \ldots, x_u) : C = g_{i_1}^{x_{j_1}} \cdots g_{i_v}^{x_{j_v}} \wedge C' = g_{i_1'}^{x_{j_1'}} \cdots g_{i_{v'}'}^{x_{j_{v'}'}}\}(M),$$

where indices $i_1, \ldots i_v, i_1', \ldots i_{v'}' \in \{1, \ldots, t\}$ refer to the bases $g_1, \ldots, g_t$, and indices $j_1, \ldots j_v, j_1', \ldots, j_{v'}' \in \{1, \ldots, u\}$ refer to the secrets $x_1, \ldots, x_u$. This SPK can be extended for different groups G and G' with the same order p, as follows.

$$SPK\{(x_1, \ldots, x_u) : C = g_{i_1}^{x_{j_1}} \cdots g_{i_v}^{x_{j_v}} \wedge C' = g_{i_1'}'^{x_{j_1}} \cdots g_{i_{v'}'}'^{x_{j_{v'}'}}\}(M),$$

where $C, g_1, \ldots, g_t \in G$, and $C', g_1', \ldots, g_t' \in G'$.

In the random oracle model, the SPK can be simulated without the knowledge using a simulator in the zero-knowledge-ness of the underlying PK. Moreover, the SPK has an extractor of the proved secret knowledge given two accepting protocol views whose commitments are the same and whose challenges are different.

4   Proposed Scheme

4.1   Idea

The scheme of [7] is intuitively as follows. For group public key $gpk = (g, g^\gamma)$, an SDH pair $(A_i = g^{1/(\gamma+x_i)}, x_i)$ is secret key $gsk[i]$ of member i, which is unforgeable without γ. Then, group signature of member i consists of $T_1 = u^r A_i$ and $T_2 = v^r$, where $u, v \in_R G$ and $r \in_R Z_p^*$, and the SPK proving the correctness. The revocation token of member i is A_i. By checking $e(T_1/A, v) = e(u, T_2)$ for all revocation tokens A, it can be checked whether T_1 includes a token of a revoked member.

The proposed scheme is an extension of [7]. To the public key, we add $h_j \in G$ for all $1 \le j \le T$, and the secret key is the same. Then, the group signature is modified into $T_3 = e(g^{x_i}, h_j)^r$, $T_4 = g^r$ and the SPK proving the correctness and the ownership of A_i corresponding x_i. The revocation token at interval j is $B_{ij} = h_j^{x_i}$. Then, by checking $T_3 = e(T_4, B)$ for all revocation tokens B at interval j, it can be checked whether T_3 includes a token of a revoked member. On the other hand, the revocation tokens at different interval j' do not satisfy the above checking. Moreover, the computation from a token $h_j^{x_i}$ at j to another $h_{j'}^{x_i}$ at j' is infeasible. Therefore, backward unlinkability is achieved.

4.2   Proposed Algorithms

KeyGen(n, T): This key generation algorithm is given the number of members and the number of time intervals, and computes keys as follows.

1. Select a generator $g \in G$ and $\tilde{g} \in_R G$. Additionally, select $h_j \in_R G$ for all $j \in [1, T]$.
2. Select $\gamma \in_R Z_p^*$ and compute $w = g^\gamma$.
3. Select $x_i \in_R Z_p^*$ and compute $A_i = g^{1/(\gamma+x_i)}$ for all $i \in [1, n]$.
4. Compute $B_{ij} = h_j^{x_i}$ for all i and j.

The group public key gpk is $(g, \tilde{g}, h_1, \ldots h_T, w)$. Each member's secret key $gsk[i]$ is (A_i, x_i). The revocation token at interval j of member with secret (A_i, x_i) is $grt[i][j] = B_{ij}$. Output (gpk, gsk, grt).

Sign$(gpk, j, gsk[i], M)$: The inputs of this signing algorithm are $gpk = (g, \tilde{g}, h_1, \ldots h_T, w)$, the current time interval j, the signer's secret $gsk[i] = (A_i, x_i)$ and a signed message $M \in \{0, 1\}^*$. Hereafter, we assume that M includes the time interval j in order to bind the signature to the interval. The algorithm is as follows:

1. Select randoms $\alpha, \beta, \delta \in_R Z_p^*$.
2. Compute $T_1 = A_i \tilde{g}^\alpha$, $T_2 = g^\alpha \tilde{g}^\beta$, $T_3 = e(g^{x_i}, h_j)^\delta$, and $T_4 = g^\delta$.
3. Compute

$$V = SPK\{(\alpha, \beta, \delta, x_i, A_i) : T_1 = A_i \tilde{g}^\alpha \wedge T_2 = g^\alpha \tilde{g}^\beta$$
$$\wedge T_3 = e(g^{x_i}, h_j)^\delta \wedge T_4 = g^\delta$$
$$\wedge e(A_i, wg^{x_i}) = e(g, g)\}(M).$$

The detail of this SPK is shown in Section 4.3.

Output the group signature $\sigma = (T_1, T_2, T_3, T_4, V)$.

Verify(gpk, j, RL_j, σ, M): The inputs are $gpk = (g, \tilde{g}, h_1, \ldots h_T, w)$, the current time interval j, the revocation list RL_j that consists of $\mathbf{grt}[i][j]$ for all revoked i at the interval j, a target signature $\sigma = (T_1, T_2, T_3, T_4, V)$ and the message $M \in \{0, 1\}^*$.

1. **Signature check.** Check that σ is valid, by checking the SPK V.
2. **Revocation check.** Check that the signer is not revoked at the interval j, by checking $T_3 \neq e(T_4, B_{ij})$ for all $B_{ij} \in RL_j$.

4.3   Detail of the SPK

The SPK V in the algorithm **Sign** is computed as the following SPK V'.

$$V' = SPK\{(\alpha, \beta, \delta, x_i, \epsilon, \zeta, \eta) : T_2 = g^\alpha \tilde{g}^\beta \wedge 1 = T_2^{x_i}(1/g)^\epsilon (1/\tilde{g})^\zeta$$
$$\wedge e(T_1, w)(1/e(g, g)) = (1/e(T_1, g))^{x_i} e(\tilde{g}, w)^\alpha e(\tilde{g}, g)^\epsilon$$
$$\wedge T_3 = e(g, h_j)^\eta \wedge T_4 = g^\delta \wedge 1 = T_4^{x_i}(1/g)^\eta\}(M).$$

This SPK can be computed by the SPK for the representations, where $\epsilon = x_i \alpha$, $\zeta = x_i \beta$, and $\eta = x_i \delta$ are adopted.

What we require is to prove that the SPK V is equivalent to V'. The following lemma ensures the equivalence.

Lemma 1. V' is an SPK of knowledge $(\alpha, \beta, \delta, x_i, A_i)$ s.t.

$$T_1 = A_i \tilde{g}^\alpha \wedge T_2 = g^\alpha \tilde{g}^\beta \wedge T_3 = e(g^{x_i}, h_j)^\delta \wedge T_4 = g^\delta \wedge e(A_i, wg^{x_i}) = e(g, g).$$

Proof. Since V' is an SPK of knowledge $(\alpha, \beta, \delta, x_i, \epsilon, \zeta, \eta)$ s.t.

$$T_2 = g^\alpha \tilde{g}^\beta \tag{1}$$
$$1 = T_2^{x_i}(1/g)^\epsilon (1/\tilde{g})^\zeta \tag{2}$$
$$e(T_1, w)(1/e(g, g)) = (1/e(T_1, g))^{x_i} e(\tilde{g}, w)^\alpha e(\tilde{g}, g)^\epsilon \tag{3}$$
$$T_3 = e(g, h_j)^\eta \tag{4}$$
$$T_4 = g^\delta \tag{5}$$
$$1 = T_4^{x_i}(1/g)^\eta, \tag{6}$$

such knowledge can be extracted. From the equations (1), (2), the equation $g^\epsilon \tilde{g}^\zeta = g^{x_i \alpha} \tilde{g}^{x_i \beta}$ holds, and thus $\epsilon = x_i \alpha$ holds. Then, consider the following equation transformed from (3).

$$e(T_1, w) e(T_1, g)^{x_i} / e(\tilde{g}, w)^\alpha e(\tilde{g}, g)^{x_i \alpha} = e(g, g).$$

Then, from

$$e(T_1, w) e(T_1, g)^{x_i} = e(T_1, w g^{x_i}) \text{ and } e(\tilde{g}, w)^\alpha e(\tilde{g}, g)^{x_i \alpha} = e(\tilde{g}^\alpha, w g^{x_i}),$$

we obtain $e(T_1 / \tilde{g}^\alpha, w g^{x_i}) = e(g, g)$. Thus, setting $A_i = T_1 / \tilde{g}^\alpha$, we can extract knowledge x_i, A_i s.t.

$$T_1 = A_i \tilde{g}^\alpha \text{ and } e(A_i, w g^{x_i}) = e(g, g).$$

On the other hand, from equations (5), (6), we obtain $g^\eta = g^{x_i \delta}$. Therefore, from equation (4), we can extract knowledge x_i, δ s.t. $T_3 = e(g^{x_i}, h_j)^\delta$.   □

4.4 Details of Sign and Verify Algorithms

For efficiency consideration, this subsection describes the **Sign** and **Verify** algorithms of the proposed scheme in Section 4.2, where the SPKs for representations shown in Section 4.3 are described in details. The construction of each SPK for a representation is similar to that in [7] or Schnorr based SPKs on groups with known orders. Thus, we omit the proof that underlying PKs of following SPKs are zero-knowledge proofs of knowledge.

Sign$(gpk, j, \boldsymbol{gsk}[i], M)$:

1. Select randoms $\alpha, \beta, \delta \in_R Z_p^*$, and set $\epsilon = x_i \alpha$, $\zeta = x_i \beta$, and $\eta = x_i \delta$.
2. Compute $T_1 = A_i \tilde{g}^\alpha$, $T_2 = g^\alpha \tilde{g}^\beta$, $T_3 = e(g^{x_i}, h_j)^\delta$, and $T_4 = g^\delta$.
3. Compute SPK V' (i.e., V) as follows.
   (a) Pick blinding factors $r_\alpha, r_\beta, r_\delta, r_{x_i}, r_\epsilon, r_\zeta, r_\eta \in_R Z_p$.
   (b) Compute

$$R_1 = g^{r_\alpha} \tilde{g}^{r_\beta},$$
$$R_2 = T_2^{r_{x_i}} (1/g)^{r_\epsilon} (1/\tilde{g})^{r_\zeta},$$
$$R_3 = (1/e(T_1, g))^{r_{x_i}} e(\tilde{g}, w)^{r_\alpha} e(\tilde{g}, g)^{r_\epsilon},$$
$$R_4 = e(g, h_j)^{r_\eta},$$
$$R_5 = g^{r_\delta},$$
$$R_6 = T_4^{r_{x_i}} (1/g)^{r_\eta}.$$

   (c) Compute a challenge $c \in Z_p$ using a hash function H that is regarded as a random oracle.

$$c = H(gpk, j, M, T_1, T_2, T_3, T_4, R_1, R_2, R_3, R_4, R_5, R_6).$$

   (d) Compute $s_\alpha = r_\alpha + c\alpha$, $s_\beta = r_\beta + c\beta$, $s_\delta = r_\delta + c\delta$, $s_{x_i} = r_{x_i} + cx_i$, $s_\epsilon = r_\epsilon + c\epsilon$, $s_\zeta = r_\zeta + c\zeta$, and $s_\eta = r_\eta + c\eta$ in Z_p.

Output the group signature $\sigma = (T_1, T_2, T_3, T_4, c, s_\alpha, s_\beta, s_\delta, s_{x_i}, s_\epsilon, s_\zeta, s_\eta)$.

Verify$(gpk, j, RL_j, \sigma, M)$:

1. **Signature check.** Check that σ is valid, by checking the $SPK\ V'$, as follows.
   (a) Retrieve

$$
\tilde{R}_1 = g^{s_\alpha} \tilde{g}^{s_\beta} (1/T_2)^c,
$$
$$
\tilde{R}_2 = T_2^{s_{x_i}} (1/g)^{s_\epsilon} (1/\tilde{g})^{s_\zeta},
$$
$$
\tilde{R}_3 = (1/e(T_1, g))^{s_{x_i}} e(\tilde{g}, w)^{s_\alpha} e(\tilde{g}, g)^{s_\epsilon} ((1/e(T_1, w))e(g,g))^c,
$$
$$
\tilde{R}_4 = e(g, h_j)^{s_\eta} (1/T_3)^c,
$$
$$
\tilde{R}_5 = g^{s_\delta} (1/T_4)^c,
$$
$$
\tilde{R}_6 = T_4^{s_{x_i}} (1/g)^{s_\eta}.
$$

   (b) Check the challenge c:

$$
c = H(gpk, j, M, T_1, T_2, T_3, T_4, \tilde{R}_1, \tilde{R}_2, \tilde{R}_3, \tilde{R}_4, \tilde{R}_5, \tilde{R}_6).
$$

2. **Revocation check.** Check that the signer is not revoked at the interval j, by checking $T_3 \neq e(T_4, B_{ij})$ for all $B_{ij} \in RL_j$.

Signature Length. This group signature includes 3 elements from G, 1 element from G' and 8 elements from Z_p. When an elliptic curve is used as well as [7], p is 170 bits, elements of G are 171 bits, and elements of G' is 1020 bits. In that case, this group signature is 2893 bits or 362 bytes.

Performance. The signature generation requires 10 multi-exponentiations and 1 bilinear map computation (plus 3 bilinear map computations that can be pre-computed). The verification requires 6 multi-exponentiations and $2 + |RL_j|$ bilinear map computations (plus 4 bilinear map computations that can be pre-computed).

5   Security

Since the correctness is straightforward, only BU-anonymity and traceability are shown.

5.1   BU-Anonymity

Theorem 1. *The proposed scheme satisfies the BU-anonymity in the random oracle model under the DBDH assumption.*

The following lemma implies the above theorem.

Lemma 2. *Suppose adversary $\mathcal{A}$ breaks the BU-anonymity of the proposed scheme with the advantage ϵ and q_H hash queries and q_S signature queries. Then, we can construct $\mathcal{B}$ that breaks the DBDH assumption with the advantage $(1/nT - q_S q_H/p)\epsilon$.*

Proof. The input of $\mathcal{B}$ is $(g, g_1 = g^a, g_2 = g^b, g_3 = g^c, Z)$, where $a, b, c \in_R Z_p^*$ and either $Z = e(g, g)^{abc}$ or $Z = e(g, g)^d$ for $d \in_R Z_p^*$. $\mathcal{B}$ decides which Z it is given by communicating with $\mathcal{A}$, as follows.

Setup. $\mathcal{B}$ simulates **KeyGen**(n, T) as follows.

1. $\mathcal{B}$ picks $i^* \in_R [1, n]$ and $j^* \in_R [1, T]$.
   Furthermore, $\mathcal{B}$ selects $\tilde{g} \in_R G$. Additionally, $\mathcal{B}$ selects $r_j \in_R Z_p^*$ and computes $h_j = g^{r_j}$ for all $j \in [1, T]$ except j^*. For j^*, $\mathcal{B}$ sets $h_{j^*} = g_2 = g^b$.

2. As usual, $\mathcal{B}$ selects $\gamma \in_R Z_p^*$ and computes $w = g^\gamma$.

3. As usual, $\mathcal{B}$ selects $x_i \in_R Z_p^*$ and computes $A_i = g^{1/(\gamma + x_i)}$ for all $i \in [1, n]$ except i^*. For i^*, define $x_{i^*} = a$ and $A_{i^*} = g^{1/(\gamma + a)}$, which are unknown for $\mathcal{B}$.

4. As usual, $\mathcal{B}$ computes $B_{ij} = h_j^{x_i}$ for all i except i^* and all j. For i^*, $\mathcal{B}$ sets $B_{i^* j} = g_1^{r_j} = g^{a r_j} = h_j^a$ except for j^*. For i^* and j^*, define $B_{i^* j^*} = g^{ab} = h_{j^*}^{x_{i^*}}$, which is also unknown.

   Note that simulated h_j and B_{ij} have the same distributions as the real, since $a, b, x_i, r_j \in_R Z_p^*$.

Hash queries. At any time, $\mathcal{A}$ can query the hash function used in SPK. $\mathcal{B}$ responds with random values with consistency.

Phase 1. $\mathcal{A}$ can request signing queries, corruption queries, and revocation queries at any time interval j. If $i \neq i^*$, then $\mathcal{B}$ uses the secret key of i to respond to the query as usual. If $i = i^*$, $\mathcal{B}$ responds as follows.

Signing queries: $\mathcal{B}$ computes a simulated group signature of i^*, as follows.

1. $\mathcal{B}$ selects $\delta \in_R Z_p^*$.

2. $\mathcal{B}$ selects $T_1, T_2 \in_R G$. Furthermore, $\mathcal{B}$ computes $T_3 = e(g_1, h_j)^\delta = e(g^a, h_j)^\delta = e(g^{x_{i^*}}, h_j)^\delta$, and $T_4 = g^\delta$.

3. $\mathcal{B}$ computes the simulated SPK V by using the simulator of the perfect zero-knowledge-ness, which includes the backpatch of the hash function. If the backpatch is failure, $\mathcal{B}$ outputs a random guess $\omega' \in_R \{0, 1\}$ and aborts.

   Then, $\mathcal{B}$ responds signature $\sigma = (T_1, T_2, T_3, T_4, V)$ to $\mathcal{A}$. Note that each value in σ has the same distribution as the real, since $\alpha, \beta \in_R Z_p^*$ in the real and $T_1, T_2 \in_R G$ in the simulation, and due to the perfect zero-knowledge-ness of SPK.

Revocation queries: If $j \neq j^*$, $\mathcal{B}$ responds $B_{i^* j}$. Otherwise (i.e., $j = j^*$), $\mathcal{B}$ outputs a random guess $\omega' \in_R \{0, 1\}$ and aborts.

Corruption queries: $\mathcal{B}$ outputs a random guess $\omega' \in_R \{0, 1\}$ and aborts.

Challenge. $\mathcal{A}$ outputs a message M, the current time interval j and two members i_0, i_1 to be challenged. If $j \neq j^*$, $\mathcal{B}$ outputs a random guess $\omega' \in_R \{0, 1\}$ and aborts. Otherwise, $\mathcal{B}$ picks $\phi \in_R \{0, 1\}$. Then, if $i_\phi \neq i^*$, $\mathcal{B}$ outputs a random guess $\omega' \in_R \{0, 1\}$ and aborts. Otherwise, $\mathcal{B}$ responds the following simulated group signature of i^* and j^*.

1. $\mathcal{B}$ regards c as δ, which is unknown.
2. $\mathcal{B}$ selects $T_1, T_2 \in_R G$. Furthermore, $\mathcal{B}$ sets $T_3 = Z$ and $T_4 = g_3 = g^c$.
   Note that if $Z = e(g,g)^{abc}$, $T_3 = e(g^a, g^b)^c = e(g^{x_{i*}}, h_{j*})^\delta$.
3. $\mathcal{B}$ computes the simulated $SPK\ V$ by using the simulator of the perfect zero-knowledge-ness.

Phase 2. This is the same as Phase 1.

Output. $\mathcal{A}$ outputs its guess $\phi' \in \{0,1\}$. If $\phi = \phi'$, $\mathcal{B}$ outputs $\omega' = 1$ (implying $Z = (g,g)^{abc}$), and otherwise outputs $\omega' = 0$ (implying $Z = (g,g)^d$).

Now, we evaluate the advantage of the guess of $\mathcal{B}$. Let $\omega \in \{0,1\}$ denote whether the input Z is $e(g,g)^d$ ($\omega = 0$) or $e(g,g)^{abc}$ ($\omega = 1$). Let **abort** be the event that $\mathcal{B}$ aborts. Then, we have $\Pr[\omega = \omega' | \textbf{abort}] = 1/2$. On the other hand, assume that $\mathcal{B}$ does not abort. If $\omega = 0$, i.e., $Z = e(g,g)^d$, then the challenged signature has no information on x_{i*}. Thus, $\Pr[\omega' = 0 | \overline{\textbf{abort}} \wedge \omega = 0] = 1/2$. If $\omega = 1$, i.e., $Z = e(g,g)^{abc}$, then $\mathcal{B}$ perfectly simulates the real and thus $\mathcal{A}$ guesses correctly with the advantage ϵ. Therefore, we obtain $\Pr[\omega' = 1 | \overline{\textbf{abort}} \wedge \omega = 1] = 1/2 + \epsilon$.

Putting everything together, we obtain the advantage of $\mathcal{B}$'s guess, as follows.

$$\begin{aligned}
&|\Pr[\mathcal{B}(g, g^a, g^b, g^c, e(g,g)^{abc}) = 0] - \Pr[\mathcal{B}(g, g^a, g^b, g^c, e(g,g)^d) = 0]| \\
&= |\Pr[\omega' = 0 | \omega = 1] - \Pr[\omega' = 0 | \omega = 0]| \\
&= |(1 - \Pr[\omega' = 1 | \omega = 1]) - \Pr[\omega' = 0 | \omega = 0]| \\
&= |1 - \Pr[\textbf{abort}]\Pr[\omega' = 1 | \textbf{abort} \wedge \omega = 1] \\
&\quad - \Pr[\overline{\textbf{abort}}]\Pr[\omega' = 1 | \overline{\textbf{abort}} \wedge \omega = 1] \\
&\quad - \Pr[\textbf{abort}]\Pr[\omega' = 0 | \textbf{abort} \wedge \omega = 0] \\
&\quad - \Pr[\overline{\textbf{abort}}]\Pr[\omega' = 0 | \overline{\textbf{abort}} \wedge \omega = 0]| \\
&= |1 - \Pr[\textbf{abort}](\frac{1}{2} + \frac{1}{2}) - \Pr[\overline{\textbf{abort}}]((\frac{1}{2} + \epsilon) + \frac{1}{2})| \\
&= \Pr[\overline{\textbf{abort}}]\epsilon.
\end{aligned}$$

In the rest, we evaluate $\Pr[\overline{\textbf{abort}}]$. If the guesses of i^* and j^* are correct, $\mathcal{B}$ aborts only when the backpatch is failure in the signing query. The probability that a specific signature causes the failure is at most q_H/p, as well as [7]. Thus, for all signature queries, the probability that $\mathcal{B}$ aborts due to the failure of the backpatch is at most $q_S q_H/p$. On the other hand, since $\mathcal{A}$ has no information on i^* and j^* and $\phi \in_R \{0,1\}$, the probability that $\mathcal{B}$ correctly guesses i^* and j^* is at least $1/nT$. Thus, $\Pr[\overline{\textbf{abort}}] \geq 1/nT - q_S q_H/p$.

Therefore, the advantage that $\mathcal{B}$' guesses ω is at least $(1/nT - q_S q_H/p)\epsilon$. $\square$

5.2   Traceability

Theorem 2. *The proposed scheme satisfies the traceability in the random oracle model under the SDH assumption.*

The following lemma implies the above theorem.

Lemma 3. *Suppose adversary $\mathcal{A}$ breaks the traceability of the proposed scheme with the advantage ϵ and q_H hash queries and q_S signature queries. Then, we can construct $\mathcal{B}$ that breaks the $(n+1)$-SDH assumption with the advantage $(\epsilon/n - 1/p)/(16q_H)$.*

Proof sketch. This is similar to the proof in [7]. Consider the following framework with $\mathcal{A}$.

Setup. It is given g, $w = g^\gamma$, and n pairs (A_i, x_i). For each $i \in [1, n]$, either $s_i = 1$ indicating that an SDH pair (A_i, x_i) is known, or $s_i = 0$ indicating that x_i is known but A_i is unknown. Furthermore, as usual, choose $\tilde{g}, h_j \in_R G$ for all $j \in [1, T]$ and compute $B_{ij} = h_j^{x_i}$ for all i, j. Then, run $\mathcal{A}$ on $gpk = (g, \tilde{g}, h_1, \ldots, h_T, w)$ and $\boldsymbol{grt} = (B_{11}, \ldots, B_{nT})$.

Hash queries. At any time, $\mathcal{A}$ can query the hash function used in SPK. Respond with random values with consistency.

Signing queries. $\mathcal{A}$ queries a signature on message M at member i and interval j. If $s_i = 1$, respond a signature using the secret key (A_i, x_i). If $s_i = 0$, pick $T_1, T_2 \in_R G$ and $\delta \in_R Z_p^*$ and compute $T_3 = e(g^{x_i}, h_j)^\delta$ and $T_4 = g^\delta$. Furthermore, obtain a simulated SPK V using the simulator of the SPK, which includes the backpatch of the hash function. Respond (T_1, T_2, T_3, T_4, V).

Corruption queries. $\mathcal{A}$ requests the secret key at member i. If $s_i = 0$, then abort. Otherwise, respond requested key (A_i, x_i).

Output. Finally, $\mathcal{A}$ outputs a forged signature $\sigma^* = (T_1^*, T_2^*, T_3^*, T_4^*, V^*)$ including a secret key A^*. Using all B_{ij}, we can identify the member. If the identification fails (i.e., the member is outside of all i), output σ. Otherwise, some i is identified. If $s_i = 0$, then output σ. Otherwise (i.e., $s_i = 1$), abort.

Then, there are two types of forger on the above framework. Type 1 forger forges a signature of the member who is different from all i. Type 2 forger forges a signature of the member i whose corruption is not requested.

For q-SDH instance $(g, g^\gamma, \ldots, g^{\gamma^q})$, we can obtain $g, w = g^\gamma$ and $q - 1$ SDH pairs (A_i, x_i) s.t. $e(A_i, g^{x_i} w) = e(g, g)$, using the technique of [5]. On the other hand, any SDH pair besides these $q - 1$ pairs can be transformed a solution of the q-SDH instance, which means that the q-SDH assumption is broken, using the same technique. As well as [7], we treat two types of forger differently.

Type 1. Given $(n+1)$-SDH instance, obtain n SDH pairs (A_i, x_i) with (g, w). Then, perform the framework with Type 1 forger $\mathcal{A}$ (i.e., all $s_i = 1$). $\mathcal{A}$ finally outputs a signature with secret key A^* s.t. $A^* \neq A_i$ for all i. In this case, the simulation is perfect, and thus $\mathcal{A}$ succeeds with advantage ϵ.

Type 2. Given n-SDH instance, obtain $n-1$ SDH pairs (A_i, x_i), which distributes n pairs, and set $s_i = 1$. For the unfilled entry at random index i^*, select $x_{i^*} \in_R Z_p^*$ (A_{i^*} is unknown), and set $s_{i^*} = 0$. Then, perform the framework with type 2 forger $\mathcal{A}$. In this case, it succeeds only if $\mathcal{A}$ never requests the corruption of i^*, but forges the signature including A_{i^*}. As discussed in [7], the value of i^* is independent $\mathcal{A}$'s view. Thus, the probability that $\mathcal{A}$ outputs the signature of i^* is at least ϵ/n.

Now we show how to obtain another SDH pair beyond the given $q-1$ SDH pairs, using the framework with Type 1 or Type2. We can rewind the framework to obtain two forged signatures on the same message M and the same interval j, where the commitments in the $SPK\ V$ are the same but the challenges and responses are different. As shown in [7], by the forking lemma, the successful probability is at least $(\epsilon'-1/p)^2/(16q_H)$, where ϵ' is the probability that the framework on each forger succeeds. Thus, using the extractor of the $SPK\ V$, we can obtain a pair (A^*, x^*) s.t. $A^* \neq A_i$ and $x^* \neq x_i$ for all i with the probability $(\epsilon'-1/p)^2/(16q_H)$.

Putting everything together, we have shown the following. Using Type 1 forger, we can solve the $(n+1)$-SDH instance with $(\epsilon-1/p)^2(16/q_H)$. Using Type 2 forger, we can solve the n-SDH instance with $(\epsilon/n-1/p)^2(16/q_H)$. We can guess the type of forger with the probability $1/2$. Therefore, the pessimistic Type 2 forger proves the theorem.   □

6   Extension

In practice, the revocation tokens $B_{ij} \in RL_j$ are published at the beginning of each interval j, where the group manager adds the revocation tokens to a public directory. Verifiers fetch needed RL_j from the directory on demand. Since the revocation can be performed only at the beginning of each interval, parameter T should be large. Furthermore, it is general that the list RL_j becomes longer as interval j proceeds. Therefore, all data in the public directory at a proceeded interval j, i.e., $RL_1, \ldots, RL_j$ becomes very long.

In this section, we propose an extended scheme, where the data size of the published revocation tokens in the public directory is reduced at the sacrifice of the signer's slight cost.

At first, modify $h_1, \ldots, h_T$ as follows. Consider a k-ary tree with two levels for an integer k s.t. $T \leq k^2$ (see Fig. 1). Although we show only the case of two levels, the extension to more levels is easy. In the tree, the root node is N_0, N_{j_1} is the j_1-th child of N_0, and $N_{j_1 j_2}$ is the j_2-th child of N_{j_1}, for $j_1, j_2 \in [1, k]$. Each node N_{j_1} is assigned to $h_{j_1} \in_R G$, and each node $N_{j_1 j_2}$ is assigned to

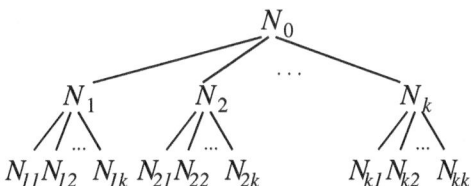

Fig. 1. A k-ary tree with two levels

$h_{j_1 j_2} \in_R G$. In this situation, every interval $j \in [1, T]$ can be correspondent to a pair of two indexes j_1 and j_2 for $j_1, j_2 \in [1, k]$ such that $j = j_1 k + j_2$. Then, the next interval of (j_1, j_2) is $(j_1, j_2 + 1)$ unless $j_2 \neq k$, and if $j_2 = k$, the next interval is $(j_1 + 1, 1)$. In each interval (j_1, j_2), the values h_{j_1} and $h_{j_1 j_2}$ along the path are used.

A group signature on message M by member i at interval (j_1, j_2) is computed as $T_1 = A_i \tilde{g}^\alpha$, $T_2 = g^\alpha \tilde{g}^\beta$, $T_3 = e(g^{x_i}, h_{j_1})^\delta$, $T_4 = g^\delta$, $T_3' = e(g^{x_i}, h_{j_1 j_2})^{\delta'}$, and $T_4' = g^{\delta'}$ for $\alpha, \beta, \delta, \delta' \in_R Z_p^*$, together with the following SPK V.

$$\begin{aligned} V = SPK\{(\alpha, \beta, \delta, \delta', x_i, A_i) : & T_1 = A_i \tilde{g}^\alpha \wedge T_2 = g^\alpha \tilde{g}^\beta \\ & \wedge T_3 = e(g^{x_i}, h_{j_1})^\delta \wedge T_4 = g^\delta \\ & \wedge T_3' = e(g^{x_i}, h_{j_1 j_2})^{\delta'} \wedge T_4' = g^{\delta'} \\ & \wedge e(A_i, wg^{x_i}) = e(g, g)\}(M). \end{aligned}$$

The difference between the basic scheme and this extended scheme is the parts T_3, T_4, T_3', T_4' and V. On the other hand, revocation token $B_{i(j_1, j_2)}$ for member i at interval (j_1, j_2) is a pair $(B_{ij_1} = h_{j_1}^{x_i}, B_{ij_1 j_2} = h_{j_1 j_2}^{x_i})$. Then, for $B_{ij_1 j_2}$, by checking $T_3' = e(T_4', B_{ij_1 j_2})$, it can be detected whether a group signature was made by member i at interval (j_1, j_2). On the other hand, for B_{ij_1}, by checking $T_3 = e(T_4, B_{ij_1})$, group signatures of i at intervals $(j_1, *)$ can be detected, where $*$ means any value of $[1, k]$. Namely, one level of tokens (the upper level, tokens of the form B_{ij_1}) allows to revoke an user during $k \approx \sqrt{T}$ time intervals at once.

Consider how to publish the revocation tokens as follows. Assume that member i is revoked at interval (j_1^*, j_2^*). Then, if $j_2^* \neq 1$, the manager publishes $B_{ij_1^* j_2^*} = h_{j_1^* j_2^*}^{x_i}$ in the public directory. Afterward, at each interval (j_1^*, j_2) s.t. $j_2^* < j_2 \leq k$, the manager similarly publishes $B_{ij_1^* j_2}$. After that, at every interval $(j_1, 1)$ s.t. $j_1^* < j_1 \leq k$, the manager publishes $B_{ij_1} = h_{j_1}^{x_i}$. Note that the manager does not publish $B_{ij_1 j_2}$ any longer. If $j_2^* = 1$, B_{ij_1} is only published at every interval $(j_1, 1)$ for $j_1^* \leq j_1 \leq k$.

In the extended scheme, the manager has only to publish revocation tokens per $k \approx \sqrt{T}$ intervals, except for the initial overhead (i.e., the publication of $B_{ij_1^* j_2^*}$). Thus, the total size of revocation tokens in public directory is sufficiently reduced. On the other hand, the signer has to compute T_3', T_4' and the corresponding SPK additionally. The communication overhead is 1531 bits and the computational overhead is 6 exponentiations (plus 1 bilinear map computations that can be pre-computed). The security of the extended scheme can be easily proved in the similar way to the basic one.

7   Concluding Remarks

Based on the bilinear maps, we have proposed a VLR group signature scheme with the backward unlinkability, and extended it to a scheme where the published revocation tokens are reduced.

In the proposed scheme, after a revocation, the revoked member remains excluded forever. However, it is easily extended to the scheme where the member is excluded only for specific intervals. This property is useful in some applications.

An open problem is to construct a shorter VLR group signature scheme with the backward unlinkability. Our group signature includes an elements of G', which is longer than elements of G. It is better to construct a signature from only elements of G.

Acknowledgments

We would like to thank the anonymous reviewers for helpful comments.

References

1. G. Ateniese, J. Camenisch, M. Joye, and G. Tsudik, "A practical and provably secure coalition-resistant group signature scheme," Advances in Cryptology — CRYPTO 2000, LNCS 1880, pp.255–270, Springer–Verlag, 2000.
2. G. Ateniese, D. Song, and G. Tsudik, "Quasi-efficient revocation of group signatures," Proc. 6th Financial Cryptography Conference (FC 2002), LNCS 2357, pp.183–197, Springer–Verlag, 2003.
3. M. Bellare, D. Micciancio, and B. Warinschi, "Foundations of group signatures: Formal definitions, simplified requirements, and a construction based on general assumptions," Advances in Cryptology — EUROCRYPT 2003, LNCS 2656, pp.614–629, Springer–Verlag, 2003.
4. D. Boneh and X. Boyen, "Efficient selective-ID secure identity-based encryption without random oracles," Advances in Cryptology — EUROCRYPT 2004, LNCS 3027, pp.223–238, Springer–Verlag, 2004.
5. D. Boneh and X. Boyen, "Short signatures without random oracles," Advances in Cryptology — EUROCRYPT 2004, LNCS 3027, pp.56–73, Springer–Verlag, 2004.
6. D. Boneh, X. Boyen, and H. Shacham, "Short group signatures," Advances in Cryptology — CRYPTO 2004, LNCS 3152, pp.41–55, Springer–Verlag, 2004.
7. D. Boneh and H. Shacham, "Group signatures with verifier-local revocation," Proc. 11th ACM Conference on Computer and Communications Security (ACM-CCS '04), pp.168–177, 2004.
8. J. Camenisch and M. Stadler, "Efficient group signature schemes for large groups," Advances in Cryptology — CRYPTO '97, LNCS 1294, pp.410–424, Springer–Verlag, 1997.
9. J. Camenisch and A. Lysyanskaya, "Dynamic accumulators and application to efficient revocation of anonymous credentials," Advances in Cryptology — CRYPTO 2002, LNCS 2442, pp.61–76, Springer–Verlag, 2002.
10. D. Chaum and E. van Heijst, "Group signatures," Advances in Cryptology — EUROCRYPT '91, LNCS 547, pp.241–246, Springer–Verlag, 1991.
11. D. Chaum, J.H. Evertse, and J. van de Graaf, "An improved protocol for demonstrating possession of discrete logarithms and some generalizations," Advances in Cryptology — EUROCRYPT '87, LNCS 304, pp.127–141, Springer–Verlag, 1988.
12. D. Chaum and T.P. Pedersen, "Wallet databases with observers," Advances in Cryptology — CRYPTO '92, LNCS 740, pp.89–105, Springer–Verlag, 1993.

13. A. Kiayias, Y. Tsiounis, and M. Yung, "Traceable signatures," Advances in Cryptology — EUROCRYPT 2004, LNCS 3027, pp.571–589, Springer–Verlag, 2004.
14. L. Nguyen and R. Safavi-Naini, "A trapdoor-free and efficient group signature scheme from bilinear pairings," Advances in Cryptology — ASIACRYPT 2004, Springer–Verlag, 2004.
15. D.X. Song, "Practical forward secure group signature schemes," Proc. 8th ACM Conference on Computer and Communications Security (ACM-CCS '01), pp.225–234, 2001.
16. G. Tsudik and S. Xu, "Accumulating composites and improved group signing," Advances in Cryptology — ASIACRYPT 2003, LNCS 2894, pp.269–286, Springer–Verlag, 2003.

Modular Security Proofs for Key Agreement Protocols

Caroline Kudla* and Kenneth G. Paterson

Information Security Group,
Royal Holloway, University of London, UK
{c.j.kudla, kenny.paterson}@rhul.ac.uk

Abstract. The security of key agreement protocols has traditionally been notoriously hard to establish. In this paper we present a modular approach to the construction of proofs of security for a large class of key agreement protocols. By following a modular approach to proof construction, we hope to enable simpler and less error-prone analysis and proof generation for such key agreement protocols. The technique is compatible with Bellare-Rogaway style models as well as the more recent models of Bellare *et al.* and Canetti and Krawczyk. In particular, we show how the use of a decisional oracle can aid the construction of proofs of security for this class of protocols and how the security of these protocols commonly reduces to some form of Gap assumption.

1 Introduction

Background

The first works formalizing the notion of security for key agreement were those of Bellare and Rogaway [7,8]. Extensions have been made to these models, most notably by Blake-Wilson *et al.* [9] and later Bellare *et al.* [6]. Although these models are generally accepted as being reasonable approaches to modelling the security of key agreement protocols, in general it appears to be rather difficult to prove key agreement protocols secure in such models and only relatively few protocols have full proofs of security in these models.

A more "modular" approach to constructing key agreement protocols was advocated by Bellare, Canetti and Krawczyk [5]. This approach entails constructing a secure protocol for ideally "authenticated links", and then applying "authenticators" to all the protocol flows to obtain a protocol secure in the standard "unauthenticated links" model. A library of basic protocols and authenticators may be built up, from which many different secure key agreement protocols may be constructed.

The disadvantage of using this modular approach is that it says nothing about the security of certain very efficient protocols that are not constructed in this modular way. In addition, cryptographic primitives such as encryption, signatures or MACs are usually required to build these "authenticators" and

---

* This author is funded by Hewlett-Packard Laboratories.

B. Roy (Ed.): ASIACRYPT 2005, LNCS 3788, pp. 549–565, 2005.

the application of these "authenticators" often increases the round complexity of a protocol. Therefore the resulting protocols are also often less efficient than protocols designed without the modular approach in mind. Of course protocols constructed using this modular approach may be modified to be more efficient using various techniques, but then the security proof may no longer be valid.

However, due to the ease of designing secure protocols using this modular approach, it has subsequently been advocated in later models such as [15,16] and has been used in the design of various key agreement protocols such as [12,13,11,22]. Although the security models of [5,15,16] do not mandate a modular approach in that their definitions of security apply directly in the standard unauthenticated network model, they do not consider protocols that are not constructed in this modular fashion. Direct proofs for non-modular protocols in the standard unauthenticated network models of [5,15,16] seem to be difficult to construct.

In many environments, the benefits of being able to easily design secure protocols outweigh the possible disadvantages. However there exist environments in which efficiency is of utmost importance, and most key agreement protocols optimized for efficiency are not constructed in a modular way. Indeed we can find several efficient key agreement protocols in the literature which do not have formal proofs of security (such as protocols in [9,19,23,24,27]) or have only proofs of security in weakened models (such as protocols in [2,3,17]. Since the structure of these protocols is not compatible with the modular approach in [5], complete proofs of security for such protocols appear to be difficult to construct.

Contributions

In this paper, we consider protocols which are not designed in a modular way but which we nevertheless wish to prove secure. Since such protocols are not designed in a modular way, the proofs of security are often complicated and error-prone. We present a technique by which the proof process of a large class of key agreement protocols can be simplified.

Informally, our technique for proving the security of a protocol Π works as follows. The first step is to prove that protocol Π has a property that we call "strong partnering" (which is defined in Section 4.1). The second step is to prove that a related protocol π is secure in a highly reduced security model. Finally, as the main result of the paper, we show how the proof of security of π in the reduced model can be translated into a proof of security for Π in the full security model using a Gap assumption.

Each step above is far simpler than a single proof of security in the full security model. The result is a modular technique for constructing proofs of security for a large class of key agreement protocols which are not constructed using the modular approach presented in [5].

We then use this technique to consider various key agreement protocols in the literature previously without proofs or with incomplete proofs of security. It is possible, using our techniques, to provide full proofs of security for protocols such as [2,3,9,17,27] (possibly after slight modifications to the protocols if necessary). Due to lack of space, we focus in detail only on the long-standing Protocol 4 in [9] which was previously without proof.

We also hope that our methods will aid future designers of lightweight key agreement protocols in the formal analysis of their protocols in simplifying their task by breaking it up into components.

Related Work

Since the pioneering work of Bellare and Rogaway [7,8], many extensions and modifications have been made to the definition of secure key agreement [6,5,9,15,16,26]. The model of security in which work is a slightly modified version of the model of Bellare *et al.* [6], although analogous versions of our results also hold in the models of [7,9,15].

Our technique also makes use of Gap assumptions, as defined by Okamoto and Pointcheval [25]. Informally, a Gap problem is the problem of solving some computational problem (e.g. computational Diffie-Hellman) with the help of a corresponding decisional oracle (in this case a decisional Diffie-Hellman oracle). The decisional problem may be easy or hard; irrespective of this a Gap problem may still be defined.

Gap assumptions have recently found several applications in cryptography. In particular, Gap assumptions have been used in [1,14,20] to prove the security of certain key agreement protocols.

In this paper, we show that, if a protocol satisfies some weakened notion of security and has a specific form, then using the Gap assumption, a full proof of security can be constructed. This result holds for protocols analyzed in the Bellare-Rogaway model [7] (or its extensions [6,9]) or in the Canetti-Krawczyk model of SK-security [15].

2   Preliminaries

Following the notation of Okamoto and Pointcheval [25], we informally define a family of Gap problems.

Let $f : X \times Y \to \{0,1\}$ be any relation on sets X and Y. The *computational* problem (or *inverting* problem in the language of [25]) of f is, given $x \in X$, to compute any $y \in Y$ such that $f(x,y) = 1$ if such a y exists, or to return Fail otherwise.

The *decisional* problem of f is, given $(x,y) \in X \times Y$, to decide whether $f(x,y) = 1$ or not.

Definition 1. *The Gap problem of f is to solve the computational problem of f using an oracle which solves the decisional problem of f.*

As an example, we define the computational, decisional and Gap Diffie-Hellman problems.

Let p and q be primes where $q|p - 1$. Let G be a multiplicative subgroup of $\mathbb{Z}_p^*$, of order q, and let $g \in G$ generate G. We denote by $DL(g,h) \in \mathbb{Z}_q$ the discrete logarithm of $h \in G$ with respect to base g. So $g^{DL(g,h)} = h \bmod p$.

Given $a, b, c \in \mathbb{Z}_q$, we define the Diffie-Hellman relation f_{DH} as follows:

$$f_{DH} : (G \times G) \times G \to \{0,1\}, \text{ where } f_{DH}(g^a, g^b, g^c) = \begin{cases} 1 & \text{if } g^{ab} = g^c \\ 0 & \text{otherwise} \end{cases}$$

We can now define the computational, decisional and Gap problems of f_{DH}, better known as the computational, decisional and Gap Diffie-Hellman problems.

Computational Diffie-Hellman (CDH) Problem: Given $g^a, g^b \in G$, where $a, b \in_R \mathbb{Z}_q$, compute $g^c \in G$, such that $f_{DH}(g^a, g^b, g^c) = 1$. That is, compute $g^c = g^{ab} \bmod p$.

Decisional Diffie-Hellman (DDH) Problem: Given $g^a, g^b, g^c \in G$, where $a, b \in_R \mathbb{Z}_q$, determine whether $f_{DH}(g^a, g^b, g^c) = 1$ or not. That is, determine whether $c = ab \bmod q$ or not.

Gap Diffie-Hellman (GDH) Problem: Given $g^a, g^b \in G$ where $a, b \in_R \mathbb{Z}_q$, as well as an oracle that solves the DDH problem on G, compute $g^{ab} \bmod p$.

The corresponding assumptions are that the above problems are *hard*, that is, they are infeasible to solve in polynomial time in a security parameter used to define the problem instances.

3   The Modified Bellare-Rogaway Model

We start by defining a modified Bellare-Rogaway (mBR) model for authenticated key agreement protocols. The model follows closely the model of Bellare *et al.* [6] which extends the original Bellare-Rogaway model [7]. However we present our model in the public key setting as in the model of Blake-Wilson *et al.* [9].

The model includes a set of participant IDs $\{U\}$, where each participant has a distinct ID U, a long-term public key P_U and a long-term private key S_U. We use Π_U^i to denote the oracle modelling the ith instance of participant U. An oracle Π_U^i may accept at any time, and once accepted it should hold a role *role* $\in \{initiator, responder\}$, a partner ID *pid* (the ID of the oracle with which it assumes it is communicating), a session ID *sid* and a session key *sk*. We note that the value i is not the *sid* but rather an internal session counter for each oracle. This may act as an internal identifier for the session until the *sid* is established.

Oracles follow the rules of the protocol, responding to input messages (from the adversary). Each oracle maintains a public transcript $T_{\Pi_U^i}$ which records all messages they have sent or received as a result of queries they have answered.

3.1   The mBR Game

The security of a key agreement protocol is modelled via the following game between a challenger C and an adversary E.

C runs a Setup algorithm on a security parameter k to create the public parameters, a set of participants $\{U\}$ and oracles Π_U^i to model instances of each participant U, and to distribute long-term keys to each participant. C also randomly selects a bit b.

The model also includes an adversary E who is given all the participants' public keys and has access to all the participants' oracles as well as any random oracles in the game. E can make the following queries:

Send(U, i, M): E can send the oracle Π_U^i a message M. If oracle Π_U^i has $pid = U'$, then Π_U^i assumes that M has come from U' and responds according to the protocol. E may also make a special Send query λ to an oracle Π_U^i which instructs U to initiate a protocol run with its partner U'. An oracle Π_U^i sets $role_U = initiator$ and is called an *initiator oracle* if the first message it has received is λ. If Π_U^i did not receive a message λ as its first message, then it sets $role_U = responder$ and is called a *responder oracle*.

Reveal(U, i): this allows E to ask the oracle Π_U^i to reveal the session key (if any) it currently holds to E.

Corrupt(U): this allows E to ask participant U to reveal its long-term private key.

Oracle States. An oracle exists in one of the following possible states:

Accepted: an oracle has accepted if it decides to accept, holding a session key, after receipt of properly formulated messages.

Rejected: an oracle has rejected if it decides not to establish a session key and to abort the protocol.

State ∗: an oracle is in state ∗ if it has not made any decision to accept or reject.

Revealed: an oracle is revealed if it has answered a reveal query.

Corrupted: an oracle is corrupted if it has answered a corrupt query.

Partners. When running the protocol, if oracles Π_U^i holding (sk, sid, pid) and $\Pi_{U'}^j$ holding (sk', sid', pid') have both accepted and the following conditions hold:

1. $sid = sid'$, $sk = sk'$, $pid = U'$ and $pid' = U$,
2. $role_U = initiator$ and $role_{U'} = responder$ or vice versa,
3. No oracle in E's game besides Π_U^i or $\Pi_{U'}^j$ accepts with session ID equal to sid,

then Π_U^i and $\Pi_{U'}^j$ are said to be *partners*.

Freshness. An oracle Π_U^i is called *unfresh* if it is revealed, or it has a revealed partner, or if its partner $\Pi_{U'}^j$ was corrupted. If an oracle is not unfresh, then the oracle is *fresh*.

Test Query. E may make a polynomial number of queries in k. Then at some point E makes a special Test query to an oracle Π_U^i. This oracle must be accepted and fresh, and it answers as follows. If $b = 0$, then Π_U^i randomly chooses a session key sk and outputs it, otherwise if $b = 1$ it outputs its own session key sk_U^i.

After this point E can continue querying the oracles except that E cannot reveal or corrupt the test oracle or its partner (if it exists). Finally E outputs a guess b' for b.

E's advantage, denoted $advantage^E(k)$, is the probability that E outputs a bit b' such that $b = b'$.

3.2   Definition of Security

We define a *benign adversary* as in [7]. Informally, a benign adversary is one who simply relays messages between parties without modification. We then define secure authenticated key agreement (AKE) protocols as follows:

Definition 2. *A protocol is an mBR-secure AKE protocol if:*

1. *In the presence of the benign adversary, two oracles running the protocol both accept holding the same session key and session ID, and the session key is distributed uniformly at random on $\{0,1\}^k$; and*
2. *For any adversary E, $Advantage^E(k)$ is negligible.*

We say that protocol Π is *mBR-insecure* if it is not mBR-secure. That is, there exists an adversary E which, with non-negligible probability (in k), wins the game against challenger C. We say that such an adversary E can successfully *mBR-attack* protocol Π.

3.3   Notes on the Security Model

Our model of security is closely related to that of Bellare *et al.* [6]. However we do not explicitly distinguish between acceptance and termination as is done in [6], and we do not model perfect forward secrecy. Both of these properties can be added as in [6]. We omit them for simplicity of presentation, but our results still hold if these properties are included.

Notice that corruption in our model is simply a query to an oracle which reveals the long-term secret key held by the oracle. The adversary does not learn other internal state of the oracle and does not gain control of the oracle. Therefore a corrupted oracle may still be considered to be fresh and can therefore still be chosen as a Test oracle. This is important in order to model key compromise impersonation attacks as defined in [9], since these attacks involve oracles whose long-term private keys have been compromised but which are not under adversarial control.

The main differences between our model and the original models of Bellare and Rogaway [7] and its public key version [9], are that our model is adaptive (that is, the adversary may continue making queries after the Test query), and we define partnering via session IDs and partner IDs (as in [6]) rather than by matching conversations. We also include the possibility for corrupted oracles to be considered fresh, allowing us to model key compromise impersonation attacks. As mentioned before, our model can easily be extended to model perfect forward secrecy as well.

We direct the reader to [6] for further details of the model presented here and to [5,6,7,9,15] for details of other models illustrating different methods for dealing with partnering, corruptions and freshness.

4   Modular Construction of Security Proofs

From now on, we assume that we are only dealing with key agreement protocols that produce a *hashed session key* on completion of the protocol. By this we mean that the key agreement protocol Π specifies that the session key be computed as the hash H of some string which we call the *session string* ss_Π. We define the session string for a particular oracle $\Pi_{U'}^i$ to be $ss_{\Pi_U^i}$. We will model H as a random oracle in our security analysis.

This reliance on hashing to produce a session key does not seem to be too strong a restriction since it is fairly common to use a key derivation function to obtain a session key from a secret value established during a key agreement protocol, and this key derivation function is usually implemented via a hash function.

4.1 Protocol Partnering

When trying to establish that a protocol Π is secure in the BR-style model, we need to ensure that an adversary cannot trivially win the game defined in Section 3.1 by an attack on the partnering properties of Π.

Definition 3. *Suppose Π is a key agreement protocol. If there exists an adversary E, which when attacking Π in an mBR game defined in Section 3.1 and with non-negligible probability in the security parameter k, can make any two oracles Π_U^i and $\Pi_{U'}^j$ accept holding the same session key when they are not partners, then we say that Π has weak partnering. If Π does not have weak partnering, then we say that Π has strong partnering.*

If a protocol Π had weak partnering against an adversary E, then E could make oracles Π_U^i and $\Pi_{U'}^j$ accept holding the same session key but without being partners. The rules of the mBR game would then allow the adversary to reveal the session key held by Π_U^i, and then choose $\Pi_{U'}^j$ as the test session, allowing E to can trivially win the game.

Therefore, for Π to be a secure key agreement protocol as defined in Definition 2, Π must have strong partnering.

The observations above apply equally to our BR-style model as they do to the Canetti-Krawczyk model [15], even though the concept of partners are slightly different in the two models. In our security model, partnership is defined via session keys, session IDs and partner IDs. For oracles Π_U^i and $\Pi_{U'}^j$ to accept holding the same session key but without being partners, they must have different $sids$ and/or $pids$. To ensure that the protocol Π has strong partnering, we must ensure that (with overwhelming probability) $sk_U^i = sk_{U'}^j$ only if $role_U^i \neq role_{U'}^j$, $sid_U^i = sid_{U'}^j$ and $pid_U^i = pid_{U'}^j$. This can be ensured by including $role_U^i$, sid_U^i and pid_U^i in the session string $ss_{\Pi_U^i}$ (and therefore in the computation of the session key sk_U^i).

This idea of including the "partnering information" in the session string ensures strong partnering in other models as well. For example, in the models of [7,8,9], partnering is defined via matching conversations, or transcripts. Therefore a key agreement protocol secure in these models can never allow two oracles to share the same key without having identical transcripts. Strong partnering in these models can therefore be ensured by including the protocol transcript in the session string of each oracle.

4.2   Reduced Games

We now consider two reduced mBR games. The first game is identical to the mBR game defined in Section 3.1 except that the adversary E is not allowed to make any Reveal queries. We call this reduce game a No-Reveals mBR (NR-mBR) game. The second game is identical to the NR-mBR game, except that the adversary no longer makes a Test query. Instead, to win the game, the adversary must select an accepted and fresh Test oracle at the end of its computation and output the session key for this oracle. Since the adversary in this game must actually compute the session key of an oracle (instead of having to decide between a session key and a random value from the key space), we call this game a computational NR-mBR (cNR-mBR) game. We define E's advantage, denoted $Advantage^E(k)$, in the cNR-mBR game to be the probability that E outputs a session key sk such that $sk = sk_{\Pi_U^i}$ where Π_U^i is the Test oracle selected by the adversary.

Definition 4. *A protocol Π is a (c)NR-mBR-secure key agreement protocol if:*

1. *In the presence of the benign adversary, two oracles running the protocol both accept holding the same session key and session ID, and the session key is distributed uniformly at random on $\{0,1\}^k$; and*
2. *For any adversary E, $Advantage^E(k)$ in the (c)NR-mBR game is negligible.*

We say that protocol Π is *(c)NR-mBR-insecure* if it is not (c)NR-mBR-secure. That is, there exists an adversary E which, with non-negligible probability (in k), wins the (c)NR-mBR game against challenger C. We say that such an E can successfully *(c)NR-mBR-attack* protocol Π.

As part of our proof process for a given protocol Π which produces hashed session keys on completion of the protocol, we will consider a related protocol π. Protocol π is defined in the same way as Π except that the session key generated by π will be the session string of Π. That is, $sk_{\pi_U^i} = ss_{\Pi_U^i}$. It will then be necessary to prove that protocol π is cNR-mBR secure. Since the cNR-mBR game is a highly reduced game, it is usually fairly easy to establish a protocol's security in this model. Although it may not be obvious how a proof of security in this reduced model may be helpful, in Section 4.3 we present a theorem which shows how a proof of cNR-mBR security for π can be transformed into a proof of mBR security for Π using a Gap assumption, provided that Π has strong partnering.

The reason we defined NR-mBR security when cNR-mBR security is our focus is that, although it is a more complex game than the cNR-mBR game, a number of recent papers presenting new key agreement protocols prove that their protocols meet such a weakened definition of security [2,9,17,3]. That is, they take an appropriate security model, and prove the security of their protocols in the No-Reveals (NR) variant of the security model.

It is trivial to see that if protocol Π is NR-mBR secure, then it is also cNR-mBR secure. We also have the following result relating the NR-mBR security of Π and the cNR-mBR security of the related protocol π.

Theorem 1. *If a protocol* Π *produces a hashed session key via hash function* H *and is NR-mBR secure, then the related protocol* π *is cNR-mBR secure.*

A sketch of the proof of this theorem is in Appendix A. We note that in the proof of the above theorem, no assumption is required concerning the properties of H.

4.3   Handling Reveal Queries Using Gap Assumptions

We now consider a protocol Π which has strong partnering and for which the related protocol π is cNR-mBR secure. In order to translate these results into a proof of mBR security for Π, we need to be able to construct a challenger C in an mBR game for Π which is able to answer an adversary E's Reveal queries.

At first glance, it seems that C needs to be able to compute the session key sk_U for any oracle Π_U^i that E may wish to reveal during the mBR game. However this is not the case if Π produces a hashed session key (via hash function H) and if H is modelled as a random oracle. We will see below in Theorem 2 that in this case, C only needs to be able to solve the following decisional problem:

Given the transcript T_U^i of oracle Π_U^i in an mBR game, as well as the P_U and $P_{U'}$ (the public keys of U and U' where $pid_U^i = U'$) and s, where s is a string, decide whether $s = ss_{\Pi_U^i}$, where $ss_{\Pi_U^i}$ is the session string of oracle Π_U^i.

We call this decisional problem the *session string decisional problem for protocol* Π.

We now present our main result.

Theorem 2. *Suppose that key agreement protocol* Π *produces a hashed session key on completion of the protocol (via hash function H) and that Π has strong partnering. If the cNR-mBR security of the related protocol π is probabilistic polynomial time reducible to the hardness of the computational problem of some relation f, and the session string decisional problem for Π is polynomial time reducible to the decisional problem of f, then the mBR security of Π is probabilistic polynomial time reducible to the hardness of the Gap problem of f, assuming that H is a random oracle.*

Proof. Since the cNR-mBR security of π is probabilistic polynomial time reducible (in security parameter k) to the hardness of the computational problem of some relation f, there exists an algorithm A that, on input a problem instance of the computational problem of f and interacting with an adversary E which has non-negligible probability η of winning the cNR-mBR game for π in time τ, is able to solve the computational problem of f with some non-negligible probability $g(\eta)$ and in time $h(\tau)$, where g and h are polynomial functions.

We now define an algorithm B which, given an adversary D which has non-negligible probability η' of winning the mBR game for Π in time τ', is able to solve the Gap problem of f with some non-negligible probability $g'(\eta')$ and in time $h'(\tau')$ where g' and h' are polynomial functions. B will act as a challenger for D. B will also run algorithm A and will simulate an adversary for A. Since B attempts to solve the Gap problem of f, B will also have access to a decisional oracle for f.

Since Π has strong partnering, we know that if two oracles share the same session key, then they must be partners (with overwhelming probability). We therefore know that D will never reveal a session key sk where sk is equal to the Test oracle Π_T^i's session key $sk_{\Pi_T^i}$. This is because D is not permitted to reveal the session key of the Test oracle or its partner (if it exists).

We also assumed that the session string decisional problem for Π is polynomial time reducible to the decisional problem of f. That is, there exists some algorithm C which, given a decisional oracle for f, is able to solve the session string decisional problem for Π in polynomial time τ''.

B runs A on the problem instance of the computational problem of f and simulates an adversary for A. A sets up a cNR-mBR game for B and gives all the public parameters to B. B in turn passes these public parameters to adversary D. B now answers all of D's queries as follows.

B passes all D's queries besides Reveal and H queries to A. Since, in any session, protocol π is identical to protocol Π until the session is completed and the session key is computed, these queries will all be answerable by A. B passes A's responses back to D.

In order for B to answer D's Reveal queries, B maintains a Guess session key list (G-List). Each element on the G-List is a tuple of the form $(T_V^j, P_V, P_{V'}, R_V^j)$ where T_V^j is the transcript of oracle Π_V^j, P_V is the public key of V, $P_{V'}$ is the public key of V' where $pid_{\Pi_V^j} = V'$, and R_V^j is a random guess for the session key sk_V^j of oracle Π_V^j. Initially the G-List is empty.

In order for B to answer E's H queries, B maintains an (initially empty) H-List containing tuples of the form (s_i, sk_i, str). For each H query on string s that D makes, B checks whether s is on the H-List as the first component in some tuple (s_i, sk_i, str). If it is, then B outputs sk_i. If s is not on the H-List then B uses the algorithm C to determine whether s is a valid session string for any oracle Π_V^j on the G-List. If $s = ss_{\Pi_V^j}$ is the session string for some oracle Π_V^j on the G-List, then B outputs R_V^j and adds the tuple (s, R_V^j, str) where $str=$"V,j" to the H-List. Otherwise B selects a random sk from the session key space, adds the tuple (s, sk, str) (where str is the empty string λ) to the H-List, and outputs sk.

When D makes a Reveal query on any oracle Π_U^i which has accepted, B proceeds as follows. If Π_U^i has an entry on the G-List of the form $(T_U^i, P_U, P_{U'}, R_U^i)$, B outputs the value R_U^i. Otherwise B checks whether any entry on the H-List of the form (s_i, sk_i, str) where $str = \lambda$ has $s_i = ss_{\Pi_U^i}$ using algorithm C. If such an entry (s_i, sk_i, str) exists, then str is set to "U,i" on the H-List and the entry $(T_U^i, P_U, P_{U'}, R_U^i)$ is added to the G-List, where $R_U^i = s_i$, T_U^i is the transcript of Π_U^i, P_U is the public key of U and $P_{U'}$ is the public key of U' where $pid_{\Pi_U^i} = U'$.

Otherwise a random session key R_U^i is selected and the entry $(T_U^i, P_U, P_{U'}, R_U^i)$ is added to the G-List. To answer the Reveal query, B outputs the value R_U^i in every case.

In this way, B can consistently answer D's Reveal and H queries. At some point D selects a Test oracle Π_T^i. B selects a random element sk from the session key space and gives this to D.

If D does not query H on the Test oracle's session string $ss_{\Pi_T^i}$, then D can only win with probability $1/S_H$ where S_H is the size of the output space of H, which we assume is negligible in security parameter k. So with overwhelming probability $1 - 1/S_H$, D queries H on $ss_{\Pi_T^i}$. B can detect this value by checking which of the tuples (s_i, sk_i, str) on the H-List with $str = \lambda$ has $s_i = ss_{\Pi_T^i}$ using algorithm C. B gives this s_i to A.

Since $ss_{\Pi_T^i} = sk_{\pi_T^i}$, B has simulated a valid adversary E for A with non-negligible probability $\eta = \eta' \cdot (1 - 1/S_H)$ and in polynomial time $\tau = \tau' + \tau'' \cdot N_H \cdot (N_R + 1)$, where N_H and N_R are the number of H and Reveal queries that D makes respectively. So A outputs the solution to the instance of the computational problem of f with non-negligible probability $g(\eta)$ and in time $h(\tau)$.

Therefore B solves the Gap problem of f with non-negligible probability $g(\eta)$ and in time $h(\tau)$.

$\square$

4.4 Different Security Models

Analogous results to Theorem 2 can be obtained for the security models of [6,7,8,9,15].

For each of these models, an equivalent definition of strong partnering can be made. In the models of [7,8,9] partnering is defined via the concept of matching conversations, so strong partnering would be defined in this context as well.

For each of these models, NR and cNR versions can be defined in the same way as for our mBR model. The definition of the related protocol π is independent of the model used.

It is then possible to prove analogous versions of Theorem 2 for these models. These in turn illustrate how proofs in these models can be constructed in a modular way.

We notice that analogous versions of Theorem 1 for alternative security models are also easy to formulate and prove.

Further details will be provided in the full paper.

5 Applying the Technique to Existing Protocols

We are now able to apply our results to key agreement protocols in the literature. We find numerous protocols [2,3,9,17] which use a hash function to derive a session key and which have proofs of security reducing to some computational assumption but only in the NR version of the security model used[1]. For each such protocol Π, full proofs of security in the relevant model can be obtained as follows.

1. It must be shown that the protocol Π has strong partnering. If Π does not have strong partnering, this can be achieved by modifying the protocol to include the appropriate partnering information (for the security model used) in the session string. It should be checked that such modifications do not affect the existing proof of security.
2. The appropriate version of Theorem 1 can now be applied to Π to guarantee that the related protocol π is secure in the cNR version of the security model used.
3. It must be shown that the appropriate decisional oracle can be used to solve the session string decisional problem of Π. In general this is a trivial reduction.
4. The appropriate version of Theorem 2 may now be used to obtain a complete security proof for Π in the full version of the security model used.

For example, the proof of security for Protocol 3 of [9] can be completed in the manner described above, although the protocol does require some modifications to achieve strong partnering. A suitably modified version of this protocol is in fact presented in [21] together with a proof of security. Interestingly, Protocol 3 of [9] and the modified version in [21] are vulnerable to a key compromise impersonation attack. However this does not affect the proof of security since the model of [9] does not capture security against these attacks.

5.1   A Concrete Example

We now consider Protocol 4 in [9], which was conjectured to be secure in [9] but has never been proven secure. We modify the protocol slightly to guarantee strong partnering and then prove this protocol secure in our mBR model. It is possible to prove the unmodified protocol secure in the model of [9] using the method described above, but the proof of strong partnering is more complicated.

We now present our modified version of Protocol 4 of [9].

Protocol 1

The *Setup* algorithm generates primes p and q where $q|p-1$. It then chooses G to be a multiplicative subgroup of $\mathbb{Z}_p^*$, where G has order q, and element $g \in G$ generates G. It also sets the session ID space $S = G^4$ and selects a hash function $H : G^2 \times S \to \{0,1\}^k$. Each participant I selects a private key x_I randomly from Z_q and sets their public key to be $X_I = g^{x_I} \bmod p$.

Suppose that A and B are participants with public keys $X_A = g^{x_A} \bmod p$ and $X_B = g^{x_B} \bmod p$ respectively. A and B run the protocol as follows:

---

[1] A proof for the protocol of [17] appearing in [10] allows the adversary to make some but not all Reveal queries.

A, as initiator will receive some input $(X_B, initiator)$ and initiates session Π_A^i, setting $pid_A = X_B$ and $role_A = initiator$.

A randomly picks a value $a \in \mathbb{Z}_q$, computes $T_A = g^a \bmod p$ and sends the following to B:

$$A \rightarrow B : T_A, X_A, X_B.$$

On receipt of the message from A, B initiates session Π_B^j with $pid_B = X_A$ and $role_B = responder$. B randomly picks a value $b \in \mathbb{Z}_q$ and computes $T_B = g^b \bmod p$. B then sends the following to A:

$$B \rightarrow A : T_B, T_A, X_B, X_A.$$

B computes $sid_B = X_A, X_B, T_A, T_B$ and $K_B = H(T_A^{x_B} \bmod p, X_A^b \bmod p, sid_B)$ and accepts with session key $sk_B = K_B$.

On receipt of the message from B, A computes $sid_A = X_A, X_B, T_A, T_B$ and $K_A = H(X_B^a \bmod p, T_B^{x_A} \bmod p, sid_A)$ and accepts with session key $sk_A = K_A$.

If the protocol completes correctly, it is easy to see that $K_A = K_B$.

The modified version of Protocol 1 in which the session key is equal to the session string of Protocol 1 is denoted by Protocol 1'.

Theorem 3. *The cNR-mBR security of Protocol 1' is probabilistic polynomial time reducible to the hardness of the CDH problem in G.*

This is proved in Appendix A. It is interesting to note how short the proof of this theorem is; this is due to the simplicity of the cNR-mBR model.

We note that a common error when proving that a protocol Π is mBR-secure (or even NR-mBR or cNR-mBR secure) is to make the assumption that the Test oracle Π_U^i has a partner, and that the input to Π_U^i comes from this partner. In fact the challenger has no control over the input to Π_U^i since the adversary controls all communications between oracles. This error can be seen in papers such as [4,18] where proofs of security were attempted in the full security model. Their corrected versions [3,17] provide proofs in the NR versions of the original models.

Theorem 4. *Protocol 1 has strong partnering in the random oracle model.*

The simple proof of this theorem is left to the reader.

Corollary 1. *Protocol 1 is secure in the random oracle model assuming the hardness of the Gap Diffie-Hellman problem.*

Proof. This result comes immediately from Theorems 2, 3 and 4 and the observation that a decisional Diffie-Hellman oracle can be used to solve the session string decisional problem for Protocol 1. Therefore the session string decisional problem for Protocol 1 is reducible to the decisional Diffie-Hellman problem (in constant time). □

We note that Protocol 1 can easily be extended to have perfect forward security by including the value $T_A^b \bmod p$ into the computation of the hash function

H. This extended Protocol 1 can then be proven secure in an extended mBR model which models perfect forward secrecy.

The protocol of [27], after slight modifications to ensure strong partnering, can also be proven secure in the random oracle model in a similar way to our Protocol 1.

6   Special Gap Groups

The Gap assumptions may not be acceptable to all, since in developing security proofs, one must assume the use of an oracle which is not known to exist: a decisional oracle. For instance, for Protocol 1, the proof of security ultimately requires an oracle which solves DDH in the group G. This is thought to be a hard problem, so there is no known method of constructing such an efficient oracle.

However there do exist groups in which the computational problem is thought to be hard but where the decisional problem is known to be easy. For instance, groups of points on an elliptic curve on which an efficient bilinear map (or pairing operation) is defined. In such groups, the pairing operation can be used to construct an efficient DDH oracle, and the Gap problem is in fact equivalent to the computational problem. Therefore if Protocol 1 had been defined over such a group, then its security would in fact reduce to the CDH problem.

7   Conclusions

We have presented a modular technique that makes use of Gap assumptions for simplifying proofs of security for key agreement protocols which are not built using the modular approach of [5]. Protocols of this type have traditionally been notoriously hard to prove secure, and we have indicated how the proofs of security of many such protocols in the literature may be constructed or completed using our technique. Our technique works not only with the model presented in this paper, but also with the models of [7,8,9,15].

We considered in detail a long-standing protocol presented in [9] which previously lacked a proof of security. We then provided a full proof of security for a slightly modified version of this protocol using the techniques introduced in this paper. We also indicated how full proofs of security for protocols in [2,3,9,17,27] may be constructed using our techniques.

References

1. M. Abdalla, O. Chevassut, and D. Pointcheval. One-time verifier-based encrypted key exchange. In S. Vaudenay, editor, *Public Key Cryptography - PKC 2005*, volume 3386 of *LNCS*, pages 47–64. Springer-Verlag, 2005.
2. S.S. Al-Riyami and K.G. Paterson. Authenticated three party key agreement protocols from pairings. In K.G. Paterson, editor, *Proceedings of 9th IMA International Conference on Cryptography and Coding*, volume 2898 of *Lecture Notes in Computer Science*, pages 332–359. Springer-Verlag, 2003.

3. P.S.L.M. Barreto and N. McCullagh. A new two-party identity-based authenticated key agreement. Cryptology ePrint Archive, Report 2004/122, 2005. http://eprint.iacr.org/.

4. P.S.L.M. Barreto and N. McCullagh. A new two-party identity-based authenticated key agreement. In *Topics in Cryptology – CT-RSA'2005*, volume 3376 of *Lecture Notes in Computer Science*, pages 262–274. Springer-Verlag, 2005.

5. M. Bellare, R. Canetti, and H. Krawczyk. A modular approach to the design and analysis of authentication and key exchange protocols. In *Proceedings of the 30th Annual Symposium on the Theory of Computing*, pages 419–428. ACM, 1998.

6. M. Bellare, D. Pointcheval, and P. Rogaway. Authenticated key exchange secure against dictionary attacks. In B. Preneel, editor, *Advances in Cryptology – EUROCRYPT 2000*, volume 1807 of *Lecture Notes in Computer Science*, pages 139–155. Springer-Verlag, 2000.

7. M. Bellare and P. Rogaway. Entity authentication and key distribution. In *Advances in Cryptology - CRYPTO '93*, volume 773 of *LNCS*, pages 232–249. Springer-Verlag, 1994.

8. M. Bellare and P. Rogaway. Provably secure session key distribution: The three party case. In *Proceedings of the 27th Annual ACM Symposium on Theory of Computing STOC*, pages 57–66. ACM, 1995.

9. S. Blake-Wilson, D. Johnson, and A. Menezes. Key agreement protocols and their security analysis. In *Cryptography and Coding*, volume 1355 of *LNCS*, pages 30–45. Springer-Verlag, 1997.

10. C. Boyd, K.-K.R. Choo, and Y. Hitchcock. On session key construction in provably-secure key establishment protocols. In *Proceedings of International Conference on Cryptology in Malaysia - Mycrypt 2005*, volume 3715 of *LNCS*, page 116131. Springer-Verlag, 2005. http://eprint.iacr.org/2005/206.

11. C. Boyd, W. Mao, and K. Paterson. Key agreement using statically keyed authenticators. In *Applied Cryptography and Network Security: Second International Conference, ACNS 2004*, volume 3089 of *Lecture Notes in Computer Science*, pages 388–401. Springer-Verlag, 2004.

12. C. Boyd, J.M. González Nieto, and Y. Hitchcock. Tripartite key exchange in the Canetti-Krawczyk proof model. In *Proceedings of 5th International Conference on Cryptology in India INDOCRYPT 2004*, volume 3348 of *Lecture Notes in Computer Science*, pages 388–401. Springer-Verlag, 2004.

13. C. Boyd, J.M. González Nieto, Y. Hitchcock, P. Montague, and Y.S.T. Tin. A password-based authenticator: Security proof and applications. In *Proceedings of 4th International Conference on Cryptology in India INDOCRYPT 2003*, volume 2904 of *Lecture Notes in Computer Science*, pages 388–401. Springer-Verlag, 2003.

14. C. Boyd, J.M. González Nieto, and Y.S.T. Tin. Provably secure mobile key exchange: Applying the Canetti-Krawczyk approach. In *Information Security and Privacy, 8th Australasian Conference, ACISP 2003*, volume 2727 of *Lecture Notes in Computer Science*, pages 166–179. Springer-Verlag, 2003.

15. R. Canetti and H. Krawczyk. Analysis of key-exchange protocols and their use for building secure channels. In B. Pfitzmann, editor, *Advances in Cryptology – EUROCRYPT 2001*, volume 2045 of *LNCS*, pages 453–474. Springer-Verlag, 2001.

16. R. Canetti and H. Krawczyk. Universally composable notions of key exchange and secure channels. In L.R. Knudsen, editor, *Advances in Cryptology – EUROCRYPT 2002*, volume 2332 of *Lecture Notes in Computer Science*, pages 337–351. Springer-Verlag, 2002.

17. L. Chen and C. Kudla. Identity based authenticated key agreement from pairings. Cryptology ePrint Archive, Report 2002/184, 2002. http://eprint.iacr.org/.

18. L. Chen and C. Kudla. Identity based authenticated key agreement from pairings. In *IEEE Computer Security Foundations Workshop – CSFW-16 2003*, pages 219–233. IEEE Computer Society Press, 2003.

19. W. Diffie, P. C. van Oorschot, and M. J. Weiner. Authentication and authenticated key exchange. *Designs, Codes and Cryptography*, 2:107–125, 1992.

20. M. Jakobsson and D. Pointcheval. Mutual authentication and key exchange protocol for low power devices. In *Financial Cryptography, 5th International Conference, FC 2001*, volume 2339 of *Lecture Notes in Computer Science*, page 178195. Springer-Verlag, 2002.

21. I.R. Jeong, J. Katz, and D.H. Lee. One-round protocols for two-party authenticated key exchange. In *Applied Cryptography and Network Security: the Second International Conference, ACNS 2004*, volume 3089 of *Lecture Notes in Computer Science*, pages 220 – 232. Springer-Verlag, 2004.

22. J. Katz and M. Yung. Scalable protocols for authenticated group key exchange. In D. Boneh, editor, *Advances in Cryptology – CRYPTO 2003*, volume 2729 of *LNCS*, pages 110–125. Springer-Verlag, 2003.

23. L. Law, A. Menezes, M. Qu, J. Solinas, and S.A. Vanstone. An efficient protocol for authenticated key agreement. *Designs, Codes and Cryptography*, 28(2):119–134, 2003.

24. T. Matsumoto, Y. Takashima, and H. Imai. On seeking smart public-key-distribution systems. *Electronics Letters*, E69(2):99–106, 1986.

25. T. Okamoto and D. Pointcheval. The gap-problems: A new class of problems for the security of cryptographic schemes. In K. Kim, editor, *Public Key Cryptography – PKC 2001*, volume 1992 of *LNCS*, pages 104–118. Springer-Verlag, 2001.

26. V. Shoup. On formal models for secure key exchange. IBM Technical Report RZ 3120, 1999. http://shoup.net/papers.

27. N.P. Smart. An identity based authenticated key agreement protocol based on the Weil pairing. *Electronics Letters*, 38(13):630–632, 2002.

Appendix A

Proof of Theorem 1. We provide a sketch of the proof of this theorem. The details are left to the reader. We show that if there exists an adversary E that can cNR-mBR attack π, then we can build an adversary A that can NR-mBR attack Π.

Suppose that an adversary E wins the cNR-mBR game for protocol π with non-negligible probability η. Suppose also that A runs an NR-mBR game with challenger C. A in turn acts as a challenger for E in a cNR-mBR game. A passes E's queries to C and returns C's outputs to E. Finally E will output the session key $sk_{\pi_U^i}$ of some fresh oracle π_U^i. Recall however that $sk_{\pi_U^i} = ss_{\Pi_U^i}$.

A then chooses Π_U^i as the Test oracle and receives a challenge key sk. If $sk = H(sk_{\pi_U^i})$ then A outputs 1, otherwise it outputs 0. A wins the NR-mBR game with probability η. □

Proof of Theorem 3. We assume that for security parameter k there exists an adversary E for Protocol 1′ who can win the cNR-mBR game with advantage η which is non-negligible in k and in polynomial time τ of k. Suppose that the number of participants is n_P and the number of sessions each participant may be involved in is n_S, where n_P and n_S are polynomial functions of k.

We now construct from E algorithm F which solves the CDH problem in G with non-negligible probability. That is, given as input elements $g^x, g^y \in G$, F's task is to compute and output the value $g^{xy} \bmod p$.

F simulates a challenger in a cNR-mBR game with E. F sets up the game with the group G and generator $g \in G$. F generates a set of participants of size n_P. For each participant I, F sets I's private key to be a randomly chosen $x_I \in \mathbb{Z}_q$ and sets their public key to be $X_I = g^{x_I} \bmod p$. However for some participant P, F sets P's public key to be $X_P = g^x$. F also picks a random participant $Q \neq P$, a session number $t \in \{1, .., n_S\}$ and a number $l \in \{1, .., n_H\}$. F starts E and answers E's queries as follows.

Send: E may make a special **Send** query Π_I^s which sets $pid_I = X_{I'}$ and instructs I to initiate a protocol run with its partner I'. E can also send any oracle Π_I^s a message M, and the oracle responds according to the protocol. However if E initializes or sends a message to oracle Π_Q^t, then Π_Q^t outputs g^y.

Corrupt(U): If E corrupts participant P, then F aborts. Otherwise F gives E the long-term private key of the participant.

Test: When E asks a **Test** query to an oracle Π_I^s, F outputs a random element from the key space $G^2 \times S = G^6$.

The probability that E queries oracle Π_Q^t for the Test session and that $pid_Q = X_P$ is $\frac{1}{n_P^2 \cdot n_S}$. In this case, we note that E could not have corrupted participant P, and so F would not have aborted.

E finally outputs a session key of the form (a, b, c) where $a, b \in G$ and $c \in G^4$. If Π_I^s was an initiator, then F outputs b as its guess for the value $g^{xy} \bmod p$, otherwise F outputs a as its guess. It is now easy to see that F solves the CDH problem on input (g^x, g^y) with probability $\eta' = \eta.(\frac{1}{n_P^2 \cdot n_S})$ which is non-negligible in k, and in time τ. $\qquad \square$

A Simple Threshold Authenticated Key Exchange from Short Secrets

Michel Abdalla[1], Olivier Chevassut[2],
Pierre-Alain Fouque[1], and David Pointcheval[1]

[1] Departement d'Informatique,
École normale supérieure,
45 Rue d'Ulm, 75230 Paris Cedex 05, France
{Michel.Abdalla, Pierre-Alain.Fouque, David.Pointcheval}@ens.fr
http://www.di.ens.fr/~{mabdalla,fouque,pointche}
[2] Lawrence Berkeley National Laboratory,
Berkeley, CA 94720, USA
OChevassut@lbl.gov
http://www.dsd.lbl.gov/~chevassu

Abstract. This paper brings the password-based authenticated key exchange (PAKE) problem closer to practice. It takes into account the presence of firewalls when clients communicate with authentication servers. An authentication server can indeed be seen as two distinct entities, namely a gateway (which is the direct interlocutor of the client) and a back-end server (which is the only one able to check the identity of the client). The goal in this setting is to achieve both transparency and security for the client. And to achieve these goals, the most appropriate choices seem to be to keep the client's password private even from the back-end server and use threshold-based cryptography. In this paper, we present the Threshold Password-based Authenticated Key Exchange (GTPAKE) system: GTPAKE uses a pair of public/private keys and, unlike traditional threshold-based constructions, shares only the private key among the servers. The system does no require any certification except during the registration and update of clients' passwords since clients do not use the public-key to authenticate to the gateway. Clients only need to have their password in hand. In addition to client security, this paper also presents highly-desirable security properties such as *server password protection* against dishonest gateways and *key privacy* against curious authentication servers.

Keywords: Threshold Protocols, Password-based Authentication.

1 Introduction

Problem Description. Consider the familiar scenario where you are at the airport waiting for your flight. You have checked-in and have now half an hour to kill. What do you do? Turn on your laptop, switch on your wireless card, and pick up the airport wireless LAN. You are prompted for a password to authenticate

B. Roy (Ed.): ASIACRYPT 2005, LNCS 3788, pp. 566–584, 2005.

yourself and upon successful authentication a port is opened for you to browse the Internet and/or read your e-mails. Now you may wonder what happens under the hood. We have indeed talked to an airport gateway, often termed hotspot, that has in turn talked to your mobile-Internet provider. T-Mobile is an example of such a provider in the United States. The gateway has passed in an encrypted form your password to the provider for authentication and gets back a yes/no depending whether or not the authentication was successful.

Although this model is very attractive in practice, existing security solutions implementing it have major drawbacks since the gateway gains some amount of information about your password. The ideal solution is a cryptographic algorithm allowing the client to securely exchange a session key with the gateway, but the gateway does not gain any information about the password and the authentication server does not gain any information about the session key. Additional problems also occur if too many people, from the same provider, try to connect to various gateways at the same time. The authentication check from the provider would become a bottleneck. Various authentication points are very desirable. Nevertheless, the password of the client cannot be stored at several places, otherwise the job of hackers would be made much easier.

Scenario. To formally define a model for the above scenario, we propose a model in which one can design a protocol among three parties (the client, the gateway and the authentication server) which protects both the session keys and the passwords. We indeed require the three following security notions which capture dishonest behaviors of the client, the authentication server and the gateway respectively: the *semantic security* of the sessions keys, which we model by a Real-Or-Random (ROR) game [2] (it has been proved strictly stronger than the more classical Find-Then-Guess (FTG) model [4]); the *key-privacy* notion [2] which entails that the session key exchanged by two parties with the help of an authentication server is unknown to the authentication server (and also to any other party, granted the semantic security); the *server password protection* which basically means that the gateway cannot learn any information about clients' passwords from the authentication server.

The ultimate goal of this paper is to achieve the highest level of security in the PAKE setting. With the above security notions, breaking into the gateway would not help to gain any information about the passwords, however the authentication server is a security hole. Breaking into the latter would leak the authentication information. Furthermore, according to the above motivation example, a unique authentication point may be a bottleneck. When data information is crucial, a usual solution to protect it is to distribute it among several servers such that a majority of them is needed to recover the initial data. Moreover, when we want to protect a cryptographic service we can split the private information into several parts, each known by one server, so that a majority of them is required to maintain the service without reconstructing the secret key in a single place. Threshold cryptography is the field that provides such solutions and allows to take into account adversaries that can break into any minority of parties. It furthermore solves the bottleneck problem.

Contribution. Our contribution in this paper is a provably-secure protocol satisfying the previously mentioned requirements. We have constructed it by defining a simple protocol, called the gateway PAKE (GPAKE) protocol, among three parties (the client, the gateway and the authentication server). GPAKE protects the session keys and the passwords according to a formal security model which we specify in this paper. It provides the additional property to be a variant of AuthA [5] perfectly *transparent* to the client. Transparency means that a client does not (need to) know whether he is talking to a server directly or whether the server is implemented as a gateway, an authentication server, or even an application server. The gateway does not also (need to) know whether the authentication server is distributed. A non-transparent protocol indeed raises real concerns on the utilization of the protocol in practice since clients need to first update their cryptographic stack in order to take advantage of the threshold PAKE feature. A transparent protocol on the other hand lets only domain administrators worry about deploying the threshold PAKE feature to their users. We have developed a threshold version (called gateway threshold PAKE (GTPAKE)) that does not break the transparency property of GPAKE, and defined its execution in our security model. Clients already running the two-party AuthA protocol (e.g, OMDHKE [8]) will not have to upgrade their stack when administrators add an extra layer of protection with GTPAKE!

Related Work. Several password-based key exchange protocols in the threshold setting have been proposed in the past by MacKenzie et al. [14] and by Di Raimondo and Gennaro [10], to name a few. In particular, the protocol by Di Raimondo and Gennaro in Eurocrypt 2003 [10], which is a threshold version of the 2-party KOY protocol [12], is proven secure in the standard model. In that paper, they have introduced the notion of *transparent* protocols, where the initial protocol and its threshold version are the same from the point of view of the client. Unfortunately, their solution is not very efficient from a practical point of view since it requires several rounds of communication between the client and the server and among the servers themselves. Moreover, like previous proposals of threshold password-based key exchange protocols, their protocol requires the password to be shared among all the servers.

The solution we propose in this paper does not require passwords to be shared across different servers. Instead, we only share the secret decryption key for a public-key encryption scheme under which all passwords are encrypted. This provides an additional feature: it is quite easy for a client to modify his password. He just needs to send the new one encrypted under the authentication servers' public key.

Moreover, contrary to the hybrid model of Halevi and Krawczyk [11], where the server has a public/secret key pair and the client only knows a password, the client is not required to check the authenticity of the public key during the execution of the protocol. Integrity is required only during the registration or when the user wants to update his password.

Organization of the Paper. In Section 2, we present the formalization used to define the execution of the GPAKE and GTPAKE protocols. Our formalization extends that of Abdalla et al. to the threshold setting [2]. In Section 3, we present the intractability assumptions used throughout the paper. In Section 4, we describe the GPAKE system and show that it achieves *semantic security* and *key privacy* in a provable secure way. In Section 5, we describe the GPAKE system's threshold version and show that it is secure —via a reduction from the security of GTPAKE to the intractability assumptions— against dictionary attacks.

2   Security Model

In this section, we present the security model we will use in the rest of the paper to define the execution of our protocol for threshold password-authenticated key exchange.

2.1   Overview

GATEWAY-ORIENTED PASSWORD-BASED KEY EXCHANGE. A gateway-oriented password-based key exchange is a three-party protocol among a client, a gateway, and an authentication server. The goal of protocol is to establish an implicitly authenticated session key between the client and the gateway with the help of the authentication server, where the authentication is done by means of a short password. In our model, the password is known to both the client and the authentication server, but not to the gateway. In fact, no long-term secrets are stored in the gateway. The authentication server, on the other hand, is assumed to know the password. While the communication channel between the gateway and the authentication server is assumed to be authenticated and private, the channel connecting the client to the gateway may be insecure and perhaps under the control of an adversary.

The security goals of our gateway-oriented password-based key exchange model are also somewhat different from those of previous models for password-based schemes. In particular, we ask that the session key shared between the gateway and the client should remain private to the authentication server (see Section 2.2 for more details). Moreover, we also ask that the chances of the gateway learning some information on the password after multiple interactions with the server, perhaps concurrently, should be negligible.

PROTOCOL PARTICIPANTS. The participants in a gateway-oriented password-based key exchange are the client $C \in \mathcal{C}$, the gateway $G \in \mathcal{G}$, and the authentication server $S \in \mathcal{S}$. We denote by $\mathcal{U}$ the set of all participants (i.e., $\mathcal{U} = \mathcal{C} \cup \mathcal{G} \cup \mathcal{S}$) and by U a non-specific participant in $\mathcal{U}$. Each client $C \in \mathcal{C}$ holds a password pw_C. Each server $S \in \mathcal{S}$ holds a vector of passwords $\mathsf{PW}_S = \langle pw_C \rangle_{C \in \mathcal{C}}$ with an entry for each client.

2.2   Security Model

Since we assume an authenticated and private channel between the gateway and the server, the communication model is similar to previous one for 2-party authenticated key exchange. In particular, we adopt the Real-Or-Random (ROR) security model of Abdalla *et al.* [2] for password-based authenticated key exchange protocol, which in turn implies that of Bellare *et al.* [4]. As in the standard model, all the interactions between an adversary $\mathcal{A}$ and the protocol participants in the ROR model are done via oracle queries. Let U^i denote the instance i of a participant U. The list of oracles available to the adversary are as follows:

- Execute(C^i, G^j): This query models passive attacks in which the attacker eavesdrops on honest executions among a client instance C^i and a gateway instance G^k. The output of this query consists of the messages that were exchanged during the honest execution of the protocol.
- Send(U^i, m): This query models an active attack against the client or gateway instance U^i, in which the adversary may intercept a message and then modify it, create a new one, or simply forward it to the intended recipient. The output of this query is the message that the participant instance U^i would generate upon receipt of message m.

The Real-Or-Random Model [2]. In the ROR model, in addition to the above-mentioned oracles, an attacker is also given access to a less restrictive Test oracle. Let b be a bit chosen uniformly at random at the beginning of the experiment defining the semantic security of session keys. The Test oracle in the ROR model is defined as follows:

- Test(U^i): If no session key for instance U^i is defined, then return the undefined symbol $\perp$. Otherwise, return the session key for instance U^i if $b = 1$ or a random of key of the same size if $b = 0$.

As in standard models, the Test oracle in the ROR model also tries to capture the adversary's ability (or inability) to tell apart a real session key from a random one. The main difference is that it does so not only for a single session but for all sessions. More precisely, the adversary in the ROR model is not restricted to ask a single Test query, but it can in fact ask multiple ones. All Test queries in this case will be answered using the same value for the hidden bit b that was chosen at the beginning of the experiment defining the semantic security of the session keys. That is, the keys returned by the Test oracle are either all real or all random. However, in the random case, the same random key value is returned for Test queries that are asked to two instances that belong to the same session (see notion of partnering below). The goal of the adversary in the ROR model is still the same: to guess the value of the hidden bit b used to answer Test queries. The adversary is considered successful if it guesses b correctly.

PARTNERING. As in [2], we use the notion of partnering based on session identifications (sid), which says that two instances are partnered if they hold the same non-null sid. More specifically, a client instance C^i and a gateway instance G^j are said to be partners if the following conditions are met: (1) Both C^i and G^j accept; (2) Both C^i and G^j share the same session identifications; (3) The partner identification for C^i is G^j and vice-versa; and (4) No instance other than

C^i and G^j accepts with a partner identification equal to C^i or G^j. In practice, the *sid* is taken to be the partial transcript of the conversation among the client and the gateway instances before the acceptance.

FRESHNESS. Differently from [2], we opt not to embed the notion of freshness inside the definition of the oracles. Instead, we take the more standard approach of explicitly defining the notion of freshness and mandating the adversary to only perform tests on *fresh* instances. The two approaches are however equivalent. In particular, we say that a *instance* of a client or gateway is *fresh* if it has accepted.

FORMAL DEFINITION. Let SUCC denote the event in which the adversary is successful. The ake − ror-**advantage** of an adversary $\mathcal{A}$ in violating the semantic security of the protocol P in the ROR sense and the **advantage function** of the protocol P, when passwords are drawn from a dictionary Dict, are respectively

$$\mathbf{Adv}^{\text{ake}-\text{ror}}_{P,\text{Dict}}(\mathcal{A}) = 2 \cdot \Pr[\,\text{SUCC}\,] - 1 \text{ and}$$

$$\mathbf{Adv}^{\text{ake}-\text{ror}}_{P,\text{Dict}}(t, R) = \max_{\mathcal{A}}\{\, \mathbf{Adv}^{\text{ake}-\text{ror}}_{P,\text{Dict}}(\mathcal{A}) \,\},$$

where the maximum is over all $\mathcal{A}$ with time-complexity at most t and using resources at most R (such as the number of queries to its oracles). The definition of time-complexity that we use henceforth is the usual one, which includes the maximum of all execution times in the experiments defining the security plus the code size.

Please note that, as proven in [2], any scheme proven secure in the ROR model is also secure in the model of Bellare *et al.* [4]. The converse, however, is not necessarily true (see [2] for more details).

AUTHENTICATION. The notion of semantic security does not guarantee the existence of a partner, but only the secrecy of the session key (implicit authentication). In order to address this problem, one usually adds mechanisms for explicit authentication of client and gateway instances. In this paper, we only consider *unilateral authentication* of the gateway, by which a client instance can be ensured that it has in fact established a key with the gateway instance it intended to. As in [7], we denote by $\text{Succ}^{\text{G}-\text{auth}}_{\mathcal{A}}$ the probability that adversary $\mathcal{A}$ successfully impersonates the gateway in an execution of the protocol. This is the probability with which a client instance accepts without having a gateway partner. The advantage function of the protocol can be defined as in previous cases.

Key Privacy. The notion of key privacy was introduced in [2] to capture the idea that the session key computed by two parties with the aid of an authentication server should only be known to those two parties and not to the server. The goal in this case is to reduce the amount of trust one puts into the server. In order to meet this goal, one has to consider an adversary with access to all the secret information stored in the server and then show that such adversary cannot distinguish actual session keys from random ones if we restrict this adversary to test sessions in which the keys are shared between two oracles. The latter restriction is important since an adversary with access to the secrets of the authentication server could always establish a key with a client by playing the roles of the gateway and authentication server. Since one of our main goals is to show that the key shared between the client and the gateway is not known to the authentication server, we also use the notion of key privacy.

To capture the above intuition more formally, [2] considers an adversary which has access to all the secrets held by the authentication server and to the oracles used in the experiment defining semantic security. They then introduce a new type of oracle, called TestPair, whose goal is to capture the adversary's ability to distinguish the real session key shared between any two oracle instances from a random one. The inputs to the TestPair oracle are the specific oracle instances whose shared session key the adversary thinks it can tell apart from a random key.

FORMAL DEFINITION. Consider an execution of the key exchange protocol P by an adversary $\mathcal{A}$ with access to all the secret held by the authentication server as well as to the Execute, Send, and TestPair oracles. Let SUCC denote the event in which the adversary is successful in guessing the hidden bit used by TestPair oracle when only asking TestPair queries to instances pairs that have accepted. The kp-**advantage** of an adversary $\mathcal{A}$ in violating the key privacy of the protocol P in the ROR sense ($\mathbf{Adv}_{P,\mathsf{Dict}}^{\mathrm{ake-kp}}(\mathcal{A})$) and the **advantage function** of P ($\mathbf{Adv}_{P,\mathsf{Dict}}^{\mathrm{ake-kp}}(t,R)$), when passwords are drawn from a dictionary Dict, are then defined as in previous definitions.

Server Password Protection. As we mentioned earlier, one of the goals of our protocol is to guarantee that the gateway is not capable of learning the user's password that is stored in the server. Clearly, as in the case of semantic security, one cannot hope for much since, in each interaction, the adversary may be able to eliminate one candidate password from the list of possible passwords. However, we ask that the adversary should not be able to do much better than. That is, if the adversary interacts q times with the server, then the probability that it can distinguish the true password from a random one in the dictionary should be only negligibly larger than $O(q/N)$, where N is the size of the dictionary. The hidden constant in this case should be as small as possible (preferably 1). Note that, in this definition, the dictionary is assumed to be uniformly distributed.

2.3   Threshold Security Model

THRESHOLD GATEWAY-ORIENTED PASSWORD-BASED KEY EXCHANGE. A (t, k, n)-threshold gateway-oriented password-based key exchange is an extension of the basic gateway-oriented password-based key exchange in which the authentication server is a distributed entity. More specifically, the clients' passwords are no longer known to any single server. Instead, each server in the set of n authentication servers is assumed to hold a share of the secret key of a public-key encryption scheme, under which clients' passwords are encrypted. The authentication of any client will require the cooperation of some size-k subset of honest servers. In addition, any adversary who learns t or fewer shares of the secret key should not learn any information about the clients' passwords.

PARTICIPANTS. The participants in a threshold protocol are the client $C \in \mathcal{C}$, the gateway $G \in \mathcal{G}$, the set of authentication servers $\{S_1, \ldots, S_n\}$ with $S_i \in \mathcal{S}$, and a trusted dealer.

Semantic Security. The definition of semantic security of threshold protocols follows the one given above for gateway-oriented protocols. At the beginning of the semantic security experiment, the adversary selects a subset of at most $t = k - 1$ servers to corrupt. We say that the adversary is *static* when it chooses the set of servers to corrupt in advance, before seeing anything. A special server, called the combiner, will be used to perform some tasks that do not require any secret. The combiner is also in charge of all communications between the gateway and the other servers.

The dealer generates a public key pk and a secret key sk for an encryption scheme. Then, he performs the secret sharing of sk and sends the part sk_i to P_i along with a verification key vk_i. The adversary obtains the secret key shares of the corrupted servers, along with the public key and the verification keys.

After this phase, the adversary is given access to the same set of oracles used in the standard security model for gateway-oriented password-based authenticated key exchange protocols.

Robustness. We say that a threshold scheme is *robust* when it takes into account *malicious* adversaries whose behavior can be different from the protocol. To force the servers to correctly perform their job, we use proofs of validity in our protocol. This also enables the combiner to correctly decrypt.

3   Diffie-Hellman Assumptions

In this section, we recall the definitions of standard Diffie-Hellman assumptions and introduce some new variants, which we use in the security proof of our protocol. We also present some relations between these assumptions.

3.1   Classical Assumptions

Henceforth, we assume a finite cyclic group G of prime order p generated by an element g. We also call the tuple $\mathbb{G} = (G, g, p)$ a represented group.

Computational Diffie-Hellman Assumption: CDH. The CDH assumption, in a represented group $\mathbb{G}$, with respect to the basis X, states that given two elements $X' = X^u$ and $Y = X^v$, where u and v were drawn at random from Z_p, it is hard to compute $Y' = Y^u = X^{uv}$. This can be defined more precisely by considering an experiment $\mathbf{Exp}_{\mathbb{G}}^{\mathrm{cdh}}(\mathcal{A}, X)$, in which we select an exponent u

in Z_p, an element Y in G, compute $X' = X^u$, and then give both X' and Y to $\mathcal{A}$. Let Y' be the output of $\mathcal{A}$. Then, the experiment $\mathbf{Exp}_{\mathbb{G}}^{\mathrm{cdh}}(\mathcal{A}, X)$ outputs 1 if $Y' = Y^u$ and 0 otherwise. We define the *advantage* of $\mathcal{A}$ in violating the CDH assumption with respect to X as $\mathbf{Adv}_{\mathbb{G}}^{\mathrm{cdh}}(\mathcal{A}, X) = \Pr[\mathbf{Exp}_{\mathbb{G}}^{\mathrm{cdh}}(\mathcal{A}, X) = 1]$, the *advantage* of $\mathcal{A}$ in violating the CDH assumption (with a random basis) as $\mathbf{Adv}_{\mathbb{G}}^{\mathrm{cdh}}(\mathcal{A}) = \mathbf{E}_X\left[\mathbf{Adv}_{\mathbb{G}}^{\mathrm{cdh}}(\mathcal{A}, X)\right]$, and the *advantage functions*, $\mathbf{Adv}_{\mathbb{G}}^{\mathrm{cdh}}(t, X)$ and $\mathbf{Adv}_{\mathbb{G}}^{\mathrm{cdh}}(t)$, as the maximum values of $\mathbf{Adv}_{\mathbb{G}}^{\mathrm{cdh}}(\mathcal{A}, X)$ and $\mathbf{Adv}_{\mathbb{G}}^{\mathrm{cdh}}(\mathcal{A})$ over all $\mathcal{A}$ with time-complexity at most t.

It is also often assumed that, *independently of what the value of X is (as long as it is a generator, of order p)*, the CDH problem with respect to the basis X is hard: the maximal value of $\mathbf{Adv}_{\mathbb{G}}^{\mathrm{cdh}}(t, X)$ over all generators X is small for any reasonable t.

Decisional Diffie-Hellman Assumption: DDH. Roughly, the DDH assumption, with respect to the basis X, states that the distributions $(X, X' = X^u, Y, Y' = Y^u)$ and $(X, X' = X^u, Y, Z = Y^v)$ are computationally indistinguishable when Y is drawn at random from G, and u and v are drawn at random from Z_p. As before, we can define the DDH assumption more formally by defining two experiments, $\mathbf{Exp}_{\mathbb{G}}^{\mathrm{ddh\text{-}real}}(\mathcal{A}, X)$ and $\mathbf{Exp}_{\mathbb{G}}^{\mathrm{ddh\text{-}rand}}(\mathcal{A}, X)$. In both experiments, we compute two random values $X' = X^u$ and Y as before. But in addition to that, we also provide a third input, which is Y^u in $\mathbf{Exp}_{\mathbb{G}}^{\mathrm{ddh\text{-}real}}(\mathcal{A}, X)$ and Y^v, for a random v, in $\mathbf{Exp}_{\mathbb{G}}^{\mathrm{ddh\text{-}rand}}(\mathcal{A}, X)$. The goal of the adversary is to guess a bit indicating the experiment he thinks he is in. We define the *advantage* of $\mathcal{A}$ in violating the DDH assumption, with respect to the basis X, $\mathbf{Adv}_{\mathbb{G}}^{\mathrm{ddh}}(\mathcal{A}, X)$, as $\Pr[\mathbf{Exp}_{\mathbb{G}}^{\mathrm{ddh\text{-}real}}(\mathcal{A}, X) = 1] - \Pr[\mathbf{Exp}_{\mathbb{G}}^{\mathrm{ddh\text{-}rand}}(\mathcal{A}, X) = 1]$, and *advantage* of $\mathcal{A}$ in violating the DDH assumption (with random basis) as $\mathbf{Adv}_{\mathbb{G}}^{\mathrm{ddh}}(\mathcal{A}) = \mathbf{E}_X\left[\mathbf{Adv}_{\mathbb{G}}^{\mathrm{ddh}}(\mathcal{A}, X)\right]$. The *advantage functions* $\mathbf{Adv}_{\mathbb{G}}^{\mathrm{ddh}}(t, X)$ and $\mathbf{Adv}_{\mathbb{G}}^{\mathrm{ddh}}(t)$ are then defined in a similar manner as above.

Again, it is also often assumed that, *independently of what X is (as long as it is a generator, of order p)*, the DDH problem with respect to the basis X is hard: the maximal value of $\mathbf{Adv}_{\mathbb{G}}^{\mathrm{ddh}}(t, X)$ over all generators X is small for any reasonable t.

3.2   Password-Based Chosen-Basis Diffie-Hellman Assumptions

The actual proofs of security of our protocol use password-related versions of the above Diffie-Hellman assumptions, in which the adversary has some control over the basis, hence the name *password-based chosen-basis decisional/computational Diffie-Hellman* assumptions. They make use of a dictionary $\mathcal{D} = \{U_1, \ldots, U_N\}$ of size N. Then, we assume that when the adversary has not correctly predicted the password (1 chance over N), he has no significant advantage. Hence, its overall advantage cannot be significantly larger than $1/N$.

We start by presenting the password-based chosen-basis computational Diffie-Hellman assumption.

Definition 1 (PCCDH). *Let* $\mathbb{G} = (G, g, p)$ *be a represented group and let* $\mathcal{A}$ *be an adversary. Consider the following experiment, where* $\mathcal{D}$ *is a dictionary of* N *elements in* G.

$$\textbf{\textit{Experiment}} \; \textbf{Exp}_{\mathbb{G}}^{\text{pccdh}}(\mathcal{A}, \mathcal{D})$$
$$(X, s) \leftarrow \mathcal{A}(\mathsf{find}, \mathcal{D})$$
$$\Pi \xleftarrow{R} \mathcal{D} \; ; \; Y \xleftarrow{R} G$$
$$K \leftarrow \mathcal{A}(\mathsf{guess}, s, Y, \Pi)$$
$$\textbf{\textit{return}} \; 1 \; \textit{if} \; K = \text{CDH}(X/\Pi, Y)$$

We define the advantage of $\mathcal{A}$ *in violating the* PCCDH *assumption with respect to the dictionary* $\mathcal{D}$, $\textbf{Adv}_{\mathbb{G},N}^{\text{pccdh}}(\mathcal{A}, \mathcal{D})$, *the advantage of* $\mathcal{A}$ $\textbf{Adv}_{\mathbb{G},N}^{\text{pccdh}}(\mathcal{A})$, *and the advantage functions,* $\textbf{Adv}_{\mathbb{G},N}^{\text{pccdh}}(t, \mathcal{D})$ *and* $\textbf{Adv}_{\mathbb{G},N}^{\text{pccdh}}(t)$, *as above.* ◇

In our security proofs, we actually need a simple variation of the above problem, in which the adversary, in the second stage, outputs a set of s candidates for the CDH value. The adversary wins if the set indeed contains K. This problem is thus named *Set Password-based Chosen-basis Computational Diffie-Hellman Problem* (SPCCDH).

We define the *advantage* $\textbf{Adv}_{\mathbb{G},N}^{\text{spccdh}}(\mathcal{A}, \mathcal{D}, s)$ of $\mathcal{A}$ in violating the SPCCDH assumption with respect to the dictionary $\mathcal{D}$, the *advantage* $\textbf{Adv}_{\mathbb{G},N}^{\text{spccdh}}(\mathcal{A}, s)$ of $\mathcal{A}$, and the *advantage functions* $\textbf{Adv}_{\mathbb{G},N}^{\text{spccdh}}(t, \mathcal{D}, s)$ and $\textbf{Adv}_{\mathbb{G},N}^{\text{spccdh}}(t, s)$ as in previous definitions.

Fortunately, the two new assumptions are not so strong, since one can prove that the SPCCDH problem is equivalent to the CDH problem as proven in Appendix B. The general result proven in Appendix B can be simplified in the particular case of not so large dictionaries:

Lemma 2. $\textbf{Adv}_{\mathbb{G},N}^{\text{spccdh}}(t, s) \leq \frac{1}{N} + N^2 s^2 \times \textbf{Adv}_{\mathbb{G}}^{\text{cdh}}(2t + \tau_e)$.

In addition to the computational assumptions above, we also make use of the following decisional assumption in our security proofs.

Definition 3 (PCDDH). *Let* $\mathbb{G} = (G, g, p)$ *be a represented group and let* $\mathcal{A}$ *be an adversary. Consider the following experiment, defined for* $b = 0, 1$, *where* $\mathcal{D}$ *is the dictionary of* N *elements in* G.

$$\textbf{\textit{Experiment}} \; \textbf{Exp}_{b}^{\text{pcddh}}(\mathcal{A}, \mathcal{D})$$
$$(X, Y, s) \leftarrow \mathcal{A}(\mathsf{find}, \mathcal{D})$$
$$\Pi \xleftarrow{R} \mathcal{D} \; ; \; s_0, s_1 \xleftarrow{R} \mathbb{Z}_p$$
$$Y' \leftarrow Y^{s_0} \; ; \; X' \leftarrow (X/\Pi)^{s_b}$$
$$b' \leftarrow \mathcal{A}(\mathsf{guess}, s, X', Y', \Pi)$$
$$\textbf{\textit{return}} \; b'$$

We define the advantage of $\mathcal{A}$ *in violating the* PCDDH *assumption with respect to the dictionary* $\mathcal{D}$, $\textbf{Adv}_{\mathbb{G},N}^{\text{pcddh}}(\mathcal{A}, \mathcal{D})$, *the advantage of* $\mathcal{A}$, $\textbf{Adv}_{\mathbb{G},N}^{\text{pcddh}}(\mathcal{A})$, *and the respective advantage functions of* $\mathbb{G}$ *for a given value* N, $\textbf{Adv}_{\mathbb{G},N}^{\text{pcddh}}(t, \mathcal{D})$ *and* $\textbf{Adv}_{\mathbb{G},N}^{\text{pcddh}}(t)$, *as above.* ◇

Fortunately again, this problem is not new. It has already appeared in [3] under the name PCDDH2. In that paper, the authors have also shown that $\mathbf{Adv}_{\mathbb{G},N}^{\text{pcddh}}(t, \mathcal{D})$ and $\mathbf{Adv}_{\mathbb{G},N}^{\text{pcddh}}(t)$ cannot be significantly larger than $2/N$.

4   The Gateway PAKE System

In this section, we describe GPAKE, the underlying gateway-oriented password-based protocol used in the construction of our threshold gateway-oriented password-based protocol.

4.1   Description

Our gateway-oriented password-based protocol, GPAKE, builds upon previous password-based key exchange protocols in [5,8,13], which in turn are based on the encrypted key exchange of Bellovin and Merritt [6]. Its description is given in Figure 1, where $\mathbb{G} = (G, g, q)$ is a represented group; ℓ is a security parameter; and $\mathcal{G} : \mathcal{U}^2 \times \text{Dict} \to \mathbb{G}$, $\text{Hash}_1 : \mathcal{U}^2 \times \mathbb{G} \times \mathbb{G} \to \{0,1\}^\ell$, and $\text{Hash}_2 : \mathcal{U}^2 \times \mathbb{G} \times \mathbb{G} \to \{0,1\}^\ell$, are random oracles.

The protocol consists of four message exchanges, two between the client and the gateway and two between the gateway and the authentication server. Since the channel connecting the gateway to the server is assumed to be authenticated and private, from the client perspective, the protocol resembles almost exactly the 2-party protocol OMDHKE in [8]. The only difference is in the key derivation function, which does not include the password.

The protocol starts with the client choosing a random element $x \in \mathbb{Z}_p$ and computing $X = g^x$, and encrypting it using $\mathcal{G}(C, G, \text{pw})$ as a mask to obtain

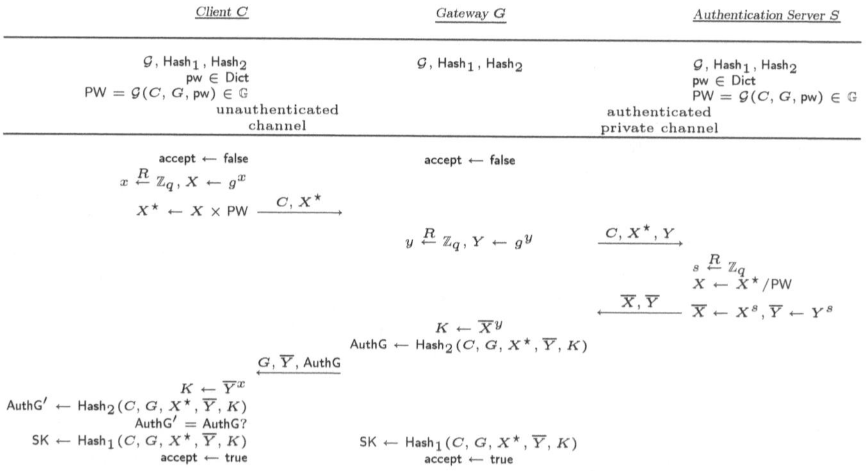

Fig. 1. GPAKE: A gateway-oriented password-based authenticated key exchange protocol

$X^\star$. The client then sends to the gateway both $X^\star$ and its identity string C. Upon receiving a message from the client, the gateway chooses a random element $y \in Z_p$ and computes $Y = g^y$, and forwards to the server both Y and the value $X^\star$ that it has received from the client. Upon receiving the values $(X^\star, Y)$ from the gateway, the server computes $X = X^\star / \mathcal{G}(C, G, \mathsf{pw})$, chooses a random element $s \in Z_p$, computes $(\overline{X} = X^s, \overline{Y} = Y^s)$, and sends it back to the gateway. Upon receiving $(\overline{X}, \overline{Y})$, the gateway computes the Diffie-Hellman key $K = \overline{X}^y$, the authenticator $\mathsf{AuthG} = \mathsf{Hash}_2(C, G, X^\star, \overline{Y}, K)$ and the session key $\mathsf{SK} = \mathsf{Hash}_1(C, G, X^\star, \overline{Y}, K)$, and sends $(G, \overline{Y}, \mathsf{AuthG})$ to the client. Upon receiving $(G, \overline{Y}, \mathsf{AuthG})$, the client computes the Diffie-Hellman key $K = \overline{Y}^x$, checks whether $\mathsf{AuthG} = \mathsf{Hash}_2(C, G, X^\star, \overline{Y}, K)$, and sets the session key to $\mathsf{SK} = \mathsf{Hash}_1(C, G, X^\star, \overline{Y}, K)$ if the test passes. The session identification is defined to be the transcript $(C, G, X^\star, \overline{Y})$ of the conversation between the client and the gateway.

4.2   Security

Semantic security. As the following theorem states, GPAKE is a secure gateway-oriented password-based key exchange protocol as long as the SPCCDH problem is hard in G. As shown in Section 3, this is equivalent to assuming that CDH problem is hard in G. The proof can be found in the full version of this paper [1]. Nevertheless, we note here that the proof of security assumes Dict to be a uniformly distributed dictionary and of size smaller than 2^ℓ.

Theorem 4. *Let* $G = (G, g, q)$ *be a represent group of prime order* q *and let* Dict *be a uniformly distributed dictionary of size* $N = |\mathsf{Dict}|$. *Let* GPAKE *describe the gateway-oriented protocol associated with these primitives as defined in Figure 1. Then,*

$$\mathbf{Adv}^{\mathrm{ake-ror}}_{\mathsf{GPAKE},G,\mathsf{Dict}}(t, q_{\mathrm{exe}}, q_{\mathrm{fake-C}}, q_{\mathrm{fake-G}}, q_{\mathrm{active}}, q_{\mathrm{test}}, q_{\mathsf{Hash}_1}, q_{\mathsf{Hash}_2}, q_{\mathcal{G}}) \leq$$

$$\frac{q^2_{\mathrm{active}} + q^2_{\mathcal{G}}}{q} + \frac{q^2_{\mathrm{exe}}}{q^2} + 2\,\frac{q^2_{\mathsf{Hash}_1} + q^2_{\mathsf{Hash}_2}}{2^\ell} +$$

$$2\,(q_{\mathsf{Hash}_1} + q_{\mathsf{Hash}_2}) \cdot \mathbf{Adv}^{\mathrm{cdh}}_G(t + (4q_{\mathrm{exe}} + 4)\tau_e) +$$

$$2 \cdot q_{\mathrm{active}} \cdot (q_{\mathsf{Hash}_1} + q_{\mathsf{Hash}_2}) \cdot \mathbf{Adv}^{\mathrm{cdh}}_G(t + 2\tau_e) + 4 \cdot q_{\mathrm{fake-C}}/N +$$

$$2 \cdot q_{\mathrm{fake-G}} \cdot \mathbf{Adv}^{\mathrm{spccdh}}_{G,N}(t, q_{\mathsf{Hash}_1} + q_{\mathsf{Hash}_2}),$$

where $q_{\mathcal{G}}$, q_{Hash_1}, *and* q_{Hash_2} *represent the number of queries to the* $\mathcal{G}$, Hash$_1$ *and* Hash$_2$ *oracles, respectively;* q_{exe} *represents the number of queries to the* Execute *oracle;* $q_{\mathrm{fake-C}}$ *and* $q_{\mathrm{fake-G}}$ *represent the number of attempts of the adversary to fake the client and the gateway, respectively;* q_{active} *represents the total number of queries to the* Send *oracle;* q_{test} *represents the total number of queries to the* Test *oracle; and* τ_e *denotes the exponentiation computational time in* G.

Remark 5. In the security model presented in Section 2, the adversary is not allowed to corrupt gateway instances. Consequently, the proof of Theorem 4 does not guarantee the security of GPAKE in that scenario. Even though GPAKE appears to be secure in the presence of such adversaries, a new proof of security would be required in this case.

Key Privacy. As the following shows, GPAKE achieves the goal of key privacy as long as the DDH problem is hard in $\mathbb{G}$.

Theorem 6. *Let* $\mathbb{G} = (G, g, q)$ *be a represent group of prime order* q *and let* Dict *be a uniformly distributed dictionary of size* $N = |\text{Dict}|$. *Let* GPAKE *describe the gateway-oriented protocol associated with these primitives as defined in Figure 1. Then,*

$$\mathbf{Adv}^{\text{ake-kp}}_{\text{GPAKE},\mathbb{G},\text{Dict}}(t, q_{\text{exe}}, q_{\text{test}}) \leq 2 \cdot \mathbf{Adv}^{\text{ddh}}_{\mathbb{G}}(t + (4q_{\text{exe}} + 4)\tau_e),$$

where q_{exe} *and* q_{test} *represent the total number of queries to the* Execute *and* TestPair *oracles; and* τ_e *denotes the exponentiation computational time in* $\mathbb{G}$.

The proof of Theorem 6 is in [1]. It is worth mentioning that, when proving the security of GPAKE, we do not give the server access to a Send oracle since we assume the server to be honest but curious. We do so because, in the actual implementation of GPAKE, the server is distributed and we assume the majority of them to be honest (see Section 5). We also note that, in order to prove key privacy in scenarios where the majority of servers is corrupted, additional modifications would need to be made to GPAKE. These modifications would include the addition of an authenticated Diffie-Hellman protocol between C and G as done in [2] and a proof that the pair $(\overline{X}, \overline{Y})$ is well formed.

Server Password Protection. The server password protection of GPAKE follows directly from the password-based chosen-basis decisional Diffie-Hellman assumption (PCDDH) introduced in [3] and recalled in Section 3. More specifically, it is easy to see that the interaction between the gateway and the server corresponds exactly to the security experiment for PCDDH. Since the security of the latter was shown in [3] to be only negligibly larger than $2/N$, where N is the size of the dictionary, it follows (via a standard hybrid argument as in [3]) that, in each interaction with the server, an adversarial gateway cannot do much better than eliminating two passwords from the list of possible candidates with each interaction. As a result, after q interactions with the server, the advantage of a malicious gateway would be only negligibly larger than $2q/N$.

5   The Gateway Threshold **PAKE** System

In this section, our goal is to distribute the authentication server in the previous gateway-oriented password-based protocol to prevent malicious adversaries that can corrupt up to k out of n servers. The solution is robust against static adversaries. The threshold version is *transparent* from the point of view of the client since it communicates only with the gateway. The threshold version is also *transparent* from the point of view of the gateway since a special authentication server, called the *combiner*, is the only server with which the gateway communicates. We also assume that the channel between the gateway and the combiner is authenticated and private. We can use signature and encryption schemes in order to fulfill this requirement using threshold signature and encryption.

Description. Let $\mathbb{G}$ is a cyclic subgroup of prime order q. We assume that the authentication servers $\{S_1, \ldots, S_n\}$ share a secret ElGamal encryption key $\mathsf{sk} = x$ using Shamir scheme with threshold k. Server i knows $\mathsf{sk}_i = x_i$ and has a verification key $\mathsf{vk}_i = v^{x_i}$, where v is a generator of $\mathbb{G}$. The encryption of the password $c = \mathbf{E}_{\mathsf{pk}}(\mathsf{PW}) = (e_c, f_c)$ under the public ElGamal encryption key $\mathsf{pk} = (g, y)$ is authenticated in a public file. At the beginning of the protocol, the combiner, S_1 wlog, receives $X^\star = X \times \mathsf{PW}$, and $Y = g^y$.

First Stage. The combiner encrypts $X^\star$ into (e, f) and proves the validity of the encryption using a zero-knowledge proof of equality of discrete-log $\mathsf{EDLog}_{y,g}(e/X^\star, f)$. Given $X^\star$ and (e, f), where $e = X^\star \times y^r$ and $f = g^r$, then we have to show that $\log_y(e/X^\star) = \log_g(f)$. Then, he broadcasts to all servers $Y, X^\star, (e, f)$ and the proof of validity $\mathsf{EDLog}_{y,g}(e/X^\star, f)$.

Second Stage. Each authentication server S_i checks the proofs and chooses a random value $s_i \in \mathbb{Z}_q$. Then, he computes $Y_i = Y^{s_i}$, $e'_i = (e/e_c)^{s_i}$ and $f'_i = (f/f_c)^{s_i}$ along with a proof of validity that Y_i and the two parts of (e'_i, f'_i) have been raised to the same power s_i: $\mathsf{EDLog}_{Y,e/e_c}(Y_i, e'_i)$ and $\mathsf{EDLog}_{Y,f/f_c}(Y_i, f'_i)$. All these values are broadcast to all the servers.

Third Stage. They check all proofs and they compute the values $e'^s = \prod_i e'_i = e'^{\sum_i s_i}$, $f'^s = \prod_i f'_i = f'^{\sum_i s_i}$, and $Y^s = \prod_i \tilde{Y}_i$. Then, they perform a threshold decryption of (e'^s, f'^s) by computing $g_i^s = (f'^s)^{x_i}$. Next, they prove the validity of the decryption by computing $\mathsf{EDLog}_{f'^s,v}(g_i^s, \mathsf{vk}_i)$. Finally, they broadcast the proof along with their decryption share g_i^s.

Forth Stage. The combiner, without any secret, can compute $f'^{xs} = \prod_{i \in S} g_i^{s\lambda_{0,i}^S}$ by using Lagrange interpolation formula and $\overline{X} = X^s = e'^s/f'^{xs}$ using k valid decryption shares. He sends to the gateway $\overline{X}$ and $\overline{Y} = Y^s$ using the authentication and private channel.

For a pictorial description of our threshold protocol, please refer to Figure 2.

Security. We now analyze the security of the threshold variant we just presented. To this end, we show a reduction between an adversary $\mathcal{A}$ against the threshold scheme and an attacker $\mathcal{B}$ against the underlying provably-secure GPAKE protocol described in the previous section.

Theorem 7. *If the underlying* GPAKE *protocol is semantically secure and the DDH assumption holds in* $\mathbb{G}$, *then* GTPAKE *is a semantically secure threshold protocol against a static adversary.*

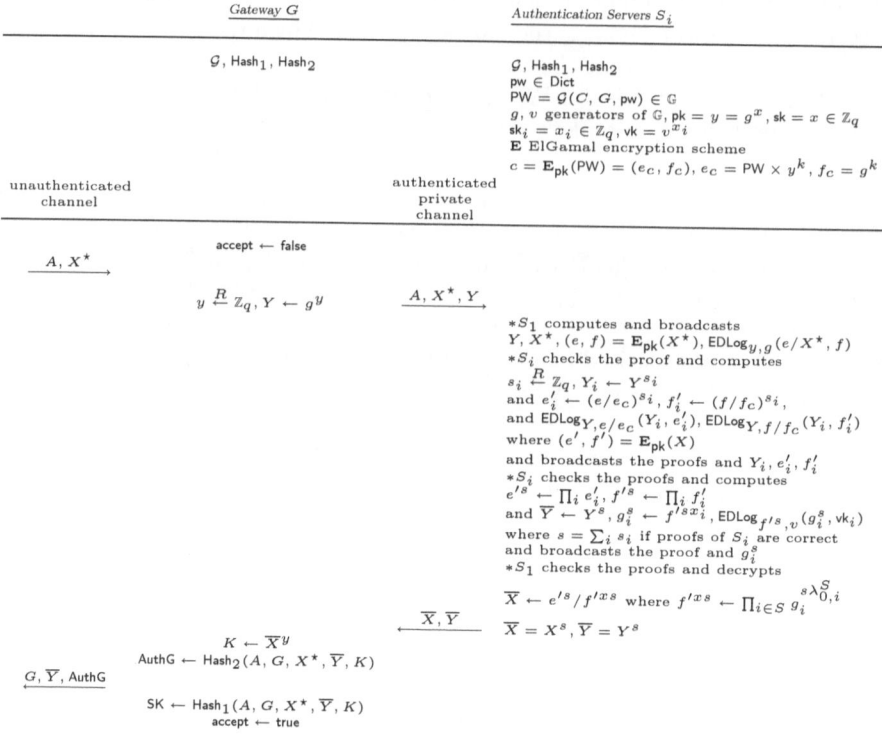

Fig. 2. Threshold version of the gateway-oriented password-based authenticated key exchange protocol. Since no change is required on the client side with respect to the non-threshold protocol in Figure 1, the client side has been omitted in the diagram.

Proof. Our goal is to reduce an adversary $\mathcal{A}$ against the GTPAKE protocol to an attacker $\mathcal{B}$ against the GPAKE protocol. We need to simulate the threshold environment for $\mathcal{A}$ that can corrupt any subset of size at most $k-1$ servers from the environment of the attacker $\mathcal{B}$. We essentially need to simulate the communications among the servers, *i.e.* the decryption parts at the end of the protocol and the proofs of validity.

Let $i_1, \ldots, i_{k-1}$ be the set of corrupted servers. Recall $x_i = F(i) \bmod q$ for all $1 \le i \le n$, and $x = F(0) \bmod q$.

To simulate the adversary's view, we simply choose the x_{i_j} belonging to the set of corrupted servers at random from the set $\mathbb{Z}_q$. This allows us to simulate all the messages, proofs of validity and decryption shares coming from the corrupted servers.

Once these values are chosen, the values x_i for the uncorrupted servers are also completely determined modulo q, since we have k points (the $k-1$ points of the corrupted servers and the point 0). The value at point 0 is the decryption value f'^{sx}. However, they cannot be easily computed since $F(0)$ is secret and corresponds to the secret key of the ElGamal scheme. The ElGamal secret key cannot be chosen by the attacker $\mathcal{B}$. Indeed, as all the passwords are encrypted using the ElGamal public key in a public file, $\mathcal{B}$ cannot know it, unless he recovers the passwords and can easily break the semantic security of the GPAKE scheme. However, we can easily compute the decryption parts $g_i^s = f'^{sx_i}$ of the uncorrupted server by using the value f'^{xs}:

$$g_i^s = f'^{sx\lambda_{i,0}^S} \times \prod_{j \in S \setminus \{0\}} g_j^{s\lambda_{i,j}^S}$$

where $S = \{0, i_1, \ldots, i_{k-1}\}$.

For the "proofs of validity", one can invoke the random oracle model for the hash function H to get soundness and perfect zero-knowledge. The soundness is similar to that in Appendix A.

Moreover, the interactive proof system is zero-knowledge against an *honest* verifier since the adversary's view can be simulated without knowing the values x_i. This view includes the values of the random oracle at those points where the adversary has queried the oracle, so the simulator is in complete charge of the random oracle. Whenever the adversary makes a query to the random oracle, if the oracle has not been previously defined at the given point, the simulator defines it to be a random value, and returns the value to the adversary. When we have to perform a fake proof for $(u_i, \bar{u}_i)$, since the simulator does not know x_i, he chooses at random $c \in \mathbb{Z}_q$ and $z \in \mathbb{Z}_q$ and defines the values of the random oracle at $(p, q, g, \bar{g}, u_i, \bar{u}_i, g^z/u_i^c, \bar{g}^z/\bar{u}_i^c)$ to be c. With all but negligible probability, the simulator has not defined the random oracle at this point before, and so it is free to do so. It is easy to verify that the distribution produced by this simulator is perfect.

Finally, as we need the semantic security of ElGamal encryption scheme, the security is based on the DDH assumption.   □

Acknowledgements

The authors would like to thank Raymond Choo for pointing out a flaw in a previous version of our schemes that made them susceptible to attacks by corrupted gateways. Such attacks are not currently taken into account by our security model. The first, third, and fourth authors have been supported in part by France Telecom R&D as part of the contract CIDRE, between France Telecom R&D and Ecole Normale Supérieure. The second author is supported by the Director, Office of Science, Office of Advanced Scientific Computing Research, Mathematical Information and Computing Sciences Division, of the U.S. Department of Energy under Contract No. DE-AC03-76SF00098. This document is report LBNL-58175. isclaimer available at `http://www-library.lbl.gov/disclaimer`.

References

1. Michel Abdalla, Olivier Chevassut, Pierre-Alain Fouque, and David Pointcheval. A simple threshold authenticated key exchange from short secrets. Full version of current paper. Available from authors' web pages.
2. Michel Abdalla, Pierre-Alain Fouque, and David Pointcheval. Password-based authenticated key exchange in the three-party setting. In Serge Vaudenay, editor, *PKC 2005: 8th International Workshop on Theory and Practice in Public Key Cryptography*, volume 3386 of *Lecture Notes in Computer Science*, pages 65–84, Les Diablerets, Switzerland, January 23–26, 2005. Springer-Verlag, Berlin, Germany.
3. Michel Abdalla and David Pointcheval. Interactive Diffie-Hellman assumptions with applications to password-based authentication. In Andrew Patrick and Moti Yung, editors, *Financial Cryptography 2005*, volume 3570 of *Lecture Notes in Computer Science*, pages 341–356, Roseau, The Commonwealth Of Dominica, February 28 – March 3, 2005. Springer-Verlag, Berlin, Germany.
4. Mihir Bellare, David Pointcheval, and Phillip Rogaway. Authenticated key exchange secure against dictionary attacks. In Bart Preneel, editor, *Advances in Cryptology – EUROCRYPT 2000*, volume 1807 of *Lecture Notes in Computer Science*, pages 139–155, Bruges, Belgium, May 14–18, 2000. Springer-Verlag, Berlin, Germany.
5. Mihir Bellare and Phillip Rogaway. The AuthA protocol for password-based authenticated key exchange. Contributions to IEEE P1363, March 2000.
6. Steven M. Bellovin and Michael Merritt. Encrypted key exchange: Password-based protocols secure against dictionary attacks. In *1992 IEEE Symposium on Security and Privacy*, pages 72–84, Oakland, CA, May 1992. IEEE Computer Society Press.
7. Emmanuel Bresson, Olivier Chevassut, and David Pointcheval. Security proofs for an efficient password-based key exchange. In *ACM CCS 03: 10th Conference on Computer and Communications Security*, pages 241–250, Washington D.C., USA, October 27–30, 2003. ACM Press.
8. Emmanuel Bresson, Olivier Chevassut, and David Pointcheval. New security results on encrypted key exchange. In Feng Bao, Robert Deng, and Jianying Zhou, editors, *PKC 2004: 7th International Workshop on Theory and Practice in Public Key Cryptography*, volume 2947 of *Lecture Notes in Computer Science*, pages 145–158, Singapore, March 1–4, 2004. Springer-Verlag, Berlin, Germany.
9. David Chaum and Torben P. Pedersen. Wallet databases with observers. In Ernest F. Brickell, editor, *Advances in Cryptology – CRYPTO'92*, volume 740 of *Lecture Notes in Computer Science*, pages 89–105, Santa Barbara, CA, USA, August 16–20, 1992. Springer-Verlag, Berlin, Germany.
10. Mario Di Raimondo and Rosario Gennaro. Provably secure threshold password-authenticated key exchange. In Eli Biham, editor, *Advances in Cryptology – EUROCRYPT 2003*, volume 2656 of *Lecture Notes in Computer Science*, pages 507–523, Warsaw, Poland, May 4–8, 2003. Springer-Verlag, Berlin, Germany.
11. Shai Halevi and Hugo Krawczyk. Public-key cryptography and password protocols. *ACM Transactions on Information and System Security*, 2(3):230–268, August 1999.
12. Jonathan Katz, Rafail Ostrovsky, and Moti Yung. Efficient password-authenticated key exchange using human-memorable passwords. In Birgit Pfitzmann, editor, *Advances in Cryptology – EUROCRYPT 2001*, volume 2045 of *Lecture Notes in Computer Science*, pages 475–494, Innsbruck, Austria, May 6–10, 2001. Springer-Verlag, Berlin, Germany.

13. Philip D. MacKenzie. The PAK suite: Protocols for password-authenticated key exchange. Contributions to IEEE P1363.2, 2002.
14. Philip D. MacKenzie, Thomas Shrimpton, and Markus Jakobsson. Threshold password-authenticated key exchange. In Moti Yung, editor, *Advances in Cryptology – CRYPTO 2002*, volume 2442 of *Lecture Notes in Computer Science*, pages 385–400, Santa Barbara, CA, USA, August 18–22, 2002. Springer-Verlag, Berlin, Germany.
15. David Pointcheval and Jacques Stern. Security arguments for digital signatures and blind signatures. *Journal of Cryptology*, 13(3):361–396, 2000.

A   Basic Tools

A.1   Threshold Secret Sharing

Let q be a prime and $1 \leq k \leq n < q$. Shamir secret sharing over $\mathbb{Z}_q$ is a k-out-of n sharing where any subset of at least k parties can recover the secret, but any subset of strictly less than k parties cannot gain any information about the secret. It is defined as follows: the dealer knows a secret $x \in \mathbb{Z}_q$, chooses $k - 1$ random points $f_1, \ldots, f_{k-1} \in \mathbb{Z}_q$, sets $f_0 = x$ and define the polynomial $F(X) = \sum_{j=0}^{k-1} f_j X^j$. For $1 \leq i \leq n$, let $x_i = F(i) \in \mathbb{Z}_q$ be the i-th share of x. Thanks to the Lagrange equality, we can show that if k shares are revealed, x is completely and can be determined by interpolation. For $S \subset \mathbb{Z}_q$ of cardinality k, any $i \in \mathbb{Z}_q$ and any $j \in S$, there exists an element $\lambda_{i,j}^S = \prod_{j' \in S \setminus \{j\}} (i - j') / \prod_{j' \in S \setminus \{j\}} (j - j') \in \mathbb{Z}_q$ such that

$$F(i) = \sum_{j \in S} \lambda_{i,j}^S F(j) \bmod q$$

A.2   Zero-Knowledge Proof of Equality of Discrete Logarithm

Let $\mathbb{G}$ be a group of prime order q with generators g and $\bar{g}$. Let $\mathsf{EDLog}_{g,\bar{g}}$ be the language of pairs $(u, \bar{u}) \in \mathbb{G}^2$ such that $\log_g u = \log_{\bar{g}} \bar{u}$. We will use a zero-knowledge proof *of membership* for the language $\mathsf{EDLog}_{g,\bar{g}}$. It is not a proof of knowledge since we only want to prove the correctness of the values computed by the authentication servers. We use the zero-knowledge proof system due to Chaum and Pedersen[9]. Although it happens to also be a proof of knowledge, we will not use this property. We describe here the non-interactive version using the Fiat-Shamir heuristic in the random oracle model.

Let $(u, \bar{u}) \in \mathsf{EDLog}_{g,\bar{g}}$ be given, so there exists $r \in \mathbb{Z}_q$ such that $u = g^r$ and $\bar{u} = \bar{g}^r$.

– The prover chooses $t \in \mathbb{Z}_q$ at random, computes $w = g^t$ and $\bar{w} = \bar{g}^t$. He computes $c = H(p, q, g, \bar{g}, u, \bar{u}, w, \bar{w})$ where H is modeled as a random oracle. Finally, he computes $z = t + rc \bmod q$ and sends to the verifier, (c, z)
– The verifier checks whether the following equality holds

$$c = H(p, q, g, \bar{g}, u, \bar{u}, g^z/u^c, \bar{g}^z/\bar{u}^c)$$

It is well-known that the interactive version of this proof is sound since a cheating prover can be accepted only with probability at most $1/q$. Assume that $(u, \bar{u}) \notin \mathsf{EDLog}_{g, \bar{g}}$, then $u = g^r$ and $\bar{u} = \bar{g}^{\bar{r}}$ where $r \neq \bar{r}$. If a proof is correct, then there exists a unique z such that $w = g^z/u^c$ and $\bar{w} = \bar{g}^z/\bar{u}^c$, then $z - rc = t$ and $z - \bar{r}c = \bar{t}$. Therefore, we get $t - \bar{t} = (\bar{r} - r)c \bmod q$ and since $\bar{r} - r \neq 0 \bmod q$, there is a unique value for $t - \bar{t}$ and so with probability $1/q$, the cheating prover is detected.

Finally, the interactive proof system is zero-knowledge against an *honest* verifier

B   Proof of Lemma 2

In this section, we show that the Set Password-based Computational Diffie-Hellman SPCCDH problem is equivalent to the (basic) computational Diffie-Hellman problem CDH: For proving this relation, one simply applies the splitting lemma [15]:

Lemma 8 (Splitting Lemma). *Let $S \subset A \times B$ such that $\Pr[(a, b) \in S] \geq \alpha$. For any $\beta < \alpha$, define*

$$T = \left\{ (a, b) \in A \times B \;\middle|\; \Pr_{b' \in B}[(a, b') \in S] \geq \alpha - \beta \right\}$$

Then   (i) $\Pr[T] \geq \beta$ (ii) $\forall (a, b) \in T, \Pr_{b' \in B}[(a, b') \in S] \geq \alpha - \beta$.

Let $\mathcal{A}$ be an adversary against the SPCCDH problem, with success probability $\alpha = 1/N + \varepsilon$. Then, we can use the splitting lemma, with $\beta = \varepsilon/2$, on

$$A = \{(\omega, X, \mathcal{D})\} \text{ and } B = \{1, \ldots, N\} \approx \mathcal{D}.$$

Our adversary $\mathcal{B}$ receives as input a random CDH instance (U, X). It chooses a random tape ω for $\mathcal{A}$, as well as N random distinct exponents $u_i \in \mathbb{Z}_p$. It defines $U_i = U^{u_i}$, which specifies the dictionary $\mathcal{D}$: with probability greater than $\varepsilon/2$, the success probability is greater than $1/N + \varepsilon/2$, over the probability space $B = \{1, \ldots, N\}$. It is thus a multiple of $1/N$, not smaller than $1/N + \nu$, where ν is the maximum in $\{1/N, \varepsilon/2\}$. One first simply runs $\mathcal{A}$ with a random k, and with probability greater than $1/N + \nu$, one gets a first set S_1 with $K = \mathrm{CDH}(X/U_k, Y) = \mathrm{CDH}(X/U^{u_k}, Y)$. One runs $\mathcal{A}$ again, with another random $k' \neq k$, and with probability greater than ν, one gets a second set S_2 with $K' = \mathrm{CDH}(X/U_{k'}, Y) = \mathrm{CDH}(X/U^{u_{k'}}, Y)$. Then, $\mathrm{CDH}(X, U) = (K/K')^{1/(u_k - u_{k'})}$. By choosing two elements at random in S_1 and S_2, one gets $\mathrm{CDH}(X, U)$ with probability $1/s^2$.

Examining Indistinguishability-Based Proof Models for Key Establishment Protocols*

Kim-Kwang Raymond Choo, Colin Boyd, and Yvonne Hitchcock

Information Security Institute,
Queensland University of Technology,
GPO Box 2434, Brisbane, QLD 4001, Australia
{k.choo, c.boyd, y.hitchcock}@qut.edu.au

Abstract. We examine various indistinguishability-based proof models for key establishment protocols, namely the Bellare & Rogaway (1993, 1995), the Bellare, Pointcheval, & Rogaway (2000), and the Canetti & Krawczyk (2001) proof models. We then consider several variants of these proof models, identify several subtle differences between these variants and models, and compare the relative strengths of the notions of security between the models. For each of the pair of relations between the models (either an implication or a non-implication), we provide proofs or counter-examples to support the observed relations. We also reveal a drawback with the original formulation of the Bellare, Pointcheval, & Rogaway (2000) model, whereby the Corrupt query is not allowed.

1 Introduction

Key establishment protocols are used for distributing shared keying material in a secure manner. However, despite their importance, the difficulties of obtaining a high level of assurance in the security of almost any new, or even existing, protocol are well illustrated with examples of errors found in many such protocols years after they were published. The treatment of computational complexity analysis adopts a deductive reasoning process whereby the emphasis is placed on a proven reduction from the problem of breaking the protocol to another problem believed to be hard. Such an approach for key establishment protocols was made popular by Bellare & Rogaway [6] who provide the first formal definition for a model of adversary capabilities with an associated definition of security (which we refer to as the BR93 model in this paper). Since then, many research efforts have been oriented towards this end which have resulted in numerous protocols with accompanying computational proofs of security proposed in the literature.

The BR93 model has been further revised several times. In 1995, Bellare and Rogaway analysed a three-party server-based key distribution (3PKD) protocol [7] using an extension to the BR93 model, which we refer to as the BR95 model. A more recent revision to the model was proposed in 2000 by Bellare,

---

* This work was partially funded by the Australian Research Council Discovery Project Grant DP0345775. The full version of this paper appears in [14].

B. Roy (Ed.): ASIACRYPT 2005, LNCS 3788, pp. 585–604, 2005.

Pointcheval and Rogaway [5], hereafter referred to as the BPR2000 model. Collectively, the BR93, BR95, and BPR2000 models will be referred to as the Bellare–Rogaway models. In independent yet related work, Bellare, Canetti, & Krawczyk [4] built on the BR93 model and introduced a modular proof model. However, some drawbacks with this formulation were discovered and this modular proof model was subsequently modified by Canetti & Krawczyk [12], and will be referred to as the CK2001 model in this paper.

Proof Models. There are several important differences between the BR93, BR95, BPR2000, and CK2001 models (which have a significant impact on the security of the models), as follows:

1. the way partner oracles are defined (i.e., the definition of partnership),
2. the powers of the probabilistic, polynomial-time (PPT) adversary,
3. the modular approach adopted in the CK2001 model, and
4. the provable security goals provided by the models.

DIFFERENCE 1: Security in the models depends on the notions of partnership of oracles and indistinguishability of session keys. The BR93 model defines partnership using the notion of matching conversations, where a conversation is a sequence of messages exchanged between some instances of communicating oracles in a protocol run. Partnership in the BR95 model is defined using the notion of a partner function, which uses the transcript (the record of all Send oracle queries) to determine the partner of an oracle by providing a mapping between two oracles that should share a secret key on completion of the protocol execution. However, such a partner definition can easily go wrong. One such example is the partner function described in the original BR95 paper for the 3PKD protocol [7], which was later found to be flawed [15].

The BPR2000 model and the CK2001 model define partnership using the notion of session identifiers (SIDs). Although in the BPR2000 model, the construction of SIDs is suggested to be the concatenation of messages exchanged during the protocol run, protocol designers can construct SIDs differently. There is no formal definition of how SIDs should be defined in the CK2001 model. Instead, SIDs are defined to be some unique values agreed upon by two communicating parties prior to the protocol execution. We observe that the way SIDs are constructed can have an impact on the security of the protocol in the model.

DIFFERENCE 2: The CK2001 model enjoys the strongest adversarial power (compared to the Bellare–Rogaway models) as the adversary is allowed to ask the Session-State Reveal query that will return all the internal state (including any ephemeral parameters but not long-term secret parameters) of the target session to the adversary. In contrast, most models only allow the adversary to reveal session keys for uncorrupted parties. In the original BR93 and BPR2000 models, the Corrupt query (that allows the adversary to corrupt any principal at will, and thereby learn the complete internal state of the corrupted principal) is not allowed.

In this paper, we consider the BR93 model which allows the adversary access to a Corrupt query because later proofs of security in the BR93 model [2,8,9,13,16,17,19] allow the Corrupt query. However, we consider the original BPR2000 model without Corrupt query because the basic notion of BPR2000 freshness restricts the adversary, $\mathcal{A}$, from corrupting anyone in the model (i.e., effectively restricting $\mathcal{A}$ from asking any Corrupt query). However, we show that the omission of such a (Corrupt) query in the BPR2000 model allows an insecure protocol to be proven secure in the model.

DIFFERENCE 3: A major advantage of the CK2001 model is its modular approach whereby protocols may be proven secure in an ideal world (AM) model in which the passive adversary is prevented from fabricating messages coming from uncorrupted principals, and translating such a protocol proven secure in the AM into one that is secure in the more realistic real world model (the UM). As Boyd, Mao, & Paterson [10] have pointed out, the CK2001 modular approach facilitates an engineering approach to protocol design, where protocol components may be combined by "mix and match" to tailor to the application at hand (analogous to a Java API library).

DIFFERENCE 4: Both the BR93 and BPR2000 models provide provable security for entity authentication & key distribution, whilst the BR95 model provides provable security for only the key distribution. Intuitively, protocols that provide both entity authentication and key distribution are "stronger" than protocols that provide only key distribution. In this paper, we refer to the BR93 and BPR2000 models that provide provable security for only key distribution as BR93 (KE) and BPR2000 (KE) respectively, and the BR93 and BPR2000 models that provide provable security for both entity authentication & key distribution as BR93 (EA+KE) and BPR2000 (EA+KE) respectively.

Motivations. We are motivated by the observations that no formal study has been devoted to the comparisons of relations and relative strengths of security between the Bellare–Rogaway and the Canetti–Krawczyk models. Although Shoup [18] provides a brief discussion on the Bellare–Rogaway models and the Canetti–Krawczyk model, his discussion is restricted to an informal comparison between the Bellare–Rogaway model and his model, and between the Canetti–Krawczyk model and his model. To the best of our knowledge, no distinction has ever been made between the Bellare–Rogaway proof model and its variants shown in Table 1.

Table 1. The Bellare–Rogaway proof model and its variants

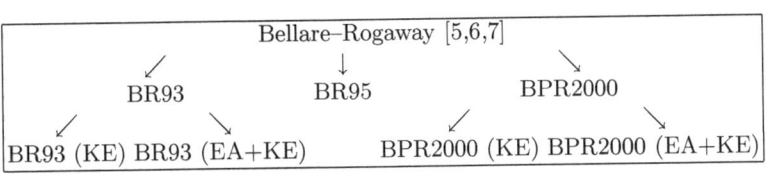

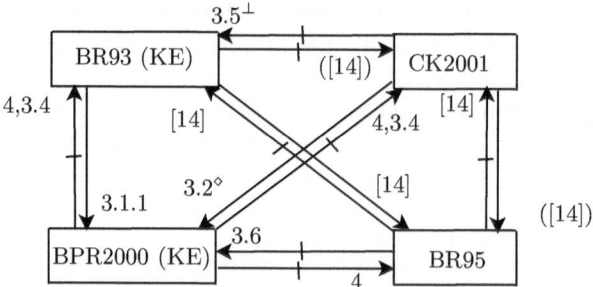

◇ holds if SIDs are constructed in the same manner in both models.
⊥ holds if SIDs are not defined to be the concatenation of messages exchanged during the protocol run.

Fig. 1. Notions of security between the Bellare–Rogaway and Canetti–Krawczyk key establishment proof models

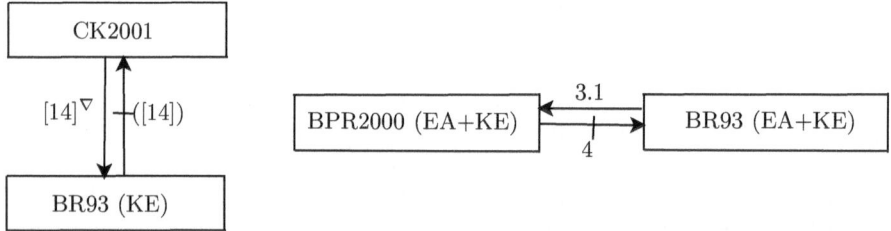

∇ holds if SIDs are defined to be the concatenation of messages exchanged during the protocol run.

Fig. 2. Additional comparisons

Contributions. We regard the main contributions of this paper to be of three-fold significance:

1. contributing towards a better understanding of the different flavours of proof models for key establishment protocols by working out the relations between the Bellare–Rogaway proof model (and its variants) and the Canetti–Krawczyk proof model,
2. demonstrating that the Bellare–Rogaway (and its variants) and the Canetti–Krawczyk proof models have varying security strength by providing a comparison of the relative strengths of the notions of security between them, and
3. identifying a drawback in the BPR2000 model (not identified in any previous studies) which allows an insecure protocol to be proven secure in the BPR2000 model, as presented in Section 4.

This work may ease the understanding of future security protocol proofs (protocols proven secure in one model maybe automatically secure in another model), and protocol designers can make an informed decision when choosing an appropriate model in which to prove their protocols secure. Our main results are summarized in Figures 1 and 2. We observe that if SIDs in the CK2001 model are defined to be the concatenation of messages exchanged during the protocol run, then the implication CK2001 → BR93 holds, and the CK2001 model offers the strongest definition of security compared to the BR93 model.

The notation $x \to y$ denotes that protocols proven secure in model x will also be secure in model y (i.e., implication relation where x implies y), $x \nrightarrow y$ denotes that protocols proven secure in model x do not necessarily satisfy the definition of security in model y. The number on the arrows represent the section in which the proof is provided, and the numbers in brackets on the arrows represent the sections in which the implication relation is proven.

Organization. Section 2 provides an informal overview of the Bellare-Rogaway and Canetti–Krawczyk models. Section 3 provides the proofs of the implication relations and counter-examples the for non-implication relations shown in Figures 1 and 2. In these counter-examples, we demonstrate that these protocols though secure in the existing proof model (in which they are proven secure) are insecure in another "stronger" proof model. Due to space constraints, some of the proofs and counter-examples appear in the full version [14]. Section 4 presents the drawback in the original formulation of the BPR2000 model by using a three-party password-based key exchange protocol (3PAKE) due to Abdalla & Pointcheval [1] as a case study. Section 5 presents the conclusions.

2   The Proof Models

In this section, an overview of the Bellare-Rogaway [5,6,7] and Canetti–Krawczyk models [4,12] is provided primarily for demonstrating the gaps in the relations and the relative strengths of security between the variants of the Bellare–Rogaway and the Canetti–Krawczyk models.

Adversarial Powers. In the Bellare-Rogaway and Canetti–Krawczyk models, the adversary $\mathcal{A}$ is defined to be a probabilistic machine that is in control of all communications between parties via the predefined oracle queries described below:

Send: This query computes a response according to the protocol specification and decision on whether to accept or reject yet, and returns them to $\mathcal{A}$.

Session-Key Reveal(U_1, U_2, i): Oracle $\Pi^i_{U_1,U_2}$, upon receiving a Session-Key Reveal query, and if it has accepted and holds some session key, will send this session key back to $\mathcal{A}$. This query is known as a Reveal(U_1, U_2, i) query in the Bellare–Rogaway models.

Session-State Reveal: Oracle $\Pi^i_{U_1,U_2}$, upon receiving a Session-State Reveal (U_1, U_2, i) query and if it has neither accepted nor held some session key, will return all its internal state (including any ephemeral parameters but not long-term secret parameters) to $\mathcal{A}$.

Table 2. Summary of adversarial powers

Oracle Queries	BR93	BR95	BPR2000	CK2001
Send	*Yes*	*Yes*	*Yes*	*Yes*
Session-Key Reveal	*Yes*	*Yes*	*Yes*	*Yes*
Session-State Reveal	*No*	*No*	*No*	*Yes*
Corrupt	*Yes*	*Yes*	*No*	*Yes*
Test	*Yes*	*Yes*	*Yes*	*Yes*

Corrupt: The Corrupt(U_1) query allows $\mathcal{A}$ to corrupt the principal U_1 at will, and thereby learn the complete internal state of the corrupted principal.

Test: The Test(U_1, U_2, i) query is the only oracle query that does not correspond to any of $\mathcal{A}$'s abilities. If $\Pi^i_{U_1,U_2}$ has accepted with some session key and is being asked a Test(U_1, U_2, i) query, then depending on a randomly chosen bit b, $\mathcal{A}$ is given either the actual session key or a session key drawn randomly from the session key distribution.

Table 2 provides a comparison of the types of queries allowed for the adversary between the various BR93, BR95, BPR2000, and CK2001 models.

Definition of Freshness. The notion of freshness of the oracle to whom the Test query is sent remains the same for the Bellare–Rogaway and Canetti–Krawczyk models. Freshness is used to identify the session keys about which $\mathcal{A}$ ought not to know anything because $\mathcal{A}$ has not revealed any oracles that have accepted the key and has not corrupted any principals knowing the key. Definition 1 describes freshness, which depends on the respective partnership definitions.

Definition 1 (Definition of Freshness). *Oracle $\Pi^i_{A,B}$ is fresh (or holds a fresh session key) at the end of execution, if, and only if, (1) $\Pi^i_{A,B}$ has accepted with or without a partner oracle $\Pi^j_{B,A}$, (2) both $\Pi^i_{A,B}$ and $\Pi^j_{B,A}$ oracles have not been sent a* Reveal *query (or* Session-State Reveal *in the CK2001 model), and (3) A and B have not been sent a* Corrupt *query.*

The basic notion of freshness (i.e., does not incorporate the notion of forward secrecy) in the BPR2000 model requires that no one (including A and B in requirement 3 of Definition 1) in the model has been sent a Corrupt query. This effectively restricts $\mathcal{A}$ from asking any Corrupt query in the (BPR2000) model.

Definition of Security. Security in the Bellare–Rogaway and the Canetti–Krawczyk models is defined using the game $\mathcal{G}$, played between a malicious adversary $\mathcal{A}$ and a collection of $\Pi^i_{U_x,U_y}$ oracles for players $U_x, U_y \in \{U_1, \ldots, U_{N_p}\}$ and instances $i \in \{1, \ldots, N_s\}$. The adversary $\mathcal{A}$ runs the game $\mathcal{G}$, whose setting is explained in Table 3.

Success of $\mathcal{A}$ in $\mathcal{G}$ is quantified in terms of $\mathcal{A}$'s advantage in distinguishing whether $\mathcal{A}$ receives the real key or a random value. $\mathcal{A}$ wins if, after asking a Test(U_1, U_2, i) query, where $\Pi^i_{U_1,U_2}$ is fresh and has accepted, $\mathcal{A}$'s guess bit b'

Table 3. Setting of game $\mathcal{G}$

Stage 1: $\mathcal{A}$ is able to send any oracle queries at will.
Stage 2: At some point during $\mathcal{G}$, $\mathcal{A}$ will choose a fresh session on which to be tested and send a Test query to the fresh oracle associated with the test session. Depending on the randomly chosen bit b, $\mathcal{A}$ is given either the actual session key or a session key drawn randomly from the session key distribution.
Stage 3: $\mathcal{A}$ continues making any oracle queries at will but cannot make Corrupt and/or Session-Key Reveal and/or Session-State Reveal queries (depending on the individual proof model) that trivially expose the test session key.
Stage 4: Eventually, $\mathcal{A}$ terminates the game simulation and outputs a bit b', which is its guess of the value of b.

equals the bit b selected during the Test(U_1, U_2, i) query. Let the advantage function of $\mathcal{A}$ be denoted by $\mathsf{Adv}^{\mathcal{A}}(k)$, where $\mathsf{Adv}^{\mathcal{A}}(k) = 2 \times \Pr[b = b'] - 1$.

2.1 The Bellare-Rogaway Models

2.1.1 The BR93 Model
Partnership is defined using the notion of matching conversations, where a conversation is defined to be the sequence of messages sent and received by an oracle. The sequence of messages exchanged (i.e., only the Send oracle queries) are recorded in the transcript, T. At the end of a protocol run, T will contain the record of the Send queries and the responses. Definition 2 describes security for the BR93 model.

Definition 2 (BR93 Security). *A protocol is secure in the BR93 model if for all PPT adversaries $\mathcal{A}$, (1) if uncorrupted oracles $\Pi^i_{A,B}$ and $\Pi^j_{B,A}$ complete with matching conversations, then the probability that there exist i, j such that $\Pi^i_{A,B}$ accepted and there is no $\Pi^j_{B,A}$ that had engaged in a matching session is negligible, and (2) $\mathsf{Adv}^{\mathcal{A}}(k)$ is negligible. If both requirements are satisfied, then $\Pi^i_{A,B}$ and $\Pi^j_{B,A}$ will also have the same session key.*

Requirement 1 of Definition 2 implies entity authentication, whereby entity authentication is said to be violated if some fresh oracle terminates with no partner.

2.1.2 The BR95 Model
Partnership in the BR95 model is defined using the notion of a partner function, which uses the transcript (the record of all Send oracle queries) to determine the partner of an oracle. However, no explicit definition of partnership was provided in the original paper since there is no single partner function fixed for any protocol. Instead, security is defined predicated on the existence of a suitable partner function. Definition 3 describes security for the BR95 model.

Definition 3 (BR95 Security). *A protocol is secure in the BR95 model if both the following requirements are satisfied (1) when the protocol is run between* two oracles $\Pi^i_{A,B}$ and $\Pi^j_{B,A}$ in the absence of a malicious adversary, both $\Pi^i_{A,B}$ and $\Pi^j_{B,A}$ accept and hold the same session key, (2) for all PPT adversaries $\mathcal{A}$, $\mathsf{Adv}^{\mathcal{A}}(k)$ is negligible.

2.1.3   The BPR2000 Model

Partnership in the BPR2000 model is defined based on the notion of session identifiers (SIDs) where SIDs are suggested to be the concatenation of messages exchanged during the protocol run. In this model, an oracle who has accepted will hold the associated session key, a SID and a partner identifier (PID). Definition 4 describes partnership in the BPR2000 model.

Definition 4 (BPR2000 Partnership). *Two oracles, $\Pi^i_{A,B}$ and $\Pi^j_{B,A}$, are partners if, and only if, both oracles have accepted the same session key with the same SID, have agreed on the same set of principals (i.e. the initiator and the responder of the protocol), and no other oracles besides $\Pi^i_{A,B}$ and $\Pi^j_{B,A}$ have accepted with the same SID.*

In the BPR2000 model, security is described in Definition 5. The notion of security for entity authentication is said to be violated if some fresh oracle terminates with no partner.

Definition 5 (BPR2000 Security). *A protocol is secure in the BPR2000 model under the notion of*

- *key establishment if for all PPT adversaries $\mathcal{A}$, $\mathsf{Adv}^{\mathcal{A}}(k)$ is negligible.*
- *mutual authentication if for all PPT adversaries $\mathcal{A}$, the advantage that $\mathcal{A}$ has in violating entity authentication is negligible.*

2.2   The Canetti-Krawczyk Model

In the CK2001 model, there are two adversarial models, namely the unathenticated-links adversarial / real world model (UM) and the authenticated-links adversarial / ideal world model (AM). Let $\mathcal{A}_{UM}$ denote the (active) adversary in the UM, and $\mathcal{A}_{AM}$ denote the (passive) adversary in the AM. The difference between $\mathcal{A}_{AM}$ and $\mathcal{A}_{UM}$ lies in their powers, namely $\mathcal{A}_{AM}$ is restricted to only delay, delete, and relay messages but not to fabricate any messages or send a message more than once. Prior to explaining how a provably secure protocol in the AM is translated to a provably secure protocol in the UM with the use of an authenticator, we require definitions of an emulator and an authenticator, as given in Definitions 6 and 7.

Definition 6 (Definition of an Emulator [4]). *Let π and π' be two protocols for n parties where π is a protocol in the AM and π' is a protocol in the UM. π' is said to emulate π if for any UM-adversary $\mathcal{A}_{UM}$ there exists an AM-adversary $\mathcal{A}_{AM}$, such that for all inputs, no polyomial time adversary can distinguish the cumulative outputs of all parties and the adversary between the AM and the UM with more than negligible probability.*

Definition 7 (Definition of an Authenticator [12]). *An authenticator is defined to be a mapping transforming a protocol π_{AM} in the AM to a protocol π_{UM} in the UM such that π_{UM} emulates π_{AM}.*

In other words, the security proof of the UM protocol in the CK2001 depends on the security proofs of the MT-authenticator used and that of the AM protocol. If any of these proofs break down, then the proof of the UM protocol is invalid.

Definitions 8 and 9 describe partnership and security for the CK2001 model.

Definition 8 (Matching Sessions). *Two sessions are said to be matching if they have the same session identifiers (SIDs) and corresponding partner identifiers (PIDs).*

Definition 9 (CK2001 Security). *A protocol is secure in the CK2001 model if for all PPT adversaries $\mathcal{A}$, (1) if two uncorrupted oracles $\Pi^i_{A,B}$ and $\Pi^j_{B,A}$ complete matching sessions, then both $\Pi^i_{A,B}$ and $\Pi^j_{B,A}$ must hold the same session key, and (2) $\mathsf{Adv}^{\mathcal{A}}(k)$ is negligible.*

3   Relating the Notions of Security

In our proofs for each of the implication relations shown in Figure 1, we construct a primary adversary, $\mathcal{PA}$, against the key establishment protocol in $\mathcal{PA}$'s model using a secondary adversary $\mathcal{SA}$ against the same key establishment protocol in $\mathcal{SA}$'s model. $\mathcal{PA}$ simulates the view of $\mathcal{SA}$ by asking all queries of $\mathcal{SA}$ to the respective Send, Session-Key Reveal, Session-State Reveal, Corrupt, and Test oracles (to which $\mathcal{PA}$ has access), and forwards the answers received from the oracles to $\mathcal{SA}$. The specification of the simulation is given in Figure 3.

Note that Shoup [18–Remark 26] pointed out that an adversary $\mathcal{A}$ in the Bellare–Rogaway model wins the game if $\mathcal{A}$ is able to make two partner oracles accept different session keys without making any Reveal and Test queries. His findings are applicable to only the BR93 and CK2001 models where the definitions of security requires two partner oracles to accept with the same session key, as described in Definitions 2 and 9 respectively. However, this is not the case for the BR95 and BPR2000 models.

The notation in this section is as follows: $\{\cdot\}_{K^{enc}_{U_1 U_2}}$ denotes the encryption of some message under the encryption key $K^{enc}_{U_1 U_2}$, the notation $[\cdot]_{K^{MAC}_{U_1 U_2}}$ denotes the computation of MAC digest of some message under the MAC key $K^{MAC}_{U_1 U_2}$, and $Sig_{d_U}(\cdot)$ denotes the signature of some message under the signature key d_U, $\mathcal{H}$ denote some secure hash function, $\|$ denote concatentation of messages, and pwd denote some secret password shared between two users.

3.1   Proving Implication Relation: BR93 (EA+KE) → BPR2000 (EA+KE)

Recall that the Corrupt query is not allowed in the BPR2000 model but is allowed in the BR93 model as shown in Table 2. Intuitively, the model with a greater

Queries	Actions
Send	$\mathcal{PA}$ is able to answer this query pertaining to any instance of a server or player by asking its Send oracle.
Session-Key Reveal	$\mathcal{PA}$ is restricted from asking a Session-Key Reveal query to the target test oracle or its partner in its own game. Similarly, $\mathcal{SA}$ faces the same restriction[R]. Hence, $\mathcal{PA}$ is able to answer this query by asking its Reveal oracle and is able to simulate the Session-Key Reveal query perfectly.
Corrupt	$\mathcal{SA}$ is disallowed from asking a Corrupt query to the principal of the target test session or whom the target test session thinks it is communicating with in its own game. Similarly, the $\mathcal{PA}$ faces the same restriction. Hence, $\mathcal{PA}$ is able to answer this query by asking its Corrupt oracle and simulates the Corrupt query perfectly.
Test	If the following conditions are satisfied (under the assumption that both $\mathcal{PA}$ and $\mathcal{SA}$ choose the same Test session), then $\mathcal{PA}$ queries its Test oracle. The Test oracle randomly chooses a bit, b_{Test}, and depending on b_{00}, the Test oracle either returns the actual session key or a random key. $\mathcal{PA}$ then answers $\mathcal{SA}$ with the answer received from its Test oracle. Let b_{SA} be the final output of $\mathcal{SA}$ and $\mathcal{PA}$ will output b_{SA} as its own answer. $\mathcal{PA}$ succeeds and wins the game if $\mathcal{SA}$ does. – The Test sessions in both $\mathcal{PA}$'s and $\mathcal{SA}$'s simulations have accepted, and must be fresh. • Since $\mathcal{PA}$ is able to answer all Send, Session-Key Reveal, and Corrupt queries asked by $\mathcal{SA}$ as shown above, if the Test session in $\mathcal{SA}$'s simulation has accepted, so does the same Test session in $\mathcal{PA}$'s simulation. • Since $\mathcal{PA}$ faces the same restriction as $\mathcal{SA}$ of not able to reveal or corrupt an oracle or principal associated with the Test session, if the Test session in $\mathcal{SA}$'s simulation is fresh, so is the same Test session in $\mathcal{PA}$'s simulation.

R: subject to the following requirements:

1. non-partners in the simulation of $\mathcal{SA}$ are also non-partners in the simulation of $\mathcal{PA}$ so that whatever we can reveal in the simulation of $\mathcal{SA}$, we can also reveal in the simulation of $\mathcal{PA}$. Alternatively, we require that partners in the simulation of $\mathcal{PA}$ are also partners in the simulation of $\mathcal{SA}$ so that whatever we cannot reveal in the simulation of $\mathcal{PA}$, we also cannot reveal in the simulation of $\mathcal{SA}$.
2. a fresh oracle in the simulation of $\mathcal{SA}$ is also a fresh oracle the simulation of $\mathcal{PA}$ so that whatever we cannot reveal in the simulation of $\mathcal{SA}$, we also cannot reveal in the simulation of $\mathcal{PA}$.

Fig. 3. Specification of simulation between the primary adversary and the secondary adversary

adversarial power, especially one that allows the adversary access to the entire internal state of a player (i.e., via the Corrupt query), has a tighter definition of security than the model with a weaker adversarial power.

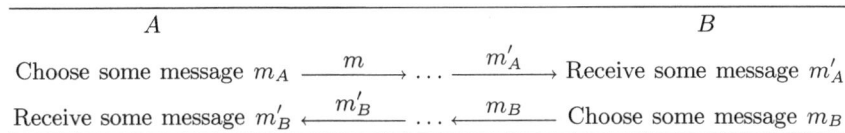

Fig. 4. An example protocol execution

3.1.1 Proof for the Key Establishment Goal

Let the advantage of some PPT adversary, $\mathcal{A}_{00}$, in the BPR2000 (EA+KE) model be $\mathsf{Adv}^{\mathcal{A}_{00}}$, and the advantage of some PPT adversary, $\mathcal{A}_{93}$, in the BR93 (EA+KE) model be $\mathsf{Adv}^{\mathcal{A}_{93}}$.

Lemma 1. *For any key establishment protocol, for any $\mathcal{A}_{00}$, there exists an $\mathcal{A}_{93}$, such that* $\mathsf{Adv}^{\mathcal{A}_{00}} = \mathsf{Adv}^{\mathcal{A}_{93}}$.

Proof (Lemma 1). An adversary $\mathcal{A}_{93}$ against the key establishment protocol in the BR93 (EA+KE) model is constructed using an adversary $\mathcal{A}_{00}$ against the same key establishment protocol in the BPR2000 (EA+KE) model, as shown in Figure 3. In other words, let $\mathcal{A}_{93}$ be the primary adversary and $\mathcal{A}_{00}$ be the secondary adversary where $\mathcal{A}_{93}$ simulates the view of $\mathcal{A}_{00}$. $\mathcal{A}_{93}$ asks all queries by $\mathcal{A}_{00}$ to the respective Send oracles, Session-Key Reveal oracles, and Test oracle (to which $\mathcal{A}_{93}$ has access), and forwards the answers received from the oracles to $\mathcal{A}_{00}$. Eventually, $\mathcal{A}_{00}$ outputs a guess bit b_{00} and $\mathcal{A}_{93}$ will output b_{00} as its own answer. $\mathcal{A}_{93}$ succeeds and wins the game if $\mathcal{A}_{00}$ does.

In order to demonstrate that the primary adversary, $\mathcal{A}_{93}$, is able to answer the queries asked by the secondary adversary, $\mathcal{A}_{00}$, we need to satisfy requirements 1 and 2 described in Figure 3. Using the example protocol execution shown in Figure 4, B is said to have a matching conversation with A if, and only if, message m'_A received is the same message m_A (i.e., $m'_A = m_A$) sent by A, and A is said to have matching conversation (in the BR93 model) with B if, and only if, message m'_B received is the same message m_B (i.e., $m'_B = m_B$) sent by B. In the context of Figure 4, $sid_A = m_A||m'_B$ and $sid_B = m'_A||m_A$ (in the BPR2000 model), and $sid_A = sid_B$ if message m'_A received by B is the same message m_A (i.e., $m'_A = m_A$) sent by A, and message m'_B received by A is the same message m_B (i.e., $m'_B = m_B$) sent by B. Hence, if both A and B have matching conversations, then $sid_A = m_A||m'_B = m'_A||m_A = sid_B$. If A and B are BR93-secure protocols, then A and B will also accept with the same session key.

Recall that the BPR2000 definition of partnership requires two oracles to accept with the same SID, corresponding PID, and the same key, in order to be considered partners. Now, if A and B do not have matching conversations, then A and B are not BR93 partners. This also implies that A and B are not BPR2000 partners since $sid_A \neq sid_B$. Since non-partners in the simulation of the secondary adversary, $\mathcal{A}_{00}$, are also non-partners in the simulation of the primary adversary, $\mathcal{A}_{93}$, requirement 1 (described in Figure 3) is satisfied.

An oracle is considered fresh in the BPR2000 model if it (or its associated partner, if such a partner exists) has not been asked a Reveal query and an oracle is considered fresh in the BR93 model if it (or its associated partner, if such a partner exists) has not been asked either a Reveal or a Corrupt query. Hence, it follows easily that a fresh oracle in the BPR2000 model is also fresh in the BR93 model. Hence, both requirements 1 and 2 (described in Figure 3) are satisfied.

To analyse $\mathsf{Adv}^{\mathcal{A}_{93}}$, we first consider the case in which the Test oracle associated with $\mathcal{A}_{93}$ returns a random key. The probability of $\mathcal{A}_{00}$ guessing the correct b_{00} bit is $\frac{1}{2}$ since it cannot gain any information about the hidden b_{93} bit. We then consider the case where the Test oracle associated with $\mathcal{A}_{93}$ returns the actual session key. In this case, the proof simulation (of $\mathcal{A}_{00}$) is perfect and $\mathcal{A}_{93}$ runs $\mathcal{A}_{00}$ exactly in the game defining the security of $\mathcal{A}_{00}$. Therefore, if $\mathcal{A}_{00}$ has a non-negligible advantage, so does $\mathcal{A}_{93}$ (i.e., $\mathsf{Adv}^{\mathcal{A}_{93}} = \mathsf{Adv}^{\mathcal{A}_{00}}$). This is in violation of our assumption and Lemma 1 follows. $\square$

3.1.2 Proof for the Entity Authentication Goal

By inspection of Definitions 2 and 5, the definitions for entity authentication in both the BR93 and BPR2000 models are equivalent, whereby entity authentication is said to be violated if some fresh oracle terminates with no partner. Following from our earlier proofs in Section 3.1.1, we define $\mathcal{A}_{93}$ to simulate the view of $\mathcal{A}_{00}$. In other words, $\mathcal{A}_{93}$ does anything that $\mathcal{A}_{00}$ does. Since non-partners in the simulation of $\mathcal{A}_{00}$ are also non-partners in the simulation of $\mathcal{A}_{93}$, therefore if $\mathcal{A}_{00}$ has a non-negligible probability in violating mutual authentication, so does $\mathcal{A}_{93}$. This is in violation of our assumption and the proof for entity authentication follows.

3.2 Proving Implication Relation: CK2001 → BPR2000 (KE)

Recall that one of the key differences between the BPR2000 and the CK2001 models is that the Canetti–Krawczyk adversary is allowed to ask the additional Session-State Reveal and Corrupt queries, as shown in Table 2. Intuitively, the model with a greater adversarial power has a tighter definition of security than the model with a weaker adversarial power. To support our observation, let the advantage of some PPT adversary in the BPR2000 (KE) model be $\mathsf{Adv}^{\mathcal{A}_{00KE}}$, and the advantage of some PPT adversary in the CK2001 model be $\mathsf{Adv}^{\mathcal{A}_{01}}$.

Lemma 2. *For any key establishment protocol and for any $\mathcal{A}_{00KE}$, there exists an $\mathcal{A}_{01}$, such that $\mathsf{Adv}^{\mathcal{A}_{00KE}} = \mathsf{Adv}^{\mathcal{A}_{01}}$.*

Proof. An adversary $\mathcal{A}_{01}$ against the security of a key establishment protocol in the CK2001 (UM) model is constructed using an adversary $\mathcal{A}_{01}$ against the security of the same key establishment protocol in the BPR2000 (EA+KE) model. The primary adversary, $\mathcal{A}_{01}$, runs the secondary adversary, $\mathcal{A}_{00KE}$, and has access to its Send oracles, Session-State Reveal oracles, Session-Key Reveal oracles, Corrupt oracles, and Test oracle.

Recall that we assume in Figure 1 that this relation holds if, and only if, SIDs for both the BPR2000 (KE) and CK2001 model are constructed in the same manner. If A and B are BPR2000 partners, then $sid_A = sid_B$ and A and B will also be partners in the CK2001 model, since $sid_A = sid_B$ implies that both A and B will have matching sessions. Hence, we can say that all CK2001 partners are also BPR2000 partners (under the assumption that SIDs for both the BPR2000 (KE) and CK2001 model are constructed in the same manner) and all partners of CK2001-secure protocols are also BPR2000 partners (recall that in CK2001 security, two partners within a secure protocol must accept the same session key). This implies requirement 1.

An oracle is considered fresh in the BPR2000 model if it (or its associated partner, if such a partner exists) has not been asked a Reveal query and an oracle is considered fresh in the CK2001 model if it (or its associated partner, if such a partner exists) has not been asked either a Reveal or a Corrupt query. Hence, it follows easily that a fresh oracle in the BPR2000 model is also fresh in the CK2001 model. Hence, both requirements 1 and 2 (described in Figure 3) are satisfied.

To analyse $\mathsf{Adv}^{\mathcal{A}_{01}}$, we first consider the case in which the Test oracle associated with $\mathcal{A}_{01}$ returns a random key. The probability of $\mathcal{A}_{00KE}$ guessing the correct b_{01} bit is $\frac{1}{2}$ since it cannot gain any information about the hidden b_{01} bit. We then consider the case where the Test oracle associated with $\mathcal{A}_{01}$ returns the actual session key. In this case, the proof simulation (of $\mathcal{A}_{00KE}$) is perfect and $\mathcal{A}_{01}$ runs $\mathcal{A}_{00KE}$ exactly in the game defining the security of $\mathcal{A}_{00KE}$. Therefore, if $\mathcal{A}_{00KE}$ has a non-negligible advantage, so does $\mathcal{A}_{01}$ (i.e., $\mathsf{Adv}^{\mathcal{A}_{00KE}} = \mathsf{Adv}^{\mathcal{A}_{01}}$ is also non negligible). In other words, if such an adversary, $\mathcal{A}_{00KE}$, exists, so does $\mathcal{A}_{01}$. This is in violation of our assumption and Lemma 2 follows.   □

3.3 Proving Implication Relation: CK2001 → BR93 (KE)

This proof follows on from Section 3.2. Let the advantage of some PPT adversary in the BR93 (KE) model, $\mathcal{A}_{93KE}$, be $\mathsf{Adv}^{\mathcal{A}_{93KE}}$.

Lemma 3. *For any key establishment protocol and for any $\mathcal{A}_{93KE}$, there exists an $\mathcal{A}_{01}$, such that $\mathsf{Adv}^{\mathcal{A}_{93KE}} = \mathsf{Adv}^{\mathcal{A}_{01}}$.*

Proof. We construct an adversary $\mathcal{A}_{01}$ against the security of a key establishment protocol in the CK2001 model using an adversary $\mathcal{A}_{93KE}$ against the security of the same key establishment protocol in the BR93 model. Since we assume that SIDs in the CK2001 model are defined to be the concatenation of messages exchanged during the protocol run (similar to how SIDs are defined in the proof that appears in Section 3.1), the discussion on the notion of partnership between the BPR2000 and BR93 models apply in the discussion on the notion of partnership between the CK2001 and BR93 models. Hence, we can say that all BR93 partners are also CK2001 partners and all CK2001 partners are also BR93 partners (under the assumption that SIDs in the CK2001 model are defined to be the concatenation of messages sent and received during the protocol execution). Therefore, $\mathcal{A}_{01}$ is able to simulate the view of $\mathcal{A}_{93KE}$. Note that since $\mathcal{A}_{93KE}$ is not allowed to ask any Session-State Reveal in the BR93 model, $\mathcal{A}_{93KE}$ will not be asking any such queries in the simulation.

To analyse $\mathsf{Adv}^{\mathcal{A}_{01}}$, we first consider the case in which the Test oracle associated with $\mathcal{A}_{01}$ returns a random key. The probability of $\mathcal{A}_{93KE}$ guessing the correct b_{01} bit is $\frac{1}{2}$ since it cannot gain any information about the hidden b_{01} bit. We then consider the case where the Test oracle associated with $\mathcal{A}_{01}$ returns the actual session key. In this case, the proof simulation (of $\mathcal{A}_{93}$) is perfect and $\mathcal{A}_{01}$ runs $\mathcal{A}_{93KE}$ exactly in the game defining the security of $\mathcal{A}_{93KE}$. Therefore, if $\mathcal{A}_{93KE}$ has a non-negligible advantage, so does $\mathcal{A}_{01}$ (i.e., $\mathsf{Adv}^{\mathcal{A}_{01}} = \mathsf{Adv}^{\mathcal{A}_{93KE}}$ is also negligible), in violation of our assumption. Lemma 3 follows. $\square$

3.4   Proving Non-implication Relation: BR93 (KE) / CK2001 $\nleftrightarrow$ BPR2000 (KE)

As a counter-example, we revisit and use the improved (Bellare–Rogaway) three-party key distribution (3PKD) protocol due to Choo et al. [15] which has a proof of security in the BPR2000 (KE) model. We then demonstrate that this protocol fails to satisfy the functional requirement. Consequently, the protocol is insecure in the BR93 (KE) and CK2001 models. Figure 5 desribes the CBHM-3PKD protocol, which was proven secure in the BPR2000 model. In the protocol, there are three entities, namely: a trusted server S and two principals A and B who wish to establish communication.

Figure 6 depicts an example execution of the CBHM-3PKD protocol in the presence of a malicious adversary. At the end of the protocol execution, both uncorrupted prinicpals A and B have matching sessions according to Definition 8. However, they have accepted different session keys (i.e., A accepts session key SK_{AB} and B accepts session key $SK_{AB,2}$). This violates Definitions 2 and 9, which implies that the 3PKD protocol is not secure under the BR93 (KE) and the CK2001 models. However, according to Definition 4, both A and B are not BPR2000 partners since they do not agree on the same session key and hence, the protocol does not violate the BPR2000 security (i.e., Definition 5).

3.5   Proving Non-implication Relation: BR93 (KE) $\nleftrightarrow$ CK2001

Canetti & Krawczyk prove the basic Diffie–Hellman protocol secure in the UM [12]. In order to prove BR93 (KE) $\nleftrightarrow$ CK2001, we modified the (Canetti–Krawczyk) Diffie–Hellman protocol to include a redundant nonce N_{BA}, as shown in Figure 7. The modified Diffie–Hellman protocol does not authenticate the redundant nonce N_{BA}. Although N_{BA} is not authenticated, addition of N_{BA} does not affect the security of the protocol.

1. $A \longrightarrow B : R_A$
2. $B \longrightarrow S : R_A, R_B$
3a. $S \longrightarrow A : \{SK_{AB}\}_{K_{AS}^{enc}}, [A, B, R_A, R_B, \{SK_{AB}\}_{K_{AS}^{enc}}]_{K_{AS}^{MAC}}, R_B$
3b. $S \longrightarrow B : \{SK_{AB}\}_{K_{BS}^{enc}}, [A, B, R_A, R_B, \{SK_{AB}\}_{K_{BS}^{enc}}]_{K_{BS}^{MAC}}$

Fig. 5. Choo, Boyd, Hitchcock, & Maitland provably secure 3PKD protocol

1. $A \longrightarrow B :$	R_A
2. $B \longrightarrow S :$	R_A, R_B
3a. $S \longrightarrow A :$	$\{SK_{AB}\}_{K_{AS}^{enc}}, [A, B, R_A, R_B, \{SK_{AB}\}_{K_{AS}^{enc}}]_{K_{AS}^{MAC}}, R_B$
3b. $S \longrightarrow B :$	$\{SK_{AB}\}_{K_{BS}^{enc}}, [A, B, R_A, R_B, \{SK_{AB}\}_{K_{BS}^{enc}}]_{K_{BS}^{MAC}}$

$\mathcal{A}$ intercepts and deletes $\{SK_{AB}\}_{K_{BS}^{enc}}, [A, B, R_B, \{SK_{AB}\}_{K_{BS}^{enc}}]_{K_{BS}^{MAC}}$.

2. $\mathcal{A}_B \longrightarrow S :$	R_A, R_B
3a. $S \longrightarrow A :$	$\{SK_{AB,2}\}_{K_{AS}^{enc}}, [A, B, R_A, R_B, \{SK_{AB,2}\}_{K_{AS}^{enc}}]_{K_{AS}^{MAC}}, R_B$

$\mathcal{A}$ intercepts and deletes $\{SK_{AB,2}\}_{K_{AS}^{enc}}, [A, B, R_A, \{SK_{AB,2}\}_{K_{AS}^{enc}}]_{K_{AS}^{MAC}}$.

3b. $S \longrightarrow B :$	$\{SK_{AB,2}\}_{K_{BS}^{enc}}, [A, B, R_A, R_B, \{SK_{AB,2}\}_{K_{BS}^{enc}}]_{K_{BS}^{MAC}}$

Fig. 6. Execution of CBHM-3PKD protocol in the presence of a malicious adversary

A		B
$x \in \mathbb{Z}_q$	$\xrightarrow{A, sid, g^x}$	$y \in \mathbb{Z}_q$
Verify Signature	$\xleftarrow{B, sid, g^y, Sig_{d_B}(B, sid, g^y, g^x, A), N_{BA}}$	$y, N_{BA} \in \mathbb{Z}_q$
$SK_{AB} = g^{xy}$	$\xrightarrow{A, sid, g^y, Sig_{d_A}(A, sid, g^y, g^x, B), N_{BA}}$	$SK_{AB} = g^{xy}$

Fig. 7. A modified (Canetti–Krawczyk) Diffie–Hellman protocol

A	$\mathcal{A}$	A
$\xrightarrow{A, sid, g^x}$		$\xrightarrow{A, sid, g^x}$
$\xleftarrow{B, sid, g^y, Sig_{d_B}(B, sid, g^y, g^x, A), N_A}$	$\mathcal{A}_A$	$\xleftarrow{B, sid, g^y, Sig_{d_B}(B, sid, g^y, g^x, A), N_{BA}}$
$\xrightarrow{A, sid, g^y, Sig_{d_A}(A, sid, g^y, g^x, B), N_A}$	$\mathcal{A}_B$	$\xrightarrow{A, sid, g^y, Sig_{d_A}(A, sid, g^y, g^x, B), N_{BA}}$

Fig. 8. Execution of the modified (Canetti–Krawczyk) Diffie–Hellman protocol in the presence of a malicious adversary

Figure 8 depicts an example execution of the (Canetti–Krawczyk) Diffie–Hellman protocol in the presence of a malicious adversary. Recall that we assume that the non-implication relation: BR93 (KE) $\nleftarrow$ CK2001 holds if, and only if, SIDs in the CK2001 model are not defined to be concatenation of messages exchanged during the protocol run, as shown in Figure 1. Let $\mathcal{A}_U$ denote $\mathcal{A}$ intercepting message and sending fabricating message impersonating U.

At the end of the protocol execution, both A and B are partners according to Definition 8, since they have matching SIDs and corresponding PIDs (i.e., $PID_A = B$ and $PID_B = A$). In addition, both uncorrupted A and B accept the same session key, $SK_{AB} = g^{xy} = SK_{BA}$. The CK2001 definition of security is not violated (in the sense of Definition 9). However, both A and B did not receive all of each other's messages (recall that messages in message round 2 and 3 are fabricated by $\mathcal{A}$) and neither A's nor B's replies were all in response to genuine messages by B and A respectively. Hence, both A and B are not BR93 partners.

$A\ (pwd_A)$	$S\ (pwd_A, pwd_B)$	$B\ (pwd_B)$

$$x \in_R \mathbb{Z}_p, X = g^x$$
$$pw_{A,1} = \mathcal{G}_1(pwd_A)$$
$$X^* = X \cdot pw_{A,1}$$
$$\underrightarrow{A, B, X^*}$$

$$r \in_R \mathbb{Z}_p$$
$$R \in_R \{0,1\}^{l_R}$$
$$pw_{A,1} = \mathcal{G}_1(pwd_A)$$

$$y \in_R \mathbb{Z}_p, Y = g^y$$
$$pw_{B,1} = \mathcal{G}_1(pwd_B)$$
$$Y^* = Y \cdot pw_{B,1}$$
$$\underleftarrow{B, A, Y^*}$$

$$pw_{B,1} = \mathcal{G}_1(pwd_B)$$
$$X = X^*/pw_{A,1}, Y = Y^*/pw_{B,1}$$
$$\overline{X} = X^r, \overline{Y} = Y^r$$
$$pw_{A,2} = \mathcal{G}_2(R, pwd_A, X^*)$$
$$pw_{B,2} = \mathcal{G}_2(R, pwd_B, Y^*)$$

$$\underleftarrow{S, B, R, Y^*, \overline{Y}^*} \quad \overline{X}^* = \overline{X} \cdot pw_{B,2}, \overline{Y}^* = \overline{Y} \cdot pw_{A,2} \quad \underrightarrow{S, A, R, X^*, \overline{X}^*}$$

$$pw_{A,2} = \mathcal{G}_2(R, pwd_A, X^*)$$
$$\overline{Y} = \overline{Y}^*/pw_{A,2}, K = \overline{Y}^x = g^{xry}$$
$$T = (R, X^*, Y^*, \overline{X}^*, \overline{Y}^*)$$
$$SK_A = \mathcal{H}(A, B, S, T, K)$$

$$pw_{B,2} = \mathcal{G}_2(R, pwd_B, Y^*)$$
$$\overline{X} = \overline{X}^*/pw_{B,2}, K = \overline{Y}^x = g^{xry}$$
$$T = (R, X^*, Y^*, \overline{X}^*, \overline{Y}^*)$$
$$SK_B = \mathcal{H}(A, B, S, T, K)$$

Fig. 9. Abdalla–Pointcheval 3PAKE

Hence, $\mathcal{A}$ can obtain a fresh session key of either A or B by revealing non-partner instances of B or A respectively, in violation of BR93 security (Definition 2).

3.6   Discussion on Non-implication Relation: BPR2000 (KE) $\nleftarrow$ BR95

Recall that security in the models depend on the notion of partnership. However, no explicit definition of partnership was provided in the BR95 model and there is no single partner function fixed for any protocol in the BR95 model. The flawed partner function for the 3PKD protocol described in the original BR95 paper was fixed by Choo *et al.* [15]. However, as Choo *et al.* has pointed out, there is no way to securely define a SID for the 3PKD protocol that will preserve the proof of security. Hence, protocols that are secure in the BR95 model may not necessarily be able to be proven secure in the BPR2000 (KE) model.

4   A Drawback in the Original Formulation of the BPR2000 Model

4.1   Case Study: Abdalla–Pointcheval 3PAKE

We revisit the protocol 3PAKE due to Abdalla & Pointcheval [1], which carries a proof of security in the BPR2000 model, as shown in Figure 9. Let A and B be two clients who wish to establish a shared session key, SK, S be a trusted

$A\ (pwd_A)$	$\mathcal{A}$	$S\ (pwd_A, pwd_B, pwd_C)$	$\mathcal{A}$	$B\ (pwd_B)$

$\mathcal{A}$ corrupt C and obtain all internal states of C, including pwd_C

$\xrightarrow{A,B,X^*}$ Intercept Intercept $\xleftarrow{B,A,Y^*}$

$$e \in_R \mathbb{Z}_p, E = g^e \text{ s.t. underlying value } E \neq 1$$
$$E^* = E \cdot \mathcal{G}_1(pwd_C)$$

$\xrightarrow{A,C,X^*}$ $\xleftarrow{C,A,E^*}$

$$pw_{A,1} = \mathcal{G}_1(pwd_A)$$
$$pw_{C,1} = \mathcal{G}_1(pwd_C)$$
$$X = X^*/pw_{A,1}, E = E^*/pw_{C,1}$$
$$\overline{X} = X^r, \overline{E} = E^r$$
$$pw_{A,2} = \mathcal{G}_2(R, pwd_A, X^*)$$
$$pw_{C,2} = \mathcal{G}_2(R, pwd_C, E^*)$$
$$\overline{X}^* = \overline{X} \cdot pw_{C,2}, \overline{E}^* = \overline{E} \cdot pw_{A,2}$$

Intercept $\xleftarrow{S,C,R,E^*,\overline{E}^*}$

$\xleftarrow{S,B,R,E^*,\overline{E}^*}$ $\xrightarrow{S,A,R,X^*,\overline{X}^*}$

$pw_{A,2} = \mathcal{G}_2(R, pwd_A, X^*)$ $\qquad\qquad$ $pw_{C,2} = \mathcal{G}_2(R, pwd_C, E^*)$

$\overline{E} = \overline{E}^*/pw_{A,2}, K = \overline{E}^x = g^{xre}$ $\qquad$ $\overline{X} = \overline{X}^*/pw_{C,2}, K = \overline{E}^x = g^{xre}$

$T = (R, X^*, E^*, \overline{X}^*, \overline{E}^*)$ $\qquad\qquad\qquad$ $T = (R, X^*, E^*, \overline{X}^*, \overline{E}^*)$

$SK_A = \mathcal{H}(A, B, S, T, K)$ $\qquad\qquad\qquad$ $SK_C = \mathcal{H}(A, B, S, T, K)$

Fig. 10. Execution of 3PAKE in the presence of a malicious adversary

server, pwd_A (and pwd_B) denote the password shared between A and S (B and S respectively), $\mathcal{G}_1, \mathcal{G}_2$, and $\mathcal{H}$ denote random oracles, and l_r and l_k denote security parameters.

4.2 New Attack on Abdalla–Pointcheval 3PAKE

Figure 10 describes an execution of 3PAKE in the presence of a malicious adversary, $\mathcal{A}$. Let C be another client who has a shared password, pwd_C, with the server, S. Prior to the start of the communication initiated by A, $\mathcal{A}$ corrupts a non-related player, C (i.e., static corruption), thereby learning all internal states of C (including the shared password with S, pwd_C).

In the attack outlined in Figure 10, $\mathcal{A}$ intercepts the first message from A and changes the identity field in the message from A, B to A, C. $\mathcal{A}$ impersonates A and sends the fabricated message A, C, X^* to S. $\mathcal{A}$ impersonates C and sends another fabricated message C, A, E^* to S. S, upon receiving both messages, will respond as per protocol specification. At the end of the protocol execution, A believes that the session key, $SK_A = \mathcal{H}(A, B, S, T, K)$, is being shared with B. However, B is still waiting for S's reply, which will never arrive, since $\mathcal{A}$ has intercepted and deleted the message from the network. However, $\mathcal{A}$ is able to compute the fresh session key of A, since $\mathcal{A}$ is able to decrypt and obtain $K = g^{xre}$ and $SK_A = \mathcal{H}(A, B, S, T, K)$, since parameters A, B, S, and T (T is the transcript of the protocol execution) are public.

Consequently, protocol 3PAKE is insecure. However, this attack[1] cannot be detected in the existing BPR2000 model since Corrupt query is not allowed. Protocols proven secure in a proof model that allows the "Corrupt" query (in the proof simulation) ought to be secure against the unknown key share attack, since if a key is to be shared between some parties, U_1 and U_2, the corruption of some other (non-related) player in the protocol, say U_3, should not expose the session key shared between U_1 and U_2. In other words, protocol 3PAKE will be insecure in the BR93, BR95, and CK2001 models, since $\mathcal{A}$ is able to trivially expose a fresh session key (i.e., $\mathsf{Adv}^{\mathcal{A}}(k)$ is non-negligible) by corrupting a non-partner player.

5   Conclusion and Future Work

We examined the Bellare–Rogaway and Canetti–Krawczyk proof models. We analysed some non-intuitive gaps in the relations and the relative strengths of security between both models and their variants. We then provided a detailed comparison of the relative strengths of the notions of security between the Bellare–Rogaway and Canetti–Krawczyk proof models. We also revealed a drawback with the BPR2000 model and a previously unpublished flaw in the Abdalla–Pointcheval protocol 3PAKE [1]. However, such an attack would not be captured in the model due to the omission of Corrupt queries. Our studies concluded that (1) if the session identifier (SID) in the CK2001 model is defined to be the concatenation of messages exchanged during the protocol run, then CK2001 model offers the strongest definition of security compared to the Bellare–Rogaway model and its variants, and (2) the BPR2000 model is the weakest model.

As a result of this work, we hope to have contributed towards a better understanding of the different flavours of proof models for key establishment protocols (whether protocols proven secure in one model are also secure in another model). While our studies focus only on the Bellare–Rogaway and Canetti–Krawczyk models, it would be interesting to extend our work to other computational complexity proof models (e.g., the proof model due to Shoup [18]) or other simulation-based proof models (e.g., the universal composability approach and the black-box simulatability approach due to Canetti et al. [11] and Backes et al. [3] respectively).

---

[1] Informally, it appears that this attack can be avoided by including the identities of both A and B when computing $pw_{A,2}$ and $pw_{B,2}$.

References

1. M. Abdalla and D. Pointcheval. Interactive Diffie-Hellman Assumptions with Applications to Password-based Authentication (Extended version available from http://www.di.ens.fr/~pointche/pub.php). In *FC 2005*, pages 341–356. Springer-Verlag, 2005. Vol. 3570/2005 of LNCS.
2. S. S. Al-Riyami and K. G. Paterson. Tripartite Authenticated Key Agreement Protocols from Pairings. In *9th IMA Conference on Cryptography and Coding*, pages 332–359. Springer-Verlag, 2003. Vol. 2898/2003 of LNCS.
3. M. Backes, B. Pfitzmann, and M. Waidner. A General Composition Theorem for Secure Reactive Systems. In *TCC 2004*, pages 336–354. Springer-Verlag, 2004. Vol. 2951/2004 of LNCS.
4. M. Bellare, R. Canetti, and H. Krawczyk. A Modular Approach to The Design and Analysis of Authentication and Key Exchange Protocols. In *STOC 1998*, pages 419–428. ACM Press, 1998.
5. M. Bellare, D. Pointcheval, and P. Rogaway. Authenticated Key Exchange Secure Against Dictionary Attacks. In *Eurocrypt 2000*, pages 139 – 155. Springer-Verlag, 2000. Vol. 1807/2000 of LNCS.
6. M. Bellare and P. Rogaway. Entity Authentication and Key Distribution. In *Crypto 1993*, pages 110–125. Springer-Verlag, 1993. Vol. 773/1993 of LNCS.
7. M. Bellare and P. Rogaway. Provably Secure Session Key Distribution: The Three Party Case. In *STOC 1995*, pages 57–66. ACM Press, 1995.
8. S. Blake-Wilson, D. Johnson, and A. Menezes. Key Agreement Protocols and their Security Analysis. In *6th IMA International Conference on Cryptography and Coding*, pages 30–45. Springer-Verlag, 1997. Vol. 1355/1997 of LNCS.
9. S. Blake-Wilson and A. Menezes. Security Proofs for Entity Authentication and Authenticated Key Transport Protocols Employing Asymmetric Techniques. In *Security Protocols Workshop*, pages 137–158. Springer-Verlag, 1997. Vol. 1361/1997 of LNCS.
10. C. Boyd, W. Mao, and K. Paterson. Key Agreement using Statically Keyed Authenticators. In *ACNS 2004*, pages 248–262. Springer-Verlag, 2004. Vol. 3089/2004 of LNCS.
11. R. Canetti. Universally Composable Security: A New Paradigm for Cryptographic Protocols. Cryptology ePrint Archive, Report 2000/067, 2000. http://eprint.iacr.org/2000/067/.
12. R. Canetti and H. Krawczyk. Analysis of Key-Exchange Protocols and Their Use for Building Secure Channels (Extended version available from http://eprint.iacr.org/2001/040/). In *Eurocrypt 2001*, pages 453–474. Springer-Verlag, 2001. Vol. 2045/2001 of LNCS.
13. L. Chen and C. Kudla. Identity Based Authenticated Key Agreement Protocols from Pairings (Corrected version at http://eprint.iacr.org/2002/184/). In *CSFW 2003*, pages 219–233. IEEE Computer Society Press, 2003.
14. K.-K. R. Choo, C. Boyd, and Y. Hitchcock. Examining Indistinguishability-Based Proof Models for Key Establishment Protocols (Full version available from http://eprint.iacr.org/2005/270). In Bimal Roy, editor, *(Accepted to appear in) Asiacrypt 2005*. Springer-Verlag, 2005. LNCS.
15. K.-K. R. Choo, C. Boyd, Y. Hitchcock, and G. Maitland. On Session Identifiers in Provably Secure Protocols: The Bellare-Rogaway Three-Party Key Distribution Protocol Revisited (Extended version available from http://eprint.iacr.org/2004/345). In *SCN 2004*, pages 352–367. Springer-Verlag, 2004. Vol. 3352/2005 of LNCS.

16. P. D. MacKenzie and R. Swaminathan. Secure Network Authentication with Password Identification. Submitted to the IEEE P1363 Working Group, 1999.
17. N. McCullagh and P. S. L. M. Barreto.   A New Two-Party Identity-Based Authenticated Key Agreement (Extended version available from http://eprint.iacr.org/2004/122/). In *CT-RSA 2005*, pages 262–274. Springer-Verlag, 2005. Vol. 3376/2005 of LNCS.
18. V. Shoup. On Formal Models for Secure Key Exchange (Version 4). Technical Report RZ 3120 (#93166), IBM Research, Zurich, 1999.
19. D. S. Wong and A. H. Chan. Efficient and Mutually Authenticated Key Exchange for Low Power Computing Devices. In *Asiacrypt 2001*, pages 172–289. Springer-Verlag, 2001. Vol. 2248/2001 of LNCS.

Server-Aided Verification: Theory and Practice

Marc Girault and David Lefranc

France Telecom, Research and Development,
42 rue des Coutures, F-14066 Caen, France
{marc.girault, david.lefranc}@francetelecom.com

Abstract. We introduce the server-aided verification (SAV) concept, which consists in speeding up the verification step of an authentication/signature scheme, by delegating a substantial part of computations to a powerful (but possibly untrusted) server. After giving some motivations for designing SAV protocols, we provide a simple but realistic model, which captures most situations one can meet in practice (note that this model is much more general than the one recently proposed by Hohenberger and Lysyanskaya, who require the server to be made of two softwares which do not communicate with each other [14]). Then, we analyze and prove in this model the security of two existing SAV protocols, namely the Lim-Lee [15] modification of Schnorr scheme [28] and the Girault-Quisquater variant [10] of GPS scheme [7,24]. Finally, we propose a generic method for designing SAV versions of schemes based on bilinear maps, which can be applied to the Boneh-Boyen signature schemes [3], the Zhang-Safavi-Naini-Susilo [32] signature scheme and the Shao-Lu-Cao identification scheme [30].

Keywords: identification protocol, digital signature, interactive proof, zero-knowledge, discrete logarithm, non-repudiation, bilinear map, pairing.

1 Introduction

Designing efficient signature and identification (or authentication) schemes is one of the main challenges of public key cryptography. Indeed, with the development of smart cards and RFID tags, or more generally low cost chips with small computation capabilities, it becomes crucial to propose schemes suited to such devices.

Until now, research has essentially focused on speeding up the prover/signer computations. In particular, zero-knowledge (ZK) paradigm [11] has led to very efficient schemes, including Fiat-Shamir [6], Guillou-Quisquater [13], Schnorr [28] and GPS [7,24] protocols. Another research direction was to speed-up RSA [26] private operation by sharing the computation task with a powerful but untrusted computer [16]. The latter approach, usually named "server-aided RSA", is delicate and many proposals have been broken (see e.g. [19,20,22]).

On the other hand, speeding up the verification task has been relatively few scrutinized. One reason may be that RSA is very efficient from this point of view.

B. Roy (Ed.): ASIACRYPT 2005, LNCS 3788, pp. 605–623, 2005.

Indeed, the use of a small public exponent leads to a few modular multiplications to perform, and even only one in the variant from Rabin [25]. Furthermore, the task of doing a modular reduction can be reduced to a still lighter operation by using various tricks (e.g. [31]). Finally, batch verification allows a server to verify many RSA signatures in an optimized manner ([1]).

Nevertheless, RSA leaves open the problem of designing an identification scheme which is efficient at both ends. A first valuable solution may be ZK factorization-based schemes, as they generally involve a moderate and well-balanced computational task at each end. However, in many environments, this task still remains too heavy. For instance, if the prover's device is a low cost smart card and/or if the transaction must take place in very few milliseconds, then significantly faster computations are required.

Discrete-logarithm-based schemes, when used in their "coupon mode" ([18]), allow the signer to compute the signature in a particularly fast manner. A coupon is essentially a precomputed exponential, leaving the signer with an ultra-light task (typically a modular multiplication with a small modulus or even less) at the time of signing. The verifier has a price to pay, since he must compute the exponential of a rather large number. As a consequence, speeding up verification step in a discrete-logarithm-based scheme is a very significant challenge, both from theoretical and practical points of view.

In a client-server environment, this challenge can be solved by using pre-computation techniques, which allow to decrease the average time of verification by a factor close to five [4]. A more general approach would consist in sharing the computations with a powerful but untrusted server. Since it is the analogue of "server-aided RSA" at the verifier's side, we call it "server-aided verification". The main difference between these two notions is that the verification does not involve private keys, so that there is no concern with *confidentiality*. On the other hand, there is a major concern with *integrity*: the output of verification step must be trusted by the verifier -or it has no value at all.

In real world there are many situations in which a secure but not powerful chip is connected to a powerful but not secure powerful device. For example, in a GSM mobile telephone, the more sensitive cryptographic operations are performed in the so-called SIM (Subscriber Identification Module), which is already aided by the handset chip, mainly to decipher the over-the-air enciphered conversation. In a payment transaction, a so-called SAM (Secure Access Module) is embedded in a terminal already containing a more powerful chip. We can also mention the example of a smart card plugged into a personal computer, seeing that many PCs will be equipped with smart card readers in a near future.

This paper is about server-aided verification in general, applied to discrete-logarithm-based schemes in particular. While not using this name, nor providing formal definitions and proofs, a few authors have already addressed this problem. In the late 80's, at Cardis 2000 conference, Quisquater and De Soete proposed tricks to speed up RSA verification with a small exponent [31]. At Eurocrypt'95 conference, Lim and Lee gave a generic method, based on the "randomization" of the verification equation [15]. This equation is only known to the verifier, so that a cheater can solve it only if he guess it: security is unconditional. The counterpart of this nice method is that the verifier must perform a heavy pre-computation before carrying out the transaction.

A completely different approach has been proposed by Girault and Quisquater [10] and described in European NESSIE project final proceedings [9]. While no precomputation nor randomization is required, the security remains computational, based on the hardness of a sub-problem (namely factorization) of the initial underlying problem (namely composite discrete logarithm).

Recently, at TCC'05, Hohenberger and Lysyanskaya addressed the situation in which the server is made of two untrusted softwares, which are assumed not to communicate with each other [14]. While this assumption is very particular and much stronger than ours (since, in essence, we assume that the verifier does not trust anybody nor anything except himself), it allows a very light public computation task (typically one modular multiplication in the Schnorr scheme).

Starting from this background, the motivation of this paper was two-fold: first, clarify the properties that server-aided verification must satisfy and classify the different approaches to achieve them; second, extend the class of protocols for which verification can be server-aided. The result is as follows: in section 2 we define our model and identify three possible approaches to achieve the main property. In section 3 we prove in this model the security of the two state-of-the art protocols mentioned above. In section 4 we propose a generic method applicable to signatures schemes based on bilinear maps (in particular Boneh-Boyen [3] and Zhang-Safavi-Naini-Susilo [32]), and prove them secure in our model. Finally, we provide a conclusion.

2   Model

2.1   An Illustrative Example

Let us illustrate the notion of server-aided verification with RSA signature scheme. In this scheme, the signer computes a signature σ of the message m by extracting an eth root modulo n of $f(m)$, where f is specific to the exact scheme which is used (typically f is a combination of some hash-function(s) and some redundancy function(s)). The verifier checks that $\sigma^e \bmod n = f(m)$. If the equality holds, σ is accepted; otherwise, it is rejected.

If the verifier has only a small computation capability, he may want to be aided when checking the equality. So let us suppose that he has access to a more powerful, but untrusted server or, equivalently, to a trusted server via a non authenticated communication link. (If the server and the communication link were both trusted, then the verifier would just ask the server for the verification of $\sigma^e \bmod n = f(m)$ and the server would reply with OK or NOK). For instance, the verifier may think of the two following possibilities:

- Ask the server to compute the value $Y = \sigma^{\frac{e-1}{2}} \bmod n$. Then, the server returns the value Y and the verifier finally checks if $f(m) = Y^2 \sigma \bmod n$.
- If the value $e = e_1 \times e_2$, with $e_1 < e_2$, then ask the server for the computation of $Y = \sigma^{e_2} \bmod n$ so that the verifier only has to check if $f(m) = Y^{e_1} \bmod n$.

For each of these protocols, even if it deviates from its assigned part, the server cannot fool the verifier as long as it does not collude with the (legitimate or not) prover. Indeed, given n, m and σ, finding Y such that the final verification equation is satisfied requires the ability to extract (square or e_1^{th}) roots mod n.

Now, what about a possible collusion between a cheating prover and the server? In the first protocol, an illegitimate prover and the server can easily collaborate in order to let the verifier accept a fake signature: the cheater can choose randomly $0 < \tilde{Y} < n$ and computes $\tilde{\sigma} = f(m)\tilde{Y}^{-2} \bmod n$. The cheater first provides the value $\tilde{\sigma}$, and then asks the server to answer with the value $\tilde{Y}$. Obviously, $\tilde{\sigma}$ and $\tilde{Y}$ fulfill $\tilde{Y}^2\tilde{\sigma} = f(m) \bmod n$ and, as a consequence, the signature is accepted. Since the solution to be chosen must at least resist a collusion between the server and an illegitimate prover (which in practice, may be represented by the same entity), this implies that this first protocol cannot be used.

Fortunately, this attack does not apply to the second protocol. Indeed, it remains secure against a coalition between a cheating prover and the server since finding the right value of Y given n and m requires to be able to extract an e_1^{th} root modulo n.

Nevertheless, a more subtle attack remains possible if the legitimate prover and the server collaborate. Instead of providing the verifier with the right signature σ, the legitimate prover may send a value $\tilde{\sigma}$, correlated to σ in a way known by the server (e.g. by adding it to a random value). Later, when the verifier wants to check the signature, he sends a request to the server. The latter reconstructs σ from n, m and $\tilde{\sigma}$, which allows him to reply with the right value Y. The verifier is satisfied and stores the pair $(m,\tilde{\sigma})$. Unfortunately, the stored signature is wrong and the legitimate prover can easily repudiate it. Here, the point is that the verifier does not check in any way the consistency between $\tilde{\sigma}$ and Y.

This leads us to distinguish, in the model that we propose, two kinds of deviating provers: on one hand the cheaters (who do not know the signature private key); on the other hand the legitimate provers (who misbehave in order to make some kind of repudiation possible).

Note however that the latter attack may be of very little significance in the case of an authentication protocol or more generally when non-repudiation property is not required.

2.2   Definitions

In this subsection, we formalize the server-aided verification concept. We deliberately restrict our model to the situation in which the modification of the basic protocol does not impact prover's view of the initial protocol. Indeed, the prover should not matter whether verification is server-aided or not. Of course, such an assumption does not prevent the prover from playing himself the role of the server if both parties find convenient to do so.

We also assume for simplicity that verification in the initial protocol consists in checking a predicate at the end of the protocol. Most of the protocols we are aware work that way, or can be replaced by equivalent protocols which work that way. First, we precisely define the different types of provers we consider.

Definition 1 (Legitimate/Misbehaving/Cheating). *Let π be an interactive proof of knowledge between a (so-called) prover $\mathcal{P}$ and a (so-called) verifier $\mathcal{V}$. As usual, we denote by $\tilde{\mathcal{P}}$ a prover which deviates from the protocol. The (non-deviating) prover $\mathcal{P}$ is said legitimate, while $\tilde{\mathcal{P}}$ is:*

cheating *if he does not hold the knowledge he claims to hold (and we denote him $\tilde{\mathcal{P}}_1$);*
misbehaving *if he holds this knowledge (and we denote him $\tilde{\mathcal{P}}_2$).*

We model the prover $\mathcal{P}$, the verifier $\mathcal{V}$ and the server $\mathcal{S}$ with polynomial probabilistic Turing machines (PPTM) with respective random tapes ω_P, ω_V and ω_S. We also consider that the verifier owns an additional tape denoted ω'_V on which precomputed values can be written. The *computational cost* of the verifier is defined as the number of steps performed by the Turing machine $\mathcal{V}$. In practical examples, our computation unit is the n-bit modular multiplication, which is a $\mathcal{O}(n^2)$ operation if using a standard algorithm to make it.

We now give the definition of a SAV protocol taking into account an optional property.

Definition 2 (SAV protocol). *Let π be an interactive proof of knowledge between a prover $\mathcal{P}$ and a verifier $\mathcal{V}$, with a common input $\mathcal{I}$ of size $|\mathcal{I}|$, and which halts by verifying a predicate $\mathcal{E}_\pi$ (we denote $\mathcal{E}_\pi = 1$ if the predicate is satisfied, $\mathcal{E}_\pi = 0$ if not). Let π-cost denote the computational cost of $\mathcal{V}$ during the execution of π.*

Let π^* be an interactive protocol between the prover $\mathcal{P}$, the verifier $\mathcal{V}$ and a server $\mathcal{S}$, equal to the composition of two protocols π^- and π' such that:

- *the protocol π^- is equal to the protocol π without the verification of $\mathcal{E}_\pi$;*
- *the protocol π' is an interactive protocol between $\mathcal{V}$ and $\mathcal{S}$;*
- *$\mathcal{V}$ finally accepts (π^*-accepts) or rejects (π^*-rejects) $\mathcal{I}$ by verifying a final predicate $\mathcal{E}_{\pi^*}$ (we denote $\mathcal{E}_{\pi^*} = 1$ if the predicate is satisfied, $\mathcal{E}_{\pi^*} = 0$ if not).*

*Let π^*-cost denote the computational cost of $\mathcal{V}$ during the execution of π^*. The protocol π^* is said to be a **server-aided verification (SAV) protocol** for π if:*

1. *(auxiliary completeness)*
   - *$\forall \mathcal{I}$, $\Pr\limits_{\omega_S, \omega_V} (\mathcal{V}\ \pi^*\text{-accepts}\ \mathcal{I} \mid \mathcal{E}_\pi = 0)$ is negligible in $|\mathcal{I}|$.*
   - *$\forall \mathcal{I}$, $\Pr\limits_{\omega_S, \omega_V} (\mathcal{V}\ \pi^*\text{-rejects}\ \mathcal{I} \mid \mathcal{E}_\pi = 1)$ is negligible in $|\mathcal{I}|$.*

2. *(auxiliary soundness)* $\forall \mathcal{I}$, $\forall \tilde{\mathcal{P}}_1$, $\forall \tilde{\mathcal{S}}$, $\Pr_{\omega_{\tilde{\mathcal{P}}_1}, \omega_{\mathcal{V}}, \omega_{\tilde{\mathcal{S}}}}$ $(\mathcal{V} \ \pi^*\text{-}accepts \ \mathcal{I} \mid \mathcal{E}_\pi = 0)$ is negligible in $|\mathcal{I}|$.

3. *(computational gain)* The computational cost π^*-*cost is strictly less than* π-*cost*.

If non-repudiation is required, π^* must also verify:

(auxiliary non-repudiation) $\forall \mathcal{I}$, $\forall \tilde{\mathcal{P}}_2$, $\forall \tilde{\mathcal{S}}$, $\Pr_{\omega_{\tilde{\mathcal{P}}_1}, \omega_{\mathcal{V}}, \omega_{\tilde{\mathcal{S}}}}$ $(\mathcal{V} \ \pi^*\text{-}accepts \ \mathcal{I} \mid \mathcal{E}_\pi = 0)$ *is negligible in* $|\mathcal{I}|$.

Remark 1. From the definition, proving the auxiliary non-repudiation also proves the auxiliary soundness which also proves the first condition of the auxiliary completeness.

2.3   Achieving the Auxiliary Soundness

We currently distinguish two ways to achieve the auxiliary soundness.

Final Predicate Hard to Know. The final predicate $\mathcal{E}_{\pi^*}$ is constructed from the predicate $\mathcal{E}_\pi$ by (secretly) randomizing it, so that only the verifier knows it. As a consequence, if the prover is a cheater $\tilde{\mathcal{P}}_1$ (and the predicate $\mathcal{E}_\pi$ is false), there is no way for the server $\tilde{\mathcal{S}}$ to fool the verifier, even if colluding with $\tilde{\mathcal{P}}_1$. The better strategy consists in guessing the randomizing parameter(s), the probability of which can be easily controlled by choosing the adequate size. Moreover, this case can be subdivided into two sub-cases:

- *Unconditionally* unknown predicate: even with unlimited resources, an enemy has no better strategy to retrieve the final predicate than guessing it.
- *Computationally* unknown predicate: it is computationally hard for the enemy to retrieve the final predicate.

Final Predicate Hard to Solve. The final predicate $\mathcal{E}_{\pi^*}$ is constructed from $\mathcal{E}_\pi$ such that the final predicate is computationally hard to solve. As a consequence, if the prover is a cheater $\tilde{\mathcal{P}}_1$ (and the predicate $\mathcal{E}_\pi$ is false), there is no feasible way for the server $\tilde{\mathcal{S}}$ to fool the verifier, even if colluding with $\tilde{\mathcal{P}}_1$. Note that the hard problem used in $\mathcal{E}_{\pi^*}$ is necessarily easier than (i.e. can be reduced to) the one used in $\mathcal{E}_\pi$, since auxiliary completeness implies that a solution for the initial predicate can be turned into a solution for the final one.

2.4   Achieving the Auxiliary Non-repudiation.

A SAV protocol based on an unconditionally unknown predicate verifies the auxiliary non-repudiation since the security is unconditional (even w.r.t. $\tilde{\mathcal{P}}_2$).

In the case of a SAV protocol π^* based on a hard-to-solve predicate, if the hard-computational problem used for π^* can be broken using the private key involved in the basic protocol π, then a misbehaving prover can obviously break the SAV protocol so that the auxiliary non-repudiation is not verified.

2.5 Security Model in the Case of Signature Scheme

To prove that the auxiliary soundness (respectively the auxiliary non-repudiation) of a protocol π^*, we assume that $\tilde{S}$ communicates with $\tilde{P}_1$ (respectively $\tilde{P}_2$). In the case of signature schemes, to make a message m and an invalid signature $\tilde{\sigma}$ be π^*-accepted, as in classical proofs [12] of signature scheme, we distinguish different type of attacks. Thus, we assume that $\tilde{P}_1$ (respectively $\tilde{P}_2$):

(**No message attack**) has no access to valid signatures.

(**Known message attack**) obtains a set of valid signatures associated to a given set of messages.

(**Generic message attack**) obtains a set of valid signatures associated to a set of messages of his choice, before knowing the public key.

(**Directed chosen message attack**) obtains the set of valid signatures associated to a set of messages of his choice, before knowing the public key.

(**Adaptive chosen message attack**) obtains valid signatures for messages of his choice, after knowing the public key.

In all these attacks, the message m, on which $\tilde{P}$ sends an invalid signature $\tilde{\sigma}$, does not belong to the set of messages for which a valid signature is known.

3   SAV Protocols for Identification Schemes

In this section we apply our model to two formerly suggested methods to delegate computations during the verification step. The first one is a generic method proposed by Lim and Lee [15] and applicable to many discrete-logarithm-based schemes. The second one is a modification by Girault and Quisquater [10] of the GPS scheme, which is particularly interesting in the so-called RSA-like version of GPS, as proposed by Girault and Paillès [8]. We prove that these two solutions are both SAV protocols in the sense of section 2.2.

3.1   An Unconditionally-Unknown-Predicate-Based SAV Protocol

At Eurocrypt'95, Lim and Lee suggested a general method to delegate computations during the verification step of discrete-logarithm-based schemes (signature and identification) [15]. In this paper, the computations are not delegated to any server, but to the prover himself. Our approach is more general but their results can be easily adapted to it. To validate (or not) their generic method, we analyze it when applied to the Schnorr identification scheme; the results presented below remain valid for the Schnorr signature scheme.

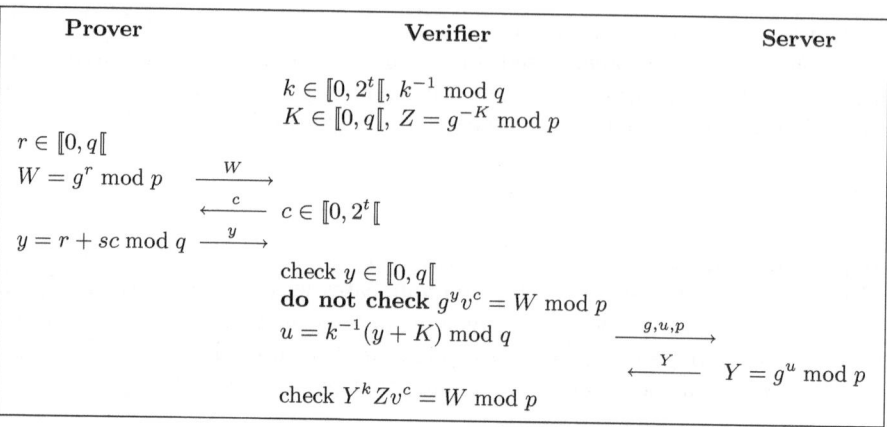

Fig. 1. The Lim-Lee modification of the Schnorr identification scheme

The Lim-Lee Protocol. In the Schnorr identification scheme, a prover owns a private key s and a public key (g, p, q, v) such that g is of prime order q modulo a prime integer p and $v = g^{-s} \bmod p$ (generally, g, p and q are system parameters). The Lim-Lee protocol is described in Fig. 1. In particular, it requires the precomputations of two values Z and $k^{-1} \bmod q$.

Theorem 1. *Let $\mathcal{I}$ be a public key (g, p, q, v) and t the security parameter for the Schnorr scheme. The Lim-Lee protocol is a SAV protocol for the Schnorr Scheme if $|q| > t$ and $\log_2 |\mathcal{I}| = o(t)$.*

Proof. Let $\mathcal{E}_\pi$ and $\mathcal{E}_{\pi^*}$ denote respectively the verification of $(y \in [0, q[$ and $g^y v^c = W \bmod p)$ and $(y \in [0, q[$ and $Y^k Z v^c = W \bmod p)$.
Auxiliary completeness. In the Lim-Lee method, $(\mathcal{E}_\pi = 1) \Longleftrightarrow (\mathcal{E}_{\pi^*} = 1)$ stands so that $\Pr_{\omega_S, \omega_V} (\mathcal{V}\ \pi^*\text{-accepts } \mathcal{I} \mid \mathcal{E}_\pi = 0) = 0$ and $\Pr_{\omega_S, \omega_V} (\mathcal{V}\ \pi^*\text{-rejects } \mathcal{I} \mid \mathcal{E}_\pi = 1) = 0$.

Auxiliary soundness. We assume $\mathcal{E}_\pi = 0$. From the given values u and y such that $u = k^{-1}(y + K) \bmod q$, with $k \in [0, 2^t[$ and $K \in [0, q[$, the entropy over k, in the sense of the Shannon theory, is then exactly equal to t so that k is unconditionally unknown. Since only one value k satisfies the final equation $\mathcal{E}_{\pi^*}$, the probability that $\mathcal{V}\ \pi^*$-accepts is equal to to 2^{-t} (the probability of guessing the right k). This probability is negligible if $\log_2 |\mathcal{I}| = o(t)$.

Computational gain. In section 2.2, we assumed that the Turing machine associated to the verifier owns an additional tape to store precomputed values so that, when considering the computational cost of the verifier, these precomputed values are not taken into account.

Remark 2. As described in [28], by using an extension of the square and multiply algorithm with the precomputed value gv, the computation of $g^y v^c \bmod p$, with $|y| = l$, $|c| = t$ requires on average $1.5l + 0.25t$ modular multiplications.

In the Schnorr scheme, since $|y| = |q|$ and $|c| = |k| = t$, π-cost is equal to $1.5|q| + 0.25t$ modular multiplications. In the Lim-Lee protocol, computing $Y^k v^c$ requires $1.75t$ modular multiplications and multiplying by Z requires one more, i.e π^*-cost is equal to $1.75t + 1$ modular multiplications. If we omit the negligible cost of the modular multiplication $k^{-1}(y + K) \bmod q$, the difference of computational costs, given by $1.5(|q| - t) - 1$, is greater than 0 if $|q| > t$.

Auxiliary non-repudiation. As the security of the SAV relies on the perfect privacy of k, i.e the unconditional security of the transformation over y, even the misbehaving prover has no advantage over a cheater to determine this value k. □

Example 1. Typically, q is a 160-bit number and t is equal to 32. Thus, the Lim-Lee protocol decreases by around 75% the computational cost of the verifier.

Remark 3. If, for one reason or another, the size of q is significantly larger than 160 bits, we can also design a SAV protocol based on a computationally unknown predicate. The verifier precomputes $h = g^K \bmod p$ with K typically a 160-bit number; the server computes $Y = h^y \bmod p$ and the verifier finally checks if $Y = (W v^{-c})^K \bmod p$. This SAV protocol does not verify the auxiliary non-repudiation.

3.2   A Hard-to-Solve-Predicate-Based SAV Protocol

The Protocol. The RSA-like GPS identification scheme was presented by Girault and Paillès at WCC'03 [8]. It is a variant of the GPS identification scheme [7,24], based on the intractability of the RSA problem. In this scheme, a prover $\mathcal{P}$ owns a public key (n,g,f,e) and a private key s such that e is a prime integer and $es = 1 \bmod \phi(n)$, $f = g^{-s} \bmod n$ and, as a consequence, $g = f^{-e} \bmod n$.

In the same paper [8], Girault and Paillès suggest a method to delegate to a server some computations of the verification step. This protocol, called *server-aided RSA-like GPS identification scheme*, is described in Fig. 2. This method is essentially the same as the one proposed by Girault and Quisquater at Eurocrypt 2002 rump session and applied to the basic GPS identification scheme; it can be found in [9].

In the following, we denote π the RSA-like GPS identification scheme and π^* the server-aided RSA-like GPS identification scheme.

Theorem 2. *Let $\mathcal{I}$ be a public key (n,g,f,e) for π. Under the intractability of the RSA problem, π^* is a SAV protocol for π if $\log_2 |\mathcal{I}| = o(\log_2 e)$.*

Proof. We denote $\mathcal{E}_\pi$ and $\mathcal{E}_{\pi^*}$ the respective verification of equations of $\big(y \in [\![0, 2^R + en[\![$ and $g^y f^c = W \bmod n\big)$ and $\big(y \in [\![0, 2^R + en[\![$ and $Y \in]\!]0, n[\![$ and $Y^e f^c = W \bmod n\big)$.

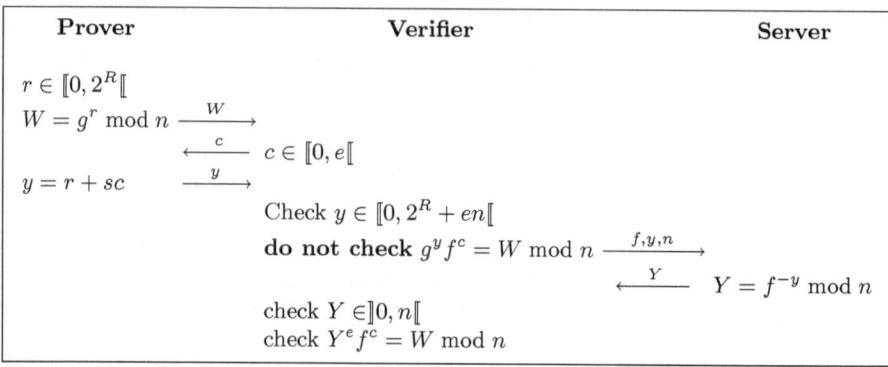

Fig. 2. The server-aided RSA-like GPS identification scheme

Auxiliary completeness. $(\mathcal{E}_\pi = 1) \Longleftrightarrow (\mathcal{E}_{\pi^*} = 1)$ stands so that, using the same argument as in the proof of the Lim-Lee protocol, the auxiliary completeness is verified.

Auxiliary soundness. We assume $\mathcal{E}_\pi = 0$. The proof relies on the following lemma.

Lemma 1. *Assuming $\mathcal{E}_\pi = 0$, if $\mathcal{I}$ is π^*-accepted with a probability greater than $\varepsilon' = \frac{1}{e} + \varepsilon$, then, an eth root of the public key f can be computed in time less than $4\tau/\varepsilon'$, with a probability greater than $\frac{\varepsilon^2}{6(\varepsilon')^2}$, τ denoting the average running time of π^*.*

Proof. Assuming $\mathcal{E}_\pi = 0$, with a classical consideration (see e.g [13]), the probability of success in π^* is at least $1/e$. This probability is negligible in $|\mathcal{I}|$ if $\log_2 |\mathcal{I}| = o(\log_2 e)$. Let us assume that

$$\Pr_{\omega_{\tilde{P}_1}, \omega_V, \omega_{\tilde{S}}} (\mathcal{V} \ \pi^*\text{-accepts} \ \mathcal{I} \mid \mathcal{E}_\pi = 0) \geq 1/e + \varepsilon = \varepsilon'.$$

In appendix A, we describe an algorithm which returns, in time less than $4\tau/\varepsilon'$ and with a probability greater than $\frac{\varepsilon^2}{6\varepsilon'^2}$, two triplets (W, c_1, Y_1) and (W, c_2, Y_2) with $c_1 \neq c_2$, $Y_1 \neq 0$ and $Y_2 \neq 0$.

These two triplets verify $Y_1^e f^{c_1} = Y_2^e f^{c_2} \mod n$. Without loss of generality, we assume that $c_2 > c_1$ so that $0 < c_2 - c_1 < e$. Since e is a prime integer, $\gcd(e, c_2 - c_1) = 1$, so that there exist two integers a and b such that $a \times e + b \times (c_2 - c_1) = 1$. Then, we obtain $f = \left(f^a (Y_1/Y_2)^b \right)^e \mod n$ so that $f^a (Y_1/Y_2)^b \mod n$ is an eth root of the public key f. $\square$

Computational gain. Let l denote the binary size of y; using Remark 2, the computation cost of the verifier in π^* is equal to $1.75|e|$ whereas in π, it is equal to $1.5l + 0.25|e|$. Due to the absence of modular reduction in y, the difference of computational costs, given by $1.5(l - |e|)$, is greater than 0.

Auxiliary non-repudiation. A misbehaving prover $\tilde{\mathcal{P}}_2$ involved in π^* knows the inverse s of e modulo $\phi(n)$. Thus, for this prover, solving the RSA problem is easy, and the auxiliary non-repudiation cannot be verified.   □

Example 2. Typically, n is a 1024-bit number, e is a 32-bit number and s is a 1024-bit number. No modular reduction is required so that y is around a 1050-bit number. Using the server-aided RSA-like GPS scheme, the computational cost of the verifier is decreased by around 95%.

Remark 4. Two other SAV protocols for GPS family can be considered; the first one verifies the auxiliary non-repudiation and is in the Lim-Lee article [15]; the second one is the same as in Remark 3.

4   First SAV Protocols for Pairing-Based Schemes

In this part, we present a generic SAV protocol applicable to several signature schemes based on bilinear maps (or pairings): in particular, the ZSNS signature scheme from Zhang, Safavi-Naini and Susilo [32] and the Boneh-Boyen signature schemes [3] (it also applies on the identification scheme from Shao, Lu and Cao [30] which is constructed from one of the Boneh-Boyen signature schemes).

4.1   The Generic SAV Protocol

We assume the existence of a bilinear map $e : G \times G \rightarrow G_1$. The groups G and G_1 are cyclic groups of prime order p and $e(g,g) \neq 1$.

The method applies on schemes in which the verifier checks if $e(\sigma, f(\mathcal{I}, m, r)) = e(g,g)$, such that f is a public function specific to the scheme, $\mathcal{I}$ the public parameters including the public key, $(r, sigma)$ defines the signature of a message. Depending of the scheme, r exists or not.

The basic idea of our generic SAV protocol is to delegate the (expensive) pairing execution to the server, the verifier being left with two (relatively much faster) exponentiations, one of them being precomputable. On the whole, it consists in first executing the signature scheme and, instead of verifying the equation $e(\sigma, f(\mathcal{I}, m, r)) = e(g,g)$, in running the following protocol with a server.

1. The verifier randomly picks an integer $t \in [\![0, p[\![$, and precomputes $e(g,g)^t$.
2. After receiving a message and its signature, the verifier computes the value $\alpha = \left(f(\mathcal{I}, m, r)\right)^t$ and sends it with σ to the server.
3. The server computes the value $\beta = e(\sigma, \alpha)$ and sends it back to the verifier.
4. The verifier finally checks if $\beta = e(g,g)^t$.

Auxiliary completeness. The equivalence $e(\sigma, f(\mathcal{I}, m, r)) = e(g,g) \Longleftrightarrow e(\sigma, \alpha) = e(g,g)^t$ stands and using the same argument as in the proof of the Lim-Lee protocol, the auxiliary completeness is verified.

Auxiliary non-repudiation. Our SAV construction allows the misbehaving prover $\tilde{\mathcal{P}}_2$ to send any value $\tilde{\sigma}$. Then, during the computation of β, $\tilde{\mathcal{P}}_2$ transmit the right value σ to $\tilde{\mathcal{S}}$ so that $\mathcal{I}$ is finally π^*-accepted. The hard computational problem involved in the SAV protocol can be easily solved using the private key of the basic protocol. The auxiliary non-repudiation cannot be verified.

4.2   Application to the ZSNS Signature Scheme

In the ZSNS scheme [32], the signer owns public parameters $(g,p,e(g,g))$, a public key U and a private key x such that $U = g^x$. To sign a message m, the signer computes the signature $\sigma = \frac{1}{H(m)+x}$, with H a hash function from $\{0,1\}^*$ into $[0,p[$. The verifier accepts the signature if $e(\sigma, g^{H(m)}U) = e(g,g)$ (in the generic description, $f(\mathcal{I}, m, r)$ corresponds to $g^{H(m)}U$). This scheme is secure against an adaptive chosen message attack in the random oracle model, under the intractability of the k-CAA problem introduced by Mitsunari et al. [17]:

given g, g^x, h_0, $h_1 \ldots$, h_k (h_i all different), $g^{\frac{1}{h_1+x}},\ldots, g^{\frac{1}{h_k+x}}$, output $g^{\frac{1}{h_0+x}}$.

We define the k-*Bilinear CAA problem* (k-*BCAA*) as follows:

given g, g^x, $h_0,\ldots$, h_k (h_i all different), $g^{\frac{1}{h_1+x}},\ldots, g^{\frac{1}{h_k+x}}$, output $e(g,g)^{\frac{1}{h_0+x}}$.

In appendix B, we prove this problem is harder than the $(k+1)$-Bilinear Diffie Hellman Inversion problem $((k + 1)$-BDHI$)$ introduced by Boneh and Boyen in [2].

Let π denote the ZSNS signature scheme, π^* the generic protocol presented in section 4.1 applied to π, $\mathcal{E}_\pi$ the verification of the equation $e(\sigma, g^{H(m)}U) = e(g,g)$ and $\mathcal{E}_{\pi^*}$ the verification of equation $\beta = e(g,g)^t$.

Theorem 3. *The protocol π^* is a SAV protocol for π, secure against adaptive chosen message attacks in the random oracle model under the intractability of the k-BCAA problem.*

Proof. The auxiliary completeness is already proved in section 4.1.

Auxiliary soundness. Using the model of security of section 2.5, it relies on the following lemma.

Lemma 2. *(With the above notations) Assuming $\mathcal{E}_\pi = 0$, if the server $\tilde{\mathcal{S}}$, communicating with a cheater $\tilde{\mathcal{P}}_1$ which asks q_H queries to the hash oracle and q_S ($< q_H$) queries to the signing oracle, makes $\mathcal{I}$ be π^*-accepted with a probability greater than ε, then the q-BCAA problem, $q \geq q_H + q_S - 1$, can be solved with a probability of success greater than $\frac{(1-\varepsilon')\varepsilon}{q_H}$ and in time $O(\tau)$; with τ denoting the average running time of π^* and ε' the probability of success of a q_S adaptive chosen message attack against the ZSNS signature scheme.*

Let us consider the following random instance of the q-BCAA problem: given g, g^x, h_0, $h_1,\ldots$, h_q (h_i all different), $g^{\frac{1}{h_1+x}},\ldots, g^{\frac{1}{h_q+x}}$, output $e(g,g)^{\frac{1}{h_0+x}}$.

We now construct an algorithm $\mathcal{A}$ which interacts with $\tilde{\mathcal{P}}_1$ and $\tilde{\mathcal{S}}$, and which solves the above instance of the q-BCAA problem. We assume that $\tilde{\mathcal{P}}_1$ never repeats two same queries to each oracle but can ask a same query to both oracles.

S1 $\mathcal{A}$ prepares a set of answers for the hash oracle: $\mathcal{H} = \{w_0, w_1, \ldots, w_{q_H-1}\} \subset \{h_0, h_1, \ldots h_q\}$ such that $h_0 \in \mathcal{H}$. $\mathcal{A}$ also establishes a list l_H, initially empty, of queries with the corresponding answered hash value.

S2 When $\tilde{\mathcal{P}}_1$ makes a hash query m_i, for $0 \le i \le (q_H - 1)$, $\mathcal{A}$ answers w_i and adds the couple (m_i, w_i) in l_H. We denote by $\tilde{m}$ the hash query for which the answer is h_0. If m_i has already been queried to the signing oracle, there exists a couple (m_i, w_i) in l_H and $\mathcal{A}$ answers w_i.

S3 $\mathcal{A}$ also establishes a set S_H, initially empty. When $\tilde{\mathcal{P}}_1$ makes a signing query m_i, two cases are possible: if m_i has already been queried to the hash oracle, there exists a unique couple (m_i, w_i) in l_H; if $m_i = \tilde{m}$, then $\mathcal{A}$ fails, otherwise $\mathcal{A}$ answers $g^{\frac{1}{w_i+x}}$. If m_i has not been queried to the hash oracle, then $\mathcal{A}$ randomly chooses $h_i \in \{h_0, h_1, \ldots, h_q\} \setminus (\mathcal{H} \cup S_H)$, answers $g^{\frac{1}{h_i+x}}$, adds the couple (m_i, h_i) in l_H and adds h_i in S_H.

S4 After making all the queries to the oracles, $\tilde{\mathcal{P}}_1$ outputs a couple (m^*, σ^*). If the message m^* is not equal to $\tilde{m}$ and if (m^*, σ^*) is such that $\mathcal{E}_\pi = 0$, then $\mathcal{A}$ sends to $\tilde{\mathcal{S}}$ the value $\alpha = g^t = g^{(h_0+x) \times \frac{t}{h_0+x}}$ for a random value $t \in [0, p[$; otherwise, $\mathcal{A}$ fails and then stops.

S5 Finally, $\tilde{\mathcal{S}}$ answers a value β. $\mathcal{A}$ π^*-accepts the couple (m^*, σ^*) if $\beta = e(g,g)^{\frac{t}{h_0+x}}$.

Let n_H denote the number of queries first asked to the random oracle and then asked to the signing oracle. Assuming the hash function behaves like a random oracle, the cheater $\tilde{\mathcal{P}}_1$ cannot distinguish the algorithm $\mathcal{A}$ from a real attack scenario. Moreover the server $\tilde{\mathcal{S}}$ cannot distinguish the value g^t from a value $g^{t'(h_0+x)}$ since t is randomly picked in $\in [0, p[$. Finally, $\mathcal{A}$ ends if :

1. in step S3, the messages queried to the signing oracle are all different from $\tilde{m}$ which occurs with a probability equal to $\frac{q_H - n_H}{q_H}$,
2. in step S4, the message m^* is equal to $\tilde{m}$ and (m^*, σ^*) is such that $\mathcal{E}_\pi = 0$ which occurs with probability greater than $(1 - \varepsilon')/(q_H - n_H)$,
3. in step S5, $\tilde{\mathcal{S}}$ answers a value β such that $\beta^{t^{-1}} = e(g,g)^{\frac{1}{h_0+x}}$, which happens with a probability greater than ε.

As a consequence, the probability of success of the algorithm is greater than $\frac{(1-\varepsilon')\varepsilon}{q_H}$.

Computational gain. The hash value $H(m)$ is assumed to be of size $|p|$ so that, using the Remark 2, computing $(Ug^{H(m)})^t$ requires $1.75|p|$ modular multiplications which corresponds to the verifier cost (since $e(g,g)^t$ is precomputed).

Remark 5. It is often complained that a pairing evaluation is too computational expensive to be used in practice. If we consider that such an evaluation is equivalent to the computation of around 4 group exponentiations, then it requires in average $6|p|$ group multiplications.

Using the above remark, and considering that the computation of $Ug^{h(m)}$ requires $1.5|p|+1$ modular multiplications, we obtain a final cost for the verifier equal to $7.5|p|+1$ modular multiplications for the basic ZSNS signature scheme. The computation cost in π^* is obviously less than in π such that the computational cost of the verifier is decreased by around 70%.   □

5   Conclusion

We have first formalized the concept of a server-aided verification (SAV) protocol, and introduced three properties for such a protocol. Two of them, called auxiliary completeness and auxiliary soundness, are mandatory, while the third one, called auxiliary non-repudiation, must be satisfied only when non-repudiation is required.

In a second time, we have analyzed in this new model two already existing SAV protocols, which both happen to reach the mandatory properties. The first one, proposed by Lim and Lee [15], verifies the auxiliary non-repudiation at the price of requiring the verifier to precompute some values. The second one, initially suggested by Girault and Quisquater [10], is easy to plug into protocols of GPS family, but do not achieve the optional property.

Finally, we have presented a generic SAV protocol for pairing-based schemes, applicable in particular to the Zhang et al. [32] and the Boneh-Boyen [3] signature schemes. Our new method consists in making the server perform the heaviest computation, namely the pairing evaluation, so that the scheme becomes almost as efficient as a "classical" discrete-logarithm-based signature scheme. But since only the mandatory properties are satisfied, it remains an open problem to find SAV protocols for pairing-based schemes which verify the auxiliary non-repudiation. The Fig. 3 compares the two main characteristics of the different protocols considered in this article.

SAV protocol	Auxiliary non-repudiation	Computational gain
The Lim-Lee method	yes	85%
Server-aided RSA-like GPS scheme	no	95%
Our generic SAV protocol	no	70%

Fig. 3. The different SAV protocols of this article

Acknowledgements

The authors wish to thank David Pointcheval and Aline Gouget for valuable and helpful discussions and comments.

References

1. M. Bellare, J. A. Garay, and T. Rabin. Fast Batch Verification for Modular Exponentiation and Digital Signatures. In Nyberg [21], pages 236–250.
2. D. Boneh and X. Boyen. Efficient Selective-ID Secure Identity Based Encryption Without Random Oracles. In Cachin and Camenisch [5], pages 382–400.
3. D. Boneh and X. Boyen. Short Signatures without Random Oracles. In Cachin and Camenisch [5], pages 382–400.
4. E. F. Brickell, D. M. Gordon, K. S. McCurley, and D. B. Wilson. Fast Exponentiation with Precomputation (Extended abstract). In Rueppel [27], pages 200–207.
5. C. Cachin and J. Camenisch, editors. *Advances in Cryptology - Eurocrypt '04*, volume 3027 of *Lecture Notes in Computer Science*. Springer-Verlag, 2004.
6. A. Fiat and A. Shamir. How to Prove Yourself : Practical Solutions to Identification and Signature Problems. In A. M. Odlyzko, editor, *Advances in Cryptology - Crypto '86*, volume 263 of *Lecture Notes in Computer Science*, pages 186–194, 1986.
7. M. Girault. Self-Certified Public Keys. In D. W. Davies, editor, *Advances in Cryptology - Eurocrypt '91*, volume 547 of *Lecture Notes in Computer Science*, pages 490–497. Springer-Verlag, 1991.
8. M. Girault and J. C. Paillès. On-line/Off-line RSA-like. In *International Workshop on Coding and Cryptography 2003*, 2003.
9. M. Girault, G. Poupard, and J. Stern. Some Modes of Use of the GPS Identification Scheme. In *3rd Nessie Conference*. Springer-Verlag, 2002.
10. M. Girault and J. J. Quisquater. GQ + GPS = new ideas + new protocols. Eurocrypt '02 - Rump Session, 2002.
11. S. Goldasser, S. Micali, and C. Rackoff. The Knowledge Complexity of Interactive Proof Systems. In *19th Annual ACM Symposium on the Theory of Computing*, pages 210–217, 1985.
12. S. Goldwasser, S. Micali, and R. L. Rivest. A Digital Signature Scheme Secure against Adaptive Chosen-Message Attacks. *SIAM Journal on Computing*, 17(2):281–308, 1988.
13. L. C. Guillou and J. J. Quisquater. A Practical Zero-knowledge Protocol Fitted to Security Microprocessor Minimizing both Transmission and Memory. In C. G. Günther, editor, *Advances in Cryptology - Eurocrypt '88*, volume 330 of *Lecture Notes in Computer Science*, pages 123–128. Springer-Verlag, 1988.
14. S. Hohenberger and A. Lysyanskaya. How to Securely Outsource Cryptographic Computations. In Joe Kilian, editor, *Theory of Cryptography, Second Theory of Cryptography Conference*, volume 3378 of *Lecture Notes in Computer Science*, pages 264–282. Springer-Verlag, 2005.
15. C. H. Lim and P. J. Lee. Server (prover/signer)-Aided Verification of Identity Proofs and Signatures. In L. C. Guillou and J. J. Quisquater, editors, *Advances in Cryptology - Eurocrypt '95*, volume 921 of *Lecture Notes in Computer Science*, pages 64–78. Springer-Verlag, 1995.
16. T. Matsumoto, K. Kato, and H. Imai. Speeding up Secret Computations with Insecure Auxiliary Devices. In S. Goldwasser, editor, *Advances in Cryptology - Crypto '88*, volume 403 of *Lecture Notes in Computer Science*, pages 497–506. Springer-Verlag, 1988.
17. S. Mitsunari, R. Sakai, and M. Kasahara. A New Traitor Tracing. *IEICE Trans.*, E85A(2):481–484, 2002.
18. D. M'Raihi and D. Naccache. Couponing Scheme Reduces Computational Power Requirements for DSS Signatures. In *CardTech*, pages 99–104, 1994.

19. P. Q. Nguyen and I. E. Shparlinski. On the Insecurity of a Server-Aided RSA Protocol. In C. Boyd, editor, *Advances in Cryptology - Asiacrypt '01*, volume 2248 of *Lecture Notes in Computer Science*, pages 21–35. Springer-Verlag, 2001.

20. P. Q. Nguyen and J. Stern. The Béguin-Quisquater Server-Aided RSA Protocol from Crypto '95 is not Secure. In K. Ohta and D. Pei, editors, *Advances in Cryptology - Asiacrypt '98*, volume 1514 of *Lecture Notes in Computer Science*, pages 372–379. Springer-Verlag, 1998.

21. K. Nyberg, editor. *Advances in Cryptology - Eurocrypt '98*, volume 1403 of *Lecture Notes in Computer Science*. Springer-Verlag, 1998.

22. B. Pfitzmann and M. Waidner. Attacks on Protocols for Server-Aided RSA Computation. In Rueppel [27], pages 153–162.

23. D. Pointcheval and J. Stern. Security Proofs for Signature Schemes. In U. M. Maurer, editor, *Advances in Cryptology - Eurocrypt '96*, volume 1070 of *Lecture Notes in Computer Science*, pages 387–398. Springer-Verlag, 1996.

24. G. Poupard and J. Stern. Security Analysis of a Practical "on the fly" Authentication and Signature Generation. In Nyberg [21], pages 422–436.

25. M. O. Rabin. Digitalized Signatures and Public-Key Functions as Intractable as Factorization. Technical Report MIT/LCS/TR-212, Massachusetts Institute of Technology - Laboratory for Computer Science, January 1979.

26. R. Rivest, A. Shamir, and L. Adleman. A Method for Obtaining Digital Signatures and Public-Key Cryptosystems. *Communication of the ACM*, 21(2):120–126, 1978.

27. R. A. Rueppel, editor. *Advances in Cryptology - Eurocrypt '92*, volume 658 of *Lecture Notes in Computer Science*. Springer-Verlag, 1993.

28. C. P. Schnorr. Efficient Identification and Signatures for Smart Cards. In G. Brassard, editor, *Advances in Cryptology - Crypto '89*, volume 435 of *Lecture Notes in Computer Science*, pages 239–252. Springer-Verlag, 1990.

29. C. P. Schnorr. Efficient Signature Generation by Smart Cards. *Journal of Cryptology*, 4(3):161–174, 1991.

30. J. Shao, R. Lu, and Z. Cao. A New Efficient Identification Scheme Based on the Strong Diffie-Hellman Assumption. In *International Symposium on Future Software Technology*, 2004.

31. M. De Soete and J. J. Quisquater. Speeding Up Smart Card RSA Computations with Insecure Coprocessors. In *Smart Card 2000*, pages 191–198, 1989.

32. F. Zhang, R. Safavi-Naini, and W. Susilo. An Efficient Signature Scheme from Bilinear Pairing and its Applications. In F. Bao, R. H. Deng, and J. Zhou, editors, *Public Key Cryptography*, volume 2947 of *Lecture Notes in Computer Science*, pages 277–290. Springer-Verlag, 2004.

A   Algorithm from Lemma 1

Let us consider the following algorithm, constructed from [29].

To analyze this algorithm, we first recall a well-known probabilistic lemma (see [23] for the proof).

$i := 0$
do $i = i + 1$
    Choose a random tape $\omega_{\tilde{\mathcal{P}}_1}$ and compute W
    Send $\tilde{\mathcal{P}}_1$ a random c_1 in $[\![0, e[\![$
    Obtain from $\tilde{\mathcal{P}}_1$ the answer y_1 and check $\mathcal{E}_\pi$
    Ask the server $\tilde{\mathcal{S}}$ the computation of Y_1
until $((\mathcal{E}_\pi = 0) \text{ and } (Y_1^e v^{c_1} = W))$
$j := 0$
do $j = j + 1$
    Send $\tilde{\mathcal{P}}_1$ a random $c_2 \neq c_1$ in $[\![0, e[\![$
    Obtain from $\tilde{\mathcal{P}}_1$ the answer y_2 and check $\mathcal{E}_\pi$
    Ask the server $\tilde{\mathcal{S}}$ the computation of Y_2
until $\left(((\mathcal{E}_\pi = 0) \text{ and } (Y_2^e v^{c_2} = W)) \text{ or } (i == j) \right)$
if $((\mathcal{E}_\pi = 0) \text{ and } (Y_2^e v^{c_2} = W))$
    then return (W, c_1, Y_1) and (W, c_2, Y_2)
    else return FAIL.

Lemma 3. *Let A be an event defined on $X \times Y$ such that $\Pr_{x,y}\big(A(x,y)\big) \geq \varepsilon$ and let $\Omega = \{a \in X;\ \Pr_{x,y}\big(A(x,y)\big) \geq \varepsilon - \alpha\}$, then: $\Pr_x(x \in \Omega) \geq \alpha$ and $\Pr_x\big(x \in \Omega | A(x,y)\big) \geq \alpha/\varepsilon$.*

We assume $\Pr_{\omega_{\tilde{\mathcal{P}}_1}, \omega_\mathcal{V}, \omega_{\tilde{\mathcal{S}}}} (\mathcal{V}\ \pi^*\text{-accepts } \mathcal{I} \mid \mathcal{E}_\pi = 0) \geq 1/e + \varepsilon = \varepsilon'$. Let Ω be the set of random tapes $\omega_{\tilde{\mathcal{P}}_1}$ such that $\Pr_{\omega_\mathcal{V}, \omega_{\tilde{\mathcal{S}}}} (\mathcal{V}\ \pi^*\text{-accepts } \mathcal{I} \mid \mathcal{E}_\pi = 0) = 1/e + \varepsilon/2$.
Let us now consider the probability of success of this algorithm. Since the GPS RSA-like identification scheme is sound, the probability of success (i.e $\mathcal{E}_\pi = 1$) of a cheater $\tilde{\mathcal{P}}_1$ is less of equal to $1/e$ so that the probability that $(\mathcal{E}_\pi = 0)$ is great or equal than $(1 - 1/e)$.

The probability of success of the first loop is, by definition of $\tilde{\mathcal{S}}$ and $\tilde{\mathcal{P}}_1$, greater than $(1 - 1/e)\varepsilon'$; and for any integer N, i is equal to N with a probability equal to $\varepsilon'(1 - 1/e) \times (1 - \varepsilon'(1 - 1/e))^{N-1}$.

The probability that the first loop succeeds with a random tape $\omega_{\tilde{\mathcal{P}}_1}$ lies in Ω is greater than $\varepsilon/(2 \times \varepsilon')$ (using lemma 3).

If $\omega_{\tilde{\mathcal{P}}_1}$ in Ω, the second loop ends with $(\mathcal{E}_\pi = 0)$ and $(Y_2^e v^{c_2} = W)$ with a probability greater than $\varepsilon/2(1 - 1/e)$; otherwise, $\Pr_{\omega_{\tilde{\mathcal{P}}_1}, \omega_\mathcal{V}, \omega_{\tilde{\mathcal{S}}}} (\mathcal{V}\ \pi^*\text{-accepts } \mathcal{I} \mid \mathcal{E}_\pi = 0) \leq \varepsilon'$. Thus, finding this second value c_2 before $j = N$ occurs with a probability greater than $1 - \big(1 - \varepsilon/2(1 - 1/e)\big)^N$. Then, the full probability of success of the algorithm is:

$$\sum_{i=1}^{+\infty} \varepsilon'(1 - \frac{1}{e})\left(1 - \varepsilon'(1 - \frac{1}{e})\right)^{i-1} \times \frac{\varepsilon}{2\varepsilon'} \times \left(1 - \left(1 - \frac{\varepsilon}{2}(1 - \frac{1}{e})\right)^i\right)$$

which can be rewritten as :

$$\frac{\varepsilon}{2}(1-\frac{1}{e})\left(\sum_{i=0}^{+\infty}\left(1-\varepsilon'(1-\frac{1}{e})\right)^i-(1-\frac{\varepsilon}{2}(1-\frac{1}{e}))\sum_{i=0}^{+\infty}\left((1-\varepsilon'(1-\frac{1}{e}))(1-\frac{\varepsilon}{2}(1-\frac{1}{e}))\right)^i\right)$$

Using the equality $\sum_{i=0}^{+\infty}x^i=\frac{1}{1-x}$, we obtain

$$\frac{\varepsilon}{2}(1-\frac{1}{e})\left(\frac{1}{\varepsilon'(1-\frac{1}{e})}-\frac{\left(1-\frac{\varepsilon}{2}(1-\frac{1}{e})\right)}{\varepsilon'(1-\frac{1}{e})\left((1+\frac{\varepsilon}{2\varepsilon'})-\frac{\varepsilon}{2}(1-\frac{1}{e})\right)}\right)$$

$$=\frac{\varepsilon^2}{4\varepsilon'^2\left((1+\frac{\varepsilon}{2\varepsilon'})-\frac{\varepsilon}{2}(1-\frac{1}{e})\right)}$$

Since $\varepsilon'>\varepsilon$, we obtain $(1+\frac{\varepsilon}{2\varepsilon'})-\frac{\varepsilon}{2}(1-\frac{1}{e})\leq 1+\frac{\varepsilon}{2\varepsilon'}\leq(1+\frac{1}{2})\leq 3/2$, so that the algorithm succeeds with a probability greater than $\frac{\varepsilon^2}{6\varepsilon'^2}$. The running time of the algorithm is $\frac{2\tau}{(1-1/e)\varepsilon'}\leq\frac{4\tau}{\varepsilon'}$ with τ the average running time of the SAV protocol.

B k-BCAA is a Stronger Problem Than $(k+1)$-BDHI

We recall that the k-BCAA problem is defined by:

given g, g^x, h_0, $h_1,\ldots,h_k$ (h_i all different), $g^{\frac{1}{h_1+x}},\ldots,g^{\frac{1}{h_k+x}}$, output $e(g,g)^{\frac{1}{h_0+x}}$.

The $(k+1)$-BDHI problem from [2] is defined by:

given f, f^y, $f^{y^2},\ldots,f^{y^{k+1}}$; output $e(f,f)^{\frac{1}{y}}$.

We assume there exists an algorithm which solves the k-BCAA problem and we consider the following given input for the $(k+1)$-BDHI problem: f, f^y, $f^{y^2},\ldots,f^{y^{k+1}}$ for a non zero y.

First, we need to construct a valid input for the k-BCAA problem. Let A_i denote f^{y^i} $\forall i\in[\![0,k+1]\!]$ and let B_i denote $e(f,f)^{y^i}$ $\forall i\in[\![0,2k-1]\!]$.

Construction of the input of the k-BCAA problem. The method used here is inspired by Mitsunari et al. [17]. Let $h_0,h_1,\ldots,h_k$ be $k+1$ distinct random values in $[\![0,q[\![$ and let $P(Y)$ be the polynomial given by $\prod_{i=1}^{k}(Y-h_0+h_i)$. This polynomial is of degree k in Y and can be expanded into $P(Y)=\sum_{i=0}^{k}\alpha_iY^i$.

Let g be the value $f^{P(y)}$ which is obtained by computing $\prod_{i=0}^{k}(A_i)^{\alpha_i}$ and let P_K be the value $g^{-h_0}\prod_{i=0}^{k}(A_{i+1})^{\alpha_i}$ which is also equal to g^{y-h_0}.

Moreover, $\forall j\in[\![1,k]\!]$, let $P_j(Y)$ be the polynomial given by $\prod_{i=1;i\neq j}^{k}(Y-h_0+h_i)$, so that $(Y-h_0+h_j)P_j(Y)=P(Y)$; each $P_j(Y)$ can be expanded into $\sum_{i=0}^{k-1}\beta_i^jY^i$. Then, $\forall j\in[\![1,k]\!]$, we denote by S_j the value $\prod_{i=0}^{k-1}(A_i)^{\beta_i^j}$ which is equal to $f^{P_j(y)}=f^{P(y)/(y-h_0+h_j)}=g^{1/(y-h_0+h_j)}$.

If we finally denote $x = y - h_0$, we then obtain $h_0, h_1, \ldots, h_k, g, P_K = g^x$, $S_1 = g^{1/(x+h_1)}, \ldots, S_k = g^{1/(x+h_k)}$ so that we have constructed a valid input for the algorithm solving the k-BCAA problem: we obtain the solution $e(g,g)^{1/(x+h_0)}$ for the current instance of the k-BCAA problem.

Recovering the solution of the $(k+1)$-BDHI. The output value of the k-BCAA problem $e(g,g)^{1/(x+h_0)}$ is equal, by definition, to $e(g,g)^{1/y}$ and more precisely, to $e(f,f)^{P^2(y)/y}$ (we have assumed y is a non zero value).

Let $P'(Y)$ be the rational fraction $P^2(Y)/Y$ which can be written as $\frac{\gamma_{-1}}{Y} + \sum_{i=0}^{2k-1} \gamma_i Y^i$; γ_{-1} is a non zero value equal to $\prod_{i=1}^{k}(h_i - h_0)$. Thus,

$$e(g,g)^{1/(x+h_0)} = e(f,f)^{P^2(y)/y} = e(f,f)^{\frac{\gamma_{-1}}{y} + \sum_{i=0}^{2k-1} \gamma_i y^i} = e(f,f)^{\frac{\gamma_{-1}}{y}} \prod_{i=0}^{2k-1} B_i^{\gamma_i}.$$

As a consequence, we obtain:

$$e(f,f)^{\frac{1}{y}} = \left(e(g,g)^{1/(x+h_0)} \prod_{i=0}^{2k-1} B_i^{-\gamma_i} \right)^{\gamma_{-1}^{-1}}$$

Errors in Computational Complexity Proofs for Protocols

Kim-Kwang Raymond Choo, Colin Boyd, and Yvonne Hitchcock

Information Security Institute,
Queensland University of Technology,
GPO Box 2434, Brisbane, QLD 4001, Australia
{k.choo, c.boyd, y.hitchcock}@qut.edu.au

Abstract. Proofs are invaluable tools in assuring protocol implementers about the security properties of protocols. However, several instances of undetected flaws in the proofs of protocols (resulting in flawed protocols) undermine the credibility of provably-secure protocols. In this work, we examine several protocols with claimed proofs of security by Boyd & González Nieto (2003), Jakobsson & Pointcheval (2001), and Wong & Chan (2001), and an authenticator by Bellare, Canetti, & Krawczyk (1998). Using these protocols as case studies, we reveal previously unpublished flaws in these protocols and their proofs. We hope our analysis will enable similar mistakes to be avoided in the future.

1 Introduction

Despite cryptographic protocols being fundamental to many diverse secure electronic commerce applications, and the enormous amount of research effort expended in design and analysis of such protocols, the design of secure cryptographic protocols is still notoriously hard. The difficulty of obtaining a high level of assurance in the security of almost any new or even existing protocols is well illustrated with examples of errors found in many such protocols years after they were published. The many flaws discovered in published protocols for key establishment and authentication over many years, have promoted the use of formal models and rigorous security proofs, namely the computational complexity approach and the computer security approach.

Computer Security Approach: Emphasis in the computer security approach is placed on automated machine specification and analysis. The Dolev & Yao [13] adversarial model is the de-facto model used in formal specifications, where cryptographic operations are often used in a "black box" fashion ignoring some of the cryptographic properties, resulting in possible loss of partial information. The main obstacles in this automated approach are undecidability and intractability, since the adversary can have a large set of possible actions which results in a state explosion. Protocols proven secure in such a manner could possibly be flawed – giving a false positive result.

B. Roy (Ed.): ASIACRYPT 2005, LNCS 3788, pp. 624–643, 2005.

Computational Complexity Approach: On the other hand, the computational complexity approach adopts a deductive reasoning process whereby the emphasis is placed on a proven reduction from the problem of breaking the protocol to another problem believed to be hard. The first treatment of computational complexity analysis for cryptography began in the 1980s [14] but it was made popular for key establishment protocols by Bellare & Rogaway. In fact, Bellare & Rogaway [4] provided the first formal definition for a model of adversary capabilities with an associated definition of security. These human-generated proofs provide a strong assurance that the security properties of the protocols are satisfied. However, it is often difficult to obtain correct proofs of security and the number of protocols that possess a rigorous proof of security remains relatively small. Furthermore, such proofs usually entail lengthy and complicated mathematical proofs, which are daunting to most readers [20]. The breaking of provably-secure protocols after they were published is evidence of the difficulty of obtaining correct computational proofs of protocol security. Despite these setbacks, proofs are invaluable for arguing about security and certainly are one very important tool in getting protocols right.

Importance of Specifications and Details: Rogaway [24] pointed out the importance of robust and detailed definitions in concrete security. In fact, specifications adopted in the computer security approach are expected to be precise (without ambiguity) and detailed, as such specifications are subjected to automated checking using formal tools. Boyd & Mathuria [7] also pointed out that it is the responsibility of the protocol designers and not the protocol implementers to define the details of protocol specifications. Protocol implementers (usually non-specialists and/or industrial practitioners) will usually plug-and-use existing provably-secure protocols without reading the formal proofs of the protocols [20]. Bleichenbacher [6] also pointed out that important details are often overlooked in implementations of cryptographic protocols until specific attacks have been demonstrated. Flaws in security proofs or specifications themselves certainly will have a damaging effect on the trustworthiness and the credibility of provably-secure protocols in the real world.

In this work, we advocate the importance of proofs of protocol security, and by identifying some situations where errors in proofs arise, we hope that similar structural mistakes can be avoided in future proofs. We use several protocols with claimed proofs in the Bellare–Rogaway model as case studies, namely the conference key agreement protocol due to Boyd & González Nieto [8], the mutual authentication and key establishment protocols (JP-MAKEP) due to Jakobsson & Pointcheval [18] and WC-MAKEP due to Wong & Chan [26]. We also examine an encryption-based MT authenticator due to Bellare, Canetti, & Krawczyk [2].

In the setting of the reductionist proof approach for protocols, the security model comprises protocol participants and a powerful probabilistic, polynomial-time (PPT) adversary $\mathcal{A}$, where the latter is in control of all communication between all parties in the model. The original BR93 proof model was defined only for two-party protocols. In subsequent work, the model is extended to analyse three-party server-based protocols [5] and multi-party protocols [9].

Boyd–González Nieto Protocol: An inappropriate proof model environment is one of the likely areas where protocol proofs might go wrong. In the existing proof of the Boyd–González Nieto conference key agreement protocol [8], we observe that the proof model environment has the same number of parties in the model as in the protocol, which effectively rules out a multi-user setting in which to analyse the signature and encryption schemes. Consequently, this shortcoming fails to include the case where $\mathcal{A}$ is able to corrupt a player that does not participate in the particular key agreement protocol session, and obtains a fresh key of any initiator principal by causing disagreement amongst parties about who is participating in the key exchange.

The attack we reveal on Boyd–González Nieto conference key agreement protocol is also known as an *unknown key share attack*, first described by Diffie, van Oorschot, & Wiener in 1992 [12]. As discussed by Boyd & Mathuria [7– Chapter 5.1.2], $\mathcal{A}$ need not obtain the session key to profit from this attack. Consider the scenario whereby $\mathcal{A}$ will deliver some information of value (such as e-cash) to B. Since B believes the session key is shared with $\mathcal{A}$, $\mathcal{A}$ can claim this credit deposit as his. Also, a malicious adversary, $\mathcal{A}$, can exploit such an attack in a number of ways if the established session key is subsequently used to provide encryption (e.g., in AES) or integrity [19].

In the attack on Boyd–Gonzalez-Nieto protocol, $\mathcal{A}$ is able to reveal the key of a non-partner oracle whose key is the same as the initiator principal, thus violating the key establishment goal. The existence of this attack means that the proof of Boyd–González Nieto's protocol is invalid, since the proof model allows Corrupt queries. Protocols proven secure in a proof model that allows the "Corrupt" query (in the proof simulation) ought to be secure against the unknown key share attack, since if a key is to be shared between some parties, U_1, U_2, and U_3, the corruption of some other (non-related) player in the protocol, say U_4, should not expose the session key shared between U_1, U_2, and U_3. In the proof simulations of the protocols on which we perform an unknown key share attack, $\mathcal{A}$ does not corrupt the owner or the perceived partners of the target Test session, but instead corrupts some other (non-related) player in the protocol that is not associated with the target Test session or a member of the "attacked" protocol session.

JP-MAKEP: We also describe an unknown key share attack on the JP-MAKEP which breaks the reduction of the proof from JP-MAKEP to the discrete logarithm problem. Similarly to the Boyd–González Nieto protocol, the proof model allows Corrupt queries for clients, and hence secure protocols ought to be immune to unknown key share attacks.

WC-MAKEP: An attack against WC-MAKEP is described where an adversary $\mathcal{A}$ is able to obtain a fresh key of an initiator oracle by revealing a non-partner server oracle sharing the same session key. The proof was sketchy and failed to provide any simulation.

Encryption-Based Authenticator: In the Bellare–Canetti–Krawczyk encryption-based authenticator, we demonstrate that an adversary $\mathcal{A}$ is able to use a Session-State Reveal query to find the one-time MAC key and use it to authenticate a fraudulent message. We identify the problem (in its proof) to be due to an incomplete proof specification (**Session-State Reveal** queries not adequately considered), which results in the failure of the proof simulation where the adversary has a non-negligible advantage, but the MAC forger, $\mathcal{F}$, does not have a non-negligible probability of forging a MAC digest (since it fails). This violates the underlying assumption in the proof. We also demonstrate how the flaw in this MT authenticator invalidates the proof of protocols that use the MT-authenticator using protocol 2DHPE [16] as a case study.

Organization of Paper: Section 2 briefly explains the Bellare-Rogaway and the Canetti–Krawczyk models. Section 3 revisits the Boyd–González Nieto conference key agreement protocol, the JP-MAKEP, and the WC-MAKEP. Previously unpublished attacks on these protocols are demonstrated and flaws in the existing proofs are revealed. We conclude this section by proposing fixes to the protocols. Fixed protocols are not proven secure, and are presented mainly to provide a better insight into the proof failures. Section 4 revisits the encryption-based MT-authenticator proposed by Bellare, Canetti, & Krawczyk [2]. Finally, Section 5 presents the conclusions.

2 Informal Overview of the Bellare-Rogaway and Canetti–Krawczyk Models

Throughout this paper, the Bellare & Rogaway 1993 model, 1995 model [4,5], the Bellare, Pointcheval, & Rogaway 2000 model [3], and the Canetti & Krawczyk 2001 model [2,10] model will be referred to as the BR93, BR95 BPR2000, and CK2001 models respectively. Collectively, the BR93, BR95, and BPR2000 models are known as the Bellare-Rogaway model.

2.1 Bellare-Rogaway Models

In the Bellare-Rogaway model, the adversary, $\mathcal{A}$, is defined to be a probabilistic machine that is in control of all communications between parties and is allowed to intercept, delete, delay, and/or fabricate any messages at will. $\mathcal{A}$ interacts with a set of $\Pi^i_{U_u,U_v}$ oracles (i.e., $\Pi^i_{U_u,U_v}$ is defined to be the ith instantiation of a principal U_u in a specific protocol run and U_v is the principal with whom U_u wishes to establish a secret key). Let n denote the number of players allowed in the model, where n is polynomial in the security parameter k. The predefined oracle queries are shown in Table 1.

The definition of security depends on the notions of partnership of oracles and indistinguishability. The definition of partnership is used in the definition of security to restrict the adversary's **Reveal** and **Corrupt** queries to oracles that are not partners of the oracle whose key the adversary is trying to guess. An important difference between the three Bellare–Rogaway models is in the way partner oracles are defined (i.e. the definition of partnership). The BR93 model defines partnership using the notion of matching conversations, where a conversation

Table 1. Informal description of the oracle queries

A Send(U_u, U_v, i, m) query to oracle $\Pi^i_{U_u, U_v}$ computes a response according to the protocol specification and decision on whether to accept or reject yet, and returns them to the adversary $\mathcal{A}$. If the client oracle, $\Pi^i_{U_u, U_v}$, has either accepted with some session key or terminated, this will be made known to $\mathcal{A}$.
The Reveal(U_u, U_v, i) query captures the notion of **known key security**. Any client oracle, $\Pi^i_{U_u, U_v}$, upon receiving such a query and if it has accepted and holds some session key, will send this session key back to $\mathcal{A}$.
The Corrupt(U_u, K_E) query captures **unknown key share attacks** and **insider attacks**. This query allows $\mathcal{A}$ to corrupt the principal U_u at will, and thereby learn the complete internal state of the corrupted principal. Notice that a Corrupt query does not result in the release of the session keys since $\mathcal{A}$ already has the ability to obtain session keys through Reveal queries. In the BR95 model, this query also gives $\mathcal{A}$ the ability to overwrite the long-lived key of the corrupted principal with any value of her choice (i.e. K_E).
The Test(U_u, U_v, i) query is the only oracle query that does not correspond to any of $\mathcal{A}$'s abilities. If $\Pi^i_{U_u, U_v}$ has accepted with some session key and is being asked a Test(U_u, U_v, i) query, then depending on a randomly chosen bit b, $\mathcal{A}$ is given either the actual session key or a session key drawn randomly from the session key distribution.

is defined to be the sequence of messages sent and received by an oracle. The sequence of messages exchanged (i.e., only the Send oracle queries) are recorded in the transcript, T. At the end of a protocol run, T will contain the record of the Send queries and the responses. Definition 1 gives a simplified definition of matching conversations.

Definition 1 (BR93 Matching Conversations). *Let n_S be the maximum number of sessions between any two parties in the protocol run. $\Pi^i_{A,B}$ and $\Pi^j_{B,A}$ are said to be partners if they both have matching conversations, where*

$$C_A = (\tau_0, 'start', \alpha_1), (\tau_2, \beta_1, \alpha_2)$$
$$C_B = (\tau_1, \alpha_1, \beta_1), (\tau_3, \alpha_2, *), \text{ for } \tau_0 < \tau_1 < \ldots$$

Partnership in the BR95 model is defined using the notion of a partner function, which uses the transcript (the record of all SendClient and SendServer oracle queries) to determine the partner of an oracle. However, no explicit definition of partnership was provided in the original paper since there is no single partner function fixed for any protocol. Instead, security is defined predicated on the existence of a suitable partner function. Two oracles are BR95 partners if, and only if, the specific partner function in use says they are.

BPR2000 partnership is defined based on the notion of session identifiers (SIDs) where SIDs are suggested to be the concatenation of messages exchanged during the protocol run. In this model, an oracle who has accepted will hold the associated session key, a SID and a partner identifier (PID). Note that any oracle that has accepted will have at most one partner, if any at all. Definition 2 describes the definition of partnership in the BPR2000 model.

Definition 2 (BPR2000 Partnership). *Two oracles, $\Pi_{A,B}^i$ and $\Pi_{B,A}^j$, are partners if, and only if, both oracles have accepted the same session key with the same SID, have agreed on the same set of principals (i.e. the initiator and the responder of the protocol), and no other oracles besides $\Pi_{A,B}^i$ and $\Pi_{B,A}^j$ have accepted with the same SID.*

2.2 Canetti-Krawczyk Model

In the CK2001 model, there are two adversarial models, namely the unathenticated-links adversarial model (UM) and the authenticated-links adversarial model (AM). Let $\mathcal{A}_{UM}$ denote the adversary in the UM, and $\mathcal{A}_{AM}$ denote the adversary in the *AM*. The difference between $\mathcal{A}_{AM}$ and $\mathcal{A}_{UM}$ lies in their powers. Table 2 provides an informal description of the oracle queries allowed for both $\mathcal{A}_{AM}$ and $\mathcal{A}_{UM}$. Let n denote the number of players allowed in the model, where n is polynomial in the security parameter k.

Table 2. Informal description of the oracle queries allowed for $\mathcal{A}_{AM}$ and $\mathcal{A}_{UM}$

Oracle Π_{U_u,U_v}^i, upon receiving a Session-State Reveal(U_u, U_v, i) query and if it has neither accepted nor held some session key, will return all its internal state (including any ephemeral parameters but not long-term secret parameters) to the adversary.
Session − Key Reveal, Corrupt, and Test are equivalent to the Reveal, Corrupt, and Test queries in Table 1 respectively.
Send(U_u, U_v, i, m) is equivalent to the Send query in Table 1. However, $\mathcal{A}_{AM}$ is restricted to only delay, delete, and relay messages but not to fabricate any messages or send a message more than once.

A protocol that is proven to be secure in the AM can be translated to a provably secure protocol in the UM with the use of an authenticator. Definition 3 provides the definition of an autheticator.

Definition 3 (Definition of an Authenticator). *An authenticator is defined to be a mapping transforming a protocol π_{AM} in the AM to a protocol π_{UM} in the UM such that π_{UM} emulates π_{AM}.*

In other words, the security proof of a UM protocol depends on the security proofs of the MT-authenticators used and that of the associated AM protocol. If any of these proofs break down, then the proof of the UM protocol is invalid. CK2001 partnership can be defined using the notion of matching sessions, as described in Definition 4.

Definition 4 (Matching Sessions). *Two sessions are said to be matching if they have the same session identifier (SIDs) and corresponding partner identifier (PIDs).*

2.3   Definition of Freshness

Freshness is used to identify the session keys about which $\mathcal{A}$ ought not to know anything because $\mathcal{A}$ has not revealed any oracles that have accepted the key and has not corrupted any principals knowing the key. Definition 5 describes freshness, which depends on the respective notion of partnership. The following definition of freshness does not incorporate the notion of forward secrecy, or the notions of session expiry and exposure in the Canetti–Krawczyk model since these notions are not necessary to explain our attacks.

Definition 5 (Definition of Freshness). *Oracle $\Pi_{A,B}^i$ is fresh (or holds a fresh session key) at the end of execution, if, and only if, (1) $\Pi_{A,B}^i$ has accepted with or without a partner oracle $\Pi_{B,A}^j$, (2) both $\Pi_{A,B}^i$ and $\Pi_{B,A}^j$ oracles have not been sent a* Reveal *query (or* Session-State Reveal *in the CK2001 model), and (3) A and B have not been sent a* Corrupt *query.*

2.4   Definition of Security

Security in the models is defined using the game $\mathcal{G}$, played between a malicious adversary $\mathcal{A}$ and a collection of Π_{U_x,U_y}^i oracles for players $U_x, U_y \in \{U_1, \ldots, U_{N_p}\}$ and instances $i \in \{1, \ldots, N_s\}$. The adversary $\mathcal{A}$ runs the game $\mathcal{G}$, whose setting is explained below:

Stage 1: $\mathcal{A}$ is able to send any oracle queries at will.
Stage 2: At some point during $\mathcal{G}$, $\mathcal{A}$ will choose a fresh session on which to be tested and send a Test query to the fresh oracle associated with the test session. Depending on the randomly chosen bit b, $\mathcal{A}$ is given either the actual session key or a session key drawn randomly from the session key distribution.
Stage 3: $\mathcal{A}$ continues making any oracle queries at will but cannot make Corrupt or Session-State/Key Reveal queries that trivially expose the test session key.
Stage 4: Eventually, $\mathcal{A}$ terminates the game simulation and outputs a bit b', which is its guess of the value of b.

Success of $\mathcal{A}$ in $\mathcal{G}$ is measured in terms of $\mathcal{A}$'s advantage in distinguishing whether $\mathcal{A}$ receives the real key or a random value. $\mathcal{A}$ wins if, after asking a Test(U_1, U_2, i) query, where Π_{U_1,U_2}^i is fresh and has accepted, $\mathcal{A}$'s guess bit b' equals the bit b selected during the Test(U_1, U_2, i) query. Let the advantage function of $\mathcal{A}$ be denoted by $\mathsf{Adv}^{\mathcal{A}}(k)$, where $\mathsf{Adv}^{\mathcal{A}}(k) = 2 \times \Pr[b = b'] - 1$.

The notions of security for entity authentication are client-to-server authentication, server-to-client authentication, and mutual authentication. An adversary is said to violate client-to-server authentication if some fresh server oracle terminates with no partner. Similarly, an adversary is said to violate server-to-client authentication if some fresh client oracle terminates with no partner. An adversary is said to violate mutual authentication if some fresh oracle terminates with no partner.

Definitions 6, 7, and 8 describes the definition of security for the BR95 model, the BPR2000 model, and both the BR93 and CK2001 models respectively.

Definition 6 (BR95 Definition of Security). *A protocol is secure in the BR95 model if both the following requirements are satisfied: (1) When the protocol is run between two oracles $\Pi^i_{A,B}$ and $\Pi^j_{B,A}$ in the absence of a malicious adversary, both $\Pi^i_{A,B}$ and $\Pi^j_{B,A}$ accept and hold the same session key. (2) For all probabilistic, polynomial-time (PPT) adversaries $\mathcal{A}$, $\mathsf{Adv}^{\mathcal{A}}(\mathsf{k})$ is negligible.*

Definition 7 (BPR2000 Definition of Security). *A protocol is secure in the BPR2000 model if both the following requirements are satisfied: (1) When the protocol is run between two oracles $\Pi^i_{A,B}$ and $\Pi^j_{B,A}$ in the absence of a malicious adversary, both $\Pi^i_{A,B}$ and $\Pi^j_{B,A}$ accept and hold the same session key. (2) For all probabilistic, polynomial-time (PPT) adversaries $\mathcal{A}$, the advantage that $\mathcal{A}$ has in violating entity authentication is negligible, and $\mathsf{Adv}^{\mathcal{A}}(\mathsf{k})$ is negligible.*

Definition 8 (BR93 and CK2001 Definitions of Security). *A protocol is secure in the BR93 and CK2001 models if both the following requirements are satisfied: (1) When the protocol is run between two oracles $\Pi^i_{A,B}$ and $\Pi^j_{B,A}$ in the absence of a malicious adversary, both $\Pi^i_{A,B}$ and $\Pi^j_{B,A}$ accept and hold the same session key, and (2) For all PPT adversaries $\mathcal{A}$, (a) If uncorrupted oracles $\Pi^i_{A,B}$ and $\Pi^j_{B,A}$ complete matching sessions, then both $\Pi^i_{A,B}$ and $\Pi^j_{B,A}$ must hold the same session key, and (b) $\mathsf{Adv}^{\mathcal{A}}(\mathsf{k})$ is negligible.*

3   Flawed Proofs in the Bellare–Rogaway Model

3.1   Boyd–González Nieto Conference Key Agreement Protocol

The conference key agreement protocol [8] shown in Figure 1 carries a claimed proof of security in the BR93 model, but uses a different definition of partnership than that given in the original model description. Although this protocol was proposed fairly recently, it has been widely cited and used as a benchmark. In the protocol, the notation (e_U, d_U) denotes the encryption and signature keys of principal U respectively, $\{\cdot\}_{e_U}$ denotes the encryption of some message under key e_U, $\sigma_{d_U}(\cdot)$ denotes the signature of some message under the signature key d_U, N_U denotes the random nonce chosen by principal U, $\mathcal{H}$ denotes some secure one-way collision-resistant hash function, and SK_U denotes the session key accepted by U. The protocol involves a set of p users, $\mathcal{U} = \{U_1, U_2, \ldots, U_p\}$.

The initiator, U_1, randomly selects a k-bit challenge N_1, encrypts N_1 under the public keys of the other participants in the protocol, signs the encrypted nonces $\{N_1\}_{e_{U_2}}, \ldots, \{N_1\}_{e_{U_p}}$ and broadcasts these messages in protocol flows 1 and 2 as shown in Figure 1. The other principals, upon receiving the broadcasted messages, will respond with their identity and a random nonce. All principals are then able to compute the shared session key $SK_{U_i} = \mathcal{H}(N_1||N_2||\ldots||N_p)$. The session identifier (SID) in the protocol is defined to be the concatenation of messages received and sent. Note that the adversary, $\mathcal{A}$, is allowed to capture and suppress any broadcasted messages in the network.

1. $U_1 \rightarrow * : \mathcal{U} = \{U_1, U_2, \ldots, U_p\}, \sigma_{d_{U_1}}(\mathcal{U}, \{N_1\}_{e_{U_2}}, \ldots, \{N_1\}_{e_{U_p}})$
2. $U_1 \rightarrow * : \{N_1\}_{e_{U_i}}$ for $1 < i \leq p$
3. $U_i \rightarrow * : U_i, N_i$

The session key is $SK_{U_i} = \mathcal{H}(N_1 || N_2 || \ldots || N_p)$.

Fig. 1. Boyd–González Nieto conference key agreement protocol

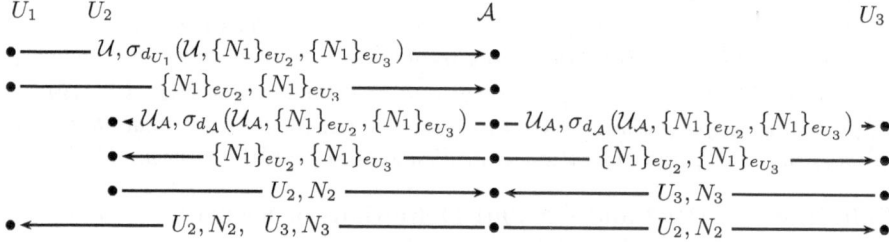

Fig. 2. Unknown key share attack

3.1.1 Unknown Key Share Attack

Figure 2 shows the execution of the Boyd–González Nieto conference key agreement protocol in the presence of a malicious adversary, $\mathcal{A}$. For simplicity, let $\mathcal{U} = \{U_1, U_2, U_3\}$ and $\mathcal{U}_\mathcal{A} = \{\mathcal{A}, U_2, U_3\}$, which denote two different sessions. In Figure 2, the actions of the entities are as follows:

1. The initiator, U_1, encrypts N_1 under the public keys of the other participants in the protocol (i.e., $\mathcal{U} \setminus U_1$), signs the encrypted nonces $\{N_1\}_{e_{U_2}}, \{N_1\}_{e_{U_3}}$ together with $\mathcal{U}$, and broadcasts these messages in protocol flows 1 and 2.
2. A malicious adversary, $\mathcal{A}$, intercepts the broadcasted messages sent by U_1. In other words, the broadcasted messages sent by U_1 never reach the intended recipients, U_2 & U_3.
   - $\mathcal{A}$ then signs the intercepted encrypted nonces $\{N_1\}_{e_{U_2}}, \{N_1\}_{e_{U_3}}$ together with $\mathcal{U}_\mathcal{A}$ (instead of $\mathcal{U}$) under $\mathcal{A}$'s signing key
   - $\mathcal{A}$ now acts as the **initiator** in a **different session** and broadcasts these messages in protocol flows 1 and 2.
3. U_2 & U_3 upon receiving the broadcasted messages, will reply to $\mathcal{A}$ with their identity and a random nonce.
4. $\mathcal{A}$ impersonates U_2 & U_3 and forwards the messages from U_2 & U_3 to U_1.
5. U_1, U_2 & U_3 are then able to compute the shared session key $SK_{U_i} = \mathcal{H}(N_1 || N_2|, |\ldots || N_n)$.

Table 3 describes the internal states of players U_1, U_2 & U_3 at the end of the protocol execution shown in Figure 2. We observe that U_1 is not partnered with either U_2 or U_3 according to Definition 2, since U_1 does not have matching SIDs or agreeing PIDs (Krawczyk termed such an attack a *key-replication attack* [22] whereby $\mathcal{A}$ succeeds in forcing the establishment of a session, S_1, other than the Test session or its matching session that has the same key as the Test session. In this case, $\mathcal{A}$ can distinguish whether the Test-session key is real or random by asking a Reveal query to the oracle associated with S_1.).

Table 3. Internal states of players U_1, U_2, and U_3

U	sid_U	pid_U
U_1	$U, \sigma_{d_{U_1}}(U, \{N_1\}_{e_{U_2}}, \{N_1\}_{K_{U_3}}), \{N_1\}_{e_{U_2}}, \{N_1\}_{e_{U_3}}, U_2, N_2, U_3, N_3$	$\{U_2, U_3\}$
U_2	$U_A, \sigma_{d_A}(U_A, \{N_1\}_{e_{U_2}}, \{N_1\}_{e_{U_3}}), \{N_1\}_{e_{U_2}}, \{N_1\}_{e_{U_3}}, U_2, N_2, U_3, N_3$	$\{A, U_3\}$
U_3	$U_A, \sigma_{d_A}(U_A, \{N_1\}_{e_{U_2}}, \{N_1\}_{e_{U_3}}), \{N_1\}_{e_{U_2}}, \{N_1\}_{e_{U_3}}, U_2, N_2, U_3, N_3$	$\{A, U_2\}$

U_1 believes that the session key SK_{U_1} is being shared with U_2 and U_3, but U_2 (and U_3 respectively) believes the key $SK_{U_2} = \mathcal{H}(N_1\|N_2\|N_3) = SK_{U_3} = SK_{U_1}$ is being shared with $\mathcal{A}$ and U_3 (and U_2 respectively), when in fact, the key is being shared among U_1, U_2, and U_3. However, $SK_{U_1} = SK_{U_2} = SK_{U_3} = \mathcal{H}(N_1\|N_2\|N_3)$. Although the adversary $\mathcal{A}$ does not know the value of the session key (since $\mathcal{A}$ does not know the value of N_1), $\mathcal{A}$ is able to send a Reveal query to the session associated with either U_2 or U_3 and obtain $SK_{U_2} = \mathcal{H}(N_1\|N_2\|N_3) = SK_{U_3}$, which has the same value as SK_{U_1}. Hence, the Boyd–González Nieto conference key agreement protocol shown in Figure 1 is not secure in the BR93 model since the adversary $\mathcal{A}$ is able to obtain the fresh session key of the initiator U_1 by revealing non-partner oracles of U_1 (i.e., U_2 or U_3), in violation of the security definition given in Definition 8.

3.1.2 An Improved Conference Key Agreement Protocol
It would appear that by changing the order of the application of the signature and encryption schemes, the attack shown in Figure 2 can be avoided. However, at a first glance, this may appear to contradict the result of An, Dodis, & Rabin [1] that no matter what order signature and encryption schemes are applied, the result can still be secure. A closer inspection reveals that our observation actually supports the findings of An *et al.*, since the protocol operates in a multi-user setting. Although An *et al.* found that signature and encryption schemes can be applied in either order in the two user setting, they found some further restrictions in the multi-user setting. These restrictions are that the sender's identity must be included in every encryption and the recipient's identity must be included in every signature. In this case, swapping the order of the encryption and signature schemes happens to cause the protocol to fulfil these requirements.

An alternative way to prevent the attack is to include the sender's identity in each encryption and also the session identifier, *sid*, in the key derivation function. We use the same construct for *sid* (i.e., the concatenation of all messages received) as used by Boyd & González Nieto. In the improved protocol, the adversary $\mathcal{A}$ will not be able to "claim" ownership of the encrypted message $\{N_1, U_1\}_{e_{U_i}}$ since the identity of the initiator is included in the encryption. Since the construct of the session key in the improved protocol comprises the associated *sid*, a different *sid* will imply a different session key. Hence, the attack shown in Figure 2 will no longer be valid against this improved protocol.

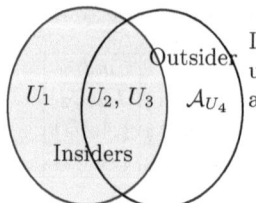

In the proof simulation of the protocol execution shown in Figure 2, $\mathcal{A}$ corrupts U_4, an outsider in the target session, and assumes U_4's identity.

Fig. 3. Insiders vs outsider

3.1.3   Limitations of Existing Proof

In the existing proof, the security of the protocol is proved by finding a reduction to the security of the encryption and signature schemes used. The number of protocol participants in the proof simulation, p, is assumed to be equal to the number of players allowed in the model, n, where n is polynomial in the security parameter k. In its reductionist approach, the proof assumes that there exists an adversary $\mathcal{A}$ who can gain a non-negligible advantage, $\mathsf{Adv}^{\mathcal{A}}(k)$, in distinguishing the test key from a random one. An attacker is then constructed that uses $\mathcal{A}$ to break either the underlying encryption scheme or the signature scheme.

In the context of the attack shown in Figure 2, assume that the number of protocol participants in the proof simulation is three. The proof then assumes that the number of parties in the model is also three. However, in order to carry out the attack, we have to corrupt a 4th player (i.e., U_4, an outsider as shown in Figure 3) to obtain the signature key of U_4.

Since U_4 does not exist in the model assumed by the proof, the attacker against the encryption and signature schemes cannot simulate the $\mathsf{Corrupt}(U_4)$ query for $\mathcal{A}$ and the proof fails since although $\mathcal{A}$ succeeds, it cannot be used to break either the encryption or signature schemes. Our observation is consistent with the above results of An *et al.*, which highlight the underlying cause of the proof breakdown – the proof environment effectively did not allow a multi-user setting in which to analyse the signature and encryption schemes.

3.2   Jakobsson–Pointcheval MAKEP

Figure 4 describes the published version of JP-MAKEP [18], which was designed for low power computing devices[1]. JP-MAKEP carries a claimed proof of security in the BR93 model but uses the notion of SIDs in the definition of partnership. There are two communicating principals in MAKEP, namely the server B and the client of limited computing resources, A. The security goals of the protocol are mutual authentication and key establishment between the two communicating principals. A and B are each assumed to know the public key of the other party (i.e., g^{x_B} and g^{x_A} respectively).

---

[1] The original version appeared in the unpublished pre-proceedings of Financial Crypto 2001 with a claimed proof of security in the BR93 model. Nevertheless, a flaw in the protocol was discovered by Wong & Chan [26]. In this published version, the flaw found by Wong & Chan in the original version has been fixed.

Client A (x_A, g^{x_A})		Server B (x_B, g^{x_B})
$a, t \in_R \mathbb{Z}_q, c = g^a, T = g^t, K = (g^{x_B})^a$		
$r = \mathcal{H}_1(T, g^{x_B}, c, K), A' = \mathcal{H}_2(g^{x_B}, c, K) \xrightarrow{\quad ID_B, c, r \quad}$		$K = c^{x_B}, A = \mathcal{H}_2(g^{x_B}, c, K)$
$A' \overset{?}{=} A$	$\xleftarrow{\quad A, e \quad}$	$0 \le e < 2^k$
$d = t - e x_A \bmod q$	$\xrightarrow{\quad ID_A, d \quad}$	$r \overset{?}{=} \mathcal{H}_1(g^d(g^{x_A})^e, g^{x_B}, c, K)$
$sid = (ID_B, c, r, A, e, ID_A, d)$		$sid = (ID_B, c, r, A, e, ID_A, d)$
$sk = \mathcal{H}_0(g^{x_B}, c, K)$		$sk = \mathcal{H}_0(g^{x_B}, c, K)$

Fig. 4. Jakobsson–Pointcheval MAKEP

A (x_A, g^{x_A})	$\mathcal{A}$ (x_A, g^{x_A})	B (x_B, g^{x_B})
$\xrightarrow{\quad ID_B, c, r \quad}$	$\xrightarrow{\quad ID_B, c, r \quad}$	
$\xleftarrow{\quad A, e' = 0 \quad}$	Fabricate	$\xleftarrow{\quad A, e \quad}$
$\xrightarrow{\quad ID_A, d = t \quad}$	Fabricate	$\xrightarrow{\quad ID_A, d - e x_A \bmod q \quad}$
		$r \overset{?}{=} \mathcal{H}_1(g^{d-e x_A}(g^{x_A})^e, g^{x_B}, c, K)$
	$sid_{BA} = (ID_B, c, r, A, e, ID_A, d - e x_A \bmod q)$	
	$sid_{AB} = (ID_B, c, r, A, e', ID_A, d) \ne sid_{BA}$	
$sk_{AB} = \mathcal{H}_0(g^{x_B}, c, K)$		$sk_{BA} = \mathcal{H}_0(g^{x_B}, c, K)$

Fig. 5. Unknown key attack on Jakobsson–Pointcheval MAKEP

3.2.1 Unknown Key Share Attack

Figure 5 depicts an example execution of JP-MAKEP in the presence of a malicious adversary $\mathcal{A}$. At the end of the attack, B believes he shares a session key, $sk_{BA} = \mathcal{H}_0(g^{x_B}, c, K)$, with the adversary $\mathcal{A}$, when in fact the key is being shared with A (i.e., unknown key share attack). A and B are not partners since they have different SIDs, $sid_{BA} = (ID_B, c, r, A, e, ID_A, d - e x_A \bmod q) \ne sid_{AB}$, and different perceived partners (i.e., $PID_A = A$ and $PID_B = \mathcal{A}$).

From Figure 5, we observe that A has terminated the protocol without any partners, in violation of the server-to-client authentication goal. On the other hand, the server, B, has terminated the protocol with the adversary, $\mathcal{A}$, as its partner. Hence, the client-to-server authentication is not violated. Consequently, JP-MAKEP is not secure since the adversary is able to obtain a fresh session key of A by revealing a non-partner oracle of A (i.e., an oracle of B), in violation of the security definition given in Definition 8. A fix for JP-MAKEP is to change $0 \le e < 2^k$ in the protocol specification to $0 < e < 2^k$.

3.2.2 Flaws in Existing Proof

In the proof simulation of the protocol, let P be another client where $P \ne A, B$. P is clearly the "outsider" in the target session of Figure 5 that $\mathcal{A}$ is attacking.

$\mathcal{A}$ then corrupts P, the outsider, and assumes P's identity. This is allowed in the existing proof [18–Lemma 3] for the server-to-client authentication, since it is claimed that the JP-MAKEP provides partial forward-secrecy whereby corruption of the client may not help to recover the session keys.

The proof assumes that the probability of $\mathcal{A}$ violating the server-to-client authentication is negligible. In the context of the attack shown in Figure 5, $\mathcal{A}$ managed to violate the server-to-client authentication by corrupting a non-partner player, P. By violating the server-to-client authentication, $\mathcal{A}$ is then able to distinguish a real key or a random key by asking a Reveal query to a non-partner server oracle of A, and hence violate the server-to-client authentication with non-negligible probability. The discrete logarithm breaker $\mathcal{A}_{\mathcal{DL}}$ (which is constructed using $\mathcal{A}$) is unable to obtain a non-negligible probability of breaking the discrete logarithm problem, contradicting the underlying assumption in the proof. Consequently, the proof simulation fails (the result of Reveal and Corrupt queries were not adequately considered in the simulation).

3.3   Wong–Chan MAKEP

Figure 6 describes WC-MAKEP [26], which was proposed as an improvement to the original unpublished version of JP-MAKEP. Note that Figure 6 describes the corrected version of WC-MAKEP, where the computation of $\sigma = (r_A \oplus r_B)$ by A is replaced by $\sigma = (r_A \oplus r_B) \| ID_B$.

3.3.1   A New Attack

Figure 7 depicts an example execution of WC-MAKEP, where at the end of the protocol execution, A and B accept with the same session key, $SK_{AB} = \mathcal{H}(\sigma) = SK_{BA}$.

However, according to Definition 1, both A and B are not partners as B's replies are not in response to genuine messages sent by A (i.e., both A and B will not have matching conversations given in Definition 1). Since two non-partner oracles, $\Pi_{A,B}$ and $\Pi_{B,A}$, accept session keys with the same value, the adversary $\mathcal{A}$ can reveal a fresh non-partner oracle, $\Pi_{B,A}$, and find the session key accepted by $\Pi_{A,B}$, in violation of the security definition given in Definition 8. In addition, both oracles of A and B have terminated the protocol without any partners, in

$A\ (a, g^a)$		$B\ (SK_B, PK_B)$
$r_A \in_R \{0,1\}^k, x = \{r_A\}_{PK_B}$		
$b \in_R \mathbb{Z}_q \setminus \{0\}, \beta = g^b$	$\xrightarrow{\ Cert_A, \beta, x\ }$	Decrypt x
$\sigma = (r_A \oplus r_B) \| ID_B$		
$y = a\mathcal{H}(\sigma) + b \bmod q$	$\xleftarrow{\ \{r_B, ID_B\}_{r_A}\ }$	$r_B \in \{0,1\}^k$
$SK_{AB} = \mathcal{H}(\sigma)$	$\xrightarrow{\quad y \quad}$	$g^y \overset{?}{=} (g^a)^{\mathcal{H}(\sigma)}\beta, SK_{BA} = \mathcal{H}(\sigma)$

Fig. 6. Wong–Chan MAKEP

A	$\mathcal{A}$	B
$\xrightarrow{\ Cert_A, \beta, x\ }$	Fabricate message	$\xrightarrow{\ Cert_A, \beta \cdot g^e, x\ }$
$\xleftarrow{\ \{r_B, ID_B\}_{r_A}\ }$		$\xleftarrow{\ \{r_B, ID_B\}_{r_A}\ }$
$\xrightarrow{\ \ \ y\ \ \ }$	$y' = y + e \bmod q$	$g^{y'} \stackrel{?}{=} (g^a)^{\mathcal{H}(\sigma)}(\beta \cdot g^e)$
$SK_{AB} = \mathcal{H}(\sigma)$	$\xrightarrow{\ \ \ y'\ \ \ }$	$SK_{BA} = \mathcal{H}(\sigma)$

Fig. 7. Attack on Wong–Chan MAKEP

violation of the mutual authentication goal. Hence, WC-MAKEP is insecure in the BR93 model since the attack outlined in Figure 7 shows that both the key establishment and mutual authentication goals are violated.

3.3.2   Preventing the Attack

A possible fix to WC-MAKEP is to change the construction of the session key to $SK = \mathcal{H}(A, B, \beta, x, y, \sigma)$. The inclusion of the sender's and responder's identities and messages (β, x, y) in the key derivation function effectively binds the session key to all messages sent and received by both A and B [11]. If the adversary changes any of the messages in the transmission, the session key will also be different. Intuitively, the attack shown in Figure 7 will no longer be valid against WC-MAKEP.

3.3.3   Flaws in Existing Proof

The existing (sketchy) proof fails to provide a proof simulation. In the absence of a game simulation in the existing proof, we may only speculate that the proof fails to adequately consider the simulation of Send and Reveal queries (in the same sense as outlined in Section 3.2.2).

In the flaws in the AMP protocol [23] and EPA protocol [17] revealed by Wan & Wang [25], both proofs fail to provide any proof simulations. These examples highlight the importance of detailed proof simulations, as the omission of such simulations could potentially result in protocols claimed to be secure being, in fact, insecure.

4   Flaw in the Proof of an Encryption-Based MT-Authenticator

In this section, we reveal an inadequacy in the specification of the encryption based MT-authenticator proposed by Bellare, Canetti, & Krawczyk [2] and identify a flaw in its proof simulation. We then demonstrate with example protocol (the protocol 2DHPE [16]) how the flaw in the proof of the encryption-based MT-authenticator results in the violation of the key establishment goal in the protocol 2DHPE where a malicious adversary is able to learn a fresh session key.

In fact, the attack we reveal on the protocol 2DHPE also applies to protocol 14 that appears in the full version of [15]. Surprisingly, the inadequancy in the specification was not spotted in the proof simulation of the MT-authenticator, and has not previously been spotted in other protocols [15,16] using this MT-authenticator.

We may speculate that if protocol designers fail to spot this inadequancy in the specification of their protocols, the protocol implementers are also highly unlikely to spot this inadequancy until specific attacks have been demonstrated, as suggested by Bleichenbacher [6].

Having identified the flaw in the proof of the MT-authenticator, we provide a fix to the MT-authenticator specification. As a result of this fix, protocols using the revised encryption based MT-authenticator will no longer be flawed due to their use of this MT-authenticator. The notation used throughout this section is as follows: the notation $\{\cdot\}_{K_U}$ denotes an encryption of some message m under U's public key, K_U, and $MAC_K(m)$ denotes the computation of MAC digest of some message m under key K.

4.1 Bellare–Canetti–Krawczyk Encryption-Based MT-Authenticator

Figure 8 describes the encryption based MT-authenticator, which is based on a public-key encryption scheme indistinguishable under chosen-ciphertext attack and the authentication technique used by Krawczyk [21]. Note that the specification of the encryption-based MT-authenticator does not specify the deletion of the received nonce v_A (incidentally, v_A is also the one-time MAC key) from B's internal state before sending out the last message.

4.2 Flaw in Existing Proof of MT-Authenticator

In the usual tradition of reductionist proofs, the existing MT-authenticator proof [2] assumes that there exists an adversary $\mathcal{A}$ who can break the MT-authenticator, and an encryption-aided MAC forger, $\mathcal{F}$ is constructed using such an adversary $\mathcal{A}$ against the unforgability of the underlying MAC scheme. Subsequently, the encryption-aided MAC forger, $\mathcal{F}$, can be used to break the encryption scheme. $\mathcal{F}$ who has access to a MAC oracle, is easily constructed as follows:

– guess at random an index i,

A		B
Choose nonce v_A	$\xleftarrow{\quad sid, m \quad}$	Choose message m
	$\xrightarrow{\quad sid, m, \{v_A\}_{K_B} \quad}$	Decrypt $\{v_A\}_{K_B}$
Verify $MAC_{v_A}(m, A)$	$\xleftarrow{\quad sid, m, MAC_{v_A}(m, A) \quad}$	Compute $MAC_{v_A}(m, A)$

Fig. 8. Bellare–Canetti–Krawczyk encryption-based MT-authenticator

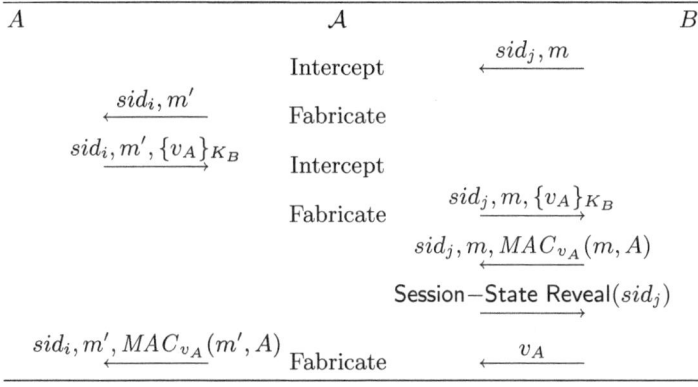

Fig. 9. Execution of encryption-based MT-authenticator in the presence of a malicious adversary, $\mathcal{A}$

- for all but the i-th session, generate a key v_k and answer queries as expected,
- if $\mathcal{A}$ calls a Session-State Reveal[2] on any session other than the i-th session, the response can easily be simulated,
- if $\mathcal{A}$ calls a Session-State Reveal on the i-th session, $\mathcal{F}$ aborts.

The assumption is that if $\mathcal{A}$ has a non-negligible advantage against the underlying protocol, then $\mathcal{F}$ has a non-negligible probability of forging a MAC digest.

Consider the scenario shown in Figure 9. When $\mathcal{A}$ asks for the one-time MAC key (i.e., v_k) with a Session-State Reveal query, it is perfectly legitimate since this session with SID of sid_j is not the i-th session with SID of sid_i. Recall that sessions with non-matching SIDs (i.e., $sid_i \neq sid_j$) are non-partners.

Clearly, $\mathcal{F}$ is unable to answer such a query since v_A is a secret key (note that the MAC oracle to which $\mathcal{F}$ has access is associated with v_A, but $\mathcal{F}$ does not know v_A). Hence, the proof simulation is aborted and $\mathcal{F}$ fails. Consequently, $\mathcal{F}$ does not have a non-negligible probability of forging a MAC digest (since it fails) although $\mathcal{A}$ has a non-negligible advantage against the security of the underlying protocol, in violation of the underlying assumption in the proof.

4.3 Proposed Fix to the Encryption-Based MT-Authenticator

In this section, we provide a fix to the encryption-based MT-authenticator by requiring that the party concerned delete the received nonce from its internal state before sending out the MAC digest computed using the received nonce. With the fix, the adversary will not be able to obtain the value of v_A using a Session-State Reveal query. Hence, in the proof of the security of the MT-authenticator, $\mathcal{F}$ will be able to answer such a query because $\mathcal{F}$ is no longer required to return the value of v_A. Therefore, the attack shown in Figure 9 will

---

[2] Note that in the original paper of Bellare, Canetti, & Krawczyk [2], a Session-State Reveal is known as a Session-Corruption query.

$A\ (\pi_{A,B})$		$B\ (\pi_{A,B})$
$x \in_R \mathbb{Z}_q, v_A \in_R \{0,1\}^k$	$\xrightarrow{A, sid, g^x, \{v_A\}_{K_B}}$	$y \in_R \mathbb{Z}_q$
		$v'_A = \mathcal{D}_{d_B}(\{v_A\}_{K_B}), N_B \in_R \{0,1\}^k$
$SK_{A,B} = (g^y)^x$	$\xleftarrow{B, sid, g^y, N_B, MAC_{v'_A}(B, sid, g^y, A)}$	
	$\xrightarrow{sid, \{A, sid, g^x, N_B, \pi_{A,B}\}_{K_B}}$	$SK_{B,A} = (g^x)^y$

Fig. 10. Hitchcock, Tin, Boyd, González Nieto, & Montague (2003) protocol 2DHPE

no longer be valid, since $\mathcal{A}$ will no longer be able to obtain the value of v_A and fabricate a MAC digest.

4.4   An Example Protocol as a Case Study

Figure 10 describes a password-based protocol 2DHPE due to Hitchcock, Tin, Boyd, Gonzalez-Nieto, & Montague [16]. Using the protocol 2DHPE as an example, we demonstrate that as a result of the flaw in the proof of the encryption-based MT-authenticator, the proof of protocol 2DHPE is also invalid. In the example protocol, both A and B are assumed to share a secret password, $\pi_{A,B}$, and the public keys of both A and B (i.e., K_A and K_B respectively) are known to all participants in the protocol. The protocol uses the encryption-based MT-authenticator to authenticate the message B, sid, g^y from B. Figure 11 describes an example execution of protocol 2DHPE in the presence of a malicious adversary $\mathcal{A}$ (in the UM). We assume that $\mathcal{A}$ has a shared password with B, $\pi_{A,B}$. At the end of the protocol execution shown in Figure 11, oracle $\Pi_{A,B}^{sid}$ has accepted a shared session key $SK_{A,B} = g^{xz}$ with $\Pi_{B,A}^{sid}$. However, such an oracle (i.e., $\Pi_{B,A}^{sid}$) does not exist. By sending a Session-State Reveal query to oracle $\Pi_{B,A}^{sid_A}$, $\mathcal{A}$ learns the internal state of $\Pi_{B,A}^{sid_A}$, which includes v'_A. With v'_A, $\mathcal{A}$ can fabricate and send a MAC digest to A. Hence, the adversary is able to obtain a fresh session key of $\Pi_{A,B}^{sid}$ (i.e., $SK_{A,B} = g^{xz}$) since $\mathcal{A}$ knows z (in fact, z is chosen by $\mathcal{A}$).

However, if the encryption-based MT-authenticator requires B to delete the received nonce v'_A from B's internal sate before sending out message 3, then $\mathcal{A}$ will not be able to obtain the value of v'_A with a Session-State Reveal query and fabricate $MAC_{v'_A}(B, sid, g^y, A)$. Consequently, protocol 2DHPE will be secure.

5   Conclusion

Through a detailed study of several protocols and an authenticator with claimed proofs of security, we have concluded that specifying correct computational complexity proofs for protocols remains a hard problem. However, we have identified three areas where protocol proofs are likely to fail, namely: an inappropriate proof model environment, Send, Reveal and Corrupt queries not adequately considered in the proof simulations, and omission of proof simulations.

$$A \qquad\qquad\qquad \mathcal{A} \qquad\qquad\qquad B$$

$$A, sid, g^x, \{v_A\}_{K_B} \qquad \mathcal{A}, sid_A, g^x, \{v_A\}_{K_B}$$
$$\xrightarrow{\hspace{3cm}} \qquad \xrightarrow{\hspace{3cm}}$$
$$v'_A = \mathcal{D}_{d_B}(\{v_A\}_{K_B})$$
$$B, sid_A, g^y, N_B, MAC_{v'_A}(B, sid, g^y, A)$$
$$\xleftarrow{\hspace{3cm}}$$

$$\text{Session} - \text{State Reveal}(B, sid_A)$$
$$\xrightarrow{\hspace{3cm}}$$

$$B, sid, g^z, N_B, MAC_{v'_A}(B, sid, g^z, A) \qquad v'_A$$
$$\xleftarrow{\hspace{3cm}} \qquad \xleftarrow{\hspace{2cm}}$$

$$sid, \{A, sid, g^x, N_B, \pi_{A,B}\}_{K_B}$$
$$\xrightarrow{\hspace{3cm}}$$

$$SK_{A,B} = g^{xz}$$

Fig. 11. Execution of protocol 2DHPE in the presence of a malicious adversary

We also observe that certain constructions of session keys may contribute to the security of the key establishment protocol. This observation supports the findings of recent work of Choo, Boyd, & Hitchcock [11], who describe a way of constructing session keys, as described below:

- the identities and roles of the participants to provide resilience against unknown key share attacks and reflection attacks since the inclusion of the identities of both the participants and role asymmetry effectively ensures some sense of direction. If the role of the participants or the identities of the (perceived) partner participants change, the session keys will also be different.
- the unique SIDs to ensure that session keys will be fresh, and if SIDs are defined as the concatenation of messages exchanged during the protocol execution, messages altered during the transmission will result in different session keys (and prevents the key replicating attack [22] in the Bellare–Rogaway and Canetti–Krawczyk models).

Acknowledgements

This work was partially funded by the Australian Research Council Discovery Project Grant DP0345775. The first author would like to thank Dr. Juan Manuel González Nieto of Information Security Institute for his insightful discussions on the conference key agreement protocol.

References

1. J. H. An, Y. Dodis, and T. Rabin. On the Security of Joint Signature and Encryption. In *Eurocrypt 2002*, pages 83–107. Springer-Verlag, 2002. Vol. 2332/2002 of LNCS.
2. M. Bellare, R. Canetti, and H. Krawczyk. A Modular Approach to The Design and Analysis of Authentication and Key Exchange Protocols. In *STOC 1998*, pages 419–428. ACM Press, 1998.

3. M. Bellare, D. Pointcheval, and P. Rogaway. Authenticated Key Exchange Secure Against Dictionary Attacks. In *Eurocrypt 2000*, pages 139 – 155. Springer-Verlag, 2000. Vol. 1807/2000 of LNCS.
4. M. Bellare and P. Rogaway. Entity Authentication and Key Distribution. In *Crypto 1993*, pages 110–125. Springer-Verlag, 1993. Vol. 773/1993 of LNCS.
5. M. Bellare and P. Rogaway. Provably Secure Session Key Distribution: The Three Party Case. In *STOC 1995*, pages 57–66. ACM Press, 1995.
6. D. Bleichenbacher. Breaking a Cryptographic Protocol with Pseudoprimes. In *PKC 2005*, pages 9–15. Springer-Verlag, 2005. Vol. 3386/2005 of LNCS.
7. C. Boyd and A. Mathuria. *Protocols for Authentication and Key Establishment.* Springer-Verlag, June 2003.
8. C. Boyd and J. M. González Nieto. Round-optimal Contributory Conference Key Agreement. In *PKC 2003*, pages 161–174. Springer-Verlag, 2003. Vol. 2567/2003 of LNCS.
9. E. Bresson, O. Chevassut, and D. Pointcheval. Provably Authenticated Group Diffie–Hellman Key Exchange — The Dynamic Case. In *Asiacrypt 2001*, pages 209–223. Springer-Verlag, 2001. Vol. 2248/2001 of LNCS.
10. R. Canetti and H. Krawczyk. Analysis of Key-Exchange Protocols and Their Use for Building Secure Channels (Extended version available from http://eprint.iacr.org/2001/040/). In *Eurocrypt 2001*, pages 453–474. Springer-Verlag, 2001. Vol. 2045/2001 of LNCS.
11. K.-K. R. Choo, C. Boyd, and Y. Hitchcock. On Session Key Construction in Provably Secure Protocols (Extended version available from http://eprint.iacr.org/2005/206). In *Mycrypt 2005*, pages 116–131, 2005. Vol. 3715/2005 of LNCS.
12. W. Diffie, P. C. van Oorschot, and M. J. Wiener. Authentication and Authenticated Key Exchange. *Journal of Designs, Codes and Cryptography*, pages 107–125, 1992.
13. D. Dolev and A. C. Yao. On the Security of Public Key Protocols. *IEEE Transaction of Information Technology*, pages 198–208, 1983.
14. S. Goldwasser and S. Micali. Probabilisitic Encryption. *Journal of Computer and System Sciences*, pages 270–299, 1984.
15. Y. Hitchcock, Y.-S. T. Tin, C. Boyd, and J. M. González Nieto. Tripartite Key Exchange in the Canetti-Krawczyk Proof Model (Extended version available from http://sky.fit.qut.edu.au/~boydc/papers/). In *Indocrypt 2004.* Springer-Verlag, 2004. Vol. 3348/2004 of LNCS.
16. Y. Hitchcock, Y.-S. T. Tin, C. Boyd, J. M. González Nieto, and P. Montague. A Password-Based Authenticator: Security Proof and Applications. In *Indocrypt 2003*, pages 388–401. Springer-Verlag, 2003. Vol. 2904/2003 of LNCS.
17. Y. H. Hwang, D. H. Yum, and P. J. Lee. EPA: An Efficient Password-Based Protocal for Authenticated Key Exchange. In *ACISP 2003*. Springer-Verlag, 2003. Vol. 2727/2003 of LNCS.
18. M. Jakobsson and D. Pointcheval. Mutual Authentication and Key Exchange Protocol for Low Power Devices. In *FC 2001*, pages 169–186. Springer-Verlag, 2001. Vol. 2339/2002 of LNCS.
19. B. S. Kaliski. An Unknown Key-Share Attack on the MQV Key Agreement Protocol. *ACM Transactions on Information and System Security (TISSEC)*, pages 275–288, 2001.
20. N. Koblitz and A. Menezes. Another Look at "Provable Security". Technical report CORR 2004-20, Centre for Applied Cryptographic Research, University of Waterloo, Canada, 2004.

21. H. Krawczyk. SKEME: A Versatile Secure Key Exchange Mechanism for Internet. In *NDSS 1996*, pages 114–127. IEEE Internet Society Press, 1996.
22. H. Krawczyk. HMQV: A High-Performance Secure Diffie-Hellman Protocol (Extended version available from `http://eprint.iacr.org/2005/176/`). In *Crypto 2005*. Springer-Verlag, 2005. Vol. 3621/2005 of LNCS.
23. T. Kwon. Authentication and Key Agreement via Memorable Passwords. In Ari Juels and John Brainard, editors, *NDSS 2001*. Internet Society Press, 2001.
24. P. Rogaway. On the Role Definitions in and Beyond Cryptography. In *ASIAN 2004*. Springer-Verlag, 2004. Vol. 3321/2004 of LNCS.
25. Z. Wan and S. Wang. Cryptanalysis of Two Password-Authenticated Key Exchange Protocols. In *ACISP 2004*. Springer-Verlag, 2004. Vol. 3108/2004 of LNCS.
26. D. S. Wong and A. H. Chan. Efficient and Mutually Authenticated Key Exchange for Low Power Computing Devices. In *Asiacrypt 2001*, pages 172–289. Springer-Verlag, 2001. Vol. 2248/2001 of LNCS.

Universal Designated Verifier Signature Proof (or How to Efficiently Prove Knowledge of a Signature)

Joonsang Baek, Reihaneh Safavi-Naini, and Willy Susilo

Centre for Information Security,
School of Information Technology and Computer Science,
University of Wollongong,
Wollongong, NSW 2519, Australia
{baek, rei, wsusilo}@uow.edu.au

Abstract. Proving knowledge of a signature has many interesting applications. As one of them, the Universal Designated Verifier Signature (UDVS), introduced by Steinfeld et al. in Asiacrypt 2003 aims to protect a signature holder's privacy by allowing him to convince a verifier that he holds a valid signature from the signer without revealing the signature itself. The essence of the UDVS is a transformation from a publicly verifiable signature to a designated verifier signature, which is performed by the signature holder who does *not* have access to the signer's secret key. However, one significant inconvenience of all the previous UDVS schemes considered in the literature is that they require the designated verifier to create a public key using the signer's public key parameter and have it certified to ensure the resulting public key is compatible with the setting that the signer provided. This restriction is unrealistic in several situations where the verifier is not willing to go through such setup process. In this paper, we resolve this problem by introducing a new type of UDVS. Different from previous approach to UDVS, our new UDVS solution, which we call "Universal Designated Verifier Signature Proof (UDVSP)", employs an *interactive protocol* between the signature holder and the verifier *while maintaining high level of efficiency*. We provide a formal model and security notions for UDVSP and give two constructions based on the bilinear pairings. We prove that the first construction is secure in the random oracle model and so is the second one in the standard model.

1 Introduction

1.1 Motivation

Consider a situation where Alice, who has graduated from the University ABC, would like to apply for a job online. In this situation, Alice has to convince the employer that she indeed holds the diploma that has been signed by the registrar of the University ABC. However, she does not want to send her diploma away, since she feels that anyone else might be able to use it for a different purpose.

B. Roy (Ed.): ASIACRYPT 2005, LNCS 3788, pp. 644–661, 2005.

A normal digital signature cannot satisfy her requirement as anyone who has obtained a message (in the above example, Alice's diploma) and a signature on it (the registrar's signature on Alice's diploma) can easily *copy* them. For this reason, Alice seeks a new type of digital signature that can provide a property that the signature on Alice's diploma is *non-transferable* meaning that Alice can convince Bob that she is in possession of a valid diploma awarded by the University ABC but having talked to Alice, Bob cannot convince any other parties about the truth of the statement.

At a glance, it seems that Alice's need can be met by the Universal Designated Verifier Signature (UDVS), introduced By Steinfeld et al. in Asiacrypt 2003 [25]. In UDVS, a "designator (signature holder)" who has obtained a valid signature from a "signer" can convince a "designated verifier" that he holds a valid signature obtained from the signer but other parties including the designated verifier himself cannot convince other parties of the validity of the same statement. In spite of their elegant structures, the difficulty of adopting the UDVS schemes proposed so far including those from [25,26,28] to the Alice's diploma verification problem is that they require designated verifiers to create private/public key pairs *using the same public key parameter that has been set by the signer* and have them certified. (Indeed, the protocol for conducting such a task, "Verifier Key-Registration", is included as a sub-algorithm of UDVS [25]). This is sometimes hard to be realized especially when proving knowledge of a signature obtained from the original signer is only a designator's interest. – In the above scenario, for example, the employer will be less likely to agree on creating a private/public key pair according to the public parameter set by Alice's university just only to verify her diploma, as this key setup involving management of Public Key Infrastructure (PKI) may incur significant cost. Hence, although the UDVS seems to be a good candidate to solve Alice's diploma verification problem, the public key setup requirement for verifiers remains as a problem.

Motivated by the above problem of the UDVS schemes considered in the previous literature, we would like to obtain a new type of UDVS that eliminates the assumption of having the verifier generate a private/public key pair to verify the signature holder's claim. In order to achieve this, the natural methodology one can envision is to adopt the *interactive* proof [15] style protocol. However, interactive protocols sometimes significantly degrade the system efficiency. So another important requirement of the new UDVS is *high level of efficiency*. Our new UDVS proposed in this paper will satisfy both requirements.

1.2   Our Contributions

In this paper, we propose a new type of UDVS, which we call "Universal Designated Verifier Signature Proof (UDVSP)" and provide two highly efficient constructions based on the bilinear pairings [4,18]. Informally, our UDVSP system has the following characteristics: 1) The signer signs a message and provides the message/signature pair to the designator (signature holder); 2) the designator *transforms* the signer's signature and, using an interactive protocol that takes this transformed signature as common input, convinces the designated verifier that he has indeed obtained the *valid* signature on the message from the signer; and 3) the designated verifier does not have to setup a private/public key.

In terms of security, we formalize the security of UDVSP against *impersonation* attack: The system should not allow the attackers including the designated verifier to convince any other person that the designator indeed holds a valid signature from the signer. Our two concrete constructions of UDVSP are proven to be secure under the proposed security model relative to known computational assumptions related to hardness of the discrete-logarithm problem. The security proof for the first construction needs the random oracle model [2] while the second one does not depend on this assumption.

Our two constructions of UDVSP are highly efficient. The signing algorithms of them are the same as those of underlying signature schemes [5,7], which are very efficient. The transformation algorithms just need one exponentiation and the interactive verification protocols only require two bilinear pairing operations on top of the Schnorr identification protocol [23]. (Note that the details of these algorithms and protocol will be given in Section 3).

We remark that throughout this paper, the term "designated" has a literal meaning that a *specified* verifier participates in the protocol run by the signature holder. This does not mean that it provides *explicit* authentication of the verifier's identity, which is provided in the non-interactive designated signature [17] where the verifiers are authenticated by checking the certificate of their public keys. Note that as mentioned in [17], the advantage of the non-interactive designated verifier signature is that it can prevent somewhat strong attacks such as mafia (a.k.a. man-in-the-middle) attacks [12] and blackmailing [16] as the verifiers are explicitly authenticated by their public keys (which come with the certificates issued by the trusted third party).

1.3   Related Work

The concept of UDVS was proposed by Steinfeld et al. [25], who constructed a concrete scheme that realizes the concept using the bilinear pairings. They also observed that Boneh et al.'s [6] ring signature [24] converted to two-signer ring signature can be viewed as UDVS. The UDVS schemes based on the RSA and Schnorr signatures were soon followed [26]. Very recently, the UDVS scheme based on the bilinear pairings whose security can be analyzed without the random oracle assumption was proposed by Zhang et al. [28]. Although these schemes are elegant, as discussed earlier, the assumption of having designated verifiers to generate their own private/public key pairs according to the signer's public key parameter setting is strong and even unrealistic in some situations. We note that the reason why one needs such a key registration process for verifiers in the UDVS schemes is that *non-transferability* of a signature obtained from the original signer is achieved via the technique of trapdoor commitment [8] non-interactively as widely adopted in the various designated-verifier signature schemes [17,19,27].

In contrast, undeniable signature proposed by Chaum and Antwerpen [9] achieves non-transferability (of the original signer's signature) via an interactive protocol although non-interactive version of the protocol is also be possible using the trapdoor commitment. (We note that the security analysis of Chaum's undeniable signature is given only recently by Ogata et al. [22]). However, as discussed in [25], the crucial difference between the UDVS and the undeniable signature (including other designated-verifier signatures) is that in the latter, only the *signer* who possesses the secret signing key can designate a signature while in the former, *any* legitimate user who possesses the signature from the signer can perform designation.

Another related area of UDVS is anonymous credential system [20,9,10]. However, as mentioned in [25], this areas of research focuses more on user privacy such as "selective disclosure" of attributes and "unlinkability" of user transaction. Our work (and the work related to UDVS [25,26,28] in general) focuses more on providing an *efficient* mechanism to convince designated verifiers about the truth of the statement that a signature holder is in possession of a valid signature from the original signer. Consequently, we can avoid *heavy* zero knowledge proof protocols used in many credential systems such as [20,9,10]. Interestingly, our first construction of UDVSP shows that if proving knowledge of a signature is only concern, one can simply use Boneh, Lynn and Shacham (BLS)'s [5] pairing-based signature scheme whose security against chosen message attack is relative to the *standard* Computational Diffie-Hellman (CDH) problem, as opposed to the one used in [20], whose security against chosen message attack is based on the fairly complex and non-standard assumption called "LRSW assumption".

Moreover, in order to precisely establish the end goal of security of our UDVSP systems, the security analysis given in this paper does not depend on the auxiliary properties such as proof of knowledge [1], witness indistinguishability [13] and honest verifier zero knowledge and so on.

Finally, we remark that Naor [21] also pointed out that it is not desirable to assume that the verifier of the authentication is part of the system and has established a public key. This is because it is often difficult to assure the independence of keys in the PKI and there is no reason to assume that the verifier has chosen his key properly.

2   Preliminaries

2.1   Symbols and Notations

We use the notation $\mathsf{A}(\cdot, \ldots, \cdot)$ to denote an algorithm, with input arguments separated by commas. (Note that our underlying computational model is a probabilistic Turing Machine). The notation $\mathsf{A}^{\mathsf{O}(\cdot)}(\cdot, \ldots, \cdot)$ denotes that algorithm A makes calls to an oracle $\mathsf{O}(\cdot)$. We use $a \leftarrow \mathsf{A}(x_1, \ldots, x_n)$ to denote the assignment of a uniformly and independently distributed random element from the output of A on input $(x_1, \ldots, x_n)$ to the variable a.

We use the notation $\mathsf{Prot}[P(\underbrace{\cdot, \ldots, \cdot}_{\text{private input}}) \leftrightarrow V(\underbrace{\cdot, \ldots, \cdot}_{\text{private input}})](\underbrace{\cdot, \ldots, \cdot}_{\text{common input}})$ to

denote an interactive protocol Prot between a prover P and a verifier V, both of which are modeled as probabilistic Turing Machines. *Private* inputs for P and V are presented inside the parentheses immediately followed by the letters "P" and "V". *Common* inputs for P and V are presented inside the parentheses followed by the square brackets "[ ]".

Given a set S, we denote by $b \xleftarrow{\text{R}} S$ the assignment of a uniformly and independently distributed random element from the set S to the variable b.

We say a probability function $f : \mathbb{N} \to \mathbb{R}_{[0,1]}$ is negligible in k if, for all $c > 0$, there exists $k_0 \in \mathbb{N}$ such that $f(k) \le \frac{1}{k^c}$ whenever $k \ge k_0$. Here, $\mathbb{R}_{[0,1]} = \{x \in \mathbb{R} | 0 \le x \le 1\}$.

2.2   Computational Primitives

The bilinear pairing e that will be used throughout this paper is the *admissible* bilinear pairing [4,18], which is defined over two groups of the same prime-order q denoted by $\mathbb{G}_1$ and $\mathbb{G}_2$. (By $\mathbb{G}_1^*$ and $\mathbb{Z}_q^*$, we denote $\mathbb{G}_1 \setminus \{1\}$ where 1 is the identity element of $\mathbb{G}_1$, and $\mathbb{Z}_q \setminus \{0\}$ respectively.) Suppose that $\mathbb{G}_1$ is generated by g. Then, $e : \mathbb{G}_1 \times \mathbb{G}_1 \to \mathbb{G}_2$ has the following properties: 1) Bilinear: $e(g^a, g^b) = e(g, g)^{ab}$, for all $a, b \in \mathbb{Z}_q$ and 2) Non-degenerate: $e(g, g) \ne 1$.

For convenience, we define an atomic bilinear pairing parameter generation algorithm that will be used in many parts of the paper.

– $\mathsf{PramGen}_a(k)$: This algorithm generates two groups $\mathbb{G}_1$ and $\mathbb{G}_2$ of order $q > 2^k$ and creates bilinear map $e : \mathbb{G}_1 \times \mathbb{G}_1 \to \mathbb{G}_2$. It also chooses a generator g of the group $\mathbb{G}_1$. It outputs a parameter $(q, g, e, \mathbb{G}_1, \mathbb{G}_2)$.

We now review the definition of "One More Discrete-Logarithm (OMDL)" problem used to analyze the security of the Schnorr identification protocol [23] against impersonation under active attack in which an attacker can participate in the execution of the protocol as a cheating verifier [3].

Definition 1 (OMDL). The corresponding experiment for this problem, denoted $\mathbf{Exp}^{omdl}(k)$, is defined as follows. Firstly, the atomic parameter generation algorithm is run and parameter $(q, g, e, \mathbb{G}_1, \mathbb{G}_2)$ is generated. A polynomial-time attacker A now makes n queries to the challenge oracle $\mathcal{C}(\cdot)$ and m queries to the Discrete-Logarithm (DL) oracle $\mathcal{DL}_{q,g}(\cdot)$. Upon receiving a query (null input), the challenge oracle $\mathcal{C}(\cdot)$ returns a random point $h \in \mathbb{G}_1$. Upon receiving a query z, $\mathcal{DL}_{q,g}(\cdot)$ returns s such that $g^s = z$. However, a restriction here is that $m < n$. Namely, the number of queries to the DL oracle should be strictly less than the number of queries to the challenge oracle. A's final goal is to output *all* the discrete logarithms of the n challenges returned from $\mathcal{C}(\cdot)$. Formally, we describe $\mathbf{Exp}^{omdl}(k)$ as follows.

– Experiment: $(q, g, e, \mathbb{G}_1, \mathbb{G}_2) \leftarrow \mathsf{PramGen}_a(k)$; $(s_1, \ldots, s_n) \leftarrow A^{\mathcal{C}(\cdot), \mathcal{DL}_{q,g}(\cdot)}(q, g, e, \mathbb{G}_1, \mathbb{G}_2)$
– Output: If $(g^{s_1} = h_1) \wedge \cdots \wedge (g^{s_n} = h_n)$, where $h_1, \ldots, h_n$ are random points in $\mathbb{G}_1$ output by the challenge oracle $\mathcal{C}(\cdot)$, and $m < n$, where m denotes the number of queries to the DL oracle, then return 1. Otherwise, return 0.

We define A's advantage as $\mathbf{Adv}_A^{omdl}(k) = \Pr[\mathbf{Exp}^{omdl}(k)] = 1$. We say that OMDL problem is hard if $\mathbf{Adv}_A^{omdl}(k)$ is negligible in k.

Other computational problems that we use in this paper are the Computational Diffie-Hellman (CDH) and the Strong Diffie-Hellman (SDH) problems, which are reviwed in Appendix A.

3   Universal Designated Verifier Signature Proof System

3.1   Model

As informally outlined in Section 1, there are three parties involved in Universal Designated Verifier Signature Proof (UDVSP) system: a *signer*, a *designator* (signature holder) and a *designated verifier*. After creating a secret (signing) key and public (verification) key pair, the signer signs a message and transmits the resulting signature together with the message to the designator. It is important that transmission of the signature should be done in a secure manner, e.g. via secure channel. (This is similar to the private key generation process in identity-based cryptography in which a trusted party generates a private key associated with user's identifier information and sends the resulting key via secure channel). Having obtained the valid signature from the signer, the designator creates a transformed signature by generating a random mask and *hiding* the original signature using it. The designator then convinces the designated verifier via an interactive protocol that the transformed signature has been generated from the valid signature obtained from the signer. Below, we formally define UDVSP system.

Definition 2 (Universal Designated Verifier Signature Proof). A Universal Designated Verifier Signature Proof system consists of the following five polynomial-time algorithms and a protocol:

- SigKeyGen: Taking a security parameter $k \in \mathbb{N}$ as input, this algorithm generates a signer's public/secret (verification/signing) key pair (pk, sk). We write $(pk, sk) \leftarrow \mathsf{SigKeyGen}(k)$.
- Sign: Taking signer's secret key sk and a message m as input, this algorithm generates a signature σ on m. We write $\sigma \leftarrow \mathsf{Sign}(sk, m)$.
- Verify: Taking a signer's public key pk, a signature σ and a message m as input, this algorithm outputs 1 if σ is a valid signature on m and outputs 0 otherwise. We write $d \leftarrow \mathsf{Verify}(pk, \sigma, m)$, where $d \in \{0, 1\}$.
- Transform: Taking a signer's public key pk and a signature σ as input, this algorithm picks a secret mask $\tilde{sk}$ and generates a transformed signature $\tilde{\sigma}$ using $\tilde{sk}$. It outputs $\tilde{\sigma}$ and $\tilde{sk}$. We write $(\tilde{\sigma}, \tilde{sk}) \leftarrow \mathsf{Transform}(pk, \sigma)$.
- IVerify: This is an interactive verification protocol between a designator and a designated verifier, denoted P and V respectively. Common inputs for P and V are a signer's public key pk, a transformed signature $\tilde{\sigma}$ and a message m. P's private input is a secret mask $\tilde{sk}$ used to create $\tilde{\sigma}$. V does not have any private input. In this protocol, P tries to convince V that $\tilde{\sigma}$ has been

generated from the valid signature σ obtained from the signer, with the knowledge of $\tilde{sk}$. The output of this protocol is verification decision 1 or 0 depending on whether V accepts or rejects. We write $d \leftarrow \mathsf{IVerify}[P(\tilde{sk}) \leftrightarrow V](pk, \tilde{\sigma}, m)$.

Notice that in the above definition, SigKeyGen and Sign are run by the signer; Verify and Transform are run by the designator. We emphasize that Verify *is not publicly available* in UDVSP system.

We require two *consistency* properties from UDVSP system. One property is that the signature σ on the message m, produced by the signer should be accepted as valid by the Verify algorithm. The other property is that the transformed signature $\tilde{\sigma}$ produced by the designator using the valid signature σ from the signer and his secret mask $\tilde{sk}$ should be accepted as valid in the IVerify protocol.

3.2   Security Notions

The first essential security requirement for UDVSP system is that a signature created by the signer should be existentially unforgeable under (adaptive) chosen message attack, which is a standard requirement for digital signature schemes. Below, we review the formal definition of unforgeability of chosen message attack [14].

Definition 3 (Unforgeability against Chosen Message Attack). Suppose that SigKeyGen, Sign and Verify are as defined in Definition 2. Consider the following experiment $\mathbf{Exp}^{f-cma}(k)$ in which a polynomial-time attacker A after making queries to the signing oracle $\mathsf{Sign}(sk, \cdot)$, outputs a *new* message and valid signature pair:

- Experiment: $(pk, sk) \leftarrow \mathsf{SigKeyGen}(k) : (m, \sigma) \leftarrow A^{\mathsf{Sign}(sk,\cdot)}(pk)$
- Output: If $1 \leftarrow \mathsf{Verify}(pk, m, \sigma)$ and m has not been queried to $\mathsf{Sign}(sk, \cdot)$ then return 1. Otherwise return 1.

We define A's advantage in the above experiment as $\mathbf{Adv}_A^{f-cma}(k) = \Pr[\mathbf{Exp}^{f-cma}(k) = 1]$. We say that the underlying signature scheme of UDVSP system is existentially unforgeable under chosen message attack if $\mathbf{Adv}_A^{f-cma}(k)$ is negligible in k.

The second essential security requirement for UDVSP system is resistance against impersonation attack. That is, UDVSP system should prevent an attacker who does not hold a valid signature created by the signer from impersonating the honest designator who holds a valid signature created by the signer.

We divide this impersonation attack further into two categories, "Type-1" and "Type-2" attacks. In Type-1 attack, an attacker who has obtained a transformed signature participates in the IVerify protocol as a *cheating designated verifier* and interacts with an honest designator a number of times. The attacker then tries to impersonate the honest designator to other honest designated verifier. Below, we give a formal definition for security against the Type-1 attack.

Definition 4 (Security against Impersonation under Type-1 Attack).
Assume that SigKeyGen, Sign, Verify, Transform and IVerify are as defined in
Definition 2. Suppose that a polynomial-time attacker A consists of two sub-
algorithms $\hat{V}$ and $\hat{P}$, which represent a cheating designated verifier and a cheating designator respectively. Let P denote an honest designator. Let $\mathsf{Conv}_{\mathsf{IVerify}}$
be a function that outputs a conversation transcript T of the IVerify protocol
between P and $\hat{V}$. Note here that T is a random variable afreshed by P and $\hat{V}$'s
random coins. We write $T \leftarrow \mathsf{Conv}_{\mathsf{IVerify}}[P(\tilde{sk}) \leftrightarrow \hat{V}](pk, \tilde{\sigma}, m)$.

Now consider an experiment $\mathbf{Exp}^{im-type1}(k)$. Firstly, in this experiment, a
signer's public/secret key pair (pk, sk) is generated using a security parameter
$k \in \mathbb{N}$. pk is then given to the honest designator P and the attacker $A = (\hat{V}, \hat{P})$.
Next, an arbitrary message m is chosen and a signature σ on m is generated.
Also, a designator's secret mask $\tilde{sk}$ is chosen based on pk and a transformed
signature $\tilde{\sigma}$ is created using $\tilde{sk}$. $\tilde{\sigma}$ is then given to $A = (\hat{V}, \hat{P})$ while $\tilde{sk}$ is given
only to P. $\hat{V}$ now interacts with P in the IVerify protocol $p(k)$ times, where $p(\cdot)$
denotes a polynomial-time computable function. Having accessed to transcripts
of these interactions and $\hat{V}$'s random coins used in them, which are denoted
T_i and $r_i^{\hat{V}}$ respectively for $i = 1, \ldots, p(k)$, $\hat{P}$ tries to *impersonate* the honest
designator P to an honest designated verifier V in the IVerify protocol. Formally,
$\mathbf{Exp}^{im-type1}(k)$ can be described as follows.

- Experiment: $(pk, sk) \leftarrow \mathsf{SigKeyGen}(k);\ m \leftarrow \{0,1\}^*;$
  $\qquad \sigma \leftarrow \mathsf{Sign}(sk, m);\ (\tilde{\sigma}, \tilde{sk}) \leftarrow \mathsf{Transform}(pk, \sigma);$
  $\qquad T_i \leftarrow \mathsf{Conv}_{\mathsf{IVerify}}[P(\tilde{sk}) \leftrightarrow \hat{V}](pk, \tilde{\sigma}, m)$ for $i = 1, \ldots, p(k):$
  $\qquad d \leftarrow \mathsf{IVerify}[\hat{P}((T_1, r_1^{\hat{V}}), \ldots, (T_{p(k)}, r_{p(k)}^{\hat{V}})) \leftrightarrow V](pk, \tilde{\sigma}, m)$
- Output: d

We define A's advantage in the above experiment as $\mathbf{Adv}_A^{im-type1}(k) =$
$\Pr[\mathbf{Exp}^{im-type1}(k) = 1]$. We say that UDVSP system is secure against impersonation under Type-1 attack if $\mathbf{Adv}_A^{im-type1}(k)$ is negligible in k.

In Type-2 attack, the attacker simply *ignores the transformed signature that
he has obtained before* but tries to create a new transformed signature on his
own and use this to impersonate the honest designator to an honest designated
verifier in the IVerify protocol. In what follows, we formally define the security
against Type-2 attack.

Definition 5 (Security against Impersonation under Type-2 Attack).
Assume that SigKeyGen, Sign, Verify, Transform and IVerify are as defined in
Definition 2. Let A be a polynomial-time attacker. Consider an experiment
$\mathbf{Exp}^{im-type2}(k)$. Firstly, in this experiment, a signer's public/secret key pair
(pk, sk) is generated using a security parameter k and pk is given to A. Then, an
arbitrary message m is chosen and is given to A. A then generates a designator's
secret mask $\tilde{sk}'$ and a transformed signature $\tilde{\sigma}'$ on its own and participates in the
IVerify protocol with an honest designated verifier V. Formally, $\mathbf{Exp}^{im-type2}(k)$
can be described as follows.

- Experiment: $(pk, sk) \leftarrow$ SigKeyGen(k); $m \leftarrow \{0,1\}^*$; $(\tilde{\sigma}', \tilde{sk}') \leftarrow A(pk, m)$:
  $$d \leftarrow \text{IVerify}[A(\tilde{sk}') \leftrightarrow V](pk, \tilde{\sigma}', m)$$
- Output: d

We define A's advantage in the above experiment as $\mathbf{Adv}_A^{im-type2}(k) =$ $\Pr[\mathbf{Exp}^{im-type2}(k) = 1]$. We say that UDVSP system is secure against impersonation under Type-2 attack if $\mathbf{Adv}_A^{im-type2}(k)$ is negligible in k.

4   Our Universal Designated Verifier Signature Proof Systems

4.1   UDVSP System Based on BLS Signature

Our first UDVSP system is based on Boneh, Lynn and Shacham (BLS)'s [5] signature scheme. Each sub-algorithm and protocol of this system can be described as follows.

- SigKeyGen(k): Compute $(q, g, e, \mathbb{G}_1, \mathbb{G}_2) \leftarrow$ PramGen$_a(k)$. Choose $x \xleftarrow{\text{R}} \mathbb{Z}_q^*$ and compute $y = g^x$. Specify a hash function $H : \{0,1\}^* \to \mathbb{G}_1$. Output $pk = (k, q, g, e, \mathbb{G}_1, \mathbb{G}_2, H, y)$ and $sk = (k, q, g, e, \mathbb{G}_1, \mathbb{G}_2, H, x)$.
- Sign(sk, m), where $m \in \{0,1\}^*$: Compute $\sigma = H(m)^x$. Output σ.
- Verify(pk, m, σ): Check $e(\sigma, g) \overset{?}{=} e(H(m), y)$. If the equality holds, output 1. Otherwise, output 0.
- Transform(pk, σ): Choose $z \xleftarrow{\text{R}} \mathbb{Z}_q^*$ and compute $\sigma^z (= H(m)^{xz})$. Output $\tilde{\sigma} = \sigma^z$ and $\tilde{sk} = z$.
- IVerify$[P(\tilde{sk}) \leftrightarrow V](pk, \tilde{\sigma}, m)$:
    Both P and V compute $v_1 = e(\tilde{\sigma}, g)$, and $v_2 = e(H(m), y)$.
    1. P chooses $t \xleftarrow{\text{R}} \mathbb{Z}_q^*$, computes $w = v_2^s$ and sends w to V.
    2. V chooses $c \xleftarrow{\text{R}} \mathbb{Z}_q^*$ and sends it to P.
    3. P computes $t = s + cz \bmod q$ and sends t to V.
    4. V checks $v_2^t \overset{?}{=} w v_1^c$. If the equality holds then output 1. Otherwise, output 0 otherwise.

If the hash function H is assumed to be the random oracle [2], one can prove that the Sign algorithm above is unforgeable under chosen message attack assuming that the CDH problem (Definition 6) is hard [5] (in $\mathbb{G}_1$).

Notice that the above IVerify protocol is a protocol for proving knowledge of z satisfying the relation $e(\tilde{\sigma}, g) = e(H(m), y)^z$. From this, P can convince the designated verifier that he possesses a valid BLS-signature $H(m)^x$. More precisely, if there exists a knowledge extractor [1] that extracts z, one can use this extractor to construct another knowledge extractor that outputs $\tilde{\sigma}^{1/z}$ as a valid signature. Indeed, this value is a valid BLS-signature as $e(\tilde{\sigma}, g) = e(H(m), y)^z$ implies $e(\tilde{\sigma}, g)^{1/z} = e(H(m), y)$ and hence $e(\tilde{\sigma}^{1/z}, g) = e(H(m)^x, g)$. However, as mentioned earlier, we do not use this auxiliary property to analyze the security of the proposed system as the zero-knowledge or witness-indistinguishability required to provide the security against impersonation under *active* attacks (i.e. attacks other than eavesdropping attack) often compromises the efficiency of protocol [4].

It is important to notice that in the IVerify protocol, the designated verifier does not need to setup his private/public key pair, which is a crucial difference compared to previous UDVS schemes.

4.2   UDVSP System Based on BB Signature

Our second UDVSP protocol is based on Boneh and Boyen (BB)'s [7] signature scheme. Each sub-algorithm and protocol of this system can be described as follows.

- SigKeyGen(k): Compute $(q, g, e, \mathbb{G}_1, \mathbb{G}_2) \leftarrow \mathsf{PramGen}_a(k)$. Choose $x \overset{\mathrm{R}}{\leftarrow} \mathbb{Z}_q^*$
  and $y \overset{\mathrm{R}}{\leftarrow} \mathbb{Z}_q^*$. Compute $u_1 = g^x$ and $u_2 = g^y$. Output $pk = (k, q, g, e, \mathbb{G}_1,$
  $\mathbb{G}_2, u_1, u_2)$ and $sk = (k, q, g, e, \mathbb{G}_1, \mathbb{G}_2, u_1, u_2, x, y)$.
- Sign(sk, m) where $m \in \mathbb{Z}_q$: Choose $l \overset{\mathrm{R}}{\leftarrow} \mathbb{Z}_q^*$ and compute $\delta = g^{1/(x+m+yl)}$.
  (If $x + m + yl = 0$, try different l). Output $\sigma = (\delta, l)$.
- Verify(pk, m, σ): Check $e(\sigma, u_1 g^m u_2^l) \overset{?}{=} e(g, g)$. If the equality holds, output
  1. Otherwise, output 0.
- Transform(pk, σ): Choose $z \overset{\mathrm{R}}{\leftarrow} \mathbb{Z}_q^*$ and compute $\tilde{\delta} = \delta^z (= g^{z/(x+m+yl)})$.
  Output $\tilde{\sigma} = (\sigma^z, l)$ and $\tilde{sk} = z$.
- IVerify$[P(\tilde{sk}) \leftrightarrow V](pk, \tilde{\sigma}, m)$:
  - Both P and V compute $v_1 = e(\tilde{\delta}, u_1 g^m u_2^l)$, and $v_2 = e(g, g)$.
    1. P chooses $s \overset{\mathrm{R}}{\leftarrow} \mathbb{Z}_q^*$, computes $w = v_2^s$ and sends w to V.
    2. V chooses $c \overset{\mathrm{R}}{\leftarrow} \mathbb{Z}_q^*$ and sends it to P.
    3. P computes $t = s + cz \bmod q$ and sends t to V.
    4. V checks $v_2^t \overset{?}{=} w v_1^c$. If the equality holds then output 1. Otherwise,
       output 0.

The above UDVSP system is structurally similar to the previous one presented in Section 4.1. However, a nice feature of this second construction is that it does not depend on random oracle due to the underlying signature scheme can be proven unforgeable against chosen message attack without employing the random oracle assumption [7].

Similarly to the previous construction, the IVerify protocol in the above UDVSP system can be viewed as a protocol for proving the knowledge of z satisfying the relation $e(\tilde{\sigma}, u_1 g^m u_2^l) = e(g, g)^z$.

5   Security Analysis

As mentioned in the previous section, the unforgeability of the underlying signature schemes of our two UDVSP systems were proven under the assumption that the CDH and SDH problems are hard respectively [5,7]. Therefore, we only analyze the security of the two UDVSP systems under impersonation attack.

The first theorem is concerned with the security of our UDVS system based on the BLS signature against impersonation under Type-1 attack.

Theorem 1. *The UDVSP system based on the BLS signature is secure against impersonation under Type-1 attack in the random oracle model assuming that the OMDL problem is hard in $\mathbb{G}_1$.*

Proof. Let $A = (\hat{V}, \hat{P})$ be an impersonator that tries to break the UDVSP system based on the BLS signature under Type-1 attack. Let B be an OMDL attacker. Suppose that B is given $(q, g, e, \mathbb{G}_1, \mathbb{G}_2)$. First, B queries its challenge oracle $\mathcal{C}(\cdot)$ to obtain a challenge point h_0. Suppose that $h_0 = g^{s_0}$ for some random $s_0 \in \mathbb{Z}_q^*$. Now, B chooses an arbitrary string $m \in \{0,1\}^*$. B also chooses $x \xleftarrow{R} \mathbb{Z}_q^*$ and computes $y = g^x$. B then outputs $pk = (k, q, g, e, \mathbb{G}_1, \mathbb{G}_2, H, y)$ as the signer's public key, where a random oracle $H : \{0,1\}^* \to \mathbb{G}_1$ can be constructed as follows. B sets $H(m) = g^l \in \mathbb{G}_1$. For $m' \neq m$, B chooses $l' \xleftarrow{R} \mathbb{Z}_q^*$ and returns $H(m') = g^{l'} \in \mathbb{G}_1$. Finally, B computes $\tilde{\sigma} = h_0^{lx}$ and gives this to A as a transformed signature. B proceeds to simulate the n times of execution of the IVerify protocol between $\hat{V}$ and an honest designator P as follows. (Below, $i \in \{1, \ldots, n\}$).

- Make a query to $\mathcal{C}(\cdot)$ and get the response h_i. Compute $w_i = e(h_i^{lx}, g)$ and send this to $\hat{V}$. When $\hat{V}$ sends c_i, make query $h_i h_0^{c_i}$ to $\mathcal{DL}_{q,g}(\cdot)$ to get the response t_i and send this back to $\hat{V}$. $\hat{V}$ then checks $e(H(m), g)^{t_i} \stackrel{?}{=} w_i e(\tilde{\sigma}, g)^{c_i}$.

Notice that the distribution of the transformed signature $\tilde{\sigma}$ constructed in the simulation above is the same as that in the real attack: Since $h_0 = g^{s_0}$ for random $s_0 \in \mathbb{Z}_q^*$, $\tilde{\sigma} = h_0^{lx} = g^{lxs_0} = H(m)^{xs_0}$ for random $l, x \in \mathbb{Z}_q^*$.

We now show that the simulation of IVerify is correct. Firstly, w_i in the above simulation and the one sent by P in Step 1 of the real protocol are identically distributed: Since $h_i = g^{s_i}$ for some random $s_i \in \mathbb{Z}_q^*$, we have

$$w_i = e(h_i^{lx}, g) = e(g^{s_i l}, g^x) = e(g^l, g^x)^{s_i} = e(H(m), y)^{s_i}.$$

Secondly, since t_i is the discrete-logarithm of $h_i h_0^{c_i}$, we have $t_i = s_i + c_i s_0 \bmod q$ and hence

$$
\begin{aligned}
e(H(m), y)^{t_i} &= e(H(m), y)^{s_i + c_i s_0} = e(H(m), y)^{s_i} e(H(m), y)^{c_i s_0} \\
&= e(g^l, g^x)^{s_i} e(g^l, g^x)^{c_i s_0} = e(g^{s_i lx}, g) e(g^{s_0 lx}, g)^{c_i} \\
&= e(h_i^{lx}, g)^{s_i} e(h_0^{lx}, g)^{c_i} = w_i e(\tilde{\sigma}, g)^{c_i}.
\end{aligned}
$$

After performing the above simulation n times, B now attempts to extract s_0, the discrete-logarithm of h_0. Using this value, B can compute the discrete-logarithms of other points $h_1, \ldots, h_n$. To do so, B runs $\hat{P}$ to get w in

Step 1 of IVerify, selects $c \stackrel{R}{\leftarrow} \mathbb{Z}_q^*$ and runs $\hat{P}$ to obtain its response t and checks $e(H(m), y)^t \stackrel{?}{=} we(\tilde{\sigma}, g)^c$. If the equality holds, B runs $\hat{P}$ again with the same state as before but with different challenge $c' \in \mathbb{Z}_q^*$, obtains its response t' and checks $e(H(m), y)^{t'} \stackrel{?}{=} we(\tilde{\sigma}, g)^{c'}$. If the equality holds, B computes $\frac{t-t'}{c'-c} \bmod q$. (Note that this part is due to the "reset lemma" formulated in [3]). We show that $\frac{t-t'}{c'-c} \bmod q$ is the discrete-logarithm of h_0. Observe that

$$
\begin{aligned}
e(g^{lx(t-t')/(c-c')}, g) &= e(g^{lx(t-t')}, g)^{1/(c-c')} = (e(g^l, g^x)^t e(g^l, g^x)^{-t'})^{1/(c-c')} \\
&= (e(H(m), y)^t e(H(m), y)^{-t'})^{1/(c-c')} \\
&= (we(\tilde{\sigma}, g)^c (we(\tilde{\sigma}, g)^{c'})^{-1})^{1/(c-c')} \\
&= e(\tilde{\sigma}, g)^{(c-c')})^{1/(c-c')} = e(h_0^{lx}, g) = e(g^{lxs_0}, g).
\end{aligned}
$$

From the above equation, we obtain $\frac{t-t'}{c'-c} = s_0 \bmod q$. Since we have s_0, we can compute $s_i = t_i - c_i(s_0 f_i)$ for $i = 1, \ldots, n$. Finally B outputs $s_0, s_1, \ldots, s_n$.

Now we prove the security of our first UDVS system against impersonation under Type-2 attack.

Theorem 2. *The UDVSP system based on the BLS signature is secure against impersonation under Type-2 attack in the random oracle model assuming that the CDH problem is hard in $\mathbb{G}_1$.*

Proof. We present a reduction from the unforgeability of the original BLS signature scheme to the security of our UDVSP system under Type-2 attack. The above theorem then follows since the BLS scheme is shown to be (existentially) unforgeable under chosen message attack in the random oracle model assuming that the CDH problem in $\mathbb{G}_1$ is hard [5].

Let A be an impersonator that tries to break the UDVSP system based on the BLS signature under Type-2 attack. Let B be a forger that tries to break the BLS signature scheme under chosen message attack. Suppose that B is given a public key $(q, g, e, \mathbb{G}_1, \mathbb{G}_2, y, H)$, where $y = g^x$ and $H : \{0,1\}^* \to \mathbb{G}_1$ is a hash function modeled as a random oracle [2]. Firstly, B outputs $pk = (k, q, g, e, \mathbb{G}_1, \mathbb{G}_2, H, y)$ as the signer's public key. B then chooses an arbitrary string $m \in \{0,1\}^*$.

B now runs A to get $\tilde{\sigma}'$. B continues to run A to get w in Step 1 of IVerify. Upon receiving w, B picks $c \stackrel{R}{\leftarrow} \mathbb{Z}_q^*$, runs A to obtain its response t and checks $e(H(m), y)^t \stackrel{?}{=} we(\tilde{\sigma}', g)^c$. If the equality holds, B runs A again with the same state as before but with difference challenge $c' \in \mathbb{Z}_q^*$, obtains its response t' and checks $e(H(m), y)^{t'} \stackrel{?}{=} we(\tilde{\sigma}', g)^{c'}$. If the equality holds, B outputs $\tilde{\sigma}'^{\frac{c-c'}{t-t'}}$ as a forgery. (Similarly to the proof of the previous theorem , this part is due to the "reset lemma" formulated in [3]).

In remains to show that $\tilde{\sigma}'^{\frac{c-c'}{t-t'}}$ is a valid signature on m. From the above two equations, we get

$$e(H(m), y)^t / e(H(m), y)^{t'} = we(\tilde{\sigma}', g)^c / we(\tilde{\sigma}', g)^{c'}$$
$$e(H(m), y)^{t-t'} = e(\tilde{\sigma}', g)^{c-c'}$$
$$e(H(m), g^x)^{t-t'} = e(\tilde{\sigma}', g)^{c-c'}$$
$$e(H(m)^x, g) = e(\tilde{\sigma}', g)^{\frac{c-c'}{t-t'}}$$
$$e(H(m)^x, g) = e(\tilde{\sigma}'^{\frac{c-c'}{t-t'}}, g).$$

Thus we have $\tilde{\sigma}'^{\frac{c-c'}{t-t'}} = H(m)^x$, which is a valid signature on m.

The following two theorems are concerned with the security of our second UDVSP system against impersonation attack.

Theorem 3. *The UDVSP system based on the BB signature is secure against impersonation under Type-1 attack assuming that the OMDL problem in hard in* $\mathbb{G}_1$.

Proof. Let $A = (\hat{P}, \hat{V})$ be an impersonator that tries to break the UDVSP protocol based on the BB signature scheme under Type-1 attack. Let B be an OMDL attacker. Suppose that B is given $(q, g, e, \mathbb{G}_1, \mathbb{G}_2)$. First, B queries its challenge oracle $\mathcal{C}(\cdot)$ to obtain a challenge point h_0. Suppose that $h_0 = g^{s_0}$ for some random $s_0 \in \mathbb{Z}_q^*$. B then chooses an arbitrary string $m \in \{0, 1\}^*$. B also chooses $x \overset{R}{\leftarrow} \mathbb{Z}_q^*$ and $y \overset{R}{\leftarrow} \mathbb{Z}_q^*$ and computes $u_1 = g^x$ and $u_2 = g^y$. B then outputs $pk = (k, q, e, g, \mathbb{G}_1, \mathbb{G}_1, \mathbb{G}_2, u_1, u_2)$ as the signer's public key. Finally, B computes $\tilde{\sigma} = h_0^{\frac{1}{x+m+yl}}$ and publishes this as a transformed signature. B proceeds to simulate the steps of IVerify as follows. (Below, $i \in \{1, \ldots, n\}$).

- Make a query to $\mathcal{C}(\cdot)$ and get the response h_i. Compute $w_i = e(h_i, g)$ and send this to $\hat{V}$. When $\hat{V}$ sends c_i, make query $h_i h_0^{c_i}$ to $\mathcal{DL}_{q,g}(\cdot)$ to get the response t_i and send this back to $\hat{V}$. $\hat{V}$ then checks $e(g, g)^{t_i} \overset{?}{=} w_i e(\tilde{\sigma}, u_1 g^m u_2^l)^{c_i}$.

Notice that the distribution of the transformed signature $\tilde{\sigma}$ constructed in the simulation above is the same as that in the real attack as $h_0 = g^{s_0}$ for random $s_0 \in \mathbb{Z}_q^*$ and hence $\tilde{\sigma} = h_0^{\frac{1}{x+m+yl}} = g^{\frac{s_0}{x+m+yl}}$ for random $x, y, l \in \mathbb{Z}_q^*$.

We now show that the simulation of IVerify is correct. Firstly, w_i in the above simulation and the one sent by P in Step 1 of the real protocol are identically distributed: Since $h_i = g^{s_i}$ for some random $s_i \in \mathbb{Z}_q^*$, we have $w_i = e(g^{s_i}, g) = e(g, g)^{s_i}$. Secondly, since t_i is the discrete-logarithm of $h_i h_0^{c_i}$, we have $t_i = s_i + c_i s_0 \bmod q$. Hence,

$$e(g, g)^{t_i} = e(g, g)^{s_i + c_i s_0} = e(g, g)^{s_i} e(g, g)^{c_i s_0} = w_i e(g^{\frac{s_0}{x+m+yl}}, g^{x+m+yl})^{c_i}$$
$$= w_i e(h_0^{\frac{1}{x+m+yl}}, u_1 g^m u_2^l)^{c_i} = w_i e(\tilde{\sigma}_i, u_1 g^m u_2^l)^{c_i}.$$

After performing the above simulation n times, B now attempts to extract s_0, the discrete-logarithm of h_0. Using this value, B can compute the discrete-logarithms of other points $h_1, \ldots, h_n$. To do so, B runs $\hat{P}$ to get w

in Step 1 of IVerify, selects $c \overset{R}{\leftarrow} \mathbb{Z}_q^*$ and runs $\hat{P}$ to obtain its response t
and checks $e(g, g)^t \overset{?}{=} we(\tilde{\sigma}, g)^c$. If the equality holds, B runs $\hat{P}$ again with
the same state as before but with different challenge $c' \in \mathbb{Z}_q^*$, obtains its response t' and checks $e(g, g)^{t'} \overset{?}{=} we(\tilde{\sigma}, g)^{c'}$. If the equality holds, B computes
$\frac{t-t'}{c'-c} \bmod q$. (Note that this part is due to the "reset lemma" formulated in
[3]). We now show that $\frac{t-t'}{c'-c} \bmod q$ is the discrete-logarithm of h_0. Observe
that

$$
\begin{aligned}
e(g^{\frac{t-t'}{c-c'}}, g) &= e(g^{t-t'}, g)^{\frac{1}{(c-c')}} = (e(g, g)^t e(g, g)^{-t'})^{\frac{1}{(c-c')}} \\
&= \left(we(\tilde{\sigma}, u_1 g^m u_2^l)^c (we(\tilde{\sigma}, u_1 g^m u_2^l)^{c'})^{-1} \right)^{\frac{1}{(c-c')}} \\
&= e(\tilde{\sigma}, u_1 g^m u_2^l)^{\frac{c-c'}{c-c'}} = e(h_0^{\frac{1}{x+m+yl}}, g^{x+m+yl}) = e(g^{s_0}, g).
\end{aligned}
$$

From the above equation, we obtain $\frac{t-t'}{c'-c} = s_0 \bmod q$. Since we have s_0, we
can compute $s_i = t_i - c_i s_0$ for $i = 1, \ldots, n$. Finally B outputs $s_0, s_1, \ldots, s_n$.

Theorem 4. *The UDVSP system based on the BB signature is secure against
impersonation under Type-2 attack in the random oracle model assuming that
the SDH problem is hard in $\mathbb{G}_1$.*

Proof. Similarly to the proof of Theorem 2, we present a reduction from the
security of the original BB signature scheme to the security of our UDVSP system
under Type-2 attack. The above theorem then follows since the BB scheme is
shown to be unforgeable under chosen message attack (in the standard model)
assuming that the SDH problem in group $\mathbb{G}_1$ is hard [7].

Let A be an impersonator that tries to break the UDVSP system based on
BB under Type-2 attack. Let B be a forger that tries to break the BB signature
scheme under chosen message attack. Suppose that B is given a public key
$(q, g, e, \mathbb{G}_1, \mathbb{G}_2, u_1, u_2)$, where $u_1 = g^x$ and $u_2 = g^y$ for random $x, y, \mathbb{Z}_q^*$. Firstly,
B outputs $pk = (q, g, e, \mathbb{G}_1, \mathbb{G}_2, u_1, u_2)$ as the signer's public key. B chooses an
arbitrary string $m \in \{0, 1\}^*$.

B now runs A to get $\tilde{\sigma}' = (\tilde{\delta}', l)$. B continues to run A to get w in Step 1
of IVerify. Upon receiving w, B picks $c \overset{R}{\leftarrow} \mathbb{Z}_q^*$, runs A to obtain its response
t and checks $e(g, g)^t \overset{?}{=} we(\tilde{\delta}', u_1 g'^m u_2^l)^c$. If the equality holds, B runs A again
with the same state as before but with difference challenge $c' \in \mathbb{Z}_q^*$, obtains
its response t' and checks $e(g, g)^{t'} \overset{?}{=} we(\tilde{\delta}', u_1 g^m u_2^l)^{c'}$. If the equality holds, B
outputs $\tilde{\sigma}^{\frac{t-t'}{c-c'}}$ as a forgery. (Note that this part is due to the "reset lemma"
formulated in [3]).

We now show that $\tilde{\sigma}'^{\frac{t-t'}{c-c'}}$ is a valid signature on the message m. From the
above two equations, we get

$$e(g,g)^t/e(g,g)^{t'} = we(\tilde{\sigma}',g)^c/we(\tilde{\sigma}',g)^{c'}$$

$$e(g,g)^{t-t'} = e(\tilde{\delta}',u_1g^mu_2^l)^{c-c'}$$

$$e(g,g)^{t-t'} = e(\tilde{\delta}',u_1g^mu_2^l)^{c-c'}$$

$$e(g,g) = e(\tilde{\sigma}',g^{x+m+yl})^{\frac{c-c'}{t-t'}}$$

$$e(g,g) = e(\tilde{\sigma}'^{\frac{c-c'}{t-t'}(x+m+yl)},g).$$

Thus we have $\tilde{\sigma}'^{\frac{t-t'}{c-c'}} = g^{\frac{1}{x+m+yl}}$, which is a valid signature on m.

6   Concluding Remarks

In this paper, we proposed an alternate method to realize Universal Designated Verifier Signature (UDVS) [25], called Universal Designated Verifier Signature Proof (UDVSP). We constructed two *efficient* and *provably-secure* UDVSP systems based on the pairing-based signature schemes proposed in [5] and [7]. The important feature of our two constructions compared to previous UDVS schemes [25,26,28] is that the verifier is no longer required to generate his private/public key pair for verifying that the signature holder is in possession of a right signature from the original signer.

Additionally, we observe that *when a designator and a signer are the same entity*, the UDVSP system becomes an undeniable signature scheme with a confirmation protocol only. As an example, using the UDVSP system based on BLS signature, one can construct an undeniable signature scheme as follows.

- SigKeyGen(k): Compute $(q,g,e,\mathbb{G}_1,\mathbb{G}_2) \leftarrow \mathsf{PramGen}_a(k)$. Choose $x \xleftarrow{\mathrm{R}} \mathbb{Z}_q^*$ and compute $y = g^x$. Specify a hash function $H : \{0,1\}^* \to \mathbb{G}_1$. Output $pk = (k,q,g,e,\mathbb{G}_1,\mathbb{G}_2,H,y)$ and $sk = (k,q,g,e,\mathbb{G}_1,\mathbb{G}_2,H,x)$.
- Sign(sk,m), where $m \in \{0,1\}^*$: Choose $z \xleftarrow{\mathrm{R}} \mathbb{Z}_q^*$ and compute $\tilde{\sigma} = H(m)^{xz}$. Output $\tilde{\sigma}$.
- Confirmation$[P(sk,z) \leftrightarrow V](pk,\tilde{\sigma},m)$:
  - Both P and V compute $v_1 = e(\tilde{\sigma},g)$, and $v_2 = e(H(m),y)$.
    1. P chooses $t \xleftarrow{\mathrm{R}} \mathbb{Z}_q^*$, computes $w = v_2^s$ and sends w to V.
    2. V chooses $c \xleftarrow{\mathrm{R}} \mathbb{Z}_q^*$ and sends it to P.
    3. P computes $t = s + cz \bmod q$ and sends t to V.
    4. V checks $v_2^t \overset{?}{=} wv_1^c$. If the equality holds then output 1. Otherwise, output 0.

Notice that in the above scheme, anyone cannot verify the validity of a signature without the help of the signer, which is essentially a main requirement of undeniable signature.

Designing a disavowal protocol for the above scheme and its formal analysis under the new security model for undeniable signature proposed in [22] are our future work.

Acknowledgement

The authors are grateful to the anonymous referees of Asiacrypt 2005 for their helpful comments.

References

1. M. Bellare and O. Goldreich, *On Defining Proof of Knowledge*, In Crypto '92, LNCS 740, pp. 390–420, Springer-Verlag, 1993.
2. M. Bellare and P. Rogaway, *Random Oracles are Practical: A Paradigm for Designing Efficient Protocols*, In ACM-CCS, pp. 62–73, 1993.
3. M. Bellare and A. Palacio, *GQ and Schnorr Identification Schemes: Proofs of Security against Impersonation under Active and Concurrent Attacks*, In Crypto '02, LNCS 2442, pp. 162–177, Springer-Verlag, 2002.
4. D. Boneh and M. Franklin, *Identity-Based Encryption from the Weil Pairing*, In Crypto '01, LNCS 2139, pp. 213–229, Springer-Verlag, 2001.
5. D. Boneh, B. Lynn and H. Shacham, *Short Signatures from the Weil Pairing*, In Asiacrypt '01, LNCS 2248, pp. 566–582, Springer-Verlag, 2001.
6. D. Boneh, C. Gentry, B. Lynn and H. Shacham, *Aggregate and Verifiably Encrypted Signatures from Bilinear Maps*, In Eurocrypt '03, LNCS 2656, pp. 416–432, Springer-Verlag, 2003.
7. D. Boneh and X. Boyen, *Short Signatures Without Random Oracles*, In Eurocrypt '04, LNCS 3027, pp. 56–73, Springer-Verlag, 2004.
8. G. Brassard, D. Chaum and C. Crpeau, *Minimum Disclosure Proof of Knowledge*, In Journal of Computer and System Sciences, 37 (2), pp. 156–189, 1988.
9. D. Chaum and H. Antwerpen, *Undeniable Signatures*, In Crypto '89, LNCS 435, pp. 212–216, Springer-Verlag, 1990.
10. J. Camenisch and A. Lysyanskaya, *An Efficient System for Non-Transferable Anonymous Credentials with Anonymity Revocation*, In Eurocrypt '01, LNCS 2045, pp. 93–118, Springer-Verlag, 2001.
11. J. Camenisch and A. Lysyanskaya, *Signature Schemes and Anonymous Credentials from Bilinear Maps*, In Crypto '04, LNCS 3152, pp. 56–72, Springer-Verlag, 2004.
12. Y. Desmedt, C. Gourtier and S. Bengio, *Special Uses and Abuses of the Fiat-Shamir Passport Protocol*, In Crypto '87, LNCS 293, pp. 21–39, Springer-Verlag, 1988.
13. U. Feige and A. Shamir, *Witness Indistinguishability and Witness Hiding Protocols*, In 22nd Symposium on the Theory of Computing (STOC), pp. 416–426, ACM, 1990.
14. S. Goldwasser, S. Micali and R. Rivest, *A Digital Signature Scheme Secure Against Adaptive Chosen- Message Attack*, In SIAM Journal on Computing, 17 (2), pp. 281–308, 1988.
15. S. Goldwasser, S. Micali and C. Rackoff, *The Knowledge Complexity of Interactive Proof System*, In SIAM Journal on Computing, 18 (1), pp. 186–208, 1989.
16. M. Jakobsson, *Blackmailing Using Undeniable Signatures*, In Eurocrypt '94, LNCS 950, pp. 425–427, Springer-Verlag, 1994.
17. M. Jakobsson, K. Sako and R. Impagliazzo, *Designated Verifier Proofs and Their Applications*, In Eurocrypt '96, LNCS 1070, pp. 143–154, Springer-Verlag, 1996.
18. A. Joux: *The Weil and Tate Pairings as Building Blocks for Public Key Cryptosystems*, Algorithmic Number Theory Symposium (ANTS-V) '02, LNCS 2369, pp. 20–32, Springer-Verlag, 2002.

19. H. Krawczyk and T. Rabin, *Chameleon Hashing and Signatures*, Network and Distributed System Security Symposium (NDSS) '00, pp. 143 – 154, The Internet Society, 2000.
20. A. Lysyanskaya, R. Rivest, A. Sahai and S. Wolf *Pseudonym Systems*, In Selected Areas in Cryptography (SAC) '99, LNCS 1758, pp. 184–199, Springer-Verlag, 1999.
21. M. Naor, *Deniable Ring Authentication*, In Crypto '02, LNCS 2442, pp. 481–198, Springer-Verlag, 2002.
22. W. Ogata, K. Kurosawa and S. Heng, *The Security of the FDH Variant of Chaum's Undeniable Signature Scheme*, In Public Key Cryptography (PKC) '05, LNCS 3386, pp. 328–345, Springer-Verlag, 2005.
23. C. P. Schnorr, *Efficient Identifications and Signatures for Smart Cards*, In Crypto '89, LNCS 435, pp. 239–251, Springer-Verlag, 1990.
24. R. Rivest, A. Shamir and Y. Tauman, *How to Leak a Secret*, In Asiacrypt '01, LNCS 2248, pp. 552 – 565, Springer-Verlag, 2001.
25. R. Steinfeld, L. Bull, H. Wang and J. Pieprzyk, *Universal Designated-Verifier Signatures*, In Asiacrypt '03, LNCS 2894, pp. 523–542, Springer-Verlag, 2003.
26. R. Steinfeld, H. Wang and J. Pieprzyk, *Efficient Extension of Standard Schnorr/RSA Signatures into Universal Designated-Verifier Signatures*, In Public Key Cryptography (PKC) '04, LNCS 2947, pp. 86–100, Springer-Verlag, 2004.
27. W. Susilo and Y. Mu, *Deniable Ring Authentication Revisited*, In Applied Cryptography and Network Security (ACNS) '04, LNCS 3089, pp. 149–163, Springer-Verlag, 2004.
28. R. Zhang, J. Furukawa and H. Imai, *Short signature and Universal Designated Verifier Signature without Random Oracles*, In Applied Cryptography and Network Security (ACNS) '05, LNCS 3531, pp. 483–498, Springer-Verlag, 2005.

A   Definitions of CDH and SDH

Definition 6 (CDH).   Let A be a polynomial-time attacker. Consider the following experiment $\mathbf{Exp}^{cdh}(k)$:

- Experiment: $(q, g, e, \mathbb{G}_1, \mathbb{G}_2) \leftarrow \mathsf{ParamGen}_a(k); (a, b) \xleftarrow{\text{R}} \mathbb{Z}_q^* : \kappa \leftarrow A(g^a, g^b)$
- Output: If $\kappa = g^{ab}$ then return 1. Otherwise, return 0.

We define A's advantage as $\mathbf{Adv}_A^{cdh}(k) = \Pr[\mathbf{Exp}^{cdh}(k)] = 1$. We say that CDH problem is hard if $\mathbf{Adv}_A^{cdh}(k)$ is negligible in k.

It is believed that the above CDH problem in group $\mathbb{G}_1$ is hard (computationally intractable). On the contrary, the Decisional Diffie-Hellman (DDH) problem in this group can be solved in polynomial time with the help of the bilinear pairing. We note that the security of Boneh, Lynn and Shacham's [5] short signature scheme is relative to CDH.

We now review the definition of the Strong Diffie-Hellman (SDH) problem in group $\mathbb{G}_1$ as follows.

Definition 7 (SDH). Let A be a polynomial-time attacker. Consider the following experiment $\mathbf{Exp}^{sdh}(k)$ (Below, n is polynomial in k).:

– Experiment: $(q, g, e, \mathbb{G}_1, \mathbb{G}_2) \leftarrow \mathsf{PramGen}_a(k); \; x \xleftarrow{\mathrm{R}} \mathbb{Z}_q^*$:
$$\kappa \leftarrow A(g, g^x, g^{x^2}, \ldots, g^{x^n})$$
– Output: If $\kappa = (c, g^{1/(x+c)})$ where $c \in \mathbb{Z}_q$ then return 1. Otherwise, return 0.

We define A's advantage as $\mathbf{Adv}_A^{sdh}(k) = \Pr[\mathbf{Exp}^{sdh}(k)] = 1$. We say that SDH problem is hard if $\mathbf{Adv}_A^{sdh}(k)$ is negligible in k.

We note that the security of Boneh and Boyen's [7] signature scheme is relative to SDH.

Efficient Designated Confirmer Signatures Without Random Oracles or General Zero-Knowledge Proofs (Extended Abstract)

Craig Gentry[1], David Molnar[2], and Zulfikar Ramzan[1]

[1] DoCoMo USA Labs
{cgentry, ramzan}@docomolabs-usa.com
[2] University of California, Berkeley
dmolnar@eecs.berkeley.edu

Abstract. Most prior designated confirmer signature schemes either prove security in the random oracle model (ROM) or use general zero-knowledge proofs for NP statements (making them impractical). By slightly modifying the definition of designated confirmer signatures, Goldwasser and Waisbard presented an approach in which the Confirm and ConfirmedSign protocols could be implemented without appealing to general zero-knowledge proofs for NP statements (their Disavow protocol still requires them). The Goldwasser-Waisbard approach could be instantiated using Cramer-Shoup, GMR, or Gennaro-Halevi-Rabin signatures.

In this paper, we provide an alternate generic transformation to convert any signature scheme into a designated confirmer signature scheme, without adding random oracles. Our key technique involves the use of a signature on a commitment and a separate encryption of the random string used for commitment. By adding this "layer of indirection," the underlying protocols in our schemes admit efficient instantiations (i.e., we can avoid appealing to general zero-knowledge proofs for NP statements) and furthermore the performance of these protocols is not tied to the choice of underlying signature scheme. We illustrate this using the Camenisch-Shoup variation on Paillier's cryptosystem and Pedersen commitments. The confirm protocol in our resulting scheme requires 10 modular exponentiations (compared to 320 for Goldwasser-Waisbard) and our disavow protocol requires 41 modular exponentiations (compared to using a general zero-knowledge proof for Goldwasser-Waisbard). Previous schemes use the encryption of a signature paradigm, and thus run into problems when trying to implement the confirm and disavow protocols efficiently.

1 Introduction

Digital signatures allow one party to sign a message and have the resulting message-signature pair be verifiable by anyone. There are, however, situations when the signer may want to limit signature recipient's ability to present the

B. Roy (Ed.): ASIACRYPT 2005, LNCS 3788, pp. 662–681, 2005.

signature to others. Chaum and van Antwerpen [9] introduced the notion of *Undeniable Signatures* to help achieve this aim. Such signatures require the involvement of the original signer each time they are verified. Of course, this approach places excessive responsibility on the signer to be available and to not act maliciously. As an alternate approach, Jakobsson et al. [18] introduced *Designated Verifier* signatures which can only be validated by a specific user (who the signer can designate). However, the recipient cannot convince another party of the signature's validity, which is a desirable feature in many situations.

Chaum [7] introduced the notion of a *designated confirmer signature* (DCS), which overcomes both these limitations. Such signatures require the assistance of a trusted third party called the *confirmer*. Given a signature σ that the signer issues, the confirmer can execute a special Confirm protocol to prove that a signature σ is a valid signature on a message m, or a Disavow protocol to show that σ is not a valid signature on a message m. Without the confirmer, however, no party can determine whether σ is a valid signature for m or not.

APPLICATIONS OF DESIGNATED CONFIRMER SIGNATURES. Designated confirmer signatures have several cryptographic applications. For example, Asokan et al. demonstrate their use for "optimistic" fair exchange, in which a trusted third party need be involved only if cheating is suspected; the third party plays the role of confirmer [1]. Chaum notes that they are useful for integrity-critical content, such as virus updates, which is updated as part of a subscription service. In this application, without the assistance of the confirmer (for a fee), the content cannot be verified [7]. Therefore, efficient designated confirmer schemes are of practical as well as theoretical interest.

DEFINITIONAL ISSUES IN DCS SCHEMES. Okamoto provided the first formal definition of a designated confirmer signature [21]. His scheme is simple to describe: use an ordinary signature scheme to sign a message, then use an ordinary public-key encryption scheme to encrypt the resulting signature with the designated confirmer's public key. General zero-knowledge proofs for NP statements can be used to provide the Confirm and Disavow protocols. Of course such proofs involve a reduction step to an NP-complete language (e.g., the language representing graphs that are three colorable), and cannot really be used in practice. Work on designated confirmer schemes continued, and it became clear that the correct definition had numerous subtleties, involving issues including coercion of the signer, handling multiple signers with the same confirmer, and others. We focus on two key issues in the definition of designated confirmer signature schemes that will affect our construction. Firstly, we must consider whether to require designated confirmer signatures to be simulatable. Michels and Stadler, following Okamoto, adopt a definition that requires "invisibility" of designated confirmer signatures [26,21]; i.e., there exists a simulator who can create a "valid-looking" designated confirmer signature for any message m. Secondly, we must consider whether the Confirm and Disavow protocols are required to be zero-knowledge or instead may satisfy some weaker property. Previous definitions, such as those of Michels and Stadler, have included both these requirements [26]. Subsequent designated confirmer schemes were proposed by Camenisch and Michels [4], and by Camenisch and Shoup [6]. Other than the Okamoto scheme just mentioned, the remaining schemes all have security proofs in the random oracle model [2].

Goldwasser and Waisbard were interested in coming up with schemes that were provably secure without appealing to random oracles and without appealing to generic zero-knowledge proofs [17]. They found a clever way to approach this goal. They first argued that the previous definitions are too strong and do not capture the motivating applications of designated confirmer signature schemes. They modified Okamoto's original definition to require only that an adversary cannot verify signatures unless specifically assisted by the designated confirmer. Following the definition, they then show constructions of designated confirmer signatures for some specific signature schemes using strong *witness hiding proofs of knowledge* as a tool.

While Goldwasser and Waisbard can completely circumvent the use of random oracles, their Disavowal protocol still requires a generic zero-knowledge proof. Also, their witness hiding proofs of knowledge have soundness error $\frac{1}{2}$ and so are repeated λ times, where λ is the security parameter, to reduce the error. The efficiency of their protocols depends on the specific signature scheme. For example, with Cramer-Shoup as the underlying signature scheme each repetition costs 2 exponentiations in the underlying group [17].

CONFIRMER COMMITMENTS REVISITED. Our approach is to use a Paillier-based instantiation of the confirmer commitment idea of Michels and Stadler [26]. A *confirmer commitment* is a special type of commitment scheme with a public key. Anyone can use the public key to create a commitment to a message m, but only the holder of the corresponding secret key can prove or disprove the resulting commitment is a commitment to the message m.

Michels and Stadler noted that signing a confirmer commitment would be an "obvious" approach to building a designated confirmer signature scheme [26]. This is because the confirmer commitment can only be matched to a message m by the confirmer, who holds the secret key. Unfortunately, their definition required "invisibility" for confirmer signatures, namely that given any message, there exists a simulator that can produces a "valid-looking" designated confirmer signature on that message. This ruled out the approach *a priori*, because signatures from the underlying signature scheme cannot be simulated for an existentially unforgeable signature scheme; any such simulator would imply the existence of a forger. As Goldwasser and Waisbard have argued, however, such requirements are too strong when we only care that no adversary can convince others that a signature is valid. We show in this paper that replacing the simulation requirement with the more natural non-verifiability of signatures requirement allows us to prove that the "obvious" scheme is secure.

We stress that, by itself, this observation is *not* enough. A more serious problem with the approach of confirmer commitments, as shown by Camenisch and Michels [4], is that the construction of confirmer commitments proposed by Michels and Stadler is actually not secure when multiple signers share the same confirmer [26]. Therefore it is not trivial to create a secure designated confirmer signature scheme from confirmer commitments, even with the weakened definition. While Camenisch and Michels sketch a fix for the Michels and Stadler construction, they do not give a full proof of security. Finally, while Camenisch and Michels define a generic transformation and prove it secure, efficient instantiation depends on the details of the underlying signature scheme; we analyze their suggested instantiation, which uses RSA with Full Domain Hash, in Section 5 [4]. We give a transformation in Section 4 that achieves security and efficiency given any signature scheme existentially unforgeable against chosen message attack. Instead of giving a new definition for confirmer commitments, however, we simply prove directly in Section 4 that the resulting scheme is a secure designated confirmer scheme.

CAMENISCH AND SHOUP'S APPROACH. Camenisch and Shoup introduced new protocols for verifiable encryption and proving inequality of discrete logarithms [6]. Goldwasser and Waisbard note that these protocols are of interest in the designated confirmer setting [17]. Indeed, Camenisch and Shoup sketch a construction of designated confirmer signatures as part of their work on verifiable encryption. While we will use the protocols of Camenisch and Shoup in our construction, the way in which we use them is different. We sign a commitment and then encrypt information needed to open the commitment, while Camenisch and Shoup perform a verifiable encryption of a signature directly.

Because the Camenisch-Shoup approach encrypts a signature directly, the efficiency of Confirm and Disavow depends essentially on the underlying signature scheme. Their sketch suggests the use of Schnorr signatures [24], together with a trick for reducing the validity of a Schnorr signature to an equality of discrete logarithms. Details of the resulting scheme are not given, but are due to appear in a forthcoming paper. Since this paper is not yet available, in Section 5 we flesh out what we suspect the details to be to allow for comparison between our approach and theirs.

We highlight one such detail that affects our construction of DCS schemes: the Camenisch-Shoup protocols as described satisfy only special honest-verifier zero-knowledge. Special honest-verifier is not a strong enough property in the context of an adversary for DCS schemes, because the DCS adversary may act as a cheating verifier during Confirm and Disavow protocols. We show how to use techniques of Cramer, Damgard, and MacKenzie to fix this problem [13].

Finally, we note that the Camenisch-Shoup sketch suggests the use of Schnorr signatures, which require random oracles. Adapting their approach to a new signature scheme without random oracles is not trivial. We briefly outline difficulties with several such schemes in Section 5. Our approach, in contrast, works for any signature scheme without modification and easily yields a designated confirmer signature that does not need random oracles.

OUR CONTRIBUTIONS. We make three contributions. First, we show that adopting the Goldwasser-Waisbard definition [17] allows us to prove that the approach of signing a commitment yields a designated confirmer signature scheme using any secure signature scheme as a building block. We specify a generic construction (based on any signature scheme, encryption scheme, and commitment scheme) and prove it secure *without* the use of random oracles. Second, we give

	Random Oracle	Signature	Confirm	Disavow
GW [17]	No	Cramer-Shoup [10]	2λ exps	generic ZKP
GW [17]	No	GMR [16]	2λ exps	generic ZKP
GW [17]	No	GHR [14]	2λ exps	generic ZKP
CS [6]	Yes	Schnorr [24]	10 exps	41 exps
CM [4]	Yes	RSA-FDH	24λ exps	60λ exps
Our scheme	No	Any	10 exps	41 exps

Fig. 1. Comparison of our approach to Goldwasser-Waisbard, Camenisch-Shoup, and Camenisch-Michels. Here λ is a security parameter. We achieve efficient Confirm and Disavow protocols without using random oracles. Section 5 explains these results in detail.

an instantiation using Pedersen Commitments [23] together with Camenisch and Shoup's [6] variant of Paillier's cryptosystem [22]. This approach achieves Confirm and Disavow protocols without appealing to generic zero-knowledge proofs and without appealing to random oracles independent of the choice of signature scheme. The resulting Confirm protocol requires 5 exponentiations (compared to 320 for Goldwasser-Waisbard) and our Disavow protocol requires 17,000 modular multiplications (whereas Goldwasser-Waisbard require a potentially very expensive generic zero-knowledge proof). Of course, we base our security on the security of Paillier's cryptosystem and on the security of Pedersen commitments, whereas Goldwasser and Waisbard require different assumptions than we do; we elaborate on this, and other aspects of the comparison, in Section 5. Third, we show that the resulting Confirm and Disavow protocols are zero-knowledge (whereas Goldwasser-Waisbard provide strong witness hiding proofs of knowledge), even against cheating verifiers, by combining the Camenisch-Shoup protocols with techniques of Cramer, Damgard and MacKenzie [13].

2   Preliminaries

Throughout λ is a positive integer denoting the security parameter. The security parameter is an implicit input to the algorithms discussed throughout the paper (and we omit it from the list of inputs when it might be otherwise clear from context). Let $\mathsf{negl}(\lambda)$ denote a negligible function; i.e., one that grows smaller than $1/\lambda^c$ for all c and all sufficiently large λ. For a positive integer a, we let $[a]$ denote the set $\{0, \ldots, a-1\}$. If $\mathsf{Alg}(\cdot, \cdot, \ldots)$ is a probabilistic algorithm, then $\mathsf{Alg}(x_1, x_2, \ldots)$ is a probability space over the random choices made by Alg. We let $x \leftarrow \mathsf{Alg}(x_1, x_2, \ldots)$ denote the experiment of running Alg on inputs $x_1, x_2, \ldots$, where x is a discrete random variable denoting the outcome. Note that Alg implicitly induces a distribution on the possible outputs. For a set S, we let $|S|$ denote the number of elements in S. If S is defined by a mathematical group, then $|S|$ is the group order. If S is equipped with a probability distribution D, we let $x \xleftarrow{D} S$ denote the experiment of choosing $x \in S$ according to D. We typically let the underlying distribution be the uniform distribution R. In our context an adversary (denoted by $\mathcal{A}$, $\mathcal{F}$, etc. depending on the situation) is a probabilistic polynomial time random access machine with oracle access to some number κ of oracles, each of which is capable of computing some specified function. If $(f_1, \ldots, f_\kappa)$ is a κ-tuple of (oracle implemented) functions, and $\mathcal{A}$ is a κ-oracle adversary, then $\mathcal{A}^{f_1, \ldots, f_\kappa}$ denotes the adversary augmented with its oracles. An adversary may also have oracle access to a *protocol*, in which case the adversary provides protocol inputs from one side of the protocol (e.g., a verifier in an interactive proof system) and has oracle access to the responses from the other side of protocol (e.g., a prover in an interactive proof system). As above, the adversary on a given set of inputs induces a probability space, and we can associate a discrete random variable to the output of the experiment of running the adversary on a given set of inputs equipped with a given set of oracles. We now describe some of the tools required for our construction.

PROOFS OF KNOWLEDGE. Some of our protocols will be proofs of knowledge (PoK), as defined by Bellare and Goldreich [3]. Informally, an interactive proof (P, V) for a relation $R = \{\alpha, \beta\}$ is a proof of knowledge if there exists a probabilistic polynomial time knowledge extractor E who can extract a witness β given oracle access to a (possibly cheating) prover. The knowledge extractor is allowed to rewind the prover if necessary. The *knowledge error* of a ZKPoK quantifies the success probability of the extractor in terms of the prover's probability of convincing the verifier. Specifically, let P be a prover with respect to α. We say that the proof of knowledge has knowledge error $\kappa(\alpha)$ if, when the prover succeeds with probability $\epsilon(\alpha)$ the knowledge extractor E^P succeeds with probability at least $\epsilon(\alpha) - \kappa(\alpha)$.

ZERO-KNOWLEDGE PROOFS. The well-known Chaum-Pedersen protocol for proving equality of discrete logarithms and the Camenisch-Shoup protocols (which we describe below), are *special honest-verifier zero-knowledge Σ-protocols* [19] (SHVZK). This means that the protocols are public-coin and can be simulated assuming an honest verifier (i.e., a verifier that picks challenges uniformly at random). The *special* property means there is a simulator that, given the challenge of a verifier, can create the prover's messages.

The zero-knowledge proofs in our DCS scheme, however, must be zero-knowledge even against arbitrarily cheating verifiers. Moreover, we must be careful that our ZK proofs in our scheme not only reveal nothing about the witness, but also that the transcripts of a "real-world" interaction between the prover and a verifier in the ZK proof are indistinguishable from a transcript that a probabilistic polynomial-time simulator can generate using rewindable black-box access to the verifier. Such ZK proof protocols can be found in [15,13]. For our efficient instantiation, we prefer the Cramer-Damgard-Mackenzie (CDM) approach, in which a prover P proves knowledge of a witness w for x to verifier V using SHVZK Σ-protocols in both directions, roughly as follows:

- Part 1: V commits to a value e and proves knowledge of e;
- Part 2: P gives a witness-indistinguishable proof of knowledge of either the verifier's value e or the witness w.

When applied to SHVZK 3-round proofs of knowledge, this approach yields a zero-knowledge proof of knowledge (ZKPoK) with negligible knowledge error, neglible soundness error, and which remains perfect zero-knowledge even against malicious adversaries. Specifically, there exists a simulator $S^{V'}$ that, given access to an arbitrary verifier V', outputs a transcript identically distributed to the transcript of interactions between the prover and V'. We will use this simulator extensively in the reduction algorithm of our DCS scheme's proof of security. Strictly speaking, the SHVZK 3-round proof of knowledge must satisfy an additional condition, namely that an associated "commitment relation" also have a 3-round proof of knowledge. Fortunately, as we will see, this is the case for our efficient instantiation, because we can leverage an efficient discrete logarithm protocol given by Cramer et al. [13]

CAMENISCH-SHOUP VERIFIABLE ENCRYPTION. We use an adaptation of Camenisch and Shoups's Paillier-based encryption scheme, which allows verifiable encryption of discrete logarithms. The scheme relies on the decisional composite residuosity assumption (DCRA). Let P, Q be Sophie-Germain primes – i.e., $P = 2p + 1$ and $Q = 2q+1$ for primes p, q. Let $N = PQ$. The DCRA states, roughly, that it is hard to distinguish random elements of $\mathbb{Z}_{N^2}^*$ from random elements of the subgroup consisting of all N-th powers of elements in $\mathbb{Z}_{N^2}^*$. The original DCRA introduced by [22] does not require the use of Sophie-Germain primes, though they are required by [6] and by us for technical reasons. As pointed by [6], it is clear that as long as Sophie-Germain primes are sufficiently dense in the set of primes (as is believed to be true), then the DCRA without the Sophie-Germain restriction implies the DCRA with the Sophie-Germain restriction.

We give a sketch of the encryption scheme; details can be found in [6]. The user creates a composite modulus $N = PQ$ as above. The user's public key includes a collision-resistant hash function H, $h = 1 + N$, a random $g' \in (\mathbb{Z}/N^2\mathbb{Z})^*$, and values $g = g'^{2N}$, $y_1 = g^{x_1}$, $y_2 = g^{x_2}$, and $y_3 = g^{x_3}$ for secrets $x_1, x_2, x_3 \in [N^2/4]$.

To encrypt r with a "label" $L \in \{0, 1\}^*$, the sender chooses $t \in_R [N/4]$ and computes (u, e, v) with $u = g^t$, $e = y_1^t h^r$, and $v = \text{abs}((y_2 y_3^{H(u,e,L)})^t)$, where $\text{abs}(a) = N^2 - a \mod N^2$ if $a > N^2/2$ else $\text{abs}(a) = a \mod N^2$. The ciphertext is (u, e, v, L). A user with the private key can decrypt (u, e, v, L) as follows. First, it checks that $\text{abs}(v) = v$ and $u^{2(x_2+H(u,e,L)x_3)} = v^2$. If the check fails, the user outputs $\perp$ and halts. Otherwise, it computes $\hat{r} = (e/u^{x_1})^{2k}$ for $k = 2^{-1} \mod N$. If $\hat{r}$ is of the form h^r for some $r \in [N]$, it outputs r; otherwise, it outputs $\perp$.

To obtain a verifiable encryption scheme from the basic encryption scheme above, one uses an additional composite modulus $N_2 = P_2 Q_2$, where $P_2 = 2p_2 + 1$ and $Q_2 = 2q_2 + 1$ are safe primes, along with elements $g_2, h_2 \in \mathbb{Z}_{N_2}^*$ of order $p_2 q_2$. Optionally, one may use a third group – e.g., a group Γ of prime order ρ with generators γ and δ for which the discrete logarithm problem is not known to be vulnerable to subexponential attacks – to improve efficiency. We view $(N_2, g_2, h_2, \Gamma, \gamma, \delta)$ as a common reference string. We require $N_2 \neq N$ and $|\Gamma| < N2^{-k-k'-3}$ for security parameters k and k' as described in [6].

Now, suppose that $\alpha = \gamma^r$ for $r \in [\rho]$; then, r can be verifiably encrypted as follows. The sender computes (u, e, v) as before, generates $s \in_R [N_2/4]$, sets $\ell = g_2^m h_2^s$, and then provides the following ZKPoK:

$$PK\{(t,r,s) : u^2 = g^{2t} \wedge e^2 = y_1^{2t} h^{2r} \wedge v^2 = (y_2 y_3^{H(u,e,L)})^{2t} \tag{1}$$
$$\wedge \, \alpha = \gamma^r \wedge \ell = g_2^m h_2^s \wedge r \in [\rho]\} \; . \tag{2}$$

The verifiability aspect of the encryption scheme relies on the strong RSA assumption – namely that, given N_2 and $z \in \mathbb{Z}_{N_2}^*$, it is hard to find $x \in \mathbb{Z}_{N_2}^*$ and $e \geq 2$ such that $x^e = z \bmod N_2$. One could alternatively avoid using the third group Γ by setting requiring $N_2 < N2^{-k-k'-3}$, setting $a = g_2^r$, and prove the same equalities as above except those involving ℓ. Notice, however, that if we do use the third group, then the last proof simply becomes a group membership check.

3 Model and Definition of Designated Confirmer Signatures

We describe designated confirmer signatures (DCS) following the exposition of [17]. The model comprises three parties: a signer $\mathcal{S}$, a verifier $\mathcal{V}$, and a designated confirmer $\mathcal{C}$. A designated confirmer signature scheme supports the following (probabilistic polynomial-time) algorithms:

- DCGen: takes as input 1^λ, and outputs two pairs of keys $(\mathsf{SGk}_\mathcal{S}, \mathsf{VFk}_\mathcal{S})$ and $(\mathsf{Pk}_\mathcal{C}, \mathsf{Sk}_\mathcal{C})$. The first pair constitutes $\mathcal{S}$'s signing and verification keys, and the second consists of $\mathcal{C}$'s public and private keys. For simplicity of exposition we denote DCGen as a single algorithm; in an actual implementation, the signer and confirmer would generate their key pairs separately, using distinct algorithms SGen and CGen, so that $\mathcal{C}$ does not learn $\mathsf{SGk}_\mathcal{S}$ and $\mathcal{S}$ does not learn $\mathsf{Sk}_\mathcal{C}$.
- Sign: takes as input a message m and $\mathsf{SGk}_\mathcal{S}$. It outputs a signature σ such that $\mathsf{Verify}(m, \sigma, \mathsf{VFk}_\mathcal{S}) = \mathsf{Accept}$.
- Verify: takes as input $m, \sigma, \mathsf{VFk}_\mathcal{S}$ and outputs Accept if σ is an output of $\mathsf{Sign}(m, \mathsf{SGk}_\mathcal{S})$.

Further, a DCS scheme must support the following protocols:

- ConfirmedSign$_{(\mathcal{S},\mathcal{V})}$: an interactive protocol between $\mathcal{S}$ and $\mathcal{V}$ with common input $(m, \mathsf{VFk}_\mathcal{S}, \mathsf{Pk}_\mathcal{C})$. The output is a pair (b, σ') where $b \in \{\mathsf{Accept}, \perp\}$ and σ' is $\mathcal{S}$'s designated confirmer signature. For some $\mathcal{V}$, the ConfirmedSign protocol must be complete and sound. For completeness, we require that there is some $\mathcal{S}$ such that for any (valid) signer and confirmer keys, and for any message m, the ConfirmedSign protocol outputs a $(\mathsf{Accept}, \sigma')$ where $\mathsf{Verify}(m, \mathsf{Extract}(m, \sigma', \mathsf{Sk}_\mathcal{C}, \mathsf{VFk}_\mathcal{S}), \mathsf{VFk}_\mathcal{S}) = \mathsf{Accept}$. For soundness, we require that for all signers $\mathcal{S}'$, if the result of running ConfirmedSign results in an Accept, then

$$\Pr[\mathsf{Verify}(m, \mathsf{Extract}(m, \sigma', \mathsf{Sk}_\mathcal{C}, \mathsf{VFk}_\mathcal{S}), \mathsf{VFk}_\mathcal{S}) = \perp] < \mathsf{negl}(\lambda).$$

In other words, $\mathcal{S}'$ cannot convince $\mathcal{V}$ that an "un-extractable" designated verifier signature is valid.

- ReconfirmedSign$_{(S,V)}$: an interactive protocol between S and V with common input $(m, \mathsf{VFk}_S, \mathsf{Pk}_C, \sigma')$ for designated confirmer signature σ'. The output is $b \in \{\mathsf{Accept}, \bot\}$. The completeness and soundness requirements are similar to those of Confirm$_{C,V}$ below. In our scheme, the ReconfirmedSign protocol is identical to ConfirmedSign (except that ReconfirmedSign takes σ' as input) and to the Confirm protocol (except that a signer takes the place of the confirmer); so, we omit further discussion of ReconfirmedSign.
- Extract: takes as input $m, \sigma', \mathsf{Sk}_C, \mathsf{VFk}_S$ and returns a string σ such that Verify$(m, \sigma, \mathsf{VFk}_S)$ outputs Accept if σ is an output of Sign(m, SGk_S), and outputs $\bot$ otherwise.
- Confirm$_{(C,V)}$: an interactive protocol between C and V with common input $(m, \sigma', \mathsf{VFk}_S, \mathsf{Pk}_C)$. The output is $b \in \{\mathsf{Accept}, \bot\}$. The protocol must be both complete and sound. For completeness, we require that there is some C such that if Verify$(m, \mathsf{Extract}(m, \sigma', \mathsf{Sk}_C, \mathsf{VFk}_S), \mathsf{VFk}_S) = \mathsf{Accept}$ then $b = \mathsf{Accept}$. For soundness, we require that for all confirmers C' if

$$\mathsf{Verify}(m, \mathsf{Extract}(m, \sigma', \mathsf{Sk}_C, \mathsf{VFk}_S), \mathsf{VFk}_S) = \bot,$$

then $\Pr[\mathsf{Confirm}_{(C',V)}(m, \sigma', \mathsf{VFk}_S, \mathsf{Pk}_C) = \mathsf{Accept}] < \mathsf{negl}(\lambda)$.
- Disavowal$_{(C,V)}$: an interactive protocol between confirmer C and verifier V with common input $(m, \sigma', \mathsf{VFk}_S, \mathsf{Pk}_C)$. The output is $b \in \{\mathsf{Accept}, \bot\}$. The protocol must be complete and sound. For completeness, we require that there is a confirmer C such that if Verify$(m, \mathsf{Extract}(m, \sigma', \mathsf{Sk}_C, \mathsf{VFk}_S), \mathsf{VFk}_S) = \bot$ then Disavowal$_{(C,V)} = \mathsf{Accept}$. For soundness, we require that for all confirmers C', if Verify$(m, \mathsf{Extract}(m, \sigma', \mathsf{Sk}_C, \mathsf{VFk}_S), \mathsf{VFk}_S) = \mathsf{Accept}$, then $\Pr[\mathsf{Disavowal}_{(C',V)}(m, \sigma', \mathsf{VFk}_S, \mathsf{Pk}_C) = \mathsf{Accept}] < \mathsf{negl}(\lambda)$.

For the purposes of the security model, we also define OutputDCS$_{(S,V)}$, a two-move stunted version of ConfirmedSign$_{(S,V)}$ in which V queries m and S outputs a DCS σ' on m (without "confirming" its correctness).

We now state the security requirements of a DCS scheme in detail.

Definition 1. *Below, we assume that the adversary has access to a collection $\mathcal{O} = \{\mathsf{ConfirmedSign}_{(S,A)}, \mathsf{ReconfirmedSign}_{(S,A)}, \mathsf{Confirm}_{(C,A)}, \mathsf{Disavow}_{(C,A)}, \mathsf{Extract}_{(C,A)}\}$ of five oracles for: 1) receiving a confirmed signature on an message of its choice (via the ConfirmedSign$_{(S,A)}$ oracle); 2) executing the prover's role in the ReconfirmedSign$_{(S,A)}$ interactive protocol; 3) executing the prover's role in the Confirm$_{(C,A)}$ interactive protocol; 4) executing the prover's role in the Disavow$_{(C,A)}$ interactive protocol; and 5) extracting an ordinary signature from a designated confirmer signature.*

1. **Security for verifiers.** *Security for verifiers follows from the soundness requirement above – informally, that an adversary must not be able, even if the adversary compromises the private keys of S and C, to create a (m, σ') that will be confirmed (either in ConfirmedSign or Confirm) even though Verify$(m, \mathsf{Extract}(m, \sigma', \mathsf{Sk}_C, \mathsf{VFk}_S), \mathsf{VFk}_S) = \bot$ ("Case 1"), or that will be disavowed even though Verify$(m, \mathsf{Extract}(m, \sigma', \mathsf{Sk}_C, \mathsf{VFk}_S), \mathsf{VFk}_S) = \mathsf{Accept}$*

("Case 2"). Formally, we define the advantage of the adversary $\mathsf{Adv}^{\mathsf{fool}\mathcal{V}}(\mathcal{A}):=$ $\Pr[b_{\mathsf{fool}\mathcal{V}1} = 1 \vee b_{\mathsf{fool}\mathcal{V}2} = 1 \vee b_{\mathsf{fool}\mathcal{V}3} = 1]$, where $(b_{\mathsf{fool}\mathcal{V}1}, b_{\mathsf{fool}\mathcal{V}2}, b_{\mathsf{fool}\mathcal{V}3})$ are defined by the experiment in Figure 2. For compactness, use "Case 1" and "Case 2" to refer to the verification condition that the adversary's output (m, σ') must satisfy. We say a scheme is secure for verifiers if $\mathsf{Adv}^{\mathsf{fool}\mathcal{V}}(\mathcal{A}) <$ $\mathsf{negl}(\lambda)$ for all probabilistic polynomial time algorithms $\mathcal{A}$.

2. **Security for signers.** *Informally, an adversary should be able to create a DCS (m, σ'_0) that is extractable or confirmable (either in ConfirmedSign or Confirm) only if σ'_0 is somehow "equivalent" to a DCS (m, σ'_1) that it received in response to a ConfirmedSign query on m. We say (m, σ'_0) and (m, σ'_1) are equivalent if $R(m, \sigma'_0, \sigma'_1) = 1$ for some specified efficiently computable relation R. For example, if DCS signatures are strongly existentially unforgeable, it may be appropriate to say $R(m, \sigma'_0, \sigma'_1) = 1$ only when $\sigma'_0 = \sigma'_1$. However, R need not be that restrictive; it depends on the DCS scheme. In the experiment in Figure 2, L_{sig} is a list that is viewed as containing the (m, σ'_1) associated to the ConfirmedSign output, as well as all (m, σ') for which $R(m, \sigma', \sigma'_1) = 1$. In the figure, for compactness, we say (e.g.) $\sigma' \notin L_{sig}$ rather than the more accurate $(m, \sigma') \notin L_{sig}$, since m will be clear from the context. Formally, we define $\mathcal{A}$'s advantage $\mathsf{Adv}^{\mathsf{imp}\mathcal{S}}(\mathcal{A})$ to be the probability that the experiment returns 1. We say a scheme is secure for signers if $\mathsf{Adv}^{\mathsf{imp}\mathcal{S}}(\mathcal{A}) < \mathsf{negl}(\lambda)$ for all probabilistic polynomial time algorithms $\mathcal{A}$.*

3. **Transcript Simulatability.** *The confirmation or disavowal of a designated confirmer signature σ' should not be transferable – e.g., the transcript of a proof of knowledge in $\mathsf{Confirm}_{\mathcal{C}, \mathcal{V}_1}(m, \sigma', \mathsf{VFk}_{\mathcal{S}}, \mathsf{Pk}_{\mathcal{C}})$ should not convince $\mathcal{V}_2$ $(\neq \mathcal{V}_1)$ that σ' signs m. To ensure that $\mathcal{V}_1$'s transcript is unconvincing, we require that transcripts be simulatable. To model this in the experiment in Figure 2, first $\mathcal{A}_0$ outputs two messages m_0 and m_1 and some state s, next a DCS σ' on one of the messages is output, and then $\mathcal{A}_1$, $\mathcal{A}'_1$ and $\mathcal{A}_2$ play a game in which $\mathcal{A}'_1$ tries to make its output (when the DCS signs m_1) look indistinguishable from $\mathcal{A}_1$'s output (when the DCS signs m_0); $\mathcal{A}_2$ attempts to distinguish whether its input τ came from $\mathcal{A}_1$ or $\mathcal{A}'_1$. In the game, $\mathcal{A}_1$ gets almost complete access to the oracles $\mathcal{O}$; the only restriction is that $(m, \sigma') \notin L_{ext}$, where L_{ext} is a list that is viewed as containing each (m_i, σ'_i) that has been queried by $\mathcal{A}_1$ to the Extract oracle, as well all (m'_i, σ''_i) for which $R(m, \sigma'_i, \sigma''_i) = 1$; otherwise $\mathcal{A}_1$ could trivially give $\mathcal{A}_2$ indisputable proof that m_0 was signed – the extraction of σ'. On the other hand, we give $\mathcal{A}'_1$ very limited access to $\mathcal{O}$; it can make only q OutputDCS queries, where $\mathcal{A}_1$ makes at most q ConfirmedSign queries. We give $\mathcal{A}_2$ access to a limited set of oracles $\mathcal{O}_{lim}$ – specifically, $\mathcal{A}_2$ cannot make any $\mathcal{O}$ query on (m_0, σ'') if $R(m_0, \sigma', \sigma'') = 1$ or on (m_1, σ'') if $R(m_1, \sigma', \sigma'') = 1$; otherwise, its distinguishing task becomes trivial. If $\mathcal{A}_2$ has negligible advantage, this suggests that $\mathcal{A}_1$'s potentially authentic transcript that m_0 was signed is no more convincing or informative than $\mathcal{A}'_1$'s simulated transcript that (falsely) "proves" that m_0 was signed. In the security proof, $\mathcal{A}'_1$ will use $\mathcal{A}_1$ as a subroutine, and will simulate correct responses to $\mathcal{A}_1$'s $\mathcal{O}$ queries on σ' and equivalent*

Exp-NoFoolVerifier:
1. $(\mathsf{SGk}_S, \mathsf{VFk}_S, \mathsf{Sk}_C, \mathsf{Pk}_C) \leftarrow \mathsf{DCGen}(1^\lambda)$
2. $(m, \sigma_1', \tau_1, \tau_2, \tau_3) \leftarrow \mathcal{A}_0^\mathcal{O}(\pi, \mathsf{SGk}_S, \mathsf{Sk}_C)$
3. $(b_{\mathsf{fool}V1}, \sigma_0') \leftarrow \mathsf{ConfirmedSign}_{(\mathcal{A}_1(\tau_1), \mathcal{V})}(\pi, m)$ in Case 1
4. $b_{\mathsf{fool}V2} \leftarrow \mathsf{Confirm}_{(\mathcal{A}_2(\tau_2), \mathcal{V})}(\pi, m, \sigma_1')$ in Case 1
5. $b_{\mathsf{fool}V3} \leftarrow \mathsf{Disavowal}_{(\mathcal{A}_3(\tau_3), \mathcal{V})}(\pi, m, \sigma_1')$ in Case 2
6. Return $b_{\mathsf{fool}V1} \vee b_{\mathsf{fool}V2} \vee b_{\mathsf{fool}V3}$.

Exp-NoImpSigner:
1. $(\mathsf{SGk}_S, \mathsf{VFk}_S, \mathsf{Sk}_C, \mathsf{Pk}_C) \leftarrow \mathsf{DCGen}(1^\lambda)$
2. $(m, \sigma') \leftarrow \mathcal{A}^\mathcal{O}(\pi, \mathsf{Sk}_C)$
3. $b_{\mathsf{imp}S} \leftarrow \mathsf{Verify}(m, \sigma, \mathsf{VFk}_S)$
   for $\sigma = \mathsf{Extract}(m, \sigma', \mathsf{Sk}_C, \mathsf{VFk}_S)$
4. Return $(b_{\mathsf{imp}S} \wedge (\sigma' \notin L_{sig}))$.

Exp-TranscriptSimulatability:
1. $(\mathsf{SGk}_S, \mathsf{VFk}_S, \mathsf{Sk}_C, \mathsf{Pk}_C) \leftarrow \mathsf{DCGen}(1^\lambda)$
2. $(m_0, m_1, s) \leftarrow \mathcal{A}_0^\mathcal{O}(\pi, \mathsf{SGk}_S)$
3. $b \xleftarrow{R} \{0, 1\}$
4. $(\flat, \sigma') \leftarrow \mathsf{ConfirmedSign}_{(S, \mathcal{V})}(\pi, m_b)$
5. If $b = 0$, $\tau \leftarrow \mathcal{A}_1^\mathcal{O}(\flat, m_0, m_1, s, \sigma')$;
   else, $\tau \leftarrow \mathcal{A}_1'^{\mathsf{OutputDCS}}(\flat, m_0, m_1, s, \sigma')$
6. Return 1 iff $b = \mathcal{A}_2^{\mathcal{O}_{lim}}(m_0, m_1, \tau, \sigma')$
   and $\sigma' \notin L_{ext}$.

Fig. 2. Experiments for definition of DCS security. Above, π is shorthand for $(1^\lambda, \mathsf{VFk}_S, \mathsf{Pk}_C)$.

DCS's. Formally, we define the advantage of the adversary $\mathsf{Adv}^{\mathsf{trans}}(\mathcal{A})$ *to be* $\max\{0, \Pr[\text{experiment returns } 1] - 1/2\}$.

In our model, we allow that σ' may convince verifier $\mathcal{V}_2$ above that the signer indeed signed *some* message m. In this sense, the transcript is not perfectly simulatable; only the ZK proofs are. Accordingly, in the security model, $\mathcal{A}_1'$ needs access to ConfirmedSign; without *some* DCS's generated by $\mathcal{S}$, $\mathcal{A}_1'$ has no hope in our scheme of making its output indistinguishable from $\mathcal{A}_1$ (which has almost unrestricted access to $\mathcal{O}$). Thus, our model is weaker than that in [21]. However, we believe that our model, especially given our very efficient instantiation, is suitable for real-world settings, where it would be easy (e.g.) for the confirmer to publish a few "dummy" signatures by the signer during each time period to camouflage the presence or absence of a "real" (meaningful) signature. Again, we are inspired here by the discussion of Goldwasser and Waisbard [17], which emphasizes capturing only the "non-verifiability" of a DCS, although our definition differs from theirs.

HOW THE MODEL PREVENTS CONFIRMER IMPERSONATION. Of course, for a DCS scheme to be secure, it should be infeasible for an adversary $\mathcal{A}$ (even if it has SGk_S) to *impersonate the confirmer* by performing an Extract, Confirm, Disavowal, or ConfirmedSign associated to a pair (m, σ') contained in $L_{sig} \setminus L_{ext}$. Interestingly, this requirement is already covered by a combination of our Exp-NoFoolVerifier and Exp-TranscriptSimulatability experiments. For example, suppose that there is an adversary $(\mathcal{B}_0, \mathcal{B}_1, \mathcal{B}_2)$ that "breaks" Confirm in that $(m_0', s') \leftarrow \mathcal{B}_0^\mathcal{O}(\pi, \mathsf{SGk}_S)$, $(\sigma'', \tau') \leftarrow \mathcal{B}_1^\mathcal{O}(\pi, s')$, $\mathsf{Confirm}_{(\mathcal{B}_2(\tau'), \mathcal{V})}(\pi, m_0', \sigma'') = $ Accept for $(m_0', \sigma'') \in L_{sig} \setminus L_{ext}$ with non-negligible probability, where (s', τ')

is state information that is forwarded, and where B_1 makes only a polynomial number q of $\mathcal{O}$ queries. Then, $(\mathcal{A}_0, \mathcal{A}_1, \mathcal{A}_2)$ can use $(\mathcal{B}_0, \mathcal{B}_1, \mathcal{B}_2)$ to break Exp-TranscriptSimulatability with non-negligible probability, as follows. $\mathcal{A}_0$ runs $\mathcal{B}_0$, relays $\mathcal{B}_0$'s $\mathcal{O}$ queries and the responses, sets $m_0 = m_0'$ and outputs (m_0, m_1). If $b = 0$ in Exp-TranscriptSimulatability, $\mathcal{A}_1$ runs $\mathcal{B}_1$ and relays $\mathcal{B}_1$'s $\mathcal{O}$ queries and the responses, except that it responds to one of $\mathcal{B}_1$'s ConfirmedSign queries on m_0 by using a ReconfirmedSign query on (m_0, σ'). $\mathcal{B}_1$ outputs (σ'', τ') and $\mathcal{A}_1$ sets $\tau = \tau'$; σ'' is equivalent to σ' with probability at least $1/q$. Finally, if σ'' is equivalent to σ', $\mathcal{A}_2$ runs $\mathsf{Confirm}_{(\mathcal{B}_2(\tau), \mathcal{V})}(\pi, m_0, \sigma'')$. If the output is Accept, $\mathcal{A}_2$ outputs '0'; otherwise, it outputs a random bit. Since the output is Accept with non-negligible probability, and since an output of Accept implies $\mathsf{Verify}(m', \mathsf{Extract}(m', \sigma', \mathsf{Sk}_C, \mathsf{VFk}_S), \mathsf{VFk}_S) = \mathsf{Accept}$ with overwhelming probability assuming $\mathsf{Adv}^{\mathsf{fool}\mathcal{V}}(\mathcal{A}) < \mathsf{negl}(\lambda)$, $\mathcal{A}_2$'s advantage is non-negligible.

Using the approach above, one can show that, for any (m_0', m_1') adaptively chosen by $\mathcal{B}_0$, $\mathcal{B}_1$ has a negligible probability of outputing a DCS σ'' on m_0' that $\mathcal{B}_2$ can disavow on m_1'. However, for the special case of Disavowal, one may want to require something stronger: that for any m_0' adaptively chosen by $\mathcal{B}_0$, $\mathcal{B}_1$ has a negligible probability of outputing an m_1' and a DCS σ'' on m_0' that $\mathcal{B}_2$ can disavow on m_1'. *Our scheme satisfies this requirement*, but it may not be necessary in general. If the message space is super-polynomial, and if a verifier $\mathcal{V}$ could merely check that m_1' was generate randomly and independently of (m_0', σ''), it would already believe that the probability that σ'' is a DCS on m_1' is negligible. Thus, it does not seem unreasonable to allow that $(\mathcal{B}_1, \mathcal{B}_2)$ may be able to disavow *some* message with respect to a DCS σ'' in $L_{sig} \setminus L_{ext}$ on m_0'. It is an open question whether a more efficient DCS exists that meets the weaker requirement.

4 Our Transformation

THE GENERIC CONSTRUCTION. We first describe a generic scheme that transforms any traditional signature scheme into a DCS scheme; the transformation also requires an IND-CCA2 secure encryption scheme and a statistically-hiding computationally-binding commitment scheme C. The scheme also uses zero knowledge proofs secure against cheating verifiers, as discussed in Section 2. After describing our scheme generically, we provide an efficient instantiation.

- DCGen: $\mathcal{S}$ uses a secure digital signature scheme $\mathsf{DSS} = (\mathsf{SGen}, \mathsf{Sign}, \mathsf{Verify})$, and creates a key pair $(\mathsf{VFk}_S, \mathsf{SGk}_S) \leftarrow \mathsf{SGen}(1^\lambda)$. C uses an IND-CCA-2 encryption scheme $\mathsf{PKE} = (\mathsf{CGen}, \mathsf{Enc}, \mathsf{Dec})$, and creates key pair $(\mathsf{Pk}_C, \mathsf{Sk}_C) \leftarrow \mathsf{Gen}(1^\lambda)$. Note that C need not participate in any setup other than creating and publishing a key pair.
- Sign: To sign a message m with auxiliary information c, $\mathcal{S}$ creates a statistically hiding and computationally binding commitment $\psi = C(m, r)$ to the message m using randomness r and creates $\sigma^* = \mathsf{Sign}((\psi, c, \mathsf{VFk}_S), \mathsf{SGk}_S)$. The basic signature is $\sigma = (\sigma^*, c, r)$. $\mathcal{S}$'s verification key VFk_S is signed

together with the commitment to prevent a signature issued by one signer from being fed to the Confirm oracle with a different signer's public key.

- ConfirmedSign: In addition to the above steps in the Sign procedure, S also computes the ciphertext $c = \mathsf{Enc}(\mathsf{Pk}_C, r)$. The designated confirmer signature is $\sigma' = (\sigma^*, \psi, c)$ for $\sigma^* = \mathsf{Sign}((\psi, c, \mathsf{VFk}_S), \mathsf{SGk}_S)$. The signer also performs a ZK proof of knowledge of a value r such that $\psi = C(m, r)$ and $c = \mathsf{Enc}(\mathsf{Pk}_C, r)$.

- Confirm: C first checks that $(\psi, c, \mathsf{VFk}_S)$ has been signed with SGk_S using the provided VFk_S, and aborts if the check fails. Then, C performs a ZK proof of knowledge of a value r such $\psi = C(m, r)$.

- Disavow: To disavow a purported signature $\sigma' = (\sigma^*, \psi, c)$ on message m, C does the following. C first checks if c is a valid encryption of some r. If not, it performs a ZK proof of knowledge that the string is not a well-formed encryption. Otherwise, C computes $r' = \mathsf{Dec}(\mathsf{Sk}_C, c)$. If $\psi \neq C(m, r')$, then C provides a ZKPoK of a value ρ such that $\psi \neq C(m, \rho)$ and $\rho = \mathsf{Dec}(\mathsf{Sk}_C, c)$.

- Extract: On input $\sigma' = (\sigma^*, \psi, c)$ and m, C computes $r' = \mathsf{Dec}(\mathsf{Sk}_C, c)$ and confirms that $\psi = C(m, r')$ and $\sigma^* = \mathsf{Sign}((\psi, c, \mathsf{VFk}_S), \mathsf{SGk}_S)$. If so, it outputs r'; else, it outputs $\perp$.

Notice that all the statements involving zero-knowledge proofs can be expressed as NP statements (and have a short witness). Therefore, we can, in theory, instantiate the above scheme in polynomial time for any suitably secure encryption scheme, commitment scheme, and signature scheme. Of course using generic zero-knowledge proofs for NP-statements is not very practical. Therefore, we now describe how to instantiate the encryption and commitment schemes so that the resulting zero-knowledge proofs of knowledge are simple and efficient.

EFFICIENT INSTANTIATION FOR ANY SIGNATURE SCHEME. We show how to efficiently instantiate the above scheme. The underlying encryption scheme PKE is the scheme by Camenisch and Shoup discussed in Section 2. The commitment scheme $C(m, r)$ will be a Pedersen-type commitment scheme over group Γ of prime order ρ, with generators γ and δ, as described in Section 2. We can use any secure signature scheme. Then, our confirm and disavow protocols use the CDM ZK proofs as described in Section 2. With these choices, the underlying zero-knowledge proofs are efficient (using the CDM techniques for proving equality and inequality of discrete logarithms together with the Camenisch-Shoup verifiable encryption of the randomness used for the Pedersen commitment). Moreover, we can plug in *any* secure signature scheme and the complexity of the Confirm, Disavow, and Extract are essentially independent of this choice.

SECURITY ANALYSIS. We now state a theorem that our generic transformation yields a secure designated confirmer signature scheme. We require that the signature schemes be existentially unforgeable under chosen message attack, that our commitment schemes be hiding and binding, and the encryption scheme be secure against chosen ciphertext attack. The security for our efficient Paillier-based instantiation follows.

Theorem 1. *Let* DSS = (SGen, Sign, Verify) *be any signature scheme existentially unforgeable against chosen message attack, and let* PKE = (Gen, Enc, Dec) *be any IND-CCA2 secure encryption scheme and* $C(M, r)$ *be any statistically-hiding computationally-binding commitment scheme with perfect zero-knowledge proofs of knowledge for committed values secure against cheating verifiers. Then the DCS scheme obtained by our generic conversion is a secure DCS scheme.*

Proof. (Sketch). In this proof, we say that the relation $R(m, \sigma', \sigma'')$ equals 1 in our scheme if $\sigma' = (\sigma^*, \psi, c)$, $\sigma'' = (\sigma^{*\prime}, \psi', c')$, and $(\psi, c) = (\psi', c')$; otherwise, it equals 0. Also, below, a second algorithm (say, $\mathcal{B}$) will construct the necessary zero knowledge proofs in response to to $\mathcal{A}$'s $\mathcal{O}$ queries by using a (possibly rewinding) simulator. For example, assuming we use the CDM protocol [13] for our ZK proofs, $\mathcal{B}$ proceeds as follows: upon receiving $\mathcal{A}$'s commitment to its value e together with a proof of knowledge of e, $\mathcal{B}$ extracts e by using the knowledge extractor E together with $\mathcal{A}$. Then $\mathcal{B}$ can complete Part 2 of the CDM protocol by using its knowledge of e. As Cramer et al. argue, B's proof in Part 2 is witness indistinguishable; so, $\mathcal{B}$'s simulation is sound.

Now, suppose the theorem is false. Then there exists a probabilistic polynomial time adversary $\mathcal{A}$ that can break the security of the DCS scheme. Specifically, at least one of $\mathsf{Adv}^{\mathsf{impS}}(\mathcal{A})$, $\mathsf{Adv}^{\mathsf{impC}}(\mathcal{A})$, $\mathsf{Adv}^{\mathsf{foolV}}(\mathcal{A})$, or $\mathsf{Adv}^{\mathsf{trans}}(\mathcal{A})$ is not negligible in the security parameter. We consider the resulting cases.

THE $\mathsf{Adv}^{\mathsf{impS}}(\mathcal{A})$ CASE. If $\mathsf{Adv}^{\mathsf{impS}}(\mathcal{A})$ is not negligible, then the adversary has a non-negligible probability of successfully outputting a DCS (m, σ') for which $\mathsf{Verify}(m, \mathsf{Extract}(m, \sigma', \mathsf{Sk}_C, \mathsf{VFk}_S), \mathsf{VFk}_S) = \mathsf{Accept}$ and $\sigma' \notin L_{sig}$. From $\mathcal{A}$, we can construct an algorithm $\mathcal{B}$ that either constructs an existential forgery of the underlying signature scheme, or violates the binding property of the commitment scheme as follows.

The algorithm $\mathcal{B}$ generates $(\mathsf{Sk}_C, \mathsf{Pk}_C)$ and gives (π, Sk_C) to $\mathcal{A}$. Then $\mathcal{B}$ responds to $\mathcal{A}$'s ConfirmedSign query on a message m' by choosing a random r', setting $\psi = C(m', r')$, generating an appropriate ciphertext c that encrypts r', and then using its oracle access to Sign to obtain a signature on (ψ, c). For Confirm, Extract and Disavowal queries, $\mathcal{B}$ uses Sk_C. Suppose that $\mathcal{A}$ outputs a pair (m, σ') with $\sigma' = (\sigma^*, \psi,)$ with $(m, \sigma') \notin L_{sig}$. $\mathcal{B}$ uses Sk_C to perform Extract on σ', thereby obtaining $\sigma = (\sigma^*, r, c)$. If $(m', \sigma') \in L_{sig}$ for some m', then $\mathcal{B}$ must have responded to $\mathcal{A}$'s ConfirmedSign query on m' by generating a random r' for which $\psi = C(m', r') = C(m, r)$; since $m' \neq m$, this violates the binding property of the commitment scheme. Otherwise, if there is no message m' for which $(m', \sigma') \in L_{sig}$, $\mathcal{B}$ outputs σ as an existential forgery of the signature scheme (on the message $(\psi, c, \mathsf{VFk}_S)$).

THE $\mathsf{Adv}^{\mathsf{impC}}(\mathcal{A})$ CASE. Suppose that $\mathsf{Adv}^{\mathsf{impC}}(\mathcal{A})$ is not negligible. Then, from $\mathcal{A}$, we can construct an algorithm $\mathcal{B}$ that breaks the chosen-ciphertext security of the underlying encryption scheme.

The algorithm $\mathcal{B}$ runs as follows. It picks two random messages r_0 and r_1 for the "find" stage of the encryption game, and receives a challenge ciphertext $\mathsf{Enc}(r_b)$ for a random b. Then $\mathcal{B}$ runs $\mathcal{A}$ as a subroutine. $\mathcal{B}$ responds to $\mathcal{A}$'s Extract queries by using its access to the decryption oracle of the encryption scheme.

Then $\mathcal{B}$ responds to *one* of $\mathcal{A}$'s q ConfirmedSign queries by flipping a coin b', setting $\psi = C(m, r_{b'})$ and $c = \mathsf{Enc}(r_b)$, querying the Sign oracle for a signature σ^* on $(\psi, c, \mathsf{VFk}_S)$, and setting $\sigma' = (\sigma^*, \psi, c)$. To construct a (potentially false) "proof" that the $r_{b'}$ embedded in ψ is identical to the r_b embedded in c, $\mathcal{B}$ uses the simulator $S^{\mathcal{A}}$ for the ZK proof of knowledge of r_b, treating the adversary as a cheating verifier. Because the ZK proof of knowledge is complete and because the transcripts output by the simulator are identically distributed to the interaction between the real prover and the adversary, the adversary will accept the "proof."

For *other* ConfirmedSign queries by $\mathcal{A}$, $\mathcal{B}$ acts as follows: $\mathcal{B}$ generates a random r as in the actual scheme, sets $\psi = C(m, r)$ and $c = \mathsf{Enc}(r)$, and queries the Sign oracle for a signature σ^* on $(\psi, c, \mathsf{VFk}_S)$; it responds with (σ^*, ψ, c) and the appropriate proofs of knowledge.

$\mathcal{B}$ responds to a Confirm or Disavowal query on $(\sigma^*, \psi, c, \mathsf{VFk}_S, m)$ by determining whether σ^* is a valid signature on $(\psi, c, \mathsf{VFk}_S)$.

If so, and if $\mathcal{B}$ has not queried $(\psi, c, \mathsf{VFk}_S)$ to the Sign oracle, $\mathcal{B}$ aborts. If $(\psi, c, \mathsf{VFk}_S)$ has already been signed, then $\mathcal{B}$ recovers its log of the action it performed in the ConfirmedSign query corresponding to $(\psi, c, \mathsf{VFk}_S)$; in particular, it recovers the values of (r', m') that it used to generate ψ. Then, if $m = m'$ (and Confirm is therefore appropriate), it proves (using a "false" proof via the simulator, if necessary) that this value of r' is encrypted in c. Analogously, if $m \neq m'$ (and Disavowal is therefore appropriate), $\mathcal{B}$ can provide a proof of knowledge of an r' such that r' is encrypted in c and $C(m, r') \neq \psi$.

Eventually, with non-negligible probability, $\mathcal{A}$ outputs some $(m, \sigma') \in L_{sig} \setminus L_{ext}$. Let $\sigma' = (\sigma^*, \psi, c)$. If $\mathcal{A}$ performs a successful Confirm, Disavowal or ConfirmedSign using (m, σ'), $\mathcal{B}$ uses $\mathcal{A}$ together with the knowledge extractor E to extract the value r encrypted in c. Now there are two cases. In the first case, $c = \mathsf{Enc}(r_b)$ – i.e., the challenge ciphertext for $\mathcal{B}$ – with probability negligibly close to $1/q$. Notice that because the zero-knowledge proof is perfect zero-knowledge, the use of the simulator to construct proofs does not affect this probability. If $c = \mathsf{Enc} r_b$, then $\mathcal{B}$ outputs b as its guess; otherwise, $\mathcal{B}$ selects b uniformly at random. In the second case, $c \neq \mathsf{Enc}(r_b)$. In this case, we can violate the soundness of the underlying ZKPoK: the execution of Confirm or ConfirmedSign on c constitutes an interaction that violates soundness of the proof of knowledge.

THE $\mathsf{Adv}^{\mathsf{trans}}$ CASE. We construct $\mathcal{A}'_1$ by using $\mathcal{A}_1$ as a subroutine; later, we show that if $\mathcal{A}_2$ can distinguish which output came from $\mathcal{A}_1$, this violates the IND-CCA2 security of the encryption scheme.

We construct $\mathcal{A}'_1$ as follows. To generate τ, $\mathcal{A}'_1$ runs $\mathcal{A}_1$ on input (m_1, s, σ'). $\mathcal{A}'_1$ responds to $\mathcal{A}_1$'s permitted $\mathcal{O}$ queries by using its access to $\mathcal{O}$. For Confirm queries on (m_1, σ') (or on (m_1, σ'_1) for which $R(m_1, \sigma', \sigma'_1) = 1$) and disavowal queries on (m_0, σ') (or equivalent DCS's), $\mathcal{A}'_1$ uses the rewinding technique to construct the needed (false) ZK proofs. Eventually, $\mathcal{A}_1$ outputs a string τ'; $\mathcal{A}'_1$ outputs $\tau = \tau'$ and terminates. Let $1/2 + \epsilon_0$ be the probability that $\mathcal{A}_2$ outputs b when $\mathcal{A}'_1$ generates its output in this manner.

Now, consider the following modified experiment ModExp, whose only difference from the experiment in Figure 2 is that we replace $\mathcal{A}_1$ with $\mathcal{A}_1''$. We construct $\mathcal{A}_1''$ as follows. To generate τ, $\mathcal{A}_1''$ runs $\mathcal{A}_1$ on input (m_0, s, σ'). $\mathcal{A}_1''$ responds to $\mathcal{A}_1$'s permitted $\mathcal{O}$ queries by using its access to $\mathcal{O}$. For Confirm queries on (m_0, σ') (or equivalent DCS's) and disavowal queries on (m_1, σ') (or equivalent DCS's), $\mathcal{A}_1''$ uses the simulator to construct the needed ZK proofs. Eventually, $\mathcal{A}_1$ outputs a string τ'; $\mathcal{A}_1''$ outputs $\tau = \tau'$ and terminates. Let $1/2 + \epsilon_1$ be the probability that $\mathcal{A}_2$ outputs b when $\mathcal{A}_1''$ generates its output in this manner.

The only difference between the two experiments is $\mathcal{A}_1$'s view; in ModExp, $\mathcal{A}_1$ obtains simulated proofs of true statements in response to its Confirm query on (m_0, σ') and disavowal query on (m_1, σ'). Thus, if $|\epsilon_0 - \epsilon_1|$ is non-negligible, then $\mathcal{A}_2$ distinguishes interactions with the simulator from interactions with the true prover, contradicting the zero-knolwedge property of the ZK proofs.

The only difference between the algorithms $\mathcal{A}_1'$ and $\mathcal{A}_1''$ in ModExp is that the former simulates a (false) Confirm on (m_1, σ'), while the latter simulates a true Confirm (and similarly for Disavowal queries). Thus, if $|\epsilon_1|$ is non-negligible, an adversary $\mathcal{B}$ can use $(\mathcal{A}_0, \mathcal{A}_1, \mathcal{A}_1', \mathcal{A}_1'')$ to break the IND-CCA2 security of the encryption scheme. Specifically, $\mathcal{B}$ runs $(\mathcal{A}_0, \mathcal{A}_1, \mathcal{A}_1', \mathcal{A}_1'')$ and obtains the messages m_0 and m_1. Then $\mathcal{B}$ selects m_0 and m_1 in the find stage of the IND-CCA2 encryption game. Finally, $\mathcal{B}$ guesses the bit b. We see that if $|\epsilon_1|$ is non-negligible, then $\mathcal{B}$ wins the encryption game with non-negligible probability.

THE $\mathsf{Adv}^{\mathsf{foolV}}(\mathcal{A})$ CASE. Finally, if $\mathsf{Adv}^{\mathsf{foolV}}(\mathcal{A})$ is not negligible, then the adversary can generate fake valid zero-knowledge proofs with non-negligible probability, violating soundness.

5   Evaluation

OUR EFFICIENT INSTANTIATION. For our efficient instantiation, Confirm requires proving equality of discrete logarithms, specifically proving knowledge of an r such that $\frac{e}{u^{x_1}}^2 = \gamma$. This can be accomplished using protocols of Chaum and Pedersen in four exponentiations. To achieve general-verifier ZK, the techniques of Cramer et al. result in a 4-round protocol with 10 total exponentiations [8,13].

The Disavow protocol requires proving inequality of discrete logarithms, which we do by using the techniques of Camenisch and Shoup [6]. From the Preliminaries, the resulting proof consists of five clauses, four of which prove statements about discrete logarithms and the final clause shows that a committed value r is in a specified range. Because we work over a group with public prime order and the range is just the order of the group, the range test reduces to a simple group membership test costing one exponentiation. For the other four clauses, we can apply the optimized protocol of Cramer et al. to obtain general-verifier ZK at the cost of 4 rounds and 10 exponentiations per clause; with sequential composition this gives us 16 total rounds and 41 total exponentiations. We remark that a more efficient protocol appears possible by using the results of Cramer et al. on monotone composition of SHVZK protocols, but this result is already better than a generic zero-knowledge proof [13].

COMPARISON TO GOLDWASSER-WAISBARD. Both our approach and Goldwasser-Waisbard use a weakened definition of designated confirmer signatures which requires non-verifiability of unconfirmed signatures. Goldwasser-Waisbard use this weakening to explore strong witness hiding proofs of knowledge (WHPOKs) for Confirm protocols, and we use this weakening to explore a different way of creating designated confirmer signatures [17].

While the strong WHPOKs constructed by Goldwasser and Waisbard are more efficient than generic zero-knowledge proofs, they still require substantial practical overhead. For example, the strong WHPOK described for the case of Cramer-Shoup signatures uses a zero-knowledge proof of knowledge (ZKPOK) of an ith root as a subroutine. Each such proof of an ith root requires an exponentiation; with the suggested parameters this uses a 161-bit exponent. Two proofs are needed for the WHPOK, which then must be repeated λ times to reduce the soundness error. As a result, Confirm requires 2λ exponentiations. Further, Disavow still requires a generic ZKPOK; Goldwasser and Waisbard note that there appears to be no easy way to extend their approach to obtain an efficient Disavow, since it is not clear what witness is supposed to be "hidden." The efficiency requirements for the strong WHPOK exhibited for the GMR and Gennaro-Halevi-Rabin signatures are similar. While Goldwasser and Waisbard do exhibit a more efficient WHPOK for the case of RSA signatures, the resulting DCS signatures are existentially forgeable.

Our Confirm, in contrast, requires 10 exponentiations. Further, our Disavow protocol is more efficient than the generic ZKPOK used by Goldwasser-Waisbard, although less efficient than Confirm. Finally, our protocols are zero-knowledge instead of witness-hiding.

The main advantage of Goldwasser-Waisbard is that they have exhibited efficient strong WHPOK using the same assumptions as the underlying signature scheme. Our approach, in contrast, requires the "extra" composite residuosity assumption for the Paillier scheme. We note, however, that for each new signature scheme, new effort must be exerted to find efficient strong WHPOK without adding new assumptions. Conversely, one could look for protocols in our framework that require different assumptions for Confirm and Disavow. For example, if one were willing to live with an inefficient Disavow , we could replace the Camenisch-Shoup encryption with an arbitrary IND-CCA2 scheme and construct an efficient Confirm assuming only hardness of discrete logarithms.

COMPARISON TO CAMENISCH-MICHELS. Camenisch and Michels give a generic scheme for constructing designated confirmer signatures. They propose a specific instantiation with RSA signatures and Cramer-Shoup encryption [4]. Security for the underlying RSA signature is achieved by using full-domain hash, so the resulting scheme has a proof of security only in the Random Oracle model. Their Confirm protocol requires proving 12 statements regarding equalities and proofs that committed numbers are in a specific interval, while their Disavow protocol has 20 such statements. They note in their Remark 4 that because these proofs involve double discrete logarithms the verifier uses only binary challenges. As a result, the proof must be repeated λ times for soundness [4]. We optimistically estimate that each clause takes 3 exponentiations, leading to a total of 36λ exponentiations for Confirm and 60λ for Disavow.

COMPARISON TO CAMENISCH-SHOUP. In their paper on verifiable encryption, Camenisch and Shoup observe that, following Asokan et al., a designated confirmer Schnorr signature can be created where Confirm requires proving only a single equality of discrete logarithms [6,1]. The details are due to appear in a forthcoming paper. Because this paper is not yet available, we speculate on the details to make a reasonable comparison to our work. Let (γ, γ^x) be a public key for a Schnorr signature, where γ is a generator of a group G and x is the secret key. Then a Schnorr signature on m is the triple (β, c, s), where $\beta = \gamma^r$ for a random r, $c = H(\beta, m)$, and $s = r + xc \bmod \rho$, for ρ the order of G. The DCS Schnorr output is then the 4-tuple (β, c, δ, ψ), where $\delta = \gamma^s$ and ψ is an encryption of s with the confirmer's public key. Anyone can check that $\delta = \beta\gamma^c$ to verify the consistency of the signature. Then the confirmer need only prove or disprove that $\psi = E(\log_\gamma \delta)$ to Confirm or Disavow.

In this special case, the Camenisch-Shoup approach is as efficient as our scheme for Confirm and Disavow; indeed, we use their protocols for proving inequality of discrete logarithms. Unfortunately, the Schnorr scheme requires random oracles, so as sketched the approach does not produce a scheme with a proof in the standard model.

If we review the Cramer-Shoup, Goldwasser-Micali-Rivest, and Gennaro-Halevi-Rabin signature schemes with proofs of security in the standard model, then we see that these schemes do not appear to have the same reduction as Schnorr from validity to equality of discrete logarithms. For example, Cramer-Shoup requires proving knowledge of an i'th root, which does not translate straightforwardly to a statement about equality of discrete logarithms. In contrast, our use of a commitment adds a "layer of indirection" that allows us to achieve efficiency for every signature scheme. As a result, we can use any of these signature schemes to obtain an efficient designated confirmer signature with a proof in the standard model.

Finally, we note that the Camenisch-Shoup approach requires, as we do, a Paillier-type encryption and the associated composite residuosity assumption for efficient implementation. Therefore both their approach and ours require possibly introducing extra assumptions beyond those of the underlying signature scheme.

6   Conclusion

We have shown that weakening the definition of designated confirmer signatures, as suggested by Goldwasser and Waisbard, can yield a big payoff in the efficiency of generic designated confirmer signature schemes. By using a commitment scheme to add a "layer of indirection," we used the techniques of Camenisch and Shoup to exhibit efficient Confirm and Disavow protocols for any underlying signature scheme. Going further, we could look for commitment schemes and efficient protocols based on different assumptions. For example, can we adapt the techniques of Camenisch and Lysyanskaya [5] to obtain an even more efficient instantiation based on bilinear mappings? We could also investigate the strong witness hiding proofs of knowledge approach of Goldwasser and Waisbard with an eye towards weakening the assumptions required for efficient instantiation.

Acknowledgments

We thank Phil MacKenzie for his careful review and assistance. We thank Jan Camenisch for answering our questions regarding Schnorr designated confirmer signatures. We also thank the anonymous referees for useful comments. This work was carried out while David Molnar was visiting NTT DoCoMo Labs USA.

References

1. N. Asokan and V. Shoup and M. Waidner. "Optimistic fair exchange of digital signatures." IEEE Journal on Selected Areas in Communications 18 (2000) no. 4 591-610.
2. M. Bellare and P. Rogaway. Random oracles are practical: A paradigm for designing efficient protocols. *ACM CCS 1993.*
3. M. Bellare and O. Goldreich. On defining proofs of knowledge. In CRYPTO '92. Lecture Notes in Computer Science, no. 740 390-420.
4. J. Camenisch and M. Michels. "Confirmer Signature Schemes Secure Against Adaptive Adversaries." *EUROCRYPT 2000.*
5. J. Camenisch and A. Lysyanskaya. "Signature Schemes and Anonymous Credentials from Bilinear Maps." *CRYPTO 2004.*
6. J. Camenisch, V. Shoup. "Practical Verifable Encryption and Decryption of Discrete Logarithms" *CRYPTO 2003.* Full version available from www.shoup.net.
7. D. Chaum "Designated Confirmer Signatures," *EUROCRYPT 1994.*
8. D. Chaum and T. P. Pedersen "Wallet Databases with Observers." *CRYPTO 1992.*
9. D. Chaum and H. Van Antwerpen. Undeniable Signatures. *CRYPTO 1989.*
10. R. Cramer and V. Shoup "Signature Schemes Based on the Strong RSA Assumption" *ACM CCS 1999.*
11. I. Damgard. "Efficient concurrent zero-knowledge in the auxiliary string model." *EUROCRYPT 2000.*
12. R. Cramer and V. Shoup. "A Practical Public Key Cryptosystem Provably Secure Against Adaptive Chosen Message Attack." *CRYPTO 1998.*
13. R. Cramer, I. Damgard and V. Shoup. "Efficient Zero-Knowledge Proofs of Knowledge without Intractability Assumptions." *PKC 2000.*
14. R. Gennaro, S. Halevi, and T. Rabin. "Secure Hash-and-Sign Signatures Without the Random Oracle." *Proc. EUROCRYPT 1999.*
15. O. Goldreich and A. Kahan. "How to Construct Constant-Round Zero-Knowledge Proof Systems for NP." *Journal of Cryptology,* 9(3):167–189.
16. S. Goldwasser, S. Micali, and R. Rivest. "A Digital Signature Scheme Secure Against Adaptive Chosen Message Attacks." *SICOMP Vol 17, No 2, April 1988,* pp. 281–308.

17. S. Goldwasser and E. Waisbard. "Transformation of Digital Signature Schemes into Designated Confirmer Signature Schemes," *Theory of Cryptography Conference, 2004.*
18. M. Jakobsson, K. Sako, R. Impagliazzo. "Designated Verifier Proofs and Their Applications." *EUROCRYPT 1996.*
19. R. Cramer, I. Damgard, and B. Schoenmakers. Proofs of partial knowledge and simplified design of witness hiding protocols. *CRYPTO 1994.*
20. M. Naor and M. Yung. "Public-key cryptosystems provably secure against chosen ciphertext attacks." *STOC 1990.*
21. T. Okamoto "Designated Confirmer Signatures and Public Key Encryption Are Equivalent," *CRYPTO 1994.*
22. P. Paillier. "Public-key cryptosystems based on composite degree residue classes." *EUROCRYPT 1999.*
23. T. P. Pedersen. "A threshold cryptosystem without a trusted third party." *EURO-CRYPT 1991.*
24. C. P. Schnorr. "Efficient Identification and Signatures for Smart Cards." *CRYPTO 1989.*
25. A. Shamir, Y. Tauman "Improved Online-Offline Signature Schemes," *CRYPTO 2001.*
26. M. Michels and M. Stadler. "Generic constructions for secure and efficient confirmer signature schemes." *EUROCRYPT 1998.*
27. J. Garay and P. MacKenzie and K. Yang "Strengthening Zero-Knowledge Protocols Using Signatures." EUROCRYPT 2003, LNCS 2656, pp. 177–194
28. P. MacKenzie and K. Yang. "On Simulation-Sound Trapdoor Commitments." EU-ROCRYPT 2004, LNCS 3027, pp. 382–400.

Universally Convertible Directed Signatures

Fabien Laguillaumie[1,3], Pascal Paillier[2], and Damien Vergnaud[1]

[1] Laboratoire de Mathématiques Nicolas Oresme,
Université de Caen, Campus II, B.P. 5186,
14032 Caen Cedex, France,
{laguillaumie, vergnaud}@math.unicaen.fr
[2] Gemplus Card International, Cryptography Group,
34, rue Guynemer, 92447 Issy-les-Moulineaux Cedex, France
pascal.paillier@gemplus.com
[3] Projet TANC - INRIA Futurs,
Laboratoire d'informatique (LIX),
École polytechnique, 91128 Palaiseau cedex, France

Abstract. Many variants of Chaum and van Antwerpen's undeniable signatures have been proposed to achieve specific properties desired in real-world applications of cryptography. Among them, *directed signatures* were introduced by Lim and Lee in 1993. Directed signatures differ from the well-known confirmer signatures in that the signer has the simultaneous abilities to confirm, deny and individually convert a signature. The *universal* conversion of these signatures has remained an open problem since their introduction in 1993. This paper provides a positive answer to this quest by showing a very efficient design for universally convertible directed signatures (UCDS) both in terms of computational complexity and signature size. Our construction relies on the so-called *xyz*-trick applicable to bilinear map groups. We define proper security notions for UCDS schemes and show that our construction is secure in the random oracle model, under computational assumptions close to the CDH and DDH assumptions. Finally, we introduce and realize *traceable* universally convertible directed signatures where a master tracing key allows to link signatures to their direction.

1 Introduction

Digital signatures were introduced to identify the source of digital data. In particular they are *non-repudiable* and *universally verifiable*. For centuries, seals and handwritten signatures were attached to documents to indicate the issuer's identity. To determinate the authenticity of this identity, the *original scripts* have to be validated in some sense. In the electronic world, however, the ease of recopy and thereby distribution of digital signatures associated to the *self-authenticating* property may pose a serious threat to the signer's privacy. The concept of *undeniable signature* was first addressed at Crypto'89 by Chaum and van Antwerpen [12]. These signatures have the appealing property that a purported signature cannot be checked without the cooperation of the signer and cannot be denied if the latter has indeed generated the signature. They have

B. Roy (Ed.): ASIACRYPT 2005, LNCS 3788, pp. 682–701, 2005.

found numerous applications in applied cryptography, but the obvious problem with this idea is that in any setting where the signer becomes unavailable, nothing can be determined. Hence, Boyar, Chaum, Damgård and Pedersen [7] proposed *convertible undeniable signatures* which provide the additional feature of converting (individually or universally) the undeniable signatures to ordinary signatures. Another approach has produced various flavors of undeniable signatures which may also be verified by interacting with an entity which has been designated by the signer. *Directed signatures* introduced in 1993 by Lim and Lee [21], *(designated) confirmer signatures* [11], or *limited verifier signatures* [1] are among the best known examples. All of them, which we gather under the generic name of *delegated undeniable signatures*, guarantee to the recipient of a signature the ability to verify it, even when the signer cannot (or refuses to) do so. Directed signatures find a prominent application in the realization of complete peer-to-peer secure messaging systems and are a powerful tool to devise protocols for contract signing [2] or verifiable signature sharing [15]. They propose an individual conversion operation, but up to now *none of them* provides a mechanism for *universal* conversion[1].

From a formal point of view, directed signatures and confirmer signatures are quite similar, the only notable difference, apart from the signer's ability to convert signatures, being the real-world applications the authors had in mind. In brief, a universally convertible directed signature scheme enjoys the following properties. Assuming a signer A and a confirmer B, seen as registered users of the system, A produces signatures that only B (and A her/himself) can verify. Signatures of that type are called (A, B)-directed signatures. Now both A and B have the ability to

- prove in a non-transferable way the validity or invalidity of an (A, B)-directed signature to any other party.
- convert a given (A, B)-directed signature into a regular, universally verifiable signature. This operation does not affect other (A, B)-directed signatures and is carried out independently of the signed message.
- publish a universal trapdoor $\mathcal{T}$ by the means of which all (A, B)-directed signatures become universally verifiable. The trapdoor has no impact whatsoever on (A', B')-directed signatures for $(A', B') \neq (A, B)$.

These operations are independent and performed concurrently, meaning that A and B do not have to interact with each other to achieve either one of these operations.

The literature on confirmer signatures is inconsistent on whether the signer is able to confirm and/or deny signatures. In the recent formalization of confirmer signatures [9,17], in order to protect the signer from a coercer, this ability is delegated only to the designated confirmer. However, the signer's ability to confirm, deny and sometimes convert signatures is requested or strongly desirable in many contexts,

---

[1] The limited verifier signature scheme, introduced in 1999 by Araki *et al* [1], provides the universal conversion operation. However, this protocol was broken by Zhang and Kim [23].

and this is supported by a number of schemes (*e.g.* [11,12,21]) including directed signatures. Again, none of these supports universal conversion of signatures.

Contributions of the Paper. The main contribution of this paper is an efficient and secure directed signature scheme featuring for the first time the universal conversion property. Our design relies on a simple observation known as the *xyz*-trick [20] which applies to bilinear map groups and allows to realize new cryptographic protocols achieving tradeoffs between authenticity and privacy.

We propose a security model for universally convertible directed signatures that captures and extends the strongest notions of unforgeability and signature invisibility. We prove that our signatures are existentially unforgeable, in the random oracle model, under chosen-message attacks with respect to a new computational assumption closely related to the Diffie-Hellman assumption.

We also show that our signatures are invisible, in the random oracle model, in a weak sense assuming the Decisional Tripartite Diffie-Hellman (DTDH) problem is intractable, and in a strong sense under a non-standard yet well-defined assumption. The scheme supports many variations, and it is easy to achieve invisibility under the DTDH assumption.

In addition to that, we introduce *traceable universally convertible directed signatures* by which a (master) tracing key enables a Tracing Authority (TA) to link signatures to their direction i.e. their issuer and confirmer (we also use the term receiver). We realize the concept using an efficient variation of our basic scheme. We show that the obtained signature scheme inherits the security properties of the basic scheme and that the power conferred to the TA by the tracing key is computationally limited to the tracing procedure.

2   Preliminaries

2.1   Bilinear Group Systems

Recently, bilinear maps have allowed the opening of a new territory in cryptography, making possible the realization of protocols that were previously unknown or impractical. We now recall the definition of bilinear group systems. In the sequel, we make use of a bilinear group pair $(\mathbb{G}_1, \mathbb{G}_2)$ for which there is an efficiently computable isomorphism ρ from $\mathbb{G}_2$ to $\mathbb{G}_1$.

Definition 1 (Bilinear group system). *A* bilinear group system *is a tuple* $(q, P_1, P_2, g_t, \mathbb{G}_1, \mathbb{G}_2, \mathbb{G}_t, \langle \cdot, \cdot \rangle, \rho)$ *where* q *is a prime number,* $\mathbb{G}_1, \mathbb{G}_2, \mathbb{G}_t$ *are groups of order* q *with efficiently computable inner laws,* $\langle P_1 \rangle = \mathbb{G}_1$, $\langle P_2 \rangle = \mathbb{G}_2$, $\langle g_t \rangle = \mathbb{G}_t$, $\langle \cdot, \cdot \rangle : \mathbb{G}_1 \times \mathbb{G}_2 \to \mathbb{G}_t$ *is an efficiently computable map such that for all* $(x, y) \in \mathbb{Z}^2$, $\langle xP_1, yP_2 \rangle = \langle P_1, P_2 \rangle^{xy}$ *holds and* $\langle P_1, P_2 \rangle \neq 1$ *and* $\rho : \mathbb{G}_2 \to \mathbb{G}_1$ *is an efficiently computable isomorphism with* $\rho(P_2) = P_1$.

Definition 2 (Bilinear group system generator). *A* bilinear group system generator *is a probabilistic algorithm* SETUP *that takes as input a security parameter* k *and outputs a bilinear group system* $(q, P_1, P_2, g_t, \mathbb{G}_1, \mathbb{G}_2, \mathbb{G}_t, \langle \cdot, \cdot \rangle, \rho) \xleftarrow{\$}$ SETUP(k) *such that* q *is a* k-*bit prime number.*

2.2 Computational Problems in Bilinear Group Systems

Depending on its practical embodiment, a bilinear group system may or may not provide an efficiently computable isomorphism from $\mathbb{G}_1$ to $\mathbb{G}_2$. In particular, ρ may not be efficiently invertible. In this case, there is a computational separation between problems defined over $\mathbb{G}_1$ and $\mathbb{G}_2$. For instance, the Decisional Diffie-Hellman problem DDH $[\mathbb{G}_2]$ on $\mathbb{G}_2$ is trivial since $\langle \rho(xP_2), yP_2 \rangle = \langle P_1, xyP_2 \rangle$ for any $x, y \in \mathbb{Z}_q^*$, but the same problem defined over $\mathbb{G}_1$ may remain somewhat intractable. Several new computational problems of various flavors have recently been defined over bilinear groups. We now give the definition of the complexity assumptions we will be using in this paper.

Tripartite Diffie-Hellman (TDH): Let $(q, P_1, P_2, g_t, \mathbb{G}_1, \mathbb{G}_2, \mathbb{G}_t, \langle \cdot, \cdot \rangle, \rho)$ be a bilinear group system. Given group elements $(xP_1, yP_1, zP_2) \xleftarrow{\$} \mathbb{G}_1^2 \times \mathbb{G}_2$, compute $xyzP_1 \in \mathbb{G}_1$.

This computational problem is at least as difficult as the computational bilinear Diffie-Hellman problem [6]. Similarly, Decisional Tripartite Diffie-Hellman is defined as the problem of distinguishing the distribution of (co-)Diffie-Hellman tuples $\{(xP_1, yP_1, zP_2, uP_1) \mid x, y, z \xleftarrow{\$} \mathbb{Z}_q^*\}$ from the uniform distribution over $\mathbb{G}_1^2 \times \mathbb{G}_2 \times \mathbb{G}_1$:

Decisional Tripartite Diffie-Hellman (DTDH): Let $(q, P_1, P_2, g_t, \mathbb{G}_1, \mathbb{G}_2, \mathbb{G}_t, \langle \cdot, \cdot \rangle, \rho)$ be a bilinear group system. Given group elements $(xP_1, yP_1, zP_2, uP_1) \in \mathbb{G}_1^2 \times \mathbb{G}_2 \times \mathbb{G}_1$, decide whether $u \equiv xyz \pmod{q}$.

The security of our signatures also relies on the following new computational problem:

Flexible Square Diffie-Hellman (FSDH): Let $(q, P_1, P_2, g_t, \mathbb{G}_1, \mathbb{G}_2, \mathbb{G}_t, \langle \cdot, \cdot \rangle, \rho)$ be a bilinear group system. Given $xP_2 \in \mathbb{G}_2$, output a tuple $(Q, xQ, x^2Q) \in \mathbb{G}_1^3$ for some freely chosen $Q \in \mathbb{G}_1$.

Remark 1. Even though not really considered as classical, the KEA1 assumption[2] was introduced in 1991 by Damgård [14]. Roughly speaking, KEA1 captures the intuition that any algorithm which, given a pair $(P, xP) \in \mathbb{G}^2$, computes a pair $(Q, xQ) \in \mathbb{G}^2$ must "know" $\log_P Q$. It is easily seen that under KEA1, the FSDH assumption is equivalent to a co-Diffie-Hellman assumption defined over $\mathbb{G}_1$ and $\mathbb{G}_2$.

2.3 Designated-Verifier Proofs of Equality of Two Discrete Logarithms

To make our security reductions complete, the executions of the confirming/denying protocols have to be simulated in the random oracle model. Therefore we rely in the design of our scheme on a procedure allowing to prove in a non-transferable way the equality (or the inequality) of two discrete logarithms

---

[2] This assumption and some variants are formally analyzed in [3] and have been used to prove that 3-round protocols were zero-knowledge.

without revealing information on their value. We make use of non-interactive designated-verifier zero-knowledge proofs [18] of equality of discrete logarithms $\log_\alpha \beta = \log_g y$. The notation is DVPK $[x : \beta = \alpha^x \wedge y = g^x]$, where α and g are two elements of same prime order in their respective groups. We use the notation DVPK $[x : \beta \neq \alpha^x \wedge y = g^x]$ for the dual proof of inequality. Designated-verifier proofs form the basis of denying and confirmation protocols in many undeniable and confirmer signature schemes in the literature. We refer the reader to [18] for further details.

3   Universally Convertible Directed Signatures

3.1   Definition

Given an integer k, a *universally convertible directed signature scheme* DS with security parameter k is formally defined by the following:

- **generation of public parameters:** DS.Setup is a probabilistic algorithm which takes as input k and outputs public parameters (which include a description of the signature space);
- **key generation for signer A and confirmer B:** DS.Signer.KeyGen is a probabilistic algorithm which takes as input the public parameters and outputs a signing key pair (pk_A, sk_A). DS.Confirmer.KeyGen is a probabilistic algorithm which takes as input the public parameters and outputs a confirmer key pair (pk_B, sk_B);
- **key-registration:** DS.Register is a protocol between a user and a "Key Registration Authority" which takes as input the public parameters and the user's public key pk, and outputs a pair (pk, notif) where $\text{notif} \in \{\text{accept}, \text{reject}\}$ is the registration authorization decision. The fact that a given public key has been properly registered with the authority, is guaranteed by a signature of it by the authority.
- **signature generation:** DS.Sign is a probabilistic algorithm which takes as input a bitstring $m \in \{0,1\}^*$, the signer's private key sk_A, the confirmer's public key pk_B and the public parameters. The output bitstring σ is called *an (A, B)-directed signature on m*;
- **signature verification by confirmer B (resp. signer A):** DS.Confirmer.Verify (resp. DS.Signer.Verify) is a deterministic algorithm which takes as input two bitstrings m and σ, the signer's public key pk_A, the confirmer's private key sk_B (resp. the signer's private key sk_A, the confirmer's public key pk_B) and the public parameters and checks whether σ is a valid (A, B)-directed signature on m;
- **confirming/denying protocols with confirmer B (resp. signer A):** DS.Confirmer.{Confirm, Deny} (resp. DS.Signer.{Confirm, Deny}) are protocols between a confirmer (resp. a signer) and a third party which takes as input two bitstrings m and σ, the signer's public key pk_A, the confirmer's private key sk_B (resp. the signer's private key sk_A, the confirmer's public key pk_B) and the public parameters. The output is a non-transferable proof that σ is a valid or an invalid (A, B)-directed signature on m;

- **individual conversion by confirmer B (resp. signer A):** DS.Confirmer.Convert (resp. DS.Signer.Convert) is a deterministic algorithm which takes as input a bitstring σ, the signer's public key pk_A, the confirmer's private key sk_B (resp. the signer's private key sk_A, the confirmer's public key pk_B) and the public parameters, and outputs a bitstring $\tilde{\sigma}_B$ called a B-*converted signature* (resp. $\tilde{\sigma}_A$ called an A-*converted signature*);
- **verification of a B-(resp. A-)converted signature:** DS.User.VerifyConfirmer (resp. DS.User.VerifySigner) is a deterministic algorithm which takes as input two bitstrings m and $\tilde{\sigma}_B$ (resp. $\tilde{\sigma}_A$), the signer's public key pk_A, the confirmer's public key pk_B and the public parameters and checks whether $\tilde{\sigma}_B$ (resp. $\tilde{\sigma}_A$) is a valid B-converted (resp. A-converted) signature on m;
- **generation of a universal trapdoor by confirmer B (resp. signer A):** DS.Confirmer.Trapdoor (resp. DS.Signer.Trapdoor) is a deterministic algorithm which takes as input the signer's public key pk_A, the confirmer's private key sk_B (resp. the signer's private key sk_A, the confirmer's public key pk_B), the public parameters and outputs a universal trapdoor $T_{A,B}$ which makes it possible to universally verify all (A, B)-directed signatures;
- **universal signature verification:** DS.User.Verify. is a deterministic algorithm which takes as input three bitstrings m, σ and T, the signer's public key pk_A, the confirmer's public key pk_B and the public parameters, and tells whether σ is a valid (A, B)-directed signature on m.

Moreover, a universally convertible directed signature scheme must satisfy the following (informally defined, precisely detailed in the next section) properties:

1. **correctness:** properly formed (A, B)-directed, A-converted and B-converted signatures must be accepted by the verification algorithms;
2. **unforgeability:** it is computationally infeasible, without the knowledge of the signer's private key, to produce a directed signature that is accepted by the verification algorithms or by the confirming protocols;
3. **completeness and soundness:** the verification protocols are complete and sound, where completeness means that valid (invalid) signatures can always be proven valid (invalid) and soundness means that no valid (invalid) signature can be proven invalid (valid).
4. **invisibility:** given a message m and a purported (A, B)-directed signature σ on m, it is computationally infeasible, without the knowledge of the confirmer's or the signer's private key, to ascertain that σ is a valid (A, B)-directed signature of m.
5. **non-transferability:** a user participating in an execution of the confirming/denying protocols does not obtain information that could be used to convince a third party about the validity/invalidity of a signature.

3.2 Security Notions for Universally Convertible Directed Signatures

Unforgeability against adaptive chosen message attacks. The *de facto* standard notion of security for digital signatures was formalized by Goldwasser,

Micali and Rivest [16] as existential unforgeability under adaptive chosen message attacks (EF-CMA). For universally convertible directed signatures, the unforgeability security is defined along the same lines, with the notable difference that the adversary can be any of the confirmers chosen by the signer. Therefore, in the attack scenario, the forger $\mathcal{A}$ is allowed to request signatures directed to any registered user of her choice (whose secret key might be known to her). Besides, signer individual/universal conversion algorithms might also leak information to the adversary. We therefore suppose that the adversary knows the confirmers' private keys, the associated signer-generated universal trapdoors, and we allow her to request the individual conversion of any signature of her choice. As usual, the forger has the natural restriction that the returned forgery (including a message, a directed signature and a confirmer's identity) has not been returned by the signing oracle during the game.

Invisibility of signatures. The strongest security notion for undeniable and confirmer signatures is the one of invisibility introduced by Chaum, van Heijst and Pfitzmann in [13]. We precisely define the notion of signature *invisibility* under adaptive chosen message attacks in our context, introducing two flavors of invisibility, weak-Inv-CMA and Inv-CMA.

We consider an adversary $\mathcal{A}$ that runs in two stages: in the find stage, $\mathcal{A}$ takes as input the public keys pk_A and $pk_B^\star$, and outputs a message $m^\star$ together with some state information $\mathcal{I}^\star$. In the guess stage, $\mathcal{A}$ gets as input $\mathcal{I}^\star$ and a challenge signature $\sigma^\star$ either formed by signing the message $m^\star$ or chosen at random in the signature space. Then $\mathcal{A}$ returns her guess as to whether $\sigma^\star$ is a valid (A, B)-directed signature on $m^\star$ or not.

In the weak-Inv-CMA-model, the adversary has access in both stages to the signing oracle Sign and to the confirming/denying oracle Confirm and Deny. In the Inv-CMA-model, $\mathcal{A}$ is also given access to the individual conversion oracle Convert, and to the universal trapdoor generation oracle Trapdoor. In both cases, she is allowed to invoke these oracles on any message and any confirmer of her choice with the restriction of not sending $(m^\star, \sigma^\star, pk_B^\star)$ to the oracles Confirm, Deny and Convert in the second stage and not sending $pk_B^\star$ to the oracle Trapdoor at any stage.

Let $t \in \mathbb{N}^{\mathbb{N}}$, $\boldsymbol{q} = (q_{\text{Sign}}, q_{\text{Confirm}}, q_{\text{Deny}}, q_{\text{Conv}}, q_{\text{Trap}}, q_{\text{Reg}}) \in [\mathbb{N}^{\mathbb{N}}]^6$ and $\varepsilon \in [0,1]^{\mathbb{N}}$. An algorithm $\mathcal{A}$ is a $(k, t, \boldsymbol{q}, \varepsilon)$-forger (*resp.* a $(k, t, \boldsymbol{q}, \varepsilon)$-distinguisher) against DS if for all integer k, it runs in time at most $t(k)$, makes at most $q_{\text{Sign}}(k), q_{\text{Confirm}}(k), q_{\text{Deny}}(k), q_{\text{Conv}}(k), q_{\text{Trap}}(k), q_{\text{Reg}}(k)$ queries to the given oracles, and has forgery success (*resp.* distinguishing advantage) $\geq \varepsilon(k)$ against DS with security parameter k.

4   Efficient Universally Convertible Directed Signatures

We now describe our first universally convertible directed signature scheme which for readability is denoted again by DS.

Generation of public parameters
DS.Setup: Given a security parameter k, the public parameters are $(q, P_1, P_2, g_t, \mathbb{G}_1, \mathbb{G}_2, \mathbb{G}_t, \langle \cdot, \cdot \rangle, \rho) \xleftarrow{\$} \text{SETUP}(k)$ as well as a hash function H mapping arbitrary bit strings to $\mathbb{Z}_q^*$.

Key generation
DS.Signer.KeyGen: Signer A picks random $x_1, x_2 \xleftarrow{\$} \mathbb{Z}_q^*$ and computes $X_1 = x_1 P_1$ and $X_2 = x_2 P_2$. A's public key is $(X_1, X_2) \in \mathbb{G}_1 \times \mathbb{G}_2$. A's private key is (x_1, x_2).

DS.Confirmer.KeyGen: Confirmer B picks a random $y \xleftarrow{\$} \mathbb{Z}_q^*$ and computes $Y = y P_1$. B's public key is $Y \in \mathbb{G}_1$. B's private key is y.

DS.{Signer, Confirmer}.Register: A confirmer public key $pk_B = Y = y P_1$ is registered by letting B prove (possibly non interactively) the knowledge of y to the registration authority by engaging in DVPK $[y : Y = y P_1]$. Similarly, a user registers his signing public key $pk_A = (X_1, X_2) = (x_1 P_1, x_2 P_2)$ by proving in zero-knowledge her/his knowledge of x_1 and x_2. The fact that a given public key has been properly registered with the authority, is guaranteed by a signature of the it by the authority.

Signature generation
DS.Sign: Given a message $m \in \{0, 1\}^*$ and the public key Y of a confirmer, A picks a random $r \xleftarrow{\$} \mathbb{Z}_q^*$, and computes $U = r P_2$ and $V = (r x_1)(x_2 + H(m, U, Y))^{-1} Y$. In case $x_2 + H(m, U, Y) \equiv 0 \pmod q$, A restarts the signing procedure with a new value for r. The signature is $\sigma = (U, V)$.

Verification by confirmer/signer
DS.Confirmer.Verify: Given a message $m \in \{0, 1\}^*$ and a signature $\sigma = (U, V)$, B checks whether $\sigma \in \mathbb{G}_2 \times \mathbb{G}_1$ and $\langle V, X_2 + H(m, U, Y) P_2 \rangle = \langle X_1, U \rangle^y$.

DS.Signer.Verify: Given a message $m \in \{0, 1\}^*$ and a signature $\sigma = (U, V)$, A checks whether $\sigma \in \mathbb{G}_2 \times \mathbb{G}_1$ and $\langle V, X_2 + H(m, U, Y) P_2 \rangle = \langle Y, U \rangle^{x_1}$.

Confirmation and disavowal protocols
DS.Signer.{Confirm, Deny}: Given a message $m \in \{0, 1\}^*$ and a signature $\sigma = (U, V)$, A proves to any third party that

$$\text{DVPK} \left[x_1 : \langle V, X_2 + H(m, U, Y) P_2 \rangle = \langle Y, U \rangle^{x_1} \wedge X_1 = x_1 P_1 \right]$$

$$\text{or DVPK} \left[x_1 : \langle V, X_2 + H(m, U, Y) P_2 \rangle \neq \langle Y, U \rangle^{x_1} \wedge X_1 = x_1 P_1 \right].$$

DS.Confirmer.{Confirm, Deny}: Given a message $m \in \{0, 1\}^*$ and a signature $\sigma = (U, V)$, B proves to any third party that

$$\text{DVPK} \left[y : \langle V, X_2 + H(m, U, Y) P_2 \rangle = \langle X_1, U \rangle^y \wedge Y = y P_1 \right]$$

$$\text{or DVPK} \left[y : \langle V, X_2 + H(m, U, Y) P_2 \rangle \neq \langle X_1, U \rangle^y \wedge Y = y P_1 \right].$$

Individual conversion and verification algorithms

DS.Signer.Convert: Given a purported (A, B)-directed signature $\sigma = (U, V)$, A computes $W = x_1 U \in \mathbb{G}_2$ and outputs $\tilde{\sigma}_A = (U, V, W) \in \mathbb{G}_2 \times \mathbb{G}_1 \times \mathbb{G}_2$ as an A-converted signature on m.

DS.User.VerifySigner: Given a message $m \in \{0, 1\}^*$ and a converted signature $\tilde{\sigma}_A = (U, V, W)$, any user checks whether $\langle X_1, U \rangle = \langle P_1, W \rangle$ and $\langle V, X_2 + H(m, U, Y)P_2 \rangle = \langle Y, W \rangle$.

DS.Confirmer.Convert: Given a purported (A, B)-directed signature $\sigma = (U, V)$, B computes $W = yU \in \mathbb{G}_2$ and outputs $\tilde{\sigma}_B = (U, V, W) \in \mathbb{G}_2 \times \mathbb{G}_1 \times \mathbb{G}_2$ as a B-converted signature on m.

DS.User.VerifyConfirmer: Given a message $m \in \{0, 1\}^*$ and a converted signature $\tilde{\sigma}_B = (U, V, W)$, any user checks whether $\langle Y, U \rangle = \langle P_1, W \rangle$ and $\langle V, X_2 + H(m, U, Y)P_2 \rangle = \langle X_1, W \rangle$.

Universal trapdoor generation and verification algorithms

DS.{Signer, Confirmer}.Trapdoor: A or B computes $\mathcal{T} = yX_1 = x_1 Y = x_1 y P_1$ and makes $\mathcal{T}$ public.

DS.User.Verify: Given a message $m \in \{0, 1\}^*$ and a signature $\sigma = (U, V)$, any user uses the trapdoor $\mathcal{T}$ to check whether $\langle V, X_2 + H(m, U, Y)P_2 \rangle = \langle \mathcal{T}, U \rangle$.

The correctness of DS is obvious, and the completeness and soundness of all protocols are classical results [10]. We now discuss a few facts about our scheme.

EFFICIENCY. An (A, B)-directed signature σ is a pair of elements in $\mathbb{G}_2 \times \mathbb{G}_1$, being in that comparable to Boneh and Boyen's recent signature scheme [5]. Signature generation requires an inversion modulo q followed by one exponentiation in $\mathbb{G}_1$ and one exponentiation in $\mathbb{G}_2$. Therefore no pairing is required. Signature verification by the confirmer is a bit more demanding as a couple of pairings have to be computed. We note that conversion procedures, as well as the generation of a universal trapdoor require a single exponentiation in $\mathbb{G}_1$ or $\mathbb{G}_2$ and are therefore pairing-free.

VERIFIABILITY PROPERTIES. We note that our scheme is fully verifiable in the sense that all private operations are independently verifiable by third parties. These properties are desirable even though not requested in our definitions. If our system serves as a basic primitive in a cryptographic protocol typically, full verifiability may allow early detection of cheating behaviors and localization of malicious parties.

SECURITY. We note first that the property of non-transferability is fulfilled by our scheme as a direct consequence of the use of designated-verifier proofs in confirmation/disavowal protocols. Further, we state that our scheme resists existential forgeries and that signatures are invisible. Both security reductions stand in the random oracle model.

Theorem 1 (Unforgeability of DS). *Let $t, q_H \in \mathbb{N}^\mathbb{N}$, $q = (q_{\text{Sign}}, q_{\text{Confirm}}, q_{\text{Deny}}, q_{\text{Conv}}, q_{\text{Trap}}, q_{\text{Reg}}) \in [\mathbb{N}^\mathbb{N}]^6$ and $\varepsilon \in [0, 1]^\mathbb{N}$. Assume there exists a (k, t, q, ε)-forger $\mathcal{A}$ against DS, in the random oracle model.*

Further assume that $\mathcal{A}$ is limited to q_H executions of H. Then there is an algorithm that solves the FSDH problem in the bilinear group system generator SETUP *with probability $\varepsilon'(k) \geq 1 - 1/2^k$ within time*

$$t' \leq t \cdot \frac{(q_H + q_{\mathrm{Confirm}} + q_{\mathrm{Deny}} + q_{\mathrm{Convert}} + 2)}{\varepsilon} + (\|\boldsymbol{q}\| + q_H) \cdot p_1,$$

where p_1 is a explicit polynomial and $\|\boldsymbol{q}\| = q_{\mathrm{Sign}} + q_{\mathrm{Confirm}} + q_{\mathrm{Deny}} + q_{\mathrm{Conv}} + q_{\mathrm{Trap}} + q_{\mathrm{Reg}}$.

Proof. The proof relies on the Forking Lemma [22] and is in spirit rather similar to the security proof of known discrete-log-based signature schemes such as Schnorr. Assume $\mathcal{A}$ is a forger that $(k, t, \boldsymbol{q}, \varepsilon)$-breaks DS. Here, q_H stands for the number of queries submitted by $\mathcal{A}$ to H since H is viewed as a random oracle. We construct a reduction algorithm $\mathcal{B}$ that, by interacting with $\mathcal{A}$, solves the FSDH problem with time bound and success probability as claimed in Theorem 1. Algorithm $\mathcal{B}$ is given bilinear map parameters $(q, P_1, P_2, g_t, \mathbb{G}_1, \mathbb{G}_2, \mathbb{G}_t, \langle \cdot, \cdot \rangle, \rho)$ generated by SETUP(k) and an instance xP_2 of the FSDH problem. $\mathcal{B}$'s goal is to produce a tuple $(Q, xQ, x^2 Q)$ for some $Q \in \mathbb{G}_1$. $\mathcal{B}$ does so by interacting with the forger $\mathcal{A}$ as follows. First, $\mathcal{B}$ picks a random $x_1 \xleftarrow{\$} \mathbb{Z}_q^*$ and sets $X_1 = x_1 P_1$ and $X_2 = xP_2$. The knowledge of x_1 in the simulation will be used intensively in the simulation of DS.Signer.Confirm and DS.Signer.Deny}

FIND STAGE. We define a probabilistic subroutine $\mathcal{B}_0(\varpi)$ of $\mathcal{B}$. Given an arbitrary input ϖ, $\mathcal{B}_0(\varpi)$ runs $\mathcal{A}$ with random tape ϖ, transmits $(q, P_1, P_2, g_t, \mathbb{G}_1, \mathbb{G}_2, \mathbb{G}_t, \langle \cdot, \cdot \rangle, \rho)$ as public parameters to $\mathcal{A}$, as well as the public key $pk_A = (X_1, X_2)$. Then $\mathcal{B}_0(\varpi)$ simulates the scheme's oracles H, DS.Sign, DS.Signer.{Confirm, Deny}, DS.Signer.Convert and DS.Signer.Trapdoor as follows.

Simulation of H. Given $m \in \{0, 1\}^*$ and $(U, Y) \in \mathbb{G}_2 \times \mathbb{G}_1$, if $H(m, U, Y)$ is defined, output its value. Otherwise, pick a random $h \xleftarrow{\$} \mathbb{Z}_q^*$, define $H(m, U, Y) = h$ and output h.

Simulation of DS.Sign. Given $m \in \{0, 1\}^*$ and a confirmer's public key $pk_B = Y$, pick a random $r, h \xleftarrow{\$} \mathbb{Z}_q^*$. Set $V = rx_1 Y$ and $U = rX_2 + rhP_2$. If $H(m, U, Y)$ is defined and is $\neq h$, $\mathcal{B}_0(\varpi)$ aborts. Otherwise $\mathcal{B}_0(\varpi)$ defines $H(m, U, Y) = h$ and outputs $\sigma = (U, V)$.

Simulation of DS.Signer.{Confirm, Deny}. Since $\mathcal{B}_0(\varpi)$ knows x_1, $\mathcal{B}_0(\varpi)$ is able to verify any given directed signature and consequently, to engage successfully in one of the two protocols   DVPK $[x_1 : \langle V, X_2 + H(m, U, Y) P_2 \rangle = \langle Y, U \rangle^{x_1} \wedge X_1 = x_1 P_1]$ or DVPK $[x_1 : \langle V, X_2 + H(m, U, Y) P_2 \rangle \neq \langle Y, U \rangle^{x_1} \wedge X_1 = x_1 P_1]$ for any given $m \in \{0, 1\}^*$, $\sigma = (U, V) \in \mathbb{G}_2 \times \mathbb{G}_1$ and $Y \in \mathbb{G}_1$. Note that a simulation of H is required in either case.

Simulation of DS.Signer.Convert. Given $\sigma = (U, V)$, output $\tilde{\sigma}_A = (U, V, x_1 U)$.

Simulation of DS.Signer.Trapdoor. Given $Y \in \mathbb{G}_1$, output $\mathcal{T} = x_1 Y$.

If $\mathcal{A}$ returns a forgery $(Y, m, \sigma = (U, V))$, $\mathcal{B}_0(\varpi)$ simulates H once again to get $h = H(m, U, Y)$ and checks whether $\langle V, X_2 + H(m, U, Y) P_2 \rangle = \langle Y, U \rangle^{x_1}$. If the equality holds, and if σ does not appear in the transcript of DS.Sign, $\mathcal{B}_0(\varpi)$ is said to *succeed*.

Algorithm $\mathcal{B}$ restarts $\mathcal{B}_0(\varpi)$ for random values of $\varpi \xleftarrow{\$} \{0,1\}^*$ until $\mathcal{B}_0(\varpi)$ succeeds. Let $(Y, m, \sigma = (U, V))$ be the last output of $\mathcal{A}$. Then $\mathcal{B}$ memorizes ϖ, the index j of $(m, U, Y) \mapsto h$ in H's transcript (sorted in chronological order), and the first j outputs of H noted $h_1, \ldots, h_j$. If ℓ denotes the index in the transcript of DS.Sign of the last signature output *before* H returns h_j, $\mathcal{B}$ also memorizes $\ell, \sigma_1, \ldots, \sigma_\ell$.

REPLAY STAGE. As is classical with forking-based reductions, we define a second probabilistic subroutine $\mathcal{B}_1(\varpi)$ of $\mathcal{B}$ which role is essentially to replay the last and successful execution of $\mathcal{B}_0(\varpi)$ until the moment when H is about to output h_j, and then simulate all oracles with fresh random values from that moment on. The tape ϖ being given by the find stage, $\mathcal{B}_1(\varpi)$ runs $\mathcal{A}$ with random tape ϖ, transmits the same public parameters $(q, P_1, P_2, g_t, \mathbb{G}_1, \mathbb{G}_2, \mathbb{G}_t, \langle \cdot, \cdot \rangle, \rho)$ to $\mathcal{A}$, as well as $pk_A = (X_1, X_2)$. Then $\mathcal{B}_1(\varpi)$ simulates the oracles as follows, using its own random tape π.

Simulation of H. If the query index is $i < j$, output h_i. Otherwise, simulate as in the find stage with fresh random values.

Simulation of DS.Sign. If the query index is $i' \le \ell$, output $\sigma_{i'}$. Otherwise, simulate as in the find stage with fresh random values.

All other oracles are simulated exactly as in the find stage. If $\mathcal{A}$ returns a forgery $(Y', m', \sigma' = (U', V'))$, $\mathcal{B}_1(\varpi)$ queries its own simulation of H to verify σ' the same way $\mathcal{B}_0(\varpi)$ verified σ. If σ' is invalid or was output by the simulation of DS.Sign or if the index of $(m', U', Y') \mapsto h'$ in the transcript of H is $j' \ne j$, then $\mathcal{B}_1(\varpi)$ is said to fail.

Algorithm $\mathcal{B}$ restarts $\mathcal{B}_1(\varpi)$ with random values for π until $\mathcal{B}_1(\varpi)$ succeeds. Let then $(Y', m', \sigma' = (U', V'))$ be the last output of $\mathcal{A}$.

KEY RETRIEVAL STAGE. We perform a specific stage that allows $\mathcal{B}$ to retrieve the confirmer private key y' associated to the find-stage forgery (Y', m', σ'), i.e. such that $Y' = y' P_1$. To this end, $\mathcal{B}$ replays $\mathcal{B}_1$ once with a slightly modified random tape $\pi' \approx \pi$ such that replaying the registration stage of Y' by $\mathcal{A}$ allows to extract y'. As registration is performed via a non-interactive DVPK of a discrete log, modifying the 'challenge' value returned by the internal hash function of the protocol yields y' by knowledge extraction[3]. $\mathcal{B}$ then stops $\mathcal{A}$ and memorizes y'.

FINAL OUTCOME. $\mathcal{B}$ disposes of two valid forgeries $(Y, m, \sigma = (U, V))$ and $(Y', m', \sigma' = (U', V'))$. Since $(m', U', Y') \mapsto h'$ and $(m, U, Y) \mapsto h$ have the same index in the transcript of H, we must have $(m', U', Y') = (m, U, Y)$ by a causality argument. In particular, $\mathcal{B}$ knows $y = y'$. $\mathcal{B}$ then computes $\Delta = x_1^{-1} y^{-1} V$ and $\Delta' = x_1^{-1} y^{-1} V'$. From the simulation, there exists $r \in \mathbb{Z}_{q-1}^*$ (unknown to $\mathcal{B}$) such that $\Delta = r(x+h)^{-1} P_1$ and $\Delta' = r(x+h')^{-1} P_1$. $\mathcal{B}$ poses $R = rP_1$ and $Q = (h'-h)^{-1}(\Delta - \Delta') = r[(x+h)(x+h')]^{-1} P_1 = [(x+h)(x+h')]^{-1} R$, or aborts if $h' - h \equiv 0 \pmod{q}$. Finally, one has $\Delta = (x+h') Q$ so that

---

[3] This technique is classical and we therefore do not enter into more details here.

$\Delta - h'Q = xQ$. Since $R = (x+h)(x+h')Q$, we get $R - (h+h')xQ - hh'Q = x^2Q$ and $\mathcal{B}$ outputs (Q, xQ, x^2Q) to its own challenger.

REDUCTION COST. We start with a preliminary observation. The transcript of H contains exactly $q_{tot}(k)$ hash definitions, where $q_{tot} = q_H + q_{Sign} + q_{Confirm} + q_{Deny} + 1$, since the simulation of H is invoked by the simulation of other oracles (the constant term 1 comes from the verification of the forgery). Among these hash values, exactly $q_{Sign}(k)$ were defined by the simulation of DS.Sign and by construction, the j-th hash definition $H(m, U, Y)$ cannot be one of these.

Let us denote by $\mathcal{H}_j$ the set of vectors $(h_1, \ldots, h_{q_{tot}(k)})$ leading to a forgery of index j and $\varepsilon_j = \Pr\left[(h_1, \ldots, h_{q_{tot}(k)}) \in \mathcal{H}_j\right]$, the probability being taken over all the values of $h_1, \ldots, h_{q_{tot}(k)}$ over $\mathbb{Z}_q^*$. Note that the ε_i's may depend on $\mathcal{A}$ and w but in any case $\sum_j \varepsilon_j = \varepsilon(k)$ must hold. Following our remark above, there must be at least $q_{Sign}(k)$ values of j for which $\varepsilon_j = 0$. We now invoke the

Lemma 1 (Splitting Lemma [22]). *Noting $\mathcal{X}_j$ the set of vectors $(h_1, \ldots, h_{j-1})$ such that*

$$\Pr\left[(h_1, \ldots, h_{j-1}, h'_j, \ldots, h'_{q_{tot}(k)}) \in \mathcal{H}_j\right] \geq \frac{\varepsilon_j}{2},$$

where the probability is taken over $h'_j, \ldots, h'_{q_{tot}(k)} \xleftarrow{\$} \mathbb{Z}_q^*$, one has

$$\Pr\left[(h_1, \ldots, h_{j-1}) \in \mathcal{X}_j \mid (h_1, \ldots, h_{q_{tot}(k)}) \in \mathcal{H}_j\right] \geq \frac{1}{2}.$$

where the probability is taken over $h_1, \ldots, h_{j-1} \xleftarrow{\$} \mathbb{Z}_q^*$.

We expect the find and key retrieval stages to require at most $\varepsilon(k)^{-1} + 1$ executions of $\mathcal{A}$. Suppose that the transcript of H when $\mathcal{B}_0(\varpi)$ succeeds is $(h_1, \ldots, h_{q_{tot}(k)}) \in \mathcal{H}_j$ for some j. This event occurs with non-zero probability $\varepsilon_j / \varepsilon(k)$ as soon as $\varepsilon_j \neq 0$. Further assume that $(h_1, \ldots, h_{j-1}) \in \mathcal{X}_j$; the probability that this occurs is at least $1/2$. Then the expected number of executions of $\mathcal{B}_1(\varpi)$ is $2/\varepsilon_j$. Putting it all together, and taking into account the abortion case $h' \equiv h \pmod{q}$, $\mathcal{B}$ succeeds with probability $\geq 1 - 1/2^{-k}$ after

$$\frac{1}{\varepsilon(k)} + 1 + \sum_{1 \leq j \leq q_{tot}(k), \varepsilon_j \neq 0} \frac{\varepsilon_j}{\varepsilon(k)} \cdot \frac{1}{2} \cdot \frac{2}{\varepsilon_j} \leq \frac{q_{tot}(k) - q_{Sign}(k) + \varepsilon(k)}{\varepsilon(k)}$$

executions of $\mathcal{A}$, i.e. in time at most $[t \cdot (q_H + q_{Confirm} + q_{Deny} + q_{Convert} + 2)/\varepsilon](k)$. The term $(\|\mathbf{q}\| + q_H) p_1$ comes from the time needed to simulate all oracles. $\square$

Remark 2. The simulation of the DVPKs imposes the random oracle model and we therefore must allow the adversary to query the internal oracles used to compute proofs. The simulation cost induced by these queries are included into q_H.

We also state that DS is weakly invisible under the assumption that the Decisional Tripartite Diffie-Hellman problem is intractable:

Theorem 2 (Weak Invisibility of DS). *Let* $t, q_H \in \mathbb{N}^{\mathbb{N}}$, $q = (q_{\mathrm{Sign}}, q_{\mathrm{Confirm}}, q_{\mathrm{Deny}}, 0, 0, q_{\mathrm{Reg}}) \in [\mathbb{N}^{\mathbb{N}}]^6$ *and* $\varepsilon \in [0, 1]^{\mathbb{N}}$. *Assume there exists a* $(k, t, \boldsymbol{q}, \varepsilon)$-*distinguisher* $\mathcal{A}$ *against* DS, *in the random oracle model. Then there exists an algorithm that solves the DTDH problem in the bilinear group system generator* SETUP *with probability* $\varepsilon' = \varepsilon/2 - o(1)$ *within time* $t' \leq q_{\mathrm{Reg}} \cdot t + (\|\boldsymbol{q}\| + q_H) \cdot p_2$, *where* p_2 *is an explicit polynomial.*

Proof. We show that, assuming the hardness of the Decisional Tripartite Diffie-Hellman DTDH, DS is weakly invisible under an adaptive chosen-message attack. Our reduction is in essence similar to previously known reductions in the standard model, and we therefore skip minor details. Note that H needs not be seen as a random oracle. The fact that we require the random oracle model only stems from the need to simulate zero-knowledge proofs.

Assume $\mathcal{A}$ is an attacker that $(k, t, \boldsymbol{q}, \varepsilon)$-breaks the weak invisibility of DS as defined earlier. We construct a reduction algorithm $\mathcal{B}$ that, by interacting with $\mathcal{A}$, solves a DTDH instance with time bound and advantage as claimed in Theorem 2. The outline of the reduction is as follows. Algorithm $\mathcal{B}$ is given an bilinear group system $(q, P_1, P_2, g_t, \mathbb{G}_1, \mathbb{G}_2, \mathbb{G}_t, \langle \cdot, \cdot \rangle, \rho)$ generated by SETUP(k) and an instance $(\alpha P_1, \beta P_1, \gamma P_2, \delta P_1) \in \mathbb{G}_1^2 \times \mathbb{G}_2 \times \mathbb{G}_1$. $\mathcal{B}$'s goal is to decide whether $\delta \equiv \alpha\beta\gamma \pmod{q}$. $\mathcal{B}$ does so by interacting with the forger $\mathcal{A}$ as follows. First, $\mathcal{B}$ picks a random $x_2 \xleftarrow{\$} \mathbb{Z}_q^*$ and sets $X_1 = \alpha P_1$ and $X_2 = x_2 P_2$. Then $\mathcal{B}$ sends the public parameters to $\mathcal{A}$ as well as the signer public key (X_1, X_2) and the challenge confirmer public key $Y^* = \beta P_1$. $\mathcal{B}$ attempts to simulate all oracles throughout the find stage, as shown later. $\mathcal{A}$ then returns a challenge message m^*. $\mathcal{B}$ then picks a random bit $b \in \{0, 1\}$ and sets $U = \gamma P_2$. If $b = 0$, $\mathcal{B}$ sets $h^* = H(m^*, U, Y)$ and $V = (x_2 + h^*)^{-1}(\delta P_1)$. If $b = 1$, $\mathcal{B}$ initializes $V \xleftarrow{\$} \mathbb{G}_1$. Then $\mathcal{B}$ defines $\sigma^* = (U, V)$ and σ^* is returned to $\mathcal{A}$ as the signature challenge. Throughout the guess stage, $\mathcal{B}$ simulates the oracles the same way it did in the find stage. $\mathcal{A}$ finally outputs a guess $b' \in \{0, 1\}$ and $\mathcal{B}$ returns 1 to its own challenger if $b' = b$ or 0 otherwise.

When $\delta \equiv \alpha\beta\gamma \pmod{q}$, signature simulations will all be correct and the advantage of $\mathcal{A}$ in guessing b is at least $\varepsilon(k)$. In the case $\delta \not\equiv \alpha\beta\gamma \pmod{q}$, the signatures output by $\mathcal{B}$ are simply invalid and $\mathcal{A}$ may then behave arbitrarily. Overall, $\mathcal{B}$ correctly guesses its own challenge with probability negligibly close to $\varepsilon(k)/2$.

Key Retrieval for $Y \neq Y^*$. When $Y \neq Y^*$, $\mathcal{A}$ must have registered the public key $Y = yP_1$ prior to requesting any signature of type (m, Y), so that $\mathcal{B}$ recovers y via registration replay as in the proof of unforgeability. This requires to reboot and replay A with the same random tape up to the point in executing the DVPK when bringing fresh randomness in the 'challenge' hash value allows to extract the discrete log y. Knowing y, $\mathcal{B}$ continues the second execution of A until a new confirmer key Y' is registered, and so forth. This strategy ensures that $\mathcal{B}$ can actually recover all the confirmer private keys matching the public keys registered by $\mathcal{A}$. The price to pay is a factor $q_{\mathrm{Reg}}(k)$ in the number of times $\mathcal{A}$ has to be executed. Note that, since we make use of non-interactive DVPK of a discrete logarithm, there is no concurrent interleving of registrations and therefore the "reboot and replay" technique applies readily.

Simulation of Signatures for $Y \neq Y^\star$. Signatures are simulated in the following way. Given (m, Y), $\mathcal{B}$ first recovers $y = \log_P Y$ in its transcript. Then $\mathcal{B}$ picks a random $r \xleftarrow{\$} \mathbb{Z}_q^*$ and sets $U = rP_2$ and $V = ry(x_2 + h)^{-1}(\alpha P_1)$, where $h = H(m, U, Y)$. $\mathcal{B}$ memorizes (σ, m, Y, r) in its transcript and returns $\sigma = (U, V)$.

Simulation of Other Operations Involving $\mathcal{B} \neq \mathcal{B}^\star$. As $y = \log_P Y$ is known to $\mathcal{B}$ whenever $Y \neq Y^\star$, $\mathcal{B}$ can individually convert any (A, B)-directed signature $\sigma = (U, V)$ given by $\mathcal{B}$ to $\mathcal{A}$ by simply computing $W = rX_1$ where r is the randomness used to construct σ. Similarly, $\mathcal{B}$ can generate universal trapdoors $\mathcal{T} = yX_1$.

Simulation of Confirmation/Denial Protocols. $\mathcal{B}$ simulates the DVPK of $x_1 = \log_{P_1} X_1$ (that $\mathcal{B}$ does not know) or $y = \log_{P_1} Y$ (that $\mathcal{B}$ knows from the key retrieval stage). This requires to simulate the internal random oracle of DVPK in the first case. The proof is then returned to (the user corrupted by) $\mathcal{A}$.

Simulation of Signatures for $Y = Y^\star$. Given m, $\mathcal{B}$ picks a random $r \xleftarrow{\$} \mathbb{Z}_q^*$, sets $U = r(\gamma P_2)$ and $V = \frac{r}{x_2 + h}(\delta P_1)$ where $h = H(m, U, Y^\star)$. $\mathcal{B}$ returns $\sigma = (U, V)$.

REDUCTION COST. As discussed above, $\mathcal{B}$'s own challenge is solved with probability $\varepsilon'(k) \geq \varepsilon(k)/2 - \Pr[\text{DVPK fails}]$ within time bound $q_{\text{Reg}}(k) \cdot t(k) + \|q\|(k) \cdot p_2(k)$ where p_2 is an explicit polynomiaml and the second term comes from the simulations of all oracles. This is as claimed in Theorem 2.   □

INVISIBLE UNIVERSALLY CONVERTIBLE DIRECTED SIGNATURES. We refer the reader to Appendix A for a proof that DS is invisible under a non-standard complexity assumption referred to as the q_s-Tripartite-DCAA problem.

Because of its simplicity, however, our scheme admits many variations. A possible direction to reach invisibility under a weaker assumption consists in replacing the individual conversion algorithms by standard non-interactive zero-knowledge (NIZK) proofs of knowledge of equality/inequality of discrete logarithms. The NIZK proof is then appended to the directed signature as a replacement of the third signature part W. It is then possible to obtain invisibility under the Decisional Tripartite Diffie-Hellman assumption. The proof is very similar to the one of Theorem 2 except that signature conversions are provided to the adversary by simulating the corresponding NIZK proofs for signatures issued by the reduction. The other cases are upper bounded in probability by the unforgeability property of our scheme.

5   Universally Convertible Directed Signatures with Traceability

Directed signatures find a prominent application in the realization of complete peer-to-peer secure messaging systems. In such a system, users have a unique key pair $\{pk = (X_1, X_2), sk = (x_1, x_2)\}$ where $X_1 = x_1 P_1, X_2 = x_2 P_2$ and x_1 plays simultaneously the role of a signing and of a confirming key. By misuse of language, we sometimes call x_1 the *anonymity key* and x_2 the *signing key* for reasons that will appear clearly in what follows. We view a confirmer more like a regular receiver of a signed message and preferably adopt this term in the sequel. In authenticated messaging systems, putting a restriction on the ability to verify signatures is of a certain interest towards the users' privacy. The property of invisibility guarantees this privacy until one of the two parties wishes to end it.

There are real-life contexts, however, in which conferring this ability to a trusted authority acting in extreme circumstances is desirable. One may think of private contract signing for instance, where criminals make use of the system to sign illegal contracts that are not publicly verifiable. What is really desired is a traceability mechanism[4] enabling a tracing authority (TA) to link upon request directed signatures to their direction i.e. the identities of their signer and receiver. We now introduce an extension of our scheme that supports signature tracing.

5.1   Description of the Scheme DST

Setup and Key generation

The generation of public parameters and keys in the system is essentially the same as above, except that we include $Z = zP_2 \in \mathbb{G}_2$ into the system public parameters. The tracing key is $z \in \mathbb{Z}_q^*$. Moreover, we require users to (securely) submit their anonymity keys x_1 to the Key Registration Authority (KRA). A receipt is returned to the registering user after that, under the form of a NIZK proof $\psi(X_1)$ that the KRA knows x_1.

Signature generation

Now, given a message $m \in \{0, 1\}^*$ and the public key Y of the receiver, signer A picks random $r, s \xleftarrow{\$} \mathbb{Z}_q^*$, and computes $U = rP_2$, $W = rZ + sP_2$, $T = s^{-1}Y$, and $V = rx_1(x_2 + H(m, U, W, T, Y))^{-1}Y$. Again, when $x_2 + H(m, U, W, T, Y) \equiv 0 \pmod{q}$, A restarts the signing procedure with new values for r, s. Next, signer A computes a NIZK proof of consistency $\pi = $ NIZK$[(r, s, h, X_1, X_2, Y) : \psi(X_1) \wedge \psi(Y) \wedge \langle P_1, W \rangle \langle \psi(Z), U \rangle^{-1} = g_t^s \wedge Y = sT \wedge \langle \psi(V), X_2 + hP_2 \rangle = \langle \psi(X_1), T \rangle^{rs}]$. The signature is $\sigma = (U, W, T, V, \pi)$.

Other operations

The verification procedure and the confirming/denying protocols are unchanged, except that the non-interactive proof π is verified. Signature conversions are done the same way i.e. by appending $x_1 U$ or yU, or a NIZK proof of knowledge of x_1 or y to the signature. The generation of trapdoors is unchanged. Universal verification requires the additional check that π is correct.

---

[4] In [19], Kiayias, Tsiounis and Yung propose a similar traceability mechanism in the context of group signatures.

Signature Tracing

A prerequisite for signature tracing is the recovery of the anonymity key x_1 of the suspected user. This is done by the Key Registration Authority upon judicial request. Now the TA is given a signature $\sigma = (U, W, T, V, \pi)$ of some message m and is asked to decide whether σ was issued by the given user and if so, to whom the signature was directed. The TA first ascertains that π is correct and searches in the public key database a key Y for which $\langle T, W - zU \rangle = \langle Y, P_2 \rangle$. The search is always successful, because a proof that Y lies in the set of registered keys is included in π and is known to be correct. Now given Y and x_1, the TA checks whether $\langle V, X_2 + H(m, U, W, T, Y)P_2 \rangle = \langle Y, U \rangle^{x_1}$. We note that in case of mismatch, the TA is left with anonymous material meaning that if the signature was issued by some user A' then the identity of A' is preserved. This property is in fact computationally guaranteed, as stated later.

5.2 Security Analysis

We state that (A, B)-directed signatures are existentially unforgeable and invisible under adaptive chosen-message attack for any user $\neq A, B, \text{TA}$. We rely again on the FSDH and the DTDH assumptions in the random oracle model.

Theorem 3 (Unforgeability and Weak Invisibility). *Let* $t, q_H \in \mathbb{N}^\mathbb{N}$, $q = (q_{\text{Sign}}, q_{\text{Confirm}}, q_{\text{Deny}}, q_{\text{Conv}}, q_{\text{Trap}}, q_{\text{Reg}}) \in [\mathbb{N}^\mathbb{N}]^6$ *and* $\varepsilon \in [0, 1]^\mathbb{N}$.

1. *Assume there exists a* $(k, t, \boldsymbol{q}, \varepsilon)$-*forger* $\mathcal{A}$ *against* DST, *in the random oracle model. Further assume that* $\mathcal{A}$ *is limited to* q_H *executions of* H. *Then there is an algorithm that solves the FSDH problem in the bilinear group system generator* SETUP *with probability* $\varepsilon'(k) \geq 1 - 1/2^k$ *within time*

$$t' \leq t \cdot \frac{(q_H + q_{\text{Confirm}} + q_{\text{Deny}} + q_{\text{Convert}} + 2)}{\varepsilon} + (\|\boldsymbol{q}\| + q_H) \cdot p_3,$$

where p_3 *is a explicit polynomial.*
2. *Assume there exists a* $(k, t, (q_{\text{Sign}}, q_{\text{Confirm}}, q_{\text{Deny}}, 0, 0, q_{\text{Reg}}), \varepsilon)$-*distinguisher* $\mathcal{A}$ *against* DST, *in the random oracle model. Then there exists an algorithm that solves the DTDH problem in the bilinear group system generator* SETUP *with probability* $\varepsilon' = \varepsilon/2 - o(1)$ *within time* $t' \leq q_{\text{Reg}} \cdot t + (\|\boldsymbol{q}\| + q_H) \cdot p_4$, *where* p_4 *is an explicit polynomial.*

Proof. The proof is similar to those of the security of the scheme DS and will be given in the full version of the paper.   □

We also state two important properties fulfilled by the tracing mechanism. They tell us in essence that beyond traceability, the Tracing Authority has no 'hidden powers' over standard users of the system.

Theorem 4 (Abuse-free Traceability). *Signatures issued by user* A *remain invisible to the tracing authority itself as long as the anonymity key* x_1 *of user* A *is undisclosed to the TA.*

Theorem 5 (Tracing-Proof Unforgeability). *After x_1 is disclosed to the TA to enable tracing, the tracing authority is still unable to existentially forge signatures on behalf of A.*

We argue that these properties come from the computational separation between the anonymity key x_1 and the signing key x_2. In fact, after the x_1-part of the secret key of a traced user has been revoked, signatures from that user remain unforgeable because x_2 has not been compromised. The revoked user could even be rehabilitated and a new anonymity key generated to replace the revoked one. This allows a clear separation of powers invested in users and authorities of the system. Due to lack of space, the complete proofs will be given in the full version of the paper.

5.3 Technical Considerations

Implementation of the nizk proof π. The NIZK proof π is implemented as a Fiat-Shamir-transformed conjunction of interactive proofs of the predicates forming π. We rely on prior art [8] to provide an efficient procedure to generate π in practice.

Performances. Signature generation requires 2 exponentiations over group $\mathbb{G}_1$ and 2 over group $\mathbb{G}_2$, and no pairing. Here too, off-line/online signature generation trade-offs are possible by appending a third key part $X_3 = x_3 P_2$ in the user key. Signature conversions and the generation of trapdoors require a single exponentiation over $\mathbb{G}_2$ or $\mathbb{G}_1$ respectively. All verification algorithms require at least two evaluations of the bilinear map. We note that the tracing procedure requires $O(N)$ bilinear map evaluations where N is the number of registered (non-revoked) users. We leave as an open problem to find similar schemes admitting a tracing procedure in polylog complexity in all parameters.

Extensions. Invisibility under the Decisional Tripartite Diffie-Hellman assumption is obtained by replacing the individual conversion procedures by standard NIZK proofs. All operations within the scheme (signature conversion, trapdoor generation) are easily adapted to be verifiable. Among other possible extensions, we cite multi-receiver directed signatures.

6 Conclusion

We properly defined security notions for directed signatures that support the additional property of universal conversion. Using the xyz-trick, we realized the first scheme featuring both individual and universal conversion of signatures, thereby addressing a problem left open since 1993. The new scheme offers attractive practical advantages in terms of signature length and performances. In comparison with previous works, the computational costs for the signer in the signature generation, the confirmation/disavowal protocols and the conversion algorithms, are among the smallest of all delegated undeniable signature schemes. We have proved the security of our scheme in the random oracle model under computational assumptions closely related to the Diffie-Hellman and Decision Diffie-Hellman assumptions on bilinear map groups.

Finally, we introduced traceable directed signatures as a powerful extension to allow a Tracing Authority within the system to link signatures to their direction i.e. issuer and receiver. We believe that our signature schemes are simultaneously efficient and customizable, and we expect to see new cryptographic applications of our work in the future. The xyz-trick will certainly have other applications in future works as well. For example, our scheme is easily extended to achieve the time-selective conversion property as in [20].

References

1. S. Araki, S. Uehara, K. Imamura: The Limited Verifier Signature and Its Application. IEICE Trans. Fundamentals, Vol. E82-A (1), 63–68 (1999)
2. N. Asokan, V. Shoup, M. Waidner: Optimistic Fair Exchange of Digital Signatures. Proc. of Eurocrypt'98, Springer LNCS Vol. 1403, 591–606 (1998)
3. M. Bellare, A. Palacio: The knowledge-of-exponent assumptions and 3-round zero-knowledge protocols. Proc. of Crypto'04, Springer LNCS Vol. 3152, 273–289 (2004)
4. M. Bellare, P. Rogaway: Random Oracles are Practical: a Paradigm for Designing Efficient Protocols. Proc. of 1st ACM Conference on Computer and Communications Security. 62–73 (1993)
5. D. Boneh, X. Boyen: Short Signatures Without Random Oracles. Proc. of Eurocrypt'04, Springer LNCS Vol. 3027, 56–73 (2004)
6. D. Boneh, M. Franklin: Identity-based Encryption from the Weil Pairing. SIAM J. Computing, 32 (3), 586–615 (2003)
7. J. Boyar, D. Chaum, I. B. Damgård, T.P. Pedersen: Convertible Undeniable Signatures. Proc. of Crypto'90, Springer Vol. LNCS 537, 189–205 (1991)
8. E. Bresson, J. Stern: Proofs of Knowledge for Non-Monotone Discrete-Log Formulae and Applications. Proc. of ISC'02, Springer LNCS Vol. 2433, 272–288 (2002)
9. J. Camenisch, M. Michels: Confirmer Signature Schemes Secure against Adaptive Adversaries. Proc. of Eurocrypt'00, Springer LNCS Vol. 1807, 243–258 (2000)
10. J. Camenisch, M. Stadler: Efficient Group Signature Schemes for Large Groups. Proc. of Crypto'97, Springer LNCS Vol. 1296, 410–424 (1997)
11. D. Chaum: Designated Confirmer Signatures. Proc. of Eurocrypt'94, Springer LNCS Vol. 950, 86–91 (1995)
12. D. Chaum, H. van Antwerpen: Undeniable Signatures. Proc. of Crypto'89, Springer LNCS Vol. 435, 212–216 (1989)
13. D. Chaum, E. van Heijst, B. Pfitzmann: Cryptographically Strong Undeniable Signatures Unconditionally Secure for the Signer. Proc. of Crypto'91, Springer LNCS Vol. 576, 470–484 (1992)
14. I. Damgård: Towards Practical Public Key Systems Secure Against Chosen Ciphertext Attacks. Proc. of Crypto'91, Springer LNCS Vol. 576, 445–456 (1991)
15. M. K. Franklin, M. K. Reiter: Verifiable Signature Sharing. Proc. of Eurocrypt'95, Springer LNCS Vol. 921, 50–63 (1995)
16. S. Goldwasser, S. Micali, R. Rivest: A Digital Signature Scheme Secure against Adaptive Chosen-Message Attacks. SIAM J. Computing, 17 (2), 281–308 (1988)
17. S. Goldwasser, E. Waisbard: Transformation of Digital Signature Schemes into Designated Confirmer Signature Schemes. Proc. of TCC'04, Springer LNCS Vol. 2951, 77–100 (2004)

18. M. Jakobsson, K. Sako, R. Impagliazzo: Designated Verifier Proofs and their Applications. Proc.of Eurocrypt'96, Springer LNCS Vol. 1070, 142–154 (1996)
19. Aggelos Kiayias, Yiannis Tsiounis, Moti Yung: Traceable Signatures. Proc. of Eurocrypt'04, Springer LNCS Vol. 3027, 571–589 (2004)
20. F. Laguillaumie, D. Vergnaud: Time-Selective Convertible Undeniable Signatures. Proc. of CT-RSA'05, Springer LNCS Vol. 3376, 154-171 (2005)
21. C. H. Lim and P. J. Lee: Modified Maurer-Yacobi's Scheme and its Applications. Proc. of Auscrypt'92, Springer LNCS Vol. 718, 308–323 (1993)
22. D. Pointcheval, J. Stern: Security Arguments for Digital Signatures and Blind Signatures. J. Cryptology, Vol. 13 (3), 361–396 (2000)
23. F. Zhang, K. Kim: A Universal Forgery on Araki *et al.*'s Convertible Limited Verifier Signature Scheme. IEICE Trans. Fundamentals, Vol. E86-A (2), 515–516 (2003)

A   Invisibility of DS

The invisibility of DS relies on the difficulty of solving the following ℓ-*Tripartite-DCAA Problem* in connection to the *xyz*-trick. It is similar to a class of problems recently introduced by Laguillaumie and Vergnaud [20]:

ℓ-Tripartite-DCAA Problem: Let $(q, P_1, P_2, g_t, \mathbb{G}_1, \mathbb{G}_2, \mathbb{G}_t, \langle \cdot, \cdot \rangle, \rho)$ be a bilinear group system. Given $(x_1 P_1, x_2 P_2, y P_1, z P_2, Q, h) \xleftarrow{\$} (\mathbb{G}_1 \times \mathbb{G}_2)^2 \times \mathbb{G}_1 \times \mathbb{Z}_q^*$ and for some $\ell \geq 0$,

$$\left(h_i, x_1(x_2 + h_i)^{-1} P_1, x_1 y(x_2 + h_i)^{-1} P_1 \right)_{i \in [\![1, \ell]\!]} \in \left(\mathbb{Z}_q^* \times \mathbb{G}_1^2 \right)^{\ell}$$

with $h \notin \{h_1, \dots, h_\ell\}$, decide whether $Q = x_1 y z (x_2 + h)^{-1} P_1$.

We state that, assuming the hardness of the ℓ-Tripartite-DCAA problem and that of the Flexible Square Diffie-Hellman problem, the schemes DS and DST are invisible under chosen-message attack in the random oracle model.

Theorem 6 (Invisibility of DS and DST). *Let* $t, q_H \in \mathbb{N}^{\mathbb{N}}$, $q = (q_{\text{Sign}}, q_{\text{Confirm}}, q_{\text{Deny}}, q_{\text{Conv}}, q_{\text{Trap}}, q_{\text{Reg}}) \in [\mathbb{N}^{\mathbb{N}}]^6$ *and* $\varepsilon \in [0, 1]^{\mathbb{N}}$. *Assume there exists a* $(k, t, \boldsymbol{q}, \varepsilon)$-*distinguisher* $\mathcal{A}$, *in the random oracle model, against* DS *(or* DST*). Then there exists an algorithm* $\mathcal{B}$ *that solves the* q_s-*Tripartite-DCAA problem in the bilinear group generator* SETUP *with advantage* ε' *and a* $(k, t'', \boldsymbol{q}, \varepsilon'')$-*forger* $\mathcal{C}$ *against* DS *such that*

$$\varepsilon' + (q_{\text{Confirm}} + q_{\text{Deny}} + q_{\text{Convert}}) \cdot \varepsilon'' \geq \varepsilon$$

where $\mathcal{B}$ *runs in time at most* $t' = (q_{\text{Reg}} + 1) \cdot t$ *and* $\mathcal{C}$ *runs in time* $t'' = t + \mathcal{O}(1)$.

Proof. Assume $\mathcal{A}$ is an Inv-CMA-adversary that $(k, t, \boldsymbol{q}, \varepsilon)$-distinguishes the signatures of DS. As in the unforgeability proof, q_H represents the number of queries submitted by $\mathcal{A}$ to H since H is again viewed as a random oracle. We construct two reduction algorithms $\mathcal{B}$ and $\mathcal{C}$ that interact with $\mathcal{A}$ and respectively solve the q_s-Tripartite-DCAA problem and produce an existential forgery with time and success probability as claimed in Theorem 6.

ALGORITHM $\mathcal{B}$: Algorithm $\mathcal{B}$ is given public parameters $(q, P_1, P_2, g_t, \mathbb{G}_1, \mathbb{G}_2, \mathbb{G}_t, \langle \cdot, \cdot \rangle, \rho)$ generated by SETUP(k) and an instance

$$\left((x_1 P_1, x_2 P_2, y P_1, z P_2, Q, h), \left(h_i, R_i = \frac{x_1}{x_2 + h_i} P_1, S_i = \frac{x_1 y}{x_2 + h_i} P_1 \right)_{i \in [\![1, q_s]\!]} \right)$$

in $(\mathbb{G}_1 \times \mathbb{G}_2)^2 \times \mathbb{G}_1 \times \mathbb{Z}_q^* \times (\mathbb{Z}_q^* \times \mathbb{G}_1^2)^{q_s}$ of the q_s-Tripartite-DCAA problem. $\mathcal{B}$'s goal is to decide whether $Q = x_1 y z (x_2 + h)^{-1} P_1$ and $\mathcal{B}$ proceeds to use forger $\mathcal{A}$ to do so. $\mathcal{B}$ sets $X_1 = x_1 P_1$, $X_2 = x_2 P_2$, $Y^* = y P_1$, initializes a counter $i = 1$ and simulates $\mathcal{A}$'s environment as follows:

Simulation of H. Same simulation as in the unforgeability proof.

Simulation of DS.Register. Each time the adversary registers a new public key $Y = y' P_1$, the reduction rewinds $\mathcal{A}$ from the beginning without changing anything but the challenge in the proof-of-knowledge of the discrete logarithm y' of Y in base P_2 (see the proof of unforgeability). Therefore, we can suppose wlog that the reduction knows the secret key of all the users registered by $\mathcal{A}$, at the expense of running $\mathcal{A}$ at most $q_{\text{Reg}}(k)$ times.

Simulation of DS.Signer.{Confirm, Deny}. If the signature has been produced by $\mathcal{B}$ in the simulation then use the same simulation as in the unforgeability proof. Otherwise, simulate a designated-verifier proof of invalidity.

Simulation of DS.Sign. Given $m \in \{0,1\}^*$ and a confirmer's public key Y, pick a random $r \xleftarrow{\$} \mathbb{Z}_q^*$. If $Y = Y^*$ set $U = r P_2$ and $V = r S_i$. Otherwise $Y = y' P_1 \neq Y^*$, and $\mathcal{B}$ sets $U = r P_2$ and $V = r y' R_i$. Now if $H(m, U, Y)$ is defined and is $\neq h_i$, the reduction restarts with a new value for r. Otherwise the reduction defines $H(m, U, Y) = h_i$, outputs $\sigma = (U, V)$ and increments i.

Simulation of DS.Convert.{Signer, Confirmer}. Given $Y \in \mathbb{G}$, $m \in \{0,1\}^*$ and $\sigma = (U, V) \in \mathbb{G}^2$, invoke the simulation of H on (m, U, Y). If σ has been obtained by the simulation of DS.Sign then retrieve the randomness r such that $U = r P_2$ and output $\tilde{\sigma}_A = (U, V, r X_1)$ or $\tilde{\sigma}_B = (U, V, r Y)$. Otherwise, output Invalid.

Simulation of DS.Signer.Trapdoor. Given $Y \in \mathbb{G} \setminus \{Y^*\}$, output $\mathcal{T} = y' X_1$ where $Y^* = y' P_2$.

In this simulation $\mathcal{B}$ simulates perfectly $\mathcal{A}$'s environment unless at some point in time $\mathcal{A}$ queries a valid signature (U, V) not produced by $\mathcal{B}$ to the oracles DS.Signer.{Confirm, Deny} or DS.Convert.{Signer, Confirmer}. Let us denote Bad this event. We have $|\varepsilon'(k) - \varepsilon(k)| \leq \Pr(\text{Bad})$ and the running time of $\mathcal{B}$ is at most $t'(k) = (q_{\text{Reg}}(k) + 1) \cdot t(k) + \mathcal{O}(1)$.

ALGORITHM $\mathcal{C}$: We claim that there exists an EF-CMA-adversary $\mathcal{C}$ which $(k, t'', q, \varepsilon'')$-breaks DS, where $t'' = t + \mathcal{O}(1)$ and $\varepsilon'' \geq (q_{\text{Confirm}} + q_{\text{Deny}} + q_{\text{Convert}})^{-1} \Pr[\text{Bad}]$. Basically, $\mathcal{C}$ runs $\mathcal{A}$ and outputs as a forgery one of the signatures (selected at random) queried by $\mathcal{A}$ during the Inv-CMA game, to one of the oracles DS.Signer.{Confirm, Deny} or DS.Convert.{Signer, Confirmer} which was not obtained by the oracle DS.Sign.

This directly leads to the above claims for the scheme DS and the proof extends readily to the invisibility of the scheme DST. □

Author Index

Lecture Notes in Computer Science

For information about Vols. 1–3708

please contact your bookseller or Springer